REPORT

OF

A MISSION TO YARKUND IN 1873,

UNDER COMMAND OF

SIR T. D. FORSYTH, K.C.S.I., C.B.,

BENGAL CIVIL SERVICE,

WITH

HISTORICAL AND GEOGRAPHICAL INFORMATION

REGARDING THE

POSSESSIONS OF THE AMEER OF YARKUND.

CALCUTTA:
PRINTED AT THE FOREIGN DEPARTMENT PRESS.
1875.

CONTENTS OF BOOK.

CHAPTER I.

	Page.
Narrative of progress of mission to Káshghar and back to India	1

CHAPTER II.

	Page.
General description of Káshghar by Dr. Bellew and Captain Chapman, comprising—	23
Names of the Region	ib.
Geographical position	24
Superficial extent	ib.
Area in square miles	ib.
Comparative Topography	ib.
Physical Features	25
Highland	ib.
Lowland	ib.
Desert	26
Swamp	29
Lake	30
Political Divisions	31
Khutan	32
Yárkand	34
Yángí Hissár	36
Káshghar	38
Úsh Turfán	41
Aksú	42
Kúchá	43
Kúrla	44
Karáshahr	45
Kalmáks	46
Turfán	49
Lob	51
Marálbáshí	54
Dolán	ib.
Sirikol	55
Kirghiz of Alátágh and Pámir	57
Pukhpúlúk of Múztágh	61
Population	62
Climate and Seasons	63
Salubrity	66
Natural Productions	69
Animal	ib.
Vegetable	74
Mineral	75
Industrial productions	76
Agriculture	ib.

Manufactures	79
Inhabitants	80
Manners and Customs	84
Marriage	ib.
Birth	86
Circumcision	87
Education	ib.
Games and Amusements	88
Etiquette	89
Occupations	ib.
Women	ib.
Dress and Ornaments	90
Death	92
Funeral	ib.
Food	ib.
Habitations	94
Language	95
Government of the country under the Chinese	ib.
Government of Káshghar under the Amir	97
The King	ib.
Rule and Policy	98
The Court	99
Administration of Government	100
Administration of justice	ib.
Punishments	ib.
Religious Institutions	102
Finance	ib.
Police	103
The Army	104

CHAPTER III.

History of Káshghar by Dr. Bellew ... 106

CHAPTER IV.

Narrative of expedition to Chádirkúl and the Tian Shán Range by Lieutenant-Colonel Gordon ... 214

CHAPTER V.

Narrative of expedition to Marálbáshí by Captain Biddulph ... 217

CHAPTER VI.

Narrative of expedition over the Pámír to Wakán by Lieutenant-Colonel Gordon ... 222

CHAPTER VII.

Narrative of geographical explorations made by Captain Trotter, R.E., and his Assistants ... 233

		Page.
Geographical Appendix —		
Section A. Latitudes	...	295
,, B. Longitudes	...	327
,, C. Heights	...	339
,, D. Alphabetical list of latitudes, longitudes and heights	...	361
,, E. Magnetic observations	...	369
,, F. Meteorological observations	...	373
,, G. Routes	...	417

CHAPTER VIII.

Geological notes by the late Dr. Stoliczka ... 460

CHAPTER IX.

Commerce by Capt. Chapman ... 474

CHAPTER X.

On Photography by Captain Chapman ... 491

CHAPTER XI.

Memorandum on Sheep carrying by Captain Biddulph ... 492

CHAPTER XII.

Memorandum on Money, weights, and measures by Dr. Bellew ... 494

CHAPTER XIII.

The Calendar ... 512

CHAPTER XIV.

Record of Meteorological Observations by Dr. Bellew ... 513

CHAPTER XV.

Vocabulary by Dr. Bellew and Captain Biddulph ... 534

LIST OF NEGATIVES, TAKEN BY CAPTAINS E. F. CHAPMAN, AND H. TROTTER, ON THE EXPEDITION TO YARKUND, 1873-74.

CAPTAIN CHAPMAN'S SERIES.

No.
1. Camp in the Nusseem Bagh, Kashmir, August 1873.
2. Embassy Camp, Kashmir.
3. Durbar Tent, visit of the Maharajah to the British Envoy.
4. Lama Yuru, Buddhist Monastery and Chortens.
5. Camp Nimmoo, in Ladak.
6. Tartar Women at Nimmoo in Ladak, September 1873.
7. Leh, the Capital of Ladak, View of the Bazar and Palace.
8. Leh, the Capital of Ladak, View from Joint Commissioner's Garden.
9. The Indus Valley from Leh, Eln. 11,500 feet, View from Joint Commissioner's Garden.
10. The Ex. Raja of Ladak and family.
11. "Kolon," No. 1, Head of the family entitled by Treaty to conduct a caravan every third year from Kashmir Territory to Lhassa the Capital of the Grand Lama.
    No. 2, Heera Munshi of Ladak.
    No. 3, Kolon's Son.
12. Shémurs of Ladak, Group of Ladies taken at Leh.
13. Professional dancers of Leh.
14. The Nubra Valley from Panamik, looking S. E. Buddhist Chortens in the foreground.
15. Buddhist temple at Panamik, Gods of the Buddhists.
    1 Chakna Durge.
    2 Sangias Shukia Tuba.
    3 Pakpa Chingre Zik.
    4 Dekhna Karpo, goddess.
16. Heads of Oves Ammon, &c., shot by Capt. Molloy, Joint Commissioner of Ladak, 1873.
17. Crossing the Sasser Pass, Breakfast above Tooti Aylak, elevation 16,300 feet.
18. Camp at Shahidulla Khwoja, the frontier outpost of Yarkund Territory towards Kashmir, 22nd October 1873.
19. Shahidulla Khwoja, October 1873.
    Camp at the frontier outpost of His Highness the Maharajah of Jummoo and Kashmir.
20. Men of the Pakpoo tribe living in the Valleys bordering that of the Tisnaf river.
21. Men of the Pakpoo tribe.
22. Group of Natives of Kargullik, November 1873.
23. Officers in the service of the Dadkhwah of Yarkund.
24. Dastarkhwan at Kargalik, 3rd November 1873.
25. Street Hawkers in the square of the Mess Room of the British Embassy in Yarkund, November 1873.
26. Street Hawkers, Yarkund.
27.   Ditto   ditto.
28.   Ditto   ditto.
29. Snuff and Tobacco Shop, Yarkund.
30. Flour Cleaner and Oil Sellers.
31. Yaghach-chi. The Carpenter.
32. The Knife Grinder.

(2)

No.
33 Verandah of interior Court yard of the Urda of the Dadkhwah of Yarkund, shewing the Hall of Audience.
34 Guard of Artillery Sirbaz, and group of officers assembled in the Court yard of the Urda of the Dadkhwah of Yarkund.
35 Soldiers from Aksu.
36 Soldiers from Kuchar.
37 Soldiers from Kashghar.
38 Soldiers—Kashgaris.
39 Soldiers from Kuchar. Aksu and Khoten.
40 Players on Longhorn and Mir-i-Shub.
41 Musicians of Yarkund.
42 Sikh Merchants in Yarkund.
43 Baltistanis from near Skardo resident in Yarkund.
44 Tunganis, resident in Yarkund.
45 Yarkundis.
46 Yarkundis, Specimens of goitre.
47 Hospital, British Embassy in Yarkund.
48 A Doulan from the Maralbashi.
49 The Pamir Mountains from Yangi Hissar and the Tagharma Peak.
50 Guard of Honor under Panjsad Khal Mahomed. (Bahatur Batcha) sent out to meet the Envoy from Yangi Hissar.
51 Kirghiz Felt (Akoe) occupied by officers of the mission at Yangi Hissar.
52 Soap, Tape, Oil and Sweetmeat Sellers of Yarkund.
53 Coppersmiths manufacturing water vessels.
54 Bootmaker, Bread seller and Cotton cleaner.
55 Snuff Seller.
56 The Fortune-teller.
57 Derwishes, professional beggars.
58 Saddle maker.
59 The Forge.
60 Silk Reeling.
61 Cotton Spinning.
62 Opium Smokers.
63 Andijani and Child by a Yarkund Woman.
64 Cradle Scene, Yangi Hissar.
65 Children and Toy, Yangi Hissar.
66 Presents made to the Amir of Kashghar in the name of Her Majesty the Queen, and of His Excellency the Viceroy.
67 Yuz-bashi, Panjabashi, and Dah-bashi, at attention.
68 Ditto ditto at Ease.
69 Attendants at the Embassy.
70 Tungani troops of the Amir.
71 Ditto ditto.
72 Ditto ditto.
73 Oves Polii.
74 Oves Polii Lyre horned Antelope, frozen specimens.
75 Present of game and fruit in Kashghar.
76 Female Patients attending the Embassy Hospital, January 1874.
77 Patients attending the Embassy Hospital.
78 A Nogai from Omsk and a Native of Sirikul, Pamir.

No.
79 Bhokara and Khokandi Merchants.
80 Party deputed to Kabul, 1st January 1874.
81 Shrine of Sultan Satuk Bogra Khan at Artush, North of Kashgar.
82   Ditto   ditto   ditto.
83 Karawal (Frontier outpost), at Tangi Tar in the Thian Shan 60 miles N. of Kashgar.
84 The Kirghiz of Tiggur Matti and Bash Sugun in the Tian Shan.
85 Group at Kalti Aylak in the Artush District.
86 Moosa Khwoja, Son of the Hakim of Artush, with hawks.

CAPTAIN TROTTER'S SERIES.

87 Winter Quarters in Kashghar, Dr. Stoliczka on left and Captain Biddulph on right.
88 Scinde Valley, Cashmere.
89 The "Dadhkwahs" band, Yarkund.
90 Scinde Valley, Cashmere.
91 Polo players, Ladakh.
92 Scinde Valley, Cashmere.
93 Sonamarg.
94 A Hadji of Karghalik.
95 Tash-khoja, an Andijani Yazbashi.
96 Two natives of Sanjwa.
97 Group of Yarkundis of the lower classes.
98 Group of natives, Yarkund.
99 } Chinese Troops, Kashghar.
100 }
101 A Chinese Slave, and a Fakir of the Country.
102 Chinese Troops, Kashghar.

REPORT

OF

A MISSION TO YARKUND IN 1873,

UNDER COMMAND OF

SIR T. D. FORSYTH, K.C.S.I., C.B.,

BENGAL CIVIL SERVICE.

Corporal Rhind, Her Majesty's 92nd Gordon Highlanders, Camp Sergeant and Clerk.

Jemadar Siffat Khan, in charge of escort furnished by the Corps of Guides which consisted of—

10 Sowars, 1 Naick, and 10 Sepoys.

Lieutenant-Colonel Gordon as second in command had superior charge of all camp arrangements, and issued the necessary orders for daily routine, the entire control of the escort and ammunition was in his hands. He also commanded sundry separate expeditions.

Dr. Bellew had charge of all medical arrangements and was President of the staff mess.

Captain Chapman was appointed Secretary to the Mission, and had charge of the mule equipment, camp equipage, treasure chest, and postal arrangements.

Captain Biddulph had charge of the Toshakhana when he was with the head-quarters of the Mission, it being placed under Captain Chapman's care at other times. He commanded the advance party to Shahidulla, and was employed on a separate expedition to Maralbashi, and accompanied Lieutenant-Colonel Gordon to Wakhan.

Captain Trotter and Dr. Stoliczka had charge of their special departments.

Of the native Government employés selected to serve, Ressaidar Mahomed Afzul Khan, 11th Bengal Lancers, was appointed Attaché in charge of the native portion of the camp, Ibrahim Khan, Inspector of Police, was another Attaché, and was employed on special duty.

Abdool Subhan, Assistant Surveyor, attached to the Survey Department, assisted Captain Trotter, and conducted separately an exploration of Shignan, returning by Badakshan and Cabul. Colonel Walker, R.E., Superintendent G. T. S., further placed at my disposal seven of the Survey Pundits.

Experience having shown the necessity for rendering the expedition independent in the matter of carriage, one hundred mules of a very fair stamp were purchased, through the agency of Tara Sing, at a moderate price. These were equipped with saddles nearly resembling those of the Otago pattern used in Abyssinia, which were made in the Government workshops at Cawnpoor, mule trunks of a special pattern being supplied with them. The saddles and trunks were productions that would be considered highly creditable to any manufactory, and proved most serviceable.

As some delay occurred in the return of Syud Yakub Khan, the Yarkand Envoy, from Constantinople, it was thought advisable to send an advance party to examine carefully the routes between Leh and Shahidulla. Accordingly on the 15th July 1873, Captains Biddulph and Trotter and Dr. Stoliczka left Murree and journeyed to Shahidulla. The head-quarters party left on 19th July, but halted for some time at Srinuggur till I joined them, when we all proceeded to Leh which we reached on the 20th September. Here, in addition to what is usually known as warm clothing, each follower received fur socks, leggings, boots, and a chogah lined with sheep-skin, a warm cap covering the ears, and thick gloves, besides a good felt and blankets. Meat and tea formed part of the daily ration, and the whole were comfortably sheltered in tents.

The road as far as Leh is too well trodden to require any description here. The route taken by the advance party by the Chargbchemo Valley is sufficiently well detailed in the Geographical chapter, and I need only here remark that the inclemency of the season was such as to prevent anything like an extensive exploration, and in fact its effects were speedily visible on our lamented companion Dr. Stoliczka. However, though the hardships undergone by this advance party deserve passing mention, there is not much loss to geographical science to record, for the route taken by them had been fully examined and reported on, first by that intrepid but unfortunate traveller Mr. Hayward, and afterwards by Dr. Cayley, and by the first expedition to Yarkand in 1870.

Captain Trotter and Dr. Stoliczka rejoined our camp at Aktagh on the 13th October, whilst Captain Biddulph pursued his enquiries down the Karakash River and met us at Shahidulla on the 18th October.

If space permitted, it might be interesting to give a detailed account of a journey to Shahidulla from Leh over the highest passes in the world. Suffice it however to say that the journey of 240 miles was accomplished in 15 marches, with no other accident than the loss of eight baggage animals, and this with 300 souls and 400 animals in camp. The Glacier Pass of the Sasser, and the icy region of the Shyok Valley and the Karakorum Pass were fortunately crossed without snow, which however attacked us on the northern side, and accompanied with an eager nipping air added much to the discomfort inseparable from travelling sustained for many days at an elevation varying from 15,000 to 18,000 feet. Some idea of the cold may be formed from the fact that our minimum thermometer recorded a temperature of 15° below zero inside a tent, whilst in Captain Biddulph's camp it descended to 26° below zero in the open air.

At Shahidulla we were met by Yuzbashi Mahomed Zareef Khan, a Captain of the Amir's army, who had been deputed with some soldiers to await our arrival, and who gave us a hearty welcome. Here too we were joined by Ibrahim Khan, whom I had sent ahead to Yarkand to report our approach. After a halt of four days at Shahidulla, during which time Captain Trotter and his subordinates explored the surrounding country, and Drs. Stoliczka and Bellew paid a visit to the jade mines at Balakchi, Lieutenant-Colonel Gordon moved on with the chief part of the camp to Sanju, the nearest village in the Yarkand plain, and Syud Yakub Khan joining us two days after we followed over the Grim Pass. This Pass was not crossed without great difficulty owing to a fresh fall of snow. The ascent for the last 100 feet to the summit was up a wall of ice. The Kirghiz who had met us at Shahidulla, their farthest point, rendered great assistance in roughing the ice with pickaxes, laying down felts, and dragging the animals up. It was impossible for men or beasts to keep a firm footing on the icy zigzags, and many were precipitated over the snowy sides some hundreds of feet below. The loss amounted to eight mules and three ponies, none of the horses belonging to the Cavalry escort being in the number of casualties. When we reached Sanju on the 30th October, we found the country just beginning to put on its wintry appearance. The yellow look of the leaves and the frosty ground reminded us of European lands.

Here we were met by a special messenger bearing a letter of welcome from the Atalik Ghazi. Another letter came at the same time to Syud Yakub Khan, congratulating him on the success of his mission to Constantinople. I mention this to notice the manner in which such letters are received. The recipient taking it in both hands raises the letter to his forehead, and stands with his face in the direction whence it was sent, while he reads it most respectfully. He then presses the seal upon both eyes, and having folded it up, places it in his turban. This is a literal fulfilment of the Persian saying, "on my head and eyes" and seems to have been a custom in Eastern Turkestan from a very early time.*

After a halt of two days at Sanju we resumed our march towards Yarkand on the 2nd November crossing low ranges, long flats, and stony desert here and there at long intervals intersected with streams from the mountains, on the sides of which and wherever watercourses could be carried signs of cultivations were abundant.

On the 5th November we reached Kargalik, the first place of importance we had seen, and were struck by the signs of prosperity and civilization exhibited to us at every turn. An eating-house, with its clean table and forms and piles of China plates and bowls, at once took us back across the seas to the recollection of many a country restaurant in France. We were conducted through the bazaar to quarters built expressly for our accommodation; much to our gratification we found them far superior to anything we expected to find in the country, and our surprise at the neatness of the carpentry and clean regularity of the walls was surpassed by the comfort of the apartments and their good though somewhat scanty furniture. Thick felts and handsome carpets from Khoten covered the floors, and high backed chairs but no tables were provided. Fire-places, like our own, warmed the rooms without filling them with smoke, roof ventilators completing our requirements. The quarters for

---

* In Remusat's History of Khoten this is alluded to as a custom in the 6th century. Quand quelqu'un reçoit une lettre, il la met d'abord sur sa tête avant de la décacheter, p. 17.

ourselves were enclosed within walls and ranged on two opposite sides. A third side was covered in by a raised verandah through which were doors leading to a spacious kitchen and out-offices. In another quadrangle was an open court and covered stables, with mangers for one hundred horses. Altogether the arrangements were very good, and as we found in our subsequent travels similar accommodation at nearly all the chief halting places, this detailed description will answer for all.

I may here also notice the system of hospitality which is such a marked feature in Eastern Turkestan. It is said that in England we never can transact business satisfactorily without dining over it, but here in the East it seems as if good living and perpetually entertaining one's guests were the chief end of life. The dastarkhwan (literally table cloth) generally a gaudy chintz-lined coverlet is spread at each village of any size, under some clump of trees or, if in winter, in a house, where a good blazing fire offers a warm welcome, and the guests are invited to dismount; cups of hot tea are handed round, and then a number of trays varying from 20 or 30 to 100 laden with fruit, delicious bread, and sweets and cooked meats are brought in. No matter what be the hour of the day, or how frequently similar halts may have been made previously, it is a point of honor for the local magnate to lead the travellers to this feast, and it is equally a point of honor for the traveller to show his politeness even at the risk of ruining his digestion, by drinking numberless cups of tea and dipping his hands into the steaming dish. One part of their customs struck us with surprise and unfeigned pleasure; be the host Turk or British, he and his guests eat alike from the same dish and hand food to the surrounding attendants, who are troubled with no scruples of caste to interfere with their hearty appetite. It is the duty of the guest first to break bread and present a portion to his host.

We halted one day at Kargalik, and on the 7th November marched to Posgam 25 miles, most of the way across a highly cultivated and populous plain through which flows the River Tisnaf. This we crossed at about the fourteenth mile, and a little further on came to Yakshamba Bazaar, a considerable village, where as the name implies a market is held every Sunday mostly for the barter of farm produce. Here we alighted for a dastarkhwan at a newly built rest-house, on the same general plan as that at Kargalik, but smaller. Here too the Turkish officers, who had come from Constantinople in the suite of the Atalik's Envoy, made their appearance in military uniform and somewhat puzzled the curious villagers as to their identity, for their Turkish is almost as difficult of comprehension to the people here as is their own vernacular in the form we not unfrequently offered it to them.

From this place to Posgam and from that on to Yarkand the road lies over a thickly populated country, highly cultivated and freely irrigated by numberless small canals drawn off from the Zarafashan or Yarkand River. We crossed this river at a few miles from Posgam. It was even then a large stream, and in summer is only passable by boat.

Beyond the river, at about ten miles from Posgam, we alighted at Zilchak, where some tents and a dastarkhwan had been prepared for us. Whilst here the Yussawal Bashi or Chamberlain with a party of the Governor's body-guard* arrived with messages of welcome from the Dadkhwah. The dastarkhwan disposed of, we brushed the dust off our uniforms and set out towards Yarkand, five miles distant, in two parties closely following each other—the returning Envoy with his Turkish suite and the British Envoy with his staff of officers. As we approached the city, we were met by successive troops of citizens and merchants, who saluted us in a very friendly way, and, joining our cavalcade, soon swelled it to upwards of three hundred horsemen. And so we went on to the city, observing here and there that the road had been levelled, holes filled in, pools and puddles covered with earth, and "eyewash" generally put on pretty thick.

---

* The guard consisted of 30 men, and their mode of salutation was somewhat singular. They came forward in batches of five, and knelt on one knee. This appears to be the true Eastern Turki fashion, for M. Remusat in his History of Khoten says —" Quand ils se recontrent ils s'agenouillent, cést a dire qu'ils mettent un genou en terre."

1.—Camp in the Nusseem Bagh, Kashmir, August 1873.

The crowds lining the road near the city gate were generally very well and warmly clad and behaved with remarkable quietness. The variety of race types was a very marked feature in the general appearance of the multitude, and next to this the almost universal prevalence of goitre. We passed into the city through its main bazaars, and out again, then across an open space of about a couple of furlongs to a detached fort, the Yangishahr or New Town. Here we were saluted at the gate by the guard and presently found ourselves in the quarters prepared for us. They were the same as those occupied by me on the occasion of my former visit, but the accommodation had been increased by the erection of five or six new quarters within the same area.

All the rooms were nicely furnished and everything was done to make us comfortable, not to forget the dastarkhwan, which here grew to ninety-two dishes and trays.

The day following we paid a visit to the Dadakhwah, the Governor of this city and district. His palace adjoined our own quarters, and was approached through three courtyards, each with its own guard of matchlockmen, great burly figures, all boots and bundle, for such was the appearance of their forms gathered in about the middle as their flowing robes of stark bright patterns were by the loose folds of a waistband.

The Dadkhwah, Mahammad Yunus Jan, on our approaching his audience chamber, a spacious hall with a gaudily painted roof, the decorations bearing the impress of Khokundi art, came out into the verandah to meet us, and after the usual introduction conducted us up the length of the hall to the cushions ranged at its upper end. After the interchange of the customary compliments and ceremonies, the presents were brought in, admired and examined. The court officials then brought in fruits and sweets, and tea was served round. A brief conversation then closed the interview and we returned to our quarters.

From my former experience of our relations with the people of Yarkand, I was curious and rather anxious to see how we should be treated. Hitherto it had not been the custom to allow foreigners to move about with unrestricted freedom. Messrs. Shaw and Hayward had been kept close prisoners to their quarters during the whole period of their sojourn in the country, and when the former expedition of 1870 entered the city of Yarkand an attempt was made to prevent the English officers from going out. The most disquieting rumours and sinister prophesies had been promulgated regarding the reception which awaited this mission, and though we had been able to trace them to their source, still it was just possible that there was some foundation of truth. It was with no small anxiety then that I watched the slightest action of our hosts, and I found it advisable to issue the strictest orders to prevent any sort of offence being given by our followers.

We had come provided with every kind of scientific apparatus, but it was more than probable that theodolites, photographic cameras, &c., might be looked on as only instruments of the black art. I therefore enjoined on one and all the utmost caution, and decided that until we reached the royal presence, and had an opportunity of explaining the harmless nature of our scientific instruments, they should not be used. I also gave orders, which were strictly enforced during our whole stay in the country, for a roll-call of all followers to be held twice a day, and none were allowed to be out of camp after half-past 7 P.M., nor were any permitted to go into the bazaars without permission from Ressaidar Afzul Khan, whose duty it was to see that the men were decently dressed and behaved themselves properly. To these precautions and to the sense of being kept under tight discipline, I attribute in a great measure the remarkable freedom from trouble which we enjoyed. The total number of followers was 120, and I am happy to be able to record that, during a period of seven months we were in Kashghar territory, not more than twenty-two punishments were inflicted.

Our first appearance in the streets of Yarkand excited the lively curiosity of the inhabitants, and the scene was particularly interesting. Entering the city by the Altun or golden gate, we turned to the right and passed down the butcher's street, where, suspended in front of the shops, such as may be seen in a butcher's stall at home, we saw good beef, mutton, yak's and horse flesh, the head or tail of the animal being left attached to the carcase to indicate the kind of meat.

Thence, passing on through street of shops, we came to an open chouk or square, where a crowd of people was collected round two Durweshes, who sang with not too melodious voice some song which afforded much amusement. From the earliest times all travellers who have visited these countries have been impressed with the gay merry character of the people and, though the present ruler has enjoined a more severe demeanour, there is still much of the old love of gaiety left. We then proceeded through a covered bazaar where all kinds of wares were displayed—here and there China cups and articles of jade, English and Russian chintzes, broadcloth from India, &c. Taking another turn to the right we found ourselves in what is called the Shám or evening bazaar where, as its name indicates, crowds of men and women collect every evening round booths and stalls at which boots, caps, dresses, and other articles of daily use are exposed in large quantities for sale. Everywhere the people treated us quite as of themselves, though of course they collected round us in good humoured curiosity to examine closely the first Europeans they had ever seen.

On no single occasion throughout our whole stay in the country did we ever meet with the slightest rudeness or incivility; no scowling looks nor angry taunts were levelled at us; on the contrary, wherever we went we always found people pleased to meet and converse with us.

The cloth merchants live in the chief bazaar which is larger and altogether of a superior description, being covered over as in Cairo or Stambul and the shops presenting a very similar appearance to shops in those cities.

Immediately beyond this is the bakers' street, where every shop is for bread or food of some kind. There was a restaurant which particularly attracted our notice from its extreme cleanliness and the neatness of all its arrangements. In front was the cooking range, with a fire below, over which a large cauldron was placed; the steam from this passed through a series of sieves in each one of which was meat or vegetables or other food, which was thus cooked to a nicety by steam. By the side were the vegetables cut into shreds ready for cooking, whilst a man was busy preparing flour for pastry. Inside we saw forms and tables at which the customers sat. I have been in similar restaurants in Stambul, but have seen nothing so clean and tempting as is to be found in Yarkand or Kashghar. In the streets we saw wheel-barrows with trays, on which patés, rolls of bread, fruit and cooked vegetables were hawked about, exactly as apples and pies are sold from carts in the streets of London. The bread rolls are made of the finest white flour and are pleasant to the taste as to the eye.

There was an air of comfort even among the lower classes, and a something decidedly more in common with our ideas than is encountered elsewhere in the East. To see the poorer people going to a shop and buying loaves of bread and meat pies, was pleasanter than seeing each individual seated separately on the ground cooking an indigestible-looking chupattee in selfish solitude as in India.

One curious sight witnessed by some of our party deserves mention here. At intervals the Kazí of the city goes round the shops inspecting weights or measures. On this occasion he detected a butcher using short weight. The culprit was at once seized, his neck and legs bound together, and repeated blows were laid on his back with a thick broad leather strap; on another occasion a man detected in using false measures had the measure tied round his neck and he was flogged through the chief bazaars and streets. There is no Penal Code in Yarkand but, if it be allowable to offer a suggestion on such matters, I think Indian society would rejoice if the Yarkand method of summarily punishing such rascals could find an appropriate section in the Indian Penal Code.

I have here given my first impressions of a ride through the city, but there is much more of interest which will be detailed hereafter in another part of this report.

Various rumours were spread abroad about the ultimate destination of the mission; one day we heard we should have to go to Aksu; again it was said that the ruler of the country was coming to see us at Yarkand on his way to Khoten; then it was that we were to be hurried off to Kashghar. Finally the truth came out that His Highness the Atalik Ghazi having determined to receive us with all due honor, had caused an entirely new suite of buildings to be erected for our accommodation, and as they would not be ready for some days, the fact of it being the month of fast, the Ramazan, afforded a reasonable excuse for asking us to delay our onward progress. We therefore spent a very pleasant three weeks in visiting Yarkand and the vicinity. Just outside the city on the east are extensive marshes, where ducks, geese and snipe abound and afford ample occupation to the sportsman and the naturalist. Some of our party went out for a two days excursion to shoot pheasants, and returned with the veritable burgoot, golden eagle, or bear coot as called by Atkinson whose stories about the bird, nay its very existence, have been seemingly called in question. This bird is said by Atkinson to kill bears.

We were told it would kill deer, wolves, and even large game, and, being impatient to try its powers, we took several burgoots with us to the Yarkand jheels to fly them at the large geese and herons which abound there. To our surprise and disappointment the eagles would tamely alight from the falconer's arm on to the ground and take no notice of the game. Subsequent experience taught us that the story of these birds attacking large four-footed game was perfectly true, and I shall hereafter record how I saw a large wild boar brought to bay entirely by the attack of a burgoot.

On the 22nd November we were awoke at early dawn by hearing six guns fired in honor of the Eed, and music and dancing were kept up for some hours. Syud Yakúb Khan then came to take leave of us, having been summoned by the Atalik to Kashghar. We were to follow on the 28th, and it was arranged that we should send on our heavy baggage at once by carts, we ourselves following with a light camp. Carts were supplied for this purpose. These are good substantial vehicles, on two wheels six feet in diameter, and drawn by four or six horses; one horse only is in the shafts, the leaders being harnessed abreast and driven with reins by a man sitting on the front of the cart. We were much struck by the business-like way in which the carts were loaded, every box being weighed, and the number written down, and only a certain load—ten hundredweight, allowed to be put on the cart. The animals used were the ordinary Yarkand ponies, very strong and willing, who would pull through the heaviest ground in a steady determined way, performing stages of 20 and 25 miles without apparent fatigue. When one thinks of one's experience with Indian hackeries and even dák gharries, the inevitable feeling comes over one's mind that even Indian civilization has something to learn from the wrongly called barbarous Yarkand. We afterwards found that these carts are used as omnibuses for the transport of passengers from time to time, and from our embassy quarters at Yangi Shahr we used to see such an omnibus go to and from the city of Kashghar several times a day. There are also travelling carts running regularly between Yarkand and Kashghar, making five stages in which seats are obtained at a fixed rate.

During our stay at Yarkand our relations with the Dadkhwah were of the happiest kind. By degrees he became accustomed to the idea of photography, and allowed Captains Chapman and Trotter to take likeness of his soldiers, and even admitted the camera into the court-yard of his palace, taking good care however to preserve even the skirt of his garment from falling within the range of the photographer's lens. Captain Trotter put up a sun-dial in his court-yard, and Dr. Bellew gained the hearts of the Dadkhwah and his people by his skillful operations on blind and sick patients. The day before our departure the Dadkhwah invited us to an early dinner, when the number of the respective dishes sorely tasked the appetites of the hungriest or most polite.

Sergeant Rhind won no small applause by his performance on the Highland bagpipes, but I observed that the worthy Governor of Yarkand did not bestow as much attention on the Highland costume as I expected he would do. On asking the reason, I was told that he did not like to take notice of his appearance, as evidently in his hurry to attend the Sergeant had forgotten to put on his trowsers!

Winter had quite set in when on the morning of the 28th November the British Mission left Yarkand for Kashghar. At the first 'sang' or five mile-post we crossed a wooden bridge, and rode for an hour through a well inhabited and wooded country till we came to the edge of the Karakum, literally black sandy desert. Here we were invited to alight and warm ourselves by a confortable fire in a peasant's house, and after the usual hospitality we took leave of the Dadkwah's high officials and rode across a desolate tract of sandy hillocks and marshy plain till we reached the flourishing village of Kok Robat (Blue Post-house). Here we put up in the royal oorda, or rest-house. Next morning we pursued our way prepared as we thought to face the cold, but we had not gone above a mile into the desert plain before a keenly cutting wind proved that the ordinary winter costume of Englishmen was not suited to a Yarkand climate.

A few days before, when wandering about the Yarkand bazaar, we were offered for sale fur leggings, socks, and caps, which were not sufficiently tempting to induce us to purchase, whereupon the disappointed tradesman said, in a warning voice; you will want these and more before very long. Now we had to repent the little heed we gave to his words. For three hours we had to endure the most cutting cold. As we approached Ak Robat (White Post-house) which is a hostelerie in the desert much similar to one of the rest-houses in the Egyptian desert, we were met by Khal Mohamad, the Military Governor of Yangi Hissar, with 20 horsemen who had ridden out two days' journey to escort us in with honor. Khal Mohamad is a remarkably smart looking and as we afterwards found a very intelligent and distinguished officer, and the neat martial appearance of his men and the precision with which they wheeled round and trotted ahead of us excited the approval of my military companions. The uniform of these men consisted of green velvet caps with fur inside, yellow leather coats lined with fur and trowsers of the same, neatly embroidered. The officer had a curious patch of the fur on his back in the form of a heart. This is supposed to be a distinguishing mark to his followers when he leads in battle. On alighting at Ak Robat we found, as usual, a well carpeted room with a good fire to welcome us, and soon afterwards Khal Mohamad and his followers having doffed their uniform came in, bearing smoking dishes for breakfast, and waited on us. We were now in a land of surprises, but nothing perhaps was more striking than the versatility of the soldiers of the Amir's army. When not employed on actual military duty, they turn their hand to cooking, carpentry, or any work that may require to be done, and when they march they are encumbered by no heavy baggage train. Each man carries his blanket or choga tied behind his saddle, or, when boxes or saddle bags are necessary or cooking utensils have to be carried, they are slung across the saddle, on the top of which the soldier mounts and makes a march of 30 or 40 miles a day.

From Ak Robat we rode on over the desert tract, here and there meeting signs of habitation, till we came to the village of Kizil, where we put up for the night in the royal caravanserai. As we entered the village we saw the furnaces for smelting iron which Mr. Shaw describes in his book. Dr. Stoliczka visited them; he found the ore much impregnated with lime which acts as a flux and renders possible the peculiarly simple process described by Mr. Shaw. Our next day's march was through cultivation, past the village of Toplok, and over the River Shahnoz which we crossed by a good wooden bridge built by the Atalik. Mills were worked by this stream, and here and elsewhere we saw water-power used for husking rice and other purposes. After crossing a low sandstone and conglomerate ridge, we entered the town of Yangi Hissar. The gardens and private houses here are surrounded by mud walls with crenellated tops, giving the appearance of fortifications. Passing through the main street of the bazaar, which resembles those in Yarkand, we came by the fort, which is in a plain about 300 yards from the town, and is built in the form of a rectangle, and presents a somewhat imposing appearance.

Leaving this fort to the right we were taken to a large walled garden, in which a comfortable set of quarters had been prepared for us, while Kirghiz tents were pitched inside the enclosure. The walls of the largest rooms had been neatly painted, good carpets and silk musnuds were on the floor, and tables and stools, covered with red baize and supposed to suit our English tastes, had been specially made for us.

We halted two days at Yangi Hissar, the Atalik having sent a special messenger to say that he feared we must be tired with our long march, and he therefore wished us to take rest. This was a polite form of letting us know that the arrangements for our proper reception at the capital had not been quite completed.

At Yangi Hissar we found ourselves close to the lofty range of mountains in which the Tagharma, Chish Tagh, and other towering peaks looked conspicuously grand and made us long

2.—Embassy Camp, Kashmir.

for the time to come when the Pamir should be explored. It is dangerous to advance ideas regarding geographical problems without going fully into all the details of proof, which I must reserve for some other occasion, but I think I can give reasons for supposing that the Tagharma Peak and its surrounding country is alluded to in a passage in Ezekiel, Chapter 27-14—"They of the House of Togarmah* traded in thy fairs with horses and horsemen and mules;" also Chapter 38-6—"The House of Togarmah of the north quarters, and all his bands."

We left Yangi Hissar on the 3rd December and halted for the mid-day dastarkhwan at a very picturesque kind of shooting lodge in the village of Soghlak, on the banks of a stream which was at that season dry. We passed the night at the village of Yepchan in the oorda or royal resting place.

Next morning was to see the British Mission enter the capital of Eastern Turkestan. It was a cold brisk day, and all the streams were frozen with a thin coating. The atmosphere, so often clouded by a thick impalpable dusty mist, was fortunately beautifully clear and we had a magnificent view of the giant peaks on the Alai to our left, whilst before us extended the long and comparatively speaking low range of the Tian Shan which separates Khokand and Russia from the Atalik's dominions.

At Karasu, about 5 miles from our destination, we halted to have breakfast and to put on our uniforms, after which we remounted and crossing a small bridge were met by Mirza Ahmed Kúsh-begí, one of the highest officials in the Atalik's Court who had come out with an escort of cavalry to bring us in. Mirza Ahmed is a man of some note in Central Asian history and took part in the wars with Russia which ended so disastrously for the Khokand army.

He was mounted on a fine bay horse of Andijani breed, with a saddle and bridle of remarkably neat and somewhat European pattern. As we rode along over the undulating slopes, the fort of Yangi-Shahr, the residence of the Atalik, came in view, and further on in the far distance we could discern the long low walls of the City of Kashghar, a place till then unvisited, and in fact I believe unseen, by any Englishman. As we approached Yangi-Shahr, we passed several separate enclosures which were the residences of some of the Atalik's officers, answering in a way to our barracks. At the entrance to one we saw two 9-pounder guns drawn up, in front of which a soldier with an Enfield rifle stood sentry.

Passing by the north-east corner of the fort we came in sight of the royal gateway, on the right of which and distant about 80 yards is the new Elchi Khana or embassy quarters, recently erected for our reception. Crowds of spectators here thronged the road and scanned with eager looks this novel apparition.

It is a mark of politeness in these countries to dismount in the street and not to ride inside a gateway; so, following the example of Mirza Ahmed, we left our horses outside and entered a spacious gateway, inside which on three sides were raised platforms with a fire-place to accommodate the guard. Through this we passed into a spacious quadrangle round all sides of which a broad verandah ran. On two sides doors opened into good sized rooms; a passage at the opposite side led into the inner quadrangle, on three sides of which sets of rooms for the accommodation of the members of the embassy had been neatly fitted up. The floors were well carpeted with rugs from Khoten. English velvet or broadcloth lined the walls up to the wainscoat, above which were neatly built recesses for shelves. The ceiling was papered with English or Russian paper, and the outer windows, for they were double, had neat frames with paper doing duty for glass,—an article as yet but little known to the present race, though as I afterwards found in my exploration of a buried city, glass was known and used by the inhabitants of the land 1,000 years ago. The fire-places were large and well built with gypsum plaster and had the inestimable merit of giving out a good heat without emitting smoke at the same time.

---

* Togarmah was grandson of Japhet.

The kitchen arrangements and accommodation for servants, the stables for 50 horses, and the enclosure for our baggage animals, were all in keeping and excellent, and I fear the comparison we drew between the method and ingenuity of these so-called barbarian people and of their more civilized neighbours across the Himalayas was not in favour of India.

Whilst we were settling ourselves in our new quarters, Ihrar Khan Tora, the same person who came to India as Envoy from the Atalik in 1871-72, called to enquire after our health and to request that we would at once present ourselves before his master. Fortunately our baggage animals, which being always lightly loaded were accustomed to keep pretty well up with us, soon arrived and we were speedily ready to obey the summons. Mounting on horses, we rode across the moat and inside the large gateway, and after passing a small quadrangle found ourselves in an open space, on one side of which was a large mosque and other buildings, and in the left front the Atalik's palace. According to etiquette we dismounted at about 40 paces from the gateway and walked slowly along with Ihrar Khan, the Yasawal-bashi or head chamberlain with white wand in hand going ahead. In the outer gateway soldiers were seated on a dais, with their fire-arms laid on the ground before them, their arms folded and their eyes cast on the ground. We then crossed obliquely an empty court-yard and, passing through a second gateway filled with soldiers, crossed another court on all sides of which soldiers in gay costumes were ranged seated. From this court we passed into the penetralia, a small court, in which not a soul was visible and everywhere a deathlike stillness prevailed. At the further end of this court was a long hall with several window doors. Ihrar Khan then led us in single file, with measured tread, to some steps at the side of the hall, and, entering almost on tip-toe, looked in and returning beckoned with his hand to me to advance alone. As I approached the door he made a sign for me to enter, and immediately withdrew. I found myself standing at the threshold of a very common looking room, perfectly bare of all ornament and with not a very good carpet on the floor: looking about, I saw enter at a doorway on the opposite side, a tall stout man, plainly dressed. He beckoned with his hand and I advanced thinking that it must be a chamberlain who was to conduct me to 'the presence.' Instinctively however I made a bow as I advanced and soon found myself taken by both hands and saluted with the usual form of politeness, and I knew that I was standing before the far-famed ruler of Eastern Turkestan. After a few words of welcome the Atalik led me across the room and seated me near him by the side of a window. At this moment a salute of 15 guns was fired. His Highness asked in an eager tone after the health of Her Majesty and of the Viceroy, and soon afterwards called in a low voice to Ihrar Khan to bring in the other officers. They came in one by one, and each was shaken by the hand and made to sit down by my side. Then there was a long and somewhat trying pause, during which the Atalik eyed each one of us with intent scrutiny; I had been told that etiquette forbade the guest to speak much on the first interview, and that it was a point of good manners to sit perfectly still, with downcast eyes.

When it is remembered that the oriental posture requires the visitor to sit upon his heels, with feet well flattened under him, the excrutiating agony of having to keep perfectly unmoved in this position for perhaps half an hour will be appreciated.

After this silent ordeal had been undergone for some time, at a sign from the Atalik 16 soldiers came in with the dastarkhwan, and the Atalik breaking a loaf of bread shared it with us. After the cloth was removed, we, remembering our lesson in manners, rose up and stroking our beards said 'Allah o Akbar,' soon after which the Atalik said 'Khush-amadeed' 'you are welcome.' This was the signal for us to be released from our agonising position, and we shook hands and departed. During the interview Ihrar Khan stood by the door at the further end of the room, it not being etiquette for any one to be near enough to hear any thing that passes between the ruler and his guest.

According to the etiquette of the country, after having thus paid our respects to the ruler, it was considered proper for us to remain quiet in our own quarters for a few days. Some of our followers however went to the city of Kashghar to make purchases, and found themselves the object of eager curiosity, while crowds thronged round calling them 'English.' The fact is that so very little intercourse has taken place between India and the people of Kashghar that they knew scarcely anything of us.

On the day following our first interview, His Highness went out to pay his devotions at the shrine of a celebrated Saint Huzrat Afák, and, a day or two later, returned with the new dignity of Amir and title of Khan which had been brought to him by Syud Yakúb Khan from Constantinople. Henceforth then the Atalik Ghazi, Yakúb Beg, was to be known as the Amir Mohamad Yakúb Khan of Kashghar, coins were struck and prayers recited in the name of Sultan Abdul Aziz Khan, and on the name of the coin the words Zurb-i-Mahrusa-i-Kashghar 'Mint of the protected country of Kashghar,' were struck.

The 11th December having been fixed for the formal reception of the British Mission, Ihrar Khan came over from the palace with one hundred men to carry the presents, and himself to conduct us to the presence chamber. Her Majesty's letter, enclosed in a magnificent casket of pale yellow quartz clamped with gilt bands and handles and bossed with onyx stones, was carried by Sergeant Rhind, who was followed by the Havildar of the Guide Escort bearing His Excellency the Viceroy's letter in a richly enamelled casket, officers and escort followed in procession on horseback. On dismounting and approaching the gateway, all the Amir's guard stood up. The ceremony of approaching the Amir was the same as on the former occasion. His pleasure at receiving this mark of Her Majesty's favor was visible in his brightened countenance, and, as the letters were delivered, he frequently repeated Alhumdulilla, 'God be praised,' adding "you have conferred a great favor on me. I am honored by the receipt of a letter from the Queen. I am highly gratified." The presents were then passed before him in review and conveyed into an inner apartment. The usual dastarkhwan was spread before us, and in course of conversation the Amir remarked—"Your Queen is a great sovereign. Her government is a powerful and beneficent one. Her friendship is to be desired as it always proves a source of advantage to those who possess it. The Queen is as the sun in whose genial rays such poor people as I flourish. I particularly desire the friendship of the English. It is essential to me. Your rule is just. The road is open to every one, and from here to London any one can come and go with perfect freedom."

The Amir then desired us to consider his country as our home, and to do just what we liked without any hesitation; all his officers had been warned, he said, to show every attention to the royal guests. On my expressing a desire to see his troops, he said, you have only to name the day and you can see whatever you like.

On the 13th December we paid our first visit to the City of Kashghar.

The distance is about five miles through a cultivated and populous tract all the way. At first the road passes amongst a number of detached and semi-fortified enclosures used as barracks for the Amir's troops and their families. They are neat quadrangular structures, with crenellated walls and defensible gateways, and are capable of accommodating from fifty to sixty families each. Between them are corn-fields and parade-grounds intersected by irrigation canals and dotted in all directions by butts for musketry practice.

Beyond these the road drops in the wide bed of the Kizil Sú, or "Red River," and is here carried across a long stretch of water-logged land by a wide causeway built of faggots laid with earth and planted with willow trees. It conducts to the bridge across the river, a rough wooden structure supported on two piers between the banks and protected by railings on each side. Beyond the bridge the road lies over higher ground to the city, about a mile distant, and leaves some ancient ruins a little way off to the right. They attract attention from the height and massive structure of the fortifications of the old citadel, the outlines of which are still very fairly represented in the existing remains.

Aski Shahr, or "Ancient city" (the ruins, amidst which are gardens and orchards and huts)—in contradistinction to Kuhna Shahr, or "Old City" (the present town of Kashghar), and Yangi Shahr, or "New City" (the residence of the Amir and his Court)—was a flourishing seat of trade with China in the time of Wang Khan, the predecessor in these parts of Chengiz Khan. It was noted for the strength of its fortifications and for many centuries successfully resisted the attacks of successive conquerors. At this time the ramparts are about thirty feet high, and twelve paces wide at top; the bastions, which were built up of successive layers of mud cement, project some forty paces from the rampart walls and still show the marks of connection with them by means of covered passages or galleries one above the other. At least such was our solution of the meaning of the regular lines of rafter sockets (decayed wood was found *in situ* in one of them) that at intervals of six or seven feet run horizontally round these bastions.

To Iskandar Mirza, a grandson of the Amir Timur, is assigned the credit of having reduced this famous stronghold by diverting the Kizil Sú against its walls. A main branch of the river certainly does flow where the east face of the city walls ought to stand, and so far accounts for their disappearance, and gives support to a tradition connected therewith. It is to the effect that the defenders, on seeing the means resorted to by the enemy for their reduction, gave up all for lost, and at once sought means of escape from the vengeance their obstinate resistance had provoked. By a counterstratagem on the part of their Chiefs, they were enabled under cover of darkness to escape to the cities in the direction of the Marálbáshi and Táklamakán unobserved by the enemy, who too late discovered that the sounds of activity proceeding from within the walls were produced by the only living creatures left there—a number of camels with rattle-drums fixed on their necks, scampering wildly through the deserted streets—the unwitting agents of their own protracted terror, the people's hurried escape, and the enemy's destructive rage. And so the celebrated Káshghar of the time of Wang Khan was reduced to ruins.

From the bridge we passed through a thin suburb to the city, which is considerably smaller than that of Yarkand. It is enclosed within high walls strengthened by buttress bastions at short intervals, and surrounded by a deep ditch. The entrance on the south side is through three gateways, one within the other and at different angles, into the main bazar. The centre gate has folding doors plated with iron, and is kept by a guard of fifty soldiers, whom we found seated on each side of the roadway with prong-rest rifles set before them. Our progress through the bazaar was slow owing to the dense crowd of market people thronging the thoroughfare, and the circumstance afforded us a good opportunity for judging of the condition of the general community and observing the different types of nationality. Compared with similar scenes in Yarkand, one is struck by the remarkably robust and healthy look of the people and the almost entire absence of goitre which is there nearly universal: and next, by the large proportion of pure Chinese faces amongst the general crowd of Uzbaks, Tajiks, and Tunganis: whilst here too, as there, the generally excellent clothing, the good-will, the order and the activity characterizing the crowd did not fail to attract our notice.

Arrived at the Dadkhwah's residence, we passed through a succession of courts similar to those of the Governor's residence at Yarkand and the Amir's palace here—each with its guard of soldiers clad in the national *choga* and loose silk robe splashed boldly broadly and bluntly with all the colours of the brightest rainbow and seated along the walls with downcast heads and solemn looks, amidst silence perfect.

The Dadkhwah met us in the verandah of his audience-hall and after salutation conducted us to the seats prepared expressly for us at the upper part of the room. These were high-backed arm-chairs, cushioned and covered with scarlet cloth or purple plush. All were ranged round two sides of a large square table covered with the rainbow pattern silks before alluded to. Our host took his seat on a divan near us, welcomed us warmly to Kashghar, and begged we would pardon any omissions on his part, as he had never had the pleasure of meeting any of our people before and was consequently ignorant of our customs, and assured us it was his desire to please and do us honour.

Alish Beg is an active little man, of very pleasing manners, and bright intelligent features of a strongly Tartar cast. His hospitality was so profuse that our united efforts made small impression on the array of five score and five dishes and trays and bowls of stews, pilaos, pastry, sweets and fruits, &c., set before us. The fact did not escape the notice of our host and drew from him the remark that we would probably address ourselves more freely to the feast before us if relieved of the ceremonial restraints of his presence, and he consequently withdrew on the plea of some pressing business to transact, begging us the while to consider his house and grounds as our own.

With this liberty we passed an agreeable afternoon in the garden attached to the Residency, though its trees were leafless, its tanks frozen, and kiosks deserted. In the full foliage of summer it must be a delightful retreat. In this garden we found a heap of copper ore recently brought in from some hills to the north of the city. A sample of it was subsequently submitted for Dr. Stoliczka's opinion, and was found by him on analysis to be a copper pyrites capable of yielding twenty-five per cent. of the pure metal.

Towards sunset we took leave of our host, highly gratified at the cordial reception and hospitable entertainment he had provided for us, and galloped back to our quarters, passing on the road an active tide of traffic to and fro between the old and new cities. Most were on horseback, or mounted on donkies, and very few on foot, whilst no small number found accommodation in the "omnibus" carts that ply daily on this road. These are covered waggons, drawn by four horses, one between the shafts and three abreast in front: they carry from twelve to sixteen passengers huddled together any fashion: they make three or four journeys a day, and the charge is thirteen *pul*, or about two pence English, each way.

On the 18th instant, we attended a review of the Khatai or Chinese troops in the service of the Amir. There are, we were told, some three thousand odd of these representatives of the recently ruling race now in the Amir's army. They are of course all forcible converts to Islam, have been deprived of their "pigtails," amongst several other privileges, and are kept separate from the other troops in a fortified barrack of their own. Their arms, organization, and discipline too are quite distinct, and maintained in their own Chinese fashion under a Chief called Kho-dalai.

At the review we found twenty-eight companies, of fifty men each, on the ground. They were disposed in two divisions opposite to each other, and at the head of each company were carried two standards of triangular shape and bright colour, one at the head of each file of twenty-five men. Their only weapon is a large, heavy smooth-bore, set in a wooden socket, and very much like an ordinary duck-gun. It is called *tyfu*, is carried on the shoulders of two men, the foremost acting as a rest or support, and is served by three others, *viz.*, one to carry ammunition and load, a second who carries a long ramrod tipped with a bunch of horse hair to clean the gun and complete loading, and the third as supernumerary and stop-gap in case of casualty. There are ten of these *tyfu* guns with each company.

In front of each division, as they stood facing each other drawn up in contiguous columns of companies, were posted a half company each of spearmen, with their heads bound with handkerchiefs, the ends fluttering in the wind, of archers helmeted after the fashion of the stage, and of "tigers," men clad throughout in yellow, streaked with broad bars of black, and topped above with a pair of neat ears. These last carried large circular shields gaudily painted with dragons and other hideous monsters on one side and concealing on the other a gunbarrel set in a socket of wood, and serving also as a handle whereby to carry the shield. All these three classes wore short side-swords.

Midway between the two divisions stood the band, composed of a big drum carried in a framework sedan by two porters, and attended on each side by lesser drums, with players of flageolet, bugle, and cymbals. With the band stood the commandant, the Kho-dalai, attended by a number of fuglemen, one of whom carried a large flag and the rest small ones.

Such was the appearance and disposition of the Khatai force as we found it on reaching the parade ground. At a signal from the Kho-dalai, the head fugleman waved his flag and all the little flags ran out to their proper places and waved likewise. And presently, without any sound being uttered, the kaleidoscope began to work. Companies, following their standards, crossed, recrossed, and interlaced and finally resolved themselves into a long straight line. Another wave of the flags, and the javelin-men, archers and "tigers" bounded to the front, gesticulating, capering and cutting antics in an absurdly grotesque manner, ending with the line of "tigers" dispersing the enemy's cavalry by crouching under cover of their shields, and suddenly starting up with a yell and flourish of their dragons. The enemy's horse is supposed to have re-formed and again come to the charge, and the "tigers" run together in small groups of five or six within a circle of their shields: suddenly the shields part asunder with a volley, arms and legs and darting dragons flash before one's sight, and the whole line of skirmishers disappears behind the main line, from which the *tyfu* men now come into action. A rapid and well-maintained fire runs up and down the line for a few minutes, and then the "tigers," &c. again appear in the front, playing their swords upon stragglers and wounded of the repulsed enemy, and stopping now and again to scare away some rallying horseman with a crouch and a bound, or with a roll and a shout.

In this style a variety of manœuvres were performed, such as forming line, changing front, volley and independent firing, skirmishing, &c., whilst a retreat was covered by rockets and fuse torpedoes. The expenditure of powder was unstinted, and the *tout ensemble* of the spectacle highly dramatic. On the conclusion of the review, we were entertained by the Kho-dalai at a very *recherché* Chinese *dejeuner* in a marquee on the ground.

Whilst thus engaged, the athletes and mountebanks of the regiment went through some of their performances for our amusement. The exercises with the sword, battle-axe, and javelin were very cleverly performed and with extreme rapidity, though their merit was not apparent since they seemed dangerous only to the performer. The single stick, cudgelling, kicking and tumbling were laughable, as much by reason of the dumpy forms and squab features of the actors, as by their activity and merry gestures. The performances ended with a burlesque acted by the "tigers." A champion engages one of them. He is put to flight and takes refuge behind the barricades of his comrades' shields. The victor pursues and boldly rushes up the sloping bank of shields. A puff of smoke, a rolling body, and a corpse, theatrically stiff, borne away by head and heels, ushers in the finale. The band plays, the standards come to the front, the companies range themselves in their places and there we left them. Groups of them afterwards attended at our Residency to be photographed and sketched. At our Christmas games, we had an opportunity of seeing their target practice with the *tyfu*. Their shooting at two hundred and fifty yards' range was remarkably good, considering the nature of the weapon and its mode of use, and is no doubt attributable to the daily practice that goes on at the numerous butts in the vicinity.

We also witnessed the artillery practice of a battery under the command of a Panjabi, who has for many years been a naturalized subject of Khokand and latterly of Kashghar. Amongst his men are many Kashmiris, Panjabis and Afghans, and oddly enough the words of command are given in English.

The small escort of guides, cavalry and infantry, attached to the Embassy, were present on the ground, and everywhere conspicuous in the crowd of troops, by their smart set-up and soldierly bearing. They drew to themselves no small share of attention, and by the deference paid to them were evidently looked upon as friends. The Snider practice of the infantry was only appreciated by the few who knew the weapon, but the *neza-bazi* and sword-cutting of the cavalry excited a lively interest, and many were the murmurs of applause that greeted the successful passes, as trooper after trooper carried away the peg, or sliced the turnips set up in a row. Fortunately for our credit, the men entered keenly the lists and acquitted themselves very creditably.

The Khokandi horsemen are strangers to this mode of using the spear and sword: and on this occasion unreservedly expressed their admiration. We had in the early part of the day seen their practice at a cap stuck on a short stick. It consists in loading and firing at full gallop at the mark indicated, but the movements were so clumsy and slow, and the aim so very much at random, that it barely deserves mention. The Khokand soldier, though nearly always seen on horseback, does not fight except on foot, and even for this his native arms and dress are but ill-adapted, and consequently they are not skilful in feats of arms. A game more to their taste however is *ulak*, a scramble on horseback, for the possession of a sheep on its passage from the starting point to the goal. It is carried in the lap, and is snatched from one to another with more roughness and energy than with skilful horsemanship.

At the conclusion of the games, we were entertained at luncheon by the commandant of artillery before mentioned, Nabbi Bakhsh, Jemadar, who received us in his own house, and seemed as well pleased with the day's proceedings as we were, all the result of a well-timed compliment on the excellence of his mortar practice. The afternoon was well advanced when we took our leave and sought the shelter of our own quarters, for the keen frosty air we had been exposed to since the morning had become painfully numbing.

On the 20th December the Treaty of commerce was presented for the Amir's acceptance, on which occasion His Highness expressed very warmly his desire to avail himself of European science for the improvement of his country, and his determination to render every facility to traders.

Up to the time of our arrival at Kashghar, the daily wants of our camp had been supplied by our hosts with the most profuse liberality. But now that we had taken up our quarters for the winter, I considered it proper, in accordance with the instructions received from the Viceroy, to endeavour to relieve the Amir from the heavy burdens of such unbounded hospitality. This caused a lively negotiation, it being a point of honor with our kindly hosts to allow us to incur no expense of any kind; they were even anxious to supply gratis all the articles of curiosity &c., which we purchased in the bazaar. Let me not be understood however to imply that in such a case the tradespeople would have been the sufferers, for it is a fact well worthy of prominent notice, that on all occasions, wherever we went and drew supplies from the Ameer's officials, the people were always properly paid, the Yuzbashi or other officer in charge of our party having been provided with cash for the purpose. I shall have occasion to mention hereafter, an instance, which came under our immediate observation, of the people being paid fully for work done for the State, thus justifying the opinion we had formed that there is less oppression practised on the peasants in the kingdom of Kashghar than probably in any other country in Asia.

After much discussion the daily Zyafat or allowance for our mission was fixed as follows :—

  60 charaks* Indian corn,
  50 donkey loads straw, } for our horses and baggage mules.
  200 bundles Lucerne grass

  10 charaks rice
  6 ditto flour } for our followers.
  20 loads firewood
  3 sheep
  300 Tungas† for the officer's mess.

Besides this liberal allowance of food, suits of furs and other warm clothing were supplied to every member of the embassy, and once or twice a week a profusion of every kind of fruit, game (deer, pheasants, partridges, ducks,) and fish, &c., was sent to the mission.

As the Amir had given permission for us to go where we liked, and suggested the idea of our going to some of his outlying forts on shooting excursions, accompanying this offer with permission to make free use of our scientific instruments, Lieutenant-Colonel Gordon left Kashghar on the 31st December accompanied by Captain Trotter and Dr. Stoliczka, on a visit to Chadyr Kul in the Tian Shan range; whilst Captain Biddulph went off in another direction to visit the forest of Maralbashi. A full account of these excursions is given in another part of this report, so I need not enter upon the details here.

If space permitted me, it would be interesting to the general public to give a lengthened description of our ordinary life during a most pleasant sojourn of nearly four months at the capital of the Amir. But I can only here give a passing notice of our friendly intercourse with the chief officers of his Court, who entertained us at their houses, and accepted our hospitality in return. The intensity of the winter, with a thermometer which for many weeks descended some degrees below zero, and frequently did not mount above freezing point in the sun, prevented us from moving about very freely, but it afforded us a good opportunity of shewing to the astonished inhabitants the skill of some and the clumsiness of others of our party in the science of skating.

---

* Charak = 16lbs.   † 4½ Tunga = 1 Rupee.

Our relations with our good friends the Kashgharians were of the pleasantest nature, unmoved by a single contretemps, and it is with pleasure and pride I record the fact that no single instance of altercation occurred between any of our followers and the people of the country. The system which I had enforced from the outset, of having the roll called twice a day, and of not allowing any of our followers to leave the precincts of the embassy quarters without permission, had an admirable effect in checking misconduct, and inspired confidence in the Amir's officials that no abuse of their kind hospitality would be allowed.

A remarkable proof of their confidence was afforded in the popularity of the dispensary which Dr. Bellew established in one of the courts of our embassy. As we travelled along from Sanju to Yarkand, Syud Yakúb Khan shrewdly observed that the skill of an English physician would do as much as anything else to cause the people to look favorably on our mission, and as we rode past the villages on our route, he would enquire what sick there were, and brought them out for Dr. Bellew's inspection. This was somewhat a trial for medical skill, for in the majority of cases, the patients suffered from diseases inseparable from old age, and the gift of renovating youth is denied to human skill. But in the treatment of eye diseases and in performing sundry surgical operations at Yarkand, Dr. Bellew was happily successful so that his fame preceded him to Kashghar, and when we had erected two spacious Kirghiz tents in the embassy quarters, patients of both sexes flocked daily for treatment. Dr. Bellew's account of his work in this department will be read with great interest.

Syud Yakúb Khan, whose enlightenment and freedom from all prejudice, facilitated greatly all our proceedings, and augurs well for the advancement of this interesting country, was particularly desirous to avail himself of the scientific knowledge of our lamented friend Dr. Stoliczka, though I regret to say that untoward circumstances prevented our geologist from having full scope for the prosecution of his pursuits. And I lament that his hand no longer remains to record the result of such enquiries as he was enabled to make. From some notes however, which he gave at my request to the Amir, I am able to give the following analysis of coal and metals, &c., which were brought for his inspection.

I. Copper ore brought from the Alai range.

This proved to be sulphuret of copper and iron, generally known as copper pyrites. It contains—

Copper 30%
Iron 35%
Sulphur 35%

It is a good copper ore, being brittle, and yielding easily to the hammer. The impurities of the ore are small, silica, alumina, mica and magnetic iron. These may be calculated at 20 per cent. So that out of 100 lbs. of rock, 80 lbs. of pyrites ought to be got, and from this again 23 lbs. of pure copper.

II. Coal from the range west of Kashghar.

This contains:—

Ash 13%
Volatile matter including water ... 40%   } Total combustible
Fixed carbon ... ... 47%   } matter 87%

This is good coal, exceeding the average of Indian coal by having a comparatively moderate proportion of ash. This is a fine pale reddish powder the color being caused by a small quantity of iron oxide. The coal is deep shining black with a splintery fracture. The large quantity of volatile matter would make it a fair coal for obtaining gas, but it is very slightly caking.

III. Coal from Turfan:

Ash 20%
Volatile matter, *i.e.*, water ... 39% } Combustible matter
Fixed carbon ... ... 41% } 80 per cent.

3.—Durbar Tent, visit of the Maharajah to the British Envoy.

This is a fair coal, black with a somewhat dull earthy fracture. The ash is greyish white with bluish specks, a caking coal. Both these coals are particularly free from pyrites.

IV. Copper from west of Kashghar.

A piece of soft sandstone of a pale reddish color poorly disseminated with carbonate of copper, not more than 24 per cent. of copper being procurable.

V. Galena from west of Kashghar.

A remarkably pure galena evidently occurring in a white quartoze comparatively soft rock which adheres to the ore only in small quantities. The pure galena is composed of 85·55 per cent. of lead and 13·45 of sulphur. In the most perfect process as much as $84\frac{3}{4}$ per cent. of lead was obtained from galena, but the usual yield is from 75 to 80 per cent. This includes silver, if any be present, which is very often the case; in fact galena is generally argentiferous, but the process to ascertain the percentage of that precious metal is complicated and lengthy, and larger specimens than those submitted are required for examination.

On the 2nd February His Highness the Ameer put his seal to the Treaty of Commerce which had been prepared for his acceptance, and thus the object of our mission was happily accomplished. But as the winter season was still in all its severity, it was necessary to delay our departure for India for some time. Meanwhile, I determined to take advantage of the Amir's offer to show us somewhat of his country, and on the 14th February Dr. Bellew, Captains Chapman and Trotter, and Dr. Stoliczka started with me on an excursion to the Artysh District north of Kashghar. Snow had fallen a day or two before, and the cold was intense, but the bright clear atmosphere enabled us to have a magnificent panoramic view, and was useful to Captain Trotter in disclosing sundry peaks and ranges of hills.

As far as Awat, about six miles, we rode through thick cultivation. Awat itself is a large village. Here we came upon saline soil and passed over barren ground till we reached the shrine of Mahram Khoja, daughter of Sultan Satuk Boghra Khan, who was buried here about 800 years ago and regarding whom mention will be found in the history of Kashghar. The present Amir has erected a very neat tomb over her grave and built a set of houses or rooms for pilgrims. This he has done in the case of all saints and martyrs of note all over his country, thus acquiring a character for sanctity. Fine tall poplars grow in the shrine enclosure. After a short halt here, we resumed our ride over undulating ground, leaving the village of Beshkirim to our left, and crossing two streams till we came to the foot of a low gravel and sandstone ridge, which we crossed and then descended into the Artysh valley. This valley is studded with small hamlets, and in the centre is the bazar of Altun or Golden Artysh, where is the tomb of Satuk Boghra Khan, the first Chief of the country who embraced Islamism in the tenth century and imposed the new religion on the inhabitants. His mausoleum, a rather imposing structure of sun-dried bricks faced with green tiles, was built in its present form about 44 years ago. Several masonry buildings have been erected by the present Amir for the priests and pilgrims who frequent the shrine, and there is a large school attached to it.

The Governor of the Artysh district, Mohamad Khan Khoja, a descendant of Satuk Boghra Khan, received us very politely and conducted us to comfortable quarters in the royal oorda. On the following day, the usual weekly bazar was held at Artysh and we witnessed a lively scene. As we passed through the streets on the day of our arrival, the place looked deserted with its closed shops, empty verandahs, and not a soul stirring. To-day everything was changed.

About 2,000 people thronged every street and lane, and all intent on business: blacksmiths shoeing horses, mending spades and vessels; women selling cotton, raw and in thread; sheep and oxen being sold, and meat in large quantities hung up for sale. The restaurants opened for the day drove a thriving trade. The most lively scene was in the cloth markets, where merchants from Kashghar were to be seen purchasing cotton cloths for export to Almaty (Fort Vernoye in Russia). These cloths are of rather coarse texture, but very strong and useful. Hundreds of men were offering these for sale, and the trade though most brisk was conducted in a much less noisy manner and with less haggling than one is accustomed to find in an Indian bazar. Traders in Russian chintzes and Khokand cutlery occupied the veranda in one street and did business in a more leisurely manner. All transactions were for cash an Tungas were the circulating medium. The whole business of the market was over and ever body had left the place by early evening.

These weekly markets are a remarkable feature in Central Asia. Colonel Yule in h 'Book of Marco Polo,' remarks that "market days are not usual in Upper India or Cabul b are universal in Badakshan and the Oxus Provinces. The bazars are only open on those da and the people from the surrounding country then assemble to exchange goods, generally l barter." Marco Polo in his Chapter LIII. mentions a great market held at a large place the road to the kingdom of Mien, when the people of the country round come on fixed da three times a week and hold a market. In the Shan towns visited by Major Sladen, he fou markets held every fifth day. This custom, he says, is borrowed from China and is gener throughout Western Yunan. Burnes, in his travels to Bokhara, mentions arriving at Karra a village 16 miles distant from Kursbee on a market day, "for in the towns of Turkista they hold their bazars on stated days as in Europe. We met many people proceeding to th thing, but not a single individual on foot—all were equestrians. A stranger is amused seeing a horse literally converted into a family conveyance, and a man jogging along with h wife behind him. The ladies are of course veiled like most females in this country: the prefer blue cloths to white as in Cabul, and are sombre looking figures." This correspon very much with the Kashghar custom, except that the ladies, who have the reputatio of being independent and disposed to have the upper hand, are not content to ri meekly behind their husbands, but generally have their own pony, on which perhaps ma be seen paniers full of melons, on top of which the woman rides astride with a child behin while the husband follows more humbly mounted on a donkey.*

Having expressed a desire to see something of Kirghiz life in the interior, we found ever arrangement made for a ten-days' trip, by our friend Mohamad Khan Khoja, who sent h younger son, Moosa Khan, to take care of us. Moosa Khan is a fine manly intelligent yout of two and twenty, a keen sportsman, and, as we found, a most pleasant companion.

Leaving the valley of Artysh, we passed through a gorge into an immense valley whic comes down from the Terek pass, and then entered the Tungi Tar or narrow defile as its nam implies. Here we found a good line of fortifications erected on a well selected point, where few resolute men could keep a large body of invaders in check.

Passing through this defile, along the frozen river bed, over which the wintry blast cam with cutting force, we emerged upon a very broad valley almost wide enough to be called plain, on the other side of which rose the snow clad peaks of the Aksai range, and we saw t Tian Shan mountains before us in all their glory. It was impossible not to feel a strong thri when beholding this magnificent scene. On the lofty plateau, and on the nothern slopes, li Atbashi, the great grazing ground of the Kirghiz tribes, and there was the trysting place the nomad Chiefs, who every spring, as we are told by the author of the *Rozaat-i-sufa*, assen bled to hold their *kurultai*, or open air parliament, to settle their affairs, and to arrange plan for the summer's campaign. The plain on which we found ourselves was said to be we grassed in summer, but at the time of our visit was covered with snow. Here and there a fe scattered domes of mud or sun-dried bricks told the last resting place of Kirghiz Chiefs. I the sheltered corner of a valley, a cluster of round felt tents might be seen, and as we rod

---

* NOTE.—In America the conversion of the animal into a family conveyance seems to be more complete tha anywhere else, if we may believe the following account given in the *Times*:—A FAMILY PONY.—"Yesterday says a Southern Colorado paper, "we saw a man, a woman, a goodsized boy, two babies, five or six blanket a buffalo robe, and two strings of chili on a single pony. Every available inch from his ears to the ro of his tail was 'taken.' The poor animal was very small; thin as a towel rack; of a sickly, pale colou and one fore leg was about five inches shorter than the others—the knee joint of that leg was very larg and we supposed that the missing part of the leg was driven in there by the weight above, so that whe it was relieved the leg would stretch out again like a turtle's head. In fact, nearly all his legs were shor and the crookedest convention of legs that we ever saw. Taken altogether, it was the most amusing horse an load we ever saw. Incredible as it may seem, the wiry little animal passed us on a trot."

through the encampment the elders and the women would come forward with friendly curiosity to watch the novel invasion and to offer milk.

With ready hospitality they pitched felt tents for our reception, and kindled large fires, and then began the usual drinking of innumerable cups of tea. At night the cold was intense, the thermometer falling to 20° below zero, and was considerably aggravated by a cutting wind which found its way through the well-worn felt walls of the tents.

In this way we journeyed for several days, whiling away the time on the march with hawking hares (one hawk killed seven hares in one morning), till we came to Ayak Sughun, where we joined the direct road from Kashghar to Ush Turfan. Here Captain Trotter and Dr. Stoliczka left us to explore the country in the direction of Ush, and an account of their travels will be found elsewhere. We descended the valley leading to the plain of Artysh and came to the village of Kulti Yailak, and thence returned by Altun Artysh to Kashghar. At Kulti Yailak, while wandering through the dense grass jungle in search of pheasants, we suddenly came upon a splendid wild boar, in size far surpassing any that could be seen in India, and then it was that we had ocular proof of the powers of the burgoot. Flying at his prey he struck the boar on the hind quarters with his talons and so completely bothered and perplexed the animal, that he was brought to bay, when our Kashghar companions with young Moosa Khan at their head eagerly belaboured him with sticks, till he received his *coup de grace* from a rifle. Hunting with the spear is not known to these people and those which some of our party brought with them in the hope of sport were broken on the road.

But pleasant though our sojourn had been at Kashghar, we looked anxiously forward to the time when we could resume our ordinary travels. At one time we had hopes of making an extended exploration of the country in the north-east as far even as Lake Lóp. But various reasons combined to prevent the prosecution of these plans, and as all our business had been satisfactorily concluded, and we were a heavy expense to our generous host, I took occasion, soon after our return from Artysh to Kashghar, to press for permission to depart.

During our absence from Kashghar, the heir-apparent, Beg-Kuli-Beg, had returned from the north-east frontier, where he had successfully commanded his father's troops in engagements at Manass and other places. On my offering to pay my respects to him, an invitation was sent for all the officers to a *dejeuner* at his house in the fort, at which Syud Yakúb Khan also was present and acted as Turki interpreter for me, though I may mention that Colonel Gordon and Dr. Bellew, and notably the latter, had acquired a fair knowledge of that language during our stay. Beg-Kuli-Beg is a fine young man of about 27 years, somewhat like his father in build and height. He seemed rather shy at first, but displayed intelligence in his remarks, and was evidently interested to learn all about the first *Feringees* whom he had seen.

On the 16th March we had an interview with the Amir to take formal leave, on which occasion he reiterated his expressions of friendship and his earnest desire to cement the alliance thus favorably begun.

On the following day we took our departure from Kashghar, under the usual salute, and were accompanied part of the first stage by Syud Yakúb Khan and Ihrar Khan. On the 18th we reached Yangi Hissar, whence I despatched Lieutenant-Colonel Gordon, Captains Biddulph and Trotter and Dr. Stoliczka to proceed to Wakhan; Ressaidar Afzul Khan went ahead to announce their approach. I had sent Ibrahim Khan on the 1st January to Cabul with letters to Amir Sher Ali, in the hope that it might have been arranged that the mission should return to India *viâ* Badakshan and Cabul, but was in ignorance of the threatened troubles arising out of the disagreement between the Amir and his son Yakúb Khan. Lieutenant-Colonel Gordon was instructed by me to proceed no further than Wakhan till joined by me, and in the event of an unfavorable reply being received from Affghanistan, to retrace his steps to India by Yarkand and Ladakh. How well Lieutenant-Colonel Gordon carried out the expedition entrusted to his charge will be seen from his own account which is appended to this narrative.

It is no easy matter to arrange for the transport of so large a party as ours was across the Karakorum, and the month which was spent by Dr. Bellew, Captain Chapman and myself at Yangi Hisar was not more than sufficient time to enable me to complete my arrangements.

To Captain Chapman, in addition to his work as Secretary, had fallen the duty of providing the carriage and making all other necessary arrangements such as are comprehended in the Quarter-Master-General's department, and it is only due to this officer that I should prominently notice the complete success of his careful management. He thoroughly equipped Lieutenant-Colonel Gordon's party for the Pamir expedition, and aided by Tara Sing laid out all supplies and provided animals for our return journey to India. Owing to the judicious care taken of our bagagge mules and ponies, and the strict supervision exercised, we were able to bring our animals over the severe passes to Ladakh, not only without serious loss, but even in fair condition, thus proving that this journey, though unquestionably one of the most difficult undertakings, can be accomplished without any of the disasters which render the Karakorum route so generally abhorred.

During a month's stay at Yangi Hissar, we visited all the places of local interest in the vicinity, and on one occasion Dr. Bellew accompanied me on an excursion to Oordum Padshah, one of the most celebrated places of pilgrimage in the country. Riding for three hours in a N.-E. direction through a well cultivated country to the village of Saigoon, we suddenly were plunged into the great desert. Our route then lay over hilly ground and wide plains. Here and there we saw small wells covered over with huts to protect them from sand storms. The water in all was very brackish. At one well there was a large tomb and kind of hospice, where the man in charge, following the usual custom, came out with a large loaf of black bread on a trencher, and offered tea. At 5 P.M., after a ride of 35 miles we came to the shrine of Huzrat Begum, said to be the daughter of a 'Rúm' Padshah. Here we found a regular hospice, with an inner court-yard and four or five rooms for the better class of pilgrims. Outside are numerous rooms in a spacious court-yard for common folk, and a separate cluster of houses for the servants of the shrine. The Sheikh, or head of the establishment, is Shah Muksood, an old man of 87, very hale and jovial looking. He said he had never been beyond the first village in his life, and certainly therefore could never have tasted a drop of sweet water.

We learned that there was a ruined city not far off which belonged to Tokta Rashid, an Uigur Chief, and which had been destroyed by Arslan Khan more than 800 years ago. Starting next morning with spades and pickaxes, we determined to see what remains of former civilization could be dug up, and after a weary search found broken pieces of pottery, bits of copper, broken glass and China, and two coins, one of which is partly decipherable, and appears to belong to a very early period. The discovery of glass here is remarkable, for there is none used now-a-days, and the art of making it seems wholly unknown. We then rode in a N.-W. direction for about 12 miles to Oordum Padshah. Our route lay first over a low sandstone ridge, whence we descended into a genuine sea of sand. The billows of sand, sometimes 50 and 70 feet high, flowed like a storm-tossed sea over the hard desert; here and there dry land as it were, in the shape of hard soil, appearing. The invariable direction of the sand was from N.-W. to S.-E. About half way we came to a deserted 'Lungur,' or traveller's rest-house, partially buried in a huge sand hill which was gradually creeping over it. This Lungur was built about 90 years ago, and has been abandoned for 30 years, but has all the appearance of having been used and kept in fresh repair till lately.

Further on we passed one or two more rest-houses with wells of brackish water, and many buildings partially buried in the sand. Arriving at the shrine we found a spacious oorda, or royal caravanserai, built of bricks and lime, with white-washed walls. This had been erected by the present Amir. Here we had excellent accommodation provided for us by old Sheikh Muksood, who told us many interesting tales of the olden time. He informed us that the sand came from the N.-W. in one steady unvarying line, and was gradually advancing over the country. A serai which he had built some 30 years ago had been completely buried in one of these sand waves. Arslan Khan is buried here with all his army, who were killed fighting with Tokta Rashid, the Uigur Chief, more than 800 years ago. At that time there were habitations and cultivations, now all one sea of sand. It is said that as these sands progress in their course, cities become buried, and after centuries of entombment reappear as the sand wave passes on.

4.—Lama Vuru, Buddhist Monastery and Chortens.

5.—Camp Nimmoo, in Ladak.

The buried cities near Khoten and Takla Makan are constantly spoken of, and wonderful stories are related of the valuable property recovered therefrom. It was not our good fortune to visit them, and travellers' tales must always be accepted *cum grano*, but some good gold coins of Justin and Constantine's time were brought thence to me, and some gold ornaments similar to those worn by Hindoo women of the present day were dug out of one city, and we saw quantities of black bricks of tea which had come from the same locality. We heard just the same kind of stories about the great desert as are related by Marco Polo :—"There is a marvellous story related of this desert, which is, that when travellers are on the move at night, and one of them chances to lag behind, or to fall asleep, or the like, when he tries to join his company again, he will hear spirits talking, and will suppose them to be his comrades. Sometimes the spirits will call him by name, and thus shall a traveller oft times be led astray, so that he never finds his party, and in this way many have perished. Sometimes the stray traveller will hear as it were the tramp and hum of a great cavalcade of people away from the real line of road, and taking this to be their own company, they will follow the sound and when day breaks they find that a cheat has been put upon them, and that they are in an ill plight. Even in the day time one hears these spirits talking. And sometimes you shall hear the sound of a variety of musical instruments and still more commonly the sound of drums."

Stories are told of showers of sand being rained down on cities and burying them in an incredibly short space of time. It is said that no animal life is to be found in these inhospitable tracts, and though the wild camel is said to inhabit the desert, I have never yet come nearer to a verification of the story, than to hear a man say he had met others who had shot it. One witness went so far as to declare he had seen one, and another promised to produce the skin of one, but it was not forthcoming, and the existence of the wild camel is still a problem to be solved for the satisfaction of those who are unwilling to accept popular belief as conclusive evidence.

It was near the end of March before the winter broke, and on the 21st of that month the thermometer at night rose above freezing point for the first time since we left Leh on 29th September. By the middle of April the trees were in full leaf, and the whole country was green with the springing crops. As all cultivation depends entirely on irrigation, great activity is displayed at this season in clearing out the canals and opening out new watercourses. The system of irrigation adopted here seems much akin to that in force in the submontane districts in the Punjab, where the whole management of the canals and the distribution of the water has from time immemorial been in the hands of the villagers, wholly independent of the action of the Government, and if I may be allowed to say so infinitely more effective and popular than where the irrigation is conducted through official agency. But in one instance I saw workmen, in the vicinity of Yangi Hissar, being employed to construct or restore a canal which brought water to the fort, and as I was passing by towards evening I observed the men seated in knots of 50, receiving their daily hire; one tunga, about six pence, being given to each.

On the 3rd May news having come that the proposed plan of a return through Cabul could not be carried out, and that Lieutenant-Colonel Gordon's party were returning to Yarkand, Dr. Bellew, Captain Chapman and I commenced our homeward journey. We reached Yarkand on the 6th, and halted there till the 18th May, in order to receive the letters for Her Majesty and for the Viceroy, which the Amir sent by the hand of our good friend Syud Yakúb Khan. He also brought with him an European traveller, M. Berczenczey, who had given himself out on arrival at Kashghar as an old friend of mine, but on reaching Yarkand he changed his story, and said he had come to search for the cradle of the Hungarian race. He represented himself as having been ill treated at Kashghar by the Amir's officials, and as being prevented from pursuing his intention of proceeding *viâ* Aksu and Kara-Shahr to Kokonor. I ascertained that the extent of his ill-treatment was his being placed under surveillance whilst in Kashghar, as he acknowledged that he did not belong to Russia, England, or Turkey, the only three European nations with whom the Amir had any dealings. But he acknowledged that he was well fed and clothed, and he certainly was not subjected to more restraint than was experienced by Messrs. Shaw and Hayward.

f

However, I advised Syud Yakúb Khan to accord to this gentleman perfect liberty. The Syud took occasion, when we were his guests one day in a charming garden just outside the city, to ask M. Berczenczey whether he had any ground of complaint, and I particularly remarked to him that now was the proper time for him to speak out if he had received any sort of ill-treatment. He expressed himself as perfectly satisfied, and signed a written paper to this effect. Syud Yakúb Khan then accorded in writing free permission to the traveller to go where he pleased, and I assumed that he would pursue his journey to Kokonor. But M. Berczenczey now abandoned the professed object of his visit to Kashghar, and begged to be allowed to accompany my camp to India. As this arrangement could not be complied with, he made his way by the Sanju route to Ladakh, and I deputed one of my escort to accompany and take care of him, and provided him with a tent, ponies, and supplies.

Before leaving Kashghar I had obtained the Amir's consent to my taking the Kogiar route on our return to India. This route had the reputation of being very much shorter and easier than that by Sanju and the Karakash. But it had been closed for many years to travellers, partly owing to the attacks of the Kunjút robber tribe, and there was some difficulty at first about supplies. This was however overcome by the energy and ability of Tara Sing, who, by purchasing and hiring baggage animals laid out provisions as far as Burtsi, 14 marches from Kogiar, and to within four days of the fertile Nubra valley in Ladakh.

Leaving the old Sanju track at Kargalik we made a march up the Kogiar valley and crossing the Topa Dewan, a short and low pass, we came into the valley of the Tisnaf stream. Our road thence for four days was up the bed of this river, at that time swollen by the melting snows to such an extent as to make the frequent passage of the stream a constant difficulty and not infrequent danger.

We found the Yangi Dewan a very easy pass to ascend, but on descending the valley on the south, leading to the broad bed of the Yarkand river, we experienced considerable difficulty in passing our animals over the crevasses of the ice beds which filled the valley. For three days our journey was along the broad Yarkand River, which had to be crossed frequently, but at no point was troublesome. At Aktagh on the 4th June we rejoined the old road between Ladakh and Shahidulla on the Karakash, and thence retraced our last year's steps over the Karakorum.

Between the Karakorum and the Sasser Passes, the summer route crosses the high Dipsang Plain, and then follows the rocky bed of a stream till the Shyok is reached. Here we were met by Mr. Johnson, the Wazir of Ladakh, who made most complete and comfortable arrangements for crossing the Sasser and Digur Passes, and on the 17th June the head-quarters of the mission entered Leh.

Lieutenant-Colonel Gordon's party followed in our wake, and found supplies and all necessaries at each stage. He arrived at Leh on 29th June, but I grieve to have to record the melancholy fact, that when all the difficulties and dangers of a year's travel were just at an end, our friend and companion, Dr. F. Stoliczka, fell a sacrifice to his zeal in the cause of science. On the road to Yarkand last year this intrepid and indefatigable savant endangered his life by over exertion, when pursuing his geological researches at an elevation of nearly 19,000 feet and in spite of intense cold. The journey across the Pamir was a severe trial to his enfeebled constitution, and on reaching the lofty Karakorum Dr. Stoliczka exhibited signs of great distress. Undaunted however by all suffering, and too little heeding the warnings thus given, he overstrained his lungs and heart by toiling on foot up a mountain-side to make some scientific observation, and then, when he consented to be treated as an invalid, the injury was past all human skill to remedy, and he rapidly passed away.

Truly has it been said by His Excellency the Viceroy:—

"Eminent scientific attainments and great natural abilities were in Dr. Stoliczka combined with persevering industry and enthusiastic devotion to the pursuit of physical science. He had already worthily earned a wide reputation by his work in the Palæontologia Indica.

"Throughout the scientific world Dr. Stoliczka's loss will be deeply deplored, and nowhere and by none more sincerely than in India and by the Government of India whom he so ably and honorably served."

Exd.—J. M.

CHAPTER II.

GENERAL DESCRIPTION OF KÁSHGHAR.*

Names of the Region.—The country now most commonly called Káshghár or Káshgharia has at different periods of its history been known under different names. By the early historians of the Arab conquest the country, which in the time of the ancient Persian sovereignty was known as Túrán or Mulki Tártár, was generally denominated Turkistán, and its different natural divisions were distinguished by appropriate appellations.

Amongst these the province now represented by Káshghár was called—to distinguish it from the proper Bukhárá in the corresponding basin to the west—Kichik Bukhárá or "Little Bukhárá," and it is described under this name by Juwení, the author of the *Jahánkushá*; though it appears that at the time of the Arab conquest it was generally spoken of either simply as Turkistán or "the country of the Turk," or, to distinguish it from the Turkistán proper—the northern portion of the region populated by that widely extended race—as Bilád-us-Shirk or "the eastern cities;" and by Rashíduddín, the Wazír of Ghazán Khan and author of the *Táríkh Rashídí*, it is called Mashrik Turkistán or "Eastern Turkistán."

The Moghol invasion, without entirely displacing these names, gave it another—that of Mogholistán or "the country of the Moghol"—and it was generally known by this name during the period of the rule of the Chaghtáy Khans. In the time of the later Princes of that dynasty, however, the name of Káshghar, their capital, came into use to designate the plain country south of the Alátágh in contradistinction to Mogholistán proper, which was applied in a more restricted sense to the home of the nomad Moghol on the elevated plateaux of that mountain range and in the valleys at its northern base. And this name of Káshghar has ever since been the one most commonly used to represent the great basin of the Tárim River, though other names have been applied to it in whole or in part by foreigners. Thus by the Chinese conquerors—under whose rule it was included in the great western frontier province of Ila—it is called Tianshan Nan Lu or "the way south of Tianshan," and by modern European authors Chinese Turkistán.

Finally, by its western neighbours of the present day—by Khokand and Bukhárá—it has since the period of the Chinese conquest been called Alty Shahr or "the six cities," and Yatty Shahr or "the seven cities;" terms which apply properly only to the western half of the country, in which are situated the six or seven cities to which the Chinese Emperor had conceded certain privileges of trade and local government on behalf of the Khokand State. And it is by these last names that the province is generally alluded to by the Russians.

As has been mentioned in the preceding history of this region, it was in the time of Changiz—when he divided his empire amongst his sons—allotted under the name of Mogholistan, together with the countries of Turkistán and Máwaránahar on the west and Kará Khitáy in the east, to his son Chaghtáy. All these countries collectively have been styled "the middle Tartar Kingdom" as distinct from the northern and western Tartar Kingdoms which were the portions of his other sons. This Mogholistán—according to the *Táríkhi Rashídí* of Mirzá Hydar—was in the time of Chaghtáy also denominated Mangláy Súba or "Front Province" or "direction of sunrise." And its limits are given as from Shásh or Táshkand on the west to Jálish on the east, and from Isigh Kol on the north to Sárígh Uighur on the south.

At the same time the limits of Káshghar, according to the same authority, were Shash and the Bolor mountains on the west; the country beyond Turfán to the borders of the Kalmák territory on the east; Artosh on the north; and Khutan on the south. These limits, with the exception of the extension to Shásh itself, hold good to the present day; for the Shásh territory extends eastward to Atbáshí on the Upper Nárín where Artosh begins.

---

* The portions of sections relating to horses, page 71; marriage, page 85; birth and onwards, page 86; women, page 89; death, page 92; punishments inflicted in Eastern Turkestan, page 100; and Chinese punishments, page 101, are by Captain Chapman—the rest by Dr. Bellew.

Geographical position.—As above defined Káshghar is comprised between 36° and 43° north latitude, and between 73° and 92° east longitude. Between these parallels its limits may be thus described. The north boundary runs obliquely between 39° and 43° north latitude from the Tirik Dawán in 73° east longitude to Pichán in 92° east longitude, and is formed by the southern watershed of the Celestial or God Mountains, called Alátágh (Allah-tagh?) Tangrí Úla, and Tianshán in Turki, Moghol, and Chinese respectively.

The south boundary runs obliquely between 38° and 36° north latitude from Sárígh Kúl or Sirikol in 74° east longitude to Cháchan of the Sárígh Uighúr in 83° east longitude, and is formed by the northern slopes of the great Tibet range of mountains which is known in different parts of its extent by the names of Kuenlún or "Blue Mountains," Súnglún or "Onion Mountains," Karákoram or "Black Shale," and the Múztágh or "Ice Mountains" of Bolor.

The east boundary cuts the parallels of 92° and 85° of east longitude from Pichán on the north to Cháchan on the south between the parallels of 43° and 36° north latitude, and presents an undefined border formed by the shifting sands of the Gobí Desert.

The west boundary cuts the parallels of 73° and 74° east longitude from Tirik Dawán on the north to Sárígh Kúl on the south between 40° and 37° north latitude, and is formed by the eastern slopes of the Aláy and Pamír plateaux and the eastern watershed of the Bolor mountains or Bolortágh.

These are the natural geographical boundaries of Káshghar, or the valley of the Tárim River, and they closely correspond with the present political limits of the country.

Superficial extent.—As above limited, the greatest length of Káshghar, from Tirik Dawán to Pichán along its northern frontier, is about a thousand miles. Its least length, from Sárígh Kúl to Cháchan along the southern border, is about five hundred miles.

Its greatest breath, from Turfán to Cháchan on the eastern frontier, is about five hundred miles. And its least breadth, from Tirik Dawán to Táshkorghán in Sárígh Kúl on the western boundary, is about a hundred and fifty miles.

Area in square miles.—If we multiply the means of the above assumed measurements of length and breadth, we shall get 243,750 square miles as an approximate representation of the area of Káshghar. But it must be borne in mind that by very much the greatest part of it is an uninhabited waste, as is to be described presently.

Comparative topography.—Káshghar is separated from the neighbouring regions on the north, the west, and the south by the lofty highland ranges of the great mountain system of the Asiatic continent, and on the east is divided off from China by the desert of Gobí.

In the time of the Chinese rule it formed the southern division of the Ila province which included the great basins on the north and south of the Tiánshán range, and was limited on the east and west by the vast deserts of Gobi and Kapchák respectively.

The division to the north of the separating range is called by the Chinese *Tianshan Pe Lu*, or "the way north of the Celestial Mountains," and by the Moghol natives Zúnghár—the Songaria of European writers. Similarly the division to the south of the range is called *Tianshan Nan Lu*, or "the way south of the Celestial Mountains," and Káshghar by the Chinese and Moghol respectively. The former division lies between the Altai—the great mountain range of Mongolia—and the Tiánshán, and drains westward to the desert of Kapchák. Whilst the latter, with which only we are here concerned, lies between the Tiánshán and the Kuenlún—the great mountain range of Tibet—and drains eastward to the desert of Gobí.

On its north are the Russian possessions of Turkistán, and the Túrgút country of the Yuldúz and Orúmchí Kalmák—the Zúnghár above referred to. On its west are the Khanate of Khokand, and the independent petty chiefships of Karátakin, Shighnán, and Roshán, and the Afghan held province of Badakhshán, with the elevated plateaux of Pámir, Kizil Art and Aláy intervening. On its south are the Kashmir provinces of Ladákh and Báltistán, or Bolor, on the one hand, and Great Tibet or Hlassa or Úcháng on the other. And on its east, beyond Gobí, is the Chinese province of Kánsuh.

6.—Tartar Women at Nimmoo in Ladak, September 1873.

7.—Leh, the Capital of Ladak, View of the Bazar and Palace.

Physical features.—The prevailing character of the region thus surrounded is a vast plain surface extending east and west. But it may be conveniently described under the natural divisions of Highland, Lowland, Desert, Swamp, and Lake. And we will now briefly notice each in turn.

Highland.—This portion is constituted by the elevated plateaux and deep valleys of the lofty mountain barriers which form three sides of its area, and is characterized as much by the rigour of its climate as by the nakedness of its hills. Glaciers are found on its more elevated ranges, and there is everywhere an absence of forest trees.

Nevertheless its glens and hollows are the home of numerous tribes who are mostly nomads in their habits—who during the winter nestle in the nooks and sheltered gullies that border on the lowlands, and in summer migrate with their flocks and herds to roam over the rich pastures that sprout so soon as the snow melts off the wide plateaux or steppes which buttress the main ranges.

The peculiar features of these highlands are the general barrenness of the hill slopes and the narrowness of the channels by which they drain into the central plain or basin, not less than the steppes of rich pasture and tablelands of inhospitable waste which constitute the progressively higher parts of the several mountain ranges up to their water-sheds.

The mineral resources of these tracts are not well known, though there is ample evidence to prove that the rocks contain rich veins of the most useful and precious metals, besides mines of some highly prized minerals. These will be noticed in detail hereafter under the head of Natural Productions.

The vegetable kingdom is, as a rule, very sparsely represented, and, except on the northern slopes of the Alátágh—which indeed is beyond the limits of the country—there is a notable absence of forest trees everywhere. The deep valleys through which the mountains drain, however, and the elevated steppes or plateaux between their parallel ridges are clothed with a more or less rich vegetation which in some respects is peculiar to the region.

In the valleys, along the river courses, it is met with in the form of thickets of brushwood which line the banks in narrow belts with patches of tall reed grass interspersed; or where, as in the higher altitudes, the river courses expand into wide and more level channels, it is found in long island strips in the river bed itself. The composition of these brushwood thickets varies in different localities, but the characteristic and most generally diffused plants are species of tamarisk, myricaria and buckthorn; different species of the willow, the poplar and the rose; the dwarf juniper, arbor vitæ, with several species of the astragalus, and some of the barberry. Varieties of hedysarum, sedum, clematis, &c., and many other plants of herbal growth are found in the lower valleys where, too, pasture is the most abundant, and the poplar and the willow grow as forest trees in small clumps of few or many. For the rest the mountains may be described as a vast wilderness of desolation with glaciers on the highest ranges and snow for half the year on the next subordinate ridges.

Animal life at these elevations is most scarce if not absent entirely. The wild ox = *cútás*, the ibex = *takka*, two species of wild sheep—the ovis Poli = *ghúlja*, and ovis Ammon = *raós*—and a species of antelope = *jirán* haunt the snow line where, too, the marmot = *sughúr*, and rats of sorts have their burrows. In the more sheltered glens, lower down the river courses, are found the wild horse = *cúlán*, and the hare = *cúyán*. The bear = *arik* is found on the Alátágh, where it is said to dig out and devour the marmot whilst in its state of hybernation, and troops of wolves = *borí* with the stealthy leopard = *caflán* hunt on the Atbáshí plateaux of Alátágh and the Pámir of Bolortágh where the wild sheep do most abound.

Birds are represented by the solitary raven and the only less so chough at the highest altitudes, where too the eagle loves to soar. In the lower valleys the Grecian or red-legged partridge = *kiktik* is common everywhere, as are sparrows, finches, larks, wagtails, tits, rock martins, &c., &c., but the snow pheasant = *úlár* is only found at the snow line.

Lowland.—This division comprises the belt of hill skirt lying at the base of the bounding ranges, and varies in width in different localities. It is the most populous part of the country, and is the only portion of it which is permanently settled and cultivated. In it are situated all the cities and towns of the country together with their respective suburban settlements.

In its general aspect this division partakes of the characters of the two others between which it forms the connecting medium—of the hills on one side and of the desert on the other. Near the former it presents an uneven surface on which are prolonged the subsiding terminal offshoots of spurs from the mountain boundaries till they merge into the general level of the plain. Whilst towards the latter it rapidly expands into an undulating plain which insensibly sinks and becomes continuous with the desert.

The soil everywhere is characterized by its aridity and barrenness. Contiguous to the hills it consists of stony detritus intermixed with rolled boulders; further off it becomes coarse gravel; and finally, on the verge of the desert it assumes the form of pure sand. Everywhere it is more or less highly charged with salines which in the depressions of the undulating surface form sheets of white efflorescence, or spongy encrustations on which flourish a variety of saltworts. In many places these salines retain sufficient moisture to form mud bogs and marshes on which grow coarse reeds and dwarf tamarisks.

But the peculiar features of this tract are the numerous rivers which traverse its surface to their point of ultimate junction with the main stream—the Tárim River—which is the great drainage channel for the whole country. They are the seats of the fixed population and the entire productive industry of the country. Their number and names are many as they issue from the mountains on three sides of the basin, but they all converge at different points to form four principal rivers which are named after the settlements founded upon them. They are the Khutan, Yárkand, Káshghar, and Aksú Rivers; and they all converge and unite far out on the desert to the south of Aksú to form the Tárim River, which afterwards receives as tributaries the Kúchá and Káidú Rivers and thus completes the drainage of the valley.

These streams in their passage across this tract mostly flow in wide channels between low banks of sand. The larger ones flow upon firm pebbly bottoms, and the smaller ones in a bed of sand. The volume of their streams varies according to the seasons. Thus in winter even the largest of them are so much shrunk as to be crossed dry footed by stepping from stone to stone; whilst the smaller ones, which are mostly bridged, are at this season generally frozen over. In summer on the contrary they are all so swollen by the melting snows, that they fill the whole of their wide channels and, as in the case of the Yárkand River, form a stream nearly a mile broad and only passable by boat.

None of these rivers is navigable, but they are otherwise profitably utilized for purposes of irrigation. Numerous canals are drawn off from them to the lands on each side, and thus convert considerable tracts of what would otherwise be desert waste into fertile and populous settlements. The extent of these is at present limited, but were the means existing fully developed a much wider area might be settled and brought under cultivation.

All these rivers contain fish, and in the case of the larger streams they are a source of food to the inhabitants on their banks. Some of them, as the rivers of Khutan, yield the jade stone which in the time of the Chinese proved a source of considerable wealth to the country. And others, as the Yárkand or Zarafshán="Gold disperser," yield gold. Under the Chinese rule its sands were washed for the precious metal; but now this industry in common with others has quite died out.

Desert.—This division occupies the whole of the Káshghar basin beyond the lowland belt skirting the mountains, and as the two insensibly merge a line of demarcation is not easily recognized. In general aspect it presents a vast undulating plain of sand which slopes gently to the eastward. Its elevation is estimated to vary between 2,500 feet at Lob Nor and 4,000 feet on the Yárkand border. Its surface is traversed by the four rivers which go to form the Tárim, and by that stream itself. The banks of these rivers are fringed by broader or narrower belts of forest composed mainly of poplar, willow and tamarisk, amongst which is an impenetrable growth of tall reeds. In the covert of these thickets lurk the tiger, leopard, lynx, and wolf, together with the wild pig; and a species of stag—called *bocá* or *búghá* for the male, and *marál* for the female—pastures on their skirts.

Further out in the desert towards the east, the high banks and sand dunes which break the uniformity of its level towards the west and south either disappear or greatly diminish

8.—Leh, the Capital of Ladak, View from Joint Commissioner's Garden.

9.—The Indus Valley from Leh, Eln. 11,500 ft., View from Joint Commissioner's Garden.

in height, and then the river spreads broadcast over the surface forming wide lagoons or marshes, belted by reeds and tamarisk brushwood, till the waters again find a defined channel between banks. And this occurs at intervals over an extent of some three hundred miles beyond which the river flows in a clear channel five days' journey in length to the Lake Lob.

The greatest portion of this desert tract is an unmitigated waste with a deep coating of loose pulverulent salines on which only the wild camel finds a footing. Horses cannot traverse it owing to their sinking knee-deep in the soft soil; whilst to man the dust raised proves suffocating, and the glare from the snow white salts blinding.

The only parts that are inhabited are the immediate banks of the Tárim River, and the angles of junction formed by its tributaries from Kúchá and Karáshahr. The latter is a considerable river called Káidú. It drains the Yuldúz valley and at Karáshahr falls into the Lake Baghrásh—the Bostáng of the maps. From this it issues to the south and, winding round the west of the Kúrúgh Tágh sand hills which separate its lake from that of Lob, at seven days' journey from the city joins the Tárim. At its point of junction a road goes across the desert to Khutan, but to the east of it are the lagoons and marshes abovementioned. For two or three hundred miles on this part of its course the Tárim River is the seat of some primitive tribes who dwell in reed huts on its banks and in boats upon its stream. They will be described hereafter under the head of inhabitants of the country.

It may be here noted as a remarkable object on this desert tract that on the road to Khutan south of this peopled district of Lob is the site of an ancient city of that name now buried in sand; and at three days' journey further to the south are the ruins of Katak, another ancient city of this region, which has been overwhelmed by the shifting sands.

During our stay in the country we had an opportunity of witnessing the manner in which such a catastrophe is brought about. Whilst the embassy was halted at Yangi Hissar we paid a visit to the shrine of Ordám Pádshah in the Kúm Shahídán or "Martyrs' Sands" on the verge of the desert, and there saw some buildings actually undergoing the process of submergence by the shifting sands.

It is effected in this wise. During the spring and summer months a north or north-west wind prevails. It blows with considerable force and persistence for many days consecutively. As it sweeps over the plain it raises the impalpable dust on its surface, and obscures the air by a dense haze resembling in darkness a November fog in London; but it drives the heavier particles of sand before it, and on the subsidence of the wind they are left on the plain in the form of ripples like those on a sandy beach washed by an ebbing current.

In process of time under the continued action of this wind the ripples grow in size, and at the same time progress gradually over the plain in the direction of the wind. As they grow in size the more defined and uniform becomes their shape, and the more exact their direction with that of the wind.

At Kúm Shahídán these moving sands presented a most remarkable uniformity in their direction and in the regularity of their wave lines. The wave lines were formed by a series of three to six or more semilunes ranged over the plain in rows one behind the other in the direction whence the wind blew, that is, to the north or north-west.

All the semilunes in every series and in all the rows exactly resembled each other in every particular except dimensions, and all faced the direction to which the wind blew, that is to the south or south-east.

Each semilune towards the north or north-west sloped up gently from the plain, and reached its greatest height—from twelve to sixty or eighty feet—in the centre of the curve which faced to the south or south-east. From this centre the loose sand sloped down gently along

the projecting horns of the crescent to the plain, but in the arc of the crescent itself t
drop was very sudden, as shown in this diagram :—

The wind blowing from N. drives the loose sand up to S., beyond which it toppl
over and passes down the slope out of its further action. And a continuance of this proces
without changing the form, is always shifting its particles from the direction of N.
that of S., and thus advancing the sand across the plain.

From some partially buried buildings we examined at this place, and from the data fu
nished to us regarding the period of their construction, and the distance of the sand dunes
the time, we calculated that these sands were advancing over the plain between S. ar
S.E. at the rate of about a foot a year or rather more at this spot. But from simil
data regarding a half submerged post-house, eight miles off to the south, we calculated th
rate of advance at fully three feet a year at that spot. This post-house occupied the summ
of a low mound on the plain (the surface of which here presented a wide shallow hollo
encrusted with salines and covered with reeds, as appeared in the intervals between the su
cessive rows of sand waves) which had a very distinct slope towards a great drainage gull
some few miles further to the south; and this inclination of the ground may account for th
more rapid rate of advance at this spot, though the varying force of the wind would not b
without its aiding effects.

From these instances it may be concluded that the rate of advance of these moving sand
is a varying measure dependent on the velocity of the wind and the nature of the surface
and that under any circumstances the process is a gradual one. Consequently it may b
assumed that the burial under them of the cities of Lob and Katak—though a sudden catas
trophe for individual houses as they successively became overwhelmed—was on the whole a slo
process extending over many years, and thus afforded the inhabitants ample leisure to abando
their doomed abodes and migrate to safer localities.

This view is supported by an incidental reference to a whirlwind of sand which sul
merged a considerable portion of the city of Katak about the middle of the 14th century i
the *Tárikhi Rashidi* of Mirza Hydar. In his account of this storm he describes the sand a
falling from the sky as does a shower of rain; and probably it was blown off the overtower
ing sand dunes which in their progressive advance had encroached upon the outer walls of th
city. But beyond recording the flight of two or three individuals from the limited area o
this convulsion of nature he does not mention any general exodus of the population, thoug
he alludes to the circumstance of their having been frequently warned to depart from the cit
doomed to destruction. And this indicates that the impending calamity was foreseen and it
nature understood.

Wandering shepherds and huntsmen who now frequent the vicinity of these buried citie
report that the houses and domes and minarets of Katak are seen to reappear from under th
sands in all their pristine perfection; and they tell marvellous tales of the undisturbed repos
and uninjured state of their furniture and contents; and they even describe the skeleton form
of the occupants as still retaining the exact positions they happened to be in at the time the
were overwhelmed, by the sudden fall and subsidence of some great encroaching sand dun
most probably, the regular form of whose loose agglomeration of particles was broken by th
obstruction to its symmetrical advance offered by the house it buried in its own dissolutio
and subsidence. This, I may here note, is easily understood from what we witnessed at Kúr
Sháhidán. Here we saw a sand wave of three contiguous semilunes which in its advanc
across the plain had come upon the court wall of a tenement in the way of its progress
One of the side semilunes which overtopped the wall by five or six feet had broken over it

obstruction and half filled the court area with the loose sand of its substance; whilst the other two not so obstructed continued their steady advance in unbroken form by the side of the tenement.

In illustration of the carelessness with which we found this accustomed danger treated it is worthy of note that we saw the house thus threatened with submergence actually occupied by its tenants, although the sands had approached to within a few feet of its verandah. Doubtless had the sand dune met the back of the house and broken over its roof, instead of over its front court wall, the occupants would have been entombed in their dwelling, as were those of Katak, according to the veracious statements of the unsophisticated shepherds of the country.

These wanderers about Katak further state that the houses, &c., of the buried city which they have seen reappear from under the sand are no longer to be found when they again visit the place in their migrations, though their position is recognized by the minaret tops projecting from the fresh sands under which they have passed. This, too, is easily to be understood if we remember that the sand travels in wave lines the rows of which follow each other at intervals of twenty or thirty to a hundred yards.

The first line will break over an obstructing house and bury it; but, the wind continuing, its loose particles are driven on and resume their original form on the clear ground beyond; whilst the submerged house reappears from under the advancing wave till it is again buried by the one next following it; and so on with the successive rows until the whole of the moving sands have passed on beyond its site.

Consequently, in process of time, provided the sands be limited in extent, the buried cities of Lob and Katak ought to reappear in the world much in form of their first state when submerged some four hundred years ago. With the requisite data an interesting calculation could be made as to the period when this resurrection might be expected to occur. Unfortunately for this we have no knowledge of the extent of the moving sands in their vicinity. Those of Kúm Shahídán extend across the plain in an unbroken series of wave lines for about fifteen miles from east and north-east to west and south-west and have a width of about eight miles more or less from north and north-west to south and south-east from Ordám Pádshah towards Yángí Hissár; and within these limits they cover an area of about a hundred and twenty square miles. Till all this has moved on to the east of the site of Ordám Pádshah the shrine is not free from the risk of submergence—the fate that has long since overtaken the city of that name which is said to have been buried eight hundred years ago; though we could get no history of the occurrence. Whilst on the spot we could find no traces of this buried city, but as the sands extend many miles eastward of the shrine on to the desert they may be there, inasmuch as we were assured there was such a buried city albeit none of our informants could indicate the site.

Swamp.—This natural division of the country with the next that is to be described forms one of the characteristic features of the general aspect of the preceding division or desert tract, and taken as a whole constitutes no small portion of its general area.

The swamp or marsh land is principally concentrated on the course of the Tárim River in the eastern part of its course before it joins Lake Lob. Little is known regarding this tract, owing to its inaccessibility, beyond that it extends over two or three hundred miles of country from west to east, and that the Tárim River passes through it to Lake Lob. It is described as a vast expanse of impenetrable reeds fringed by a forest belt of poplar and tamarisk trees. The people of Lob are said to move about the swamps in their boats, and find a way through them in five days to the lake. They are said to yield great abundance of fish, on which the people mainly subsist, and to swarm with water-fowl of all sorts, as well as musquitoes and venemous gnats, together with other horrid insects and snakes. The white swan and a species of otter are also found here, and their skins are articles of barter between the Lob people and the traders of Kúchá and Karáshahr. A certain number of otter skins also form part of the annual tribute paid by these people to Káshghar.

There is no cultivation here nor any fixed settlement. The people live in transportable reed-frame huts or in boats, and possess great herds of horned cattle. The produce of these and of the chase constitutes their entire wealth, as will be described hereafter. The shor[e] of these marshes produce a rich pasture, and the reed belts around harbour great numbers [of] wild pig, wolves, leopards, and tigers. The climate of this tract is described as extreme[ly] insalubrious to strangers though not so to the natives. The heat in summer is said to be ve[ry] great, but the winter, as compared with the rest of the valley, is a mild season and frosts la[st] only for a few days.

Besides this great swamp tract in the eastern part of the valley there is another simil[ar] tract of considerable extent on the shores of the Baghrásh Lake near Karáshahr to the nort[h]. The two are separated by the Kúrúgh Tágh range of sand hills, amongst the ridges of whi[ch] the wild camel=*túga* is said to breed. On the western half of the plain there are numberle[ss] minor swamps and marshes scattered about on the hollows of the surface. S[o]me of the[m] assume the form of pools or small lakes and are called *Kol*=Lake by the natives, as Áy K[ol] on the Aksú road, &c.

Lake.—Like the swamps the lakes are in the eastern half of the valley, and very little [is] known about them. Three principal ones are spoken of, *viz.*, Baghrásh, Lob, and Karya.

Baghrásh is situated to the south and east of Karáshahr, and receives the Káidú River as [it] debouches from the Yuldúz valley on to the Káshghar plain, and gives it exit to join the Tári[m] River, which it does at a point seven days' journey from Karáshahr by winding round Kúrúg[h] Tágh, a wide range of clay and sand hills that separate this lake from the district of Lob. Th[e] Lake Baghrash, also called Káidú Kol, may be considered as a mere expansion of the Káidú Riv[er] over a hollow basin in the way of its course. It is described as a shallow sheet of water s[ix] days' journey in length, covered with floating islands of reeds amongst which the river flows, a[nd] bordered on each side by a belt of tall reeds, poplars, and tamarisk trees. Along its souther[n] shore in all its length runs the Kúrúgh Tágh ridge, and between the two is a road from Kur[la] to U'sh Aktál—a journey of seven days.

Lob Lake is described as situated on the edge of the Gobi desert at the extreme east lim[it] of the Káshghar plain. In the *Tárikhí Rashídí* of Mirzá Hydar it is mentioned as covering a[n] area four months' journey in circuit, and as giving exit to the great Kará Morán River of Chin[a]. In this calculation of its extent the swamp tract to the west would seem to be included. Whil[e] at Káshghar I made enquiries regarding this lake from some Kirghiz and Kalmák shepherd[s] who professed to be familiar with the locality, and also from some of the Amir's officers who ha[d] visited Lob district during the Turfán campaign. The accounts of all, though varying cons[i]derably in details, corresponded remarkably as to the facts of the existence of the lake, and i[ts] connection with the swamps to the west, and as to the general characteristics of the place an[d] people. My most intelligent informant was a native of Karáshahr who had visited the Lo[b] settlement on the Tárim just below the junction of the Káidú River repeatedly during five suc[c]essive years. His description may be briefly given thus—" Lob is a succession of lakes alon[g] the Tárim River. Each lake gives off five or six streams which spread over the plain and reunit[e] lower down to form the next lake, and so on for a journey of thirty days by the road. Beyon[d] this is the Great Desert of which nobody knows anything. All the lakes are fringed by reed[y] marshes and forests of tamarisk and poplar, but there are no willows. The people live in hut[s] of wattle or in boats on the river. They are rich in cattle, sheep, and horses, but do not culti[ti]vate the soil, which is all sand, and forms undulating ridges between the several lakes and th[e] forests on their shores. Tigers, wolves, and wild pig abound in the thickets, and fish are pler[n]tiful in the river. Venemous insects, and a large species of scorpion swarm all over the place."

Another intelligent informant was a Kirghiz of Kákshál. He had travelled all over Ila an[d] Kánsuh during nearly thirty years, and was in Bajin or Pekin at the time the city was take[n] by the allied French and English armies in 1860. He had resided as a shepherd for three year[s] at Lob itself and professed to know every settlement in the whole tract. His statement[s] on this subject correspond in the main with those of the informant above quoted, an[d] add thereto the following particulars:—" Lake Lob or Lop Kol is situated in a grea[t] salt desert. It is entirely uninhabited, and is five days' journey in circuit. Nobod[y] can go more than three or four days' journey to the east of the lake owing to th[e] depth of the soft powdery saline soil on which neither man nor beast can find a footing[.]

From the lake a river goes out to the south-east across an immense desert of thin salt and sand. At fifteen or twenty days' journey it passes under a mountain and re-appears on the other side in China or Khitá. In olden times a young man of Lob went in his boat to explore the river beyond the lake. After going down the stream for seven days he saw a mountain ahead, and on going closer found the river entered a frightful black and deep chasm in the rocks. He tried to stop his boat, but the swiftness of the current carried it into the chasm. At its further end he saw a small black hole under the mountain, and had only time to lie down in the bottom of his boat when it was drawn into this dark passage. The top of the boat scraped the roof of the channel, and bits of stone continually fell upon him. After a long time he emerged from the darkness into light and found the bottom of his boat strewed with nuggets of gold. He went down the river for some days and landed in a country where the people had only one eye, and this one eye was in the middle of the forehead, and brighter than any two of other people. He wandered amongst them for six years and was then seized by some Khitá soldiers and taken prisoner to Bájin. He lived there many years, and gradually worked his way back with caravans stage by stage to Kámol and Karáshahr, and finally returned to his own home an old grey bearded man after an absence of 22 years. All this is quite true, and is known to everybody in Lob, where this man's descendents still live in the settlement of Arámahalla or Arámyla as it is called. It is at the junction of the Aksú and Kúchá River with the Tárim."

Karya Lake or Karya Kol is similar in general characters not to those above described, but to the lesser lakes on the western half of the plain. It is said to be situated on the desert south-west of Lob on the road to Khutan, beyond an intervening tract of sand hills, and to receive the Karya River. It has no outlet, and in seasons of drought becomes a mere boggy marsh. Its shores are covered with reeds and thickets of tamarisk and poplar, and are frequented by shepherds who camp here for the sake of the pasture. Its reeds are the breeding place of innumerable wild fowl.

Such are the chief physical features and natural divisions of the Káshghar territory, and that their peculiarities materially determine the character of its climate and the nature of its seasons will be readily understood. But before we proceed to consider these it will be profitable first to describe the political divisions of the country, because the artificial changes wrought in them by the industry of man are not entirely without their share of influence in modifying the effects of natural causes.

Political divisions.—The present political or governmental divisions of the Káshghar territory are the same as those of ancient times, and have been determined by the natural features of the country. They are all separated from each other by greater or less strips of intervening arid desert waste; and each within its own limits forms a separate little State, with its capital, and district towns, and rural settlements, the position, number and extent of which are dependent on the course and distribution of its water supply. Each little State too, notwithstanding the corrupting effects of foreign rule and intermixture, has its own peculiarities of dialect, of dress, of social customs, and domestic habits. During a prolonged government under a single rule the intercommunication between neighbouring States operates to blend or obliterate these peculiarities, and consequently the distinctions are not so readily observable between adjoining States as between those more widely separated. Yet they are observable as a relic of the isolation that prevailed prior to and during the rule of the Chaghtáy Khans, when in the recurring periods of anarchy of that time each little State formed an independent principality at war with its neighbour, and was supported entirely by its own internal resources of food, clothing, and means of defence. Moreover, although under the Chinese rule the movements of troops and trade caravans backwards and forwards all over the country afforded the people of the several States greater facilities of intercommunication than they ever enjoyed before or have found available since, the natural obstacles of the road were sufficient to deter any but men bound on business from the risks, and fatigues, and expenses of the journey. Consequently even under favouring conditions the social isolation of these States has been only a degree less than their local isolation.

In general appearance and plan of arrangement all these little States bear a comm[on] resemblance. Thus each has its central fortified city or capital with its suburbs more or le[ss] extensive, its district or market towns, and its rural settlements, and around all its lit[tle] frontier outposts. In each the capital alone is fortified and surrounded by walls. The mark[et] towns or bázárs are, as the name indicates, mere markets thronged on the market day a[nd] deserted for the rest of the week, except of course by the permanent residents, who are most[ly] tradesmen, victuallers, and handicraftsmen. Their open collection of tenements gradual[ly] expand, and in clusters of two or three or more spread far and wide along the water-cours[es] around, and form the rural settlements. These consist of a number of scattered homestea[ds] along the main canal or river of the settlement, and each homestead is surrounded by its ow[n] fields and orchards, and gardens and vineyards. They thus spread over a considerable tract [of] country which, from the willows, poplars, æleagnus, and mulberry trees planted along the wate[r] courses, wears the appearance of population and plenty. Each of these settlements is separat[ed] from the next by an intervening strip of waste land varying in width from only a few hundr[ed] yards to twelve or more miles, in which latter case the waste becomes blank desert. The produ[ce] of these settlements is carried weekly to the market towns for barter and thence to the capita[l] which is the seat of trade and manufacture.

The rural settlements, it will thus be seen, are purely agricultural; the market tow[ns] mere centres of exchange, though not exclusively so, for some have special industries—as iro[n] smelting at Kizilí—besides the trades supported by the market people; and the capitals t[he] recipients of their produce. The separation of the homesteads in the rural settlements, an[d] the isolation of these from their neighbours proves most advantageous in respect to police an[d] hygiene. It prevents combination for tumult or sedition, and operates to render the peasant[ry] unusually docile and timid if not entirely peaceable; and whilst it checks the growth [of] epidemics and spread of contagion, it affords the people the most favourable conditions f[or] maintaining good health, a blessing which they in fact enjoy as freely as most peop[le] similarly situated. On the other hand, however, this arrangement proves nugatory as regar[ds] self-defence against an organized army, or small disciplined force; but rather favours th[e] enemy who has effected his entrance by placing at his disposal just the supplies he requires f[or] the maintenance of his troops engaged in besieging the capital. It is owing to these ci[r]cumstances, coupled with the unwarlike character of the peasantry, that the country ha[s] always succumbed quickly to the arms of the invader, and in times of anarchy been th[e] easy prey of adventurers, till partitioned off into independent little principalities under loc[al] chiefs who ruled within the limits of their own petty States as sovereign lords, or wh[o] confederated with their neighbours under an acknowledged head to repel a foreign foe, or [to] check the ambition of an internal rival.

With these preliminary remarks on the general characters and arrangements of all th[e] petty States comprising the Káshghar territory, we will now proceed to describe them several[ly] in detail. They are in the order of their sequence, on the lowland tract skirting the moun[tains] that bound three sides of the country, Khutan, Yárkand, Yángi Hissár, Káshghar, U'c[h] Turfán, Aksú, Kúchá, Kúrla, Karáshahr, and Turfán. There are besides the highland distri[ct] of Sárígh Kúl, the desert military post and Dolan settlement of Marálbáshí, and the swam[p] colony of Lob. And finally, there are the Kirghiz steppes of Alátágh and Pámir, and th[e] mountain retreats of the aboriginal Pakhpúlúk of Múztágh.

Khutan.—This little State is situated at the northern base of the Kuenlun mountain, an[d] includes the deep valleys which drain its slopes into the river on which the capital stands. [It] has from remote times been in more or less continuous communication with China either as [a] tributary ally or a subject State, and has from the earliest ages been celebrated for its mus[k] and its silk, for its gold and its jade.

According to Remusat, its ancient Chinese name was Kiu-sa-tan-na from the Sanskr[it] Kustaná = "Pap of the World," and at different periods it has been described in the anna[ls] of that empire under the names of Iu-thian, Iu-tun, Iu-siun, Hou-an-na, Khiou-tan, an[d] Hou-tan. In the tenth century, at the time of the Baghra Khan crescentade, it was calle[d] Chín or Máchín by the Musalmans, and its capital Chínshahr or "Chín City." At th[e] present day it is locally known as Ilchí or Ilsa, and the name is applied in a restricted sense to the capital city in distinction to the fort or military city adjoining it. But the whole State is known as Khutan or Alty Shahri Khutan = "Six cities of Khutan" from the six towns composing it, viz., Ilchí, Karákásh, Yúrungkásh, Chira, Karyá or Kiryá, and Náya.

Each of these townships, to which is added a seventh called Koh-tágh or Kuránghotágh, forms a separate government under a Beg, who is subordinate to the Hákim Beg or "Ruling Beg" at the capital. Collectively the population of these several townships is reckoned at 18,000 houses, and they are distributed as follows.

Ilchí or Khutan, the capital, 6,000 houses. Close opposite is the Gulbágh Fort, which in the time of the Chinese had a garrison of 2,000 men. The city is walled and stands on the Khutan river, on both banks of which are its suburbs. Its people are mostly Turk and Tártárs with a considerable mixture of foreign blood, principally Chinese; and amongst them are settled many emigrants from Andiján or Khokand, together with natives of Tibet, Kashmir, and the Punjab, and also of Kabul. There is besides a small fluctuating population of merchant traders.

The principal manufactures of the city are silk fabrics, carpets, and a coarse cotton cloth called *khám*. These, together with the other chief products of the country, viz., gold, jade-stone, musk, raw silk, and raw cotton, form the staples of its trade and its most valuable exports. Under the Chinese rule all these industries flourished, and attracted a large number of merchants to the country; but, with the exception of the cotton trade, they are now all in a very languishing state, owing, it is said, to the great number of workmen who perished in the late massacres and wars. A trustworthy resident of the city who had witnessed the whole revolution, from the overthrow of the Chinese to the establishment of the Amír, informed me that the whole country was now completely impoverished, and that it had lost nearly half of its male population. His account of the state of trade was much thus—"The jade trade, which formerly supported several thousand families in its collection and manufacture, had now entirely disappeared. So the gold mines, which under the Chinese employed whole settlements, are now deserted, excepting only one or two which are worked as a close monopoly by the Amír. The carpet trade has similarly declined, and the rare productions of gold wire, silk, and wool combined, which under the Chinese found eager competitors, are now never seen, for there is nobody left to buy them. The cotton industry is the only one that flourishes, for we must all wear clothes, and the *khám* (a sort of buckram) which the weavers turn out is so cheap and durable that everybody buys it. The silk is good enough, though not to compare with that of Andiján; but where ten men wore it before hardly one can afford to do so now."

Karákásh. This is a settlement of 1,000 houses on the lower course of the river of that name, scattered in clusters of three or four homesteads together. In this district there are both jade and gold mines, and the people have lots of horses and cattle.

Yúrungkásh, 1,000 houses. It comprises several settlements on the Khutan River between the city and the mountains. At Jíyá, which is a collection of 150 homesteads on the sandy plain, about 4 *tash* from the mountains, a good deal of silk is produced; and at Kúmbát and Táshmalik, two small villages in the hills about 4 *tash* from Yúrungkásh, there are jade quarries and gold diggings.

Kuránghotágh, 1,500 houses. This district comprises several glens on the upper course of the Khutan River up to its sources on the Kang Dawán, and is contiguous to the northward with Yúrungkásh. Its principal settlements are Chorash, Chamand, Ambár, Chukár, Achyán, Soktyán, and Zabirá or Mazár Chár Imám. They are all in separate glens, and Chorash is the residence of the Beg. From Chamand to Kang Dawán is a day's journey to the south-west with no habitation. Gold is washed in streams from the mountain, but only in summer. In this direction too is Chákil; it is four days' journey from Ilchi, and the boundary of its territory, for there is no road beyond it as the mountains here join those of Karákoram and Sásir. This is a very wild district, and as the name implies the glens are narrow, deep, and dark.

Chíra, 4,000 houses. This is a market town, and has many populous settlements along the river of the same name. The soil is sandy but productive, and most of the silk of the country is produced here. A strip of arid sandy desert separates this district from Khutan and Yúrungkásh on one side and Karyá on the other. The river of Chíra flows through the settlement in several streams which get lost on the desert. The mulberry and æleagnus grow here to perfection, and their fruits are esteemed better than those in any other part of the country. The people are rich in cattle, sheep and camels, and manufacture excellent felts which they sell at Khutan. There are gold mines in the hills to the south.

Karyá, 4,000 houses. This district resembles the last, and is a market town on the river bearing its name. Its settlement extends for several miles up and down the stream till it is lost on the Tákla Mukán desert to the north. Its productions are the same as those of Chíra. At a day's journey to the south is the Soghrak settlement of 200 houses in a long glen. There are gold mines here similar to those at Chamand on the other side of the hills in the Kurái ghotágh district. Further on in the mountains, at Kalakúm, where there is no habitation, there are other gold mines, and mines of native sulphur. There is a road, two days' journey through narrow defiles, from Kalakúm to Chamand which is a settlement of 200 houses.

Náya, 500 houses. This is a small district on the edge of the desert, and ends toward the east at Mazár Bíbí Injila, or as it is commonly called Imám Ja'far Sadík. This is the boundary, too, of the Khutan State in that direction, and is considered to be the limit of the Amír's territory, although he claims possession of Cháchan, and has a Governor there. The settlements of Náya are dispersed along the foot of the hills upon the streams issuing from them, and are all of small extent, few containing 50 houses. There are gold mines in the district, and more productive than elsewhere. Across a desert waste to the east is Cháchan. This is a flourishing settlement of 500 houses on the banks of two rivers which unite on the plain, and flow in a single stream towards Lob. The town is situated at the foot of a mountain to the south, and a river flows on its west and its east. On these are planted the farmsteads of the settlement. By the Chinese this place was used as a penal colony for Khutan. It now belongs to the Amír, who has sent Daulat Beg of Khutan as his Governor there. The people are very prosperous and industrious, and are fond of good living and merriment. They are Musalmans, but very lax in their observance of the *Shara* or "Law."

A white stone called *mánoh* is quarried in the hills here and sent in large quantities to China. Formerly Cháchan was a very important place on the caravan route from Khutan to China. The ruins of the ancient city still exist on a ridge of hill overlooking the present town. They cover a great extent of surface, and are mostly buried under drift sand, but here and there their walls stand out, and are substantially built of brick and stone. Nobody knows anything of their history except that the city anciently belonged to infidels and was destroyed by the Musalmans. At the present day people dig in the ruins for the sake of the bricks and stones, and sometimes find great treasure in gold and precious stones. There is a road north from this to Lob, three or four days' journey across the desert by shepherd camps.

Inclusive of Cháchan the population of Khutan, according to the Chinese revenue returns, is reckoned at 18,500 houses. This at seven persons per house will give the total population of the State as 129,500 souls. But this, from all accounts, is much above the actual number now to be found within its limits. Khutan communicates with Tibet and Kashmir by the Sánjú road, with Yárkund by the Gúmá road, and with Lob by the Marján Uldí road along the course of the Khutan River. Its frontiers are Sánjú on the west, Múnjí near Gúmá on the north-west, Marján Uldí on Táklá Makán to the north, and Imam Ja'far Sadík on the east.

Yárkand.—This is the most populous and most extensive of all the States of Káshghar and its city, which was in ancient times the capital of the country, is still the largest and most wealthy in the whole valley. It is enclosed within fortified walls which are supported at intervals by buttress bastions topped with loopholed turrets. The length of the city is from north to south, but the walls describe an irregular figure, and have no surrounding ditch. The circuit is about four miles, and they are pierced by five gates or *dábza = darwaza*, viz., *Altún* or "Gold (gate)" on the south, *Cáwughat* or "Melon" on the west, *Tera-bágh* or "Hide garden" on the north, *Mascí* or "Jester" on the east, and *Kháncáh* or "Monastery" on the south-east.

The city stands on the open plain, and is surrounded by wide spreading and populous suburbs, which consist of farmsteads scattered about in small clusters amongst the fields and

10.—The Ex. Raja of Ladak and family.

11.—"Kolon," No. 1, Head of the family entitled by Treaty to conduct a caravan every third year from Kashmir Territory to Lhassa the Capital of the Grand Lama; No. 2, Heera Munshi of Ladak; No. 3, Kolon's Son.

gardens, and orchards, and timber trees. At five hundred yards or so to the west of it stands the Chinese fort or *Mángshín*, which is called Yangishahr or "New City" in distinction to the Kuhna shahr or "Old City." It is a strong square fort surrounded by a deep ditch, and entered over a drawbridge by a single gate which faces the Káwughat Gate of the city on the east. Between these two gates is a street of cook shops behind which are the cattle market and gallows on one side, and the horse market on the other. In the time of the Chinese it is said to have been a lively scene of activity and trade, but, as we found it, full three-fourths of the space were in ruins, and the rest a miserable collection of cook shops and grocers' stalls almost as dilapidated as the ruins themselves. The Yangishahr is the residence of the Governor of the State with his staff of officials and troops. Under the Chinese he was called *Khán Ambán* and now he is called *Shagháwul Dádkhwáh*. He lives in a spacious *orda* or "palace," which is shut off from the rest of the area by high walls, and is surrounded by the barracks and artillery gunsheds of the garrison. In the Yangishahr are also several commodious residencies for the higher officers of government or for foreign visitors and guests. One of these had been fitted up for the reception of the Embassy. It is in the centre of the fort area, and though closely crowded by other buildings was comfortably furnished for our special benefit, and we were allowed free liberty of ingress and egress. The garrison is said to number 1,800 men, who live with their families in the fort; but fully half the number are generally absent on detachment duty in the district, or in the frontier outposts, though their families remain behind. According to the Chinese revenue returns the population of the Yarkand State is estimated at 32,000 houses spread all over its area. This at seven persons per house will give the total population of the State as 224,000 souls. The limits of the State are, along the south frontier, Sánjú to Shahídulla, Kilyán to Yangi Dawan, Kokyár to Kulánúldi, and Kosharáb to the Múztágh of Kunjut. Along the west frontier are the highland district of Sárigh Kúl and the Kirghiz steppes of Pámir and Aláy; but these are beyond the present reckoning which only includes the country up to the foot of the hills, from Yakka Arik to Cháechiftlik or Chachiklik pass; north of this line the country is a desert waste. The north border of the State is a blank arid desert on which the boundary is marked by a small post house, where are two wells of brackish water 98 feet down. It is called Ak Rabát or "White Stage" and separates Yarkand territory from that of Yángí Hissár. The east border also is desert, and is marked by a line from Gúmá on the south by Mihnat Ortang on the east to Shamál on the north. In this area the settlements of Gúmá, Sánjú, Kilyán, Kokyár, Kosharáb, and Yakka Arik are the limits of cultivation; all beyond—and a good deal within—is sterile desert or mountain skirt. The above reckoned population is thus distributed.

Yárkand city, 5,000 houses, inclusive of mosques, colleges and saráes; and the immediate suburbs, including Yangishahr, 5,000 houses. Total 10,000 houses. The rural settlements of Sánjú 2,000, Kilyán 800, Kokyar 800, Yakka Arik 700, Kárghalik 2,000, Besharik 1,800, Posgám 1,600, Boryá 600, Gúmá 3,000, Kosharáb 500, Orpa 1,000, Tagharchí 200, Otúnchilik 2,000, Mirsháh 500, Islámbágh 500, Rabátchi 600, Tonguzlik 300, Arámang 100, and all other minor settlements 3,000. Total 32,000 houses. These figures are only approximate, and, from personal observation in respect to several of the most populous settlements, may I believe be taken as fairly correct.

The city itself having a circuit of four miles outside the walls may be considered as covering an area of 3,097,600 square yards. If we deduct one-fifth for fortifications, streets, courts, bazars, and tanks, of which last the number is said to be 120, we shall have 2,478,080 square yards left for the houses. And this, if we take 25 by 20 yards as the average measurement, will give the number at 4,956 or about 5,000 houses, which at seven persons per house represents a population of 35,000 souls. The calculation is certainly fully up to the mark, and I believe much above the actual fact, for compared with Peshawar, which has a population of something under 60,000 souls, Yarkand is an insignificant city. I don't think its population much exceeds 20,000 souls at the present time.

The citizens are mostly Turk with Tartar and Chinese converts and half breeds, and they have amongst them a large number of foreign settlers who are reckoned at two thousand

---

NOTE.—40,000 is the figure at which I should be disposed to put the population from the statements given by the local authorities.—T. D. F.

families. They are emigrants from Andiján, Badakhshán, and Kashmír in nearly equal proportions, besides a few Hindustani and Kabuli outcastes. They bear a character for all sorts of knavery and debauchery in common with the Tartar residents, who are besides characterized as seditious and turbulent. They belong to the Karátághlúk faction, whose doings have been mentioned in the preceeding history.

Under the Chinese rule Yárkand was the seat of government and a most flourishing centre of trade. Besides the garrison of 5,000 men, there was a floating population of nearly ten thousand followers, suttlers, artificers, pedlars, and merchants whose activity brought life, wealth, and prosperity to the city.

"What you see on market day now," as a citizen informed me, "is nothing to the life and activity there was in the time of the *Khitáy*. To-day the peasantry come in with their fowls and eggs, with their cotton and yarn, or with their sheep, and cattle and horses for sale; and they go back with printed cottons, or fur caps, or city made boots, or whatever domestic necessaries they may require, and always with a good dinner inside them, and then we shut up our shops and stow away our goods till next week's market day brings back our customers. Some of us go out with a small venture in the interim to the rural markets around, but our great day is market day in town. It was very different in the Khitáy time. People then bought and sold every day, and market day was a much jollier time. There was no Kázi Rais with his six *muhtasib* armed with the *dira* to flog people off to prayers, and drive the women out of the streets, and nobody was bastinadoed for drinking spirits and eating forbidden meats. There were musicians and acrobats, and fortune-tellers and story-tellers, who moved about amongst the crowds and diverted the people. There were flags and banners and all sorts of pictures floating at the shop fronts, and there was the *jallab*, who painted her face and decked herself in silks and laces to please her customers."——"Yes. There were many rogues and gamblers too, and people did get drunk, and have their pockets picked. So they do now, though not so publicly, because we are now under Islám, and the *Shariát* is strictly enforced.

The city contains several large colleges—there are thirty-eight in all—and mosques, and a number of saráes. None of them are of architectural note, except perhaps the new Andiján Saráe, which is a brick and mortar building with commodious vaults and lodges. A peculiar feature of the city are its *kol* or "tanks" of drinking water. There are, it is said, 120 within the walls. They are filled from canals on the outside, and are mere excavations in the soil, and are in no way protected from the impurities of the streets, or from wind drifts. In other respects of municipal arrangement and general conservancy, as well as in the appearance of the bazars, streets, and tenements, the city may be compared with a third rate Musalman town in which the houses are for the most part built of raw brick and mud plaster.

The principal industry here is the leather trade. Excellent boots and shoes of the European pattern are manufactured in the city; as are all sorts of saddlery and harness gear, together with sheepskin cloaks, and fur caps of the Tartar fashion. And these are exported to the neighbouring districts. The coarse cotton called *khám* is also woven here, and exported with that from Khutan to Andiján. For the rest the industrial trades are such as supply the domestic requirements of the people, and produce nothing for export.

The Yárkand division is traversed by several rivers on the course of which, and on canals drawn from which, its settlements are situated. They are the Sánjú or Gúmá river, the Kilyán, the Tiznáf, and the Zarafshán. The two first are lost on the desert, and the two last unite to form the Yárkand river. The Tiznáf waters the settlements of Kokyár, Besharik, and Kárghalic. The Zarafshán irrigates those of Yakka Arik and the city and south suburbs of Yárkand. The Orpa river flows through its western suburbs and joins the Yárkand river to the north. The Orpa is the only river which is bridged in this division, though most of the canals are so too. It and they flow on sandy bottoms; the other rivers on firm pebbly beds.

Yángi Hissár.—This division lies to the north-west of Yárkand and connects it with Káshghar. It is a flourishing and populous settlement extending some twenty miles from west to east along the course of the Sháhnáz river. The city and fort, however, are separated from the river by an intervening ridge of sand stone and gravel heights called Káyrágh; and with their suburbs are watered by six *ustang* or "canals," which are brought from the Ak Kay reservoir at the Mazár Khoja Baglán, 30 miles to the west of the town, where it is filled from streams coming down from the hills. The settlements to the south of Káyrágh are watered from the Sháhnáz which is lost on the desert to the east; and those on the north border of the division by the Kosán river which joins the Káshghar stream.

The limits of Yangí Hissár are Ak Rabát on the south, and Yapchang on the north; Egízyár Karawul, or outpost to the Chishtágh mountain on the west, and Ordám Pádsháh, or Kúm Shahídán on the east. The general character of the country is arid desert, with here and there small saline pools, or more extensive reedy wastes; and everywhere the soil is highly charged with salts which cover the ground with a white efflorescene even under growing crops. On the southern half of the division is a wide waste of this saline soil. It is covered with salt worts and a coarse reedy grass, and is so soft and spongy that cattle cannot traverse it off the beaten track.

Within the above limits, the population is reckoned at 8,000 houses, of which 2,000 constitute the city and its immediate suburbs. The rest are thus distributed. Along the south tract—Kizilí 200 houses, Chamalung 200, Kudúk, Tamyari, and Kosh Gumbaz 150, Topoluk 400, Kilpichim, Kálpín, and Toghochi 250, Egizyar 300, Tishiján, Sugat, and Piliz 100, Domshún, Yangíyar, and Ditir 100, and Kíng Kúl 600—total 2,300 houses. Along the middle tract—Konosák, Altúnchi, and Kásh Arik 200 houses, Tawiz 200, Karágho 100, Atimchágh and Campá 100, Shimlá 150, Mángshín 200, Khoja Arik 300, Syghán 300, and Arába 250—total 1,800 houses. Along the north track—Oktay and Cholpangarik 100 houses, Cháharshamba Bázár and Sáylik 250, Altúnlúk 200, Súgholúk 250, Tonglúk 250, Súnolúk 200, Yapchang 250, and other small settlements as Hazrat Begum, Ordam Pádsháh, Kárí Atám, &c., 400—total 1,900 houses. Total population of the division 56,000 souls.

The Yangi Hissár settlements are entirely agricultural. The city is a small town of about 600 houses composed of dilapidated tenements and decayed fortifications, and its people and surroundings wear an air of poverty, neglect, and decadence; yet the suburbs are flourishing gardens and cornfields. On the plain a few hundred yards to the north of the town is the Yangishahr, a strong fort with high turreted walls and a deep ditch. And between the two are the barracks of the garrison and their families, small fortified enclosures with crenelated walls.

In the time of the Chinese this was, as it is still, an important military post, and there are now more Chinese converts here than in any other part of the country, except at Káshghar itself. The Amír has a garrison of 500 men here, who are mostly quartered outside the fort, which is the depository of his treasure and the residence of some State prisoners and refugees. Amongst the latter Hydar Tora, son of Amír Muzaffaruddín of Bukhárá, who has been kept here under strict supervision for some years as a guest living on the bounty of Yákúb Beg.

Yángi Hissár is an interesting place historically as the scene of the grand struggle for mastery between Budhism and Islám; and though the former was overthrown, it was not without a heavy price paid by the victors in their best blood, as has been mentioned in the History. The place abounds in the tombs and sacred shrines of the early champions of the Faith, and a few miles to the west of the town, at Chúchám Padshah, is a vast cemetery consecrated to the dust of ten thousand warrior martyrs to the cause. It is a desolate waste spread far and wide over a dreary wilderness of sand hills and hollows, and even now its sepulchral odours and deep solitude impress the visitor with the magnitude of the contest and the fierceness of the fight. In this struggle—which it appears lasted for a quarter of a century before Budhism was stamped out by the conquest of its most flourishing seat at Khutan—several little fortified cities in this division were reduced to ruins. The largest of these, Ordám Padshah = "My King's palace," is now only known by name, for the site of its existence has for eight centuries been buried under the shifting sands; where still stands the shrine of Ali Arslán Khán and his 300 fellow martyrs, surrounded by a billowy sea of sand dunes which, as the venerable custodian solemnly informed us, "have hitherto, out of respect to the sacred resting place of the holy martyrs, passed on in their course giving the hallowed spot a wide berth; and please God they will always do so to all eternity."

About twelve miles to the south of this shrine, near that of Hazrat Begum on the desert are the indistinctly traceable fortifications of a castellated city now called Shahri Nuktá Rashíd. It is more or less completely buried under sand, but the mound tops are wind swept, and strewed thickly with bits of pottery, China, and glass; coins too are said to be found here, and Sir Douglas Forsyth got one of them from the keeper of the neighbouring shrine. In the opposite direction, to the west of the present town, are the ruins of another city, apparently very ancient and strongly fortified by high battlemented mounds the substantial walls of which are in parts still fairly traceable. As an instance illustrative of the dry character of the climate here, I may mention that we found sheets of matting, such as are used at the present day in the foundations of walls, still in excellent preservation under the layers of raw bricks composing the structure of the battlements; although, as we were assured and as history tends to prove, the place has been in ruins for eight hundred years. The original name of this city is lost, and it is now known simply by the name Tam = "Wall," and the people know no more of its history than that it formerly belonged to the Kingdom of Nuktá Rashid, the *Káfir*, and was destroyed by Ali Arslán Khan, the *Ghází*. Further north than Tam, near Chárshamba Bázár are the ruins of Oktú or Oktay. They are described as built of stone, and as being more substantial and more extensive than any others in the division. This is probably that Ota through which in early ages passed the caravan road from Kashghar over the Bolor range and through Karátakin to Balkh for the outlets west and south by the Oxus and Bamian respectively. The other great trade route was from Káshghar over the Tirik pass to Úsh or Osh and on along the Jaxartes. It is still in use as the caravan road to Orenburgh. The first has been long since abandoned as a trade route.

Yángí Hissár = "Newcastle," as the name and etymology indicate, dates only from the Muhammadan conquest; but from its appearance and the remains of walls in the vicinity it would seem to occupy the site of some more ancient city.

Every street has its *bang* shop, generally a mean little shed, in which two or three pipes are at the disposal of the passers by. There are besides, several opium divans, places more like pawnbroker's shop than anything else. Obscure chambers, dimly lighted by a row of flickering lamps along the floor, on which lie the somnolent devotees of this "thief of reason and riches." On shelves ranged round the walls are neatly folded and labelled bundles of their household chattels even to the clothes off their backs, all kept in pawn till released by cash payment. We shall return to this subject under the head of agricultural products. Suffice it here to say that the abuse of these deleterious drugs is prevalent throughout the country. I have thus referred to it in this place, because I observed that the people of Yángí Hissár were more generally addicted to these forms of intoxication than those of Yarkand or Káshghar; a point in which they do not belie the character given them by common report.

Káshghar.—This State is situated in the angle of junction between the great mountain ranges of Alátágh and Bolórtágh, and for purposes of government includes the steppes of Pámir and the glens of Sárigh Kúl. But these last, being beyond its proper limits, are excluded from the present reckoning, and will be described separately hereafter.

Its limits are: On the north—Balauti Hill which separates it from the canton of Úsh Turfán; Tirikti Fort and Tásh Rabát on Alátágh which separate it from the Kirghiz of Isígh Kol; Chakmák Fort and Kará Aylák of Atbáshi which separate it from the Russian outpost on the Nárín; and the Aktágh range which separates it from Úzkand in Andiján; Mingyol outpost at foot of the range. On the west—Tirik Dawán which separates it from Úsh in Andiján and Karátágh and the hills down to Chíshtágh = "Tooth Hill," north of the Chachiklik Pass which form the eastern border of the Aláy Pámir. On the south—the Khan Arík canal (from Yamányár branch of Kosán River), Tazghún and Yapchang. On the west—the desert from Fyzábád to Kol Táylák and Súghún.

Within these limits the population is estimated at 16,000 houses, or at seven per house, at 112,000 souls. Of these 5,000 houses are allotted to the city and its immediate suburbs, and the remainder are thus distributed amongst a number of considerable market towns and agricultural settlements. Along the hill skirt to the west—Opal 800 houses, Táshmalik 700, and Múshí 400. Along the hills to the north—Mingyol 200 houses, Sarman 300, Artosh 2,000,

12.—Shémurs of Ladak, Group of Ladies taken at Leh.

13.—Professional dancers of Leh.

and Arghú 400. On the plain to the east—Beshkirim 800 houses, Daulat Bágh 600, Yangabad 600, and Fyzábád 600. On the plain to the south—Kizil 800 houses, Khánarik 800, and Tázghún 500. And all other lesser settlements 1,500. Total 16,000 houses.

The general character of the country is level plain quite up to the foot of the hills, where it becomes broken by low ridges of clay and conglomerate. The soil is mostly sandy and charged with salts, but it is said to be more productive than that of the other divisions already described. It is watered by several streams from the hills to the north, and from springs at the foot of those to the west. They are the Tirikti or Súghún river on the banks of which are Kirghiz pasture grounds; the Artosh river on which is the populous settlement of that name; the Túman river on which stands Káshghar city with the settlements of Sarman, Beshkirim, and Daulat Bágh; the Kizil river on which are the market town of Fyzábád, the southern suburbs of the city, and the Mushi settlement; the Yamányár, and its great canal of Khánárik with their settlements; and the Tázghún, and its canals, and their settlements. Those to the north of the city unite to form the Artosh river, and those to the south to form the Fyzábád river; and the two unite near Kol Táylák to form the Káshghar river.

Káshghar is the present capital of the country, the seat of its government, and the most active centre of its trade, which is exclusively with Russia by the caravan route to Almáti. It consists of the Kuhna Shahr, or "Old City," on the right bank of the Túman river, and Yángishahr, or "New City," on the plain five miles to the south of it. Between the two flows the Kizil river on which are several fortified barracks, and small farms, with the conspicuous shrines of Sayyid Jaláluddin Bughdádí and Hazrat Padsháh, and the ruins of Aski Shahr or the "Ancient City;" and the communication is by a wood bridge across the river.

Kuhna Shahr is a small fortified city on high ground overlooking the river. Its walls are lofty and supported by buttress bastions with loopholed turrets at intervals. The glacis is protected by a covered way, and the whole is surrounded by a deep ditch, which is crossed by a timber bridge leading to each of the two gates, viz., the "Kúm Darwáza or "Sand Gate" on the south, and the Sú Darwáza or "Water Gate" on the north. The fortifications are all of hard clay, and much out of repair. The eastern quarter of the city is occupied by the palace of the Dádkhwáh or "Governor," and near it is a substantial new built saráe; and the main line of bazar passes between the two from one gate to the other. The city covers about half the area of Yárkand, and may contain probably 2,500 houses, if as many. But its shops are better stocked with merchandise, and there is altogether an air of brisker activity in the place. The people too are physically far superior, and one is only reminded of goitre by an occasional bulbous throat here and there in the crowd. Their general appearance too is far more prosperous, and, though the strange diversity and blending of race types is as noticeable here as at Yárkand, a more pleasing feature in the contrast are the fair complexions, rosy cheeks, and look of robust health that pervade the crowd, in place of the sallow complexion and sickly looks of the citizens of the older capital.

This city, as has been mentioned in the history, was built in 1513 A.D. by Mirzá Abákakar when he destroyed the ancient capital or Aski Shahr on the approach of Sultán Sa'íd's invading army. In its interior arrangement and general appearance of the houses and bazars it no way differs from Yárkand. The gates however are double, and the outer one to the south is plated with sheet iron studded with boss headed nails. Between the two at each side is a small row of barracks and gun-sheds for the guards of Tungáni troops; about thirty men at each gate.

About two miles to the north of the city, beyond the Túman river which is crossed by bridge, is the shrine of Hazrat Afák, the Saint King of the country who died and was buried here in 1693 A.D. It is a well kept and handsome mausoleum faced with blue and white glazed tiles, and stands under the peaceful shade of some magnificent silver poplars called *tárik*. About it are a commodious college, and mosque, and monastery. These have all been recently built by the Amír, and are the most substantial and superior structures in the country. The whole stand on their own rent-free grounds and are surrounded by rich orchards, fruit gardens, and vineyards. Beyond these again, down to the river in the direction of the city, is a vast cemetery of neatly kept tombs. Many of them are covered with dome vaulted chambers open towards the east; and in these take up their abode in their filth and their rags a number of *calandar* and *darvesh*—demented ascetics and abandoned mendicants—who with their hags and a few wretched children here lead a life of idleness and folly, the cause and effect at once of their love of *bang*—veritable "dwellers amongst the tombs," impudent claimants of charity from every passer by, and equally ready with curse or blessing as their loud appeals may require. By the Amír's favour we were permitted to visit this sacred shrine, and were received with marked attention and hospitality by Eshán Mahmúd Khan, the *Mutawalli Báshí* or "Head Custodian," a quiet and deferential priest who had received his education at Constantinople, and on parting informed us that we were the first Europeans, nay the first Christians, who had ever set foot within the hallowed precincts.

A few hundred yards to the west of Kuhna Shahr are the ruins of the Chinese fort called Gulbágh. It was destroyed in 1825 A.D. by Jahángír Khoja, and on the recovery of the country by the Chinese they built the several forts or *mángshin* which are now called Yangishahr at Yárkand, Yángi Hissár and this place.

The Yangi-shahr of Káshghar was built in 1838 when Zuhúruddín or Zoruddín was the Hákim Beg or "Chief Governor" of the division. It stands on the plain five miles south of the city and near the right bank of the Kizil river, and is nearly as large as the city itself. It is of oblong shape running north and south, and is entered by a single gateway with three portals at cross angles one within the other in the north face. The walls are lofty and massive and topped by loopholed turrets at intervals, and on each side is a projecting bastion to protect the curtains by flank fire. The glacis is protected by a covered way, and the whole is surrounded by a deep and wide ditch which can be filled from the river; at the risk, however, of bringing down the whole structure, for the walls are of mud and stand upon a porous sandy soil.

In the time of the Chinese it held a garrison of six thousand men, and was the residence of the Ambán and other Khitáy officials, with a number of families and followers. It is now the residence of the Amir whose *orda* occupies the site of the Ambán's palace, and the officers of his Court who each have their residencies within the area. The other principal buildings are the Friday Mosque or *Jumá Masjid* built upon the ruins of the Chinese temple, and the harem of which the long blank line of tall walls is all that can be seen, and, coupled with the stillness around, all that prompts conjecture as to the nature of the life within. In the middle line of the area is a military bázár, and on each side is a row of soldiers' huts, but the bulk of the troops are quartered under their respective commandants in separate barracks outside the fort; and each of these is enclosed within crenelated and loopholed walls, entered through a fortified gateway; and they are disposed within gunshot of each other between the fort and river to the north, and on the road to Yangí Hissár on the east. Amongst those in the former direction is another harem. A commodious enclosure said to accommodate two hundred ladies whom "the king delights to honour."

The *orda* or "palace" is a succession of courts one beyond the other up to the fourth in which are the Amir's private apartments. The third is occupied in the width of one side by the audience hall—a spacious chamber spread with carpets and felts and provided with a fire-pit in the centre—and in the length of one contiguous wall by a covered and raised verandah in which on State occasions the body-guard take their seats. The opposite walls are a blank spread of mud plaster singularly in keeping with the simplicity and absence of adornment around, and wonderfully suited to the aweful silence and studied stillness that characterize the discipline of the court. The second court runs parallel to the third only a wall intervening. Its short sides are occupied by a row of offices in each. One set are cook-rooms and store-rooms for the *dusturkhwan* or "table cloth of ceremony" which forms so important a feature of the social customs of this country. The other set communicate with the King's private court and are for pages in waiting and other domestics. On the long sides of this court are verandahs similar to that in the preceding. Each is matted and occupied along the wall by a long row of solemn looking figures, seated with downcast eyes, motionless and silent. Each wears a snow white turban; each has a long prong-rest gun placed on the floor in front of him; and each has his baggy robes gathered in at the waist by a buff leather belt from which hangs a sword and a multitude of the paraphernalia belonging to his gun. For the rest no two in the row are alike. Each wears a robe of different pattern, but all of the same strikingly attractive character—silk or cotton print—and all in brightest colours mixed in stark contrast. Here is a gigantic Afghan with nut brown complexion, handsome countenance, and flowing beard of glossy black; and next him is a fellow countryman of the same stalwart proportions, but bowed by the weight of his grey beard and scarred cheek; both in the midst of the subservient crew show in their looks the natural independence of the race, and, in defiance of etiquette, raise their heads to survey the stranger at their leisure, and, I must record, with a look of unmistakeable "rapprochement" too.

There sits a square-faced, flat-nosed, skew-eyed Kalmák, with cheek bones as high as his shoulders, and a body as square as his face; his ruddy features, without a hair to ornament them, are respectfully bowed, and wear an expression of seriousness only equalled by that of timid submission. Next him sits a fair, full, round faced Andijáni, with short trimmed beard, bright eyes, and an air of complacent self satisfaction supported by the stolidity with which he plants his Dutch built frame amongst his fellows. His looks of natural confidence and ready activity contrast strongly within the cunning mien and crouching seat of his Kirghiz neighbour, whose angular eyes and angular cheeks and angular face—all suffused with a healthy glow of red, and all together on one plane prolonged to a point at the chin by a short whispy tuft of beard—present a no less strange divergence from the rotund features and form beside him. But here a very different form interposes like a full stop in a sentence topped with a stroke of surprise. He is our familiar black skinned and oily faced Hindustani Musalmán, whose beard shines as bright as his eyes, and both by contrast more pronounced in colour, whilst his obsequious smiles have grown none the less by distance, despite the disguise he appears in. Beyond him again come forms more in consonance with their garb, at least according to our associations, and then another type that arrests attention by its peculiar hard lineaments, its deep sunk eyes, narrow retreating forehead, and naked projecting jowl. It is owned by the muddy skinned, withered, opium smoking Khitáy whose repulsive physiognomy is the reflexion of his cowed spirit and forced servility. Like him too, but with more oblique eyes, more prominent cheek bones, and more fleshy features is his Tungání confrére. And different from all, though strongly allied to the first, is the brown skinned, bewhiskered, and gentle looking Badakhshi, with high full forehead, long arched finely carved nose, and oval face of the true Aryan stamp. He sits with respectful pose and downcast eyes, and only looks up to show a ready obedience on his countenance.

Such was the odd medley of garbs and grimaces that composed the guard in waiting in this second court of the King's palace. The next, a much smaller one, is covered in and shelters a similar guard which holds the gateway. Everywhere within the palace courts a perfect silence prevails, so much so that even the sociable and homely sparrow shuns the stillness and chirrups not where men dare not speak.

The population of Káshghar is almost entirely Turk and employed solely in agriculture. They are said to be restless under control and inclined to tumult, and have a character for neglecting those courtesies and conventionalities of society so carefully observed by their neighbours. Further they are taxed with a want of hospitality and denounced as but poor Musalmans considering the many priests and sacred shrines in their midst. They belong to the Aktághlúk faction and, as their detractors are the rival Karátághlúk, perhaps they are not so bad as they are painted. Under the lax rule of the Chinese, however, they were notorious for indulgence in all sorts of forbidden pleasures, meats, and drinks, and amongst them flourished whole colonies of the gay and accommodating *Chaucán*. All these are now strictly repressed, and their loss is supplied by a more general resort to hemp and opium, and a most degrading vice.

Úsh Turfán.—This little division lies to the north-east of Káshghar from which it is separated by the Balauti range. This is an irregular chain of hills which, emanating from the Tirikti Peak near Chádir Kol, projects eastward parallel to the Alátágh and shuts off the Úsh Turfán valley from the plain. The western half of the valley is occupied by the Kirghiz pastures of Kákshál, through which flows the Aksáy river from Chádir Kol. Its banks, as the river approaches Safarbáy, are studded by dense forests of poplar trees, and the road passes through them for a distance of thirty miles. From Safarbáy a caravan road goes north over the Bedal Pass to the head waters of the Nárín river, and beyond, across the Zauka Pass, to Isigh Kol. The Bedal Pass marks the north boundary of U'sh Turfán and the Amir's territory, and at the entrance to the gorge leading up to it is an outpost called Bedal Karáwul.

From Safarbáy eastward the valley widens, and is studded with little farm settlements on the streams coming down the glens on either side. They form two streams called Aksáy and Táoshkán which unite and join the Aksú River south of that city. The population of this division is altogether agricultural, and estimated at 2,000 houses, or 14,000 souls at seven per house.

The capital had formerly a strong little castle, but it was destroyed with the town in 1765 A.D., and its people massacred by the Chinese for revolt in favor of the Khoja rebellion. It is now an open market town of 800 houses commanded by a fort on a hill overlooking it from the north-west. The garrison consists of 300 men, and the townspeople are the descendants of *taranchi* or "labourers" planted here by the Chinese after the massacre.

Farmsteads are scattered all over the valley, but the principal settlements are Safarbáy, Karáwul, Akyár, Achítágh, and Aral. Sheep, cattle, and horses are very numerous. The fine wool of the first is woven by the Kirghíz into a variety of materials for home use, and with the tobacco and cattle of the town finds its way to the Aksú market. The limits of the division are Kákshál on the west and the Aksú River on the east, the Bedal mountain on the north, and the Balauti ridge on the south. Its communication and trade are entirely with Aksú of which by some it is considered to form a part.

Aksú.—This is the central division of the country, and is situated at the base of Alátágh or Tangrí Ula at the southern entrance to the Múzárt or "Glacier Pass." Under the Chinese it was an important military post at the junction of the roads from Ila by the Múzárt, and from Kánsúh by Khámil and Turfán. It was the centre of the Chinese trade and formed the division between the eastern and western cities of the province, and was the limit of the trade privileges accorded by the Chinese Government to the Khokand Khan over the cities of the western division.

Its limits are from the Aksú River on the west to the Kizil or Nárinj stream beyond Sáyrám on the east, and from the water-shed of Tangrí U'la on the north to Sáy Arik, and the Aksú and Tárim rivers on the south. Its population is reckoned at 12,000 houses, of which 6,000 are allotted to the city and immediate suburbs. The rest are distributed thus. Settlements to the north—Chodá 60 houses, Kázghán 100, Sirilmá 40, and other homesteads 300. On the west—Aykol 20, Sáyarik 40, Kálpín 60, Chílán 60, Súgat 40, Marákala 20, Besh Digarman 60, and other homesteads 400. On the south—Súbalik 80, Sagfarcha 50, Daulatbágh 200, Kará Moghcha 20, Bálaring 20, Amarjama 50, Kúmbásh 200, Dolán 50, and others 630. On the east—Jám 100, Tázlung 100, Kará-yúlghún 150, Yakka Arik 150, Koshtami 250, Báy 600, Karábágh 100, Sáyrám 800, and others 1,250. Total of all 12,000 houses, at seven per house 84,000 souls.

Aksú is a very ancient city, and was formerly called Arpadíl or Ardabíl. It covers two ridges of gravel heights on the left bank of the Aksú river where it is joined by the Úsh or Kákshál river, and has a citadel on each. The city is surrounded by fortified walls, and has two gates—that on the west Sú Darwáza or "Water Gate," and that on the east Tumurchi Darwáza or "Blacksmith's Gate." The climate is described as very salubrious, though the winter is an extremely rigorous season; and the natives I have seen bear testimony in confirmation by their clear healthy looks and robust frames. The citizens are said to be peaceable and industrious, to be very sociable, and fond of gaiety and the pleasures of life generally. They are more purely Turk in physiognomy, judging from the few I saw in the Amír's service, than the citizens of either Yárkand or Káshghar, and are supposed to be the purest representatives, together with the people of Artosh north of Káshghar, of the ancient Ayghúr or Uighúr conquerors.

Aksú is celebrated for its manufactures of saddlery and harness, its pottery, and its raw hide jars called *dabba* for oil, butter, &c. Its tobacco also is considered the best that is produced in the country. All these, together with cattle and the shawl wool of U'sh Turfan, are exported to the neighbouring cities and countries. The mineral resources of the country are considerable, and in the time of the Chinese mines of lead, and copper, and sulphur were systematically worked, whilst coal was generally used in the city as fuel. The lead mines are in Tájik Tágh, five tásh north-east of Jám, and those of copper at Onbásh on the Múzárt river. The sulphur mines are on a low ridge of hills bordering the Aksáy river at Kálpín, and the coal is found in the hills near Karábágh, where are hot sulphur springs which are resorted to by the inhabitants for medicinal purposes. Coal is also found in the adjoining hills drained by the Kizil or Nárin river; and further on is an active volcano from the base of which are collected alum, and salammoniac, and blue vitriol or sulphate of copper. The asbestos mentioned by Marco Polo as a utilized product of this region is not now so known in the country.

The Múzárt pass connects this division with Ila or Kúlja. The road is described as very difficult now, though in the time of the Chinese it was kept open for troops and caravans by a regular establishment of labourers posted at intervals of three miles along the road across the glacier, which is within the Amír's territory. The glacier is four days' journey from Aksú, and two days obliquely across it to a clump of trees and a post house which mark the limit of Káshghar territory. Beyond this is a journey of eight days to Ila down the valley of the Takas River. The glacier is said to fill a long winding valley which extends three or four days' journey east and west. In the latter direction it gives rise to the Narin river, and in the former it gives rise to a river which ends in a swamp at Sháhyár and is called Múzárt Daryá. The road across the glacier is interrupted by vast fissures and moraine banks, and is covered with snow till the beginning of July. The Chinese kept the road clean swept and marked by piles of stone, but these are now all destroyed, and the road is almost impassable. It is closed to caravans by the Amír, who has built a fort for a garrison of 500 men in the Yakka Arik glen at the entrance to the defile leading up to the pass, and has diverted the current of trade to the route through Káshghar by the Narin passes to Almati or Vernöe.

That portion of this division which skirts the base of the mountains is said to be populous and productive, and to abound in gardens and rivulets. The population is mostly employed in agriculture and the breeding of cattle, and, towards the east of the capital, are massed in the two principal market towns of Báy and Sáyrám, which are only 15 miles apart on the course of the Múzárt river. In the midst of the farmsteads of the latter is a square fort built by the Chinese. It is now the residence of the Amír's Governor with a garrison of 300 men. To the north-west of Sáyrám is the Karábágh settlement and its hot springs. The place is said to be one of the most delightful residences in the whole country, and its gardens wonderfully productive.

The southern portion of the division partakes much of the character of the desert beyond, and its saline sandy soil is covered with great wastes of reed grown marsh and impassable tracts of swamp which are bordered by a brushwood of poplar and tamarisk bushes.

Kúchá.—This is a small State situated at the foot of the mountains in continuation eastward from Aksú. In ancient times it was an important little principality, and a flourishing seat of Budhism. On a hill to the north of the city are the ruins of an ancient temple and monastery. They are described as of considerable extent, and very substantially built of stone on the ledges and rocks of a precipitous hill. Fragments of sculptures are found among the *débris*, and in some galleries sunk in the rock there are said to be paintings of men and animals on the walls as fresh and bright in colour as if new. Precious stones, gems, and trinkets are occasionally found in the rubbish of the crumbled walls, and marvellous tales are told of the lustre and size of some that have been picked up here by wandering shepherds. A large figure is said to exist here, carved on the face of a rock overlooking the road to Kúrla. It is described as having the tongue lolled out and right shoulder depressed with extended arm, as in the fashion of Kalmák salutation. It acknowledges the salutes of passers by a return wag of the tongue and wink of the eye, and has often been seen to smile, by credulous Kalmáks at least.

In the mountains to the north is a volcano, and from its base a river called Zamcha issues. On its banks are dug alum and a salt of zinc called *zamch*, which is used as a mordant with alum in dying. The rocks at the foot of the hill are hot to the touch, but the water of the river is cold. Loud rumblings and explosions are constantly heard in the interior of the mountain, which is very high, and whose top is always covered with snow. It is called Khán Khurá Tágh, and forms the boundary between Yuldúz of the Kalmák and Zúnghár of the Kirghiz and Kazzák who are also called Jattah Moghol.

Zúnghár is also called Mogholistán, and extends from this mountain along the north slopes of Alátágh to Tashkand in the west. Khán Khurá Tágh is the western boundary of the Yuldúz territory. It has a volcano which emits smoke and vomits up streams of pebbles and hot mud. At the foot of the volcano is the Tolaman river which further on is called Koksú or "Blue Water." Tolaman is four days' journey from Kurla and three from Karásháhr; and Khán Khurá Tágh is two days' journey from Básh Ayghúr; and Tolaman is a day's journey further north. On the top of this mountain are the remains of hundreds of ovens which were used for the funeral feast of the Great Zúnghár Khán, Moghol, who died a thousand years ago, and was deposited in a box on the summit of the mountain. Beyond this mountain, to the north of Yaldúz, is the range of Boghdo Isin Ula, which is quite impassable owing to snow and glaciers. It separates Yuldúz from the Ila country. The above is what I learned from an intelligent native of Kúchá, which was formerly called Kúsán. The population of this division is reckoned at 6,000 houses, including 2,000 allotted to the city and suburbs, or at seven per house, 42,000 souls. The city itself is enclosed within fortified walls, and contains about 800 houses, and is divided into equal parts by a wall running through the length of the city. In the time of the Chinese one of these divisions was occupied by the Khitay garrison, traders, and Kalmák, and the other by the Musalmans; and in the suburbs dwelt a numerous and influential colony of Khoja priests. They took a prominent part in the overthrow of the Chinese rule, and almost all themselves perished in the ensuing conquest of the country by the Amír.

The people here in physique, character, and mode of life much resemble those of Aksú. Their farmsteads are described as models of neatness and thrift, and their orchards produce the finest apples and pears and pomegranates in the country. They are exported to all the neighbouring cities. The pears are of a peculiar excellence, of light colour, soft granular structure, and very juicy; for export each fruit is wrapped separately in paper, and packed in wood boxes, covered with felt, two of which make a horse load. The apples too are of a peculiar kind called *Múzalmá* or "Ice Apple;" their skins are semi-transparent, and the substance the same as if iced. The pomegranates are of large size and have juicy, sweet, red grains.

The rural population numbers 4,000 houses thus distributed. On the north—there is no habitation on this side of the city; the space between it and the mountains is occupied by patches of brushwood and reed grown swamp. On the west—Shamál Bágh 100, Daulat Bágh 150, Kútlúgh Orda 50, Bihisht Bágh 100, Chíníbágh 150, Kurol 50, Tawádin 50, Fyzábád 200, and Sháhyár 400. On this side separating Kúchá from Aksú is a wide waste of clay and sand hills in the hollows of which are reeds and swamps, quite impassable during summer floods. On the south—Yuldúz Bágh 100, Ashk Sáydí 50, and Bughúr 250, on the borders of the desert on which are the wild camel, stag, and wild pig. On the east—Uchár 30, Sáy Bágh 50, Kará Bocá 20, Yangábád 100, Uzúm 50, Mazár Bágh 150, Saksáb 20, Ashkala 30, Tora 30, Yaka Tokonáy 60, Cholábád 20, Yángi Hissár 150, Chedir 60, Súlúk Ashma 50, Chárchú 100, and Durwúl 80. These are situated on numerous little streams from the mountains; the principal of them are the rivers Zamcha, Karátál, and Shákúr. All other settlements 1,250. Total 4,000 houses.

The limits of Kúchá are from the Múzárt and Nárin rivers on the west to Durwúl on the east, and from the water-shed of the Khán Khurá Tágh range on the north to the Tárim river on the south.

Kúrla is the next division at the foot of the Alátágh or Khán Khurá range. It is a small agricultural and pasture country more than half covered by swamps and reed marshes. Its population is reckoned at 2,000 houses, or at seven per house, 14,000 souls. The capital is an open market town of 700 houses. It is commanded by a fort built by the Amír at Sáy Bágh on the road north-east to Karáshahr, three miles from the town. The river Kálgha, a tributary of the Káidú or Karáshahr river flows through the town, which is said to be smaller than Yangi Hissár.

Its suburbs to the west on the Kúchá road are Conghrát, Langar, and Shinághí to Durwúl; to the north-east on the Karáshahr road, Ukát, Sáy bégh, and the new fort to Lámpú-tásh hill; to the east on the road to Kúrúgh Tágh, Tuwúnki, Chárchú, and Shánko; and to the south on the road to Kará Kochún, Cosh Arik, Tobrachi, Taskan, Doghár, Chambola, Langar, Sháh Calandar, and Uzan.

Its limits are Durwul on the west, and Básh Ayghúr, on the right bank of the Karáshahr river which comes from the Tolaman hills where coal is worked, on the east; on the north the mountains, and on the south the Tárim river to Konchi below the junction of the united stream of the Kúcha and Kúrla rivers. This is the limit eastward of the Turk tribes of Káshghar and Yárkand; and beyond the Káidú or Karáshahr river comes the Tartar race, the Kalmak, and Khitay element in preponderance. The road from Kúrla to Karáshahr goes along the right bank of the river between it and the mountains, and beyond Dangzil, where in a reedy marsh are the ruins of Kutyághan, crosses it to the city by boat.

Karáshahr.—This division occupies a valley between the Ayghúr Bulák hills to the north, (a continuation eastward of the Alátágh or Tangri Ula range), and the Kúrúgh-tágh range of sand hills to the south. These coalesce towards the east and close the valley in that direction at Gumish Akma, about 90 miles from the city; but towards the west the valley is open and gives passage to the Káidú river, which on issuing from the Yuldúz valley spreads over the southern portion of this basin and forms the Baghrásh Kol or lake. It is described as a long sheet of water five days' journey in length, and covered with floating islands of tall reeds amidst which the river flows, in the western end of the lake only. It is separated from the Lob District to the south by the Kurúghtágh, a wide range of sandy and gravelly ridges, amongst the hollows of which the wild horse and wild camel breed. There is a road between the lake and this range, seven days' journey from Kúrla to Ush Aktál; and there is another along its southern side, between it and Lob, a seven days' journey from Kará Kochún to Turfán. There is no habitation on either route, and the soil is sandy and marshy, and covered with great spreads of reed, and tamarisk, and poplar forest. The city of Karashahr stands near the left bank of the river to the north of the lake. Between the city and the river is the Musalman settlement of farms, and from it north-east goes the road to Turfan along a wide plain between the hills and the lake. It is about six days' journey in length, and was covered with a succession of Khitay homesteads; but these were all destroyed by the Amir, and the whole way up to Ush Aktal, a distance of fifty miles, is now a mass of ruined farms and deserted homesteads. At Kará Kizil, 20 miles beyond Ush Aktál and about the same distance from Gumish Akma where the road enters the hills, there are the ruins of an ancient city called Kará Kizil in the midst of a sandy waste. They are supposed to be the remains of the ancient Chálish or Jálish.

Karáshahr is a walled city of 1,000 houses, formerly peopled by Kalmák tribes who always lived in their *Khargáh* tents (putting their cattle into the houses) and every summer emigrated to Yuldúz. It was originally founded by the Khitay with twelve Musalmán families from Kúrla and twelve from Bughúr; and it was afterwards settled by the Kalmák of the Turgut and Koshot camps, and by traders from Kámol. Since the Amír's campaign here the city is almost entirely deserted, and all the suburbs, except the Musalman settlement on the river, are now in ruins.

The population of the division was formerly reckoned at 8,000 houses or 56,000 souls, but now, excepting the Musalman settlement of 300 houses on the river and the new fort built by the Amír, there is hardly anybody in the country. The Yuldúz Kalmák who used to camp and pasture here, and who kept up a constant communication with Lob, now seldom quit their own valley. The Yuldúz Kalmák are Turgut and Koshot. Those of Ila are Olot and Mánjhú; and amongst them are many Solon and Shiba, the offspring of a Kalmák father and Khitay mother. They are a mean and beggarly set, and wear no other clothing but a loin-clout; their language is a mongrel dialect mixed up with many Arabic words; they have no other weapons besides the bow and arrow. There are also in Ila a great many *champan;* these are enslaved criminals brought and settled here from all parts of China;

they are mostly employed as soldier farmers, and to prevent their leaving the country are scored on the left cheek with a razor; they are a despicable set, and speak mixed languages, such as Khitáy, Mánjhú, Kalmák, &c. There are none of these in Yuldúz, only Kalmák and Khitay. Yulduz produces wheat=*sagántaran*, barley=*khárataran*, rice=*tuturgho*, maize = *ardanshishi*, millet=*carásuc-tirik*, melon=*gho*, water-melon=*turbuz*, cucumber=*tamshak*, opium =*khartamki*, egg plant=*petingán*, pear=*kermin*, apple=*almin*, &c. All these were grown by the Kalmák and Khitay in Karáshahr in quantity to supply their own wants and all Lob and the Yuldúz camps.

The only cultivation now, besides the Musalmán settlement on the river, is that around the new fort by the soldiers of the garrison. This fort was built by the Amir at Tawulgah three and a half *tásh* north-east from the city and half a *tásh* from the river. It is on the plain two days' journey from Lake Baghrásh on the south, and four days' from the mountains to the north. It is of square shape and built of red bricks of which the Chinese left immense piles here; the fort has one gate on the south side, and is surrounded by a deep ditch all round, and on each of its four sides are eight high turrets. It is the best fort in the country; between it and the river is a settlement of 300 farms held by families originally from Kámol; and to the west of the fort is the Shitán settlement, which is now deserted and in ruins.

The Kalmák are a distinct people from the Turk tribes of Káshghar, and differ from them in origin, physiognomy, language, religion, manners, customs, and mode of life. They belong to the great Monghol Tártár race from the north, and their principal divisions in this region are the following, *viz.*, Monghol in Mongholáy, sixteen days' journey north-east from Karáshahr; Chokúr at Issik; Tánghút in the Tánghút valley; Olot and Mánjhú in Ila; Turgút in Ila, Yuldúz, Karáshahr and Lob; Koshot in Yuldúz; Kará Kalmák in Yuldúz, Lob, Cháchan, and Tibet; Sárígh Kalmák in Yuldúz, Lysun, Orúmchí, and Turfán; and Tuwat in Tuwat or Tubat or Tibet which is also called Joh. All these originally came from Kok Nor, which is seven days' journey north of Mongholáy, and Mongholáy is twelve days' journey north-east of Orúmchí. There are besides two other countries of the Kalmák also called Kok Nor. One is five days' journey north of Orúmchí, and the other is, beyond Lob, five days' journey to the south of Kúchá. This last is continuous with Cháchan on the east of Khutan, and in it are the ruins of several ancient cities of which nobody knows anything. The principal of these is called Kok Nor. "Kok Nor means 'blue lake,' and these several countries are so called, because they have such sheets of water in different parts of their surface. But these ruins of Kok Nor I have myself seen." So says my informant whom I have before introduced as the traveller during thirty years all over this region. "They are on the desert to the east of the Katak ruins, and three days' journey from Lob in a south-west direction along the course of the Khutan River. The walls are seen rising above the reeds in which the city is concealed."——"No. I have not been inside the city, but I have seen its walls distinctly from the sandy ridges in the vicinity. I was afraid to go amongst the ruins because of the bogs around, and the venomous insects and snakes in the reeds. I was camped about them for several days with a party of Lob shepherds who were here pasturing their cattle. Besides it is a notorious fact that people who do go amongst the ruins almost always die, because they cannot resist the temptation to steal the gold and precious things stored there."——"You may doubt it, but everybody here knows that what I say is true; and there are hundreds of Kalmáks who have gone to the temple in the midst of these ruins to worship the God there."——"Yes. There is a temple in the centre of the ruins, and in it is the figure of a man. It is of the natural size, and the features are those of a Kalmák, and the whole figure is of a bright yellow colour. Ranged on shelves all round the figure are precious stones and pearls of great size and brilliancy, and innumerable *yámb* or ingots of gold and silver. Nobody has power to take away anything from here."——"This is all well known to the people of Lob. And they tell of a Kalmák who once went to worship the God, and after finishing his salutation and adorations secreted two *yámb* of gold in his fob, and went his way. He had not gone very far when he was overpowered by a deep sleep and lay down on the road side to have it out. On awaking he discovered that his stolen treasure was gone, though the fob of his *debit* or frock was as he had closed it. So he went back to the temple to get others, but to his astonishment found the very two he had taken returned to the exact spot from which he had removed them. He was so frightened that he

14.—The Nubra Valley from Panamik, looking S. E. Buddhist Chortens in the foreground.

15.—Buddhist temple at Panamik, Gods of the Buddhists.—1.—Chakna Durge; 2.—Sangias Shukla Tuba; 3.—Pakpa Chingre Zik; 4.—Dekhna Karpo, goddess.

prostrated himself before the God and confessing his fault begged forgiveness. The figure looked benignly on him and smiled, and he heard a voice warn him against such sacrilege in future. He returned to Lob and kept his story secret for a long time till a Lamma discovered and exposed him, and he was so ashamed that he left the country."

The Kalmáks are entirely a nomadic or pastoral people. They have no towns or cities of their own. They live in *Khargáh* camps, which they shift about from place to place according to the seasons and the requirements of their flocks and their crops. Their camps are always pitched in a circle around their patron God who is set up in the centre as their presiding deity and protector. Every tent besides has its own household God who receives the worship of only the occupants of the tent; but the central God is worshiped by the whole camp, and nobody passes it without a low bow and always keeping the figure on the right hand; to pass it on the left is sure to bring down some calamity on the whole community. Should anybody so offend, the whole camp is struck and pitched in some other spot. Cattle are excluded from the centre of the camp lest they should so offend the God.

The Kalmáks are all of the Budhist religion. Their idols are called *Burkhun* collectively, but the chief idol of the camps is called *Madári*. It is the figure of a man, and is of copper gilded; its size is that of a boy twelve years old. Once a year it is fixed against a pole in front of the Khan's *Khargáh* for three days at the commencement of spring; and the people come and adore by prostrating themselves on the ground before it, and pressing their foreheads against the body of the figure. Every *Khargáh* has its own idol, and everybody carries a small one suspended by a thread round the neck, and concealed on the breast inside the frock. They are mostly made of copper, though some are of brass.

Their religion is kept up by the priesthood called Lamma, and nobody knows their books but themselves. The head Lamma of each country is appointed from Tuwat or Joh and usually comes from that country. Every Kalmák father is bound to give up his second or third son to be educated as a Lamma. When a Lamma dies his body is fleshed, and the bones are broken up and tied in a bundle, and kept for transmission to Joh, which is a six months' journey from Karáshahr (my informant in these matters is a Karáshahr Kalmák) by the annual caravan.

At the yearly festival held at Joh, the bones of defunct Lammas, brought from all quarters, are boiled in a huge cauldron. On this occasion two or three aged Lammas always sacrifice themselves by jumping into the boiling liquor, and become converted into soup which is called *Sholun-arshan*. At the conclusion of the festival, this soup is distributed amongst the attendant Lammas, who fill it into copper vessels covered with red cloth; these copper vessels are called *lónkha*, and are carried about the person suspended on one side from the girdle. When all these Lammas disperse and return to their own homes they distribute their store of *Sholun-arshan* to the other Lammas who receive it in little copper vessels the size of a thimble and similar in shape to the *lónkha*. They are always worn slung at the waist from the girdle; and when he eats the Lamma first dips a wood pencil into the little copper bottle and passes it across his tongue.

The Kalmák language is different entirely from the Turki spoken by the Kirghiz, and Uzbak, and Tártár of Kásbghar; and it differs in dialect as spoken by the Mánjhú of Ila, the Kalmák of Yuldúz, and the Tuwat of Joh; the Tánghút and the Monghol too have peculiar languages, and in fact every tribe has its own speech, which is more or less unintelligible to his neighbours, though of the same race. The Mánjhú write their language in characters like the Chinese, but the Kalmák don't write their language, unless the Lamma do it for them, and then they must read it too.

A sample of the Kalmák language will be found in the comparative vocabulary appended to this general description. They appear to be entirely illiterate, for I could hear of no books amongst them.

The Kalmák people are divided into tribes and clans like the Kirghiz, whom they resemble in their wandering mode of life. The ruler of a whole province comprising many tribes is called *Ghaldan*, which is the same as Khán; and the head or chief of a tribe is called *Noyún*, which is the same as Beg; the latter titles in each case being those current amongst the Uzbak people.

The Noyún of each tribe administers the government by the aid of a staff of officers the principal of whom are the following, *viz.*, *Byla* or military governor; *Bysa* or civil governor; *Guzda* or chief justice, *Zangi* or Magistrate, under whom are a certain number of *Bodukchi* or policemen; *Maran* or military commandant, under whom are the *Cherik* or infantry, and *Murta-Cherik* or cavalry; *Padinda* or controller of water supply, who distributes the streams for irrigation of crops and watering of flocks, &c.; *Lamma* or priest; and *Gelin* or chaplain. This last is subordinate to the Lamma; he investigates and settles all minor disputes and offences. He has no power to inflict any punishment, his office being of a spiritual nature and his discipline entirely moral. In the case of serious offences—murder and theft are considered the gravest crimes—the investigation is made by the Zangi. His sentence must be approved by the Guzda, and the sanction of the Noyun must be obtained prior to its execution. For abuse or assault, or similar misbehaviour five to twenty stripes are laid on the bare buttocks with a *camchi* or horsewhip. For injury to cattle, crops, or other property equitable recompense is exacted after reference to the Guzda from whom the appeal lies to the Noyun. If the Noyun rejects the appeal, the appellant may claim the benefit of *Andaghar*. This is a very sacred ordeal, only resorted to when all other means of redress have failed, and if properly carried out, is held to be conclusive proof of the innocence of the accused. It is always carried out in the presence of the Noyun, supported by the Guzda and Zangi, under the direction of the Lamma and his Gelin. These last assemble the accused and his family and the accuser and his family, and seating them on the ground opposite each other light a fire between them. The Zangi then recapitulates the case briefly and sums up his reasons for awarding judgment against the defendant. The Gelin then appeals to plaintiff whether he will force accused to perform *Andaghar*, or acquit him without putting him to the test. If he assents to the latter course, as is often the case, the suit is dismissed and the parties disperse. Otherwise the Gelin calls on the accused to clear himself, and he does so by simply rising and making water on the fire. This act at once frees him from all odium or blame. But if at the bidding of the Gelin he rises with this intent, and there is no flow within a reasonable time, he is unhesitatingly pronounced guilty and condemned to the original sentence. So great is the dread of this ordeal, simple as it appears, that frequently the accused of murder willingly resigns himself to the extreme penalty rather than face this chance of escape.

The punishment for murder is death, but without the shedding of blood by cutting instruments or by hanging. Casting blindfold from a high rock is the common mode of execution, or in plain districts harnessing by a noose round the neck to an unbroken horse and driving it across country. The knife is never used in executions, and very often the capital punishment is commuted to fine in cash or cattle paid to the murdered one's heirs. One thousand to two thousand *tangas* or from two hundred to four hundred rupees is the usual sum paid.

Next to murder theft is held to be the most heinous offence, whilst adultery seems to be unknown as a crime. For theft, on conviction of the first offence, the Zangi inflicts from 20 to 40 stripes with a horsewhip. On second conviction the criminal is shut up in a *cará oe* or "Black Chamber" for three or four months, and then liberated on signing a written paper to forfeit a foot on the next conviction. If so convicted a third time, his foot is cut off at the ankle joint, and the stump plunged into boiling fat to staunch the hemorrhage.

The Kalmáks as a rule live in peace amongst themselves, and always treat their Lamma with great deference. Their common greeting amongst each other is *Munda wánchi* or "How d'ye do!" but they salute a superior by straightening the right arm towards the ground in advance, dropping the shoulder, and lolling out the tongue to the same side.

The common people intermarry only in their own camps, but the Chiefs get wives from the neighbouring tribes as well. There is no limit to the number of a rich man's wives, but the common people only marry one at a time. When a girl arrives at a marriageable age, from fifteen to eighteen years generally, the parents tie a red piece of cloth outside the door of their *khargáh* to announce the fact of their readiness to part with her. The suitors, with much show of modesty, vie with each other for the possession of the cloth, which is generally carried off stealthily by night; and the successful possessor declares himself by affixing it to the door of his own tent. The girl's parents now go to him, and bargain the amount of dower—sheep and horses for themselves, and clothing, &c., for the bride—and fix a day for the wedding. On the appointed day the suitor with his friends goes in procession from his own to the bride's tent. He is attended by a Lamma to perform the ceremony of marriage, and is preceded by two men carrying the *Coshugha*, which is a broad ornamented screen stretched between two poles. He is received by the girl's parents with greetings of welcome and sounds of music. The bride and bridegroom—who are not unacquainted, for women here are as free as in Europe—then take seats side by side on the ground. The Lamma repeats a certain formula of prayers, and the couple are then declared man and wife. The bride's parents feast the company, and entertain them with music and dancing, and archery and horse exercises, &c., for three days. The husband then takes his bride home and for three days similarly entertains her parents and bridal party. After this the friends disperse and the married couple settle down to their domesticity. The celibate Lamma according to custom lives with them till the wife becomes a mother, after which he gets his *congé*. The bride after quitting her parent's tent is not again allowed to enter till she becomes a mother, but in all her visits, to which there is no restriction, must remain outside the door. The Kalmák as a rule only marry one wife at a time, and do not practice polyandry, though till the birth of a child the Lamma is always the husband's partner. The morality of married couples is said to be extremely loose, and the common prostitute or *jallab* is found in every camp.

The birth of a child is always celebrated with rejoicings, but not till the forty days of impurity are passed. The mother then comes out from her seclusion, and receives the congratulations of her friends. The Lamma attends and blesses and names the infant, and the occasion is made one of feasting and rejoicing with music and games. If the babe be a son, his head is now shaved, unless he is dedicated to the church. In this case, when old enough to quit his mother's care, he is made over to the charge of a Lamma to be educated. He is never allowed to wear trowsers, only a loin clout under the frock, and in winter cloaks and furs. The common Kalmák names for men are Jirghál, Zanjirá, Kormashún, Balding, Boyún Jirghál, Chambil, Tarmashín, Keshit, Dava, Kaynja, Kishikta, Jap, Jowa, Borak, Jaymin, Lima, Khara, Záloh, Táybing, and Aywa; and of women Chagan, Shayap, Nohoy, Mánokhoy, Kharap, Sáykhin, Kharamok, Chagan Bilak, Dáh, Mohkúban, Jími Gelin, Jámoh, Dangzil, Aghih, Shám, Delbir, Sáykhin Sanan, Khaŕah, Bághder, Jimbel, Dila, Bor, and others.

On the death of a Kalmák, the hands and feet are tied together, and the body, slung on a pole, is carried to the desert or wilderness, and cast on the ground. The relatives and friends then retire to a little distance and watch for three or four hours to see if any wild animal or bird of prey comes to feed upon it. If so, they return, and carry off the body, and deposit it carefully on some hill top or other exposed place, and there leave it. Sometimes they raise a pile of stones over the corpse, but never bury it under ground; on leaving the body they wring their hands and wail and praise the deceased, recounting all his virtues as a good and worthy man. If, on the other hand, no wild animal or bird of prey attacks the body in the allotted time, they return and, stripping off the clothes from the corpse, treat it with every indignity, and casting it from them abuse the deceased as a worthless fellow, not even fit food for the vulture. Chiefs and grandees are disposed of with more ceremony. Their bodies are placed in coffins with their bows and arrows and a supply of food, and carried to some mountain top and there deposited in a lonely and inaccessible spot.

The Khan of a tribe is always so disposed of, and is carried to his last resting place by a large concourse of his subjects. The Kalmák of Yuldúz have no Khán now. He went to Bajin several years ago, and has never since been heard of. His wife rules the tribe in his absence. She is called Khátón Khán, and is guided in the government by an old man, who is a magician. Her age is about thirty years, and she has two sons, one aged ten years and the other eight.

Turfán.—This is the easternmost division of the Káshghar country along the foot of the hills, and borders on the desert of Gobi. It differs from the other divisions in having no rivers, except two or three insignificant streams which become short lived torrents in seasons of flood. The water supply is derived from subterranean conduits brought down from under ground springs at the foot of the hills; and where these flow on the surface are planted the farm settlements. These conduits are called *karez* by the Musalmans, and *khhin* by the Khitáy, and *nukhun-bukhá* by the Kalmák; some of them flow in a considerable stream for many miles and irrigate and fertilize wide tracts of otherwise bare desert.

Turfán extends from Gumish Akma hills separating it from Karáshahr valley on the west to Chíktam or Chightam on the borders of the desert on the east, a distance of forty *tásh* or 200 miles. Chightam is the limit of the Amír's territory eastward. The north boundary is an irregular range of hills called Ayghúr Bulák Tágh on the west and Kará Bulák Tágh on the east; whilst the southern border is an undefined line on the desert waste separating it from Lob. Within these limits the population is reckoned at 18,000 houses, or at seven per house 126,000 souls; but it does not contain anything like that number now.

After the capture of Kúchá and the destruction of the Khoja power there by the Amír, the Turfán State for a brief period formed part of the principality ruled by Dáúd Khalífa, till it was wrested from him by the conqueror as mentioned in the History. Under the Chinese this division was one of the most populous and flourishing of all the States of Káshghar, but it has suffered frightfully during the late revolution of the Tungani and succeeding conquest by the Amír, and now it is described as a long succession of ruined farmsteads and barely tenanted settlements.

Its city, which is called Kuhna Turfán or "Old Turfán" in distinction to U'sh Turfán in the west, was a thriving commercial city on the great caravan route between China and Western Asia, and the several lesser towns of the division were active seats of life and industry, but both their merchants and their wealth alike have disappeared in the recent troubles.

Turfán is described as a strong walled city surrounded by populous suburbs all watered by numerous *Karez* streams. Its population were mostly Khitáy and Tungáni, and numbered 6,000 houses in and around the city, which was protected by a citadel with a garrison of 3,000 men. It was the emporium for the silks and teas of China, and had manufactures of leather and woollen fabrics of its own. The common fuel of the city was coal brought from the Sirkip hills to the north-east. It is of brown colour and much inferior to that found at Aksú, which is black, and burns well. The city is now in a decayed state with less than half its former population, and is entirely cut off from communication with China, whence it derived its wealth. It is held as a military post by a strong garrison of the Amír's troops who, to the number of 5,000 men, are quartered in the citadel, and a new fort built on the Khokand model close to the city.

The other principal places in this division are the following, *viz.*, Tokhsún, a small fortified town on the Karáshahr road, 600 houses including the suburbs. Dabánchí, a hill castle, on the road north to Orúmchí, 500 houses with the suburbs. Súbáshi, a market town of 300 Khitáy homesteads, now in ruins. Kará Khoja, a Musalmán settlement of 500 houses. Mazár Abul Fattáh, 300 houses, Musalmán market town. Lukchun, 2,000 houses, on the Gochang River which in floods reaches Lob; this is a market town, and its farmsteads spread many miles north and south along the course of the rivulet; though the fields are irrigated by *Karez* streams. Up to this the country all the way from Turfán, a distance of fifty miles, is a succession of farmsteads held by Musalmáns. Beyond, across a strip of desert waste, is another Musalmán settlement (as in fact are all the peopled places, though many of the holdings in each are tenantless), Pichán, 500 houses, and a Khitáy fort on a small stream from Gochang Tagh; and beyond again is the frontier outpost of Chightam, 100 houses. Gochang, at the foot of the hills to the north, is a market town of 400 houses. Yangi-Khhín to its south 100 farms. Sirkip at foot of hills 200. And all the other settlements 6,500. Total 18,000 houses.

The soil of Turfán is described as similar to that of Káshghar, but more gravelly, and the productions are the same, though the climate is said to be much milder. The cotton produce here

16.—Heads of Oves Ammon, &c., shot by Capt. Molloy, Joint Commissioner of Ladak, 1873.

17.—Crossing the Sasser Pass, Breakfast above Tooti Aylak, elevation 16,300 feet.

is exported to China. Excellent melons are produced in all parts of the division, and its grapes and green raisins are the finest in the country. They are exported to Káshghar and preserved in the fresh state for winter use. In the desert to the south the wild camel and wild horse are said to be plentiful. The former is described as a small, thin limbed, double humped animal with a very soft warm wool of light brown colour. Huntsmen declare it to be a very vicious animal and extremely swift, and state that it flies at its pursuers with boldness when brought to bay, and attacks with great ferocity, biting and kicking, and when wounded vents its rage upon itself. It is always at enmity with its fellow partners in the wastes of the desert, and hunts the wild horse off its own grazing grounds.

Lob.—This is the name of a district on the banks of the Tárim River, which is formed by the union of all the rivers from Yuldúz of Ila round by the western circuit of Káshghar to Khutan and Cháchan. It is a vast region of swamps which succeed each other from the junction of the united streams of Kúcha and Kúrla with the Tárim on the west, and extend thirty days' journey east and south on to the Gobi desert. On the edge of this desert, beyond the inhabited swamp tract, is a lake five days in circuit, and from it a great river goes out to the east. The lake is quite uninhabited, and is in the midst of a desert of white salt at three days' journey from the Lob settlements.

"There are no mountains in Lob, but the ground between the bends of the river and the swamps is thrown into cliffs, and banks, and ridges of sand and gravel. Between these the country is undulating sand, and near the water is covered with reeds and forests of poplar and tamarisk, but there is no willow. Some of the gravel ridges are higher than Kayrágh at Yangí Hissar (about 300 feet), and higher than the Hazrat Begum ridge (about 600 feet), but they are all lower than the Kúrúgh Tágh which separates Lob from Karáshahr on the north, and lower too than the hills which separate it from Cháchan on the south; but these last are a great way off on the desert, and nobody ever goes there or knows anything about them. Why ask what they consist of ? Everything here is sand, and salt, and nothing else." Such in substance is what I learned from a Kalmák of Karáshahr who knew Lob well. I shall quote him and a fellow tribesman, and two officers in the Amir's service, who visited the country during the Turfán campaign, as I proceed with this brief notice of the district:—

"Lob is reached from all directions along the course of the several rivers flowing to it. Thus from Khutan by the Khutan Daryá; from Maralbashí by the Yarkand Darya through Dolan settlements nearly all the way; from Aksú to Ara Mahalla by the Aksú Darya; from Kúcha to the same settlement by the Múzárt Darya, and so on. From Kúrla I know the road well, as I have travelled it several times. It is four days' journey. The first stage is Yárkúrúl, four *tash*, over a sandy waste with reeds, pools, and poplars here and there on the route. Second stage Konchi, five *tash*, across similar country to the Tárim river below where it is joined by a river coming from Kúcha and Kúrla. Third stage, four *tash*, on the desert of sand hills, salt wastes, reeds, and pools. Fourth stage, Karákochun, five *tash*, across similar desert to the reed huts of Kalmák and Kirghiz Musalmáns on the river bank. Here Lob begins, and goes east and south along the course of the Tárim. It consists of many settlements on the marshy lakes and their connecting channels. The whole tract is called Lob, but this is Lob Proper. The other settlements to the west form distinct districts and are called Karákochun, Lyso, and Ara Mahalla. There are others, but these are the principal seats of population. Everywhere the river banks are low, hardly raised above the river stream, and are covered with broad or narrow belts of *jangal*. This consists of a tall reed called *comush*, and a shorter and different reed called *chigh*, and of the poplar or *toghrác*, and the tamarisk or *yúlghún*; the willow or *súgat* is not seen here.

"Lob was only peopled a hundred and sixty years ago by emigrant families of the Kará Kalmák, Koshot, Túrgut, &c., to the number of a thousand houses. They are now all professedly Musalmáns, and have *Mullá* and *Imám* priests amongst them, but they don't know much about Islam. We look on them with contempt as only half "Musalmán."——"No, I am not a Kalmák, thank God."——"Yes, my ancestors were, but I am a Musalmán, God be praised ! And my father was before me."——"Yes, there were other people in Lob before these Kalmák emigrants came, but nobody knows who they are or anything about them. They are called *Yáwa Kishi* or "wild people" and delight to live with the wild beasts and their cattle in the thickets and brakes about the marshes."——"No; I have never seen any of them, but I have heard the Lob people talk of them. They are small black men with long matted hair and shun the society of other men. Whenever they see any of the Lob people they run away and hide in the reeds and thickets. Nobody knows where they come from or where they live, and nobody understands their language. They are said to have boats like the Lob people, but they never mix with them. They are supposed to have some settlement in the marshes to the south-east."——"Yes, the country is a very large one, and nobody knows its extent or boundaries, for the people never go out of their own limits, but they cannot be very many, or they would band together and drive out the Musalmán settlers. These people are very timid amongst other men, but, though only armed with bow and arrow and a long pike, they are brave hunters. They keep cattle, but have no cultivation whatever. They wear clothes of a material called *lúf*. It is very coarse and strong, and is also worn by the people of Lob who weave it into cloths of varying texture, some of which are very light and fine."——"Yes. As you say so, the name of the country may be derived from this material, but nobody here ever said so. God only knows the truth! though the distinction is plain enough. We call the country Lob, and the material lúf."——"No, I never heard the name Lob Nor. I have heard the names Lop and Lop Kol; they are only the Kirghiz pronunciation of Lob."——"Yes. There are hundreds of families of Kirghiz shepherds scattered all about the Lob camps. They came originally from the Kákshál and Búghú camps away to the north, and are very good friends with the Kalmák."——"The stuff called *lúf* is the fibre of a plant called *toça-chígha* which grows in plenty all over the sandy wastes bordering the marshes. It is not found here (Yángi Hissár), and only grows in Lob. The material made from it too is never seen anywhere but in Lob, and is only worn by the people of that country. It protects the wearer from the attacks of gnats and musquitos, which never alight on this cloth. The plant has a flower and bears a pod like the wild liquorice here. The *lúf* is thus prepared. The stalks are cut close to the ground and stripped of leaves; they are then thrown into a pit full of water, and left there till they rot; they are now pounded with a mallet, and the bark torn off in long shreds; bundles of this bark are again thrown into a pit of water till it ferments and stinks; the stuff is then taken out and pounded till it separates into fibres; these are shaken clear, and spread in the sun to bleach; and finally they are spun into thread and woven into cloth for shirts and trowsers. It is the dress of all the people of Lob, and is made in every campment."

The population of Lob Settlement is reckoned at 1,000 houses, but that of the whole swamp region eastward from the borders of Marálbáshí to the Gobi desert is about 10,000 houses, or, at seven per house, 70,000 souls. There are no permanent dwellings here, nor are there any of the *Khargáh* tents which the Kirghiz call *óe-oe*. The people live in reed huts or else in boats. The reed hut is called *Kippa*, and is a mere frame work of reeds, sometimes plastered with mud. They are dotted about in clusters of three or four or more, and are usually broken up and deserted when the tenants migrate to some other spot. The people are mostly Kirghiz and Kalmák, and their language is a corrupt dialect of the Kirghiz Turki. The Karákochún District is entirely peopled by Cochín Kirghiz originally from the Nárín valley.

"There is no cultivation in Lob. The people live on fish, and the produce of their flocks and of the chase. In April and May they collect, and eat raw the soft young shoots of a water plant called *súya*; it has a long stem like a reed, but is different both from the *comush* and the *chígh*. The people have immense numbers of sheep, cows, and horses; but the mule, the donkey, and the cat are unknown in the country. They are all now subjects of the Amír, but only pay an annual tribute of twenty-two otter skins, and nothing else. They govern themselves according to their own customs, and have no officer on the part of the Amír to interfere with them. The Governor of Turfán every year sends an agent to collect the tribute and revenue; but the people drive off their cattle into the mazes of the reed swamps, and take to their boats, and the tax gatherers wander about for a few days, and then go away frightened of the country. The arms of the people are the bow and arrow, matchlock, gun, pike, and sword. They always swear upon the gun which, as here, they call *miltic*. If any one wishes to free himself from an accusation, he appeals to the accuser to produce his gun, and kissing the muzzle places it against his left nipple and bids him fire. This throws the responsibility upon the accuser, who on this proof of innocence retracts his calumny. All the people here are brave huntsmen, but they have a great respect for human life, and are very much afraid of death.

"They are a very hardy and healthy people, and have no diseases except a kind of ague called *bazgak*. They have a great horror of small-pox, which they call *yamán* = 'the evil.' If the disease should appear amongst them, the whole community immediately abandon the locality and leave the afflicted with only one attendant and a supply of food. If the patient recovers, he is not admitted to society till the expiry of forty days. When the Amír conquered the country he summoned the Chief of Lob to Káshghar; the old man had never seen the disease and got it there; and he was so frightened that he set out to return home, but died on the road; and when his attendants returned with the intelligence the people all ran away from them till the forty days were passed. Snake bites are very common, and the people have an efficient remedy for it; they catch a frog, rip open its belly, and tie it over the wound; this affords immediate relief. Another remedy is a sort of gum or fungus found at the stumps and on the boughs of the *toghrác* or "poplar" tree; there are two kinds called *cará* and *ác* or "black" and "white" *toghrágho* respectively; the black is the kind used; it is powdered and mixed into a paste with water or spittle and so applied to the wound; it affords immediate relief. There is one kind of snake called *dúr*; its bite is immediately fatal; nothing cures it. People say that if the *Mullá* repeats the *Kalima* and breathes *dam* upon the wound, a cure is certain. God only knows; but in Lob he never arrives till the snake-bitten is dead.

"The wild animals of Lob are the wild camel = *yáwa thuga*."——"Yes. I have seen the animal myself."——"No, I never killed one myself. I have seen one which was killed by huntsmen of the camp to which I belonged. It is a small animal, not much bigger than a horse, and has two humps. It is not like a tame camel; its limbs are very thin, and it is altogether slim built. I have seen them on the desert together with herds of wild horses. They are not timid, and don't run away at the sight of a man. They do nothing unless attacked; they then run away, or else they turn and attack the huntsman; they are very fierce, and swift in their action as an arrow shot from the bow; they kill by biting and trampling under foot, and they kick too like a cow. They are hunted for the sake of their wool, which is very highly prized, and is sold to Turfán merchants.

"Another animal is the wild horse = *cúlán*. It is the size of a pony, has high withers and a narrow barrel. It is only hunted for sport. Another is the stag = *úghú*. It is hunted for its autters, which are taken to Turfán for the Bajin market. There are besides, the tiger = *bar*, the wolf = *chona*, the panther = *molún*, the lynx = *súlesún*, the fox = *aratu*, and the otter = *súyup*. All these are hunted for their furs, as are the swan = *codáy*, and the pelican = *caráchílán*."——"Yes. This is a swan's skin (shewing one bought at Káshghar), and comes from Lob. It is the only place in this country where the bird is found. There are immense numbers of wild fowl of all sorts on the lakes, and they breed there.

"The customs of the people of Lob are much the same as those of the Kirghiz, but there is one which is met nowhere else. During the spring and summer seasons the young people are in the habit of racing along the river. A party of six or eight maids forms up on the river, each in her own skiff; and a party of as many youths forms up on the bank, each on his own horse. At an agreed signal they all start off to an appointed goal, the maids paddling down the stream, and the youths galloping along the bank. If the maids win, they select a partner for the night from amongst the youths, each in the order of her arrival at the winning post; similarly if the youths win, they chose their companion in turn from amongst the maids. The contract only lasts for that night, and the couplings vary with the chances of each successive race, though often the same partners meet. If a girl becomes pregnant, she points out the author, and he marries her.

"There are innumerable camp and pasture grounds in Lob, but the principal permanent camps are Ara Mahalla, Lyso, Karákochún, Jarálik, Sálih-Akhún, Kalmák Úldi, Khitáy Keldí, and Khatt Koydí. This last is towards the south-east, and is the limit of Khitáy territory and authority. In the time of the Khitáy lots of traders used to come to Lob from Turfán, and Karáshahr, and Kúchá; they used to bring flour, sugar, honey, tea, cotton cloths, old clothes, spices, knives, needles, and such like, and barter them for otter skins, camels' wool, stags' horns, swans' down, furs of sorts, sheep, horses, and cows. All this trade has ceased now, but occasionally the Lob people bring their cattle, furs, &c., to Kúchá and Kúrla and go back with corn, flour, and cotton cloth."

Such is the result of my enquiries regarding the Lob division, and I have put it very much in the form I received it. It is certainly not without interest.

Marálbáshí.—This division occupies a wide extent of desert plain, and lies between the territories of Lob and Káshghar. Its north limit is at Kalpin on the Acsáy river, and its south at Mihnat *Ortang* on the Yarkand river, which to its junction with the Tárim also forms its east border; its west border is a wide sandy desert which joins the Káshghar territory at Yangabad. Its population is reckoned at 5,000 houses, or, at seven per house, 35,000 souls, and they are almost exclusively of an outcast Tartar tribe called Dol or Dolan, a term which is said to signify "boor." The general character of the country is an arid sandy waste, and the poverty of the people is in keeping with that of their country. Their principal settlement and headquarters are at Marálbáshí, which is also an important military post commanding the approaches to Káshghar and Yarkand from the north-east. The Chinese had a strong fort and garrison of 3,000 men here, and the Amír maintains the post with a garrison, however, of only 300 men.

The other settlements of the Dolan are mostly along the course of the Yarkand river, and next to their capital at Marálbashí, which only contains 400 houses, is Bárchak in importance. It is situated at the junction of the Yarkand river with the Tárim, and contains 300 houses, and is an important military post, as it commands the routes from Aksú and Kúchá to the southward. The other principal settlements are Chárbágh or Jabbak, Tumshuk (where are the extensive ruins of an ancient city with stone walls and fragments of sculpture), Chílán, and Kalpin to the north, and Aksak Marál, Taskama, Markit, Mughol Tárim, Laelak, &c., to the south.

A peculiar feature of the Dolán settlements is the nature of their dwellings, which are all underground; a point in which they resemble the Dolpá of Tibet, as described in the *Táríkhi Rashidi* of Mirzá Hydar. These dwellings of the Dolán are described by my informants as consisting of oblong pits dug in the ground, and roofed with a thatch of reeds supported upon poplar beams. The roofs rise very little above the surface of the ground, and their settlements are consequently not discernible till the traveller is actually moving over the roofs. They are miserable hovels in which the family consorts with its cattle, sheep, and asses, but prove an efficient shelter from the keen frosts of winter, and afford a grateful retreat from the scorching heats of summer.

The Dolán, owing to the sterile nature of the soil, have next to no cultivation. They own small herds of oxen and flocks of goats and sheep; but their principal wealth is in asses of which humble, and in this country most useful, drudge they possess incredible numbers. Their trade and communications are almost exclusively with Yarkand, whither they carry to market fuel, potashes, salt, butter, and a sort of curd cheese called *Súzma*, together with the skins of foxes and birds, and a coarse cordage or rope made of the fibre of the poplar tree, as also another production from the same source, called *toghrágho*; it is a sort of fungous decay of the trunk of the poplar, and is sold in the bazars as a ferment in baking. They carry back in exchange for these cotton cloth (generally dyed of a drab colour) flour, bread, and the biscuits, called *cúlcha*, beef, horseflesh, boots, shoes, caps, &c.

The Dolán are a very poor and illiterate people. Their chief occupations are tending their herds, collecting fuel and impure desert salt for the city market, and trapping foxes and birds for their skins. Their arms are the matchlock and pike, but they are looked on as a mean and despicable set. They nominally profess Islam, and call their priests *Khoja*, and worship them instead of *Khuda*. They have no jealousy with respect to their women, and it is the custom for the master of the house to place his wife at the disposal of his guest and retire to a neighbour's hovel till his departure. So common, it is said, is this custom that the wife receives her guests at discretion, and the shoes placed outside the door is the sign for the husband that he must not enter.

The Dolán are said to be of Kalmák origin. I saw several of them at Yarkand. They are physically a very inferior race and their mental capacity of the meanest. They are short in stature and small in limb, with retreating forehead and repulsive features of dark complexion, and Tartar cast of countenance. In general appearance they resemble the Bot of Tibet, though, as Musalmáns, they shave the head. They talk a dialect of Turki, but amongst themselves use a language nobody understands. They are said to be a very timid and simple people, and generally shun society. This last trait may be attributed to the treatment they receive from society, for the name of Dolán is sufficient to condemn the owner to every kind of drudgery much on a par with the ass he owns, and which too he perpetually rides.

Sirikol of the maps and *Sárígh Kúl* or Sirikul of native writers is a small highland division on the south-west frontier of Káshghar. Its name signifies "Yellow Glen," and the hills are described as of a light coloured rock similar to those about Shahídulla Khoja on the south frontier of Yarkand, which are of micaceous schist, friable trap, and granite. It is separated on the west from the Wakhán District of Badakshan by the Shindu range, which is crossed by a pass or *kotal* of the same name down to Aktash="White Rock" at its western base. This is the limit of Sárígh Kúl or Sirikul territory in this direction and the commencement of Wakhán; and it marks the boundary between the possessions of Amír Sher Ali Khan Afghan of Kabul and Amír Muhammad Yakúb Khan Uzbak of Káshghar.

Sárígh Kúl or Sirikul is an entirely mountainous district wedged in at the point of junction of the Bolortagh range with that of the Hindú Kush, where it joins the great Himalaya chain. To the northward and westward it is separated from the Pamir by the Tagharma mountain and its emanations, and to the southward and eastward from the independent little States of Yasín and Kunjud by the Múztágh or "Glacier Mountain" and its lofty western peaks called Taghning Bash or Taghdumbash or "Mountain Head," where meet, as in the point of section of a cross, the four great mountain systems of the Central Asian Continent, *viz.*, the Himalaya and Hindu Kush separating Tartary from India, and the Suleman and Bolor ranges dividing those two great countries into their respective distinct geographical regions; the tablelands of Khurasan and the plains of India on the one hand, and the valley of the Oxus and the basin of the Tárim on the other.

In its central part Sárígh Kúl forms an open valley of some twenty miles by five into which the glens around conduct their drainage. The several streams coalesce at different points to form the Sárígh Kúl river, which winds eastward and joins that of Yarkand in the vicinity of Kosharab on the hill skirt. In this plain is settled the bulk of the population in a number of villages dotted along its mountain borders and on the course of its river. The capital amongst these is Tashkorghan or "Stone Fort" described as a small square structure defended by a turret bastion at each angle, and supported by an adjacent village of some 200 houses. It stands on the river bank and its name is sometimes used to designate the whole district.

"The population of Sárígh Kúl is entirely different from that of the rest of the country, and is purely Aryan. It is reckoned at 2,500 houses, or at seven per house 17,500 souls. Their principal villages in the Tashkorghan valley are Shindí, Taghnam, Barangsál, Kesarov, Baldír, Armalagh, Máryang, Wácha, Kichik Túng, Túng, Chushmán, and Tizuif, and others in the glens around. At the foot of Taghárma mountain, about two *tash* north-west of Tashkorghan, in a small glen, are the hot springs called Sím Kang. Though there is a great glacier—here called *Pir-yakh*—on the top of this mountain, fed annually by four months' constant snow from December to March, these springs are boiling hot and emit clouds of steam as they issue from the rock; they have been conducted into covered tanks a short distance off, and are used by the people as medicinal baths for the cure of rheumatism and allied diseases; anybody can use them, and the custom is for the bathers to strip and lie in the water for two or three hours daily during several days."

The climate of this division is very salubrious, though the winter is a long and rigorous season during which much snow falls. Spring, summer, and autumn are one season here and last from May to October; during this period rain falls occasionally in July, but storms of thunder and lightning are unknown in the country. "I have lived in the country all my life," says my informant, a native of Túng, aged about forty years, "but I have never seen such a storm as you describe in which the sky flashes fire and the clouds make a noise."——"Yes, I know what a cloud is, and what a fog is. They often hide the mountains and everything else from view. I know what an earthquake is too; they sometimes shake the ground, and tumble down our walls, but the mountains never growl, nor do the clouds grumble.

"When there is no snow on the ground pasture is abundant everywhere, but trees are scarce all over the country. At Túng there are some mulberry trees=*uzma*, and the apricot=*nosh*; and there are no other fruit trees in the country, nor any of other kinds except the juniper=*umbárts* and the arbor vita?=*tít* which only grow in the mountains; the willow=*wanoj* is common on all the water-courses."

"All the villages have their cultivated fields. The crops are wheat and barley, two kinds of bean, and a pulse called *makh*. Carrots and turnips are also grown. The people have lots of cattle such as sheep=*gath*, goats=*vaz*, horse=*vorj*, camel=*shutur*, cow=*zau*, grunting ox=*cotás*, hybrid ox=*staur*, the dog, cat, and fowls. The sheep, hybrid cattle, and *cotás* are the most numerous. Their wool and their butter are bartered with Yarkand traders for cotton cloth and silk cloaks, &c. The rate is one sheep for three pieces of *karbás* or *khám* of 10 yards each; that is one sheep for thirty yards of cloth. Wheat and barley are bartered with the Kirghiz for felts and horses. No coin is current in Sárígh Kúl, everything is by barter. The people have no need of money. They live on the produce of their cattle and fields, and make their own clothing. Only two materials are made in the country, viz., a thick sort of felt called *jayn*, and a warm woollen stuff called *galim*, for cloaks, blankets, &c. It is very strong and warm, and is the common dress of the people. It is made in every village and almost by every family for itself.

"The people of Sárígh Kúl came originally from Shighnán, and their language is the same as that spoken by the Shighní. They have no special tribal name, but simply call themselves Sárígh Kúlí. By the people of Kashghar they are called *Tájik*, and the neighbouring Kirghiz call them *Sárt*, but they never apply these terms to each other. The Wákhí and Badakhshí, who are similarly denominated *Tájik* and *Sárt* by their neighbours of Káshghar and Bukhárá on either hand, always call us Sárígh Kúlí; and this is our proper appellation just as Wákhí is that of the people of Wakhán, and Badakhshí is that of the people of Badakhshan, or Shighní that of those of Shighnán, and Rosháni that of those of Roshan.

"The Sárígh Kúlí and the Shighní are one people. We speak the same language and have the same customs. The Wákhí and Badakhshí are a different people, and we don't understand each other's speech."——"Yes. They are called Tájik as we are, and like us too they are of the *Shia* sect, but we consider them different, and only our Chiefs intermarry with them."——"Yes. There is a sort of brotherhood of all the *Shia* tribes of Badakhshán, Roshán, Shighnán, Wakhan, Chitral, Yásin, Kunjud, Gilgit, and Yághistán down to Kashmír itself, because our *Sunni* neighbours revile us and call us *Rafizi*="Heretic"; and some of them don't allow that we are Musalmáns unless we call ourselves *Cháryárí*."——"There are lots of *Sunni* families living amongst the *Shia* everywhere, and there are about a hundred *Sunni* families in Sárígh Kúl. The Chiefs and Nobles everywhere call themselves *Cháryárí* and thus become *Sunni*, but I don't know what the difference is. They are our rulers and can do as they like; we are only poor people and don't know anything about these matters; we only do as our fathers did before us.

"Formerly our Chiefs used by way of punishment to sell some of us into slavery, and in our wars with our Sunni neighbours—the Kirghiz especially—such as fell into their hands were always enslaved, and we used to retaliate by treating their captives in like manner. No. We never ill treat slaves unless they rebel or try to escape, but we could dispose of them in barter as we pleased. If the slave is clever and docile, we give him a wife and settle him amongst us, but he is always the property of his original captor or purchaser. All this is changed now since the rule of Atálik Ghází. Formerly lots of slave boys and girls as well as men used to pass up from Kunjud and Chitrál to Badakhshán for the Bukhárá market, but this too is now stopped by the Russians. There are about a hundred slaves in Sárígh Kúl now, mostly from Kunjud and Gilgit and Chitrál. The people of Kunjud are different from us, Sárígh Kúlís, and speak quite a different language."——"Yes, I have been in Kunjud. I know the capital; it is called Hunza; it is a large city of 1,000 houses on the river which goes to Gilgit. It has a strong fort in which the King resides. His name is Ghazan Khan, and he is the son of Sháh Ghazanfar, son of Sálim Khán, son of Khisro Khán, son of Háyish Khán. He is a *Sunni* and a friend of Mír Futh Ali Sháh of Fyzábád, but his people are almost all *Shia*.

"The Kunjudi are enemies of the Sárígh Kúlí; but now we are under the rule of Atalík Ghází our warfare has ceased with them as it has with with the Kirghiz. In the time of Khán Kúlí, who died nine or ten years ago, we always had an outpost at Júd Bay to watch the Kunjud road, and one at Tágharma against the Kirghiz, because they were constantly making plundering raids into our territory. Since the Atálik's rule the people of Sárígh Kúl are prosperous and live in peace. His Governor, Sain Sháh (Toksábéy Husen Sháh, Andijání), is a just Ruler, and does not oppress the people as his predecessor, Muhammad Arif, did. He collects the revenue and governs the country through the elders of the people.

"These are called *Aksakál*, and there are two in each village. They collect the *Zakát* or one in forty of cattle and live stock, and the *'ushr* or tithe of the crops and produce of the fields, and pay it over to the Governor for the Atálík. They control the conduct of their villagers, settle disputes by fine and maintain order amongst the people. Theft is punished by confiscation of cattle or ejection from their lands in favour of the plaintiff. Adultery is punished by the death of both parties. Murder is unknown in the country. When a man dies his estate is divided into three equal parts. Half of one of these thirds goes to the King, and the remainder is divided equally amongst the heirs male.

"The marriage customs are these. The suitor pays the girl's father 30 *tilás* = Rupees 175, in sheep, cattle, horses, &c., and then a day is fixed for the wedding. The ceremony is performed by the *mullá* or priest in the presence of the assembled relatives and neighbours, and the occasion is celebrated by a *toè* or feast, with music and dancing. The bride and bridegroom sit down on the floor side by side, and the priest standing opposite repeats a short prayer, and then in the presence of the assembled witnesses, three several times asks the bride in a slow and solemn voice—'Dost thou accept this man as thy husband?' And she each time replies 'I do.' He then three successive times asks the bridegroom—'Dost thou take this woman as thy wife?' And he each time answers 'I do.' The priest then takes a bit of roast mutton, divides it into two morsels, repeats a prayer over them, breathes upon each bit, and then dipping them separately into a dish of salt, puts that in his right hand into the man's mouth, and that in his left hand into the woman's. He then turns to the witnesses and says 'These two are man and wife. Whom God has joined let no man separate.' This ends the ceremony. The bride and bridegroom rise and receive the congratulations and offerings of their friends, and during three days entertain the guests with music, dancing, games, &c. Camels, horses, and sheep, according to the rank and means of the party, are slaughtered for the feast, and on the third day the guests disperse, and at sunset the bridegroom takes his bride to his own home.

"For every wedding the father of the bride pays two *tilá* to the King, and the bridegroom one *tilá*, but nothing is paid on the birth of a child. The event, however, is celebrated by a feast to the relatives and friends. Divorce is not known, nor, except by the Chiefs, is a second wife taken during the life of the first. Widows can re-marry after one year of mourning, and the occasion is celebrated by a feast. If she do not re-marry on the expiry of the year, she leaves the protection of her deceased husband's relatives, and returns to her father's home. Women take part in the field labour, and have the entire control of the household arrangements, and as a rule they are treated with every respect and confidence by the men. In society they are as free as the men and know not the veil. Only the wives and daughters of the Chiefs are veiled and secluded.

Kirghiz of Alátágh and Pámir.—This division of the country comprises a very extended curve of highland plateaux, and the valleys conducting from them to the lowlands, all round the western frontiers of the country from Kákshál on the north, round by Tirik Dawán and Taghárma, to Karákash on the south. Its continuity is interrupted in the south-west by the Sárígh Kúl division above described, but for the rest its most notable peculiarity is the utter absence, other than military outposts, of fixed habitation or cultivation. Yet it has a permanent population which, within the limits of its several divisions, regularly migrates from the low to the high lands according to the seasons, and on each roams as the necessities of its requirements may dictate. And this periodical movement from one region to the other is attended by a noteworthy, though temporary, transfer of allegiance from one ruler to another, except in the southern portion of the division which is wholly within the Amir's limits.

This anomalous arrangement is the result of the existing distribution of this natural home of the Kirghiz between three different rulers—the Russians, the Khan of Khokand, and the Amír of Káshghar. Their respective shares in this partitioned territory are not very accurately defined, but this much appears to be certain that the summer and winter quarters of certain of the nomad camps are in the territories of different rulers. Thus the Kirghiz of Kákshál, which is Káshghar territory, in summer pasture on the upper Narin and Atbáshi beyond Chádir Kol, which is Russian territory, and are there joined by the nomads of Aktágh, which is the name of that part of the Alátágh range between Chádir Kol and Tirik Dawán; now the camps in the southern valleys of Aktágh are Káshghar subjects right up to the sources of the Tuman river on which the capital stands, whilst those in the northern valleys draining to Uzkand are Khokand subjects; and both in summer pasture on Russian territory.

Similarly the Kirghiz of Karátágh, the range extending from the Tirik Dawán to Tágharma, who are all Káshghar subjects, roam the plateaux of Aláy and Kizil Art with the Kirghiz of Osh and Andiján, who are Khokand subjects, as their common summer pastures; though the territory belongs to Káshghar, and has done so since its first annexation, together with Sárígh Kúl, by Mirza Abábakar at the period of the Uzbak invasion about the end of the fifteenth century, as is recorded in the *Tarikhi Rashídi*. The author of that book states that Abábakar conquered all this hill region up to Sárígh Chopán or Tangi Wakhán and annexed it to the *diwan* or "Civil jurisdiction" of Káshghar, but left the low valleys of Badakshán on the west to the Uzbak invaders.

In our maps this elevated tableland is called "Pámir steppe," but it is not known specifically by this name to the Kirghiz, who are its only frequenters. So far as I can judge from the descriptions given to me by several Kirghiz whom I have questioned on the subject the general configuration of the country would seem to resemble that of the Khurásán range of tablelands extending from Mashhad to Mekrán, or the tablelands of Belochistán from Khozdár to Shál, both of which I have seen. This Pámir steppe (which in this account, though the name is not known to the Kirghiz, I have designated Bolortágh, as that is the name by which the region is spoken of in the *Tárikhi Rashidi*) bears some noteworthy points of topographical resemblance to the Khurásán range. Both are cross ranges running north and south to connect parallel mountain systems whose main direction is east and west, and both separate wide plains or river basins. Thus the Khurásán tablelands connect the Alburz range with that of Mushti in Belochistán, and separates the hydrographic basin of Sístán from the corresponding basin in the desert of Yezd and Kirmán. So the tablelands of Bolor connect the Alátágh range with that of Himalaya, and separate the basin of the Tárim from that of the Oxus.

These latter, too, from the descriptions I have heard, would seem to resemble the Khurásán highlands in their general features of arrangement. Thus they are characterized as consisting of a number of subordinate ranges which run parallel to each other, and enclose between them those open spreads of pasture plateaux, here called *pámir* and in Khurásán *Julaga* or *Jilga*. These drain according to the direction of the hills and the lie of the land either to the east or to the west, by insignificant streams which coalesce and form considerable rivers only after they have passed beyond the plateaux. In one respect the *pámir* and the *jilga* differ; the former owing to the prohibitory nature of the climate and altitude have no fixed habitations whatever, whereas the latter, not as a rule, but only where climate and elevation admit, have such permanent abodes as villages, gardens and fields. Many of these plateaux,

18.—Camp at Shahidulla Khwoja, the frontier outpost of Yarkund Territory towards Kashmir, 22nd Oct. 1873.

19.—Shahidulla Khwoja, Oct. 1873.
Camp at the frontier outpost of H. H. The Maharajah of Jummoo and Kashmir.

however, both in the highlands of Belochistán and Khurásán, have no permanent dwellings, and in no respect differ from the *pámir*, like which, too, they are in summer the scenes of busy life and activity, crowded by the camps and cattle of nomad tribes, who there is reason to believe are not so separate in race as they are in territorial distribution. The *tuman* of the Bráhoe in Belochistán, the *aul* of the Ilyát in Persia, and the *ayil* of the Kirghiz in Káshghar, and even the *Kizdi* of the nomad Afghán, all bear a common family resemblance; and through the very words designating their camps, whilst suggesting a common origin, offer a most inviting field for historical and philological investigation. The plateaux shared in summer by the Káshghar Kirghiz of Karátágh and the Khokand Kirghiz of Osh and Andiján are called Aláy in the northern half and Kizil Art in the southern, and are bordered on the west by an interrupted chain of mountains similar to those on the east. It has no general name, but each more prominent ridge is called separately, just as each separate *pámir* has its distinguishing appellation known only to the Kirghiz, and not very definitely or generally even to them, for half a dozen different men will give each a different name to one and the same peak. "What's the use of writing down so many names?" said an impatient Kirghiz whom I had worried with interrogatories a whole forenoon, till he was sore from shifting his seat from heel to heel, and escaped from further torture on the plea that his horse was left starving in the cold. "We call one country Aláy and another Kizil Art, and we call every spread of pasture *pámir*, just as we call a stony plain *sáy*, and a slope at the foot of the hills *sirt*." "No. The *chol* is different; there is none in our country; it is only on this plain of Káshghar; any place is *chol* where the ground is arid, and bare, and slightly raised above the general level." "There are numberless camp grounds on Aláy and Kizil Art too. We call each *ayil* = camp by the name of the *Bí* = Chief." "Every place too has its name, but I don't know them. Its four years since I was on Aláy, and people give their camp grounds different names. We call a place such and such a *tágh* = hill, or *tásh* = rock, or *kol* = pool, or *cúl* = glen, or *sú* = stream, or *árt* = valley pass, or *tár* = straight or gorge, or *dawán* = hill pass, or *corghán* = fort, or *caráwul* = picket, and so on, and everybody knows the place; it does for three or four *tásh* all round or up and down." "No, the Osh Kirghiz are not subjects of Atálik Ghází. They come over Tirik Dawán every year with the Kapchák of Mádi and roam down to Chádir-tash, and Neza-tásh, and Aktásh, but they don't pay *Zakát* except to the Khan of Khokand. My father is a subject of Atálik; his camps are in Kirmán Kúl and Egizak on the Koksú at foot of Tirik Dawán; he keeps a picket on the pass; I am a *jigit* = trooper, and have served Atálik four years. I get no pay, only food and clothing for self and horse. These arms all belong to Badaulat, and I received them from my *Pansad*. I belong to the Náymán tribe. There are 1,000 houses in the hills from Sárigh Kúl to Chádir Kol, all Náymán. There are others besides as Bárga, Monác, &c. We only pay *Zakát* to Atálik, and our Chiefs are charged with the protection of the frontier against marauders from the Khokand side. There are only eight of us here in service with Badaulat. He can't keep more because we run away, or get ill and die here. We are constantly employed going backwards and forwards with orders to the frontier outposts."

The population of all this Kirghiz division is very variously estimated. By some the number is stated at 30,000 houses, but this figure, it would seem, includes all the camps on both sides the Alátágh. Of those who are recognized subjects of the Káshghar State, I don't think the number can exceed 3,000 houses, *viz.*, 800 in Kákshál and Artosh, 1,600 in the Aktágh and Karátágh valleys, and 600 on the upper waters of the Yárkand and Karákásh rivers. Counting seven for each *ac-oe* or "white house"—the name of their portable frame work and felt covered tents—this will give 21,000 souls as the Kirghiz population of the Káshghar State.

The Kirghiz occupy the whole of Megholistan proper or Zúnghár which extends from Yúlduz on the east to Táshkand on the west. Like the Kalmák they have no cities or towns but migrate from the lower to the higher valleys and plateaux according to the seasons. On the north their neighbours are the Kazzák or Cossack of Isígh Kol and Koba and Ila, on the west the Kapchák or Kipchák, on the south the Uzbak of Khokand and Turk of Káshghar, and on the east the Kalmák of Yuldúz.

They consist of two main divisions called Tagháy and Adigina, and are also called Kará-Kirghiz. The Tagháy are nearly all Russian subjects. Their principal divisions are Sultán on the Chú and Talas rivers, Búghú on the south of Isigh Kol, Sárighbaghish on the east of Isighkol, Chirik in Kákshál and Aksáy, Chongbaghish on Atbáshi and Aktágh to Tirik Dawán, Sáyak on Karátagh and on the Nárín and Jumghál rivers, Kochí in Kákshal and Artosh and Nárín. All these are Russian subjects, but some of each, except the two first, are Káshghar subjects; as are all the Náyman and Kará Khitay, who extend with some Sáyak and Kochí from Aktágh all round to Karákásh and the Khutan frontier.

The Adigina comprise the camps of Bárga, Bakal, Munák, Sawáy, Jorú, Josh, Kokehíla, &c., and are partly Khokand and partly Russian subjects. They are in Osh, Andiján, Marghilán and the Farghana mountains, and in summer roam Aláy and Kizil Art with the Sáyak, Kará Khitay, and Náymán of Káshghar. Amongst the Adigina are many Kapchák and Kazzák camps who have separated from their own Chiefs. The wealth of the Kirghiz consists in their horses and cattle. They have numbers of camels and oxen, and sheep innumerable. They sow wheat, barley, and maize here and there on the lower valleys, but they have no regular fields or gardens. They make excellent felts and carpets, and a soft woollen cloth, as well as tapes, and caps, and a variety of domestic clothing and tent gear; all from the wool of their flocks and herds. They bring their felts and carpets, and cattle and skins of butter, &c., to market for sale, and take back cotton cloth, boots, snuff, tea, tobacco, needles, cauldrons of iron, cotton prints, and such like, as silks, furs, &c.

The Kirghiz profess Islám and are *Sunní* Musalmáns, but they are very ignorant of the doctrines of the faith, and very careless in the observance of its ordinances. In fact many of them are yet pagans, though different from the Kalmák. They are said to be much given to drunkenness by a strong spirit they distil from mare's milk. It is called *nasha* and is distilled from *cumis* which is fermented butter milk of the mare. What we tasted at Káshghar was a slightly vinous, subacid drink of very agreeable flavour and mildly exhilarating effect in the dose of a pint. It is the national drink of the Kirghiz, and reputed to possess all sorts of wonderful virtues and properties. It is a tonic and aid to digestion, prevents fever, cures dysentery, retards old age, restores virility, and makes the barren fertile, besides many other benefits it confers on its consumers. The spirit distilled from it is a colourless fluid apparently the same as alcohol, for very little suffices to produce senseless intoxication. The Kirghiz of Karákochún in Lob are noted for the superiority of this spirit turned out of their stills. It is usually made from mare's milk, but any other or a mixture of milks is also used for the purpose.

The Kirghiz have many customs peculiar to themselves, and treat their women with the greatest confidence and deference. They are very fond of hunting and are robbers by nature. Until the establishment of the Atálik's rule they systematically levied black mail on all caravans passing through their lands, and habitually plundered unprotected travellers. Their camps are under the government of a Chief or *Bí*, who settles disputes in consultation with the *ácsacál* or "grey beards"="elders." The chief of a whole tribe is called *Sultán*, and he is the referee in cases of appeal against the decision of the *Bí*, but as a rule the people are very much their own masters and keep the law in their own hands. They are described as extremely impulsive and impatient of control, and in cases where an aggrieved party considers himself unjustly treated by his judges it is not an uncommon thing for him to kill himself, or to tear open his shirt and gash his chest and stomach with a knife, or to snatch up his own child and dash out its brains on the ground, thereby throwing the responsibility of his ruin upon his unjust judges.

Their marriage customs and ceremonies are very similar to those of the people of Sárigh Kúl, though they don't intermarry with them at all; but their observance of the marriage ties is from all accounts very lax, and adultery and elopement are a fruitful source of discord. The bride is always purchased from the father at a price varying according to the rank of the parties, but whatever the sum agreed to, it is paid in cattle or clothing and always in nine of each kind. Thus nine horses, and nine sheep, and nine camels, &c., &c. A rich man may give more, but it must be in the same ratio—a multiple of nine, and no fractional quantity—and the reckoning is made by that figure all the way through, as four nines of horses, and four nines of sheep, &c., or twelve nines of horses, and so on. A poor man may give only a nine of sheep but he cannot give less than that number. Similarly the presents given by the father to the bride must be in the same number or its multiple of each kind, as nine frocks, nine mantles, nine carpets, &c., and the presents made by friends too must be in the same number, as nine pieces of silk, nine veils, nine caps, &c., &c. The origin of the selection of this particular number, called *tocúz*, is not known, but the custom is observed by all the Turk and Tartar tribes of Central Asia.

The language of the Kirghiz is a dialect of the Turki spoken in Káshghar, but they are mostly an illiterate people, though their Chiefs have books recording the history of the tribes, and others of poetry. They are fond of music, and there are many travelling minstrels and story tellers, called *bacsí*, in the camps. The common names of Kirghiz men are Sikkan, Súránchi, Táylak, Cholpang, Músá, Atantay, Turdá, Sádík, Khidir, Sáydin, Pokbasar, Yobasar, Sultay, Sadir, Anizar, Tilaka, Khán, Tora, &c. And of women, Ganjika, Sárah, Sholpanáy, Orún, Orúzághácha, Olja, Irancha, Ariján, Shachán, Shakar, Toctághácha, 'Ayim, Bakhtághácha, Tolkun, Zácha, Munsághácha, Búrúlúsh, &c.

Pakhpúlúk of Múztágh.—This division—the last and least of those of Káshghar—belongs to the district of Kokyár in the jurisdiction of Yárkand, and comprises the narrow glens and defiles of the head waters of the Tiznáf and Zarafshán, or Yárkand river on the northern slopes of Múztágh. It consists of two principal divisions, *viz.*, Khalistán which extends from Topa Dawán to Yangi Dawán and contains the upper course of the Tiznáf river, and Shanshú, with its sub-divisions of Apat Bulong, Mámok, and Molong Bulong, on the upper course of the Yárkand river up to the glaciers of Torághil which separate it from the Bálti country to the south.

It is a very poor and inhospitable country, very little known even to the people of Yárkand, but remarkable as the retreat of a most interesting and purely Aryan people who only require to be put into coat and trowsers to pass, so far as outward appearance goes, for the fairest Englishman.

On the return journey of the embassy, we marched through the length of Khalistán, and had the opportunity of meeting some of these people, and Captain Chapman took a photograph of two of them who were employed in our camp. Their tall figures, fair skins, light eyes, and sandy whiskers and hair, coupled with their pronounced Caucasian features, at once marked them as of an entirely different race to any of the many our journey had brought us in contact with. Unfortunately, the temerity of these people had carried their camps and families into the recesses of the glens and mountain hollows far out of the line of our march, and we were consequently deprived of the opportunity of learning much about them by personal observation.

By the people of Yárkand they are called Pápú, but to me they called themselves Pakhpá and their country Pakhpúlúk—a Turkí adjectival form signifying "belonging to the Pakhpá"—and corresponding to the noun and adjective forms of *Briton* and *British* respectively. They profess Islám—the *Shia* doctrine—and speak the Turki of Yárkand, but in a corrupt and not easily intelligible form even to natives of that city. They denied having any other language of their own, and their undisguised fear led them to conceal all information regarding themselves, though they were by no means so reticent in replying to questions regarding their Kunjud neighbours on the south side of the mountain. The names of the camp grounds in their country are all Turki, but those of the subdivisons of the country itself, as will be seen from the examples above given, are not so, though to what language they may be referred I have no means of ascertaining.

The two Bulong, Mámok, Aghil, Khalistán, &c., in their distinct etymology resemble the unintelligible names of localities peculiar to the adjoining hill tract designated by the Turki appellation Sárigh Kúl or Táshkorghán, such as Wáchá, Maryang, Kesarov, &c., and denote a separate origin from the several different *aric, cádúc, yár, tásh, corghan, úldí, sáldí,* &c., of the later Turk possessors, so common on the plain, and on the beaten tracks of their goings and comings. Yet they appear not to have anything in common, for these Pakhpúlúk assured us that the languages of Kunjud, Sárigh Kúl, and Wakhán were unintelligible to them.

They are said to number altogether 2,000 houses, which at seven for each will give their total population at 14,000 souls. They are a very poor people, and seldom quit the recesses of their hills. They have several little villages to which they retire for shelter in winter, but during summer they spread in small camps amongst the mountains with their small flocks of sheep and cattle, and in favouring spots grow crops of barley and wheat. Their arms are the matchlock and sword, and their clothing a course woollen material made from the fleece of their sheep.

They seem to have been hunted by all their neighbours, and were at perpetual war with the Chinese. But under the strong rule of the Amír they enjoy, if not prosperity, at least peace and immunity from the slave hunting raids of their Kunjud enemies. Until six or eight years ago they were annually harrassed by robber bands from Kunjud who drove off their cattle and carried away their people as slaves for the markets of Bukhára and Yárkand. Their Chief village in Khalistán is said to be Chúkchú, 200 houses, at two days' journey west from Chighligh camp ground on the Tiznáf river at the foot of Topa Dawan.

Population.—From the data furnished in the preceding description the population of the Káshghar State may be tabulated and summed thus :—

Khutan	18,500 houses		129,500 souls.
Yárkand	32,000 ,,		224,000 ,,
Yangi Hissár	8,000 ,,		56,000 ,,
Káshghar	16,000 ,,		112,000 ,,
Ush Turfán	2,000 ,,		14,000 ,,
Aksú	12,000 ,,		84,000 ,,
Kúchá	6,000 ,,		42,000 ,,
Kúrla	2,000 ,,		14,000 ,,
Karáshahr	8,000 ,,		56,000 ,,
Turfán	18,000 ,,		126,000 ,,
Lob	10,000 ,,		70,000 ,,
Marálbáshí	5,000 ,,		35,000 ,,
Sárígh Kúl	2,500 ,,		17,500 ,,
Kirghiz	3,000 ,,		21,000 ,,
Pakhpúlúk	2,000 ,,		14,000 ,,
Total	145,000 ,,		1,015,000 ,,

Such are the results of a careful enquiry into the population of the several divisions of the country, and the numbers given are mostly those represented to be the revenue reckonings of the Chinese rulers. My personal observation, however, leads me to the belief that this one million and fifteen thousand is very considerably above the actual numbers which a proper census would disclose as the true population of the country in the possession of the Amír as defined in the preceding pages, and I have been enabled to form this estimate for the whole country from experience of its western divisions.

Two circumstances conspire to mislead the mere traveller in his calculations. One is the sudden transition from a region of solitude and desolation to another of society and habitation; and the other is the striking contrast between the desert wastes around and the flourishing settlements that spread far and wide between them. Thus the traveller approaching the country from the south has to cross a vast uninhabited region utterly devoid of trees and verdure; and after ten or twelve days of such desolation he suddenly plunges into a flourishing settlement extending over as many miles along a river course, and thickly planted with trees in all its extent. His first impression is one of dense population and plenty, but a closer investigation shows him that abundance of trees does not necessarily prove numbers of population; and he discovers that the houses are widely scattered either as single homesteads or in clusters of two or three together; and if he counts them, he will find that within a radius of a couple of miles all round hardly fifty tenements visible. He quits this settlement on his onward journey and, whichever way he goes, he traverses a wide waste of blank desert to the next which, may be, is a market town and entered on market day. He here finds a closely packed and busy crowd blocking the streets with their numbers; and extricating himself from their midst he goes his

20.—Men of the Pakpoo tribe living in the Valleys bordering that of the Tisnaf river.

21.—Men of the Pakpoo Tribe.

way impressed by the density and activity of the population. But if he halt here, he will find the illusion dispelled. The morrow instead of a struggling and jostling crowd will show him lonesome streets with long rows of silent forges, empty cook shops, deserted grocers' stalls, and the tenantless sheds of the shoe-maker, hatter, and draper; and if he enquires, he will learn that the multitude of yesterday is dispersed far and wide over this and the adjoining settlements till next week's market day brings them together again.

I have no data on which to base an approximate estimate of the area of land under cultivation in each division; but considering the limited water supply and the barren nature of the soil, and comparing the spreads of cultivation with those of other countries where the population is known, it does not appear to me that the soil is capable of feeding the alleged population in the western divisions of the country which I have seen, particularly if it is borne in mind that they are entirely self supporting and receive no extraneous supplies of breadstuffs and similar food. It is for these reasons that I am disposed to estimate the actual normal population at a lower figure than that produced by the reckoning in the time of the Chinese as above given; and independent of the great diminution that is said to have occurred by the war losses and massacres attending the revolution that overthrew their rule, and transferred the possession of the country to other hands.

Climate and seasons.—The preceding description of the natural and political divisions of the country will have prepared us for a diversity in the character of its climate and seasons corresponding with the physical peculiarities of the several divisions themselves. And though I can only speak from personal knowledge of what prevails in the western districts, there are some special characteristics which by common consent are applicable to the whole region. These I may here briefly notice before proceeding to detail the meteorological observations recorded during our stay in the country.

The chief and most notable peculiarities in the climate of Káshgharia are the extreme dryness of its atmosphere at all times, the trifling amount of its rain fall, and the more or less dense haze which nearly always obscures the air; the periodical winds which sweep its surface, the intensity of the sun's rays, and, finally, the very great range of temperature between summer and winter.

The first is the result of the vast expanse of arid sandy desert which forms so large a portion of not only this region itself but of the Central Asian Continent both on its east and on its west, and is intensified by the second; for what rain does fall is caught by the mountain ranges bounding the country on three sides (and even then mostly in the form of snow), and rarely reaches the plain country in any appreciable quantity; whilst the third would seem to be the effect of both the other causes combined; the impalpable dust of the desert, unweighted by a trace of moisture, floating up into an atmosphere equally void of its presence and there obscuring its transparency till the general haze be dissolved, not by wind alone, for that only intensifies it, but by moisture either in the form of cloud or rain or snow. These atmospheric peculiarities characterize the climate of Káshghar in greater or less development and with more or less persistence in all its extent and during all seasons.

The remaining three characteristic peculiarities of the climate are more of a seasonal nature, and prevail in their proper periods with greater or less intensity according to the determining influences of locality. The winds on the plain blow only in the spring and autumn months, and then persistently, with diurnal lulls only, from the north or north-west as a rule; and for the rest of the year the atmosphere may be considered as still. For though whirlwinds and eddies do circle over the desert wastes during the spring and summer months as they do over the plains in India, the spheres of action of the several currents are very limited and rarely produce any extensive or general disturbance of the atmosphere beyond their own little isolated tracts. In the eastern borders of the desert and on Gobi itself, however, these whirlwinds are described as assuming vast proportions and raging over wide tracts with overwhelming violence; but they are not known in this form in the western portions of the plain.

As on the plains so on the mountains, the spring and autumn months are those in which regular winds do most prevail. According to native reports those on Alátágh are mostly from the north or north-west; those on the Pámir steppes are mostly from the west; and those on the Karákoram and Kuenlun are mostly from the south and south-east. These may be taken as the main directions whence the winds blow in each region respectively, but their currents must be diverted by every obstructing ridge and conducting defile. This is well exemplified on the passes of the Karákoram and Tibet range, and at each camp ground may be seen stone walls, raised as a protection to the traveller from the keen blasts of the prevailing winds; but in no two of them will they be found in the same general direction, except on the wide tablelands; and there the general turn of the curved walls to the north and west corroborates the popular report as to the prevalence of winds from the opposite directions.

The general absence of wind in the summer and winter seasons on the plain is a condition favourable to the country as a habitable region. For otherwise the perpetual clouds of dust and sand in the one season would materially interfere with the operations of agriculture and the daily pursuits of life; whilst the intensified cold in the other would prove inimical to all forms of life under the existing circumstances.

The intensity of the sun's rays on the plains of Káshghar is a notable feature of its climate and a phenomenon that requires explanation, because its effects upon the sensibility of man are out of all proportion more perceptible than on that of mercury. The highest temperature recorded during our stay in the country from 1st November to 24th May was 140°F. by a maximum thermometer placed in the direct rays of the sun, yet the exhaustion produced in man by exposure to a sun which indicated considerably less than that degree by the thermometer, I observed was much greater than anything I had ever noticed in India. None of our camp followers could walk a march even in an early sun, and our cattle exhibited more distress than is usual in India. The natives of the country, too, are equally prone to its effects, and cannot endure toil in the sun. It was a subject of common remark amongst us that in all our marches we rarely met a traveller on foot and rarer still, if ever, saw one carrying a load. Everybody in the country rides, either on horse, camel, ox, or ass, or he travels by cart. Judging from my personal experience I am disposed to attribute this inordinate action of a by no means tropical sun to the combined effects of a very dry atmosphere and refraction of caloric with blinding glare from an arid soil of salines and sand.

Not less notable than this action of the sun's rays is the wide range of the atmospheric temperature in the circle of the seasons. July is said to be the hottest month of the year by the natives. I have no data whereby to judge of its temperature. From the observations recorded by Dr. Geo. Henderson, during his visit to Yarkand with Mr. Forsyth in 1870, the temperature of the air on the plain country towards the close of August may be taken at 79°F. In May, according to my own observations, the maximum temperature in the shade was recorded at 97°F. on the 19th of the month at Yakshamba Bazar, two marches to the south of Yárkand city. The minimum temperature of the air was recorded at 20°F. below zero on the 19th February at Tigarmiti near the Súghún valley at the foot of the mountains north of Artosh.

These may be taken as the extremes of heat and cold in the course of the year, but are no criterion for the diurnal alternations, which as a rule are very equable; whilst at the same time the transition from one season to the next is a gradual process, singularly free from the sudden and great variations of temperature that characterise the climate of some parts of the Punjab. This will be seen by an examination of the meteorological records appended to this report.

The seasons in the plain country are distinguishable into four of equal duration, but in the mountain regions there are only two seasons—a summer and a winter—for the spring, summer, and autumn in those elevated tracts run rapidly together, and may be considered as lasting only from the beginning of June to the end of September. The other eight months are winter, of greater or less rigour according to altitude, during which frosts prevail and vegetation is dormant.

The winter or *cish* extends over the months of December, January, and February. It is a cold, still season, with a more or less constantly overcast sky, and an atmosphere rarely disturbed by winds; whilst the humidity of the air, notwithstanding the continued frosts, is greater than at any other period of the year, as will be seen by the meteorological records above referred to. The climatic elements of this season are represented in the following abridged table of meteorological observations recorded at Káshghar:—

	December.	January.	February.
Thermometer, Maximum	+60° F.	+40°	+49°
,, Minimum	− 3°	− 4°	− 5°
Days of cloud	27	29	28
,, wind	2 W., 2 E.	1 N., 1 E.	3 N. E., 2 N.
,, snow	0	0	3

These observations were taken in a small court-yard in which were two occupied *khargah* tents, and about which were our dwellings and stables. The temperature on the open plain outside was considerably less than the minima above recorded, and on the 19th February a temperature of 20° below zero was observed at Tigarmiti north of Artosh by Captain H. Trotter of the Royal Engineers.

The spring or *arta-yáz* gradually emerges from winter and towards its close suddenly lapses into summer. It extends over March, April, and May, and is characterised by greater atmospheric changes than either of the other seasons. March is a frosty, cloud-cast month with occasional clear days towards its close. Vegetation shows no signs of activity till the middle of this month, when the willow by several days precedence begins to unfold its leaf buds, and wave in the breezes which now dispel the clouds of winter, and make way for the haze which gradually, during the next month, takes possession of the air, and by the end of the season completely obscures the hills and distant prospect around. The climate of this season in the western portion of the plain is represented in the annexed table of recorded observations:—

	March.	April.	May.
Thermometer, Maximum	79°	88°	95°
,, Minimum	16°	31°	40°
,, Sun's rays	122°	140°	135°
Days of cloud	20	26 Haze.	24 Haze.
,, wind	20 N. W., 6 S. E.	22 N. W., 2 S. W.	16 N. W., 6 S. E.
,, rain and snow	3 S., 2 R.	0	0

The summer or *yáz* extends over the months of June, July, and August. I have no data for the illustration of the characters of this season. It is the period in which agricultural operations are matured, and is described as hot and sultry even in the settlements, where the abundant growth of trees and numerous running streams, by their grateful shade and refreshing moisture, considerably mitigate its scorching heats, which are only experienced in their intensity by the traveller across the arid deserts around. Whirlwinds and circular currents now and again career across the plain in fitful eddies, but there are no rain storms, though dust or sand storms with thunder and electric disturbance do occasionally occur. They clear the atmosphere, and are succeeded by a brief lull, and occasionally by a slight rain shower, before the sun resumes its power, much as in Northern India.

The autumn or *káz* like the winter is a more or less still season ushered in with northwestern breezes which disperse the summer haze, and correct the aridity of its air by the diffusion of cloud moisture, till gradually the sky becomes overcast as in winter. It is reckoned the most healthy season of the year and that in which the sky is most uniformly blue and clear, though the diurnal range of temperature is very considerable. Frosts set in early and the latter half of the season is little distinguishable from winter. It comprises the months of September, October, and November. The meteorology of the last month is the only one for which I have recorded observations on the plain country, and they may be thus abridged:—November. Thermometer, Maximum 58°; Minimum 13°. Days of cloud, 16; of wind, 3 N. W., and of rain, 0.

The observations above recorded, it should be borne in mind, were made in the midst of habitation and population, and the indications of temperature have no doubt been considerably affected by the influence of surrounding conditions. Thus the recorded heat of summer, in the thickly planted and freely watered settlements, may be fairly presumed to be less than it is in reality on the bare, arid, sandy wastes around. And similarly the degrees of frost recorded in the former situations may be considered to be considerably less than what prevails on the open plains and desert tracts outside.

The long duration and intensity of the season of frost is indicated by the furs developed by the wild animals, and in a lesser degree by the domestic, as well as by the ordinary clothing of the inhabitants. This subject will be noticed hereafter, but it may be here stated that all the wild animals during winter are protected by a soft warm coat of woolly down growing next the skin at the roots of the coarser fur, and that man during the same seasons envelopes his body in thick felts, or silks, or furs.

Salubrity.—The influence of climate upon the health of the inhabitants is in all countries altered and varied in a greater or less degree by the operations of a multitude of diverse agencies associated with the conditions and employments of the people; and, consequently, without long continued and careful study of all the circumstances of each particular case it is impossible to say what is solely the result of climatic agency and what the result of mode of life; or where one begins and the other ends, or how the one cause re-acts upon the other, and to what exent the results are attributable to each, or either, or both, combined with some local peculiarity of soil, or water, or air.

During our stay in the country we had many opportunities of judging of the prevalent diseases amongst the people, and these were extended by the establishment of a charitable dispensary in connection with the Embassy. Subjoined is a classified list of the numbers of each disease treated in the dispensary. It speaks for itself, and needs no special analysis in this place, beyond a few general remarks on its more characteristic indications, as exponents of the health state in western Káshghar during its most rigorous season of cold—a season which with the preceeding months of autumn is considered the most healthy portion of the year.

The rarity of febrile diseases is very notable, and so far as I could ascertain the people of Káshghar (my remarks only apply to the western districts) enjoy an uncommon immunity from this class of diseases. The eruptive fevers of childhood are certainly known, but rarely prevail as epidemics, and small-pox is deprived of much of its destructive violence, owing to the free exposure to air and the isolation of the sick. The people have a greater dread of this disease than any other, and on its appearance amongst them immediately vacate the house or camp, leaving the afflicted with a single attendant, and do not return till forty days have elapsed. Malarious fevers it would appear are hardly known, though a form of typhoid or enteric fever is said to prevail in the early spring and winter seasons. Cholera is unknown in the country, but a fatal epidemic, which by some is described as that disease, and by others as a malignant form of typhoid, is said to have visited Khutan in 1872 as an importation from Kashmir. It did not spread beyond the city, and since its cessation has not again re-appeared. The scattered tenements of a settlement are usually so isolated by a surrounding of fields and orchards and plantations that the spread of infectious diseases from one to the other is reduced to a minimum, whilst the separation of each settlement from the next by an intervening strip of arid desert secures it an almost complete immunity from invasion by disease from its neighbour.

The frequency of diseases of the eye, and particularly of the internal humours, is very remarkable, and is mostly attributable to the combined effects of climate and soil. The extreme dryness of the atmosphere, which in April shows a difference of 26 degrees between the indications of the wet and dry bulbs of the hygrometer, coupled with the intense glare of the sun from a white sandy saline soil, and the particles of dust constantly set afloat in the air, must be a prolific source of discomfort, and a severe trial of the powers of so delicate an organ.

Another set of diseases whose origin is due to effects of climate are those of the respiratory system, and the frequency of their prevalence in a chronic form is a fair index of the severity of the winter season. With this category too may be included the muscular forms of rheumatism.

More notable than any of the above, as much on account of its extraordinary prevalence as on account of its limitation to certain localities is the disease called goitre or bronchocele. It is met with in all the country from Káshghar to Khutan, but attains its maximum of frequency and development at Yárkand itself. Here it is the exception to escape this hideous deformity and most inconvenient disease. It is seen in all forms and stages of growth, and in all classes and ages from the teething infant to the toothless grey beard, and does not appear materially to shorten life. In examining promiscuous groups of the people about our Residency and in attendance at the dispensary, I, on different occasions counted 7 out of 10, 11 out of 13, 5 out of 7, 3 out of 12, 9 out of 15, and on one occasion an entire group of 7 goitrous subjects. Their numbers in the bazar crowds is surprising and the enormous development and deformity in some cases are as astonishing as they are repulsive. I did not see a single case of cretinism, though I was told that idiotcy was not uncommon amongst children in whom the disease attained a rapid development. The people call goitre *búcác* or *búghác* and attribute it to the water they drink. The city, where the disease is far more common than in the rural districts or hills, is supplied with water by canals from the Zarafshan or Yárkand River, which takes its rise, and in its upper course flows, amongst mountains of micaceous schist and slate shales. On the plain, too, it flows over a sandy soil largely mixed with mica, as do the canals drawn from it. These last are conducted into the city and there from time to time replenish a number of uncovered tanks or reservoirs sunk in the loose soil of the ground for the supply of the citizens. Their water is more or less stagnant and full of confervæ, and all sorts of impurities derived from the bordering roadways. Some of the people more than usually affected by this disease applied at the dispensary for relief, but the great majority hardly considered it a disease, and none but children in whom the growth was incipient were treated with any hope of benefit.

Another class of diseases, owing their origin to the habits of the people, as distinct from the effects of climate, deserves a brief notice, inasmuch as they afford a pretty correct idea of the state of morals, domestic habits and vicious practices amongst the people. Venereal affections though not uncommon are still far less frequent than the known lax morality and promiscuous intercourse of the sexes would lead one to expect, unless indeed such cases have not so freely shown as others free from any stigma of reproach have done. But such as were seen included some of the most repulsive and destructive forms of secondary syphilis, aggravated apparently by abuse of mercurial remedies.

The frequency of skin diseases may be recognized as an exponent of the dirty habits of the people, and their little habitude to ablution. But the last of the more prevalent afflictions we need here notice is the dyspepsia produced by the abuse of opium and Indian hemp. Amongst the city people everywhere it is met in a very aggravated form too frequently, and marks very surely the destructive effects of those poisons. The haggard, hungry, dolorous and discontented looks of these wretched victims of their passion tell but too truly the loss of all pleasure in life to them, and speak for the necessity of their continuance in the vice to eke out to its bitter end the short span of aimless existence left for them.

Record of sick, out-door and in-door patients, treated at the Dispensary of the Káshghar Embassy from the 1st November 1873, at Sánjú, to the 24th May 1874, at Kokyar.

General diseases.		Local diseases.	
Agues	20		
Influenza	16	*Nervous system.*	
Mumps	13		
Erysipelas	5	Paraplegia	9
Rheumatism	83	Epilepsy	3
Lumbago	23	Neuralgia	89
Gout	7	Mania	5
Syphilis, Primary	16	Dementia	8
,, Secondary	68	Hysteria	9
Scrofula	16		123
Phthisis, Pulmonary	6		
Hœmoptysis	5	*Diseases of the Eye.*	
Scurvy	5	Conjunctivitis	321
Anœmia	13	Pterygium	13
Anasarca	7	Ulcer of cornea	6
	303	Albugo	15

Disease of the Eye.—(concluded.)

Onyx	2
Iritis	5
Cataract	33
Amaurosis	11
Glaucoma	5
Entropium	11
Ectropium	1
Trichiasis	7
Hordeolum	13
Staphyloma	3
Cancer	5
Melanosis	3
	454

Diseases of the Ear.

Abscess of Ext. Meatus	2
Inflammation ,,	37
Perforated Tympanum	16
Obstruction by wax	5
	60

Diseases of the Nose.

Lupus	4
Ozœna	2
Polypus	26
	32

Diseases of the Heart.

Palpitation	5
	5

Diseases of Thyroid Glands.

Goitre or bronchocele	168
Exopthalmic bronchocele	11
Pulsating bronchocele	8
	187

Respiratory system.

Croup	10
Bronchitis	328
Asthma	103
Pneumonia	2
Pleurisy	32
	475

Digestive system.

Thrush or Aptha	13
Ranula	2
Decayed tooth	86
Relaxed Tonsils	105
Enlarged ,,	5
Elongated Uvula	3
Dyspepsia	378
Gastrodynia	21
Pyrosis	18
Dysentery	33
Diarrhœa	5
Colic	28
Hernia, Inguinal	17
Hœmorrhoids	63
Prolapsus Ani	12
Condyloma Ani	14
Fistula Ani	3
Hepatitis	6
Jaundice	2
Splenitis	7
Ascites	5
	826

Urinary system.

Calculus Vesicœ	6
Gonorrhœa	58
Strictura urethrœ	3
	67

Generative system.

Hydrocele	2
Orchitis	9
Spermatorrhœa	37
Ovarian dropsy	3
Amenorrhœa	12
	63

Diseases of Bones.

Periostitis	13
Necrosis	6
Synovitis	4
	23

Cutaneous system.

Pityriasis capitis	25
Psoriasis	7
Herpes	11
Eczema	15
Acne	6
Frostbite	11
Boil	9
Carbuncle	3
Ulcer	206
Whitlow	13
Ringworm	5
Itch or scabies	173
Fatty tumor	4
Fibrous ,,	2
Sebaceous ,,	11
	501

Debility, general.

From opium smoking	19
,, Indian hemp smoking	25
	44

Intestinal worms.

Ascarides	5
Tape-worm	7
	12

Injuries.

Fracture of skull	1
,, ,, humerus	2
,, ,, patella	1
,, ,, tibia and fibula	2
Dislocation of shoulder	2
,, ,, elbow	1
,, ,, wrist	1
Incised wound	5
Gunshot wound	3
	18

Surgical operations.

Entropium, excision	2
Cataract, extraction	9
Cancer, excision	3
Polypus Nasi, extraction	5
Enlarged tonsils, excision	2
Dislocation shoulder, reduction	1
Tumors, excision	3

Surgical operations.—(concluded.)			Congenital deformity.		
Bullet, excision	...	1	Harelip	...	5
Calculus vesicæ, lithotomy	...	3	Hypospadia of urethra and fissure of scrotum	...	1
Teeth, extraction	...	34			6
Ulcer sinus, incision	...	8			
		71			

The above table shows the numbers of sick of each disease who applied for medical aid at the Embassy Dispensary from the day of entering the settled country at Sánjú, and during our stay at Yárkand, Yangi Hissár, and Káshghar, up to our arrival at Kokyár, and departure thence for India. Whilst it testifies to the eagerness with which European medical aid is sought by the people of Káshghar, it may also be taken as a fair exponent of the diseases from which they suffer.

Natural productions.—These may be very briefly noticed here under the heads of Animal, Vegetable, and Mineral.

Animal.—Káshgharia, in its wide expanse of desert plain, and its long ranges of elevated mountain plateaux, is the native home of the primæval parent stocks of some of man's most useful domestic animals on the Asiatic Continent. Here are found on the soft saline deserts, where no other foot can tread, the double-humped wild camel of Tartary, the *yáwatúga* of the natives. It is described as a small animal but little larger than a horse, and with neat slim built limbs: particulars in which it differs little from its domestic congener here. I was surprised at the diminutive size, and clean formed limbs of many of the camels we saw in the Kirghiz camps (so different from the tall ungainly brutes one is familiar with in India), and noticed that their cry is as different as their form from that of the Indian variety of the species. The wild animal, according to the concurrent testimony of independent witnesses and authorities, is hunted in the vicinity of Lob and Turfán for the sake of its wool.

The wild horse or *cúlán* breeds in the hollows of the sandy ridges bordering the desert, and in the valleys of the great mountain ranges bounding it; and in the latter situations not unfrequently shares the pasture with the Kirghiz herds of its domesticated kindred species.

The wild ox or *cútás* (bos grunniens) is only found at the highest elevations under the snow line, and is a huge animal with long shaggy hair. The domestic animal in the possession of the Kirghiz of Múztágh and Sárigh Kúl is a much smaller brute, and nearly as vicious and intractable as his untamed brother. The hybrid between the wild male and the domestic cow, however, is a highly valued, most useful, and productive creature with all the virtues of the domestic breed improved by the stamina of the wild blood. The wild *cútás* is occasionally hunted, but with great caution owing to its ferocity and courage when brought to bay.

The Ovis Ammon or *ráos* is said only to be found on the Tibet border about the Tághdumbásh and Múztágh, and the Ovis Poli or *ghúlja* on all the Pámir steppes and the plateaux of Alátágh. Sárigh Kúl seems to be the limit between them, the one not going further north, and the other not coming further south. But the Ibex or *takka* has no such limitation, and is found on Alátágh to the north as on the Báltí mountains to the south.

The stag or *búghú* male, and *marál* female, haunts the forest borders along the river courses on the mid plain, and is hunted for its antlers, which are an article of commerce with China. The deer or antelope, called *kiyik*, herds in the lower valleys and on the sand hills bordering the desert; in the former localities it often gets mixed up with the flocks of the Kirghiz shepherds. There is another antelope, called *júrán*, which is only found on the higher plateaux of the Karákoram and Aláy, and is usually seen in couples or singly. It is probably the Lyre horned antelope of Tibet.

The hare, called *táoshcán* by Káshgharis and *cúyán* by Andijánis, is common in the brushwood of the lower valleys, and in the pasture wastes bordering the settlements on the plain.

The other wild animals are the tiger=*yolbárs*, the panther=*molún*, the lynx=*sulésun*, the wolf=*borí*, the fox=*túlkí*, and a similar animal called *Sarigh Cúyurugh* or "yellow-tail." These are with the wild pig=*tongúz* all found on the plain country, and, excepting the first, in winter all develop a thick coat of fur; for the sake of which, excepting the last, they are hunted. We saw some specimens of the wild pig in the thickets on the Fyzabad River, beyond Kol Taylak near Artosh, in the month of February, and found they were coated with a thick layer of soft crispy wool under the long bristles of their ordinary covering. Besides the above, in the hills are found the bear=*arík*, and the marmot=*súghúr*.

Amongst birds, those deserving mention either on account of their utility or frequency, are the following, *viz.*, the swan=*codáy* in Lob, the goose=*cáz*, the Brahmani duck of India, called *anget*, and wild duck=*úrdak*, in vast numbers and variety on the pools and marshes in all parts of the country. These, with the crane, heron, peewit, snippets of sorts, and other water birds, all breed here in the summer, and mostly go across the mountains to India on the approach of winter. On our passage across the Karákoram range in October we found several stragglers of these birds frozen to death in the migration; and at Aktágh our lamented comrade, the late Dr. F. Stoliczka, rescued a benumbed landrail from immolating itself in our camp fire into which it was struggling its way from the cold shelter of a neighbouring rock, and preserved it instead to adorn the shelves of the Calcutta Museum. At this place, too, I picked up a frozen snipe whose eyes stared from their sockets like bright round pearls—by the congelation of their humours.

The hooded crow=*álacárgha*, the rook=*carácárgha*, the jackdaw=*zághcha*, the magpie=*saghizghán*, the starling=*carácúchcach*, the dove=*pakhtak*, the blue pigeon=*coshkil*, the horned owl=*yapalak*, the swallow=*kalaghach*, the sparrow=*cúchcách*, together with the blackbird, thrush, lark, robin, wren, and a variety of wagtails and finches are common about the settlements, as are their enemies the kestral, harrier, and sparrow hawk.

In the mountains are found the raven=*cúzghún*, and the chough, the black eagle=*cáracosh*, and the golden eagle=*búrghút*. This last is taken from the nest, and trained, for purposes of hunting, to strike the stag, deer, pig, and wolf, and even the bear. Several varieties of the hawk species are trapped and trained for sport; their native names are *carchaghay*=falcon (peregrine), *lachin*, *shuncar*, *turumti*, *tulak*, *italgha*, and others.

Other characteristic birds of the country are the pheasant=*cirghawul*, partridge (francolin)=*kiklik*, quail=*bodna*, podoces=*cúm saghazac*, snow pheasant=*ular*, and the florican bustard or obarah=*tughdarra*; but of this last we saw no specimens. The buzzard is common about the settlements, but I saw no vulture in all the country.

The domestic animals are the ox, horse, sheep, and goat, the ass, the dog, the cat, and the rabbit; fowls, ducks, and pigeons are also kept; and the camel, grunting ox or *yák*, and the hybrid cow are found mostly amongst the Kirghíz and Kalmák, and in the southern settlements of the country, where only the mule is abundant; whilst the dog and the cat are man's companions everywhere.

Oxen are not very plentiful, and judging from the droves we saw, the breed is of inferior size and productive quality; probably the consequences of a long winter confinement, and scanty pasture at all times. The best milch kine are said to yield from six to nine quarts of milk daily. In the agricultural districts bullocks are used in the plough and as beasts of burthen. And everywhere they supply the butcher's stall with very fair beef.

The horse is raised in great numbers all over the country, and is of a breed peculiar to the country, though very much resembling the *yábú* of Afghanistan. Its chief points are short or medium height, round barrel and deep chest, with full quarters and thick limbs. It is inured to carry heavy loads at a peculiar jog amble of about five miles an hour, and is said to be very enduring if not urged beyond its natural pace. This is the common animal in the possession of nearly every family in the country. It is called *topichác* or "roadster," in distinction to the *arghúmác* or "thorough bred," which is either of Andiján or Turkman breed, and is only used by the wealthy or by the Chiefs. Generically all horses are called *át*, but they have distinguishing names according to colour; thus the white horse is called *bóz*, the chestnut *túrúk*, the bay *chilán*, the roan *chokur*, the dun *jard*, the piebald *ála*, the brown *kok*, the grey *cúl*, and the iron grey *caráboz*. The *túrúk* or "chestnut" is supposed to be the most common and hardy of all. The horse is here used in the plough and in harness as freely as under the saddle and pack, and horseflesh is an article of daily consumption amongst all classes. Mules are not

22.—Group of Natives of Kargullik, Nov. 1873.

23.—Officers in the service of the Dadkhwah of Yarkund.

often met with except in the Khutan division, where, it is said, they are numerous. Asses of a diminutive breed abound everywhere, and in the cities are found in surprising numbers, and perform the work which elsewhere is done by porters. The sheep is raised here in immense numbers, and is of a very superior breed, both as regards flesh and fleece. It is of the *dumba* or "fat-tailed" variety, and is a large animal, standing higher and longer than its English fellow. It is pastured with the goat in large flocks in the valleys all along the foot of the hills, and in winter both throw up a thick coat of soft downy wool under the longer fleece and hair respectively. This fine wool is woven by the Kirghiz into a variety of warm fabrics for home wear, and much of it is exported to Kashmir for the use of the shawl weavers there. The dog is found here under a variety of forms. There is the sheep dog and watch dog of the Kirghiz—a wolfish, savage animal, and a very efficient protector against surprise by man or beast. The pariah, as in other cities of the East, has his home in the streets; by day he hangs about the butchers' stalls, and at night reposes on the dungheaps; and such of them as have owners, testify their acknowledgments of favours conferred by howling dismally all night from the housetops. The spaniel and terrier and curs of sorts, strangely like their brethren about any European barrack in India, now and again attract attention like strangers on the scene.

The camel, with the horse and sheep, constitutes the wealth of the Kirghiz. They are not so numerous as one might be led to imagine, partly owing to the more general use of the horse as the transporter of merchandise, and partly to the fact of their being only reared by the Kirghiz and Kalmák. They are all of the double-humped variety, and some of them are very handsome creatures grandly arrayed in bushy shags of deep soft wool, who step a proud leisurely pace fully conscious of the imposing dignity of their form and bearing.

The grunting ox and the hybrid cattle are mostly, if not altogether, limited to the southern borders of the country, and flourish best in the lower valleys of the Múztágh and Karákoram ranges. We saw none of them on the plain beyond Sanjú. They are common in Sárígh Kúl and Wakhán and with the Kirghiz of Kíng Kúl and Cháchiklik. Finally in the time of the Chinese, there was the domestic pig, but with the reign of Islám, he has disappeared from the scene entirely.

Regarding the fishes of Káshghar I have little information. Most of the lesser streams, and all the main rivers are stocked with different kinds. In Lob fish form the main diet of the people, and to a limited extent this form of food is consumed in the principal cities. But there are no fisheries for a regular supply of fish to the market. Some were occasionally brought for our table, and they were of two different species. One of which was the barbel, weighing up to eighteen or twenty pounds or more.

The following extracts from Burnes serve to preface a few short notes on the different kinds of horses met with in Eastern Turkestan:—

Horses.—Burnes, Volume III., Chapter IV.—"The horse attains a noble perfection in Turkestan and the countries north of Hindu Koosh. The climate is favorable to its constitution, and the inhabitants exhibit the most patient solicitude in its breeding and food; so that its best qualities are developed. The Toorkman horse is a large and bony animal, more remarkable for strength and bottom than symmetry and beauty. Its crest is nobly erect, but the length of body detracts from its appearance in the eye of a European; nor is its head so small, or its coat so sleek as the brood of Arabia. This want of ornament is amply compensated by its more substantial virtues, and its utility is its beauty.

*   *   *   *   *

"The peculiar manner in which a Toorkman rears his horse arrests attention, and will perhaps account for its stamina and superiority; since education, whether of the beast or the man, leaves the most permanent impression. The diet is of the simplest kind and entirely free from the spices and sugars, the 32 and 42 mussalahs (condiments) of the Indians. Grass is given at stated periods of the forenoon, evening, and midnight; and after feeding on it for an hour, the horse is reined up and never permitted to nibble and eat as in Europe. Dry food is preferred at all times, and if green barley and jerwarree are given in its stead, the animal then receives no grain. At other times a horse has from 8 to 9lbs of barley once a day. Clover and artificial grasses are cultivated in Bukhara and on the banks of the Oxus; and, when procurable, always used in a dry state. The stalk of the jerwarree, which is as thick as a walking stick, and contains much saccharine juice, is a more favorite food. The long intervals between the times of baiting inures these horses to great privations; the supply of water allowed is also most scanty. Before a Toorkman undertakes a foray or chupao, he trains, or, to use his own words, "cools his horse," with as much patience and care as the most experienced jockey of the turf, and the animal is sweated down with a nicety which is perhaps unknown to these characters. After long abstinence from food, the horse is smartly exercised and then led to water. If he drinks freely, it is a sign that his fat has not been sufficiently brought down, and he is starved and galloped about till he gives this required and indispensable proof. A Toorkman waters his horse when heated, and then scampers about with speed to mix the water and raise it to the temperature of the animals body. Under this treatment the flesh of their horses becomes firm, and their bottom is incredible; I have had authentic accounts of their performing a journey of 600 miles in seven and even six days. Speed is at all times looked on as an inferior quality to bottom.

* * * * *

"The breed of the Toorkman horse is of the purest kind; when the animal is overheated, or has performed great work, nature bursts a vein for it in the neck, which I did not credit till I had become an eye-witness of the fact.

"The Toorkmans cut their horses, as it is a popular belief among them that they are then more on the alert and undergo more fatigue than stallions. The Toorkmans believe their horses to be exceedingly nice in hearing, and will often trust to their steeds for the alarm of an approaching enemy. I was particularly struck with the fine crests of the Toorkman horses; and I heard, though I could not authenticate its truth by observation, that they are often confined in a stable with no other aperture than a window in the roof which teaches the animal to look up, and improves his carriage. The contrivance seems fitted for such an end. The finer horses of the Toorkmans are seldom sold, for their owners may be truly said to have as much regard for them as their children. It must not, however, be imagined that all the horses of Toorkestan are equally renowned, for as most persons beyond the Oxus have a mount of some kind, a great portion of them are very inferior animals.

"In Bukhara there are many Kazzak horses, a sturdy and little animal, with a shaggy coat and very long mane and tail, much and deservedly admired. They are brought from the deserts between Bokhara and Russia."

The Toorkman horse, as described by Burnes, may be considered a great rarity throughout the Káshghar territory. There are regular importations of horses from Andijan and Badukshan; these are of two distinct kinds, the Andijanee horse having, in comparison with the Badukshanee one, the more rounded form and the symmetry of the Arab breed; while the Badukshanee horse is no doubt an inferior breed from the Toorkman stock. In every sense both breeds appear to turn out admirable hacks: they are hardy and enduring, and very bold and active, without possessing great speed. I cannot ascertain that there are any long priced horses in the possession of the Amir, or of any of the officials of his Court, and I doubt whether such are brought into the country. I have seen a very fair Badukshanee horse purchased for 13 tillahs: prices may run up to 30 tillahs or 40 tillahs, there being a slight preference for the Andijanee breed amongst the purchasers on account of association. The Andijanee horses, however, are rarely brought in as an article of trade apart.

With each kafila there will probably be a few horses which have been ridden by the merchants, which are offered for sale on arrival at Káshghar, or are presented to the Amir. From Badakshan, however, horses for sale are regularly brought over the passes. No foreign horse enters the country and finds its way to the market until after inspection by the Amir's officials, often by himself, and in Yárkand by the Dadkdwah; he claims the right of pre-emption, and a good animal invariably finds its way into his stable, or is presented to one of the officers of his army.

The breed of the country, which is so often spoken of as "the Yárkand pony," presents quite a different type: this is a short horse so to speak, the larger animals approaching what we know as the "cob." This nag is an excellent roadster, but his qualities are distinctly those of the pack-animal. He must be separated from the Kazzak horse alluded to by Burnes, and from the Kalmák pony whose home lies to the north-east in the direction of Kuldja, but which is met with frequently in the provinces of Káshghar; these ponies are exceedingly hardy; they are peculiarly vicious in stable and resent grooming, but if a bridle is held out to them, they readily allow it to be put on and are quiet when mounted.

The Yárkand pony, with his long mane and tail, seems more nearly allied to the Kazzak horse.

Both breeds are not usually shod, if they are only used in the plain country, but all ponies that have to cross the mountains are regularly shod. Nearly all the Yarkandees who travel are familiar with the art of putting on shoes. Both ponies of the Yárkand and of the Kalmák breed resist being shod; they have either to be slung or thrown for the purpose. In Káshghar and elsewhere, there are regular slinging arrangements in front of the smithies.

The stable treatment, diet, and rearing of the Toorkmans horse alluded to by Burnes is in force throughout Káshghar; remedies for sickness are few, and veterinary treatment appears to be of Chinese introduction, and to be rather of Kalmák origin than to have come from the west; the horse doctor's wallet, however, commonly contains, salamoniac which is administered for retention of urine, Kwang Chia, a Chinese compound, applied for healing wounds, Kwang Chi, a medicine for fever, and a mixture of alum, lime, and vermilion which serves as a second healing application, together with the instruments necessary for bleeding and for cutting out ossification, and an iron tube for administering medicine.

In gelding, the entire testicle is extracted and the wound is washed with salt and water, the horse being put on low diet, and kept constantly moving.

Well-bred ponies are constantly relieved of surfeit or during heat by the bursting of small veins near the surface of the body. Burnes refers to the bursting of a vein in the neck of the Toorkman horse as a special provision of nature under similar circumstances.

The best Yárkand ponies are purchased at Yárkand itself, where they are cheaper than at Káshghar and elsewhere. The prices range from 120 tangas = Rupees 25 to 400 tangas = Rupees 80. Kalmák ponies are not so common in the market, as they are preferred for riding.

The load placed on the Yárkand pony by the trader is rarely under $2\frac{1}{2}$ maunds = 200℔s, and is usually 3 maunds or 240℔s; this in addition to a heavy felt and pad (palán). It is customary for the Yarkandee to balance the load by taking a seat on the top, so that, if the weight of a man be added to the above, the limit of endurance is probably reached.

At extreme altitudes the baggage animals often suffer from congestion—the remedy usually adopted is to throw the sufferer, pierce a hole through the cartilage of the nostril, pass a few hairs of the tail through this, which are tied in a knot, give a sharp cut with the whip, and the animal rising tears out the cartilage. The long mane and tail of the Yarkandee pony have already been noticed; when crossing streams and frequently in stable the tail is tied in one or two knots and kept from trailing.

Stabling lighted by a single hole in the roof is referred to by Burnes as a possible means of causing a horse to acquire an erect carriage by teaching him to look up. The ordinary method of lighting and ventilating, not only stabling, but dwelling-houses in Turkestan, is by a hole in the roof, and does not appear to have its origin in any idea of affecting the carriage of the horse. The practice of confining animals in very dark stabling seems, however, to act injuriously and make them addicted to shying.

The very large number of ponies in Eastern Turkestan might appear a matter of great surprise, but from the earliest time this animal seems to have been applied to every possible use; the climate is favorable to him and he is well cared for as a matter of course. The limited number of old ponies in work and in the market is striking in comparison with other countries: the fact is that the Yarkandee gets as much as he possibly can out of his pony during the years of his prime, and when he is old or stricken, readily disposes of him at the butcher's shop. The practice of eating horse-flesh thus, in some measure, does away with the necessity for veterinary practice. The price of horse-flesh is usually something more than what is paid for beef or mutton, and the dish is by very many deemed a luxury.

The usual grain upon which the Yárkand pony is fed is Indian-corn, but dry fodder (Lucerne grass) is the chief article of diet. Barley is given to the better class of horses by those who can afford it.

The use of ponies in ploughing is referred to elsewhere.

With Mahomedans Solomon is the special protector of horses; before gelding or administering medicine, prayers are addressed to Solomon, the horse doctor also takes the name of Duldul, the horse of the Divinity and Mahomed's horse. Stroking his beard and saying:— "Ba birkut-i-Hazrat-i, Solomon Nubbi, ba hormut-i-burak-i-Mahomadee, ba hormut-i-Duldul-i-Allee, ba in Asp Sehut shavad."

Vegetable.—Káshghar is singularly deficient in the variety of its indigenous flora, and the distribution of vegetation generally, as the preceding description will have foretold, is very limited and sparse; yet there are some peculiar features of vegetable growth generally in this country which may be now briefly noted. In the western parts of the country all vegetation is dormant from October till April. It is not till the early days of the latter month that the ground begins to green on the plain, whilst in the hills, according to the elevation, the period of activity is variously postponed to as late as June. We found no wild plants in flower on the plain during all our stay in the country, excepting a few common field herbs in the settlements, and a few wild plants at the foot of the hills as we left the country towards the end of May. Everywhere on the plains we found either the withered stalks of the preceding summer's growth, or the fresh sprouts of the new season.

For convenience of description I propose to notice the flora of this country very briefly under different heads, according to habitat in the hills, or deserts, or plains, or cultivated settlements.

In the hills, and the valleys and plateaux spreading between them, there is a more or less abundant vegetation which supports numerous herds of domestic cattle, as well as an unknown number of their wild congeners. On the Pámir and Alátágh it is described as a rich growth of pasture grasses and flowering herbs with few shrubs and fewer trees. From the description given to me by some Kirghiz shepherds these pastures would appear to resemble those of the Khurásán highlands, and to be mainly composed of different varieties of Artemisia and Astragalus, with the Calligonum, Hedysarum, and Peganum, the Ephedra, Berberis, and Tamarix, with a smaller growth of thistles, trefoils, crowfoots, &c.; with the crocus, lily, and onion, dispersed amidst the general spread of grasses and sedges. On the hill slopes grows the juniper, and along the watercourses are found the willow, tamarisk, rose, honeysuckle, and its climber, the clematis.

The description is not far out from our own experiences of the valleys at the foot of Alátágh on the north, and the Muztágh range on the south. In the former we found the wider pasture valleys very much as above described in point of vegetation, and in the narrower ones, drained by a river, as the Súghún north of Artosh, we found belts of tall reeds and grasses with detached clusters of poplar, and willow, and celeagnus; and at intervals, in the bed of the stream, thickets of tamarisk, rose, barbery and honeysuckle with its entwining clematis. In the valleys of the Kárákash, Tiznáf, and Yarkand rivers on the south, we found the vegetation with much the same general character. Thickets of tamarisk, buckthorn, myricaria, rose, honeysuckle, clematis, &c., set the banks on each side, or covered the uneven ground with a scattered brushwood, in the spaces of which grew spreads of tall grasses of the arundo and andropogon species, with now and then fields of carex, sedge, or tufty patches of poagrass. Scattered bushes of the barbery and the thorny Astragalus, with the Ephedra and another species of short tufty Astragalus dotted the hill slopes, with a more or less thick sprinkling of the Artemisia and the Peganum Harmali. In the lower valleys are found the poplar, willow, occasionally the wild fig or *pipal* of India, and generally the Hololachne, with the tamarisk and rose everywhere. At the higher elevations the brushwood dwindles and disappears, and the surface is either bare gravel and clay, or it is dotted with tufts of the Eurotia

24.—Dastarkhwan at Kargalik, 3rd Nov. 1873.

25.—Street Hawkers in the square of the Mess Room of the British Embassy in Yarkund, Nov. 1873.

salsola, and a Caryophyllaceous Arenaria, both of which are called *burtsi* by the natives of Thibet, to whom, in common with other travellers in this region, they are the only sources of fuel; or else, at some springhead, there is an oasis of green grasses and sedges with crowfoots and gentian. On the slopes and hollows where the soil is slaty, rhubarb grows in plenty, and where granite more predominates are found two or three varieties of large leafed Umbellifer, Saxifrages, and the Saussurea, whilst thistles and the prophet flower or Arnebia are met as common roadside plants in the intermediate elevations at almost every bed of gravel or sand.

On the deserts, vegetation of every kind is extremely scanty. Wide patches of tall reeds, species of Arundo and Andropogon, are found where the surface is water-logged by marsh or pool; and where there are desiccated hollows, deep with loose pulverulent salines, the Hololachne, Salsola, Halicornia, and other saltworts, with a degenerate sort of dwarf tamarisk, luxuriate in proportion. For the rest the surface is a sheer waste of bare arid sand, till its continuity is cut by some river bed, when vegetation again appears in belts of thick forest along each bank. Here the chief constituents are tall reeds, called *comush* (Andropogon) and *chigh* (Arundo), the poplar, called *toghrac* (Populus balsamifera), and the tamarisk, called *yúlghún*.

On the plains, or waste tracts between the cultivated settlements, is a very scanty and widely dispersed scrub of camels thorn, wild liquorice (on both of which are seen the tangled skeins of the dodder), Calligonum, Lycium, and Peganum, with here and there patches of Hololachne, and spreads of tribulus terrestris, with trefoils and melilots; the convolvulus, goosefoot, chamomile, artemisia, dandelion, thistle, and other common herbs of every English roadside.

In the cultivated settlements vegetation reaches its greatest development, and, by comparison with the wastes around, flourishes in rich abundance. The wild herbs of the fields and meadows are those of England. The corncockle and poppy, the tare and trefoils, with the plantain and polygony, peep out amidst the growing crops with familiar habitude; whilst the fumitory, marsh mallow, amaranth, and darnel spread a carpet on the foot-paths, and conduct to the meadows of rich clover and grass, radiant with buttercup and daisy, potentil and tormentil, anemone and geranium; and fragrant with mint and thyme, and sage and centaury.

All the settlements are well stocked with trees for fuel, timber, and fruit. The common roadside trees are the poplar and the willow, and there are two kinds of each, the *toghrác* or "populus balsamifera" and the *tarik* or "populus alba," the *bed* or "weeping willow," and the *sugat* or "common willow." The *toghrác* yields a gum and a fungoid growth called *toghrághú* which is used in medicine and as a ferment in baking; and the *tarik* furnishes the timber used in house-building. The *bed* is an ornamental tree, not very common, and with its relative, the *sugat*, which is always polled for the purpose, is the principal source of fuel during winter. The other common trees are the *uzma* or mulberry, the *sadda* or elm, the *jighda* or celeagnus, and the *chilán* or jujube. I saw the *sadda* only in the Yarkand division, but the others are common everywhere, and their fruits are largely consumed; those of the two last never fail to appear on every *dastúrkhwán;* and I must record never seem to grow less, so long at least as there is anything more palatable and satisfying at hand. The walnut grows at Yarkand and in the southern divisions, but I did not see it at Káshghar, whither the fruit is carried to market from Yarkand.

For the rest, the vegetation of the settlements may be included under the head of agricultural products, and will be noticed hereafter when describing the agricultural industry of the country.

Mineral.—The mineral products of Káshghar are varied, and from all accounts abundant, though lamentably neglected and undeveloped. The gold-diggings and jade-quarries of Khutan have long been famous in history, the iron furnaces of Kizili are still in operation, and the coal of Aksú and Turfán continues to burn on the domestic hearth in those places. That found in the former locality is described as of excellent quality and very black; whilst that of Turfán is said to be of a reddish-brown color and of very inferior burning power, owing to its gritty and earthy impurities. The Aksú coal is said to come from the vicinity of Karábágh, and that of Turfán from the hills about Sirkip near Ghochang. The Turki name of the mineral is *tásh kúmúr* or "stone charcoal."

From the volcanic region between Kúchá and Karashahr the markets of the western cities are supplied with alum, sal ammoniac, sulphate of copper, and yellow ochre; and mines of lead and copper which are worked by the Chinese are indicated in this vicinity; *viz.*, those of lead at Tajik Tágh, ten *tásh* north-east of Aksú, and those of copper at Onbásh on the Múzárt river near Báy. Lead and sulphur are, it is said, still procured for the Káshghar market from the former Chinese workings in some low hills near Kalpin on the Aksay river south of Aksú, and a lead mine, now unworked, is said to exist in the hills near Oksalor on the Mingyol road to the Tirik Dawán. The ore is also brought in, with crude sulphur from the hills to the west of Opal, by the Kirghiz of that vicinity, as is metallic antimony picked up on the surface in the form of small rolled pebbles.

Iron is brought to the Kizili smelting furnaces from Kiziltágh and Túmur Tágh, or "Red Hill" and "Iron Hill," respectively, at the sources of the Shahnaz river. Further south again, at Kosharab, are old forsaken mines of lead and silver, whilst at Khoja Mazár on the Tiznáf river south of Kokyár are the copper mines discovered and worked by the Chinese. On our way up this valley we saw the ruins of the smelting furnaces on the river bank, where fuel was in plenty, a little below Khoja Mazár; but none of the people with us could point out the site of the mines which had been abandoned since the disappearance of the Chinese from the country.

An impure kind of alimentary salt is gathered on the surface of desiccated pools on the desert south and west of Marálbáshi; and gypsum, or plaster of Paris, is found in extensive beds in many localities along the hill skirts. It is the cement generally used instead of lime for plastering walls, &c., in all the western towns of the country.

Industrial productions.—These may be briefly noticed under two separate heads of agriculture and manufacture.

Agriculture.—This is the most important and most widely spread industry of the country, and the one on which the inhabitants depend for existence, as there are no imports of breadstuffs from neighbouring countries. Consequently all the settled population, other than urban, is agriculturalist and nothing else. Cattle-breeding is the care of the wandering Kirghiz and Kalmák, and manufactures are the business of the city people.

The agriculturalists or peasantry are spread over the settlements and city suburbs in a fashion peculiar to the country. Each family has a separate homestead, called *oe*, and these homesteads stand either singly or in clusters of two or three or more together, in the midst of the fields and plantations and orchards by which they are surrounded. None of the homesteads, or clusters of them, is enclosed, or in any way protected by fortified walls of defence; nor in any settlement are the tenements massed together as in an Indian village. Generally from four to sixty or eighty homesteads are planted at short intervals of a hundred to two or three hundred yards or more along the course of a rivulet or canal, and each such group forms a parish or ward called *mahalla*, and its community is superintended by an elder, called *ácsacál* or "grey-beard." A collection of these *mahalla* forms a village or *yaz*, and a succession of two or three or more of these form a township or *kand*. In each *kand* there is a market or *bazar*; it usually consists of a main-street of stalls and cross-streets opening into it, and about them are crowded together the residences of the Government officials, and of the resident shopkeepers, victuallers, artizans, &c. The several residences are enclosed within walls and are called *hauli*; towards the exterior they separate from each other and gradually merge into the homesteads scattered around. The *bazar* is never fortified, but in some of the strategically important townships there is a separate little fort. The Government of each *kand* is supervised by a district governor, who is called *beg*, or *mir*, or *sarkár*, according to his rank and the importance of his charge; and he has under him a staff of officials for the maintenance of order, collection of revenue, &c. A market is held once a week in the bazar, and is attended by the peasantry of the township and neighbouring settlements, who here barter their farm produce for the productions of the city, and lay in a stock of provisions for the ensuing week, and at sunset disperse to their homes. Each *kand* has its mosque, and school, and guest-house, with their respective priests, tutors, and servitors, and is, in fact, so far as the requirements of life are concerned, a complete integer of the many that go to form a division or provincial Government; or in other words, the bazar is to the constituent elements of the township what the capital is to the component parts of the province. In its shops are found all the domestic requirements of the peasantry, whilst the journeymen cobblers, saddlers, farriers, &c., who attend on market-day, perform all the necessary little jobs necessitated by wear and tear. On these busy days little coin is current; all exchanges are by barter. Farm produce, such as grain, fruits, cotton, fodder, poultry, &c., with home-spun yarn, and home-woven cloth, and a coarse cotton fabric called *khám* or *karbás*, and live-stock, such as horses, plough-oxen, cows, sheep, &c., are brought in and exchanged with the city traders or bazar shopkeepers for ready made clothing, as fur trimmed hats, printed scarves, embroidered boots, silk frocks or glazed cloaks, latticed veils, &c., for the fair sex, and fur coats and top boots, fur caps, coats of quilted cotton, &c., for the men; or they are exchanged amongst each other, as a horse for so many sheep, &c. The *khám* is the material most in demand by the city traders, and is generally purchased for cash after brisk competition.

The produce of the farms may be classed under the three heads of field, garden, and orchard. The operations in each are all begun and completed during six months of the year— from April to October—and for the remainder, the ground, as its tiller, lies idle. All cultivated land is irrigated; without water no crop matures. The distribution of water is superintended by a Government officer called *miráb*, and there are several of them in each township, according to size and extent. The *miráb* in turn makes over the stream under his charge, or a portion of it, to the *ácsacál* of the several *mahalla*, and he allots the water proportionally to each homestead. At each harvest the *miráb* receives as fee from each *ácsacál* one part in fifty of the total outturn of corn in his *mahalla*. Of the whole which the *miráb* thus collects, he keeps one-half for himself, and the other half he makes over to the *beg* for Government; or if the land be held in fief by a *pánsad*, or other feudatory of the king, he delivers it to such feoffee. For the rest, agricultural operations are much the same as elsewhere. Horses and oxen are used indifferently in the plough, and manure of the dung-heaps is freely mixed with the soil, which is everywhere very poor and requires much attention. As the crops sprout, it is customary to give them two or three successive top-dressings of clean, dry sand, to counteract the injurious effects of the white saline encrustations which continually form on the surface.

The principal field crops are the following:—

Wheat *(Bughdáy)*.—It is sown in two seasons, *viz.*, in August and September, for the winter crop, called *Kúzluk bughdáy*, and in March and April for the summer crop, called *Yázluk bughdáy*. The autumn sowing lies in the ground through the winter, and sprouts in March, about the time of the spring sowing. Both crops ripen together and are cut in July; but the winter seed returns fourteen-fold, or fourteen *chárak* for every *chárak* sown, whereas the spring seed returns only seven-fold. This crop is consequently mostly sown in autumn. In spring, during April, they receive two or three top-dressings of manure and sand, and are not irrigated till in ear.

Barley *(Arpa)*.—Is not grown in Káshghar and Yangi Hissar, and but sparingly in Yarkand. It returns ten-fold, and is sown in spring at the same time as wheat. Its ten-fold return is said to be actually less than the seven-fold of wheat, owing to the lighter weight of its seed.

Maize *(Conác)*.—Generally grown everywhere. Sown in April and harvested in September. Returns sixty-fold. The corn and stalks are used as winter food for horses and cattle instead of barley, and the meal very generally as a bread stuff.

Rice *(Shál)*, the plant, and *gurunj*, the grain.—Principally grown in Yarkand division. Sown in April and cut in September and October. Returns six to eight-fold. The seed is husked on the banks of the canals by a pounder-mill worked by water. It is called *sucana*, and consists of a horizontal axle-beam, in the middle of the shaft of which are four immovable flanges or paddle-boards against which the water plays. The shaft is supported at each end by an upright socket post on each side of the mill-stream, and at one end of it are two long clappers which project six or eight inches on opposite sides. As the shaft revolves, by the water playing against the paddles, these clappers alternately, in turn, catch and release the handle of the pounder, which works on a fulcrum block, and is so adjusted that the clapper in revolving with the shaft shall catch and depress the short hand of the lever, and thus raise the pounder, which projects down at right angles from its other end, and let it fall again as in course of revolution it releases the depressed lever head. The pounder is a round-ended bar of wood fixed at right angles into the head of the long hand of the lever, and plays upon the rice in a wooden mortar. The *súcana* may be built by anyone on a suitable stream by permission of the district governor, and on payment of a fee to Government of sixty *tanga* (fourteen rupees about) and this clears him of all further taxation on its operations. The miller's charge is one *chárak* in fifteen of husked rice. The entire mechanism of the mill is in wood-work, and the several parts are very neatly put together. We saw several of these mills at work on the canals in the line of our march, and were impressed by the stride in civilization in advance of what we had left behind us in Kashmir, where the laborious and by no means graceful operations of the pole pestle and mortar are a prominent feature in the scene peculiar to the banks of the Bidasta.

Lucerne (*Yúrúshca*), green, and *beda*, dry.—Sown in August and September; sprouts in March and April. Is cut three times in six months, and after each receives a top-dressing of manure, and free irrigation, one sowing lasts three years, after which the roots decay. When sown, the seed is mixed with an equal quantity of barley, otherwise the lucerne does not thrive. It is extensively grown as a fodder crop, and is stored in bundles for winter use.

Millet (*Joári*)—Is grown in the southern districts, mostly at the same time as maize. Grain and stalks used as winter fodder for cattle, and the meal as a bread stuff.

Cotton (*kiwaz*).—Largely cultivated in Khutan, Yarkand and Turfán, and exported east and west in both the raw and manufactured state, and also extensively consumed for home use. The seed is sown in April and May, flowers in July, and pods continue forming till the end of October. They are gathered three times in the season, and after the last gathering the stalks are cut away close to the ground. The plant does not grow higher than two to three feet, and bears much more fruit than foliage. Fresh seed is sown every year. Two *chárak*=forty pounds of seed are allowed to each *tanáb* of land=560 yards square, and yield eight *tártam*=twenty pounds of cotton, and twenty-four *tártam*=sixty pounds of seed. The Government tax is five *tanga*=about one rupee on each *tanáb*, or less according to quality and selling price. The seed is separated from the cotton by an ingenious roller gin, worked by pedal and eccentric wheel; it is called *chighric*. The seeds are pressed for oil, and the cake given to fatten cattle. The cotton is considered of excellent quality, and is in great demand for the Khokand and Tashkand markets.

Flax (*Zighir*).—Extensively cultivated for its seed in all the western divisions. The seed is the chief source of the oil used in the country, and the cake is given to stall-fed cattle. The oil-mill or press is worked by horses or oxen, and is similar to that used in the Punjab. The seed is sown in April and May, and the crop is cut in October.

Indian hemp (*Kandir*).—Grown largely in the Yarkand division. The resin is collected in October and packed in bags of raw hide for export, principally to India; and hemp is prepared from the stalks, but it is a very coarse fibre and only used for twisting into rope by the peasantry. The resin packed for exportation is usually pounded up with a varying proportion of the green leaves, and the adulteration is carried to such an extent that in the Yarkand bazar the drug sells at only twelve or twelve and a half *jing* to the *chárak*, instead of sixteen which is the proper measure. That is to say, a fourth part or thereabouts is struck out of the calculation for payment. For example, the selling price of *chars* (the resin) is from thirty to fifty *tanga* the *chárak* of sixteen *jing*; the seller, who is the producer too, weighs out sixteen *jing* and takes payment for only twelve, receiving twenty-two and a half to forty-two and a half *tanga* instead of thirty to fifty. There are different qualities of the drug according to the manner and period of its collection, and they are carefully scrutinized by connoisseurs. The Government tax on the drug is two *tanga* (eight annas nearly) per *chárak*. Hemp resin is very generally consumed by all classes, and in the cities it is abused to excess with very injurious effects upon the health of the people. It is generally called *bang*, and is smoked mixed with tobacco, or eaten in the form of a confection. The confection is thus prepared :—to ten *tolas* of *bang* add ten pints of water, and boil; then remove from the fire, and on cooling, strain through muslin. To the strained liquor add five *tolas* of mutton fat, and boil again till the suet is melted; then remove from the fire and pour in cold water till the fat cakes with the *bang* and subsides and clear liquor only remains. Pour this off, and to the fat add saffron one *mithcál*, zedoary one *mithcál*, and cinnamon one *tola*, all finely powdered, and honey, ten *tolas*, and thoroughly mix together.

Opium (*Afim.*).—The poppy is cultivated in Yarkand and Káshghar, but not largely. The opium got from it is of very inferior quality and only used to mix with the foreign drug which comes from India. Poppy-heads and the seeds are sold in the bazar by druggists for medical purposes. Opium is either eaten or smoked. In the former case, either raw as purchased, or in the form of extract. This is prepared thus:—Steep the opium in water over night, then wash into a thick solution, and strain through muslin. Boil the liquor to evaporation in a greased saucepan to prevent the opium sticking to the sides and getting burned. Cool and dry, and the extract is ready for use, either to eat or to smoke. In the latter case, the smoker lies down on one side with his head on a pillow close to the lamp, at which he lights his pipe. This is a china or metal tube some sixteen inches long, with a jade or other mouthpiece, and is called *ghāza*. At the far end (which is closed), on one side, is a small aperture large enough to admit a goose-quill. In the aperture a small quantity of the soft extract, about the size of a pea, is applied to its sides by a pencil of wood, which is twirled between the finger and thumb, so that the extract sticks to the sides and orifice of the aperture without blocking it. The pipe is then turned to the candle, and the aperture with the opium brought close up to the flame. The smoker now draws several sharp full inhalations till the opium is consumed, and puffing out the smoke from his lungs, goes off into a dreamy stupor. This habit is extremely prevalent in the cities, and in private houses too. Both sexes are equally addicted to it as to *bang*.

The garden produce of Káshghar may be considered essentially the same as that of European countries.

The cabbage, turnip, and radish, the carrot, beet, and lettuce, the onion, capsicum and tobacco, and peas, and beans, and the egg plant, are grown in the suburbs of all the western cities and towns; as are the pulses, cicer and phaseolus, and melons and cucumbers of excellent quality, together with the pumpkin and the gourd. These last are scooped out and used as water jars, and some of them are larger in capacity than an ordinary bucket; the gourd is generally of the long bottle-necked kind, and is called *kapak*.

Many kinds of flowering plants are also cultivated, such as the rose, the tuberose, the lily, the wall-flower, china aster, marigold, &c. With the orchards are included the vineyards and plantations. In them are found the plum, apricot, peach, pear, apple, and quince; the fig, the walnut, the pomegranate, the celeagnus, jujube, and mulberry. The vines are trained on trellises, and produce excellent grapes of many different varieties. They are preserved for winter use by hanging the bunches on rope lines stretched across deep cellars. The raisins, of small seedless variety, are more or less green and of excellent flavour, whilst those prepared from the Turfán grape are noted for their size and sweetness, though in appearance they look uninviting.

Manufactures.—Since the overthrow of the Chinese rule, the manufacturing industries of Káshghar have declined, and in the case of some profitable arts have altogether disappeared. The workings at almost all the metalliferous mines, as at those of coal and the quarries of jade, have ceased with the continuance of their rule. The manufacture of jade ornaments has disappeared, and the art itself is said to be lost with the workmen who perished in the revolt. The trade in the unwrought mineral is gradually reviving, and choice samples of the stone now slowly find their way to China through Almati on the one side and Leh on the other. The gold mines of Khutan are worked on a small scale, as a strict monopoly by the Amir, and the coal of Aksú and Turfán is collected on the surface by the peasantry and carried for sale to the cities; but its consumption now is, from all accounts, as nothing to what it used to be under the Chinese. The iron mines of Shahnáz are the only ones which continue in full operation. The collection and smelting of the ore, which is all done at Kizili, provides employment and means of support to some four or five hundred families. The metal which is considered of very superior and ductile quality, supplies the markets of all the western cities, and is entirely used up in the manufacture of domestic utensils and articles for home use.

The silk culture and manufacture of different textures from it at Khutan was in a very depressed state, but the Amir is making efforts to revive it. What is produced is for the greater part exported to Khokand in the form of a coarse spun fibre, or it is used at home for purposes of embroidery, &c. It is sold in the bazars of Káshghar side by side with Khokand silk (which is of far finer and softer quality) in the form of loose hanks dyed in a variety of bright colours. Formerly most of this coarse silk was used up at Khutan in the weaving of a strong parti-coloured material from which robes were made, and much, too, was used in the manufacture of carpets, for which the place has long enjoyed celebrity.

The carpet manufacture of Khutan is of a kind peculiar to the place. The ordinary wool carpets are of very good quality, and the patterns and colours are simple, and combined with harmonious effect; but they don't approach the carpets of Persia, such as those of Gháyn and Kirmánsháh, either in the elaborateness of design, the superior soft quality of the wool, the excelling fineness of the dyes, or in general evidence of artistic skill. The special manufacture of the place, however, has excelling qualities peculiar to itself. The silk carpets are highly prized, and in the time of the Chinese were much in demand, but they are not now made, except to special order. Another kind of carpet, in which the wool pattern stands on a ground of gold or silver, formed of three-plait threads, is an admirable novelty, and wears a look of superb richness which fit it for the king's chamber. The weight of this carpet is surprising, and its cost heavy in proportion. Its disadvantage is that the metals are apt to tarnish in damp weather and mar the effects of its proper brilliance. One of these carpets was spread in the residency prepared for us at Káshghar. It had evidently seen much rough service, yet even in its worn state it commanded admiration. For the rest, the manufactures of Káshghar may be considered as merely the handicraft trades which are found to flourish amongst all organized societies of civilized men. A strong coarse cotton cloth called *khám* is woven in all the western settlements, though more abundantly in Khutan. It is the dress of the common people, and for winter wear is padded with cotton and quilted. Much of it is exported to Khokand and Badakhshán and Thibet. The loom used resembles that seen in the Punjab. In Yarkand boots and shoes are made, and hides are tanned, for the supply of the markets of Khutan and Káshghar. Very good saddlery and harness, as used in this country, are also made here and at Aksú. Felts are made at Khutan, and also amongst the Kirghiz.

Furs, mostly sheep-skins, trimmed with imported otter skins from Russia, and ibex skins from Kashmir, are cured in all the towns and made up into cloaks, &c., for the home trade. But most of the furs got into the country are exported to Russian territory. A kind of buff leather, of which are made the loose "overall" trowsers called *shim*, is prepared at Yarkand and also at Aksú. That made in the latter city is the best, and its excellence is attributed to the superior quality of the pomegranate rind used in the process of curing. Ironsmiths and carpenters, each in their own line, turn out a number of articles of domestic use, and they occupy a prominent place in the bazar shops.

Inhabitants.—From previous remarks it will have been gathered that the inhabitants of Káshghar consist of a mixture of tribes or races which belong to one or other of those two great principal families of the Central Asia continent, namely the Turk and the Tartar.

Of the many new sights and scenes that meet the eye of the traveller in Káshghar, none more fixes his attention than the singular varieties of physiognomy and race type that are crowded together in the cities; a feature which distinguishes them in a marked manner from the inhabitants of the rural districts. Yet, with all the variation in stature, build, and facial lineament, he sees there is a common semblance pervading the mass which declares the natural affinity of its constituents, and no less distinctly warns him that he has come amongst a different people to those he has left behind him in India.

In the first place, he finds there is not a black skin, nor even a dark complexion amongst them. Then he observes that their features are different modifications of one and the same type, and as different from that of the Hindu, as is their clothing from that of the natives of India. On further acquaintance he learns that their language is of an entirely separate stock; that their manners and morals are of a stamp diverse to the ethical system obtaining south of the passes; and that their mental qualities are of a peculiar character too. He notices that they are averse to sustained physical exertion, or to the endurance of toil, and everywhere sees the horse and the ass saving all the labour of walking and carrying burdens; whilst a variety of mechanical aids meet him at almost every turn, in witness to the ingenuity of the devices adopted to reduce the operations of necessary work to a minimum. He is struck by the punctilious ceremonies that regulate their society; and by the universal degradation of their amatory instincts, and its concomitant indifference to the chastity of their women. And finally, he is struck by their complete freedom from all those caste-prejudices and restrictions which form so important a character of the system of society in India, and finds them omnivorous, in point of indifference as to meats and drinks; cosmopolitan, as regards citizenship, and carelessly tolerant in matters of religious sentiment, if not of doctrinal ascendancy.

For the sake of description, the inhabitants of the country may be classed under the heads of urban and rural, and between the two, in the western divisions at least, to which my remarks will be now confined, there is a marked difference; as there is between the two great divisions of the rural population itself.

As regards the urban population, I will not attempt to describe in detail the several typical forms of its race representatives, nor the hybrid gradations and half-caste varieties produced by their indiscriminate intermixture. To convey a tolerably correct notion of the heterogenous elements that have combined to produce the homogeneous whole of the city population, it will be sufficient here to indicate the principal tribes of the two typical forms of man—the Mongolian and the Caucasian—which meet and commingle in these centres of life and activity. Thus of the former stock we find the Manjhu, the Moghol or Mongol, the Kalmák, the Kirghiz, the Noghay, the Kapchak, and the Uzbak. All of whom are designated Tartar, together with the Kara Khitay, the Khitay, and the Tungani, who are excluded from that category, though of the same stock. Of the latter typical form we find the Tajik of Hindu Kush, represented by the Wakhi, Badakhshi, Shighni, &c., the Kashmiri, the Kabuli, and the Punjabi, all of whom are included in the appellation Aryan, together with the Syad and the Arab, who are not so included.

In these several tribes the typical form is most aberrant only in the Uzbak of the one stock, and in the Syad of the other, owing to their more thorough intermixture, the first with a Tajik element, and the other with a Moghol element. The remaining tribes of each original stock, having maintained a more or less complete isolation in their native homes, possess a proportionately perfect typical resemblance to the parent form. The hybrid offspring between a male and female of the opposite stocks, between Mogholian and Caucasian, is called Arghun, and always takes after the superior stock, whether the Caucasian parent be male or female. This is exemplified as fully in the exterior form of body and cast of features as in the superior development of the intellectual faculty and improved standard of morality. Frequently the Arghun in physiognomy and growth of beard is not to be distinguished from the pure Aryan, whilst in stature and bulk of body he certainly equals, if he does not excel, the average of the superior stock. His quick intelligence, fertility in resource, and ready organization are acknowledged in the fact of his often rising to the most important offices under Government, and in the character he bears as a shrewd man of business, successful manager, and good accountant. But as rule his better qualities are suppressed by the nature of the society in which his lot is cast, and his inferior social status has made him cautious and crafty, and gained him an unenviable character for treachery, at least, in the lower ranks of the class.

The half-caste offspring between different cognate tribes of the Mogholian stock differ little from the typical form of the original race, except in the very varied modifications of the family type; and their tendency is to degenerate in intellectual as well as moral and physical qualities. To this mixed class belong those nondescript, ill-favoured creatures who compose the rabble of the streets; untutored in mind, dissolute in habits, and tattered in garments, veritable street Arabs, ready at every corner to hold a horse, carry a bundle, or run a message; and equally ready, too, to pick a pocket, filch a steak, or rob a baker's board. Many of them are hawkers about the streets of meat pies, pastry, biscuits, and sweetmeats, which they trundle about on hand-barrows, just as their counterparts do in London; or they hang about the more frequented thoroughfares with a tray of buns and cakes, supported against the stomach in front by a sling round the neck. Some go about with a knife-grinder's cart exactly similar to those seen in any English town, and accompany it with a cry that twangs familiar to the English ear; others carry flat baskets of cucumber, melon. &c., on their heads, and cry them in the streets as the cadger does in the London by-ways. But whatever their occupation they all have the same perplexing Tartar features, which partake of Khitay and Manjhu, and Kalmák, and Kirghiz semblance, yet are distinctly referable to neither one or the other. They are said to be the offspring of Chinese troops and traders of the abovenamed and other tribes by half-caste women of the cities. In Ila, these half-castes by a Manjhu father and Kalmák mother are called Solon, as those by a Khitay father and Kalmák mother are called Shiba; but the terms, though known, are not commonly used in Káshghar.

Similar to these half-castes in some respects, but strangely different in physiognomy, is the Chálgurt, or offspring of an Uzbak father by a woman of Káshghar. The range in variety of feature in this class is very great, and its most notable peculiarity is that it presents an equal blending of the typical characters of the prime stocks, a point in which it differs remarkably from the Arghun. In the Chálgurt the cast of countenance and the small round head are decidedly Tartar features, but the full beard up to the ears is as markedly Tajik. The explanation may possibly be found in the aberration of the Uzbak type from its parent form, for in external appearance the Uzbak differs little from the Chálgurt he produces; and the tendency of the latter to take after the father indicates that the superiority he has acquired by Caucasian intermixture has, through long continuance, become innate, and formed for his tribe a race sub-type similar to that of the Persian or the Othmanli further west. The Chálgurt class has received an immense impetus to its growth since the conquest of the country by the Amir, for his Andijan and Tashkand troops have taken very freely to the women of the country, and their barracks and military lines swarm with little children, the offspring of their alliances. Many of these children, as indeed are their mothers, are perfectly fair and rosy cheeked, and might pass for robust English children, but for the rotundity of their features and figures.

At Yarkand I selected thirty men and nine women out of the crowd one morning attending at the Embassy dispensary and measured their height and circumference of the head. The former measurement was taken standing against a graduated post with the boots on, consequently an allowance of from half an inch to an inch should be made for the thickness of the heels. The head measurement in the men was on a shaven scalp, and in the women over the smoothed hair; and in each by a measuring tape passed round above the ears, and meeting in front between the supra orbital arches above the root of the nose. The results are thus tabulated:—

Men.—Height and Circumference of head.—Thirty subjects.

	Inches.	Inches.	
Tallest	68·40	23·0	Maximum.
Medium	64·37	21·43	Medium.
Shortest	60·20	20·40	Minimum.

Women.—Height and Circumference of head.—Nine subjects.

	Inches.	Inches.	
Tallest	62·20	21·50	Maximum.
Medium	60·00	20·625	Medium.
Shortest	57·40	20·10	Minimum.

All the above were natives of the city and of Tartar race, and do not include any Andijani, Kashmiri, Badakhshi, or other foreigners. In almost all the bodies were well-formed and of square build.

The measured heights of individuals natives of other cities were these, *viz.*:—

A man of Kúchá, 71·60″; of Khutan, 72·10″; two men of Aksú, 71·10″ and 71·50″; two men of Káshghar, 69·60″; and a Dolan of Taskama, 65·40″.

The urban population of the western cities, it will be gathered from the preceding remarks, is a confused mixture of Turk and Tartar, or Moghol and Tájik, and the offspring of their several alliances one with the other. Their appearance as a whole baffles description, because the special characteristics of the several types are incapable of general

26.—Street Hawkers, Yarkund.

27.—Street Hawkers, Yarkund.

application. All that can be distinctly stated is that Tartar blood predominates with a greater or less admixture of the Turk element, and a sprinkling here and there, more or less thick, of the foreign Tajik forms; such obtains in the cities only.

In the rural districts the case is very different. Here the population consists of two distinct classes, the settled or agricultural, and the wandering or nomad.

The settled population is everywhere in the western divisions of the country of Turk descent, and represents the ancient Hiungnú or Uighúr, the Hun of Hyatila or Attila's invading armies. Time and circumstances have completely changed their personality, and now they differ but little in external appearance from their cousins, the heirs of the Saljuk conquest of Asia Minor and Byzantium, where, in the west as in the east, they have given their name to the country of their adoption; Turkey on the one side, and Turkistan on the other.

They are a fine, well-grown people, with a more or less distinct trace of northern origin which has not been quite obliterated by their Caucasian development of beard and stature. This Tartar cast of countenance is more noticeable in some districts than in others, and especially in Yangi Hissar, where the effects of the Tajik innervation are less developed than in the divisions to the north and south. In physical constitution the rural population is superior to that of the cities; but, though diligent and orderly in their avocations, they are equally incapable of enduring continued or severe labor. This may be partly accounted for by the life of inactivity they lead during the long winter, from November to March, during which period all agricultural operations are in abeyance. It is said that they only have three months of real work in the year, the season of ploughing and the season of reaping. For the rest, they have an easy time of it, and are seen stretched before their homesteads basking in the sun, or sleeping away the heavy hours under the shade of their plantations, as the case may be. They are not given to athletic exercises, nor to sport generally, and the weekly market-day is the only event that rouses them to activity.

At Karghalik I took the measurements of height and circumference of the heads of thirty men as at Yarkand. They were taken indiscriminately from the crowd of spectators gathered about our quarters; the subjoined are the results:—

Height and Circumference of head in inches.

		Inches.	Inches.	
Tallest	...	70·40	21·00	Maximum.
Medium	...	66·75	20·66	Medium.
Shortest	...	61·50	20·40	Minimum.

The nomad population is represented by the Kirghiz. They are of distinct Moghol type, but of a different family from their kinsmen and neighbours on the north, and west, and east, *viz.*, the Kazzak, Kapchak, and Kalmák, respectively. Their occupation is entirely that of shepherds and breeders of cattle. They are a hardy race, and fond of field sports and hunting. The tribes most in contact with the fixed population show signs of the intermixture with the superior stock in increased growth of body and some show of beard. Their intellectual qualities and morality, however, are described as of a low order. They are said to be quarrelsome, indolent, and filthy in habits; to be much addicted to drunkenness, robbery, and petty theft. Their women are said to do all the domestic labor in the camps, and manufacture the felts, carpets, tapes, &c., for which the race is celebrated. In complexion they are fair, and some of them are rosy; but their type of beauty is only suited to the Kirghiz taste, and for ugliness is not to be matched in many countries. Yet some of the younger girls, though with no pretensions to beauty, according to the European standard, have comely features, and simple, modest manners, which, if common report be true, is more than can be said of the matrons and wives of either the nomad or the fixed population.

The foregoing remarks apply to the representative inhabitants of the country. The special tribes found located amongst them have been already mentioned in the notice of the several governmental divisions.

Manners and customs.—These vary more or less widely amongst the several distinct peoples composing the general population; but those that control the conduct of the communities massed together in the cities and settlements may be taken as a guide to the whole.

Islam is the religion of the land, and has been for eight centuries. Consequently the mode of life of the people is in the main in accordance with the precepts of that doctrine. During the last century of Chinese rule, the observance of the prophet's law fell into neglect owing to the absence of State authority amongst the priesthood, and a general laxity of morals and disregard of religious ordinances soon spread amongst the people, and even pervaded the ranks of the priesthood itself. Most prominent amongst these innovations was the restoration of woman to her former state of freedom and equality in general society. But now on the re-establishment of a purely Islamite rule, and the strict enforcement of the *Shari'at*, this liberty is taken from her, and she is accorded no other privileges than those allowed by the Mahomedan law.

In the rural districts women enjoy much of their wonted freedom, but in the cities their seclusion and the use of the veil is strictly enforced. The system of *mata'* or "mariage de convenance" which was of universal prevalence, together with public prostitution, under the Chinese rule, is now entirely suppressed, and any infraction of the new order is punished with exemplary severity. Though the regulation of society and the administration of the Government are based on the *Shari'at*, there are many national customs that remain unaffected by the trammels of that inelastic and unalterable code. For convenience sake, we will now notice the more characteristic traits of the people under separate heads in detail.

Marriage.—Amongst the higher classes and the peasantry, parents usually betroth their children in infancy, but the ceremony is not performed till they arrive at puberty, the age of which varies from fourteen to sixteen years. Amongst grown up people the contract is one of mutual consent. In either case it is made binding by the *nikáh* of the Mahomedan *Shari'at*. In the first case, in which the parents make the contract, the boy's parents fix the dower or *mahr* for the girl, and the parents of both provide the wedding clothes, ornaments, and household equipment for each respectively. When the marriage terms are agreed to, the girls' parents get a letter of permit from the governor of the city to the effect that "such a one, the daughter of so and so, son of so and so, of such a place, marries with their consent such a one, the son of so and so, of such a place." The fee for this letter of permit and registry is one *tanga* = about sixpence, to the city governor. After this, the day is fixed, and all the relations and friends assemble at the bride's house, where the *nikáh* is read by the priest, who receives as his fee from one to two or more *tanga* according to the rank and means of the parties. With the rich the wedding festivities are prolonged over three or four days, with music and feasts and games; but with the poor the newly married couple go to the bridegroom's house the same night, and the festivities are confined to dancing and singing amongst the guests, and the disposal of a sheep or two slaughtered for the feast. Amongst the common people, where the parties are grown up men and women, the bride merely gets a suit of clothes and such ornaments as she can persuade the suitor to give her, and, after the performance of the *nikáh*, they feast a few friends and go home together, till they disagree and separate.

Prior to the adoption of Islam by the Moghol, woman held a more exalted position amongst them, and in the relations of matrimony often exercised a supreme authority in the affairs of the household. This is indicated by the terms they applied to married woman, viz., *Khátún Aghá*, *Khánim*, *Begim*, "mistress lady," "my chief," "my lord" respectively. Numerous instances are recorded in the history of the Emperor Babar and other Moghol chiefs, illustrative of the important position held by woman in the society of the early Moghol power. In these days the sex, it would seem, commanded a far greater deference and respect than it is accorded in the present day. The effect of the Mussalman system of seclusion has been to deprive the wife of her just right and freedom, and the consequence has been to debase the noblest qualities and most prized virtues of the sex. That they are impatient of their treatment as mere chattels is evinced by their very frequent resort to the loophole of escape the law permits in divorce. The custom is extremely prevalent, and by some women is systematically worked as a means of securing an independence and provision for old age. For example, a woman will marry in Yarkand, and, if dissatisfied, will, after a short time, quarrel and divorce her husband before the *Cázi*, whose fee for the letter of divorce is only one *tanga*. By the act of divorce she gets rid of a master and profits by the amount of dowry, clothes, &c., she received on marrying him. The dowry is not a fixed sum, but varies according to terms agreed on prior to marriage. A woman, after divorcing her husband, cannot re-marry till the expiry of the *'iddat*, which is a period of three months and ten days; but the divorced husband may re-marry after the expiry of forty days. This woman, after the days of *'iddat*, will marry another husband in Yarkand, producing the letter of divorce to show that she is free to do so. Him, too, she will divorce as she did the first, keeping the wedding clothes, outfit, and dowry. She now has two letters of divorce, and is thus enabled to evade the law and escape the restraint of the *'iddat*, during which she would have to live upon her dowry, and commences a system of divorcing by which she secures an independence, and finally settles down with the man of her choice. And she works it thus: having divorced her second husband in Yarkand, she at once goes off to Yangi Hissar, and there contracts a marriage on the strength of the letter of divorce of the first husband, the date of which shows that the *'iddat* is no bar. As the others, so him, too, she divorces, and securing the dowry, moves on to Káshghar, and there plays the same game, and gradually works her way back to her home with the accumulated profits of some eight or ten such transactions.

Should she bear any children, they belong to the husband who is the father. If he so choose, he may resign his claim and give the child to the mother, and if not, he leaves the infant with the mother till weaned, and then takes possession of it. During this period, according to the decision of the *Cázi*, he pays the mother from one to four *tanga* a month for the child's keep.

Marriage.—The girl desired by a son is demanded for him by his father and mother, who visit the girl's family and ask that she may be given. Refusal is, as a matter of form, twice given, but the third time the girl's parents consent. When this happens, the father and mother of the youth present the girl with a ring and a pocket handkerchief. The parents of the youth are, on this occasion, given tea and sugar, and return home.

The engagement thus formed may be continued for ten or twelve days, or even for six months, without marriage.

Whenever the ceremony has been determined on, the bridegroom elect gets ready clothes for his bride:—a hat; a chogah; a kurpa; a tukin, a marjan, (bead ornament); a lahore (indoor hat); munchak (a thread of pearls); dandi (zéra) (earrings); belánzak (bracelets); sách tatma (chignon for plaits of hair); toomár (charms); oitak (boots); juráb (socks); tshtán (pyjama); tshtán bag (pyjama strings); agabanoo (a cloth thrown over the shoulders); frinjee (an overcoat with large sleeves in which the arms are not inserted); koilik (a chemise). The trousseau prepared as above is conveyed by the bridegroom, with a sheep, rice, and sheep's fat, to the house of the bride and presented to her parents; on this occasion he is accompanied by his father and mother and immediate relatives, who remain as guests in the bride's house for three days, during which feasting and dancing and singing go on at the expense of the girl's parents.

On the fourth day the girl's parents present the bridegroom with an entire suit of clothing, boots, &c. The bride then selects a man of their acquaintance as Padr Wakeel (Toyata) (Marriage Father). This is arranged as follows: Two grey beards of the party approach the girl and ask her whom she selects as her Toyata, when she names an individual. The mullah then arranges with the Toyata and the dowry is fixed and marriage settlement. The mullah then asks the bridegroom if the settlement is agreed to. When this is announced to the assembled relatives they shout mubarik. This is done with the reading of the kulmah, and thus completes the marriage ceremony.

The woman cannot be taken from one city to another without her consent: this is agreed to by the husband, being demanded by the Toyata; he further declares that he will not chastise her without fault; that he will not take another wife without her consent; that for six months after marriage he will not undertake a journey. If he then starts on a journey, that he will advance a subsistence allowance of six months; that he will allow his wife free intercourse with her father and mother and near relations.

After the agreement is given, water and salt are produced, and the salt is dissolved in a small cup. The parents of the contracting parties then dip bread into the salt water. It is a point of emulation between the bride and bridegroom's representatives to first dip the bread into the cup; if the bride's father is first successful, and puts the saturated bread into the daughter's mouth, it is considered a good omen by the bridegroom. The wife is then conveyed to the husband's house. The children and others of the mohulla, if it is in the city, put a rope across the road and make a pretence of stopping the party; they are, however, bribed with a present to let the procession pass. The wife is called for two or three months Kelim, and the husband Kiayo: "the bride and bridegroom" during the first few months are not called by their proper names. As the bride leaves her father's house it is considered proper for the relations to weep. When she reaches the house of the bridegroom, before she enters in, a carpet or felt is first put outside the door on which she is seated, and a *fire* is lighted, and women of the husband's family, who are respectable matrons, hold the four corners of the felt or carpet upon which the bride is seated, and carry her round the fire three times, after which she is taken into the house across the threshold. The female relatives (usually unmarried) who have accompanied her, remain with her for three days in the house of the bridegoom (her own house). After the three months she ceases to be called Kelim, and goes by the name of Chaukan until she becomes pregnant, when she is called Jewan, and at this period the fact of her pregnancy is celebrated by feasting and singing with her female acquaintances; at the same time she puts on the bands in front of her dress, which mark the mother, retaining them henceforward;

these are four short cross-bars fastened to the dress where it closes over the bosom; they are either green or red as long as the husband is living, and during widowhood are covered with black.

Birth.—Is celebrated by a feast to the neighbours and friends in the case of a boy, but no demonstration is made for the birth of a girl. It is popularly believed, or stated at least, that two girls are born to one boy in this country, and certainly the very apparent preponderance in numbers of women which attracts the traveller's notice supports the assertion. There are no midwives in the country. The woman's mother or the neighbour women attend and do all the necessary service. The navel string is turned up to the forehead, and cut off at that length; wrapped in cotton wool, coiled on the belly, and there secured by a band; it is anointed daily with melted cow's fat, and falls off on the seventh or eighth day. Some take the skin of the sheep slaughtered for the feast to celebrate the event, and rubbing a mixture of one part *kachur* and two parts turmeric, finely powdered, on its inner surface, spread it whilst yet warm over the mother's back and belly, and keep it on for a night and day before removal. The skin contracts very firmly and, it is said, speedily restores the natural slim form. There is no music or dancing or rejoicing on the occasion of a birth as in India. The rich usually employ a wet nurse to suckle the child. The mother remains in seclusion till the fortieth day, on which she takes a bath and puts on new clothes, and receives her guests and friends at an entertainment. On this day the child is named, sometimes without ceremony, but usually the astrologer is called in to cast its horoscope and foretell its future. The child is on this day rolled up in swaddling bands, and for the first time put in the cradle which is to be its home till weaned. The cradle or *bechuc* is a wood frame on rocking boards, is covered with a curtain canopy, and spread with a mattress, in the centre of which is a hole for the *shumuc*. This is a wooden urinal, exactly like a common tobacco pipe; the bowl is adjusted above—it is wider for girls—and the tube passes vertically down through the hole. It effectually keeps the bedding dry, and is of universal use. Strings of them are exposed for sale in the bazars.

Birth and onwards.—A new-born child, after being washed, &c., has a lump of sugar put into its mouth. The mother keeps the child near her for 7 days, but on the 8th day it is taken

28.—Street Hawkers, Yarkund.

29.—Snuff and Tobacco Shop, Yarkund.

from her, excepting at the time of suckling. As soon after birth as is possible, a mullah is called in to whisper the azan into the child's ear. With a son, after 40 days, whatever hair may have grown is removed from the head. The hair is weighed and a corresponding weight of silver is given to the naie (barber). After this a feast is given to relatives. Until the boy is mature, he is called Ogul Bala; similarly a girl is called Kiz Bala. He is then called Yiggit, and the girl, Chaukan. All children are sent to school to the mullah at the age of 4 or 5. After leaving school a boy is usually apprenticed to a trade. During the time of his apprenticeship, he is clothed and fed by his master. When he has mastered the trade, his parents present the master with an entire suit of clothes, and a feast is given to the *trade*, in whose presence the master is clothed. The master presents the pupil on this occasion with a set of working tools used in his particular trade, and henceforward he starts a shop of his own.

CRADLE SONGS.

Over boys.

Yating Bullum,	Sleep my babe.
Yating Bullum,	Sleep my babe.
Khan Bulling Bullum,	A Khan you shall become.
Beg Bulling Bullum,	A Beg most sure shall be.
Yurtunieggasi Bulling Bullum,	Broad lands possess and wealth besides my babe.

Over girls.

Khanim Pudsha, Bulling Bullum	Spouse of King and baby mine.
Aiduk Yeshnub, Bulling Bullum	Fairy moonlight! baby mine.
Yating Bullum!	Sleep my babe.

Circumcision.—This rite is considered one of the most important of the "five foundations" of Islam, and its observance is now encouraged with a revival of the ceremonies which fell into neglect under the Chinese. The age for its performance varies between the second and eighth or tenth year, and the day is fixed after consulting the stars and a book of lucky days and omens, in which every day of every month has its special prognostic qualities. The operation is performed by the barber or *Sátirách (Sartarásh)* in the presence of the assembled women of the family, and neighbours and friends. The occasion is celebrated with a feast. Amongst the wealthy it is prolonged to two or three days, with music, dancing and games, and the distribution of largess to the poor and priests. On the conclusion of the feast, the friends present eggs and clothes for the boy, who is attended till the wound is healed by the barber. About the tenth or twelfth day, when this occurs, the boy is bathed and dressed, the barber is dismissed with his fee according to the means of the parents, generally two to four *tanga*, and the beggars and priests are collected for a feast.

Education.—When eight or ten years old, children are sent to school. Boys and girls together are seated closely packed on forms, of which the back of one forms the desk for the form behind it. The boys are all on one side of the room, and the girls on the other, and between is an alley, at the top of which is the seat of the teacher. The children are taught the creed and prayers from books set before them, and all gabble out their lessons with constant repetition and great volubility, and the din produced is confusing. There are several of these schools in each city, and one or more in all the market-towns of the rural settlements. The school, or *maktab*, is a low, ill-ventilated room, generally under the upper story of some private house, which is conveniently situated near a crowded thoroughfare, and some of them are amongst the shops in the bazar. Girls older than ten or twelve years don't attend, but boys are not limited to age. They are taught reading and writing, and use as text-books the Gulistan of Sádí, and the Sikandar Nama amongst others of less reputation. The pupils are all day scholars and pay the teacher from half a *tanga* to a *tanga* a month. Education is not compulsory, but a certain coercion is exercised on the parents to make them send their children to school. For the higher forms of education, as it is by the Mahommedan standard, the pupils go from the *Maktab*, to the *Madrassa* or college. Here they study theology, law, medicine, poetry and history, with writing and accounts. Physics are unknown, and altogether the standard of knowledge is very inferior. Much too great importance is attached to theology and metaphysics, to the neglect of more practically useful studies. There are several colleges in each city, and all the shrines and more sacred tombs in the country have either a college or a school attached to them. The colleges are charitable foundations which have been established at different periods by pious individuals, and are supported by grants of rent-free land. Under the Amir's rule, all these establishments have been restored to their original prosperity, and many which had fallen to decay have been entirely rebuilt and enlarged. Most of them have cloisters, with accommodation for from twenty to eighty students or more, and a chapel and hospice are attached to each, with a considerable establishment of priests, teachers, and servitors. In all of them the teaching is strictly that of Islam, to the exclusion of everything not allowed by the *Shari'at* or unprovided for in the *hadith*, and they are all under the special patronage of the Amir, who from time to time visits some of the more important ones, and on all occasions of public rejoicing or festivity distributes bounty to the establishments and resident scholars.

Games and Amusements.—Those played by young people are *corchác*, = "wrestling," "romps;" *Bád-parg*, = "kite-flying;" *Mucca warstarídí*, = "marbles;" *Khanjar oyáudí*, = "pitch-and-toss" into a hole with walnuts or pice; *Uzuc oyándí*, = "knuckle bones," dice playing with four bones; *Top chatáng*, = "ball-and-bat" or "rounders," in which the player is put out by a catch, and has to go out and carry in the winner on his back; and *Tushe Anasi Bálási*, = "mother and children in the hole," a sort of tip-cat played with bat and ball from a little pit.

Those played by grown-up people are *Shatranj*, chess; *takhna*, draughts; *kághaz-oyándí*, cards, called *kaphi* by the Khitay; *Tukhm chicḱi*, cracking eggs by tapping small ends together for wager; *Dah chín oyándí*, gymnastics, athletics, &c., by professionals. Other amusements are *kaptar-oyándí*, = "pigeon-flying;" *Tukh* or *Cochcár* or *Kiklik-warstarídí*, = "cock or ram," or "partridge-fighting." There are besides other sports and exercises, such as single-stick, cudgelling, fencing, wrestling, archery, &c., but they are only practised by professionals of Chinese or Kalmák race who are now enlisted in the Amir's army. Amongst the athletic exercises occasionally indulged in by the troops are *úlak*, a sort of chevy chase on horseback to gain possession of a slaughtered lamb carried away by an acknowledged champion, by pursuit and snatching from his lap; and *Millic chicdí*, = "target practice," loading and firing on horseback at a cap stuck on a stake, whilst at full gallop.

The more refined amusements in which both sexes meet for society are tea-parties and musical concerts and dances, each of which is conducted with the observance of much ceremony and etiquette, according to rules and conventionalities appropriate to each. The dances are performed by women only, and not in public; only in the presence of invited guests, and are conducted with proper decorum. The musical concerts are performed by professional artists and singers, and the principal instruments used are the guitar; a sort of harp or violin called *cánún*; a sort of violin called *rabáb*; the flageolet; the cymbal; the triangle; and the tambour and the trombone. The musician or *naghmáchí* does not play in public, only at private houses to which he is called to grace an entertainment. There is a class of mendicant minstrels and actors who go about the streets, and wander from place to place to make a living. They are of two distinct orders, viz., the *calandar* or *darvesh*, and the *bácchí*. The two first are religious beggars and vagabonds, and go about in companies of five or six. They sing and dance and dress in a grotesque fashion, and affect a demented character, with dishevelled hair and patched garments, often covered with a cape of some wild animals' skin, such as of the tiger, bear, leopard, or wolf. They always carry a staff topped with a tuft of *yák-tail* hair, or an iron mace on which is fixed a string of steel rings. This they jingle in keeping time with their vociferous songs and dances of gesticulation. The *bácchí* is a musician, conjuror, improvisatore, and actor. He professes acquaintance with the world of spirits, and glibly calls on Michael and all the angels who throw him into a cataleptic state, and the spectators are persuaded into the belief that he does all sorts of marvels.

Etiquette.—Ceremony is an important feature of Káshghar society, and its forms are observed with punctiliousness on the most trivial occasions. Respect and obedience to parents and superiors is held to rank in the first place of duty. The young and inferiors always stand in a respectful and submissive attitude, with the head bowed and hands folded in front, at a distance from their superiors, and always address them with the word *tacsír*="fault," and equivalent in use to our "Sir." Children never take the names of their parents so long as they are alive, but speak of them as *Atám* or *Anám*—"my father" or "my mother." On receiving any attention or favour, the recipient carries the right hand to the heart and forehead, and with a bow says, "*ashk-ulla*—"God's love;" or he takes the thing presented and raises it to his eyes with the same gesture and expression; or if the gift is not placed in his hands he, if seated, rises and with a comprehensive sweep of the arms strokes his beard, either real or more frequently imaginary. When seated at an entertainment this ceremony is gone through on each occasion that he is addressed by a superior, or is handed a morsel from the "table cloth," and one may be seen constantly getting up and down from and on to his heels in acknowledgment of civilities and commands from a superior. In matters of duty, commands are received standing, and acknowledged by bending on one knee, sweeping the arms in a circle to stroke the beard, and with the words *yakhshi tacsir*="Very good Sir."

The salutation on meeting is *Sálam-álaikúm*="Peace be to you," with a low bow, and the hands folded across the stomach. The reply is *a'laikúm as-salám*="And to you be peace." A friend passing another on the road says *Hármáng*—"Be not fatigued;" and the other replies *Yol-bolsún*—"may you have the way," or "may your way prosper." On parting in the streets, friends bow politely several times with polite expressions for each other's welfare. Visitors are received with more or less ceremony, according to rank, either at the outer gate, or in the court, or at the threshold, and conducted to their seats by the host. After the mutual health enquiries, either tea or the *dastúrkhwán* is invariably brought in, and to omit both is considered a mark of disrespect. The *dastúrkhwán*—"Tray of ceremony," varies according to the rank and state of the visitor, and may comprise anything from two or three trays of dry fruits and biscuits, to two or three hundred trays and an elegant and varied dinner. It is customary for the host to help his honored guest to the first morsel with a *Bismillah*—"In the name of God," and then the others help themselves. At the conclusion, the sign for the removal of the cloth is a simultaneous move to rise, with a sweeping stroke of the beard and sonorous *Alláhú Akbar*—"God is most Great" by all the guests. The table-cloth is a long sheet of printed cotton, or figured silk, and is spread on the floor.

The recipient of a letter from the king or other superior takes it in both hands, and raises it to the heart and forehead before reading. After reading he faces the direction whence it came, and pressing it to his lips and eyes places it securely in the folds of his turban or in his cap. Women courtesy by bending the knees, and bowing low with the hands folded in front.

Occupations.—There are no restrictions of caste as in India to fetter either sex in the choice of a means of livelihood. The father may be a blacksmith and the son a tailor; the mother may keep a shop, and the daughter may be a sempstress. In Yarkand we found many of the grocers and bakers shops kept by women; and I was told some of them were sole mistresses, and owned the shops in their own right, free from the control of the husband. The chief occupations of the women are spinning, lace-work, and embroidery, and in the rural districts they sometimes take part in the field labours of harvesting, and in caring for the cattle at home. The occupations of the men include all the ordinary handicrafts, special manufactures, trade, accounts, &c., &c. Amongst the Kirghiz, however, the women do all the weaving, carpet and felt-making, &c., as well as looking after the cattle and domestic arrangements.

Women.—The number of women in Káshghar, and the facilities of marriage and divorce, as well as the absence of absolute poverty throughout the country, mitigate the hardships, and obviate the crimes which follow on the adoption of a plurality of wives. The expense of marriage consists in the provision of marriage garments by the husband; these vary in quality according to the wealth of the man; a poor man may, however, content himself with the presentation of a hat and a pair of boots, costing no more than 10 tangas.

The cazi's fee amounts to no more than one tanga, though much larger sums are paid by those who can afford it. The ceremonial of marriage is given in detail elsewhere; it may be curtailed to the reading of the nika by the cazi, in the presence of three or four witnesses.

There appears to be no difficulty attending marriage between men and women of different ranks in life; nor does a woman who has been the wife of a rich man, and has obtained a divorce, object to marriage with a man of small means. Two wives represent the average number; but the limit of four is not even strictly adhered to. The ceremony of divorce amounts to no more than the affixing of the cazi's seal to the talaknamas, which are kept one by the man, and one by the woman, in proof of their release from the marriage tie. The divorce may be with mutual consent, or by the man, who declares his intention before the cazi. By the woman, the discharge may be obtained as follows: she declares her intention publicly to her husband three times of leaving his house; if he is willing, or if he hastily says "go" three times, the woman then goes to the cazi and claims dismissal, on which the cazi calls for the husband and enquires of him whether he has given her her divorce.

A more simple method for the wife to adopt is to present herself before the cazi weeping, and taking off the shoes (which come over the feet of her boots) to place them turned over before the cazi. This is taken to mean an accusation against the husband of his having committed an unnatural offence against her; no other evidence is required, the man is sent for and the talaknamas are ordered. The smallest fee on a divorce is half a tanga. It is a matter of pride with many women to have been the wife of several husbands; this, however, may be said to be chiefly the fashion with a certain set of women in the towns: the general population having more settled homes than such customs imply.

After divorce the children are usually divided, the boys going with the father, and the daughters with the mother. Subsistence may be ordered for the wife if she be pregnant, or is suckling a child, or a present may be made by the husband, or a fixed sum be paid down. Marriage is possible to the woman three months after the divorce. These rules are those of the Shariat; also, if a husband divorce his wife, and regret having done so, so as to seek to marry her again, he cannot do so without her having contracted another marriage.

The above customs imply more than the usual freedom allowed to women in Mahomedan countries being the rule, and, in Káshghar, women mix freely in the daily life of their husbands, and are to be seen on all occasions sharing in their pursuits, for the most part unveiled, except when some representative of authority is passing. They are admirable riders, being as familiar with the saddle as the men.

Dress and Ornaments.—Owing to the nature of the climate, the summer and winter costume differ in proportion to the opposite extremes of the seasons. In the former it consists of light gauze materials, or silks of very bright and staring colours for the rich, and of common white cotton cloth of home-manufacture for the poor. In winter it consists of warm furs, and padded silks for the rich, and of sheepskin cloaks and padded cotton robes, usually dyed of a drab or ash grey colour, for the poor. All classes, and both sexes wear boots, which in winter are lined with a casing of thick felt, and all, too, put on two, three, or up to six robes and trowsers one over the other. Men in travelling wear loose, baggy overalls of buff leather called *shim*. Sometimes the robes are tucked into the *shim*, like a shirt into the trowsers, and the effect is provocative of merriment to the stranger, though it is surprising how the arrangement frees the rotund and ungainly forms from the encumbrance of their multifarious flowing robes.

The dress of the men consists of the following costumes, *búc*, a quilted cap or bonnet, generally of silk material, or embroidered or printed cotton; *báshlic*, a hood with long lappets worn in travelling, generally of woollen material, sometimes of fur or sheepskin; *dopa*, an embroidered skull-cap, quilted and padded, of silk or printed cotton; *talpac*, a fur cap, generally of lamb's fleece, edged with otter or other fur, and sometimes covered with velvet or brocade; *dastár*, a shawl turban, only worn by the wealthy and nobility; *salla* a muslin turban of pure white, only worn by the priesthood and soldiers and officers of Government; *sarpech*, an ordinary turban worn by merchants clerks, &c. The common people and peasantry all wear the Tartar cap, called *talpac*; and it is said, are prohibited from wearing the turban; *kómlak* a shirt, loose in body and sleeves, usually of coarse cotton; *tambál*, trowsers loose and baggy, generally of cotton, and sometimes padded and quilted; *ishtán*, trowsers of a different material, such as silk or wool; *tambál bagha*, the trowsers-band round the waist; *shim*, overall trowsers, loose and baggy, generally of buff leather, embroidered with silk and edged below with fur usually lined with printed cotton, and open for six inches on the outside of each leg below; *otak*, boot reaching to the knee, and of European pattern; *másá*, goloshes or slippers worn over foot of boot in wet weather, left at the door on entering the house; *kepish*, (kafsh) a common shoe; *Páylay*, gloves of worsted or fur; *dabkú*, fur over-boot; *páypák*, a felt stocking worn inside the boot; *chapan*, a loose long robe, open in front, with long sleeves, four or five sometimes worn one over other; *ton*, a loose over-cloak. This and the preceding are usually of silk or printed cotton in bright colours and staring patterns; *belwagh*, waist-band or sash; *juba*, fur coat, mostly of sheepskin. Soldiers wear besides the *kamar*, a leather waist-belt; to it are attached a multitude of the paraphernalia of their arms; they are collectively styled *yarác*, and comprise powder-bag, tinder-box, shot-bag, flint-and-steel case, knife, hammer, priming pin, &c., &c.

The dress of the women consists of the following; *búc*, quilted cap, edged with fur; *orá búc*, a high bonnet of mitre shape, usually of silk, and ornamented with a tassel and embroidery; *talpac*, fur cap or hat of sheepskin covered with gold brocade, and edged all round with a deep border of otter fur; *salla*, a muslin turban folded into the shape of a high cap or hat, with the end hanging behind, or over one shoulder; *chumbal* and *chimat*, different kinds of veil: they are square, and about fourteen inches each way, and are worn tied round the hat: they are mostly white, of wide lattice pattern, but some are black and of horse hair, just like the texture of a sieve; *kómlak*, shirt, or loose shirt, of cotton or silk; *tambál*, trowsers, loose and baggy; *tambál páychá*, leggings, embroidered and edged with fur, worn attached to the trowsers so as to show below the upper robes; *chapan*, a loose frock, open in front; *lechak*, a scarf or shawl of muslin or light gauze worn over other clothes without passing the arms through the sleeves; *ác-peja*, a mantle of white muslin like the last. These two are worn by young married women, who are called *chaucán* till they become matrons, when they are called *juwán*, and wear by way of distinction the *paraja*, an over-cloak which has four bars of braid on the breast. Unmarried girls are called *ayghachi*, and dress as the *chaucán*. *Otak*, boot, similar to that worn by men; *kirm-otak*, a shorter high-heeled boot, ornamented with gold and silk embroidery; *ormada-otak*, another kind of ornamented boot; *kepish*, shoes; *payzár-kepish*, shoe or slipper, embroidered and ornamented; *juba*, fur coat. The dress of women differs little from that worn by the men, except in respect to head-dress and mantles, and the *shim*. Neither sex wear night clothes; they merely take off the boots, and go to sleep on the floor. Bedsteads, or the charpoy of India, are not known in the country. The rich have sleeping places in a corner of the room, where the *copa* (mattrass) is spread, with a *kirgiz* (felt) over it. The pillow is called *takya*, and the coverlet *yotcan*. In winter the bedding is spread upon the *sandal*, which is a wide platform supported on masonry parapets, or low walls, and heated by a fire of dry stable refuse which lies smouldering below.

Ornaments.—Very few are used except as additions to the garments, and only by the fair sex. They consist ordinarily of the earring = *zira*. It consists of a string of pearls and red coral beads strung together in alternation. Some wear these plaited into the back tresses; they are then called *chichanghac*. The *uzúc*, or finger ring, is worn by both sexes; by men as a signet, and by women as an ornament; in the latter case the settings are the diamond, ruby, pearl, turquoise, &c. Women also wear a gold or silver wristlet, *beluzúc*; it is usually chased with ornamental patterns, and studded with pearls and rubies. No other ornaments are now usually seen, though in the time of the Chinese there was a great variety of gold and silver jewellery used, mostly as ornaments for the head; but they have now entirely gone out of fashion. Women ornament the hair now only with the pearl and coral beads before mentioned. During girlhood, when they are called *ciz* or *ayghachi*, they have the head shaved over the crown, or as they grow older they wear the hair in a plain loose queue tied by a ribbon at the back of the head; and so they wear it, as virgins, till married, when they plait it into two long three-ply tresses, which, with the aid of foreign locks are prolonged down the back nearly to the heels. As staid matrons they discard the aid of art, and are content to plait their natural locks into two short twists behind each ear.

Death.—At death the chin of the corpse is tied up with a chin cloth, and the thumbs of the hands are tied together and the big toes of the feet, the body being washed and laid out.

If a wife lose her husband, she wears mourning (a black cloth over her shoulders, and on the red cloth of the stripes worn in virtue of her having become "Jewan" a small cross bar of black) for 40 days, the black cross bar on the stripes remains until she marries again. No cooking is done in the house of the dead for three days; all that is required being supplied by relatives or friends. On the fourth day a feast is prepared for mullahs who speak in praise of the dead. The corpse is, however, only retained in the house during 24 hours. After her husband's death, the wife uses his name in her prayers on every Thursday and daily.

If the wife dies, the husband wears a white cloth (chitta) as a kummerbund.

The following derges are in common use:—

For husband.—Wai Khwojum Eéh; Wai Humrahim Eéh; Wai Akhoonun Eéh; Sun Munnitashlub Kitting Mun; Kaida Kelsum Khwojum Eéh.

For wife.—Wai Humrahim Eéh; Wai Khanim Eéh; Bullalu Yatin Kalding Khanim Eéh.

For father.—Wai Dadum; Mecca Um Dadum; Medina Um Dadum; Yatini Kalding Akhoon Dadum.

For mother.—Wai Amun Eéh; Mecca Um Amun; Medina Um Amun.

For son.—Wai Bullum Eéh; Wai Bullum Eéh; Kaida Kelsum Bullum Eéh.

For daughter.—Wai Bullum Khanim Bullum; Cherailik Bullum.

The following short account of a funeral witnessed at Yangi-Hissar and of the ceremonies which followed, will explain the customs in force:—On the 29th of April a mullah died in Yangi Hissar; he left two women in his house, the one his wife and the other his sister, besides one daughter and two sons. At the funeral the two women preceded the corpse, wearing each a black robe down to the heels, with white kummerbunds; immediately behind the corpse came the two boys, and after them the daughter (who was about ten years of age), riding a pony and dressed in the patched-garment of a Kullah Darvesh, to signify that owing to her father's death she had become a fakir. The following day two elderly females established themselves in the house for three days to console the bereaved. On the night of the funeral, and the following night, two mullahs remained at the cemetery reading the Koran. On the 7th day the women took off their black robes and placed a black cloth over the bars on their dresses, which implied their being "Jewans." On this day an ásh was distributed amongst the acquaintances of the deceased, and a large iron vessel, containing one dearak of ásh, was conveyed to the cemetery, a mullah being in attendance to read a portion of the Koran. The mullah and the bereaved women partook at the grave, after which they returned home and the mourning was at an end; the women then having remained for seven days in the house were at liberty to move about. Mourning for father or mother on the part of a woman is indicated by covering the upper part of the head dress with a piece of white cloth.

Food.—The crops noted under the head of agricultural productions will have indicated that the nature of the food of the people of Káshghar differs but little from that of most European countries. Flesh is very freely consumed, and so cheap as to be within the reach of all classes as a constituent of the daily meal. In the time of the Chinese, there were no prohibitions in the matter of eating and drinking, and consequently the flesh of all animals was eaten without distinction, and drinks and liquors of all sorts found a ready sale in the markets. This is now all changed; the flesh of ass, swine, dog, &c., is strictly prohibited, and only that of those animals is allowed to be used which are pronounced lawful by the *Shariat*. Thus excellent beef, mutton, and horse-flesh are exposed for sale in the butchers' stalls, and the variety is occasionally increased by that of the camel and goat, and *cutás* or yak ox, and to a more limited extent by that of the wild sheep, the wild stag, the wild goat, and the antelope. Wild-fowl and game are also occasionally exposed for sale, but more generally they are limited to the royal court and the courts of the district governors. They comprise the wild-goose, teal and ducks in great variety, partridges, quail, and the pheasant, both snow and desert, together with the sand grouse, florican, pigeons, &c., and the hare.

The common cereals and vegetables, as in Europe, form important items of the daily food. The wheat bread is always leavened, and is of very superior quality. A kind of fungoid growth found on the poplar tree, and called *toghraghu*, is habitually used as a ferment, and sold in every bazar. Vegetables and fruits are preserved fresh for winter use, by storing out of the reach of frost and damp in deep underground vaults and cellars.

Milk is little used, and butter is rarely seen in the fresh state. Mutton fat or that of beef is used in culinary operations in its place, as a rule, though skins of preserved butter, by boiling, are sold in the bazar. They are brought in by the Kirghiz, and are not to be found amongst the agricultural population.

Of the varieties of food I will not attempt a description. The dishes comprise a mixture of the Musalman and the Chinese cuisine, with perhaps a touch of the French and Italian. Roast and boiled joints, soups, ragouts, and bouillis; the *palao, corma, cima,* and *kabab* with salads, pickles, jelly and syrup are some of the forms of food usually set before the guest, together with pastry of all sorts, puffs, patties (meat and jam) cakes, sweets, candied-fruits, and fruit fresh and fruits dry. The beverages are water, or *eau sucré*, or sherbet of pomegranate juice, &c. Tea is the ordinary drink of all classes, usually with sugar and always without milk. It precedes and follows every meal, and is offered to the visitor at all hours of the day. The use of wine or spirits is strictly prohibited, and none are made in the country, though small bottles of Russian liqueurs are found on sale in the shops of Káshghar and Yarkand. The Kirghiz distil a strong spirit from the fermented liquor of mare's milk called *cumis*, but neither one or other ever find their way to market.

Tobacco is not much smoked, except as a vehicle for *bung* or "hemp," and is not much esteemed by itself for quality, though that produced at Aksú is credited with a mild and superior flavour. In the form of snuff, however, its use is almost universal, both by the ordinary method and by mastication. In the former case it is, I believe, the cause of the remarkable prevalence of polypus in the nose in Káshghar, though it is necessary to state that in some cases of the disease which came under my notice, the patients denied the use of snuff at all. In the latter case it certainly is the cause, in common with opium and hemp, of much of the dyspepsia which is the general complaint of the country. The snuff of Káshghar is different from any other that I have seen. It is of a bright green colour, and extremely hot and pungent. The powdered stalks of the *chicandar*, a species of ephedra, and powdered quicklime are habitually added to it. This snuff is seen exposed for sale everywhere in the cities and settlements, and is very generally indulged in by women past their prime. The snuff of Peshawar, called Marghozi, after the village where it is produced, is in much demand, and is reputed the best that reaches Káshghar.

Death.—The following is the procedure observed when death closes the career on earth. When the last moment is near, the arms are folded across the chest, the legs are straightened out, and the great toes are tied together. The death is at once reported to the *mulla*, or "priest" of the parish, who hastens to the death-bed. The relations and friends now assemble, and the women lament with loud wails and cries, slapping their faces and breasts with open palms. The winding-sheet is then brought, and the priest, after washing the body according to the Mahomedan rites, puts it on the corpse. The women again break into lamentations, and then the body is placed on a bier, and carried in procession to the grave. Sometimes a party of *darvesh* and *calandar* are hired to precede the procession and chaunt funeral dirges. The people of the house in which the death has occurred put off their usual clothes, and for two or three days wear those of beggars, and follow the corpse to the grave. The *janazah*, or funeral-prayers, are repeated by the priest, the people around saying *Amin* or "Amen." During three days no food is cooked in the house in which a death has occurred, but is brought to the mourners by their friends and neighbours.

On the third day the *zakatchi*, "tax collector," comes and makes an inventory of the deceased's estate, and after paying his debts, divides the remainder into forty equal parts. One of these he takes for the king, and the remaining thirty-nine he divides equally amongst the heirs male. These now, according to their means, cook food and feast the beggars, ascetics and divinity students, together with the relatives and friends of the deceased. They appoint a priest to perform a "complete recital of the Koran," and give him the deceased's shoes and stockings as his perquisites, together with a suit of new clothes and a small sum of money. They pay the gravedigger two or three *tanga*, and sacrifice a sheep over the grave, and its carcase is taken by the officiating priest as his perquisite. This ends the funeral ceremony as observed by the common people. The wealthy retain a priest to recite the Koran daily over the grave for forty days, and feast the relations and friends, and the poor and priests on the third, the seventh, and the fortieth days.

The grave and side sepulchre are on the Musalman plan, but tombstones are not used except for saints and grandees, and in such cases the epitaph is found written on glazed tiles. Most graves are seen with merely a heap of earth piled along their length, but some have tombs raised over them. Generally the tomb is an oblong platform, two or three feet high, and supports a cylindrical figure along its length, something in the shape of a coffin, and the whole is built of raw bricks or clay, coated with a plaster of mud. Grave-yards are generally enclosed, and their area held as sacred ground.

Habitations.—The cities and towns in general appearance and plan of arrangement much resemble those of Afghanistan, and some parts of Persia to the west. They are surrounded by fortified walls, and are everywhere built of clay, stone being never seen, and baked bricks only in the more important buildings, such as mosques, colleges, and saraes. The streets are unpaved, and wind irregularly amongst the blocks and rows of tenements, and are mostly narrow and more or less filthy. There are no large open spaces, nor any public gardens or plantations. The drains and gutters are mostly open, or indifferently covered for footway in front of the shops; and empty on to some low ground only a few yards beyond the city walls, or else stagnate within their enclosure. In some of the quarters, shut off from the main bazars and thoroughfares, are open tanks 40 to 60 or 100 feet square; they are mere superficial excavations, and, as their contents indicate, a collection of all the impurities of the vicinity dissolved in the water. The main bazars are in parts covered in by a frame-work of rough beams and rafters, thatched with a loose layer of straw and reeds, through which are numerous gaps. The shops themselves are mean, low, and dark hovels, with a platform in front raised some three or four feet above the level of the street. They are of small dimensions and have no pretension to regularity, neatness, or decoration. In fact they cannot compare either in build or in the display of stores to the shops of any cantonment bazar in India, far less to those of the commercial cities of the Panjab.

The style of building is entirely devoid of architectural character, and the only structures that attract attention amidst the jumble of mud walls and flat roofs, are some mosques and colleges of ancient date, and one or two newly-built masonry saraes. The former are as notable for their state of neglect and decay as are the latter for the opposite characters.

The dwelling-houses are mostly single-storied, in long rows, on each side of the streets; but off the main lines of traffic the tenements are found more frequently double-storied. Those of the gentry are enclosed with a court or garden plot inside high walls, the entrance to which is through a double portal, between the gates of which is a roofed space for horses to stand, and a raised platform on one side for the gatekeeper. The arrangement of the interior is more regular, and consists of low chambers opening on to a central hall, which again conducts to an open verandah covered in from the court and slightly raised above its level. The walls are seldom white-washed, and are furnished with numerous little alcoves or recesses which serve the purpose of shelves and cupboards. In the roof there is always a light and air-ventilator, usually a simple square opening, 20 inches to 2 feet each way, protected by a grating of wood-work for the interior apartments, but much wider and unprotected for the central hall. The fire-places are similar to those in English houses in their plan, and have chimney-flues and pieces, and a low line of masonry for fender. The doors are plain boards, single or double, and work on pivot-sockets, and are secured by a bolt of wood which passes into a hole in one side bracket, and is unlocked by an ingenious catch-key, also of wood. The windows are large and double, and resemble the doorways. The outer one is of lattice-work covered with paper, and opens by two folds; the inner one is of boards, and resembles the door in

30.—Flour Cleaner and Oil Sellers.

31.—Yaghach-chi. The Carpenter.

make; between the two is the thickness of the wall. Above the door and window, there is sometimes a small lattice window covered with paper in winter, and open in summer. Few houses have a well in the court or garden, but each house has it cess-pit, over which is built the privy. None of the houses are raised much above the level of the ground, and in most the lower rooms are sunk a little below the level of the ground. It is usual to lay the foundations upon a layer of rolled stones from the river beds; over these is spread a layer of matting, and then the clay wall is built upon it, either with bricks or in forms between boards. In their lines and angles most houses are superior to those of the same class of people in India; but in their surroundings, and the utter neglect of conservancy, they are no ways different.

Such are the main characters of the Káshghar dwellings, which are everywhere roofed with poplar beams and rafters, overlaid with a layer of plastered earth spread upon matting. They are warmed with the fire-places mentioned, or, as is the case in most of the better houses, the sleeping-room is provided with a *sandal*. This is a square space enclosed by low walls two feet high; in its centre is a round flat-topped pillar of the same height; from this pillar to the walls pass a series of boards which form a floor above the enclosed space; they are removable, and are now and again taken off to prepare the *sandal* for use; this is done by spreading its floor three or four inches deep with dry horse-dung, and setting it on fire to smoulder through the night; the boards are replaced, and the bedding spread on the floor, which is shared by the whole family.

The king's palace, and those of the city governors, with other public buildings which have been erected since the Amir's accession to the Government, are of a different character, and in the superiority of their structure and general plan, more resemble the houses of the Persian nobility than anything I can compare them to. They are not Indian and they are not European, nor are they Chinese, but they may be on the Khokand model.

Language.—The language of the people of Káshghar is the Uighúr dialect of Turki. It is spoken with greater or less difference of idiom and patois in the several divisions of the country, and that of Aksú is said to be the purest. In the appendix will be found a vocabulary of the dialect spoken in Yarkand. Formerly the language was written in a character peculiar to itself, but the Arabic letters have long since displaced it, and none of the old books are now to be met with. The literature of the country is very little known, though some poetical and historical works which have been examined by European *savants*, prove, by the purity and perspicuity of style, that the language in the palmy days of the Uighúr empire must have attained a high degree of culture—no doubt as one consequence of the Islam supremacy and the contact with Persian civilization. I have no practical knowledge, however, of the subject, and our opportunities in the country were not such as to favour research in this direction.

Government of the country.—Under the Chinese rule Káshghar was governed as a non-regulation province by a *Jáng jung* or Viceroy, whose capital was at Ila or Khúlja. He held the country by a purely military occupation to maintain order, realise the revenue, and protect trade, and left the internal administration of the government in the hands of Musalman natives of the country, who received their appointments from himself, subject to confirmation from Pekin; and were in all cases immediately subordinate and responsible to superior officers of the ruling race who were, for the higher grades, appointed direct from Pekin.

The system bears some points of resemblance to that of our own in India—at least so far as concerns the administrative and executive offices. Thus the Viceroy of Ila appointed over each of the two provinces of his government a *Khákan* or *Khán Ambál* (or as it is written *Ambán*), or Lieutenant-Governor. That of Zúnghár was styled *Ong Ambál*, or Lieutenant-Governor of the Right, and that of Káshghar, *Sól Ambál*, or Lieutenant-Governor of the Left. The latter resided at Yarkand, as the seat of government and capital of the province. In him was vested the entire administration of the country, and his authority was supreme except in matters connected with foreign policy, or in questions which required the sanction of the Pekin or Home Government through the Ila Viceroy. He resided in a palace in the Yangishahr of Yarkand with his officers of state, and a special body-guard of Khitay troops.

His administrative staff consisted of a *Kichik Ambán*, " Little Governor" or Deputy Governor, a sort of Private and Foreign Secretary combined, who was the medium of communication for all the next subordinate ranks; a *Yáng Táy Dáláy*, "Chief Military Commandant," who had the control of all the troops in the country; a *Yáng Pang Dáláy*, or "Chief Civil Administrator," who superintended the trade, post, and intelligence departments; the *Sang Dáláy*, "Chief Finance Minister," who supervised the revenue returns, trade imports, and municipal taxes; and *Khóbóy Dáláy*, "Chief Judicial Administrator," with whom rested the control of the Law Department; cases affecting only Khitay subjects he settled himself, but those occurring between Musalman and Khitay he referred, in conjunction with the *Wáng*, for the decision of the Khán Ambán. Each of these *Dáláy* or "chiefs" had under him a *Ghaldáy* or "Deputy," who really did all the work, and brought it in each case to his *Dáláy* for confirmation; and each *Ghaldáy* had under him a staff of subordinates, such as messengers, writers, policemen, &c., whose chief was called *Doghobeg*. A similar staff formed the Government establishment under an *Ambán* in each division of the province, and each of those divisional *Ambán* reported direct to the *Khán Ambán* at Yarkand. The divisional Ambáns always resided at the chief city or capital town of their respective divisions, in a separate citadel called Yangishahr, which was held by the Khitay troops, under the command of a Dáláy, who was next in rank to the Ambán. The *Dáláy* commandants were of different ranks, distinguished by the colour of the balls on their hats, and in the larger garrisons, as those of Yarkand and Káshghar, there were two or three of them. The highest was called *Changtáy Dáláy*, and the next in order *Khó*, and *Má*, and *Yé*, &c. The *Má Dáláy* held command of the Trengani troops. The second in command of these *Dáláy* was called *Ghaldáy*, and under him were the *Zúngyá* or Captain (*Júzbáshí*), the *Konyá*, or Lieutenant (*Pinjábáshí*), the *Linyá* or Serjeant (*Onbáshí*), and the *Chirik*, or Private (*Jigit*). These were the principal Chinese officers, and all the higher grades were changed every two or three years for new incumbents, sent either from Ila, or from Pekin.

The Musalman officers held their appointments at the option of the Khán Ambán who usually received heavy bribes from time to time to retain them in their posts, though in the first place, the highest grades were always appointed from Ila, and the officer selected was always a native of some other city than that in which he held office; thus a native of Aksú would be sent to Khutan, one of Turfán to Yarkand, and so on.

The highest rank was called *Hákim Beg*, or "Governor Commandant," and corresponded with that of the divisional *Ambán*. The Chinese called this officer *Wáng* or "chief." He carried out the details of Government over the Musalman subjects of the division; he ruled and was responsible directly to the *Ambán* for the maintenance of order, collection of the revenue, and protection of the frontier. He had no authority whatever over Khitay or Kalmák subjects, and very little over the foreign Musalmans, as will be presently seen, and was in all respects subordinate to the *Ambán*. The *Wáng*, Commissioner of Division, resided in a palace inside the city or town, with a considerable staff of officials attached to his court, and a guard of Khitay troops, under a *Zúngya*, which was periodically relieved from the Yangishahr. He had a "Deputy Commissioner" called *Ishikághásí*, who superintended the details of the Municipal Government, and reported direct to the *Wáng*. The executive staff comprised a number of officers who acted under a chief called *Beg*. There was a *Beg* or "Assistant Commissioner" appointed to the charge of each district of the division, and his duties were, to maintain order, keep the roads, and collect the revenue. His staff comprised a *Cazí* or "judge," a *Zakátchi*, or "customs officer," a *Jebachí* or "revenue collector," together with a treasurer, secretary, and a number of messengers and policemen, and in certain localities a guard of Khitay troops under a *Zungyá* or *Linyá* according to its strength.

The subordinate Musalman officials had no dealings with the Khitay, who were under officers of their own nation; nor had the Khitay officials any direct dealings with the Musalmans. The latter were entirely governed by their own *Hákim Beg* or *Wáng*, who decided their law-suits amongst themselves on his own authority. But cases affecting both Musalman and Khitay were adjudicated conjointly by the *Wáng* and *Khobóy Dáláy*, or referred for final decision to the *Ambán*. The chief duty of the *Wáng*, so far as the Chinese were concerned, was the collection of the revenue and customs duties and trade taxes; and so long as these were punctually paid, he was very little interfered with; unless indeed his exactions and irregularities threatened to produce riot and revolt, in which case he was deposed and sent elsewhere to buy himself into office to the profit of some other *Ambán*. The *Wáng* and his *Ishikághási*, and the *Beg* of each district, held in addition to their salaries, each of them, in proportion to rank, certain estates in fief from the Ila Viceroy. Some of these were of considerable extent and value, and in the aggregate formed no trifling portion of some of the divisions. On the conquest of the country by the Amir, all these feudal tenures escheated to him, and he has distributed them on the same terms amongst his adherents and deserving officers from Khokand.

In each of the western cities to which the Chinese Government had granted trade privileges in favor of the Musalmans of Khokand, there grew up colonies of emigrants, and merchant settlers from Andijan. These, as they grew in numbers and importance, formed a distinct community governed by a chief of their own nationality. He was called *Aksakál*, and got his appointment on lease from the Khán of Khokand, to whom he paid a sum annually in return for the revenue he collected from the Andijan subjects. These foreigners in the details of their government as citizens were under the authority of the *Wáng* through their *Aksakál*, who was subordinate to him; but in all matters of revenue and trade they were solely under their *Aksakál* who was consul on the part of the Khokand Khán. The Andijan colony in each city had a separate *Aksakál*, and each farmed his post separately from the Khokand Khán, but all were subordinate in authority and rank to a chief consul, or *Chaung Aksakál*, who had his headquarters at Káshghar.

This system of double government under a third supervisor led to a succession of disagreements between the Aksakáls and the Wángs in the division of their authority; whilst the weak measures adopted by the Chinese to check such irregularities only increased the arrogance of the foreigners, and gradually took them more and more out of the control of the Wángs, till in the end they were constantly rebelling, and finally acknowledged no authority but that of their Aksakál.

The other foreign settlers in the country, as the Badakhshi and Kashmiri of Yarkand, were similarly governed by an *Aksakál* of their own nationality, and the Badakhshi enjoyed the same privileges as the Andijani; but the Kashmiri having no trade relations with the Chinese Government, paid their taxes through their *Aksakál* direct to the Wáng. The fixed taxes were the '*ushr* or "tithe" of land produce, and the *zakát* or fortieth of live-stock and merchandise; there were, besides, a tax of two to seven or eight *tanga* per *tanáb* on garden produce, such as vegetables, fruits, drugs, &c., and a tax on cotton, both raw and manufactured; this was usually levied in kind from the grower and weaver at a varying rate according to quality; another was the house-tax or *khán áylic*, generally one tanga per month, but in the time of the Tangani revolt it was raised to four *tanga* to supply the deficiency caused by non-receipt of treasure from Ila for the pay of the troops. These were the recognised taxes, but there were many others, such as on fuel brought for sale to market, on milch kine kept in the city, &c.; and they proved a ready means of oppression and a prolific source of that discontent which left the rulers without a single helping hand, or sympathising heart, in the hour of their distress and destruction.

Government of Káshghar under the Amir.—The events connected with the conquest of the country by its present ruler have been detailed in the historical sketch. It remains now to state what is known regarding the ruler himself, and to describe briefly the nature of the Government under which he holds the country. This may be done under separate heads as hereunder follows:—

The King.—Amir Muhammad Yákúb Khán, was born at Piskat near Taskand in 1235 H., =1820 A.D. His mother was the sister of Shekh Nizamuddin Kazi of Piskat, and the second wife of Pur Muhammad Mirza of Dihbíd near Samarcand.

Pur Muhammad is also called Muhammad Latif, and is said to be of Tymur lineage. His family was originally settled in Karatakin on the borders of Badakhshan, but moved to Dihbíd at the time of the Uzbak invasion, where he was born. In the time of Muhammad Ali Khán of Khokand, he emigrated to Khujand, and there entered a college to study for the church. After some years he was appointed to the office of Kazi at Karamma, and whilst there married a lady of the place, by whom he had a son named Muhammad Arif. He then removed to Piskat, and there married the mother of Amir Muhammad Yákúb Khán. Muhammad Arif is now residing at Káshghar with the rank of *Tocsabay* in the court of his half-brother. About four years ago he was sent to govern the district of Sarigh Kul, but was soon recalled and has remained unemployed ever since.

The Amir has also two sisters, one of whom was married to Nar Muhammad Khán, the Governor of Tashkand, who then got his brother-in-law appointed to the charge of Akmasjid, with the rank of Koshbegi. At this place the Amir married a Kapchak lady of Juelik, and she bore him his eldest son, Beg Kuli Beg, or Beg Bacha, as he is called, in 1265 H.=1848 A.D.

The Amir was brought up in his native village; and instead of following the religious calling of his father, he was led away by the stirring events of the times, and the disordered state of the country, to seek his fortunes at the capital. And there we find him at the age of twenty-five years as a *Mahram* or "court chamberlain," an office of trust, in the service of the youthful Khudayar Khán, on his elevation to the throne of Khokand in 1845 by the Kapchak chief, Musalman Kuli. It was shortly after this that Nar Muhammad, the Kapchak Governor of Tashkand, married his sister, and through his influence with the regent Mussalman Kuli, obtained for the *Mahram* promotion to the rank of *Koshbegi*, or "lord of the family," and the office of Governor at Akmasjid. The *Koshbegi* held this post for five or six years, till the capture of the fort by the Russians in August 1853, and he was soon after appointed *Mír* or "chief" of the Kilaochi fort.

In 1858 his patron, Musalman Kuli, was executed by Khudayar in a very barbarous manner. This act roused the hostility of the Kapchak and Kirghiz against the Khán; and espousing the cause of his elder brother, they drove Khudayar from the country, and set Mullah Khán on the throne at Khokand. Amongst the most active of the supporters of the new Khán was the *Mír* of Kilaochi; and for his services he was raised to the rank of *Shaháwal* or "intendant," and attached to the court. Shortly after, however, he was appointed Governor of the frontier fort of Kuramma, with the rank, once more, of Koshbegi. From this, at the end of 1860, he was transferred with Kaná'at Shah, the *Náyb* of Khokand, to Tashkand to watch the Russians who were advancing upon Turkistan. Whilst he was on this frontier, Mullah Khán was assassinated in his bed by a plot of the nobles, and Khudayar hearing the news, at once issued from his retreat at Jizzak, and hastened to secure Tashkand. On arrival there he was welcomed and set on the throne as Khán by the *Koshbegi* and *Náyb*, and for this service Khudayar retained Yákúb Beg in his post as Governor of Kuramma fort.

In the meantime Mullah Alim Kuli, Kirghiz of Osh, had set Shah Murád Khán, grandson of Sher Ali Khán, on the throne at Khokand, and marched with him against Khudayar at Tashkand. On their approach, Yákúb Beg left Khudayar, and, joining Alim Kuli, retired with him to Kuramma, there to equip and organise their forces. From this they set out and besieged Khudayar in Tashkand; but after a month of desultory skirmishing, failing to make any progress, they retreated to Khokand. From this shortly afterwards, Alim Kuli sent Yákúb Beg to hold Khujand, which was threatened by Khudayar and his allies from Bukhárá. On their approach, Yákúb Beg surrendered his charge, retired to Bukhárá with the returning army, and resided there some time as a *bi* or "noble" attached to the court of the Amir.

In 1863 the Amir Muzaffaruddin of Bukhárá marched to Khokand to set his new brother-in-law, Khudayar, on the throne there against the usurper Alim Culi, and Yákúb Beg returned with his army to the scene of his former activity. On the departure of the Bukhárá troops, Yákúb Beg and some other leading men joined Alim Kuli who, having executed Sultan Murád, had set up Syad Sultan as Khán. This rival Khán at once restored Yákúb Beg to his former rank and office, and sent him to hold the fort of Kuramma; and shortly afterwards he joined his benefactor with his contingent to aid in the capture of Khujand.

32.—The Knife Grinder.

33.—Verandah of interior Court yard of the Urda of the Dadkhwah of Yarkund, shewing the Hall of Audience.

Following this, the Regent, Alim Kuli, proceeded by Kuramma to secure and settle Tashkand. Here he executed the Governor, Shádmán Mirzá, and reinstated his own father-in-law, Nar Muhammad, *Parwánchi*. On his return towards the capital he placed the *Hudáychi*, Hydar Kuli Kapchák, in command of the Kuramma Fort, and took the *Koshbegi*, Yákúb Beg with him to Khokand for attendance at court. Whilst here, about April 1864, news arrived of the advance of the Russians against Chamkand, and Alim Kuli at once sent forward Yákúb Beg to secure and strengthen the defences of Tashkand. On his arrival there he was joined by Mirza Ahmad, Koshbegi, retreating with his troops from Chamkand. In October the Russians appeared before Tashkand. Yákúb Beg issued to fight them, but was defeated and driven back into the fort; and the Russians on their part, having lost several men, retired on Chamkand. Alim Kuli now hurried up with reinforcements, and set to work to fortify the place. Whilst so engaged, the envoys of Sadik Beg Kirgniz arrived with news of the revolt in Káshghar, and the want of a Khoja to fill the vacant throne there. Alim Kuli sent off Buzurg Khán, with *Koshbegi* Yákúb Beg as his *Bátor báshi*, but could spare no troops to help them to take the country. The rest of Yákúb Beg's career has been given in the history, up to the date of his assuming the title of Amir Muhammad Yákúb Khán.

He has ten sons and several daughters living. Only two of his Khokand sons are with him in Káshghar, *viz.*, Beg Kuli Beg, aged twenty-six years, and Hacc Kuli Beg, aged twenty-three years. The other sons, born in Káshghar and brought up in the palace, are children, the eldest of whom are now learning to read their lessons; their names are Abdulla Beg, Rahmán Kuli Beg, Karîm Kuli Beg, Khadayár Beg, &c.

The Court.—The Amir's court is said to be formed on the model of that of Khokand. It certainly contains many of the former courtiers of the late Mallah Khán, and not a few refugees from the court of the ruling Khudayar Khán; all of whom, with rare exceptions, have left their families and property on their patrimonial estates in Khokand, or in the districts now incorporated with the Russian empire.

The Amir, however, has no fixed establishment, nor regular gradation of ranks, such as formed the court of the Khokand Khán. The principal of these officers attached to the palace were the *zinbardár*, groom in waiting; the *dasturkwánchi*, butler; the *hudáychi*, chamberlain; the *yasáwul*, mace-bearer; the *mirákhor*, master of the stables; the *muhram*, confidential messenger; the *khazinachi*, treasurer; the *aftábachi*, cup-bearer; the *bacáwalbáshi*, chief provisioner; and a number of other minor grades of court domestics.

The principal officers of state were the *mihtar*, prime minister; the *parwánchi*, chancellor; the *dádhkwáh*, district governor; the *atálik*, preceptor or controller of the state; the *koshbegi*, lord of a tribe or lieutenant of a country; the *shaghawal*, foreign secretary; the *ishikágha*, lord warden; the *tocsáwá* or *tocsábáy*, lord of a standard or leader of an army in the field; *carawulbegi*, intendant of frontier defences; the *corchi*, master of ordnance; the *jabachi*, revenue collector; the *zakátchi*, custom officer; the *mirzábáshi*, chief secretary; the *umara*, courtier, and some others of lower rank. Besides these officers there were certain ranks of nobility such as *sudúr*, *orác*, *inác*, *khoja*, *torah*, and *eshán*, the possessors of which periodically attended court and gave the king the benefit of their advice in matters referred for their judgment.

The military officers under the direct authority of the king were the *mingbáshi*, "commandant of a thousand;" but in reality the office is equivalent to general of a division; the *amîrilashkar*, brigadier; the *bátorbáshi*, detachment or troop leader; the *náyb*, deputy or second in command; the *pansadbáshi*, commandant of five hundred, or regimental colonel; the *yúzbáshi*, commandant of a hundred, or captain; the *pinjúbáshi*, commandant of fifty, or lieutenant; the *onbáshi*, commandant of ten, or sergeant; the *yáwur*, aide-de-camp; the *corbáshi*, provost marshall; and the *jallád*, the executioner. The foot soldier was called *sarbáz*, and the horse soldier *jigit*.

The ecclesiastic department, which includes that of law, comprised the following officers, namely, *shekh-ul-islám*, elder of the faith, or bishop; *cazi-kalán*, chief justice; *cázi askar*, judge of criminal causes; *cázi-ul-cúzát*, judge of civil causes; *cázi raís*, judge of religious causes; *cázi muhtasib*, judge of offences against public morals; *mufti*, judge of decrees; *'álim*, judge of appeal; *mukarrir*, notary; *mudarris*, schoolmaster; *khátíb*, preacher; *imám*, chaplain; *muazzin*, caller to prayers; *mujáwir*, sweeper, &c. There were, besides, the *mullá*, *'álim* or *'ulama*, *ákhún*, &c., doctors of divinity and law, usually on the establishment of some college; as were the *shekh*, superior; *mutawalli*, custodian; *cárí*, koran reader; and *farrásh*, servitor attached to the shrine connected with it. Of the above departments of governments only the two last are found fully organised in Káshghar, *viz.*, the army and the church, though neither can be considered to work efficiently, nor in their present state, to be capable of resisting serious opposition. With respect to the first two, the court itself is managed with an affectation of extreme simplicity, without parade or pomp of any kind; and this absence of ostentation is counterbalanced by the punctilious observance of a very minute etiquette and strict discipline; all conducted within the precincts of the royal residence, with a solemnity of behaviour and severity of silence which are most impressive in effect; and are heightened by the gravity of deportment habitually observed by the Amir in his behaviour towards his courtiers.

The distance between the Amir and his courtiers is wide. Very few are allowed to be seated in his presence, and then at a considerable interval between. Even his highest and most trusted nobles and adherents, in his presence, display a manner of humility and deference which is not assumed, but is the natural effect of the fear inspired by the knowledge of his absolute authority, and the experience of the trifling causes which may evoke his displeasure and call forth the tyranny of his wrath. Few words are ever spoken in the presence, and then only in reply, with an expression of timidity and tone of deprecation. The Amir carries on the government of the country through his own direct authority by means of officials immediately in correspondence with himself in all matters other than those of trifling detail.

Administration of government.—This is conducted through a staff of governors of division, who are styled *dádhkwáh*. Each receives his orders from the Amir direct, and is responsible for the revenue of the country committed to his care, as well as for the maintenance of order and the security of the roads and frontiers. The *dádhkwáh* resides in an *orda* or palace in the fort of the capital of his division, with the garrison which is under his orders, and an establishment of officials for the different offices of the executive government, such as the administration of justice, collection of revenue, management of police, &c. And he has in each district of his division a *beg, or mir*, or *sarkár*, according to the size of the district, who is a governor subordinate to himself, and has a staff of officers corresponding to those at the capital. These district governors correspond direct with the *dádhkwáh*, and are responsible to him for the revenue, and the safety and the good order of their several charges. The *dádhkwáh* has no power to remove or appoint these district governors without the sanction of the Amir; but within prescribed limits he is the supreme authority in his own division, and holds a court daily for the despatch of public business; the confirmation and execution of the sentences passed by the law courts, the reception of petitions, enquiry into the wants of traders, &c., &c. In all matters of extraordinary occurrence, as well as in cases in which capital execution is sentenced by the judges, he refers to the Amir for final orders.

Administration of Justice.—This is conducted by a staff of judicial officers called *cázi, mufti, 'alim*, &c., according to the *Shariat*, and is the same as in other Musalman governments. Each *dádhkwáh* has such a staff as part of his governing establishment, as has each of his district governors or superintendents; only in the latter cases the department is represented by a minor official, who transfers all cases beyond his powers for settlement by the higher officers at the capital of the division; where such sentences as mutilation, torture, flogging, and execution are carried out in the presence of the *dádhkwáh*.

Punishments inflicted in Eastern Turkestan. Ancient punishments before the 10th century (Moghul).—Under the Moghuls, a noble was entitled to forgiveness nine times, but, for the tenth fault, was imprisoned; when taken before his Chief on this occasion for enquiry, such noble would be mounted on a white horse (of 2 years of age); on his arrival before the hakim nine white felts were placed under the horses feet; during the enquiry a second noble acted as spokesman between the hakim and the offender. If his fault was proved and he was pronounced worthy of the punishment of death, the offender with considerable state was placed on a seat.

Two men of rank then supported him, taking him by the shoulders, when the executioner, who was then termed *Kanchi*, approached. This man tied both arms with bandages, both above and below the elbow, and when the large vein was discovered in each arm, it was opened, and the offender was allowed to bleed to death, the bandages being removed. It was a rule that at his death the two dignitaries who assisted should weep and lament him publicly, and that they should superintend his burial. Sentence of death thus administered was termed *ulderub*. If sentence short of death was awarded, what was termed *yarghú* was ordered; this involved confiscation of property, and degradation from rank or title of nobility.

On common people death was inflicted either by cutting the throat with a sword, or by bricking up the living man in a wall (burial alive).

For adultery, women were punished by cutting off the breasts and by severing the main sinew behind the ankle. They were, however, usually imprisoned and subjected to hard labour for smaller offences.

Men guilty of murder or of high treason (offence against the reigning Khan) were buried up to the waist in a public manner, and an address, putting forth the offence of the culprit, was read by the Torachi-Tora (act); after which death was inflicted by spearing, a body of mounted troops being drawn up for the purpose. If a man was accused of murder, theft, or other important offence and denied the charge, he was subjected to the following torture to extract confession; boiling oil was sprinkled over his body, but chiefly over his neck and shoulders. This torture was called Kín, other inferior punishments were *kulta*—scourging with a thick short stave. *Teyak.*—Flogging with pomegranate branches. The pomegranate tree is revered by Fire-worshippers, and this punishment would appear to have come from their rule.

Sultan Satúk Bogra Khan introduced punishments according to the Shariat, but the old custom of cutting the throat with the sword was retained; the custom of death by burying to the waist and killing with a spear was altered to burial up to the waist and public stoning.

Chinese Punishments. (*Theft.*)—Imprisonment, but the offender had a collar of

wood known as shál placed round his neck. On the weekly bazar days the prisoner was taken into the city to beg, when he obtained subsistence for the week. If he was chained, it was with a double chain and a long iron bar connecting them; one of the chains being fastened to the neck and the other to the ankle, progression became possible by the prisoner holding the iron bar in his hands. This chain was termed ishkal. Offenders accused of murder or offence against the State were distinguished by confinement in a cage until sentence was passed. If *death* was awarded, the head was cut off with a sword, the executioner wearing a red dress: before the execution he was primed for his task with intoxicating drink. In cases of *crim. con.* the man and woman were placed on donkeys and taken through the street, the man having his face blackened and turned towards the donkey's tail; the woman with a sack thrown over her head. *Rape* was punished with death, the head being cut off at a place where four roads meet. Minor offences among men were punished with the lash. The Chinese had an establishment at Charchend for those undergoing sentence of banishment, where they were watched by a military force and were subject to regulations as convicts. At the present time the punishments are as follows:—For *Murder.*—Death in public on the bazar day by the cutting of the throat; the body being left on the spot for eight pahar as a warning or *Hanging*. For *Highway Robbery.*—If accompanied by violence, death by public execution, or mutilation of hand or foot. Death is inflicted on both sexes, but the hands and feet of women are not struck off.

For *Theft.*—The first offence, and sometimes the second, are forgiven; but for the third offence the hand of a man is cut off. A woman, if convicted of theft, and sentenced to punishment, is put on a donkey with the stolen article on her neck and taken through the city, or is publicly flogged with the dira, the long leather strap of the kazee's attendant; the offender, however, is not stripped. If a woman is convicted when pregnant she cannot be punished till 40 days after the birth of a child; six women are said to have been publicly executed in Kashghar since the Amir's rule commenced. The use of the torture known as Kín is said still to be employed.

If a woman, unmarried, keeps company with a man, without going through the form of marriage, she is subject to 100 strokes of the dira; but for *adultery proper*, proved by eye-witnesses, two being sufficient, neither of whom must be a slave, death by cutting of throat or stoning is inflicted.

The cutting of the throat is usually carried out in the larger cities, and hanging is adopted in provincial places. Thieves are sometimes punished by cutting off nose or ear, as well as hand or foot; punishments are usually inflicted in the districts where the offence is committed, but occasionally public execution is ordered in Kashgar or elsewhere. Hanging is simply carried out by putting a noose over the neck and pulling the body by means of a rope from the ground, the rope running over a plain pully. Minor punishments are fine and the lash. Imprisonment is but little resorted to. Cases of theft under Rupees 10 worth of property, and not accompanied by violence, are invariably punished by strokes of the dira (a flat leather strap).

All cases of important crimes, or relating to important individuals, are at once reported to head-quarters, and a mubariknama is forwarded from Kashghar, ordering sentence to be carried out in conformity with the Shariat and without further reference or giving detailed instructions. With people of any importance sentence of death further requires the confirmation of the Amir. In addition to all this the Amir has his own executioners and holds his own Court for the trial of State offences. Petty offences about the palace and amongst the soldiery are tried by the Kazi Ushkur.

Religious institutions.—These are the same as in all Mahommadan countries, and are under the direct patronage of the Amir and the special care of the divisional governors, who see to the protection of their rights and the promotion of their objects, the nature of which has been already described.

Finance.—The fixed sources of revenue are the *'ushr*, or tithe of all cereal produce of the land, and the *zakát* or customs duty. The *'ushr* is levied from all cultivated land not sequestered for church purposes, or granted in exemption as fiefs. On the conquest of the country by the Amir he issued a decree with the sanction of the *'alim*, to the effect that the whole of the soil vested in himself as sole and absolute proprietor; but that hereditary owners and leaseholders could renew their rights by purchase through the *'alim* of the division to which they belonged. This order applied equally to the freehold tenants by purchase, who were mostly Andiján emigrants. The majority of the landholders redeemed their rights by payment to the *'alim*, from whom they received a document bearing his seal in testimony of the transaction. The lands which under the Chinese rule were held as crown property, and had been given in fief to the several divisional governors in their time (the *Wáng, Ishikághá, Beg, &c.*,) were exempted from this order, and the Amir reserved them for distribution amongst his adherents and officers. Church lands also were similarly exempted, and their glebe rights were renewed in favour of the original bequests. But all waste land, including the pasture tracts around the settlements were decreed the absolute property of the Amir, and before they could be brought under cultivation it was incumbent on the farmer to purchase or rent it. All land, whether waste or cultivated, other than orchard and vineyard, appears to sell alike at the fixed rate of forty *tanga* or ten rupees, for as much as is sown with one *chárak* or twenty pounds of wheat.

Generally the landowner or holder does not cultivate his estate himself, but lets it out to tenants, who, after paying the Government demands, render three-fourths of the net produce to the landlord, and retain the remaining share for themselves. The Government demands on the land are the *'ushr*, or one in ten parts of the gross produce of all cereal crops; and the *tanábi* or tax on a measured area of fruit and vegetable gardens, and other crops not cereal. The *tanáb* is a linear measure of nearly 47 yards, and any space on two sides by a line of that length is called a *tanáb* of land. The tax varies from one or two, to eight or ten *tanga* the *tanáb*, according to the nature and value of the crop. Such are the legal demands, but in practice much more is exacted by the Collectors for their own benefit, and whilst at Yangi Hissar we saw Government orders upon certain settlements for the collection of the *'ushr* at the rate of three parts in ten.

The *zakát* is a Mahommedan tax like the *'ushr* sanctioned by the *Shari'at*. It is one part in forty of all live-stock, and of merchandise entering the country. In the former case it is levied yearly in kind, but in the latter at an *ad valorem* rate in cash, at the custom house where the goods are examined. There are no data as to the receipts under these heads, and no accounts appear to be kept. Seemingly the Amir leaves this to the *dádkhwáh*, and makes no enquiry so long as the flow into the imperial treasury does not flag, or does not come short of the roughly estimated capabilities of the division. There are, besides the above, some municipal imposts and taxes on drugs, &c., but their amount is trifling. And there is the produce of the gold mines of Khutan, of which no details are known. Previous to the treaty of trade with Russia, merchants other than Musalmans paid the *zakát* at the rate of one in twenty *ad valorem*, as in other Mahommadan States, and Hindus further paid a monthly tax of two *tanga* per head so long as they resided in the country, and were prohibited from wearing the turban or riding on horseback in the streets. These restrictions have been all rescinded by the terms of the treaty concluded with the British Government, and British subjects, irrespective of creed, are now only subject to the same imposts as the Musalmans.

Police.—The system of police is very intricate, and its ramifications pervade all society, with the effect of creating a profound mistrust of each other amongst the people, without materially improving the state of public morals; for though some vices and abuses are put down with severely repressive measures (as prostitution and spirit or wine drinking), others of a worse nature are taken no notice of (as sodomy and opium or hemp-smoking), whilst others again, as gambling and obscenity, are little interfered with, unless the censor of public morals should come in contact with them in his rounds.

The police may be divided into two classes, *viz.*, the secret and municipal. The first are everywhere, and amongst all classes, and nobody knows who they are, or how they act, but everybody feels their presence and is carefully on his guard.

The municipal police comprises the urban and suburban divisions. The first is under the management of a superintendent called *Corbáshi*, whose office corresponds to that of the *kotwál* in Indian cities; and he has under him a body of policemen called *tarzagchi*. These have their beats in the city by day, and patrol it in small parties called *pasban* by night. Thieves, beggars, and wanderers found in the streets at night are lodged in prison till morning; beggars are then set free with a warning, and others on bail. But if a plaint is lodged against any so taken, he is carried before the *cázi* who investigates the case and gives judgment; and the case is then taken to the *mufti* who passes sentence, and then to the *'alim* who confirms, and finally to the *dádhkwáh*, who sees it carried into execution without further reference, except in cases in which death is the sentence, and for this he must first obtain the sanction of the Amir. Execution is usually by hanging, though by slaughter, that is, cutting the throat, is not unfrequent. The gallows is a fixture in some open space near the city, and is furnished with three or four pulleys and long ropes. A noose at one end of the latter is passed round the neck of the condemned, and he is hauled up by the executioners till dead, and left to hang several days as a warning to others. The *tarzagchi* of the night patrol collect one *dárchin*=two *pysa* every week from each shop in the city.

Once every day the *Cázi Rasi's*, attended by a staff of four to six *muhtasib*, each of whom carries a *dira*, or leather thong fixed to a wooden handle, goes the round of the bazars and main thoroughfares on horseback. He examines the weights in the retail shops, and flogs such as have short weights; or in serious cases sends the offenders before the *mufti* for judgment. His own powers do not exceed the summary infliction of 20 to 40 stripes of the *dira*, and these are freely bestowed on women appearing unveiled in the streets, on gamblers, drunkards, brawlers, and disorderly characters, and such as neglect the stated hours of prayer, and others. The weights are inspected once a fortnight, as also the stores of flour exposed for sale, and where earth is found mixed with it, the offender is flogged in front of his shop.

The city gates are held always by a military guard, and at night a Khitay watchman beats the *yang*, a sort of wooden gong, from a post over the gateway. This is a Chinese custom, and is still kept up. The *yang* is a hollow triangular case of wood, and is sounded with a drumstick at short intervals all through the night. The night patrol of the *tarzagchi* also sound a drum on their rounds. It is called *dúmbac*, and is like a tambour in shape, but covered on both sides.

The suburban police have the same duties as the urban, and occupy posts on the roads leading from the suburbs to the city, and at night keep a guard of two men at particular spots and cross-roads. They examine travellers and see that those passing the limits are provided with passports. Nobody is allowed to pass from one division to another, or from one district to another, without a passport, and if he does so, he is stopped and sent back for inquiry at the first police station on the road. In every city and market town there is an office for the issue of passports. It is a mere bit of paper, stating the bearers name, where he goes from and to where he goes, and on what business, and on what date. It is granted free of charge, and on return of the bearer to his original place, he must get it stamped or signed at the office of the place he leaves. This office is in charge of a secretary, who is under the orders of the *Pánsadbáshi* or other military commandant of the division or district.

The Army.—The Chinese held the country with an organized force of about twenty thousand men, of which five thousand were Kalmák cavalry, including the body-guards of the several divisional Ambáns, which were composed of Mánjhú Tartars from the Ila country. These guards varied in strength from fifty to two hundred men, according to the rank of the Ambán, and the extent of his command, and were all armed with the lance and sword, and were uniform in dress and horse equipments. The Kalmák were an irregular body, only armed with the bow and arrow, and mounted on their own horses; they were mostly employed as foragers and scouts.

The army is under the direct command of the Amir through *Pánsadbáshi* officers appointed by him. There are twelve of this rank at Káshghar, two at Yangi Hissar, and two at Yárkand. Each *Pánsadbáshi* is supposed to have five hundred men under him, with five *Yúzbáshi* or commandant of a hundred. Each of these has two *Pinjabáshi* or commandant of fifty under him; and each of these has five *Onbáshi* or commandant of ten under him. This is not, however, carried out in practice, and the *Yúzbáshi* and *Pinjabáshi* are usually directly under the orders of the Amir, and if not employed in independent duties, are shifted about from one *Pánsadbáshi* to another.

CHAPTER III.

HISTORY OF KÁSHGHAR.*

By H. W. Bellew.

The ancient history of this region, which constitutes no mean portion, as regards superficial extent at least, of that vast territory indicated by the comprehensive term Central Asia, is enveloped in the doubts of obscurity that surround all ancient history.

For several centuries anterior to the Christian era it formed part of the empire of Túrán swayed by a long line of Scythian Kings who are referred to a common descent from the great family of Afrásyáb. Of the wealth, power, civilization and laws of this ancient and most remarkable people who figure in the early records under the various Tártár, Chinese, Indian, and European appellations of Kinto Moey, Sai, Su, Sácá, Sákyá, Xaca, Sacœ, Scythœ, Tokhárí, Yueichi, Yuchi, Yetœ, Getœ, Jattah, Jath, Jat, Jotun, Gothi, Guti, Goths, Guttones, Massagetœ, Caucasians, Tentones, Venden, Vandals, Germans, &c., &c., and who are all classed under the generic appellation of Aryan from Ariavartha, the old Sanskrit name of the region now known as that group of mountain ranges concentrating in Hindú Kush—the Kohi Káf of Orientals, the Caucasus of occidentals—and recognized as the primæval abode or location of the Caucasian stock of the Man family, we have many historic records; but none more significant than the yet enduring consequences of their early foreign conquests from this cradle of their race extending from the valley of the Syhon on the west to the basin of Lake Balkash on the east.

The successive irruptions of their vast colonizing hordes into northern and eastern Europe during the centuries just preceding and following the Christian era, as history teaches, thoroughly revolutionized the old form of society, and planted a new

---

* There are several histories of the life and career of Yakúb Khan, the Amír of Kashghar, besides those to be found in Vambery's and Von Hellwald's published works.

But no one has gone into the History of Eastern Turkistan from the earliest times with such deep and careful research as Dr. Bellew. He has spent many months in reading voluminous Persian and Turki manuscripts, and owing to his remarkable linguistic attainments he has enjoyed better opportunities than any one else of conversing with the learned men of the country. I have therefore adopted his history for incorporation in this work.

(Sd.)   T. D. Forsyth.

The following sketch of the history of Káshghar, and supplementary description of the country, have been prepared for submission to Government at the request of Sir Douglas Forsyth, late Envoy to the Court of Káshghar.

The work has been compiled from such authorities and materials as were accessible at the time, coupled with the results of personal enquiry and observation on the spot during the stay of the Embassy in the country.

These from the nature of the case, it will be understood, were found as limited as the time itself at my disposal and, though no labour has been spared in reducing the mass of materials collected into a consecutive and at the same time brief form, there has consequently been no attempt to enter into lengthy detail. This last result could only have been accomplished had I enjoyed the advantage of a reference to European and Oriental libraries, and a sufficient leisure to study the subject.

34.—Guard of Artillery Sirbaz, and group of officers assembled in the Court yard of the Urda of the Dadkhwah of Yarkund.

35.—Soldiers from Aksu.

set of languages, with a new blood on the soil of their conquests there. Whilst to the south and east the Indian peninsula similarly in its language, religion, and feudalism bears testimony to the earlier and as complete transplantation of the ancient Scythian element in that direction. Between these two great waves of migration are the Persians.

Their historians romance on the theme of the wars of the early sovereigns of Iran against the incursions of those kindred races, the terrible Scythians of Túrán. Their poets sing the heroic combats and deeds of valour of their champions against this northern tyrant, and tell of his final repulse beyond the Oxus, the limit between the two empires.

The power of the Scythians in their native seat appears to have been first broken by their western neighbours and old enemies of Irán, and finally extinguished by the Macedonian conquest.

M.P.   Syáwush, about 580 B.C., fleeing from his father, Kaikáos, crossed the Jyhon and sought refuge with the enemy of his family, Afrásyáb, whose capital—near
N.   the site of the modern Bukhárá—was Rámetan, not very long afterwards celebrated
M.P.   for its magnificent *átashkadah* or "fire temple." The Scythian King received the Persian refugee with kindness and, granting him an honorable asylum, gave him his daughter, the beautiful Farangís, in marriage, with the provinces of Khutan and Chín as her dowry. Thither Syáwush retired with his bride, and settling at Kung—probably Katak, the ruins of which now exist near Lob at 12 or 14 days journey north-east of Khutan—made it the capital of his government of Khutan and Chín, or as it is usually styled Máchín which, together, comprised the southern and eastern portion of the great basin known as Eastern Turkistan.

I trust, however, that the history and description of this, to us, new region, such as they are, will be found to contain some interesting and useful information, and serve to convey a correct knowledge of the past events and present condition of the country to which they relate.

It is necessary for me here to state that the published authorities from whose works I have drawn my information are noted in the margin of the text by initials according to the subjoined detailed list. For the rest and for the later history I am indebted to the statements of various individuals, actors, or participators in the events they described, such as Afghans, Hindustanis, Audijánis, Kalmác and other residents. Whilst for the information brought together in the general description I am indebted to the statements made by natives of the country, compared and tested, or modified and enlarged according to my own personal observation and enquiry.

The following authors have been made use of in the compilation of this history of Káshgharia, namely:—

    Malcolm's History of Persia. M.P.
    Yule's Cathay and the way thither. Y.C.
    Beal's Fah Hian. B.F.H.
    Remusat's Khoten. R.K.
    Michell's Russians in Central Asia. M.V.
    Vambery's History of Bukhára. V.B.
    Hamilton Smith's Natural History of the Human Species. S.H.S.
    Wells William's Middle Kingdom. W.W.
    Romanoffski's Turkestan. Rom.
    Rauzat-us-Safá of Mír Kháwind Sháh. R.S.
    Zafar Náma Tymúrí of Sharífuddín 'Alí Yazdí. Z.N.T.
    Tabcáti Násari of Minhájuddín 'Uthmán Jáuzjání. T.N.
    Tárikhi Narshakhi written 332H.=943 A.D. by Abúbakar Muhammad bin Ja'far al Narshakhí, and translated from the Arabic by Muhammad bin Za'far bin 'Umar into Persian in 522H.=1127A.D. N.
    Tazkira Bughra Khan, translated from the original Persian into Turki by Shekh Najmuddín Attár. T.B.K.
    Tárikhi Rashídí of Mirzá Hydar Gúrikán. T.R.
    Tárikhi Sighár, monograph of 'Abdulla *Pánsad* in the service of the Ruler of Káshghar. T.S.
    Tazkira Hidáyat of Mír Kháluddín Yárkandi. T.H.
    Personal observation or enquiry. P.

SIMLA,   (Sd.) H. W. BELLEW, *Surgeon-Major*,
The 22nd August 1874.   *Yárkand Embassy.*

Garshewáz became jealous of the rising power of Syáwush, and persuading his brother, Afrásyáb, that he aimed at independence so excited his suspicions that he summoned him to his capital and there killed him. Popular tradition points to the Darwáza Ghoryán of Bukhárá as the spot on which he was slain; and the site was long held sacred by the Mughán or "fire-worshipers," the followers of Zarathustra or Zoroaster, who used to assemble there every New Year's day at sunrise, each man bringing a cock which he sacrificed on the spot in commemoration of the murder. N.

The murder of Syáwush created intense excitement in Persia, and Kaikáos bending to the popular demand sent his general, the celebrated Rustam, with a great army to avenge his death. He besieged Rámetan for two years, built Rámish opposite to it, and finally driving Afrásyáb from the country occupied it for seven years with his Persians. M.P. / N.

Syáwush left a posthumous son by Farangís, named Kaikhusro, or Cyrus, who after a romantic career of infancy became King of Persia, and warred with his grandfather to avenge the death of his father. His general, Rustam, after many prodigies of valour against the troops of Chín and Khutan, drove Afrásyáb from his capital, and dividing his country amongst the Persian commanders returned to the Court of Kaikhusro. Afrásyáb, however, again recovered his capital, and waged an indecisive warfare against the Persian Sovereign till Kaikhusro finally conquered Bukhárá and Samarcand, and capturing Afrásyáb slew him. His grave is said to be at the Ma'bad gate of the city where these events are commemorated amongst the people of Bukhárá in the popular ditties known as "The songs of Syáwush." M.P. / N.

Kaikhusro now resigned his crown and government to his adopted son, Lohrasp, the son-in-law of Kaikáos, and he soon exacted homage from the rulers of Tártary and China, and thus established his authority over the country of the Afrásyáb Kings. The Persian sovereignty thus established in Túrán was destroyed in the person of Dáráb II., the fifth in succession from Lohrasp, by the conquest of Alexander the Great about 330 B.C. And the Greek Bactrian kingdom founded by him in Saghd was in its turn overthrown by the invasion from the north of the Great Yuchi. M.P.

During the period from the overthrow of the Afrásyáb dynasty to the subsequent establishment of the Greek Bactrian empire the region to the east, known as Chinese Tartary, or locally as *Kichik Bukhárá* or "Little Bukhárá," was the theatre of contest between conflicting races—the early Caucasian possessors, and invading Moghol or Mongol hordes from the extreme north. These numerous tribes of hardy mountaineers, pressed by the barbarian hosts from the north—who in later times have become prominent on the pages of history under the names of Moghol, Mánjhú or Mánchúr, Kalmák or Kalmuck, Kirghiz or Kirguise, Noghay, Báshkir, Uzbak, &c.—during the long period of the Chow dynasty from 1122 to 250 B.C., when the Chinese Empire was divided into a fluctuating number of petty principalities—from 125 at one time to 41 at another—made repeated incursions into the more tempting territories of their eastern and southern neighbours, until in 253 B.C., Che Hwangti, the first universal monarch of the empire, built the Great Wall against their destructive inroads. P. / B.F.H.

Of these northern tribes the Yuchi or Tokhár, a branch of the Tungnu or Eastern Tártár people, were the most warlike and formidable. They had been driven from their lands westward to the banks of the Ila River just anterior to 200 B.C. by the Hiungnu, or Huns, under their Chief Mothe who, in his victorious career, finally conquered all the country from the borders of China on the east to the banks of the Volga on the west. The rapid rise to power of the Hiungnu alarmed the Chinese, and in the reign of Kaou-tsu, the first Emperor of the Han dynasty, from 202 to 194 B.C., they sent an army against Mothe. But it hastily retired before the vast superiority of his numbers, and the Hiungnu for 50 years maintained their supremacy.

At this time the Yuchi, pressed by the Hiungnu, separated. The lesser division or Little Yuchi passed into Tibet, whilst the greater division or Great Yuchi—the Táy Yuchi—descended upon Káshghar, Yárkand, and Khutan where, about 163 B.C., they displaced the original occupants called Sáká or Sú by the Chinese.

B.F.H.   Some years later—139 B.C.—the Emperor Wooti, of the Han dynasty, sent an Envoy to the Great Yuchi for the purpose of arranging a combined movement against the Hiungnu, the common enemy of both. But at the time of his arrival, the Yuchi, being pressed by the Ussun tribe, were urged forward to the invasion of Saghd, and Tahia—the country of the Dahœ—and they carried the Chinese Envoy, Chang Kian, along with them.

On this new ground the Yuchi gradually made good their stand, and—about 126 B.C.—having overthrown the decaying Greek Bactrian kingdom, drove out the Saka across the Oxus and the mountains beyond into the country drained by the Kabul river, and, establishing themselves in their place, soon spread over the province that has since been named, after their tribal appellation, Tokháristán; which includes Balkh, Cundúz, Hissár, Bolor, Wakhán, and Badakhshán.

The Envoy, Chang Kian, after a detention of ten years effected his release, and returned to China after an absence of 16 years, during which he experienced a variety of remarkable and perilous adventures, with only two survivors of the original company of 100 with which he set out. His return was welcomed with rejoicings, and, on account of the knowledge he had acquired of the western nations, he was raised to high rank, and, with Hou Kiuping as General, entrusted with the conduct of an expedition against the Hiungnu who were at that time—123-121 B.C.—contesting the possession of the several little States from Khámil round by Káshghar to Khutan against the Ouigour or Uyghúr who, since 200 B.C., had, under the name of Kuisse, taken possession of the country from the direction of Khámil.

The expedition failed, and Chang Kian was reduced from his high position to the ranks. But during this campaign his troops first saw the golden statue of Budha which was worshiped by the King of Hieai-to or Kartchou, and which was destined hereafter to be the means of introducing the new faith into China. The statue was taken and carried to the Emperor, and afterwards served as the model for others when the doctrine of Budha gained a footing in the country, as will be mentioned further on.

Wooti, though at first unsuccessful, prosecuted the war against the Hiungnu, and materially checked their career. His successor, Chaouti, followed the same policy, and finally broke their power by a singal defeat. This disaster was followed by dissensions and anarchy amongst the tribes, whilst a plague and famine coming in the wake of their protracted warfare completed the reduction of the turbulent Hiungnu, who in 60 B.C. passed under subjection to the Chinese.

Y.C.   They subsequently, however, rebelled and for a season recovered their former independence, but were again subdued in 83 A.D., and, following this, the whole country was annexed to China by—94 A.D.—the capture of Káshghar. These successes were achieved by the celebrated soldier Panchao who from this crossed the mountains of Bolor, attacked the Yuchi or Tokhári, killed their King, and a few years later pushed his arms as far as the Caspian; for in 102 A.D. he sent an expedition thus far westward under Kanyng in the vain-glorious attempt to conquer the Roman Empire.

From this time forward till the period of the Arab conquest, the history of this region belongs to that of the Chinese Empire.

Whilst the Chinese were thus engaged in subjugating the territory of Káshghar, the Great Yuchi, relieved from the pressure of their old enemies, consolidated their power in their new possessions, and during the century of their settlement in Saghd and Tábia became a very numerous and powerful nation with their capital at Bukhárá.

N.   This ancient city is said to have been built by Afrásyáb on the site of a former marsh formed by floods from the Másaf River, and the country around to have been settled by tribes originally coming from Turkistán under a Chief named Abrawy. He settled the country, built Bekand as his capital, and Dabosy as his castle, and planted the settlements of Núr, Kharcán, Fardánsa, Safina, Taráwjak, and Ayswánsa.   N.

After a time this Abrawy oppressed the people, and many of them, under a leader named Hamok=*Buzurg*=Great, emigrated to Turkistan, and there built the town of Hamokat; whilst the others, unable thus to escape from their toils, sought aid from the King of Turkistan, one Caráchorin Turk, surnamed *Byágho*=Great. He sent a vast army under his son, Sher Kishwar, who seized Abrawy in Bekand, and killing him by tossing in a sack of red felt, assumed the government of the country on the part of his father.

Sher Kishwar recalled the emigrants from Hamokat, and settled them on their former lands under their own Chiefs who were called Bukhár Khidát, because they were the original possessors of the country. He restored Bukhárá from the state of ruin to which it had fallen and improved the city, and planted the suburbs of Mástí, Mumástí, Sacmatín, Satmín and Farb.

After a reign of 20 years, he was succeeded by Iskajakt who built the towns of Rámetan, Darkhashi, and Sahrá. He received in marriage a daughter of the Emperor of China, and when she arrived at Bukhárá there came in the train of her dowry a costly idol temple resplendent in jewels, and the rarest gems which he caused to be set up at Rámetan with great ceremony and pomp.

Bukhárá at this period was a principal centre of the Zoroastrian religion, and abounded in temples for the worship of fire; whilst in the region adjoining to the east Hindoo Brahmanism flourished vigorously. The idol temple above referred to indicates the importation of a new element by the introduction of the Chinese Pantheon of mythology. Be this as it may, all three forms of worship were now shortly to be supplanted by a different religion which was pressing its way up through the passes to the south.

The Yuchi, the last Caucasian race that left the north central high land of Asia,   S.H.S.
on being pressed by the Mongolians or Huns from the north-east—about 200 B.C.— were driven from Shensi upon the Sai or Saka of Khutan and Káshghar, whom they, in turn, propelled forward to the west and south. One of these divisions from southern Tibet fell upon the Greek Bactrian State—90 B.C.—then ruled by Mithridates, and about the same time came into conflict with the Parthians whose King, Artaban, they slew. From Bactria they crossed the Paropamisus, and subdued another Greek sovereignty in Afghanistan, on the south side of the range, and passing onwards, formed a province of Sind; but, in an attempt to advance further eastward, they were routed and driven back by Vikramaditya, King of Avanti—56 B.C.

Following the repulse of the Scythians south of the passes, Khiu-tsiu-hi,   B.F.H.
recognized as the Hyrcodes of the coins—39-26 B.C.—King of the Kwai-tchang, or Gouchang, or Gushan, the strongest of the five tribes into which the Great Yuchi had divided, united the other four under his rule, and pushing across the mountains, conquered Cabul, Ariana, and Gandhára. His son, Hima Kadphises of the coins, continued the father's conquests, and subdued all India west of the Jamna, and ruled from 35 to 15 B.C. His son, the celebrated Kanishka, with his brothers, Hushka and Jushka, ruled over Kashmír for sixty years.

This Kanishka adopted the religion of Budha—which, though it had for three centuries before flourished in India, was only in the reign of Asoka—250B.C.— established as the State religion here—and became its ardent supporter, so that the new doctrine was rapidly spread throughout all the Tokhárí dominion. During his reign—15 B.C. to 45 A.D.—the third great Synod of Budhist clergy was held in Káshmír, and some of the finest *stupa* or "tope" in Kabul and the Panjab were erected.

In the fourth year of the reign of Mingti, second Emperor of the Han dynasty, the capital of which was established by his predecessor, Kwangwu, at Loyang or Honanfu, His Majesty saw in a vision the apparition of a resplendent figure entering

36.—Soldiers from Kuchar.

37.—Soldiers from Kashghar.

B.F.H.   his palace. A conclave of astrologers and priests was assembled to interpret the dream, and they unanimously referred the personage to Budha, of whom a golden image, as before mentioned, had already, 121 B.C., reached the country; and a mission was forthwith deputed to the Great Yuchi and to India for the purpose of studying the doctrine. The mission returned, after an absence of eleven years, with a number of Budhist priests and books. These last were translated about 76 A.D., and thus the doctrine of Budha, already firmly established in Tokháristán and the adjoining countries, was now fairly introduced into China. It was eagerly adopted, and spread rapidly, so that in Loyang alone there were in 350 A.D. forty-two richly embellished pagodas, besides others of inferior note.

The discipline of the monks, however, was yet very imperfect; a source of sorrow to the devout disciples of the great teacher, and a cause of trouble to those charged with the maintenance of public order. To remedy these evils, one of the former class, Chi Fah Hian, set out on a pilgrimage to India to study in its native seat the law of which he was an enthusiastic follower. About the same time the Emperor, Yao Hing, 397-415 A.D., sent an army to Koutche=Kúchá, a petty principality at the foot of the mountains, and to the north-west of Lake Lob, to fetch one Kumárajivá, a learned Indian priest residing there, to instruct the native priesthood in the right way.

P.   Kúchá, in early times, appears to have been the site of a large Budhist monastery. I have been informed of the existence there at the present day of very extensive ruins, originally built of great blocks of dressed and sculptured stone. A series of chambers or galleries is said to be excavated in a hill hard by, and their interior is described as decorated with a rich variety of paintings, remarkable alike for the superiority of their execution, and the freshness of their colours. Some figures, too, are mentioned as carved on the rocks in the vicinity, and numerous sculptured fragments are found about the ruins; whilst tales are told of the marvellous size and rare excellence of the gems that are occasionally picked up amongst the *debris*.

One of these, described as '*áin-ul-harr*, or " cat's eye," the size of a hen's egg, and of a lustre equal to that of a lamp in a dark room, is said to have been found here some years ago by a poor shepherd who was murdered for the possession of the gem through the instrumentality of a China merchant by whom the ill-gotten treasure was sold to the Emperor for a fabulous sum. The unscrupulous trader, however, as the story goes, did not long enjoy his wealth; for on his return journey homeward, to spend the rest of his days in the thus ill-purchased ease, he was overtaken by a whirlwind in the passage of the desert of Gobi, and overwhelmed in a storm of sand, amidst the wild cries, shouts, and jeering laughter of the evil spirits that haunt this dread region, and, by such convulsions of the elements they rule over, flourish upon the destruction of their victims.

B.F.H.   Fah Hian set out on his journey in 400 A.D., and passed from the frontier town of Chang Yeh in Kansu to Tun Wang, the Sachion of Marco Polo, in Tangut. From this he crossed the desert of Gobi to Shenshen in seventeen days, and thence in fifteen days, through the country of the Uighúr, he came to Khutan, where he arrived in deplorable plight, after experiencing inconceivable hardships and dangers from the difficulties of the roads and rivers. At Khutan he met an hospitable reception, and found a highly flourishing Budhist community, with ten thousand priests, many magnificent temples, commodious monasteries, and a general devotion to the rites of the religion.

With these two instances of Kúchá on the north and Khutan on the south, we may fairly understand that the Budha doctrine here found a congenial soil, took firm root, and made a rapid growth. It was not so, however, further to the east. Fah Hian returned from India by way of Ceylon and Java in 415 A.D., after an absence of fifteen years. A few years later, in 420 A.D., the Tsin dynasty was overthrown by that of the northern Wei Tartar, and during the first years of their rule Budhism was persecuted, and images and temples of the faith prohibited. These restrictions, however, were relaxed in 451 A.D., and one temple was allowed in each city, with permission for forty or fifty of its people to become priests. But they were placed under the special supervision of the police, since it had become a too frequent occurrence for criminals to assume the priestly garb in order to escape the punishment of their offences; and for agitators under its protecting cloak the more conveniently to prosecute their seditious schemes. The fresh impetus now acquired by the new doctrine aroused the hostility of the followers of the system of Confucius, which had been from of old the orthodox religion of the land, and many attempts were made to banish it; but, though persecuted and patronized by turns, Budhism continued slowly and steadily to spread throughout the Wei kingdom, and finally became established with an endurance commensurate with its very gradual growth. In 518 A.D. Tai Han, Empress Dowager of the Great Wei, commissioned Sung Yun, a native of Tan Wang in Little Tibet, to proceed to India for books of the Budha doctrine; and he returned after an absence of three years with 175 volumes. But the religion had at this time become corrupted by the use of charms and magic, an innovation that found favour mostly in the camps of the ignorant Tartar nomads, and the new importation effected apparently but little amelioration. B.F.H.

Consequently, about a century later, 629 A.D., in the reign of Tae Tsung, second Emperor of the Tang dynasty, 620 to 904 A.D., another celebrated pilgrim set out from China to seek the true and pure doctrine in India. This was Hiouen Thsang. He set out from Liang Cheu by the old caravan route through Khámil, Turfán, and Karáshahr to Aksú. Here he crossed the Múz-art="glacier pass" to Lake Isigh Kol, and thence went on to Taráz=Turkistán, and Shásh=Táshkand, Samarcand, and Balkh. From this he continued his way by Bámyán, and Lampáka=Lamghán or Lughmán into India, whence, after an absence of sixteen years, he returned to his home by the outward route of Fah Hian through Khutan.

Whilst the Budhist doctrine, already fast decaying in India, was thus working its way to a new growth in China, the Christian religion, as represented by the Nestorian Church, was steadily advancing across the continent from the west. The activity and zeal of the early missionaries had already carried the Word far eastwards, and, so early as the fifth and sixth centuries, they had established bishoprics at Herat, Marv, and Samarcand; later at Yarkand, and finally in China itself. That of Yarkand still flourished in 1260 A.D., or 1272 A.D., when Marco Polo visited the country, and probably fell at the same time as the bishopric of Almalik or Almáligh in 1339-40 A.D., under the bigoted zeal of the usurper 'Ali Sultan, as will be noted hereafter. Y.C.

The Chinese rule established over this region up to Bolor in 94 A.D., continued without interruption under Imperial Governors at the cities of Peshbalik or Beshbaligh ="The five towns," Karáshahr, Káshghar, and Khutan, until the decline of the Thang dynasty in the latter part of the ninth century when, owing to the internal divisions of the empire on the one hand, and the pressure of the conquering Arabs on the other, the border States of its distant western province gradually fell away, and became the possessions of petty local Chiefs who, to maintain the semblance of their assumed independence, preyed upon each other until they were in turn themselves swallowed up by more powerful enemies. P.

Khutan, however, favoured perhaps by its position, appears to have maintained a more continuous communication with China than the other States of this frontier province, and we read of Envoys with tribute going to the Imperial capital through successive centuries almost up to the period of the recovery of the ancient frontier of the empire.

In the reign of Wooti, of the Han dynasty, 140-87 B.C., Chinese officers were first sent to Khutan, whose King resided in the western town, called Changan, which contained 2,300 families, or 19,300 souls, and had an army of 2,400 men. R.K.

In the seventh year of Hian-ti, 202 A.D., Khutan sent caparisoned elephants as tribute. And in the following century, when China was divided into three

R.K. kingdoms, the States of Jounglou, Iumi, and Soule, which constituted Káshghar, belonged to Khutan.

In the ninth year of Wooti, of the Liang dynasty, 509 A.D., Envoys went with tribute to the Chinese capital, and in the annals of this reign, Khutan was then thus described:—"The people are Budhists, and their women are in society as amongst other nations. They (the women) braid the hair into long plaits, and wear pelisses and loose trowsers. The people are very ceremonious and polite, and curtsy on meeting by bending one knee to the ground. They write with pencils of wood, and carry

P. stone seals, and on receiving a letter raise it to the head before opening it." This description, it may be here noted, applies equally to the people of Khutan at the present day, excepting only that they are no longer Budhists, and with the addition that, when they have read their letters they invariably carry them in the folds of their turbans, or in their Tatar caps. Less than a century earlier than the above period, however, they received a very different character, and one, so far as morality is concerned, by no means inapplicable at the present day, from the officers of an expeditionary force that entered the country in pursuit of a fugitive rebel.

R.K. In the sixth year of Tae Wooti, of the north Wei dynasty, 445 A.D., an expedition was sent to punish the Tartars of Tangut. Their Prince, Mouliyan, fled to Khutan, and, coming into collision with its King, killed him. He was pursued, overtaken, and defeated at Yen-phing-pelan, whence he fled for refuge to the west of Khutan. The force it seems stayed here some time, and on their return the officers gave the following description of the country:—"The district of Khutan is very fertile in all sorts of grains, and abounds in mulberry and fruit trees. It possesses good horses, camels, and mules. According to the law of the country, murderers are punished by death, and other offenders according to the gravity of their crimes. For the rest the manners of the people—as the productions of the country—are analogous to those of the Koueitseu (the Kuisse or Uighúr). They are devoted Budhists, and have a great number of temples and religious towers for the service of which they support large establishments of priests. These people, however, know neither justice nor civility, and amongst them are many thieves, and adulterers, and other villainous reprobates."

In 518 A.D., amongst the tribute offerings sent from Khutan were *vases de verre*, and in the tribute of 541 A.D. was an image of Budha, carved in jade in some foreign country. In £32 A.D., the sixth year of the reign of Tae Tsung, Khutan sent as tribute a splendid jade zone, which the Emperor acknowledged with a special letter of thanks. The State at this period appears to have considerably extended its borders, for it is described as including the regions known under the Han dynasty as Jounglou, Kanmi (Khámil), Kiule (Kúrla), and Pichán. Its rivers were noted for their jade, which was discovered by its shining in the water at night. It was fished out by diving, after the subsidence of the floods produced by the melting of the snows on the mountains.

The description of the country in the annals of this reign goes on to say that the people were Budhists, ceremonious and polite, and distinguished as clever artificers. They were fond of music and dancing, and the enjoyments of life generally. In the deserts to the west was found a species of rat, the size of a hedgehog, which travelled in troops and yielded a gold coloured fur. This little animal, I may here note, has probably long since been exterminated by the fur hunters, for it is not now known in the country. The only animal approaching its description found there at the present day is the jerboa. There was neither silk here formerly nor the mulberry tree. Both were introduced by an Eastern Princess, who secreted their seeds in her bonnet when she went as bride to the King, who had long vainly sought to get possession of them by other means. The letters, literature, and laws of Khutan are derived from the Hindus, and their influence has been to civilize the people. The ancient name of Khutan is Kiusa-tan-na from the Sanskrit Kustana, which signifies "Pap of the world," in connection with the Hindu legend regarding the importation of the Brahma creed to this region. The other names under which Khutan appears in Chinese writings are Iuthian, Iu-tun, Iu-siun, Hou-an-na, Khiou-tan, and Hou-tan or Hotan.

In the reign of Kao-tsung, 650-655 A.D., an expedition under Assena Cheni against the Kouei-tseu of Beshbaligh terrified all the States on the western frontier, and Fou-che-siu, the King of Khutan, went in person to the capital with a tribute-offering of three hundred camels. He was well received and granted the title of "General of the Right," whilst his son was appointed "Commander of the Cavalry of the Right." After a detention of some months he was sent back to his government, but his son and younger brothers were detained as hostages at the Imperial Court.

In 665 A.D. the Koung-youei of Káshghar and the Tibetans made a joint attack on Khutan and Sitcheou, but the places were delivered from them by the aid of the "General of the Left," whose Government was most probably, I may here note, at Almáligh on the north of the Tian-shan range. About this period envoys with tribute were sent more frequently and regularly, and in 717 A.D., the fifth year of Yuan Sung, presented, amongst other native products, a wild camel "swift as the wind." In 760 A.D. the son of the King of Khutan, who was an officer in the Emperor's palace, was made administrator of his native country. And again in 780 A.D., the first year of Kian Chang, an officer of the palace was sent to Khutan for $iu=$"jade" ornaments. He made a great collection, and, loading the precious freight on camels, set out on his return, but was misled on the route, and plundered by his ruffianly Hoi-he guides. He himself managed to escape to Eu-cheu, where he died from the effects of the hardships endured on the journey. It was long after this period that these prized objects of art, hitherto only attainable by royalty and nobility, began to reach China as articles of commerce.

In 938 A.D., the third year of Kao-tsu, of the second Tsin dynasty, the King of Khutan, Li-ching-thian, sent with his tribute red salt, native gold, $li=$"yák" or wild ox tails, $iu=$jade, and cotton-cloth. The Emperor in return sent a high court official, Kao-khiu-hoei, to notify his confirmation in the Government of "the very precious" kingdom of Khutan. He journeyed by the Chachan route, found the King dressed in the Chinese fashion, and the religion Budhism. He noted that the country produced several good kinds of wine; that the people cultivated gardens and flowers; and that they ate rice cooked with honey. He observed, too, that there were many Tibetans in the country, and that they were always at hostility with the natives.

In 961 A.D. the Khutan tribute included jade and crystal; and ten years later an elephant captured in war against Káshghar; most likely, I may here note, in the war against Sultan Satoc Bughra Khan, King of Káshghar, the first notable convert to the doctrine of Muhammad in this region, and its most violent propagandist, as will appear further on. In 1081 A.D. the tribute from Khutan comprised pearls, coral, ivory, camphor, and mercury; all for the first time now sent, and indicating an increase of trade with India. Four years later, a live tiger, captured in the country, accompanied the tribute for the Emperor's acceptance; but as no body about the palace could be found to manage the savage brute, the offering was declined. Later, in 1406 A.D., during the Ming dynasty, Khutan, whose King was now entitled He-han=Kho-han=Khácán, sent Envoys with tribute; and in the annals of the reign, recording this fact, the country is described as a royal kingdom which, from the time of the Han dynasty to that of the Sung, has not ceased to be *en rapport* with China.

In 1420 A.D. Khutan, Haliei, and Patahechang=Badakhshán, sent horses as tribute. At this period such embassies from the extreme frontier States were of very frequent occurrence owing to the facilities they afforded for smuggling merchandize through the frontier Custom-Houses. Their real object, as a mere cloak for purposes of trade, was soon recognized by the Chinese Government, and, since the large number of foreigners entering the country in the train of the Envoys gave rise to

R.K. numerous disputes, and much inconvenience, orders were issued for placing them under severe restrictions; and the operation of these regulations soon led to their discontinuance.

Towards the close of the Youan dynasty, about the middle of the fourteenth century, the country was disturbed by anarchy, and the trade route remained closed till the restoration of order in the beginning of the following century, when trade again flowed in the old channels. It was the re-opening of the commercial intercourse which had been closed for half a century, and the insecurity attending the journey by caravan at first, that led to the device of the trading embassies abovementioned.

I have introduced the preceding notes on the history of Khutan, as furnished by Chinese records, because they serve in some measure to dispel the general obscurity that veils the course of events in this region during the long period of its rule under the Chinese Governors, and, subsequently, under the petty independent Princes who had thrown off their subjection to that Empire; and because they help to elucidate and confirm the later history of the region, which only begins to clear up on the arrival of the Arabs in the fertile and populous valley of the Oxus, when the chain of events becomes more connected with the succeeding establishment of their rule and religion there.

The astonishing successes of these wild sons of the desert in their conquering career through Persia were hardly more wonderful than the rapid domination of their arms, and its concurrent supremacy of creed in the very heart of Asia. So early as the 53rd year of the *Hijra*=673 A.D., the Khálif M'uáwya sent forward his General, 'Abdulla Ziyád, to the conquest of Khurásán, which at that period included Bukhárá, notwithstanding its position beyond the Oxus, the recognized ancient limit of the province.

N. The city of Bukhárá, which in ancient times was known by the names of Namajkat, and Barmaskat, and Cuhnduz, was at this period in the hands of a Turk Prince called Baydon, and entitled Bukhár-Khidát. He died about the time of the appearance of the Arabs on the borders of Khurásán, and was succeeded in the Government by his widow, the Queen Kháton, who reigned fifteen years during the infancy of her son Tughsháda. She was celebrated alike for her beauty, wealth, and talents, and, as history records, for her amours. Her rule was popular, her Court magnificent, and her wealth prodigious. She is described as daily riding out from her palace to her Court in the Registán, forenoon and afternoon, attended by a gorgeous retinue of slave-girls and eunuchs, for the transaction of public business, the dispatch of justice, and the distribution of rewards and punishments. In the interval between the two sessions she retired to her palace, whence long files of servants presently issued with trays of food and delicacies for the refection of her courtiers. The royal guard at the Court comprised a choice band of two hundred noble youths, all richly clad and fully armed, who came in rotation daily from the townships around, so that it fell to the lot of each to attend the Court on this duty four times in the year.

It was during the reign of this Queen that the Arabs first crossed the Jyhon or Oxus. The rapid approach of 'Abdulla Ziyád with his terrible warriors filled the people with apprehension and alarm. Queen Kháton sent off messengers in hot haste for aid from Turkistan, north and east, and meanwhile sought to keep off the invader by rich gifts and sweet words. Her summoned allies arrived opportunely, and at once fell upon the enemy, who was already in the suburbs of the capital spreading fire and sword amongst the unwarlike and terrified farmers. The Arabs were now vastly outnumbered by the hosts of their assailants, but the impetuous fury of their warriors counterbalanced the paucity of numbers, and the Turk army in this their first encounter with the soldiers of the west received an unexpected check, and defeat.

'Abdulla captured Bekand and Rámetan, and then set siege to Bukhárá. The Queen, who had escaped from the battle field with the loss of a richly bejewelled boot, valued at 10,000 *diram*, fortified herself in the citadel, whilst her allies from without pressing around, the Arab Commander was content to retire on payment of a million *diram*, and recrossed the Oxus, carrying away with him 4,000 captives.

For his failure at Bukhárá, 'Abdulla Ziyád was removed from the command in Khurásán in 56 H.=676 A.D., and Sáíd bin Uthmán appointed in his place. He immediately renewed the campaign against Bukhárá. Again her allies rallied round the Queen with a host of 120,000 men collected from all Turkistan and Káshghar, but, in their first encounter with the Arabs, they were seized with a panic and dispersed in confusion. The Queen offered to buy off the invader with most liberal terms, but S'aíd left the money in her keeping for safe custody till his return from Saghd, whither his victorious troops were pursuing the fugitives to Samarcand, and meanwhile took eighty hostages as security. Amongst these, the historian records, Queen Kháton got rid of some obnoxious nobles who had spoken disparagingly with reference to her familiarity with one of the late King's domestics, and had threatened to oust the bastard Tughsháda in favour of a legitimate Prince. S'aíd, on his return from Samarcand, and departure for Khurásán, carried these hostages away with him, together with a thousand other captives taken in the war. They were ultimately taken to Medina, and there set to till the land as slaves, but, rising in rebellion, they killed S'aíd, and were themselves slain in revenge.

M'uáwya was succeeded as Khálif by his son Yazíd. He appointed Muslim bin Ziyád Viceroy of Khurásán, and he at once proceeded with vigour to prosecute the war across the Oxus. On this Queen Kháton sent her agents abroad to summon her allies, and by way of determining the hesitation of Tarkhon, the Prince of Saghd, who had so severely suffered at the hands of S'aíd, sent him a proposal to share her bed, and the government of the country, on conditions that he came and drove back the Arabs. Tempted by the offer, he joined the army coming from Turkistán under Bandon, the *Malik* or Prince of that country, and with it camped on the Kharcám Rud River in the vicinity of the city. But the Queen in the interim had opened the gates to Muslim, and submitting herself to him secured, by the grant to him of the favours she had offered to others, a measure of leniency for her followers and subjects that excited surpise, and brought no little ridicule upon the rough Arabian soldier's susceptibility to the charms of the sex. The allies, however, disapproving the Queen's conduct, attacked the Arabs with all their force, but were discomfited with the loss of 400 slain, and their leader, Malik Bandon, amongst the number. They rallied, however, under Malik Tarkhon, and renewed hostilities till the invaders, finding it unsafe to remain longer without support, were content to exact a profession of *Islám*, and a heavy indemnity; on the payment of which they again retired across the Oxus.

Following this Kutaiba bin Muslim was appointed Viceroy of Khurásán. He continued the war against Bukhárá, and conquered all Tokháristán. He crossed the Oxus in 88H.=707 A.D. to Bekand, which he took after a siege of fifty-days, and, leaving a garrison under Warca to hold it, marched on towards the capital. The Arabs left behind, following the example of their commandant, who had laid violent hands on the two beautiful daughters of one of the most influential Chiefs of the place, worried the citizens so by their lawlessness that they rose in revolt, and slew Warca and many of his men. On hearing of this Kutaiba hastened back, and took a summary vengeance by a general massacre of all those capable of bearing arms, and the plunder and destruction of all their temples. He sacked the town, and levelled its walls, and, finally, carried off the survivors captive in his army, amongst the soldiery of which they were distributed.

At the time of this destruction of Bekand many of its most wealthy merchants and other heads of families were absent on their trading business at Káshghar and the cities on the Chinese frontier; and when they returned, they sought out and ransomed their families, their wives, and their daughters from the Arab captors, and rebuilt their ancient town upon its ruins. The circumstance is noted as a remarkable occurrence, owing to the rapidity with which a town of such extent, and so thoroughly

N. destroyed, was restored to its former comfort and prosperity; and, whilst it is certainly indicative of the persevering industry and enterprise of the people, suggests the possession of wealth and the existence of an extensive and profitable trade with China.

In the plunder of this prosperous commercial town Kutaiba took a vast store of gold and silver, and, amongst other valuables, two rare pearls, each the size of a pigeon's egg, found in one of the idol temples. These last he sent as an offering to Hajáj with the letter announcing his victory. The Khálif in acknowledgment gracefully expressed his astonishment more at the rarity of his General's honesty than of his precious offering.

After the destruction of Bekand, the Arabs successively reduced Khabnon, Fáráb, and Wardána; and then Kutaiba found himself surrounded, and cut off from communication with Khurásán, by the numerous armies pouring in from the east and north to the aid of Bukhárá. Amongst the leaders of these troops were Malik Tarkhon of Saghd, the Jand Khidát, and the Wardána Khidát, and Malik Gormughánon, Turk, who was sister's son of the *Faghfur* = Emperor of China.

Kutaiba was thus hemmed in for four months, and was finally extricated from his difficulty by the address of one of his councillors—the *Maula* Hayán Nabti, who opened a communication with Tarkhon, and so artfully played upon his fears, by representing in exaggerated terms the dangers that threatened him from the vast numbers of his foreign allies, that he soon succeeded in obtaining from him a nominal tender of submission with the payment of 2,000 *diram* as tribute, and thus effected a dissolution of the Turk confederation. The allies, finding that Tarkhon had retired from the field, broke from each other, and retraced their steps to their respective countries, plundering all the way; and the Arabs, thus set free, marched upon Bukhárá, where they levied a heavy indemnity, and then returned across the Oxus to Marv.

Kutaiba made four successive campaigns against Bukhárá, with whose deposed Queen he carried on an amour, that has supplied the historians of the time with many amusing anecdotes. His last campaign was in 94H. = 712 A.D., when he established Tughsháda in the government, and fixed the yearly tribute at 40,000 *diram* for the Khálif, and 10,000 *diram* for the Amír of Khurásán. At this time, too, owing to the habitual relapsing of the people from the newly enforced faith to their old idolatary, he distributed his Arabs amongst the citizens—one in each household—the more effectually to convert the people by example and to teach them the rites and doctrines of the new religion. He ordered also that they should share equally with the family in food and raiment, to be supplied free of cost at the expense of the town. These measures proved extremely distasteful to the citizens, who naturally at first opposed them; but the force of summary and severe examples speedily cowed them to submission, though 700 families of a sect called Kashkasha, who are described as a wealthy mercantile community, abandoned their dwellings in the city, and formed a settlement of huts outside its walls. These in the course of years grew into a suburb called afterwards *Kosh Mughan* = "Dwelling of fire-worhippers." It is probable, I may here note, that these Kashkasha (query *Kashisha* = Christian priest) were Christians, and not, as the name afterwards given to their settlement would imply, Zoroastrians, because in this last campaign Kutaiba destroyed every emblem of idolatry in the place, and on the site of the great idol temple built the Jumá Masjid or Friday Mosque, whilst he suppressed any outward signs of adherence to idolatry by the only arguments known to *Islam,* by death or tribute.

V. B. In the year following this settlement of Bukhárá, Kutaiba invaded the province of Farghána, and thence crossing the Tirik Dawán or "Sweating Pass" into Káshghar—at that time occupied by the Uighúr—ran his expedition as far as Turfán on the Chinese frontier of Kánsuh. Here he received intelligence of the death of the Khálif Walíd, and consequently, retracing his steps, returned to Marv where he was killed in a plot by his enemies at the end of 98H. = 716A.D., aged 47 years.

The new convert Tughshada, who was appointed Bukhár-Khidát by Kutaiba, in gratitude for the favour, named his first born son after his patron. This Kutaiba bin Tughshada was in after years executed at Samarcand by Abú Muslim, in the time of Nasr bin Sayyár, the Viceroy of Khurásán, for apostacy and rebellion in joining the insurrection of the Shía against the Sunni, which marked the early rivalry of these great Muhammadan sects in the early period of their progress here. And ten years later, Tughshada himself, who had always been but a doubtful convert, was assassinated at the instigation of the same Abú Muslim in the presence of Nasr, who was at that time at Samarcand; and the historian records that his servants coming in cut the flesh from the body and carried away the bones to Bukhárá. Nasr Sayyár, at this period, subjugated Farghána, and pushed an expedition across the pass into Káshghar, but without any more stable result than a useful reconnoissance of the country.

Tughshada, at the time of his death, had reigned 32 years, and was succeeded in the government of Bukhárá by his second son, Sukán, who was assassinated in his palace at Farakhsha by his Arab Wazír on account of his relapse to idolatry and drunken habits. His brother, Banyát, then became Bukhár-Khidát. He joined the rebellion of the *Sufed Jamahgán*="White clads," the followers of the "Veiled Prophet" or Mucanna, in the time of the Khálif Mahdi, and was captured and slain in his palace at Warkhshi in 166 H.=782 A.D.

In that year Abúl 'Abbás was appointed Viceroy of Khurásán by the Khálif Mahdi, the father of the famous Harún Arrashid. He held his Court at the then capital of the province—Marv, and received many complaints of the frequent inroads of the pagan Turk upon the Saghd and Bukhárá lands. They had recently raided Sámdún and carried off many of its people into slavery, and a deputation of the Chiefs consequently went to Marv to represent their grievance and seek protection. Abúl 'Abbás consulted them as to the best means of providing against the evil, and on the suggestion of Yazíd bin Ghorak, Malik of Saghd, who said that an ancient Princess of the country had protected her territories from such inroads by a great barrier wall built along the frontier, gave orders for the construction all along the frontier of a defensive wall, with a gate and turret at every half mile. The wall was at once commenced by Amir Muhtahid bin Hamadi, the Governor of Bukhárá, and was finished in 215 H.=830 A.D., when Amir Muhammad bin Mansúr was the Governor. It was maintained in repair by the labour of the people till the time of the Amir Ismáíl Sámání, who relieved them of the burthen, and the wall then soon fell to neglect and decay.

After the death of Banyát the government of Bukhárá fell to the hands of successive members of the family. The last of the Bukhár-Khidát was Abú Ishák, bin Ibráhim, bin Khálid, bin Banyát, from whom the government passed into the hands of the Sámání family.

The founder of this great family was a Zoroastrian of the village of Sámán, and traced his descent from the celebrated Bahrám Chobín. He had been ousted from the government of Balkh, and sought redress at the hands of the Viceroy of Khurásán, Asad bin 'Abdulla. He restored him to the government on his professing *Islám*, and the Sámání, in proof of his sincerity and gratitude, named his first son after his patron and friend. This Asad had four sons, *viz.*, Núh, Ahmad, Yahyá, and Ilyás, who all subsequently took prominent positions in the government.

When Rafí bin Laith of Sístán seized Samarcand, Hárún Arrashíd sent Harithma bin Ayán with an army against him. He failed, however, to recover the city, and Mámún—at this time joining Hárún in Khurásán—called on the sons of Asad to aid his General. They in consequence intervened, and effected a settlement between Rafí and Harithma, and thus pacified Hárún, who feared the loss of all Khurásán.

Shortly after this Hárún died at Tús=Mashhad, and Mámún succeeded as Khálif. He appointed 'Asá bin 'Ubád Viceroy of Khurásán, and bid him provide for the sons of Asad in reward for their good service. Accordingly Núh was made

38.—Soldiers—Kashgaris.

39.—Soldiers from Kuchar, Aksu and Khoten.

N. Governor of Samarcand, Ahmad of Farghána, Yahya of Táshkand, and Ilyás of Herat. On the death of Núh in 192 H.=807 A.D., Ahmad succeeded to the Government of Samarcand, and on his death, 250 H.=864 A.D., his son, Nasr, succeeded, and, on the first of *Ramazán* in the following year, was appointed Viceroy of the newly-constituted province of Máwaránahar, or Transoxiana, by the Khalif Wáthic Billah.

In the revolt of Yakúb bin Laith of Sístán, Nasr, aided by his younger brother, Ismáíl, recovered Bukhárá from the rebel, and in Ramazán 260 H.=873 A.D. appointed him its Governor. By this victory Nasr established his authority over all Turkistán, and in the same year received, from the Khálif Muwaffic Billah, a new patent, appointing him Viceroy of Máwaránahar, from the Jyhon or Oxus to Acsá-i-Bilád-i-Mashric or "The extreme cities of the East."

The two brothers after this quarrelled, and each had the *Khutba*="Friday prayer for the reigning family," read in his own name, and Ismáíl further withheld the revenue of 50,000 *diram* due yearly from Bukhárá. On this Nasr at Samarcand summoned his brothers from Farghána and Táshkand with their troops and Turk levies, and marched against Bukhárá in *Rajab* 272 H.=winter of 885-6 A.D., but, before coming into collision, they were reconciled by Harithma, who had crossed the Oxus on the ice to the aid of Ismáíl, and now persuaded them all to return to their respective Governments; a step they were the more ready to adopt on account of the severe losses they had experienced in men and cattle from the intense cold and scarcity of supplies.

Three years later, however, the brothers again broke into hostilities, and Nasr, marching against Bukhárá, was met and defeated by Ismáíl at Dih Wárz on Tuesday, 15th *Jamádi Akhir* 275 H.=888 A.D. On this occasion Nasr fell into the hands of Ismáíl who, treating him with an unlooked-for deference and respect, begged his speedy return to his own Government, lest the people hearing of his disaster should rise in revolt against him. Nasr lauded his brother's magnanimity in tears, and avowing that he had expelled from his heart all feeling of animosity against him, hastened back to Samarcand, where he died four years later.

Ismáíl now advanced and took possession of Samarcand, and from that as a base prosecuted a *ghazát*="crescentade" on the Turk frontier. In 280 H.=893 A.D. he captured and annexed Taráz=Turkistán, a populous and wealthy frontier city that had long been frequented as a mart of exchange by Turk, Christian, Muhammadan, and Chinese merchants, and, exacting a general profession of Islám converted its great *Kalisiya*="Christian Church" into a "Friday Mosque," in which he had the *khutba* read in the name of the Khalif M'utasid Billah, and finally returned to Bukhárá laden with a rich plunder. Whilst he was engaged in this "meritorious" war for the difflusion of Islám, Ismáíl, in *Muharram* 280 H., received a patent from the Khálif confirming him as Viceroy in succession to Nasr. Its arrival was opportune, and stimulated the Muslims to the successes above indicated, and to less successful efforts to force the creed across the passes to the eastward; in which direction the way for the Faith was prepared by the persuasive eloquence of their merchant Missionaries years before its forcible establishment at the point of the sword.

Seven years of active religious propagandism on the Turkistán frontiers had elapsed, when Ismáíl, who during this period had acquired an undefined sort of authority over the States of Káshghar, was involved in the war against 'Umro Laith, whom, after a short and decisive campaign, he captured at Balkh, 288 H.=901 A.D., and two years later sent prisoner to Baghdad. For this service he received from the Khalif M'utasid Billah a fresh patent of sovereignty over the countries of Khurásán to the frontiers of Sind and Hind, and Máwaránahar and Turkistán. Following this he prosecuted a campaign in Tabaristán, and annexing the province returned to Bukhárá, 291 H.=903-4 A.D., the sovereign of an empire that extended from Ray, Cazwín, Ispahan, and Shiráz on the west to the vallies of the Tián-shán on the east, and from the borders of the great desert on the north to the Persian Gulf on the south.

Ismail Sámání was a just and firm ruler, and, though a sincere Muhammadan, a liberal patron of his native literature; and during his reign the Persian language was revived in its former purity, after two centuries of suppression by the Arabs. After a prosperous and glorious rule of thirty years, the last eight as Viceroy of Khurásán and Máwaránahar, he sickened, and died at Zarmán, whither he had been carried for change of air, on the 15th *Safar* 295 H.=907 A.D. He is known in history as the Amír Mází=past Prince. His son, Ahmad, succeeded to the throne. He subdued a revolt in Sístán, and on his return, whilst on a hunting excursion on the banks of the Jyhon, received intelligence of the revolt of Tabaristán. The news so disturbed his mind that it disarmed his usual precaution, and the tiger, habitually chained at the entrance to his chamber as a guard at night, was on this occasion forgotten; and his slaves, seizing the opportunity, entered and beheaded him, at the instigation of one of his own family, on Thursday, 11th *Jamadi Akhir* 301 H.= 913-4 A.D. He reigned six years and four months, and is called Amír Shahíd= martyr Prince.

Abúl Hasan Nasr, his son, succeeded at the age of ten years. His reign was disturbed by revolts in the western provinces, and noted for a conflagration at the capital, which lasted three days, *Rajab* 325 H.=936 A.D., and was seen at Samarcand. The greater part of the city was destroyed, together with the palace, full of treasures and rarities of art, which all perished in the flames. Bukhárá has never since, it is said, recovered its former magnificence. Abúl Hasan Nasr died after a reign of thirty-one years in *Shabán* 331 H.=942 A.D. He is called Amír Sáíd =prosperous Prince. His son, Núh, succeeded. His reign was disturbed by anarchy, and a serious revolt at Marv. Order was not restored till 341 H.=952 A.D., and he died, having reigned twelve years, a couple of years later in *Rabí Akhir* 343 H. He is called Amír Hamíd=laudable Prince.

He was succeeded by his son, 'Abdul Malik, aged ten years, who reigned seven, and was killed by a fall from horseback at the game *Chaugán*="hockey" in *Shawál* 350 H.=961 A.D. He is called Amír Rashíd=intelligent Prince.

His brother, Mansúr, succeeded, but was at first opposed by Ulaptakin, the Governor of Níshábor, who seized Balkh. He relinquished this "material guarantee," however, and consented to the succession, on the tribute of 50,000 *diram* being paid, as before, to Nishábor. Mansúr, on the other hand, subsequently exacted from the Dailami or Dilami Chief of Fars and Irác a similar annual tribute. He died after a disturbed reign of fifteen years and five months on Sunday, the 16th *Muharram* 365 H.=976 A.D., and is called Amír Shadíd=impetuous Prince.

His son, Núh, called Amír Sàíd Abúl Kásim, succeeded. His reign was characterised by general anarchy and confusion. The border province revolted, and the Samání power quickly declined. Abú Alí Samchor, the Governor of Khurásán, revolted, and joining with Faik, the deposed Governor of Herat and Balkh, invited Bughra Khán, Chief of the Uighúr Tartár of Káshghar, to attack Bukhárá. This he did, and, driving Abúl Kásim out, took possession of his capital. He did not long enjoy his success, however, for he almost immediately sickened with a fever, and, hastening to regain his native air, died a few stages out from the city. His army retraced its steps to Farghana and Káshghar, and Abúl Kásim on its departure returned to his capital, and, recovering his power, drove his refractory nobles out of the country into Khurásán. Here they raised a strong party, and, securing the aid of the Dilami Prince, renewed their hostility. Abúl Kásim, on this, unable alone to cope with their combined forces, called to his aid Subuktakin, the newly established independent Prince of Ghazni, and with him attacked and routed the rebels at Herat. After this Abúl Kásim was forced once more to seek the aid of Subuktakin against a threatened attack by the rising Iylik Khan, son of Bughra Khan, at the instigation of the restless Faik. On this occasion the threatened

N. invasion was staved off, and Faik provided for by the Government of Samarcand. Peace did not long endure, for on the death of Abúl Kásim a contested succession, and intestine broils soon led to the division of the Sámáni empire, or what remained of it, between the two great Tartar Chiefs of the time, between Mahmúd, the son of Subuktakin of Ghazni, and Iylik Khan, the son of Bughra Khan of Kashghar. The latter, who had extended his possessions to Khiva or Khwáhrizm, now seized Bukhárá, and taking prisoner Abdul Malik, the last reigning Prince of the Sámáni dynasty, sent him to his capital at Organj, where he died.

P. It will be seen by the preceding sketch of the history of the Muhammadan power during the first three centuries of its rule in Máwaránahar, that it from the very commencement, notwithstanding the opposition the Arabs here experienced, and the check the rapid progress of their arms through Persia here received, made its weight felt upon the independent States of Turkistan to the north and east; and thus acquired a steadily growing influence, which aided, as it materially was, through the channels of trade, in after times facilitated the spread of the faith and rule over those wide regions, whence the former ultimately penetrated to, and took root in the furthest limits of the Chinese Empire; where it has so flourished that in our own day we find it aspiring to seize the supreme control of the Government, and the sovereignty of the country, a struggle that is still proceeding at this day.

The first expedition of Kutaiba along the southern skirts of the Allah Tágh, or Tianshán, or Tangrí Ula, or God Mountains, as they are called in Arabic, Chinese, Mongol, and English respectively, the "Celestial Mountains" of European Orientalists, up to Turfán, opened the way to Islám; and the next expedition of Nasr bin Sayyár kept it so, till, in the time of the native Sámáni rule, the relations thus commenced were naturally more freely extended and improved, and presently, 260 H. = 873 A.D., led to the subjugation of the country in the reign of Nasr, the first Prince of that dynasty, which on the decline of the Khiláfat or Khálifat rose to divide the Persian soil with the Dilami.

The nature of this subjugation, however, appears to have been more nominal than real, and, in the absence of an absolute authority, the creed made but little general progress against the quiet and resolute opposition of the Budhists and Christians; and this even in the cities where its forcible profession was more easy of accomplishment; whilst in the rural districts and nomad camps it found no footing whatever.

We find, indeed, that Islám was not even nominally established in the country till nearly the last quarter of the next century, when a Prince of the hereditary ruling family of Bughra Khan at Káshghar, becoming a convert to the faith, enforced it upon his subjects at the point of the sword, in the face of a determined and protracted opposition which prevented its spread beyond the limits of his own territory and immediate authority. It was only now, on the downfall of the Sámáni dynasty, that Islám, through the proselitizing zeal of the successors of that family—of Mahmúd in the direction of Hindustan, and of Iylik Khan in the direction of Turkistan—received a fresh impetus, and was extended south, east, and north with a rapidity only equalled by the violence employed, and with an endurance not less remarkable.

T.B.K. The account of the first introduction of this religion into Káshghar, as given in the *Tazkira Bughra Khan*, which is a history of the Islamite martyrs and saints in this country translated into Uighúr Turki from the original Persian by Shekh Attar, is an absurdly distorted figment of the preisthood built upon a foundation of fact. The eighth chapter of this book is devoted to the history of Abú Nasr Sámáni, at whose hands, it is said, the Prince above alluded to was converted; and as its style is characteristic, I here introduce a summarized version of it.

"Abú Nasr Sámáni was a very devout and holy man, and versed in all sorts of kingly knowledge. He was virtuous and gentle, and a strict *Musalman*, who never diverged from the way of the law of the Prophet. He was a merchant, and devoted all the profits of his trade to charity amongst the Musalmáns, of whom he fed and clothed the destitute and homeless. One day he purposed starting on a journey to replenish his funds and extend the sphere of his charities, but the Prophet came to him in a vision, and bid him postpone his departure till such time as he should appoint, when he would also indicate the direction he should take. Abú Nasr, greatly rejoiced and highly honored by the Prophet's favour, abandoned his proposed journey, and for six years devoted himself to the service of God and the performance of religious exercises. At the end of this time the Prophet again appeared before him, and bid him prepare for a journey to Turkistán, where was a chosen servant of God, one Sátuk Bughra Khan, who would convert the people to Islám. Abú Nasr, again, for six years devoted himself to the rigid worship of God, and was aided, comforted, and supported by the pure spirit of the Prophet who, at the end of this time, once more visited him in a trance, and giving him his blessing bid him rise, and depart for Turkistan.

Abú Nasr took his son, Khwajah Abúl Fattáh, and set out on his way, and, going from city to city, arrived at Andiján. Everywhere he asked for Sátuk Bughra Khan, and at last a certain person informed him that a youth of that name resided at Káshghar, and was notorious on account of his wisdom, for, though as yet but a mere child, none of the elders and wise men could controvert his speech.

From Andijan Abú Nasr set out with a caravan of three hundred merchants, and after some days arrived at Káshghar, where he found the object of his search, and, after a short conversation, brought him into the fold of Islám.

Abú Nasr devoted ten years to the instruction and conversion of Sátuk, and in this period made seven thousand of the people Musalmans, and taught seventy of them to be priests. He lived eighty years, and followed the teachings of the "Commander of the Faithful" Abúbakar Sadíc, and attained to the dignity of *Uwais*, which is a spiritual quality inferior to that of Prophet, but superior to that of Saint. He also towards the end of his life attained to the rare quality of *Cutub*, and became endowed with all knowledge both visible and invisible, temporal and spiritual. The number of this special rank is limited to forty at any one time throughout the world.

Shekh Najmuddin Attár was the first to discover that Abú Nasr had attained this exalted dignity. The new *Cutub* now retired from the world, and spent six months in seclusion as an ascetic. At length one day *Cábiz-ul-arwáh* = "the seizer of souls," that is the angel Isráíl, appeared and bid him restore his soul to God. "Take me," said Abú Nasr, "My wish is to go to God. I have no business with this earthly frame." He drew his mantle over him, and, stretching his legs out straight, faced towards Mecca. His servants, surprised at the unusual attitude, drew near, and, finding him dead, broke into loud wails and sore laments. They informed his son, Abúl Fattáh, and his adopted child, Sátuk Bughra Khan, and they all assembled, and mourned over the corpse. A disciple asked of Sátuk, who was to wash the body. He replied "the body itself knows." That disciple knelt by the corpse, and repeated the question. And a voice from its chest said "let Najmuddin, with my sons, wash me." They accordingly washed and laid out the body, and buried it at Mashhad in Artosh 350 H. = 960 A.D. The funeral was attended by 10,700 common people, and the prayers were recited by 5,000 dervishes and ascetics."

Such are the most noteworthy points in the history of Abú Nasr Sámání, as given in this eighth chapter of the book above mentioned. The following chapter gives the history of Hazrat Sultan Satuk Bughra Khan Ghazí, and may be summarized in this wise :—

"Hazrat Sultan Satuk Bughra Khan Ghazi was born in 333 H. = 944 A.D. At the age of twelve years he accepted Islam, and was the first convert in Turkistan. On the day of his birth, though it was midwinter, the earth quaked, and springs burst forth and flowed on the surface of the ground; flowers bloomed and trees budded. The wise men and elders were concerned at these signs of commotion in nature, and predicted the destruction of their religion by the new-born Prince, and the establishment of Islam in place of their ancient native institutions. They consequently

40.—Players on Longhorn and Mir-i-Shub.

41.—Musicians of Yarkund.

T.B.K. sought to kill him. The infant's mother bid them wait till he grew up, and then to kill him if he turned Musalmán.

Sátuk was six years old when his father, Tangri Kadír Bughra Khan, died (during an expedition against Bukhárá). His widowed mother and himself then passed to the protection of Harún Bughra Khan, the surviving brother and successor to the throne. He educated his nephew as an idolator till he was twelve years old. At this time Satuk, with forty attendants, one day went out a hunting. A hare started from under a thorny bush, and Sátuk, bow in hand, giving chase, got separated from the others. The hare now suddenly stopped, and assumed the form of a man, and thus addressed the youth :—"Come, my son! I am waiting for you. God be praised! I have found you alone. Come nigh me. I have a few words to say. Dismount." Satuk, amazed at what he saw and heard, dismounted, and knelt before the figure, which speaking, said, "My son! Why continue in such idolatry? You know that your Creator's name is Muhammad. Walk in his way."

Sátuk considered within himself "What man is this who speaks thus? There is no such person here. Where does he come from?" Wondering in this fashion he turned to the figure and said, "What have you been saying to me? Oh venerable sage!" The figure replied, "My son! Oh blessed youth! I wish not your tender body in hell fire. The thought grieves me." Sátuk enquiring asked, "Oh venerable sage! What sort of place is hell?" And the sage replied, "My child! Hell is a place of much fire, and full of scorpions, where unbelievers and sinners are consigned, and tortured in all manners of ways."

Fear seized the heart of Sátuk, and he said, "Speak! Venerable sage! I will repeat what you say." The sage pronounced the form of creed, "there is no God but God, and Mahomed is the prophet of God." Sátuk in return asked, "What are these words, and what do they mean?" The sage, in answer, said, "My son! Repeating these words you become a Musalmán, and go to Paradise, where are beautiful maids and youths, and wine. Refusing them you go to hell, and suffer all its terrible torments." Sátuk thereupon repeated the creed, and accepted Islám. The sage then informed him that there was much to learn as he grew up, and that his teacher would shortly arrive and conduct him into the perfect way. Some say that this sage was *Dajál-ul-ghaib Khoja Zinda*, the *Wazír* or Minister of Iskandar Pádsháh, and others that he was an angel; but the truth is, he was the prophet Khizr. And he suddenly vanished from the sight of the bewildered Sátuk, who was now rejoined by his attendants, from whom he kept the occurrence secret.

Some days later Sátuk again went a hunting with his forty attendants to the Uston Artosh or "Upper Artosh," and at Búcú found a caravan of well clad and highly favoured foreigners camped on the meadow. He drew near to see who they were, and one of their party, followed by a few attendants, came forward to meet him. This was Abú Nasr who, at once recognizing the object of his search, turned to his followers, and, praising God, told them that the sole purpose of his journey was to meet this noble youth, and that now the whole desire of his heart was accomplished. He bid them open their loads and bring out some offerings worthy the acceptance of the illustrious Prince. In the midst of this was heard the sonorous chaunt of the '*azán* or Muhammadan "call to prayer." The boxes and loads were instantly left open as they happened to be, and the strangers assembled round a leader to perform their devotions. Abú Nasr, on their conclusion, returned to Sátuk, whom he found dismounted, and standing lost in mute amazement. He approached and gave him the *salám*, and then, respectfully embracing the noble youth, invited him to his tent, where he presented some rarities as an offering of good-will.

Sátuk accepted the presents, and asked the donor's name. On hearing it he at once knew him as "the teacher" the prophet Khizr had spoken of, and he straightway sought an explanation of the extraordinary and impressive sight he had witnessed; asking what was the meaning of the prayers and genuflexions, and adorations which the whole company, leaving their property open and unguarded in a strange place and foreign country, had assembled to perform together.

Abú Nasr, in reply, briefly explained the tenets and ordinances of Islám. He then described this world as transitory, man as a frail being, riches as his bane, and infidelity as the cause of his ruin. He expatiated on the delights and pleasures of Paradise, and enlarged in comparison therewith upon the pains and torments of Hell. The one, he told his listener, was the reward of the Faithful who performed their five daily prayers; the other, he warned him, was the punishment of the Infidel, who neglected these prayers.

Sátuk was gravely impressed by the speaker's words and earnest manner. A solemn awe took possession of his mind, and he wished forthwith to be of the Faithful. Abú Nasr bid him repeat the creed after himself. He did so, and straightway became a Musalmán. "Who is Muhammad?" then enquired Sátuk. "He is the friend of God, and the guide to all people in the right way to eternity," replied Abú Nasr. "He saves them from Hell, obtains God's pardon for their sins, and secures their entry into Paradise." Sátuk was next taught the doctrines of the faith, and then, in the first promptings of his zeal for it, summoned his forty attendants, and invited them to follow his example and become Musalmáns. Some did so of their free-will, and others through fear of Sátuk's sword; but that same day they all accepted Islám, and became Musalmán, and, returned to the palace, agreed to conceal the fact for fear of the revenge of the infidels.

During six months Sátuk and his forty, stealthily by night, used to visit Abú Nasr, and from him learn the Kurán, the prayers, and the ordinances of the religion, and to worship God according to the law of Muhammad. At this time Hárún Bughra Khan was troubled in mind by a dream he saw, in which he was seized and worried by a tiger cub. He assembled his wise men, priests, astrologers, and nobles, and consulted them as to its interpretation. They unanimously referred it to the apostacy of the King's nephew, and agreed on the necessity of killing him before he destroyed them and their religion.

The mother of Sátuk here interposed, and demanded that her son should first be put to the proof, and if, as suspected, he turned out to be a Musalmán, she would not oppose his execution. Her claim was acceded to as a just one, and it was decided to test the sincerity and loyalty of Sátuk by inviting him to lay the foundation of an idol temple they were about to build. Sátuk, warned of this, consulted Abú Nasr as to how he should escape the difficulty before him. His teacher bid him be of good cheer, and told him that, where personal safety was imperiled, the perpetration of certain prohibited acts was lawful, and that in the case of himself, provided he mentally avowed the foundations to be those of a mosque, the setting of the bricks would be an act meritorious in itself, and acceptable to God.

Thus fortified, Sátuk attended the assembly of the Royal Court, the grandees, nobles, priests, troops, and citizens at the time and place appointed, and, at the bid of Hárún, stepped forward, and with all solemnity set the first brick of the idol temple, mentally, the while, considering it to be a mosque. At the third brick Hárún, extending his arms, exclaimed "Hold! My son! No need to labour more. My mind is at rest now. You are free to act as you please." The assembly dispersed, and that same night Sátuk repaired to the residence of Abú Nasr, and asked how long it would be before they might openly acknowledge Islám. "That," he replied, "is best known to yourself." Sátuk, on this, proposed to attack the idolators immediately without further delay, content for himself to trust in God's aid for the victory. Abú Nasr applauded his zeal, but pointed to the paucity of their numbers.

Sátuk, nothing daunted thereby, now declared his resolve to at once make war upon the infidels, for his trust was in God, and, though few in numbers, their boldness would bring many to the standard of Islam. Seeing the zeal of his pupil for the cause Abú Nasr consented to his proposal. During six months, by converting two and three at a time, he had, on this night, about six hundred converts and followers about him, and it was decided that they should make their attack on the following night.

Accordingly, Sátuk and Abú Nasr, and all the Musalmáns set out together to surprise Hárún in his palace. Arrived at the city walls, Abú Nasr stretched forth

T.B.K.   his hands to Heaven and prayed "Oh God! Of thy excellence and mercy vouchsafe victory to the Faithful, and grant that a deep sleep oppress the infidel." His prayer was answered, and a profound slumber overpowered the idolators. The Musalmáns entered the palace, took from the King's stables four hundred horses, equipped themselves with armour of his troops, slew some of them as they slept at their posts, and, collecting a store of provisions, issued from the city, and marched off to Dava Tágh=Camel Hill, where they took up a position for war. The date of Hárún's death is 380 H.=991 A.D.

In the morning Hárún, enraged at the violation of his palace, moved out with an army of forty thousand men to attack the revolutionists. The fight lasted from the forenoon till sunset, and infidel blood flowed in rivers. Five thousand idolators were sent to hell, and two Musalmáns were wounded. Next day six thousand men joined the army of Islám, and, taken two by two, and three by three, were made Musalmáns. The fight was resumed next morning, and continued for seven days and nights, with a terrible loss to the infidels, whose blood flowed in torrents. The victorious army of Islám grew daily by fresh accessions, and now numbered twelve thousand men.

After some days, provisions ran short, the horses were worn out, and the men reduced to straits. The soldiers now grew discontented, and, complaining, demanded of Abú Nasr how long their hardships were to endure. "That is best known to yourselves" he replied; and added—"You will see what comes from God. All will be well." That same night he took a force of ten thousand men, all Musalmáns, and set out to surprise Hárún. As before, on arrival at the city he prayed to God for victory to the Faithful, and confusion to the idolator.

The infidels were sunk in so deep a sleep, that they knew not their hands and feet. Sátuk made his way into the palace, and found Hárún sound asleep, with a lamp burning at his side, and a slave reclining thereby. He drew his sword to take his uncle's head, but was restrained by the consideration that it was unmanly to slay him in his sleep, and by the remembrance of "the claims of his salt," for, though an infidel, he had been his protector and guardian for several years. He consequently roused him by a prod on the foot with the point of his sword, and offered to spare his life on his accepting Islám.

The haughty Hárún, in wrath at his nephew's insolence, peremptorily refused, and began to upbraid his treachery and ingratitude; but Sátuk cut short his reproof and his life by a single stroke of his sword, and, casting the severed head out of the window on to a dung heap, came out of the palace, and, taking possession of the city, at once proclaimed the establishment of himself as King, and of Islám as the religion of Káshghar. On this day, it is said, by the grace of God and the blessing of his Prophet, twenty thousand converts were added to the fold of the Faithful.

Sátuk warred against the infidels during the whole of his long reign, and acquired the honorable title of *Ghází*="Crescentader." His miraculous acts were many, but the two most notable were these: First, his sword, in its sheath, was like those used by other men, but when he drew it against the infidels, it lengthened to forty yards, and mowed down whole fields of them. Second, on ordinary occasions Sátuk was like other men, but when he warred against infidels, and charged their ranks, long flames of fire issued from his mouth and consumed crowds of them. Other infidels, on seeing this terrible power, became terrified and flocked to him to be made Musalmáns.

Sátuk was twelve and a half year's old when he first entered on war against the infidels. He used to fight them every summer, and spend the winter in the worship of God. By the time he was ninety-six years old he had subdued and converted to Islám all the country from the Amú Daryá=Oxus, beyond Balkh and Cish or Kark, to Karákoram in the north, and everywhere established the religion of Muhammad according to his *Shariat*=Law.

P.   The above statement, I may here note, would seem to identify Sátuk with Iylik Khán or Iylik Mázi, as he is usually styled, the son of the Bughra Khan who has been before mentioned as having invaded Bukhárá, where he died in the reign of the Amír Sáid Abul Kásim. This Iylik Mází, whose early seat was at Uzkand in the province of Farghana, was the first Tártár Prince who brought the Uighúr people together as a nation. And his empire extended from the shores of the Caspian on the west to the Desert of Gobi and the frontiers of China on the east.   P.

Towards the close of his reign, Sátuk made an expedition to the borders of Khitá, and established Islám over all the country up to Turfán. Here he became ill, and was conveyed back to Káshghar, where he lay sick a whole year and then died. In his last hours he summoned his friends around him, made his will; committed his family and government to the charge of Abúl Fattáh, the son of Abú Nasr, gave directions for his burial, and exhorted his sons to follow in his own steps, and adhere to the faith of the Prophet, and serve God truly. Then from a tray set before him he took a rose and smelled it, next he took an apple and ate it, and finally he took a goblet of sharbat and drank it. After this he stood up and repeated the creed, next he revolved in a circle three times, and sang a Persian couplet to the effect that, " a drop taken from the ocean makes it none the less. A soul on quitting its body rends but its covering veil." He then sat down and resigned his life with the close of day, 430 H.=1037 A.D. He was buried at Mashhad in Alton Artosh or Lower Artosh, and the funeral was attended by two *Walí*="Saint," seventy thousand *Alim*="learned men" or "clergymen," twenty-two thousand *Ghází*="Crescentader," and fifteen thousand *Awwám-un-nás*="Common people."   T.B.K.

Such, omitting absurdities and miraculous incidents, is the history of the Prince who introduced Islám at Káshghar, as given in the book mentioned at the outset of the quotation. It further states that his successor, Abúl Fattáh, died three years later, and gives the following particulars regarding the family of Sátuk:—   P.

Hazrat Sultan Sátuk Bughra Khan Ghází left four sons and three daughters. The former were Hasan Bughra Khan, Husen Bughra Khan, Yúsuf Kádir Khán, and   . The latter were Nasab Turkán Khánim, Hadya Turkán Khánim, and Álá Núr Khánim. The last was a lady noted for her beauty, piety, and chastity. Her history briefly is this, and resembles that of Hazrat Miryam=Lady Mary. Álá Núr Khánim, on reaching the age of maturity, was one night engaged in the worship of God, when the Angel Gabriel came to her and poured a drop of light into her mouth. It produced a feeling of comfort, and for a while she became insensible. After this, one night, she went out at the gate, and, seeing the figure of a tiger, fainted. Some months and days after this again, at the time of the "Friday prayers," on the 10th *Muharram*   H., she gave birth to a son with ruddy complexion, gazelle eyes, and sweet voice. The King was wrathful, and the people wondered, saying, "What manner of event is this?" He ordered an investigation of the mystery, and the divines and priests, the judges and lawyers, the grandees and nobles, all assembled and examined Álá Núr Khanim. Her explanation was considered satisfactory, and she was pronounced innocent, and the boy, in reference to the apparition she had seen, was named Syad Ali Arslán Khán. He was brought up by his mother, and at the age of seven years betrothed to Toc Bùbù, a daughter of Bughra Khán. She bore him three sons, *viz*., Muhammad Arslán, Yúsuf Arslán, and Kizil Arslán, and several daughters, one of whom married Syad Jaláluddin, the son of Syad Baháuddin Shámi, and the others different Muhammadan divines of note. Hadya Turkán Khánim married Syad Jaláluddin, the son of Syad Alauddin, and bore him three sons and several daughters, from whom proceeded a number of Káshghar, Táshkand, and Samarcand relationships.   T.B.K.

Sultan Hasan Bughra Khán, with the title of Hazrat Padshah Ghazi, succeeded his father at Káshghar. In his reign the idolators from Khutan, called also Chinshahr, invaded Káshghar with an army of thirty thousand men, under the leaders Bocta Rashid, Nucta Rashid, and Jagálú Khalkhálú of Máchín. They devastated several of its settlements, and for several months besieged the suburbs of the capital, and caused a famine in the country. At length Hasan, with his brother,

T.B.K. Yusuf Kadir, and nephew, Ali Arslán, issued from the city with an army of forty thousand men, and took the field against them.

Bocta Rashíd, the champion of the infidel army, came forward for combat, and Ali Arslán, on the side of the Faithful, advanced to meet him. Each was attended by his supporters, and as they closed in combat, the two armies joined in battle. A hard fight ensued till nightfall, when the Musalmáns were forced to retire within the city, though they sent five hundred idolators to hell, in return for a few Musalmáns of note, who left the scene of their earthly troubles for the joys and delights of Paradise.

The battle was resumed next day, under the lead of Yúsuf Kadir, and with a more decided success, for he routed the enemy with the loss of seven hundred killed and the whole of their camp, which was plundered by the victorious Musalmáns. Following up this advantage, Hasan appointed Husyún Fyzulla, with a garrison of fifteen thousand men, to the charge of the city, and nominating Syad Jalaluddín as his minister, himself with fifty thousand men took the field in pursuit of the enemy, who had rallied and taken up a position on the Tázghún river. A desultory and indecisive skirmish at nightfall left the hostile armies camped opposite to each other.

Next morning, Hasan, having assembled the army, performed the prayers with great ceremony and all solemnity, and then appointing Yúsuf Kadir to the charge of his camp went out to the battle. His heralds preceding blew their horns, and announced his royal titles and high lineage, and as he entered the field called for a champion from the other side worthy to meet the King. Jagálú Khalkhálú of Máchín answered the challenge, and came out against him. Both armies *en suite* clashed in conflict, and after a hard struggle, with success changing from side to side, the Khutan army was finally routed with great loss, and driven to retreat at Yángí Hissár. Hasan now returned triumphant to Káshghar, and celebrated his victory by public rejoicings, feastings, and largesses to the poor. But finding the infidels were still in force at Yángí Hissár, he raised an army of ninety thousand men and sent it, under the command of Ali Arslán, to drive the enemy out of the country.

Ali Arslán and his host found the Khutan and Máchin troops, thirty thousand men, strongly posted amongst the gravelly ridges of Bocsha-socsha, and Ortang Kará in the vicinity of Yángí Hissár. Several indecisive engagements followed with more or less encouraging success to the Musalmán arms, and the Káshghar troops pressed closer around their enemy with each successive skirmish. Finally Jagálú Khalkhálú, finding he could make no head against the superior numbers of his opponent, offered a rich reward in gold to any one who should devise a means of defeating and destroying Ali Arslán, whose noted bravery and impetuosity in fight had inflicted considerable loss and dispirited his men.

A poor and aged *Játlic* = Christian priest—at this period the Nestorian church was numerously represented all over the Káshghar territory, and for two centuries later the Christians held their own, and flourished side by side with their brethren of the rival, and subsequently dominant, faith, till their persecution and suppression by the Muhammadan rulers about the middle of the fourteenth century—who was in the habit of passing from one camp to the other came forward as a candidate for the offered reward. The Máchín leader took the *Játlic*, from his mean and poverty stricken appearance, to be a hungry vagrant merely attracted by the value of the offered prize, and was inclined to dismiss him summarily, but the man's speech impressed him in his favour, and he gave him a hearing. The *Játlic* now disclosed his scheme to attack the enemy at daybreak, when they were less on the alert and more sleepy than at any other time, and assured Jagálú Khalkhálú of success, provided he fell upon the Musalmáns at the moment they were engaged in the performance of their prayers, for they then laid aside their arms.

Accordingly, on the 10th *Moharram* 489 H. = 1096 A.D., at dawn of day, when the army of Islám was engaged in prayer, the Máchín Commander fell upon the

Musalmáns with the whole of his force, and routed them with immense slaughter. Ali Arslán was killed and beheaded, and the victors, pursuing the vanquished, chased them into Káshghar, under the walls of which they paraded the head of their victim, the renowned hero and favourite champion of the Musalmáns, and then cast it to the dogs.

This hero martyr has, consequently, two shrines erected to his memory. One at Ordám Pádsháh, called also *Kúm Shahídán* = "Martyrs' Sands," about fifty-six miles east of Yángi Hissár, over his body where he was killed, and the other at Daulat Bágh, close to Káshghar city, where his head is supposed to have been buried.

The Khutan and Máchín army invested Káshghar for several days and thoroughly devastated the suburbs. In one of the skirmishes during this time Alá Núr Kháním was killed. The account given in the book from which the preceding history is taken runs much to this effect:—Alá Núr Khánim, called also Bíbí Miryam from the circumstances attending the birth of Alí Arslán, in the anguish of sorrow at the death of her son resolved to avenge his loss, and, accompanied by a body of her maids, rushed into the fray against the infidels. She slew twenty-five of them, and then, being overpowered, took to flight. The ground miraculously opened in her course, and disclosed some caverns, and she and her maids sought shelter in their recesses. Their pursuers, however, presently discovered them in their retreat, and put them all to death.

The shrine of Bíbí Miryam, it may be here noted, stands near a deep ravine about ten miles north by east from the city of Káshghar. It has been recently restored by the present ruler, Amír Muhammad Yákúb Khan, who has enclosed its sacred precincts, and built a substantial mosque and commodious college on its grounds, and appointed a suitable establishment of custodians, priests, and teachers for their respective services.

After this disaster Hasan and his brothers, Husen and Yusuf Kádir, performed the funeral ceremonies of the slain with solemnity and magnificence. Camels, horses, oxen, and sheep were slaughtered without stint, and the whole of Káshghar, great and small, rich and poor, were feasted. A fresh army of sixty thousand men was raised, and Hasan again took the field, and, after a succession of victorious engagements, drove the enemy into the hills at Kokyár. From this he returned by way of Yárkand. The city submitted to him without resistance, and the people, coming out with their arms suspended from their necks in token of subjection, presented a rich array of gifts as peace-offering. Hasan halted here some time to settle the district and levy a contribution for his army. He then appointed Abdussamad of Káshghar his Governor over the city, and returned to his capital to enjoy a season of peace and plenty, now ushered in by this successful campaign. The country during this period of rest became so prosperous and productive that one *chárak* = twenty pounds weight of corn, did not cost a single *púl* = a penny.

Hasan Bughra Khan had reigned twelve years when Khoja Abdulla from Turkistán and Khoja Abábakar from Táshkand arrived over the Tirik Dawán, as envoys, to seek the aid of Hasan in restoring order in their country. He forthwith assembled his army, committed Káshghar to the charge of Husyún Fyzulla Khoja and Abúl Kásim, Káshghari, as his Minister, and with his brothers, Hasan and Yúsuf Kádir, and a great host set out for Turkistan. He spent the summer and winter there in subjugating the country, and in the spring celebrated his nuptials with Bíbí Chah Miryam, a noble lady and noted beauty of the place, the *jayn* = niece, of Khoja Ahmad Yasaví, whose tomb there is the most sacred shrine in the country. He then set out on a campaign over the whole country to the westward, and penetrated to Madáyn in Persia. From this, after a prolonged stay, he returned by the Culzum Daryá or Caspian Sea, and converting the infidels, re-established Islám, city by city and tribe by tribe, up to Káshghar, where he arrived after an absence of several years. Here he found his progress checked, for in his absence the city had passed into the hands of the Khutan infidels, and the people had relapsed into their old idolatry.

(129)

T.B.K. He, consequently, sent Yúsuf Kádir back as envoy to the Imám Nasiruddín at Madáyn for assistance in a *Ghazát* = "crescentade," and meanwhile with his army of sixty thousand men, amongst whom were many Arab adventurers and Persian mercenaries, laid siege to the city. After five months of skirmishing and blockade the garrison, pressed for food, came out with all their force to drive off the enemy and raise the siege. They were cut off from the city, defeated with great loss, and pursued across the Kosán river, whilst Hasan, taking possession of Káshghar, received the submission of the people, and made them anew publicly profess Islám.

Hasan now re-established the *Sharíat* in all its severity, prohibited the use of wine, and flesh of dog, ass, and swine as unlawful; levied a ruinous contribution for his army, and, after a complete plunder of the city, mounted the throne as King. Having thus settled and secured the city, he assembled his army and marched against the infidels who had taken post at Yangí Hissár up to which point they held the country. After some severe engagements, he drove them out of the town on to the Cáyrghághitágh or Cáyrághitágh, a ridge of sand hills close to the south. In a subsequent engagement with Jagálú Khalkhálú beyond this ridge, Hasan Bughra Khán and three hundred of his warriors were cut off from their supports, and slain to a man. As most of them were men of rank and note from Tabríz, the village in the vicinity was called, in commemoration of the slaughter, Tabrízí, or as it is locally pronounced Tawiz. This disaster is dated Wednesday, *4th Muharram*, H.

P. Bíbí Chah Miryam Khánim, who accompanied the King on this campaign, now entered the field to avenge her husband's death. But she was quickly put to flight and pursued into the sandy desert, where she was overtaken and killed four days later. Her grave is marked by a lonely unpretending shrine, in connection with which is a poor monastery and alms-house, far away from habitation, on the borders of the sandy desert, thirty-six miles to the south-east of Yángí Hissár, and sixteen miles south of Ordám Padsháh. Half a mile to the south of the shrine, which is called Mazár Hazrat Begum, are the indistinctly traceable ruins of a town, said to have been the city of Nucta Rashid. It presents nothing to view but the outlines of the foundations of rampart walls, and bastions, now mostly buried by the drifting sands. Here and there, where the sands have been swept away by the winds, the surface is strewed with fragments of pottery and glass, and occasionally coins are found amongst the *débris*.

T.B.K. Husen Bughra Khan, the brother of Hasan, now made a desperate effort to retrieve the day. But Nucta Rashid, elated by his successes, fought with an equal fury, and Husen was killed not far from the spot where his brother fell. His army was routed with terrible slaughter, and pursued to Káshghar, which again fell into the hands of the Khutan Chiefs.

The two brothers, Hasan and Husen, were buried in one grave on the field of their martyrdom, and the spot is marked by the shrines and attached monastery of Chúchám or Khojám Pádshah three miles west by south of Yangí Hissár, amidst the ruins of a vast cemetery.

Shortly after this, Yúsuf Kádir, who had been sent to Madáyn for aid, returned with an army of twenty-four thousand men, and accompanied by Syad Aláuddín. As he crossed the Andiján Pass, or Tirik Dawán, the infidels, abandoning the city, retired to Chín Shahr—called also Ilchi and Khutan—and Yúsuf Kádir, taking possession of Káshghar, mounted the throne as King. He added to his Arab force by the levy of a fresh army at the capital, and set out to conquer Khutan. His campaign proved successful, and Islám was now for the first time established in this flourishing seat of Budhism. Jagálú Khalkhálú was killed in the course of the campaign near Cúmáb or Gúmá, and his country subdued and annexed to Káshghar, after a war, from first to last, of twenty-four years.

P. Such is a brief sketch of the history of the Bughra Khan family in the Káshghar territory, and whilst it gives an insight into their own ambitious designs under the tutelage of their Muhammadan preceptors, it, at the same time, conveys a fair idea of the resistance at first opposed to the establishment there of the new religion. We may now return from this digression to review the part played by this family in the politics of the country adjoining it on the west before proceeding to follow up the course of events that again bring us to the theatre of action at Káshghar. P.

On the death of Bughra Khán at Bukhárá, the fugitive Abúl Kásim returned, and was re-established in the government by Subuktakin, the ruler of Ghazni, who then passed westward to the conquest of Nisháboꞓ and Herat. Meanwhile Iylik Khán, the son of Bughra Khán, from Káshghar repeatedly invaded Bukhárá against Abúl Kásim, until he was finally defeated by Subuktakin, and peace restored. Abúl Kásim died 387 H. = 997 A.D. and was succeeded by his son, Abúl Hárith Mansúr. He was soon blinded by a rival noble in favour of his brother, Abdúl Malik who, too, was a mere youth. He was for a while supported against the hostility of Mahmúd, the son of Subuktakin, by Begtakin and Faik, but was ultimately driven to seek refuge with Iylik Khan at Káshghar, who then himself marched to Bukhárá, and threw Abdúl Malik and the rest of his family into prison, 389 H. = 999 A.D. V.B.

Abdúl Malik died in prison, but his brother, Muntazir, a third son of Abúl Kásim, effected his escape, and attempted the recovery of Bukhárá. Iylik Khan, however, whose empire now extended from the borders of China to the Caspian, drove him from the country into Khurásán. From there he wandered into Sistán, where he was killed by some petty robbers, Rabí Awwal 395 H. = 1004 A.D.

With the death of Muntazir ended the Sámání dynasty, which had, from 260 H. = 873 A.D., during a period of one hundred and thirty years, ruled over all Central Asia, and founded the Islám polity there on the orthodox *Sunní* model.

The Uighúr, who under their Chief Iylik Khan, rose to power during the declining years of the Sámání rule, did not long enjoy their career of prosperity. Iylik Khan had his capital at Káshghar, and only held Bukhárá during the last years of the Sámání rule. Jand, a fertile country, eighty *farsakh* = "league" from Bukhárá, was seized by Saljúk, a partizan of the deposed Muntazir, who now became independent. He was the son of Tomak, and had been expelled from the northern steppe with Súbásh, the General of the Prince Begú. With their following and new adherents they settled in the vicinity of Bukhárá. Here the grandsons of Saljúk, Toghrul and Chákar, warred with Iylik Khan, and after his death, with the Bughra Khan family of Káshghar.

Alitakin, the ruler of Samarcand, in alliance with Iylik Khan, quarrelled and warred with Kádir Khán, the son of Bughra Khán. On this Mahmúd marched to the latter's aid, and, driving out Alitakin, protected Kádir from Saljúk and other enemies. In 524 H. = 1129 A.D. Sultán Sanjar seized Samarcand, and carried its Governor, Muhammad bin Suleman, prisoner to Khurasán, but afterwards reinstated him. Subsequently in 534 H. = 1139 A.D. Khwáhrizm Shah captured Bukhárá, destroyed its fort, and killed Ali Khalicat, the Governor of Sultán Sanjar. And again, following this, the next year Samarcand revolted under Ahmad, and Sultán Sanjar, subduing it, appointed Nasr, the son of Ahmad, to its government; but this led to more war, and the decline of the Sanjar rule. For at this time the government of the Uighúr had passed into the hands of Gorkhán. N.

V.B.

Gorkhán = Khánán Khán, Lord of Lords, was the title of the King of the Kará Khitáy, a people who came originally from Khitá, the northern provinces of the Chinese empire. They were at first a party of eighty emigrant families, who, on leaving their own country, found a refuge amongst the border Kirghiz. They soon, however, disagreed with these nomads, and moving on gradually made their way to Ayl or Ila, where they built a city. Here they were joined by a number of Turk wanderers, and their number soon exceeded forty thousand families. On the death of their first Gorkhán, his widow, Goyánik, assumed the government, but, owing to her profligacy, was soon deposed by her late husband's brother, who then succeeded to the government by the murder of a rival brother. And he, on his death, was succeeded by his son as Gorkhán. R.S.

42.—Sikh Merchants in Yarkund.

43.—Baltistanis from near Skardo resident in Yarkund.

Y.C.　　　According to D'Ohsson, as quoted by Yule, the Kará Khitáy Empire was founded by a Prince of the Leao dynasty, who, on its fall before the Kin, in the beginning of the twelfth century, escaped from North China. He is the Yelin Táshí of the Chinese, and the Fushi Taifu of Rashíduddín. He was well received by the Uighúr and others, subjects of the Khita Empire to the west of the desert, and ultimately, acquiring power and strength, conquered all the country up to Khwáhrizm, and in 1125 A.D. took the title of Gorkhán. His capital was Balásághún, and his religion was Budhist.

He was succeeded in turn by a son and grandson, and the latter was reigning, when in 1208 A.D. the son of the last Khán of the Christian Náymán sought refuge at the Court of Kará Khitáy, and married the daughter of Gorkhán. He plotted against his benefactor, ultimately captured him, and took possession of most of his country. He abandoned Christianity at the bid of his wife, and in the end was slain in the mountains of Badakhshán by the Moghol under Changiz in 1218 A.D.

According to the French Monk William de Rubruquis, who was sent to Tatary on a mission to Bátú Khan by Louis IX of France when that sovereign was in Palestine, and who extended his travels to the Court of Mangú Khan, and the city of Karákoram, as quoted by the same author, Kará Khitáy was a name used in distinction from the proper Khitay. They dwelt in an alpine country north of Khitá, where in a plain amongst the mountains dwelt the Náymán tribe of Nestorian Christians. Their Chief, on the death of Gorkhán, the Kará Khitáy Ruler, rose to be King in his place, and was called by the Nestorians "King John," the Prester John of Europe. He was known by this name but to few in the time of Rubruquis when Kin Khan held the country.

This King John had a brother, who, like himself, was a great shepherd, and dwelt three weeks journey off on the other side of the Kará Khitáy mountains, where his capital was the small town of Karákoram. His name was Aong Khan, and his people the Karait and Makrit, who were also Christians, though their Lord became an idolator. Beyond his pastures, at from ten to fifteen days' journey, were the Moghol tribe, a poor people, without a leader or religion, except that of soothsayers and sorcerers. Beyond the Moghol or Moal was another poor tribe, the Tártár.

This Aong Khan, or Une Cham, the Chief of the Karait of Karákoram, is the Tuli of the Chinese writers, and the Toghrul of the Persian. He got the title Une, or Aong, or Wáng, as it appears in different authors, and which is equivalent to Khán = "Chief," "Lord" from Kin, the sovereign of North China. Aong Khan, on the death of his brother, King John, became Khán, and his flocks spread over the country to the Moghol borders. At this time there was amongst the Moghol tribes a blacksmith, Tamújin or Tamúrchi, who used to lift the cattle of Aong Khan's people; and they complaining to him, he invaded the Moghol lands, and drove Tamújin to refuge amongst the Tátár.

T.N.　　　According to the Tabeáti Násirí, written by Minhájuddín 'Uthman, Jauzjaní in 658H. = 1259 A.D., Tamúrchi Tártár, Chief of the Moghol tribe, was the father of Changíz. One day out a hunting he got a *toghrul* or "crane" or "crested heron," and stuck its plumes in his cap by way of ornament. From this circumstance he was named Toghrultakin = "Toghrul by name." The Turk tribe had a separate Chief, but both Turk and Moghol were the subjects of Altán Khan of Tamgháj. They were a thieving, adulterous, and reprobate people and altogether wicked.

Such in brief is what is known of the antecedents of Gorkhán, who now, on the decline of the Sanjar rule, appears upon the scene.

R.S.　　　About this period there was at Balásághún, the Kúbalígh of the Moghol, a Khán or Ruler of Afrásyáb descent. His power was declining, and he was constantly harassed by the incursions of the neighbouring predatory tribes of Cárlígh, Cánculí, and Kapchák. And in his distress he turned for aid to the Gorkhán of the Kará Khitáy.

Gorkhán marched to Balásághún on his invitation. But he took the place for himself, and subjugating the offending tribes to his own rule, appointed the Afrásyáb *Malik* or King to rule over the Turkmán people. Gorkhán next subdued the Kirghiz, and, taking the cities of Beshbáligh and Almáligh (the present Almátí or Almá Atá, as it is written in books), extended his conquests over Káshghar and Khutan, which were then at mutual hostility, and brought the adjoining province of Farghána under his rule. R.S.

At this time the Kará Khitáy nomads, who wandered over the country to the north of Khokand, now occupied by the Kará Kirghiz and Kapchac, appealed to Gorkhán against the heavy taxes exacted by Sultan Sanjar. V.B.

According to the Tabcáti Násiri, the Kará Khitáy were a people who, having revolted against the King of Tamgháj, came to the cities of Cubáligh and Balásághún, and pastured on the Islamite borders, where the Musalmáns were ruled by Afrásyáb Princes descended from Iylik Márzi, under subjection to the Saljúk Kings. They at first paid tribute, but, on getting strong, revolted, and were attacked by Sultan Sanjar, whom they defeated, and whose wife, Turkán Kháton, they captured under their leader Táynko Taráz, who restored her on peace being made. The Sanjar power declined after this defeat, and the Turkistán Princes, being distracted and weakened by wars amongst themselves, sought the aid of the Kará Khitáy, who came and took the government for themselves, and kept it for eighty and odd years. Their rulers were in succession Ayma, and Sangam, and Arbar, and Tana, and Táynko, and then a queen who was succeeded by Gorkhán. His army invaded the country repeatedly, and conquered all up to the Jyhon, including Talicán, Balkh, Amúy, and Tarmiz, and made Khwáhrizm tributary, and Khurásán too, excepting only the Sultáns of Ghor and Bámyán. Gorkhán was deposed by the Shúncár Tártár, Koshluk, and with him ended the rule of the Kará Khitáy. Before him Táynko Taráz was defeated and captured by Sultán Muhammad Khwáhrizm Sháh, at whose hands he accepted Islám. He had won forty-five battles before, and had never been defeated, till on this occasion Sultán Muhammad assailed his *banga*="fortified camp" three several times, and finally captured him and his whole army. T.N.

When, as abovementioned, the Kará Khitáy nomads on the Khokand frontier complained to their King of the exactions of the Sanjar Governors, he took up their grievances and demanded redress, but failed in obtaining satisfaction. Consequently Gorkhán, in 536 H.=1141 A.D., assembled his forces, and, being joined by the Chiefs of the country, invaded Máwaránahar, whence he drove out Sultán Sanjar across the Oxus to Andkhúy, where he died a lunatic not many years later. He destroyed the fugitive King's army, and appointed Aymautakin as his Governor of Bokhárá, from which he then pushed on to Khwáhrizm, where he made its King, Atsiz, tributary in 30,000 *diram* yearly. The *diram* may be reckoned as equal to about six pence. V.B.

N.

A couple of years later, Háshim Araba attacked Bukhárá, drove out Carácha Beg, the Governor of Gorkhán, and killing his Wazir, one Shahab, plundered the city and destroyed its fortifications. They were restored in 560 H.=1164 A.D. by the Kará Khitáy Governor of Gorkhán, who was in turn ousted by Muhammad bin Sultantakin Khwáhrizm Shah in 564H.=1168 A.D., who re-built and improved the fortifications. Finally they were destroyed in 616H.=1219 A.D., when Changiz took the place.

On the death of Sultan Sanjar, his nephew, Mahmúd, succeeded, and reigned for six years, when he was blinded by Bughra Khan of Káshghar, or one of the family of that name, to whom he was related on the mother's side. And thus the Saljúk empire fell to pieces; the Khwáhrizm King dividing Khurásán with him of Ghor, whilst Máwaránahar and Farghana fell to the hands of Gorkhán. With this division of the eastern portion of the Saljúk empire ended the first Turk dynasty in Máwaránahar, where the Persian literature and culture still flourished, the Turk element forming only the military class. V.B.

V.B. During the next fifty years the States of Bukhárá and Samarcand were contested by Gorkhán of the Uighúr country on the east, and Khwárizmsháh of the Khiva on the west.

Khwárizm or Khivá was given in fief by Malik Sháh Saljuk to his General, Nushtakin Garcha, who was succeeded in 491 H.=1097 A.D. by his son, Muhammad Kutubuddin. He ruled thirty years, and assumed the title of Khwáhrizm Sháh, and in 521 H.=1127 A.D. was succeeded by his son Atsiz. He rebelled against Sultan Sanjar, and in the anarchy thus produced Gorkhán seized Máwaránahar, and made the Khwárizm Sháh tributary as stated above. Atsiz died at Kochán or Khaboshán in 551 H.=1156 A.D., and his son, Arslán Khan, who succeeded, continued the tribute to Gorkhán. He died in 560 H.=1164 A.D.

The succession was now contested between Takish, the eldest son, and Sultántakin, the younger nominated one. Civil war continued for ten years, when by the aid of Gorkhán, on the promise of continued tribute, Takish was established on the throne of Khwáhrizm. He died on the 10th *Ramazán* 596 H.=1199 A.D., and left an empire nearly equal to that of the Sámáni and Saljúki to his son, Muhammad Kutubuddin Khwáhrizm Shah. He continued the tribute to Gorkhán, and with the aid of the Uighúr defeated Shahábuddín, King of Ghor, and on his death annexed Ghor, Herat, and Sístán in 612 H.=1205 A.D. He next subdued Irán, and in 616 H.=1209 A.D., proud in the consciousness of his strength, refused the tribute to Gorkhán, and invaded Bukhárá. He defeated the Uighúr army and captured Atrar, whence he returned to Khwáhrizm.

On this Gorkhán, now ninety-two years of age, at once took the field, recovered Atrar and other places, and set seige to Samarcand. Meanwhile Kutubuddín Khwáhrizmsháh hurried back, and a fight ensued with the Uighúr army at Banákat, in 620 H.=1213 A.D., but the action was indecisive and both armies retired. In this battle Gorkhán was opposed by Koshluk Khán, the son of Tayúng Khán, Náyman, who now turned traitor to his patron and benefactor, and revolted against him.

R.S. This Koshluk, chief of the Náyman tribe of Christians, was a Budhist, but his wife was a Christian. He had been forced to flee from Beshbálígh by the hostility of Changíz, and coming to the westward found an asylum with Gorkhán, who received him well, and attached him to himself as an ally, and strengthened the connection by giving him his daughter in marriage. When Khwáhrizmshah, elated by his successes in Irác, refused the tribute to Gorkhán and invaded Bukhárá, he entered into a plot with Koshluk to divide the Uighúr empire by a simultaneous attack from the east and west. The agreement come to was that if Khwáhrizm Shah were first successful, he should have the country up to Káshghar and Khutan, but that if Koshluk first succeeded, he should take the country up to Banákat on the Syhon or Jaxartes river as his share.

Khwáhrizm Sháh, from his vicinity, was first in the field, and took the country up to Atrár, as before mentioned. And he now recovered the place after the battle at Banákat, from which Gorkhán retreated in disorderly haste to his capital, where, on arrival, he found the gates closed against him. He beseiged Balásághún for sixteen days, and, then taking it, gave the city up to plunder and massacre for three days, during which, it is said, forty-seven thousand souls perished.

Koshluk following up now appeared on the scene of riot and bloodshed. He soon routed the demoralized army, and captured Gorkhán, whom he consigned to an honorable captivity, in which he died two years later aged ninety-five. He next attacked Almáligh (Almábáligh), and killed its ruler, and then for successive years campaigned Káshghar and Khutan, and spread devastation and famine over the land. He was a Budhist, and his wife a Christian, and each proselytized to his or her own creed, and everywhere persecuted the Muhammadan. At Khutan, an ancient and most flourishing seat of the creed of his adoption, Koshluk took an ample revenge upon the hostile creed for the destruction its professors had wrought upon the temples and monasteries of the place, and requited the massacres and persecutions of their monks and priests at the hands of Yúsuf Kádir and his Arab allies by like reprisals. He assembled three thousand of their clergy, and demanded a summary recantation of their false doctrine, and on their refusal to deny their "Pure Prophet," he executed their chief priest, Sheikh Jaláluddín, by suspending him head downwards from the bough of a tree in front of the principal mosque; whilst he let loose his soldiery amongst the rest to slay and torture, and finished with the destruction of their mosques and desecration of their tombs.

Whilst Koshluk was running this violent career in the south-west of the Uighúr country, another Budhist chief, Aydy Cút, Tártár, had risen to power at Balásághún in the north-east of the same region, and with only less violence persecuted the Muhammadans up to the Táshkand frontier, and destroyed their town of Kásán belonging to the province of Farghána. (Abúl Fidá).

At this time the growing power of Changíz had made itself felt on the Uighúr border, and Aydy Cút, alive to his own interests, tendered an early submission to the rising conqueror. He was in consequence highly favoured, and Changíz gave him one of his daughters to wife. Koshluk, on the other hand, mistrustful, and continuing the old antipathy, did not so submit. Changíz, consequently, sent a strong force of his Moghol, under Jattah Noyán, to exterminate him and his Náymán.

The Moghol invaders fell upon and slew all the Náymán troops they could lay hands on at Káshghar, where they found them scattered amongst the peasantry, from whom they had taken forcible possession of their houses; and then followed in the track of Koshluk to Khutan, subjugating and settling the country as they went on.

Koshluk, on hearing of the destruction of his army and the approach of his dread enemies, abandoned Khutan, and fled in haste with only a few attendants into the mountains of Badakhshán, and the Moghol, pursuing, got some Wákhí or Wakhán huntsmen, amongst whom he was concealed, to deliver him up to them. They straightway killed him, and sent his head to Changíz, who then annexed Káshghar and Khutan, and the country up to the Syhon.

This brings us to the period of the Moghol invasion under Changíz, and that occupation of the country which has given to it the name of Mogholistan; just as in anterior ages a similar irruption from the north, under Ayghúr Khán, gave to it, and the adjoining region to the west, the name of Turkistán, from the designation of the main division of the great Tártár invaders of that period, after whom the whole of the Central Asian plateau takes the general name of Tartary. To understand this it is necessary to go back to the early history of these peoples. The oriental version as given by Mír Kháwind Sháh, the Mirkhond or Khondemir of European authors, whose opportunities of acquiring reliable information on the traditions of the country were, from his position at Herat during the glorious reign of the great Sultán Husen Mirzá in the latter half of the fifteenth century, probably as good as those of other historians, may be briefly summarized much as follows:—

Yáfath or Japhet, which signifies "ancestor," was the forefather of the Turk race. When the ark rested on the mountain Júdí, Noah sent forth Japhet to the countries of the east, and gave him the *yada-tásh* = jade stone, which signifies "rainstone," for by its possession was secured a timely rain for the crops in their seasons. From him sprung the following peoples:—

Chín. He was the inventor of painting, silk culture, the art of weaving, and many other useful arts.

Seláb. He warred with Rús, and Kharz, and Kamárí for the possession of the land, and finally settled in the country bearing his name. It is in 64° N. Lat. and beyond the *haft iclím*, where, owing to the intensity of the cold, the houses are sunk underground.

Kharz or *Khazar.* He settled on the River Amil = Volga, and built the city of Khazar there, and cultivated the soil.

Rús. He settled on the tracts adjoining Khazar; introduced punishment by fine and confiscation, and heritage by daughters, the sons receiving only their fathers' weapons of war.

44.—Tunganis, resident in Yarkund.

45.—Yarkundis.

R.S.   *Ghaz.* He settled in Bulghár, and warred with Turk. They are both the worst and most turbulent of the sons of Japhet.

Kamári were huntsmen on the borders of Bulghár, and were clad in the furs of weasels and other animals. They separated into the divisions of Bartás and Bulghár.

Turk. Settled at Baligh = "City" in Silingáy, which is a mountainous region, with small rivers, and many springs. Here houses were first built, of reeds and logs. Turk had four sons, *viz.*, Codak, Chagal, Parskhar, and Aylác. Codak discovered the use of salt by his bread falling on saline ground out a hunting.

Other sons of Japhet from whom nations sprung are Manshij, Sadsan, and Yarij. They were all at first nomads, and to this day they all prize most highly the *yada-tásh*.

Turk became the first Khán of Turkistán. He was the cotemporary of Kyámurth, the first sovereign of Persia. At eighty years of age he resigned his kingdom in the east to his eldest son, Amalgha Khán, who in his old age resigned it to Bátú Khán. He was a really great Prince, and was succeeded by his son, Kúyúk, who, also, was a wise, just, and powerful sovereign. On his death he was succeeded by his son, Alinja Khan. In his reign the Turk became a powerful nation, and relapsed from their ancient form of religion. He had twin sons, Tátár and Mughol, and in his old age he divided his empire between them, and they lived in harmony after his death. Tátár from father to son gave a succession of eight Kings, the last of whom was Báydú Khan. The kingdom then became dismembered by internal dissensions.

Mughol similarly gave a succession of nine Kings, the last of whom was Ayl or El Khán. From him is continued the line of the Turk. Mughol had four sons, *viz.*, Kará, Azar, Kaz, and Uz. Kará Khán succeeded to the throne, and is the ancestor of the Moghol tribes. His home was at Karákoram = "Black Shale," between two mountains called Artak and Kartak. He had a son named Aghor, who first married the daughter of his uncle Kaz; but not agreeing with her he next married the daughter of his uncle Uz; and not agreeing with her either, finally married the daughter of his uncle Azar. She accepted the new religion he preached to her, and they loved each other and lived happily together. His first wives became jealous, and plotted to poison him, but the vigilance of his favourite guarded him. The discontented wives then complained to Kará Khan of being neglected and despised by his son, because they had refused to desert their faith for his new religion, which he wished them to adopt.

On this Kará Khan, fearful of the spread of the new doctrine amongst his people, marched to attack his apostate son on his hunting grounds. He was forewarned by his faithful wife of the design against him, and was consequently on his guard, and in the fight that followed, Kará Khan was killed. Aghor Khan now (about 650 B.C.) ascended the throne, and converted the people to the new faith. He reigned seventy-three years. Some of his tribes rebelled and sought aid from Chín, whose King sent an army to their assistance. Aghor marched against it, defeated it, and subdued all the Tártár and Moghol tribes in that country.

After this he invaded Bukhárá, and subjugated all Turkistán, and then held a grand national assembly or *Curultay* of all his princes, and nobles, and chiefs, called together from every part of his empire. They came over journeys of one or two years, with their families and flocks, with their *Khargáh* or "circular framework huts" and waggons, and formed a vast camp such as had never been seen, and made high festival. On this occasion, in counsel with his nobles, Aghor Khan framed a code of laws for the government of his empire, at the wisdom of which the mind is wonder-struck, and which raised him to the same exalted position amongst the Turk nations that was held by Jamshed amongst those of Persia. He gave distinctive appellations to the several tribes of Turk, such as Uighur = "joining," because this tribe sided with him against the hostility of his father, Cánculi = "waggon," because of their wealth in, and use of those vehicles; Calich = "sword," because of their distinction in its use, &c., &c. Aghor Khan, after seventeen years' war subdued the Burác tribes, and after the campaigns of Ghor and Ghurjistán returned to his own seat at Karákoram, where he died. He left six sons, viz., *Gún* = Sun, *Ay* = Moon, *Yuldúz* = Star, *Kók* = Sky, *Tágh* = Mountain, and *Dangíz* = Sea. From these in twenty-four divisions, from sons and grandsons, are descended all the Turkmán tribes.

Turkmán is a recent name for those Turk tribes who settled in Máwaránahar, and, though not intermarrying with foreigners, became altered in appearance by the effects of change of climate, and mode of life, and were called by their neighbours Turkmánind or Turkmán = "Turklike." Aghor Khan, in his western conquests, took Khurásán and both Irác, and extended his power over the countries of Misr = Egypt, Shám = Syria, Rúm = Turkey or the Roman Empire, and Afrásig = Africa? On his return to Artak Kartak he held a grand national assembly, and celebrated his conquests by magnificent festivities. Nine hundred mares and nine thousand ewes, according to the rule of ten sheep to one horse for feasts, were slaughtered, and wine and delicacies of every sort and country were lavishly expended on the feast, whilst rich robes and presents were distributed to the nobles.

On this occasion Aghor Khán divided his empire amongst his six sons. The right wing amongst the three eldest, and the left wing amongst the three youngest, and he gave them his bow and three arrows between them. The three eldest broke the bow and shared its pieces, and are in consequence collectively known by the term *Buzúc* = "Destroyer." The three youngest shared the arrows between them, and are collectively styled *Uchúc* = "Three arrows."

Shortly after this assembly Aghor Khan died, and his son, Gún, succeeded to the throne, with his father's Minister, Arcíl, as councillor. He represented that each of the six brothers had now four sons, making in all twenty-four royal princes, and proposed that they should be all provided for so as to prevent discord. Accordingly each was allotted his own province, and city, and rank, and standard, and privileges. The six brothers shared the government for seventy years, and then the son of Dangiz, named Manglay, became ruler of Mogholistán, and reigned one hundred and ten years.

Manglay was succeeded by his son El Khan. At this time Turkistán and Máwaránahar belonged to Túr bin Farídún. He allied with Sonj Khan, the Tátár Chief, and they warred with El Khan, whose camp they surprised, and captured to a man, excepting only his son, Cayán, and his maternal uncle's son, Tukoz, who, each with his wife, effected their escape.

These four fugitives escaped to a mountain fastness, inaccessible on all sides but by a single track, called Arkana Cúl (in the Cobdo District), and these in course of time multiplied to many families. Those of Cayán were called Cayát, and those of Tukoz, Daralkín. After this, by melting and digging a way across an iron mountain barrier, they issued from their retreat, and recovered their ancestral seats from the Tártár possessors, and were joined by the other Moghol tribes.

The Moghol country extends from that of the Uighúr on the west to the frontiers of Khitá on the east, and from Silingay (in Cobdo) and Carcar on the north to Tibet on the south. The food of the people is the flesh of their flocks and the chase, and their clothing furs.

Yuldúz, the son of Mangláy Khwája, the son of Tymúr Tash = "Ironstone," a descendant of Cayán, when he ruled the Moghol, raised their name to the highest fame, and annually celebrated the mode of escape from the iron mountains of Arkana Cúl by the erection of furnaces, and melting and hammering of iron, and singing and feasting all night.

Such, in brief summary, is the history of the origin of the Turk people, whose career in this region through the Uighur period has been sketched in the preceding pages, as given by Mír Kháwind Sháh. His account of the Moghol people may be briefly summed up as follows:—

Alan Coá, the granddaughter of Yuldúz Khán, Cayát, was the wife of her father's brother's son, and she bore him two sons, named Yalkadi and Yakjadi; and after his death she ruled the tribe, and educated her sons. At length, like the

R. S. self-breeding women of the Northern Isles, and the mother of Hazrat Isá = Lord Jesus, she became pregnant without the intervention of a father, by means of a ray of light entering her *Khargáh* at night, and passing into her mouth as she slept. She was a noted beauty, and was now naturally charged with unchastity; but at a convocation of the Moghol chiefs and nobles she satisfied them of her innocence by shewing some of them the light as it again entered her tent at night, to witness which phenomenon a party of them had been appointed to keep watch. She was in due time delivered of three sons, *viz.*, Yacún Caycay, from whom descend the Caycay tribes; Yasfya Sáljí, from whom descend the Sáljút tribes; and Buzúnjar Muthcán, from whom come all the Moghol Kháns. The progeny of these three sons are collectively styled Buzún, and those of the two sons by her cousin and husband are styled collectively Daralkín, and they hold an inferior rank.

Buzúnjar Khán succeeded to the throne. He conquered Túrán, which was divided amongst many rival Turk Chiefs, and adopted the title of Khácán or Cá'án, which signifies "Sovereign Lord." On his death he left two sons, Bocá, the eighth ancestor of Changíz, and Tocá, the ancestor of Máchín.

Bocá was succeeded by his son Domín Khan; and he in turn left a widow, named Manolán, and nine sons. She was very wealthy and wise, and dwelt in a strong castle on the Arkaby mountain, at the foot of which flowed a swift river. Here she stored her riches, and from here she ruled her people, and got wives for her sons from the neighbouring tribes. At this time seventy *gorán* = "a camp of one thousand tents" of the Jaláyr tribe, camped on the Great Kalorán river near Khitá, with whose people they were always at war. At length the Khitáy crossed the river, and drove off the Jaláyr from their border, and they retreated and came on to the pastures of Manolán.

Manolán collected her people, and issued from her retreat to drive them off, but was overpowered and killed with eight of her sons and many of her men, and her castle was captured by the invaders. The ninth son escaped the fate of his family through his absence on a visit to his uncle, Máchín, to whose daughter he was betrothed. Máchín now prepared to avenge the loss of his relatives upon the Jaláyr, but was appeased by their rendering up seventy culprits for execution, and excusing the disaster as the act of some lawless bands contrary to the desire of the tribe; and peace was restored.

Káydú Khan now ascended the throne. He is the sixth ancestor of Changíz and Caráchar Noyan. He dug the canal of Jaralúm, and warred with the Jaláyr. He had three sons, *viz.*, Báyncar, Harca Lingam, and Khárchín. From Báyncar are descended Changíz and Tymúr; from Harca Lingam, the Tanjút tribe; and from Khárchín, the tribe of Sájyút. On the death of Káydú his eldest son, Báyncar, succeeded to the throne; but he soon died, and his son, Tomna Khan, took his place. He was a great Prince, and largely extended the empire. He had nine sons, seven by one wife, and twins by the other. These last were Kabl Khan, the third ancestor of Changíz, and Cáchúly Khán, the eighth ancestor of Tymúr.

Kabl Khan ascended the throne on the death of his father. He is called Alanjik Khan by the Moghol. He appointed Cáchúly his regent when he went to visit Altán Khán, the King of Khitá. On his death he was succeeded by his son, Kúbla Khan. He warred with Altán Khán, and, defeating his Tártár and Khitáy, plundered his country, and returned home with his Mughol laden with a rich booty. He died soon after, and was succeeded by his brother Buznán. His uncle, Cáchúly Bahádur, having died, Buznán appointed his son, Ardúnchi Birlás, to the command of the army. On his death, Buznán was succeeded by his son, Mysoka Bahádur, and he, on the death of Ardúnchi, appointed his son, Súghanchín, to the command of the army in succession to his father. Mysoka warred with the Tártár, and, defeating them, captured their Chiefs Tamújin = Tamurchi or Tymurchi = "blacksmith" or "ironsmith," and Kará Bocá = "black stag." From this campaign he returned to Dylon Yulduc, where his wife, Aolún, gave birth to Changíz, on the 26th

Zicada 549 H.=1154 A.D. Mysoka called him Tumúrchi or Tamújin, because that Tártár Chief's rule ended at the time of his birth. Aolún bore Mysoka two other sons, *viz.*, Jújí = "stranger," and Casar = "wild beast." Mysoka died in 562 H.= 1166 A.D., and his General, Súghanchín, soon after.

The recently subjugated tribes now revolted, and joined the Tanjút or Tangút tribe, and both Moghol and Tártár became divided by internal dissensions, and soon separated under rival Chiefs. The Birlás tribe too, the family in which the command of the army was hereditary, now revolted against Changíz, who was aged sixteen years.

Changíz, on succeeding to his father's rule, suffered many reverses at first, and was opposed by the tribes of Jámocá, Tanjút, Cunghrát, Jaláyr, and others, consequently he sent Karáchár Noyán, the son of Súghanchín, to seek the aid of Aong Khán, who had been an old ally of Mysoka, and was at this time the most powerful Prince in all Turkistán. He treated the envoy well, invited Changíz to his court, received him with cordial hospitality, and adopted him as his son; and Changíz in return did him good and faithful service. He defeated the Makrít Chiefs, Borkin and Tocyá Begi, who had joined the brother of Aong Khán in rebellion against him. On this the Tanjút, Sáljút, Cunghrát, Jaláyr, Tátár, and other tribes, joining in revolt, confederated against Aong Khán and Changíz, and swore on slaughtered horse, cow, sheep, and dog to overcome them or die in the contest. Accordingly both sides prepared for war. The hostile hosts met in battle at Byor Náwar, and after a bloody engagement the troops of Aong Khan and Changíz were victorious.

After this, owing to old enmity and jealousy of his power, Búyurúc Khan, brother of Táyáng Khan, the ruler of the Náymán, attacked Aong Khan, but his army was destroyed by the cold and snow. Changiz had now served Aong Khan seven years, and, having risen to great favour and authority, was envied by all the courtiers, and looked on with jealousy by the nobles. The ruler of the Jájrát tribe, named Jámocá, was the most active against him, and instigated Sanjún, the son of Aong Khan, to hostility against him on the pretence that he was in league with Táyáng Khan to seize the government. At first Aong Khan refused to credit the charges brought against the fidelity and loyalty of his favoured confidant, but the perseverance with which they were reiterated finally shook his faith, and he was persuaded to make an attempt to seize him.

Accordingly with his son's army, on the pretence of a hunting excursion, he marched to the territory held by Changíz, and there pitched its tents in the vicinity of his camp. Changíz was soon after informed of the plot to surprise his camp at night by one of his soldiers, who brought with him two boys, from whom he had heard of the intentions of their neighbours; and they, on being questioned, asserted they had overheard what they had reported at the tent of a soldier in the opposite camp, where they had gone to sell milk. Accordingly Changíz, satisfied as to the truth of the boys' statements, quietly abandoned his camp at nightfall, and, leaving the tents standing, moved with Karáchár Noyán and his troops into the hills hard by. Aong Khan fell upon the camp towards day light, and, finding it empty, followed in the track of the fugitives. A fight ensued, Sanjún was wounded, and Aong Khan put to flight, leaving many of his Karait dead on the field.

Changíz after this remained sometime at the salt springs of Báljúna, and assuming independence established a code of discipline for the government of his adherents. It was known as *yásá-yúsún* = "established custom," and owing to its severity led to the desertion of many of his followers. He now rewarded the two lads, who had informed of the plot, by attaching them to his court with the rank of *Tarkhán*, the privileges of which were free access to the royal presence, and immunity from punishment for criminal offences up to nine convictions; and the dignity was made hereditary. The descendants of these Tarkhán were still met with in Khurásán in the fifteenth century.

From Báljúná Changíz moved to the banks of a river flowing at the foot of a mountain on the border of Khitá, and here he mustered his army, which numbered only four thousand six hundred men. From this he moved on to the Nor or Náwar = "Lake," and from there sent envoys to treat with the Kúnghrát tribe, who came and joined him. He next sent envoys to arrange a peace with Aong Khán, but they returned unsuccessful, and war followed. Changíz defeated Aong Khán, who fled for asylum to Táyáng Khán, but he was attacked on the way by some nomad robbers, who killed him and sent his head to their Chief; and he had the skull set in a gold frame, and in memory of their old enmity used to address it with words of reviling. Sanjún, on this occasion, escaped to Tibet, and thence made his way to Káshghár, where he was executed by its Chief in 599 H. = 1202 A.D.

Changíz by this victory subjugated all the Mughol tribes, and at the age of forty-nine years ascended the throne at Shamán Gara, his favourite camp ground in the same year 1202 A.D. According to Mughol custom he was raised aloft on a pile of felt carpets, and putting on the crown with magnificent ceremony, changed his name from Tamúgin to Changíz.

Now, in the following year, 1203 A.D., Táyáng Khán, Náymán, dreading the power of the rising conqueror, sent envoys to arrange an alliance with Alácosh Namugin, the King of the Angait, but he refused the advances made, and joined Changíz, who was already on the march against the Náymán. His army camped on the Gulbaty plain till the end of the summer harvest, and then the vanguard advanced to the Altáy river, where it came up with the army of Táyáng Khan, and his allies, the Makrit, Karait, Awrát, Jájrát, and other tribes.

Changíz defeated them all. Táyáng died of his wounds, and Koshluk, his son, escaped to his uncle, Búyurúc Khan. The tribes of Tátár, Caycay, Durmán, and Sáljút submitted, but that of Makrit held out. Changíz returned for winter to Shamán Gara, and in the spring marched against Toctá Begi, the ruler of the Makrit. He, with his son, Kará Namoda, fled to Búyurúc Khán, the brother of Táyáng Khán, and Changíz subjugated the Makrit. He then went against Tangút or Cáshmín, destroyed its fort, and slew all who offered resistance, as was his established rule.

Changíz after these victories extended his *yásá-yúsún* code over all the subjugated tribes, whom he now incorporated into his military organization, framed on the decimal system, by which the whole population capable of bearing arms was enrolled in his army. They were divided into companies of ten called *ón*; of a hundred, called *yúz*; of a thousand, called *ming*; and of ten thousand, called *túmán*. And each of these was under a commander, called respectively *Onbáshi*, *Yúzbáshí*, *Mingbáshí*, and *Túmán Aghá*, who was directly subordinate to the commander next in superiority to him, so that each commander had direct control of only ten units: thus the Túmán Aghá of ten Mingbashi, the Mingbashi of ten Yúzbáshi, the Yúzbáshi of ten Onbáshí, and the Onbáshí of ten men. The system was rigidly enforced, and governed by strict regulations for the conduct and responsibility of each rank. And practically it worked with that success which enabled its originator to achieve the surprising conquests that in less than ten years laid the whole of Asia at his mercy, of which alas! it knew not even the semblance.

In the following spring he held a grand national assembly, or *Curultáy*, and, mounted on a magnificent throne, confirmed the change of his name from Tamújin to Changíz; established the *yásá-yúsún*, written now for the first time in the Uighúr character, as the law of his realm; held high festival, and then set out on a campaign against the resisting Búyurúc Khán. He was killed, and his country ravaged, but his nephew, Koshluk, escaped to Toctá Begi, and they both retired to the country of Arwish. Changíz returned from this campaign to quell a revolt in Tangút, and then turned his arms against the Kirghíz on his western borders. They, however, met him with a prompt tender of submission and tribute, and were in return granted the privilege of holding their lands in *Séyúrghátmish*, or "military fief," and Changíz retraced his steps triumphant to Shamán Gara.

After a brief repose there, he again, at the end of 604 H.=1207-8 A.D., took the field, and went against Koshluk and Toctá Begi in Awrish, and on the way received the submission of the Awrát, who acted as guides to the hiding place of the fugitive Chiefs. Toctá Begi was killed in the fight at Arwish, but Koshluk again escaped by flight, and found refuge with Gorkhán, Chief of the Kará Khitáy, and ruler of Turkistán, who received him well, and gave him his daughter to wife. After this victory Changíz received the submission of Arslán Khán, the El or "Chief" of the Cárlúc tribe, and of Aydy Cút, the Chief of the Uighúr, whom he treated with great favour, and to whom he gave one of his daughters in marriage. Following this he sent envoys to demand the submission of Altán Khán, the King of Khitá. The King refused, and Changíz marched against him, defeated his army with terrible slaughter, sacked and destroyed many cities, and pursued the King—in those days the Kings of Khitá were always called Altán Khan, just as they were afterwards called Ayming Khán—to Khánbáligh or Chunkad, the Cambalay of Marco Polo. R.S.

On the approach of the invader, Atlán Khán sued for peace, and sent his daughter to him as wife. Changíz accepted her and turned back, but Altán Khán, leaving his son with a strong army in Khánbáligh, removed his Court to Taming, which he made his capital. This city had been built by his father on a very wide river, and was protected by three lines of fortified walls one inside the other, and was adorned by handsome palaces, and gardens in which were produced the fruits of both hot and cold climates.

At this time, however, the Kará Khitáy, who had revolted and seized some Khitá territory, submitted to Changíz and sought his aid, and he consequently sent an army with them against Khánbáligh. The King's son fled to Taming, and the city, reduced by famine and siege, was taken and plundered of an immense treasure. Altán Khán poisoned himself, and Changíz, after a campaign of two years, conquered most of Khitá, and leaving strong garrisons in Tughúr and its frontiers returned to his Yúrt or "country seat" at Shamán Gara = "The Shaman's home."

The Náymán country now revolted, and Changíz sent an army, provided with carts, to subdue and settle it. It marched to the Kara Morán river in Mogholistán, and there came up with the enemy under Codo, the brother of Toctá Begi. He was slain and his son taken prisoner. The youth was a noted archer, and displayed his skill before Júji, who having seen him put one arrow on the other at a mark, interceded with his father to spare the life of so skilful a bowman. Changíz, however, refused, and with the lad's death the ruling family of Makrit became extinct, 613 H.=1216 A.D. At this time the Comát tribe on the Khitá frontier having revolted were also subjugated.

Whilst this force was operating against the Makrit on the Cúmkichik = "Little Sands" on the east of Mogholistan, another force was hunting to the death Koshluk, and settling the country of Káshghar and Khutan up to the Syhon on its west, as has been before related. And this brings us back to the course of our narrative of events. P.

About this period then, with the submission of Aydy Cút of Balásághún and Arslan Khan of Almáligh on the north, and with the death of Koshluk and the annexation of Káshghar and Khutan on the south of the Tianshán, the territory of Changíz extended from the east borders of the desert of Gobi to the west slopes of Tianshan mountains, where it marched with the frontiers of Máwaránahar, ruled by Khwáhrizm Sháh, and included the whole of Mogholistán proper.

The anarchy prevailing in this region just prior to the Moghol invasion had led Sultan Muhammad Kutubuddin Khwáhrizm Sháh to meditate the conquest of Khitá, but the fame of the conquering Changíz caused him to restrain his ambition, and instead thereof he sent a friendly mission to the conqueror of the east to spy out the land. T.N.

On the return of this embassy, one of its members, Syad Baháuddín, related to the author of the *Tabcáti Násiri*, the work from which I am quoting, at Tolak of Ghor in the year of the Mughol invasion of Khorasan, 617 H. = 1220 A.D., that as the mission approached the capital of Tamgháj (Changíz was at the time prose-

T. N. cuting his Khitá campaign), they marched for three days along a hill white as snow with the bleached bones of the slain in its siege, whilst the ground between to the city was black and grimed with their gore, the stink of which killed some and poisoned most of their party. At the city itself, under one of its towers, he saw a pile of bones, said to be those of twenty thousand virgins, who had been cast from it to escape by such death the fury of the Moghol soldiers.

Khwáhrizm Sháh's embassy was well received by Changíz, who dismissed the envoy with rich presents, and the following brief message of his master :—" I am King of the East. Thou art King of the West. Let merchants come and go between us, and exchange the products of our countries." A caravan of merchants accompanied the returning envoy, who amongst the other presents from Changíz carted away a block of native gold the size of a camel's neck. On arrival at the frontier city of Atrár, 1218 A.D., the Governor, Kádir Khán, by order of Khwáhrizm Sháh, detained the caravan, and soon after murdered all the merchants to the number of four hundred, and plundered their property.

This treacherous act brought down upon the country the savage vengeance of Changíz. He collected his forces from Turkistán, Chin, and Tamgbáj, under eight hundred standards of a thousand men each; eight hundred thousand horsemen. He appointed, besides, three hundred thousand horses for the baggage of the army, its carts, and families, &c., including one horse to every ten men, with its load of three sheep made into *cadíd*=" sundried salt-meat," a skin of *Cumiz*=" mare's milk wine," and a *Kazghan*=" iron cooking pot." Thus provided his hardy soldiers marched three months across deserts, and rivers, and mountains, and towards the end of 616 H. =1219 A.D. arrived at Atrár. Here he left Júji and Aoktay with their troops, who on its capture after a siege of five months, in revenge for the murder of their merchants there, destroyed every living thing in it. Meanwhile Changíz himself with a strong force hurried on to Bukhárá, the capital.

P. We need not here follow the career of his frightful butchery and devastation. It is sufficient for our purpose to note here that the cities of Káshghar escaped these calamities, and that a strong contingent of their Uighúr soldiery under Aydy Cút and other leaders were in the conqueror's army; that Khwáhrizm Sháh, flying before the storm his savagery had raised, was chased into Mazandarán, and escaped his pursuers by ship on the Caspian to disappear from the scene; that the populous cities of Bukhárá, Balkh, Nishabor, Herat, Ghazni, and many another in this region were utterly destroyed with their inhabitants; that the vaunted impregnable castles and fortresses of Tokháristán, Kábul, Ghor, Sístán, Khurásán, and Khiva were without exception captured and dismantled or razed; that the entire region from Azarbíján on the west to the Indus on the east, and from Dasht Kapchák on the north to Sistán on the south, was in the short space of only six years so thoroughly wasted and ruined that more than as many centuries has not sufficed to obliterate the effects and marks of the havoc then worked, far less to restore the region to its former state of prosperity and population; and finally, that having chased Sultán Jaláluddin Khwahrizm Sháh, the son and successor at Ghazni of the fugitive King, across the Indus, he was called back from his mad career of devastation to quell a revolt in his own home at Tungút.

T. N. Changíz, the author from whose work these records are taken states, had in 615 H. = 1218 A.D., just at the time he was preparing to set out against Khwáhrizm Shah, received envoys from the Khálif Násir of Baghdad urging him to do so, in revenge for the independence of the Khálifat assumed by this ruler of Máwaránahar. He was joined on the way by Arslán Khán of Almálígh, and by Aydy Cút from Beshbálígh with his Uighur contingent. On arrival at Atrár he left Aoktáy and Chaghtáy, with Júji in support to take the place, and sending Alác Noyán and Mangú Bocá to Banákat and Khujand, himself hurried on against Bukhárá, the *Cutub-ul-islám*=" centre prop of Muhammadanism." In the Mugh or Parsi language *Bukhár* is said to signify "collection of knowledge," but with the Uighúr and Khitáy it means "idol temple." The city was now completely sacked and ruined, and its population massacred and enslaved. At Atrár, which was garrisoned by fifty thousand of Khwáhrizm Sháh's troops—he himself fled from the capital by Nishábor to Absukún, where he died 22nd *Zi Hijj* 617 H.=1220 A.D., (Vambery)—not a soul was left alive, the whole population being led out in batches of fifty and butchered on the plain outside the walls. T.N.

On his return march from the Indus, Changíz sent his son Aoktáy in mid-winter to Ghazni and Ghor, there to wipe out in the blood of the people the disaster his troops had suffered at the hands of Jaláluddín in the fight at Parwán.

He did this so effectually during a campaign of two years, that not a trace of the aboriginal Aryan stock, the *Gabar* or fire-worshiper of Irán, is now to be found in the country. The only inhabitants of that mountain tract—the real Kohi Káf of Orientals, the Paropamisus of the Greeks, the Indian Caucasus of Europeans—at the present day, are the descendants of the army of occupation left there by him. And though still pure Moghol in race type, and many of their customs, they know nought of their antecedents. They have entirely lost their language before that of their subsequent Persian rulers, and are now only known amongst their Afghan neighbours as the poor, mean, despicable, and heretic *Hazára* (evidently the designation of their original military divisional settlements), whom as being *Shia* it is lawful to oppress, enslave, and sell. The remarkable persistence of the race type of these Moghols during six hundred years is easily explained by the isolation of their position in an inaccessible and easily defended mountain country, whose natural outlets and affinities are more with the cognate races of the Oxus valley than with the foreign Aryan tribes of the Kabul highlands and the basin of Kandahar. But to return to our subject. P.

Whilst Aoktáy was marching to Kabul on this errand, Changíz went into winter quarters in Gabari or the Gabar country (the country of the fire-worshipers, now known as Pakli and Swat) to wait the return of his envoys to the Emperor of Hindustán, Sultán Sáid, at Delhi, to ask his permission for a passage to Chín through Farájál and Kámrúd. During these three months he sent out parties in all directions to forage the country and reduce the forts held by the Irác troops amongst the mountains, whilst he spent his time in consulting the fates by burning the *Shána* or "Sheep scapula," a custom still common amongst the Hazára or Moghol of the Ghazni highlands. The omens by these were unpropitious, and his envoys, at the same time, returning with an unfavourable reply, Changíz at once set out across the snowy mountains, whilst it was yet winter, and, with great difficulty and loss of life made his way by Kabul and Káshghar to Turkistán. T. N.

His route was probably across the Swát country into the Kúnar valley, where Chagán Saráe, or "white hostelry," from its name attests Moghol occupation, and thence up the Chítrál valley, called also Káshkár through the easy Barogil Pass, which is practicable for half of the year, on to the plain of Káshghár. Such at least was the route taken by part of his army, if not by Changíz himself, who, according to the author of the Tabcáti Nasiri (a personal actor at Tolak in the defence against his invasion of Ghor), rejoined his camp with the heavy baggage, left at Naman Pushta in Tokharistan, and took it on with him to Samarcand, where he spent the spring and summer. P.

Here in 621 H.=1224 A.D. he held a *Curultáy*, and divided his conquests amongst his sons. To Aoktay he gave the Eastern Tártár country, comprising China and Mongolia; its capital was Khanbaligh=Pekin. To Batu, the son and successor of Júji, he gave the Northern Tártár country, including Dasht Kapchak; its capital was Saray on the Volga. To Chaghtáy he gave the middle Tártár kingdom, which comprised Mogholistan, that is Zunghár on the north, and Káshghar on the south, Máwaránahar, Khwahrizm, and Afghanistan; its capital was Almaligh. And to Tuli he gave Khurásán and Iran; its capital was Tabriz. V.B. & Y.C.

Having thus disposed of his empire Changíz returned to his seat at Karákoram, or Shamán Gara, and in Zi Hijj 621 H.=1225 A.D., after an absence of seven years, R.S.

46.—Yarkundis, Specimens of goitre.

47.—Hospital, British Embassy in Yarkund.

R.S. rejoined his family. He here held a *Cúrultáy*, and celebrated his conquests by magnificent festivities. After these rejoicings he marched against Shandarca, the rebel Chief of Tangút, devastated his country and reduced him to subjection, but, restoring him to favour, gave him one of his daughters in marriage. This Chief, however, it appears, again rebelled, and Changíz taking the field against him was wounded by an arrow, and died from its effects in *Ramzán* 624 H.=18th August 1227 A.D. (Y.C.), aged seventy-three years, having reigned twenty-five. He was buried, by his own desire, without ostentation, at the roots of a tree in his favourite hunting grounds. He had more than five hundred wives, but only five were noted for birth and beauty combined. They were Parta Cochín, a noble lady of the Cúnghrát tribe, the mother of his noted sons. In his early wars she was taken prisoner by the Makrít, and delivered to Aong Khán. He kept her sometime, and on a cessation of hostilities restored her to Changíz, whom, shortly after her return, she presented with the son named Jújí=stranger. A stigma always attached to his parentage, and was the cause of his disagreement with his brothers, and subsequent separation from them. He died during the life of Changíz, and his son, Bátú Khán, inherited his share of the empire. Parta Cochín after him bore Changíz three sons, viz., Aoktáy, Chaghtáy, and Túlí, and five daughters.

The other noted wives were Konjú, daughter of Altán Khan, King of Khitá; Kormay Sún, daughter of Táyáng Khán; Mysolon, the daughter of Jámkabúd; and Cúlán, the daughter of Táyrasún. The offspring of Changíz in a few generations exceeded ten thousand souls. He first instituted his celebrated *Yasá-Yúsún* code after the death of Aong Khán. On his coronation he confirmed it, and had it written in the Uighúr character, which he adopted for the Moghol language. He first established the decimal system of military organization, and the several ranks and offices for the civil administration of the Moghol empire, and instituted the hunting circles, called *Jirga*, with the rules and regulations for their conduct, and the pains and penalties for their infraction. He was a just ruler, protected merchants and encouraged commerce, tolerated all religions, and was liberal to those who unconditionally surrendered to his authority; but to those who opposed him his only course was one of utter ruin and extermination. On the death of Changíz some confusion followed in the succession to the Chiefship, and it was not till the spring of the third year after, that Aoktáy was acknowledged *Khán* at a *Cúrultáy* held in his camp. At this assembly he was crowned King, and divided the treasures left by Changíz amongst his sons, and nobles and chiefs and troops. He performed the funeral obsequies of the departed conqueror, and sacrificing forty noble virgins to his manes consigned them to his grave as companions in the world he had gone to. On this occasion Aoktáy received the homage of his brothers and nobles nine times on bended knee (according to the Tártár observance of that number), after which they went out and knelt three times to the sun as witness to their sincerity. All criminals were pardoned up to date, and the *Yasá-Yúsún* of Changíz ordained as the rule of government. And thus was inaugurated the succession to the throne of Changíz.

After this *Cúrultáy*, in the spring of 627 H.=1229 A.D., Aoktáy with Chaghtáy, and Túlí, marched to the conquest of Khitá. Túlí died during the campaign from the effects of a fever contracted through an act of brotherly devotion, of which instances are not uncommon amongst Tártár tribes. He had, to save the life of the sick Aoktáy, voluntarily taken his disease to himself by drinking a cup of water in which it had been typically washed away from his afflicted brother. The Moghol army suffered great losses in this campaign from the effects of climate and disease, but their booty in captured women was so great that the districts depopulated from these causes were soon repeopled by their offspring.

From the conquest of Khitá, Aoktáy returned to Karákoram, and in the spring of 633 H.=1235 A.D. sent his son Kúyúk, and Batú, the son of Jújí, and Mangú, the son of Túlí, and all the sons of Chaghtáy to the conquest of Rús, Charkas, and Bulghar, whilst he devoted his time to the restoration of the principal cities destroyed by his father, and the erection, at Karákoram, of a magnificent palace for himself.

It is said to have covered several square miles of surface, and to have comprised R.S.
separate suits of apartments for his several brothers and their families, besides hunting
parks, flower gardens, fish ponds, &c., and all sorts of resorts for pleasure and amusement, with gorgeous pavilions and halls for music, dispersed over the grounds. In
all these the workmanship was of the most elaborate and costly kind, and the
handiwork of the most skilful artificers and masters from China and the countries
of the west. On the return of the victorious armies from the latter direction, he
held a *Curultáy* here, and in the midst of its magnificent ceremonies, and varied
displays, its pleasures and festivities, the Great Lord of all the Tártár nations, the
most puissant sovereign of the age, the Great Aoktáy Cáán, the successor of Changíz,
died suddenly in 639 H.=1241 A.D. as King of Irán and Turán on the west,
and Mogholia and Khitá on the east.

Chaghtáy succeeded, and ruled the country from Irán to Karákoram. He was V.B.
a bigotted Budhist and a confirmed drunkard, nevertheless the country during his
rule flourished and prospered. He held his Court at Almálígh, between which and
Bukhárá he established a post of express couriers for speedy intelligence. He died
in the same year after Aoktáy, and left many sons, of whom Bísú, Borí, Bydar, and
Basan Bocá were present at the Curultáy, when Kúyúk, son of Aoktáy, succeeded to
the Kháni.

Chaghtáy had nominated his grandson Kará Huláku, a minor, to succeed him,
and his mother, Abúskún, acted as regent, and put to death many State officers in the
way of her ambition. On this Kúyúk deposed her, and disposing of other rivals,
in 645 H. = 1247 A.D., appointed Bísú as successor to Chaghtáy.

This, however, led to anarchy at the capital, Almálígh, and disorder soon spread Y.C.
all over the country, and led ultimately to the dismemberment of the Chaghtáy
empire, on the ruins of which, after the lapse of a hundred years of anarchy, usur-
pations, depositions, and murders amongst the Moghol Princes contending for power,
was constructed the new kingdom of Mogholistán, or Jattah Ulús, by a Chaghtáy
descendant. This kingdom of Mogholistán comprised the countries of Zúnghár and
Káshghar on the north and south respectively of the Allah Tágh or Tianshán range
of mountains.

Kúyúk, after three years' reign, was succeeded by Mangú Khan, the eldest son V.B.
of Túlí. He reinstated Kará Huláku and Abúskún, and, deposing Bísú for rebellion
against his authority, ordered Kará Huláku to kill him; but both died before the
mandate could be carried out. On this Mangú appointed Organa, the widow of Kará
Huláku, to the government of the Chaghtáy empire. She ruled in peace for ten
years at Almálígh, and there, in 1254 A.D. (Y.C.) received Huláku Khan, the
second son of Túlí, and the Lord of the Western Tátár, when he was on his march
from Karákoram against the *muláhid* or "assassins" in Persia, where, after the conquest of Baghdád, he died at Maragha in Azarbiján, not long after his brother,
Mangú, who died in 658 H. = 1259 A.D. at the siege of Tangtásh from the
effects of excessive drinking during his campaign against China. On his death war
broke out between his son and successor Cubláy Cáán, whose capital was at Khán-
bálígh, and Arik Búghá in the west.

Organa was now deposed by Algú, who fixed his seat at Almálígh as the protegé
of Arik Búghá. But he soon revolted and joined Cubláy, who, whilst Arik Búghá
was engaged against him in the west, advanced and seized Karákoram. Arik Búghá
now took Almálígh and drove out Algú, who fled first to Káshghar, and then to
Khutan, and finally to Samarcand. Meanwhile Almálígh was devastated, famine
followed, and thousands perished. Arik Búghá was now deserted by his Chiefs, and
proposed peace provided he held the Chaghtáy country. Algú agreed to this, married
Organa, and appointing Masáúd Beg, the Chaghtáy Governor of Máwaránahar, to act
as Wazir, thus restored peace.

Algú now repelled the invasion of Turkistán by Kaidú, the grandson of Aoktay,
who, aided by Bátú, contested the succession to the paramount *Khání* against Cubláy,
and died soon after his wife in 662 H. = 1263 A.D. Cubláy then appointed

V.B. Mubárak Sháh, the son of Kará Huláků, Khan of the Chaghtáy *ulús* = tribes, and Búrác, the great grandson of Chaghtáy as his Wazir.

P. In Mubárak Sháh we find the first Musalmán name amongst the Moghol rulers. The invasion of Changíz had given a decided check to the advance of that Islám, which had made such rapid progress in the conversion of this country to its doctrine in the two preceding centuries; for under his policy, which was followed by his immediate successors, of an impartial toleration of all creeds, the Muhammadan divines, deprived of their convincing argument with the sword, were brought down to the level of equality with the other religious propagandists of the time. And we find accordingly that for many years after the death of Changiz the diverse doctrines of Budha, Christ, and Muhammad flourished side by side, not, however, without emulous jealousy and rivalry. Yarkand itself, when Marco Polo visited the country in the reign of Cubláy Cáán, was a Bishop's see, as was Almálígh.

In the anarchy that soon divided the Changíz descendants, the professors of Islám gradually acquired the political ascendancy, and with it the advance of their religion gained a fresh impetus accompanied by all the enthusiasm and fanaticism that marked its earlier career here under the guidance of saintly teachers and miracle mongers, who claimed descent from their Prophet. Their success amongst the settled population in the cities and towns, and in the rural districts generally, was rapid and enduring, and led in the end, as will be seen in the sequel, to the government of the country passing into the hands of the priesthood.

This was more especially the case in the Western States of Káshghar up to Kúchá, which were nearer to Bukhárá, the centre of the Islam polity in Central Asia. Whilst beyond it, to the east, owing to the more immediate influence of the Budhism of China, the religion of the Prophet has never taken so firm a hold of the people, and even amongst the nomad tribes, who are more or less in direct contact with or dependent on the Musalmán population of the settled country, is more nominal than real unto the present day.

In the struggle for supremacy between these two religions here, Budhism and Muhammadanism, the Christianity, which in the early centuries of their rivalry held such a prominent and prior position in all the vast region of Central Asia, has left not a trace by which its former existence here can now be recognized. This is not to be wondered at if we consider the jealous intolerance of the Musalmán rulers, and the vigilant hostility that has even up to the present day enabled them to exclude all professors of the rival and superior doctrine from the pale of their subjects, and too often to prevent their even living in their countries as mere sojourners for a period. Let us hope, however, that brighter days are in store for the Christian in Central Asia, and that the enlightened toleration of the west may yet ere long extend its blessings of religious liberty to this region of blind bigotry and ignorant fanaticism.

V.B. Mubárak Sháh, the first Musalmán on the throne at Almálígh, was soon ousted by his Wazír, Búrác, the next heir to the Chaghtáy *Kháni*, who then, as a partizan of Cubláy, renewed the war with Kaidú, till ultimately, in 667 H. = 1269 A.D., they swore mutual peace and friendship in a cup of mingled gold and blood on the plain north of the Jaxartes, and became *anda* = allies (a term of relationship applied to men who are married to sisters), and shared the country between them. Bukhárá and Samarcand were held by Búrác, and Káshghar and Yarkand up to Kará Khoja, with the Talas river valley, and the country from Lake Balkash to Chagán Nor, that is Zungharia and Káshgharia, were held by Kaidú.

After this Búrác warred with Abaka, son and successor of Huláku, as King of Persia, but was defeated near Herat, and returning to Bukhárá, died there in the spring of 669 H. = 1270 A.D. And Kaidú then became master of the whole territory of Máwaránahar and Turkistán. He appointed Nekbay, the son of Sarban, to the *Kháni* of the Chaghtáy *ulús*.

On this the sons of Búrác and Algú united in revolt. Nekbay too revolted and was killed, and Toctymúr was appointed to govern the Chaghtáy *ulús*. He was

presently ousted by Dava = camel, the son of Búráo, who held Khutan (where he was V.B.
buried) as an ally of Kaidú, by whom he was now, in 671 H. = 1272 A.D., set on the
throne of Chaghtáy (Y.C.).

Dava Khan after this put an end to all other Aoktáy rivals, and added Turkistán
north of the Jaxartes to the Chaghtáy dominions. On the return of Tymúr Cáán,
the son and successor of Cubláy (under whose glorious reign the indolence and
barbarity of the Moghol character was greatly improved and softened by their
contact with the industry and polish of the Chinese), from his raid down to Lahore
Dava joined Kaidú against him. The hostile armies met and fought 701 H. = 1301
A.D. in the country between Karákoram and the Tárim river of Lob (in the vicinity
probably of Karáshahr the modern site of the ancient Jálish). Kaidú was defeated,
and, dying on his way home, was succeeded by his son Chaba or Shabar. He and
Dava now united in submission to Tymúr Cáán, but they soon after quarrelled.
Tymúr Cáán attacked Chaba, 703 H. = 1303 A.D., between Samarcand and Khujand,
whilst Dava seized all the Chaba territory and reunited the Chaghtáy empire as
before its division by Kaidú (Y.C.).

This did not last long, however, for Dava died in 706 H. = 1306 A.D., and the Y.C.
people of Eastern Turkistán, who had been under Kaidú rule, such as the Uighúr
of Káshghar, Yarkand, and Allahtágh (Alatagh), preferred a separate rule to that of
the Musulmáns of Mawaránahar, and, finding no Chaghtáy descendant amongst them,
invited Aymil Khoja, the son of Dava Khán, to be their ruler. He was succeeded
in 1347 A.D. by Toghlúc Tymúr, who thus once more re-established the eastern
branch of the Chaghtáy *Kháni*, known as the kingdom of Mogholistán or the Jattah
ulús, whose capital was at Káshghar first, then at Yárkand, and later at Aksú, with
the summer quarters at Atbashi on the Upper Nárín to the north of the Allahtágh.

Meanwhile in Máwaránahar another son of Dava, named Konjuk, had ascended V.B.
the throne. He died very shortly, and then Talikada, a descendant of Moaltakin, a
Chaghtáy, who was killed at Bámyán, succeeded. He accepted Islám, and was the
second convert amongst Moghol rulers. He was soon killed by his nobles, who then
set Kabak, another son of Dava, on the throne. Chaba warred with him, and was
defeated. Kabak now resigned the Government to an elder brother, Eshan Boghá,
who was chief of the Chaghtáy *ulús* from 709H. = 1309 A.D. to 716H. = 1316 A.D.
He conquered Khurásán up to the Murgháb river in 1315 A.D. In retaliation for
this Oljátú, the Moghol King of Persia, under the name of Khudá Banda, sent an
army with a convert brother of Eshán Boghá, named Yasavar (and a refugee with him)
to ravage Máwaránahar. They massacred, pillaged, and captivated the population
up to Samarcand in the depth of winter. Eshán Boghá now disappeared, and Kabak,
resuming the Government, punished his rebel brother, and died 721H. = 1321 A.D.

After this followed many years of rivalry and anarchy under successive Chiefs,
till the time of Kábil Sháh in 1363 A.D. During this period, since the invasion of
Changíz, the Moghol character succumbed to the superior physique and innervation
of their subjects of the Caucasian stock, and their manners and religion declined
before the advancing force of a revived Islám.

After the death of Kabak, the Kháni of the Chaghtáy empire in 1321 A.D. Y.C.
fell to the hands of Elchi Gadáy, who was succeeded by Tarmashirin Khán. He
became a convert to Islám, and, adopting the name 'Aláuddín, abandoned Almáligh,
the later capital of the Moghols—the first and original capital was Beshbáligh—and
removed his Court to Máwaránahar. He was dethroned 1334-35 A.D. by his
brother Búzún Khán. He persecuted the Musálmans, who at this time everywhere
displayed a remarkable activity and zeal in propagating their polity and creed; but
was very soon deposed by Chansi, or Jinkshi Khan, also of the Chaghtay line, to
whom Pope Benedict XII. in 1338 A.D. addressed a letter of thanks for the protection
he afforded to Christians.

He in turn was shortly ousted from the Government by Yesuntimur, and he
again, in 1338-39 A.D., by 'Alí Sultán, that "certain villain of a falconer, a Saracen

48.—A Doulan from the Maralbashi.

49.—The Pamir Mountains from Yangi Hissar and the Tagharma Peak.

Y.C. of the blood royal," by whose orders the Christian Missionaries and the Bishop of the See were martyred at Almáligh (in 1339-40 A.D.), where presently he was ousted by the Amír Kazghan, or Kazan, who reigned till 1346 A.D., and was the last effective Khán of the main Chaghtáy branch.

After his death in that year, the successive rulers of the Chaghtáy *úlús* were mere puppets in the hands of the Amírs, or Provincial Military Governors, who set up and knocked down much at their pleasure, till the time of Tymúr. And even he at the height of his power maintained a titular successor to the Chaghtáy throne. The last of these, Sultán Muhammad Khan, died on active service in Tymúr's Anatolia campaign in 1403 A.D.

T.R. The first of these rulers of the Chaghtáy *úlús*, or Moghol Khans, as they are called, was Toghlúc Tymúr, who was set on the throne in succession to the Amír Kazghan by the Amír Boláji of Aksú. His history, as given in the *Tárikhi Rashídi*, a history of the Moghol Khans, written by Mirza Hyder in Kashmír, 952 H = 1544 A.D., may be thus summarized.

Toghlúc Tymúr Khán was the son of Eshán Boghá, the son of Dava, the son of Bárác, the son of Kará Bisú, the son of Mangú, the son of Chaghtáy, the son of Changiz. Eshán Boghá had many wives. Of these Sátelmish Kháton was the chief, but she was barren. He went on an expedition into Máwaránahar, and left her in charge of his other wives. According to the ancient custom of the country the chief wife, in the absence of her husband, had supreme control of his other wives, and power to dispose of them as she pleased. Sátelmish now found one of Eshán Boghá's wives, Minílik Kháton by name, was pregnant, and, becoming jealous, gave her away in marriage to a noble, named Sharáol Dukhtoy.

On his return home Eshán Boghá was grieved to learn this, and soon after died, leaving no successor to the Government. The Moghol tribes consequently soon became divided by anarchy and dissension till Amir Boláji, Doghlát, produced the rightful heir. He sent one Tásh Tymúr = " Iron stone," with a flock of sheep for his sustenance, to wander amongst the Moghol tribes, discover the camp of Sharáol Dukhtoy, and find out if Minilik had borne a son. And if so, to steal and bring him away. Tash Tymúr, after long wandering, arrived at the camp of Sharáol, when only one blue goat of his flock of three hundred remained. He found that Minílik had two sons : the one by Eshan Boghá called Toghlúc Tymúr; and the other by Sharáol, called Anjú Malik.

He stole away Toghlúc, and joining a caravan, brought him by way of the Múzárt, or " Glacier Pass," to his master at Aksú. In crossing the glacier his youthful charge fell into a crevasse, and was extricated from his perilous position in the bottom of the chasm by means of a ladder of ropes, through the aid of the merchants of the caravan, headed by their leader Begjik. For his success in this enterprise, and the circumstance of the one remaining goat when he found Toghlúc, the adventurous Tásh Tymúr got the soubriquet of *Kok Ajku* = Blue goat.

Amír Boláji was originally of an Aksú family. When Chaghtáy divided his kingdom into military commands, he gave the Mangaláy Súbah = " the Front division" to Aortobá, the grandfather of Boláji. Its boundaries on the east are Kohistán and Tábogor; on the west Sám and Jáh Cásman, which is the end of the Farghána country ; on the north Isíghkol ; and on the south Cháchan and Sárigh Uighúr.

Amír Bolají succeeded to this command, and its chief cities, in his time, were Khutan, Yárkand, Kásán, Uzkand, Andiján, Atbáshi, Kosán, and Aksú. This last was the capital of Boláji.

Toghlúc Tymúr was sixteen years old when he arrived at Aksú, and two years later, about 1332 A.D., Boláji set him up as Khán; and he was so acknowledged by all Mogholistán and most of the Chaghtáy country. He became a convert to Islám, and the author I am quoting gives the following account in connection with the event :—

When Changiz took Bukhárá he slew most of the Musalmán clergy there, with their High Priest Khoja Háfizuddín; but he spared Mauláná Shujáuddín Mahmúd and his family, and sent them to Karákoram. On the fall of that city, his sons went and settled at Lob and Katak, large cities between Turfán and Khutan. Here they left large families. The last representative of these was Shekh Jamáluddín. He resided in Katak, and fled from it when the place was buried by a hurricane of sand, which fell from the sky as does rain.

The wind sometimes blows away this sand, and exposes to view domes and minarets, which again become buried by fresh drifts of sand. At times houses, too, are thus exposed, and wandering shepherds relate that their furniture is discovered intact, and the occupants are seen standing as bleached skeletons, or lying prostrate as desiccated bodies just in the attitudes in which they were overwhelmed; and all uninjured by decay.

The Shekh foresaw the impending calamity, and warned the citizens of it a week beforehand, and taking leave of his congregation at the Friday prayers, quitted the city and escaped the approaching destruction. He came to Aksú by way of Ay Kol two years after the arrival there of Toghlúc Tymúr, and met the young Chief on a hunting excursion in the vicinity as he approached the city. He was seized, and taken before Toghlúc for infringing the rule to fall in with the *jirga*="hunting circle" on meeting it, and in excuse pleaded ignorance as a stranger coming from Katak. Toghlúc was at the time feeding one of his hounds on boar's flesh, and turning scornfully towards the Musalmán thus addressed him—"Ho! Tájik! Art thou the better or this dog? "The Shekh promptly replied—"Since I have the faith I am the better. Without it the dog is better than me." This bold answer made an impression on Toghlúc, and on his return home he sent for the Tájik, and enquired of him what the faith was that made him better than a dog. The Shekh explained the *imán*="Faith," and set before him the tenets of Islám. Toghlúc was struck by the merits of the doctrine, and promised to accept the "Faith" on becoming King, as he now feared the hostility of his people.

The Shekh soon after died, and committed the charge of converting the Moghol Prince to his son, Arshaduddín. Following this Toghlúc went to Mogholistan to receive the allegiance of the Kirghíz, Jattah, &c., and was there proclaimed King. Arshaduddín, in obedience to his father's behest, set out for the royal camp, and at daylight after arrival there chaunted the Muhammadan call to prayer near the King's tent. He was seized and taken before the Khán for making such an untimely noise and disturbing his slumber. Toghlúc asked him who he was, and what he meant. "I am," replied the Musalmán priest with characteristic fervour and independence, "the son of him to whom you gave your word to accept Islám on becoming King, and, by his dying injunction, I have come for its fulfilment. Toghlúc, true to his promise, welcomed him cordially, treated him with marked deference, and accepting Islám at his hands, summoned his nobles one by one and invited them to follow his example.

Amír Tolak, the brother of Boláji, who at that time held the rank of Doghlát, and had three years before, when Governor of Káshghar, secretly become a Musalmán, was now the first to make a public profession of the Faith; and others following the example, they went from tent to tent and speedily converted most of the Chiefs. The Jarás nobles, however, refused to follow suit, unless their champion, one Sanghoy Bocá, was first thrown in wrestling with the Tájik. The new converts opposed the demand on the grounds of the manifest inequality of the combatants; but the Shekh, interposing, accepted the challenge, saying that his trust was in God for the victory. The Jarás champion scornfully, in the pride of his strength, seized the puny Tájik to throw him, but the priest of Islám solemnly planted the palm of his hands on his adversary's breast, and repeated an appropriate text from the Kurán touching the repulsion and overthrow of the unbeliever, and the pagan champion fell senseless to the ground. On his recovery he acknowledged his discomfiture as a divine warning and without hesitation accepted the Faith; and one hundred and sixty

T.R. thousand people followed his example. Toghlúc Tymúr was at this time twenty years of age, and he died ten years later in 764H.=1362 A.D.

V.B. In the anarchy following on the death of Amír Kazghan, the Jaláyr north of Samarcand, and the Suldoz in Kish and Nakhshab became independent, and others set up for themselves in different parts of the country.

T.R. Toghlúc Tymúr on becoming King of the Chaghtáy *ulús* found this anarchy reigning in Máwaránahar, and in Rabí Tháni 761H.=1359-60 A.D., thirty years after the death of Tarmashirín Khán, invaded the country, and restored a short lived order. At Khujand he received the submission of Amír Báyzíd Jaláyr, and at Kárshí drove Amír Hájí Birlás, to retreat across the Oxus into Khurásán. Tymúr, who now first appears on the scene of Asiatic politics, in the history of which his career fills so eventful a page, appealed to him not to desert the country without a struggle, and himself, collecting a force at Kish, advanced to Khazár to oppose the enemy who were coming on plundering the country under the guidance of Hájí Muhammad Sháh Yasaví.

But Toghlúc meantime had reached the capital, and Tymúr, unable to check the invaders, turned and repairing to him there, tendered submission. Toghlúc was favorably impressed by the rising conqueror, and reinstating him in the Government of Kish and its dependencies, retired from the country. On his departure the Amírs Hájí Birlás, Khizr Yasaví, and Tymúr united in revolt against the Moghol. Consequently Toghlúc again invaded Máwaránahar with a numerous army in *Jamádi Awwal* of the following year. The Amírs Báyzíd and Bayán Suldoz submitted, and accompanied the Moghol army to Samarcand, but Hájí Birlás and his brother, Aydko, opposing, were driven into Khurásán. They escaped to Sabzwár, and were there slain by the people of Karásha, in the Juwen *buluk* or "district." In after years, when Tymúr conquered Khurásán, he avenged their death by a massacre of the people, and grant of the country in fief to the heirs of his murdered kinsmen. In this second campaign, Toghlúc, on the recommendation of the Amír Hamid, Kurulkút, one of the wisest and most influential of the Jattah nobles, re-confirmed Tymúr in the Government of Kish, and, in the same winter, took the field against Amír Husen, who held out at Kundúz. Toghlúc crossed the Wakhsh river, and passed through the narrow and difficult pass of Darband Ahanín="iron barrier," beyond which he was joined by Kaikhusro of Khatlán, who had deserted from Amír Husen, then in full flight down the Oxus. Toghlúc crossed the river to Kundúz, and passed the spring and summer in subjugating the country up to Hindú Kush. He returned to Samarcand in the autumn; executed Bayán Suldoz, and many other troublesome Chiefs, and having established his son, Ilyás Khoja, as governor of Máwaránahar, with Begjik, a Jattah noble, as minister, and Tymur as councillor, returned to Mogholistán.

V.B. On the departure of the Moghol army, Tymúr disagreed with Begjik, and, effecting his escape with his wife, Olja Turkán, joined Husen in the Khivá desert. From this date commenced that extraordinary career of this second world conqueror of modern times—the "scourge of God" over the whole Asiatic continent, the China region excepted. Here we are only concerned to notice that portion of his devastating career connected with the history of this country.

Tymúr was born in the Shahrisubz suburb of Kish on Tuesday, 5th *Sha'ban* 736H.=1333 A.D., and was the son of Turgháy, the Chief of the Birlás tribe, and Governor of Kish on behalf of the Amír Kazghan. His father sent him for service to the Court, and Kazghan being favorably impressed by the bearing of the youth, gave him in marriage the celebrated Olja Turkán Kháton (the daughter of his son, Salah Khán), the devoted partner of his early adventures and misfortunes; and appointing him *Ming-báshi*="commander of a thousand," took him along with his army on the campaign against Husen Kurd of Khurásán.

Both Amír Kazghan and Turgháy died soon after this expedition, and Husen, succeeding his father in the Government, appointed Tymúr to the charge of Kish in succession to Turgháy. But anarchy and disorder soon spread all over the country, and brought about the invasion of Toghlúc above noticed. Tymúr, after his escape from Samarcand, wandered a toilsome and adventurous month in the desert, where he was captured by the slave-hunting Turkmán. He, however, effected his escape with Olja, and returning secretly to Kish, raised a band of adventurers, and sought a career for himself by a raid into Sístán. Here he was wounded by an arrow in the right foot and lamed for life, and thus got the name of Tymúr Lang = "Tymúr the Lame," the famous Tamerlane of history. V.B.

Whilst he was laid up with this wound Amír Husen seized Balkh, and Tymúr joined him there. At this time their united forces numbered only fifteen hundred men. Ilyás Khoja sent a force against them, but it was defeated near Kundúz in 765 H. = 1363 A.D., and as he presently heard of the death of his father, Toghlúc, Ilyás hurried off from Samarcand to secure the throne at Almáligh. Tymúr on this drove the Jattah out of Máwaránahar, and returning from Táshkand entered Samarcand, and was well received. He held a *Curultáy* and set Kábil Sháh on the throne.

In the following spring Ilyás returned with a large army to recover Máwaránahar, and was met in opposition by the Amírs Husen and Tymúr. A battle ensued on the muddy plain of Láe = "Mud" on the banks of the Bádám river between Chinás and Táshkand in *Ramazan* 766 H. = 1364 A.D. In the fight Husen quarrelled with Tymúr, and quitting the field, retired to Sále Saráe. Tymúr thus deserted withdrew to Karshí and Balkh, whilst Ilyás advancing set siege to Samarcand. A plague now broke out in his camp, and he was forced to retreat as best he could, having lost many men and most of his cattle. T.R.

Tymúr and Husen now warred for the mastery, and, finally, after years of alternate reconciliations and hostilities, Husen surrendered at Balkh, and was there executed 771 H. = 1369 A.D. Tymúr now held a *Curultáy*, and in Turk fashion was raised aloft on a white felt, and proclaimed King of Máwaránahar as Amír Tymúr Gúrikán, with the title of Sháh Sáhibi Karán, on Wednesday, 12th *Ramazan* of the same year (Z.N.T.). From this he crossed to Samarcand, and fixing it as the capital of the Chaghtáy Empire now revived in his person, built its fort, and established the *Yúsáo* of Changíz as the law of the land (T.R.). V.B.

In the winter following this the restless Jattah again invaded Máwaránahar. Tymúr drove them across the Syhon, and subjugating the Kumza and Ortagtamúr tribes on the frontier, returned to his capital. Whilst he was absent on this expedition the Sháh of Badakhshán, Shekh 'Alí, invaded Kundúz, and plundered the country; consequently Tymúr at once set out again to punish him. T.R.

He marched by way of Tálkhán and Kishm, forced the obstinately defended passes of Gokus and Jurm, and came up with the Badakhshí Sháh in the deep and strongly barricaded glen of Artunj-darra, at the junction of two swift torrents. Tymúr drove him from this position to Canagh Aolang, where crossing the head waters of the Jyhon, the fugitive King stood to defend its passage. Sheik 'Alí was here taken prisoner, and his army dispersing for the most part escaped into the neighbouring glens. In the pursuit Tymúr got entangled in the mountains, and was surrounded and nearly captured in a deep and winding defile by a party of the Badakhshí highlanders. Z.N.T.

His escape was merely due to the impudent temerity of his few attendants, who rushing in amongst the ignorant Tájik, slapped them in the face, and with affronted dignity demanded if they knew who it was they dared to press around so disrespectfully. On hearing the already dread name of the rising conqueror, the simple mountaineers at once tendered submission, and suing for pardon, restored the prisoners and captives they had captured. Tymúr in after years often referred to this fight as the hardest and most perilous of the many he had engaged in, and the country as the most rugged and difficult of any he had seen in all his varied experiences. Yet he did not fail to punish in an exemplary manner his soldiers who, on this occasion, allowed themselves to be captured by the enemy.

T. R.   On the death of Toghlúc Tymúr his son, Ilyás Khoja, hastening up from Samarcand, as stated, succeeded to the throne at Almáligh in 1364 A.D.; but, on his return to Mogholistán in the following year from his disastrous attempt to recover Máwaránahar, he was seized and killed by Amír Kamaruddín, who had usurped the Government and murdered all the descendants of Toghlúc he could lay hands on. Eighteen Moghol Princes were killed by him in one day; but, Khizr Khoja, the youngst son of Toghlúc, a boy of twelve years, and the only surviving member of the family, was rescued by Khudádád, the Amír of Káshghar and nephew of the usurper, and sent away by him with his mother, Mír Aghá, and some trusty adherents for concealment in the mountains of Bolor.

This Kamaruddín was one of five brothers who held district Governments in Mogholistán as heirs of former Amírs originally appointed by Changiz. They were Tolak at Káshghar, Boláji at Aksú, Kamaruddín at Atbáshí, Shamsuddín, who was present at the battle of Láe, and Shekh Daulat, of whom there is no trace. Tolak, the eldest, was succeeded in the *úlús-begi* by Boláji; and he by his son, Khudádád, who was seven years old when his father died.

Z.N.T.   Whilst Amír Kamaruddín was thus securing his usurped rule in Mogholistán, the Amírs Husen and Tymúr were contesting the mastery in Máwaránahar; and, on the final accession of the latter to the throne at Samarcand, his first care was to repel the encroachments of the Jattah Moghol on the Táshkand frontier, as before mentioned. The submission then exacted did not prove effective, and the Jattah, taking advantage of Tymúr's absence in the campaigns against Badakhshán and Khwárizm, made repeated incursions across the border into Máwaránahar.

Whilst engaged in his first campaign against Khívá, Tymúr in the spring of 773 H.=1371 A.D. sent a force under Bahrám Jaláyr and Khítáy Bahadur to repel the Jattah incursions. They drove the enemy across the border, and pursuing, devastated the country up to Almátú or Almáti, where, defeating the Karait, they concluded peace. It did not last long, however, and Tymúr, on his return from Khwárizm, took the field with a numerous army against Kamaruddín, the Jattah Chief. He took flight to the mountains, and Tymúr, after ravaging the country up to Sikiz Aghach="Eight trees" in the vicinity of Isigh Kol, returned with innumerable captives and cattle.

Following this came Tymúr's second campaign against Khiva in 774 H.=1372 A.D., whence he brought away Súyún (daughter of Yúsúf Súfí, who died in the first siege), whose marriage with his son, Jahángír, he celebrated on return to the capital. Meanwhile the irrepressible Kamaruddín continued his incursions on the borders of Táshkand. Consequently, Tymúr took the field on his third campaign against the Jattah.

He set out from Samarcand on Thursday, 1st *Shábán*, 776 H.=1374 A.D., but was forced to return after a few marches owing to the intensity of the cold, and loss of men and cattle in the frosts, winds, and snows. He set out again two months later with a recruited army, and sent Jahángír ahead with the vanguard by Syrám to Kok-tappa, where Kamaruddín was camped. He drove the Jattah army from this position, and pursued them to their stronghold, Barka Kurghán, a small castle in the highest of three dark and deep glens, each of which was occupied by a swift and copious torrent. Kamaruddín and his nomads, scared by the boldness of their pursuers, fled during the night, and Jahángír then, plundering the country along the Ayla River, took whole camps of the Jattah prisoners, and marched them off under escort to Samarcand by order of Tymúr, who next sent him in pursuit of Kamaruddín to Pae-tágh="Mountain Base."

The Chief escaped into the mountains, but his principal settlement at Úch-Burhán or Úch Turfán, together with his treasures and family, fell into the hands of Jahángír, who, returning thence, joined his father, after an absence of fifty-three days, at Kará Kasmác, and rendered up his captives and plunder. Tymúr distributed these amongst his soldiers, but reserved the prize of all,—the lovely Dilshád Agha="Lady

Heart's Joy," the daughter of the fugitive Jattah Chief—for himself, and a few days Z.N.T.
later, crossing Atbáshi to Arpa Yázi plain, there celebrated his marriage with her
by magnificent ceremonies, and a round of splendid festivities, amidst which he was
sumptuously entertained by Mubárak Shah, the Makrit Chief of the country, who
presented gifts in the customary rotation of nine of each kind. After these rejoicings Tymúr crossed the 'Ucba Yási Pass to Uzkand, where he was joined by his first
wife, Olja Turkán; and thence, with a succession of festivities and entertainments, in
which he escaped more than one plot against his life, returned to his capital.

In the spring of the next year, 777H. = 1375 A.D., Tymúr detailed a force of
thirty thousand horse under Amír Sárboghá with 'Adilsháh Jaláyr, Khitáy Bahádur,
and Elchiboghá, to hunt down and kill Kamaruddin, who had again renewed his
attacks on the frontier; and, appointing Acboghá to the Government of Samarcand,
himself set out on his third expedition against Khiva.

On his departure Sárboghá and 'Adilsháh revolted, and, seizing the other two,
besieged Samarcand. Tymúr hastened back to the relief of the capital, but the
rebels, escaping into the Kapchák country, there, in the absence of Urús Khan
amongst his nomads, killed his minister Uji Báy, and passing on, joined Kamaruddin.
With him they invaded Andiján, held by 'Umar Shekh as Governor for Tymúr, and
drew off the Kazzák tribes from him to their own party.

In consequence of this Tymúr, having secured Samarcand, set out on his fourth
campaign against the Jattah of Mogholistán. Kamaruddin retired to Atbáshi, and,
sending off his people and cattle to Isigh Kol, lay in ambush with four thousand horse
at Sóng Kol. He surprised Tymúr and a small escort with him, but was driven back
and pursued to Sikiz Aghach. Here Tymúr heard of the death of his favourite son,
Jahángir, at Samarcand, and, leaving a force under 'Umar Shekh, with Acboghá,
Khitáy Bahádur and others to carry on the war, himself hurried back to the capital,
where he was met by the populace in ashes and mourning.

Kamaruddin, after a long chase, again escaped his pursuers to the Korátu Desert;
and they returned having plundered the country thus far, and executed the rebellious
'Adilsháh, whom they captured wandering in a demented state in the hills near the
Acsúmá tower—a red brick pillar built on the Kará Chác hill as an outlook upon the
Kapchák plain.

After the funeral obsequies of his son, Tymúr, in 778H. = 1376 A.D., set out
on his fifth campaign against the restless Kamaruddin. The advance was led by
Muhammad Beg, the son of Amír Músá, and he came up with the enemy at Boghám
Isigh Kol. The Chief was not found, but his army and camp, after a short struggle,
were captured. In this expedition Tymúr learned that Toctamish, the son of Urús
Khan, was coming to seek his protection. He left an *Amíri tumán* = "Commander of
ten thousand" to meet and escort the refugee from Kapchák, and meanwhile pursued
his return march to the capital by the route through Cochcár and Jumghál to Uzkand
in Farghána. At Samarcand he received Toctamish, and, loading him with favors,
adopted him as his son, and gave him Atrár and Syrám to hold as a frontier against
his brother Toctá Káyá.

In this last campaign against the Jattah, Kamaruddin, who was of such vast
size that a child of seven years could stand in one of his boots, was unable to keep his
saddle owing to dropsy and a foul disease in the groin. His people, on the close
approach of Tymúr, concealed him in a forest at Kolmá Cájor, with a supply of food
and a couple of slaves to attend him; but he was never again seen or heard of. On
his disappearance peace and order were once more restored to the Jattah of Mogholistán.

During the period Kamaruddin held rule over Mogholistán, Khizr Khoja, the T.R.
heir of Toghlúc Tymúr, was wandering in exile amongst the mountains on the opposite
borders of the country, moving from place to place as his hiding was discovered by
the pursuing emissaries of the usurper. From Bolor he was successively carried out
of harm's way to the mountain retreats of Badakhshán, Khutan, and Sárígh Uighúr,

and finally to the Kalmák settlements about Katak and Lob. And thus he spent the twelve years from the death of his father to that of his persecutor.

On the disappearance of Kamaruddín, his nephew, Khudádád, the Amír of Káshghar, assumed the Government of the Jattah tribes; and, after restoring order amongst them, recalled Khizr from his retreat at Lob, and, in 1383 A.D. (Y.C.), set him on the throne at Káshghar as Khán of Mogholistán. Khizr now allied with Tymúr, and sent him as a gift the beautiful Tokal Khánim, one of the widows of the late enemy of both.

He enforced a strict observance of the Muhammadan *Shariat* amongst the Jattah nomads, who were still mostly Budhists; and next to Káshghar he made Turfán the second capital of the Moghol Khácán—the title he revived on ascending the throne. Tymúr died in his reign, and then Khizr, becoming more independent, restored the old Moghol form of government, which, during the disordered rule of his predecessor, had fallen to neglect. He now granted to his benefactor and friend, the Amír Khudádád, the rank and privileges that had been originally accorded by Changíz to his ancestor, Aortúbo, with the additions made thereto by Toghlúc Tymúr on behalf of Boláji, and by himself, now, in favour of his faithful adherent.

The privileges originally granted by Changíz were the following:— First, *Túmán-togh* = "Banner of ten thousand men." Second, *Nacára* = "Kettledrum." Third, *Cushún-togh* = "Camp-banner," of which two were allowed. Fourth, *Cúr* = "Armour," which none but the Khán had the power to remove from the person. Fifth, *Jirga* = "Hunting circle," with power to punish according to rule those who infringed its regulations. Sixth, *Amiri-úlús* = "Commander of his tribe." Seventh, *Sar-dúwán* = "Top seat in Court," at a bow length on either side of the Khán. To these Toghlúc Tymúr added two others, namely: Eighth, *Amiri Cushún* = "Command of a camp of one thousand men," with power to promote and reduce without reference to the Khán. Ninth, *Tarkhán* = "Pardon of crime to the ninth conviction," for Amír Boláji and his direct heirs; on conviction of the tenth crime to be bled to death from both arms. Khizr Khoja now added another for Amír Khudadád, namely, tenth, *Yasáwul* = "Provost," at feasts and entertainments. One *Yasáwul* of the Khán to be mounted on his right hand, and one *Yasáwul* of the Amír to stand on his right hand at Court. After drinking the cups to be sealed with their respective signets by the *Yasáwul*. He gave the title of *Gúrikán* also to Khudádád and made it hereditary.

These privileges and ranks descended from Amír Khudádád to his son Muhammad Sháh, and from him to his nephew Syad Ali, and then to his son Muhammad Hydar, and his son Muhammad Husen, and his son Mirzá Hydar (the author of *Tárikhí Rashídí*), and to his son Syad Muhammad, in whom they became extinct 940 H. = 1533 A.D.

Previous to the assumption of this royal prerogative, however, Khizr had to experience the weight of Tymúr's vengeance, when, in 791 H. = 1389-90 A.D., owing to the obstinate hostility of the Jattah, he undertook his final campaign for the subjugation of Mogholistán, after his return from the conquest of Afghánistán.

He took its capital, Almáligh, and ravaged the whole country up to Kaidú, where he fixed his head-quarters. Here, in the charming and productive valley of Yuldúz, he enjoyed the delights of its climate, and the pleasures of its attractive scenery of clear streams, fresh meadows, and umbrageous forests, amidst a succession of feasts and hunting excursions; whilst his vast army in four grand divisions swept the whole country north and south of the Tianshán range, and finally rejoined him there with the world of their plunder and captives.

Of the two southern divisions, one ravaged the country from Andiján and Káshghár along the southern skirts of Allah-tágh or Alatágh to Kará Khoja beyond Turfán; whilst the other did likewise from Sárigh Kúl and Kokyár, along the north base of the Khutan and Sárigh Uighúr country, across by Katak and Lob to the appointed rendezvous. At Yuldúz Tymúr divided the spoil amongst his troops, transported whole tribes of the population to Samarcand, restored Khizr to the

government of his crushed and crippled people, married his daughter, and, leaving T.R.
the main army with its train of captives to follow, set off with a party of light
horse on the 15*th Shábán* and arrived at Samarcand 7*th Ramazán* 791H., thus
accomplishing a journey of three months in as many weeks.

In this campaign the divisions operating on the north of the Alátágh overran
the whole country between the sandy steppes on the north and the green vallies of
Yuldúz on the south. They took the royal city of Aymil Guja, which, according to
Yule, was probably built on the bank of the Aymil river from the Alákol, and was
the original capital of the refugee Khitáy, who founded the Kará Khitáy empire, and
is now represented by, probably, Chughuchak of Turbaghátai.

One more expedition was sent in the following spring against Anga Tora of Z.N.T.
Karátál, an active ally of Khizr in the last campaign. The invaders devastated
afresh the country up to Almálígh, and, driving Anga Tora from his capital, pursued
him to the River Irtish, beyond which he escaped into the county of Tolus, whence
come the *Sumúr* = sable, *Cácúm* = otter, and other furs.

After this Tymúr was occupied for many years in his western conquests, and
the invasion of India. On his return to Samarcand, for the nineteenth time, with
the spoils and treasures of one-half the Asiatic continent, his insatiable pride and
ambition led him to undertake the conquest of the other.

Amongst the vast preparations set on foot for the conquest of China, he sent T.R.
orders to Khizr Khoja, his feudatory in Mogholistán, to sow the land at Kok-tappa
with corn, and there to collect cattle for his army about to march that way.
Khizr was there with the Amír Khudádád, in the early spring of 807 H. =
1405 A.D., to superintend the collection of supplies for the advancing host.
One day as he and his friend were seated in their camp discussing affairs
over a social cup of *cumiz* = fermented mare's milk, a figure in white, mounted
on a black horse, suddenly dashed past the guards, and galloping into camp
made for the spot where they were seated, and announcing in a loud voice
" Amír Tymúr lies dead at Atrár," suddenly disappeared from sight before the guards
running up from all sides could stop him. " A *jinn* = ' ghost' most likely" remarks the
historian I quote, " for confirmation of the fact was not received till forty-five days
later." Tymúr crossed the Syhon on the ice, and was obliged to halt at Atrár, also
called Táráb, on account of an inflammation of the lungs. The disease rapidly
increased, and after a delay here of seven or eight days he died from its effects on
the 7*th Shábán* 807 H. = 17th February 1405 A.D. (V.B.)

Khizr Khoja ruled independently for several years after this, and was succeeded
by his son, Muhammad Khan, who was the last of the Moghol Khácán. He was
a wealthy, just, and powerful Prince, and converted all his people to Islám, yet so
jealous was he of the turban, the outward emblem of the Faith, being worn by any
but the priesthood and his own officials, that he punished any of the Tartar peasantry
who dared to desecrate the sacred head-piece, by securing their own national fur caps
upon their heads by horse shoes pegged to their skulls.

The Moghol have no record of the date of his birth or death; but, Ulugh Beg
in Máwaránahar, and Sháhrúkh in Khurásan, were his contemporaries. He was
succeeded by his son Sher Muhammad Khan, during whose reign the country
enjoyed security and prosperity. His brother, Sher Ali Oghlán, died aged eighteen
years during his life, and left a son named Wais Khán. He rebelled against his
uncle, and formed a band of *cazzác* = robber, with whom he harried the Máwaránahar
border. He was joined by adventurers and discontents from all parts of the country,
and, amongst others of note, by Syad Ali, the grandson of Khudádád, as will be
presently related.

On the death of Tymúr, his only surviving son, Sháhrúkh, was at Herat, so he V.B.
appointed his grandson, Pir Muhammad, as his successor. But, whilst he was
debauching at Kabul, Sultán Khalil, the son of Miránsháh, who happened to be
with the army, got possession of Samarcand. Pír Muhammad now contested the

50.—Guard of Honor under Panjsad Khal Mahomed, (Bahatur Batcha) sent out to meet the Envoy from Yangi Hissar.

51.—Kirghiz Felt (Akoe) occupied by officers of the mission at Yangi Hissar.

V.B.　throne, but was slain at Shuborghán, in 809 H.=1406 A.D., by his own *Wazír*, Pir Ali Táz.

Khudádád then opposed Khalíl, who had estranged the nobles from his support by his unseemly and infatuated love for Shádulmulkh="the country's joy;" on whom, whilst neglecting for her service the affairs of his government, he squandered, to the just indignation and disgust of the royal ladies of the harem, the vast treasures left by Tymúr. Khalíl by his folly, and the discontent it gave rise to, soon fell under the power of his rival, to whom he was delivered by his own Generals. Khudádád sent him to Káshghar, and, taking possession of the capital, exposed to ridicule and insult in its streets the luxurious and fascinating Shádulmulk, the former slave of Háji Syfuddín and now the wife of the infatuated Khalíl, who, in his exile, instead of exerting himself to recover his independence and lost power, did nothing but waste his time in maudlin versification of the idol of his love. Sháhrukh, hearing of the downfall of his nephew, marched from Herat against Khudádád, who fled to Táshkand and sought the aid of the Moghol King; but he killed him, and sent his head to Sháhrúkh as a token of friendship. Sháhrúkh, having thus secured the submission of all Máwaránahar, recalled Khalíl from Káshghar, and, restoring to him his love, sent him to the government of Irác, on the way whither he died, 812 H.=1409 A.D.; and appointed his own eldest son, the celebrated Ulugh Beg, to the government of Máwaránahar.

T.R.　At this time the Amír Khudádád was in attendance on Muhammad Khan in Mogholistán, and had left his son, Syad Ahmad, to govern at Káshghar. He was deaf and had an impediment in his speech, and was altogether a weak and unpopular ruler; and was soon deposed by Khoja Sharif, one of the city magnates, who invited Ulugh Beg over, and delivered the city to him.

Ahmad fled to his father in Mogholistán, and died there soon after; and the aged Khudádád then adopted his son, Syad Ali as his favourite. He was a fine soldierly youth, and a noted hunter, but, seemingly, as liable as others to the tender emotions of love. When Ahmad Mirzá of the Tymúr family fled from Sháhrukh, he sought asylum with Amír Khudádád in Mogholistán. He was accompanied by his sister, and with this young lady Syad Ali fell in love. When they left on their return homewards he accompanied the refugees on a promise of marriage with the object of his affections. When they reached Andiján, however, they were all seized by order of Ulugh Beg, who killed Ahmad, married his sister, and sent Ali to prison at Samarcand. He nearly died there of dysentery, but recovered on getting some of his accustomed *cumiz*, after he had been given up by the doctors; and when Ulugh, a year later, went to see his father at Herat, he took this gigantic Moghol with him as a specimen of the sort of people he had to deal with on the frontier. On the way, however, he took alarm at the size of his weapons, his arrows measuring sixteen palms, and, fearful lest they should be turned against himself, sent him back to the capital with secret orders for his execution.

Syad Ali, however, managed to effect his escape to Táshkand, whence he found his way to Amir Khudádád, who, to get him out of the way, sent him to Wais Khan, at that time wandering amongst the Kalmák of Lob and Katak, and the Sárigh Uighúr. Wais received him well, and gave him his sister, Oron, in marriage, and Ali, with his bow, shot two stags for the wedding feast. From this region Wais and his new ally found their way to Turkistan. Here Wais allied with, and married, Sikanj, the sister of the Governor Shekh Núruddín, the son of Sárboghá, Kapchák, and the enemy of his uncle Sher Muhammad Khan, with whom he waged war, till on his death he succeeded to the government.

The reign of Wais Khán was characterized by a succession of unprofitable campaigns against the Budhist Kalmák. He fought 61 actions against their Chief, Eshán Táyshí, and only gained a single victory. He was on one occasion captured by the Kalmák Chief, who not only spared his life, but saved him from drowning whilst crossing a river in retreat.

In proof of his gratitude, Wais gave his sister, Makhtúm Kháním, in marriage   T.R.
to his chivalrous adversary on condition of his accepting Islám, and henceforward
recognized him as an ally. This Eshán Táyshi had his seat in the vicinity of Turfán,
where he excavated several *kárez* or subterranean aqueducts for the irrigation of his
fields. He was very fond of hunting the wild camel, and annually made an excursion
to Lob and Katak in pursuit of the game for the sake of their wool, which his
mother used to weave into cloth for his vestments. And he wore none other but
these.

His wife, Makhtúm Kháním, bore him two sons, namely, Ibráhím Aong, and
Ilyás Aong, and a daughter, Kádir Birdí, who married Mír Karim Birdi. Owing to
their new creed these brothers warred with the Kalmák, whose Chief, Amá Sánjí
Táyshí, and his three hundred thousand people, drove them and their hundred and
seventy thousand people to Mogholistan, whence again, in the time of Dost Muhammad, they pressed them on to the Khitá border. Ibrahím left a son, Bábolay, the
Chief of the tribe of that name there, and they subsequently warred with Mansúr on
the Khitá border.

In April-May 1420 A.D. Amír Khudádád received and entertained the embassy   Y.C.
under Shádi Khoja, with Ghyáthuddín and five hundred followers, from Sháhrúkh to
the Emperor of China. Their route from Herát was by Balkh and Samarcand to
Táshkand and Syrám; and thence to Asferah, where the Amír met them and forwarded their progress by Yuldúz to Turfán, whence they went on by Kará Khoja to
Atsáfí, and Kámil on the Chinese frontier. They returned two years later by the
desert route to Khutan, and thence to Káshghar; and on by Andiján to Samarcand
and Herat, owing to the Moghol route on the north of the Alátágh being closed by
disturbance amongst the tribes. Amír Khudádád was a pious, beneficent, and
popular governor, and administered the government of Mugholistan during the
reigns of four Chaghtáy Kháns.

The cities of Káshghar, Yárkand, Khutan, Aksú, Báy, and Kusan or Kúchá   T.R.
were held by his sons, grandsons, and nephews, and his dependents numbered twenty-four thousand families. Yet he had neither flocks nor herds, but lived frugally and
simply in a single *Khargah*, and for a journey depended on the loan of his neighbour's
horses. He spent his wealth in ransoming and liberating the Musalmáns enslaved by
the Moghols, who habitually raided Turkistán, Táshkand, and Andiján in this pursuit.
In his old age seeing no prospect of restoring order in the country under the rule of
Wais, he favored the schemes of Ulugh Beg, and inviting him to Chuí, there made
the Moghol over to him.

The tribes, however, disapproving the transfer of their liberties, dispersed to
their steppes, and Khudádád, no longer able to stay amongst them, decided on making
the pilgrimage to Mecca, which even in his time seems to have been, as now, the last
resort of unsuccessful statesmen and rulers. For this purpose he returned with
Ulugh Beg to Samarcand, and was thence forwarded by him with every mark of
attention and hospitality to Herat. From this, after a short stay, he went on to Mecca,
and died at Medina, where he was buried, aged ninety-seven years.

Meanwhile Ulugh sent a force under Sátuk Khán to reduce Mogholistán. He
met and engaged the Moghol under their Chief near Isígh Kol; and, the nomads
being put to flight, Wais endeavoured to rally them by heading a charge against the
Samarcand troops, but, his horse stumbling at a ditch, he was thrown, and instantly
beheaded by one of Sátuk's attendants. On this his army dispersed to their camps,
and Sátuk then led his troops against Káshghar, where he was killed by Karákúl
Ahmad, a grandson of Khudádád.

Ulugh then despatched an army against Káshghar to avenge his death. Carákúl
was seized, and sent prisoner to the capital, where he was executed; whilst the
district, as Andiján had been before, was annexed to Samarcand, and governed by
officers of the Doghlát family appointed by Ulugh. But Aksú, Báy Kúsán, Turfán,
Yárkand, Khutan, &c., continued in the hands of Khudádád's family.

T.R.   On the death of Wais Khan, the government of Mogholistán became divided. The northern States of Zúnghár fell successively to his sons Eshán Boghá and Yúnus, whilst the southern States of Káshghar fell to Syad Ali (whose capital was at Aksú), the Minister of Wais, and to his successors, heirs of the Amír Khudádád. As the events occurring in these regions during the rule of these rival governors has not been hitherto published, so far as I am aware, I here introduce an abridged record of them as gathered from the *Tarikhi Rashidí*.

Wais left two sons, Yúnus and Eshán Boghá, each of whom was supported by his own faction in claiming the succession. The nobles who favoured Yúnus, then a lad of thirteen years, carried him off to Ulugh at Samarcand to gain his recognition and support; but he, in 832 H.=1428 A.D., sent him out of the way to his father at Herat. Here Sháhrukh placed him under the charge of Mauláná Sharífuddín Ali, Yazdi, the most celebrated scholar, poet, and divine of the time, to be educated. Yúnus remained under his tuition for twelve years, till the great teacher's death. And then during another twelve years, after travelling in Persia and Arabia, he settled at Shiráz.

Meanwhile Eshán Boghá ruled the Moghol tribes amidst a scene of unmitigated disorder, ushered in at the very commencement of his reign by the murder of Tymúr, Uighúr, his Governor of Turfán. He was torn to pieces by the nobles, who then, terror struck at their own rash barbarity, fled the country. In this disorder Syad Ali, the grandson of Amír Khudádád, and *Wazir* of Wais—who, for his services in the wars with the Kalmák, had been granted by the latter the country of Khutan in fief—seized Aksú from his brothers, Adil Momin and Syad Muhammad, both of whom he killed, and, bringing Eshán Boghá from Mogholistán, established him in it as the capital of his government, with himself as Minister.

From this Syad Ali waged a predatory warfare against Ulugh on the borders of Turkistán and Farghána, and ultimately succeeded in recovering for himself all the country under his grandfather's government, which, during the fourteen years since his departure, had become divided amongst his descendants, and partly annexed by Ulugh to Samarcand.

When Ulugh Beg, on the death of his father, came to the throne at Samarcand, in 850 H.=1446 A.D., he confirmed Amír Khudádád in his hereditary government, and the Amír appointed his son, Syad Ahmad, to the charge of Káshghar; but on his deposition by Khoja Sharif, as has been before mentioned, Ulugh appointed one Sultán Malik, Doghlát, to the government on the part of Samarcand. He was in turn succeeded by, first, Hájí Muhammad, Sháysta, and then by Pír Muhammad, Birlás, the nominees of Ulugh. Syad Ali, the son of Syad Ahmad, now attempted to recover the city from the Hájí with a force of only seven thousand men, but, suffering an ignominious defeat at the hands of the Bukhárá troops, fled back in disorder to Aksú. He renewed the attack in the following year during harvest time, and, laying waste the country, plundered the suburbs, and hastily retired before he could be brought to action by the Samarcand Governor. Owing to his remissness on this occasion the Sháysta was replaced by a Birlás, one Pír Muhammad, surnamed *Bangí* from his constant intoxication by the drug called *bang* (the resin of the hemp plant); and, Syad Ali again appearing under the walls during the third harvest, the citizens, to avert the famine threatened by another destruction of the crops, seized the worthless *Bangí*, and delivered him to the invader, who at once executed him, and took possession of Káshghar, to the joy of the populace who had been greatly oppressed by the foreign governors.

Syad Ali now restored order, and, during a rule of 24 years, proved a just and popular governor. The people prospered and multiplied, and cultivation and cattle increased with amazing rapidity. He left three sons and two daughters, and the share of heritage falling to the lot of one of the former, Muhammad Hydar, the grandfather of the author from whom this account is derived, included one hundred and twenty thousand sheep.

The rest of the country, however, still continued in a very disordered state. The Jarás nobles, with the Báren tribe and Konji nobles, joined the Kalmák in plundering Mogholistan north of the Tianshan; the Cáloji and others joined Abúlkhyr in Uzbakistán; whilst the Kirghiz of Atbáshi and Isigh Kol harried the Farghána and Táshkand borders. During this period of disturbance, Eshán Boghá, in 855 H. = 1450 A.D., being joined at Atbáshi by Mír Muhammad Sháh, the son of Khudádád, carried an incursion across the borders, and plundered the districts of Turkistán, Táshkand, and Syrám. And again, taking advantage of the absence of Abú Sáid Mirzá, the great grandson of Tymúr and successor of Ulugh at Samarcand, in his campaign against Khurásán (on the death of Sháhrúkh), he invaded Andiján, seized the fort, and, liberating its governor, Ali Kochak, on ransom, plundered the country, and retired to the hills.

From this secure retreat he repeated his incursions till Abú Sáid, powerless to check him, recalled Yúnus from his exile, and, making a treaty of alliance with him, set him up with an army, and sent him to recover his patrimony from his younger brother. Yúnus at this time, 860 H. = 1455 A.D., was forty-one years of age. He set out on his enterprise without delay, and on arrival in Mogholistan was joined by the Konji tribe under their Chief, Pir Hájí, whose daughter, Doulat Begum, he married. She bore him three sons. At Isigh Kol he was joined by the Begjik tribe with their Chief, Mir Ibráhim, the nephew of Pír Hace Birdí. With these adherents to his cause Yúnus marched against Káshghar.

Here the aged Syad Ali summoned to his aid Eshán Boghá, who at the time was in Yuldúz. He hastily collected sixty thousand Jattah, and arrived at Káshghar in eleven days with but six thousand of his men. Yúnus, nevertheless, was defeated and driven back to Mogholistan, where his lately made friends, deserting him, returned to their own camps and pastures; and his borrowed army, following their example, took their own ways back to their homes. Yúnus, with only a few trusty servants, wandered awhile in distress and disguise, and finally returned to Abú Sáid in Khurásán, attended by a single slave, whom, in the absence of any other property, he presented as an offering on first admission to his patron's presence. Abú Sáid, on learning the deplorable state of his affairs, restored the faithful slave to him, and, setting him up afresh, gave him a residence at Banikand, called also Sháhrúkhi. Here he provided him with a fresh army, and once more sent him to renew the attempt to recover his throne.

Syad Ali died at Káshghar in 862 H. = 1457 A.D., and left two sons, Sániz Mirzá, by a Jarás wife, and Hydar Mirzá, by Oron Nishin Khánim, the aunt of Yúnus and sister of Wais Khan. According to Moghol custom, Sániz, the eldest, succeeded to the government; but he was a mild and timid Prince, and, resigning Káshghar and Yángí Hissár to his brother, retired to the less disturbed Yárkand, which he made his capital.

Hydar was married to Daulat Nigár Khánim, the daughter of Eshán Boghá, and his sympathies were, consequently, with him instead of with Yúnus. And on the death of his father-in-law, in 866 H. = 1461 A.D., he allied with his son and successor Dost Muhámmad. Sániz on the contrary allied with Yúnus.

The brothers did not agree, and Yúnus, after his return from Abú Said set up with a fresh army, now again coming to Káshghar as rightful King, Hydar left the place and joined Dost Muhammad at Aksú. After some stay at Káshghar, during which he contracted a marriage with the daughter of the King of Badakhshán, his nomads fretting under the restraints of city life, and deserting him with increasing frequency, Yúnus was afraid of being left alone in his newly recovered capital, and, consequently, appointing Sániz to the Government of Káshghar, he returned to Mogholistan with his restless wanderers.

Sániz died at Káshghar, after a reign of seven years, by a fall from his horse, in 869 H. = 1464 A.D., and Hydar at once took possession of the city from Aksú. Dost Muhammad at the same time made an attempt to seize Yárkand, but, the gates being

52.—Soap, Tape, Oil and Sweetmeat Sellers of Yarkund.

53.—Coppersmiths manufacturing water vessels.

closed against him, he consented to retire on the surrender of the family of Sáníz, whose widow, Jamák Aghá, he forthwith married, and whose sons, Abábakar and 'Umar, and a daughter, Khan Sultán Khánim, he sent off to Aksú; whilst he himself turned off to plunder Káshghar during the temporary absence of Hydar at Yángí Hissar.

Dost Muhammad was seventeen years old when he succeeded his father at Aksú, and was supposed to be mad from his eccentricities, the most noted of which was his assumption of the character of a *darvesh* with the name Shams Abdál. He added the title *Abdal* to the names of all his courtiers and public officers, and insisted on their being so addressed in all official correspondence or business.

His treacherous conduct now at Káshghar estranged Hydar from his interests, and sent him over to the side of Yúnus; whilst Abábakar, to whom he had given his sister, Husn Nigár Khánim, in marriage, terrified by his violent bursts of temper, fled to his uncle at Káshghar; and Dost, to be rid of him entirely, sent his bride after him. Following this the mad youth insisted on marrying one of his late father's widows. His desire was prohibited by the clergy as unlawful, but he executed seven of them in turn, and then an eighth was found willing to perform the ceremony on the grounds that such a connexion was lawful only to such an infidel. Dost Muhammad was seized with a violent colic on the nuptial night with his step-mother, and died six days later, aged twenty-four years, in 873 H.=1468 A.D., having reigned seven years. The date of his death is told in the chronogram *ao khúk murd*= "that pig died."

In the disorder following, his son, Kabak Sultan Oghlán, fled to Jálish and Turfán; and Yúnus, waiting his opportunity on the frontier, came down and seized Aksú. But his nomads again deserted him to join Kabak, and he was forced to return to Mogholistán. Here, on the Ayla river, he was attacked by Amá Sánjí Táyshí, the Kalmák Chief, and, being defeated with great slaughter of his Moghol, was compelled to retreat to Karátocí on the River Syhon. His camp here, whilst Yúnus had crossed the frozen river on a hunting excursion, was surprised by Búrúj Oghlán, son of Jání Beg, son of Abúlkhyr, who with his marauding Uzbak took shelter from the inclemency of the weather in the *Khargah* tents with the Moghol women and old men. Yúnus on receiving intelligence of this hurried back, and, surrounding the enemy, attacked and slew most of them with their leader, only a few escaping back to the steppe.

Shortly after this, in the spring, Yúnus moved to Táshkand, where Shekh Jamál Khar was Governor on the part of Samarcand, which, with Hissár, Kundúz and Badakhshán, on the death of Abú Sáid in Irac, had fallen to his son, Sultán Ahmad; whilst Harí and Khurásán had passed to Husen Mirzá; and Farghána with Andiján to 'Umar Shekh, the son of Abú Sáid; to each of whom Yúnus subsequently allied himself by giving a daughter in marriage.

On his arrival now at Tashkand, in 875 H.=1470 A.D., Shekh Jamál seized Yúnus, and, imprisoning him, gave his wife to Khoja Kalan; but she and her maids set upon and killed him with bodkins and needles the first time he presumed to enter her chamber. A year later Abdul Cudús, the nephew of Karím Birdí, Doghlát, killed Shekh Jamál, liberated Yúnus, and presented him with his persecutor's head. His Moghols now gathered round their King, and excused their perfidy in delivering him up to Jamál as the result of his bringing them to city life, which to them was worse than prison. Yúnus admitted his error, and returned with them to Mogholistán, where he ruled many years in peace; Hydar at Káshghar being his tributary. On his return this time to Mogholistán, Kabak was killed at Turfán by his nobles, and his head brought to Yúnus as a token of friendship; but he punished the bearers, and reproved the nobles for slaying their Prince, even though a rebel. After he had killed Búrúj Oghlán at Karátocí, Yúnus sent his eldest daughter, Mihr Nigár Khánim, as wife to Sultán Ahmád, the son of Abú Sáid, to cement the friendship and maintain the alliance his father had initiated between the long estranged Moghol and Chaghtáy. And now on his establishment in the government of Mogholistán,

880 H. = 1475 A.D., he gave his youngest daughter, Cutlúgh Nigár Khánim, in marriage to Umar Shekh (another son of Abú Sáid), his friend and ally, the Governor of Andiján. She became the mother of the celebrated Bábur Bádsháh, the Emperor of India, and founder of the Mughol dynasty there.

Yúnus and 'Umar Shekh, being friendly neighbours, often exchanged visits in their respective dominions. On one of these occasions 'Umar sought the aid of Yúnus to oust Ahmad from Samarcand; but he refused on account of his marriage relations with both. Ahmad, however, being informed of the plot prepared to attack his brother, who at once called in the aid of Yúnus, and settling him at Akhsi, thus averted the menaced hostility.

'Umar now wished Yúnus to retire, but, as he refused, they fought, and Yúnus capturing his son-in-law, made peace, and restored him to his government. He then returned to Mogholistán. On this Ahmad renewed his preparations to attack 'Umar Shekh, and he again summoned Yúnus, and settled him at Marghilán. At this juncture Khoja Nasíruddín Ubedullah, a divine whose sanctity drew crowds to prostrate themselves in the dust before him, intervened and made peace between the three belligerents—Ahmad, Umar and Yúnus, in the last of whom the arbiter, to his surprise, instead of the uncouth, wild Moghol he expected to see, found a reverential devotee, an elegant Chief, and polished scholar, the compeer of the learned Ulugh Beg. He treated him with marked favour and patronage, pronounced him a good Musalmán, and, declaring his Moghol to be within the fold of the Faithful, prohibited as unlawful the custom of enslaving them as *Kafir* = infidels.

In Káshghar, meanwhile, another Prince was rising into power. The widow of Sániz, whom Dost Muhammad had taken to wife when he attacked Yárkand, became, after his death, the wife of Hydar, the brother of her first husband. She had borne Sániz two sons, Abábakar and Umar; and to his brother she bore two other sons, Muhammad Husen, Gúrikán (the father of the author here quoted), and Syad Muhammad Mirzá. This matron, Jamák Aghá, favoured her first born, Abábakar, who was a gigantic athlete, a brave soldier, and cunning hunter. These qualities made him very popular amongst the nobles, and his mother, deceiving Hydar as to the character of his ambition, secretly drew away the nobles from his court to the side of her son, and encouraged him to recover his birthright, and take the lead in the government. Abábakar having soon collected some three thousand followers, fled to Yárkand, and, seizing the city, set up as independent ruler in succession to Sániz Mirzá.

His brother Umar joined him there, and they shortly set out together to annex Khutan. On the way there, however, they quarrelled, and Abábakar, depriving his insubordinate and ambitious brother of sight, sent him back to Hydar at Káshghar. From this, on its fall, he went to Samarcand, but returned again after some years, and died there in 921 H. = 1514 A.D.

Khutan at this time was in the possession of two brothers, Khán Nazr and Cul Nazr, the hereditary descendants of Khizr Sháh, a brother of Amír Khudádád, who had given the place to him in the distribution of his government amongst his family. These two brothers, in the anarchy following on the death of Syad Ali, became independent, and made repeated attempts to subdue both Yarkand and Káshghar. Consequently Hydar did not now oppose Abábakar in his attempt to reduce them. His first expedition failed, but in the second, which shortly followed it, whilst swearing to terms on the Kuran, a scuffle ensued regarding the possession of the book, and in the melée both brothers were seized and killed. In the midst of the confusion Abábakar took possession of the city, and proclaimed himself King. He was for some time following this engaged in a succession of expeditions to subjugate the hill districts to the south and west of Khutan; and, having finally secured his conquests in those quarters, he next turned his arms against Hydar at Káshghar.

At this time Abdul Cudús (who had killed Shekh Jamál Khar, and liberated Yúnus, for which service he had been rewarded with the rank of Amír and title of

T.R. Gurikán, and granted the government of the Doghlat tribe in Andiján, but who had since rebelled and fled the country) was a refugee with Hydar, who had given him his daughter, Aghá Sultán Khánim, in marriage; and he now sent him against Abábakar who was plundering Yángi Hissár. The successful young soldier, however, quickly defeated him, and Cudús, with three hundred men, fled to Badakhshán. Here he joined Sultan Mahmúd, who gave him the government of Kundúz, where he was subsequently killed in a border skirmish with the Kator infidels.

After the defeat and flight of Cudus, Hydar issued with an army of thirty thousand men to oppose the advance of Abábakar, but was driven back with great loss. In this extremity he sent urgent appeals for succour to his maternal uncle, Yúnus, who, hastily collecting fifteen thousand Moghol, hurried to the aid of his tributary protegé. On his approach Abábakar called in his plundering parties and retired to his capital; and Hydar, now joined by Yúnus, followed to besiege him in Yarkand.

Abábakar, however, nothing daunted by their advance, made a vigorous sally from the city, and put them all to flight in the greatest disorder and haste. Hydar, with only two or three attendants who could keep pace with him, reached Káshghar without drawing rein in twenty-four hours, whilst the panic struck Moghol fled without ever turning to look behind them. Abábakar, proud of his success, lavished rewards on his soldiers; and Hydar, disgusted, was only too glad to get rid of the rabble who now deserted him; whilst Yúnus, full of wrath, took his way back to Mogholistán vowing condign vengeance.

He returned the following year, 885 H. = 1480 A.D. with sixty thousand Moghol, and joining Hydar and his new levy of thirty thousand men at Káshghar, they marched together to Yárkand, and completely invested the city. Abábakar, in face of the odds against him, confined himself to the defence of his capital, for which he had only five thousand men, including three thousand tried veterans; and he employed them to the best advantage, and with an unlooked for success in his sallies.

Each of his horsemen was accompanied by an archer, and a sworded shield-bearer on each side. As they neared the enemy, and their horse came to the charge, the bowmen shot their arrows, whilst the shield-bearers capered and tumbled, and, rattling their shields, performed wild antics to frighten the adversary's horse; and with such success that many of their riders were thrown and at once beheaded. In this manner Abábakar's skirmishers advanced against the besiegers, and, a sudden panic seizing the Moghol, they broke and fled in utter disorder. The efforts of Yúnus failing to rally them, he was forced to follow, and retired with his discomfited host to Aksú, where he wintered with his family and army. Hydar meanwhile was pursued by Abábakar, and hastily collecting five thousand families, abandoned his capital and joined Yúnus. On this Káshghar fell into the hands of the victor, and thousands of its people, fleeing from the vengeance of his soldiery, emigrated to Andiján.

On the first occasion of Yúnus coming to Káshghar to aid Sániz against Hydar and Dost Muhammad, he married Sháh Begum, the daughter of Sháh Sultan Muhammad, the King of Badakhshán. She bore him two sons and two daughters, namely, Mahmúd, born 868 H. = 1465 A.D., and Ahmad, and Nigár Khánim and Daulat Khánim. During his stay at Aksú this winter after the defeat at Yárkand, Hydar, having lost Káshghar and anxious to secure Aksú for himself, detached the youthful Ahmad from his father on the promise of giving him the place so soon as he recovered his own government; and they both rebelled and seized one of the two forts the place contained.

On this Yúnus summoned his eldest son, Mahmúd, who, during his absence ruled in Mogholistán, to come to his aid. He arrived in seventeen days with thirty thousand Moghol, and they then besieged the rebellious Hydar. After forty days, during which Ahmad repenting of his folly had effected his escape and gained the pardon of his parent, Hydar, finding himself deserted and hard pressed for food, surrendered unconditionally. Yúnus generously pardoned his treachery, and, on his departure in the spring, took him to Mogholistán, and there attached his son, Muhammad

Husen (the father of my author), a lad aged twelve years, as companion to Mahmúd; and they grew up together mutual friends as King and Minister.

In the summer following, Yúnus purposed another attack upon Abábakar for the recovery of Káshghar, but was called to Andiján and settled at Úsh by Umar Shekh, who was again threatened by Ahmad seeking to seize Táshkand and Sháhrukhí, which, since the death of Shekh Jamál, had fallen into his hands as part of Farghána. Yúnus passed the winter at Úsh, and thus prevented war between the quarrelsome brothers; and in spring, leaving Hydar and Muhammad Husen in the government of Úsh, rejoined the Moghol under Mahmúd. On his departure, Umar, jealous and mistrustful of the presence of Hydar, ousted him, and he went with his son as a refugee to Abábakar at Káshghar. Here he detained Muhammad Husen a year, and then sent him to Sultan Mahmúd, son of Abú Saíd, the Governor of Badakhsán, whence he subsequently was invited to rejoin Yúnus, and give him the benefit of the medical skill for which he had obtained a reputation in the country, and nurse him during his last fatal illness.

In the autumn following this, however, Ahmad, taking advantage of the absence of Yúnus, attacked Táshkand, and Umar once more recalling his trusty ally settled him at Syrám for the winter. Whilst here, his second son, Ahmad, hating the restraints of city life, deserted Yúnus, and with a number of his Moghol returned to the freedom of his steppes. His flight was unnoticed owing to the danger threatened by the advance from Samarcand of the other Ahmad, to check whose progress Mahmúd was sent out with thirty thousand men. He was joined in the vicinity of the menaced city by Umar Shekh with fifteen thousand men from Farghána, and they both attacked the enemy. After a few unimportant skirmishes the Khoja Nasíruddín Ubedulla interposed to prevent further hostility between the brethren, and made peace between the three by giving the bone of contention to Yúnus, who now in 890 H.=1484 A.D. became King at Táshkand. As a bond of friendship on assuming the government, he betrothed his son, Mahmúd, to Karákúz, the "black-eyed" daughter of Ahmad; and the belligerents then retired to their respective governments the best of friends.

Yúnus fell sick shortly following this, and, after a lingering illness of two years, died aged seventy-four years. He was the most enlightened, merciful, and just of all the Moghol Kháns, and stands amongst them an unique character for learning, liberality, and piety.

Mahmúd now succeeded to the throne at Táshkand; but the death of Yúnus was the signal for a fresh outbreak of hostilities, and Ahmad and Umar, free from the controlling influence of his superior character, at once renewed a rival contest for its possession. Mahmúd easily repulsed a force sent against him by Umar Shekh, but in the year following Ahmad attacked the city with an overwhelming force of a hundred and fifty thousand men, and would have taken it but for the treachery of his General, Sháhibeg Khán or Shaibán.

This successful adventurer, the founder of the Shaibán dynasty in Máwaránahar, was the son of Sháh Budágh, and grandson of Abúlkhyr. After the death of Búrúj Khán he experienced varied fortunes in Máwaránahar, and finally took service with Ahmad, and was classed amongst his nobles, over all of whom, except only Mír Abdul Alí Tarkhán, he held superior rank. His exalted position—which he maintained with a body-guard of three hundred devoted adherents of his own tribe— and the dislocated state of society at the time, favored the ambitious views of this Uzbak fortune hunter. During his service at Samarcand he had made several friends, and not a few jealous rivals as well, against the machinations of whom his trusty band of countrymen afforded him protection. The present opportunity offered him a chance he did not fail to take advantage of. During the three days' siege of Táshkand, he opened communications, and plotted with Mahmúd to desert Ahmad, and join him with the force under his command.

The arrangement was that Mahmúd should make a sally seemingly against him, but really throw his force against Abdul Ali, whilst he himself, feigning retreat, would fall upon and plunder Ahmad's camp. The scheme was successfully carried out. Ahmad lost his camp and army, thousands in their flight being drowned in the Parag and Khyr rivers, and himself with difficulty escaped to the capital with only a few followers. Peace was now made through the intervention of the Khoja Nasíruddín, and the luxurious and haughty Ahmad, giving the betrothed Carákúz to Mahmúd in marriage, acknowledged him as an independent King.

After this Mahmúd gave his elder sister by a year, Khúb Nigár Khánim, in marriage to Muhammad Husen, Gúrikán, the companion of his youth and the faithful friend and supporter of his father, and appointed him to the government of Oratappa. To Sháhibeg Khán at the same time, in return for his services at Táshkand, he gave the government of Turkistán.

Muhammad Husen ruled at Oratappa for nine years, during which the following important political changes occurred in the neighbouring States. Farghána, after the death of Umar Shekh, was contested by his two sons, Bábur and Jahángír. Bukhárá and Samarcand were contested by Báyncar and Sultán Ali, the sons of Sultan Mahmúd, the son of Abú Sáid, on the one hand, and by Sháhibeg on the other. Khurasán flourished under the glorious and powerful rule of Sultán Husen Mirzá. Whilst Irác, on the death of Yákúb, the son of Uzún Hasan, passed into the hands of Sháh Ismáíl, the founder of the new Saffaví dynasty. The Dasht Kapchák, meanwhile, was ruled by Búrúndúc, the Chief of the Júji *ûlús*. And Shásh = Táshkand continued the seat of Mahmúd, the son of Yúnus, who was the most noted Prince of Chaghtáy descent. He first in 889 H. = 1484 A.D. settled the Moghol, who are also called Kará Khitáy, in cities, and established the rule of their Khans who now roamed full masters of Shásh, which they held up to 908 H. = 1492 A.D.

The Moghol Khans were from father to son, Toghlúc Tymúr, who was set on the throne by Amír Boláji, Khizr Khoja, Sher Alí, Wais, Yúnus, and Mahmúd. Their ministers or hereditary governors were from father to son, Amír Boláji, who first introduced Islám amongst the Moghol, Khudádád, Syad Ahmad, Syad Alí, Muhammad Hydar, and Muhammad Husen.

The settlement of Sháhibeg at Turkistán gave offence to his enemies, the sons of Gadáy and Jáni Beg, who, at the instigation of the aggrieved Ahmad, collected the Kazzák and Uzbak, and waged war with Mahmúd. He was twice defeated by them, and then, his supporter deserting him, his court became the refuge of all sorts of adventurers and outlaws.

Umar Shekh at this time 899 H. = 1493 A.D. was crushed to death by the fall of his house, and Ahmad at once set out from Samarcand to secure Andiján from annexation by the Moghol. The nobles, however, set Bábur, the son of the deceased Chief, aged twelve years, on the throne, and called in the aid of Mahmúd for his support. Ahmad, in the interim, had advanced to Marghilán, and, falling sick there, concluded peace, and hurried back, but died on his way to the capital. On this Sultán Mahmúd from Hissár seized Samarcand. He died there after a rule of only six months, and then Báyncar Mirzá succeeded. Mahmúd Khán, with the hope of restoring his declining authority, now hastened to contest its possession with him; but, his rabble being routed at Miánkál, he returned to Táshkand, and to stave off attack from himself, incited Sháhíbeg to invade the country. This the ambitious Uzbak immediately did, and ended by conquering Samarcand and Bukhárá, an enterprise in which he was aided by Bábur.

Sháhibeg Khán now turned his arms against Mahmúd at Táshkand, and he, long since reduced to a mere semblance of independence, hastily called to his aid his younger brother, Ahmad, who was ruling the nomads in Mogholistán. He arrived in time to oppose the Uzbak attack, but their conjoined forces were defeated, and both brothers were captured with most of their men. Sháhibeg liberally set free

Mahmúd and Ahmad, but retained nearly all their troops in his own service. The brothers, with the wreck of their army and a few adherents who still clung to them, retired to Aksú, where Ahmad died in the ensuing winter 909 H.=1503 A.D.

Mahmúd after this, not being able to live in peace with his son and successor, Mansúr, retired to Mogholistán, and after five years of very varied troubles amongst the nomads there, returned to Táshkand to seek a government from Sháhibeg. But the rising conqueror, anticipating trouble from this rightful heir to the Government, killed him and all his family on the bank of the Khujánd river in 914 H.=1508-9 A.D.; and the date is commemorated in the chronogram *labi daryáe Khujand*="bank of the Khujánd river."

Ahmad, after he had quitted his father at Syrám, as before mentioned, returned to Mogholistán, and spent ten years in reducing the tribes to subjection; and he and his sons ruled there independently from 900 to 948 H.=1494 to 1541 A.D. During the first two years he destroyed the Arlát family, exterminated the Jarás and other nobles, and drove out the Cáloji tribe into the Kalmák territory. His terrible slaughters gained him the name of *Alaja*, or "the slayer," by which he is known in history. His successes against the Kazzak and Uzbak and Kalmák secured order throughout the wide extent of Mogholistán, and protected the country over a length of seven or eight months' journey from external invaders.

In 905 H.=1499 A.D., having thus settled Mogholistán, Alaja set out against Abábakar at Káshghar. On his approach Abábakar, provisioning both Káshghar and Yangi Hissár, retired to Yárkand, and there shut himself up in its fort. Alaja, after some resistance, took Yangi Hissár, and on its fall, Káshghar surrendering, he wintered there. Early next spring he marched against Yárkand, but failing to take the place, plundered the suburbs, and pursued the fugitive peasantry into the hills on the west.

On this Abábakar issued from Yárkand, and occupying the pass conducting out of the hills, there lay in wait for the enemy. He surprised and defeated Ahmad, recovered the booty taken by his troops, and drove him on from Káshghar to Mogholistán. It was a year after his return from this campaign that Ahmad, leaving his eldest son, Mansúr, to govern the Moghol, took his younger sons, Sáid and Bábájác, with him to the aid of his brother against Sháhibeg, as has been mentioned.

Ahmad, or Alaja Khan, left seventeen sons of whom Mansúr, the eldest, succeeded to the government. Iskandar died soon after his father, and finally Sáid returned from his exile, and divided the country with Mansúr. On the death of the father, however, all the sons quarrelled over the division of his territory, and Abábakar, seizing the opportunity of their discord, attacked and took Aksú, from which Mansúr had retired to Kúsán; whence, now on the fall of his capital, he fled to Mogholistán. Abábakar plundered Aksú, and, destroying its fortifications and houses, transported the population to Úsh Turfán, whither also he transferred the government; and, leaving a garrison in support, returned by way of Káshghar to his capital laden with the treasures amassed by Ahmad during a reign of twenty-five years.

Mansúr, meanwhile, fought his brothers Khalil and Sáid for the government of the Moghol, whilst their uncle, Mahmúd, unable to check the disorder or bring the brothers to reason, left the country for Tashkand, where, with all his family and followers, he was killed, as before related. Mansúr ultimately succeeded in recovering Kúsán and Aksú from his brothers Ayman and Bábájác, who, on the decline of Abábakar's rule, had taken possession of, restored, and re-peopled those ancient seats. And in 912 H.=1506 A.D., at Aksú, he met and made peace with Sáid, who, having seized Káshghar from Abábakar, now shared the country with him, and acknowledged his rights as elder brother, and "coined and prayed" in his name. They reigned in peace for twenty years, during which the country flourished, and order was so securely established that travellers journeyed singly from Khámil on the Khita border to Andiján through the length of the land without fear or care for provisions, finding hotels at every stage on the road.

Mansúr during this period waged a succession of *ghazát* or religious wars against the Kalmák and Khitáy. In one of these, the Khoja Tajúddín of Kúsán or Kúchá was killed. He was a descendant of the Mauláná Arshaduddín, who converted Toghlúc Tymúr; and was the pupil of Mauláná Ali Ghazzán of Tús=Mashhad. Tajúddín studied for some time under Khoja Nasíruddín Ubedulla, and was for fifty years in the service of Ahmad and Mansúr. He traded and farmed largely, and, acquiring much wealth and influence, took a prominent part in the government of the country.

After his campaigns on the Khitá border, Mansúr warred with the Kazzák and Uzbak at Aris in Mogholistán, where his best General, Súfi Mirzá Begjik, was killed. After this he retired to Jalish and Turfán, and seldom again took the field. On the death of Sáíd he made an attempt to recover Aksú, but was driven back, and died in 959 H. = 1542 A.D., aged sixty years, having reigned forty-three. He left two sons, Sháh Khán and Muhammad Sultan, and a daughter, whom Sáíd took for his son Rashíd. During his later years Mansúr resigned his government to his eldest son, and retired to private life for devotion to religious exercises. He is described as a pious Musalmán, and a good governor, simple in ceremony, and attentive to the wants of his people. Yet as illustrative of the sentiments of morality in his time, it is related of him that he kept as private chaplain a *Cari* or "chaunter of the Kurán." He was a man with a perfect intonation, clear voice, and unfailing memory, but he was slovenly in dress, filthy in habits, and beastly in practices—qualities that gained him the opprobious nickname of *Mangasik*. The courtiers were scandalized by his shameless depravities, and urged his dismissal on the grounds of his having been taken in an unnatural crime with a cow, but the pious King rejected their petition with the rebuke that he kept the man to teach him to read the Kurán, not to rape cattle.

Mansúr's brother Sáíd, who took Káshghar from Abábakar, has the following history:—When fourteen years old, he and his brother, Bábájác, accompanied their father to the aid of his brother Mahmúd when he was attacked at Táshkand by Sháhibeg. In the fight at Akhsi, this Sáíd was wounded in the hip by an arrow, and fell into the hands of Shekh Báyzid, the governor of the place, who imprisoned him. In the year following, Sháhibeg invaded Farghána, killed Báyzid and his brother, Ahmad Tanbal, and all their family, and annexed the country. He liberated Sáíd and took him to Samarcand, and thence with his army in the campaign against Khusro Sháh, who had seized Hissár, Kundúz, and Badakhshán. On their return to Samarcand, and the departure of Sháhibeg on his expedition against Khiva, Sáíd escaped to Uzkand, and thence joined his uncle, Mahmúd, at Yatakand in Mogholistán. In the factions then dividing the tribes there, Sáíd joined his brother, Khalíl, who ruled the Kirghiz. During four years they warred against their elder brother, Mansúr, and their uncle, Mahmúd, till, finally, the latter withdrew and returned to Táshkand where he was killed, as related.

On the departure of Mahmúd, Mansúr again took the field against Sáíd and Khalil, and marching from Jálish and Turfán, met and fought them at Járún Jalák. Each army put forward a champion for single combat. Sáíd's man, one Shekh Ali, was unhorsed in the first encounter by Cutlugh, the champion of Mansúr. On this the Kirghiz rushed forward to rescue their fallen champion, and the Moghol, too, advancing to support their hero, both sides joined in battle. Khalíl and Sáíd, unable to make head or stand against their superior numbers, both fled the field, and Mansúr, securing the Kirghiz, carried them away bodily and settled them at Jálish.

The fugitives went to join Mahmúd, but, on arrival at Akhsi, learned of his execution, and were themselves made prisoners. Khalíl was killed, and Sáíd was taken before Jánibeg, the uncle of Sháhibeg, who, having recently fallen from his horse and injured his head and reason, gave him his liberty. He at once set out to join Bábur at Kabul by way of Badakhshán, where he rested awhile with Mirzá Khán in the Zafar fort. At this time the strong highlands on the east of Badakhshán belonged to Káshghar, to which they had been annexed by Abábakar; whilst the cultivated vallies to the west were held by the Uzbak. Between the two, a few narrow glens were all that remained to a heretic king, called Sháh Ráziúddín, *Chiràghkush*, whom the Badakhshí had set on the throne. Amongst them in his little fort of Zafar, Mirzá Khán, the only Musalmán in the country, led a hard and solitary life, pinched for the bare necessaries of existence.

Sáid remained three years at Kabul, till Sháhibeg or Shaibán was killed at the battle of Marv by Sháh Ismáil, the new King of Persia, and then accompanied Bábur to Kundúz. Meanwhile, Syad Muhammad Mirzá, son of Muhammad Hydar (my author's uncle), had expelled Jánibeg and secured Andiján. And he now sought the support of Bábur, who sent Sáid and other Moghol nobles to occupy the province; and Syad Muhammad, on being relieved of the government, was appointed *úlúsbegi* of the Moghol.

Following this, Abábakar, thinking to profit by the dislocated state of affairs across the border, invaded Andiján with twenty thousand men from Káshghar, but was defeated at Tútlúgh, two *farsakh* from the city, by Sáid with only fifteen hundred men. In this interim, Bábur, having defeated the Uzbuk at Hissár and driven them out of Máwaránahar, mounted the throne at Samarcand in 917 H.= 1509-10 A.D. In the spring, however, the Uzbak returned from Táshkand under 'Ubedulla Khán, who seized Bukhárá.

Bábur went out to oppose him, but was defeated at Ghajdawán, and retiring to the capital, fled thence with his family to Hissár; and the Uzbak once more gained the ascendancy. Sa'id, too, at the same time, advanced to check the enemy at Táshkand, but he also was defeated, and driven back to Andiján by Súyúnj, who overran the border districts.

On the return of Bábur, with the Persian army sent to his aid by Sháh Ismáil, Sáid, in the spring of 918 H.=1511 A.D., went to seek the aid of Kásim, the Kapchák King. But he returned unsuccessful, and when, two years later, the Uzbak with a numberless host invaded Farghána, he quitted the country in *Rabi Awwal*, the spring of 920 H.=1513 A.D., and retired to Yatakand on the borders of Mogholistán. From this he presently invaded Káshghar where Abábakar, now aged sixty years, was as weak in authority as he was unpopular in rule.

On the approach of the invader, Abábakar, transporting the entire population to Yárkand, destroyed the ancient fort and city of Káshghar, which from remote times had been the capital of the country, and the residence of the kings of the Afrásyáb dynasty.

Regarding this ancient city, Mirzá Hydar gives the following account in the *Tarikhi Rashidi*:—Afrásyáb was a Turk, and is the Bocá Khán of the Moghol. He was the son of Pash, the son of Kharshín, the son of Túr, the son of Faridún. In later times Káshghar was the capital of Sátuk Bughra Khán, who introduced Islám. After him it was the capital of Gorkhán, the Kará Khitáy King, who ruled over all Máwaránahar; and of his successor Koshlúk, the Chief of the Náymán tribe of Christians, who was killed by the troops of Changiz in Sárígh Chopán, whither he had fled for refuge amongst the Badakhshí.

In the division of his empire, Changíz gave the countries of Mogholistán, Kará Khitáy, Turkistán, and Máwaránahar to his son Chaghtay. And similarly, in the distribution of his nobles, he gave to him the Doghlát tribe. Chaghtay settled them in the Mangláy Súba from Shásh on the west to Jálish on the east, and from Isigh Kol on the north to Sarigh Uighúr on the south. The first Doghlát who resided in the Sárígh Uighúr region was Amír Báyzid, and the government has descended from father to son to Abábakar.

Káshghar formerly produced many things that are not now known in the country, expecially the furs called *cácúm*=otter, and *sinjáb*=ermine. Its limits are, on the west, Shásh and the high mountains of Bolor, which form a chain from south to north, where they join the range of Mogholistán; on the east, the country beyond Turfán

54.—Bootmaker, Bread seller and Cotton cleaner.

55.—Snuff Seller.

T.R. to the borders of the Kalmák country, "of which nobody knows anything but the Kalmák." Its limit on the north is Artosh, and on the south Khutan. It is a month's journey from north to south, but, if one ride hard from west to east, he passes beyond cultivation and habitation in a single day.

The rivers are all between Káshghar and Khutan, and this is the only fertile part of the country; all the rest is a desert of sand, with thick jangal, and vast saline wastes, and nothing else. Many large cities have flourished on it in ancient times, but of them only Lob and Katak are now known by name. Signs of others are found, and again lost in the shifting sands, by hunters of the tiger, wild camel, and wild ox. The country produces lots of fruits and flowers, but there is no money. All trade is by barter. The soil is poor and unproductive, and requires much toil; consequently it is impossible to support an army in the country. In spring high winds obscure the air with dust, much worse than in India. Káshghar in comparison with Dashti Kapchák and Kalmák is as a populous city, with all sorts of availables; but in comparison with Samarcand it is as a bare desert. As the proverb says, "Ask those from Hell of Purgatory, and they call it Paradise." It is, however, a safe retreat from plunderers and marauders, and well suited as a place of seclusion and spiritual meditation, and has long been noted for its saints, monks, and recluses.

Abábakar now destroyed the ancient capital of this country. He demolished its fort, and levelled its suburbs, and with ten thousand men in seven days built the new fort of Káshghar on the high bank of the Túman river, a little higher up its course. Its area is 150 *jarió*=50 acres; its walls were twenty yards high, and at top wide enough for four horsemen abreast; the tower and bastions rose ten yards higher, and were all wonderfully strong.

He stored this new fort with provisions, and, leaving a garrison under his General, Yúsufyán, retired to Yángi Hissár. This, too, he put in a state for defence, and then returning to his capital fortified its defences with all haste; and having finished these preparations, he again set out to oppose the invaders, who were pressing on from Atbáshi.

Sáid left his baggage with the families at Túman-báshi, the head waters of the Túman river—the limit between Mogholistán and Káshghar—to follow afterwards, and himself pushing on with the fighting men on the third day reached Artosh. On the next day he seized the defences abandoned by Abábakar on Uch Burhán ridge, and came in sight of the newly built fort, three *farsakh* off to the southward.

Here he mustered his army, four thousand seven hundred men, all experienced soldiers who had seen twelve years' service in Máwaránahar. Amongst them were Doghlát, Caráculác, Dokhtoy, Birlás, Yarazin, Ordatagi, Atárchi, Konji, Jarás, Babarin, Begjik, Cáloji, Cárlúc, Makrit, Shoncár, and other nobles, each with his following of one hundred and fifty to two hundred men. From this Sáid crossed the Túman at the Sarman ford, two *farsakh* from the fort, and meeting the army sent by Abábakar, who himself remained at Sogholúc in support of the garrison, defeated and pursued it up to the walls, under which he camped for the night. During the darkness the garrison abandoned the fort, and fled to Yárkand, and Sáid, pushing on, laid siege to Yangi Hissár, the key to the capture of both Káshghar and Yárkand. The citadel was held by former Generals of Abábakar, who had been taken out of prison to conduct its defence.

The chief of these was Mír Wali who, in the early career of his master, had subjugated for him the country of Bolor to the borders of Cáyrtagin or Caratakin, Badakhshán, Tibet, and Kashmir; who, later, had taken Aksú and Kúsán, and, clearing them of Kirghiz and Moghol, had subdued Mogholistán; and who, finally, invaded Farghána, and ravaged Jagrák, Ush, and Uzkand. In Abábakar's second invasion of Andiján and defeat at Tútlúgh, he suspected his own people of treachery, and executed several hundred of them summarily. He reduced his General, Mír Wali, with ignominy, rooted out his beard, emasculated him and all the males of his family, subjected the females to dishonour, and cast all into prison to labour on the roads.

This Mír Wali now, through fear of his master's vengeance, held out for two months at Yángi Hissár, and then, hearing of Abábákar's flight from the capital, surrendered his trust to Sáid who, placing his own governor with a garrison in the fort, at once hurried on to Yárkand.

Here Abábakar, during the siege of Yangi Hissár, had been busy emptying his armoury of its accumulated stores, and clearing the prisons of the crowded victims of his wrath. He now distributed sixty thousand suits of armour, including twelve thousand horse trappings, amongst the population who were enrolled *en masse* for the defence of the capital. A timid peasantry, gardeners, handicraftsmen of all trades, and other peaceable citizens, who had never handled a spear, nor shot an arrow, far less wielded a sword, and who, during a generation of unexampled tyranny, had grown up cowed by despotic condemnations to dungeons, prisoner gangs, tortures, mutilations and executions, now had arms, of which they knew not the use, thrust into their unwilling hands, and were driven out to fight.

With such a pressed rabble multitude Abábakar essayed from his capital to raise the siege of Yangi Hissár. At the first stage out his disorderly mob, coming in sight of an outpost picket of Sáid's army, at once took fright, cast away the arms forced upon them, and dispersed in all directions. Abábakar was now past further explosions of wrath and torture. He returned to his palace, set his son, Jahángír, in the charge of the city, and, packing up his treasures, retired with them to Khutan. Six days later, Jahángír, on the fall of Yangi Hissár, collecting his valuables, gave the city up to plunder, and in the confusion and strife that ensued effected his escape to Sánjú.

Sáid, on receiving intelligence of these events at Yárkand, immediately sent forward Khoja Ali Bahádur to secure the place; and he took possession of the city at the end of Rajab 920 H.=1513 A.D. Sáid followed with the rest of his army largely increased by new accessions, and mounting the throne gave the place up to plunder for two months; during which his troops ransacked every corner, despoiled the citizens and their previous plunder, and secured an immense booty in rich merchandize of all sorts, together with the abandoned treasures amassed by Abábakar during a reign of forty-eight years.

Immediately on arrival at the capital, Sáid sent out parties in pursuit of the fugitives. Abábakar fled before them from Khutan to Karánghotágh. Here at Aktásh he burnt, and cast into the river what he could not carry away into the mountains, and killing the spare horses and camels fled towards Tibet. On the road his followers, scenting death ahead, plundered and deserted him.

The fugitive, after wandering hungry and demented some time over the bleak, desolate, and inhospital tablelands of the Tibet plateau, on the approach of winter, turned in search of shelter from the biting frosts of that elevated region into the sheltered valleys towards Khutan. He was intercepted, seized, and killed by a party of his many pursuers in the Karákásh valley, where a mean tomb on the river bank, two stages from Shahidulla Khoja, now marks the site of his grave.

His pursuers, after taking possession of Khutan and its treasury, sent out numerous parties on his track, and the roads leading to the mountains. One of these, at Sarpúl, found his abandoned cattle and treasures, and fishing out the sparkling gems from the clear stream, returned with a rich store of pearls, rubies, emeralds and diamonds, with rare silks and other costly treasures.

Jahángír—he was married to Khadija Sultán Khánim, full sister of Sáid and fourth daughter of Alaja Khan who fell into the hands of Abábakar when he took Aksú—was similarly pursued, and finally taken at Sánjú. He was sent prisoner to Yángi Hissár, and ultimately executed there by order of Sáid. Abábakar had many children, of whom he killed several for trivial offences. Jahángír was his eldest son, by Khánzada Begum, the sister of Mahmud.

During his long reign of forty-eight years, Abábakar subdued Tibet to the borders of Kashmir. In 905 H.=1499 A.D. he defeated Alaja Khan, and drove him from the country. He subjugated Bolor, and annexed most of the *hazáraját=*

T.R. "thousands" of Badakhshán as far as Tang; and for twelve years this region, as far as Sárigh Chopán, formed part of the Káshghar *diván*=demesne, till Sáid, on conquering the country, gave this district to his General Mír Beg. He, however, was opposed by Mirzá Khán of Wakhán, one of the *hazarachí* of the Badakhshán *hazárajat*, the limit of which is called Durwazi Wakhán by the Badakhshi, and Súrigh Chopán by the Káshghari. In the time of Sháhibeg, Abábakar invaded Andiján and annexed Ush, and Mád and Uzkand. He subdued all Mogholistán, dispersed the Moghol, and drove the Kirghiz to join Mansúr at Jálish and Turfán. And finally, on the death of Alaja, he annexed Aksú and Uch Turfán.

He excavated all the ruins and mounds about Káshghar, Yárkand and Khutan in search of buried treasure. This work was carried on summer and winter by the labour of convict gangs of men and women in separate chains; they were so punished for the most trivial offences with the worst criminals. Each gang consisted of from ten to twenty prisoners secured together by a chain running from one to the other through a collar fastened round the neck of each. They were ruled by merciless overseers who for a slight default in discipline were themselves consigned to the gang, and were fed on the scantiest fare.

By their toil Abábakar accumulated vast treasures from these ruined cities; for nothing escaped him, even the dust being sifted for gems. In a vault in some ruins near Khutan—which is described as a most ancient city, and remarkable for the absence of the *'aka*=magpie, which is common elsewhere in the country; and if perchance one should appear it is counted an ill omen, and the people turn out and drive it away—were found twenty-seven *khúm*=jar, each capable of holding a fully armed bowman, without his body touching its sides. Each *khúm* contained a copper *aftába* =ewer, with an iron spout that projected to the level of its brim. Each *aftába* was one and a half *gaz*=yard high, and when filled with water was as much as two men could lift. As found each was full of gold dust, and the space between it and the containing *khúm* was packed with silver *bálish*, each the size of an ancient brick and depressed in the centre. Each *bálish* weighed five hundred *mithcál*. (The *mithcál* of the present day weighs sixty grains). In each jar was found a paper with a Turki inscription—"For the wedding of the son of Khumár Khátón," but who or what she was nobody knows. All this wealth was deposited in Abábakar's treasury, and now fell into the possession of Sáid.

Abábakar was frightfully cruel in his punishments. He used to slay and mutilate whole families for the offence of a single member, even if accused ten years after its commission. When his troops captured Sháh Begum, and Mihr Nigár Khánim, and Muhammad Sháh (the brother of my author), and other members of the family of his own father and mother, as they came from Kabul to Badakhshán, he brought them to Káshghar and treated them shamefully. He kept Muhammad Sháh amongst his eunuchs till fifteen years old, and then staked him to a wall of his chamber by an iron rod through the belly, and thus left him to die and rot. His own sister, Khan Sultánim, he shut up in a room and fed on nothing but raw spirits, and when tortured by thirst and hunger her ravings were quieted by a fresh dose poured down by force, till at last she died. Such are only two instances that bear mention of his treatment towards his own nephews and nieces, and sons and daughters. The whole country trembled at his foul and indescribable cruelties. When he invaded Andiján, he massacred three thousand people of Jagrák, Mád, and Uzkand on the pretence that they had plotted against his life. He cut off the feet of thousands of his own subjects, simply lest, malcontent, they should go to other countries and conspire against him.

Despite his unheard-of barbarities and merciless cruelties, Abábakar affected a pious devotion to the Faith, and pretended a rigid observance of the *Shariat*. He was always attended by priests and expounders of the law, to whom he used to appeal for confirmation of his judgments; but if they dared disapprove, he straightway pronounced them worthy of death, and in his clemency and respect for their profession spared their lives, but imposed tasks worse than death itself.

He made Yárkand the capital of his kingdom, and greatly improved the city. He built its fortifications which enclosed two hundred *man* of land (that is land capable of being sown by that quantity of corn, which at fifteen pounds the *man* equals three thousand pounds), and had six gates, each protected by two bastions, and connecting walls one hundred yards in advance, a novel arrangement, by which the approach was defended by archers on each side. Inside the city he laid out twelve parks, with handsome mansions, and a hundred houses in each. He brought canals into the city, and planted twelve thousand gardens in its suburbs. All these now fell into the hands of Sáíd, and were ravaged and plundered by his soldiery.

After settling Yárkand, Sáíd returned to Káshghar, and there, in the winter of 921 H.=1514-15 A.D., received a visit from Mansúr who had come from his government of Jálish and Turfán. In the first month of the following year Sáíd went by Uch Turfán, where his brother, Ayman Khoja, was Governor, to Aksú which since its devastation by Abábákar on the death of Ahmad had remained in ruins, and at Báy met Mansúr for the return of his visit. He now acknowledged him as his elder brother and independent ruler of Jálish and Turfán, and giving Aksú to him returned to Yárkand for the winter.

In the following spring Sáíd moved to Káshghar, and there collected his forces to invade Andiján and expel Súyúnjúk. He was joined by Ayman and Bábájac with their small contingents, and on arrival at Chádir Kul mustered his troops. His brothers warned him that the army was unequal to the task undertaken, and proposed that they should change the plan of the expedition, and limit it to a raid in the hills. Consequently they spent a few weeks in the chase of wild horse and sheep, and the plunder of nomad camps, and then returned to the capital.

After this Sáíd set out on an expedition against the Sárígh Uighúr twelve days' journey from Khutan, but on arrival at the latter place he was so prostrated from the effects of a hard bout of debauchery that he was obliged to forego the meritorious duty of converting them. He sent a force, however, to explore their country, and it returned after an absence of two months without having found any traces of the pagan enemy; whilst himself in the interim was borne back to the capital in a stupid state of drunkenness.

He was roused from this ignoble course by the plain admonition of the Uzbak master of Máwaránahar, and his warning against the unchecked hostilities of the border tribes; and Sáíd, alarmed lest the vengeance of Sháhíbeg should fall upon himself, at once set out on an expedition to Isígh Kul to check the inroads of his Kirghiz there upon the lands of Turkistán, Syrám, and Andiján. He dispersed their camps, and capturing their Chief, Muhammad Báy, carried him off prisoner to Yárkand in 923 H.=1516 A.D., and thus restored quiet on the border.

During the reign of Sháhíbeg Khan, Badakhshán was divided between Khusro Sháh on the west and Abábakar on the east. Sáíd on taking Káshghar had given his share of the country up to Sárígh Chopan in fief to Mír Beg, one of his nobles; but Mirzá Khán, the Governor of Zafar fort, expelled him. Consequently Sáíd marched against him, and settling the difficulty peaceably returned to Yárkand. From this in the summer following he went to Aksú, which had recently (923 H.) been recovered from Mansúr by Ayman Khoja, who restored and resettled the place for himself. He now removed Ayman to Káshghar, whence he went to Bábur in India where he died in 938 H.=1531 A.D., and installed Mansúr in the Government; and he reigned there in peace for two years till 928 H.=1521 A.D.

In this year (926 H.) Mirzá Khan died, and his infant son, Sulemán, was put on his throne in Badakhshán. Sáíd meant to have gone against him, but a revolt of the Kirghiz pagans in Moghólistán prevented him. He sent his son, Rashíd, with the liberated Muhammad Báy to quell them, and himself followed to their support in the following year. He wintered at Kuchcár, and being there seized with a fit of piety and remorse for his many sins returned to Káshghar, and wished to abdicate in favour of his brother Aymán. His priestly adviser, Tájuddin, aided by the persuasive

56.—The Fortune-teller.

57.—Derwishes, professional beggars.

eloquence of Khoja Muhammad Yúsuf just arrived from Táshkand, however, dissuaded him from the purpose. Instead thereof he made him confess and repent his sins, and promise to expiate them by serving God and the Prophet by the prosecution of a yearly *ghazát* against the pagans and infidels on his borders.

In the spring of 931 H. = 1524 A.D., Sáid again went to the support of Rashíd at Isígh Kul, where he had his camp to control the Kirghiz. Whilst there he received intelligence of the death of Súyúnjuk and disorder amongst the Uzbak. Consequently he at once invaded Andiján, seized Uzkand, the strongest fort in the country, and razed it to the ground, captured Ush and the capital, and annexing them to Káshghar, returned to Mogholistán. Here he established Rashíd in the government against Táhir Khan and Abúl Kásim, the Uzbak leaders whose cause had failed in Máwaránahar, and returned to his own capital. On the rise of the Manghit, however, in succession to them, and their invasion of Mogholistán, Rashíd, unable to hold his own against them, returned to Káshghar.

In the winter following this, Sáid sent Rashíd and Mirzá Hydar (the author of *Tárikhi Rashídí*) on a *ghazát* against the *káfir* of Bolor. This country is bounded east by Káshghar and Yárkand; north by Badakhshán; west by Kábul; and south by Kashmír. It is altogether a mountain fastness, and has not a level *farsakh* of ground in a circuit of four months' journey. Its people have no religion, and their women do all the labour, field and domestic. The men do nothing but fight each other all day and every day, and only cease when their women interpose with food. They then enter their houses, and on the conclusion of the meal return to fight; and so it goes on from sunrise to sunset; and at night they always barricade their doors and keep watch.

These people have few oxen, but lots of goats and sheep from whose wool they make all their clothing. There is little pasture in the country; and every glen has its own peculiar language which is unintelligible to the neighbours. Honey and fruits are in plenty. The pomegranates are especially good, and have sweet white grains like those of no other country. Rashíd returned from this expedition, in which he does not appear to have effected much against the *káfir*, by way of Sárigh Chopán in the summer of 934 H. = 1527 A.D.

On the death of Mirzá Khán, his infant son, Sulemán, succeeded to the throne of Badakhshán. Bábur had him brought to Kabul, and sent his own son, Humáyún, to hold the country. He governed it from 926 to 935 H. = 1519 to 1528 A.D., when he was summoned to India. The Badakhshí now feared the Uzbak, and sought protection of Sáid. He left Rashíd in the government of Káshghar, and set out for Badakhshán in 936 H. = 1529 A.D. On arrival at Zafar, however, he found the fort already occupied by Hindál, the brother of Humáyún. It being mid-winter, and retreat impossible, Sáid negotiated a stay of three months with Hindál on the grounds that he had come to protect the place against Uzbak invasion, and with no thought of wresting it from Kábul. After a very hard time of it in deep snows, with a scarcity of provisions, Sáid was glad to turn back to his capital with the first approach of spring. Bábur on this recalled Hindál, and re-established Sulemán at Zafar.

Following this in the winter of 937 H. = 1530 A.D., Sáid resumed Aksú from Mansúr, and appointed Rashíd to its government with Mirzá Hydar as his minister. Six months later he recalled the latter, and in *Zí Híjj*, the spring of 938 H. = 1532 A.D., set out with him and an army of five thousand men on a *ghazát* against Tibet.

The rivers of Tibet on the north-east all flow to the Kok Nor Kol in the sandy desert. It is three months' journey in circuit; and from the lake flows the great Kará Morán river of Khitá.

The Dolpá tribe of Tibet trade between Khitá and Hind, and carry their merchandize exclusively on sheep. They spend one winter in Khitá and the other in Hind. Three hundred families of them live in under-ground burrows at Altúnchi, where they dig and sift gold during only forty days of the year owing to the excessive cold. Other gold mines of Tibet are in Champa.

Mirzá Hydar and Iskandar, the son of Sáid, with four thousand men led the advance, and proceeding by the direct route arrived at Nubra in *Safar* 938 H. = 1532 A.D. From this they sent off parties in all directions to convert to Islám, or to slay the recusants. They took the fort of Maryol, which was held by two Chiefs called Lacea Choghdán and Basánkol.

The cold here was intense. From this Iskandar was hastily recalled owing to the alarming illness of his father from *dam* = "breath" on the Dolpá road from Khutan. On arrival at Nubra, however, Sáid recovered, and with a thousand men turned off to winter at Bálti. Iskandar, meanwhile, rejoining Mirzá Hydar, pushed on by the Zoji Pass, where he quickly routed its four hundred defenders, to winter in Kashmír.

Bahrám Toe, the Ruler of Bálti, submitted to Sáid who at once took possession of the town, located his troops in its houses, killed the men, seized the women, and till spring waged a destructive guerilla all over the country to Maryol. During the same time Iskandar subjugated Káshmír, and married the daughter of Muhammad Sháh its King.

In the spring both parties met in Maryol. From here Sáid sent Iskandar and Mirzá Hydar, with two thousand men, to destroy the idol city of Aorsáng (or as it is colloquially pronounced Aocháng or Ucháng), which was the *cabla'* or Jerusalem of the Khitáy, and himself set out on his return to Yárkand by the Sácrí Pass into Nubra. On rising from this to the highland of the Karákoram Pass, Sáid was again taken ill with *dam*, and, though hurried along to get across the difficult parts as quickly as possible, died at a stage only four days short of the place where the *dam* is no longer felt. The spot, I may here note, is marked by the name Daulat Beg Uldi = "The Lord of the State died." It is the stage directly to the south of the Karákoram Pass, and is 16,400 feet above the sea. Sáid died at the end of 939 H., aged forty-six years, having reigned twenty. On the arrival of the corpse, Syad Muhammad Mirzá, who had repaired to the capital from his government at Káshghar on first intimation of the King's death, performed the funeral rites, and, with a strong party of nobles in support, assumed the government pending the return of Iskandar.

But Rashíd at the same time coming from Aksú, seized Syad Muhammad on the first day of the new year 940 H., and slew him over his father's grave where the unsuspecting minister had come to express the usual condolence. He then mounted the throne himself, and, sending off his agents to Káshghar, executed all the family of his victim, and confiscated his property.

Iskandar and Mirzá Hydar, meanwhile, had penetrated twenty marches towards Aorsáng, and on the *1st Safar*, having defeated the Champa Tibetans at Báryáng, captured great booty in cattle and sheep. They ravaged the country around for several months, and on the *1st Muharram* 940 H., the day on which Rashíd killed Syad Muhammad, were attacked in a narrow defile by Kárdom and the Hindú army and defeated with considerable loss; Hydar's brother, 'Abdulla, being amongst the slain.

From Maryol this expeditionary force marched altogether two months towards Aorsáng. In one month they came to the forts of Nok and Labok on the shore of a lake forty *farsakh* in circuit. Here they lost nearly all their horses from the fatal effects of *dam*, and the army had to proceed on foot with great difficulty and loss to Támluc, whence is fourteen days' journey to Bangála. At Támluc horses enough to mount ninety men were seized, and the army then advanced four days' march to Askarof, whence is a journey of twenty days to Aorsáng. From this they were forced to retire owing to the exhaustion and inefficiency of the troops. From Támluc to Maryol is twenty stages. In two stages they came to Koko, and there levied a contribution of three thousand *mithcál* of gold from the people.

Whilst here messengers arrived from Rashíd summoning Iskandar to Yárkand, and informing Hydar of the execution of his uncle and all his family, and prohibiting his return to the country. They consequently marched at once to Maryol, and arrived at its capital, Calá Shiya, in twenty-five days, and taking possession of the fort, halted for stragglers to rejoin. The season was mid-winter, and the loss in men and cattle from the intense cold was severe. In the early spring Iskandar with seven hundred men set out on a foraging expedition to replenish the exhausted supplies of the army. He plundered all the country of Rang Shigar, and after an absence of two months returned to Maryol.

By this time the messengers sent by Hydar with presents and congratulations to Rashíd, and an appeal to revise his decision of banishment for the sake of their early friendship and service together, now came back with peremptory orders for the return of Iskandar with the troops, but a strict prohibition against the return of Hydar, or even his stay in Tibet. On this the army dispersed and took their way back to Yárkand as best they could in small parties straggling all over the country.

Iskandar and Hydar were soon left with only fifty adherents. And with these they set out in the ensuing winter to make their way to Badakshan by the route of Tághdumbásh, Janác, and Sanic, and Pámír. The party was reduced to twenty-seven men by sickness and death by the time they reached the Karákoram, which they crossed in $Sumbúl$ = September—October. Here Iskandar with four men parted from his companion and friend, and took the road to Yárkand; whilst Hydar with the remaining twenty-one, following an unknown track, wandered for three days over a desolate waste of mountains and snows, on which they shot several $cutás$ = wild ox ($bos\ grunniens$) of huge proportions for food, and finally arrived at Káshgám, a populous little valley at seven days' journey from Pámír. Here the people (who, it would seem, were Musalmáns) welcomed the wanderers with hospitality, fed and clad them, and forwarded them on to Badakhshán, where Hydar found shelter with the King, Sulemán Shah, who was the son of his maternal aunt. Here he was soon after joined by his family from Yárkand, and by Iskandar, who was at the same time expelled the country by Rashíd.

In the autumn they all set out together by way of Kabul to join Kamrán, the son of Bábur, at Láhore. From this Hydar proceeded to the Court of Humáyún, and was by him equipped and sent to conquer and govern Kashmír. He entered the country over the passes on the 22nd $Rajab$ 948 H.=1541 A.D., and it was in its capital that he wrote the $Tárikhi\ Rashídí$ from which these details are derived.

Sáid, entitled Sultán Sáid Khan Gházi, was considered a generous, just, and mild prince, and pious during his later years as a disciple of Khoja Kháwind Mahmúd of the Hanáfi sect. His son and successor, Rashíd, was the child of a slave girl who, when seven months pregnant with him by Sáid, was carried off prisoner by the Uzbak when they invaded Andiján. Sáid recovered her and the infant when he returned to the country by the aid of Bábur, who was his uncle's son. At this time Mirzá Hydar's sister, Habíba Sultán Khánim, arrived in Andiján from Samarcand, and Rashíd aged three years was in 915 H.=1509 A.D. made over to her to be educated.

At the age of thirteen years Rashíd accompanied his father in the expedition against Mogholistán. He was on this occasion taken prisoner at Akhsi by Jánibeg, but was recovered on his expulsion from Farghána. He was subsequently sent to govern in Mogholistán with Mirzá Hydar as his $Wazir$, but returned to Káshghar on the invasion of that region by the Kazzák and Uzbak. At eighteen years of age he was sent with Hydar on a $ghazát$ against the pagans of Bolor in 934 H.=1527 A.D., and on his return thence was sent to the government of Aksú. After six months' stay with him there Mirza Hydar joined Sáid's expedition into Tibet as $Wazir$ to his son Iskandar.

On accession to the throne Rashíd Sultán allied with the Shaibán Khans, and killed and banished all his father's faithful adherents. Mansúr twice attacked him to recover Aksú, but was each time repulsed with loss.

He banished all his brothers and uncles, and his father's wives, and beggared the whole family. He allied with the Uzbak, and gave his sisters in marriage to their nobles. During his reign (of thirty-three years) he annexed Andiján on the one side, and Turfán on the other. In his time the Uzbak gained domination over the Moghol, who were in two great divisions called Moghol and Chaghtáy. The Moghol are the same as the Jattah and Kirghiz, and they number thirty thousand families in Turfán and Káshghar; they are mostly pagans, and the meanest of mankind. They call the Chaghtáy by way of derision Carádánás. T.R.

According to the Tárikhi Khánán Chaghtáya (a book I have not had an opportunity of examining), Rashid left two sons, Ábdul Karím and Muhammad Khan, each of whom succeeded to a divided government in turn. In the reign of the latter the Kirghiz invaded the country, and the dynasty of Chaghtáy Khans collapsed 980 H.=1572 A.D. by the dismemberment of the country between rival representatives of the family; having endured two hundred and twelve years under varying fortunes since its first establishment 761 H.=1360 A.D. by Toghlúc Tymúr. T.K.C.

During the two centuries of rule under the Chaghtáy Khans, Islám in Mogholistan recovered the check it had suffered under the invasion by Changíz, and the government of his immediate successors. And with the influx of Muhammadan divines during the reigns of the first rulers of that dynasty, soon acquired a more fanatic influence amongst the people than it had ever before exhibited. This was due to the proselitizing zeal and activity of the Musalmán merchant priests who traversed the country in all directions, and spread their doctrine more by example and persuasive devices than by force. P.

The graves of the early champions of the Faith, who fell martyrs to the cause of its propagation in this region, were everywhere diligently sought out, their occupants canonized as saints, and their tombs converted into sacred shrines endowed with all sorts of beneficent virtues. Rich grants of land were apportioned by successive Khans for the support of their establishments, whose presiding elders in return dispensed, in the name of their patron saint, endless favors and bounties to an illiterate and superstitious peasantry—by means of magic charms for the cure of disease, by professed miraculous aversions of calamity, and by promised attainment of desires. By methods such as these the priesthood gradually acquired an overwhelming influence over the minds of the people, and soon exerted it to control their domestic life, and finally to usurp the direction of their political conduct and relations.

In the reign of Rashid Sultan, the great saint and divine of the age, the celebrated Mauláná Syad Khoja Kásání, more commonly known as the Makhdúmi Ázam="The Great Master," the metropolitan of Samarcand, visited Káshghar. He was received with the most profound reverence and devotion by the citizens, and was granted rich estates by the Khan. Whilst here he married a lady of the place, Bibi Chiya, and she bore him a son, the Khoja Ishác.

Some of the Makhdúm's sons settled at Káshghar, and by virtue of their exalted parentage, which they traced up to the Prophet, enjoyed a reverential deference from all classes, and were with it accorded by the rulers a leading part in the councils of the government. This liberty they soon turned to the advancement of their personal interests, and, consequently, jealousy and rivalry divided the brotherhood; and two great factions, which exist to the present day, were formed, each supported by its own adherents and partizans amongst the people.

The party siding with the *Imámi Kalán*, Khoja Muhammad Amin (the eldest son of the Makhdúm by a daughter of the Syad Yúsuf of Kásán) whose seat was at Artosh, was styled *Aktaghluc* = "White mountaineer," from the Aktagh or "white mountains" to the north, to which they looked for extraneous support from the Kirghiz there.

The party of the younger son, Khoja Ishác, was called *Karataghluc* = "Black mountaineer," from the Karatágh or "black mountains" to the west of his seat at Khánaric, to whose Kirghiz they looked for aid.

P.	This introduction of the Kirghiz into the internal politics of Káshghar soon produced a confused state of anarchy amongst the several Chiefs ruling the country, and their ambitious rivals amongst the priesthood—between the Khan's, successors of Rashíd on the one hand, and the Khoja's, descendants of Makhdúmi Azam on the other.
	I have not met with any connected account of the events of this period. It appears, however, that in the time of Khoja Muhammad Yúsuf, the son and successor of Khoja Muhammad Amín at Artosh, the whole country was split up into independent Chiefships amongst the sons of Rashíd. Thus A'bdulla held Khutan, Muhammad Khan ruled at Yárkand, Ismáíl at Káshghar, Khudábanda at Aksú, A'bdurrashíd at Kúchá, and at Turfán, and they were all inextricably embroiled in mutual jealousies and hostilities, till Khoja Hidáyatulla, the son of Khoja Yúsuf, succeeded, by the aid of the Zúnghárí, in acquiring the supreme control of the government.
Y.C.	It was during this period of divided authority that Benedict Goës, in November 1603 A.D., arrived at Yárkand, where he found Muhammad Khán was the ruler. Goës owed his favourable reception here, and safe passage through the country to a purely fortuitous circumstance. On his way up from Lahore he was delayed several months at Kabul, and finally set out thence in the caravan of Hájí Khánim, the sister of the Káshghar ruler, to whom he was able to render a service by the loan of six hundred pieces of gold, which the lady, returning from the pilgrimage to Mecca with an empty purse and no credit, was unable to raise amongst the Kabul merchants to meet her pressing requirements and needs. On arrival at Yárkand, after a perilous and adventuresome journey through the robber-haunted passes of Badakhshán and Wakhán, the lady repaid her debt in precious jade from Khutan of which city her son was the Governor, and, in requital of his goodness, befriended the stranger and procured for him a friendly reception, and the protection of both her brother and son. Goës stayed here some months under the much needed hospitality and protection of Muhammad Khán, who ultimately forwarded the Christian Missionary on his journey by Jálish and Turfán to the Chinese frontier where he died. In connection with the religious ferment in the country at the time of this Christian Missionary's visit, it is interesting to note that Muhammad Khán bravely took the friar's part in his adherence to the truth and merits of his own saving faith, and listened to his theological arguments in a spirit of toleration, and with a liberality of mind not to have been expected amongst such a fanatic crew. Indeed, he seems to have acted exceptionally, and more than once had to interpose his protection to shield his guest from the blood thirsty fanaticism and bigotted intolerance of his subjects.
T.H.	In the struggle for ascendancy between the Aktághlúc and Karátághlúc factions, the leader of the former, Mullá Fázil of Artosh, in 1031 H. = 1618 A.D., called to his aid the Khoja Kalán of Khujand, the son of Khoja Muhammad Sáduddín of Coba in the ancient country of Kaikobád and Afrásyab. He came with a force of a thousand men, and was established at Káshghar; but the sons of Khudábanda from Aksú at once besieged the city with the aid of the Yárkand troops and their Kirghiz and Kapchák levies. They harassed the suburbs for six months till at length the Khoja, raising a force amongst the citizens, made a sortie and drove off the besiegers with severe loss.
M.V.	The Aktághlúc party now took the lead, and ultimately in the person of Khoja Hidáyatulla aspired to the direct control of the government. On this Ismáíl, the Ruler of Káshghar, drove him from the city to Kashmir. He repaired from this to the Daláy Lamma, who sent him with a recommendation for aid to the Ghaldan of Zúnghár. That Chief, however, took the opportunity to annex the country, and, establishing the Khoja as his own governor at Yárkand as the capital, exiled the family of Ismáíl to Ghuljá, the capital of his own government. Hidáyatulla, however, though supported by Kalmák authority, had a troubled rule owing to the opposition and intrigues of the rival faction.
T.H.	The following particulars regarding this remarkable character, the founder of the Khoja power in the country of which he is now venerated as the patron saint,

are gathered from the *Tazkira Hidáyat*, written by Mír Kháludddín of Yárkand shortly after the Khojá's death:—

Khoja Hidáyatulla, usually called Hazrat Afák = "Most High Presence," was the son of Khoja Muhammad Yúsuf, the son of Khoja Muhammad Amín, the son of Hazrat Makhdúmi Ázam. He held entire dominion, spiritual and temporal, over the Moghol States of Káshghar, Yárkand, Khutan, Aksú, Kúchá, and Turfán, and had many disciples in Khitá, Bulghár, Urús, and Hindustan. He held a fifth part of Mogholistán in *jágír* = demesne, and received tithes from his disciples in foreign lands; from Kashmír and Badakshán, and the Tungáni in Khitá notably.

Amongst the people of Káshghar he was held as a Prophet second only to Muhammad, and in his miraculous powers of healing the sick and restoring the dead he was reckoned the equal of Hazrat Ísá = "Lord Jesus." His bearing exercised a marvellous effect upon the people, and his appearance amongst them produced the most extraordinary manifestations of fascination. Some wept with joy, some sang with delight, others danced and leaped and whirled around, and others again fell senseless to the ground, whilst all were irresistably attracted to him by an ecstatic devotion of spiritual love. His miracles are said to be countless; yet in his early career scoffers and unbelievers were not wanting.

Abdurrashíd, the Ruler of Yárkand, was his enemy, and appointed a partizan, one Mullá A'bdulla, to the office of Cází in the city. He took every opportunity to destroy the Saint's growing influence, and in his Court of Justice used to denounce Afák as a hypocrite and rogue who, in the garb of a *darvesh*, took the property of the people to keep his retinue of slave boys in gilded crowns, and to deck his concubines innumerable in silks and brocades. The speech of the bold tongued Cází was reported to Afák, but he merely remarked with meek resignation that God would in due time visit him with due reward. Shortly after this the railer was present at an entertainment given by the object of his vituperation, and was choked by a bone sticking in his throat. His friends fell at the Saint's feet, and offering all his wealth, and the sinner's repentance, implored him to save the man's life.

Afák bid his neighbour hit the Cází a blow on the throat, and as he did so the bone was ejected to the dying man's relief. Of the company some laughed, some wept, and others fainted, but the scoffing Cází recovered, and through very shame retired into private life at Aksú. From this he afterwards returned as a partizan and favored servant of the Saint's son and successor.

Mirzá Sháh Mahmúd, a Jarás noble of Yárkand, was another prominent scoffer. He was a debauchee and opium-smoker, and reviled the sanctity of Afák, saying "were he really a man of God he would have cured me of my evil ways." His brother, Gházi Beg, was an equally infidel railer. But both very soon met a just retribution. The one died from an overdose of his favorite drug, and the other of a severe colic whilst out hunting even before they could carry him home. It was by such miracles as these that Afák's sanctity was proved and established. During his reign Afák warred twelve years with the Kirghiz and Kalmák before he acquired the sole sovereignty. Attended by Mullá Álím of Yárkand he accompanied Yolbárs Khan on his fatal campaign against Khitá, and gained many disciples amongst the Tungáni there.

In his time Muhammad Amín Khán, Ruler of Yárkand, went against his brother, Khudábanda, at Aksú. He fell sick on the way, and was brought back in a *járghál* = "horse litter," but died before reaching his home. His friends at once took the body to Afák, and the Khán's mother, Begum Pádsháh, falling at the Saint's feet, presented twenty thousand *tanga* = four thousand rupees in cash, and promising ten thousand more implored his intercession to restore her son to life. Afák was at breakfast at the time, and taking a spoonful of gruel from his bowl applied it to the mouth of the defunct. A perspiration presently broke out over the body, the limbs began to move, and on the third day the dead man was riding about as usual. It was such miracles as this that gained for Hazrat Afák the reputation of a second Hazrat Ísá.

T.H.   Khudábanda now raised an army of Kirghiz and Kalmák to avenge this attack upon Yárkand. Muhammad Amín at once appealed to Afák for protection, and the Saint thus disclosed to the ruler of the State his own ambition: "Hold! Khan! Restrain your desires. This country of Moghollistán is the garden of the Khojas. I entrust it to your care. Do no violence, nor oppression. Be the friend of God's friends. Withhold your tongue from the slander of my people, and be the enemy of my enemies. If you fail in these duties, eternal pains and tortures are your lot, for the wrath of the Saints is a reflexion of the wrath of God. Khudábanda is your vassal. He now draws his sword? Go you against him. The spirit of the Saints upholds your arms. Victory and triumph are yours. My son from Káshghar, Khoja Muhammad Yahya, goes with you."

Accordingly they set out together with a large army against Aksú. The fort was taken, Khudábanda was seized and taken before Muhammad Amín, who at once slew him. The victory was claimed by the Khoja as the result of Afák's miraculous aid; and on the return of the victorious army, he presented the deserving of the soldiers before his father for reward. Amongst the foremost of these was Khudábirdi Bí, Chongbaghish Kirghiz, who was the first to assault and force the gate of the castle. The Saint cast a benign glance on the hero, and inquired "What desirest thou? Oh Mír!" The Kirghiz saluting replied "*Tacsír Pádsháhim!* = Sire! My King! By your high favour I have no lack of worldly wealth. I have herds of horses, and strings of camels, and droves of oxen. My flocks of goats and sheep are countless, and there is no limit to the number of my slaves and wenches; but I have no son." "How many wives have you?" asked the Saint. "*Taesír!* I have two wives" replied the Mír. Afák took two apples from a tray set before him, and handing them to the Kirghiz Bí, said "Give this to the one wife, and this to the other wife." And so he dismissed him. The hero returned home and did as he was bid. Each wife conceived, and in due course each gave birth to a son. This miracle is notorious in all the Káshghar and Yárkand territory.

Following this in 1043 H.=1630 A.D., Muhammad Amín Khán, alarmed at the rapid rise of Afák and jealous of his power, declared war against him, and closing the roads to Hindustan and Badakhshán to prevent his escape, vowed to exterminate the whole Khoja race. On this Afák summoned the aid of Yahya, called also Khan Khoja, as the eldest of his sons; and on his arrival from Káshghar with a numerous army, the troops of the Khán deserted to the Khoja; and thus reduced to helplessness Muhammad Amín forgot his boasts and threats, and sought safety by flight. He was pursued, captured, and executed beyond the Yárkand river.

Afák after this gained supreme control of the government. In his later years he resigned the reins of authority to Yahya, who for fifteen years had been the custodian of the family sepulchre at Artosh and the superior of its attached monastery, and retired to spend his declining years in the society of his disciples over whom his magic influence produced a spell of servile devotion.

Afák converted nearly a hundred thousand people to Islám, not reckoning the ladies of the nobility and gentry amongst whom he exercised an influence and control of a mysterious and imperious nature. He died suddenly at Yárkand in the midst of a theological discussion with his disciples in the beginning of *Rajab* 1105 H.=1693 A.D., and was buried in the vault of his father at Altún Artosh. His funeral was attended by ten thousand relatives, disciples, and retainers. His grave is now the holiest shrine in the country, and is called *Mazár fyzulanwár Astánae Hazrat Eshán Álishán Hazrat Afák*="The shrine bounteous in lights, the threshold of His Eminent Presence, the Most High Presence."

During the life of Afák, the mausoleum and monastery built over the grave of his father, were destroyed and burned by the Kirghiz and Kazzák invaders. Yahya rebuilt them, and, adding a college and alms-houses, much enlarged the area of the shrine. And he gave the revenues of Fyzábád, Daulatbágh, and the Arwát canal in bequest for their maintenance. These buildings were completed only shortly before the death of Afák who, on being informed that all was ready for him to open and bless the institution, foretold his speedy arrival there for his last resting place. T.H.

On the death of Afák, the succession to the government was immediately contested by his sons. Yahya, who had for some years conducted the government over seventeen cities of Mogholistán, was killed within seven months, at the end of Safar 1106 H., through the intrigues of Kháním Pádsháh, the widow of Afák. She was a daughter of Rashíd, and a grand-daughter of Sultán Saíd, and now used her influence with the nobles and chiefs in favour of her own son, Mahdi, at that time aged sixteen years. This excited the jealousy of the *darvesh*, and being instigated by other members of the family, they soon after attacked her palace, and killing her, set it on fire.

In the midst of this confusion Acbásh, a brother of Yahya, came from Turfán and seizing Yárkand, drove the youthful sons of Afák, namely, Khoja Husen (called Baghra Khan by his father) aged nine years, and Calich Burhánuddin, aged five years, and other members of the family to Hindustán. Sixteen years later Husen returned from his exile, and became the Governor of Yárkand and Káshghar.

Acbásh on gaining possession of the city quarrelled with his Kirghiz and Kapchák allies, and, after some desultory warfare, was seized and executed at Yángí Hissár by Arzú Muhammad, the Kirghiz leader; who then fought to oust his rival comrade Camát Bi, the Kapchák Chief; and in the end they destroyed each other.

Afák, in his first attempt to seize the government of the country, was unsuccessful, and was driven from Káshghar by its Ruler, Ismáíl Khan, to take refuge in Kashmír. From this he repaired to the Daláy Lamma who sent him with a recommendation for aid to the Ghaldan = Khán, or Chief of the Olot Kalmák, or Eleuth of Zúnghár. M.V.

The Ghaldan, however, took the opportunity to seize the country for himself, and in 1678 A.D. appointed Afák his Governor at Yárkand as the capital, with a large staff of Kalmák officials supported by garrisons in the different towns. At the same time he carried off Ismáíl and his family into exile at Ghúlja, his own capital.

Afák distributed the several offices of government and provincial charges amongst his Aktághlúc partizans, in subordination to the Zúnghárí Chiefs who, however, themselves took no part in the internal administration of the government. They were content merely to hold the country and realize the monthly tribute of four hundred thousand *tanga* = eighty thousand rupees.

Anarchy and hostility, however, continued for several years between the two factions, till the Karátághlúc being defeated finally emigrated to Kashmír. Afák now to allay suspicion resigned the government to his brother, Ismáíl Muhammad, the Governor of Úsh Turfán, and set him to attack the Zúnghárí. He fell upon the Kalmák, and, plundering their camps, seized an immense number of captives and great booty in cattle. He then feared the vengeance of the Ghaldan, and fled to the mountains, where he was killed by his own guides. On this Afák resumed the government.

On the assassination of Yahya after the death of Afák, his brother from Turfán seized Yárkand as already mentioned. To maintain himself there against his opponents, Acbásh called to his aid from Khujand one Khoja Dányál of the Karátághlúc faction. On this the people of Káshghar brought in Khoja Ahmad, Aktághlúc, and set him up as ruler, and war then followed between the rivals.

The Aktághlúc, with their Kirghiz partizans, besieged Yárkand to seize Dányál, but were repulsed by the Kirghiz under their leader Háshim Khan in the interest of the Karátághlúc. His success, however, was short lived, for the Khoja intrigues presently drove him to retire to his steppes. Dányál now gained over the Kalmák, who joined him at Yárkand to avenge the invasion from Káshghar against which they marched together. The city surrendered after a few skirmishes, and the Kalmák chief, appointing as governor a citizen chosen by the people, took both Ahmad and Dányál prisoners to Ila or Ghúlja, and thus restored quiet to the country.

58.—Saddle maker.

59.—The Forge.

M.V.   In 1720 A.D. Zaban Raptan (Arabdán Khan of the Zúnghári?) restored Dányál to the government of Alty Shahr=six cities, but appointed his own Governors in each of them, and fixed the revenue at a hundred thousand *tanga*=twenty thousand rupees, that of Afák being a thousand *tanga*=two hundred rupees *per centum* of his subjects. He at the same time kept Chagán, the eldest son of Dányál, as a hostage at Ila, whither Dányál repaired periodically to render account of his government.

W.W.   Arabdán Khán of the Zúnghári died in 1720 A.D., and, his sons disputing the throne, the rule was seized by the rival Chiefs, Amursana and Tawats, or Davatsi. The usurpers quarrelled as to the division of authority, and Amursana going to Pekin for aid returned with a Chinese army and expelled Tawats. He then rebelled against the Chinese Emperor, and defeated two armies sent against him by Kienlung. But he succumbed to the third, and fled to Tobolsk, where he died in 1757 A.D.

His territory then fell to Kienlung, who nearly exterminated the Zúnghári and Olot, and then invited the Túrgút or Tourgouth emigrants from their settlements on the Volga, and they returned to their ancient patrimony in 1772 A.D. Meanwhile Chinese troops and colonists, with exiles and nomads soon re-peopled the country depopulated by the massacre of half a million people during the Chinese conquest. And the Mánchú authority was established by a system of conciliation and coercion judiciously combined; whilst the development of the agricultural and mineral resources of the country, and the protection afforded to commerce, soon restored prosperity.

M.V.   Ghaldan Chiring on succeeding to the throne confirmed Dányál in his appointment; but after his death, to weaken the power of the Karataghlúc faction, he divided the government of the country amongst his several sons. Thus to the eldest, Khoja Chagán, he gave Yárkand, to Yúsuf he gave Káshghar, and similarly Aksú to Ayúb, and Khutan to Ábdulla; with a Kalmák agent conjointly at each place.

The mother of Yúsuf was the daughter of a Kalmák *Noyán*="Noble," and he spent his youth in Zúnghár by the order of the Khán Tawats. Now seeing the dissension reigning there he got leave to go and defend Káshghar from a pretended attack by the Kirghiz. But on arrival there in 1754 A.D. he set to work to raise an army to free his country, at the very time that Amursana was seeking the aid of the Boghdo Khan for the rule of the Zúnghári against his rival Davatsi.

The conduct of Yúsuf excited suspicion, and the Kalmák Governor of the city plotted to assassinate him whilst at prayers in the mosque. The plot, however, was disclosed to him, and Yúsuf seizing the chief actor, Khudáyár, the *Ishikagha* or "Mayor," executed him. But his accomplices, a son of Khudáyár and Ábdussattár (a Beg of Artosh), escaped to Ila with the intelligence of the revolt at Káshghar. Meanwhile at Yárkand, the Governor, Gházi Beg, seized Chagán, and Yúsuf at once went to his aid with the cry of Islám. He at the same time sent a force of a thousand men to Barchak to intercept the road and prevent the Kalmák carrying off Chagán to Ila. Presently Sadic, the son of Chagán, appeared with aid from the opposite direction. He hurried up from Khutan with seven thousand men and some Kirghiz levies, and managed to get possession of the family of Ghazi Beg, whom he threatened with their torture and death unless he released his father. The Governor fearing for them, and dreading the vengeance of Yúsuf, set free his captive, and sought forgiveness with the Kurán on his head. And he was pardoned at the intercession of Chagán himself.

In the meantime Yúsuf had sent envoys to Khokand and Bukhárá reporting the overthrow of the Zúnghári rule, and seeking the aid of the faithful in support of Islám. The independence of these cities, however, of Káshghar, Yárkand, and Khutan, was not of long duration.

In 1757 A.D., after Amursana had returned to Zúnghár with a Chinese army, his rival, Davatsi, fled with three hundred men by the Múzárt Pass to Úsh Turfán. He was here seized by Khojám Beg, the Governor, and delivered to the Chinese who, settling Amursana at Ila with a Chinese garrison in support, thus possessed themselves of the rule in Zúnghár.

Amursana now set to re-subjugate the three revolted cities, and by the advice of A'bdul Wahháb and Khoja Syad Beg, Governors on the part of the Kalmák of Aksú and Úsh Turfán respectively, and with the consent of the Chinese General, resolved to make use of the Aktághlúc party for the purpose.

Burhánuddín and Khan Khoja, the sons of Ahmad (whose family had great influence at Káshghar), were at this time in exile at Irin Khabirghan on the head waters of the Ila river to the east of Ghúlja. They were consequently summoned to the city where Khan Khoja was retained as hostage, whilst his brother was sent with a force of Kalmák, Chinese, and Turkistání to Aksú. Here Burhánuddín was well received, and with his army reinforced by five thousand Musalmáns from Kúchá, Turfán, and Aksú itself, and by the Dolán tribe to the south, set out with his new adherents to Úsh Turfán. Here, too, he received a joyful welcome, but was detained some time owing to a coalition of the rebel States to oppose him.

The confederates were already on the march from Yárkand by way of Yángí Hissár and Artosh to check the advance of Burhánuddín, when Yúsuf died in his retreat at Yárkand. His son, A'bdulla, was at once installed as ruler at Káshghar with the title of Khoja Pádshah, and he lost no time in sending his son, Khoja Mullám, with the Káshghar contingent to join the Yárkand force, and they together besieged Úsh Turfán.

Here the Karátághlúc besiegers proposed to the besieged Aktághlúc that they should lay aside their party jealousies and combine as Musalmáns, and invade Ila. And by way of inducement they promised Burhánuddín the government of Káshghar, Aksú, and Turfán. But he, being surrounded by the Chinese and Kalmák, told the deputation to advise the Karátághlúc leaders to go to Ila, and seek the pardon of the Chinese Emperor through his Viceroy there. Meantime some of the Aktághlúc in the besieging force secretly plotted with Burhánuddín, and in the first fight went over to him in a body with the Kirghiz whom they had won to their side.

On this the besiegers dispersed, and their leaders fled back to Káshghar, where Burhánuddín, following in pursuit, was received with open arms. From this he advanced against Khoja Chagán, who held Yárkand, and in the names of the Boghdo Khan and Amursana demanded his surrender to Chinese protection. Chagán sent a reply of defiance, and with the cry of "Islám" raised the populace for a *ghazá*. Burhánuddín consequently closely besieged the city, and finally, after some skirmishing in which Ináyat, the son of Chagán, was killed, took it through the treachery of Ghází Beg, who on a pretence of famine led Chagán to make a sortie with all his force to raise the siege.

In the sally Ghází Beg took flight, and threw the defenders into confusion, and the besiegers rallying drove them into the city. During the night Chagán fled with his family, and next day Ghází Beg surrendered the city to Burhánuddín. Chagán was pursued and overtaken at the Zarafshán river, where Arka, a son of Yúsuf, was killed in the conflict, whilst Nazar with two attendants escaped to India. The rest were taken back to Yárkand, and all executed. And so the Aktághlúc replaced the Karátághlúc in the government of the country. In 1758 A.D., Burhánuddín aided by his brother, Khan Khoja, rebelled, and, consequently, in the following year a Chinese army under the Governor of Ila invaded the country, and after a succession of contests drove the rebel brothers to seek refuge in Badakhshán. Here the King, Sultan 'Sháh, killed them both, and sent their heads to the Chinese General, and Káshghar was annexed as an integral part of the Chinese Empire under the Provincial Governor of Ila. In this war four of the sons of Afák were killed in fight, and two were taken prisoners to Pekin for execution there. Only one son of Burhánuddín escaped. His name was Khoja Sáádat A'li, commonly called Sarimsak.

The Chinese to consolidate their authority in this western province of their Empire in 1764 A.D. built Hoi Yuan Chen on the River Ila, and re-settled Zúngharía, which had been depopulated by the massacre of half a million people, by Chinese emigrants and exiles from Kansuh, and with Sibo, Solon, and Daur colonists,

M.V. and a Manchú garrison of soldiers of the Green Dragon standard. In the Ila district seven thousand Musalmán families were reduced to serfdom as tillers of the soil, whilst the remnant of the Zúnghárí were granted roaming tracts in their former locale. The government was confided to a *Tzian Tziun* or *Jáng-Júng* = "Viceroy," with three Lieutenants at Ila, Túrbaghátai, and Káshghar; but the details of local government were left to be administered as before by Musalmán officers. Chinese garrisons, however, were located in the principal cities, outposts were established on the frontiers, and post stages built on all the main routes for quick communication. And thus the Chinese secured their conquest.

This success of the Chinese arms alarmed the Islám polity all over Central Asia, though the border Chiefs immediately under their influence professed vassalage to the Chinese Emperor. Ablai of the Middle Horde in 1766 A.D. submitted to the Boghdo Khán, and was granted the title of Prince. Núr 'Ali of the Little Horde in token of submission sent envoys to Pekin. Whilst Adania or Erdáná Bí, the Khan of Khocand in 1758 A.D., and then his successor, Nárbota Bí, recognized the protectorate of China. But the rest of Central Asia was panic-struck by the establishment of the Chinese rule on their very frontier.

In 1762 A.D. Chinese mandarins with an escort of a hundred and thirty men went to Ablai, and demanded horses and supplies for an army to invade Turkistán and Samarcand in the spring. On this Erdáná Bí of Táshkand, and Fazl Bí of Khujand, and the independent Kirghiz Chiefs sent envoys to seek aid from Sháh Ahmad—the Durrání who, after the death of Nadir, had raised Afghanistan into an independent kingdom, and the Afgháns to the proud position of the most powerful nation of the East.

Ahmad had, ten years before, conquered all the country on the left bank of the Oxus from Chárjúe up to its head waters in Badakhshán, and now in 1763 A.D., in answer to the call for Islámite aid, he sent a force of Afgháns to protect the frontier between Táshkand and Khokand. And at the same time he sent an embassy direct to Pekin to demand the restitution of the Muhammadan States of Eastern Turkistán. Meanwhile in 1765 A.D. the people of Úsh Turfán, forestalling the Musalmán aid reckoned on, rose in revolt, but the rebellion was at once quelled by a massacre of the citizens and the complete destruction of the town.

The Afghán deputation was not well received at the Chinese capital, and the Durrání sovereign was at the time too much engaged against the Sikhs to turn his attention in this direction. And the Chinese on their side were deterred from further conquest in the helpless States of Central Asia to the west by the presence of an Afghán army of fifteen thousand men in Badakhshán; sent there to ravage the country and execute the King, Sultan Sháh, in revenge for his murder of the two refugee Khojas in 1760 A.D. They brought under subjection, however, the Kirghiz on the north-west, and yearly sent a force from Káshghar and Turbaghatai, accompanied by Chinese traders for barter, to collect the annual revenue of one per cent. of horses and cattle and one per mille of sheep, in return for the privilege of pasturing on the steppe between Lake Balkash and the Alátágh.

After the revolt of Úsh Turfán, the Chinese rule was undisturbed till 1816 A.D., when Zi'áuddín Akhúnd, Karátághlúc of Táshmalik or Táshbaligh = "stone town," to the west of Káshghar, rebelled and with a party of Kirghiz raided the Chinese outposts. He was soon captured and executed, but his son, Ashraf Beg, carried on the war till he shared the same fate. His young brother, however, was sent to Pekin, where he was executed on attaining full age.

This quelled the Karátághlúc for a time, and the government went on without any serious outbreak till 1825 A.D., when the appearance of the Russians on the Bogú camp grounds and the seven rivers led to a decline of the Chinese prestige, which was presently confirmed by the revolt of the Khoja Jahángir.

Under the Chinese rule certain trading privileges were accorded to the city of Aksú and those to the west of it, which were not granted to Kúchá and the other cities to the east; whilst no Musalmán trader was allowed to go northward by the

Múzárt Pass. The cities to the westward of Aksú had always from their position shared a community of interests with Khokand or Andiján, anciently called Farghána (which during the time of the Moghol Khans was included in the government of Káshghar, as it was at an earlier period under the rule of the Bughra Khan family when Uzkand was the capital of one of their Princes), and the adjoining States of Máwaránahar, and in them the Khoja influence had always been greatest.

But the eastern cities on the other hand from Kúchá to Khámil had hardly felt this influence, and were from their vicinity and common interests more in unison with the Chinese. This natural tendency the Chinese authorities encouraged by a conciliating rule, and the grant of princely titles, whilst the Emperor himself, to strengthen the bonds of attachment, married a Khámil Princess.

The trading privileges enjoyed by the western towns enabled their people to maintain constant communication with their co-religionists to the west of the passes, and afforded them opportunities of intriguing with the Musalmáns there for the restoration of the Khoja rule, and the hatching of all sorts of sedition against the established government. To check the troubles and disquiet arising from this source, the Chinese in 1813 A.D. subsidized the Khan of Khokand with two hundred *yamb* = £3,660 yearly to control the hostility of the Khojas, who since their conquest of the country had emigrated to his territory.

Amongst these was Sarimsak, the last descendant of the Afác family. After many years of wandering in Central Asia he settled in his old age at Khokand, to be near Káshghar, whence he derived his revenues. He was here joined by many Karátághlúc discontents from the Chinese side of the border, who complained of the oppression of the foreign rulers, the violation of their wives and daughters by the infidel, and the suppression of their religious supremacy. These grievances, coupled with the fate of the two murdered Khojas, excited universal sympathy amongst Musalmáns, and to fan it, emissaries set out from Káshghar in 1820 A.D., and spread themselves over Central Asia to enlist the aid of Islám in a *ghazá* against the *káfir* invaders.

As a first consequence Murád Beg, the Ruler of Kundúz, on the pretence of avenging the murder of the Khoja brothers on behalf of his relative, Sarimsak, conquered Badakshán, and deported its people to sicken and die in the swamps of his own country. And as a second Jahángír Khoja invaded Káshghar.

Sarimsak had three sons, Yúsuf Khoja, who lived at Bukhárá, Bahaúddin, and Jahángír who was born in 1788 A. D. On the death of Úmar Khan of Khokand in 1822 A. D., Jahángír fled from the city to the Kará Kirghiz, and plotted against Káshghar, where the devotion of the people to the Khoja interest and the weakness of the Chinese rule were well known to him. His hostility now was the commencement of those troubles which have ever since distracted the country till its conquest by the present Ruler, Amír Muhammad Yákúb Khan, Atálik Ghází.

Jahángír first enlisted the aid of Súránchí Beg, Chongbaghish Kirghíz, who merely plundered the Káshghar suburbs and was driven back. On this failure the Khoja went to the Sáyak Kirghiz of Bolor, and securing the adhesion of their Chiefs, Atantai and Tailak, made the summer resort of the Kirghiz camps on the upper course of the Nárín river his head-quarters. Here he assumed the character of a saint and miracle worker, and made many excursions against the enemy; but without much success, till at last in 1825 A.D. a small party of Chinese who had pursued his raiders to the Nárín, and plundered the country up to Fort Kurtka, were surprized in a narrow defile on their return journey and slaughtered almost to a man.

This victory was at once noised in Khokand, and emissaries were sent to raise the Uzbak, Kazzák, and Búrút Kirghiz, many of whom with Andijání and Badakhshí adventurers flocked to the green banner of Jahánghír. In the following spring the Khoja marched against Káshghar with a considerable force under the command of 'Isa *Dádkhwáh*, lent to him as General by Muhammad Ali Khan of Khokand, and camped at Beshkirim in its northern suburbs.

The Chinese came out to attack, but were quickly routed and driven back to their citadel, whilst Jahángír entering the city amidst the acclamations of the people

60.—Silk Reeling.

61.—Cotton Spinning.

M.V. established himself in the palace with the title of Syad Jahángír Sultán, and at once organized his government on the Khokand model, substituting the Musalmán turban for the Chinese cap, balls, and feathers. He allowed most of the Begs to retain their posts, but appointed Andiján partizans to the principal offices, and executed Muhammad Saíd of Khámil, the *Wang* = Governor on the part of the Chinese, for his opposition.

On the fall of Káshghar, the people of Yangi Hissar, Yárkand, and Khutan rose simultaneously, and massacring the Chinese everywhere, razed their forts and joined the service of the Khoja. In June Muhammad Ali Khan, jealous of the Khoja's success, himself appeared at Káshghar with fifteen thousand men to join in the *ghazá*, but he was coldly received by Jahángír, who looked upon him as a dangerous rival. The Khan, however, set vigorously to work to take the Chinese fort of Gulbágh, a few hundred yards to the west of the city, in which the garrison still held out ; but his efforts proving ineffectual, and having lost a thousand men under its walls in twelve days, his ardour cooled as rapidly as it had glowed, and he returned to his principality there to make amends for the disappointment in adding a new province to his dominions by stamping the envied title of *Ghází* on his coinage.

Jahángír meantime continued the siege of the Gulbágh, and it fell to him on the seventeenth day. The Chinese Governor and principal officers committed suicide, whilst their troops fleeing in all directions were captured and massacred to the number of eight thousand men. Only four hundred of the captives were spared on their professing Islám, and they were at once distributed over Máwaránahar as an inducement to the Faithful to rally round Jahángír.

Muhammad Ali Khan now uneasy at the growing success of the Khoja, discouraged volunteers and plotted with Isa *Dádkhwáh* to raise a mutiny amongst his troops. The General's plans, however, were timely discovered, and he was reduced from his post of *Mingbáshí*, and the disorder quelled. Many other plots against Jahángír now came to light, but he was generally popular and had the support of the Musalmáns everywhere.

P. Meanwhile the Chinese Viceroy at Ila had been active in his preparations to recover the revolted cities, and despatched an immense force of Tungání, Khitáy, and Kalmák against the rebels. The Chinese army arrived at Aksú in January (six months after the fall of Káshghar), under the command of a Jáng Júng Tán, with a Jáng Júng and several Ambán. From this in the early spring a force of twelve thousand men was sent by way of Cáy Yoli to Khutan, and another of seven thousand men to Yárkand, whilst the main army of eighty thousand men assembling at Marálbáshí set out thence against Káshghar. Jahángír in the meantime had concentrated his Khutan and Yárkand levies at the capital, and on the approach of the Chinese sent out an army of fifty thousand men to oppose them.

The hostile armies met at Yangabad, and according to custom each put forward a champion for single combat. That of the Chinese was a giant Kalmák archer fantastically dressed like a devil dragon ; whilst the champion on the side of Jahángír was a noted Khokandi warrior equally versed in sword and rifle practice and clad in gaudy silks and chain armour. The two advanced to the contest on the open plain backed by their respective supporters. But whilst the Khokandi was adjusting his rifle the Kalmák shot an arrow through his chest and out between the shoulders, and his adversary fell dead on the spot. A skirmish followed between the supporting parties, but the Káshghar army, disheartened by the untoward commencement of the contest, soon broke and fled in disorder. They were pursued with great slaughter and loss in captives as far as Cazán Kul, where the Chinese army camped for the night.

Next day they advanced in three great divisions by the Yangi Hissar road on the south, Daulatbagh on the east, and Sarman on the west, and invested the city on three sides. During the night Jahángír with seven followers fled by the Chacmác Pass to the Karátakka mountain, where he was stopped by the snow, and his troops, finding themselves thus deserted, next day dispersed and took the road to Andiján. They were pursued and cut up by numerous detachments of Chinese, some of whom penetrated as far as Ush, whence they were repelled and driven back by the Kirghiz and Kapchák who rallied to the defence of their homesteads and beaten countrymen. Meantime the Chinese General sent a force under Ishác Wáng with the Chih Ambán, Dawán Ambán and others in pursuit of Jahángír. His hiding place was pointed out by some Kirghiz nomads of Karátakka, and Jahángír surrendering to his pursuers was brought back to the Jáng Júng Tán, who sent him prisoner to Pekin, where he was subsequently executed with torture. P.

In return for this service the Chinese General appointed Ishác Wáng of Úsh Turfán (whose success on this occasion was due to the treachery of Jahángír's former ally, Suránchi Beg, Chongbaghish Kirghiz, who now thought to avert the punishment due to his own hostilities by delivering up to the victors their fallen enemy, and his own acknowledged spiritual leader and king) to the government of the city, and building the Yángíshahr fort, a *farsakh* to the south of it, in place of the Gulbágh destroyed by Jahángír, established Jáh Dárín with a strong garrison in its command, and returned to Ila.

The Emperor Taukwang was delighted at the successful suppression of this revolt, and showered honors and rewards upon Changlung, his General of Ila, and upon his troops. For his good service he rewarded Ishác Wáng with the title of Prince of Káshghar. He was, however, soon after accused of treason and summoned to Pekin for trial, and though acquitted of the charge, he was detained there several years before being permitted to return. W.W.

Jahángír ruled only nine months, and in the spring of 1828 A.D. the Chinese recovering possession of the revolted cities re-established their authority by numerous executions and tortures and confiscations, and by the transportation of twelve thousand Musalmán families from Káshghar to Ghulja, or Kuldja, where they were settled as serfs under the name of *taránchí*="sweaters," "labourers." M.V.

This revolt of Jahángír, originating in Khokand, was the cause of the influence then acquired by that principality; and it has been maintained ever since to the final overthrow of the Chinese rule in Eastern Turkistán, as will be seen in the sequel. The Chinese, after quelling the revolt, punished the rebels as stated above, and avenged themselves on the Khokand Khán by stopping trade and placing restrictions on communication with his province.

On this Muhammad Ali Khán, who had recently annexed Karátakin, Darwáz and Kuláb and had made tributary the Burut and other Kirghiz, decided in 1829 A. D. to attack the Chinese. For this purpose he invited Khoja Yúsuf, the elder brother of Jahángír, from Bukhárá, and proclaimed a *ghazá* to set him on the throne of his ancestors. Yúsuf took the field in September 1830 with a force of 20,000 men, mostly Andijan and Tashkand troops, with some Karátakin levies and Káshghar refugees; all under the command of *Mingbáshí* Hacc Culí Beg, a brother-in-law of Muhammad Ali Khán.

The Chinese with 3,000 men advanced to oppose them, but were defeated at Mingyol, and the invaders pushing on seized Káshghar, where Yúsuf was at once set on the throne. Yángí Hissár, Yárkand, Khutan, and Aksu, up to the Múzárt Pass, quickly fell into his possession; and the Chinese, as before, were everywhere massacred; whilst the arrival of their troops from Ghulja was delayed for want of carriage.

This advance of the Khokand army roused the hostility of Bukhárá against Andijan, and Muhammad Ali Khán, to avert the attack threatened by Nasrulla Khán, at once recalled his General Hacc Culí Beg; and Yúsuf, unable to hold his position unsupported amongst the fickle Musalmáns of Káshghar, returned with him in November or December after a rule of only ninety days. He carried away as trophies of his success 500 Chinese captives, and was accompanied by several hundred families of Káshghar emigrants who settled in the suburbs of Khujand and Táshkand.

M.V.   During the period of this invasion, Western China was disturbed by the revolt in Shensi and the capture and massacre of Bárkúl by the Musalmáns, and consequently the Chinese troops did not concentrate at Ghúlja or Ila till the following January, after the Khokand army had retired from Káshghar.

In the spring of this year (1831), whilst they were re-occupying the evacuated towns, Muhammad Ali Khán, who had staved off his difficulty with Bukhárá, sent Hacc Culí Beg with an army of 7,000 men to subjugate the Kará Kirghiz who, during the recent troubles, had been raiding his border. He dispersed the Sáyak camps on the Upper Nárín, and took prisoners their chiefs Atantai and Tailac; whilst the Koshbegi of Táshkand at the same time pursued the Boghu tribes and penetrated beyond Ila to the military post of Sibo.

These successes of the Khocand Khán altered the policy of the Chinese Governor, who now sent four envoys to treat with Muhammad Ali Khán. He detained three of them as hostages, and with the fourth sent Alím Pádsháh, a rich merchant, as his agent to Pekin, with certain demands for the government of the Musalmán population of the towns of Eastern Turkistan. He secured the following concessions for the Khán: *first*, dues as per *shariat* on all merchandise brought by Musalmán traders to the towns of Acsú, Ush Turfán, Káshghar, Yángí Hissár, Yárkand and Khutan to go to the Khán of Khocand; *second*, the power to appoint in each of these towns an *Aksakál*,—"white-beard" or "elder" as commercial agent to collect these dues under a Khocand inspector to reside at Káshghar as political representative; and *third*, that all foreign Musalmáns residing in these towns were to be under the entire control of these agents. In return the Khokand Khán agreed to restrain the Khoja party and to prevent their invading the country, and to imprison any member attempting to do so.

The envoy on his return from Pekin, in 1832, was appointed Inspector at Káshghar on the part of Khokand, and, according to the Andijan custom, held the post on lease. His authority extended over the "six cities" to which the treaty regulations applied, and hence the country was called by the Andijan people *Alty Shahr*, or by a different reckoning (in which Marálbáshí belonging to Yárkand was counted separately) *Yatty Shahr* "seven cities." And this was the region in which Khokand influence was greatest, its effects being as yet barely perceptible in the eastern cities.

Thus were established trade and political relations between Western China and Khokand. Through them the Khokandí acquired an increasing influence in the country, and a firmer grasp on the sympathies of the people, in opposition to the rule of the Chinese, to whose prestige the revolts of Jahángír in 1826, and of Yúsuf in 1830, coupled with the influence exercised by the proximity of the Russians, proved serious blows.

After reducing the Kará Kirghiz Muhammad Ali Khán extended his frontiers, and in 1832 built the Kurtka Fort on the Nárín and that of Táshkorghan on the Pámir border, and he held besides nearly a fourth of the population of these towns under the rule of his agents. To keep this power, it was his interest to restrain the Khojas, and he consequently strictly watched their movements.

Until 1846 the country enjoyed peace under the just and liberal rule of Zuhúruddín, the Governor on the part of the Chinese. He appears to have been a native of Káshghar, and to have emigrated to Khokand in 1830. From this he went to Petropawlovsk and Kazán, and returned thence by Semipalatinsk to Ghúlja where he represented to the Chinese Governor that he had escaped from prison at Khokand. He was, in consequence, taken into favour and appointed *Ishikághá*, or "Mayor" of Káshghar, and gradually rose to the post of *Hákim Beg*, or *Sol Ambán* as he is styled in the inscription over the gate of Káshghar, of which, in 1255 H. (1839 A.D.), he restored the fortifications and built the palace. During his rule were erected the new Chinese forts, called *Mángshín* or *Yángíshahr*, outside each of the towns of this country, for the accommodation of the Chinese garrisons and arsenals, instead of the former citadels, called *Gulbágh*, which were destroyed by the rebels.

In 1845, on the accession of Khudáyár Khán to the throne of Khokand, the relations with Káshghar were violated by marauding bands of Andijání and Kirghiz; and the Khojas, taking advantage of the anarchy on all sides, and the internal strife distracting parties in Khokand, banded together and collecting a small force invaded Káshghar in the autumn of 1263 H. (1846 A.D.), and laid siege to the city and the Chinese *Mángshín*, four miles to the south. The city held out for thirteen days under its Governor, Kásim Beg, who, on its surrender to the enemy through the treachery of the citizens, then fled out by the Tuman River gate and effected his escape to the Chinese fort.

This invasion is known as the revolt of the *Haft Khojagán*, or "Seven Khojas," as it was conducted by that number of the members of the Afák family. The eldest of these was Eshan Khán Khoja, commonly called Katta Tora, "Great Lord;" and amongst the others were Buzurg Khán, Walí Khán, Kichik Khán, and Tawakkul Khán, all of whom subsequently figured in the conquest of the country by Yakúb Beg Atálik Ghází.

Katta Tora now assumed the government in Káshghar, and appointed the others to the surrounding towns and settlements. Here these worthies pillaged the houses of the government officials appointed by the Chinese, and, seizing their wives and daughters to stock their harems, at once abandoned themselves to a course of unbridled licentiousness and debauchery; their troops the while besieging the Chinese garrison shut up in the *Mangshín*.

Their reign of oppression, however, did not last long, for in seventy-five days after the fall of the city, about November, the *Jáng Júng* of Ila, the *Jáng Júng* of Orúmchí and Changtáy, the *Dowáng* of Karásháhr, and the *Dowáng* of the Kalmák, each having collected his troops of Mánchú, Túrgút, Sibo and Solon, amounting to 12,000 men, including 3,000 *Champan*, or "criminal exiles" marked with a scar on the left cheek, arrived at Marálbáshi to quell the revolt. On this Katta Tora set out from the capital to secure Yárkand, but was intercepted and brought to action by the Chinese at Kok Rabát. After a fight of two hours his army was routed, and he fled back to Káshghar; but here the citizens having had enough of his rule, and disgusted at the Khoja licentiousness and the oppression of the Andijan soldiers, closed the gates against him; and he and his *confrères* escaped back to Khokand with only a few followers, carrying with them the curses and jeers of those they left behind.

The Chinese again took possession of the city without opposition, and restoring order dismissed the Ambán and Kho Dárín who held the *Mángshín*; and Zuhúruddín, the Musalmán governor of the district on the part of the Chinese, was similarly reduced for having allowed the city to fall into the hands of such a worthless crew; and their places were filled by new nominees. The *Jáng Júng* of Ila then executed a number of principal men who had joined in the Khoja revolt, and slew many of the people in revenge for the massacre of the Chinese traders and settlers in the city, and finally, after reinforcing the several garrisons, returned to his own government.

On the re-establishment of the Chinese rule, the former trade, and political relations with Khokand were at once renewed; and Khudáyár Khán appointed as his representative at Káshghar an active partizan, Núr Muhammad Khán, who had already given proof of his devotion to the Khoja cause by delivering the city over to them in the recent revolt. And he now protected the Andijání residents, and fostered the Khoja influence. During his tenure of office the Andijan element acquired a considerable numerical accession by new immigrants from Khokand, who were encouraged to buy land, marry, and settle in the country. With this increase to the strength of their foreign supporters, the Musalmán population of the towns daily became more arrogant in their demands, and more independent in their bearing under the rule of their conquerors, till in another decade their restiveness under the Chinese yoke culminated in the last of the Khoja revolts under Walí Khán in 1857.

P.   The explanation of these successive Khoja revolts under Jahángír in 1825, under Yúsuf in 1830, under Katta Tora in 1846, and under Walí Khán in 1857, is not difficult if we consider the claims of their family and the nature of the tenure of the country by the Chinese. As to the first, the preceding pages will have illustrated the character of the Khoja government in the country from the date of its first establishment by Khoja Afák; their rule, it will be remembered, was in subordination to the authority first of the *Ghaldan* of Zúnghár, and then of the Emperor of China, and was characterized by mutual jealousies and party rivalries, and by a persistent hostility to the paramount power. Whilst as to the second, the Chinese, as has been mentioned, held the country by a mere military occupation for the maintenance of order, the realization of revenue and the protection of trade. Their garrisons were located in forts outside the several towns they commanded, and their troops were kept quite distinct from the Musalmán population inside the walls. Whilst the Chinese merchants and traders, and others following in the wake of the relieving troops came and went, or settled and traded, and worked in the market suburbs that sprang up between the forts and the cities; only a small proportion of them took up quarters amongst the Musalmán residents within the walls, and their numbers amongst the peasantry were even still less. The internal government of the Musalmán population not under the Khokand agents, both in the cities and rural districts, was everywhere conducted according to the *shariat* by Musalmán officials appointed by the Chinese Viceroy, and wearing Chinese uniforms and emblems, jointly with officers of his own nation to whom they were subordinate.

P.   The clashing of rival interests produced by this three-fold system of government,—*viz.*, the Khokand agency, the *shariat* for the Musalmáns, and Chinese law for the traders and settlers of that empire,—the venality of the officials of all three classes, coupled with the general laxity of morals and the neglect of their religious ordinances by the Musalmáns now no longer awed by the dictation of an arrogant priesthood, soon led to grave discontent amongst the influential classes of the Muhammadan population, especially those under Khokand rule. And this state of affairs, coupled with the blow given to the Chinese prestige by the establishment of the Russians at Almátí or Fort Vernoe in 1853, encouraged them once more to try and cast off the foreign yoke. Intrigues with the Khoja party in Khokand had from the commencement of the new rule been a dangerous feature in the political relations of this Chinese province with that Muhammadan State, and the opportunity now promising success they were renewed with a redoubled energy through emissaries inviting the Khojas to come and resume the possessions of their ancestors, and assuring them of the support of the population.

M.V.   Consequently, during 1855-56 A.D., Walí Khán Khoja and his brother Kichik Khán made several attempts to invade Káshghar, but on each occasion were repulsed at the frontier pickets owing to their numerical weakness. In the spring of 1857, however, Walí Khán, after performing the prayers of the *Ramazán'Íd*, 16th May, set out from Khokand with seven Káshghar emissaries and a small band of trusty adherents to carry out a preconcerted enterprise against the Chinese.

They arrived at the Ocsálár Fort belonging to Khokand (on the Ush and Káshghar road) at night, and surprising the little garrison killed the commandant and won over the soldiers to join the Khoja. Some Káshghar troops who had been sent by Núr Muhammad, the Khokand agent there, to collect the revenue from the Chongbaghish Kirghiz, and who were then encamped in the vicinity, soon joined the adventurers, and brought with them a party of the tribes to swell the Khoja's force. At the same time some scouts sent out by the Chinese were captured and brought to Walí Khán who inaugurated his bloody career by at once striking off their heads with his own hand.

He then pushed on, and crossing the Kizil ford surprised the picket there as they slumbered under the effects of their opium pipes, and slew every soul of them, and at dawn appeared before the *Kúm Darwáza*, or "Sand Gate," on the south side of the city. He set fire to the gate, and, forcing through, rushed into the city,

a 19

as the people were rousing from their sleep, with the cry of, "Welcome Buzurg Khán Torá!"—he was the only son of Jahángír, and one whom the people had been expecting as a deliverer. Núr Muhammad at once came forward to greet the Khoja with congratulations on his arrival, and delivering the city to him, installed him in the palace; whilst the citizens rising *en masse* hunted, plundered, and murdered the Chinese everywhere. In the confusion Ahmad Wáng, the Musalmán governor on the part of the Chinese, with a few others, escaped by the opposite gate and took refuge in the *Mángshía* or *Yángishahr* with the Chinese garrison.

Walí Khán inaugurated his rule in the city by appointing Andijan adherents to all the Government offices, and by executing a number of the Chinese officials and merchants who had flocked to him for protection from the mob; and by distributing their wives and daughters amongst his partizans, and confiscating their property to himself. The first to join his party were the Aktaghluc Chiefs of Artosh and Beshkirim; and Mír Ahmad Shekh, of the former place, in proof of his devotion, gave his daughter in marriage to the Khoja.

Their example was followed by the chiefs of the surrounding settlements, and Walí Khán soon had a force of 20,000 men at his command. He pressed a number of Afghan traders whom he found in the city into his army, and set all the iron-smiths and tailors in the place to work in the manufacture of arms and uniforms for his troops. At the same time he employed many thousands of the people to dam the Kizil River at Pakhtaghlic and turn its stream against the Yángishahr Fort which was held by the Bádárín and Yehdárín, *Ambáns*, with 6,000 men.

Whilst thus employed at Káshghar he sent a force under Tilá Khán to seize Yángí Hissár and Yárkand. At the former the Chinese garrison shut themselves up in the fort, and Tilá Khán passing on invested Yárkand in June 1857. The Chinese issued from their fort to drive off the besiegers, but were defeated, and fled back to the shelter of their walls. The city meantime held out, though offering to surrender on the appearance of the Khoja himself, and Tilá Khán, after plundering the suburbs, retired on the approach of Chinese succour.

In seventy-seven days after the fall of Káshghar—August—a Chinese force of 12,000 men, with the Ambáns Fákhya from Ila, Sháy Dárín from Orúmchí, Changtáy from Karáshahr, and others arrived at Marálbáshí to the relief of Yárkand. Walí Khán sent out a force to intercept them, but it was defeated and driven back to Káshghar; and the Chinese advancing relieved Yárkand of the enemy. They halted here ten days to rest their men and settle the city, and then taking most of the Yárkand troops with them proceeded against Walí Khán at Káshghar. At Kizilí they were opposed by a force sent out by him to stop their advance, but immediately attacked and defeated it. The scattered troops, however, rallied and made a stand at Sugat Bulác "Willow Spring" to contest the passage to Yángí Hissár. But they were again defeated and put to flight, and the Chinese, carrying everything before them, at once pushed on and released the garrison shut up in Yángí Hissár.

They halted here four days, and then marched to recover Káshghar. But Walí Khán, now deserted by his chiefs and his army who were already disgusted at his licentiousness and terrified by his violent tempers and capricious judgments, fled from the city with only a few followers, without even waiting their arrival. He made good his escape to Darwáz, but was there made prisoner by the ruler, Ismáíl Sháh, and delivered up to Khudáyár Khán. And thus, after a rule of only a hundred and fifteen days, in September 1857 ended the last of the Khoja revolts under the most licentious tyrant and blood-thirsty maniac of that ambitious and selfish fraternity. In his short reign he committed more bloodshed, and more oppression, and more villany than either of his predecessors, from whom he only differed in the degree of his wickedness.

Walí Khán was a degraded debauchee, and was seldom free from the intoxication of his favourite drug—*bhang*. His ruthless cruelties and capricious executions, his

P. thirst for blood and his unholy lusts soon rendered his rule intolerable, and awed even his most partial supporters into hatred. The pile of heads, to which in an unhappy moment was added that of the inoffensive scientific traveller, Adolphe Schlagentweit, raised by him on the river-bank above the Kizil Bridge for long months remained a mournful testimony of his savage cruelties; whilst the tales of his hellish barbarities are still fresh in the memory of a people for centuries accustomed to deaths and tortures in their worst forms.

On the flight of Walí Khán the Chinese recovered possession of Káshghar without opposition. The former officials, both Chinese and Khokandi, such as had escaped the clutches of Walí Khán, were dismissed and their offices given to others; whilst the leaders in the revolt were one by one captured and executed with tortures. Amongst the first was Mír Ahmad Shekh, the custodian of the Sátoc Bughra Khán shrine at Alton Artosh, for his active partizanship with the Khoja rebel. He was crimped from heel to head and disembowelled; and his heart plucked out, whilst yet beating with life, was thrown to the dogs. He was then decapitated, and his head exposed in a cage on the main road leading to the city, together with a long row of those of other victims of Chinese revenge. His eldest son, Mír Ali Cází, shared a similar fate; but three other sons, Abdurrahim, Ismáil, and Mahmúd from whom I have derived the above particulars, escaped by the Kurtka Fort to Khokand.

Many other leading men were executed with like barbarity, and their heads similarly exposed for their part in the revolt; whilst hundreds of others perished in the revenge taken for the massacre of the Chinese merchants and settlers. These executions did not cease till August of the following year, when relations on the former footing were resumed with Khokand, and Khudáyár's agent arrived at Káshghar.

M. V. In the meantime Walí Khán on his return to Khokand was arraigned by the relatives of his victims for the murder of so many innocent Musalmáns. He was formally tried by the *Ulama*, "Doctors of the Law," and with characteristic partiality acquitted as being a *Syad* or descendant of the Prophet; whilst his accusers were even fined for daring to asperse the character of one boasting such honourable lineage. He, however, met his retribution at last, and was assassinated at Káshghar, the very scene of his crime, by the present ruler, Yákúb Beg, whom he accompanied in the party of Buzurg Khán, as will be mentioned hereafter.

In the spring of 1858, Khudáyár Khán sent Nasíruddín of Shahrikhan, who had acted in the same capacity in 1847, as envoy to Káshghar to renew relations with the Chinese, to express concern for the revolt, and to report the imprisonment of the notoriously free and favoured Walí Khán. The envoy arrived at Káshghar in August with a caravan of 500 returning fugitives, and the Chinese, at once granting the former concessions, accepted him as Khokand agent with the title of *Dádkhwáh*. And thus the former relations between these incompatible people were once more resumed.

P. In 1278 H. (1862 A.D.) after the establishment of the Russian rule on the northern frontier of Káshghar, by their capture of the forts of Tokmak and Piskak which they took in August 1860, and on the eve of the Tungani revolt in Shensi, one other minor disturbance occurred in Káshghar before the final revolution that led to the severance of the whole province from its connection with the Chinese empire. The three refugee sons of Mír Ahmad Shekh returned in this year from their asylum at Tashkand with a gathering of 300 men to recover their ancient patrimony in Artosh by the aid of the border Kirghiz who were their hereditary subjects.

Near Káshghar they fell in with a caravan of Chinese merchants, and plundering it killed seventeen of the traders in revenge of the death of their father. They then went on to Artosh where they raised the standard of revolt. On this a force of 2,000 Chinese infantry from the *Mángshín* and 1,000 cavalry from the city was sent out against them by the Ambán. The brothers were deserted by their rabble crew in the first skirmish with the enemy, and themselves fled the field as fast as any of them.

They were pursued and overtaken in the Arghú Valley adjoining Artosh. Here Abdurrahím and several of his men were captured and taken prisoners to the Ambán, but the rest escaped into the hills and ultimately returned to Tashkand. Abdurrahím was kept in prison pending reference to the Viceroy at Ila; and after some months, orders arriving from Pekin, he was publicly executed.

Next followed the Tungani mutiny, and the invasion by Buzurg Khán Khoja, and the final conquest of the country by his General, the *Koshbegi* Yákúb Beg, Atálik Ghází, and now the Amír Muhammad Yákúb Khán. To understand these revolutions aright, and to appreciate the differences that mark the character and exciting causes of this last from the previous revolts in this country, it is necessary to go back and review the history of the Khokand State in regard to its political relations with this western province of the Chinese empire, and to note the important fact that, though each and all of these revolts arose from one common source in the impatient ambition of Islam, this last revolution sprang from the eastward as the act of a nation or whole people for the supremacy of their religion; whilst its several predecessors originated as the work of a single ambitious family, or of private individuals for their personal interests, in the adjoining western state of Khokand which, again, has finally interposed to replace the Muhammadan Chinese rule as represented by the Tungani rebels by the usurped authority of its own adventurers.

This last revolution in fact, the description of which is to come, in contradistinction to all the previous revolts, was an outbeak amongst the Chinese themselves. It was Chinese destroying Chinese, the Muhammadan Tungani against the Búdhist Khitay. In the midst of their contention the old Khoja claim was revived, but, as the Tungani had never been their partizans, it was nowhere supported, and hence the success of Yákúb Beg in the confusion of rival interests distracting the country—a success to which the presence of the Russians on the northern frontier was not without effect in determining the course of events.

V. B.

The province of Farghána, Andijan, or Khokand, as it is indifferently called, was during the rule of the Moghol Kháns a more or less independent principality, mostly in alliance with Bukhárá, under the rule of princes of the Tymúr dynasty. After the defeat of Babur, whose father, Umar Shekh, was its ruler, the province fell into the possession of the Uzbak, Sháhibeg Khán or Shaibán, in whose time from Osh to Khojand was the country of Yúnus Khán. His sons, with the aid of the Kirghiz and Kapchák, drove out the usurper Tanbal, and then warred with the Uzbak for possession of all the lands on the banks of the Syhon or Jaxartes, claiming these Turkistan lands as the descendants and heirs of Kaidú.

P.

On the decline of their dynasty, during the reign of Rashíd Sultán of Káshghar, the power of the Moghol Kháns succumbed to that of the Uzbak, and was shortly after usurped by the Khoja pretenders. In the anarchy characterizing the last years of the long reign of Abdúlla, and the few months of that of his son and successor, Abdúl Momin, with whose death in 1597 A.D. the Shaibání dynasty ended, the province of Farghána recovered its independence under local chiefs; and maintained it more or less continuously during the disordered reigns of princes of the Ashtarkhán dynasty which ended with Abúl Fyz who, shortly after his surrender to Nádir in September 1870, was murdered together with his son by his own *wazír*, Rahím Báy of the Manghit tribe, who then usurped the government and founded the existing dynasty of Bukhárá.

I have not met with any published account of the history of Andijan during this period of turmoil marking the decline of the Ashtar Khán dynasty, in which it appears the province regained independence under a local chief who founded the power of the present ruling family there. Whilst at Káshghar, I obtained a manuscript account of the conquest of the country by Yákúb Beg, Atálik Ghází, written for me by his General Abdúlla, *Amírilashkar*, who was a principal actor in the events he describes. He was the most trusted and most active of Yákúb Beg's adherents, and joining him at the outset, served him faithfully and well till incapacitated by an

62.—Opium Smokers.

63.—Andijani and Child by a Varkund Woman.

P. incurable affliction. His impetuous bravery and ferocity in battle soon gained him the reputation of a successful soldier, and he rose to the rank of *Amírilashkar*, "Commander of an Army" or General, before he was obliged to retire from active service to the unemployed rank of *Pansaddi*, "Commander of 500." He is said to have killed with his own hands full 10,000 of the enemy—men, women and children—during the six years of war, and was struck blind, even his admirers admit, by the direct act of God to prevent his destroying more of His innocent creatures.

In the introductory pages of this little book, which is entitled chronographically as well as significantly, *Tárikhi Sighár*, "Little History," 1290 H. (1873-74 A.D.), is a brief notice of the rise and progress of the present ruling family of Khokand. From this, with other published data and personal enquiries on the spot (Káshghar), I am enabled to compile the following account:

T.S. In 1104 H. (1692 A.D.) there resided in the suburbs of Khokand two Kapchák brothers, originally of Changíz descent, named Culún Bí and Chamách Bí. They were disciples of Maulánáí Lutfulla of Chust, which is seven *farsakh* off across the River Syhon; and they used daily to cross the river together to supply the venerated divine with curds and cream. The divine always favoured the elder brother, Culún Bí; but one day as they went to him with their daily offering they were attacked by a party of Manghít robbers who relieved Culún of his load. In the struggle Chamách escaped to Chust with his portion of the curds and cream.

Lutfulla on learning the cause of the other's absence, for being empty-handed after escape from his despoilers he returned home, told the younger brother that it was his fortune to gain his blessing; and forthwith stretching his hands to heaven the Saint prayed, "Oh God! grant that the children of Chamách Bí become kings, "and those of Culún Bí, ministers. And grant, Oh God! that the children of Manghít, "exceeding forty, be born blind."

Chamách Bí died in Khokand, and left a son named Rahím Bí who became king. On his death his son Erdáná (Edenia or Adania) succeeded to the throne. He conquered Karátakín and Darwáz and Pámir to Wakhán, and in 1758 A.D. acknowledged the protectorate of the Chinese empire bordering on his eastern frontier. He left two sons, Muhammad Amín and Shábrukh, of whom the first and eldest succeeded to the throne. He soon died, and left two sons, Nárbotá Beg and Hájí Beg. Nárbotá Beg succeeded, and he, too, acknowledged the protectorate of China, and sent his brother Hájí Beg out of the way on a pilgrimage to Mecca. On his return thence he married a Khokand lady, who bore him a son named Beg Oghaly. Afterwards he took a second wife, the daughter of a chief of the Cocheár Júmghál Kirghiz, and she bore him a son named Sher Ali. Nárbotá Beg left two sons, Alím Beg and Umar Beg, of whom the former succeeded to the Kháni.

Culún Bí left a son, Ernazar Mirzá, who was *Begibásh*, or "Commander-in-Chief," in the time of Rahím Bí, and was noted for his bravery and exploits. He died a natural death, and left a son named Abdurrahmán Mirzá. He succeeded as *Begibásh*, and soon acquired a reputation eclipsing that of his father. He captured Gharmsárán and Namangán from the Khoja rulers, and wrested Marghinán from the Uzbak possessors. He conquered the districts of Isfár and Chárkoh held by Zumurrud Sháh, and drove the Mírs from Orátappa. He also captured Khujand, and built the frontier forts of Sháhrúkhya and Kiláochí. All these enterprises he carried out as the *Begibásh* of Erdáná Bí, in whose reign the whole province was consolidated under one rule. After this he raised a large army in Khujand, and passing Jizzák laid siege to Samarcand for twenty-eight days, when he retired on the payment of a yearly tribute of one *púd* of gold by the Bukhárá King, Sháh Murád Bí, and carried away with him the Karácalpák families found there.

Whilst he was engaged on this expedition, Awlay Khán, the Governor of Táshkand, raided Gharmsárán and Namangán, and was returning with his plunder, when Abdurrahmán giving chase overtook him at Toetappa, and recovered the booty and captives. He sent these to Nárbotá at Khokand, and himself returned by

Kíláochi to Khujand to protect that frontier. Awlay Khán died at Táshkand a month after this defeat, and Yúnus Khoja, a descendant of the Khálif Umar, then became Khán in his place. Three months later, in 1214 H. (1799 A.D.) Nárbotá Beg died, and was succeeded by his son Alím Khán. At this time Abdurrahmán was lying paralytic at Khujand, and his son Abdúlla Mirzá became *Koshbegi* with the new Khán; but Alím, jealous of the great influence he had acquired and dreading his rivalry, had the infirm old man brought to him at the capital, and executed him at the Khoja Turáb *Mazár*, a shrine two *farsakh* from the city.

Alím had reigned eight years when, in 1222 H. (1806 A.D.), he went against Yúnus at Táshkand and took the city. In the assault Abdúlla *Koshbegi* was wounded, and after a month died from the effects of the injury. His son, Rahmán Culí Mirzá, succeeded as *Koshbegi* "Lord of the family," or "Controller of the household." Alím Khán stayed a year at Táshkand to settle the country, and then appointing his own governors returned to the capital.

Two years later, however, he was recalled by disturbances there, and leaving his brother Umar in charge of Khokand hurried off with a large army to Táshkand. He was detained here a year in quelling the revolt, and finally quieted the country by many executions and severe punishments. Owing to his cruelties the chief people fled from the city, and joining Umar at Khokand set him on the throne as Khán. On this Alím set out to recover his capital, but was encountered at Tocsán Cáwún by the rebel chiefs who seized and executed him, 1226 H. (1810 A.D.).

Umar Khán now ascended the throne in his own right. He had a troubled reign of twelve years, and died in 1238 H. (1822 A.D.) and was succeeded by his eldest son, Muhammad Ali Khán. On his accession to the throne Jahángír Khoja fled from Khokand and, joining the Kirghiz, raised them to hostility against the Chinese at Kashghar, and in 1825 with them seized the country. Muhammad Ali Khán joined him there in June of the following year to secure the conquest for himself, but, being coldly received and losing many men in the siege of the Chinese citadel, he hastily retreated to his capital.

Four years later he sent his General Hacc Culí Beg, with Yúsuf Khoja and a strong army, to avenge the defeat of Jahángír and annex Káshghar to his own dominions. His activity in this direction excited the jealousy of Nasrulla or Bahádúr Khán, the Amír of Bukhárá, who marched against him. Consequently Muhammad Ali Khán, in the end of 1830, recalled his General from Káshghar after he had been there only three months, and the Khoja returned with him just as the Chinese reinforcements arrived to recover the place.

Muhammad Ali Khán reigned successfully for nineteen years, and was the most powerful of all the Khokand Kháns. The states of Khutan, Yárkand, Káshghar, Uch Turfan, and Aksú, though in the possession of the Chinese, paid the *zakát* collected from Musalmán merchants to him, and he appointed his own agents in these towns for the realization of these dues, and for the protection of the interests of the Musalmáns. The Jattah country of Zúnghár up to Ila, and the whole of Mogholistan up to Kizil Jár also paid *zakát* to him. In the direction of Organj he annexed Akmasjid and Kumosh Kurghán, and in that of Bukhárá all the country up to two *farsakh* of Jizzák acknowledged his rule.

Saíd, the Amír Hydar of Bukhárá, died in the second year of his reign, in 1240 H. (1824 A.D.), and was succeeded by his son Amír Nasrulla, called Bahádúr Khán. On his accession to the throne Muhammad Ali Khán sent his *Koshbegi*, Azim Báy, to him with messages of condolence and congratulation. The new Amír acknowledged Muhammad Ali as his elder brother, and with his envoy returning to Khokand sent his own ambassador and rich presents; other envoys went and came, and a treaty of perpetual friendship between the two States was concluded. It was after this that Muhammad Ali, in 1827, undertook his campaign against the Kirghiz; and in the succeeding years made tributary all the Zúnghár country and the western cities of Káshghar, held by the Chinese, up to Aksú inclusive.

T.S. Later he destroyed the frontier fort of Peshágir, built by the Khokandis in 1819, and erected the fort of Kuramma at two *farsakh* from Jizzák, and placing his own garrison in it under *Mingbáshi* Gadáy Báy took up his residence at Orátappa where he devoted himself to wine and women.

Bahádúr Khán now jealous of his growing power, and incensed by his encroachment upon the Bukhárá frontier, in 1839 took the field and marched against the new Kuramma Fort. Gadáy Báy held out for fifteen days, and then, abandoning his charge, fled and joined his master at Orátappa. Muhammad Ali Khán, now roused from his pleasures by alarm for his throne, at once marched against the enemy, and camping at a *farsakh* from the fort, in a fit of boldness inspired by an extra dose of *bhang*, came out and challenged Bahádúr Khán to meet him in single combat. His nobles, however, intervening with professions of devotion to his service and person, persuaded him to retire, and the would-be champion, on recovery from his intoxication, being seized by sudden misgivings as to the loyalty of his nobles, abruptly quitted his army, and with only fifty followers fled to Khokand, which he reached in eight days. His army fought for three days and then followed the example of their Khán. Nasrulla pursued the fugitives, and captured the forts of Zamin and Orátappa, and planting his own garrisons in them returned to Bukhárá to watch the operations of the British army in Afghanistan.

On his departure Muhammad Ali Khán returned, and, driving out the Bukhárá troops, recovered Orátappa. But Nasrulla again took the field against him with a numerous army, and in the spring of the following year, 1840, defeated Muhammad Ali and dispersed his army. He followed up this victory by a succession of others, and between September and November annexed Kuramma, Naó, Khujand, and Táshkand, and the country beyond up to the Dasht Kapchak. He appointed his own governors in most of these places, but gave the government of Khujand to Sultán Mahmúd Khán, the brother and rival of Muhammad Ali Khán; and then fearful of the Russians who were pressing on the Jaxartes, and mistrustful of the British who held on at Kabul with Sháh Shuja-ul-Mulk, hastened back to Bukhárá where, during the preceding six years, he had received as envoys from Russia, Demaison in 1834, and Vitcovich in 1835; and as envoys from India, Stoddart in 1838, and Conolly in 1840, both of whom he at this time held prisoners, and both of whom he subsequently murdered—on the 17th June 1842.

V.B. On the departure of Nasrulla the two brothers immediately became reconciled, and revolted; consequently, again, in April 1841, Babádúr Khán set out with a powerful army, breathing wrath and vowing the destruction of Khokand, which at this time was an open town without any fortified walls. Muhammad Ali Khán here held the enemy in check for seven days, and then fled with his family towards Marghinán. At Yacca Tút they were all seized by Mahmúd Khoja, the governor, and delivered over to Nasrulla by whom they were all immediately murdered. Thus perished in 1258 H. (1841 A.D.) Muhammad Ali Khán, the most able and the most powerful of all the Khokand Kháns, his mother, his wives, his brother Sultán Mahmúd Khán, and his son Muhammad Amín Beg who was accused of incest with his mother. His other sons, Muhammad Ali, Muhammad Karím, Muhammad Rahím, Azím Beg, and Abdulla Mirzá, with many nobles and principal officers, were sent away prisoners to Bukhárá.

Satisfied with this extinction of the rival dynasty, Nasrulla spared Khokand the threat he vowed against it, and instead established Ibrahím Khyál, Manghít, formerly Governor of Marv, as his Governor in it, with a considerable garrison in support. He then returned triumphant to his capital, more than ever puffed with pride, and more than ever abandoned to his brutish lusts and inhuman cruelties.

Two months after the departure of the Amír with his Bukhárá army, Musalmán Culí, Kapchák, assembled the Kirghiz, Kapchák, Uzbak, and Tájik Chiefs, with their respective contingents, at Namangán, and by their consent set Sher Ali, the son of Hají Beg, up as Khán. On the accession of Alím Khán to the throne, he had been sent out of the way to the Kirghiz, and was now willing to accept the vacant throne under the guidance of Musalmán Culí as his *wazír*. They, consequently, at once marched against Ibráhím Khiyál, and driving him out of Khokand set to work, and in forty days surrounded the city with fortified walls. Sher Ali now established himself in the citadel as Khán of Khokand with Musalmán Culí as *wazír*, and appointed his sons to the principal provincial governments. Thus Khudáyár got Namangán, Sarimsak got Marghinán, and Súfí Beg got Andiján, whilst Mallah Khán remained at court with his father.

Meanwhile Ibráhím Khiyál, who had been pursued to Káni Bádám, escaped to Bukhárá, whence Nasrulla once more set out to recover his lost conquests. His grand preparations, fierce threats, and pompous boasts, however, did not avail him; for after a siege of sixty days, in which he lost many men by deaths and desertions, he was obliged to retire from Khokand unsuccessful. But his retreat did not restore peace to the country. The sons of the late Muhammad Ali Khán, whom he had left in prison at Bukhárá, escaped from their durance during his absence on this campaign, and returning to Khokand immediately raised a tumult in favour of their prior rights to the government.

Sher Ali did his utmost to appease them, and appointed Muhammad Karím, the most active and ambitious of them, as *Hudaychi*, or "Chamberlain," in his own court. He at once made use of his position to usurp the rule for himself, and by his overbearing conduct quickly made an enemy of the *wazír*, Musalmán Culí, who carried off Khudáyár, and fled with him to the mountains. There he raised a party of his own Kapchak and the Kírghiz, and descending upon Khokand seized and executed Muhammad Karím with a number of his partizans, and re-established Sher Ali as the Khán, with himself as *wazír* as before.

On this Sarimsak, with the support of Alím Beg and Syad Beg, *Dádkhwáhs*, and a party of Kirghiz, rebelled at U'sh or Osh. Musalmán Culí forthwith went against them, and defeating their troops at Mádí, captured and executed Sarimsak. Whilst Musalmán Culí was thus engaged in the east of the province, Murád Khán, son of Alím Khán, had come with aid from Bukhárá to Uthmaní on the west of it, and thence seizing Khokand had killed Sher Ali Khán after he had reigned three years. The Kapchák and Uzbak now combined and set up Khudáyár, aged fifteen years, as Khán with Musalmán Culí as his *wazír*, and recovering Khokand executed Murad Khán after he had ruled only three weeks. Musalmán Culí, the king-maker, now took all the power into his own hands, the youthful Khudáyár being a mere puppet on his accession to the throne in 1845.

In the time of Muhammad Ali Khán, the command of the Akmasjid Fort was given to Muhammad Ali Beg of Marghinán with a garrison of 500 men, and he continued to hold the post under the rule of Khudáyár till he was killed in its defence against the Russians in July 1852. At this time Nar or Nazar Muhammad of Karású near Osh was the Governor of Táshkand for Khudáyár. He had given a sister in marriage to Yákúb Beg of Piskat in the suburbs, and now, through his influence with Musalmán Culí, got his brother-in-law appointed to the charge of the Akmasjid Fort with the rank of *Ooshbegí*. Yákúb Beg held the post for a year till its capture by the Russians in August 1853. In the December following his expulsion from Akmasjid, Yákúb Beg set out from Táshkand with Súfí Beg, the brother of Khudáyár Khán, and a force of 600 horse to recover the fort, but they were all put to flight in the very first encounter. In the following April 1854, Khudáyár himself prepared to march against Akmasjid, but was diverted from his purpose by an inopportune attack on his frontier by Nasrulla Khán.

Khudáyár had for long been impatient of the power and control of his *wazír*, and now in 1855, having staved off the hostility of Bukhárá, he determined to get rid of his obnoxious minister; and to this end instigated a number of his nobles

64.—Cradle Scene, Yangi Hissar.

65.—Children and Toy, Yangi Hissar.

T.S. whose jealousy and hatred of Musalmán Culí were well known to him. A party of twenty of them leagued together to carry out the Khán's and their own wishes. They seized the *wazír* one morning as he came to the court for the usual salutation, and hurrying him off to the execution square there "spread-eagled" him on a board, and so left him for three days to the insults and jeers of a rabble of hired ruffians, and then gibbeted him on the gallows hard by. And such was the recompense the "king-maker" Kapchák received for setting Khudáyár Khán on the throne, and for having ruled the country for thirteen years with more moderation and justice than any of the legitimate Kháns had shown themselves capable of.

Khudáyár now took the reins of government into his own hands, and, amongst other changes, appointed *Koshbegi* Yákúb Beg to the charge of the Kiláochi Fort and made some ineffectual attempts to recover the Akmasjid Fort from the Russian grasp. Whilst absent on one of these expeditions his elder brother, Mallah Khán, with the aid of the Kapchák and Kirghiz, captured Khokand after a siege of seventeen days, and was immediately joined by most of the nobles.

Khudáyár and a younger brother, Sultán Murád, on this retired to Bukhárá for asylum and aid; whilst Mallah Khán, establishing himself at the capital, posted his own governors over the country. Thus he sent Súfí Beg to Namangán, Hasan Beg to Marghinán, Alím Beg to Andiján, Israr Culí to Chamyan, Muhammad Músá to Táshkand, Syad Beg to Khujand, and Yákúb Beg, *Koshbegi*, he raised to the rank of *Shaghául*, or "Foreign Minister," and appointed to the charge of the fort of Kuramma. Alím Culí he appointed as his own *Zinbardár*, or "Equerry," and Khadír and Beg Muhammad each as *Hadáychi*, or "Court Chamberlain," and Caná'at Sháh he kept at Khokand as his *Náib*, or "Deputy Governor," and subsequently sent him to Táshkand to watch the Russian movements in the direction of Hazrat Sultán Turkistán.

In the commotion and excitement following the murder of Musalmán Culí the Khoja Walí Khán, *Tora*, set out from Khokand on his expedition against Káshghar. Whilst he was perpetrating his barbarities there the Kirghiz and Kapchák in Khokand rose in revolt under the lead of Alím Culí, and killing Mallah Khán set Sháh Murád, a grandson of Sher Ali, on the throne. Khudáyár on this advanced from Jizzák with a Bukhárá force and seized Táshkand, where Caná'at Sháh and Yákúb Beg, *Shaghául* of Kuramma (he had been associated with the other to watch the Russians) surrendered the city, and, joining him, set him on the throne there as Khán. For this service Yákúb Beg was again taken into favour by Khudáyár Khán and re-appointed to his former office of *Koshbegi*.

Meanwhile Sháh Murád, who had been put on the throne by Alím Culí, Kapchák, set out with him as *Amirilashkar* against Táshkand. On their arrival Yákúb Beg, *Koshbegi*, joined the Kapchák leader, and they both retired to Kuramma, the fort of the former. Here they increased and fully equipped their army, and then returned and besieged Táshkand. After a month of close investment and desultory skirmishing, finding their troops disheartened and beginning to desert, they raised the siege and withdrew to Khokand, whence Alím Culí sent Yákúb Beg as Governor to Khujand.

Khudáyár, having in the meantime summoned the aid of the Bukhárá Amír, now marched against Khujand with the Bukhárá army under Muzaffar-ud-dín himself who in the previous year, 1860, had succeeded to the throne on the death of his father, Nasrulla, and now joined him on the banks of the river. Yákúb Beg surrendered the fort, and Khudáyár sent him away under surveillance with the army returning to Bukhárá with the Amír, and then went on with a detachment of it to be set on the throne for the second time at Khokand.

The Bukhárá army took the city after a siege of ten days, when Alím Culí escaped to Karású, and Sháh Murád Khán to his uncle amongst the Kirghiz in the hills. Khudáyár now took possession of his old quarters in the citadel, and sent

a 21

Suliman Khoja, the *Shekhulislám* or "high priest" of Khokand, to re-assure and conciliate Alím Culí and bring him in on a promise of pardon and kind treatment. But the wily and rough Kapchák refused to trust the "high priest's" promises, and turned a deaf ear to his honied words of persuasion; and Khudáyár in consequence sent a force to coerce him under Mullá Sultán as commander. He seized Andiján and detached Abdullá *Pánsad* (the author of the work I quote) to secure Shahrikhán whilst he fortified his own position. But on the third night Alím Culí took the fort by surprise and killed nearly a thousand of the Kirghiz and Kapchák, whilst Mullá Sultán escaped on foot and in disguise to Shahrikhan.

Khudáyár immediately took the field to retrieve this disaster, but on arrival at Karáwultappa he mistrusted his Kirghiz and Kapchák, and consequently sent 3,000 of them back to Khokand. He then advanced by Karájighda and Marghinán to Yacca Tút, where he was joined by Mullá Sultán and Abdúlla with their diminished force. Alím Culí in this interval had left Andiján and taken up a position at Aska, and Khudáyár, learning this from his scouts, left his main army standing, and with a small force advanced to attack him at Cabá Shor; but he was forestalled by his adversary who fell upon him with his whole force as he reached the ground. A severe fight followed, and lasted till sunset, with great loss on both sides.

Sultán Murád, the brother of Khudáyár, fled the field and took the road to the capital, but was stopped by the army left at Yacca Tút; and the Khán, unable to follow his example, set to work and fortified his position with carts and camp equipage for the night. He was here besieged for three days when Alím Culí, failing to force his defences with his few men, retired to Marghinán to collect his Kapchák from the hills; and Khudáyár thus set free seized the opportunity and hurried back to Yacca Tút where he halted four days, and sent off messengers reporting a great victory and the flight of the enemy, for the satisfaction of his party at Khokand.

His couriers had no sooner started, however, than Alím Culí re-appeared with a fresh army and besieged Khudáyár in his camp for forty days, and then making a dash at Khokand seized the city; here the priests and chief citizens coming out with *curáns* borne on their heads welcomed his arrival and set him on the throne as Khán.

Khudáyár now in turn resumed the offensive, and following the usurper attacked him in the capital; and here all the people again turned back to the side of their lawful chief. Alím Culí, unable to hold the place against such a combination, quitted the city taking with him seventeen cannons he found in it, and continued the war by besieging Andiján, which had been re-occupied on the part of Khudáyár by Kádir Culí Beg. He held out eight days, and then surrendering the place joined the Kapchák leader who with his new ally then attacked Marghinán held by Mullá Sultán. He was killed in a sortie, and his *Mingbáshí*, Mirzá Ahmad, then abandoning the fort fled to Khokand. Alím Culí secured the place with a garrison and then went in pursuit of the fugitive.

In this interim Khudáyár had sent his sister as wife to the Bukhárá Amír with envoys to seek his aid. Muzaffaruddín married the lady, and then in 1863 set out with a large army to the support of his new brother-in-law who was now hard-pressed by Alím Culí besieging the capital, when the relieving army opportunely arrived at Khujand. Alím Culí's outpost pickets being driven in by the advancing army, he raised the siege and retired to Dormánja to watch events, but finding that the Bukhárá army had entered Khokand he set out on the third day and retreated to Karású.

After a week's delay Khudáyár took the field in pursuit of the enemy, and his ally of Bukhárá followed a march in rear. Alím Culí was defeated at Karású and pursued to Uzkand, whence he entered the hills and fortified a very strong position in the Kará Khoja *Tar*, or "Defile." Khudáyár followed him, but, frightened by difficulties of the country, hastily retired from the hills, and joined his ally who was devastating the plain country. Muzaffaruddín, after a feast to celebrate their success

T.S. and meeting, was visited by a severe nightmare, and taking the dream as a bad omen, at once struck his camp and hastened back by Marghinán to Khokand whence, after a halt of fourteen days, he set out for his own capital, taking Sultán Murád with him. On the departure of this Bukhárá army, with which he had returned from his exile, Yákúb Beg *Koshbegi*, Bátur Culí *Shagháwul*, and Mirzá Ahmad *Koshbegi*, with several *Pánsad* officers and others, joined Alím Culí. On this Muzaffaruddín halted at Surkhsú, and sent Sultán Murád back to Khokand as Khán. But, as he could not hold the place, he left it after a week, and accompanied by Abdúlla *Pánsad* went to join Alím Culí. On arrival at Osh they were met by Tásh Khoja *Hudáychi* from Alím Culí, and he, according to his orders, killed Sultán Murád and took Abdúlla back with him to his master who robed him and took him into his own service.

From Osh Alím Culí moved to Yár Mazár, and halting a week held a consultation with his adherents, and by their consent decided on bringing Syad Sultán Beg, the son of Mallah Khán, from Namangán and setting him up as Khán, with himself as his minister.

Syad Sultán, on assuming the government, sent Yákúb Beg as *Mír* to the Kuramma Fort, and himself marched with Alím Culí to Khokand whence Khudáyár retreated to Jizzák. He here collected the relics of his deserted army, and from amongst their chiefs sent Ming Báy and Nar Muhammad *Lashkarbásh*, and several *Pánsad* officers, with a force to secure Khujand which, with the aid of Yákúb Beg from Kuramma with his contingent, they took after a siege of ten days, the Governor Dost Muhammad, Karácalpák, escaping to Bukhárá. Alím Culí arrived there a few days later, and appointing Mirzá Ahmed *Koshbegi* to the government, set out for Táshkand by Kuramma, where he was entertained by Yákúb Beg.

At Táshkand Alím Culí was the guest of the Governor Suliman Khoja, but suspecting his fidelity he killed him, and re-established Nar Muhammad, the brother-in-law of Yákúb Beg, in the government; he returned then to Khokand by Kiláochí, from which he summoned Yákúb Beg to join him, and sent Hydar Culí, Kapchák, to take his place at Kuramma.

Whilst these events were following one the other in Khokand, much more important changes were enacting in the countries bordering to the north and east. In the former direction the Russians were steadily pushing on from Uch Almá Atá or Almáti (or Fort Vernoe, as their great military post on the north of Isigh Kol is called). They took Awliyá Atá or Aulieta on the 16th June 1864, and Hazrat Turkistán on the 24th of the same month. From the latter the Governor, Mirzá Daulat, fled to Táshkand where he found Alím Culí with a large army busily fortifying the defences of the city, to which he had hastened on the first intelligence of the Russian advance.

From Táshkand Alím Culí advanced with a considerable force under Ming Báy *Lashkarbásh* to secure Chamkand, but he was met and attacked on arrival there by a Russian column from Turkistán; and after a severe encounter succeeded in driving them back. The Awliyá Atá column, however, coming up at this juncture joined that from Turkistán, and the combined Russian forces next day made an attack upon Chamkand. Alím Culí fought with his accustomed impetuosity and bravery, and forced the Russians to fall back upon Turkistán. He then put the defences of the place into repair, and leaving Mirzá Ahmad *Koshbegi* in its command with a strong garrison, hurried back to control affairs at Khokand, to recover which Khudáyár was intriguing.

Three months had hardly elapsed when news came that the Russians were again moving in great force against Chamkand. On this Alím Culí at once despatched Yákúb Beg *Koshbegi* to hold and strengthen the defences of Táshkand. On his arrival there, however, he was joined by Mirzá Ahmad just arrived from Chamkand, whence he had been driven by the Russians who took the place in the beginning of October 1864, and ten days later pushed on against Táshkand. As they approached

Yákúb Beg came out to oppose them with all his force. A severe fight took place in which the Russians lost 200 men killed, but they drove the Táshkand army back into their fort, and were then obliged themselves to retreat on the fourth day back to Chamkand. — T.S.

Whilst this struggle was going on at the frontier, Alím Culí with Syad Sultán Khán and a large army was hurrying up from Khokand to the support of Táshkand, and on his arrival there rewarded the defenders and sent the heads of the Russians slain all over the country as trophies of their success against "the cursed Urús." He then set to work to improve the defences and dispose his troops on the fortification. Whilst he was thus engaged an envoy arrived from Sadíc Beg, Kirghiz of Káshghar, announcing the destruction of the Chinese rule there and the capture of the city by himself, and asking him to send a Khoja whom he might set on the throne as king of the country.

Alím Culí, in reply to this appeal, sent Buzurg Khán Khoja, the only son of Jáhangír Khoja, to recover the throne of his ancestors, and appointed Yákúb Beg *Koshbegi* to accompany him as *Bátúr-báshí* "Leader of the braves," or General of his forces, by way of securing his own interests and maintaining the Khokand influence in the Káshghar States.

Before following the Khoja, or *Tora* as he is usually styled, and his General in their career at Káshghar, it will be profitable first to trace out, most briefly though it be, that rapid succession of conquests and victories which in the course of a few short years have extended the Russian territory and rule from Almáti Vernoe on the north-east to the very gates of Bukhárá on the south-west; because this extension of Christian rule and civilized government over the Muhammadan and barbarous States of Central Asia, favoured in its success by the wild anarchy and savage despotism rampant in those very States, whilst opening out a bright future to these too-long benighted regions, has not been without an important influence on the Islám polity of not only Central Asia, but the whole Muhammadan world; for since the days of the Khálifs, Bukhárá, the *Cubbat-ulislam*, or "Centre Prop of the Faith," has always been considered the most sacred seat of its power and doctrine, and its decadence here during the past decade is already attended by signs of its revival elsewhere; in the prime seat in fact of its origin and growth. — P.

After the retreat of the Russians from their unsuccessful attack against Táshkand in the latter days of October 1864, the Khokandi under Alím Culí were emboldened to assume the offensive, and early in December invested the village of Chilik which had been recently taken by them. A small party of Cossacks was sent to its relief from Turkistán, but on arrival at Aycán or Ikan was cut off from succour and surrounded by an overwhelming force of Khokandis who fought behind shields and moveable mantlets called *carábárá*. The devoted band fought with heroic bravery, and was nearly cut to pieces without inflicting much injury upon their assailants, and only a small remnant, fighting their way through, effected a safe return to Turkistan on the 18th December 1864. — T.S. / Rom.

With the first opening of spring the Russians again took the field to avenge this disaster to their arms, and on the 10th May 1865 General Chernayef took the fort of Nyázbeg, and on the 20th of the same month, in correspondence with a party in the city who had agreed to surrender the town, camped at eight *verst*, or about five miles from Táshkand; but Alím Culí with 6,000 men and 40 guns entering the city the same day the pre-arranged "*coup*" failed. — Rom.

On the following morning Alím Culí with 40,000 men issued to destroy "the cursed Urús" who were only 4,000 strong. My informant, one who took an active part in the fight, described how the eager Khokandis swarmed to the promised destruction of their entrapped foe; how, surging in tumultuous crowds over the low ridges that broke the general level of the plain, they closed around the thickest ranks of the enemy; how, as they pressed harder and nearer, the Russian priests raised aloft the effigy of their saint, and bare-headed prayed for his intercession and — P.

aid; and how the Russian General, taking off his hat, with earnest gesticulations and raised voice called on his men to fight bravely, and with their lives to maintain untarnished their proud name and the honour of their country. And he described how his master, Alím Culí, at this moment led a charge which was the signal for all the rest to fall on and annihilate their prey, when a few skirmishers thrown out brought him to a stop by a chance ball through his belly. His fall was followed by a short commotion, and his retreat from the field. The news was immediately spread through the assailing host, and as immediately its disorderly crowds turned and fled, each its own way; and in less than an hour not a vestige remained of that vast multitude which, in the name of Islám, had come out to devour the "infidel Urús." And thus that brave band of Russians passed from the jaws of death to the security afforded by a complete victory, with the capture of 200 muskets taken and a loss of 300 men killed inflicted upon the retiring enemy.

The wounded Alím Culí was carried off the field by his Commandant of Artillery, one Nabbí Baksh, a native of Sialkot in the Panjáb, who, since the days of the Sikh campaign, had found a livelihood here in the courts of Bukhárá and Khokand successively. He now took his master up in his lap and galloped off the field as fast as his horse could carry the double load, leaving his guns and everything else to take care of themselves. Alím Culí died in Táshkand the same evening, and an assembly of the chiefs in consultation then decided on sending for aid to Bukhárá, and in the meantime to continue the defence under Mirzá Ahmad *Koshbegi*, and Atá Beg *Dádkhwáh* who was formerly the Governor of Piskak Fort when it was taken by the Russians in August 1860.

Rom. To intercept the aid summoned from Bukhárá, the Russians on the 29th May marched to Ziuchata on the Bukhárá road and took possession of Chináz, whilst the Bukhárá army advancing to Samarcand occupied the frontier forts on the Syr Daryá (the Syhon or Jaxartes).

On this the Russians advanced against Táshkand and invested the city on three sides during the 18th-19th June. A couple of days later the Khokand Khán, Sultán Murád, with 200 followers quitted the city by night, and at the same time Iskandar Beg with a small Bukhárá force entered it. The Russians consequently stormed the town on the night of the 26th-27th June, and after a desperate resistance captured the city and during the next two days disarmed its people, 29th June 1865.

T.S. On the death of Alím Culí his chiefs, as above stated, held on in the fort, and by mutual consent sent the *Aksakál* of the city to Bukhárá for aid. The Amír Muzaffaruddín forthwith advanced to Samarcand, and sent off Allahyár Beg, Governor of Oratappa, and Sher Ali *Dádkhwáh* of Táshkand who was at the time with Khudáyár at Jizzák, to hold the place. On arrival at Táshkand they seized Syad Sultán Khán, the puppet of Alím Culí, and sent him off under escort to Muzaffaruddín who had by that time arrived at Jizzák. He kept Syad Sultán prisoner in his camp, and started off Khudáyár from his retreat there with an army to recover Khokand. He was welcomed at Náo by the Governor, Múlán *Dádkhwáh*, who surrendered the fort to him; and Khudáyár, securing it with a garrison of his own, went on to Khujand where the people hailed his return with joy, and installed him in the citadel; where Khudáyár at once set to fortify himself.

Meanwhile the usurpers in Khokand had set up Khudá Culí Beg, the son of Macsúd Beg who was the uncle of Sher Ali Khán, as Khán of the Kirghiz and Kapchák. Khudáyár consequently invoked the aid of Muzaffurudín who at once marched from Jizzák to Khujand, where he was joined by Sultán Murád fleeing from Táshkand. He detained Murád as a prisoner, and sent Khudáyár with an army against the rebels. On his arrival at Besharic, Khudá Culí with his Kapchák and Kirghiz fled to Marghinán, and Khudáyár taking possession of Khokand called up the Amír of Bukhárá to hold it while he went in pursuit of the fugitives.

As he set out from the capital the rebels retired to Mádí beyond Osh, and there held fast. Khudáyár advanced against them, and defeating their outpost of a thousand men at Achí, captured all their chiefs, except Abdurrahmán Kirghiz and Isrár Culí Kapchák, who escaped with their followers and joined Khudá Culí at Mádí. Here Beg Muhammad *Mingbáshí*, Mirzá Ahmad *Dastúrkhwánchí*, Syad Beg Kapchák, Sadíc Beg Kirghiz, and the Khoja brothers, Eshán Khán *Tora*, Walí Khán *Tora*, and Kichik Khán *Tora*, with a number of others, held a consultation, and decided on retiring with their artillery by way of Caflán Kol to Gulsha, and there holding out and barricading the approaches. From this, as will be seen in the sequel, they all joined Yákúb Beg at Káshghar. S.T.

Meanwhile Khudáyár at Osh wrote as an humble servant to Muzaffaruddín, reporting the aspect of affairs and awaiting orders. The Bukhárá Amír, uneasy at the proximity of the Russians and unwilling to be embroiled in the troubles of his neighbour, summoned Khudáyár back to Khokand, and setting him in the government there, returned to his capital by Khujand, whence he sent a minatory message to the Russian General at Tashkand demanding his evacuation of the city and retreat to Chamkand.

But the Russian General, on the contrary, with the consent of an influential party of the citizens, who on the 30th September presented him with an address of congratulation and an appeal to be taken under the protection of the Ak Pádsháh or Czár, annexed the whole territory of Tásbkand to Russia for ever. Its limits are on the east Isigh Kol="Hot Lake," and Uch Kurghán="Three Forts" to the Syr Daryá or Jaxartes; on the north, the same from Ila to Akmasjid and Fort Raim; on the west, from the beginning to the end of the Syr Daryá with its left bank and fort of Chárdarra; and on the south, the same extent along the Syr Daryá from beginning to end. Rom.

Following this, in January 1866 came General Chernayeff's unsuccessful expedition as far as Jizzák to release the Russian envoys detained at Bukhárá, and his retreat to the Syr Daryá below Chirchik. The rupture, accelerated by this hostile conduct of the Amír Muzaffaruddín, led to the advance of the Russians under General Romanoffski who, on the 20th May 1866, exactly a year after the defeat and death of Alim Culi, gained his signal victory over the whole Bukhárá host at the famous battle of Irjár; when he put the Amír to flight, routed his army in disorder, and captured all his camp and equipage.

Following up this success, the Russians next bombarded Khujand and captured it on the 5th June. And so great was the immediate effect of their triumphs, that Khudáyár voluntarily congratulated their General on the success of his arms, and declared himself the friend and ally of Russia. Orátappa and Jizzák were taken in the October following, and a treaty of friendship and protection was concluded with Khudáyár; whilst Muzaffaruddín was warned to prepare for war, unless he restored the refugee Sultán Murád, paid one hundred thousand *tilá* = six hundred thousand rupees (counting the *tilá* at six) as war indemnity, and opened out his country to Russian traders.

The subsequent negotiations with the Bukhárá Amír not proving satisfactory led to the active prosecution of the war, to his own speedy subjection to the Russian protectorate, and to the occupation by Russia of the sister city of Samarcand in August 1868—a position which brought them into direct contact with the little States of Karátakin, Darwáz, and Shighnán on the upper waters of the Oxus; and into communication with their Tajik populations, cognate in birth and speech, and confederate in creed and polity, with their Aryan brethren of Badakhshan and Wakhán and the other petty independent hill States on the southern slopes of the Hindú Kúsh Range down to Kabul on one side and Kashmír on the other. A fact of no small importance, and notable, too, as bringing Russian influence beyond the pale of Uzbak and Tártár polity in Central Asia into the sphere of the great Aryan element of the Indian continent south of the mountains.

Whilst this succession of events and transfer of governments was taking place on the west of the Bolor Range, a hardly less important revolution had been brought

Rom. to a more bloody close by the substitution of a new government in the country to its east. Here Russia had already acquired a high degree of political influence since her establishment at Almati Vernoe in 1853, and subsequent advance in 1860 to Piskak and Tokmak (the latter of which is now a flourishing Russian town with 400 *mujik* settlers brought from Moscow); and later again by the extension of her frontier to the Nárín and establishment of her outposts at only eight days' march from the capital of Káshghar; an influence which was favoured by the concessions of a commercial treaty with the Chinese government, according to the stipulations of which Russia acquired the right to establish trade agencies and build factories in the towns of Eastern or Chinese Turkistán—a privilege, however, which was very suddenly invalidated by the revolution that now in the course of sequence claims our notice.

The insurrection of the Muhammadan Chinese, called Tungání, which broke out in the province of Kánsúh in 1862, and which has in the space of a single decade shaken the stability of the ancient government of the celestial empire to its very base is, I believe, referable to that vague and ill understood revival of Islam of which so many instances have attracted attention in widely separated parts of the Muhammadan world during the last fifteen years; and may be counted as a result of the fanatic obstructiveness of the faith to the advancing civilization and knowledge of the age.

P. Be this as it may, the religious insurrection commencing at Sálár or Hochow, in Kánsúh, which was the principal seat of the Tungání sectarians, spread very rapidly over the subordinate governments of Zúnghár and Káshghar, in which the Tungání—formerly, even against their Khoja co-religionists, the most loyal, and now the sole rebel—formed an important portion of the imperial troops holding the several frontier towns. The cities of Zúnghár and the eastern cities of Káshghar were the first to join in the rebellion, and almost simultaneously to overthrow the constituted authority by the massacre of the Budhist Chinese officials and residents for the usurpation of the government under Muhammadan leaders of the Khoja or Priest class.

So rapid were the successes of these fanatic insurgents, and so weak was the authority of the Chinese governors, that by the end of 1862 all the eastern cities of Káshghar from Cámól or Khámil to Aksú had thrown off the Chinese yoke and massacred, or subjected to the *jazya* or "poll-tax," all the Budhist officials, traders, and nomads. The movement did not spread with equal rapidity, nor with a like combination in action in the western cities or Altyshahr where, though the population was more Muhammadan, it was less Chinese, and consequently had no common interest in the movement worked by the Tungání who, as belonging to the *Sháfí* sect, were rather contemned by the orthodox *cháryárí* of the western States; though when in the following year the outbreak was precipitated in Yárkand by the action of the Chinese governor there, the Musalmáns generally were not backward in joining the *ghazát* against their infidel rulers.

In these western cities under Khokand influence discontent with the Chinese rule had been rapidly on the increase since the revolt of Walí Khán in 1857, owing to the intrigues of the Andijánís through their commercial agents. At Yárkand the Chinese Governor over the Musalmáns in the city, Afrídún Wáng of Turfán, who had held the post since ten years before the attack by Tilá Khán, became jealous of the power and growing independence of these Khokand consuls, and on the arrival of a new agent with thirty followers from that State in 1859 after the resumption of commercial relations in the preceding year, he caused their assassination by the Ambán on the representation that they were circulating seditious papers inciting the Musalmáns to rise and expel the Chinese.

The internal troubles of Khokand at this time did not admit of the Khán taking a revengeful notice of this hostile act, but the Andijan interest at Khutan was brought to bear against Afrídún Wáng, and he was deposed in favour of Rustam Beg of that place, who had bought over the Ambán with a bribe of eight *chárak* of gold, equal in weight to a hundred and sixty pounds. Afrídún Wáng, on being deposed, returned to his home at Lukchun, near Turfán, and there joining the nascent Tungani revolt came back to Kúcha, and took an active part in setting Ráshuddin Khoja at the head of affairs there. He subsequently submitted to Yákúb Beg, who squeezed him of all his wealth, for he was one of the richest men in the country, and made him reside at Káshghar; where the decrepid old man died, and left two sons in poor circumstances. Afrídún was thoroughly Chinese in his interests, and aided Ráshuddin to found a Tungání government under Khoja leaders of his own family at Aksú, Yárkand, and Khutan, in opposition to the Khokand party who had got possession of Káshghar. But his efforts failed owing to the jealousies dividing the Tungání, the Khoja, and the Musalmán Chinese officials parties, and he finally succumbed to Yákúb Beg, who rose on ruins of this house divided against itself.

Rustam Beg on assuming his dear bought office at once commenced to recoup his outlay, and squeezed the people by severe punishments, fines, and exactions of sorts. They endured his tyranny for three months, and then rose in riot to expel him from the city. He at once called in the aid of the Ambán, who marched a party of Chinese soldiers from the adjoining Yángishahr Fort into the city; but quiet was not restored till Rustam Beg was deposed, and Nyáz Beg, a candidate put forward by the citizens, was appointed in his place.

Following this, an ill-feeling arose between the Musalmán Tungání and their Budhist Khitáy comrades in the garrison, and many quarrels broke out amongst them. Just at this time, too, the Ambán received secret tidings of the Tungání mutinies in the eastern cities. He kept the news secret for some time, and then his communications with the head-quarters at Ila being cut off by the rebels, he held a private council of his principal officers, and by the consent of all it was decided to disarm all the Tungání troops. Some delay and hesitation occurred in carrying out the decision, and in the interim the intention was secretly conveyed to the Máh Dáláy who commanded the Tungání by one of his spies; and he determined to be beforehand with the Ambán, and set a strict watch upon his palace.

Shortly after, a second private council was held by the Ambán, and the Máh Dáláy, learning that the morrow had been fixed for the disarming of his men, immediately took his measures to frustrate the decision. Accordingly, that same night he summoned a number of his officers privately to his quarters, briefly informed them of the Ambán's design against them, and told them to go off to their quarters and at once inform their men of the part they were to act in the plan he had arranged to prevent its execution, and to seize the government for themselves. Having done this, he left his quarters with some 50 men, surprised the Khitáy guard sleeping outside the fort gate, and cut the throats of all as they lay more or less drugged with opium. By this time he was joined by about 400 others who, according to instructions, had followed in his track, and he then set fire to the gates and dispersed them inside the fort to rouse the garrison with the alarm of fire.

The Khitáy and Tungání troops were quartered together in the outer part of the fort, whilst the inner part or citadel was occupied by the Ambán and principal officers and their Khitáy guards. And this inner fort was shut off from the outer by walls and gates of its own. As the garrison in the outer fort was roused by the alarm of fire, the men, Tungání and Khitáy, came running out of their quarters together, but for very different purposes. The Tungání were all armed, and each now, according to his instructions, slew his Khitáy comrade as he issued from his quarters.

By this stratagem the Tungání killed 2,000 of their Khitáy brethren before the day dawned, when those in the inner fort, being roused by the tumult, attacked and expelled them from the Yángíshahr.

The Máh Dáláy and his mutineers then entered the city just as the gates were opened with the rising sun, and with white scarves tied round their heads and drooping in lappets over the shoulders dispersed through the bazars, calling on the

66.—Presents made to the Amir of Kashghar in the name of H. M. The Queen, and of H. E. the Viceroy.

67.—Yuz-bashi, Paujabashi, and Dah-bashi, at attention.

P. people to join the *ghazát* and slay the infidel Khitáy. The city chiefs, fearing the vengeance of the Chinese reinforcements as on previous occasions of revolt, attempted to quell the tumult and restore order, but the mob of ruffians, gamblers, drunkards, and others who were more or less in debt to the Chinese traders, rushed all over the city and with their knives killed every Khitáy man, woman, and child they could lay hands on, and plundered their houses. So rapid was the work of their destruction, that by noon not a Khitáy was left alive in the city, except a few who had found concealment in the houses of Musalmán friends. From the city the mob, joining the Tungání mutineers, issued into the bazar connecting it with the Yángísbahr, five hundred yards to the west and wholly occupied by Khitáy and foreign traders and settlers, and there by sunset completed the rôle of death commenced in the morning. And thus on one of the hottest days of the year, 23rd *Safar* 1280 H. (10th August 1863), perished some 7,000 Khitáy souls.

The Ambán meantime barricaded the citadel in Yángíshahr, and during the next three days with his Khitáy troops drove the Tungání mutineers from the outer fort in which they had regained a footing. The Tungání, now without a leader, made a wealthy and saintly divine of the city, one Sahibzáda Abdurrahmán, their king, and appointed the merchant Nyáz Beg, the recently-elected governor, to be his *wazír*. They next sent off messengers with the news of their success to the adjacent cities, and then set to organize a force to besiege the Khitáy shut up in the Yángíshahr citadel. On receipt of this intelligence, the cities of Khutan, Yángi Hissár, Káshghar, and Aksú all rose simultaneously against the Khitáy; and within six weeks had massacred them all, of both sexes and every age, except the garrisons which held out in the forts; and then they each and all became the scenes of the most rampant discord and contention amongst rival pretenders to the government till Yákúb Beg came and reduced them all one after the other to his own subjection.

The siege of the Yángíshahr at Yárkand had lasted three months, when Khoja Isá from Kúchá and Khoja Mahmúd from Aksú, with others who had been ousted in the struggle for ascendancy in those places by more powerful leaders, arrived at the city with a numerous following of adventurers. They were welcomed by the besiegers, and a succession of unsuccessful attempts were made to take the Yángíshahr by assault. Finally, after six months' siege, having blown down a considerable portion of the outer wall by mining and powder, the besiegers stormed the breach and massacred the defenders without quarter.

The Ambán had assembled his family and principal officers in the reception hall of his palace, and on finding all was now lost emptied his pipe on a previously laid train of powder at his feet, and perished with them in the explosion. On this the soldiers rushed to the powder magazines, one on each side of the citadel square, and setting fire to them disappeared in the ruin of their explosions. For three days similar upheavals of concealed mines continued to scatter the limbs and heads of the defenders amidst the disturbed mass of ruin.

The Khitáy being now entirely destroyed, the Kúchá and Aksú Khojas soon quarreled with Abdurrahmán as to the control of the government on the grounds of the victory having been won by them; but the Tungání rallying round the king they had set up drove the Khojas from the city. After a while these Khojas were joined by reinforcements from Aksú under Khoja Burhánuddín of Kúchá, and through his mediation Abdurrahmán consented to a division of the government; the Khojas to rule in the city, and the Tungání to hold the Yángíshahr Fort. This arrangement lasted for two months, when the Tungání went to attack Khutan, but were repulsed, as will be related hereafter.

Whilst these changes were occurring at Yárkand, another somewhat similar course of events was being enacted at Káshghar. Here the Chinese *Hákim Beg*, or "District Governor," over the Musalmáns was Cútlúgh Beg of Kúchá. He had recently, owing to the stoppage of funds to pay the troops from China, by order of the Ambán, imposed a new tax of 2 per cent. on all sale transactions in the city.

a 23

The people, fretting under this imposition, sent some Aktúghlúc agents to Khokand complaining of the violation of the trade regulations established by the Khan, and seeking relief from the exactions of their oppressors. Alím Culí was at the time too much taken up with his own troubles to heed their request, and meanwhile intelligence of the Yárkand outbreak arriving, the people rose in revolt and massacred all the Khitáy traders and residents in the city. The Ambán, without attempting to quell the tumult in the city, shut himself up with his troops in the Yángíshahr, five miles to the south of it.

On this the Aktúghlúc chiefs of Artosh called in the aid of Sadíc Beg, Kirghiz, to restore order. He hastened down with his men, and joining them was put in possession of the city; but he and his men being more intent on plunder than on the restoration of order were soon expelled the city by the Governor Cútlúgh Beg, acting in the interest of the Chinese with the support of the citizens, who were already disgusted at the numerous murders and horrid barbarities perpetrated on their fellow co-religionists by the Kirghiz chief and his savages. Sadíc now was joined by the Tungání who on the first outbreak of the rebellion had escaped from the Yángíshahr and joined the rioters, whilst a number of their less fortunate brethren were seized and killed by the Ambán. With the aid of these troops he made several unsuccessful attempts to seize the city held by Cútlúgh, and after three months of desultory and ineffectual skirmishing in the suburbs he sent an envoy to Alím Culí, informing him of the state of affairs and asking for a Khoja to come and take the country. Alím Culí was at this time engaged in strengthening the defences of Táshkand against the impending attack by the Russians, and in reply to the appeal of Sadíc Beg sent off Buzurg Khan *Tora*, the heir of Jahángír, to recover the throne of his ancestors; but as he could spare no troops to send with him, he appointed Yákúb Beg *Koshbegi* to accompany him as General and raise what force he could.

Buzurg Khán and Yákúb Beg with Abdulla *Pánsad*, Muhammad Culí *Shagháwal*, and Khoja Kalán *Hudáychi*, left Táshkand towards the end of November 1864, and at once repaired to Khokand, there to complete the final preparations for their enterprize. At the capital they were joined by some officers who had been left behind by Khudáyár, and a few other adventurers, and towards the close of the year set out for Káshghar. At Osh a few others joined and raised the number of the whole party as it left Andiján to only 68 individuals. From Osh they took the road of the Tirik Dawán, and in fourteen days reached Mingyol on the outskirts of Káshghar during the first days of the new year 1865.

Sadíc Beg, after he had sent off his envoys, repented of having asked for a Khoja, and now sought to turn Buzurg back, hoping soon to take the city without the aid of his weighty name, but the citizens and villagers hearing of his arrival flocked out to welcome him. On this Sadíc raising the siege retired to Sarman, and sent forward his brother, Kádir Beg, to welcome the Khoja, and with a proffer of his service to invite him to the entertainment he had prepared for him. Buzurg and his party accordingly came to Sarman, and next day set out for the city with the Kirghiz chief. Here Cútlúgh Beg opened the gates to the Khoja, and surrendering the city installed him in the *Orda*, or "Palace," as king amidst the acclamations of the citizens.

Buzurg Khán on thus easily gaining possession of the city committed the reins of government to Yákúb Beg, and himself true to the character of his class at once launched into a succession of pleasures and debaucheries. On this Sadíc finding himself ousted from all participation in the government became discontented, and on the fourth day after the installation of Buzurg withdrew with his men to Yángí Hissár, and setting up as claimant of the throne called the Kirghiz in the hills to the west and the Pámir to rally round him. Meanwhile Yákúb Beg settled the city, and retaining most of the old officials in their posts under Andijání supervisors, secured the Tungání for the service of the Khoja, and raised a small force from amongst the Andijání, Afghán, and other residents in the city. Whilst so engaged —twenty days after the defection of Sadíc Beg, and about the beginning of

P. February—a small party arrived from Táshkand with news of Alím Culí's victory over the Russians at Aycán, and brought with them 40 heads of the slain. These were exhibited in the main bazars, to the delight of the populace and gratification of the chiefs, and were the means of soon raising Yákúb Beg's army to some 3,000 men.

Sadíc Beg meanwhile had raised a force of as many Kirghiz, and with them marching against Káshghar invested the city and demanded its surrender. He fixed his head-quarters at the shrine of Huzrát Pádsháh, a few hundred yards from the south-eastern walls, and with sacrifices of horses and sheep devoutly sought the aid of the saint against the interlopers. On this Buzurg sent out Yákúb Beg to disperse the besiegers. After a slight skirmish he drove off their detachment posted in front of the Kúm Darwáza, or "Sand Gate," and fixing his head-quarters at the shrine of Syad Jaláluddín Bughdádí, a few hundred yards off to the south and close to the shrine occupied by Sadíc Beg, next morning sent forward Abdulla *Pansad* with a small force to dislodge him. This he quickly did by the bold impetuosity of his attack, and pursued his scattered Kirghiz across the Kizil River to Pakhtaghlic, whence Sadíc escaped to Tashmalik where he rallied his dispersed followers.

Buzurg and Yákúb Beg now took the field together with 400 horse and 4,000 foot raised in the city and suburbs. They seized Farrásh, the fort of Sadíc, and Buzurg holding this sent his General to the encounter with the Kirghiz pretender. Yákúb Beg overtook the enemy next day at the foot of the hills where the Kirghiz held fast to meet their opponents. On their approach, according to custom, they put forward their champion, a gigantic fellow named Súránchí, who could fell an ox at a blow, for single combat. Abdulla volunteered to meet the adversary, and in the first charge driving his lance through the heart of the Kirghiz killed him on the spot. Sadíc seeing his champion fall, fled into the hills, and being deserted by his gathering, who now dispersed to their camps, made his way with only a few attendants to Alím Culí at Khokand.

After this successful expedition Yákúb Beg rejoined Buzurg at Farrásh, and they marched together against Yángí Hissár, where the Chinese garrison held out in its Yángíshahr Fort. They besieged the fort ineffectually for three weeks, and then leaving a force behind to continue the investment returned to Káshghar, where, three days after arrival, Yákúb Beg took up his quarters at Pakhtaghlic and laid siege to the Yángíshahr held by the Ambán and his Khitáy garrison; whilst Buzurg re-established in the *Orda* returned to his drugs and women.

Just after the siege had commenced, Nar Muhammad *Parwánchí* with a small party arrived at Mingyol, and was detained there by the outpost guard for the orders of Yákúb Beg. He sent out the *dastúrkhwán* of welcome, and directed they should all be brought in to him. Nar Muhammad now explained that his companion—Ibráhím Khán, the son of Habíbulla Khán, Pádsháh of Khutan—had come as envoy from his father to Alím Culí to announce his success against the Khitáy and seek a friendly alliance; and that Alím Culí having received him with favour had granted him the title of Sudúr Khán, and on his departure to return home had appointed himself (Nar Muhammad) to accompany him as envoy from Khokand to the Pádsháh of Khutan.

On this Yákúb Beg decided on accompanying them as far as Yárkand, because the Kúchá Khojas who were in power there, though subordinate to the Khán Khoja—that is, Buzurg Khán—had not yet tendered their submission. They set out together from Káshghar on the 1st *Maharram* 1283 H. (28th May 1865). On arrival at Kok Rabát, the Governor of Yárkand, Nyáz Beg, and some of the Tungání leaders came out to meet Yákúb Beg with presents and a promise of welcome at the city. They halted a day, exchanged civilities, and renewed mutual vows of sincerity, and then advanced towards the city. At Karábojush they encountered a Tungání picket and were refused a passage; but after a parley with their leaders and Nyáz Beg, who explained that the visit of the Koshbegi was of a friendly nature merely to convey to the Kúchá Khojas some messages from his master the Khán Khoja, they gave way, and Yákúb Beg and his party alighted in the city at quarters provided by the Governor near his own residence. Notwithstanding the good offices of Nyáz Beg, the negotiations of the Koshbegi with the Kúchá Khojas did not progress, and both they and the city chiefs studiously held aloof from him.

The Khutan party was to have gone on after a rest of three days, but in the interval news came of the arrival at Taghárchí of the Kúchá army, 2,000 men. On this Burhánuddín Khoja of Kúchá, who had become ruler of the city after the destruction of the Khitáy garrison, and who had been most determined in his opposition to the proposed negotiations with the Koshbegi for the acknowledgment of Buzurg Khán as sovereign, rode up to the house occupied by Yákúb Beg, and summoning him by name, shouted in a blunt, peremptory voice, "I give you quarter now. Depart safe and sound. Refuse, and I seize and cast you into prison." An angry altercation followed, and quickly merged into conflict between the attendants on both sides. The Khoja Burhánuddín was captured in the struggle, and sent prisoner to the house of Abdurrahmán Hazrát, the king elected by the Tungání at the commencement of the outbreak. His followers then quickly dispersed, and with the other Khojas went to join the force at Taghárchí, which now at once advanced against Yárkand.

On their approach next morning, Yákúb Beg came out of the city by the Cabáhat Gate on the west, and sent Abdulla with 50 men to reconnoitre the enemy; whilst he took up a position to the south, between Yángíshahr and the city. Abdulla having advanced too far to the north-west round the city walls was drawn into action with the advance of the Kúchá army. His little band fought with great bravery, and inflicted considerable loss upon their assailants till about two o'clock in the afternoon, when the Tungání in the Yángíshahr, false to their promises, issued from the fort and with 50 *tufú* guns joined the enemy. Abdulla was now forced to beat a retreat, and fighting all the way back beat, at sunset rejoined Yákúb Beg with 20 of his men wounded.

Yákúb Beg now held a consultation with his officers, and as his whole force numbered only 200 men, it was decided to abandon their property left in the city and retreat immediately to Káshghar. Before leaving he detached Nar Muhammad *Parwánchi*, Mír Bábá *Hudáychí*, Hamdam *Pánsad*, and other Khokand officials of Sudúr Khán's party to his own side, and on arrival at Yángí Hissár he sent them on to Buzurg at Káshghar for surveillance. Meanwhile Sudúr in return plundered their abandoned property and fled the city to Khutan.

At Yángí Hissár Yákúb Beg sat down to resume the siege of the Yángíshahr there, which was still held by the Khitáy, who found some means of getting supplies from their well-wishers in the town. During three weeks of fusilading from the walls his soldiers mined the ditch, and Yákúb Beg then sent Abdulla to Káshghar to bring Buzurg with reinforcements for the assault. The reinforcements were collected in ten days, and then Buzurg Khán set out for Yángí Hissár, and on arrival there took up his residence in the old town. At this juncture news came of the arrival at Sarígh Kúl, "Yellow Defile" (the Sirikol of the maps), of a Bádakhshí army; and it was at the same time discovered that Hamráh Khán, the brother of Sárah Khán *Mírbacha* of Kúláb, who had come over as a partizan of Sadíc Beg and had joined Buzurg Khán when the Kirghiz aspirant fled to Khokand, had secretly sent a messenger to Jahándár Sháh of Bádakhshán to send him 1,000 men and he would seize Káshghar and Yángí Hissár for him, as the troops here were very few, and the new comers very unpopular.

Jahándár Sháh in consequence of this message appointed one Sadíc *Aksakál* as commandant, and Sáhib Nazar Beg and Cútlúgh Sháh Mír as his Lieutenants, and with 1,000 men sent them to join Hamráh Khán; and they now arrived at Sárígh Kúl.

Yákúb Beg did not consider it politic at that moment to take notice of the perfidy of Hamráh Khán as he commanded a strong contingent in the besieging

68.—Yuz-bashi, Paujabashi, and Dah-Cashi at Ease.

69.—Attendants at the Embassy.

P. force, but pushed on the attack against the fort with redoubled energy; and it fell to the vigour of his assault on the fortieth day of the siege, about the beginning of July 1865, with a loss of 100 killed, and Hamráh Khán amongst the number; whilst 2,000 Khitáy were slaughtered without quarter, and 250 taken captive. The booty found in the fort was divided amongst the troops, and after a week Aziz Beg of the adjoining town was appointed its governor with a suitable garrison. Mír Bábá *Hudáychí* was now sent to Alím Culí to report the victory and present as offerings 100 Khitáy captives, 40 *tyfá* guns, 100 silver *Yámbú* = 17,200 Rs., 50 silk *túwár* (saddle cloths), and many slave girls including nine virgins.

After securing and settling the district, Buzurg and his General returned to Káshghar and celebrated their success by a week of festivity and rejoicing. After this Yákúb Beg came out of the city, and taking up his residence in the new house built for him at Pakhtaghlic, set to press the siege of the Yángíshahr which, since his departure for Yárkand, had become very slack.

Mír Bábá had arrived at Marghinán with his charge when he heard of the capture of Nyáz Beg Fort by the Russians and the departure of Alím Culí from Khokand with a large army to the support of Táshkand. He accordingly hurried on with his party towards Táshkand, and had crossed the Kandír Dawán to Tiláo, when he met the fugitive troops and learned of Alím Culí's death; so he halted where he was.

At this time Beg Muhammad, Kapchák, Governor of Andiján, and Mirzá Ahmad, Governor of Marghinán, both shamming sick, were at the summons of Alím Culí proceeding to the front leisurely together in carts. They had crossed the Chilchik River to Coylic when they met the fugitives from Táshkand and heard of the death of Alím Culí. They at once threw off their mask and mounting their horses hurried back to Toytappa, and there collecting the scattered troops consulted with the chiefs as to a successor to Alím Culí. Mirzá Ahmad, the malingerer, proposed, and the others consented, that Beg Muhammad, his fellow malingerer, be raised to the government with the title of *Mingbáshí*; and he forthwith appointed his colleague, Mirzá Ahmad, to the office of *Parwánchí*. Both reprobates then marched to Tiláo, and summoning Mír Bábá with the Káshghar offerings, divided all amongst themselves and followers, and then returned to Khokand, where they joined the upstart Khudá Culí Khán.

Meanwhile, as before mentioned, Nabbi Baksh from Táshkand had summoned the aid of Bukhárá, and on the restoration of Khudáyár to Khokand and the flight of Khudá Culí Beg thence to Mádí, these worthies deserted him and went to Gulsha with a number of others. At this place Sadíc Beg, Kirghiz, persuaded Kichik Khán *Tora* to join him in an attack to seize Káshghar from Buzurg Khán; and they set out on this enterprise with 1,000 men under the Kirghiz leaders Uthmán, Mullá Arzú, Cosh, Khadír Ali, and others.

On arrival at Táshmalik they were joined by more Kirghiz, and took the fort of Farrásh by "coup." Its governor on the part of Buzurg Khán, one Halím *Ishikaghá*, escaped and fled to Yákúb Beg with the intelligence. He at once despatched Abdulla with 100 men to attack them, and himself followed with a larger force. The advance party drove in the Kirghiz picket at the Farrásh River, and Abdulla rushing at the fort put Sadíc to flight in the hills, and captured many horses and prisoners, and, amongst other things left in the fort, all his musical instruments, by the strains of which his Kirghiz were encouraged to the fight. Yákúb Beg came up on the recovery of the fort, and sent letters promising life and pardon to Sadíc and the *Tora* on condition of their coming in and submitting to Buzurg Khán.

The Kirghiz and Kapchák on this consulted together, and seeing no prospect of a career in Khokand, decided on casting in their lot with the Khoja at Káshghar; and accordingly sent Uthmán *Dádkhwáh* to Yákúb Beg with a tender of submission and service from all their party. He was reassured, conciliated and robed, and then sent back to bring the party in. Sadíc Beg and Kichik Khán, with the other chiefs and their followers, next day made their appearance at Farrásh. They were welcomed and robed, and assigned a place in the fort as troops in the service of the Khoja Buzurg Khán, before whom Kichik was sent to pay his respects as to an eldest brother.

As before mentioned, Hamráh Khán had summoned an army from Badakhshán, which shortly after arrival at Sárígh Kúl heard of his death at the assault of Yángí Hissár. The chiefs on this consulted whether they should return empty-handed to meet the jeers of their countrymen and taunts of their wives, or advance and seek a share in the profits of war; and they decided on first offering their services to Yákúb Beg. He accepted their offer, only too glad to draw any men to his ranks, for, owing to the divided state of parties in the country, the single district of Káshghar offered but a limited field for recruiting, and sent Masúm Khán *Tora* to Sárígh Kúl to reassure the Badakhshí leaders and to bring the whole force to him at Farrásh by way of Yángí Hissár. On arrival they were feasted and robed, and quartered with the Kirghiz and Kapchák, 2,000 men altogether, who with one accord acknowledged Yákúb Beg as their leader and ruler; the first sign of the independence Yákúb Beg presently asserted, and soon after made good.

From Farrásh these new troops were shortly removed to assist in the siege of the Káshghar Yángíshahr. A few days later, about the end of July 1865, news came from Khánaric that the troops of Kúchá, Aksú, and Uch Turfán, having met at Marálbáshí, had moved on to Taghárchí, and there, in conference with the Tungání and Yárkand chiefs, had agreed to attack and destroy the Khokand invaders, to seize Káshghar and make it the capital, and then to annex Andiján. Jamáluddín Khoja of Aksú had been elected *Amírilashkar*, and being joined by the Tungání from Yárkand with 100 *tufú* and four large cannon had marched to Mughal Tárim and there mustered his force, 40,000 men including 1,500 Tungání. From this he had marched, with the Tungání in advance, and camped in the settlement of Khánaric; from which he threatened Yángí Hissár.

On learning this intelligence, Yákúb Beg appointed Kichik Khán *Tora* to continue the siege of Yángíshahr, and bringing Buzurg out of the city, where he was besotting himself with drugs and debauchery of the vilest, took him with a force of only 2,400 men to confront the enemy and divert attention from Yángí Hissár, and camped at two *farsakh* from the Kúchá army to conceal his strength. That night they offered prayers and sacrifices for victory, and next morning disposed their force in three divisions—Buzurg with 1,200 Badakhshí and Kirghiz in the centre, Yákúb Beg with 1,000 Kapchák and Andijání on the right, and Abdulla and Ghazi Beg *Pánsad* with only 200 Andijání and Kapchák on the left. They all now performed prayers, and then confessing and repenting their sins formally pardoned each the other's faults and offences, and then imploring victory from God mounted and went against the enemy's host.

The Kúchá army was in readiness, and the battle closed on all sides at once. Yákúb Beg was soon hard-pressed, and, wounded in two places by gun-shot, was obliged to retire a little. His Kirghiz and Kapchák, seeing this, turned and fled the field to take up a safe position four miles off. The Badakhshí now came in for the brunt of the enemy's attack, and losing a few men quickly followed with Buzurg at their head to join the other fugitives. At this critical juncture the Kúchá troops, oppressed by heat and thirst, slackened the attack to slake their parched throats at an intervening canal. Yákúb Beg seized the opportunity, whilst denouncing the cowardice of Buzurg, to rally some of his special adherents, and "applying to his wounds the ointment of the empire he aimed at," banished hesitation and cheered them to a renewal of the contest. "Victory is the gift of God," he said, "and depends not on mere numbers and arms. This is the moment for exertion. The least hesitation now, and all is lost." With these words he lead them afresh to the attack, and driving the enemy from the canal, slew some hundreds as they lay on its banks exhausted by the heat and fatigue.

P.   By sunset the Kúchá army was in full retreat from Khánaric, leaving 3,000 dead on the field, and nearly double the number of prisoners who were unable to follow their fugitive brethren. Amongst these last were 1,000 Tungání who, having lost nearly 500 men in the battle, now asked quarter, and tendering submission sought service with the victor. Yákúb Beg pardoned them all, and enrolling them amongst his own troops shortly afterwards employed them in the siege of the Yángíshahr. To the remaining captives, with whom he knew not what to do, he extended a like clemency, and mounting them double on stray horses running about the field sent them after their retreating comrades. After the battle the runaways with Buzurg joined the camp; but the troops now looked to Yákúb Beg as their real master.

Three days after their return to Káshghar from the victory of Khánaric, Mír Bábá *Hudáychi*, the messenger to Alím Culí with the offerings sent from Yángí Hissár, arrived at Mingyol from Khokand. He was accompanied by Yákúb Beg's son, Khuda Culí Beg, aged sixteen years, and his mother, and by Cází Ziauddin and Kádir Culí *Dádkhwáh* as envoys on the part of Beg Muhammad *Mingbáshí* and Mirzá Ahmad *Parwánchi* to seek his protection for the Kirghiz and Kapchák. Yákúb Beg approved their request and sent back a messenger to inform them that "if Khokand were too small for them, there was ample room in Káshghar, and that his own prosperity was bound up in theirs."

Just about this time, too, news came from Yárkand that the enemy defeated at Khánaric had passed on to Kúchá without coming to the city, and that a governor was wanted to maintain order. Yákúb Beg consequently sent Mír Bábá with the rank of *Dádkhwah* to secure and settle the place. With the aid of Nyáz Beg he established himself in the *Orda* there, and conciliating the chiefs who welcomed him, soon succeeded in winning over the Tungání who held the Yángíshahr to come and pay their respects and tender submission to Yákúb Beg.

Yákúb Beg now pressed the siege of Yángíshahr with redoubled vigilance, impatient to get possession of it as a starting-point for the career he had in view. The Kho Dáláy, or Commandant of the Khitáy troops, had as his Musalmán agent and interpreter one Tokhta *Ishki Beg*, "Great Lord," who, under the Chinese rule, held the Artosh Valley in fief. Some of the spies employed by Yákúb Beg got into correspondence with this Tokhta, and as a co-religionist appealed to him to surrender the fort. The faithful man, however, declined to betray his confiding master; but being persuaded that they could not much longer hold out in the fort, he pointed out to the Kho Dáláy the extremity that threatened them all; for during the two years of siege by the Kirghiz and Andijání successively, their accumulated, and from time to time as opportunity offered, replenished stores, had become exhausted. He showed him that nothing remained for them now but death by famine or the sword, except the one way of escape by surrender and safety through Islám; and this one way he urged on him to adopt. The Kho Dáláy agreed to the proposal, and sent Tokhta to bring Yákúb Beg's assurance of protection on those terms. On his return with a favourable reply, the Kho Dáláy informed Cháng Táy, the Ambán, of his decision; but he refused to accept any terms, and at 10 o'clock that same night, the first Thursday in September 1865, just a month after the victory of Khánaric, set fire to his palace and with his family and dependents perished in the flames.

Yákúb Beg, informed of the conflagration, at once came out to the assault, but first sent Abdulla with a number of *tonchi*, or "interpreters," to offer the garrison quarter on unconditional surrender. These shouted out their message under the walls, and were answered by Tokhta from a turret over the gate; and presently the Kho Dáláy with his son and three daughters and a number of attendants surrendered to Abdulla and received protection. But in the confusion the troops assembled for the assault—Andijání, Kirghiz, Kapchák, Badakhshí, and Afghán—all rushed in to the work of destruction, and during eight days massacred, sacked, and plundered. Three thousand Khitáy families, however, escaped, and on accepting Islám were granted quarter. After this guards were set at the gates and order was restored.

The fort was now cleared of nearly 4,000 corpses, and a mosque and *orda* were at once raised by Khitáy labour on the ruins of the Chinese temple and Ambán's palace respectively. Before their completion Yákúb Beg entered the Yángíshahr, and establishing himself in the *orda*, performed prayers and a complete recital of the Kurán in the new mosque. He celebrated his success by a grand feast to the poor, and by marrying the beautiful eldest daughter of the Kho Dáláy, whom for her sake he treated with marked favour. He restored him to the command of his Khitáy, now called *Yángí Musalmán* or new Musalmán, and settling them in a separate fort gave him the rule over their families with the power of life and death amongst them. The Kho Dáláy still held his position and privileges when we saw him and his people during our stay at Káshghar. They are all enrolled in the service of the present Amír Muhammad Yákúb Khán, but are rarely employed on other than sentry duty, and are not trusted generally. Indeed, it is suspected that in secret they still practise their Budhist religion.

About the end of September, following the festivities by which this success was celebrated, the outpost officer at Mingyol reported the advance of a large party from Khokand over the Tirik Dawán Pass towards Káshghar, and headed by Khudá Culí Khán, Kapchak, and many notable chiefs. On this Yákúb Beg sent Eshán Mahmúd Khán, the *Shekhulislám* of the city, out to Mingyol to ascertain whether they came as friends or foes, and with the brief ultimatum: "If friends, they are welcome. If foes, I am ready to fight them."

The high priest found the party consisted of Khudá Culí Khán with his Kapchák and Kirghiz, nearly 1,000 men; and that he was accompanied by Beg Muhammad *Míngbáshí*, Mirza Ahmad *Dastúrkhwánchi*, Eshán Khán Tora, *Tora Kalán*, Walí Khán *Tora*, his brother, Muhammad Yúnus *Shaghawul*, Muhammad Nazar Beg *Koshbegi*, Cosh *Parwánchi*, and the *Dádkhwáhs* Janak, Múlán and others, and Umar Culí *Hudáychi*, together with Náib Nabbi Baksh *Jamádar*, and a number of *Pansad* officers and court officials, such as Hakím Beg, Turdi Culi, Syad Beg, Abdurrahmán, Isa, and others. There were with them, besides, Akram Khán, the son of the Mír of Hissár, and some sons of the Mír of Orátappa. He learned that they had all rebelled and fought against Khudáyár Khán, by whom they had been defeated at Súfi Karáwal with the loss of their artillery, and the capture of most of their troops; and that they had fled to Tocáy Báshí, and thence come on by Nacára Cháldí and Ulugchát to Mingyol, where they awaited what God should provide for them.

Yákúb Beg had already sent out ample provisions to Mingyol by way of welcome to his countrymen and former associates, and the *Shekhulislám* singing his praises advised them all to come in, tender submission, and offer service. Khuda Culí Khán with his followers hesitated; but the Khoja brothers with Mirzá Ahmad, Muhammad Yúnus, and the sons of the Khokandi Mír, and most of the others joining the high priest repaired with him to the presence of Yákúb Beg, and congratulating him on his success declared themselves his devoted servants.

Two days later the Kirghiz and Kapchák left at Mingyol, hearing of the favourable reception of their fellow refugees, and seeing no other alternative than submission, seized their Khán, and bringing him before Yákúb Beg, apologized for their hesitation, and begged to be enrolled in his service as the others had been. Their request was acceded to, and they were welcomed with a feast and robes of honour. Yákúb Beg, now strong with the accession of this force, dismissed the Badakhshí army to its home, and allowed the commandant to carry away with him the corpse of Hamráh Khán from Yangí Hissár.

Three weeks later, about the end of October 1865, Mir Bábá, the *Dádkhwáh* of Yárkand, reported his inability to hold the place owing to the intrigues of the Tungání in the Yángíshahr. Yákúb Beg on this decided to go and settle the place himself, and dragging the careless Buzurg from his absorbing pleasures in the city, appointed Cosh Kapchák *Parwánchí* his own *locum tenens* in the Yángíshahr; and taking the Khoja with him set out with a strong force of Andijání, and the

P. Tungání amnestied after the Khánaric fight; having first got the blessing of the *Shekhulislam* Eshán Mahmúd Khán. Yákúb Beg had early made a special friend of this most important Church dignitary, who was one of the original party coming over from Khokand.

When Yákúb Beg with the force going against Yárkand arrived at Yángí Hissár, he discovered reasons to doubt the fidelity of the Tungání contingent. He, consequently, at once disarmed them of four cannon, 100 *tyfú*, 200 spears, and 400 swords, which they had brought with them to the Khánaric fight, and stored them all in the fort there, and then, taking them along with his army, camped at Kizili. Here the Kirghiz and Kapchák under Sadíc Beg, in connivance with Buzurg Khán, plotted to assassinate Yákúb Beg. Their design was discovered and immediately disclosed to the intended victim by Abdulla *Pánsad*, his trusty adherent.

Yákúb Beg was at the time able to do no more than increase the vigilance of his self-guard, and to summon the chiefs of the conspirators and bind them to good faith by oath on the Kurán. He then marched on by Kok Rabát to Yárkand, where he pitched his camp with the Tungání in rear, at a mile to the south of the Yángíshahr, near Chíníbágh.

On their way to camp these disarmed Tungání interviewed some of their brethren from the Yángíshahr, and immediately proposed to them a night surprise upon the camp; but to allay suspicion advised a pretence of submission without delay. The Tungání leaders, accordingly, shortly repaired to the camp, and presenting rich offerings, humbly apologized for their conduct, and swore devotion and fidelity to the Khoja, and promised to surrender the city and fort to Yákúb Beg on the morrow. Thus deceived by their professions, the *Koshbegi* robed and dismissed the deputation, and the camp, careless of security, omitted the precaution of outlying pickets.

At midnight the Tungání issued from their fort, surprised the enemy's camp, and setting fire to some of the tents, slew many and dispersed the rest in utter confusion. Yákúb Beg and Abdulla with a few devoted adherents, after a hard hand to hand fight, in which they were all wounded, cut their way through the crowd of assailants and escaped to a place of shelter hard by; whilst the Tungání, joined by their disarmed brethren, plundered the camp and at daylight returned with their booty to the Yángíshahr.

Yákúb Beg now sent Abdulla with a few men to rally the scattered army, and he returned in the course of the day with some 300 bootless and half-clad fugitives, of whom an equal number from different quarters had already gathered round their chief to the sound of bugles blown in all directions around. The Kirghiz and Kapchák, who had held by Buzurg Khán, now wished to separate, but Yákúb Beg appealing to the Khoja pointed out the folly of the step and the certain ruin it would bring upon him, and persuaded him to hold on for the capture of the city. They consequently, though with reluctance, rejoined and together returned to the original camp ground, and trenching the position awaited events. A few days later the Tungání, having gained over the city chiefs to their side, marched in and raising the populace expelled Mír Bábá and his few followers, and plundered the treasury. They then opened fire from the walls upon the Káshghar camp. On this the Kirghiz and Kapchák, in connivance with Buzurg Khán who from the commencement, through pique at his secondary position, had done all his little abilities enabled him to thwart the operations of his General and rival, and whose conduct was the cause of the failure of this enterprise, again bodily deserted the camp with their leader Sadíc Beg. Yákúb Beg, however, managed to reassure and win them back, and next day led them in person to the assault of the city. Abdulla leading the advance set fire to and forced the south gate, and driving the Tungání out of the city back to the shelter of their fort, reinstated Mír Bábá in the *orda* with a small garrison, and rejoined Yákúb Beg who, to prevent complications and a sack of the city, had withdrawn the force back to the camp.

Buzurg now no longer concealed his jealousy and displeasure, and with the aid of Sadíc Beg and his Kirghiz formed a rival party. Yákúb Beg on his own part, ever on the watch, forthwith secretly despatched Abdulla with only 20 men, all chosen adherents, to go and secure the city for him against surprise. He then appointed Nar Muhammad *Parwánchí* to the command of Abdulla's contingent, and set to win over the Tungání in Yángíshahr who were already intriguing with Buzurg.

They met his advances promptly and with equal cunning, and on the suggestion of the go-betweens sent some messengers with offerings to express their contrition for past deeds, to beg forgiveness, and offer faithful service for the future. Yákúb Beg received their deputies with marked attention, and assuring them of his good-will and clemency, robed and dismissed them to bring in their leaders. These very shortly arrived in his camp, and vowing all sorts of fidelity and service, took their leave with profuse expressions of gratitude for their very handsome reception. But they no sooner returned to their own fort, than they set to plot treachery with the rival party in camp.

A day or two later, they moved out of Yángíshahr to the shrine of Hazrát Muhammad Sharíf, and pitching tents and spreading carpets invited Yákub Beg to a feast there to ratify their compact of fidelity and service. Fully aware of the risk of assassination, Yákúb Beg saw no way of escape; so he adopted the bold course, and committing himself to God's keeping and the protection of his prophet, set out with 20 attendants to meet his hosts, who received him with every mark of honour and presented a rich array of gifts. Buzurg Khán now seized the opportunity of Yákúb Beg's absence to carry out his own designs, and as he left the camp secretly summoned Sadíc Beg to his own tent. He arranged with him that *he was to stay behind so as to check or impede the progress of Yákúb Beg in case* he pursued, whilst he himself with Beg Muhammad *Mingbáshí* and 2,000 Kirghiz and Kapchák at once set out for Káshghar.

His flight was immediately reported secretly to Yákúb Beg just as he rose from his devotions at the shrine of the saint, and he maintaining his composure took the first opportunity to leave his hosts and hurry back to camp. Here he collected and reassured the remaining troops, and despatched Nar Muhammad with Abdulla's contingent in pursuit of the deserters. He overtook them at Tázghún and captured some stragglers, but Buzurg and Beg Muhammad with most of their force escaped him, and seizing the Yángíshahr of Káshghar established themselves in Yákúb Beg's quarters there. These from the first had been a source of menace and displeasure to Buzurg who, on their capture, now assumed the direction of the government himself, and denouncing Yákúb Beg as a rebel, appointed Beg Muhammad as General in his place. And now the rupture between the *Khoja* and the *Koshbegí* became complete.

Meanwhile the Tungání at Yárkand hearing of the flight of Buzurg, with whom they were in secret treaty for the surrender of Yárkand, and being assured by Yákúb Beg that he had returned to Andiján, forthwith tendered submission, and representing that they had been duped and were now without a head, begged he would appoint a Khoja to rule over them. Accordingly, Yákúb Beg appointed Kichik Khán *Tora* their ruler with Mír Bábá as *Dádkhwáh,* and establishing them in the city with a small garrison set out to recover his position at Káshghar.

At Kizili he left his principal chiefs, such as the Tora Kalán, Sadíc Beg, Syad Beg, Hydar Culí, Mullá Turdí Culí, and Nabbi Bakhsh, to follow with the main army; whilst he pushed on with a small party to throw himself into the city of Káshghar held for him by Abdulla.

The defected Kirghiz and Kapchák had meanwhile proclaimed Buzurg in the Yángíshahr as Pádshah, and called on the people to join his standard as *murídi-mukhlís,* or "true disciples;" and the Khoja on hearing of the approach of the rebel himself issued from the fort, and riding up to the city walls with a crowd of his followers appealed with loud cries to the citizens to come out and join him as their lawful

P. king. But Abdulla, supported by the influence of the *Shekhulislám*, who in the city discountenanced any demonstration in favour of the Khoja, answered their calls with a volley from the walls, and the mob not prepared for such a reception retired to the Yángíshahr.

Next day Buzurg learning that Yákúb Beg had arrived at Yapchang with only a small party, immediately sent out a force to intercept him on the way to the city. Yákúb Beg with his handful, however, attacked them vigorously, and after a hard fight put them to flight up to the fort ditch with the capture of a few stragglers and horses; and running the gauntlet of small mounted parties hovering on his flanks passed on to the city, where Abdulla with a deputation of the citizens came out to welcome him and renew their vows of devotion to his cause.

In this interim the force left at Kizili fell out amongst themselves. Here Sadíc Beg, true to his promise of impeding Yákúb Beg's return to Káshghar, drew away Syad Beg, Hydar Culí Kapchák, Uthmán Kirghiz, and others into a plot to set up Eshán Khán *Tora*, called *Tora Kalán* or "Elder Tora," as king, and rebelling against Yákúb Beg to seize the Farrásh fort and make it the base of their operations. The Tora Kalán, however, refused the honour forced upon him, and being joined by Muhammad Nazar Beg, Nabbi Bakhsh, Turdi Culi and others, set them to watch the disaffected.

On this Sadíc Beg with his partizans and the Kirghiz and Kapchák contingent fled to Farrásh, and recovering his old fort, collected his adherents there; whilst the Tora Kalán pushing on to Yángí Hissár with the artillery and the rest of the force, sent word to Yákúb Beg of his own fidelity and approach to join him. On arrival at Tázghún, however, he was intercepted and brought to a stand by a force of 800 Kirghiz from Farrásh under the lead of Hydar Culi; but Abdulla arriving opportunely with succour from Káshghar, drove off the enemy after a stiff fight, in which they lost 100 killed left on the field, 70 prisoners, and 200 horses captured. Abdulla having thus extricated the Tora Kalán, escorted him to the city, where Yákúb Beg welcomed his arrival with feasting, drums, and music.

Yákúb Beg now consulted his friend the *Shekhulislám* on the aspect of affairs, and with his consent, installing the Tora Kalán in charge of the city, set out with all his available force to besiege Buzurg in the Yángíshahr. On the seventeenth day of the siege Beg Muhammad *Mingbáshí*, with 17 other chief men of the Kapchák, deserting Buzurg, escaped from the fort and fled to Sultán Murád Beg, the younger brother of Khudáyár Khán, at Marghinan. The Khán of Khokand, however, hearing of their arrival there, ordered his brother to seize them all; and had the whole 18 summarily executed as worthless rebels.

After their flight Yákúb Beg succeeded in winning over the Kirghiz and Kapchák, and on the fortieth day of the siege was put in possession of the fort by them. He at once seized Buzurg Khán, and deposing him from all authority committed him to an honourable captivity; but at the same time warned him that any attempt at disturbance would immediately deprive him of the consideration due to his rank and lineage.

Buzurg, however, shortly after the death of his brother Khoja, the Tora Kalán, commenced intriguing with Sadíc Beg for the recovery of the throne. Consequently Yákúb Beg sent him prisoner to Yángí Hissár, where he kept him for nearly eighteen months, and finally released him on his promising to go the pilgrimage. He deported him out of the country to Tibet, but the Khoja, instead of going to Mecca, returned to his own home at Khokand in 1869 by way of Badakhshán and Bukhárá; and still lives there with his sons on the bounty of Khudáyár Khán.

The further events have occurred too recently to form a proper subject for history.

CHAPTER IV.

VISIT TO THE THIAN-SHÁN PLATEAU, THE CHÁDIRKÚL LAKE, AND THE CHAKMÁK FORTS.

By Lieutenant-Colonel T. E. Gordon.

Dr. STOLICZKA, Captain Trotter, and I left Yangi-Shahr, Káshghar, on the last day of the old year. Having been asked to take as little baggage as possible, the local authorities undertaking to provide us with lodging and food, we started with the limited following of six servants and six baggage ponies. The first day's journey was to Bezákh (26 miles), a village in Upper Artush. The road lay in a northerly direction, past the city of Káshghar, then through about three miles of cultivation, to a stony desert, rising gently towards a depression in the low range of hills which shuts in the valley of the Artush, a broad and far extending fertile plain, studded with villages showing signs of thriving population and careful farming. This well irrigated valley, watered by never-failing streams flowing from the Thian-Shán and Alái Mountains, must produce wonderfully rich and regular harvests. Two large camel caravans were passed, going from Almáti (Vernoé) to Káshghar with Russian goods, of which cast iron cooking pots formed a considerable portion.

The second day's journey was to Chung Terek (the big poplars), or Ák-Chirgh (white reeds), 20 miles; a Kirghiz village of mud huts and felt tents. We proceeded in a general N. N. W. direction, three miles across the Artush valley, to the mouth of the Toyun valley, up which the road lay the whole way. At nine miles we passed the Khitai, or Tessiktásh Karawal (post), a small square fort used as a customs post, and occupied by a few of the Káshghar Dádkhwah's men. This was the most advanced position held by the Chinese during their occupation of the country. We saw Kirghiz scattered over the whole valley, located wherever grazing was available for their flocks and herds. Many of their felt tent hamlets show signs of settled habitation in patches of cultivated and irrigated ground, probably attended to by the elders of the families, when the summer move to the mountain pasture lands takes place. The scenery at Chung Terek must be singularly beautiful in summer.

On the third day, January 2nd, 1874, we reached Chakmák, 21 miles further up the Toyun valley. The frozen Toyun was crossed and recrossed repeatedly as on the previous day. The hills close in a short distance above Chung Terek, and at a commanding spot, 12 miles beyond, the Mirza (also called Terek and Pust) fort is placed. The valley opens out again above the Mirza fort, but to no great extent. It affords good grazing ground to Kirghiz scattered all over it in tent clumps. Nine miles higher up is the Chakmák fort. Mahmúd Beg, the Tiksobai (Chief of the Standard) in command, welcomed us warmly, and treated us most hospitably, accommodating and entertaining us in excellent quarters inside the fort.

We continued in the same general direction on the fourth day, passing the Suyúk Karawal, eight miles up the Toyun, where it is joined by the Suyúk stream, flowing from the Suyúk Pass, distant about two days' journey, and said to be impracticable for horses in winter. The valley opens out a few miles above Chakmák, and near Suyúk the hills become rounded and low. We proceeded up the Toyun almost due north from Suyúk and halted at Gúlja-báshi (the ovis poli ground), also called Búlghúm-báshi (the Myricaria wood), 10 miles from Chakmák, a sheltered valley with abundant pasturage. We were accommodated in a capital felt tent furnished by the Commandant of Chakmák. Our accompanying party of Káshghar officials, of whom the Mírakhor Inám Khoja was the principal, was joined at Chakmák by the Yúzbáshis, Mahomed Alum and Alum Kúl, and by the Kirghiz Yúzbáshi, Mahomed Saleh, with ten of his men. Mahomed Saleh is an Andijáni Kirghiz, with 100 Chirik, Alái, and Andijáni Kirghiz under him.

70.—Tungani troops of the Amir.

71.—Tungani troops of the Amir.

We reached Torugát Bela (the brown horse's back) on the fifth day. This is a grassy plain, 13 miles from the Torugát Pass, leading over the southern crest of the Thian-Shán range. We passed through an old crater, which was pointed out by Dr. Stoliczka as verifying his previously expressed belief in the existence of an old volcano in this direction. On leaving the road and wandering over the grass covered undulating hills and long sloping flats to the west, we saw several flocks of ovis poli, but were not fortunate enough to secure any. The Torugát Bela ground was occupied by Kára Kirghiz and Kazáks from the Nárin Valley with great herds of ponies, but they were moved some distance off to make way for our party. We saw about 800 of their horses being driven off as we approached our camp.

We halted on the 5th to try our fortune after ovis poli. Large flocks were seen, but none were bagged by us. A black ibex was also seen. We went about 12 miles to the west, passing along extensive valleys and over flat-topped spurs and rounded hills, all covered with grass. On our way back to camp the Kirghiz were despatched in several directions and brought in two fine male and one female ovis poli. The country to the east of the pass appears of the same character. Laden animals can pass from Torugát Bela to the foot of the Terek pass, 25 or 30 miles to the east, by paths over the pasture grounds. The pasture, even in the depth of winter, is excellent; dry, but nutritious, as shown by the good condition of the ponies which feed entirely on it. In summer it must be very rich and abundant. We were told in the evening that the arrangements would only admit of another day's stay before returning to Chakmák, and a visit to the Chádir Kúl (the Sheet Lake) was planned. Accordingly on the following day, the 6th, we rode to the lake and back, 32 miles. We crossed the pass at 13 miles from Torugát Bela, and proceeded to a ridge 3 miles beyond, from which a splendid view of the lake, plateau, and surrounding mountains was obtained. The day fortunately was remarkably clear. There was no snow on the southern, and very little on the northern, side of the pass. The lake was entirely frozen over, and thinly covered with snow. A considerable amount of snow lay on the Tásh-Róbát range and the mountains to the west. The Tásh-Róbát pass leading to Nárin, three days' march from Chádir Kúl, was however perfectly open, as we met four or five travellers who had crossed the previous day, and halted for the night at Chádir Kúl. Several parties of Kazáks and Kára Kirghiz were seen on the pass attending their herds of ponies grazing on the slopes. The Kirghiz Yúzbáshi, who accompanied us, appeared to be on the best terms possible with them all. We were told that Nárin Kazáks and Kára Kirghiz come over annually with about 5,000 ponies for winter pasture in the Amír's territories, paying revenue to His Highness. The ponies are stout and well made. Both they and the men look enduring and active, and they must be hardy to a degree to stand as they do the cold of these heights in mid-winter. In the sheltered, Torugát Bela ground the thermometer sank to 26° below zero outside, and $8\frac{1}{2}$° below zero inside our felt tent. The wind at this season on the heights is cutting in the extreme. Of this one of our party had very uncomfortable proof when in his intense eagerness to be the envied "first" to bag an ovis poli he undertook a long and slow "stalk" round the summit of a ridge about 14,000 feet and was frost-bitten on the fingers from contact with the rifle barrel before he got a shot. In the whole way from Káshghar there is literally no "hill ascent" till within a few hundred yards of the summit of the pass, and there it is easy and gradual. Grass is obtainable throughout, being particularly abundant between Chakmák and the pass. There is no scarcity of firewood to within 25 miles of the pass, and then a good substitute is always obtainable in the stunted furze and dry horse droppings to be found in the water-courses and on the pasture grounds. Baron Kaulbars, in his description of the road, makes a strange error in saying that for 67 miles from Chádir Kúl towards Káshghar no fodder is procurable.

We returned to the Chakmák Fort on the 7th, 26 miles. On the way we saw Kirghiz loading camels with blocks of ice cut in the Toyun for transport up a side valley, where they were located with their flocks, their supply of water being thus obtained till the approach of warm weather releases the frost-bound springs.

We halted on the 8th. We were shown at Chakmák the frozen carcasses of about 50 ovis poli and black ibex, stored as part of the winter meat supply for the garrison. The Toksabai presented us with nine splendid male specimens. All had been shot by the Kirghiz troops, who, judging from what we saw of the party that accompanied us, must form very valuable auxiliaries in mountain warfare in those regions. Mounted on powerful and active ponies, which are peculiarly well adapted by natural training to continued hard work and exposure, these Kirghiz, accustomed from birth to the roughest camp life, are admirably fitted for " scouting" and mounted infantry purposes.

We returned to Káshghar on the 11th. Notwithstanding the intensity of the cold, Captain Trotter, R.E., succeeded in making a complete route survey of the road, checking it by astronomical observations. He also made hypsometrical observations for the heights. Dr. Stoliczka took the fullest advantage of all the opportunities afforded for geological research and examination, the results of which he has recorded. I made a few sketches. We were invariably well received by the soldiers and others whom we met during the journey, always getting a ready salutation of friendly respect from all. The Terek Pass on the road between Káshgar and Nárin-Almáti has long been known to geographers as leading towards Khokand. We found "Terek" to be a name in frequent use in the direction we travelled. On the road to Chádir Kúl we passed Kichik Terek, Chunk Terek, and Terak Kurgán, and were told that the forts on the other road from Káshghar to Almáti are called Terek, also that the pass leading over the southern crest is similarly named. Baron Osten-Sacken in his account of the Trans-Nárin country speaks of the "Terek," a tributary of the Nárin stream. As thus applied in naming places, silver or white poplar appears to be the meaning of the word. There are small poplars in Kichik (little) Terek, large ones at Chung (big) Terek, and that tree is the most common one in the Toyun valley. Baron Osten-Sacken mentions the banks of the Terek being " wooded with poplar." The tree is doubtlessly common on the Khokan road. I go into these particulars with reference to a question raised in a discussion on Central Asian Geography, given in the Royal Geographical Society's Proceedings, dated 25th of April 1870, as to the existence of a Terek Pass north of Káshghar, as well as one to the west.

CHAPTER V.

VISIT TO MARALBASHI.

By Captain J. Biddulph.

The Amír's permission for my going to Maralbashi having been granted, I left Yangi-shahr, Kashghar, on 31st December, accompanied by Mirza Sufee, a Punjabashi, who had orders to look after me, and make all necessary arrangements.

I reached Maralbashi in seven marches, the distance from Kashghar being about 120 miles. The road runs for the entire distance along the course of the Kizzil Su or Kashghar river, which it crosses about sixty-six miles from Yengi Shahr.

Passing the villages of Barin, Randomar, Arowah, and Yandomal, we crossed by bridges two considerable streams, the Terbuchek and the Chokanak, flowing from the south into the Kizzil, about three miles apart, and darkness having come on we halted for the night in the village of Sang.

The Punjabashi knocked at the door of the first house we came to, and demanded quarters for the night. No difficulty was made, though of course we were unexpected guests, and I do not suppose any European had ever been seen in Sang. I was shown into the principal room where they were preparing for the evening meal before retiring to rest. The family teapot and soup kettle were on the fire, and a quarter of mutton hanging up, showed they were well off for eatables. The room was clean and neat, affording a great contrast to a house of like pretensions in an Indian village. The walls were truly made, with neat niches to serve as cupboards, and in front of the fire-place was a wooden block sunk level with the ground to chop wood upon. A seat was made for me by the fire, and while the master of the house went off with the Punjabashi to get ready another room, his wife produced melons and invited me to partake, and without any awkwardness or shyness kept her place by the fire, trying to keep up as much conversation as my limited knowledge of Toorkee would permit. My small dog, which sat up and begged, seemed to afford her great amusement, and she pulled a small boy out of bed to look at it.

Leaving Sang early next morning we marched to Fyzabad, a large market town, which gives its name to the flourishing district around. At two miles from Sang we crossed the Fyzabad stream flowing from the south into the Kizzil. This and the two streams crossed the previous day are united into one stream, called the Yamanyar, at no great distance from where I crossed them. Further on we passed the villages of Kazan Kul and Shaptul; a weekly market is held at the latter.

Beyond Fyzabad habitations became scarcer, and ceased altogether at Yangi Awat, forty-six miles from Kashghar. Beyond Yengi Awat the country is covered with low bush jungle and sand hills gradually changing to forest, which becomes continuous shortly after crossing the Kizzul Su. Between Yengi Awat and Maralbashi the only habitations met with are robats or post-houses at intervals of about fifteen miles, which are erected for the use of travellers: these are all of inferior construction with little accommodation, one of them only consisting of a single room. As I took no tents with me I used the post-houses during the whole time of my absence from Kashghar.

The forest, though apparently of great extent, contains no fine timber, the only tree being the poplar (tograk) of stunted growth; the undergrowth consists of a bush growing to a height of about eight feet, a thorny bramble, and camel thorn, but there is no grass. The soil is very dry, alluvial, and covered with a thin hard crust of soda, which crackles under foot at every step, and in which horses sink up to their fetlocks. The forest abounds with gazelles (*antilopa gutturosa*) and hares, but is otherwise singularly wanting in animal life. For a space of about three quarters of a mile on each side of the river there are no trees, but in their stead a belt of thick high grass, like what is known in Indian jungles as nurkut, growing to a height of from 8 to 12 feet. In this are tigers, wolves, the large deer called by the natives "bugha" or "maral," gazelles, foxes, and pheasants. This treeless belt is doubtless caused by periodical changes of the river bed of which there are many evidences. The fall of the country to the eastward is little over 500 feet in 100 miles, according to aneroid readings taken daily. The river makes frequent turns and windings, and is level with its banks, so that a very slight flush of water would cause an overflow. The current is not rapid, and the river is frozen so hard in winter that loaded carts cross it without difficulty. It is crossed in summer by a bridge, which, however, I did not see, as I was able to save several miles by taking a short cut and crossing on the ice in another place. It varies from 70 to 100 feet in width.

At one of the robats I had an interesting conversation with a traveller who was also putting up there for the night. He was an Aksu official, and had lately come from there with a presentation horse for the Amír, and having delivered it was on his way to Khoten, where his brother was a Cazee. He told me there was a direct road from Aksu to Khoten, lying through jungle the whole way. He had visited Turfan, and said he had himself seen wild camels two marches to the east of it, and spoke of them as not being very wary, but smaller than domestic ones. I questioned him as to the existence of wild horses or asses in the desert eastward, but he said he had never heard of any.

At Togha Sulookh, between 40 and 50 miles from Maralbashi, I stopped for a day's shooting. The only game I got was one very good specimen of the gazelle, or as the people there call it, djeran. The buck measures $27\frac{1}{2}$ inches at the shoulder, and greatly resembles the common Indian gazelle, except that the horns are rather longer and curve outwards, the tips being turned sharply inwards towards one another, making a very handsome head.

The next day on the march I was met by a Yuzbashi, who had been sent out to meet me. He had brought a pair of trained hawks with him, and as we marched we beat along keeping a few yards off the road, and took several hares with them. The hawks seemed to have no trouble in holding a full grown one, and the hare was often taken within 30 or 40 yards of where he was put up, even among the brambles and bushes. The trembling of the hares when taken from the hawk was very curious, they seemed quite paralysed with terror, in a way I never saw before in animals of the kind; otherwise they were quite uninjured. Just as we got to our halting place for the night, one hawk was flown at a cock pheasant, which after a flight of 150 yards through the high trees, dropped in some thick brushwood: the hawk at once took perch above him, and we put up the pheasant again. In this way we had three flights, the pheasant escaping at last in a large extent of brambles, out of which we could not put him. This was in thick forest, but the men said if both hawks had been flown, they would have killed. It was curious to see the hawk each time perching guard over the places where the pheasant dropped, waiting for us, and watching every movement while we beat. The flight of the pheasant, when once fairly on the wing, though short, is so rapid that the hawk has no chance of striking him, but by perching high above him when down is generally able to strike him as he rises a second time.

Within four miles of Maralbashi the forest ceases, and the country is covered with long grass varied by occasional patches of scrub and swamp, much resembling the Rohilcund Terai. In this are dotted about small villages with patches of cultivation round them. The grass jungle extends over a great extent of country, as well as I could gather, to the north-east, south-west, and eastward, being doubtless formed by the overflows and changes of course of the Kizzil and Yarkand rivers. The latter, I was informed, flows close to Aksakmaral, about thirty-two miles south-west of Maralbashi.

Maralbashi, which is also known as Burchuk and Lai Musjid, contains about fifteen hundred inhabitants, and is at the junction of the road from Yarkand with the Kashghar and Aksu road. It contains a fort and small garrison of about 200 men.

72.—Tungani troops of the Amir.

73.—Oves Poli.

The river Kizzil flows under the walls of the fort. Where I crossed it on the road from Kashghar it is 100 feet wide, level with the bank, but flows here in a greatly diminished stream about 25 feet wide between high banks, 20 feet below the level of the surrounding country. Its character was so altered that it was only after repeated assurances from the people that I satisfied myself as to its being the same stream.

Close outside the fort is a palace lately built by the Ameer, who often stays here on his way to and from Aksu.

The natives of the district are called Dolans: they have a more Tartar-like cast of countenance than Yarkandees and Kashgharees, and are said to be distinguished by their fondness for music and singing. They are said to be descended from prisoners brought in the fourth century of the Hijra by Haroun Bugra Khan from Transoxiana, and forcibly settled in the country between Maralbashi and Kuchar. In the jungle villages they excavate houses out of the ground, making grass roofs level with the surface. The term Dolan is, I believe, applied generally to people of mixed parentage.

The present Hakim Beg of Maralbashi, Ata Bai, has the title of Mirakhor. He is an Andijani, about 35 years of age, with especially pleasant address, and seems much liked by the people, who all speak well of him. He was not in Maralbashi when I first arrived, having been away for 10 months with the troops at Orumchi and Manass. Four days after my arrival he returned with about 120 men.

In Ata Bai's absence I was received by the Deputy Governor, Mulla Samsakh, who showed me every attention. The whole of the public robat was placed at my disposal, and all supplies I stood in need of were furnished.

On one occasion a man forced his way into my room and rather rudely demanded in Persian a turban as a present, similar to one I had given another man the day before. He told me that he was the Mulla Alayar, and a Cazee, and reiterated his demand for the turban in a very impudent way. I told him that I was not in the habit of giving turbans to people who asked for them, and he went away as abruptly as he had entered. I sent for the Punjabashi and told him that I did not like people coming into my room without invitation, and would never give anything if I was asked for it. He said it should not happen again, and half an hour afterwards I received a message from the Mulla Samsakh, saying that I should not be troubled again, and that the Cazee had been severely beaten for his insolence. I was told afterwards that the punishment had given great satisfaction in the bazaar, where Mulla Alayar was disliked on account of his constantly asking people for things which they dared not refuse.

At Maralbashi I found a Punjabee, named Gholam Khadir, serving as a soldier. His son, a sharp lad of 13 years of age, was sent over to stay in the robat to interpret for my servants. I told him I should like to see his father, who accordingly came over the same evening. I had a long and interesting conversation with him, in which he told me his history as follows:—
"Two years ago I left Sealkote with six ponies laden with merchandize to sell at Leh. When I arrived there I found no sale for my goods, so I resolved to come on to Yarkand, being advised to do so by Mr. Shaw. In crossing the Suget Pass all my ponies perished, much snow having fallen, and I lost everything. There was only my son, the boy you have seen, with me, and a servant who went mad with the troubles of the journey. Another trader helped me on to Sanju, and from there the Hakim forwarded me on to Yarkand. I was taken before the Dadkhwah, who was very good to me, and gave me two hundred tangas and some clothes, and told me I should go back to the Punjab in the spring. When I again went before him in the spring, he told me I ought to be married, that everybody in the country was married. I protested that I had a wife in Sealkote, but he said that did not matter, and sent for a Mulla, who was ordered to find me a wife, and I was married whether I would or no ("zubberdustee"). When all my money was gone, I went again to the Dadkhwah, who sent me to Kashghar, where I was recognised by Mirza Shadee who had seen me in Sealkote. I used to make medicines and give them to people at Sealkote, and gave some to Mirza Shadee when he was there. I once gave some to Ata Bai, the Hakim here, and cured him. He gave me a robe and eight tangas for it. I was taken before the Atalik, who asked me what I could do, I answered that I doctored people. He asked me if I would serve him, I dared not refuse,

so I was sent off to this place with my son. Guns were put into our hands, and we have been here ever since. Four months after my arrival my wife was sent to me here from Yarkand. Zemindars are never taken to be soldiers, but all men who can give no account of themselves are made to serve in the ranks. The Chinese used to take zemindars for soldiers. There is much petty theft here, but no burglary; robbers are not daring as they are in India. The first time a man is caught stealing he is led all round the bazaar and beaten, the second time he has one ear cut off, the third time his right hand. I have never heard of a man being hanged for stealing. I have never seen a man hanged. The gallows are put up to frighten people. The punishment of death is only inflicted for murder. I remember two murders while I was in Yarkand. Everybody is married, even all the soldiers: when one dies, his wife is given to another. All marriages are arranged by the Mullas. When a man wishes to get rid of his wife, he turns her out of his house, and has by the Sharyat to pay her ten tangas and give her clothes. At the end of three months she may marry again. All eatables except mutton are very cheap. A great deal of beef and horse flesh is eaten. Taxes on produce are paid in kind to the extent of four per cent. People are constantly saying that there used to be much fun and wine drinking in the time of the Chinese, now there is none. The women especially are continually lamenting this. When people were very poor they used to sell their children to the Chinese for a yamboo (£17). If at the end of a year they could repay the yamboo, the children were returned to them; if not, they were made 'Kunjrees.' The bazaars were full of 'Kunjrees' in those days: they were killed when the Andijanees took the country. When you arrived in Yarkand, it was rumoured that seven or eight hundred sahibs had come; that you had come in consequence of the visit of the Russian Embassy last year. I was in Kashghar then and saw them. The Amír is much pleased at your coming. When Mr. Shaw first came he was placed in 'nuzzurbundee' (under surveillance); so was the sahib who came afterwards to Yarkand: now the Amír knows you better, and you are allowed to go where you like. Mulla Samsakh was much pleased at your mending his gun to-day (I had put the lock to rights), he says the sahibs are very clever. You saw what a thing it was, they know how to make nothing here."

From Maralbashi I went to Charwagh, a village of about 250 inhabitants, 14 miles on the Aksu road. I was especially anxious to shoot a tiger, of which there were many about, but was unsuccessful in the sea of high grass with which the country is covered. From footprints and skins, and judging by what I was told, there was no doubt that the tiger here is altogether a smaller animal than the Indian one. He seems also to differ considerably in his habits, prowling round villages at night, killing dogs and sheep, and behaving more like an Indian panther than a tiger. The people spoke of men being killed by tigers occasionally, but it does not appear to be a common occurrence.

I had, however, good sport shooting gazelles and pheasants which abounded, and I also saw the burgoots* or trained eagles kill gazelles and foxes. I was not fortunate enough to see them kill a wolf, though they were twice flown, but the animals on both occasions being in thick bush jungle and at a great distance the birds did not sight them. Their owners, however, spoke of it as an ordinary occurrence. When the jungle is not too high, they sight their prey at a great distance, and sweep up to it without any apparent effort, however fast it may be going. Turning suddenly when over its head they strike it with unerring aim. If a fox, they grasp its throat with the powerful talon and seize it round the muzzle with the other, keeping the jaws closed with an iron grasp so that the animal is powerless. From the great ease with which an eagle disposes of a full grown fox, I could see that a wolf would have no better chance. Gazelles are seized in the same way, except those with horns, in which case the eagle first fastens on to the loins of the animal, and watching his opportunity transfers his grasp to the throat, avoiding the horns. The burgoot, however, is not very easy to manage, and requires the whole of one man's care. Its dash and courage are great, but if flown unsuccessfully once or twice, it will often sulk for the rest of the day. When it kills it is always allowed to tear at its game for a little time; the men told me that if prevented doing so while its blood was up, it would very probably attack our horses.

---

* The bearcoot of Atkinson.

I was enabled by sextant observations to fix the latitude of Maralbashi at 39° 46′ 25″ N.

Nine miles to the north-east of Maralbashi is a huge black rock, apparently basaltic, with a treble peak, rising to a height of some 2,500 feet above the plain. It is very rugged and quite inaccessible and forms a conspicuous landmark. It is called "Pir Shereh Kuddum Moortaza Ali Tagh," "the Prophet Ali's footstep." At its foot on the north side is a Mazar of great sanctity. The Aksu road runs within a mile of it, and travellers on catching sight of the shrine dismount and say a prayer.

From Charwagh I was asked to come on to Tumchuk, some miles further on the Aksu road. As nothing had been said about it before leaving Kashghar, I decided not to do so, and had reason to repent my decision. On returning to Kashghar I was told that at Tumchuk are the ruins of a very ancient stone city. It happened that on one occasion while shooting I came upon a hewn stone looking like part of an hexagonal pillar, but though I made several enquiries of the men with me, none of them said a word about the ruined city. I also noticed that the jungles contained many signs showing that at one time there had been considerable cultivation.

The country round Maralbashi is well watered, and the soil rich, and seems only to want population.

The stages beyond Charwagh on the Aksu road were given me as follows by the Mulla Samsakh, who told me that there was a robat at each stage:—

1. Chadirkul.
2. Yakakuduk.
3. Zoidu.
4. Chilan.
5. Chulkuduk.
6. Soi Langri.
7. Oikul.
8. Kumbash.
9. Aksu.

I returned to Kashghar on the 23rd January in five marches from Maralbashi. The day before I left I paid a visit to Ata Bai in the fort, and thanked him for all the civility I had experienced, presenting him at the same time with a pair of binoculars and a pound of English powder. He presented me in return with a pony, and the next morning a man overtook me on the march with a trained hawk, also sent me as a present.

No attempt was made at any time in any way to control or direct my movements. I received whatever supplies I was in need of, and was treated by all officials with the greatest civility.

CHAPTER VI.

SIRIKOL, THE PÁMÍRS AND WAKHÁN.

By Lieutenant-Colonel T. E. Gordon.

CAPTAIN BIDDULPH, Captain Trotter, Dr. Stoliczka and I left Yangi Hissár, Káshghar, on the 21st March. We were preceded by Resaidar Muhammad Afzal Khán, who left the previous day, travelling by rapid marches to Wakhán with a letter to Mír Futteh Ali Shah, the ruler of that country, informing him of our proposed visit. Muhammad Afzal reached Kila Panj on the 2nd April, and rendered admirable service in preparing for our arrival.

Our first day's journey was to Egiz-yar, a large village on the verge of the plain, and the last in the inhabited country towards the hills. The road lay in a south-westerly direction, passing by several flourishing villages amidst extensive cultivation. Six miles beyond Egiz-yar the road enters the hills along the course of a feeder of the Yangi Hissár river. The plain preserves its even surface right up to the high ranges and ridges which stand out, and rise from it, without any undulating or broken ground intervening. The appearance is strikingly like that of bold sea-coast scenery. The population (a very scanty one) between this and Sirikol is entirely Kirghiz. They live almost wholly by their flocks and herds, only attempting a little scattered cultivation in the lower valleys. They are the only people we observed using the horse generally in the plough, oxen being employed in the plains, and yaks in Sirikol.*

The signs of approaching spring were showing when we left Yangi Hissár, but we found ourselves here almost back in the depth of mid-winter. All the streams were frozen, and snow lay everywhere, while fresh falls were frequent the whole way to Wakhán, and during our stay there.

We followed the Yangi Hissár tributary stream by a good road up to the Kaskasú pass (13,000 feet), which we crossed on the fourth day. Snow and ice made the passage of it, which is otherwise easy, extremely difficult. Our baggage animals at the descent had to be relieved by yaks.

For about thirty miles from the plains the hills are bold and precipitous, rising abruptly from the valley, and they are almost entirely devoid of vegetation. Beyond that, they become sloping and rounded, and in summer are covered with grass, affording excellent pasture. The descent from the Kaskasú pass is to Chihil Gumbaz (forty domes), where we expected, from the name, to find some interesting ruins. The place however has evidently been so called from that number of Kirghiz clay-brick domed tombs having at one time existed there. Now only one or two, in a ruined state, remain. A road branches off here to Yárkand, (distant one hundred and ten miles) passing down the Chárling valley and stream. In the time of the Chinese occupation this passage was watched by an outpost. The road is unsuitable for any but small parties, from an absolute want of water on it for a distance of thirty-five miles. The streams from the southern side of the Kaskasú pass and the eastern of the Torut unite here and form the Chárling, which flows into the Yárkand plain.

The fifth day's journey took us over the Torut pass (13,400 feet), which, with the hills all about, was covered with an almost perfect sheet of snow, hardly a rock appearing anywhere through the surface, except on the crests and peaks. Willow and poplar trees are plentiful

---

* *Note.*—Ploughing with horses has been a custom from the earliest times throughout Eastern Turkestan. Captain Chapman made a sketch of one which he saw at Kizil in March last.—(Sd.)   T. D. F.

below the pass, and in the narrow valleys beyond. Two or three miles of the next day's march lay through the "Tangi-Tár" (the narrow way, common name for defile), over about the worst piece of road we met with throughout the journey. The Tangi-Tár is a very narrow defile, with a stream rushing over fallen boulders and blocks of rock, flowing through it, and occupying the roadway to such an extent, that in many places the stream-bed is the only available passage. Holes cut in the wall-like sides of the rock, rising from the stream at one particularly confined place, show that in former times the passage was by means of a supported stage-way above the water. The attendant Kirghiz also mentioned this. There are several hot springs in this gorge, temperature about 116°. Birch, willow and gigantic juniper are plentiful in it. This day's march took us to the foot of a great elevated slope leading to the Chichiklik pass, plain and lake (14,700 feet), below the Yámbulák and Kok-Moinok passes, which are used later in the season on the road between Yangi-Hissár and Sirikol, to avoid the Tangi-Tár and Shindi defiles. As the season advances these passes become free from snow, while the defiles are rendered dangerous and difficult by the rush of the melting snow torrents. From the Chichiklik plain we proceeded down the Shindi ravine, over an extremely bad stony road, to the Sirikol river, up the banks of which we travelled to Táshkurgán, reaching it on the tenth day from Yangi Hissár. The total distance is one hundred and twenty-five miles.

After leaving the Káshghar plain we met with Kirghiz every day, and always found their felt tents prepared for our accommodation at each halting place, till within two days of Táshkurgán, when we entered the inhabited part of the Sirikol valley. The Kirghiz tents, having roof openings, admit of fires inside, and were thus infinitely more comfortable than our own in winter weather.

The open part of the Sirikol valley extends from about eight miles below Táshkurgán to apparently a very considerable distance towards the Kunjút mountain range. Its average breadth is about three miles. Cultivation is confined chiefly to the western slopes and is the work entirely of the Tájik inhabitants, who occupy a length of about twelve miles of the valley in the immediate vicinity of the fort. The centre of the valley, through which the river flows, is used as a pasture ground, and gives rich and abundant grazing. The hamlets are at present in a wretched looking state, the houses having fallen to ruin during the late wholesale banishment of the population to Káshghar.

The ancient name of Táshkurgán is Várshidi. The ruins show it to have been of square or rectangular form, with projecting towers, and built of rough unhewn stone. It does not appear to be of great antiquity, or very remarkable in any way.

The Sirikolis are Shíah Muhammadans. They say that they have been in the valley for seven generations, as a distinct people, with a Chief of their own, and are the descendants of wanderers who came from all quarters; from Badakhshán, Wakhán, Shighnán, Hindostán, Kunjút and Túrkistán. Hence, as my informant (Dáda Ali Shah, a Sirikoli Mullah,) said, "The language peculiar to us is a mixture of what is spoken in all these countries." Persian however is also spoken by them all. The men differ from the Kirghiz, Ozbegs, and inhabitants of Eastern Túrkistán in having regular features and full beards. Their salutation of respect is made with the hand to the forehead, and not with the arms crossed in front, as among the Túrks. Dáda Ali Shah told me that the towers still standing in most of the hamlets were built for refuge and defence in the slave hunting raids, from which they had suffered cruelly for many years, and that he himself had witnessed no less than twenty of these attacks, which have entirely ceased since the establishment of the Atálik's rule.

The valley is 10,250 feet above the sea. The cultivation consists mainly of beardless barley, beans, peas, carrots, and turnips. The domestic animals are camels, yaks, ponies, cattle, sheep and goats. The yaks are smaller than the Thibetan species. A murrain carried off nearly all the oxen and cows a year ago, and fresh cattle are now being obtained from the plains and lower hills. Willows grow thickly by the streams, and poplars appear in sheltered spots close to the hamlets. The valley extends to a great distance above the Fort, the river (variously called Tághdúngbásh, Táshkurgán, Sirikol, Tisnáf and Yárkand,) which flows through it, taking its rise in the Tághdúngbásh Pámir and Kunjút range. Kirghiz occupy it for pasture as far as the Káshghar boundary, said by the Sirikol Governor to be twenty "tash" (about eighty miles) beyond the Fort. The Tághdúngbásh Pámír lies to the north of, and parallel to, the Little Pámír, from which it is separated by a broad chain of hills joining with the Neza Tásh mountains, and forming one unbroken range. The Sirikol valley, after extending south for some distance, bends towards the west, and merges into the Tághdúngbásh Pámír, which appears to be merely a continuation of the valley at a higher elevation.

The climate of Sirikol is severe. Hassan Shah, the present Governor, who has had five years' experience of it, says, that there are only two seasons, summer and winter, the former lasting but three months, the latter nine.

The Sirikol river was of considerable size when we first crossed it, March 29th. The perfect clearness of its water, the steadiness of its flow (equality of volume day and night) and the severity of the cold then, showed it to be at the usual low winter ebb. It is said to be joined, about fifty miles further down, by the "Tong," a stream as large as itself, if not larger. Should this be found to be correct, it is probable that the Yárkand river may yet be regarded as rising in the Kunjút range instead of the Kárakoram, as hitherto believed.

The Tágharma plain lies about three miles to the north-east of the Sirikol valley, and is of the same elevation. It is a fine open crescent-shaped flat, about twelve miles long by seven broad, extending from the south-west to the north-east, and is well watered by a stream which flows through it from the north-eastern end and falls into the Sirikol river. This stream is plentifully fed by numerous springs in the middle of the plain. A few Sirikolis reside and cultivate in it, but the main portion of the inhabitants consists of one hundred Kirghiz families under their Chief Krúmchi Bí, who permanently occupy the plain as a pasture land, for which it is admirably suited from the richness and abundance of its grass.

This plain is separated from the Kizil-Art by a low rounded ridge, formed by projecting spurs from the opposite mountain ranges, the Neza-Tásh to the west and the Tágharma to the east. The ridge forms the watershed between the two plains, the drainage on the Kizil-Art side flowing into the Little Kárakúl lake, said to be about twenty miles distant. The Bardish pass leads from the watershed over the Neza Tásh range into the Áktásh valley. The road over this pass is reported to be good. It emerges nearly opposite the Great Pámír.

According to the accounts given by the Kirghiz, the Kizil-Art plain extends north from the Tágharma to the Alái, from which it is separated by a mountain range. The height of the two former is about the same, and that of the latter (the Alái) somewhat greater, but still considerably less than the elevation of the Pamir, judging from Fedchenko's description. That traveller mentions the preference given by the Khirghiz to the Alái over the Pámír, by reason of lower height. The Kizil-Art is similar in character to the Tágharma plain—being well watered and abounding with grass and fuel. Its length is about one hundred and thirty miles. It is enclosed on the east by the mountain range extending, and sweeping round from the direction of the Kokand "Terek" pass and the Alái, and on the west, by the Neza Tásh. The Little Kárakúl lake lies in the lower, and the Great Kárakúl in the upper part of this plain. The former gives exit to the "Gez" stream, which flows eastward through the Gez pass, under the lofty and massive Múztágh (the Tágharma peak of the maps), into the Káshghar plain, and there joins some of the numerous branches or canals of the Káshghar river. The size of the lake is given as about fifteen miles in circumference. The Great Kárakúl is stated to be about forty miles in circumference. It receives feeders from the Alái dividing range, and gives exit to the Múrgháb, which finds its way westward through the Neza Tásh range, and flows towards Shighnán and Roshán. Four lakes on the Kizil-Art, and in its vicinity, were mentioned as giving rise to streams: the Great and Little Kárakúls already spoken of, the Rang Kúl in the Siríz Pámír, and the Yeshil Kúl in the Alichor. The two latter furnish tributaries to the Múrgháb. Further mention will be made of these Pámírs and their lakes later on in this narrative.

We left Táshkurgán for Wakhán on the 2nd April. Hussun Shah, the Governor, accompanied us part of the way out. He rode a very fine Túrkoman horse (the first and only one seen by us) with gold mounted trappings. We remarked him to be almost the best dressed and equipped officer we had met in the Atálik's service. Our first day's journey was in a westerly direction to the foot of the Neza Tásh Pass. After leaving the Sirikol valley, we entered the Shindán defile, through which a stream flows into the Sirikol river. The defile at several places is extremely narrow, with precipitous rocks towering high above it. The road through is particularly bad for about three miles. Passage is difficult in the beginning of summer when the stream rises from the snow meltings. The following day we crossed the pass (15,000 feet) and reached the Áktásh valley (12,700 feet). The pass is easy of ascent and descent, but the very heavy snow lying on it made the day's work a trying one to the baggage horses. We were joined at this day's camp by a party of Sirikolis, with ponies and yaks, carrying supplies sent by Hussun Shah to accompany us to Wakhán. On the third day we proceeded south up the Aktash valley to its head, where it merges into the Little Pámír, extending east and west; the appearance being that of the same valley making a sweeping curve from east to north. We followed up the Áktásh stream (called Áksú by the Kirghiz) through the Little Pámír to the Gházkúl lake, from which it takes its rise.

We reached the Little Pámír lake (the Ghazkul) on the fourth day from Táshkurgán, marching forty-five miles on that and the previous day. Almost the entire distance was done through deep snow, with a freezing wind from the front, cutting the face, and inflaming the eyes, in a painful manner. On the first of these two days our difficulties were increased by the track being lost in the snow, our progress being thus considerably delayed.

The Áktásh valley runs in a northerly direction from the Little Pámír across the eastern openings of the Great and Alichor Pámírs, and sweeps into the Siríz Pámír at Ákbálik, the junction of the Áksú with the Múrgháb. Its length is said to be about sixty miles, and its average breadth, judging from the twenty miles extent, over which we travelled, is about three miles. It is a pasture resort of the Kizil-Art Kirghiz.

The Little Pámír is similar in character to the Áktásh valley, and of about the same breadth. It has the same grassy downs, slopes, and flats. It is bounded on the south by the continuation of the Neza Tásh range, which separates it from the Tághdúngbásh Pámír. The range here appears to sink considerably in height. A broad chain of rounded hills lies between it and the Great Pámír. These hills are low towards the Áktásh valley, and rise gradually towards the lake. The lake is about three miles long, and a little less than a mile broad. We found it and the stream flowing from it entirely frozen. The undulating surface of the ice on the lake showed it to be frozen right through to the bottom, and indicated shallowness. It appeared to be deeper at the western end. The height of the lake is 13,000 feet and the hills on both sides rise some 2,000 feet higher, those to the south being completely covered with deep snow. Extensive glaciers and snow beds lie near the western end. The name "Barkat Yássín," applied to the lake by some native travellers, is properly that of a rocky ravine near its head, "Burgút Yursi," "the eagles' place or nest." The "r" in "Yursi" is dropped in the pronunciation as is common in many Túrki words. Our further journey lay west past the lake. At about half a mile from its head, a water-course filled with ice, appeared leading west down the valley. Six miles lower down, we came upon the ruins of Kirghiz mud huts and a burial-ground. A stream from the eastern Tághdúngbásh Pámír joins the Little Pámír affluent of the Oxus here. The valley closes in at a distance of ten miles below the lake, and the Little Pámír may be said to terminate there. The stream then runs in a deep set course, between steep banks, which rise up to the long mountain slopes along which, by the right bank, the road leads to Langar, twenty-five miles from the lake. A deserted village and traces of cultivation were observed at Langar, and yaks and cattle were seen grazing on the opposite side of the stream. A stream of considerable size joins there from the south-east.

From Langar the road continues in a general westerly direction along the stream to Sarhadd thirty miles. In the depth of winter the frozen surface of the river makes passage up and down easy. We found the ice beginning to break up here and there, and our path had to be sought across and back, over the rocky bed and up and down the high steep banks, making the journey tedious and severe to a degree. In summer the swelling of the stream makes this road extremely difficult, and it is then that the Great Pámír route is followed in preference.

We left the last fire-wood at the mouth of the ravine leading from the Neza-Tásh pass to the Aktásh valley. Up to that willow and myricaria are found. No wood of any kind grows on the Pámírs, but the Thibetian "burtzi," a small prickly shrub with woody roots, forming a good substitute for bush fuel, is found in abundance over them. Twenty-five miles below the Little Pámír lake, birch, willow and gigantic juniper appear in thick clumps, and fire-wood is plentiful from that downwards to Wakhán and Badakshán.

The valley opens out about a mile above Sarhadd and remains more or less wide to Kila Panj, and beyond. Habitation and cultivation commence at Sarhadd and continue down the valley, with large tracts of dense low thorn and willow jungle and pasture flats intervening between the villages.

A letter of welcome from Futteh Ali Shah, the Mír of Wakhán, was received at Langar, and we were met at Sarhadd by Ali Murdán Shah, the Mír's eldest son, sent to receive us, and escort us to his father's fort residence, Kila Panj. The son is very fond of field sports, and was accompanied by a number of men with his hawks and dogs. Among the dogs were a pair of ibex hounds, two spaniels from Koláb and a terrier nondescript from Chitrál, it was said, but looking uncommonly like an importation from the vicinity of the British Infantry barracks at Peshawár. The ibex hounds are said to run the ibex to a stand-still from paralysing alarm, when they are generally easily shot. Resaidar Muhammad Afzul Khán rejoined us at Sarhadd. He reached Kila Panj on the 2nd April, travelling in fourteen days from Yangi Hissár.

We reached Sarhadd on the seventh day from Sirikól, and Kila Panj on the twelfth. We were compelled by the extreme severity of the weather to make short marches the first three days from Sarhadd. A violent and blinding snow storm met us each day on the march, accompanied by a wind so intense in its coldness, as to freeze the driven snow flakes on our faces. On the fourth day we encamped at Zong, a large village on the right bank of the Oxus, immediately below the junction of the Great and Little Pámír affluents.

The majority of the inhabitants of the villages from Sarhadd to Bába Tangi, thirty-three miles down the valley, migrate with their flocks and herds in summer to extensive grazing grounds at the Baróghil, and other passes leading into Chitrál. A few people remain in each village to attend to the growing crops, which are harvested on the return from the summer pasture lands. The inhabitants of the lower part of the Sarhadd valley, Zong, Langar-Kisht and Kila Panj, similarly resort to the hills in their neighbourhood. The flocks and herds consist of sheep, goats, cattle and yaks. Most of the horses in the country are obtained from Badakshán and Kattaghán; they are small, well bred, and hardy.

The people as a rule are very poor. They appear avaricious and particularly fond of money. The Mír himself showed the same disposition, and is moreover extremely miserly in his habits. The snow storms which prevailed during our first five days in Sarhadd drove us sometimes to seek shelter in the houses of the villagers, where we had several opportunities of observing their domestic life. The houses are flat-roofed, and built of stone and mud. The outer enclosed rooms are used as stables for horses and cattle. The family occupy one large centre room, which has a large opening in the roof immediately above an oven-like fire-place, sunk in the middle. On the four sides round this room are raised platform sleeping places, one of which is partly enclosed and allotted to the women and children. The men are warlike, hardy, and enduring. They do all the field work, the women being chiefly occupied about the house. The women do not veil, and appear to have more control in the household than is usually the case in the East. We observed the same in this respect among the Kirghiz. Whenever money was given as a present in return for shelter, the female head of the house was generally called to receive it. The men are all given to field sports, and appear fond of arms. Every house showed the arms of its male occupants slung on the walls of the inner rooms. The Wakhis as a people are good looking; many faces were seen of an extreme regularity of feature. Fair hair is not uncommon. They all speak Persian in addition to their own peculiar dialect. They describe themselves as descended from wanderers who assembled and settled in Wakhán, from all quarters.

74.—Ovis Poli Lyre horned Antelope, frozen specimens.

75.—Present of game and fruit in Kashghar.

We reached Kila Panj on the 13th of April. Mír Futteh Ali Shah rode out to meet us, and conducted us to our camp, which was pitched on an open plain in the close vicinity of his fort. He is an old man, of tall form and good face, but feeble from age and infirmity. He welcomed us to Wakhán, and expressed himself in the usual oriental complimentary terms as happy to see us at Kila Panj.

Kila Panj is on the left bank of the Oxus (or the Panja as it is there called), about six miles below the junction of the two Pámír streams. The place is so named from five forts which stand together. Only two however can properly be styled forts, even according to local notions; the other three being merely towers planted on high up-standing rocks and hillocks in their vicinity. The principal fort is occupied by the Mír. It is an irregular building of stone and mud, with high walls, and many towers, situated on an eminence close to the river. We found the river about sixty yards broad and easily fordable; when in flood it is crossed by means of inflated skin rafts.

We paid a visit to the Mír in his fort in the evening. We were received in a centre room, with a roof opening, and spaces on the four sides, similar in style to the village houses, but larger and higher. The entrance was, as with them, through the stables. The Mír received us attended by many of his people. There was no attempt at display of any kind, the Mír being dressed in the plainest manner possible, his people likewise, and the room comfortless in the extreme. Everything was rough except manners, which were exceptionally good. We observed what we had seen before with the "Mír-Záda" (Ali Murdán Shah), respect paid by kissing the hand; the people kissing the Mír's hand on arrival, on departure, and on receiving an order.

We remained thirteen days at Kila Panj. The weather was very severe most of that time. Snow fell on six days, and an intensely cold wind blew regularly till within three days of our departure. Wood speaks in his book of the withering blast of the "bád-i-Wakhán" (wind of Wakhán). It prevailed during a great part of our stay at Panja, and only ceased occasionally, to be followed by an equally chilling wind from the opposite direction, Badakshán. These winds swept across the open plain on which we were encamped, with such a cutting violence, that our horses and baggage ponies were as much starved by the cold as by scarcity of fodder.

Our party was a large one, amounting with our sepoy guard of five men of the Guide Corps, and a similar number of Káshgharis, to forty-eight men and seventy-two horses. We arrived at the most unfavorable time for supplies. Most of the excess, above the wants of the inhabitants, being sold in the end of the summer and during the autumn, to the merchants who pass with their "káfilas" in those seasons, the matter of our daily supplies and a sufficiency to take us back over the Pámir was one of great difficulty.

Wheat (beardless), barley, beans, and peas are the principal crops in Wakhán. Melons and apricots ripen at Zong, the large village previously mentioned, above Kila Panj. The climate of the Sarhadd district, extending thirty-five miles down from the first village at the head of the valley, is too cold for wheat.

The only timber grown is the white poplar, and that, by reason of the violent wind of the country, requires a sheltered position. Stunted red willow and other bushes are plentiful in the sandy stretches by the river.

There appears to be little or no mineral wealth in Wakhán. Iron is procured from Badakhshán. We could not get sufficient even to make the necessary horse shoes for our animals, and had to give our iron tent pegs to the smiths to be so worked up.

The present trade between Eastern and Western Túrkistán is very limited. It consists chiefly of "churrus" (intoxicating drug) and cotton cloth of Khoten manufacture from the former, and of horses, indigo, kincob, and sundries from the latter. The indigo and kincob are obtained from India. The Mír of Wakhán levies transit dues at a uniform rate of one Muhammadshahi rupee (equal to one rupee and three annas of Indian money) per horse-load, irrespective of value. No dues are levied at Sirikol, this being done on the goods reaching their destination.

(228)

We had been told that the Great Pámír, on account of snow, is rarely passable till the end of June, and were assured that it would be impossible for a large party like ours to succeed in any attempt earlier. On the 15th April I despatched a sepoy of the Guides with two of the Mír's men towards the Great Pámír Lake to report on the depth of snow, so that we might take advantage of any possible chance of passage. They returned in eight days, bringing such an account of the road as induced us to determine on trying it. They found the snow deep and heavy in the drifts and hollows, but the fact of their having been able to reach the lake made us regard the journey as much less difficult than had been previously represented. The Mír visited us the day after the return of the Guides, and, referring to their report, said that he would give all assistance in his power to gratify our desire to see the Great Pámír Lake, and go back by a different route than that by which we came. Our baggage horses had not recovered from the effects of the severe journey over, but as the Mír undertook to give help in that way, we were able to commence preparations for return to Sirikol. The Mír also made arrangements for the provision and carriage of eight days' supply of food for men and horses.

On the 25th the weather changed suddenly from cold to mild, and a heavy fall of rain that night, succeeded by a warm day without wind, gave signs of coming spring. On the 26th we paid a farewell visit to the Mír, and left Kila Panj that day, Captain Trotter, Doctor Stoliczka and I for the Great Pámír, and Captain Biddulph, accompanied by Resaidar Muhammad Afzul Khán, for the Chitrál Passes, a spot in the Aktásh valley being appointed as our rendezvous on the 4th of May.

We (the Great Pámír party) halted the first day at Langar-Kisht, a considerable village on the right bank of the Great Pámír stream, and the last in the valley leading up to the lake. Near it is the Issár Fort, built on a solitary rock, standing out high on the plain, and said to be of very ancient date. We examined the ruins, and found them to show no signs of greater antiquity than those of Táshkurgán-Sirikol. The mud used as cement in the walls indicated no great age. No hewn stones were seen in the whole place.

The Mír's eldest son visited us in the evening at Langar-Kisht, to say good-bye and present a pair of ibex hounds, which were evidently considered a valuable gift. The sporting tastes of the Wakhis lead them not to regard the dog as a mean animal, similarly as other Muhammadans do. Wood mentions how a slave was given in exchange for a dog, and the Mír, when we took leave of him, said that he would be always glad to see the English, that even a dog of theirs would be welcomed, and he would himself rise in the night time to see food cooked for it.*

From Langar-Kisht our road lay in a general north-easterly direction, at some height along the slopes of the mountains on the right bank of the stream. The mountains on each side rise by a very gradual incline from the deep rocky gorge in which the stream flows. The Zerzamín and Mútz streams join from the north, at eight and nineteen miles from Langar-Kisht. The upper road to Shighnán leads along the latter. Bar Panja, the capital, is said to be reached in eight days by it, and Shákh Darrah in three days. Shákh Darrah was at one time a small independent Mírship, but it now forms part of Shighnán. The Kirghiz, who formerly occupied the western end of the Great Pámír, are now located in Shákh Darrah. According to the Wakhis the Mútz stream has a course of about twenty-five miles, rising near the crest of the mountains to the north, which form the boundary between Wakhán and Shighnán, the stream from the opposite side of which falls into the Murgháb.

The Great Pámír appears to begin twenty-five miles above Langar-Kisht. The valley which up to that point is narrow, the base of the mountains approaching the bed of the stream, opens out there, and the hills on either side show low and rounded. Thence the road lay in the same general direction, over flats and long easy slopes the whole way to the lake. Birch and

---

* *Note.*—This seems to be a general expression of welcome; for the Dadkhwah of Yarkand, Mahomed Yunus Khan, said the same to me in 1870.

(Sd.) T. D. F.

willow are plentiful to within twenty-five miles of the lake. From that on, the never failing "búrtzi" affords an abundant supply of fuel. Excellent grass, similar to that in the Little Pámír, and the Áktásh and Sirikol valleys, is found throughout. The lake stream in the first sixteen miles of its course flows between high gravelly banks, which rise to far extending downs, dying away in the long and easy mountain slopes.

We were remarkably fortunate in meeting with comparatively little snow as far as the lake. There was a considerable fall on the night of the 29th at Bilaur Bas, twenty-five miles below the lake.

We reached the Great Pámír or Wood's lake on 1st May. It was entirely frozen over and covered with snow. Its water is perfectly sweet, judging from what we used for two days from the stream which flows out of it. It extends east and west, and is about ten miles long by three broad. The water marks on the shores however indicate a considerable enlargement in summer. Its height is 14,200 feet. The southern shore is even, the northern broken and irregular. The shores resemble a sea beach from the sand and gravel which cover them. Many signs of considerable depth were observed.

At three miles from the foot a high promontory runs out from the northern shore and approaches the southern side to within less than a mile. The hills to the south slope very gradually from the edge of the lake, and the peaks rise to a height of four or five thousand feet above it. Broad plains and low undulations, for about three miles, lie between it and the hills to the north, which appear much lower than those to the south.

The valley closes in at the head of the lake, and continues narrow for about eight miles, when it again opens out with a steady fall to the east. Captain Trotter by examination determined the water-shed to be at this point. Two small frozen lakes were observed near the head of the lake, under the high snowy mountains, which close in there from the south. They presented the appearance of ice accumulations, and probably, after furnishing feeders to the lake for a short time, finally disappear in summer. A valley at the head of the lake leads to the Wurm pass, by which the Little Pámír, Langar, and Sarhadd are reached in one and two days.

There was a great deal of snow about the lake, and it lay so deep on the high ground at its head, and in the valley leading down east from the water-shed, that the easy regular road that way could not be followed. We were forced to find a path along the low hills to the north, and had considerable difficulty in forcing our way through the heavy snow drifts.

The snow ceased about eighteen miles from the lake. The eastern stream from the watershed is there joined by a large one from the Shash Darrah (six valleys) in the range between the Great and Little Pámírs. Several paths lead from this point to the Little Pámír and the Áktásh valley. We followed the united streams, here called the Isligh, down to the Áktásh valley, a distance of fifty-eight miles, over a very gentle fall the whole way. The hills right and left are low and rounded, with great openings and depressions appearing every where. We were accompanied by a large party of Wakhis, acting as guides and in charge of the horses carrying our supplies. On one of these guides being asked if paths lay in the direction of certain openings pointed out, the answer was "Yes, there are paths all over the Pámír. It has a thousand roads. With a guide you can go in all directions."

From the junction of the Great Pámír with the Áktásh valley we travelled eighteen miles, south-east by south, up to the halting place, which had been agreed upon with Captain Biddulph as the point of meeting on the 4th May. Both parties reached punctually on that date, we having marched thirty-seven miles that day to keep the engagement.

Captain Biddulph succeeded in visiting the Chitrál passes, and made a most valuable addition to the results of our Pámír exploration.

The Alichór Pámír runs east and west, parallel to the Great and Little Pámírs. According to Wakhi accounts it is similar in character to them, broad at the eastern, and narrow at the western end. It is connected with the Great Pámír by the "Dasht-i-Khargóshi," a desert flat which extends across from about twenty miles below the Great Pámír lake. A road passes over it and branches from the Alichór to Shighnán and Khokand. The Dasht-i-Khargóshi is about twenty miles in length. A stagnant lake called Túz, and Sussik Kúl (salt, putrid lake) lies near the western end. The water of it was described to me as being salt to the taste. Abdúl Mejid noticed this lake as at the first stage from Khargóshi, which agrees with the account given to us. To the east of the Sussik Kúl a fresh water stream rises and flows into the Yeshil Kúl lower down in the Alichór, from which another issues and falls into the Múrgháb, below its junction with the Áksú.

The Káshghari army that fled with the Khojas in the last century before the Chinese, when they gained possession of Eastern Túrkistán, passed up the Alichór Pámír in their flight to Badakshán. They were overtaken near the Yeshil kúl, and are said to have driven their women and children, mounted on camels and horses, into the lake to meet their death by drowning, rather than allow them to fall into the hands of the Chinese. The Kirghiz have a legend that the sounds of lamentation, and of people and animals in terrifying alarm at threatened death, are often heard to come out of the lake.

I have already mentioned the Siríz Pámír when speaking of the Áktásh valley. This Pámír appears to be a continuation of the Áktásh valley, similarly as the Little Pámír is, and as the Tághdúngbásh is of the Sirikol valley. It seems to run from Ák-bálik in the east, to Bartang in the west. Bartang is the beginning of the inhabited and cultivated portion of Shighnan in that direction. It is described as abounding with fruit-bearing trees, and must therefore be much lower than Kila Panj, with a very different climate. It is easy to believe this, when the long course of the Áksú, with its steady fall, is considered.

The Kirghiz spoke of the Rung (ibex) Kúla, large lake, about one day's journey from Ák-bálik, and situated in the Siríz Pámír. This probably is the Rung Kúl of Pámír Khúrd, mentioned in Colonel Yule's Essay on the Geography of the Oxus, the Áktásh valley being thus regarded as the Little Pámír, of which it is but the continuation, as I have already explained. By the Kirghiz accounts, the Great Kárakúl is four days, the Little Kárakúl three, the Rung Kúl one, and the Yeshil Kúl two and a half days' journey from Ák-bálik. I estimate the day's journey in these accounts at fifteen miles. Abdúl Mejid made seven marches from Khargóshi to the Great Kárakúl. Of these one probably was to the Alichór, two down it to Ák-bálik, and four up the Múrgháb, by the road which is said to pass along its banks.

The animals of the Pámírs are the ovis poli, ibex, brown bear, leopard, lynx, wolf, fox, marmot, and hare. These remain throughout the year. Wild fowl swarm on the lakes in summer. The wild yak is not known on or near the Pámír.

We were not fortunate in pursuit of game. On the way over the Wakhán the snow lay too deep to permit of sport, and on the journey back our limited supplies would not admit of a halt for the purpose. The only ovis poli obtained was a female shot by Captain Trotter, on a long march of thirty-seven miles. The horns of the ovis poli and the ibex lie in great numbers at many places on the Pámírs. These animals suffer heavily from the leopards and wolves, which prey almost entirely upon them. A murrain is also said to have made great havoc amongst both some years ago. The ibex are similar to the Himalayan species, and accordingly differ from those we saw in the Thian Shán range, which were of the black species, also found in the Kúen Lúen. I brought away a pair of ovis poli horns measuring sixty-five and a half inches in length round the curve, fifty-three inches in a straight line from tip to tip, and sixteen inches round the base. I purpose giving them to the National Museum of Natural History in London.

We experienced none of the usual symptoms of great height, headache and difficulty of respiration, on the Pámírs, in the degree that native travellers have described. None of our camp followers and people suffered in any way beyond breathlessness when exertion was made. All were free from the pain of "dum" as it is called, with the exception of our mess khánsámáh, who invariably became a victim anywhere at an elevation over 12,000 feet.

There was perfect health among our party throughout the journey. One of the Wakhis, who accompanied us with the supplies over the Great Pámír, died suddenly on the last march to Áktásh, and this was the only casualty, or sickness even, among the numbers of men who

76.—Female Patients attending the Embassy Hospital, January 1874.

77.—Patients attending the Embassy Hospital.

were attached to our camp when crossing and recrossing the Pámírs. All the natives of India with us bore the severe cold and hard work with remarkable endurance and courage.

The Pámír plateau may be described as a great, broad, rounded ridge, extending north and south, and crossed by thick mountain chains, between which lie elevated valleys, open and gently sloping towards the east, but narrow and confined with a rapid fall towards the west. The waters which run in all, with the exception of the eastern flow from the Tághdúngbásh, collect in the Oxus; the Aksú from the Little Pámír lake receiving the eastern drainage, which finds an outlet in the Aktásh valley, and joining the Múrgháb, which obtains that from the Alichór and Siriz Pámírs. As the eastern Tághdúngbásh stream finds its way into the Yárkand river, the watershed must be held as extending from that Pámír, down the range dividing it from the Little Pámír, and along the Neza Tásh mountains to the Kizil Art pass leading to the Alái.

We saw hot springs at Patir, thirty-five miles below Sarhadd (tem. 130 deg.) at Zong, near Kila Panj, and at Isligh, between the Great Pámír lake and the Aktásh valley.

We made repeated enquiries from Kirghiz and Wakhis, and from Mír Fatteh Ali Shah, regarding "Bólór," as a name for any mountain, country, or place, but all professed perfect ignorance of it.

I have already explained how the name of a place has been mistaken for that of the Little Pámír lake. A similar mistake appears to have been made in the name "Sirikol" given to the lake of Great Pámír. When speaking of our journey up to the lake, we were told of stages called "Bun, Bekh, and Payán-i-kúl" (base, root, foot of lake), "Miyán and Barábar-i-kúl" (middle, and half way up the lake) and "Bálá and Sir-i-kúl (above, and head of, the lake). Sir-i-kúl was most frequently mentioned, being the usual caravan stage, and it was said in such a way as to lead easily to the idea of its being the name of the lake. When the guides were asked pointedly as to the real name of the lake, they answered—"It is called Kúl-i-Kalán (the Great Lake) because there is no other lake in the country equal to it in size." Therefore the name "Victoria," given by Wood, displaces no distinctive local one, and may well continue to be used, without fear of causing confusion.

I have spoken of the Aktásh stream flowing from the Little Pámír lake as being called "the Aksú" by the Kirghiz. In Turki the "A" in "Ak" (white) is pronounced so broad, as to sound exactly like "O." Captain Biddulph, on hearing the name so pronounced "Oksu," suggested it to be the probable derivation of the Roman "Oxus."*

We asked at Táshkurgán the meaning of "Sirikol." Hussun Shah, the governor, gave his opinion that it is a corruption of Sir-i-koh, the place being at a great elevation. On finding the valley to be a continuation of the Tághdúngbásh, I looked upon Hussun Shah's explanation as probably correct, from the fact of its being a literal translation of Tághdúngbásh, both meaning "head of the mountain." Nothing seems more likely than that the Persian-speaking Sirikolis should, on settling in the valley, give it a Persian name, literally interpreting its Turki one.

Regarding the name "Pámír," the meaning appears to be wilderness—a place depopulated, abandoned, waste yet capable of habitation. I obtained this information on the Great Pámír from one of our intelligent guides, who said in explanation—"In former days when this part was inhabited by Kirghiz, as is shown by the ruins of their villages and burial grounds, the valley was not all called Pámír, as it is now. It was then known by its village names, as is the country beyond Sirikol, which being now occupied by Kirghiz is not known by one name, but partly as Chárling, Bas Robát, &c. If deserted it would be Pámír."†

---

* *Note.*—One objection to this otherwise reasonable explanation is that the word Oxus was used by the Greeks, not Romans, long before Turki had spread so far west.

(Sd.) T. D. F.

† *Note.*—The same explanation of the word was given to me at Yangi-Hissar. It is in fact a Khokandi Turki word.

(Sd.) T. D. F.

We reached Áktásh on the 4th May, having travelled one hundred and fifty-seven miles from Panja. We found provisions awaiting us there, sent out from Táshkurgán by Hussun Shah, according to request. We had experienced some difficulty in obtaining the supplies equired for our journey from Wakhán, and were nearly being starved through the avarice and greed of those entrusted by Mír Futteh Ali Shah with the order to provide. We found, after proceeding one march beyond the last habitation, that sufficient for five days only, instead of eight, had been furnished. The Mír was at once communicated with on the subject, and we were overtaken the next day by a messenger, with a letter saying how annoyed he was at the dishonesty which had been practised towards us and himself, and that extra supplies would reach us that night, which they did. Seeing horse flesh in common use for food in Káshgar, we had learnt to look upon our ponies as a last resource, always in case of extreme necessity. We halted a day at Áktásh to rest our tired animals, and to arrange for the return of the Wakhis to Panja. Fifty of them with fifty-two horses accompanied us on the journey, and did us capital service. We rewarded them liberally, and sent them back with a letter of thanks to their Mír.

We retraced our steps to Táshkurgán, where we were again most kindly received by Hussun Shah. After three days' halt we proceeded on the return journey to the plains of Yárkand. We went the first day to the foot of the Kok-Moinok pass, taking a long round by the Tágharma plain. We crossed the Kok-Moinok (15,800 feet), and joined the road by which we travelled up, at the little lake in the Chichiklik plain. There was a considerable amount of snow on the Kok-Moinok, the last we crossed on the way down. The pass is easy of ascent and descent.

We had a fall of snow at Chihil-Gumbaz on the night of the 14th May, and cold weather till the 18th, when we were at once plunged into extreme heat at Egiz-Yar, in the plains. From that we struck across country to Kizil Robát, the first stage on the road from Yangi-Hissár to Yárkand. We arrived at Yárkand on the 21st May, left on the 28th, and reached Leh on the 29th June.

Three days after crossing the Kárakoram pass, we suffered the deep affliction of losing by death one of our party, Dr. Stoliczka, a highly valued friend and talented companion. His death is a great loss to the scientific world, for had he lived, he would have added much to knowledge by his researches and discoveries in geology and natural history.

CHAPTER VII.

GEOGRAPHICAL REPORT.

When the Government of India had decided to send a diplomatic Mission to the Atálik Ghází of Káshghar it was determined to appoint an officer of the Indian Survey Department to accompany the expedition as Geographer; and Captain Henry Trotter, Royal Engineers, of the Great Trigonometrical Survey of India, was selected for the post.

The preliminary arrangements were left by Mr. (now Sir Douglas) Forsyth entirely in the hands of Captain Trotter, subject to such advice as he might receive from Colonel Walker, R.E., the Superintendent of the Great Trigonometrical Survey. The only restrictions insisted on were that everything was to be arranged for mule carriage, and the survey baggage was to be limited to three mule loads, also that the services of two khalasies (carriers) only could be allowed to assist generally in the work. Abdul Súbhán, a Sub-Surveyor in the Topographical Survey Department, was subsequently permitted to accompany Captain Trotter to act as recorder and general assistant. Two of the Great Trigonometrical Survey "Pundits"[*] with their assistants were also placed at Captain Trotter's disposal.

It has been found convenient to arrange this Chapter in the shape of a General Report by Captain Trotter, to which is added an appendix shewing in some detail the results of the observations, astronomical, meteorological, hypsometric, and magnetic, taken by that officer and his assistants. The appendix includes some observations by Captain Biddulph on the Ling-zi-thung plains and on the road to Maralbáshi, and also contains detailed accounts descriptive of the various routes followed by members of the Mission, as well as of others compiled from native information, principally by Dr. Bellew.

CAPTAIN TROTTER'S REPORT.

Introductory.

The first point to be decided was as to the instruments and equipment to be taken, and this was an anxious matter; it was impossible to say what sort of a reception we should meet with in Yárkand, and whether I should be allowed to use openly any survey instruments at all; I had also to bear in mind the, to me, totally new condition, that my instruments would have to be packed and carried on mules, and taken over the highest passes in the world. (In the Indian Survey Department delicate instruments such as theodolites, &c., are always carried by men, and even in the survey party attached to the Abyssinian Expedition this rule, I believe, was never departed from.) This condition imposed the necessity of taking only moderate sized instruments and such as were not likely to be injured by violent shakes and jars. Fortunately among the instruments of the department there was one that had already done good service at Magdála, *viz.*, a 6-inch Transit Theodolite, with micrometer eye-piece, by Troughton and Simms. On Colonel Walker's recommendation I took this as my mainstay for astronomical observations, and I may here add that I have used it constantly throughout my absence from India, and have been very much pleased with its performance. A few slight

---

[*] The term by which it has been customary to designate natives employed by the Great Trigonometrical Survey Department on Trans-Frontier Explorations.

alterations having been made in the fittings, it was carried safely in one of our leathern mule trunks for more than 3,000 miles over I suppose some of the most difficult roads in Asia, without receiving the slightest injury, or having at any time been unserviceable. For its size it is a most perfect instrument.

I had, however, also to consider what I should use in case of secrecy being necessary, and for this of course there was nothing like a sextant, so I provided myself with a 6-inch sextant by Troughton and Simms, as well as a small pocket sextant by the same maker, taking with them the ordinary mercurial artificial horizons.

I may allude to the fact that Captains Biddulph and Chapman both spent a short time at the head-quarters of the Great Trigonometrical Survey for the purpose of practising astronomical observations in anticipation of the probability of our party separating in different directions in Eastern Turkestan. It was arranged that the former should take with him a sextant and the latter a theodolite, a sister instrument to my own. There were, therefore, in camp duplicates in case of any accident happening to my own instruments.

I also provided myself with a very small light theodolite for use on high peaks (where it would be unsafe to attempt to carry the large instrument) and for traversing along roads if opportunity should occur. Besides the instruments already named I had a supply of prismatic and pocket compasses (I may mention that owing to breakage and accidents I at one time ran short of pocket compasses, and I was much indebted to Colonel Gordon during the Pámír trip for the loan of a very good little instrument), and a small light plane-table, which I had specially made to fit on to my theodolite stand. A good hand telescope was fitted to the same stand which also served, when necessary, with a slight adaptation, for a Hodgkinson's Actinometer belonging to the Royal Society and lent to me by Mr. Hennessey of the Great Trigonometrical Survey for the service of the expedition. Colonel Roberts, the Acting Quarter Master General, kindly gave me an old astronomical telescope which had been in use for many years in the Quarter Master General's Department. This telescope was presented to the Dádkhwáh of Yárkand on our return to India.

It was proposed that I should take a complete set of instruments for observation of the magnetic elements—intensity, dip, and declination; but considering the great bulk and delicacy of these instruments, as well as the time that would have been occupied in making the necessary observations—time which I could not expect to be able to snatch from more important duties—I determined to take the dip circle only, a small instrument and one not occupying very much time to observe with. Observations for declination (variation) I was able to manage with my theodolite, with sufficient accuracy for practical purposes.

With regard to chronometers and watches for astronomical purposes, it was decided that I should only take pocket chronometers, and as the Survey Department could only provide me with one good one, I had to order two from England, a gold one by *Dent*, and a silver watch by *Brock*, a maker strongly recommended by the Royal Geographical Society. These watches, I found while crossing the Himalayas, could not be depended on for very accurate results, as the sudden and enormous changes of temperature combined with other causes to make the rates very irregular (although all were professedly compensated for temperature), and for that portion of our journey I consider it better to rely upon the Pundit's pacing, checked by latitude observations, rather than on differential longitudinal observations depending on these watches. During trips in Turkestan, however, where there was considerably less variation in temperature, the results are much more satisfactory, and in my excursion towards Ush Turfán the resulting positions in longitude depend entirely upon chronometric differences of time, as also in great measure do those between Káshghar and Panjah in Wakhán.

For meteorological observations and for determinations of height I decided to run the risk of taking with me mercurial mountain barometers, feeling that the greater confidence that would be placed in results deduced therefrom would more than compensate for the risk of loss by breakage; I procured two from Bombay and one from Calcutta, and on the whole I am glad that I did so, as I succeeded in safely transporting all three over the Himalayan ranges, having been able to get them carried by men on foot. On the other side of the mountains I was not so fortunate. At Sánjú one of them was blown down in front of my tent by a sudden violent gust of wind, and the very next day another, which I had entrusted to the care of Dr. Bellew, was, on account of the length of the march, given to a horseman to carry: the horse fell in crossing a river and No. 2 was smashed. The third survived, and regular observations were taken with it throughout the winter in Yárkand. It too was broken on the return journey, its carrier falling with it in a stream.

I was also provided with numerous aneroid barometers, hypsometers and thermometers. The latter I had specially made to order in England, as none that I could procure in India were graduated low enough to register the minimum temperature to be expected in the higher ranges of the Himalayas. As was to be anticipated in a journey like ours, very many of these have been broken; loose horses getting at night amongst the tent ropes, and in the extreme cold weather even inside the tent, have much to answer for.

While at Dehra Dún* prior to starting I was occupied in making myself familiar with the instruments I was about to take with me, and in practising the observations I should probably chiefly be dependent on; in drawing up and getting lithographed portable and compact forms for registration and computation of observations, and other miscellaneous preparatory work. I prepared a large number of sheets with all the most northerly points fixed by the Great Trigonometrical Survey on the frontier of India projected thereon, as well as the latest determinations of the Russian survey; in order that by whichever route we might go or return, or wherever we might wander, I might lose nothing for want of previous preparation. These charts were not of so much service to me as I had hoped, as wherever there was a chance that they might be utilized, the vicissitudes of the climate, and the rapidity with which we had to travel, invariably interposed to prevent my making full use of them. Colonel Walker also designed, and had prepared and photozincographed, a star chart, projected on a new principle, showing only stars of the first three magnitudes, nautical almanac stars being distinguished from all others. I found this chart a very valuable practical guide while observing.

On Sir Douglas Forsyth's application to Colonel Walker four of the Great Trigonometrical Survey "Pundits," or rather two of the old Pundits with two assistants, were attached to the Mission, as it was hoped that an opening would occur for the despatch of these men from Eastern Turkestan across the Gobi Desert and through Thibet to Hindustan. It was not deemed advisable however to employ them thus, and when the Mission advanced from Yárkand to Káshghar it was necessary to leave them in Yárkand. Permission was given, however, for one of them to follow me to Káshghar, and he did useful work, of which more hereafter. The remainder were employed in Yárkand during the winter in taking meteorological observations.

Road to Yarkand.

For a few marches from Leh, in every direction, the country has been carefully and correctly surveyed and mapped in former years by parties of the Great Trigonometrical Survey under Major Montgomerie, R.E., but between this rigorously executed survey (bounded on the north by the head waters of the Núbra and Shyok, and on the north-east by the Ling-zi-thung plains) and the table-lands of Turkestan, lie vast tracts of mountainous country, parts of which, through the enterprise, zeal, and energy of Messrs. Shaw, Hayward, and Johnson, have been mapped with tolerable accuracy, while other parts have probably never yet been traversed by man, certainly not by geographers. It was my object to weld together as far as possible the existing materials into a harmonious whole and to add whatever I could to existing data.

It had been decided that the Mission should proceed to Sháhidúla in two parties, the head-quarters going by the old Kárákorum route, whilst a detached party, consisting of Captain Biddulph (in command), Dr. Stoliczka, and myself, was directed to proceed *viâ* Changchenmo by the route by which the former Mission returned from Yárkand in 1870, and as we had

---
* The Head-quarters of the Great Trigonometrical Survey.

several days' start of the main party it was hoped that we might be able to discover some alternative route by which that line of road might be shortened and difficulties avoided. The delay of the Hadji Turrah Sahib, the Yárkand Envoy, in Constantinople made it necessary for the advanced party to halt at Leh until authentic news should arrive of his departure. Authority to advance was not received until we had been there for more than a fortnight, and we left it finally on the 12th September with orders to join the main party at Shahidúla on the 20th October.

This unfortunate though unavoidable delay not only deprived us of so much time for prosecuting geographical investigation, but postponed our departure to so late a season that inclement weather proved a serious hindrance to our advance, and a still greater impediment to me in carrying out the programme I had laid down for myself.

As the best arrangement I could make, one Pundit with an assistant was left at Leh to proceed with the head-quarters camp; the other one with a better instructed assistant, capable if necessary of doing independent work, was to accompany our own party, and in the probable event of our separation was to be attached to Captain Biddulph, the assistant being attached to Dr. Stoliczka. Abdul Subhán, the Native Surveyor, or "Múnshi" as he is generally called, was to accompany me as recorder and general assistant, and to be sent out with the plane-table should opportunity occur.

It might have been expected that the presence of such a large party would have facilitated arrangements for carrying on work; but the exact contrary was the case, as the demands on the limited resources of the country were so great that it was found impossible to send out any detached parties, the Native Surveyors were therefore obliged to accompany the main camps, to march when they marched, and halt when they halted; and as the marches are arranged for the convenience of travellers and not of Pundits, some of them were found uncommonly stiff and difficult to get through before dark. As the Pundits were in pairs a great part of the way and thus able to divide the work, the ground was got over with a fair amount of accuracy: and checked and corrected by the latitude observations taken both by themselves and myself on the outward and return journeys, the routes are certainly laid down with an amount of accuracy not hitherto attained.

I should explain that in making my plans I was guided by the peculiar nature of the survey work generally done by these natives. This consists of a traverse survey, the angles of which are measured with a prismatic compass and the distances determined by the number of Pundits' paces. These paces have a slightly different unit of length, which is generally determined at the close of operations by comparing the total amount of northing or southing as shewn by the traverse, with the true corresponding distance as determined by the difference of latitude between the starting and closing points. The Pundits are all able to take latitude observations with a sextant and are instructed to do so wherever opportunity occurs. It is obvious that the accuracy of the survey depends upon their being able to keep up a continuous measure of the road; any break in it would ruin the work. Hence the necessity, if possible, of their working in couples, so that they may relieve each other in the pacing, especially where, as in the present case, they were obliged to accompany the large camps and could not select their own halting places. The days were getting short, and if darkness once overtook a man before he had concluded his work, there was every probability of his whole survey being spoiled.

Having thus arranged for the two main lines of road to be laid down with considerable accuracy, I was free to devote myself to what I considered a very important matter, *viz.*, the fixing accurately the correct positions of certain points on the line of march. I wished to do this either by triangulation in continuation of the Great Trigonometrical Survey system of triangles, or by running with the small theodolite a very careful traverse of the road. With the Munshi's help I trusted to be able to carry this traverse up to Shahidúla, a point whose position it was very important to determine with accuracy. I also hoped occasionally to place myself in position on the plane-table by means of certain trigonometrical points which were fixed years ago by the Survey Department in advance of the accurate detailed survey. Many of these points are in the main Kárákorum and Kuen Luen ranges; some of them in the heart of the *terra incognita*

78.—A Nogai from Omsk and a Native of Sirikul, Pamir.

79.—Bhokara and Khokandi Merchants.

before alluded to; and had I had more time at my disposal, and had the weather been more favourable, I might have done very valuable work. As it was, owing to the antagonism of the elements my diary shows one almost continuous succession of disappointments, most disheartening under the circumstances that it was the beginning of the journey, and that I did not know but that circumstances might prevent any work being done after entering Yárkand territory. Climbing hills at the great elevation we were then at was very hard work, and of course occupied considerably more time and labour than similar ascents at a lower level; and in nine cases out of ten when one did arrive at the top of a high hill, snow and clouds entirely obscured both distant and neighbouring peaks. This cloudy weather combined with the necessity of regulating halts and marches according to the places where supplies had been laid out, soon made it evident that it was useless to attempt a continuation of the triangulation. The length of some of the marches and the shortness of the days made the execution of a careful traverse, as impossible as the triangulation, and after some very hard work, I reluctantly came to the conclusion that nothing could be done by myself (*i.e.*, in addition to astronomical work), but to make what use I could of the plane-table. Even with this but little was done owing to the extremely unfavourable state of the weather; but I fortunately succeeded in fixing my position satisfactorily at two or three places on the road to Sháhidúla, the most northerly point where I did so was at Chíbra, south of the Sugét Pass. Throughout the journey the cold was so intense that even the Bhots* who were with me used, on arrival at the top of a hill, to lie down in hollows or crouch behind stones in order to avoid the bitter blast. Under these circumstances, satisfactory work could not be expected, and although I kept my own health in a wonderful manner, I had the misfortune to knock up more or less nearly every man who accompanied me.

From the 24th September, the day on which we reached Gogra, until the 17th October on arrival at Sugét, I was never at a lower level than 15,500 feet, and during the whole of that period the thermometer seldom rose as high as freezing point (32° F.), whereas at night the minimum would vary from zero to 26° below zero.† From 26th September to 8th October I was never below 16,300 feet, my highest camp being at Dehra Kompás‡ 17,900 feet above the level of the sea.§ Snow was frequently falling throughout the whole of this period, and for three days was the only substitute for water, for both man and beast. Captain Biddulph, who travelled by a more easterly route than Dr. Stoliczka and myself, was living at even a greater elevation.

On the 13th of October Dr. Stoliczka and myself reached Áktágh, where we joined the head-quarters camp. It had originally been arranged that Captain Biddulph, accompanied by a Pundit, was to cross the Kárákorum line of road and explore the country to the west of Áktágh towards Kufelong. Dr. Stoliczka, accompanied by the other Pundit, was to have crossed from the Kárátágh Lake by a new route to the Kárákásh River, but his illness, as well as the weak state to which the camp followers were reduced from lengthened exposure to cold and hard work, made it necessary to alter these arrangements.

I was now directed to go up the Kárákásh River, and endeavour to find the road which was believed to exist between some point up the river and the Kárátágh Lake, and which it was supposed might turn out a good alternative route. I returned from this expedition, the details of which are given in another place, on the 20th October, and left the following day with a party under the orders of Colonel Gordon for Sanjú with instructions to await Sir Douglas Forsyth's arrival at that place.

As Sháhidúla was the first point where we struck the Atálik's dominions and met his people, I briefly give the result of survey operations up to that point.

---

* *Bhots* are inhabitants of Ladakh.

† *i.e.*, 58° below freezing point.

‡ So called from having been used as a camping ground by a former Survey Officer or Kompas (compass) wala, the native designation for all surveyors.

§ It was the hardships encountered while traversing this elevated region that brought on the illness which subsequently cost Dr Stoliczka his life.

One Pundit and his assistant accompanied the head-quarters camp and were kindly looked after by Captain Chapman, who himself took some astronomical observations along the road. They ran a route survey from Leh, viâ the Khárdung Pass, up the Nubra Valley to Changlung, thence by the Sáser Pass to Sáser, from which place the Pundit proceeded by the winter route up the Shyok River and by the Remo glacier to Daulat Beguldi, while his assistant took the summer route by Murghi and the Dipsang plains to the same spot. Thence they proceeded by the regular road over the Kárákorum Pass to Áktágh, from which place they carried their traverse down the Yárkand River for three marches to Kirghiz Jangal, returning thence to Shâhidúla by the Kirghiz Pass.

Kishen Sing, the Pundit, accompanying the advanced party commenced his route survey at Chimray, two marches east of Leh. At Zingrál, the next halting place, his assistant diverged from the main road, going over the Kay La (Pass) and joined us again at Tankse. The Pundit went with the main camp over the Chang-la.* From Tankse we all proceeded to Gogra, whence the Pundit was detached to accompany Captain Biddulph, who went over "Cayley's† Pass" and the Ling-zi-thung plains, considerably to the east of the road by which the former Mission returned from Yárkand in 1870, which road, however, he rejoined at Kizil-Jilga, thence following the Kárákásh in all its bends down to Shâhidúla. Captain Biddulph took numerous observations for height on his line of march, generally using one of the mercurial barometers for that purpose. The Pundit kept up a continuous route survey the whole way and took frequent astronomical observations for latitude. Both Captain Biddulph's and Pundit Kishen Sing's observations will be found in the Appendix to this Chapter.

This Pundit's assistant, aided by the Múnshi (as soon as I became convinced that a theodolite traverse was impracticable), carried a route survey along the road I myself followed, i.e., the one by which the former Mission returned from Yárkand, by the Changlung-Pangtung Pass. This road skirts the west edge of the Ling-zi-thung plains and striking the Kárákásh River near its head, follows the course of that river until it turns off suddenly to the north-west, a point a little beyond Khush Maidán; thence the road passes viâ the Kárátágh Pass and Lake to Aktágh. From Aktágh it goes over the Sugét Pass from which place I sent the Route Surveyors up in a north-west direction to cross the hills in front and stike the path passing from the Khirghiz Pass to Shâhidúla. My object in detaching them by that road was to enable the Múnshi to fix himself in position by some of the survey peaks on the Kárákorum away to the west. He had one fine day and succeeded in doing so, but at the cost of frost-bitten fingers, from which it took him a considerable time to recover.

Throughout the march I made astronomical observations with my theodolite which have been reduced (in duplicate) in the head-quarters office of the Great Trigonometrical Survey since my return to India. They, together with my fixings by the plane-table, as well as my astronomical work on the return journey, and the Pundit's own observations, form the basis on which the whole of the Pundit's traverses have been built up. To this frame I have added such material as is available from the maps of the Trigonometrical Survey and of Messrs. Johnson, Shaw, and Hayward. The whole combined form a map more accurate and complete than anything yet published, and should, for geographical purposes, as far as the actual lines of road are concerned, leave but little more to be desired.

Descriptions of the routes traversed by various members of the Mission will be found in the Appendix, Section, *Routes*.

As regards this early portion of our journey the only new contributions I can give to science and geography are the results of a boating expedition on the Pangong Lake, and an account of the excursion, already referred to, which I made from the neighbourhood of Shâhidúla to try and discover an alternative road on to the Karatagh plain.

The Pangong Lake district has been described at considerable length by Captain Godwin Austen in the *Royal Geographical Society's Journal* for 1867, and the additional

---

* 17,590 feet.   † 19,280 feet.

information I can now supply refers to the depth of the lake, an interesting subject of enquiry, and one which has, I believe, never been investigated with reference to this or any other of the Himalayan Lakes. A portable India rubber boat, which I had procured from England in the hope of ultimately floating it on Lake Lob, was the means which enabled Captain Biddulph and myself to make a section across the bottom of the lake. We arranged to halt a day for the purpose at Lukong.

The soundings were taken by Captain Biddulph with a fishing line, which I had carefully measured and marked before starting. We fortunately had a quiet day, and owing to the entire absence of wind and current there was not the slightest difficulty in getting these soundings most accurately.

Starting from the sandy shore at the west end of the lake we made for the island, lying about two miles off and situate nearly equidistant from the two sides of the lake. At 100 yards from the shore (*N.B.*—The horizontal distances are only rough estimations) the depth was 55 feet, the bank sinking gradually; 150 yards further on, the depth was 93 feet, and 200 yards further 112 feet; at 550 yards more, depth 130 feet, the maximum depth reached between shore and island. As we approached the latter the water grew rapidly shallow. At a distance of 400 yards from it, there was only 50 feet of water, and at 250 yards only 14 feet, from this point a shelving sandy bottom stretched up to the island, which consisted of a mass of rocks, about 150 yards in length and considerably less in breadth, of irregular shape, and extending in a direction parallel to that of the lake, *viz.*, from north-west to south-east. It was composed mostly of *calcareous tuhfa*, and in no place rose to more than four feet above the surface of the lake. The rock was very brittle and jagged, and in many places was covered with masses of shells, of which I brought away specimens: these shells appeared to me to have become only recently untenanted, but they were pronounced by Dr. Stoliczka to be many centuries old and to be fresh-water specimens. The island or rather islands (a short distance from the main rock in a south-east direction is a long sandbank rising only a few inches above the water) are submerged during heavy storms, for we found many fragments of wood, weeds, and even cattle dung, which had evidently been washed ashore from the mainland. Although the water was beautifully clear we looked in vain for fish, and with the exception of a species of bug, of which myriads were swimming about, we failed to see any animal or signs of life of any description. This is the more curious, as in a small stream which flows into the lake near Lukong there is an abundance of fish. The temperature of the water, which was decidedly brackish, was 55° F.; its color, a very pure blue where deep, and green where shallow.

From the island I pulled to the north shore of the lake, which lying under precipitous cliffs I expected to find much deeper. The water deepened out gradually to 107 feet at 300 yards from the island, and at about half way across, say half a mile from shore, there was a depth of 136 feet; at 250 yards from the mainshore we found 142 feet; at 100 yards, 114 feet; at 50 yards, 95 feet; at 30 yards, 80 feet; at 20 yards, 50 feet; at 10 yards, 12 feet. The boat, 12 feet long, was very well adapted for work of the kind, and in the absence of wind I was, without violent exertion, able to pull it along, carrying one passenger, at the rate of nearly, if not quite, four miles an hour, and this at an elevation of 14,000 feet above the sea. In fact the exertion required was considerably less than would be needed for walking at the same pace. The banks of the lake, which is about forty miles in length, showed evident signs of the water having formerly stood at a much higher level than it does at present: and there can be little doubt but that the valley along which the road passes from Tánkse up to the lake, was, at no very distant period, its main outlet; for although there is now a low pass, about two miles from the head of the lake, yet it is not much more than 100 feet above the present level of the water, and is moreover chiefly formed by detritus washed down from two side ravines, and of very recent formation.

With reference to my short excursion up the Kárákásh in search of a new road, I left Sugét on the morning of the 17th October, and was accompanied as far as Balakchi (9 miles) by Drs. Bellew and Stoliczka, who were paying a visit to the *jade* mines. After leaving them I marched on for two and a half hours to Gulbáshem, where I met Captain Biddulph on his way down the Kárákásh to Sháhidúla. My syce (groom) and guide, the only man in our united camps at Sugét, who professed to know of the existence of the road I was now searching for, had led me to believe that at about one *kos* (2 miles) from Gulbáshem, by turning up a lateral ravine on the south, a journey of 3 *kos* would bring me to a very low and easy pass, with an almost imperceptible ascent, from the top of which we were to look down upon the Kárátágh plains; and the evening we were at Gulbáshem he pointed out a neighbouring spur, beyond which, he said, the road turned off. What then was my annoyance when the next day we did not reach the turning until after a long and difficult march of 13 miles up the Kárákásh River, and even then, according to his account, the pass was further off than he had stated it to be the day before. I was extremely vexed at thus partially losing a day, for my camp was so far behind (I having arranged for a short march hoping to get up to the pass and back before night) that there was no time to move it much further on that day, and I had to halt at the entrance of the valley leading to the pass. I had now only two days left in which to visit the pass and return to Sháhidúla, as it had been arranged that I should have to be there on the 20th so as to be ready to leave with Colonel Gordon on the 21st.

Starting early in the morning of the following day and quitting the Kárákásh River (at a point 12,500 feet above the sea), we went up a broad open ravine, running south for 2½ miles, to a point where it divides into two branches of which we followed the eastern for about half a mile up a steepish ascent to a point where this also divides into two smaller ravines with a steep spur running down between them. These two ravines were bounded externally by precipitous banks several hundreds of feet in almost perpendicular height. There was apparently no practicable path along the lower portion of these defiles, but the road zigzags up the spur running down between them, and then follows the left hand one. The top of this first ascent was about 2,500 higher than our camp on the Kárákásh River.

From the top of the zigzag, the road up which, though steep, was good and practicable for laden ponies, we reached a more open country and the road now followed a broad grassy ravine with a gentle but steady rise. I followed this for seven or eight miles rising to about 16,800 feet, and there was still a stretch apparently of several miles, of gently undulating ground in front. As it was getting late in the day, and there was no time for me to go further, I climbed up a hill from which I obtained a view of the water-shed. I sent on the Pundit (the one who had been accompanying Captain Biddulph, and whom I had brought back from Gulbáshem) with instructions to follow the ravine to the water-shed, and to go beyond and fix by intersection either the Kárátágh Lake or the hill at Támba camping ground between Kárátágh and Áktágh, and, if possible, to return by Áktágh and rejoin the Head-Quarters camp at Sháhidúla. He succeeded the following day in passing the crest which turned out to be not more than a couple of miles from where I had left him, and in fixing by intersections from a distance the position of the hill before alluded to; but the guide having become seriously ill and no one else knowing the country, and the whole of the Kárátágh plain being several inches deep in snow, the Pundit was obliged to return *viâ* Gulbáshem rejoining the camp after I had left with Colonel Gordon. I returned myself that same evening to my camp at Fotásh in the Kárákásh River, not reaching it, however, till late at night and getting two or three falls on the road, which, although tolerably good by daylight, was in certain places, especially at the foot of the steep zigzag, by no means easy in the dark.

I do not think that this route is likely ever to come into general use, for although it is perhaps a better road than that between Sháhidúla and Kárákorum Brangsa (*viâ* the Sugét Pass), yet it is much longer. From Sháhidúla to Brangsa the road *viâ* the Kárákásh is at least 15 miles longer than the one by the Sugét Pass. Should, however, the road *viâ* Kizil-jilga and Kárátágh come into frequent use, I believe the Fotásh route might be employed with advantage, as there is very little difference in length of road, and grass and fire-wood are to be found in abundance all the way from Sháhidúla up the Kárákásh River, and for *two* miles up the (Fotásh) ravine, after which there is plenty of grass all the way to the pass as well as any amount of *Boortsee*.* There were numerous tracks, on the higher

---

* Boortsee is a small plant with large woody roots which grows wild in large quantities, and is in many places the only fuel obtainable by travellers.

80.—Party deputed to Kabul, 1st January 1874.

81.—Shrine of Sultan Satuk Bogra Khan at Artush, N. of Kashgar.

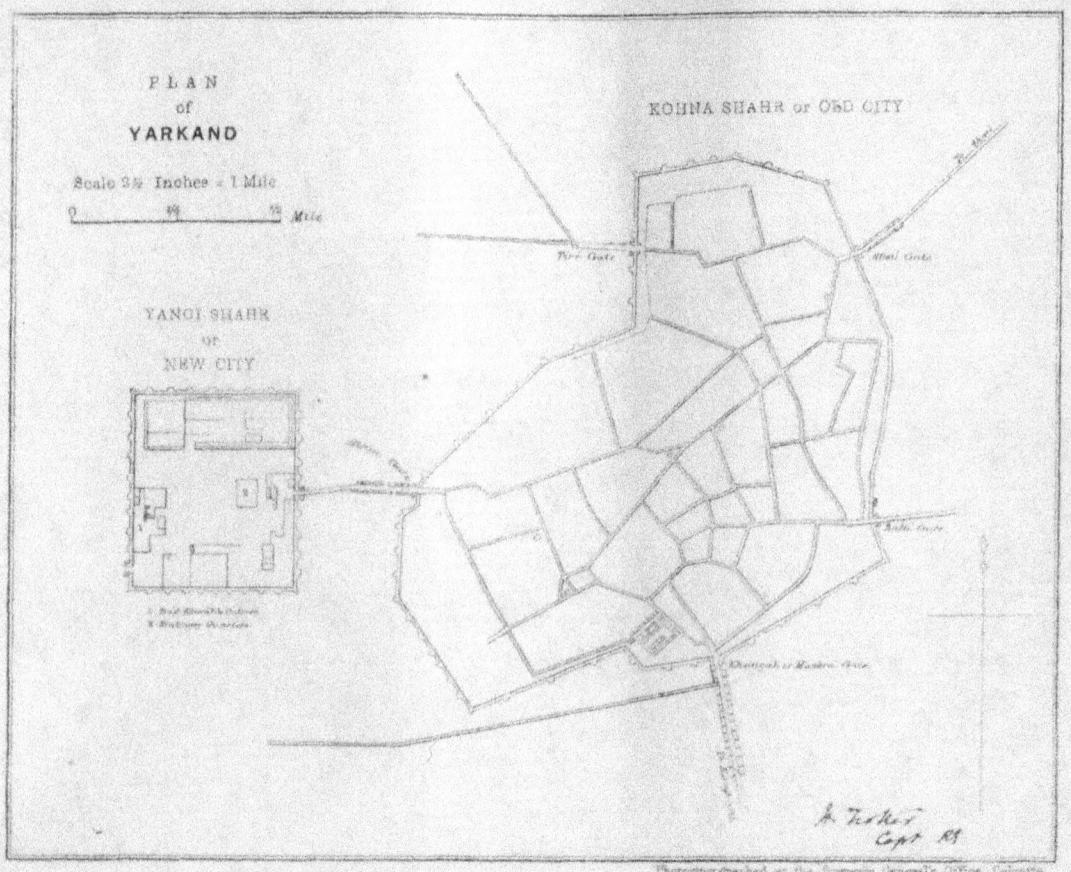

(241)

ground, of both *kiang* (wild horse) and wild yák,* a good evidence of the excellence of the grass. The road has evidently been occasionally in use, as it is marked in places where it might easily be lost in the snow by small stones placed in an upright position here and there on large rocks. My guide told me that he had only once travelled by it, when accompanying a very small caravan of not more than five or six ponies, on which occasion, there being a great deal of snow on the Sugét Pass, through which they feared they would be unable to force their way, they had resort to this alternative route to the Kárákorum. I have never met another man who was acquainted with this road, and its existence appears generally unknown to the Bhots of Ladákh.

I returned the following day to Sháhidúla (33 miles) visiting *en route* the jade mines between Gulbáshem and Balákchi. These have been described at length by the late Dr. Stoliczka.

It was deemed advisable, that from Sháhidúla onwards all open survey or display of instruments on the road was to cease. Permission was given, however, for one of the most experienced and wary of the Pundits to take observations quietly with a small pocket compass, with which he carried his route survey up to Yárkand. I also made occasional observations at night for latitude, so that a rough but tolerably correct survey of the road was obtained. On our return to India these restrictions were found to be unnecessary, and one of the Pundits proceeded from Yárkand *viâ* Sanjú and Sháhidúla, and without any attempt at concealment paced and re-surveyed the road carefully.

When we left Yárkand for Káshghar the Pundits were directed to remain behind, but one of them was permitted to follow a few days after, and made a very fairly accurate route survey up to Káshghar, the others had to stay in Yárkand until we left the country and returned (with the exception before mentioned of the man who went by Sanjú and Sháhidúla) with the advanced baggage party under Tárá Sing,† *viâ* the Kugiár and Kárákorum route. They carried a route survey from Yárkand up to Leh. The ground between Karghálik and Kúlunaldi (on the Yárkand River below Kufelong) had never before been surveyed. The Pundit who followed us to Káshghar did some good work; besides making an excursion with Tárá Sing to some of the neighbouring bazaars, whose position he was enabled to fix, he accompanied a party of the Mission on an excursion to the north of Káshghar in the Altyn Artysh Districts, making a traverse survey of the road. He also went with Colonel Gordon's party to Sirikol (Táshkurghan), and returned to Yárkand by himself, diverging from the route by which he had come at Chehil Gumbáz, whence he proceeded by the direct road to Yárkand, a distance of upwards of 100 miles, over ground that has never previously been surveyed. It was arranged for him to return to India *viâ* Khotan, a journey he accomplished most successfully. Prior to leaving the country he paid a visit to the Sorghák Gold Fields in latitude north 36°39′51″ longitude 82°42′ east of Greenwich, about 160 miles (by road) to the east of Khotan.‡ Returning thence to Kiria he found his way back to India by Polu, Noh, and the Pangong Lake, a route running from one and a half to two degrees to the east of the most easterly route we have hitherto possessed, *viz.*, that traversed in 1865 by Mr. W. H. Johnson in his journey to Khotan. Details of the route followed by the Pundit are given in the Appendix, as are also his observations for latitude and height.

Description of routes between Ládakh and Turkestan.

It is not proposed to give here a detailed description of the lines of route followed by the members of the Mission on their travels between Ladakh and Eastern Turkestan,‡ but a brief comparison of the various lines of road between the two countries may not be uninteresting.

---

* A yak is a species of mountain ox which only lives at great altitudes, and is much used for the carriage of merchandize over snow and ice. On ice they are far more sure-footed than any other beasts of burden.

† Treasurer to the Mission.

‡ Details of the roads traversed by the members of the Mission will be found in Section G. of the Appendix to this Chapter.

For practical purposes these routes may be divided into three, viz.—

The Kàràkorum route with variations (leading to Yárkand).
The Changchenmo route with variations (leading to Yárkand and Khotan).
The Rudokh (or Changthang)* route (leading to Khotan).

The Karakorum route may be subdivided into two, the Zamistáni or winter and the Tabistáni or summer road, and although these have a few marches and camping grounds in common, and cross the great water-shed between India and Central Asia at the same point, the Kárákorum Pass, yet they diverge from each other throughout the greater part of their courses. As a rule it may be laid down that the winter road passes wherever possible along and over the beds of rivers, which in the cold season contain but little water, and are generally frozen over: these streams, which form no obstacle in winter, are often impassable torrents in summer. It is therefore no matter of surprise that in spite of the intense cold and hardships of a winter journey the merchant often selects that season for his travels. The first great obstacle to be encountered after leaving Leh, both in summer and winter, is the well known Kailás range, which is said to run in one unbroken line from the sources of the Indus to the junction of that river with the Shyok. To the north of Leh this range divides the drainage of these two rivers, and is one of the most formidable obstacles to be encountered by the traveller to Turkestan. In winter it is crossed by the Digar La† (17,930 feet above sea level), a very difficult pass, in crossing which it is necessary to employ either yáks or men for the carriage of goods. A party of the Mission went over it in June, and even then there was snow lying on the top while ice and snow combined to render the passage difficult along a distance of some miles.

The summer road crosses the Khardung or Leh Pass,‡ almost north of Leh, and is 17,900 feet in height. This Pass also is impracticable for laden ponies, and is so difficult that late in June on our return journey from Yárkand, after descending the Nubra river, it was deemed advisable to go a long detour viâ the Digar Pass in order to avoid the still more formidable obstacles on the Khardung. This made the journey from Sati to Leh 42 miles instead of 29. After crossing the Kailás range and entering the Shyok valley the traveller has now before him the great Muz-tagh§ or Kárákorum Range. In the winter by following the narrow, winding, and difficult valley of the Shyok river he reaches the Kárákorum Pass, a distance of 114 miles; in the course of this portion of the journey the frozen surface of the stream has to be crossed no less than 36 times. In winter this can easily be done, as it is generally bridged by snow and ice, but in summer owing to the floods caused by the melting glaciers an entirely different route has to be adopted, and instead of ascending the Shyok the traveller descends that river to a short distance below Sati and then ascends the Nubra river, a large tributary fed from glaciers in the same mountain mass that supplies the Shyok.

The Shyok is crossed in boats near Sati, where in the summer it is a very large and rapid river. Passengers and goods are carried over in boats, while the baggage animals are made to swim across. Many of the latter are drowned in crossing.

Ascending the Nubra valley, one of the most fertile and richly cultivated in Ladakh, the traveller goes as far as Changlung (10,760 feet), almost the highest village in the valley, and situated about 40 miles above Sati. The merchant generally takes this bit very easily, advancing by short marches of ten miles each, in order to make the most of the supplies of grain and excellent lucerne grass, both of which are here obtained in abundance. The caravans from Yárkand often halt a week at Panamik (a large and flourishing village a few miles below Changlung) to feed and rest the baggage animals after the hard work and scant fare that they have had on the journey. It is here that on the outward journey the real difficulties of the march commence. Instead of following one stream right up to its source in the Kárákorum Pass, as is done in the winter route, the traveller has first of all to cross a

---

* Changthang, in the Thibetan language means 'northern plain."
† "La" is the Thibetan word for "Pass."
‡ Sometimes also called "Laoche La."
§ In Turki "Muz-tagh" means "Ice Mountain" and "Karakorum" is the equivalent of "Black gravel."

very high and precipitous hill just above Changlung village. The road ascends by a zigzag and rises rather more than 4,000 feet in a length of about five miles, the stiffest bit of ascent on the whole journey to Yárkand. After reaching the top of the *Karawal* Pass (so called from a karawal or outpost erected many years ago at this spot to enable the Ladakhis to defend their country from invasion from the north) the road descends into the Sásér stream and then passes up it to the Sásér La, a pass over a mighty ridge covered with snow and glaciers which runs down from the great mountain mass forming the eastern extremity of the so-called Kárákorum Range and separates the waters of the Nubra* from those of the Shyok. This pass (17,820 feet) is one of the most difficult on the whole road, and is rarely, if ever, free from snow, while the road passes through, over, and alongside of glaciers for many miles.† The road from the top of the pass follows the bank of a stream which enters the Shyok River at Saser Polu, a halting place on the winter road. The Shyok is here crossed with difficulty, as is proved by the fact that two Ladakhis were drowned there when returning from laying out supplies for our return journey.

The road now ascends a tributary stream on the left bank of the Shyok crosses a low pass, and at Murghi Camp joins another stream which flows from the Dipsang plains into the Shyok River. It was at this point, at a height of 15,200 feet, that the late Dr. Stoliczka breathed his last, after having traversed the Kárákorum Pass and the perhaps still more trying Dipsang plains which rise to an elevation of about 18,000 feet above the sea. The intense cold of this bleak and dreary waste prevents this route from being adopted in winter, during which season the caravans follow the Shyok River from Saser Polu up to Daulat Beguldi (Turki for "Daulat Beg died," an appropriate name for so desolate a spot). This camp, which is situated in the north-west corner of the Dipsang plain, marks the junction of the winter and summer routes, which unite here, and cross the Kárákorum Pass 11 miles above the camp, continuing together a distance of 40 miles further to Ak-tágh. The Kárákorum Pass, though 18,550 feet above the sea, is by no means so formidable an obstacle as is generally supposed. It is always free from glaciers, and in summer from snow. The ascent on both sides is gentle, and the road good, so that, although it forms the water-shed between Hindústán and Central Asia, it is less of an obstacle to the merchant than the Digar, the Khardung, the Saser or the Sanju Passes. From it the road passes along the Kárákorum stream (one of the headwaters of the Yárkand River) to Ak-tágh, traversing the comparatively open ground on the west of the Karatágh‡ plain. At Ak-tágh the roads again diverge, the winter route continues down the Yárkand river, which is crossed 18 times between Ak-tágh and Kulúnaldi,§ a distance of 74 miles. At the latter place this road ascends the range that was called by Hayward the western "Kuen Luen," and crosses it by the Yangi-Diwan (or "New Pass," 16,000 feet) into the Tiznáf River, which it follows for 41 miles to Chiklik. The road is here taken over one of the northern spurs of the Kuen Luen by the "Tupa"‖ or Ak-Korum Pass (10,470 feet), whence it descends along the banks of a gently sloping stream to Kugiar, a considerable village (containing 400 or 500 houses) on the borders of the plains of Eastern Turkestan, and 41 miles distant from Karghalik, a large town situated at the junction of the Zamistáni (*viá* Kugiar), and the Tabistáni (*viá* Sánjú) routes. It was by the Kugiar road that the Mission returned to India. The road had been closed for several years previously by order of the Yárkand authorities owing to the risk to which travellers were exposed of being plundered and sold into slavery by the wild Kanjud robbers (of Hanza and Nagar), who coming down from their fastnesses to the north of Bunji and Gilgit used to render the whole valley of the Yárkand

---

* At the head of the Nubra valley a road passes over the main Kárákorum chain by the Chorbat Pass and descends into the Yárkand river at Khufelong. It was formerly much used by the Baltistan merchants, but is now rarely employed. It is probably not less than 19,000 feet high, and is always closed for at least nine months in the year, and is at no times practicable for laden animals.

† On the return journey of the Mission several hundreds of coolies were employed for some weeks in preparing the road over this pass.

‡ "Karatagh"="Black Mountain."

§ "Kulunaldi"="the wild horse died."

‖ In Turki Tupa means "hill," and Ak-Korum "white gravel."

River from Kúlúnaldi up to Ak-tágh, utterly unsafe for travellers or merchants unless in large parties and well armed.*

It was in the month of June that the Pámír party returned by the Kugiar route somewhat too late in the season to traverse it with safety, and considerable danger was incurred from the daily increasing floods of the Tiznaf River, which after noon used to come down with such force as frequently to close the road. At this season also the southern slopes of the Yangi-Diwán (Pass) are very difficult to traverse and somewhat dangerous, as the recently dead bodies of numerous baggage animals seen by us on the return journey too surely testified. The floods of the Tiznaf are probably worse in June and July than at any other time of the year, as after that period the snow on the lower mountains has nearly all been melted. The Yárkand River, on the other hand, above Kúlúnaldi, being fed more generously by glacier streams is more difficult later on in the hot weather. We found that although there was a much larger body of water in the Yárkand than in the Tiznaf River, yet in the former the bed was broad and level, and was crossed without difficulty; whereas in the Tiznaf the bottom is narrow and generally composed of large stones and boulders which render its passage very difficult.† The road crossed it nearly 20 times in one march, or about once in every linear mile of its course. A month earlier in the season (May) the river was frozen and was ascended by an advanced party of natives without difficulty.

42. Returning to Ak-tágh, the point of divergence of the two routes, the summer road passes thence over a spur of the Kuen Luen by the Sugét, a tolerably easy pass (17,610 feet), from which the road descends along a winding stream to the Kárákásh river which it strikes a few miles above Sháhidúla.‡

At Sháhidúla the Kárákásh river winds through the Kuen Luen Range.§ The road follows along it for some 20 miles, and occasionally crosses it. In summer its passage is effected by merchants with considerable difficulty. The Kárákásh flows in the direction of Khotan, and between the river and Yárkand lies a formidable spur from the Kuen Luen, which has to be crossed. The traveller, if he be here unfettered by political obligations, has the choice of three roads before him, viz., by the Kilik, the Kilian, and the Sánjú passes. Traders are seldom or never allowed to use the former which is said to be the easiest and

---

* *Note.*—These robbers, apparently from fear of the Káshghar Amír, have of recent years ceased to infest this road, but it is reported that since the return of the Mission from Yárkand, the Kunjudis have attacked a nomadic tribe called Phakpos,¹ who inhabit numerous valleys on the west bank of the Tiznaf river. The road by which these robbers advance must pass over numerous glaciers, and crosses the Karákorum range by the Shingshal Pass, a short distance to the west of the Shigar or Muztagh Pass. The road from Shingshal descends the Kum stream and joins the road from the Muztagh Pass at a distance of one and a half marches to the north of the latter. After three short marches more the Yarkand River is reached at Dahn-i-Bazar Darah, three short marches below Kulunaldi (on the same river), a frequently used halting place on the road between Karákorum Pass and Kugiar. The Shingshal Pass is said to be easier than either the Chhorbat or the Shigar Passes, and is at times passable by laden horses. The Muztagh Pass (which was estimated by Godwin Austen at 18,400 feet, and by the Schlagentweits at 19,000 feet) road lies for a great distance over glaciers, and is difficult and dangerous. It is occasionally used by the Baltis,¹ who have a colony in Yárkand, and who traverse this pass when returning thence to their own country.

¹ Or natives of Baltistan, a mountainous district inhabited by Shiah Mussulmans, and lying to the north-west of Ladakh.

† On one occasion during the return journey, when I had gone on a couple of days ahead of Colonel Gordon's party so as to have more time for survey, I had, in order to insure security from water, placed my chronometers in my pockets instead of in the mule trunks where they were usually carried. It was the first time that I had done so, and as ill-luck would have it, I twice got parted from my horse in deep water while searching for a ford, and had to swim for my life with my chronometers in my pocket. On the same occasion my horses and baggage animals were cut off from all supplies by the floods, and were for more than 36 hours without tasting food.

‡ *Note.*—At Sháhidúla is a small fort which during the time of the disturbances in Eastern Turkestan (which resulted in the accession of the present King) was occupied by a detachment of the Maharaja's troops from Kashmir. These were subsequently withdrawn and the place is now generally recognized as belonging to the Kashghar ruler. The Kirghiz of Sanju have of late years constantly occupied the Karakash valley up as far as the great bend above Sora, and occasionally ascend some of the valleys to the south, leading up to the Karatagh plain; in many of these valleys there is abundance of grass and wood.

§ Dividing it according to Hayward's nomenclature into Eastern and Western Kuen Luen.

shortest; it follows the course of the Toghra, a considerable stream which enters the Kárákásh nine miles below Sháhidúla. The floods of this stream in hot weather often detain travellers a considerable time on its banks. The Kilik Diwan (Pass) is crossed in the 3rd or 4th march from Sháhidúla, and after going over another low pass the road joins the Kugiar route at Beshterek, one day's march to the south of Karghálik; little is known of this road, but it is said that grass and wood are to be found at every stage. It was once much used by the Baltistan merchants who are settled in Yárkand.

Nearly three miles below where the Togra-su enters the Kárákásh River is the fort of Ali Nazar, where the Kilian road leaves the Karakash valley and passes up an open ravine in a north-west direction. This road is sometimes used in the summer as an alternative to that over the Sánjú Pass; it is somewhat higher than the Sánjú Pass, but, although impracticable for laden horses, is not so difficult to traverse. The Kilian pass is crossed in the second day after leaving the Kárákásh. The road follows the stream from the pass for four marches when it debouches into the Turkestan plain at the village of Kilian, two marches to the south of Bora on the road between Sanju and Karghálik.*

The third and most frequented road from Sháhidúla is viâ Sánjú. It leaves the Kárákásh 20 miles below Sháhidúla at Mazár Abú Bakar, from which place the road ascends to the summit of the Sánjú (also happily named "Grim") pass which, although not more than 16,700 feet above sea level, was decidedly the most difficult obstacle encountered by the mission on the road to Yárkand.† Its summit is never free from snow and ice, and is impassable by laden ponies. Yaks have always to be used and are collected from all quarters for the passage of a large caravan. From the pass the road descends to the Sánjú or Sarikia River, which it follows to the large and scattered village of Sánjú, on the borders of the Great Turkestan Plain. Occasionally in the hot season the Sánjú River is so flooded in its lower course as to become impassable, in which case a detour is made by a road which crosses a small spur by the Chuchu Pass (11,800 feet), after which it follows the Arpalek stream to near Sánjú. Thence a good and level road leads to Yárkand, a distance of 122 miles, and meets the Kilian route at Bora, and the Kilik and Kugiar routes at Karghálik.

Returning now to the Changchenmo route from Leh to Turkestan, on this also the Kailás range has to be crossed, but further to the east than on the Karakorum route. The road ascends the Indus for 20 miles, and then goes up a tributary stream for 13 miles to Zingrál, from which place the range may be crossed either by the Chang La (17,600 feet), or the Kay La (17,900 feet). By the former and easier road of the two it is 23 miles from Zingrál to the large village of Tankse, situated on one of the tributaries of the Shyok River. By the Kay La foot passengers shorten the road by some six miles. The roads over both passes, although free from glaciers, are very difficult; and it is usual, although not absolutely necessary, to employ yaks in carrying goods across.

Tánkse is the last place on this road where supplies are procurable, and is, by the shortest route, 350 miles from Sánjú, the first large village encountered in Turkestan. For the whole of this distance supplies of grain, both for men and horses, have to be carried, and at a great many halting places neither grass nor fire-wood is procurable. From Tankse after passing Lukong at the head of the Pangong Lake, the road crosses a lofty mass of mountains, by the Lankar or Marsemik La (18,400 feet), a very high but in summer by no means a difficult pass. It is free from glaciers, and generally clear of snow during the summer and early autumn. Descending into the Changchenmo valley and crossing the stream, a tributary of the Shyok, the road ascends a minor stream to a point eight miles beyond Gogra, from which there is a choice of three different roads all leading on to the Ling-zi-thung‡ Plains. The most westerly path ascends the Changlung Pangtung Pass (18,900 feet), crosses the corner of the plateau and descends into a deep ravine running along the stony and very difficult bed of a stream§ (which ultimately finds its way into the Shyok River), ascends again, and skirts the

---

* In former years the Kilian would appear to have been the most frequented route, but it is now little used.
† Several mules were lost here, although their loads had all been transferred to yaks.
‡ or Ak-sai Chin.
§ The march down this ravine was one of the most trying encountered during the outward journey.

western border of the gently undulating Ling-zi-thung Plain), in traversing which the traveller crosses, almost without knowing it, the water-shed between India and Central Asia. After passing the water-shed the road crosses a small stream, one of the head waters of the Kárákásh, and then goes over a spur (Kompás La) 18,160 feet in height and descends into the bed of Kárákásh River, which it strikes, at an elevation of 17,400 feet above the sea and follows to Kizil Jilga.

The portion of the road between the Changlung Pass and Kizil Jilga is perhaps the most trying part of this route. The great elevation and consequent bitter cold is much aggravated by frequent snow and a piercing wind which blows from morning to night; the long dreary marches cause one to arrive, after dark, at camps where there are scant supplies of fuel and no grass; occasional ice beds block up the whole road, one of these extends for three miles down the Kárákásh River; all combine to try most severely both man and beast.

At Kizil Jilga the road just described joins an alternative road (taken by Captain Biddulph on the outward journey), which, leaving the usual route a few miles north of Gogra, crosses the Changlung Barma Pass (19,300 feet) on to the Ling-zi-thung plains, along which it passes at a still higher elevation than the western road. It descends into the Kárákásh River at Kizil Jilga; the greater elevation makes this road perhaps even more trying than the western route.

The third route from Gogra before alluded to leaves the Changlung valley 8 miles above Gogra and the Ling-zi-thung plain may be reached by either the Changlung Barma or the Changlung Yokma Pass a little further to the east, and of about the same elevation. This is the pass taken by Mr. (now Sir Douglas) Forsyth in his first mission to Yárkand. By it, the road followed by Captain Biddulph (striking the Kárákásh River at Kizil Jilga) may be joined, but a more northerly route passing over a succession of elevated plains was taken by the former mission, and the Kárákásh River was met a few miles above Sora at the sudden bend that the river takes when its course is turned towards the west (in north lat. 35° 55') by the Kuen Luen Range. From this point the road followed the River to Sháhidúla.

In addition to the intense cold the principal objection to all three routes skirting or passing over the Ling-zi-thung (also called Aksai Chin) is the extreme elevation at which the traveller has to remain for so many marches: the cattle are exhausted by this, and too frequently suffer in addition from the pangs of hunger and thirst. These difficulties nearly brought the first mission to Yárkand to a disastrous end, and the same causes have proved, and will probably continue to prove, sufficient to deter the experienced merchant from following this road. The older, shorter, and better known route by the Kárákorum is likely always to be preferred by the merchant even in summer, whereas in winter an attempt to traverse the Ling-zi-thung plains must almost always result in disaster.

From Kizil Jilga the road follows the Kárákásh River to Chong Tash (or "Great Stone"). From this point the eastern variation, taken by Captain Biddulph, follows the Kárákásh River right down to Sháhidúla, a distance of 166 miles, while the western or more direct road is only 113 miles in length, and although in the latter there are two high passes viz., the Kárátágh (17,700) and the Suget (17,600) to be crossed *en route*, yet they are neither of them difficult ones. The Sugét Pass may be avoided by going over the lower and still easier pass of Fotash by which the Kárákásh River is struck one march above Gulbashem. In the circuitous line from Chong-tash down the Kárákásh, the road is bad, but there is the advantage of plentiful supplies of grass and fuel which are almost altogether wanting on the Kárátágh line. The Ling-zi-thang routes meet the Kárákorum summer route at Aktágh or at Sháhidúla according as the western or eastern variation is adopted.

At the angle formed by the Kárákásh River above Sora, when turned by the Kuen Luen range, the traveller can proceed to Khotan direct (a distance of 160 miles or 11 marches) by crossing the Kuen Luen Range by the Yangi or Elchi Diwan (crossed by Mr. Johnson in his journey to Khotan in 1865), and estimated by him at 19,500 feet in height; after passing this there is another formidable glacier pass, the Naia Khan (height 18,659 according to Johnson) which has to be crossed before reaching the plains. The Elchi Diwan is said to be open for only three months in the year.

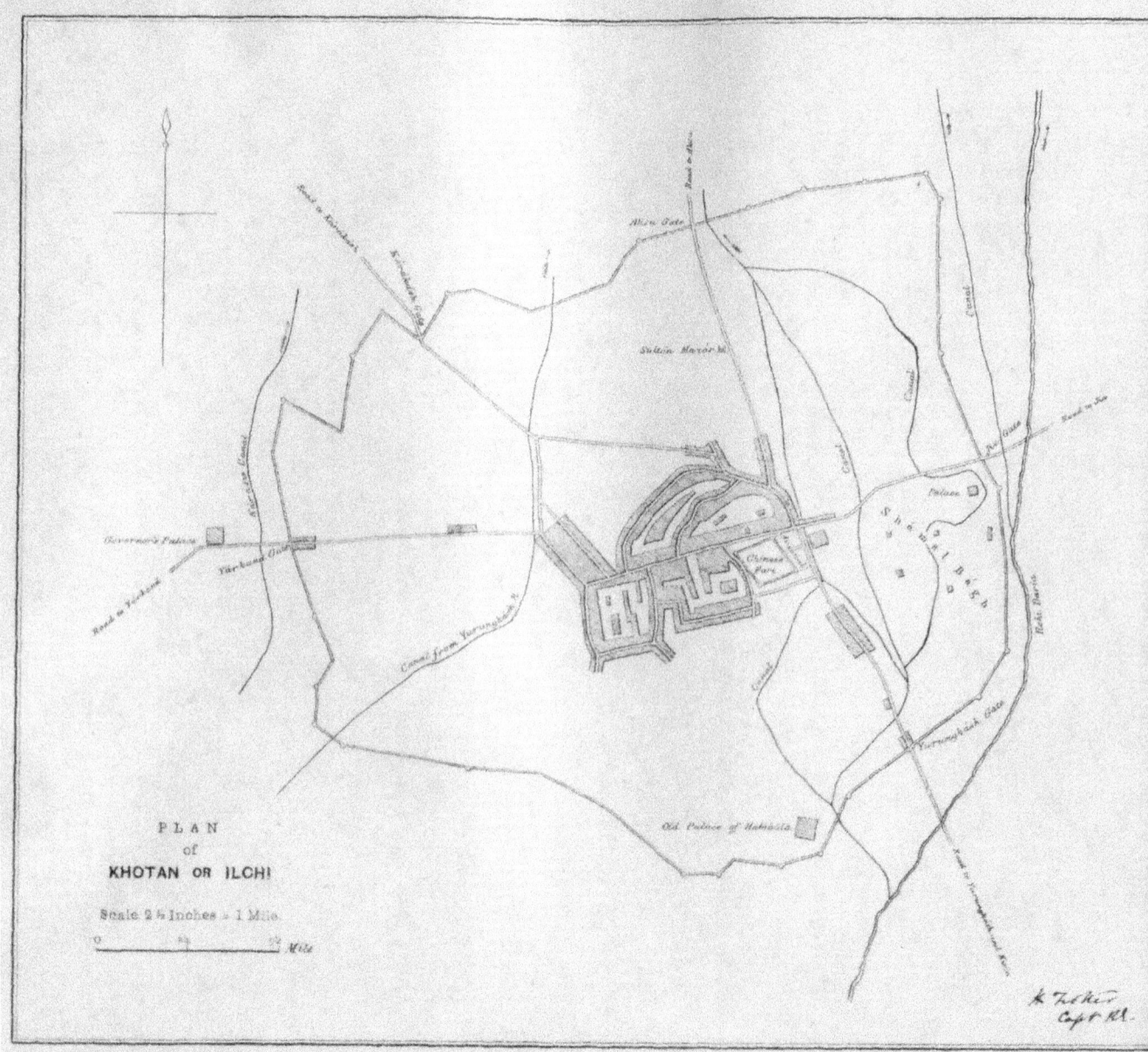

On the Kárákásh River above Fotash is a camping ground called Sumgal, from which Robert Schlagintweit crossed the Kuen Luen range by the Hindu-tásh Pass, estimated by him at 17,379 feet high. At the top of this Pass is a glacier much *crevassed* and extremely steep. It is a long and difficult march from its foot, to the village of Bushia, where are numerous tents and caves occupied by Kirghiz, and where supplies can be obtained in large quantities. It is eight marches thence to Khotan and the road is described as bad. The road by the Hindu-tásh Pass can only be used by foot passengers.

From all accounts the ordinary trade route between Khotan and Ládakh in former years was, as at present, *viâ* the Sánjú and Karakorum Passes. The road from Khotan follows that to Yárkand as far as Zanguia, whence a road goes to Sánjú village direct. Another road from Sháhidúla to Khotan lies down the Kárákásh River, and, going over an easy pass, emerges at Dúba,* a large village said to lie about 20 miles to the south-west of Piálma (on the Khotan and Yárkand road.) The road down the Kárákásh can only be used in mid winter.

We now come to consider the extreme eastern route, *viâ* the Chang-thang or "Northern plain." Of this road we have a survey by Kishen Sing Pundit, one of the most important geographical results secured by the mission.† Details will be found in Appendix, Section G., and the road itself is shown on the map accompanying this report.

A traveller from Leh to Khotan might follow the route by the Pangong Lake, along which the Pundit travelled, but he would more probably take a short cut from Lukong to the Mangtza Lake, following the ordinary Changchenmo route to Yárkand as far as the point where that road leaves the Changchenmo valley. Passing up the latter, he would make his way eastward to its head, where an easy pass is known to exist leading on to the high table land beyond. By adopting this road he would save forty miles over the more circuitous road by Noh. From Mangtza the road lies over a series of high plateaux varying from 16 to 17,000 feet in height, crossed here and there by low ridges which rise somewhat irregularly from the surface of the plain which contains numerous lakes, most of them brackish. In latitude 35° 7' north the Pundit crossed at a height of but little more than 17,000 feet the water-shed of a snowy range, which may perhaps be the true eastern continuation of the Kuen Luen. From the north of the pass the Kiria stream takes its rise; the road follows down it as far as Arash (16,000 feet), but again ascends to the Ghubolik plain, which (17,000 feet above the sea) connects the snowy range just alluded to with another somewhat lower range to the north. This last ridge is a buttress of the vast Thibetan plateau, and in descending the Polu stream from the Ghubolik. At Diwan ‡ (17,500 feet) to Polu, a distance of 28 miles (including windings), there is a fall of about 9,000 feet. Polu is a small village in the Khotan district and from it Khotan (or Ilchi) city may be reached either by the direct road (by Chihar Imám) which skirts the feet of spurs from the elevated plateau above, or the traveller may proceed down the stream to Kiria by the route followed by the Pundit.

Throughout the whole of the road from Khotan to Leh traversed by the Pundit fuel was abundant everywhere, and there was only one stage where there was not a good supply of grass. These facts would indicate the line as one well adapted for the native merchant, to whom time is of no great value. As far as I can learn however from enquiry it never has been used as a trade route on a large scale, the chief reason I believe being fear of the Chang-pas§ or Tagh-lik, wandering tribes of Tartars, nominally subject to the Chinese officials at Gartokh and Rudokh, but probably practically only so far subject to them that they would abstain from committing violent aggression on parties travelling under the protection of those authorities.

---

* Duba is shown on Klaproth's map as a large place about half way between Záwá and Sánjú.

† The only previous account we have of this road is one derived from native information supplied by Mr. R. B. Shaw, and which was published in the proceedings of the R. G. S., No. III. of 1872. This account agrees remarkably well with that given by the Pundit, and every march can be followed on the large scale map I have before me as I write.

‡ Or "Sulphur Horse Pass" so called from its being used by the Polu people when bringing sulphur to Khotan. Sulphur is excavated in large quantities from the ground near the lake in the Ghubolik plain.

§ Chang-pa in Thibetan means *Nord-man* while the Turki name for the same people is *Taghlik*, i.e. *Mountaineer*.

Habibúla, who was elected King of Khotan when the Chinese were turned out of the country, sent messengers to try and open up this route in 1864. They were seized by the Chang-pa and compelled to return to Khotan with the threat that any subsequent explorers would be put to death. The inhabitants of Keria and Polu go as far south as Ghubolik to procure sulphur. They also go west of this towards the head of the Yurung-Kash (or Ilchi) River where they search for gold and jade, but it would appear that although the Khotanese claim the country up to Lake Yeshil Kul, the head of the Kiria River, as their boundary, yet practically from fear of the Chang-pas they never go quite so far to the south. On the other hand the Chang-pas who probably have equal reason to fear the Turks from the plains, would appear not to wander further north than Rikong Chumik, the ridge to the north of which separates their grazing grounds from plains on the north, through which flows a considerable stream, passed by the Pundit, asserted by his guide to be the head of the Yurung-Kash River.* It would thus appear that owing to the mutual hostility of the two races there is a large tract of neutral ground which is never occupied by one or the other, extending from Rikong Chumik to Ghubolik; here the Pundit saw large herds of yák, antelope, and jungle sheep (*oves ammon*), which had apparently never been scared by the sight of man. Near Rikong Chumik were the remains of numerous huts; others were frequently seen along the road, but fortunately for the Pundit, he did not meet or see a single human being between Ghubolik and Noh, a distance of 244 miles, a circumstance which enabled him to complete his route survey up to Noh† without interruption.

The newly acquired knowledge of this road may perhaps lead to important practical results, but not until our relations with the Chinese Empire, and their too independent subordinates in Thibet, are placed on a more satisfactory footing than they are at present. It is apparent by combining the results of this survey with other information collected by the Survey Pundits during the past few years, that a road exists between the plains of Hindustan and Turkestan which entirely avoids the territories of the Maharaja of Cashmere, and which in the summer months may be traversed without once crossing snow, or without encountering one really difficult pass, such as we know to exist on the Karakorum and Changchenmo routes. Leaving the plains of India at the ancient city of Najibabad (between Hurdwar and Moradabad), the starting point of the old Royal Road stated by Moorcroft to have crossed these same mountain systems, a good road about 210 miles in length, and only crossing one low pass,‡ leads to the Niti Pass (16,676 feet high) over the main Himalayan range. Descending from the Niti Pass, due north into the Sutlej valley, and crossing that river at Totling (12,200 feet) by the iron suspension bridge still existing (said according to local tradition to have been constructed by Alexander the Great), and crossing by the Bogo La (19,210 feet) into the Indus valley at Gartokh (14,240 feet), the road would then follow that river to Demchok.§ Thence it would go over the Jara Pass due north to Rudokh and Noh, and by the newly surveyed route to Polu and Khotan.

Estimating the distance from Najibabad to the Niti Pass at 210 miles, thence to Noh at 275, and from Noh to Khotan (*vid* Keria) 446 miles, we have a total distance of 931 miles

---

* In the map which has been prepared for submission with this report I have not shown this stream as flowing into Yurung-Kash, but I think it not at all improbable that it may find its way through a gap which I have left in the Kuen Luen (just between the letters E. and N. of Luen). I would have inserted it, but it hardly appears consistent with Mr. Johnson's statements as to what he saw when ascending these Kuen Luen peaks in 1865, although, on the other hand, the fact that the river he crossed at Karangolak was a very large and rapid stream would indicate that it probably came from a considerable distance; knowing also as a fact how the Karakash cuts through the same range at Shahidula and how extremely difficult it is to form an accurate idea of any mountain range when viewed from a single point, I am inclined to regret that I did not show this stream in my map as the head waters of the Yurung-Kash or River of Khotan.

† From Noh he tried to get to Rudokh, but was not permitted to do so; in fact the inhabitants tried to compel him to return by the way he had come, and it was with great difficulty that he at last got permission to go to Leh direct. Anticipating a search by the first people he should encounter, he had, when nearing the village of Noh, concealed his instruments and papers in a bush. He was duly searched, but of course nothing was found, and he afterwards succeeded in again getting possession of his valuables. In Thibet the great difficulty encountered by persons entering in disguise is always on the frontier, where the examination is very strict. When once allowed to pass into the interior of the country there is little to fear.

‡ The Langar Pass 6,500 feet high which is on the 3rd day's march from the plains.

§ A more direct route exists from Totling *vid* Dankhar to Demchok.

82.—Shrine of Sultan Satuk Bogra Khan at Artush, N. of Kashgar.

83.—Karawal (Frontier outpost,) at Tangi, Tar in the Thian Shan, 60 miles N. of Kashgar.

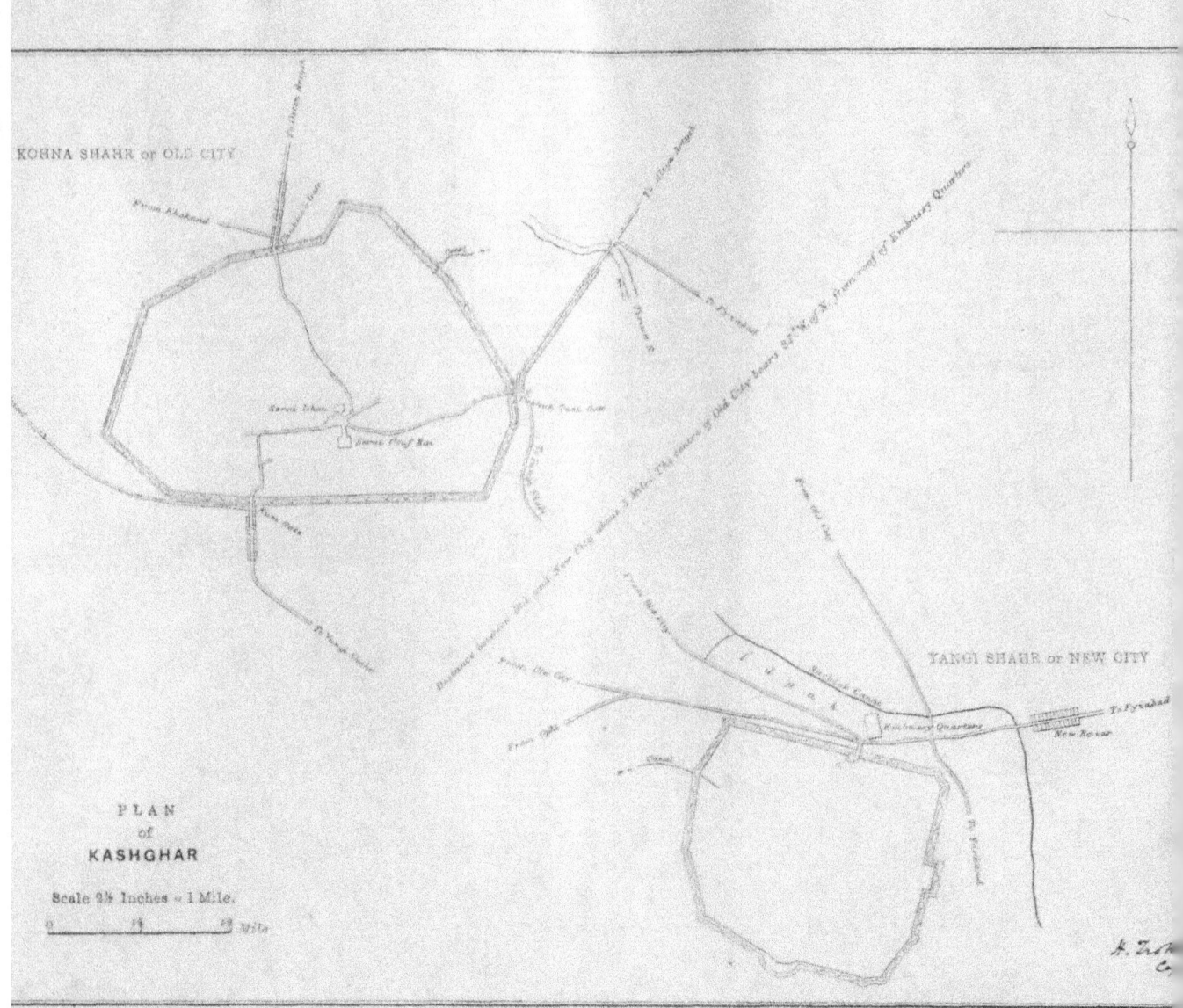

between Najibabad and Khotan, and this even might be considerably shortened by taking the direct road from Polu to Khotan.

[The ancient Royal road probably followed the above to the suspension bridge at Totling, and thence to Rudokh and Noh, whence a road now exists which passes *viâ* the head of the Changchenmo valley and Nischo into the Ling-zi-thung plains, down the Kárákásh river and over the Sánjú Pass to Sánjú (or Sarikia)* which is half way between Yárkand and Khotan.]

Summarizing our knowledge of the lengths of the various physically practicable routes from Hindustan to Turkestan we find that the distances are:—

		Miles.
From Amritsir to Leh *viâ* Rawul Pindi and Srinagar	...	635
,, ,, to ,, *viâ* Kangra	...	522
,, ,, to ,, *viâ* Sealkote and Cashmere	...	575
From Leh to Yarkand *viâ* Ling-zi-thung and Karakash River	...	584
,, ,, ,, *viâ* Changchenmo and Karatagh	...	527
,, ,, ,, *viâ* Karakorum Pass and Sanju (summer route)	...	445
,, ,, ,, *viâ* Karakorum and Kugiar (winter route)	...	472¼
,, ,, ,, *viâ* Noh, Polu, and Khotan	...	839
,, ,, Khotan *viâ* Karakorum and Sanju	...	415
,, ,, ,, *viâ* Ling-zi-thung and Elchi Pass (Mr. Johnson's route)	...	437
,, ,, ,, *viâ* Noh, Polu, and Kiria	...	637
,, Amritsar to Yarkand by the road followed by the Mission, *i.e.*, *viâ* Rawul Pindi, Srinagar, Leh and the summer Karakorum route	...	1,080
,, Najibabad to Khotan *viâ* the Niti Pass and Western Thibet	...	931

At some distant day it is not impossible that the last named road may form the highway to Turkestan, but as long as Europeans are rigorously excluded from Western Thibet we cannot hope that this consummation will be realized.

Excursions in the neighbourhood of Káshghar.

During the winter at Káshghar I was permitted to make two excursions in the neighbourhood, both of which have enabled me to add something to our geographical knowledge. The second trip was over ground, which, as far as I am aware, has never hitherto been explored, and is very incorrectly represented on existing maps.

During the first of these trips, which occupied us from the 31st December to 10th January, Dr. Stoliczka and myself, under the orders of Colonel Gordon, visited the Russian frontier at Lake Chadyr Kúl, about 110 miles north-west by north of Káshghar. We had hoped, from the extreme point reached by us, to have struck off to the Terekty Pass on the east, and to have returned by the Terekty Forts to Káshghar. Unfortunately difficulties were placed in the way of our doing this, and we had to return to Káshghar by the same road that we went.

Prior to starting, permission was given by the Ámír for me to use my instruments on the road, and I may here mention that from this time forward during the whole of my stay in Káshghar territory I was at liberty to use openly what instruments I chose. Of course a certain amount of caution was necessary. Many of the officials with whom I came in contact were doubtless very suspicious as to what it all meant, yet in no case did any one attempt to hinder my taking observations or notes, although in many cases they endeavoured to neutralize the value of my work by giving me false information on geographical subjects. I allude to this

---

* The three points that have indicated this as the line of Royal Road are:—

1st.—Moorcroft's statement that the road started from Najibabad and emerged in the Turkestan plains at Sarikia (which I identify with Sanju) half way between Yárkand and Khotan.

2nd.—The existence of an iron suspension bridge at Totling said to have been constructed by Alexander the Great (*vide* Major Montgomerie's Report on Trans-Himalayan explorations made during 1867).

3rd.—The statement made by Muhammed Amin, "Punjab Trade Report, Appendix IVA." that—"the old route taken by Moghul conquerors from Tashkend towards China passed through the Aksai Chin. Traces of it are still seen."

matter, once for all, as one which gave me much trouble and annoyance during the whole of my stay and travels in Eastern Turkestan.*

It must not be supposed, however, that because I was given permission to use instruments I have been able to turn out very accurate surveys of the countries traversed. The rapidity with which we have always travelled has made it impossible for me to do more than carry on a continuous route survey, checked by frequent astronomical observations taken at night; and even this is sometimes meagre and incomplete owing to the intense cold which we experienced throughout almost the whole of our travels, which made even the handling of a prismatic compass at times an impossibility; this, coupled with the shortness of the winter days, the occasional excessive length of the marches, many of them through snow, and the necessity on these trips of always cutting down both the baggage and the limited establishment of camp servants with which I originally started, must be held to excuse any incompleteness in the maps that I furnish.

During our first excursion the marches we made were as follows:—

From Yangí-Hissár (Káshghar) to—

		Miles.
1. Besák (Upper Artysh District)	...	26
2. Chung Terek	...	20
3. Chakmák Forts	...	20
4. Balghun Báshi	...	10
5. Turgat Bela	...	15
6. To Turgat Pass and hill above Chadyr Kul and back to (5)	...	32
7. Back to Chakmak	...	25

and back to Káshghar by the same road. I succeeded, with no little difficulty, in keeping up a continuous route survey, and took observations for latitude at four points on the line of march, the most northerly being at Turgat Bela (north lat. 40° 23′ 53″) on which occasion, while observing, the thermometer stood at 10° below zero (Fahrenheit), and an intensely bitter wind was blowing. Later on the same night the thermometer fell to 26°, while inside the *akoee*, (Kirghiz tent) where we slept, it was as low as 8½°, a temperature hardly adapted for carrying on an elaborate Survey.†

We left Yangí-shahr (the new city of Káshghar) and, going northwards, crossed the River Kizil by a good wooden bridge. At a distance of 5½ miles we passed on our left the old city of Káshghar, beyond which we crossed the River Taman by another bridge. This stream passes immediately to the north of the town, and joins the Kizil at a short distance to the east, the two forming the Káshghar Darya. At the time we passed there was but little water in either stream, that little being frozen, so that it was impossible to form any idea of the size of the vast mass of water that must come down in the summer time. The left bank of the Taman is covered by tanneries and cemeteries; the road runs nearly north and enters a narrow lane between two mud walls, on either side of which are enclosed gardens, fields, and hovels. These continue for some four miles, when the road emerges on to an open stony plain forming a very gently rising slope up to a small spur from a low range of hills running nearly due east and west, through a gap in which, formed by the river Artysh, the road passes. On the north side of the range is the wide and fertile valley of the Artysh, a name given to

---

* I may mention that in Kashghar I had been questioning a sepoy, who professed to know all about the Alai and adjacent country, on the subject of the supposed double issue from Lake Karakul. He positively assured me that the waters from it flowed west into the Oxus. A few days subsequently, when talking on the same subject, he assured me with equal confidence that he had seen the place, and that its waters flowed east to Kashghar. He subsequently admitted that he had never been within 50 miles of the lake!

† It may be imagined that taking observations in the open, to stars, with the thermometer standing below Zero, is not a very pleasant occupation. After handling the instrument for a short time, sensation, so far as one's fingers are concerned, ceases, and during a set of observations it is necessary to rush frequently into the adjacent tent to restore circulation over a fire. The recorder, on such occasions nurses the hand lantern with great care, and although the ink is placed inside the lantern, yet it would freeze on the pen between the lantern and the paper. I was eventually obliged to allow a pencil to be used on such occasions. My faithful Madras servant "Francis" also experienced no little difficulty in getting the lamps to burn properly. The oil becomes very thick from the cold. The air holes had to be carefully enlarged for high altitudes, so that while admitting more air, they might still be small enough to prevent the high winds which were frequently blowing, from extinguishing the light.

the whole district, which consists of several small townships scattered over the valley, in one of which, Besák, some five miles beyond where we crossed the river, we put up for the night.

From Besák our road lay for a few miles over fields lying in the broad Artysh valley, but we soon entered that of the Toyanda River, which flows from the Turgat Pass. This stream divides into two branches at the place where it debouches into the Artysh plain— the upper one flows nearly due east, and is extensively used in irrigating the fertile valley; the south or main branch flows into the River Artysh,* which passes along the south side of the valley, and after being joined by the Toyanda stream, cuts through the hills to the south at the gap alluded to in the preceding paragraph. On entering the Toyanda valley, here about two miles wide, we may be said to have fairly entered the Thien Shán mountains, the hills we had traversed on our previous day's journey being an isolated ridge. In marching up this open valley we had in view on our left the sharp serrated edges of the Ming-yol Hill, a prominent object in the panoramic view from the roof of the Embassy buildings in Káshghar; in front of us lay a range of snow-covered peaks also visible from Káshghar; these formed part of a small range running parallel to the main chain (east to west). We passed the old Chinese outpost of Teshek Tásh, or Khitai Karáwal, and a little beyond it the village of Tupa, (or Tapú) near which place through a large ravine on the left, is a road said to come from Kizil-boya, a fort near the head of the Káshngar River. A little further on through a broad open valley we reached the picturesque camping ground of Chung Terek, a Kirghiz village, where were a number of akoees pitched for our reception. From this place the scenery gets much bolder and the road passes between precipitious hills rising to a height of some 3,000 feet above the valley, through which a march of 20 miles brought us to the Chakmák Forts; the road goes steadily up hill, a gentle and regular ascent which continues all the way up to the Turgat Pass, and is passable by laden camels even in "mid-winter." Eight miles short of Chakmák we came across the "Mirza Terek," "Past Kurghán," or "lower fort," a carefully constructed work, which would prove a serious obstacle to an advancing foe. Here as is the case at Chakmák, the overhanging heights are so precipitous and inaccessible that it would be almost impossible for an enemy to effect a lodgment.

The road across the Russian frontier by the Turgat Pass is good, and the slope easy. The road right up to the crest of the Pass was entirely free from snow.† On the slopes near the Pass is an almost inexhaustible supply of grass.

There are two roads over this range of hills converging on a point a few miles north of the Chakmák forts—one from the Suyok Pass, two days' journey in a north-west direction, is little more than a path, and cannot be traversed by horsemen; but the other from the Turgat Pass, about 30 miles to the north of the junction (Suyok Karáwal), is now the main caravan road between Kashghar and the Russian settlement of Almáti (Fort Vernoye), and may be said to be practicable all the year round, although somewhat more difficult perhaps in summer, when there is much more water in the River Toyanda, which has to be crossed some forty times in the course of the journey.

The Suyok Pass is stated on Russian authority to be 12,800 feet above sea level. A fort called Yagachak, covers some road in the direction of the Pass, west of Chakmák, but the accounts of its position were so vague and discordant, that I was unable to fix its position even approximately. A road along a ravine about half-way between Chakmák and the Past Kúrghán was said to lead to it.

Along a ravine lying to the south of the Chakmák forts a road runs across the hills, connecting them with the Terekty Fort, nearly due north of Kashghar. It lies on the shortest road between the Náryn Fort (Russian) and Káshghar viâ the Bogushta and the Terekty Passes.

For 25 miles above Chakmák, the road took us along the course of the frozen stream, passing through volcanic rocks, to Turgat Bela, a little short of which the nature of the country alters, and the precipitous hills are replaced by gently undulating grassy slopes abounding

---

* The Artysh River is said to rise near the Terek Diwan, on the road between Kashghar and Khokand.
† In January.

with the "Ovis Poli" (Ovis Argali of the Russians).* The weather was now intensely cold; one of our party got his fingers frost-bitten from the cold contact of his rifle, and when I stopped for a few seconds on the top of a ridge to get a view of the country, and to record the reading of my aneroid, my hands and feet became entirely numbed.

From Turgat Bela (at an elevation of 11,030 feet above the sea), we rode to the Chadyr Kul Lake, and back to camp the same evening (about 32 miles). Starting early in the morning with the thermometer several degrees below zero, we rode 13 miles to the Pass up a gentle ascent through the broad and open valley, until within a mile of the crest, where the slope though still very easy, is somewhat steeper, there being a rise of about 400 feet in the last mile. On the left of our road was a range of lofty, bold, precipitous peaks, running while near the pass from north-east to south-west, but subsequently in a more westerly direction. The height of these peaks varied from 13,000 to 15,000 feet. On our right were low undulating hills extending away eastward as far as we could see. On reaching the pass (12,760 feet) we did not immediately see the lake, but had to advance for about three miles in a northerly direction, when we came suddenly into full view of the whole lake and the range of mountains beyond, a magnificent panorama. There are two nearly parallel ranges of mountains, the Turgat (sometimes called Koktaw—in Russian maps "Káshghar Daban") on which we stood, and the Táshrobát to the north, both portions of the Thien Shán range, which westward, like the Kárákorum eastwards, seems to lose its identity and merges into several comparatively unimportant chains of which it is impossible to say which is the main one. The Chadyr Kul lies between these two ridges, and, as far as one can learn from Russian sources, there is no drainage out of it, but several small streams run into it. Their maps include the lake within their boundary, which they place on the crest of the southern or Turgat range, the peaks and passes of which are of about the same average height as of the northern range. The Káshgharees (in Káshghar) claim the lake, and maintain that the Táshrobát range forms the true boundary, but their officials on the spot appeared to take a different view, and maintained that the lake was the boundary. The Ak-sai River, which rises a few miles east of the lake and between the Táshrobát and Kok-tan ranges, flows into East Turkestan, while the Arpa, which flows from a corresponding position near the west end, finds its way into the Syr Darya. This would indicate the lake itself as a good natural boundary, although it must be remembered that the Ak-sai plains to the east, the head waters of the Ak-sai River, which afterwards becomes the Kokshál, are undoubtedly occupied by Kirghiz subject to Russia.

The lake is about fifteen hundred feet below the pass, which would give the former an elevation of 11,300 feet, a result agreeing very nearly with that arrived at by the Russians. From the undulating nature of the low hills to the east of the pass, it was impossible to judge of the direction of the range.

Of course from a single view of the lake and the mountains beyond it, it was impossible to form any accurate idea as to their size, but according to the Russian maps the lake is of oblong shape, about 14 miles in length, and 5 or 6 in breadth at its widest part; its greatest length being from west by south to east by north. From where we stood about three miles north of the pass, the east extremity of the lake bore a little to west of north, while the Táshrobát Pass as pointed out by our guides lay about 17° further to the west. The lake was covered with ice, and the sleet which lay on the surface made it difficult to distinguish the edge of the lake from the nearly level plain by which it is surrounded, and which was covered with a white saline efflorescence. A single horseman near the edge was the only living object visible, a curious contrast to the other side of the pass, where within a few miles of the crest, we had seen a herd of several hundred Cossack ponies grazing at the foot of the precipitous hills before alluded to.

---

* These extensive grassy slopes, somewhat resembling the English downs, are a very curious feature of the country, and not only attract the Kirghiz as grazing grounds for their cattle, but are equally sought after by the large herds of Guljar, in one of which Dr. Stoliczka counted no less than eighty-five.

84.—The Kirghiz of Tiggur Matti and Bash Sugun in the Tian Shan.

85.—Group at Kalti Aylak in the Artush District.

The caravan road which we had followed from Kashghar lay across the plain in front of us. Beyond it is the Táshrobát Pass about the same height as the Turgat, but somewhat more difficult. A traveller who had crossed it in March told me that the road was then very bad, and difficult for equestrians, but I think his account must be somewhat exaggerated, as the camel caravans from Almáti traverse it without much difficulty, and the Russians do not write of it as a difficult pass. Between the Náryn Fort and Káshghar, a distance of 180 miles, there are only these two passes—both about 13,000 feet in height. There is a third pass, the Ák Cheta, between the At-báshi River and the Náryn Fort on the Náryn River, but this is, I believe, sometimes avoided by following the Náryn to its junction with the At-báshi, and then proceeding up the latter river to Táshrobát. When we visited the country early in January there was no snow on the ground, but we were singularly fortunate, for a traveller two months later in the year complained of a good deal of snow, while Baron Osten Sacken wrote on a former occasion that his party suffered much from cold and snow in July.

A shorter and more direct road between Náryn and Káshghar is that over the Ák Cheta, the Bogushta, and Terekty Passes, stated by Captain Reinthal to be not more than 134 miles in length, or eight days' journey. The passes, though all about the same height, i.e., between 12,000 and 13,000 feet, are more difficult than on the ordinary caravan road via Táshrobát and Turgat Bela. The Bogashta Pass is sometimes closed in winter. It is covered on the Kashghar side by the Terekty Fort. We never had an opportunity of visiting this fort, which lies, as far as I could make out, nearly due east of Chákmak and due north of Káshghar, and although we must have passed within a few miles of it during a subsequent trip in the Artysh districts, my guides studiously avoided pointing it out, and actually, on one occasion even denied its existence. The distance between Fort Náryn and Vernoe (Almati), a military district centre, with large garrison and supplies, is 180 miles by the shortest road, which goes over three passes, all between 12,000 and 13,000 feet in height.

I had hoped that we should have been able to return to Kashghar, over the undulating plateau to the east of the Turgat Pass, and by the Terekty Fort, but we had now to retrace our steps to Kashghar by the road we had come. A notice of the return journey is therefore unnecessary.

Whilst our party under Colonel Gordon was visiting the Chakmák Forts, another member of the Embassy, Captain Biddulph, paid a visit to *Maralbashi* on the direct road to Aksu. A description of his journey will be found elsewhere. During my absence Kishen Sing Pundit, was despatched in company with Sirdar Tara Sing (Treasurer to the Mission), on a visit to Khanarik and Kizil-boia, large villages lying to the south-east of Káshghar. The Pundit carried on a traverse survey wherever he went, which has thrown some light on the intricate maze of rivers and canals which irrigate the villages that are thickly scattered over the whole of the ground visited by him.

My second excursion was to the north-east of Káshghar. The Amír having granted permission for a visit to the Artysh districts, I was enabled to accompany Sir Douglas Forsyth and party during their stay there, and on their return to Káshghar, I made a rapid journey in company with the late Dr. Stoliczka towards Ush Turfán. Unfortunately on this trip, after leaving the head-quarters party the weather was much against us. Bitter cold was accompanied by snow and clouds, which combined to conceal the rocks and hills from both Dr. Stoliczka and myself, still, as the ground traversed is, as far as I am aware, entirely new to geographical science, a short account ought not to be uninteresting.

We left Yangí-hissár (Káshgar) on the 14th February for Bu Miriam Kháná, a village about 11 miles north-east of the old city of Káshghar. The first three miles of one road lay across a cultivated and well irrigated plain, and brought us to the banks of the Kizil or Káshghar River, at a place where it was easily fordable; after another four miles we reached the large village of Awát, near which large quantities of salt are collected and taken to the Káshghar market. Four miles of level plain brought us to Bu Miriam, where we learned that our baggage animals had, by mistake, taken the road to Ostyn (Upper) Artysh, and that we had no chance of seeing them that day. We accordingly pushed on to Altyn (Lower) Artysh, where we found comfortable quarters and a good dinner, provided by our host, the Hakim of the district. Both were welcome, as our own things did not come in till next morning, much to my special annoyance, as the chronometers had all run down in the night, a great misfortune, as I had been very anxious to determine a good *travelling rate* for them, and with that end in view, had taken very careful time observations before departure from Káshghar.

About a mile from Bu Miriam, we crossed the small river coming from Ostyn Artysh, the upper part of whose course I have traced in an earlier portion of this narrative. It (or rather what small portion remains after irrigating the large and fertile village of Beshkerim, which we passed on our left) falls into the Káshghár river near Khush Toghrák, about 25 miles to the east of where we crossed the stream. Five miles further on the road traverses the same low range of hills which, south of Ostyn Artysh, is pierced by the Artysh stream. This ridge, composed of clay and shales, is several hundred feet in height at Ostyn Artysh, but gradually gets lower and lower as it runs eastward, until it dwindles into nothing, and gets lost in the level plain a very short distance to the east of where we now crossed it; a few miles further on, after crossing a small stream supplied from springs on the west, we reached the village of Altyn Artysh, a march of 22 miles.

This village partakes of much the same character as Ostyn Artysh, and, indeed, nearly all the villages I have seen in East Turkestan, consisting of a number of small hamlets, scattered about the plain, at intervals from each other varying from a quarter of a mile to a mile. Each hamlet consists of a number of scattered farm-houses, each farm having its separate irrigation canal, its trees, its fields, and out-houses, and forming the residence of a family containing generally from four to a dozen souls. In a central position is the bazar, with long rows of stalls on both sides of the road, somewhat resembling that of an Indian village, but absolutely untenanted except on the weekly market day. In its neighbourhood the Hakim, who generally owns a somewhat better house than his neighbours, administers justice. Sepoys, if the village be important enough to contain any, are generally quartered near the residence of the Hakim.

The valley in which the two Artyshes are situated runs from west to east, and is throughout about eight miles in breadth; bounded on the south by the low ridge of hills before mentioned which comes to an end south-east of Lower Artysh, it is confined on the north by another and somewhat higher range, which extends eastwards from Teshek Tash on the Chakmák road, to nearly opposite the termination of the southern range, when bending towards the north-east it runs away towards Kalti Ailák, another large group of villages about 22 miles east by north of Altyn Artysh. The valley opens, where loosened from its bounds on the south, into the large desert plain which forms part of the one vast plateau of Eastern Turkestan. The one difficulty, in all this country, is want of water, and one cannot help admiring the ingenuity with which the inhabitants have made the best use of the scanty supply of this precious fluid. Where there is a sufficiency the country is one close net-work of irrigation channels, and in the spring, in these places, one unbroken mass of trees and verdure testifies to the excellence of the system. In the Artysh valley there is water in moderation, and, as far as I could learn, nearly every drop, in the spring and summer, is used in irrigation. In the winter, one sometimes comes across tracts of marshy land, but these are generally caused either by springs which rise in the neighbourhood, or by leakage from canals in autumn, at which time the water is no longer required for irrigation, and the saline nature of the soil causes breaks down and consequent leakage, which it is not considered worth while to repair until the following spring.

In Altyn Artysh, I was informed that there were in all about 3,000 houses forming the following hamlets:— 1, Meshak; 2, Sborchí; 3, Takyun; 4, Langar; 5, Kichingiz; 6, Mai or Táter; 7, Kijja; 8, Bayámát; and 9, Kukíla. It is more thickly inhabited than other parts of the surrounding country, as it forms the seat of the District Government (which includes under it Kalti Ailák and other villages). It is well watered, but the population being large, it barely produces grain sufficient for its own consumption. This deficiency is, however, made up from the neighbouring village of Kalti Ailák, where there is plenty of good rich soil, and a smaller proportionate population, due to an occasional want of water the supply of which is often insufficient to irrigate the whole of the lands. The headman of Kalti Ailák bitterly complained to me, that where there was plenty of water good land was deficient, and where little water was met it was often the reverse. This village contains about 1,000 houses, divided into the following petty districts:—Kurghán (the chief centre), Golok, Khush Toghrák, Kuyok, and Jainak.

There are two streams which enter the Artysh valley, the Toyanda before described, and the Bogoz River; a branch of the former irrigates the villages of Beshkerim and Bu Miriam, where the greater part of the water is absorbed; a small remnant however flows eastward, and in favorable seasons finds its way to Khush Toghrák, a southern hamlet of Kalti Ailák, where it mingles with the canals from the Kashghár River, employed to irrigate that village. The north branch of the Toyanda River is probably almost all expended in irrigating the fields of Upper Artysh, but it is possible that a small quantity may find its way down to Lower Artysh, or at all events may help to form the supply for certain springs which issue from the ground west of that village. The main water-supply, however, for the latter village is derived from the Bogoz River, which rises in the Chakmák range of hills, about 30 miles to the north, but derives a large portion of its water from hot springs a few miles north of the village.

On the 17th of February we started for Tangitár, making a march of about 20 miles in a northerly direction. Following the banks of the River Bogoz, a narrow but somewhat rapid stream, easily fordable, we reached after three miles the range of hills forming the north boundary of the valley. Here on a small isolated mound stand the ruins of an old Chinese fort; a mile beyond this the stream divides, the left (west) branch is the main one and comes from the snows; the temperature of its water was 42°, while that of the right hand one coming from the warm springs before mentioned was 57°. Our road followed the east branch; a path along the other goes to Chung Terek in the Toyanda valley, distant about 32 miles. Continuing our road along a ravine passing through the range of hills (which here have a breadth of about three miles from north to south), we at last emerge on to another extensive plain extending like that of Artysh from west to east, and about six miles in breadth from north to south. On the west it was bounded by the hills above Chung Terek, and extended along eastward, as far as one could see, for several miles, merging into the open plain, where the ridge to the south comes to an end. On our right, near where we entered the valley, is the village of Argu, said to contain 800 houses, but from its appearance I should not have judged it to hold half that number. Its water-supply is derived partly from springs, partly by irrigation from the Bogoz River. The road crosses in a north-west direction over a perfectly bare, stony plain, which continues away on the left as far as the eye can reach; one or two houses only near the bank of the river break the monotony and barrenness of the landscape, neither grass nor wood being elsewhere visible. After six miles we enter a gap through which the Bogoz River issues from another range of hills, also running from west to east. Here is another Chinese Karáwul* in good preservation. The road passes to the north along the Bogoz valley through the hills for about nine miles, to Tangitár, 5,800 feet above sea level. The valley was in places of considerable width, and contained much wood and grass, as a natural consequence of which numerous Kirghiz encampments were scattered over it. We passed successively those of Buábi, Budák, Kuktam, and Jai Ergiz. On our right were some very precipitous hills, forming the ends of spurs running generally from west-north-west to east-south-east.

Our camp at Tangitár, after a march of 20 miles, was at the entrance of a defile, where two small fortifications are perched up on rocks commanding the south entrance. If larger, they might possibly be of considerable use for purposes of defence, but as they cannot hold a garrison of more than 20 men, they could only be useful in keeping in check badly armed Kirghiz or bands of robbers. They are built on the limestone formation which here commences, the hills through which we had hitherto been marching having been composed of clay and gravel.

The situation of such forts, both here and in other parts of the country, are, I think, convincing proofs of the fact that the Chinese in their dealings with the Kirghiz and other robber tribes, nearly always acted on the defensive, and did not attempt to hold the hilly tracts, or claim sovereignty over them. They apparently used to content themselves with posting strong

---

* Karawul is a Turki word signifying "outpost."

guards on their frontier *inside* the lines of hills, which they appear generally to have given over entirely to the wandering tribes. The same facts apply to the hills on the west of the great Turkestan plain, where the line of fortified posts along their base was considered the boundary. This forms a striking contrast to the policy of the present Ruler, who keeps all these tribes in subjection, has disarmed them, and has replaced the former anarchy by peace and quiet.

On the 19th February we continued our way up the stream, here called Tangitár,* through a very narrow defile somewhat difficult to traverse on account of its being filled with ice. After marching a mile or so along this due north, the valley opens, and through a stony ravine on the right comes the main stream from the north-east, while opposite to it, on the left, is an open ravine along which a road is said to go to the Terekty Fort, which *I believe* lay about 10 miles off in a north-west direction. Our own road continued due north for a while, when it edged round to the east over a spur, on rounding which we discovered that we were on the borders of another large open valley, the third we had entered since leaving Káshgbar. The view from this spur was very fine; in front of us lay a vast open valley bounded on the north by the snow covered Chakmák range of hills, which, visible about 40 miles off on our left, above the forts of the same name ran in a bold irregular outline from west-south-west to east-north-east, the crest of the range passing about 16 miles to our north, and running away eastward as far as we could see, apparently getting lower and lower as it did so. The broad grass covered valley before us was about 6,000 feet above the sea, and ran parallel to the crest of the hills. Along the middle of it is a low broken ridge running in the same direction dividing the valley into two parts. Small, bare, bold isolated hills also dotted the plain, which was nearly level, draining slightly towards the south. We halted, after a short march of only 10 miles, at Túghamati, a camping ground situated in the plain, along which we continued the following day in a direction east by north for about 15 miles to another Kirghiz camping ground, called Básh Sogón (head of the Sogón). The road was so level that it was almost impossible to say where we crossed the water-shed which divides the Bogoz basin from that of the Sogón River. The latter has, at this time of the year, its chief source in springs near our camp, but as well as the Bogoz, it must in the hot season get a good supply of water from the snowy range to the north. From a high hill to the south of our camp, I obtained a fine view of the low ranges to the south, but to the north I could not see over the snowy range. The general run of the hills to the south, was from west by south to east by north. It was formed by a succession of nearly parallel ridges starting abruptly from the plain in front, and dying out gradually as they approached the east. A few miles north-west of Básh Sogón, is a largish village called Arkála, near which large numbers of ponies, sheep, and cattle were grazing. We also saw signs of cultivation, which is occasionally carried out in years when there is sufficient water-supply from the melting snow. Throughout the plain there is a good deal of grass and low jungle, and near the camp I saw some small deer (kík), whilst others of the party had good sport in hawking partridges and hares. The nights we spent on this plain were very cold; at Túghamati the thermometer outside the akoee fell 20° below zero and stood at 16° below zero when I rose in the morning. This great cold was, I think, in great measure attributable to the presence of saline matter in the soil, for our elevation was not much over 1,200 feet above that of Káshgbar, where the corresponding minimum was very much higher.

The drainage of the east portion of this large valley runs into the Sogón River, but the supply of water from the hills is apparently very small, owing I presume to the very moderate snow fall. The river, after it emerges into the plains north of Kalti Ailak, wastes away and leaks through crevices in the stony ground, and the Hakim of the latter place assured me that wells had been sunk, but had proved to be of no use, so that the whole of the water from the Sogón runs to waste, if at least we except the small quantity used by the Kirghiz higher up. This diminution in the size of rivers as they descend, is one of the chief characteristics of the country, and occurs in all minor streams that have come under my notice. Of course much of this is due to irrigation, which necessarily carries off large quantities of water, but the stony soil has also much to answer for; on the other hand the frequent appearance of large springs, giving

---

* Tangitár signifies "narrow defile."

considerable supplies of water, and often issuing from the open plains at long distances from the mountains, may account in great measure, if not fully, for the water thus lost in its early infancy.

On the 20th, our march lay in a south-east direction, following the circuitous course of the Sogón through some low hills, for about 15 miles, to Ayok Sogón (foot of the Sogón), a Kirghiz encampment situate at the east of another small plain, covered with grass and jungle and the abode of numerous Kirghiz. This camp is near the direct road from Káshghar to Úsh Túrfán, and it was here arranged that Dr. Stoliczka and myself should leave the main party, and push on in the direction of Úsh Túrfán; as far as the limited time and commissariat at our disposal would permit. It was stipulated however that we were not to go beyond the limits of the Artysh district.

The marches from Káshghar to Úsh are as follows:—

	Miles.	
Káshgar		
Altyn Artysh	22	
Kalti Ailak	22	
Kyr Bulak	33	
Jai Túpa	20	
Ui Bulak	27	
Tigarek	17	
Akchi	19	Cross the Belowti Pass between Tigarek and Ákchi.
Knyok Tokai	22	
Safr Bai	22	Road from Safr Bai to Bedul Pass across the head of the Naryn River to the Zauku Pass, and thence by Karákul to Issighkal.
Karáwul	22	
Ush Túrfán	16	
Total	242	

From Jai Tupa to Úsh there is said to be an alternative road—

Jai Túpa.
Pichan.
Piklik, over Pass to
Guljár Báshi.
Káshghar Tokai.
Kotan Serik.
Úsh Túrfán

This road is somewhat longer than the other, and strikes the Kokshal River a few miles east of Ákchi.

Leaving Ayok Sogón after an early breakfast on the 21st, we passed for a mile over the plain in a south-east direction, and struck the main road; then, turning east went up a ravine, through some hills across a low pass (5,670 feet), and found ourselves on the western edge of another of these large characteristic level plains, 15 miles across from north to south, where we entered it, and extending away eastward further than we could see. It was bounded on the north by our old acquaintance, the Chakmák range, and is probably a continuation of the Túghamatí valley, which apparently narrowed considerably to the east of our camp at Básh Sogón. The main range was here following a more northerly direction than when we had last seen it, but the peaks were involved in snow and clouds, from which they never emerged during the whole of our trip. On the north, at a distance of about 15 miles, was the Kirghiz village of Karghil, the only habitation visible. Shortly after entering the plain we passed through what proved to be the commencement of a very large forest, composed almost exclusively of poplar trees (toghrak), and a small shrub called "balghun." The poplars were stunted in growth, and although evidently in a natural state, they bore the appearance of having been pollarded. As timber I should not think the wood would be of much value, but it would furnish Káshghar with a plentiful supply of firewood, when the more convenient stocks in its neighbourhood have been exhausted.

Passing along in a north-east direction, a low range of hills at a distance of about three miles bounded the plain on the south. At about 12 miles from our last camp, still traversing forest, we passed on our left the camping ground of Kyr Bulak—inhabited in the summer by Kirghiz, but now untenanted—onwards we pushed our way over a most monotonous flat, and through the bare bleak stems of trees, until after six miles, we came to a slightly rising ground called *Dung Jigda Bulák*,* where a little water was oozing from the ground indicating a spring which, with the presence of a "jigda" or wild olive tree, gave the place its name. On over the plain, which in summer would have been pretty enough, but now was dried up and desolate. The forest ceased within about two miles of our camp at Jai Tupa, which was marked by a clump of trees standing conspicuously on an eminence above the plain. We reached it about dusk, after a march of fully 32 miles, through a very heavy sandy road which so delayed the mules carrying our baggage, that they did not arrive till eight o'clock the next morning, having stopped over night, exhausted in the jungle, about five miles short of our camp. Fortunately, we found an old Kirghiz Musjid, in which we went dinnerless to bed, protected, however, from the wind, and from the snow which fell during the night. The officials at the head-quarters' camp had assured us that we should find Kirghiz and supplies at this place, but there were neither one nor the other, and the Diwan Begi,† who accompanied us, spent his whole night (after his day's ride) in going over to the village of Karghíl beforementioned, and hunting up Kirghiz, with whom he returned about daybreak, bringing supplies for man and beast, both of whom had fasted for at least 24 hours. It snowed all the morning, but about noon we pushed on about five miles in a north-east direction to a Kirghiz camp called Jigda, where we obtained further supplies. Snow and clouds prevented our seeing any of the hills around. The forest recommenced about half way between Jai Túpa and Jigda.

The following day (23rd) we pushed on for 22 miles to Ui Bulák, having obtained from the Kirghiz two or three camel loads of grain and other supplies for our future consumption, as we were told we should not come across any more habitations. Just before starting we felt a slight shock of an earthquake, the only one I have noticed during our stay in Turkestan. Our general direction was now north-east. About two inches of snow lay on the ground, and more was constantly falling. After five miles, we saw a low ridge on our right, running parallel to the road, at a distance of about six miles. At its base in what was apparently the lowest part of the valley, was a strip of forest, a portion of the large one that extends right away to beyond Kyr Bulák, a distance of at least 32 miles. Although long, this forest is comparatively narrow, varying, as far as I could judge, from half mile to two or three miles in breadth. The southerly ridge beforementioned is said to extend easterly to Kálpin (about 15 tash)‡ a village between Ush Túrfán and Marálbáshi, and to be about five tash from the latter place. At Kálpin, like other ranges that I have traced, it gets lost in the level plain.

Our road now lay through low jungle (balgún) with little or no grass, and at about 12 miles from camp, we reached the limit of the plain and ascended a low spur running from the main range; ground bare and stony. Following this spur in a north-east direction we crossed into an open ravine, about half a mile broad. Ascending it for a short distance we arrived at our camp, near which there was a good deal of grass and plenty of fire-wood. Thermometer at night down to zero.

The next day was fortunately very fine, for we had a hard though interesting journey before us. Leaving our servants and baggage ponies behind at Ui Bulák, Dr. Stoliczka and myself continued our journey in a north-east direction, ascending the ravine, for about eight miles the road way very stony, and some inches deep in snow. Near the head of the ravine we crossed a low pass on a spur from the main range. Descending on the other side we crossed the lower slopes of the main range, passing along which for two or three miles, we came upon another large plain about six miles broad lying between two long spurs. On the further side of this plain, at Tigarek, we had the good luck to come unexpectedly across a Kirghiz encampment, belonging to Ush Túrfán. Leaving the "Dah-báshi,"§ who accompanied us as escort, to make preparations for our dinner, we procured a Kirghiz guide and started to try and reach before dark the Belowti Pass, which is on the main range that separates the drainage of the ground we had been traversing from that of the Aksai or Kokshál river, which, rising east of Chadyr-kul, flows nearly due east to Úsh Túrfán and Áksú. A march of nine

---

* In Turki *Bulák* is the equivalent for *spring*.
† The designation of the official who was deputed to make arrangements for our party.
‡ A tash here is taken at five miles, but in many parts it scarcely exceeds four miles. See note to Route XII of Section G. of Geographical Appendix.—T. D. F.
§ Or "Commander of ten (soldiers)."

miles, i.e., three miles in a north-east direction across several low projections of a spur running south, then four miles of steady ascent up a ravine to the north, followed by a sharp pull of two miles in a direction 35° east of north, brought us to the Belowti Pass, the goal for which we had been striving. From the pass itself, which is about 11,500 feet above the sea, no view was to be had, but by ascending a hill to the west, some 300 feet above it, I got a very fine view of a portion of the snowy range on the opposite side of the Kokshál river; one peak, nearly due north, stood out conspicuously, of no very great height however, its elevation being only $2\frac{1}{2}°$ from where I stood. The range appeared to run nearly due east. Parallel to it at its base lay the deep valley of the Kokshál, apparently about eight miles to the north of where I stood. The road from the pass leads down a steep ravine, at first nearly north-east, and then with a north-westerly course to the river. The position of the next camp, Ák-chai, on the big river, was pointed out to me, bearing 10° east of north, but the man who was with me could not give me a good idea of the direction of Úsh Túrfán or Áksú.

Ak-chi, the first halting-place to the north of the pass, is a Kirghiz camp close to the point where the road from the pass strikes the river. About five miles below it is Kokshál, a large Kirghiz village, between which and Úsh Túrfán, a distance of about 90 miles as far as I could learn, are numerous Kirghiz encampments, all under the orders of the Hakim of Úsh Túrfán. It was a party of these Kirghiz whom we had had the good fortune to encounter on the south of the Belowti Pass.* Near Kokshál, the alternative road from Jai Túpa, before alluded to, joins the river which takes its name from the village. The road is said to be shorter and easier than the one we had followed, but for two days there is no fire-wood. One march above Kokshál (or three marches according to another account) is the fort of Kárá Bulák, above which the Kirghiz subjects of the Amír are not allowed to pass, the ground above being held by the Russian Kirghiz, who in their turn are not allowed to cross the frontier eastward. All these Kirghiz are, I believe, of the same tribe, but being under different rulers are to a certain extent hostile; at all events they are not allowed to communicate with each other.

From Safr Bai, about 38 miles to the west of Úsh, is a road leading to Issigh-kul, by the Bedal and Zaikí Passes. The former of these is on the boundary between Russia and Káshgharia.

There are said to be about 500 Kirghiz families in the Kokshál valley, and about 350 in the valleys north and north-east of Artysh. The Kokshál valley is exceedingly rich in pasture. Its upper waters (the Aksai) were first occupied by the Russians about 10 years ago.

On the range on which I stood there were no high peaks visible, probably none more than 1,000 feet above the pass; the ground on both sides was undulating and grassy, very much resembling that to the east of the Turgat Bela Pass in the same range. It was evident that this range had, as it advanced eastward, become considerably lower, both with regard to its peaks and its water-shed. Like the smaller ranges at its base and parallel to it, I believe it to get lower still, as it goes further east, and at last to be lost in the plains near Áksú.

The sun set while I was at the top of the pass; the thermometer stood at 5° F. with a cold wind blowing, so I was glad to go back to the Kirghiz camp at Tigarek, which we reached at 9 P.M., having made good use of the only fine day we had during our trip. As it was, snow began to fall immediately after we reached the camp. The next day we returned to our standing camp at Ui Bulák; the road was three inches deep in snow, and more falling, accompanied by a bitterly cold wind; next day back to Jigda, 22 miles; weather much the same; next day 25 miles to Kyr Bulák, to which place akoees and supplies had been brought for us from the village of Karghíl, 15 miles off. The following day we marched 29 miles to the village of Kalti Ailák.

The ground we had been traversing is marked on our maps "the Syrt," and is represented as a high table-land. I took some pains to ascertain the limits of the district bearing this name, but could not arrive at very satisfactory conclusions. "Syrt" in Turki means "the back," and is therefore necessarily applied to somewhat elevated lands. The Hakim (Governor) of Artysh included under this designation the whole of the highland districts about Sonkul and

---

* From them we obtained both food and shelter.

Chadyrkul; another authority referred the name more particularly to the plains at the head of the Aksai River. The Kirghiz living in the districts we had passed through seemed to be entirely ignorant of the name, and did not recognize it; but after my return, on asking the Hákim of Kalti Ailák the whereabouts of the Syrt, he immediately replied that I had just come from it, and that the name was applicable to the whole district between Artysh and Ush Túrfán; on his evidence I think the name may remain on our maps where it is. The country can, however, by no means be considered as a high table-land rising immediately above the plains of Turkestan; it should rather be represented as a series of parallel mountain ranges, running, as a rule, from west to east, each one decreasing gradually in height, from the main ridge on the north to the lowest on the south; each subsidiary range also decreasing in height as it goes eastward. Between these ranges and running parallel to them, are extensive level plains, very little higher than the plateau of Eastern Turkestan, but gradually rising towards the north and sloping down towards the east. Thus the Túghamatí Plain, about 45 miles north of Kashghár, is about 2,000 feet higher; while the Jai Túpa plain, the same distance east of Túghamatí, is only 1,000 feet higher than Káshghar. The combined effect is to give a general slope to the south-east.

These large plains have in most cases much grass and fuel, though but little water. From the Sogón eastward we came across no flowing stream. What water is derived from the very moderate annual snowfall seems to percolate into the earth, moistening it generally, and issuing in various places in the form of springs, near which are usually to be found Kirghiz encampments. In the Tigarek plain, at the foot of the Belowti Pass, there are, I believe, no springs; and although there is good grass, the only time of the year in which the plain can be tenanted by the Kirghiz, is that at which we happened to visit it, the sole substitute for water for themselves and flocks being the actual snow, which was then lying on the ground. In the Jai Túpa valley there are water-courses running from north and east, but the supply of water is so precarious that the Kirghiz told me that it was only after years in which there was a more than average snowfall, that they attempted any cultivation at all, and under the most favorable circumstances the extent is extremely limited. There appeared to be no outlet through the hills surrounding this valley, in the lower portion of which lies the forest before alluded to. The moisture in the soil would seem to be sufficient to nourish these stunted trees. Much of the ground in the plain is covered with saline efflorescence, and from near Jai Túpa itself large quantities of crystallized salt are collected and despatched to Káshghar.

The Kirghiz who inhabited the country in the time of the Chinese appear to have led a more jovial life than at present. Under no master, they used regularly to levy black-mail from passing travellers and merchants at every camping ground; and as prompt payment always ensured a safe passage, there was seldom much difficulty in collecting their dues. Under the strict rule of the Amír they are now disarmed, and are comparatively poor, as they dare not venture on any of their old tricks. A single sepoy of the King's, selected from among themselves, is stationed in each encampment, and is responsible for the good conduct of its members; an annual present of a choga, a certain amount of grain, and remission of taxes is the remuneration he receives from the State. The Kirghiz pay as taxes annually one sheep in 40, one sheep for every two camels, and one-tenth of the agricultural produce (when there is any). In these parts horses or ponies are scarce. Nature aids the inhabitants in their poverty by a plentiful supply of a plant called locally *kuruk* or *teric*, a kind of millet which grows wild and from which they make a preparation called "*talkan*" corresponding to the Ladákhi *suttoo*, which they eat uncooked moistened with a little water. I tried some, and found it to be not unlike Scotch oatmeal, and, as it may be had for the picking it may be looked upon as a bountiful gift of Providence to these otherwise poverty stricken people.

Our march from Kyr Bulák to Kalti Ailák was for a great part of the way down the Sogón River. A kárawul, garrisoned by a few sepoys is situated where the river enters the hills south of the Ayok Sogón plain. The valley occasionally widens out into small grassy flats. After a time, the river is left (it goes off in a south-east direction and is, as before explained, soon swallowed up by the thirsty gravelly soil) and the road traverses some very bleak and desolate broken ground without a scrap of vegetation or sign of life. After passing through these hills and then over a few miles of flat stony desert we reached Kalti Ailák.

86.—Moosa Khwoja, Son of the Hakim of Artush, with hawks.

87.—Winter Quarters in Kashghar, Dr. Stoliczka on left and Captain Biddulph on right.

We spent a night there in the residence of the Hákim and went the following day to Khush Tográk, its southern township, about eight miles to the south-east. After arrival there we pushed on two or three miles to the Káshghar River, which we tried to cross in order to shoot in some jungle at the other side; but the ice was now breaking up and was so dangerous that our conductors would not venture to take us over, although the head-quarters party had crossed over a few days before on the ice without the slightest difficulty. Next day we continued our return journey, and forded the river several miles higher than where we had attempted its passage the day before. It took us nearly an hour to cross the river, the combined water, ice, and mud making the passage so difficult that our Turkestani attendants had to strip off their four or five superfluous suits of clothing and go to the assistance of our baggage animals, who, after a good deal of plunging and floundering, at last got across without accident.

Between Khush Tográk and the river there are, at this time of the year, extensive swamps, caused in the manner I have before described. Near this place the waters of the Artysh and Káshghar River mingle together; but in the hot and irrigating season the whole of the water from the Artysh River is said to be expended before reaching the junction, and the Khush Tográk village is then exclusively watered from the Káshghar River.

In the early winter when the ice first begins to form, it partially blocks up the streams and the mass of ice growing larger and larger, great frozen lakes are often formed where in summer there is merely a rapid stream of water. This makes it impossible in winter (the season of our travels) to form any accurate idea of the real size of the streams. After passing the river and crossing a few miles of salt waste we came to Faizabad, a large village on the road between Marálbáshi and Aksu. On this march I saw, for the first and only time in Turkestan, large numbers of geese and duck, all flying eastward.

It was market day in Faizabad, and the crowd attending the bazar was about as large and dense as that I had previously seen at Altyn Artysh, from which circumstance I should infer that the population of the surrounding district is about the same. On the following day (3rd of March) we returned to Káshghar, a march of 37 miles over a perfectly flat country, the road winding almost the whole way through a populous and well cultivated district. We passed successively the scattered villages of Sheaptal, Sang, and Yanduma, every village as usual composed of several hamlets, each with its separate name. At Sheaptal it was market day, but it was too early in the day to be able to form any estimate of the population attending, though on the march we met crowds of people thronging to it. The road crosses several large canals which leave the southern branch of the Káshghar River several miles above Káshghar and irrigate the whole of the ground south, south-east, and east of the city. One of them bears the name of Yamunyar, and possibly a portion of its waters comes from the river of the same name, which, rising in the Little Karakul Lake flows past Opal and Tashbalig, where it divides into numerous branches and canals, some of which probably intermingle their waters with canals from the Káshghar river. The two together form a net-work of rivers and canals which it is nearly impossible to unravel, and which is moreover constantly changing almost from day to day.

From the time of leaving the head-quarters camp at Bash Sogon, the weather was most unfavourable: snow and clouds prevented my seeing the hill tops by day or the stars by night. This lasted until our return to Uí Bulák, 26 miles west of the Belowti Pass. At Uí Bulák, Faizabad and intermediate stations I was more fortunate and was able to secure good star observations, both for latitude and time. These, combined with a rough compass survey which I made of the whole road, have enabled me to map it with a fair amount of accuracy, although the distance traversed during our absence from Káshghar, *viz.*, 340 miles, was accomplished in little more than a fortnight.

Excursion to the Pámír Steppes and Wakhán.

Shortly after our return to Káshghar from the Artysh Districts a party, under the orders of Colonel Gordon, consisting of Captain Biddulph, the late Dr. Stoliczka, and myself, was sent *viâ* Sarikol (Táshkurghán) to Wakhán, and I was instructed to take what advantage

I could of such opportunities as might offer for the increase of our geographical knowledge. The primary object with which the Mission was despatched necessitated a very rapid outward march, and the difficulty of arranging about supplies compelled our return with nearly equal rapidity, giving no time or opportunity for making detours or excursions off the road; with the exception of halts at Panjáh in Wakhán, the furthest point westward reached by the Mission, and at Táshkurghán, where we were compelled to halt for the purpose of resting our cattle, and one day at Ak-tásh for the same purpose, our journey was merely a rapid continuous march from beginning to end. I am induced to make these remarks at the outset, as I have seen paragraphs in the newspapers, and notably in the telegraphic reports of the London *Times* to the effect that "the Pámír has been completely surveyed," and other similar statements which are apt to mislead the public and induce them to expect a great deal more than has been, or could possibly have been, accomplished under the circumstances.

What I have been able to perform in the way of actual survey chiefly consists of fairly complete sets of astronomical observations, which have enabled me to fix with considerable accuracy the positions of the more important places along our line of march. These places have all been connected by a route survey, executed as carefully as circumstances would permit. I also succeeded in getting good observations with boiling point thermometers and aneroids on all the passes and at all our camps, which, combined with simultaneous barometric readings at Leh should furnish very trustworthy determinations of height. Observations for magnetic dip and declination were made at Sarikol, and for declination only at Panjah. Owing to the necessity for cutting down baggage, servants, and camp followers to the lowest possible limit, I left both my survey khlassies behind in Yárkand, as also all photographic apparatus.

From Yangi-Hissár as far as Táshkurghán I had the advantage of the Pundit's assistance, and he with the Munshi paced the whole road up to that point. The Pundit being a Hindu was not taken beyond Sirikol, but Colonel Gordon obtained permission (from Hussan Sháh, the Governor of Sirikol,) for him to return to Yárkand *viâ* Chehil Gombáz and the Chárling River. From Panjah the Múnshi was despatched on a special exploration, to be hereafter described. Up to that point I had the advantage of his services as a recorder for astronomical work. On the return journey to India the late Dr. Stoliczka kindly took his place, and recorded for me on several occasions, the last being only a few days before his death.

Before going into the details of my own reconnaissance I may, perhaps with advantage, notice the mistaken ideas* which most geographers have held, at all events until very recently, of the nature of the mass of mountains and high table-lands which separate the provinces of Eastern and Western Turkestan. The labours of the Russian Venuikof, who taking the writings of the illustrious Humboldt for his basis, and working on to them the cleverly constructed but mischievous forgeries of Klaproth, have thrown back the geography of this region into almost inextricable confusion, from which even the recondite researches of Colonel Yule and Sir Henry Rawlinson have hardly yet rescued us. The vague statements of ancient travellers such as Huen Tsán and Marco Polo, who scarcely imagined when they penned their writings, the keen interest with which they would centuries later be studied and criticized, have added to the difficulties of forming a clear and correct idea of the country. The ideas I had myself formed before my visit were vague in the extreme, but perhaps not very much more so than those of others who knew a great deal more about it. Such different descriptions as the following are difficult to reconcile:—

"The Pámír plain extends 1,000 li† from east to west and 100 li from south to north."— *Huen Tsán.*

"The centre of the plateau is 'Saryk-kul' out of which there should issue, according to all accounts, the Jaxartes, Oxus, and a branch of the Indus. This plateau, which affords excellent pasturage, extends round the lake for a distance of six days' journey in circumference, and it is said that from this elevation all the adjacent hills appear below the observer."— *Burnes.*

---

* Derived from incomplete and discordant information.
† A li is about one-fifth of a mile.

"For twelve days the course is along this elevated plain, which is called Pámír."—*Marco Polo.*

"The hills and mountains that encircle Lake Sirikól* give rise to some of the principal rivers in Asia. From a ridge at its east end flows a branch of the Yárkand river, one of the largest streams that water China, while from its low hills on the northern side rises the Sirr or river of Khokand, and from the snowy chain opposite both forks of the Oxus as well as a branch of the River Kúnúr are supplied."—*Wood.*

In the last extract, I see how an excellent, careful, and reliable observer like Wood falls into error directly he trusts to what he *hears*; and I must say that from my own experience I have little confidence in geographical information extracted from the inhabitants of Central Asia, unless from trained and educated men who are accustomed to take notes of what they see. I feel it incumbent on me therefore to discriminate clearly between what I have *seen*, and what I have *heard*, and with that end in view I propose first briefly describing that portion of the country which has actually come under my notice. I may then perhaps hazard a few remarks on what I have heard.

We started from Káshghar on our journey to Panjah on the 17th March, reaching Yangí-Hissár (36 miles to the south) on the following day. Halting a couple of days to make preparations for our journey, we left on the 21st, starting by the same route by which the "Mirza" went to Káshghar from Cabul in 1868-69. Our first march was to Ighíz-yár, eighteen miles; crossing the low broken sand hills that ran down to Yangi-Hissár from the mountains on the west, we followed for about three miles the direct road to Yárkand; then crossing the Yangí-Hissár stream at Kumbash village we passed in a southerly direction for five miles, over a flat salt waste, to the large but scattered village of Sugat, which it took us nearly half an hour to traverse. On the sandy tract a number of people were digging and collecting a very inferior kind of fire-wood, which is carried off on donkeys to Yangi-Hissár, where fuel is very scarce and dear. From Sugat none of the large mountains on the west were visible on account of the haze; the ridges before mentioned, and another low sandy ridge running parallel to, and on the other side of the Yárkand road, were all that could be seen. Sugat is situated on a slope, and our road lay up the bed of a water-course, one of many coming from the Kinkol stream, whose banks we were about to follow for several days' journey. When we passed there was but little water in the stream, and what little came was eagerly swallowed up by the thirsty soil. The villagers, on the approach of spring, were commencing to plough their lands. As the summer advances the heat increases, and with it the water-supply from the melting snow, which comes at the time when most wanted by the husbandmen for their early crops. I was informed that in summer a very small quantity of water trickles from the irrigation canals through a large ravine (which, surrounded by much broken ground, is formed at the foot of the Sugat village) and joins the Yangí-Hissár river. The chief source of supply of the river is from a number of springs situated about six miles west by south of the town from which it derives its name. I visited them the day we halted at Yangí-Hissár on our journey to Káshghar; they are surrounded by several villages, Kargoi, Kona† and Yangí Sálip, and others. At Kona Sálip the bed of the river is dry, and is formed by numerous short ravines meeting there. A little lower down, at Kargoi, the banks are fifty feet deep, and a considerable quantity of water bubbles out of the ground; fresh springs issue for a considerable way down the river, so that by the time it passes south of Yangí-Hissár there is a considerable body of water in the stream, whose bulk is also augmented by drainage from canals supplied from the River Kusán which is said to rise in the Kizil Art mountains in the neighbourhood of Tagharma Peak. The temperature of the canals from this stream was 42°, while that of the river (from the springs) was 47°. The Yangí-Hissár river, after receiving accession to its waters from the Kusán, flows eastward, and is said to lose itself in the desert near the villages of Keltarim and Chakar. The river shortly after its issue from the mountains divides into four artificial branches or canals, the Pasín, the Párách (or Kusán river), the Sailik,

---

* Wood's "Victoria Lake."
† In Turki *Kona* means *old*, and *Yangi* means *new*.

and the Tibiz, the last and southern of these it is whose waters surround the head of, and afterwards mingle with, the river of Yangí-Hissár. There is also no doubt that the waters of the northern branches mingle with, if indeed they are not identical with, the Yámunyár river (also called Tasgún, Khánárik, Oi Kubok, and a host of other names). The latter river issues from or near the smaller of the two Lakes Kárákúl (of which more hereafter) and passes from the hills near the villages of Tash-bálig and Opal. The whole of the country south of Káshghar is cut up by one net-work of canals mingled in such confusion that nothing but a careful survey can lead to a clear comprehension of them* and moreover day by day they alter, and I have often seen one canal (in appearance more like a large river than anything else) eating its way rapidly through the soft soil into another one. These changes are constantly going on, and a map constructed now would be of but little value fifty years hence.

After leaving the village of Sugat the road follows for nine miles, along the edge of a water-course through a stony plain, a narrow border of green showing signs of a scant cultivation. This brings us to our first halting-place, the good-sized village of Ighiz-yar, two miles short of which we pass on the left a conspicuous isolated conical hill with a zyarat (tomb) at top. Before reaching the village a few low hills come in sight on the west, being the ends of the low spurs coming down from the Kizil Art mountains, the first portion of these mountains that we had seen since leaving Káshghar. With our usual ill luck, from the day of our departure, the characteristic Eastern Turkestan haze entirely obscured all view of the lofty mountains on the west, preventing the possibility of forming any opinion as to the shape and direction of the spurs from the main ridge. From Káshghar on a clear day we have often seen the outlines of these hills standing out against the sky, but the distance, to the crest of the range, 70 miles, was much too great to permit of the intervening ranges or spurs being visible. I often longed to make a nearer acquaintance with them, but no opportunity ever occurred for doing so. Fortunately on the upward journey to Káshghar, the Pundit, who followed some days behind us, had some clear days, and was able to fix very satisfactorily the positions of several of the peaks of the main range.

On the second day we marched in a south-west direction, for 18 miles, to Aktala (white plain). The first four miles were up a gently rising stony plain, almost entirely destitute of vegetation, and extending to the entrance of the Kinkol valley, which runs between two spurs of which we had caught a glimpse the previous day. At a distance of two miles up the valley the road passes the foot of an old extensive fortification called "Khatt (lower) Karáwul", constructed by the Chinese on the left bank of the river, to defend themselves against incursions from the Kirghiz marauders from the Pámirs and the Alai. It is built on a commanding position running along a spur which nearly closes up the entrance of the valley. A garrison consisting of only a few sepoys, attests the fact that the Amír's rule has reduced these tribes to order and obedience. Two miles further up is Kichik (small) Karáwul, where a road along an open ravine on the left bank leads direct viá Opal to Káshghar, and a Kirghiz footpath along a ravine on the opposite side leads to Yárkand.

---

* A great source of difficulty in investigating the courses of rivers in Eastern Turkestan is their nomenclature, every portion of a stream having a different name, derived from the nearest village, by which alone is it known to the neighbouring inhabitants. In addition to these purely local designations travellers generally name the rivers after the different large towns situated on their banks, while cosmopolitans have occasionally general names which they apply to a river throughout its whole course, but which are perhaps unknown to the inhabitants of the country. Most rivers are also occasionally known by names expressive their color as Kara-Su, Kizil-Su, or Kok-Su, or Ak-Su (Turki, for black, red, blue, and white rivers), terms which may be seen broadcast in almost any map of Central Asia. No river of Eastern Turkestan carries the same name from its cradle to its grave in the big Tarim Gol or Ergol, which swallows up all the rivers of Eastern Turkestan except those that lose themselves in the desert before they reach it. The final end of the Tarim still remains, and I fear must remain, a matter of mystery. It is generally supposed to flow into Lake Lope (Lob, or Luf); but I have recently heard, on what I considered fairly trustworthy evidence, that at about 25 miles south of its junction with the Karashahr River, i.e., about 65 miles south of Kola (Koila or Kurla), it disappears in the sand near the village of Lop (Lop being I believe a Sanskrit word signifying disappearance). It is further said to reappear in the shape of a large navigable stream at the Chinese city of Saju (? Suchan). I should myself think that it more probably reappears in the marshes and lakes which are believed to exist to the eastward and south-eastward of the still somewhat mythical Lake of Lop. Perhaps Mr. Prjevalski will some day enlighten us on this matter from the east.

88.—Scinde Valley, Cashmere.

89.—The "Dadhkwahs" Band, Yarkund.

Two miles higher is the Ghijak ravine, along which a road runs to the Alai and Khokand by the Kárátásh and Kizil Art Passes*. Another seven miles up the stream brought us to our halting-place at Aktala. As we ascended, the increasing bulk of water was very appreciable, partly owing to the snow melting under the increased temperature, but also doubtless in some measure due to a large quantity being lost in the gravelly soil, which, as I have before had occasion to mention, frequently absorbs much water, that would otherwise profitably be employed in irrigation. We had crossed the river shortly before it enters the plains, and although its banks are there several feet in height, the natural bed immediately afterwards opens out on the stony plain and much water must be lost. The river divides into two main branches, the Odelang to the north, and the Ghalchak to the south. These irrigate the villages on the Grand Trunk Road between Kudok and Yangi-Hissár.

Above Ghijak the road closes in and we get several very picturesque views as we advance. The scenery is very bold, hills several hundreds of feet in almost perpendicular height enclosing the narrow valley. Fuel, water, and grass are in abundance. At Aktala the valley opens and the river branches into two streams of nearly equal size. Some miles up the western branch is the Kirghiz village of Chumbáz, by which a path is said to lead to the Kaskasú Pass. Our third day's march was to Sásak Taka, 13½ miles up stream, by a bad stony road through a very bold defile: there was plenty of wood and grass, which also appeared to be very abundant in some of the lateral valleys. About 2½ miles short of camp, a deep ravine comes in from the east, and the main stream turns to the south-west, retaining that general direction until arrival at the Kaskasú Pass, which we crossed on the 25th March. At five miles above Sásak Taka a stream joins from the south-east called Kinkol, and gives its name to the river lower down. On this day's march (fourth from Yangi-Hissár) we passed numerous Kirghiz camps containing altogether as many as 30 or 40 tents or Akoees; amongst their tenants I encountered some who came originally from the neighbourhood of Almáti. Although passing along a valley bounded on both sides by spurs from lofty hills which rose some thousands of feet above us, the scenery was not so bold as where we had passed through on the previous day; the slopes were more gentle, and numerous grassy valleys entered on both sides, up which we saw many camels, yaks and sheep.

On the fifth day (25th March), we left camp with the thermometer at 7° F. starting early in order to avoid the slush and water to be expected later on in the day from the melting snow. At first we had a bitterly cold west wind, which however moderated after an hour or so, and we had a very fine day for crossing the Kaskasú Pass. The ridge which we had to cross is a spur from the Kizil Art mountains, and separates the drainage of the Kinkol River flowing towards Yangi-Hissár, from that of the Chárling River, which goes to Yárkand. For two miles after starting our direction was a little north of west, and then for nearly three miles up to the pass nearly south of west. The road leaves the ravine (which is steep and inaccessible) and winds up the side of the valley, passsing round the head of the ravine, and over a flat ridge, at the end of which commences a steep descent of about five miles. The height of the pass is 12,930 feet, and although the length of march was only 10 miles, the baggage ponies did not arrive in camp until late in the afternoon, owing to the slippery descent on the south side, where our loads had to be transferred to yaks. There was a great deal of snow on the pass, as well as on the grassy slopes on

---

* This road is said to cross two passes before it reaches the Kizilart Diwan, and to pass, by Kichik (little) Karakul, a small lake probably not more than four or five miles in circumference, from which a road leads to Chong (great) Karakul five marches off and probably four or five days' journey in circumference. This road is said not to cross any large river but to pass mostly over high table land; abundant supplies of grass and fuel exist throughout, and I was told that camels can traverse it the whole year round. It was formerly used by merchants going from Yarkund to Khokand but is now closed. A direct road from Yangi Hissar joins it at one day's march from Ghijak at a place called Karatash. Another road leads from Opal (about 30 miles south-west from Kashghar) to the Kizilart Pass and Alai. This road was recently used by an Envoy sent from Karatigin to Kashghar one of whose suite was wounded in an encounter with the Alai Kirghiz, who are subject to Khokand. The portion nearest to Kashghar is often used as an alternative road to Khokand when the Terek Pass is closed.

either side. The view was very limited, and the deep snow prevented my leaving the road. On our return journey, about five weeks later, the snow was all melted, and there was no necessity for employing yaks.

The camp at Chehil Gombáz was at the junction of the streams coming from the Kaskasú and Torat* Passes, the two forming the Chárling River, along which a direct road goes to Yárkand, now closed against traffic "by order." On the spur between the two streams is an old Chinese building called Khitai Sháhr (Chinese city), a sort of square redoubt built on the steep slope of the hill, presenting a very curious appearance, and reminding one of the perspective pictures of Cæsar's camp, in ancient editions of that author's Commentaries. It was said to have been formerly held by a detachment of Chinese, posted to watch the Chárling passage to Yárkand.

The direct road from Chehil Gombáz to Yárkand† is 132 miles in length. The first march is to Tashkerim, a camping ground 19 miles down the Charling stream. From this place a path crosses the hills to the north, joining at Kinkol, the road we had ourselves followed. The Yárkand road continues down stream for 15 miles to Khaizak passing the villages of Bagh (30 houses), Kiok-tash (8 houses), Mirgul (25 houses), and Joya (15 houses). Between Chehil Gombaz and Bagh (the highest village in the valley) are numerous Kirghiz tents, the grassy valley affording an abundant pasturage to large herds of sheep and cattle, which remain in the valley in the cold weather, but are driven up to higher grazing grounds in the summer. Leaving the Charling stream at Khaizak, the road crosses two low spurs by the Kara Diwan and Kizil Diwan (on which there was no snow in April), and then descending to the bed of the Kizil stream‡ passes over plain and through desert § to Yakirak Kurghan, from which place to Yárkand 23½ miles further on, is a rich, thickly populated, and fertile plain. The Charling and Tashkurghán Rivers unite at Khusherab, five or six miles below Khaizak; the united stream then flows nearly due east, and is said to be met by a still larger river the Raskam (from the Karakorum Pass), at Kosherap, about 20 miles south-south-west of Yakirak.

On the sixth day (26th), we made a short march of only eight miles to Pas Robát, crossing the Pas Robát or Torat (horse's sweat) Pass, which divides the drainage of the Chárling River from that of the Tangitár, which also flows into the Yárkand river. The ascent was steep, and the descent still more so, the slope of the valley being 16° for a distance of about two miles. The height of the pass is 13,130 feet, the rise from Chehil Gombáz being about 3,000 feet, and the fall to Pas Robát about 4,000. While we were on the top the sky was cloudy and a fall of snow obscured the peaks to the north. On the return journey, however, I ascended a hill north of the pass and had a good though limited view in every direction. The ground rapidly rises towards the north and north-west, peaks rising to a height of as much as 4,000 feet above the pass, i.e., to over 17,000 feet. The mountains eastward visibly decreased in height as they approached Yárkand. On my 2nd visit the hills near the pass were covered with fresh, low, short, grass.

About half way down to camp we came upon a number of willow trees (Túrkí, Sugét), which continued in greater or less quantities down to the foot of the hill. In descending the stream we came upon some very thick river deposits having in places a thickness of 300 feet, and containing large boulders of syenite. The rock *in situ* was composed of the same materials, as that through which we had been passing for several days, viz: shales and slates.

A stream coming from the north-west had a temperature of 42°, while the temperature of the air was only 24°.

On the seventh day we continued our march up the Tangitár (Pas Robát) River; after five miles we passed on the left bank the Yámbulák stream leading to the pass of the same name, 14 miles off, situate in a direction a little north of west. Our own path lay along the main

---

* Torat or "horse's sweat."
† This road was traversed by Kishen Sing Pandit from whom the information contained in this paragraph is derived.
‡ Nearly dry in winter, but a large torrent when the snow is melting on the hills above.
§ Called "Shaitán Kum" or "Devil's sands."

stream for about five miles more to Tárbáshi, passing through a narrow and dangerous defile. The road was execrable, and we experienced great difficulty and delay in getting our baggage through. This defile would be quite impassable for field guns, and a few determined men might in places defend it against an army. The road often runs along the bed of the stream, which contains large boulders and deep holes of water. In the winter it is probably easier to traverse, but at the time of our passage we had the double difficulties of ice and water to contend with. As far as I could learn the river is never entirely frozen over, on account of the numerous hot springs which issue from the limestone rocks forming its side walls. One of these had a temperature of 125°, and the vegetation in its immediate neighbourhood was much in advance of that lower down the stream, and showed signs of approaching spring. In the summer this road is said to be rendered quite impassable by the floods from melting snow; the alternative route lies up the Yámbulák River.

On the eighth day our road lay alongside the Tangitár stream, which, from Tárbáshi, ascends a gentle slope, bounded on both sides by undulating snow covered hills. The valley rises very gradually for about nine miles, up to an almost imperceptible water-shed (14,480 feet high), by which we reached the Chichiklik plateau, a broad elevated valley whose drainage passes south, through a somewhat narrow defile, to the Táshkurghán river. On the plateau close to the water-shed were two small frozen lakes. The summer road before alluded to which goes up the Yambulak stream enters the Chichiklik plain by the Yámbulák Pass about four miles to the north of where we crossed the water-shed. On the opposite side of the valley, which was between four and five miles wide, in a south-west direction from where we entered it, is the Pass of Kok Mainák, on high spur running down from the Kizilart mountains. By this pass is the shortest road to Táshkurghán, but on our outward journey it was so deep in snow that we were obliged to take the alternative route down the Shindí valley. It is the Kok Mainák Pass that is called "Chichiklik" by the "Mirza," "Fyz Bux," and other travellers, but the correct name as given by the Kirghiz who lived in the neighbourhood is, I believe, as I have given it. Our road lay down the stream. After the first two or three miles, where the slope was very easy, the valley narrowed, and the road became exceedingly steep and difficult, passing for several miles through a succession of rocks and boulders At 10 miles below below the lakes we came to our camp at Balghun, shortly before reaching which the valley had opened considerably although surrounded on both sides by lofty mountains.

The following day (29th), we descended four miles to the junction of the Shindí with the Táshkurghán (or Sarikol or Taghdumbash) River,* just above the Sarikoli village of Shindí, inhabited by Tajiks, and containing about 15 houses, situated in a small well cultivated valley, about two miles long by one broad. Our road now lay up the Sarikol river, but I descended it for about four miles to fix the direction in which it flowed away (south-east by east)† ; returning to the junction I crossed the main stream with some difficulty owing to the rapidity of the current, and continued along its right bank, where the road passes through a very wild defile of crystalline rocks, forming almost perpendicular banks about 2,000 feet in height, through which the river winds its way with a most tortuous course. At about 10 miles above the junction we emerged on the north-east corner of the Táshkurghan or Sarikol plain. The road by which we travelled is only open in winter, as in summer the large mass of water in the Sarikol River makes it impassable. The route by the Yámbulák and Kok Mainák Passes is then used.

On entering the Sarikol valley we strike the junction of the Tagharma stream with the main river. The former comes from the plain of the same name on the north-west, and has been incorrectly described by a former traveller as the main source of the Sarikol River. When we saw it there was but little water coming down (temperature 38°), although in summer there is considerably more, but the small size of the water-course, and the evidence of

---

* Sometimes also called Yárkand River.
† From Shindí a path goes down the river, but is only practicable during two or three months in winter.

the inhabitants of the district, all tended to show that the river which flows down the Sarikol valley from the Kanjúd mountains, and through the Taghdumbash Pámír, is undoubtedly the main stream. At the point I crossed, just above the junction with the Tagharma stream, it the river was 15 yards in width, with an average depth of 1½ feet, and a velocity of four miles an hour. Two miles beyond in a southern direction brought us to the village of Chushmán, leaving only five miles for our next day's march (the 10th from Yangí-Hissár) into Táshkurghán, the chief town or rather village of the Sarikol valley. Between Chushmán and Táshkurghán (both on the left bank of the Taghdumbash River) we passed the large village of Tiznáf. It is this village that has caused much confusion to geographers by giving its name to the river, which is frequently called the Tiznáf in its lower course, and is often confounded with another river of the same name which rises on the north side of the Yangí-Díwán Pass and flows past Karghálik.

On approaching Táshkurghán (where we halted two days to rest our cattle), while passing up the valley I saw at its upper end some high peaks occasionally emerging from the clouds, but before I could get to camp they had disappeared, never to be seen again during our stay in the valley, or on our return journey, a great disappointment to me, as it is possible they were peaks in the Muz-tagh range, fixed by the Great Trigonometrical Survey. During our halt at Sarikol I took a set of magnetic as well as the usual astronomical observations, and some careful azimuthal bearings with theodolite to a large mass of snowy peaks called Muz-tagh, situated to the north of Táshkurghán. These are identical with Hayward's Taghalma mountains, which are visible from Káshghar, the highest peak of which I determined by accordant trigonometrical measurements from Káshghar and Yapchan, to be 25,350 feet above the sea.

The general outline of the Tashkúrghan valley towards its head, was fixed by bearings taken from different points on a line across it. On the return journey I was able, by ascending the ridge that separates this plain from that of Tagharma on its north (and by making a detour through the latter on the way to our camp at the foot of the Kok Mainák Pass) to lay down the borders of the northern plain with considerable accuracy. Practically the two form one large plateau divided in the middle by a low range of hills through which flows the Tagharma River. The Táshkurghán plain extends southwards from the dividing ridge before mentioned, right up to the foot of the Kanjúd passes in the Muz-tagh range, constituting in its southern portion, the Taghdumbash Pámír. The Sarikol valley may be said to have an average width of about four miles; it is bounded on the east by the snowy range of Kandár or Kandahar;* on the south-west and south are the Taghdumbash mountains; on the west the Shindí mountains; north-west the Bir-dásh, which also forms the western boundary of the Tagharma plain, to the east of which lie the Muz-tagh (or Tagharma) and the Chichiklik mountains. The Tagharma plain extends from the dividing ridge for about 12 miles in a north-north-west direction; it is only two miles in width immediately north of the ridge, but soon increases in an easterly direction to as much as 10 miles; it then narrows, being nearly closed up by spurs running down from the Bir-dásh mountains on the west and the Muz-tagh on the east. About 10 miles west of this point is the Bir-dásh Pass, over a range which divides this plain from another similar one running nearly parallel to it, viz., the Ak-tash or Ák-su. Opposite the Bir-dásh Pass the Sarikol plain again widens and extends, gently undulating, for some eight or ten miles further in the same direction.† According to statements of the Kirghiz it continues right up to the Kizil Art Pass, which separates it from the Alai, and the valley of the Surkhab River, the most northerly tributary of the Oxus. The height of the valley above sea level may be taken at Tagharma at about 10,500 feet, and I doubt whether it is very much higher in any part of its course. The drainage of the southern portion passes through the Tagharma plain into the Sarikol River;

---

* Over these mountains is a road to Yarkand, which descends into the Tung valley and after passing down it for a march or two, crosses the Arpatalek Mountains, and enters the Turkestan plain near Kosherap.

† Thus far I myself saw, from the ridge dividing the Tagharma from the Tashkurghan Plain.

and in a somewhat central position on its east edge, I would place the lake of Kichik Karakul,* about three short days' march north of Táshkurghán. Further north again, south of the Kizil, Art Pass, is the larger Lake Karakul, from which a stream is said to flow westward into the Manghábi river. I have shown in my map, what I consider the approximate positions of the various lakes and mountain ranges in those regions, but I of course cannot guarantee the accuracy of anything off our own line of march.

The Tagharma plain presented a very lively spectacle: fully 100 Kirghiz akoces were within view, scattered about in different parts of the valley; their tenants, of the Sark or Syok tribe, being subjects of the Amír of Káshghar. Open, grassy, well watered, and speckled all over with camels, yaks, horses, sheep, and goats it formed a pleasant sight after the wilds through which we had been wandering, and was a striking contrast to the Táshkurghan valley, which looked by comparison a picture of desolation, owing to the numerous uninhabited villages and tumble down houses with which it is covered. The water from the warm springs which issue in numerous places from the earth, causes the young green grass to rise (in April) in great profusion.

Formerly in the south-east portion of the Tagharma valley, at Kila-i-Tagharma or Besh Kurghan (the five forts) there were about 50 houses inhabited by Tájiks, under Sarikól. Their history has been a sad one. I got into conversation there with an old man, who told me that nearly each fort had its history. In the principal one, some thirty years ago, resided Mahomed Alum, the Hakim of Sarikól. He was attacked by a number of Andijánís from the north, himself and many of his followers killed, and the remainder carried into slavery; my informant with only one or two others escaping into the neighbouring hills. At the fort where I was standing, fifteen years later, the Kanjudis had made a raid from the south, and had killed or carried into slavery the whole of the inhabitants. Two young men standing by me had been carried off in this very raid as children, and sold as slaves in Yárkand, where they had been released shortly after the accession of the Atálik to power, but they had only within the last month been allowed to return to their homes, where four Tajik families now represent the fifty that had formerly lived there. They were doing their best, with the help of some of the neighbouring Kirghiz, to put their fields into order, and I there saw, for the first time in my travels, the yák yoked to the plough. There is much culturable ground, and it is to be hoped that this recommencement of cultivation on a small scale is only the prelude to a larger.

In the time of the Chinese rule, such was the insecurity in these parts, that the inhabitants of Sarikol dared not wander far from their villages, for fear of being seized and carried off either by the Kirghiz from the Alai, or by their neighbours of Kanjud; *now* they tell me that if a man drops his *whip* in the middle of the plain, he will find it there if he looks for it a year afterwards. This is a favourite saying amongst the people of Eastern Turkestan, which I have heard more than once employed to describe the sense of security enjoyed under the present *régime.*

On our return to Yárkand we passed along the south edge of the Tagharma plain. The direct distance from Táshkurghán to the foot of the Darschatt ravine leading to the Kok Mainák Pass is about twelve miles; thence to the pass itself (15,800 feet) is six miles, by a very difficult and stony road. The pass is four miles from the small lakes on the Chichiklik plain.

The fort of Táshkurghán, said to be of very ancient date, and to have been founded by Afrasiab, the King of Turan, has been described by former travellers who had a better opportunity for inspecting it than we had. The "Takhsobai," or Governor, evinced so great a disinclination to receive our visit there, that we had to content ourselves with inspecting it from a distance. The part at present inhabited is apparently of modern construction, and built of

---

* The waters from this lake are said to form the Yamunyar River, which flowing through the Chakar Ághil defile eastward, under the name of Gez River, enters the plains under the name of Yamunyar, and, as before mentioned, divides into several branches near the villages of Tashbalig and Opal and irrigates a great portion of the country south of Kashghar.

stones and mud, but there were in places remains of "roughed" stone facings on the sides of the rock on which the fort is built. In its neighbourhood are numerous fragments of broken wall, but I could not recognize any continuous line marking out its former limits. Taking a hint from Sir Henry Rawlinson's writings, I kept on the look-out for Buddhist remains, but could see nothing. The Pandit (who accompanied us as far as Sarikól), seemed to think that the custom which prevails throughout the whole country between Turkestan and Wakhán of heaping up skulls and horns of sheep and wild animals at the different ziárats or tombs, was a relic of ancient Buddhism. I believe that the custom is common throughout the whole of Central Asia. It certainly is so in Ladákh and Eastern Turkestan.

From Tashkúrghán to Panjah there are two roads commonly used by merchants; the first, over the little Pámir, was followed by us on the outward journey, is generally used in winter; the second is over the great Pámir and is used in summer. The latter is the easier road, but passes over much higher ground than the former and is impassable for caravans in winter, on account of the deep snow lying on it. A third alternative road is by the Tághdumbásh Pámir* at the head of the Sarikol valley. It lies high, and in midwinter is deep in snow: in former years it was much used by the Bajaori † merchants, who used to go from Bádákhshán to Yárkand by the Taghdumbash and Tung valley roads, thus keeping at the greatest possible distance from the Alai Kirghiz, whom they seem to have feared more than they did the Kunjúdis.

On the Great and Little Pámir routes the first two marches, i.e., to the west foot of the Neza Tash or Shindi Pass, are common to both lines of road, which meet again opposite the village of *Zang* at the junction of the two large streams which form the Panjah River, the most southerly branch of the Oxus.

Leaving Táshkurghán on the 2nd April, our road lay nearly due west for four miles, up a stream which issues from the Shindi mountains through a narrow and difficult defile.‡ The water, which even thus early in the season flows in considerable quantity, combines with the rocky nature of the bed of the river, which has to be crossed and recrossed in numerous places, to make the road exceedingly difficult for laden horses. After passing four miles up the defile we reached a camping ground called Jangalik situated in a well wooded open valley, about two miles long by half a mile broad. It is often used as a halting-place by travellers, but we continued up the valley to Kanshubar, a march altogether of 16 miles. Shortly before reaching camp we passed numerous hot springs. We pushed on the next day in a south-west direction until we reached the foot of the Neza Tash Diwan, where we turned westward, and passing over a low spur continued our way up the valley, entering a large basin with lofty mountains towering above us on both sides, very bold and precipitous, and of a very peculiar and striking ferruginous colour.§ A stiff pull through the snow to the top of the pass (14,915 feet above the sea level) and we were standing on the water-shed between Eastern and Western Turkestan.

I had been given to understand that we should here come in view of the "Pámírs" and was somewhat surprised at seeing in front of me nothing but a long range of low red colored hills about ten miles distant, a portion of which to the right was pointed out to me as the Great Pámír, and another on the left as the little Pámír. Nothing was visible but an irregular mass of hills whose serrated tips did not appear to rise more than 1,000 feet above the Pass on which I was standing. In front lay a large valley running in a northerly direction which subsequently turned out to be that of the Aksu River, the principal source, as now appears of the Oxus‖. The apparent continuity of the range in front of us was, as we shall hereafter see, a delusion; the hills really form the ends of broad transverse ranges, running in a westerly

---

* It is said that Alif Beg fled from Sarikol by this route.
† The district of Bajaor or Bajaur lies to the west of Swat, and its inhabitants are well known as enterprising traders.
‡ The rocks forming this defile were composed of gneiss.
§ These mountains, Dr. Stoliczka informed me, were composed of triassic limestone.
‖ Which name is perhaps derived, as Venoikof suggests, from Ak-sú.

direction, and separating the various Pamir valleys, which were concealed from our view by the low hills in front.

Descending from the Neza Tash Pass a march of a few miles in a westerly direction, through heavy snow, brought us to our camp at Kogachak, which is about three miles above the junction of the stream from the pass, with the Ak-su River. On the following day (3rd from Táshkurghán) crossing the spur between the two streams we descended into the valley of the Ak-sú, a little north of Ak-tash,* at an elevation of 12,600 feet above the sea. We continued south for six miles up the valley, which was here about two miles broad, and deep in snow. In front of us was a fine range of snow covered peaks, running in a direction a little south of west, forming the southern boundary of the little Pámír, which is really the upper portion of the Aksu valley. The latter as we advanced, gradually turns round south-west by south which direction it retains up to and beyond the lake of little Pamir.

The Little Pámír is generally considered to commence near where we entered the Ak-su stream, and consists of a long, nearly level, grassy valley, varying from two to four miles in breadth and enclosed on either side by ranges of snow covered hills sloping down rather gently towards it. Its length from east to west is about 68 miles. The Great Pámír, and all other Pámírs are as far as I could learn, of precisely similar character. The ground intervening between the Great and Little Pámírs is filled up with lofty mountains of tolerably uniform height and without any very conspicuous peaks, the hills to the west near the junction of the two main branches of the Panjah River being perhaps the highest. Our first halt in the Little Pámír was at Onkul, after a march of 25 miles for a great part of the way over snow, and with such a very bitter wind blowing in our faces, that it was almost impossible to hold an instrument in one's hand. After entering the long straight reach above the turning, near Ak-tash, several large open valleys are passed on the north, where the hills are comparatively low and undulating, those on the south side being generally much higher.

Our second day's march (4th from Táshkurghán) through this Pámír took us along an almost level road for 24 miles. As on the previous day, snow covered mountains lay on both sides as we advanced, and there was a great deal of snow in the valley itself which varied in breadth from 2 to 3½ miles. There was often a good deal of saline matter in the soil, and where this was the case the snow generally melted long before it did so elsewhere. Our camp was on the north edge of the Little Pámír Lake, which has been given by recent travellers the very different names of Barkut Yassin, Chalap, and Gez Kul or Goose Lake (Turki, Oi-kul). I made repeated enquiries as to its proper name, and found that the Wakhis generally call it the Kul-i-Pamir Khurd, or lake of Little Pamir, while the Sarikólis and Yárkandis give it the name of Oi-kul.

As some doubts had been expressed, as to the supposed double exit from this lake, I was naturally very anxious to determine the point, and in ascending the valley on this day's march I took at some twenty different points, observations with aneroid barometers to determine, if possible, the exact water-shed, which from previous accounts I had fully expected to find at the east end of the lake. The ground, however, was so level for several miles there being a rise of only 230 feet in the 24 miles between Onkul and the lake, that the aneroid was not sufficiently delicate for the purpose, and although I walked for a considerable distance on the frozen stream to enable me to satisfy myself on the subject, I arrived in camp on the banks of the lake *re-infectá*. The following morning I walked over the lake to its east end, which from a little distance off appeared entirely closed, but on walking round the head to make certain, I was soon undeceived by coming across a very narrow outlet, about nine paces across, and only a few inches deep, all ice of course. I then walked several miles down the stream (east) until I became fully convinced that its bed did slope to the east and drain into the Ak-su. This result being contrary to what I had anticipated, I then rode to the west end of the lake to see whether (as has always been supposed) a stream issued from that end also. I left my horse and started on foot to go round its head; the ice at this

---

* Three miles distant from Kogachak.

end, instead of being firm and strong, as at the other, was very brittle and would not bear my weight, so I had to wade through the heavy snow and slush on its banks. I soon came across a warm spring, from which water was decidedly flowing due east. A little further on I encountered a frozen stream, on going along which westward the barometer showed that I was walking up hill. I advanced still further, hoping to get completely round the head of the lake, so as to be *quite certain* that there was no outlet draining westward, but the walking in the deep snow at so great an elevation had completely exhausted both myself and the man who was with me, and it was with some difficulty that I got back to my horse, and hurrying on with no guide but the tracks in the snow left by the rest of the party, it was with great difficulty that I reached camp, 20 miles from the lake, shortly after dark. On the return journey, the Ressaldar came back by this road, and, according to a promise he had made me, rode completely round the head of the west end of the lake up to the foot of the steep mountain rising on the south side. The snow was then all melted, and water was flowing *into* the lake from the two sources I have just described, and nothing was flowing out. He then went to the east end, whence a stream was flowing towards Ak tásh, so this problem has been solved in a somewhat unexpected manner. The lake has only one outlet, and that eastward, and its waters flow into the Ak-sú, afterwards the Murghábi, which joins the Oxus near Wámar, *and is in all probability the longest branch of the Oxus*.

I have tried hard to discover the true onward course of this Ak-su River. On our return journey we struck it some 14 miles north-north-west of Ak-tash. It flows thence in a northerly direction for 12 miles and then turns off out of sight north-north-west. It is said to flow in a northerly direction for two marches (say 40 miles) from Ak-tash, after which it either joins, or becomes, the Murghábi River changing its course westward and flowing through the Sariz Pámir to Shighnán. It passes through Bartang, a district of Roshán and joins the river Oxus just above Kila Wámar, the chief town of Roshán.

The Little Pámir Lake is 13,200 feet above the sea level. It lies from south-west by west to north-east by east, and for a length of 3½ miles is from 1 to 1½ miles in width; it narrows considerably eastward, where, for about 1½ miles it is nowhere more than a few hundred yards in breadth. Nearly opposite the south-east corner, in a side ravine is a large glacier which drains into the Aksú stream shortly after the latter emerges from the lake.

The road passes along the north side of the lake and crosses the watershed two miles beyond the west end at a height of not more than 150 feet above the margin of the lake. Other parts of the watershed, which is nowhere well defined, are probably still lower. The descent beyond is somewhat rapid; we passed on our left a small stream which rises near the watershed, and takes the drainage of the hills to the south-west of the lake. We went for about seven miles down an open valley, (crossing several small streams flowing down large open ravines on the north), and reached some deserted Kirghiz huts and tombs called Gombaz-i-Bozai, close to where a large stream, the principal affluent of the Sarhadd branch of the Oxus, comes in from the south-east. This river has it source in the Kanjúd mountains on the west side of the Káráchunkar Pass* which crosses the Shíndi or Pámir Range, south of the Neza Tásh Pass, and separates the Taghdumbásh drainage from the head waters of the Oxus.

After passing Gombáz our path lay on the right bank of the Sarhadd stream, where we met with a constant succession of steep ascents and descents. The regular path had often to be quitted in order to avoid drifts of snow, which in places lay very deep. In the winter, when the stream is completely frozen over, its hard surface makes a capital road, which is always used by travellers. We passed at a bad season of the year, too late to be able to keep to the ice with safety as it was now breaking up, and yet before the snow on the upper road was melted. Later on in the hot weather, the lower road becomes altogether impracticable, as it is impossible

---

* The road before mentioned which was once much frequented by Bajaori merchants crosses the Karachunkar Pass. It is now but little used.

90.—Scinde Valley, Cashmere.

91.—Polo Players, Ladakh.

to cross the then swollen river.* After a while our road left the main valley which makes a detour to the left and ascends a gentle slope to a low pass, crossing which the path returns along another broad valley to our camp at Langar. This point has been considered the end of the Pamír, but I should rather be inclined to consider Gombaz-i-Bozai as the true ending. This would reduce its length from Aktash to about 56 miles.

Our next day's march (6th from Táshkurghán) was to Daráz Diwan, a distance of 15 miles; the road soon struck the main valley and continued along its northern side over a constant succession of ascents and descents, passing occasionally through snow in deep patches. We saw on the hill side a large number of juniper trees, and in some of the side ravines were birch trees and wild roses. In fact, wherever water trickled down there were signs of vegetation, but everywhere else the hills were bare. In one or two places the road descended to the river bank; in places the stream was entirely frozen over, the water flowing underneath, elsewhere it was altogether clear of ice. At two or three such places I estimated the breadth to be about 40 feet, depth 2 feet, and velocity 2½ miles per hour, temperature of water 35°. Before reaching camp was a very steep descent, having a fall of over 1,000 feet, which it only took a quarter of an hour to walk down. The river is here called by various names, Kanjúd, Sarhadd, Panjáh, and *Hamun*. The last name I have heard more than once, and it is of course the same as "Amú." Wakhán seems to be but little better off than Turkestan in the numerous names borne by the same stream. Our seventh day's march (8th April) was at first, as hitherto, on the right bank of the stream, the road crossing high spurs by very steep ascents and descents (which lead me to suppose that this was the road followed by Marco Polo). There are three roads used at different times of the year, one (in midwinter) on the surface of the frozen stream, a second which we followed, occasionally along the stream, but which generally passed over spurs, and a third, much higher up, and avoiding the stream altogether. We passed several small tributary streams and between the fifth and seventh miles we had to cross the main stream many times where it passed through very steep hills. We crossed generally over ice and snow bridges. At last we emerged into a large open gravelly plain watered by several streams and soon arrived at the village of Sarhadd (head of the boundary), the highest inhabited village of the Wakhán valley, and situated about 11,000 feet above the sea. The march was only 11 miles, but difficult. We were here met by Ali Murdan Shah, the eldest son of the Mír of Wakhán, who had marched out from Panjah to meet us. On the 8th day (from Táshkurghán) we took a very short march of only four miles to the large village of Patuch or Patur. From this day forward, in order to avoid all cause of suspicion, I took no observations on the road, but accompanied the rest of the party on the march. We were now a large detachment, as we were always escorted by the Mír Bachcha and his somewhat ragged following. This march was, while it lasted, the most trying I have ever experienced, owing to the intense bitterness of the cold wind and drifting snow which blew in our faces the whole way.

From Patuch to Kíla Panjáh, the residence of the Chief of Wakhán, there is not much of geographical interest to notice. At Yúr, 15 miles west of Patuch, a very difficult pathway crosses the mountains to Chitral, and at Vost, about seven miles short of the junction of the two Pámír streams, there is a small fort which covers the entrance of a valley up which another footpath leads to Chitral. The road from Patuch to Panjah, about fifty miles in length, lay along the valley of the Sarhadd stream, sometimes on one side of it, sometimes on the other. The valley was bounded on both sides by lofty and generally precipitous mountains, of whose height it was impossible to form any idea, as their tops and the greater part of their sides were always wrapped in clouds and mists. It was perhaps fortunate for me that I was unable to use my instruments, as I know nothing more disheartening to a surveyor than proceeding for days down a valley under such circumstances. Villages were scattered all along the road on both sides of the stream. In the whole distance from Sarhadd to Panjah there are probably about 400 houses, and their corner turrets, like those in the Sarikól valley, are evidence that the inhabitants have not fallen upon much easier times than their neighbours of Sarikól. The houses are not so good as those of Turkestan, and are apparently especially designed to keep out the wind, which seems always to be blowing violently either up or down the valley, generally speaking from west in the

---

* The road by the great Pamír is then adopted.

morning, and from east in the afternoon. On entering a house one generally passes through the stables, containing two or three horses or cows, after which one traverses a long winding narrow passage, which leads to the centre of the house which is generally very small and dirty. In the centre is a fire-place, a kind of globe-shaped stove, about 2½ feet in diameter, made of mud, and open in front for the passage of air and fire-wood. Above, is a hole in the timber roof for ventilation. The roof is dome-shaped, supported on cross-beams resting on timber uprights which surround the central fire-place, and help to support the side apartments which all open inwards towards the fire and to one another. Here the different members of the family reside. The larger portion of the house is given up to the females, who, somewhat bashful but good humoured, appear to have a very good idea of keeping the men of the household in decent subjection. The males all wear brown woollen *chogas* or cloaks of country make; *pubboes* or boots of the same kind as are worn by the Ladákhis; loose trowsers of the same material as the coat; and a generally scanty cotton turban, the almost universal colour of which is blue and white. The women, who are not over good-looking, but are pleasant and matron-like, dress very much like the men, and have long plaits of hair falling down the side of their heads. There is no artificial modesty or attempt to conceal their faces. In a cottage where we took refuge the females remained present the whole time we were there, and made some most excellent barley bread for us, kneading the flour into a cake which they plastered into the inner wall of the oven; after frequent turning a capital result was secured. Their physiognomies are very divergent, most of them have Jewish noses, but one boy I saw with a most perfect Greek profile. They all age very early, and attribute their grey hairs to the poverty of the country. The men seem affectionately disposed towards the females, always handing them fruits, sweetmeats, or any little trifles we might happen to give them. They are all poor; money and ornaments seem almost unknown, and hardly anything is seen in their houses that is not the produce of the country.

At Sarhadd the temperature of the water was 32°. At Yúr I found it to be 40° while the stream was about 60 feet in width, one and a half feet in depth, with a velocity of two and a half miles an hour. Near Yúr we passed a large stream on the right, and another on the left bank. Throughout the valley there was much jungle wood, and some old coarse grass, but up to date (April 10th) we saw no signs of spring, neither trees budding, nor grass sprouting. The road throughout is very stony, but not otherwise bad. In many places the tributary streams have brought down immense quantities of stones and *débris*, which threaten to block up the main stream. This *débris* generally spreads in a fan-like shape, from where the tributary stream opens into the main valley, and causes the river to flow round the base of the fan. At Bábátangi, the valley, which from Sarhadd had varied from three miles to one mile in width, is confined by precipitous mountains to a breadth of about one-third of a mile. It soon opens again however, and shortly after leaving Sas (about 13 miles above Panjah) it enlarges considerably, and gradually opens into a considerable plain, being joined a few miles above Panjah by the valley containing the stream from Upper Pámír. Before the junction the Sarhadd stream passes for several miles through rather dense jungle composed of red and white willows.

On our march into Zang (near the junction of the streams) we crossed the river of the Great Pámír here about 30 feet wide, one foot deep, with a velocity of about three miles per hour. It was very considerably smaller than the river we had followed from Sarhadd. Where the streams meet the valley is about three and a half miles wide and almost entirely covered with jungle. It narrows gradually towards Panjah, where it has a breadth of two miles. The height of Panjah above the sea I found to be but little more than 9,000 feet. The vegetation in the valley was very backward, much thrown back doubtless by the violent winds which tear up and down with a bitterness difficult to imagine unless it has been felt. The grass was beginning to show signs of sprouting in the middle of April, and the cultivators were then commencing to turn up the soil preparatory to sowing. The Oxus River flows on the north side of the valley, and on its left bank is Panjah, between which and the mountain range to the south, a distance of nearly two miles, the ground is almost completely covered by fields, irrigated by a stream which issues from a large ravine on the south, and is derived from a large glacier which entirely blocks up the valley in which it is situated, and whose foot merging into a snow bed, is not more than 1,000 feet higher than the Oxus valley.

At the head of the ravine containing this glacier are some snowy peaks, about six miles to the south,* which I estimated to be between 17,000 and 18,000 feet in height; they appeared to be on spurs of the Hindoo Koosh Range. It was most annoying being shut up at the bottom of a deep valley, and unable to get a nearer view of these peaks, but there was no help for it, the ravines entering the main valley from north and south were generally inaccessible, the one on the south being, as I before mentioned, blocked up by an enormous glacier, which was quite impassable, while those on the north are almost vertical chasms which looked as if the mountain had been split up by an earthquake. During our stay at Punjab, I ascended the mountains to the north to a height of about 3,000 feet above the valley only to find that I was on the lower portion of a much higher range behind, which obscured all view further north, while the hills to the south of the Oxus were so high that they intercepted the view of any peaks on the main range of the Hindoo Koosh that might otherwise have been seen beyond; in fact I could see very little more than from the ground below. On the only other fine day that we had during our stay at Panjah I went down the valley for about 12 miles, but saw little more than one or two peaks of the range to north.

Panjah itself is, or rather was, built on five small hillocks, hence perhaps its name,† and I have no doubt in my own mind that the river takes its name from the place, and not the place from the river. These five hillocks are situated near each other on the left bank of the stream, the largest is covered by a fort, the residence of the Mír Fateh Ali Sháh, and most of his followers, the other is of nearly equal size, covered by houses, and surrounded by a strong wall; on two others are small fortified buildings, while on the fifth there are nothing but ruins and graves. These fortified buildings (in one of which resides Alif Beg, ex-ruler of Sarikól) from their near proximity to each other, and commanding situation, form a position of considerable strength, and might hold out against an attacking force for some time if artillery were not brought against them. The Mírs of Wakhán have more than once held out in this stronghold against the forces of the Ruler of Badákhshán to which country they are subject. The whole population of Panjah perhaps does not exceed a hundred and fifty souls.

The district of Wakhan has been described by former travellers. It comprises the valleys containing the two heads of the Panjah branch of the Oxus, and the valley of the Panjah itself, from the junction at Zung down to Ishkashím. The northern branch of the Panjah has its principal source in the Lake Victoria in the Great Pamir, which, as well as the Little Pámir belongs to Wakhán, the Ak-tash River forming the well recognized boundary between Kashgharia and Wakhán. Both of the Pámirs were thickly inhabited by Kirghiz in former years, subject to Wákhan, but they are now unoccupied, the constant feuds

---

* Their exact distance I was unable to determine, as they could only be seen up the ravine, which has too narrow to permit of a base being measured across it of sufficient length to enable an accurate estimate to be made of the distance of the peaks.

† "Panj" is the Persian for "five." One possible derivation of the word Panjah is given above. Some authorities would derive the word from the five rivers which are supposed to form the head waters of the river on which Kila Panjah stands. There are two objections to this theory:—

1st.—It is contrary to the custom of Turkestan to name a place after a river, and to a hundred cases that I know of where the converse holds good, i.e., a river is named after a place on its banks, I do not know a single instance of a place being named after a river.

2nd.—The word is usually pronounced *Panjah*, which is nearer in sound to the Persian word "Pinjah" or fifty. The true origin of the word I believe to be from the Panjah or *palm* (of the hand) of Hazrat Ali (the son-in-law of Muhammad). In a building on a small hill about 2 miles to the south of Kila Panjah is a stone bearing the impress of a hand. Local tradition says that when this country was in the hands of the Zar-dushtis, or atash-parast (fire worshippers) the people were converted to the religion of Muhammad by a visit (in the spirit) from Hazrat Ali, who left his mark on the stone as thus described, which is an object of religious veneration in the neighbourhood. At Bar Panjah in Shighnan is a similar mark over which the Fort "Bar Panjah," "over the Panjah," has been built. Possibly this tradition has something in common with that which attributes the derivation of the word Pámir to "Pa-e-Mír," i.e., the foot of the Mír Hazrat Ali. I would myself be inclined to derive the word from "Pam," the Kirghiz word for roof, and "yer," which is both Turki and Kirghiz, for "earth" corresponding to the Persian word "Zamín." Bam-i-dunya or "roof of the world" is a name by which the Pamir is well known.

between the Shighnis, the Wakhis, the Kirghiz of the Alai, and the Kanjudis, having rendered the country quite unsafe. The highest inhabited village in the northern valley is Langar Kisht, only a few miles above the junction, and on the right bank of the stream. The Sarhadd valley (the southern branch) is inhabited from Sarhadd downwards, and there are villages scattered along both banks of the Panjah river down to Ishkashim. Wákhán formerly contained three "sads" or hundreds, *i.e.*, districts, containing 100 houses each—

1st.—Sad-i-Kila Vost or Sarhadd extending from Langar to Hissar.
2nd.—Sad Sipanj* from Hissar to Khandut.
3rd.—Sad Khandut from Khandut to Sad Ishtragh.

To these three Sads has recently been added that of Sad Ishtragh, which I believe only became a portion of Wakhan in recent times. It lies between Khandut and the State of Ishkashim.† Abdúl Subhán estimates the number of houses in Sad Ishtragh at 250, and allowing 100 for each of the other districts this gives a total of 550 houses, with a population of about 3,000 souls.

The Oxus below Wakhán.

I have now to deal with one of the most interesting geographical problems of the day, *viz.*, the probable course of the Oxus or Panjah from the point where it leaves Wakhán to where it emerges in the plains north of Said village on the frontiers of Koláb, where it has been seen and described by our countryman, Lieutenant Wood. My assistant, Abdúl Subhán, left us at Kila Panjah (the most westerly point reached by the European members of the Mission), and followed the course of the Oxus through Wakhán for 63 miles to Ishkashim, thence turning northwards he followed the same river for nearly a hundred miles, passing successively through the districts of Gháran, Shighnán, and Roshán, countries which have hitherto been known to us hardly even by name. From his report I have obtained the information following.

The small State of Ishkashim forms, together with Zebák, one of the numerous petty feudal States tributary to Badakhshán. The present ruler of both these small districts is Sháh Abdul Rahim, a Syud of Khorassan, who was placed in power by Muhammad Alum Khan, the present Governor of Balkh. It is said that the hereditary Chief of the country, Mír Hak Nazar, was ejected in order to make room for Abdul Rahim. The present territory of Ishkashim extends for about 16 miles to the north of the village of the same name, which now contains about forty houses, and consists, as is generally the case in those parts, of numerous scattered farm houses. There are small villages throughout this district on both banks of the Oxus; Sumchún and two others on the right bank, and Yákh-duru and Sar-i-Shakh on the left. These belonged to Sad Ishtragh, which was once a separate principality, but is now a district of Wakhán.

The road from Ishkashim runs along the left bank of the river up to six miles beyond Sar-i-Shakh, where the river is crossed by an easy ford. In the month of May the water flowed in a single stream, which was 3½ feet deep and about 200 yards in width. In summer it is impossible to cross the river at this point, and a very difficult path leading along the left bank is followed. Down to this point the valley is open, four or five miles in breadth and richly cultivated. The ford marks the boundary between Ishkashim and the district of *Kucheh Gharan* or "narrow caves," which has been for centuries famous for its ruby mines.

The Gháran country extends along both banks of the Oxus for about twenty-four miles, and was once upon a time rich, flourishing, and populous. Remains of large villages exist on both banks, and bear witness to the oppression that has been exercised by successive Governors of Badakhshán. The fields near these deserted villages are now cultivated by the inhabitants of the neighbouring districts of Rágh (the chief town of which is Kila Masnúj) and Sar Gholám‡ which are at a distance of a long day's journey on the further side of a range of hills, running parallel to and on the left bank of the river. *Barshár*

---

* Sad-i-Panjah.
† Written in the vernacular Shikashem.
‡ Subordinate to Badakhshán.

92.—Scinde Valley, Cashmere.

93.—Sonamarg.

or "above the river," situated four miles below the ford, is the first of these large deserted villages. A little beyond it a large stream enters the Oxus from the east deriving its name, the Boguz, from a village of some 30 houses situate ten miles up the stream. From this village a road goes to the Shákhdarah district of Shighnan. Near the junction of the Boguz with the Panjah the road crosses to the left bank of the river. Nearly opposite to Barshúr is a ravine by which a road goes over the Aghirda Pass to Faizabad, the chief town of Badakhshán. It is said to be open all the year round. Throughout the remainder of the Gháran district numerous ruins are passed on both sides of the stream, the largest of which, Shekh Beg, on the right bank, must formerly have contained about 200 houses. On the same side of the river some sixteen miles below Barshar are the celebrated ruby mines, once the source of considerable wealth to the Rulers of Badakhshán, but now apparently nearly exhausted. These mines have until lately always been worked for the immediate benefit of the Governors of Badakhshán. At the present time some 30 men are employed there under the orders of a few sepoys belonging to Muhammad Alum Khan, the Governor of Turkestan, who sends the produce to the Amír of Cabul. It was said that during the past year one large ruby about the size of a pigeon's egg was found and sundry smaller ones, the whole of which were sent to the Amír.

The rubies are found in one very large cavern to which there are three entrances, situated about 1,000 feet above the river, and about a mile up the hill side; the task of excavating appears to be not unattended with risks, as three workmen were recently killed, having fallen from the rocks while searching for the precious stones. There is a peculiar kind of soft white stone which is found imbedded in the harder rock and in this the rubies are found. In former years the inhabitants of Gháran who worked these mines paid no taxes and held their lands rent-free. The twenty men who are now employed at the mines have to furnish their own food as well as that of the guard, and also to provide lights, torches, and implements for working. The numerous deserted villages prove the possession of the mines to have been a curse rather than a blessing to the inhabitants of the valley, who have from time immemorial been under the direct rule of the Chief of Badakhshán.

Above the mines is a small village called Koh-i-Lal or "Ruby Mountain," and about one mile below them on the opposite bank of the river is the large deserted village of Shekhbeg whose ruined houses are built with stone and lime.* A small river enters at Shekhbeg on the left bank, and four miles up it lies the village of Gháran Bálá said to contain about 100 houses, invisible from the river. A few miles below Shekhbeg on the right bank of the Panjah is the village of "Garm Chashma" (hot springs) where a large stream of warm water joins the main river. On the banks of this stream the Munshi saw 20 or 30 men employed in washing the sand for gold. They were Badakhshís, and farmed the washings of the Gháran district for Rupees 200† per annum paid to the Ruler of Badakhshán. It is only within the last two years that gold has been found in this district.

Three miles beyond this is the Kuguz Parin,‡ the boundary between Gháran and Shighnán. The road throughout the Gháran district lies along the banks of the Panjah, and is in places very difficult to traverse. The valley near Barshar contracts to about one mile in width, and the road runs over large boulders alongside the river, which flows between nearly perpendicular banks; the stream is narrow and swift being not more than 200 feet across, and is almost a continuous succession of rapids. Throughout the district the Panjah valley is nowhere much more than a mile in width, and is confined by very precipitous mountains; the river is everywhere deep. In Gháran apricots of very large size and fine flavour are produced; these are held in great repute in Badakhshán. Apples and pears are met with in abundance; and but little grain is grown. There is abundance of grass and fuel to be found at the various camping grounds throughout the valley. The water of the Panjah is rarely or never used for

---

* The villages in these countries are usually built of stone and mud.

† About twenty pounds sterling.

‡ Kuguz Parin in Shighai dialect means "holes in the rock." The Persian equivalent is "Rafak-i-Somakh."

irrigation or for water mills. In the hot weather, oxen, horses, and sheep (for which the country is famous) are driven up side valleys to the tops of the mountains for grazing, returning to the valley in October in splendid condition.

Kuguz Parin consists of a tunnel passing through a mountain. On the south side, the road rises by a winding stone staircase, for a height of about 200 feet, to the mouth of the tunnel, which is excavated through solid rock, and is about 100 paces in length, and so narrow and low that it is impossible for a loaded horse to traverse it. The tunnel is said to have been constructed some three hundred years ago. Where the road emerges on the north side the path is so narrow that a projecting mass of rock often precipitates animals into the foaming torrent beneath. The river is here about 150 yards in width, and flows some 500 feet below the mouth of the tunnel.* The Shighnis boast of this place as the natural safeguard of their country, and call it their "father."

From Kuguz Parin the Oxus flows through the country of Shighnán, which extends for a distance of sixty miles down to the Darband Tower on the frontier of Roshán. This tower is situated on a high rock standing over the river, towards which it presents a perpendicular scarp of about 150 feet. The water beneath is very deep. The roadway winds round the tower,† and the ascent on both sides is very steep and difficult. The Shighnis call this place their "mother." It is a common saying in the country that if ever there should be a quarrel between Shighnan and Roshán, whichever State first seizes this tower will keep possession of both countries. The river is here barely a gunshot across, and there is no path whatever on the other side.

This country of Shighnan would appear to be richer and of much more importance than Wakhan and other districts of Badakhshán with which we are acquainted. From Kuguz Parin to Darband Tower there are numerous villages scattered along both banks of the river.‡ These are surrounded with gardens, orchards and well cultivated lands. The chief town, Bar Panjah,§ is on the left bank, and with its suburbs probably contains about 1,500 houses. The palace is inside the fort, and is built of stone; the windows have shutters outside as in Cabul and Cashmere. The fort itself is square, each side being about 500 paces in length. The walls are very strong, and about 40 feet high, built of clay, stone, and wood. There are five loopholed towers, but these contain no big guns. There is a garrison of about 400 soldiers, who are mostly armed with swords manufactured in the country itself, and with guns, said to be made by the Kirghiz, similar to those which are supplied to the Kashghar troops *viz.*, heavy rifled weapons which are fired resting on the ground, the muzzle being supported on a prong attached to the barrel of the rifle. Lead and all the materials employed in the manufacture of gunpowder are found in the country. The valley at Bar Panjah is about four miles wide and contains a great many houses and gardens. The river runs in numerous channels separated by jungle covered islands. Short punt shaped boats, similar to those in Central India, are used at the ferry. In July and August, when there is much water in the river, all travellers have to cross at Bar Panjah, to the other bank, the road on the left bank being then impracticable.

In its passage through Shignán the Oxus receives two considerable affluents on the left bank, the Shewa and Vacherv River. The former is crossed by a good bridge, and was about 25 yards in width, and unfordable, when the Múnshi passed in May. It flows from a lake in the Shewá Pamir, a favored pasture ground much frequented by herds of horses, sheep, and cattle from Badakhshán. The owners of these flocks are said to make payments to the King of Shighnán for the right of grazing there. The Vacherv River is about the same size as the Shewa stream, and joins the Panjah to the south of Bar Panjah. Along it lies a much frequented road from Shighnan, over the Shewa Pámir, to Faizabad.

---

* This portion of the route is not improbably the *Tangi Badascani* of Benedict Goez.

† At the tower was a guard of soldiers from Wamur, who examines the passports of all travellers.

‡ The names of these villages and the distances apart will be found in the Appendix.

§ Or "above Panjah" so named from having been built originally over a stone similar to the one at Kila Panjah, which was supposed to bear the impress of the *Panjah* or *palm* of Hazrat Ali.

On its right bank the Oxus receives one very large river, the Suchán, formed by two large streams, the Shákhdara and the Ghund, which unite about half a mile before joining the Panjah. The two branches are of about equal size, and the united stream is about two-thirds of the size of the main river, which continues to be called the Ab-i-Panjah. The Suchán stream enters a few miles south of Bar Panjah. The valley opens opposite the junction to a width of about four miles, forming a beautiful well cultivated plain, with a good deal of pasture land, generally covered with horses and cattle from Bar Panjah, which place forms a most picturesque addition to the landscape, situated as it is on a white rock surrounded by trees and gardens, which extend uninterruptedly a distance of about two miles north of the fort.

Both the Shákhdara and the Ghund Rivers have numerous villages on their banks. On the former at two days' march from Bar Panjah is the large fort of Rách, the residence of the Governor (Hákim) of the Shakhdara district, which is said to contain about 500 houses. The Ghund valley, the chief place on which is Chársím, is said to contain about 700 houses. Roads lie up both these valleys to the Pámir steppes. The Pamír at the head of the Ghund valley goes by the name of Bugrúmál, and is possibly a continuation of, if not identical with, the Alichúr Pámir. The direct road to Kashghar up this valley is said to be a much easier road than that by Tashkúrghán.

At Sácharv, nine miles north of Bar Panjah, in the Shighnan valley, the river narrows and becomes turbulent and the road is very bad. Sixteen miles further on is the Darband Tower before described. Beyond it lies the territory of Roshán, a dependency of Shighnan, and ruled by the same King, Yusuf Ali Khan.

Two and a half miles beyond Darband is the junction of the Murghab River with the Panjah. This is the river I have already traced from its source in the Lake of Little Pamir under the name of Ak-su. It is also said to carry away water from Lakes Karakul* and Rang-kul. The Panjah valley, which at Darband is very narrow, rapidly widens to five miles, and would be fit for cultivation, but that the ground is frequently flooded by the Murgháb River. The Munshi crossed the river about two hundred paces above its junction with the Panjah; the stream was in three channels, and the torrent was so rapid that most of the horses lost their footing. The Panjah stream was very clear, but the Murgháb was red, thick, and muddy. The volume of the latter was considerably larger and its velocity greater than that of the Panjah.† From bank to bank the width of the river bed is about one and a half miles, and of this at least one mile was covered with water. The passage was effected with great difficulty. In the summer floods the water is said to extend from mountain to mountain, a distance of not less than five miles; it can then only be crossed by boats.

This river is generally called the Murgháb, but it is also known by the name of the Darya-i-Bartang, so called from the district of that name through which it flows. Three miles below the junction, on the right bank of the now united rivers, which still bear the name of *Panjah*, is Wámur, the chief town of Roshán.

Wámur is a flourishing place; a large Fort‡ about the same size as that of Bar-Panjah, is surrounded by several hundred houses and orchards. Fruits and grain grow in abundance, and the soil is very fertile.

The Múnshi remained several days at Kila Wámur, where the King of Shighnán was residing.§ He was enabled to visit thence the *Fatíla Sang*,‖ which together with the ruby mines are described in the *Sir*¶ as the two sights of Badakhshán. It is situated about three and a half miles down the river, underlying the mountains. He extracted

---

* I am myself by no means sure as to whether this river does really receive any water from Lake Karakul.
† This statement of the Múnshi is confirmed by other sources of information which I possess.
‡ With a garrison of about 200 men.
§ The King generally spends the winter months at Kila Wámur returning for the summer to Bar Panjah.
‖ "The wick stone," probably *asbestos*.
¶ The "Sir" is a book written by Moulvi Imám Afzál, Khorassani.

some fragments from the rock *in situ* and brought them away. They consisted of a sort of soft fibrous stone which can be twisted into the shape of a wick, and when saturated with oil will burn almost for ever.* From the Fatíla stone he went two miles further down the river to the village of Pigish, the furthest point reached by him. At this point the *Oxus*, which from Ishkashim, a distance of about 100 miles, had been flowing due north, takes a sudden bend to the west, and going in that direction for a few miles turns apparently to the north.

The Roshán territory is divided into three districts—the Wámur on the right bank embracing the upper portion of the *Oxus* valley, and containing about 800 houses. The district of Pa-e-Khoja lies on the left bank of the *Oxus*, below the turn to the west before alluded to, and is said to contain about 1,000 houses. It is at a long day's journey below Wámur. This district is inhabited by *Khojahs*† who pay no tribute, but give their services as soldiers in time of war. The third district is that of Bartang,‡ which lies up the river of that name, and is said to contain about 500 houses. The direct approach to this district from the Panjah valley is very difficult, owing to the precipitous defiles through which the river passes; so that the most frequented road between Wámur and Sirich Fort, the chief place of the Bartang district, lies by the somewhat roundabout way of the Ghund valley.

The Múnshi gives the following particulars about Shighnán:—

"The country of Shighnán and Roshán is sometimes called Zuján (or two-lived); its climate and water being so good that a man on entering the district is said to have come into possession of two lives. The inhabitants state that their country is called Lubnán in the *Gulistan* of Sheikh Sádi of Shiraz, and that it is by this name that their country is known in Persia. Sheikh Sádi writes that 'there is one good Mussulman in Lubnán' (Ek-i-az-Sulhai Lubnán)."

"In time of war, the two countries combined can produce 7,000 armed men, which allowing three men from each two houses would give a present total of about 4,500 for the number of houses in Shighnan and Roshán together."

"The family of the Shah-i-Shighnán originally came from Persia. The first arrival from that country (said to have taken place about from 500 to 700 years ago) was the '*Shah-i-Khamosh*,' who was a Syud and a fakir. The country was at that time in the hands of the Zerdushtis, a very powerful and learned race. The Shah commenced to teach these people the Korán. There were already at this time Mussulmen in the neighbouring country of Darwáz, A.H. 665, and on the arrival of the Shah-i-Khamosh many people flocked thence into Shighnán. In about ten years' time he had converted large numbers of the people, and a civil war commenced which ended in the Shah-i-Khamosh wresting the kingdom from Kahakah, the then Governor of Shighnán and Roshán, under the Zerdushtis, the seat of whose Government was in Balkh. After another ten years the whole of the people were converted to the Shiah religion. The tomb of Shah-i-Khamosh now exists at Bar Panjah. Every Thursday people meet to worship there."

"The Chinese during their occupation of Kashghar used to pay to the surrounding countries a kind of subsidy, in return for which the States to whom the payments were made used to guarantee to keep the roads open, and safe for merchants. For this service the Shah-i-Shighnán used to receive an annual payment of ten *Yamboos*;§ the ruler of Sarikol used to receive six; the Kanjudis four; and the ruler of Wakhán three."

"At one period it is said that Wakhán and Darwaz and all the surrounding States were under the rule of the King of Shighnán."

The Múnshi did not succeed in bringing back much information about the course of the Oxus below Wámur. The furthest point down the river reached by him was Pigish, a village

---

* Probably *asbestos*.

† *i.e.*, whose ancestors are Syuds on one side only.

‡ Or "Above the Narrows."

§ A yamboo is a large piece of silver valued about Rupees 170 or seventeen pounds sterling.

four or five miles below Wámur. About five miles beyond Pigish on the right bank, is the village of Bar Roshán, on the frontier of Roshán. At one day's march beyond this, also on the right bank, is Waznud, the frontier village of Darwáz. Between Waznud and Bar Roshán the Pa-e-Khoja valley before alluded to enters the Panjah valley on the south. Five marches along the Panjah beyond Waznúd is Kila Khúmb, the chief town of the country of Darwáz. The road to it along the river is very difficult, and impassable for laden horses, the valley being very narrow, and the banks of the river very precipitous. Kila Khúmb is said to lie in a northerly direction from Wámur and can be reached in three days by a short summer road, which lies up the small stream which enters the Panjah (right bank) at Wámur. The boundary between Darwaz and Shighnán is the water-shed at the head of the Wámur ravine.*

The country of Darwáz possesses villages on both banks of the river Panjah. At Khúmb itself the fort is on the right bank, but some houses are on the left bank of the river. Below Darwáz is said to be the country of Khatlán, the chief town of which is Koláb.

Part of this information, which was supplied by the Múnshi as the result of enquiries made by him, is directly contradictory to the existing ideas of the geography of these regions, and I was at one time disinclined to place much reliance on it. In plotting on paper the Múnshi's route survey, it was found that the course of the Panjah river lies much to the north of the position assigned to it in existing maps. I was at first unable to reconcile this with what little authentic information we have, either from English or Russian sources, but further consideration, and study of the subject, has to a certain extent cleared the matter up. While at Simla, immediately after my return to India, I was examining some old documents in the Quarter Master General's Office, and lighted on a paper of considerable importance. It was a copy of a document well known to students of Central Asian Geography, *viz.*, the route from Khokand to Peshawur, by the Shahzada Sultan Mahomed, an Envoy who came from Khokand to India in 1854. The peculiarity of this individual copy is that it contains a marginal note that six of the halting places on the route, *viz.*, "Faizbad, Naruk, Tootkul, Buljuwan, Kulab, and Surchushma, are on the banks of the River Hamoon, which is called Panj by the natives." In the margin was a note, bearing the initials of no less a person than the present Lord Lawrence stating that the Hamoon was the same as the Oxus. The significance of the document consists in the fact that Lord Lawrence (who was then Chief Commissioner for the Punjab) was the person who originally took down the statements of the Khokandian Ambassador, who, during his stay at Murree, "lived for some weeks within a few yards of the Chief Commissioner's residence, and had frequent and intimate intercourse with him." It is evident that the document I had lighted on was a copy of the original statement as taken down by Lord Lawrence, whereas all other versions that I have seen, of the same route, omit the note that the six places abovementioned are on the banks of the Oxus.

The deduction that I made from this note was, that the Surkháb River probably joined the Oxus or Panjah somewhere above Faizabad and Naruk, and consequently that the latter river took a very considerable detour to the North, as is shown on my Preliminary Map. There were many arguments in support of this view, which it is now unnecessary to enter upon, as one of the Trans Frontier explorers, "the Havildar," has just returned from a visit to Koláb and Darwáz, and although there has not yet been time to plot the details of his work, sufficient is known to prove that the *note* to which I have alluded must be erroneous, and consequently the portion of my map which was mainly founded thereon is also erroneous. The true course of the Oxus will, I believe, be found to occupy a position intermediate between those shown on my map and on all preceding ones.

Return to Yarkánd viâ the Great Pámir.

Our return route to Yárkand lay up the north branch of the Panjah River, which flows westwards from Wood's (Victoria) Lake through a portion of the Great Pámir. Leaving

---

* Four miles above Wámur on this stream is a mine from which a rich iron ore (kurch) is obtained. At Bar Roshán also iron is found in large quantities.

Panjah on the 26th of April (the day previous to which was the first warm day we had since leaving Yangi-Hissar, the thermometer in the shade going up to 74° and in the sun to 99°) we made a short march of only six miles to Langarkish (9,350 feet), the highest inhabited spot on the road up to the lake. We passed on the left the villages of Zang and Hissar, between which is a hot spring* (temperature 120°) enclosed in a stone building and said to possess valuable curative properties, for the sake of which the old Mír occasionally visits the spot. I may note that hot springs are of frequent occurrence in these mountains; some near Patur in the Sarhadd valley have a temperature of about 160°. These springs have a sensible influence on the temperature of the rivers they flow into, a fact which tends to neutralize any argument (such as that used by Wood) that the relative elevation of the sources of the two branches of the Oxus, may be estimated from the temperature of the streams at their junction.

Where the two Pámir streams meet opposite Zang, the united river was about 40 yards wide and one and a half feet deep, with a velocity of three and a half miles per hour. This measurement was taken at 11 A.M. at which period of the day the river had not attained its full size and velocity. In the hot weather at Panjah it cannot be forded, but is crossed by rafts made of skins.

Close by the village of Hissar (or Asshor) on a small isolated rocky hill, is the ancient fort (or kila or kalhai) of Zanguebar, which I examined in hopes of finding some relic of Zoroastrian worship. The ruined walls had, within memory, been used as dwelling-houses by the inhabitants of the neighbouring village, but I could discern no relics of antiquity, except fragments of a surrounding wall, and an arch formed by large slabs of stone resting, on either side, on solid rock.

At Langar Kish, a very picturesque village, a fair sized stream from the north joined the main stream, passing through one of those characteristic fissures I have before alluded to. I tried to ascend it, but was very soon stopped by enormous boulders lying in the bed of the stream which flows between perpendicular rocky banks. From this village we had to take all our supplies for the return journey to Sarikól, and as collecting sufficient even for a rapid journey was found to be a matter of considerable difficulty, we had here reluctantly to give up all idea of halting on the road or making any detour for exploration.

Our first march from Langar Kish was about 18 miles to Yumkhana (also called Jangalik). The road follows the right bank of the river rising above it in several places as much as 1,000 feet. From both sides occasional small mountain streams help to swell the waters of the main river. We passed on our right several ruined huts formerly occupied by Kirghiz, who many years ago abandoned this part of the country. The descendants of the men who accompanied Wood on this same journey, driven away by the insecurity of life and property, are now many of them quietly settled, hundreds of miles away, in the neighbourhood of Kilian and Sanju, under the rule of the Amír of Kashghar. Not a single Kirghiz, I was given to understand, remains even under the nominal sway of the Mír of Wakhan. As we advanced the valley opened somewhat, and the mountains on the south appeared to decrease in height, radiating from a pointed peak situated between the two branches of the Panjah River. After a time we came to the Ab-i-Zer-i-Zamin, a stream flowing from the north-west through banks 1,000 feet in height. We had to descend to the bed of the stream, cross and ascend the opposite side, and then traverse a plain, formed by a broad terrace at the foot of the range on our left, and situate about 1,000 feet above the bed of the Oxus. Four miles after passing the Zer-i-Zamin River we reached our camp, where some springs and rich soil had combined to produce a profusion of grass and fire-wood. From our tents we had a very fine view down the valley, seeing in particular one very prominent snowy peak, probably 20,000 feet in height, situated near the head of the glacier opposite Panjah. Next day we continued along the right bank of the river, passing, after five miles, the Ab-i-Matz, along which

---

* Curiously enough a cold spring with a temperature of 60° F. issues from the ground within a few feet of the hot one.

is the summer road to Shighnan * from the head of the Wakhan valley. This road crosses the Joshugaz, a very high and lofty pass closed by snow throughout the winter and spring, and proceeds down the Shakh Darah (valley) to Kila Rach, the residence of the Hákim of the Shakh Darah District of Shighnan. From Rách a road continues down the stream to Bar Panjah.

On our own road, two miles beyond Ab-i-Matz, is Boharak, an occasional halting place of caravans, stated by our guide to be the commencement of the Great Pámír. Here, the valley, hitherto half a mile across, widens into a large flat open plain, one and a half miles in width, said to have abounded in former years with the magnificent Pamír sheep (Ovis Poli). Of these we saw nothing but bones and skulls. Severe murrain has within the last few years carried off not only nearly the whole of the wild sheep, but also the ibex. Six miles beyond Boharak was our camp at Yol Mazár (road-side temple), two miles short of which is a large stream joining the river on its left bank, and of equal bulk with it. Near the camp a smaller stream entered on the right bank. I ascended this for some distance and found an open grassy valley in which there were some huts in ruins, and some obvious traces of former cultivation; it was doubtless once the residence of Kirghiz. At our camp, which was at an elevation of about 12,000 feet above the sea, there was plenty of fire-wood and grass, this was the highest point in the valley at which good fire-wood was found, although further up and throughout this Pámír there was abundance of "boortsee" and grass. Two inches of snow fell at night, but the morning, though cold, was fine.

We were now fairly in the Great Pámír; the grassy valley, about a mile broad, was bounded by terraces formed by low spurs coming down in gentle slopes from the mountain ranges on both sides. On the 29th April we continued our march along the Pámír to Bilaor Bas. The road was excellent throughout, as in fact it was the whole way, from Panjah to Ak-tásh, although at starting there are numerous steep ascents and descents. This day's march was along the right bank of the river, through a grassy plain, bounded on both sides by low undulating hills. The valley gradually widens, but the flat grassy portion is nowhere much more than a mile in width, the ascent was steady, and the road everywhere first-rate. Shortly before reaching camp we passed on our left the Ab-i-Khargoshi which flows from and through the Khargoshi plain, beyond which, at a day's journey from camp, is the Alichur Pámír, which nominally belongs to Wakhán, but practically to Shighnán.† In it lies a small salt lake "Tuz-kul" from which no water flows, and beyond which the drainage goes to Shighnán. Two days' march from this lake, i.e., three days from our camp, the Alichur stream is said to fall into the Murghábi. The Alichur Pámír is reported to be higher but smaller than the Great Pámír, and to possess roads going in every direction.

On the 30th we continued along the Great Pámír for 20 miles to Mázar Tupa, the plain getting gradually wider and wider as we advanced, until a breadth of six miles is attained. The valley is not so well defined, as that of the Little Pámír, where steep mountains bordered the plain on both sides. Here low spurs from the mountain ranges north and south run into and are hardly to be distinguished from the plain. The mountains on the south are considerably higher than those on the north, the former rise to about 5,000 feet‡ and the latter to about 2,500 feet above the river bed, giving absolute heights of 18,000 and 15,500 feet, respectively.

The next day five miles of very gentle ascent brought us to the west end of Wood's Victoria Lake, which, like its sister in the Little Pámír, was supposed to have two outlets. Of that to the west there could be no doubt; through a channel some 12 paces wide, a little stream 6 inches deep, and with a velocity of 2½ miles an hour, emerged from under the ice with which the lake was covered, and flowed steadily westward. The temperature of the water was 35°, and

---

* *Vide* Appendix. Section Routes.

† i.e., according to the statement of the Wakhis who accompanied us.

‡ Elevations of hills were measured with an "Abney's clinometer," which I always used to carry in my pocket. Their positions were fixed by the intersections of compass bearings taken at different points on the line of march; the heights of the latter were determined hypsometrically.

it was thus evident that the lake was partially supplied from warm springs. A few wild fowl were congregated near this end of the lake doubtless waiting for the rapidly approaching warm weather to melt the ice and enable them to proceed with their parental duties.

The lake runs nearly due east and west, is about ten miles long, and nowhere more than two miles in breadth.

The valley in which it lies is, opposite the lake, about four miles broad. The height of the hills to the north I estimated at 3,000 feet above the level of the lake, while those on the south were at least 2000 feet higher.

The only name by which the lake is *well known* to natives is "Kul-i-Pámír Kalan," *i.e.*, lake of the Great Pámír. I have once or twice heard it called "Airán Kul," or buttermilk lake. To avoid confusion, and to make as little possible change in existing nomenclature, I purpose calling it "Kul-i-Pámír Kalan," or "Victoria Lake," the last name being the one originally bestowed by its discoverer, Lieutenant Wood. Our camp, which was about two miles east of its head was called by the "Wákhis" Sar-i-kul (head of the lake), a camp in a corresponding position at the lower end being called "Bun-i-kul" (foot of the lake). This may account for the other name erroneously given to it by Lieutenant Wood (Sir-i-kól).

After reaching camp, a distance of 16½ miles, I went to the head of the lake to investigate its drainage and determine its limits (for from a little distance off it was impossible to discriminate between the ice and snow on the lake, and the snow on shore). I was soon convinced that all the water from the hills at the east end drained *into* the lake, which therefore like its neighbour in the Little Pámír has but one outlet, although in the former case the water flows west, and in the latter east. To the East of the lake the valley opens out, and forms a large basin which extends ten or twelve miles from West to East, and six miles from North to South. At the lower portion of this basin, surrounding the head of the lake, is a great deal of marshy ground formed by the drainage which enters from numerous side valleys,* coming from the hills on the South. At the time of our visit this marsh was covered with snow and ice; but later on in the season, when the snow is melting on the surrounding hills, there is much water, and the place is said to become the favoured breeding place of thousands of geese.

Our march from Sir-i-kul lay along the Northen side of the valley, the whole of which was deep in snow, and was so level that I experienced considerable difficulty in determining the correct position of the water-shed, which was crossed at a distance of twelve miles from the east end of the lake and at a height of 14,320 feet. A frozen stream here comes down from the North, divided into two portions by a low ridge of gravel, one flowing eastward into the Aksu River, the other westward into the lake.

Eastward from the water-shed the Great Pámír valley contracts. We followed down a rivulet which, shortly before passing the camp at Shásh Tupa, joins a considerable stream coming down a broad valley from the North. The name of our camp was derived from the "Shásh Tupa" or "six hills" by which it is surrounded, and between each pair of which roads issue to different parts of the Pámír steppes.

Our road from Shásh Túpa lay for nearly eight miles due north on the right bank of the stream, and then continued down it for ten miles in a north-east direction to the camp "Dahn-i-Isligh."† On our left we passed three broad open ravines, containing streams coming from the west; one of them was nearly as large as the river we were following, and before joining

---

* Up one of these valleys is a road accross the hills to Langar in the Great Pamir. One good day's march takes the traveller over the Warram Kotal (Pass), another half day to Langar, and another half day to Sarhadd (horse marches). This is the road by which a very short time ago Jehandar Shah, the Ex-Mir of Badakhshan, when attacked by the Cabul troops, fled, accompanied by several hundred followers, to Yassin. His shorter route from Panjah would doubtless have been up the Sarhadd valley, but anticipating that he would be intercepted on that line, he made the long detour above mentioned, passing through uninhabited country the whole way from Langar Kish, and striking the Little Pamir at a considerable distance above Sarhadd, instead of having to fight his way up to the latter place.

† "Mouth of the Isligh."

94.—A Hadji of Karghalik.

95.—Tash-Khoja, an andijani Yazbashi.

96.—Two Natives of Sanjwa.

97.—Group of Yarkundis of the lower classes.

it passed through a plain some six miles long and two broad. At Dahn-i-Isligh the river is joined by two more streams, the Kizil Robat coming from the south-east, and the Karasu from the west, both of which pass through broad grassy valleys. The ground is very open, and may be traversed in almost every direction. Two or three miles north-east of our Camp the Great Pámír terminates, having extended for a distance of some 90 miles from Boharak.

From Dahn-i-Isligh I took a path which follows the Isligh stream, until it emerges into the Aksu plain; this road is somewhat circuitous, and the rest of the party took a shorter line, going over a low pass, and rejoined the main stream about 16 miles from our starting point. The path I followed is rarely used by travellers; in summer it is quite impassable on account of floods. When I went down it (in April) the ice was breaking up, and travelling was somewhat dangerous, as the river had to be crossed many times. The hills on the north are very precipitous, and in places rise nearly perpendicularly to a height of some 2,000 feet above the river bed. Where the two paths unite, the valley opens, and down it a good road leads to the Aksu plain, which is crossed diagonally in a S.-E. direction. Prior to reaching our camp at Ak-tásh we had much difficulty in crossing the Aksu River, which was much swollen by melting snow. On this march (37 miles in length) I had the good fortune to shoot an "Ovis Poli," the only one that has fallen to the rifles of our party.

At Ak-tásh we rejoined the road we had followed on our outward journey, and returned by it, to Tashkurghán and Yárkand making the slight variations in our route, to which I have already alluded.

It appears from the foregoing narrative that although the name Pámír has been inaccurately employed as a generic term covering the whole of the elevated mass lying between the Hindu Kúsh and the mountains of Khokand, yet it is rightly applied to some of the *steppes* which occupy a large portion of this region. These steppes would appear to be a series of broad undulating grassy valleys, formed on the surface of an elevated plain, by lofty ridges running more or less parallel to the equator. The general slope of the plateau is from east to west. Its eastern portion is gently undulating, and comparatively flat, while its western edge merges into spurs, which slope down gradually to the west, and are separated by bold and precipitous defiles. On the east the Pámír steppes are bounded by a transverse ridge, which has been appropriately termed the Pámír range by Pundit Manphul. This ridge runs in a direction from south-south-west to north-north-east and is the true watershed between Eastern and Western Turkestan; at the Neza Tash Pass where we crossed it, the watershed is very clearly defined; the ridge was seen trending as far north as latitude 38° 15'; it appeared to sink gradually, and I was informed by Kirghiz that it eventually subsided to the level of the Kízil-art plains a little short of the Great Karákul (lake) in which vicinity a difference of level of a few feet may probably determine the flow of water, either into the Sea of Aral in Western Turkestan, or into the semi-mythical lake of Lop, on the confines of China.

To the east of the Pámír range there is an extensive plateau, which stretches from the Muztagh range of the Himalaya mountains up to the South Khokand range—the Trans-Alai of Fedchenko—in the parallel of 39½°. Portions of it are designated in order from south to north as the Taghdumbásh Pámír, the Sarikol or Tashkurghan valley, the Tagharma, and the Kízil-art plains. This plateau is in turn bounded on the east by the range to which Hayward gave the name of the Kízil-art, the name by which it is known to the inhabitants of Kashghar, and which runs nearly parallel to Pandit Manphul's Pámír range. Fedchenko has questioned the existence of the Kízil-art range in the following words:—"Hayward's researches seem to point to a meridional range to the west of Kashgar, but he only saw these mountains in the distance, and covered entirely with winter snow, which is very misleading as regards direction. Therefore his statement regarding a meridional Kizil-art range with steep easterly declivities appears to me very untrustworthy. When you have the ends of a chain facing you they appear, when covered with snow and seen *en face* to form a consecutive chain running in a direction perpendicular to the line of sight of the beholder." But all the information I have obtained decidedly corroborates Hayward's views, which are also shared by Mr. Shaw. I have every reason to believe that the magnificent line of snowy peaks which is viewed from Kashghar, constitutes a meridional chain of mountains, instead of being composed of the tail ends of a series of longitudinal chains. It is broken through nearly at right angles by the Yamunyar river, which brings down the drainage of the Little Karakul Lake and the contiguous portion of the Kizil-art plain, just as the Kuen Luen and many of the Himalayan ranges are broken through by rivers whose sources are in the upper table-lands.

The positions of several peaks of the Kizil-art range were fixed by numerous bearings, taken from points along the road between Yárkand and Káshghar, and the four most conspicuous ones, embracing a length of 52 miles were found to lie almost exactly in one straight line having a direction of about 30° west of the true meridian. The most southerly and the highest of these, the Tagharma peak* of Hayward I ascertained trigonometrically to be 25,350 feet above sea level, while two others are at least 22,500 feet high.

From the Tagharma peak southwards the range diminishes very much in height. On our return journey we crossed the Chichiklik mountains (which may be considered as a continuation of the same range) at the Kok-Mainák Pass at an elevation of 15,670 feet; whilst further south the same mountains are pierced by the Tashkurghan river at a height of about 10,000 feet. Little is known of the range further south, but it would seem to be a connecting link with the Himalayan ranges so that the old Chinese geographers, who did indeed link together the "Bolor" and the "Karakorum" under the common name of "Tsung Ling" or "Onion mountains" were not far wrong in their ideas.

I am inclined to agree with Mr. Fedchenko in considering the Pámír steppes, within the limits by which I have defined them, to be a portion of the Thien Shán. At all events they present a very similar physical formation, the main feature of which is the existence of ranges situated on a high table-land, and running more or less east and west. We have already seen that in the only portion of the Thien Shán system visited by us, i.e., to the north and north-east of Kashghar, the mountains consist entirely of parallel ranges having an easterly and westerly direction, and that the elevated plain on which they are situated rises rapidly higher and higher as it advances northwards. It is not always easy to detect the parallelism of these ranges. On the expedition to Chadyr Kul, where we continuously ascended the bed of the Toyanda stream, I did not fully realize the fact, and it was only after our subsequent journey towards Ush Turfán, where I had an opportunity of penetrating and crossing no less than four of these ranges, that I was convinced that this southern portion was of the same physical configuration as other portions of the Thien Shán as portrayed on the Russian maps. Fedchenko, proceeding apparently solely on the basis of this theory of the parallelism of ranges, has shown in his last map the country north-east of Káshghar† in much the same way as I have myself done, and he would doubtless have been much gratified, had he lived, to find his theories so soon verified.

An examination of the map accompanying this report will show the ideas I have myself formed of the ground lying between the Great Pámir and the Alai plateau, which last has been visited by M. Fedchenko. The position and extent of the Great and Little Pámirs have been accurately laid down, and it is hoped that the mapping of the ground between them and the Alai will be found to be not very far from correct; the geographical detail shown is the result of careful study.

On the construction of the Preliminary map accompanying this report.

The positions of all places in Eastern Turkestan, and Wakhan, that have been visited by members of the Mission, depend upon the astronomically fixed position of the Yangi-shahr or new city of Káshghar, for full details of which the appendix, Sections A. and B., may be consulted.

---

* The altitude and bearings of this peak I measured with great care, with my theodolite, from both Yapchan and Kashghar, and I thus obtained two independent results of 25,364 feet and 25,328 feet.

† M. Fedchenko was never there, and, as far as I am aware, the Russians possess no survey of the ground to the north-east of Káshghar.

The final positions in longitude of Yárkand and other important places have been determined as follows:—

The true longitude of KASHGHAR (Yangi-Shahr) is ...				76° 6′ 47″
The difference of longitude between Kashghar and Yangi-Hissar as determined by Pandit Kishen Sing's pacing, corrected from latitude observations, is—				
On outward journey	+ 0° 6′ 15″	} mean 6′ 8″		+ 6′ 8″
On return journey	+ 0° 6′ 0″			
Giving for longitude of Yangi-Hissar ...				76° 12′ 55″
The difference of longitude between Yangi-Hissar and Yárkand, determined in the same manner—				
By outward journey is	1° 3′ 0″			
By return journey	1° 4′ 25″			
On the outward journey the survey was carried along the direct road, about 75 miles in length, and over a perfectly level country, whereas on the return journey the road followed a circuitous line of 180 miles, over one snowy pass and very rough ground. The first value is therefore accepted in preference, viz. ...				1° 3′ 0″
Giving a final value for YARKAND (Yangi-Shahr) of				77° 15′ 55″

which is 0° 3′ 5″ in defect of the astronomically determined value of the same place. I have determined to accept the value as deduced from Kashghar in preference to the independent results arrived at from observations to the moon.

Again, the final longitude of Yangi-Hissar (as above) is ...				76° 12′ 55″
The difference between Yangi-Hissar and Tashkurghan by Pandit's pacing corrected for latitude is	53′ 25″	}		
The difference ascertained chronometrically by Captain Trotter is	54′ 23″		mean 53′ 54″	
Giving a final value for TASHKURGHAN of ...				75° 13′ 1″

which is 4′ 59″ in defect of the value obtained from one night's observations to the moon at the same place.

The longitude of Kila Panjah (Wakhan) was determined chronometrically—

1. On outward journey, from Tashkurghan ...	72° 44′ 18″
2. On return journey, from Ighiz-yar (near to and connected with Yangi-Hissar by a traverse survey)...	72° 46′ 40″
Giving a final longitude for KILA PANJAH of...	72° 45′ 29″
Whilst the observations for absolute longitude at the same place give a result of	72° 45′ 30″
and a fourth entirely independent result obtained by Captain Trotter's route survey, corrected for latitude is	72° 44′ 10″

The mean result obtained chronometrically is adopted for the final position. The wonderfully accordant results at Kila Panjah, although highly satisfactory, must perhaps to a certain extent be regarded as fortuitous, but the admirable *rates* obtained for the watch employed in the chronometric determinations, a silver *lever watch* by Brock of London specially made for explorations, are worth recording* and ought to give results in the accuracy of which great confidence may be placed.

* Travelling rates obtained by Captain Trotter for Brock's lever watch, No. 1602, during journey from Yangi-Hissar to Kila Panjah, and return journey to Yarkand.

Stage.	Dates.	No. of days from which rate was determined.	Rate per diem gaining in seconds of time.	Remarks.
Yangi-Hissar to Ak-tala.	18th to 22nd March	4	+ 6.0	(1) Rate obtained by comparing difference of observed times with difference of longitude as derived from Pandit's pacing, corrected for latitude.
Ak-tala to Tashkurghan.	22nd to 31st March	9	+ 6.1	(2) Ditto Ditto.

(288)

I am much gratified to be able to state that after all my computations were completed and the details of routes transferred for the first time on to a correct graticule, my position of the west end of Victoria Lake (the extreme east point visited by Wood in his travels) was latitude 37° 27' north and longitude* 73° 40' 38", which is practically identical with the independent determination of the same point by Lieutenant Wood which is given at page 232, new edition of Wood's Oxus, with essay by Colonel Yule, London, 1872.

I will now indicate how the positions of points on the road between Leh (Ladakh) and Yarkand have been determined. The position of Ak-tagh (2nd camp) was fixed by myself in lat. 36° 0' 11" and long. 78° 6' 20". It was the converging point of three different route surveys (by Pandits) starting from fixed points on the south, and is in the neighbourhood of a hill above Chibra whose position was satisfactorily fixed by intersection (on the plane-table) of several rays from trigonometrically fixed peaks of the Karakorum. The position of Ak-tagh in longitude with regard to these peaks may be looked on as correct within a mile, and its position in latitude is undoubtedly correct within a few hundred feet.

From this point three traverse lines have been carried by different Surveyors to Karghalik, which, when corrected and adjusted on the proper parallel (37° 53' 15"), had a maximum divergence of 3¾ miles, the mean of the three values gives a position in (true)† longitude of 77° 25' 30."

Between Karghalik and Yarkand I had also two independent traverses, i.e., on both outward and return journey, which differed from each other in the resulting longitude of Karghalik by less than a mile. The mean of these two when referred to the value of Yárkand as determined from Káshghar places Karghalik in longitude 77° 28' 30." A mean between

Travelling rates obtained by Captain Trotter for Brock's lever watch, &c., &c.—(Concluded).

Stage.	Dates.	No. of days from which rate was determined.	Rate per diem gaining in seconds of time.	Remarks.
Yangi-Hissar to Wakhan and back to Ighiz-yar.	18th March to 18th May.	61	+ 6.1	During these 61 days almost an entire circuit was made. The difference of longitude between Yangi Hissar and Ighiz-yar, viz., 1° 45' only, was determined by Pandit's pacing.
Kogachak to Ak-tash...	3rd April to 5th May	32	+ 5.7	During these 31 days a smaller circuit was made; the difference of longitude between Kogachak and Ak-tash is 1° 35". In both these circuits allowance has been made for the stationary rate (+ 7"8) obtained during our halt in Wakhan.
Kashghar to Ighiz-yar	15th to 18th May	3	+ 5.5	Rate obtained in same manner as (1) & (2).

It should be noted that my watches and chronometers were always carried in a small box that I had specially made for them, carefully packed in cotton wool, and inserted in the middle of a large leather mule trunk, packed with clothes. They were thus kept at a tolerably uniform temperature and escaped in great measure the jerks and shakes they would otherwise have been exposed to. Of my pocket *chronometers*, having a regular chronometric escapement, one by Peter Birchall, London, No. 1096, was well suited for astronomical observations, keeping excellent time when stationary and beating half seconds very audibly. It was always used by me in my astronomical observations, but it required very careful handling, as a violent jerk was apt to make it gain several seconds suddenly. A third watch, a pocket chronometer, by Dent, unfortunately got out of order before the Pamír trip, but I had found that while travelling, neither its rate nor that of Birchall compared favorably with that obtained from Brock's watch. It is perhaps needless to add that my watches were daily carefully compared together, and also both before and after observations of stars. An omission to do this on a single occasion prevented my getting a chronometric value for the differences of longitude between Yangi-Hissar and Kashghar.

* The position in longitude in the "Preliminary map" differs slightly from this, as the latter had to be prepared prior to the completion of the computations.

† True, i.e., depending on the most recent determination of the longitude of Madras. All the Indian Survey maps are based on the astronomically determined position of the Madras Observatory. Recent observations have shown that the old value, that is the one adopted by the Survey Department, is about 3 miles too much to the east. In my map I have been compelled to make allowance for this, and have shifted three miles to the west, the whole of the positions in Northern India taken from the existing maps.

98.—Group of Natives, Yarkand.

99.—Chinese Troops, Kashghar.

this and the value previously deduced from the south gives 77° 27′ 0″ which has been assigned as its final position. The smallness of the amount of the adjustment necessary to connect my own work, depending on my own astronomical observations at Káshghar, and that depending on the Indian Survey derived from the astronomically fixed position of Madras is a gratifying proof of the general accuracy of the work.

This sketch would be incomplete without a few lines as to my connection on the north with the Russian Survey, which appears, I think, equally satisfactory with the above.

The only position in the Amir of Kashghar's dominions in Eastern Turkestan astronomically fixed by the Russians is that of Káshghar. This was done in 1872, the year prior to our own visit, by Colonel Scharnhorst of the Mission under General Baron Von Kaulbars. A comparison of results is given:—

Position of Yangi-Shahr (Káshghar) determined by English Mission, 1873—

    Latitude   ...   ...   39° 24′ 26″ North.
    Longitude   ...   ...   76° 6′ 47″ East of Greenwich.

Position of Yangi-Shahr (Káshghar) determined by Russian Mission, 1872—

    Latitude   ...   ...   39° 24′ 16″ North.
    Longitude   ...   ...   76° 4′ 42″ East of Greenwich.

As the quarters occupied by the British Mission, where the observations were made, lies outside and to the east of the fort, while those occupied by the Russians were in about the same latitude and nearly one mile to the west of the fort, the difference in longitude is reduced to about one mile, our latitudes being practically identical. I would have wished to take the mean between the two as the final position of Káshghar, but as our stay there was of much longer duration than that of the Russians, and I had opportunities of taking many more observations than they did, I prefer leaving my own values intact.* The slight discrepancy now noticed disappears on the road between Káshghar and Chadyr Kul, the only line of survey common both to the Russians and ourselves, and along which I carried a rough traverse survey in which the distances were estimated by the time occupied on the line of march. Prior to my departure from India Colonel Stubendorff, of the Russian War Office, had sent to Colonel Walker, the Superintendent of the Great Trigonometrical Survey, the positions of a number of points in Russian and in Khokandian territory that had been astronomically determined by Russian officers. Amongst them was the north-east corner of Lake Chadyr Kul. Bearing this in mind, when at the most northerly point on the road reached by us, I took a bearing tangential to the east end of the lake, which lay nearly due north at a distance of about three miles from us. On my return to India when I plotted in my work from my own astronomical position of Káshghar, I found that by adopting the Russian value of the east end of the lake, viz., latitude 40° 43′ north, our positons in longitude† of the same point exactly coincided.

In determining the position of Khotan I have made use of Pandit Kishen Sing's route from Karghalik to Khotan, and thence via Keria back to Ladakh. As a result of this route survey our previously accepted value of the longitude of Khotan has been altered by more than thirty miles. It may appear bold to make this extensive change in the position of a place that has been visited by a European explorer (Mr. Johnson), but the route survey executed by this Pandit is so consistent, and the plotted results agree so closely with the observed latitudes throughout the whole of his work, that I have no hesitation in accepting it as correct. I may further add that I have been in communication with Mr. Johnson on the subject, and that he freely admits the possibility of a large error in his longitude of Khotan.

---

* Since the above was written Colonel Walker has heard from Colonel Stubendorff that the Russian astronomical observations at Kashghar which were taken by Colonel Scharnhorst were referred to the most northern angle of the Yangi-Shahr, a position almost identical in latitude with my own, and differing by two-fifths of a mile only in longitude. Colonel Stubendorff mentions that the Russian observations depend on the eclipse of the sun on the 6th June 1872, and that corrections for error in the lunar tables have not been applied. This last remark applies to my own observations also.—H. T.

† 75° 24′ East of Greenwich.

He states that in commencing his reconnaissance from the Kuen Luen Mountains (which he carried on with the plane-table only), one of the three trigonometrically fixed points on which his work was based, turned out subsequently to have been incorrectly projected on his board. This, together with the doubt that must always exist when rapidly passing through an unknown country as to the identity of the different peaks visible from the line of march, is quite sufficient to account for the discrepancy. In my preliminary map I have assigned to Khotan a longitude of 79° 59' instead of 79° 26,' the position it has recently occupied on our maps. About its latitude there can be no doubt. Mr. Johnson took several observations there with a 14-inch theodolite and obtained a mean result of 37° 7' 35", whilst from Kishen Sing's observations with a sextant extending over nearly a month we have a mean result of 37° 7' 36". The points east of Khotan, i.e., Keria and the Sorghak gold fields, are derived from Kishen Sing's route survey, combined with his latitude observations. We also have from the same source a complete survey for the first time of the road via Polu to Noh, and thence to Leh. As a specimen of the accuracy of this Pundit's work I may mention that when the road from Karghalik to Pal, a distance of 630 miles, was plotted out on the scale of 2,000 paces to the mile, without any correction or adjustment whatever (although $4\frac{1}{2}°$ were added to each magnetic bearing in order to allow for magnetic variation) starting from my own value of Karghalik, the plot closed at Pal (fixed by the Great Trigonometrical Survey) almost absolutely correct in latitude and only eight minutes out in longitude, and in no single portion of the whole route, which passes over elevations exceeding 17,000 feet in height, did the plotted value differ by as much as three miles from his own observed astronomical latitude (vide Appendix Section A.). Of this discrepancy of eight minutes in longitude it is possible that a portion may be due to error of position in the starting point (Karghalik), but it may be noted that the amount is no more than would be accounted for by an error of $1\frac{1}{2}°$ in the assumed value of magnetic variation. It is not to be supposed that such accuracy is generally attainable, but in the present case, although the surveyor laboured under certain disadvantages from the absence of inhabitants, yet there were the compensating advantages that he was under no necessity for concealment; he was therefore able to take and record bearings when and where he pleased.

As regards the work executed to the north-east and east of Káshghar; the position of Maralbashi, on the road to Aksu, was fixed in latitude by Captain Biddulph (vide Appendix Section A.), and its position in longitude is roughly determined by a few bearings, and estimated distances taken by him on the road from Káshghar.

On the road to Ush Turfan I carried on a rough route survey wherever I went, and took observations for latitude and obtained chronometric determinations of longitude as far as Ui Bulák, in latitude 40° 26' north and longitude 77° 36' east. Thence by route survey I got a determination of the position of the Belowti Pass; calculating from this the probable position of Ush Turfan I place it about three-quarters of a degree to the east of the position given it in the last edition of Colonel Walker's Turkestan map. On examining the latest Russian map (1873) it appears that the position of Ush Turfan has been recently altered, and placed very near where I would myself locate it. I have therefore in my map adopted the last Russian values of Ush Turfan, Aksu, and all places to the east. It will be found that the cities of Aksu and Kuldja are more than twenty miles to the east of the places assigned them in all but the most recent maps.

The details inserted to the north of the map are taken almost exclusively from the Russian topographical map of Central Asia (corrected to 1873). The portion of ground to the south of Khokand, visited by Mr. Fedchenko, is derived from various maps purporting to be by that distinguished traveller, amongst others, one recently sent by Madame Fedchenko to Colonel Walker, differing materially from all others that I have seen. For the country between the Alai, visited by Mr. Fedchenko on the north, and the scene of our own explorations in the Pamírs on the south, the map is compiled from all the limited sources available* which have

---

* Including the route survey carried on by Abdul Subhan from Panjah to Kila Wamur, the chief town of Roshán, and also including a sketch map prepared by Colonel Gordon and Captain Biddulph representing their joint ideas of the geography of the Pamír.

been bound together to the best of my ability. I am by no means yet satisfied with the result, and one of my first labours, when I have finished this report, will be the preparation of a map on a larger scale of the Pámir regions, when I doubt not that further considerations will induce some changes in the map as it at present stands.

Most of the details to the south of the map, with the exception of those portions north of Leh that have been traversed by members of the Mission, have been taken from the last edition of Colonel Walker's Map of Turkestan, but all the positions in the latter have been shifted three minutes to the west in longitude in order to allow for the most recently determined value of the longitude of Madras, viz., 80° 14′ 19.5″ East of Greenwich.

In the portion of country traversed by Members and Attachés of the Mission use has been made of all the material collected by them. The maps of Messrs. Shaw and Hayward have also been called into requisition.

The reductions of the astronomical observations, and the computations of heights, have all been made in the Office of Colonel Walker, R.E., the Superintendent of the Great Trigonometrical Survey, in whose Office also, the map compiled by myself has been drawn and photozincographed. A large amount of work has been got through in a moderate space of time, and I am deeply indebted to Colonel Walker for the facilities he has given, and to Messrs. Hennessey, Keelan, and Wood in the Computing Office, and Messrs. Atkinson and Sindon in the Drawing Office for the assistance afforded by them in their several departments.

Meteorological Observations.

Whilst on the march I always took readings of thermometers, and barometer or boiling point thermometer, at our camps, and on high passes, and at other places of interest. These were taken chiefly for the purpose of determining the height above sea level of the stations of observation and where used for this object are shown in Appendix C. Where they are not required for this I have not published them, as isolated observations at different places, taken under constantly varying conditions, are not of much use to the meteorologist.

While I was at Leh Mr. R. B. Shaw, the British Joint Commissioner, commenced a regular meteorological registry, which has since been continued under the superintendence of Captain Molloy, the recorder being the Native Doctor attached to the dispensary there. At my special request Mr. Shaw kindly took extra barometrical observations at the hours of 9 A.M. and noon, whilst I was on the journey to, and during my residence and travels in, Eastern Turkestan, these being considered the most likely hours at which I should myself be able to take barometrical observations for height on passes and in camp. I have thus throughout the whole of my absence from Leh got almost simultaneous readings at the fixed Observatory of Leh, whose height has been accurately determined by the Great Trigonometrical Survey. This circumstance combined with the use by myself of mercurial barometers, enable me to compute the height of the various passes and halting-places with an amount of accuracy superior to anything yet attainable. It is hardly necessary to add that I have made at Leh, both on the outward and return journeys, numerous comparisons between my own instruments and those in use at the Leh Observatory, and that my own were previously compared with the standards at Dehra Dún (and some of them at Kew).

While on the march to Yárkand I succeeded in taking numerous sets of observations with a Hodgkinson's actinometer. I took these at the special request of Mr. J. B. N. Hennessey of the Great Trigonometrical Survey, who supplied me with an instrument belonging to the Royal Society. They were chiefly taken at considerable altitudes, but owing to cloudy weather the Chang La (Pass), 17,600 feet above sea level, was the only very high point at which I was able to take sets extending over a period of several hours in the middle of the day. These actinometric observations have been handed over to Mr. Hennessey (now in England) for reduction, and they ought to give very interesting results, which will probably be communicated to the Royal Society.

At Leh in Ladákh advantage was taken of the presence of the Pundits to get a series of continuous hourly observations of the barometer. These extended over a period of six days during which there was no break in the observations. The height of the Observatory above the sea level (11,530 feet), coupled with the extreme dryness of the air of Ladákh, and its position in the interior of a large continent, combine to render the determination of the diurnal curve of considerable value.* In the diagram accompanying the vertical scale is ten times that of the natural scale, the exaggeration being necessary in order to show clearly the curve. The actual barometer readings† have been corrected for Index Error, and reduced to a temperature of 32°, before being projected on the diagram.

The curve indicates two maxima, viz., at 1 A.M. and at 8 A.M., and minima at between 2 and 3 A.M. and between 4 and 5 P.M., which differ considerably from results obtained in other parts of the world. The daily maximum and minimum is very much more clearly marked than the nightly one.

At Yárkand also, during the winter, sets of continuous hourly observations were taken on the 20th, 21st, and 22nd of each month. Several of these sets have been reduced to a curve, which I have also shown in the same diagram.‡ It so happens that on the days that were selected for hourly observations at Yárkand there was almost always a steady fall in the barometer, as will be seen by a glance at the monthly curves in the other plate. In order to allow for this constant fall, the effect of which is to distort the true daily curve, I have applied proportionate corrections, so that the dotted line represents the true diurnal curve. The mean of six days' hourly observations, viz., on 20th and 21st of December, 20th and 21st of January and 20th and 21st of February, have been employed in constructing the curve. It will be observed that at Yárkand the night maxima and minima are much more clearly marked than at Leh, but that there is much less difference between those of the day and night. The maxima occur at 10 A.M. and 11 P.M., the minima at 4 A.M. and 3 P.M. At Yárkand, where the Pandits passed the winter, meteorological observations were commenced on the 19th November and continued without a break until the 15th March. They consisted of the readings at 9 A.M., noon, 3 P.M., 6 P.M., and 9 P.M., of a mercurial barometer, an aneroid barometer, dry and wet bulb thermometers, and direction of the wind (N.B.—There was no rainfall, but a little snow fell in March); also the maximum and minimum temperatures in the shade during the 24 hours.

At Káshghar observations were commenced on the 12th December, but were not so complete or regular as those at Yárkand, as I had fewer observers to assist me, and I was myself absent for two periods, viz., from 31st December to 11th January, and again from 15th February to 3rd March. Observations were continued up to the 16th March, and generally consisted of readings of two aneroid barometers at the hours of 9 A.M., noon, and 3 P.M., and occasionally at 6 P.M. Readings of thermometer (dry) and direction of wind were taken at the same hours, besides the maxima and minima during the 24 hours. Readings of the wet bulb thermometer were also taken during the latter half of February and March. In addition to these a series of hypsometric observations were taken, with the object of determining the relative heights of Yárkand and Káshghar.

The whole of these observations are shewn in the Appendix, Section G., to which the reader is referred. I have prepared (plate 2) a set of curves showing the connection of the barometric wave between the stations of Káshghar, Yárkand, Leh, and Dehra Dún (at the foot of the southern slopes of the Himalayas). The curve represents the height of the corrected readings of the barometer at 9 A.M., during the four months for which I was able to obtain data, with the exception of Dehra, where 9 A.M. readings not being forthcoming I have taken the observations recorded at 10-30 A.M.

---

* The Schlagintweits took hourly observations at Leh during the day, and interpolated values for the night hours. The results thus obtained cannot have anything like the same value as those derived from observations taken throughout the 24 hours.

† The instrument employed was a mercurial barometer by Casella.

‡ These diagrams have been drawn by Mr. Keelan of the Great Trigonometrical Survey, who has also rendered me great assistance in the preparation of the Appendices of this report.

Plate 1.

Curves shewing the mean diurnal variation of the Barometer

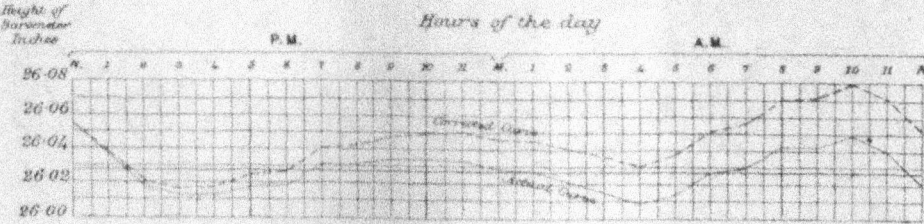

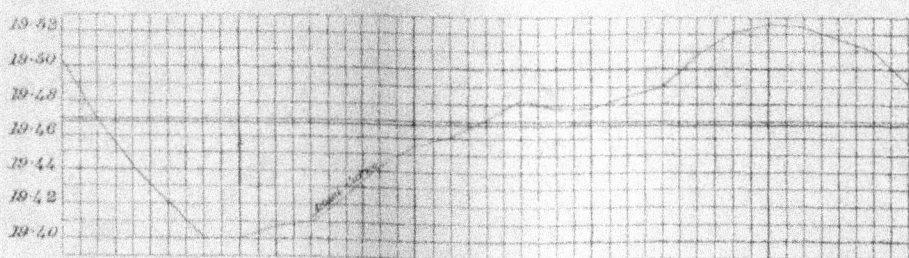

Photozincographed at the Surveyor General's Office Calcutta.

100.—Chinese Troops, Kashghar.

101.—A Chinese Slave, and a Fakir of the Country.

Magnetic Observations.

As has been mentioned in a previous portion of this report it was decided not to take from India a complete set of magnetic instruments. I took with me however a dip circle by Barrow with which observations for inclination were taken at Leh (in Ladakh), Chágra (in Ladakh), Yárkand, Káshghar, and Tashkurghán (in the Sarikol District). It has been laid down as an axiom by General Sabine, the great authority on matters of magnetism, that "the value of each new magnetic station is directly proportional to its distance from those where observations have already been made," and I may therefore hope that the record of results, *vide* Appendix, Section E., may prove of considerable value, as I am not aware that any magnetic observations have ever been taken within a very considerable distance of any of the three last named stations. The rules laid down by General Sabine were rigorously adhered to in taking the observations.

Observations for magnetic variation (declination) were taken at, and have been computed out for sixteen stations in, Ladakh, Turkestan, and Wakhan. The station furthest to the north-east was at Ui Bulák (latitude $40°\ 26'$ and longitude $77°\ 36'$) where the variation was $5°\ 40'$ east; the extreme western station was at Kila Panjah (latitude $37°$ longitude $72°\ 45'$) where the variation was $4°\ 17'$ east. Details of the results, which are very consistent *inter se*, are given in the Appendix. The instrument employed in the determination of declination was the six-inch transit theodolite, which has been described in the Appendix, Section B. It was fitted with a first-rate magnetic needle. Comparisons taken at Leh and at Dehra both prior to the departure of the Mission, and subsequent to its return, prove that no alteration has taken place in the position of its magnetic pole. The object observed was generally Polaris. In many instances, however, the sun, either near sunrise or sunset, was made use of; at important stations, such as Leh and Kashghar, the mean of several different independent determinations has been taken.

I cannot conclude this report without alluding to the sad loss we have all sustained by the recent and sudden death of our much lamented comrade, Dr. F. Stoliczka. Having been in almost daily intercourse with him from the day of leaving the Punjáb on our outward journey (through the Changchenmo, Chakmák, Artysh, and Pámír trips) up to the day of his death, and being naturally especially attracted to him as working always cordially with him to add my mite to the field of science, I most bitterly regret his loss. It is hard to think that he should not have been spared to give to the world the results of his laborious investigation and scientific research, and although he has left valuable notes behind him, yet owing to his unequalled knowledge of Himalayan geology there is probably no man living as competent as he was to do full justice to them; and it is unlikely that any one will go through his valuable zoological and other collections with the same minute care and attention that he would himself have bestowed upon them. I have special reason to regret the absence of his experience and advice while preparing my own report, in writing which I had confidently looked forward to receiving the benefit of his assistance.

(Sd.)   HENRY TROTTER, *Capt., R. E.*

102.—Chinese Troops, Kashghar.

GEOGRAPHICAL APPENDIX.

SECTION A.

LATITUDES.

(296)

Abstract of Observations for Latitude on road from LEH

Place of Observation.	Reference numbers.	Astronomical date.	Observer.	Instrument observed with.	Object observed.
Chang Lá or Sakti Pass...	3	15th Sept. 1873	Capt. Trotter...	Theodolite	Sun (*U.L.*)
Lukong Vil. Pang-gong-chu	7	19th Sept. 1873	Kalian Sing ...	Sextant No. 44	α Piscis Australis (*Fomalhaut*)
		,, ,,	Kishen Sing ...	,, 44	α Aquilæ (*Altair*)
		,, ,,	,, ,,	,, 44	α Piscis Australis (*Fomalhaut*)
		20th ,,	,, ,,	,, 44	Sun (*U.L.*)
		19th ,,	Capt. Trotter...	Theodolite	,, ,,
Chágrá	8	20th Sept. 1873	Kalian Sing ...	Sextant No. 44	α Piscis Australis (*Fomalhaut*)
		,, ,,	Kishen Sing ...	,, 44	α Ursæ Minoris (*Polaris*)
		21st ,,	,, ,,	,, 44	α Aquilæ (*Altair*)
Gográ Camp ...	12	24th Sept. 1873	Kalian Sing ...	,, 8	α Aquilæ (*Altair*)
		25th ,,	,, ,,	,, 8	α Piscis Australis (*Fomalhaut*)
		23rd ,,	Kishen Sing...	,, 44	α Aquilæ (*Altair*)
		24th ,,	,, ,,	,, 44	α Piscis Australis (*Fomalhaut*)
		,, ,,	,, ,,	,, 44	α Ursæ Minoris (*Polaris*)
E. Route *viâ* Ling-zi-thang. Bhao (Shumallung) Camp.	13	26th Sept. 1873	Kishen Sing ...	,, 44	α Aquilæ (*Altair*)
		27th ,,	,, ,,	,, 44	β Orionis (*Rigel*)
Changlung Nischu Camp.	15	27th Sept 1873	Kishen Sing ...	,, 44	α Aquilæ (*Altair*)
		,, ,,	,, ,,	,, 44	α Ursæ Minoris (*Polaris*)
Ling-zi-thang plain, camp on.	16	28th Sept. 1873	Kishen Sing ...	,, 44	α Aquilæ (*Altair*)
		,, ,,	,, ,,	,, 44	α Ursæ Minoris (*Polaris*)
		29th ,,	,, ,,	,, 44	β Orionis (*Rigel*)
Sumna Camp (E. of Kizil jilga).	18	30th Sept. 1873	Kishen Sing ...	,, 44	α Aquilæ (*Altair*)
		,, ,,	,, ,,	,, 44	α Ursæ Minoris (*Polaris*)

to YARKAND viâ *Chang-Chenmo* and *Sháhidúlla*.

Double altitudes or zenith distances corrected for index and level errors.	Elements used in computation of refraction.		Deduced Latitudes.			Remarks.
	Barometer.	Ther. Faht.	By stars north of zenith.	By sun or stars south of zenith.	Final latitudes north.	
° ′ ″	Inches.	Degrees.	° ′ ″	° ′ ″	° ′ ″	
Z. D. 30 47 40	15·8	44		34 4 49	34 4 49	In observations with the sextant the stars have been invariably taken on the meridian. In observations with the theodolite the stars have been taken on the meridian except where an asterisk has been affixed to the name of the star (in column 6). Where this occurs the numbers in the column of Remarks are the computed means of the true local times of observation used in the computation for latitude. The numbers in brackets in columns 7, 10, and 11, denote the number of pairs (face left and face right) of observations taken. The corresponding figures in column 7 give the corrected mean zenith distance.
D. A. 51 27 20	18·2	51		34 0 1		
,, 129 5 10	18·2	51		33 59 55		
,, 51 27 0	18·2	51		34 0 12		
,, 114 38 20	18·2	51		34 0 23		
Z. D. 32 17 12	18·0	61		33 59 57	34 0 6	
D. A. 51 17 20	17·6	33		34 5 4		
,, 70 55 50	17·6	33	34 5 6			
,, 128 55 40	17·6	33		34 4 40	34 4 59	
D. A. 128 24 10	17·0	44		34 20 24		
,, 50 47 10	17·0	44		34 20 4		
,, 128 23 0	17·0	44		34 21 1		
,, 50 41 40	17·0	44		34 22 49		
,, 71 27 30	17·0	44	34 21 1		34 21 4	The theodolite employed is described in the Geographical Appendix, Section B.
D. A. 128 7 0	16·3	44		34 28 59		
,, 94 21 10	16·3	44		34 29 13	34 29 6	
D. A. 127 55 53	,,	,,		34 34 33		
,, 71 56 33	,,	,,	34 35 32		34 35 3	
D. A. 127 29 33	,,	,,		34 47 45		
,, 72 23 13	,,	,,	34 48 51			
,, 93 47 23	,,	,,		34 46 10	34 47 54	
D. A. 126 32 43	,,	,,		35 16 9		
,, 73 19 43	,,	,,	35 17 9		35 16 39	

(298)

Abstract of Observations for Latitude on road from LEH

Place of Observation.	Reference numbers.	Astronomical date.	Observer.	Instrument observed with.	Object observed.
W. Route *viâ* head of Kárákásh River. — Kotajilga Camp...	19	26th Sept. 1873 ,, ,,	Capt. Trotter... ,,	Theodolite ,,	α Ursæ Minoris (*Polaris*)* ,, ,, ,, *
Sumzumlung Pa...	22	28th Sept. 1873 ,, ,, 29th ,, ,, ,,	Capt. Trotter... ,, ,, ,,	Theodolite ,, ,, ,,	α Ursæ Minoris (*Polaris*)* ,, ,, ,, γ Aquilæ α Aquilæ (*Altair*)
Dunglung or Shinglung.	26	3rd Oct. 1873 ,, ,, ,, ,,	Capt. Trotter... ,, ,,	Theodolite ,, ,,	α Piscis Australis (*Fomalhaut*) α Pegasi (*Markab*) γ Cephei
Kizil-jilga on bank of Kárákásh River.	27	5th Oct. 1873 ,, ,, 1st ,, 2nd ,, 5th ,, ,, ,,	Kalian Sing... ,, Kishen Sing... ,, ,, ,,	Sextant No. 44 ,, 8 ,, 44 ,, 44 ,, 44 ,, 44	β Ceti α Ursæ Minoris (*Polaris*) α Aquilæ (*Altair*) α Orionis β Ceti α Ur. Min. (*Polaris*)
Chúng Tash	28	8th Oct. 1873	Capt. Trotter...	Theodolite	Sun U. L.
E. Route along Kárákásh River. — Dáktod Karpo Sumdo.	30	9th Oct. 1873 10th ,, ,, ,,	Kishen Sing... ,, ,,	Sextant No. 44 ,, 44 ,, 44	α Aquilæ (*Altair*) α Orionis α Canis Majoris (*Sirius*)
Dungnagu Camp	32	12th Oct. 1873 ,, ,, ,, ,,	Kishen Sing... ,, ,,	Sextant No. 44 ,, 44 ,, 44	β Orionis (*Rigel*) α Orionis α Canis Majoris (*Sirius*)
Sorá Camp	33	13th Oct. 1873 ,, ,, 14th ,,	Kishen Sing... ,, ,,	Sextant No. 44 ,, 44 ,, 44	β Ceti α Ursæ Minoris (*Polaris*) α Canis Majoris (*Sirius*)

(299)

to YARKAND viâ Chang-Chenmo and Sháhidúlla.—(continued.)

Double altitudes or zenith distances corrected for index and level errors.				Elements used in computation of refraction.		Deduced Latitudes.			Remarks.			
				Barometer.	Ther. Faht.	By stars north of zenith.	By sun or stars south of zenith.	Final latitudes north.				
	°	′	″	Inches.	Degrees.	° ′ ″	° ′ ″	° ′ ″		H.	M.	S.
Z. D.	54	24	1(1)	18·0	16	34 29 22(1)			Mean time =	10	25	37
„	54	23	24(1)	18·0	16	34 29 27(1)		34 29 25	„	10	31	14
Z. D.	54	19	16(1)	15·9	9	34 40 39(1)			„	9	49	42
„	54	18	23(1)	15·9	9	34 40 45(1)			„	9	52	57
„	24	22	39	15·9	10		34 41 23					
„	26	8	38	15·9	10		34 41 8	34 40 59				
Z. D.	65	26	25	16·0	−3		35 10 13					
„	20	38	5	16·0	−3		35 9 53					
„	41	45	30	16·0	−5	35 9 38		35 9 51				
D. A.	71	59	0	16·5	18		35 20 33					
„	73	27	30	16·5	18	35 21 4						
„	126	25	3	16·5	18		35 19 58					
„	124	6	53	16·5	18		35 19 56					
„	71	59	33	16·5	18		35 20 10					
„	73	28	3	16·5	18	35 21 21		35 20 42				
Z. D.	41	16	37	17·0	·34		35 36 56	35 36 56				
D. A.	125	33	33	...	...		35 45 45					
„	123	15	13	...	...		35 45 47					
„	75	25	13	...	...		35 45 52	35 45 48				
D. A.	91	37	3	...	...		35 51 22					
„	123	3	23	...	...		35 51 43					
„	75	13	43	...	...		35 51 37	35 51 34				
D. A.	70	39	33	...	...		36 0 22					
„	74	49	23	...	...	36 2 0		36 1 9				
„	74	56	33	...	...		36 0 12					

(300)

Abstract of Observations for Latitude on road from LEH

Place of Observation.		Reference numbers.	Astronomical date.	Observer.	Instrument observed with.	Object observed.
E. Route along Ká- rákásh River.—(Contd.)	Jung Chidmo Camp	35	15th Oct. 1873	Kishen Sing ...	Sextant No. 44	β Ceti ...
			,, ,,	,, ...	,, 44	α Ursæ Minoris (*Polaris*)
			16th ,,	,, ...	,, 44	β Orionis (*Rigel*)
			,, ,,	,, ...	,, 44	α Orionis
			,, ,,	,, ...	,, 44	α Canis Majoris (*Sirius*)
	Gulbáshem ...	38	17th Oct. 1873	Kishen Sing ...	Sextant No. 44	β Ceti ...
			,, ,,	,, ...	,, 44	α Ursæ Minoris (*Polaris*)
			18th ,,	,, ...	,, 44	α Canis Majoris (*Sirius*)
			17th ,,	Capt. Trotter ...	Theodolite	α Ursæ Minoris (*Polaris*)*
W. Route viâ Aktágh.	Shorjilga ...	39	10th Oct. 1873	Capt. Trotter ...	Theodolite ...	α Ursæ Minoris (*Polaris*)
	Kárátágh Pass ...	41	11th Oct. 1873	Capt. Trotter ...	Theodolite ...	Sun (*U. L.*)
	Fotásh Pass (near Traverse Station No. 44.)	41A	19th Oct. 1873	Capt. Trotter ...	Theodolite	Sun (*U. L.*)
	Aktágh (1st camp)	43	13th Oct. 1873	Nain Sing ...	Sextant No. 7 ...	α Ursæ Minoris (*Polaris*)
			14th ,,	Capt. Chapman	Theodolite ...	Sun (*U. L.*)
	Chíbra Camp ...	43A	15th Oct. 1873	Kalian Sing ...	Sextant No. 8 ...	β Ceti
			,, ,,	,, ...	,, 8 ...	α Ursæ Minoris (*Polaris*)
	Sugét Camp ...	47	17th Oct. 1873	Kalian Sing ...	Sextant No. 8 ...	β Ceti
			,, ,,	,, ...	,, 8 ...	α Ursæ Minoris (*Polaris*)
	Sugét Pass ...	45	16th Oct. 1873	Capt. Trotter ...	Theodolite ...	Sun (*L. L.*)
Sháhidúlla Camp ...		48	22nd Oct. 1873	Kalian Sing ...	Sextant No. 8 ...	β Ceti
			,, ,,	,, ...	,, 8 ...	α Ursæ Minoris (*Polaris*)
			21st ,,	Nain Sing ...	,, 7 ...	,, ,, ,,
			,, ,,	,, ...	,, 7 ...	α Canis Minoris (*Procyon*)

(301)

to YARKAND viâ Chang-Chenmo and Sháhidúlla.—(continued.)

Double altitudes or zenith distances corrected for index and level errors.	ELEMENTS USED IN COMPUTATION OF REFRACTION.		DEDUCED LATITUDES.			REMARKS.
	Barometer.	Ther. Faht.	By stars north of zenith.	By sun or stars south of zenith.	Final latitudes north.	
° ′ ″	Inches.	Degrees.	° ′ ″	° ′ ″	° ′ ″	
D. A. 70 19 43	...	...		36 10 19		
,, 75 8 33	...	...	36 11 36	36 10 14		
,, 90 59 3	...	...		36 10 24		
,, 122 26 3	...	...		36 10 9	36 10 32	
,, 74 36 43	...	...				
D. A. 70 6 13	19·4	25		36 17 5		
,, 75 22 13	19·4	25	36 18 26			
,, 74 23 3	19·4	18		36 17 1		H. M. S.
Z. D. 52 42 13(3)	19·0	25		36 17 19(3)	36 17 28	Mean time = 8 36 36
Z. D. 53 47 56(3)	16·5	6	35 41 2		35 41 2(3)	Mean time = 7 27 27
Z. D. 42 30 58	15·7	30		35 42 54	35 42 54	
Z. D. 45 58 4	17·4	40		35 56 31	35 56 31	
D. A. 74 43 20	17·2	12	35 59 0			
Z. D. 43 54 37	16·6	25		35 59 6	35 59 3	
D. A. 70 26 30	15·6	25		36 6 46		
,, 75 0 20	15·6	25	36 7 38		36 7 12	
D. A. 70 3 40	18·9	25		36 18 20		
,, 75 23 40	18·9	25	36 19 10		36 18 45	
Z. D. 45 22 5	15·7	30		36 9 53	36 9 53	
D. A. 69 52 30	19·5	30		36 23 55		
,, 75 35 20	19·5	30	36 25 2			
D. A. 75 37 20	19·5	30	36 26 4			
,, 118 17 10	19·5	30		36 24 48	36 24 57	

Abstract of Observations for Latitude on road from LEH

Place of Observation.	Reference numbers.	Astronomical date.	Observer.	Instrument observed with.	Object observed.
Kárákorum Camp	48A	25th Oct. 1873 ,, ,,	Kalian Sing ,,	Sextant No. 8 ,, 8	β Ceti α Ursæ Minoris (Polaris)
Giazgia Camp	48B	29th Oct. 1873 30th ,, 24th ,, ,, ,,	Kishen Sing ,, Nain Sing ,,	Sextant No. 44 ,, 44 ,, 7 ,, 7	α Ursæ Minoris (Polaris) α Canis Minoris (Procyon) α Canis Majoris (Sirius) α Canis Minoris (Procyon)
Tám Langar	51	25th Oct. 1873 ,, ,, ,, ,,	Capt. Trotter Nain Sing ,,	Theodolite Sextant No. 7 ,, 7	α Ursæ Minoris (Polaris)* ,, ,, ,, ,, α Canis Minoris (Procyon)
Khewaz Langar	51A	26th Oct. 1873	Nain Sing	Sextant No. 7	α Canis Minoris (Procyon)
Sanjú Bazar	52	1st Nov. 1873 28th Oct. 1873 29th ,, 30th ,,	Capt. Trotter Nain Sing ,, ,,	Theodolite Sextant No. 7 ,, 7 ,, 7	α Ursæ Minoris (Polaris)* ,, ,, ,, ,, α Canis Majoris (Sirius) α Ursæ Minoris (Polaris)
Khushtagh Village	52A	2nd Nov. 1873 ,, ,, ,, ,,	Capt. Trotter Nain Sing ,,	Theodolite Sextant No. 7 ,, 7	α Ursæ Minoris (Polaris)* ,, ,, ,, ,, α Canis Minoris (Procyon)
Oi Toghrák Village	53	3rd Nov. 1873	Capt. Trotter	Theodolite	α Ursæ Minoris (Polaris)*
Boira Village	54	3rd Nov. 1873 4th ,, ,, ,,	Capt. Trotter Nain Sing ,,	Theodolite Sextant No. 7 ,, 7	α Ursæ Minoris (Polaris)* β Ceti α Ursæ Minoris (Polaris)
Karghalik Bazar	55	6th Nov. 1873 26th May 1874 6th Nov. 1873 ,, ,, ,, ,, 29th Mar. 1874 ,, ,, 30th ,,	Capt. Trotter ,, Nain Sing ,, ,, ,, ,, ,,	Theodolite ,, Sextant No. 7 ,, 7 ,, 7 ,, 7 ,, 7 ,, 7	α Ursæ Minoris (Polaris)* α Libræ α Ursæ Minoris (Polaris) β Orionis (Rigel) α Orionis Sun (U. L.) Jupiter Sun (U. L.)

(303)

to YARKAND viâ Chang-Chenmo and Sháhidúla.—(continued.)

Double altitudes or zenith distances corrected for index and level errors.	Elements used in computation of refraction.		Deduced Latitudes.			Remarks.
	Barometer.	Ther. Faht.	By stars north of zenith.	By sun or stars south of zenith.	Final latitudes north.	
	Inches.	Degrees.	° ′ ″	° ′ ″	° ′ ″	
D. A. 69 26 30	20·4	25		36 36 59		
" 76 1 20	20·4	25	36 38 0		36 37 30	
D. A. 76 12 43	20·2	32	36 43 46			
" 117 36 33	20·2	32		36 45 7		
" 73 25 50	19·9	30		36 45 37		
" 117 36 0	19·9	30		36 45 24	36 44 59	
						H. M. S.
Z. D. 51 52 38(2)	21·9	32	36 52 5(2)			Mean time = 9 19 12
D. A. 76 30 20	21·1	30	36 52 29			
" 117 23 10	21·1	30		36 51 51	36 52 4	
D. A. 117 1 20	22·5	37		37 2 47	37 2 47	
Z. D. 51 30 22(3)	24·3	19	37 11 4(3)			Mean time = 9 15 57
D. A. 77 8 0	24·5	25	37 11 12			
" 72 33 50	24·5	25		37 11 52	37 11 17	
" 77 7 30	24·5	25	37 10 58			
Z. D. 51 15 34(3)	24·7	21	37 21 40(3)			Mean time = 10 22 46
D. A. 77 28 30	23·4	33	37 21 34			
" 116 25 50	23·4	33		37 20 33	37 21 5	
Z. D. 51 12 15(3)	24·8	16	37 30 20(3)		37 30 20	Mean time = 8 58 7
Z. D. 51 2 23(3)	25·2	21	37 36 55(3)			Mean time = 11 8 11
D. A. 67 25 50	24·4	33		37 37 29	37 37 19	
" 78 0 10	24·4	33	37 37 22			
Z. D. 50 47 19(3)	26·1	22	37 53 9(3)			Mean time = 9 5 2
" 53 23 35	23·6	70		37 53 23		
D. A. 78 32 0	25·3	54	37 53 20			
" 78 35 30	25·3	54		37 52 19		
" 119 1 0	25·3	54		37 53 2		
" 111 26 50	24·9	40		37 53 43		
" 110 49 20	24·9	40		37 53 39		
" 112 13 50	24·9	40		37 53 30	37 53 15	

(304)

Abstract of Observations for Latitude on road from LEH

Place of Observation.	Reference numbers	Astronomical date.	Observer.	Instrument observed with.	Object observed.
Posgiám Bazar	56	7th Nov. 1873	Capt. Trotter	Theodolite	α Ursæ Minoris (*Polaris*)*
		,, ,,	Nain Sing	Sextant No. 7	,, ,, ,,
				,, 7	α Canis Minoris (*Procyon*)
		27th Mar. 1874	,,	,, 7	Jupiter
YARKAND. At Elchi Khaná near the centre of the Yangi-Shahr or new city of Yárkand.	57	8th Nov. 1873	Capt. Trotter	Theodolite	α Ursæ Minoris (*Polaris*)*
		11th ,,	,,	,,	Sun (*L.L.*)*
		,, ,,	,,	,,	α Cephei
		,, ,,	,,	,,	ε Pegasi
		,, ,,	,,	,,	α Aquarii
		12th ,,	,,	,,	α Ursæ Minoris (*Polaris*)
		27th ,,	,,	,,	,, ,, ,,
		9th Nov. 1873	Nain Sing	Sextant No. 7	,, ,, ,,
		10th ,,	,,	,, 7	,, ,, ,,
		26th ,,	,,	,, 7	α Canis Majoris (*Sirius*)
		30th ,,	,,	,, 7	α Canis Minoris (*Procyon*)
				,, 7	α Hydræ
		5th Dec. 1873	,,	,, 7	α Tauri (*Aldebaran*)
		,, ,,	,,	,, 7	β Orionis (*Rigel*)
		13th ,,	,,	,, 7	β Ursæ Minoris
		14th ,,	,,	,, 7	,,
		16th ,,	,,	,, 7	β Ceti
		,, ,,	,,	,, 7	Jupiter
		18th ,,	,,	,, 7	α Orionis (*Rigel*)
		,, ,,	,,	,, 7	α Canis Majoris (*Sirius*)
		19th ,,	,,	,, 7	Sun (*U.L.*)
		,, ,,	,,	,, 7	α Ursæ Minoris (*Polaris*)
		20th ,,	,,	,, 7	α Orionis
		,, ,,	,,	,, 7	α Canis Majoris (*Sirius*)
		,, ,,	,,	,, 7	α Canis Minoris (*Procyon*)
		,, ,,	,,	,, 7	α Leonis (*Regulus*)
		21st ,,	,,	,, 7	Sun (*U.L.*)
		,, ,,	,,	,, 7	α Tauri (*Aldebaran*)
		22nd ,,	,,	,, 7	Sun (*U.L.*)
		27th ,,	,,	,, 7	α Hydræ
		,, ,,	,,	,, 7	α Leonis (*Regulus*)
		6th Jan. 1874	,,	,, 7	α Ursæ Minoris (*Polaris*)
		,, ,,	,,	,, 7	Sun (*U.L.*)
		11th ,,	,,	,, 7	,, ,,
		13th ,,	,,	,, 7	,, ,,
		17th ,,	,,	,, 7	Jupiter
		,, ,,	,,	,, 7	α Virginis (*Spica*)
		19th ,,	,,	,, 7	β Ursæ Minoris
		28th ,,	,,	,, 7	α Ursæ Minoris (*Polaris*)
		30th ,,	,,	,, 7	β Orionis (*Rigel*)
		,, ,,	,,	,, 7	α Orionis
		,, ,,	,,	,, 7	α Canis Majoris (*Sirius*)
		20th Mar. 1874	,,	,, 7	Sun (*U.L.*)

(305)

to YARKAND viâ *Chang-Chenmo* and *Shahidúlá*.—(Concluded.)

Double altitudes or zenith distances corrected for index and level errors.			Elements used in computation of refraction.		Deduced Latitudes.			Remarks.
			Barometer.	Ther. Faht.	By stars north of zenith.	By sun or stars south of zenith.	Final latitudes north.	
	°	′ ″	Inches.	Degrees.	° ′ ″	° ′ ″	° ′ ″	H. M. S.
Z. D.	50	25 21(3)	26·3	29	38 11 53(3)			Mean time = 10 4 44
D. A.	79	8 30	25·4	35	38 11 32			
,,	114	42 40	25·4	35		38 12 11		
,,	110	1 0	25·8	51		38 12 1	38 11 54	
Z. D.	50	13 58(1)	26·5	28	38 24 48(1)			
,,	56	9 37(5)	26·4	47				Mean time = 10 45 0
,,	23	37 58	26·4	40	38 24 55	38 25 16(5)		,, = 12 2 29
,,	29	6 39	26·4	40			⎱38 24 57	
,,	39	20 19	26·4	40		38 24 59		
,,	50	21 50(3)	26·5	35	38 24 48(3)	38 25 5		
,,	50	13 21(4)	26·5	31	38 24 40(4)			Mean time = 11 34 50
D. A.	79	36 20	26·2	40	38 25 28			,, = 9 14 51
,,	79	36 40	26·2	40	38 25 38			
,,	70	7 30	26·2	22		38 25 4		
,,	114	16 50	,,	22		38 25 5		
,,	86	58 30	,,	22		38 25 7		
,,	135	43 40	,,	22		38 23 52		
,,	86	30 10	,,	22		38 25 3		
,,	46	14 10	,,	22	38 24 59			
,,	46	14 10	,,	22	38 24 59			
,,	65	51 10	,,	22		38 24 55		
,,	105	9 40	,,	22		38 24 57		
,,	86	29 0	,,	22		38 25 36		
,,	70	7 30	,,	22		38 24 59		
,,	56	53 0	,,	32		38 25 16		
,,	79	35 40	,,	22	38 25 16			
,,	117	55 50	,,	22		38 25 36		
,,	70	7 0	,,	22		38 25 14		
,,	114	16 10	,,	22		38 25 22		
,,	128	21 0	,,	22		38 24 55		
,,	56	50 10	,,	32		38 25 18	⎱38 25 8	Final latitude of Yárkand 38° 25′ 2″·5
,,	135	40 40	,,	22		38 25 22		
,,	56	52 30	,,	32		38 24 9		
,,	86	58 50	,,	22		38 24 51		
,,	128	21 30	,,	22		38 24 39		
,,	74	10 0	,,	18	38 25 16			
,,	58	43 0	,,	28		38 25 22		
,,	60	6 40	,,	28		38 24 57		
,,	60	45 20	,,	28		38 25 11		
,,	104	18 20	,,	18		38 25 6		
,,	82	12 30	,,	18		38 24 37		
,,	46	14 10	,,	18	38 25 7			
,,	74	9 40	,,	18	38 25 5			
,,	86	30 0	,,	18		38 25 0		
,,	117	56 10	,,	18		38 25 24		
,,	70	7 0	,,	18		38 25 6		
,,	103	19 40	,,	49		38 25 15		

Abstract of Observations for Latitude on road from LEH

Place of Observation.	Reference numbers	Astronomical date.	Observer.	Instrument observed with.	Object observed.
Panamik Village	59A	4th Oct. 1873	Nain Sing	Sextant No. 7	α Piscis Australis (*Fomalhaut*)
		,, ,,	,,	,, 7	α Ursæ Minoris (*Polaris*)
Chánglung Village	59B	6th Oct. 1873	Nain Sing	Sextant No. 7	Saturn
		,, ,,	,,	,, 7	α Piscis Australis (*Fomalhaut*)
		,, ,,	,,	,, 7	α Ursæ Minoris (*Polaris*)
		,, ,,	,,	,, 7	α Canis Majoris (*Sirius*)
		16th May 1874	,,	,, 7	α Ursæ Minoris (*Polaris*)
		17th ,,	,,	,, 7	Jupiter
		,, ,,	,,	,, 7	α Virginis (*Spica*)
		,, ,,	,,	,, 7	β Ursæ Minoris
Tútialák Camp (*Pangdong-sú.*)	59D	7th Oct. 1873	Nain Sing	Sextant No. 7	α Aquilæ (*Altair*)
		15th May 1874	,,	,, 7	Jupiter
		,, ,,	,,	,, 7	α Ursæ Minoris (*Polaris*)
Sausér-polu	59F	8th Oct. 1873	Nain Sing	Sextant No. 7	α Canis Majoris (*Sirius*)
		13th May 1874	,,	,, 7	Jupiter
		,, ,,	,,	,, 7	α Ursæ Minoris (*Polaris*)
		14th ,,	,,	,, 7	β Ursæ Minoris
		20th June 1874	Capt. Trotter	Theodolite	Sun (Centre)
Brúchse	83	17th June 1874	Capt. Trotter	Theodolite	α Serpentis
		,, ,,	,,	,,	ζ Ursæ Minoris
		,, ,,	,,	,,	δ Ophiuchi
		,, ,,	,,	,,	β Ursæ Minoris
Khúmdán Camp	60	12th May 1874	Nain Sing	Sextant No. 7	α Ursæ Minoris (*Polaris*)
Giapshan Kizil	60A	11th May 1874	Nain Sing	Sextant No. 7	Jupiter
		,, ,,	,,	,,	α Virginis (*Spica*)
		,, ,,	,,	,,	α Ursæ Minoris (*Polaris*)
Daolatbeg-uldi	61	11th Oct. 1873	Nain Sing	Sextant No. 7	β Orionis (*Rigel*)
Bálti or Kárákorum polu	62B	10th May 1874	Nain Sing	Sextant No. 7	Jupiter
		,, ,,	,,	,, 7	α Virginis (*Spica*)
		,, ,,	,,	,, 7	α Ursæ Minoris (*Polaris*)

(309)

to YARKAND viâ Karakoram and Kugiar.—(Continued.)

Double altitudes or zenith distances corrected for index and level errors.	Elements used in computation of refraction.		Deduced Latitudes.			Remarks.
	Barometer.	Ther. Faht.	By stars north of zenith.	By sun or stars south of zenith.	Final latitudes north.	
	Inches.	Degrees.	° ′ ″	° ′ ″	° ′ ″	
D. A. 117 32 20	15·6	30		35 32		
,, 87 54 40	15·6	30		35 32 50		
,, 68 24 30	15·6	30	35 33 15			
,, 101 47 30	15·6	30	35 33 22			
,, 117 58 30	16·1	25		35 33 14		
,, 68 23 50	16·1	25	35 32 56		35 33 4	
Z. D. 12 18 56	15·6	45		35 38 8		
,, 46 7 33	15·6	45		35 37 42		
,, 35 34 33	15·6	45		35 37 43		
,, 51 8 37	15·6	45		35 37 33		
,, 39 2 17	15·6	45	35 37 36			
D. A. 117 48 10	17·4	15		35 37 55		
,, 87 45 10	17·4	15		35 37 41		
,, 68 32 40	17·4	15	35 37 16		35 37 42	
Z. D. 46 30 21	16·9	31		36 0 35		
,, 51 30 46	16·9	31		36 0 15		
,, 38 40 5	16·9	31	35 59 44			
,, 44 54 45	16·9	31		36 0 9	36 0 11	
Z. D. 12 59 3	17·4	52	36 8 34		36 8 34	
D. A. 64 51 40	17·5	30		36 16 42		
,, 47 1 30	17·5	30		36 13 2		
,, 75 15 0	17·5	30	36 14 55		36 14 54	
D. A. 90 35 50	17·7	20		36 21 59		
,, 122 2 30	17·7	20		36 22 10		
,, 74 12 20	17·7	20		36 22 19	36 22 9	
D. A. 64 38 0	18·1	31		36 24 31		
,, 46 40 30	18·1	31		36 23 35		
,, 75 36 40	18·1	31	36 25 45			
,, 74 9 30	18·1	31		36 23 43	36 24 24	

Abstract of Observations for Latitude on road from LEH

Place of Observation.	Reference numbers.	Astronomical date.	Observer.	Instrument observed with.	Object observed.
Kirghiz Jangul Camp	76	10th June 1874	Capt. Trotter	Theodolite	α Virginis (*Spica*)
		,, ,,	,,	,,	α Libræ
		,, ,,	,,	,,	β Ursæ Minoris
		,, ,,	,,	,,	β Libræ
Sasak bulák Camp	78A	17th April 1874	Nain Sing	Sextant No. 7	α Hydræ
		,, ,,	,,	,, 7	α Leonis (*Regulus*)
		,, ,,	,,	,, 7	Jupiter
		,, ,,	,,	,, 7	α Virginis (*Spica*)
		,, ,,	,,	,, 7	α Ursæ Minoris (*Polaris*)
		,, ,,	,,	,, 7	β Ursæ Minoris
Teshek Tásh Camp	73A	13th April 1874	Nain Sing	Sextant No. 7	α Hydræ
		,, ,,	,,	,,	Jupiter
		,, ,,	,,	,, 7	α Ursæ Minoris (*Polaris*)
		,, ,,	,,	,, 7	β Ursæ Minoris
Duba Camp	73	5th June 1874	Capt. Trotter	Theodolite	α Coronæ
		,, ,,	,,	,,	α Serpentis
Mazár Khoja	65	12th April 1874	Nain Sing	Sextant No. 7	Sun (Upper Limb)
		,, ,,	,,	,, 7	α Leonis (*Regulus*)
		,, ,,	,,	,, 7	Jupiter
		,, ,,	,,	,, 7	α Ursæ Minoris (*Polaris*)
Chiklik	65A	31st May 1874	Capt. Trotter	Theodolite	α Libræ
		,, ,,	,,	,,	α Bootis (*Arcturus*)
		,, ,,	,,	,,	β Ursæ Minoris
		,, ,,	,,	,,	β Libræ
Ak-Masjid	63	8th April 1874	Nain Sing	Sextant No. 7	α Leonis (*Regulus*)
		,, ,,	,,	,, 7	Jupiter
		9th ,,	,,	,, 7	Sun (Upper Limb)
		,, ,,	,,	,, 7	α Hydræ
		,, ,,	,,	,, 7	Jupiter
Fusár Village	63A	6th April 1874	Nain Sing	Sextant No. 7	Sun (Upper Limb)
		7th ,,	,,	,, 7	,, ,,
		,, ,,	,,	,, 7	Jupiter

to YARKAND viâ Karakoram and Kugiar.—(Continued.)

	Double altitudes or zenith distances corrected for index and level errors.			Elements used in computation of refraction.		Deduced Latitudes.			Remarks.
				Barometer.	Ther. Faht.	By stars north of zenith.	By sun or stars south of zenith.	Final latitudes north.	
	°	′	″	Inches.	Degrees.	° ′ ″	° ′ ″	° ′ ″	
Z. D.	46	55	35	18·2	26		36 25 54		
,,	51	56	12	18·2	26		36 25 46		
,,	38	14	10	18·2	26	36 25 37			
,,	45	20	23	18·2	26		36 25 40	36 25 44	
D. A.	90	52	30	18·3	18		36 27 28		
,,	132	14	50	18·3	18		36 27 47		
,,	115	16	10	18·3	18		36 27 7		
,,	86	5	40	18·3	18		36 27 30		
,,	70	13	10	18·3	18	36 27 25			
,,	103	36	20	18·3	18	36 27 41		36 27 30	
D. A.	90	19	20	19·9	24		36 44 6		
,,	114	24	50	19·9	24		36 44 26		
,,	70	46	50	19·9	24	36 44 11			
,,	104	10	0	19·9	24	36 44 27		36 44 18	
Z. D.	9	38	13	20·2	55	36 46 37			
,,	29	56	53	20·2	55		36 46 30	36 46 34	
D. A.	124	8	20	20·9	39		36 50 50		
,,	131	30	20	20·9	30		36 50 3		
,,	114	7	30	20·9	30		36 50 52		
,,	70	59	20	20·9	30		36 50 24	36 50 32	
Z. D.	52	33	15	21·8	52		37 2 54		
,,	17	12	42	21·8	52	37 3 11			
,,	37	37	2	21·8	52	37 2 40			
,,	45	57	18	21·8	52		37 2 49	37 2 54	
D. A.	130	54	20	21·3	33		37 8 4		
,,	113	15	0	21·3	33		37 7 38		
,,	121	20	50	21·3	40		37 8 17		
,,	89	31	0	21·3	33		37 8 18		
,,	113	17	30	21·3	33		37 8 50	37 8 13	
D. A.	118	41	10	22·7	47		37 20 40		
,,	119	24	0	22·7	47		37 21 51		
,,	112	46	40	22·7	44		37 19 20	37 20 37	

(312)

Abstract of Observations for Latitude on road from LEH

Place of Observation.	Reference numbers	Astronomical date.	Observer.	Instrument observed with.	Object observed.
Kugiár Village ...	69	29th May 1874	Capt. Trotter ..	Theodolite ...	η Ursæ Majoris ...
		"	" ...	" ...	β Ursæ Minoris ...
		2nd April 1874	Nain Sing ...	Sextant No. 7	Jupiter ... ...
		3rd "	" ...	" 7	Sun (Upper Limb) ...
		"	" ...	" 7	α Leonis (*Regulus*) ...
		4th "	" ...	" 7	Sun (Upper Limb) ...
		"	" ...	" 7	α Hydræ ... ...
		"	" ...	" 7	α Leonis (*Regulus*) ...
		5th "	" ...	" 7	Sun (Upper Limb) ...
		"	" ...	" 7	α Leonis (*Regulus*) ...
Yolárik Village ...	68	27th May 1874	Capt. Trotter ..	Theodolite ...	β Ursæ Minoris ...
		"	" ...	" ...	β Libræ ...

to YARKAND viâ *Karakoram and Kugiar*.—(Concluded.)

Double altitudes or zenith distances corrected for index and level errors.			Elements used in computation of refraction.		Deduced Latitudes.			Remarks.
			Barometer.	Ther. Faht.	By stars north of zenith.	By sun or stars south of zenith.	Final latitudes north.	
	°	′	″	Inches.	Degrees.	° ′ ″	° ′ ″	° ′ ″
Z. D.	12	32	43	23·4	63	37 23 43			
,,	37	15	29	23·4	63	37 24 11			
D. A.	112	10	40	23·2	40		37 24 11		
,,	116	15	40	23·2	45		37 25 1		
,,	130	23	40	23·2	40		37 23 25		
,,	117	1	20	23·2	45		37 25 6		
,,	88	59	40	23·2	40		37 24 2		
,,	130	23	10	23·2	40		37 23 40		
,,	117	47	0	23·2	45		37 25 4		
,,	130	22	40	23·2	40		37 23 55	37 24 14	
Z. D.	37	12	41	23·6	70	37 26 59			
,,	46	21	40	23·6	70		37 27 13	37 27 6	

(314)

Abstract of Observations for Latitude on road from LEH

Place of Observation.	Reference numbers	Astronomical date.	Observer.	Instrument observed with.	Object observed.
Augche Chortan, R. bank of Nischu River.	108A.	28th July 1874 29th "	Kishen Sing... "	Sextant No. 8.. "	α Scorpii (*Antares*) β Ceti
Sumzi Ling Camp	108	26th July 1874 27th " " "	Kishen Sing... " "	" " "	α Aquilæ (*Altair*) α Piscis Australis (*Fomalhaut*) β Ceti
Chumik Lhákmo Camp...	107	23rd July 1874 " " 24th " " "	Kishen Sing... " " "	" " " "	α Scorpii (*Antares*) α Aquilæ (*Altair*) Saturn α Piscis Australis (*Fomalhaut*)
Táshliák Khiol, lake bank of.	106	22nd July 1874 " "	Kishen Sing... "	" "	Saturn α Piscis Australis (*Fomalhaut*)
Arash Camp, on right bank of Kiria river.	103	14th July 1874 15th " " "	Kishen Sing... " "	" " "	α Scorpii (*Antares*) α Piscis Australis (*Fomalhaut*) α Scorpii (*Antares*)
Ghubolik Camp, bank of Ulokshahí Khiol Lake.	102	12th July 1874 13th "	Kishen Sing... "	" "	α Aquilæ (*Altair*) Saturn
Polu Village	101	2nd July 1874 4th " " " 7th " 8th " 9th " " "	Kishen Sing... " " " " " "	" " " " " " "	α Scorpii (*Antares*) α Aquilæ (*Altair*) Saturn α Aquilæ (*Altair*) α Scorpii (*Antares*) " " " α Aquilæ (*Altair*)
Kiria Bazar	99	18th June 1874 26th " 27th " 28th " 29th " " "	Kishen Sing... " " " " "	" " " " " "	β Ursæ Minoris α Aquilæ (*Altair*) Saturn β Ursæ Minoris α Aquilæ (*Altair*) Saturn

(315)
to YARKAND viâ NOH, POLU, and KHOTAN.

Double altitudes or zenith distance corrected for index and level errors.	Elements used in computation of refraction.		Deduced Latitudes.			Remarks.
	Barometer.	Ther. Faht.	By stars north of zenith.	By sun or stars south of zenith.	Final latitudes north.	
° ′ ″	Inches.	Degrees.	° ′ ″	° ′ ″	° ′ ″	
D. A. 60 20 40	17·6	42		33 41 23		
,, 75 15 50	17·6	42		33 42 24	33 41 54	
D. A. 129 2 10	17·1	42		34 1 26		
,, 51 26 0	17·1	42		34 1 1		
,, 74 37 50	17·1	42		34 1 26	34 1 18	
D. A. 58 58 10	16·3	41		34 22 38		
,, 128 18 0	16·3	41		34 23 31		
,, 75 5 10	16·3	41		34 21 6		
,, 50 42 50	16·3	41		34 22 37	34 22 28	
D. A. 74 36 0	16·4	40		34 38 19		
,, 50 9 0	16·4	40		34 39 29	34 38 54	
D. A. 56 44 0	16·0	38		35 29 49		
,, 48 28 40	16·8	38		35 29 49		
,, 56 43 30	16·8	38		35 30 3	35 29 54	
D. A. 125 41 40	16·8	40		35 41 40		
,, 72 55 20	17·3	40		35 40 10	35 40 55	
D. A. 55 20 40	21·8	65		36 11 42		
,, 124 39 40	23·0	65		36 12 43		
,, 72 16 50	23·0	65		36 10 13		
,, 124 29 30	22·1	65		36 12 49		
,, 55 20 50	22·0	65		36 11 37		
,, 55 21 0	21·9	65		36 11 32		
,, 124 39 20	21·9	65		36 12 53	36 11 56	
D. A. 104 24 30	25·0	69	36 51 57		36 51 26	
,, 123 22 0	25·0	69		36 51 35		
,, 71 11 40	25·1	69		36 50 24		
,, 104 24 50	25·0	69	36 52 8			
,, 123 22 0	25·2	69		36 51 35		
,, 71 9 10	25·2	69		36 49 37		

a52

(316)

Abstract of Observations for Latitude on road from LEH

Place of Observation.	Reference numbers.	Astronomical date.	Observer.	Instrument observed with.	Object observed.
Sorghák Khiang Shahi Bazar.	100	22nd June 1874 23rd "	Kishen Sing "	Sextant No. 8. "	β Ursæ Minoris α Aquilæ (*Altair*)
Chíra Bazar	98	11th June 1874 " " 12th " 13th " 14th "	Kishen Sing " " " "	" " " " "	α Virginis (*Spica*) β Ursæ Minoris α Aquilæ (*Altair*) β Ursæ Minoris α Aquilæ (*Altair*)
KHOTAN CITY. Observations taken in Shamál Bagh in nearly the same latitude as the centre of the city.	93	19th May 1874 " " " " 20th " " " " " 21st " " " " " " " 26th " " " 27th " 28th " " " " " 29th " 30th " " " " " 3rd June 1874 4th " " " " " " " 5th "	Kishen Sing "	" "	α Virginis (*Spica*) α Ursæ Minoris (*Polaris*) β Ursæ Minoris α Virginis (*Spica*) α Ursæ Minoris (*Polaris*) β Ursæ Minoris α Scorpii (*Antares*) α Virginis (*Spica*) α Ursæ Minoris (*Polaris*) β Ursæ Minoris α Ursæ Minoris (*Polaris*) β Ursæ Minoris α Aquilæ (*Altair*) α Scorpii (*Antares*) α Aquilæ (*Altair*) β Ursæ Minoris α Aquilæ (*Altair*) α Virginis (*Spica*) α Ursæ Minoris (*Polaris*) β Ursæ Minoris α Virginis (*Spica*) α Aquilæ (*Altair*) α Virginis (*Spica*) α Ursæ Minoris (*Polaris*) β Ursæ Minoris α Aquilæ (*Altair*)
Kárákásh Bazar	94	23rd May 1874 24th " " " " "	Kishen Sing " " "	" " " "	α Virginis (*Spica*) α Virginis (*Spica*) α Ursæ Minoris (*Polaris*) β Ursæ Minoris
Gúmá Bazar	90	12th May 1874	Kishen Sing	"	Jupiter

to YARKAND viâ NOH, POLU, and KHOTAN.—(Concluded.)

Double altitudes or zenith distances corrected for index and level errors.	Elements used in computation of refraction.		Deduced Latitudes.			Remarks.
	Barometer.	Ther. Faht.	By stars north of zenith.	By sun or stars south of zenith	Final latitudes north.	
° ′ ″	Inches.	Degrees.	° ′ ″	° ′ ″	° ′ ″	
D. A. 104 0 40	22·9	66	36 40 5			
,, 123 45 50	22·9	66		36 39 37	36 39 51	
D. A. 85 1 20	25·4	69		36 59 49		
,, 104 41 40	25·4	69	37 0 30			
,, 123 3 50	25·4	69		37 0 37		
,, 104 41 50	25·4	69	37 0 35			
,, 123 4 0	25·4	69		37 0 32	37 0 26	
D. A. 84 47 0	25·2	70		37 6 58		
,, 71 35 0	25·2	70	37 8 20			
,, 104 56 40	25·2	70	37 7 55			
,, 84 46 50	25·2	70		37 7 3		
,, 71 34 40	25·2	70	37 8 10			
,, 104 56 50	25·2	70	37 8 0			
,, 53 29 40	25·2	70		37 7 29		
,, 84 47 10	25·2	70		37 6 53		
,, 71 34 40	25·2	70	37 8 10			
,, 104 56 40	25·2	70	37 7 55			
,, 71 34 50	25·5	70	37 8 16			
,, 104 56 30	25·5	70	37 7 51			
,, 122 50 50	25·5	70		37 7 4		
,, 53 29 10	25·5	70		37 7 43		
,, 122 50 40	25·5	70		37 7 9		
,, 104 56 30	25·5	70	37 7 51			
,, 122 50 40	25·5	70		37 7 10		
,, 84 46 40	25·5	70		37 7 8		
,, 71 34 10	25·5	70	37 7 58			
,, 104 56 20	25·5	70	37 7 48			
,, 84 46 40	25·5	70		37 7 9		
,, 122 50 20	25·5	70		37 7 22		
,, 84 46 30	25·5	70		37 7 14		
,, 71 34 10	25·5	70	37 7 59			
,, 104 56 30	25·5	70	37 7 55			
,, 122 50 30	25·5	70		37 7 17	37 7 36	
D. A. 84 29 0	25·7	70		37 15 59		
,, 84 28 30	25·7	70		37 16 14		
,, 71 54 0	25·7	70	37 17 49			
,, 105 15 0	25·7	70	37 17 5		37 16 47	
D. A. 113 52 30	25·5	69		37 37 31	37 37 31	

(318)

Abstract of Observations for Latitude on road from

Place of Observation.	Reference numbers	Astronomical date.	Observer.	Instrument observed with.	Object observed.
Kok Robát	109	20th May 1874 " " " "	Capt. Trotter " "	Theodolite " "	Jupiter β Leonis α Virginis (*Spica*)
Kizil Village	110	30th Nov. 1873 " "	Capt. Trotter "	Theodolite "	α Ursæ Minoris (*Polaris*)* " " "*
Yangi Hissar Town	111	1st Dec. 1873 18th Mar. 1874	Capt. Trotter "	Theodolite "	α Ursæ Minoris (*Polaris*)* α Leonis (*Regulus*)
Yapchan Village	112	3rd Dec. 1873 " "	Capt. Trotter "	Theodolite "	α Ursæ Minoris (*Polaris*)* γ Pegasi (*Algenib*)*
KASHGHAR—Yangi-Shahr. In Embassy Quarters just outside the gate of the Yangi-Shahr.	113	4th Dec. 1873 19th " 24th " " " " " " " 27th " " " " " 29th Jan. 1874 " " " " 3rd Feb. 1874 " " 13th " " " " " " "	Capt. Trotter " " " " " " " " " " " " " " " " "	Theodolite " " " " " " " " " " " " " " " " "	α Ursæ Minoris (*Polaris*)* " " "* " " "* α Tauri (*Aldebaran*) β Orionis (*Rigel*) ε Orionis β Orionis (*Rigel*) ε Orionis α Ursæ Minoris (*Polaris*)* δ Orionis ε Orionis α Orionis* α Canis Minoris (*Procyon*)* α Ursæ Minoris (*Polaris*)* α Canis Majoris* α Ursæ Minoris (*Polaris*)* " " "* " " "*

(319)

YARKAND to KASHGHAR.

Double altitudes or zenith distances corrected for index and level errors.				Elements used in computation of refraction.		Deduced Latitudes.			Remarks.			
				Barometer.	Ther. Faht.	By stars north of zenith.	By sun or stars south of zenith.	Final latitudes north.				
	°	′	″	Inches.	Degrees.	° ′ ″	° ′ ″	° ′ ″				
Z.D.	33	53	20	25·3	71		38 26 11					
,,	23	9	29	25·3	71		38 26 2					
,,	48	56	25	25·3	71		38 26 2	38 26 5				
										H.	M.	S.
Z.D.	50	11	57[3]	26·4	20	38 39 26[3]			Mean time =	6	19	48
,,	50	7	33[2]	26·3	20	38 39 20[2]		38 39 23	,, =	6	44	5
Z.D.	49	48	24[3]	26·3	37	38 55 58[3]			Mean time =	6	56	
,,	26	20	59	25·2	33		38 56 17	38 56 8				
Z.D.	49	32	48[3]	25·5	38	39 13 32[3]			Mean time =	6	36	15
,,	24	44	53[2]	25·5	38		39 13 30[2]	39 13 31	,, =	7	38	48
Z.D.	49	34	40	25·6	24	39 24 16[3]			Mean time =	11	7	4
,,	49	38	39[4]	25·6	14	39 24 19[4]			,, =	10	18	28
,,	49	13	25	25·5	17	39 24 5						
,,	23	8	40	,,	,,		39 24 23					
,,	47	44	30	,,	,,		39 24 36					
,,	40	40	44	,,	,,		39 24 31					
,,	47	44	19	,,	,,		39 24 24					
,,	40	40	34	,,	,,		39 24 21					
,,	49	55	38[3]	,,	20	39 24 22[3]			Mean time =	10	51	8
,,	39	47	55	,,	17		39 25 0					
,,	40	41	14	,,	,,		39 24 57					
,,	32	1	31[4]	25·7	19		39 24 26[4]		Mean time =	9	35	47
,,	33	52	43[4]	25·5	14		39 24 19[4]		,, =	7	25	33
,,	50	51	16[4]	,,	,,	39 24 13[4]			,, =	11	1	45
,,	55	56	32[6]	25·5	20		39 24 32[6]		,, =	5	53	42
,,	50	44	10[2]	,,	,,	39 24 14[2]			,, =	10	2	5
,,	50	47	47[2]	,,	,,	39 24 26[2]			,, =	10	12	48
,,	50	49	18[2]	,,	,,	39 24 33[2]		39 24 26	,, =	10	17	34

(320)

Abstract of Observations for Latitude on road from

Place of Observation.	Reference numbers.	Astronomical date.	Observer.	Instrument observed with.	Object observed.
Osten Artysh (Besak Village).	115	10th Jan. 1874	Capt. Trotter...	Theodolite ...	δ Orionis ...
Chung Tirik Village ...	116	9th Jan. 1874	Capt. Trotter...	Theodolite ...	α Ursæ Minoris (*Polaris*)
Chakmák Fort ...	118	8th Jan. 1874	Capt. Trotter...	Theodolite A.	Sun (U. L.) ...
Chakmák Station, three miles north of fort.	118A	3rd Jan. 1874	Capt. Trotter...	Theodolite ...	,, ,,
Torgat Belá ...	119	7th Jan. 1874	Capt. Trotter...	Theodolite ...	α Ursæ Minoris (*Polaris*)

Observations for Latitude on road

Viâ Uch Turfan.	Ayák Soghon ...	126	20th Feb. 1874	Capt. Trotter...	Theodolite ...	ε Orionis ...
			,, ,,	,,	,, ...	α Orionis ...
	Kyr Bulák ...	127	27th Feb. 1874	Capt. Trotter...	Theodolite ...	α Ursæ Minoris (*Polaris*)*
	Ui Bulák ...	129	25th Feb. 1874	Capt. Trotter...	Theodolite ...	β Orionis (*Rigel*) ...
			,, ,,	,, ...	,, ...	δ Orionis ...
			,, ,,	,, ...	,, ...	ε Orionis ...
Viâ Marálbáshi.	Faizabád ...	132	2nd March 1874	Capt. Trotter...	Theodolite ...	δ Orionis ...
			,, ,,	,, ...	,, ...	ε Orionis ...
			,, ,,	,, ...	,, ...	α Orionis ...
	Marálbáshi ...	137	11th Jan. 1874 17th ,,	Capt. Biddulph	Six-inch Sextant.	Sun (L. L.) ...

Observations for Latitude taken in

Place of Observation.	Reference numbers.	Astronomical date.	Observer.	Instrument observed with.	Object observed.
Tangitár ...	139	17th Feb. 1874	Capt. Trotter...	Theodolite ...	α Canis Minoris (*Procyon*)
		,, ,,	,,	,, ...	β Geminorum (*Pollux*) ...
Tughamati ...	140	18th Feb. 1874	Capt. Trotter...	Theodolite ...	β Orionis (*Rigel*)
		,, ,,	,,	,, ...	δ Orionis ...
		,, ,,	,,	,, ...	ε Orionis ...
Kizil-boia or Shamba Bazar	140A.	3rd Jan. 1874	Kishen Sing ...	Sextant No. 44	α Orionis ...
		4th ,,	,, ...	,, 44	α Canis Majoris (*Sirius*)
		,, ,,	,, ...	,, 44	α Canis Minoris (*Procyon*)
Khánárik or Khánárik Shamba Bazar.	140B.	5th Jan. 1874	Kishen Sing ...	Sextant No. 44	β Orionis (*Rigel*)
		,, ,,	,, ...	,, 44	α Orionis ...
		6th ,,	,, ...	,, 44	α Canis Majoris (*Sirius*)
		,, ,,	,, ...	,, 44	α Canis Minoris (*Procyon*)

(321)

KASHGHAR to CHADYRKUL.

Double altitudes or zenith distances corrected for index and level errors.				Elements used in computation of refraction.		Deduced Latitudes.								Remarks.
				Barometer.	Ther. Faht.	By stars north of zenith.			By sun or stars south of zenith.			Final latitudes north.		
		°	′	″	Inches.	Degrees.	°	′	″	°	′	″	°	′	″	
Z. D.	39	59	34	25·0	20				39	36	50	39	36	50	
Z. D.	48	50	36	23·0	2	39	47	0				39	47	0	
Z. D.	62	3	11	21·5	32				40	5	9	40	5	9	
Z. D.	62	41	14	21·5	10				40	8	28	40	8	28	
Z. D.	48	13	51	19·4	—10	40	23	53				40	23	53	

from KASHGHAR to AKSU.

Z. D.	41	17	5	25·5	23				40	0	47				
,,	32	35	56	25·5	23				39	59	25	40	0	6	
Z. D.	50	7	31(3)	25·2	29	40	6	7(3)				40	6	7	Mean time = 9h 21m 21s
Z. D.	48	46	1	23·8	25				40	25	57				
,,	40	49	22	23·8	25				40	26	24				
,,	41	42	41	23·8	25				40	26	20	40	26	14	
Z. D.	39	52	31	26·0	42				39	29	34				
,,	40	45	51	26·0	42				39	29	30				
,,	32	6	15	26·0	42				39	29	42	39	29	35	
Z. D.	61	50	7	26·2	28				39	46	1				
,,	60	47	12	26·3	29				39	46	46	39	46	24	

neighbourhood of KASHGHAR.

Z. D.	34	23	22	23·9	32				39	56	41				
,,	11	36	53	23·9	32				39	56	51	39	56	46	
Z. D.	48	22	0	23·7	30				40	1	54				
,,	40	24	56	23·7	30				40	1	57				
,,	41	18	8	23·7	30				40	1	46	40	1	52	
D. A.	116	1	33	25·0	20				39	22	44				
,,	68	11	23	25·0	20				39	22	59				
,,	112	21	23	25·0	20				39	22	44	39	22	49	
D. A.	84	48	33	26·0	20				39	15	46				
,,	116	16	13	26·0	20				39	15	24				
,,	68	25	53	26·0	20				39	15	44				
,,	112	35	3	26·0	20				39	15	53	39	15	42	

(322)

Abstract of Observations for Latitude on road from YANGI to KILAH

Place of Observation.	Reference numbers.	Astronomical date.	Observer.	Instrument observed with.	Object observed.
Aktala Camp	149	22nd March 1874 ,, ,,	Capt. Trotter ,,	Theodolite ,,	α Hydræ α Leonis (*Regulus*)
Kasha-sú Camp	151	15th May 1874 ,, ,, ,, ,, ,, ,,	Capt. Trotter ,, ,, ,,	Theodolite ,, ,, ,,	α Virginis (*Spica*) ζ Virginis η Ursæ Majoris α Boötis (*Arcturus*)
Tárbáshí Camp	156	27th March 1874	Capt. Trotter	Theodolite	α Leonis (*Regulus*)
TÁSHKURGHÁN, Camp near the Fort.	160	31st March 1874 ,, ,, ,, ,, ,, ,, ,, ,,	Capt. Trotter ,, ,, ,, ,,	Theodolite ,, ,, ,, ,,	α Leonis (*Regulus*)* ,, ,, ,, α Ursæ Minoris (*Polaris*)* α Ursæ Majoris* ,, ,, ,,
Kogachak Camp	163	3rd April 1874 ,, ,,	Capt. Trotter ,,	Theodolite ,,	α Hydræ α Leonis
Aktásh Camp	183	5th May 1874	Capt. Trotter	Theodolite	β Corvi
Shash Tipá Camp	181	2nd May 1874. ,, ,, ,, ,,	Capt. Trotter ,, ,,	Theodolite ,, ,,	α Ursæ Majoris δ Leonis β Corvi
Pámir-kul, Camp on N. edge of Oi-kul or lake of Little Pámir.	165	5th April 1874 ,, ,, ,, ,, ,, ,,	Capt. Totter ,, ,, ,,	Theodolite ,, ,, ,,	ι Ursæ Majoris α Hydræ α Leonis α Ursæ Majoris
Daráz Diwán Camp	167	7th April 1874 ,, ,, ,, ,,	Capt. Trotter ,, ,,	Theodolite ,, ,,	ι Ursæ Majoris α Hydræ θ Ursæ Majoris
Mazár Tipá Camp	178	30th April 1874	Capt. Trotter	Theodolite	γ Leonis

(323)

PANJAH (WAKHAN) viâ TASHKURGHAN and return journey to YARKAND.

Double altitudes or zenith distances corrected for index and level errors.				Elements used in computation of refraction.		Deduced Latitudes.			Remarks.
				Barometer.	Ther. Faht.	By stars north of zenith.	By sun or stars south of zenith.	Final latitudes north.	
		°	′	″	Inches.	Degrees.	° ′ ″	° ′ ″	° ′ ″	
Z. D.	46	35	44	22·2	29		38 29 38		
,,	25	53	42	22·2	29		38 28 57	38 29 18	
Z. D.	48	41	45	19·7	26		38 12 8		
,,	38	8	44	19·7	26		38 12 3		
,,	11	44	50	19·7	26	38 11 34			
,,	18	21	49	19·7	26	38 12 16		38 12 0	
Z. D.	25	30	55	19·0	15		38 6 8	38 6 8	
									H. M. S.
Z. D.	25	12	7(3)	20·2	23		37 46 59(3)		Mean time = 9 23 37
	25	11	37	20·2	23		37 46 50		
	53	11	31(3)	20·2	23	37 46 30(3)			,, = 9 39 20
	24	40	49(4)	20·2	23	37 46 55(4)			,, = 10 17 48
,,	24	38	49	20·2	23	37 46 48		37 46 49	
Z. D.	45	43	37	18·2	9		37 37 23		
,,	25	1	46	18·2	9		37 36 58	37 37 11	
Z. D.	60	16	18	18·6	26	37 35 13		37 35 13	
Z. D.	24	54	9	26·0	18	37 31 36			
,,	16	18	32	26·0	18		37 31 32		
,,	60	13	2	26·0	18	37 31 54		37 31 39	
Z. D.	11	17	55	18·0	4		37 14 14		
,,	45	21	48	18·0	4		37 15 33		
,,	24	38	58	18·0	4		37 14 10		
,,	25	11	49	18·0	4		37 13 49	37 14 27	
Z. D.	11	31	49	19·6	27	37 0 20			
,,	45	6	30	19·6	27		37 0 16		
,,	15	14	59	19·6	27		37 0 1	37 0 9	
Z. D.	16	59	59	1·79	20		37 28 53	37 28 53	

(324)

Abstract of Observations for Lat. on road from YANGI HISSAR to KILAH PANJAI

Place of Observation.	Reference numbers.	Astronomical date.	Observer.	Instrument observed with.	Object observed.
Yol Mazár Camp	176	28th April 1874	Capt. Trotter...	Theodolite ...	α Leonis ...
Kilah Panjah (WAKHAN)	174	18th April 1874	Capt. Trotter...	Theodolite ...	α Ursæ Minoris (*Polaris*)
		22nd ,,	,, ...	,, ...	α Virginis (*Spica*)
		,, ,,	,, ...	,, ...	ζ Virginis ...
		,, ,,	,, ...	,, ...	η Ursæ Majoris
		,, ,,	,, ...	,, ...	α Libræ ...
		,, ,,	,, ...	,, ...	α Libræ ...

(WAKHAN) viâ TASHKURGHAN and return journey to YARKAND.—(Concld.)

Double altitudes or zenith distances corrected for index and level errors.				Elements used in computation of refraction.		Deduced Latitudes.						Remarks.
				Barometer.	Ther. Faht.	By stars north of zenith.			By sun or stars south of zenith.			
											Final latitudes north.	
		°	′	″	Inches.	Degrees.	°	′	″	°	′	″	°	′	″	
Z. D.	24	42	54	19·0	32				37	18	7	37	18	7	
Z. D.	54	19	43	21·3	25	37	0	14							
,,	47	30	3	21·3	25				37	0	28				
,,	36	57	2	21·3	25				37	0	21				
,,	12	56	8	21·3	25	37	0	8							
,,	52	30	39	21·3	25				37	0	23				
,,	52	33	35(2)	21·3	25				37	0	25(2)	37	0	18	Mean time = 12 H. 51 M. 4 S.

GEOGRAPHICAL APPENDIX.

SECTION B.

LONGITUDES.

The method of observation employed in the determination of absolute longitudes was that of lunar zenith distances, as being best adapted to the largest instrument carried with the expedition, *viz.*, a six-inch transit theodolite, with micrometer eye-piece. This method of observation has not hitherto occupied a prominent position in English astronomical works, and as the results at *Kashghar* cannot but be considered satisfactory, I have thought advisable to enter somewhat at length into the subject and to give an example of the computation of a single night's observations there, drawn up on a form specially prepared from Chauvenet's *formulæ* by J. B. N. Hennessey, Esq., of the Great Trigonometrical Survey.

The subject is gone into somewhat fully in an article furnished by Colonel Walker, R.E., to *Hints to Travellers*, a publication of the Royal Geographical Society (3rd Edition, December 1871), to which the reader is referred.

The instrument employed at Kashghar is furnished with two micrometers, each moving a separate wire, the eye-piece being so arranged that the micrometer wires may be placed parallel either to the fixed vertical or to the fixed horizontal wire of the diaphragm, according as transits or zenith distances are required to be observed.

The distance between the micrometer and centre wires is adjustable at pleasure, and may be set according to the rate of motion of the celestial body observed. A complete observation of the moon, on one face of the instrument, consists in noting the chronometer times of passage of the moon's limb across each of the wires in succession and the corresponding reading of the vertical verniers; a complete pair of observations on both faces gives, altogether, six *times* and four *readings* of the vertical arc. The readings of the ends of the bubble of the level attached to the telescope, object and eye ends being alternately directed towards the object observed, give a correction to be applied to the mean of the readings of the vertical arc which gives a final zenith distance corresponding to the mean of the six chronometer times.

In the example I have given it took me just three quarters of an hour to observe ten complete pairs of zenith distances as before described. A quarter of an hour may be allowed for the observation of three pairs of zenith distances to a star for time, prior to the observations to moon, and an equal time for similar observations after. To complete the observations in the time above mentioned, however, the observer must be thoroughly familiar with his instrument, must have a good recorder, and have his lamps and apparatus in perfect order.

The weak point of the system is that it is only applicable at certain times when the moon is favorably situated for observation; still, however, even in this respect it contrasts favorably with all other methods, excepting that of "lunar distances," for determining longitudes. I give some rules which have been laid down on this subject by Colonel Walker in the *Hints to Travellers*, modified by subsequent experience: they may I hope be of use to future explorers.

"Take pairs of observations of zenith distance on a star for the determination of the local time and chronometer error, then take other pairs of observations of zenith distance on the moon; in each instance adopt the mean of the chronometer times as that of the 'complete observation' of zenith distance. Both moon and star should be as nearly easterly or westerly as possible, and not very near (say within 10° of) the horizon. The operations should commence and close with star observations, in order that the chronometer rate may be duly ascertained and allowed for. The effect of instrumental errors will be materially reduced when the stars and the moon are on the same side of the meridian and at nearly the same zenith distance; if time permits, observations should be taken both east and west of the meridian, and both before and after full moon. In north latitudes, when the moon is going from south to north in declination on any day, she is most favorably situated for observing when west of the meridian; if moving in declination from north to south, she should be observed east of the meridian. The best time for observation is *when the direction of the proper motion* of the moon is towards the zenith of the observer. The sidereal time when this occurs may be readily found, graphically, by drawing on a chart of the heavens a tangent to the moon's orbit, at some point near the mean position of the moon on the day of observing, and producing it to cut the declination circle passing through the observer's zenith; then the hour circle passing through the point of intersection gives the sidereal time of observation. For practical purposes it will suffice to drop a perpendicular from the point indicating the moon's mean position on to the ecliptic, and drawing through that point a line at right angles with the perpendicular, and prolonging it to cut the declination circle. It will be found that the most favorable times occur when the moon is on the observer's prime vertical, and the least favorable when she is on the meridian. Whenever possible a few observations should be taken daily on several days rather than a large number on a single day."

An examination of the results of the observations now published shows, at a glance, that those at Kashghar are both much more complete and satisfactory in every way than those taken at Yarkand and elsewhere. This is easily accounted for by several reasons:—

My stay at Yarkand was limited to twenty days in all, many of which were cloudy and unfavorable for observing; whereas I was at Kashghar on and off for more than two months, during which time I was enabled to select the most favorable days for observing; I was at Yarkand during the early portion of our stay in the country, and not knowing what opportunities I should have, if any, for further observations, there or elsewhere, I observed the moon whenever I could get an opportunity quite irrespective of its position being favourable or otherwise. The observations were taken in a small court-yard, where the paved flooring gave anything but a stable footing to the instrument and caused great difficulty with the levels. The noise in the small court of people moving about during the operation was, it may well be imagined, highly detrimental to such delicate work as observations for longitude, particularly where a pocket chronometer had to be used.

At Kashghar, on the other hand, the court-yard was much larger and quieter and the ground more stable, and altogether the surroundings were very much more favorable.

These circumstances, combined with the results obtained from the computations, have induced me to employ the longitude of *Kashghar* as the origin for all my positions in Turkestan.

I have merely employed the other observed longitudes as checks upon the general accuracy of the positions of those points as determined by other methods, for which *vide* the details on the construction of the map which are given in the body of the report.

(Sd.)   HENRY TROTTER, *Capt., R.E.*

Observations for Time, and resulting Chronometer corrections employed in determi[ning] Local Mean Time for the calculation of Longitude from Lunar Zenith Distances[...]

Place of Observation.	Astronomical date	Object observed.	E. or W. of Meridian	Elements employed in computation of refraction.		No. of pairs of observations.	Mean of observed Z. Ds corrected for dislevelment.	Mean of Chronometer Times.	Computed correction to Chronometer Time to [...]
				Baro.	Ther.				
				In.	(Fahrt.) °		° ′ ″	H. M. S.	H. M
KASHGHAR (Yangi-Shahr.)	1873. 6th Dec.	γ Geminorum	E.	25·7	24	3	53 8 29	10 8 32·0	—0 2[...]
	„ „	β „	„	...	...	3	41 15 19	11 43 27·3	—0 2[...]
	7th „	β „	„	25·8	...	3	47 21 5	11 7 57·6	—0 2[...]
	„ „	α Leonis	„	...	15	3	66 7 53	12 40 2·6	—0 2[...]
	27th „	α Androm.	W.	5·5	20	3	42 46 7	9 21 31·1	—0 2[...]
	28th „	α Arietis	„	25·6	18	2	50 11 53	11 39 11·7	—0 2[...]
	„ „	α „	„	...	...	2	52 26 18	11 50 45·6	—0 2[...]
	1874. 29th Jan.	β Geminorum	E.	...	31	3	47 13 25	7 40 17·9	—0 2[...]
	„ „	α Leonis	„	...	16	3	49 40 49	10 38 33·6	—0 2[...]
	31st „	α „	„	25·5	15	4	49 34 17	6 56 31·0	+3 1[...]
YARKAND	1873. 8th Nov.	β Tauri	E.	26·25	28	3	46 4 26	10 45 45·7	—0 1[...]
	„ „	β Geminorum	„	...	...	3	48 57 41	12 50 17·0	—0 1[...]
	9th „	„ „	„	26·25	23	3	39 3 6	13 36 52·9	—0 1[...]
	„ „	„ „	„	...	...	3	22 15 22	15 3 56·5	—0 1[...]
TASHKUR-GHAN.	1874. 31st March	α Bootis (Arcturus)	E.	20·2	23	3	58 51 15	9 10 9·9	+0 [...]
KILA PANJAH	24th April	β Geminorum	W.	21·4	41	3	58 26 41	10 18 29·2	—0 1[...]
	„ „	α Leonis (Regulus)	„	...	...	4	55 26 9	11 45 13·2	—0 1[...]

(331)

Observations of Lunar Zenith Distances and resulting determination of Longitude.

Place of Observation.	Astronomical date.	The moon. E. or W. of Meridian.	The moon. Upper or Lower Limb.	Mean of each pair of observed Z. Ds corrected for dislevelment.	Mean of Chronometer Times.	Resulting Longitude. Value from each pair of observations.	Resulting Longitude. Mean of each day's observations.	Approx. sidereal time of observations.
				° ′ ″	H. M. S.	H. M. S.	H. M. S.	H. M.
KASHGHAR (Yangi-Shahr). The station of observation was in the centre of the Embassy Buildings just outside of and to the north of the YangiShahr or New City.	6th Dec. 1873.	E.	L.	48 30 3 47 48 47 46 40 26 46 3 40 43 59 14 43 16 48 42 25 11 41 45 4	10 27 19·3 30 59·0 37 4·4 40 19·9 51 24·4 55 9·3 59 45·2 11 3 18·2	5 4 9 4 25 4 6 4 15 3 51 4 16 4 0 4 25	5 4 11	3 45
	7th „	E.	L.	49 1 13 48 7 59 47 2 24 46 23 50 45 7 4 44 27 30 43 33 28 42 51 23	11 24 3·1 28 46·8 34 37·3 38 2·3 44 52·1 48 23·3 53 12·9 56 58·0	5 3 59 4 10 3 56 4 19 4 20 4 21 4 7 4 5	5 4 10	4 45
	27th „	W.	L.	53 13 22 54 2 16 57 16 20 58 0 11 59 4 2 59 42 29	9 47 18·0 52 17·1 10 11 34·9 15 52·1 22 2·4 25 44·6	5 4 14 4 11 4 23 4 17 4 32 4 24	5 4 20	4 40
	28th „	W.	L.	46 56 38 47 43 14 48 33 30 49 43 0 50 17 58 51 17 43 51 53 54 52 45 57 53 23 12 54 25 40	10 25 34·8 30 10·9 35 5·8 41 48·7 45 10·3 50 52·7 54 18·5 59 13·6 11 2 44·2 8 34·2	5 4 42 4 34 4 28 4 41 4 40 4 36 4 42 4 36 4 23 4 34	5 4 36	5 15
	29th Jan. 1874.	E.	U.	42 31 24 41 49 33 41 1 42 40 14 34 39 13 27	6 33 49·5 37 32·2 41 46·0 45 57·1 51 22·2	5 4 41 4 36 4 48 4 41 4 44	5 4 47	3 25

Observations of Lunar Zenith Distances and resulting determination of Long.—(contd.)

Place of Observation.	Astronomical date.	The Moon. E. or W. of Meridian.	The Moon. Upper or Lower Limb.	Mean of each pair of observed Z Ds corrected for dislevelment.	Mean of Chronometer Times.	Resulting Longitude. Value from each pair of observations.	Resulting Longitude. Mean of each day's observations.	Approx. sidereal time of observations.
				° ′ ″	H. M. S.	H. M. S.		
KASHGHAR (Yangi-Shahr)—concluded.	29th Jan. 1874.	E.	U.	38 36 19 37 53 53 37 12 17	54 39·8 58 25·6 7 2 7·9	4 51 4 59 4 54		
	31st Jan. 1874.	E.	U.	42 21 6 41 39 0 40 2 49 38 29 9 37 54 22 36 36 42	8 31 25·7 35 12·4 43 48·7 52 15·4 55 23·6 9 2 25·1	5 4 44 4 24 4 51 4 29 4 34 4 50	5 4 39	H. M. 5 36
	Arithmetical Mean of Longitude from six days' observations, which is the value finally adopted.						H. M. S. 5 4 27·2 or ° ′ ″ 76 6 47·5	
YARKAND Station of observation in the Embassy Quarters in the centre of the Yangi-Shahr or New City.	8th Nov. 1873.	E.	L.	54 59 57 53 48 30 53 7 19 52 21 38 51 34 9 48 19 50 47 38 27 46 26 52 45 30 28	11 10 35·0 16 54·7 20 33·2 24 35·1 28 44·9 45 50·8 49 28·3 55 44·5 12 0 41·2	5 8 30 8 30 8 35 8 43 9 13 8 58 9 6 9 8 9 0	H. M. S. 5 8 51	H. M. 2 4
Ditto	" "	W.	U.	57 55 21 58 32 13 59 15 55 60 10 58 60 47 38 61 29 37 62 16 38 63 29 22	20 22 51·3 26 7·9 30 1·8 34 58·4 38 15·6 42 2·2 46 16·0 52 50·8	5 9 40 10 0 10 7 9 50 9 55 9 52 10 4 9 59	5 9 56	11 5

(333)

Observations of Lunar Zenith Distances and resulting determination of Long.—(concld.)

Place of Observation.	Astronomical date.	The Moon.		Mean of each pair of observed Z. Ds corrected for dislevelment.	Mean of Chronometer Times.	Resulting Longitude.		Approx. sidereal time of observations.
		E. or W. of Meridian.	Upper or Lower Limb.			Value from each pair of observations.	Mean of each day's observations.	
				° ′ ″	H. M. S.	H. M. S.	H. M. S.	H. M.
YARKAND. Station of observation in the Embassy Quarters in the centre of the Yangi-Shahr or New City.	9th Nov. 1873.	E.	L.	38 17 7 37 25 58 36 35 26 35 39 54 31 57 45 31 6 19 30 6 53 29 11 7	13 36 28·9 40 58·1 45 25·9 50 19·5 14 10 4·3 14 41·2 20 2·9 25 5·8	5 8 52 9 11 8 55 9 7 9 8 9 2 8 50 9 1	5 9 1	5 15
	Arithmetical mean of longitude from three days' observations*						5 9 16 or ° ′ ″ 77 19 0	
	Final longitude adopted for Yarkand, *vide* body of Report						77 15 55	
TASHKURGHAN. Station of observation about 300 yards to the east of the Fort.	31st March 1874.	E.	U.	61 44 7 60 37 23 59 59 7 59 16 52 58 4 33 57 17 40	7 27 42·3 33 51·1 37 24·3 41 20·9 48 7·2 52 32·7	5 2 16 2 4 1 44 1 26 1 7 1 1	H. M. S. 5 1 36 or ° ′ ″ 75 24 0	8 15
	Which gives the Astronomical longitude from one night's observations.							
	Final longitude adopted for Tashkurghan, *vide* body of Report						75 19 1	
KILA PANJAH. Station of observation about 300 yards to south of principal Fort of Kila Panjah.	24th April 1874.	W.	L.	44 0 53 45 13 15 46 15 41 47 3 46 50 52 43 51 40 43 52 24 10 53 3 42 55 9 16	10 23 21·7 31 0·5 34 53·5 38 59·7 58 28·8 11 2 32·8 6 13·8 9 34·9 20 14·1	4 50 55 51 17 51 7 51 2 50 43 50 57 51 8 51 9 50 56	H. M. S. 4 51 2 or ° ′ ″ 72 45 30	13 0
	Which gives the Astronomical longitude from one night's observations.†							
	Final longitude adopted for Kila Panjah, *vide* Geographical Chapter.						72 45 29	

* Observations were also taken at Yarkand on three other nights, when the moon was so unfavorably situated that these have not been employed.

† Observations were made on another night at Kila Panjah, but it appeared from the resulting time computations that the chronometer employed had been going irregularly.

(334)

SPECIMEN COPY OF COMPUTATION OF ONE DAY'S

Computation of Longitude fr

At Kashghar (Yangi-Shahr) Station, on

Moon { West of Meridian. Lower Limb observed. } | Lat. N. $= \phi =$ 39° 24′ 32″ | Assumed

Ref. No.	No. of observation (Mean of F. L. and F. R.)		1			2			3	
(1)	Chronometer Time of observation		10	47	55·2	10	52	31·3	10	57	26·2
(2)	„ Correction —			22	20·4		22	20·4		22	20·4
(3)	Local Mean Time (Ast. D.) = 28 days +		10	25	34·8	10	30	10·9	10	35	5·8
(4)	Approx. Gr. Mean Time = (3) + L_1 = 28 days +		5	20	34·8	5	25	10·9	5	30	5·8
(5)	☾'s observed Zenith Distance = ζ_0		46	56	38	47	43	14	48	33	30
(6)	Refraction (for B and T) = r = +				57			59		1	0
(7)	☾'s Semi-diameter at (4) from N. A. = S —			16	2		16	2		16	2
(8)	From Table I ΔS —				11			11			11
(9)	(5) + (6) + (7) + (8) = ζ_2		46	41	22	47	28	0	48	18	17
(10)	☾'s Horizontal Parallax at (4) from N. A. = π'' +			58	45		58	44		58	44
(11)	From Table II $\Delta \pi''$ +				5			5			5
(12)	Log. $\pi_1' = $ log. $(\pi + \Delta \pi)''$			3·54777			3·54765			3·54765	
(13)	Log. sin ζ_2			1·86192			1·86740			1·87314	
(14)	(12) + (13) = log. $(\pi_1 \sin \zeta_2)''$			3·40969			3·41505			3·42079	
(15)	$\pi_1 \sin \zeta_2$			42	49		43	20		43	55
(16)	(9) − (15) = $\zeta_2 − \pi_1 \sin \zeta_2 = \zeta_1$		45	58	33	46	44	40	47	34	22
(17)	☾'s Declination at (4) from N.A. = δ +		11	57	8	11	58	15	11	59	27
(18)	$\Delta \delta$ from Table III +				15			15			15
(19)	(17) + (18) = $\delta + \Delta \delta = \delta_1$ +		11	57	23	11	58	30	11	59	42
(20)	$\phi − (19) = (\phi − \delta_1)$		27	27	9	27	26	2	27	24	50
(21)	(16) + (20) = $\zeta_1 + (\phi − \delta_1) = 2\sigma_1$		73	25	42	74	10	42	74	59	12
(22)	(16) − (20) = $\zeta_1 − (\phi − \delta_1) = 2\sigma_2$		18	31	24	19	18	38	20	9	32
(23)	σ_1		36	42	51	37	5	21	37	29	36
(24)	σ_2		9	15	42	9	39	19	10	4	46
(25)	Log. sin σ_1			1·7765729			1·7803585			1·7843813	
(26)	Log. sin σ_2			1·2066735			1·2245847			1·2430716	
(27)	Log. sec ϕ			0·1120256			0·1120256			0·1120256	
(28)	Log. sec δ_1			0·0095255			0·0095554			0·0095876	
(29)	(25) + (26) + (27) + (28) = log. sin $2\frac{1}{2} t$			1·1047975			1·1265242			1·1490661	
(30)	Log. sin $\frac{1}{2} t$			1·5523988			1·5632621			1·5745331	
(31)	t (in arc) +		41	48	18	42	54	56	44	6	8
(32)	S. T. Gr. Mean Noon on 28 days (see (4))		18	28	5·8	18	28	5·8	18	28	5·8
(33)	Local Mean Time (same as (3))		10	25	34·8	10	30	10·9	10	35	5·8
(34)	Acceleration for (4)				52·7			53·4			54·2
(35)	(32) + (33) + (34) = local S. T. of observation = θ		4	54	33·3	4	59	10·1	5	4	5·8
(36)	t (in time) deduced from (31) +		2	47	13·2	2	51	39·7	2	56	24·5
(37)	☾'s Right Ascension or AR = $\theta − t$		2	7	20·1	2	7	30·4	2	7	41·3
(38)	Greenwich Mean Time for (37) from N. A.		5	21	1·1	5	25	47·8	5	30	51·2
(39)	(38) − (33) = Approx. Long. = L_2 —		5	4	33·7	5	4	23·1	5	4	14·6
(40)	(39) − $L_1 = L_2 − L_1$ +				26·3			36·9			45·4
(41)	At (38) change in ☾'s A R for increment of $1^m = \lambda''$ +			2·155			2·155			2·156	
(42)	Do. Do. Decn. Do. = β'' +			14·621			14·615			14·609	
(43)	Log. cos ϕ (see (27))			1·8880			1·8880			1·8880	
(44)	Log. sin t (see (31))			1·8239			1·8331			1·8426	
(45)	Log. cosec ζ_1 (see (16))			0·1432			0·1377			0·1319	

(335)

OBSERVATIONS FOR *LONGITUDE* AT KASHGHAR.

om Lunar Zenith Distances.

28th December 1873 (*Civil Date*, P.M.)

Long. E. = L_1 = −	76 15	Barometer	= B =	25·6 Inches.
=	5h. 5m. in time	Thermometer	= T =	18° (Fahrenheit.)

4	5	6	7	8	9	10
11 4 9·1	11 7 30·7	11 12 13·1	11 16 38·9	11 21 34·0	11 25 4·6	11 30 54·6
22 20·4	22 20·4	22 20·4	22 20·4	22 20·4	22 20·4	22 20·4
10 41 48·7	10 45 10·3	10 50 52·7	10 54 18·5	10 59 13·6	11 2 44·2	11 8 34·2
5 36 48·7	5 40 10·3	5 45 52·7	5 49 18·5	5 54 13·6	5 57 44·2	6 3 34·2
49 43 0	50 17 58	51 17 43	51 53 54	52 45 57	53 23 12	54 25 40
1 3	1 4	1 5	1 8	1 10	1 12	1 14
16 2	16 2	16 2	16 2	16 2	16 2	16 2
11	11	10	10	10	10	10
49 27 50	50 2 49	51 2 36	51 38 50	52 30 55	53 8 12	54 10 42
58 44	58 44	58 44	58 44	58 44	58 44	58 44
5	5	5	5	5	5	5
3·54765	3·54765	3·54765	3·54765	3·54765	3·54765	3·54765
1·88081	1·88455	1·89077	1·89443	1·89956	1·90313	1·90894
3·42846	3·43220	3·43842	3·44208	3·44721	3·45078	3·45659
44 42	45 5	45 44	46 7	46 40	47 3	47 41
48 43 8	49 17 44	50 16 52	50 52 43	51 44 15	52 21 9	53 23 1
12 1 5	12 1 55	12 3 18	12 4 7	12 5 19	12 6 10	12 7 36
15	15	15	15	15	15	15
12 1 20	12 2 10	12 3 33	12 4 22	12 5 34	12 6 25	12 7 51
27 23 12	27 22 22	27 20 59	27 20 10	27 18 58	27 18 7	27 16 41
76 6 20	76 40 6	77 37 51	78 12 53	79 3 13	79 39 16	80 39 42
21 19 56	21 55 22	22 55 53	23 32 33	24 25 17	25 3 2	26 6 20
28 3 10	38 20 3	38 48 56	39 6 27	39 31 37	39 49 38	40 19 51
10 39 58	10 57 41	11 27 57	11 46 17	12 12 39	12 31 31	13 3 10
1·7898535	1·7925646	1·7971396	1·7998761	1·8037582	1·8065019	1·8110386
1·2673721	1·2790005	1·2983804	1·3096455	1·3253301	1·3362001	1·3538172
0·1120256	0·1120256	0·1120256	0·1120256	0·1120256	0·1120256	0·1120256
0·0096314	0·0096539	0·0096912	0·0097132	0·0097457	0·0097687	0·0098076
1·1788826	1·1933346	1·2172368	1·2312604	1·2508596	1·2644963	1·2866890
1·5894413	1·5966673	1·6086184	1·6155362	1·6254298	1·6322482	1·6433445
45 43 41	46 32 24	47 55 6	48 44 55	49 56 11	50 46 55	52 11 38
18 28 5·8	18 28 5·8	18 28 5·8	18 28 5·8	18 28 5·8	18 28 5·8	18 28 5·8
10 41 48·7	10 45 10·3	10 50 52·7	10 54 18·5	10 59 13·6	11 2 44·2	11 8 34·2
55·3	55·9	56·8	57·4	58·2	58·8	59·7
5 10 49·8	5 14 12·0	5 19 55·8	5 23 21·7	5 28 17·6	5 31 48·8	5 37 39·7
3 2 54·7	3 6 9·6	3 11 40·4	3 14 59·7	3 19 44·7	3 23 7·7	3 28 46·5
2 7 55·1	2 8 2·4	2 8 14·9	2 8 22·0	2 8 32·9	2 8 41·1	2 8 53·2
5 37 15·4	5 40 38·6	5 46 26·6	5 49 44·2	5 54 47·7	5 58 35·9	6 4 10·2
5 4 33·3	5 4 31·7	5 4 26·1	5 4 34·3	5 4 25·9	5 4 8·3	5 4 24·0
26·7	28·3	33·9	25·7	34·1	51·7	36·0
2·156	2·156	2·156	2·156	2·157	2·157	2·157
14·603	14·598	14·593	14·588	14·583	14·578	14·572
1·8880	1·8880	1·8880	1·8880	1·8880	1·8880	1·8880
1·8549	1·8608	1·8705	1·8761	1·8838	1·8892	1·8977
0·1241	0·1203	0·1140	0·1102	0·1050	0·1014	0·0955

(336)

SPECIMEN COPY OF COMPUTATION OF ONE DAY'S
Computation of Longitude
At Kashghar (Yangi-Shahr) Station, on

Moon { West of Meridian. Lower Limb observed. }   Lat. N. $= \phi =$ 39° 24′ 32″ Assumed

Ref. No.	No. of observation (Mean of F. L. and F. R.)		1	2	3
(46)	$(43) + (44) + (45) =$ Log. sin q		1·8551	1·8588	1·8625
(47)	Log. tan q from (46)		0·0114	0·0190	0·0269
(48)	Log. cos δ_1 (see (28))		1·9905	1·9904	1·9904
(49)	Log. λ (see (41))		0·3334	0·3334	0·3336
(50)	Log. 15		1·1761	1·1761	1·1761
(51)	Log. sum $= (47) + (48) + (49) + (50)$		1·5114	1·5189	1·5270
(52)	Log. β		1·1650	1·1648	1·1646
(53)	$(52) - (51) =$ log. a (see Table IV.)	+	$\bar{1}$·6536	$\bar{1}$·6459	$\bar{1}$·6376
(54)	$1 + a$		1·450	1·442	1·434
(55)	$\dfrac{L_2 - L_1}{1 + a} = \Delta L_1$	+	18s.	26s.	32s.
(56)	$L = L_1 + \Delta L_1$	−	5h. 4m. 42s.	4m. 34s.	4m. 28s.

Explanation of Symbols adopted.

Ast. D.   stands for Astronomical Date.
Gr: do.   Greenwich.
S. T.   do.   Sidereal Time.
N A.   do.   Nautical Almanac.
Approx: do.   Approximate.

Rules for Computation.

Compute δ for each observation, i.e., for Nos. 1, 2, 3 ... 8.
Do. $\Delta \delta$ }
Do. S } for middle observation, and adopt this value as constant for all the other observations.
Do. $\Delta \pi$ }
Do. π and ΔS for No. 1 and No. 8, and interpolate for Nos. 2 to 6 with change in Gr. Mean Time for argument.

NOTE.—S and ΔS have the same sign and are both $\pm$ when $\frac{\text{upper}}{\text{lower}}$ limb of ☾ is observed; $\Delta \delta$ is + in N. Latitude; t is $\pm$ if ☾ is $\frac{W}{E}$ of Meridian; λ is always +; β is $\pm$ when ☾ is moving in Declination from $\frac{\text{S. to N.}}{\text{N. to S.}}$: sign of $a =$ sign of $\beta \times$ sign of t.

(337)

OBSERVATIONS FOR *LONGITUDE* AT KASHGHAR.—*(Continued.)*
from Lunar Zenith Distances.

28th December 1873 (*Civil Date*, P.M.)

Long. E. = L_1 = − 76° 15′ | Barometer = B = 25·6 Inches.
      5h. 5m. in time | Thermometer = T = 18° (Fahrenheit.)

4	5	6	7	8	9	10
1·8670	1·8691	1·8725	1·8743	1·8768	1·8786	1·8812
0·0366	0·0412	0·0488	0·0528	0·0586	0·0627	0·0689
1·9904	1·9903	1·9903	1·9903	1·9903	1·9902	1·9902
0·3336	0·3336	0·3336	0·3336	0·3339	0·3339	0·3339
1·1761	1·1761	1·1761	1·1761	1·1761	1·1761	1·1761
1·5367	1·5412	1·5488	1·5528	1·5589	1·5629	1·5691
1·1644	1·1643	1·1641	1·1640	1·1638	1·1637	1·1635
1·6277	1·6231	1·6153	1·6112	1·6049	1·6008	1·5944
1·424	1·420	1·412	1·409	1·403	1·399	1·393
19s.	20s.	24s.	18s.	24s.	37s.	26s.
4m. 41s.	4m. 40s.	4m. 36s.	4m. 42s.	4m. 36s.	4m. 23s.	4m. 34s.

Mean resulting longitude from observations on 28th December 1873—5h. 4m. 36s. or 76° 9′ 0″.

Table used to facilitate the computation.

TABLE I for ΔS			TABLE II for $\Delta \pi$			TABLE III for $\Delta \delta = D(1-f)$				
☾ = Apparent Zenith Distance	Horizontal semi-diameter.		Latitude	Equatorial Parallax.		Latitude	D		δ	f
	14′ 0″	17′ 0″		53′	61′		π			
							53′	61′		
°	″	″	°	″	″	°	″	″	″	
0	12·7	18·8	0	0·0	0·0					
10	12·5	18·6	10	0·3	0·4					
20	12·0	17·7	20	1·2	1·4	0	0·0	0·0	0	·00
30	11·0	16·3	30	2·7	3·1	5	1·8	2·1	5	·00
40	9·7	14·4	40	4·4	5·1	10	3·7	4·2	10	·02
50	8·2	12·1	50	6·2	7·2	15	5·5	6·3	15	·03
60	6·4	9·5	60	8·0	9·2	20	7·2	8·3	20	·06
70	4·4	6·5	70	9·4	10·8	25	8·9	10·3	25	·09
80	2·3	3·4	80	10·3	11·9	30	10·6	12·1	30	·13
90	0·1	0·2	90	10·6	12·2	35	12·1	13·9		
						40	13·6	15·6		
						45	14·9	17·2		
						50	16·2	18·6		

Example. $\phi = 30°·5′$
$\pi = 56′·7$, $\delta = 7°$
From Tables
$D = 11″·5$
$-fD = -1·2$
$\Delta \delta = 10$

GEOGRAPHICAL APPENDIX,

SECTION C.

HEIGHTS.

ABSTRACT OF OBSERV

Observations on road from LEH to YAR

Number in Alphabetical List.	Place of Observation.		Date.	Observer.	At Station. Reading of barometer or boiling point thermometer corrected for index error.
					Inches or Degrees.
1	Chimray village		13th Sept. 1873	Capt. Trotter	19·340(2)
2	Zingral Camp		14th „	„	16·776(4)
3	Chang La (or Sakti Pass)		15th „	„	15·635(6)
4	Tsultak village		„ „	„	16·680(2)
5	Tankse village		16th & 17th Sept. 1873	„	18·650(8)
6	Chakr Talao Camp		18th Sept. 1873	„	18·022(2)
7	Lukong village (on Pangong Lake)		19th & 20th Sept. 1873	„	17·851(7)
8	Chágrá Camp		21st Sept. 1873	„	17·217(8)
9	Lankar La (or Marsimik Pass)		22nd „	„	15·135(2)
10	Rimdi Camp		„ „	„	15·727(4)
11	Pamzal Camp		23rd „	„	17·388(4)
12	Gogra Camp		24th „	„	16·864(4)
13	East Route *viâ* Lingzi Thang.	Shummal Lung pa or Bhao	26th „	Capt. Biddulph	15·897
14		Changlung Burma Pass	27th „	„	14·596
15		Nischu (Camp near)	„ „	„	14·912
16		Lingzi Thung plain (south side of)	28th „	„	15·534
17		Lingzi Thung plain (camp on)	„ „	„	15·560
18		Súmná Camp east of Kiziljilga	30th „	„	15·729
19	West Route, *viâ* Head of Karakash River.	Kotajilga Camp	26th „	Capt. Trotter	16·149(1)
20		Pangtung Camp	28th „	„	15·725(1)
21		Pangtung or Chang Lung Pass	„ „	„	14·805(1)
22		Sumzum Lung pa Camp	29th „	„	15·714(4)
23		Dehra Compass Camp	30th „	„	15·309(1)
24		Compass Wala's Pass	1st Oct. 1873	„	A 15·18(1)
25		Karakash River near Compass La	„ „	„	15·625(1)
26		Shinglung, or Dunglung Camp	2nd & 3rd Oct. 1873	„	15·844(8)
		Ditto	„ „	„	181·60(2)
27	Kiziljilga Camp		1st, 2nd „	„	16·698(2)
28	Chungtash Camp		8th „	„	16·786

NOTE.—The figures in column (5) when given in inches are the corrected readings of a mercurial mountain barometer unless the letter A. is
The numbers in brackets following the figures in column (5) indicate the number of sets of observations, the corrected mean of which has been employed

ATIONS FOR HEIGHT.

KAND viâ *Changchenmo and Shahidúla.*

of Observation.		At Base Station Leh.*			Resulting height above mean sea level.	Remarks.
Temperature of mercury (Fahrenheit).	Temperature of air (Fahrenheit).	Corrected reading of barometer.	Temperature of mercury (Fahrenheit).	Temperature of air (Fahrenheit).		
Degrees.	Degrees.	Inches.	Degrees.	Degrees.	Feet.	
63	61	19·580	60	56	11,890	
57	51	19·580	60	56	15,780	
43	31·3	19·617	58·3	54	17,590	By Captain Biddulph, 17,395 feet.
51	38	19·617	58	54	15,950	
51	48	19·617	58	54	12,900	
61	58	19·617	58	54	13,890	
56	55	19·617	58	54	14,130	
52·3	48·8	19·617	58·3	54	15,090	
45	25	19·617	58·3	54	18,420	By Captain Biddulph, 18,530 feet.
41	42	19·617	58	54	17,500	
58	54	19·569	56	52	14,790	
47·3	45·5	19·569	56·3	54	15,570	
...	48·2	19·424	...	57·6	17,020	
...	32	19·478	...	56·5	19,280	
...	35·3	19·396	...	57·8	18,630	
...	33·3	19·522	...	56·3	17,680	
...	29·0	19·522	...	56·3	17,610	
...	22·0	19·443	...	54·2	17,150	
47	44	19·569	56	52	16,730	
24	22	19·569	56	52	17,250	
33	26	19·569	56	52	18,910	
32	28	19·569	56	52	17,330	
21	15	19·569	56·3	49·3	17,890	
...	23	19·537	49	40·6	18,160	
33	30	19·572	49	40·6	17,440	
25	25	19·572	49	40·6	17,030	} Mean height = 17,030 feet.
...	18	19·537	49	40·6	17,030	
...	26·5	19·508	...	43·1	16,590	
...	37·8	19·659	...	43·5	15,590	

attached, in which case an aneroid barometer has been used; when given in degrees the figures are the corrected means of hypsometrical readings, in determining the height.

* The height of the observatory at Leh is taken as 11,536 feet above sea level.

Observations on road from LEH to YAR

Number in Alphabetical List.		Place of Observation.	Date.	Observer.	AT STATION — Reading of barometer or boiling point thermometer corrected for index error.
					Inches or Degrees.
29	East Route along Karakash River.	Karakash River, Captain Biddulph's Camp	9th Oct. 1873	Capt. Biddulph	16·898
30		Ditto ditto	10th "	"	17·233
31		Ditto ditto	11th "	"	17·450
32		Ditto ditto	12th "	"	17·656
33		Ditto ditto (Sora)	13th "	"	17·796
34		Ditto ditto	14th "	"	18·036
35		Ditto ditto	15th "	"	18·376
36		Ditto ditto	16th "	"	18·491
37		Fotash Camp	18th "	Capt. Trotter	18·890(2)
38		Gulbashem	17th "	Capt. Biddulph	18·804
38		Ditto	17th & 18th Oct. 1873	Capt. Trotter	19·057(2)
39	West Route via Aktagh.	Shorjilga Camp	10th Oct. 1873	Capt. Trotter	16·322(3)
39		Ditto	" "	"	182·75(2)
40		Top of hill above Camp	" "	"	A 15·35(1)
41		Karatagh Pass	11th "	"	180·80(2)
42		Karatagh Lake	" "	"	182·15(2)
43		Aktagh 1st	13th "	"	16·571(2)
44		Chibra Hill	15th "	"	A 15·36(1)
45		Suget Pass	16th "	"	15·399(1)
46		Suget Hill	" "	"	A 15·36(1)
47		Suget Camp	17th "	"	18·575(1)
48		Shahidúla	21st "	"	19·477(1)
49		Sirki Angár	22nd "	"	18·290(1)
50		Sanju Pass (or Grim Pass)	23rd "	"	16·106(1)
51		Tam village	25th "	"	21·700(1)
52		Sanju village	28th "	"	24·010(2)
53		Oi Tughrak village	2nd Nov. 1873	"	24·425(1)
54		Boira village	4th "	"	24·856(1)
56		Posgiam village	7th "	"	25·931(1)
55		Karghalik Town	6th "	"	25·711(3)
57		YARKAND, Yangishahr	Dec. 1873 to March 1874.*	......	25·992 *

* The mean height of the barometer, derived from four months' observations at Yárkand, has here

KAND viâ *Changchenmo and Shahidúla*.—(Concluded.)

OF OBSERVATION.		AT BASE STATION LEH.			Resulting height above mean sea level.	REMARKS.
Temperature of mercury (Fahrenheit).	Temperature of air (Fahrenheit).	Corrected reading of barometer.	Temperature of mercury (Fahrenheit).	Temperature of air (Fahrenheit).		
Degrees.	Degrees.	Inches.	Degrees.	Degrees.	Feet.	
...	30·0	19·637	...	51·5	15,540	
...	42·9	19·572	...	53·5	14,980	
...	45	19·563	...	49·2	14,620	
...	36·5	19·471	...	50·7	14,160	
...	34·0	19·529	...	41·7	14,000	
...	47·4	19·513	...	50·5	13,670	
...	43·6	19·490	...	47·7	13,120	
...	43	19·453	...	50·7	12,910	
38	36	19·615	47	43·8	12,520	
...	41	19·512	...	51·0	12,530	} Mean height = 12,385 feet.
28	21·5	19·615	47	43·8	12,240	}
29	29	19·655	49	44	16,410	} Mean height = 16,490 feet.
...	31	19·619	49	44	16,570	
...	31	19·619	49	44	18,050	
...	30	19·620	48·5	44	17,710	
...	28	19·620	48·5	44	16,890	
22	...	19·655	48·5	44	15,960	
...	20	19·583	47	43·8	17,910	
32	13	19·615	46·5	43·8	17,610	
...	20	19·583	47	43·8	17,990	
38	38	19·615	47	43·8	12,970	
53	40	19·615	46·5	43·8	11,780	
28	30	19·615	47	43·8	13,340	
...	48	19·558	43·6	39·5	16,760	
54	52	19·584	44	39·5	8,790	
...	39	19·558	43·6	39·5	6,070	
53	49	19·666	40	36	5,760	
34	33	19·666	40	36	5,840	
36	36	19·666	40	36	4,210	
46·9	48	19·666	40·1	36·4	4,370	
32	32·6	19·439	24·6	32	3,923	

been employed; and the corresponding mean of the barometer during these same months at Leh.

Observations on road from LEH to YAR

Number in Alphabetical List.	Place of Observation.	Date.	Observer.	AT STATION Reading of barometer or boiling point thermometer corrected for index error.
				Inches or Degrees.
58	Sasser La (Pass)	8th October 1873	Nain Sing	15·419(1)
59	Sasser Pulu Camp	8th ,,	,,	17·009(1)
60	Khumdán	9th ,,	,,	16·983(1)
61	Daolatbeguldi Camp	12th ,,	,,	16·057(1)
62	Karakoram Brangsa	13th ,,	,,	15·855(1)
63	Ak Masjid	9th April 1874	,,	21·636(5)
64	Tupa or Akoram Pass	10th ,,	,,	20·392(1)
65	Mazar Khoja Camp	11th ,,	,,	21·325(2)
66	Yangi Diwan Pass	16th ,,	,,	16·672(1)
55	Karghalik Town	6th Novr. 1873	Captain Trotter	25·711(3)
55	Karghalik do.	27th May 1874	,,	203·65
				25·286
68	Yolaregh	28th ,,	,,	200·90
				23·901
69	Kugiar Village	29th ,,	,,	200·20
				23·559
64	Tupa or Akoram Pass	1st June 1874	,,	193·19(3)
70	Tiznaf River, Camp on	2nd ,,	,,	196·47
				21·799
71	Skatlich Camp	2nd ,,	,,	196·82
				21·959
65	Mazar Khoja Camp	3rd ,,	,,	195·32
				21·277
73	Dubá Camp	3rd ,,	,,	193·67
				20·547
74	Uch Ughaz or Chiragsaldi	8th ,,	,,	185·72
				17·321
66	Yangi Diwan Pass	8th ,,	,,	183·10(2)
75	Kulunaldi on Yarkand River	9th ,,	,,	188·62
				18·445
76	Kirghiz jangal Camp	10th ,,	,,	187·92
				18·168
77	Kashmir Jilga Camp	11th ,,	,,	186·92
				17·779
78	Khufelong Camp	12th ,,	,,	185·97
				17·415
79	Aktagh, 2nd Camp	13th ,,	,,	184·67(2)
80	Wahabjilga Camp	14th ,,	,,	183·12
				16·362
62	Karakoram Brangsa	15th ,,	,,	181·72
				15·867
81	Karakoram Pass	16th ,,	,,	179·32(4)
61	Daolatbeguldi Camp	17th ,,	,,	181·92(2)

KAND viâ *Karakoram* and *Kugiar*.

Of Observation.		At Base Station LEH.			Resulting height above mean sea level.	Remarks.
Temperature of mercury (Fahrenheit).	Temperature of air (Fahrenheit).	Corrected reading of barometer.	Temperature of mercury (Fahrenheit).	Temperature of air (Fahrenheit).		
Degrees.	Degrees.	Inches.	Degrees.	Degrees.	Feet.	
28	18	19·655	48·5	44	17,840 a	a Mean height = 17,820 feet.
21	15	19·655	48·5	44	15,240	
28	15	19·655	48·5	44	15,290	
15	12	19·655	48·5	44	16,700 b	b Mean height = 16,790 do.
5	15	19·655	48·5	44	17,030 c	c Do. = 17,180 do.
47	45·3	19·589	43·8	43·9	8,870	
37	35	19·589	43·8	43·9	10,450 d	d Mean height = 10,465 do.
30	30·5	19·589	43·8	43·9	9,250 e	e Do. = 9,355 do.
23	18	19·575	46	46·1	15,690 f	f Do. = 16,000 do.
46·9	48	19·666	40·1	36·4	4,370	} Do. = 4,440 do.
...	69	19·689	60	59·2	4,510	
...	60	19·689	60	59·2	6,150	
...	78	19·689	60	59·2	6,450	
...	66	19·587	63·1	60·0	10,480 d	
...	56	19·750	63·1	60·0	8,800	
...	70	19·750	63·1	60·0	8,550	
...	62	19·750	63·1	60·0	9,460 e	
...	60	19·750	63·1	60·0	10,440	
...	43	19·614	62·9	60·1	14,940	
...	49	19·451	62·9	60·1	16,310 f	
...	35	19·614	62·9	60·1	13,210	
...	35	19·614	62·9	60·1	13,620	
...	50	19·614	62·9	60·1	14,250	
...	49	19·614	62·9	60·1	14,810	
...	40	19·451	62·9	60·1	15,330	
...	42	19·614	62·9	60·1	16,490	
...	40	19·628	61·4	57·9	17,330 c	
...	40	19·469	61·4	57·9	18,550	
...	22	19·628	61·4	57·9	16,880 b	

(346)

Observation on road from LEH to YAR

Number in Alphabetical List.	Place of Observation.	Date.	Observer.	AT STATION Reading of barometer or boiling point thermometer corrected for index error.
				Inches or Degrees.
82	Dipsang Col	17th June 1874	Capt. Trotter	A15·11(1)
83	Bruchse	17th ,,	,,	183·72(2)
84	Murghi	18th ,,	,,	185·02(2)
58	Sasser Pass	21st ,,	,,	180·52(2)
85	Changlung spur, top of	22nd ,,	,,	184·97
				17·089
86	Changlung village	22nd ,,	,,	192·32(1)
87	Panamik village	23rd ,,	,,	192·57
				20·071
88	Shyok and Nubra Rivers (junction of)	23rd ,,	,,	192·72
				20·136
89	Digar La Pass	27th ,,	,,	180·42(3)

KAND viâ *Karakoram and Kugiar.*—Concluded.

of Observation.		At Base Station LEH.			Resulting height above mean sea level.	Remarks.
Temperature of mercury (Fahrenheit).	Temperature of air (Fahrenheit).	Corrected reading of barometer.	Temperature of mercury (Fahrenheit).	Temperature of air (Fahrenheit).		
Degrees.	Degrees.	Inches.	Degrees.	Degrees.	Feet.	
...	42	19·628	61·4	57·9	18,450	
...	42	19·469	61	57·9	15,920	
...	55	19·469	61·4	57·9	15,190	
...	36	19·469	61·4	57·9	17,800 *a*	
...	27	19·586	69·0	66·6	15,310	
...	52	19·413	69·0	66·6	10,760	
...	78	19·586	69·0	66·6	10,840	
...	60	19·586	69·0	66·6	10,760	
...	50	19·413	69·0	66·6	17,930	

(348)

Observations on road from YARKAND to

Number in Alphabetical List.	Place of Observation.	Date.	Observer.	AT STATION Reading of barometer or boiling point thermometer corrected for index error.
				Degrees.
90	Guma village	12th and 13th May 1874	Kishen Sing	203·51(5)
91	Muji village	14th May 1874	,,	204·0(1)
92	Zawa Kurghan	16th ,, ,,	,,	203·28(1)
93	KHOTAN City	18th ,, ,,	,,	203·24(5)
93	Ditto	19th ,, ,,	,,	203·03(3)
93	Ditto	31st ,, ,,	,,	203·16(3)
94	Karakash town	23rd ,, ,,	,,	203·78(1)
95	Borezen Yotkan village	29th ,, ,,	,,	203·40(2)
93	KHOTAN City	7th June ,,	,,	203·50(3)
96	Yurungkash town	8th ,, ,,	,,	203·30(3)
97	Dol Langar village	9th ,, ,,	,,	203·00(1)
98	Chira village	11th ,, ,,	,,	203·38(3)
98	Ditto	13th ,, ,,	,,	203·45(2)
99	Keria Town	18th ,, ,,	,,	202·57(3)
100	Sorghak Khiang Shahi Bazaar	22nd ,, ,,	,,	198·42(3)
99	Keria Town	29th ,, ,,	,,	202·92(3)
101	Polu village	8th July ,,	,,	196·33(3)
102	Ghubolik Camp, bank of Ulok Shahi Kul	12th and 13th July 1874	,,	182·1(2)
103	Arash Camp, bank of Keria River	15th July 1874	,,	183·92(3)
104	Keria River at Bas Kul	16th ,, ,,	,,	182·25(1)
105	Yeshil Kul (Lake)	18th and 19th July 1874	,,	183·58(2)
106	Tashliak Kul (bank of)	22nd July 1874	,,	182·67(4)
107	Chumik Lhakmo Camp	23rd and 24th July 1874	,,	182·63(2)
108	Sumzi Ling Camp	26th July 1874	,,	184·50(1)

LEH viâ Khotan, Polu and Noh.

OF OBSERVATION.		AT BASE STATION LEH.			Resulting height above mean sea level.	REMARKS.
Temperature of mercury (Fahrenheit).	Temperature of air (Fahrenheit).	Corrected reading of barometer.	Temperature of mercury (Fahrenheit).	Temperature of air (Fahrenheit).		
Degrees.	Degrees.	Inches.		Degrees.	Feet.	
...	75·3	19·509		51·4	4,340	
...	72·5	19·465		53·6	4,290	
...	70·0	19·465		53·6	4,430	
...	72·6	19·496		51·9	4,500 a	a Mean height = 4,490 feet.
...	76·6	19·496		51·9	4,590 a	
...	80·2	19·530		60·0	4,480 a	
...	82·0	19·481	The quantities given in the preceding column have been reduced to a temperature of 32°.	62·4	4,010	
...	84·9	19·502		62·5	4,240	
...	77·8	19·586		60·0	4,380 a	
...	67·3	19·451		60·1	4,370	
...	68·0	19·388		64·8	4,420	
...	75·8	19·451		60·1	4,260 }	
...	81·2	19·451		60·1	4,180 }	Mean height = 4,220 feet.
...	67·0	19·469		57·9	4,830 b	b Mean height = 4,575 feet.
...	77·2	19·413		66·6	7,060	
...	90·8	19·413		66·6	4,320 b	
...	70·0	19·477		65·4	8,430	
...	45·0	19·477		65·4	16,960	
...	59·7	19·533		68·5	16,020	
...	47·0	19·454		70·7	16,880	
...	54·3	19·494		71·1	16,160	
...	49·0	19·463		65·8	16,620	
...	41·3	19·463		65·8	16,600	
...	73·0	19·428		68·1	15,570	

(350)

Observations on road from

Number in Alphabetical List.	Place of Observation.	Date.	Observer.	AT STATION. Reading of barometer or boiling point thermometer corrected for index error.
				Inches or Degrees.
109	Kok Robát	28th Nov. 1873	Capt. Trotter	205·64[(2)1]
110	Kizil village	29th " "	"	205·64[(2)]
111	Yangi Hissar town	30th Nov., 1st & 2nd Dec. 1873.	"	204·71[(6)]
112	Yapchan village	4th Dec. 1873	"	204·64[(2)]
112	Ditto	17th March 1874	"	204·33[(2)]
113	KASHGHAR (Yangi Shahr)	1873. 11th Dec., 3-30 p.m.	"	25·968
		14th " 9 a.m.	"	25·026
		17th " 9 "	"	25·764
		18th " 3 p.m.	"	25·680
		21st " 3 "	"	25·971
		25th " 3 "	"	25·754
		21st Jan., noon	"	25·816
		8th Feb. 3 p.m.	"	25·576

NOTE.—The values given above as barometrical readings at Káshghar are actually the readings

	KASHGHAR (Yangi Shahr)	Dec. 1873 to March 1874.	Capt. Trotter	Corrected mean reading. A. 25·880

NOTE.—This mean reading of 25·880 inches is obtained from the reduction of

Observations on road from KASH

114	Artysh River, bed of	31st Dec. 1873	Capt. Trotter	A. 25·07[(1)]
115	Besak village (Osten Artysh)	31st " and 1st Jan. 1874	"	203·33[(1)]
116	Chungterek, Kirghiz village	1st and 2nd Jan.	"	199·13[(1)]
117	Balghun Bashi Camp	3rd Jan.	"	194·98[(1)]
117	Ditto	7th "	"	A. 21·13[(1)]
118	Chakmak Fort	3rd "	"	196·18[(1)]
119	Turgat Bela Camp	5th "	"	191·83[(1)]
119	Ditto Ditto	6th "	"	192·03[(2)]
120	Turgat Pass	6th "	"	188·83[(2)]

YARKAND to KASHGHAR.

OF OBSERVATION.		AT BASE STATION LEH OR YARKUND.			Resulting height above mean sea level.	REMARKS.
Temperature of mercury (Fahrenheit).	Temperature of air (Fahrenheit).	Corrected reading of barometer.	Temperature of mercury (Fahrenheit).	Temperature of air (Fahrenheit).		
Degrees.	Degrees.	Inches.	Degrees.	Degrees.	Feet.	
...	47	19.720	40	32.5	3,830	
...	38	19.720	40	32.5	3,910	Mean height = 4,030 feet.
...	34	19.660	39	36	4,320	See Station No. 110, page 21.
...	42	19.547	...	36.5	4,140	Mean height = 4,210 feet.
...	22	19.353	...	27.3	4,280	
		Base Station Yarkand 3,923 feet above sea level.				
...	33	26.100	43	39	4,056	
...	26	26.173	24	20	4,068	
...	23	25.195	23	20	4,074	
...	47.5	25.837	52	50	4,088	Mean value deduced from Yarkand 4,060 feet.
...	32	26.080	34	32	4,041	
...	33	25.950	36	33	4,123	
...	33	25.923	30	31	4,032	
...	39	25.648	41	40	3,997	

corresponding to the corrected mean of several boiling point observations.
Base Station Leh 11,538 feet above sea level.

...	33.8	19.446	24.6	32.2	4,027	From Leh ... 4,027
						From Yarkand ... 4,060
						Final value ... 4,043 feet.

several hundreds of observations.

GHAR to CHADYRKUL.

...	23	26.000	22	19	4,860	
...	28	25.976	22	20	5,290	Mean height = 5,160 feet.
...	30	25.951	21	19.5	7,000	
...	...	26.071	21	19	9,180	Mean height = 9,205 feet.
...	−8	26.199	20	19	9,230	
...	10	19.449	...	16.6	8,830	
...	−5	19.449	...	16.6	11,150	Mean height = 11,090 feet.
...	20	19.449	...	16.6	11,030	
...	12	19.449	...	16.6	12,760	

(352)

Observations on road from KASHGHAR

Number in Alphabetical List.	Place of Observation.	Date.	Observer.	AT STATION Reading of barometer or boiling point thermometer corrected for index error.
				Inches & Degrees.
121	Bibi Miriam village	14th Feb. 1874	Capt. Trotter.	A 25·84[2]
121	Ditto	22nd & 24th Feb. 1874	,,	A 25·52[4]
122	Artysh Altyn village	15th & 16th ,,	,,	A 25·79[8]
122	Ditto	Ditto	,,	A 25·88
123	Besh Kerim village	26th Feb. 1874	,,	A 25·57[1]
124	Kalti Ailak village	24th & 25th Feb. 1874	,,	A 25·77[2]
124	Ditto	1st March 1874	,,	204·72[2]
125	Bash Sogon Camp	19th & 20th Jan. 1874	,,	200·63[2]
125	Ditto	19th & 20th Feb. 1874	,,	A 23·84[2]
126	Ayak Sogon Camp	21st Feb. 1874	,,	A 24·97[1]
126	Ditto	Ditto	,,	202·94
127	Kyr Bulak Camp	28th Feb. 1874	,,	202·48
127	Ditto	Ditto	,,	202·48
128	Jai Tupa Camp	22nd Feb. 1874	,,	A 25·14[1]
129	Ui Bulák	23rd ,,	,,	200·12
129	Ditto	26th ,,	,,	199·54[2]
130	Jigda Camp	23rd ,,	,,	202·88[4]
130	Ditto	27th ,,	,,	202·94[2]
131	Belowti Pass	24th ,,	,,	191·28[2]
131	Ditto	24th ,,	,,	191·28

* The height of Kashghar is taken

(353)

to *AKSU* viâ *Ush Turfan*.

Of Observation.		At Base Station LEH or KASHGHAR.*			Resulting height above mean sea level.	Remarks.
Temperature of mercury (Fahrenheit).	Temperature of air (Fahrenheit).	Corrected reading of barometer.	Temperature of mercury (Fahrenheit).	Temperature of air (Fahrenheit).		
Degrees.	Degrees.	Inches.	Degrees.	Degrees.	Feet.	
	37	25·88		34	4,070	⎫ Mean height = 4,270 feet.
	31	25·96		32	4,470	
	38	25·91		29	4,150	⎫ ,, = 4,100 ,,
	33	19·386 (LEH)		20·2	4,050	
	54	25·67		35	4,130	
	45	25·79		32	4,050	⎫ ,, = 4,000 ,,
	20	25·913	41	39·4	3,950	
	8	19·460 (LEH)		21·5	6,490	⎫ ,, = 6,390 ,,
	29	26·00		31	6,390	
	22	25·93		31	5,010	⎫ ,, = 5,025
	19	26·037	40	40·2	5,040	
	20	19·436 (LEH)		27·2	5,380	⎫ ,, = 5,335 ,,
	20	25·92		34	5,290	
	24	26·128	38	38·2	4,910	
	16	26·05		40	6,680	⎫ ,, = 6,650 ,,
	16	25·811	44	42·8	6,620	
	26	19·454 (LEH)		22·2	5,190	⎫ ,, = 5,095 ,,
	25	25·986	42	40·7	5,000	
	10	19·446 (LEH)		22·9	11,430	⎫ ,, = 11,355 ,,
	10	25·88		38	11,280	

as 4,043 feet above sea level.

(354)

Observations on road from KASHGHAR

Number in Alphabetical List.	Place of Observation.	Date.	Observer.	At Station — Reading of barometer or boiling point thermometer corrected for index error.
				Inches & Degrees.
132	Faizabad town	1st Jan. 1874	Capt. Biddulph	A 26·04
133	Yangi Awat village	2nd ,,	,,	,, 26·10
134	Kashmir village	3rd ,,	,,	,, 26·37
135	Tojha Sulukh village	4th ,,	,,	,, 26·45
136	Shujeh village	6th ,,	,,	,, 26·60
137	Maralbashi town	8th ,,	,,	,, 26·56(3)
138	Charwagh village	15th ,,	,,	,, 26·57

Points in neighbourhood

139	Tangitar Kurghan	17th & 18th Feb.	Capt. Trotter	A 24·31(3)
139	Ditto	18th Feb.	,,	202·04(2)
140	Tughamati	18th & 19th Feb.	,,	A 24·05(3)
140	Ditto	19th Feb.	,,	201·54(2)

to AKSU viâ Maralbashi.

of Observation.		At Base Station KASHGHAR.			Resulting height above mean sea level.	Remarks.
Temperature of mercury (Fahrenheit).	Temperature of air (Fahrenheit).	Corrected readings of barometer.	Temperature of mercury (Fahrenheit).	Temperature of air (Fahrenheit).		
Degrees.	Degrees.	Inches.	Degrees.	Degrees.	Feet.	
...	28·5	A 26·00	...	28·5	3,990	As these results mostly depend upon single readings of an Aneroid Barometer, they can only be looked upon as approximate.
...	28·5	,,	...	28	3,930	
...	22	,,	...	22	3,670	
...	24	,,	...	24	3,590	
...	26·3	,,	...	26	3,440	
...	27	,,	...	27	3,480	
...	24	,,	...	24	3,470	

of KASHGHAR.

...	32	25·88	...	33	5,670	} Mean height = 5,730 feet.
...	27	26·29	42	39·7	5,790	
...	29	26·02	...	33	6,090	} Mean height = 5,975 feet.
...	4	26·14	33·6	33	5,860	

Observations on road from YANGI-HISSAR

Number in Alphabetical List.	Place of Observation.	Date.	Observer.	AT STATION Reading of barometer or boiling-point thermometer corrected for index error.
				Inches & Degrees.
148	Ighizyar village	22nd March 1874	Capt. Trotter	201·38(2)
149	Aktala Camp	,, ,,	,,	198·19(2)
150	Sasak Taka Camp	23rd ,,	,,	A 20·92(2)
152	Kaskasu Pass	25th ,,	,,	188·60(1)
153	Chehil Gumbaz Camp	,, ,,	,,	193·17(2)
154	Turat Pass	26th ,,	,,	188·07(2)
155	Past Robat Camp	,, ,,	,,	195·02(2)
156	Tarbashi Camp	27th ,,	,,	191·24(2)
157	Chichiklik Plain (pass leading into)	28th ,,	,,	185·67(2)
158	Balghun Camp	,, ,,	,,	192·72(2)
159	Chushman village	29th ,,	,,	193·57(2)
160	TASHKURGHAN, fort and town	31st ,,	,,	193·27(2)
		1st & 2nd April 1874	,,	193·62(4)
161	Kanshubar Camp	2nd ,,	,,	188·64(4)
162	Neza Tash Diwan (Pass)	3rd ,,	,,	185·18(2)
163	Kogachak Camp	,, ,,	,,	189·00(4)
164	Unkul Camp	4th & 5th ,,	,,	188·62(4)
165	Oikul, Káz-kul or lake of Little Pamir, north side	6th ,,	,,	188·17(2)
166	Langar Camp	6th & 7th ,,	,,	189·39(4)
167	Daráz Diwan Camp	7th & 8th ,,	,,	192·62(5)
168	Sarhadd village	8th ,,	,,	192·67(2)
168	Sarhadd village	9th ,,	,,	192·07(2)
169	Baroghil Pass		Capt. Biddulph	......
170	Patuch village	9th & 10th ,,	Capt. Trotter	192·59(4)
171	Yur village	10th & 11th ,,	,,	193·19(4)
172	Babatangi (Patur) village	11th & 12th ,,	,,	194·00(5)
173	Zung village	12th & 13th ,,	,,	195·65(4)
174	Kila Panjah (Wakhan)	13th, 14th, &25th,,	,,	195·67(6)
174A	Langarkish village	27th ,,	,,	195·17(2)
175	Yumkhana or Jangalik Camp	,, ,,	,,	191·47(2)
	Ditto ditto	28th ,,	,,	A 19·65(2)
176	Yol Mazar Camp	28th & 29th ,,	,,	189·98(4)
177	Bilnor Bas Camp	29th ,,	,,	188·65(2)

(357)

to PANJAH (WAKHAN).

OF OBSERVATION.		AT BASE STATION YARKAND.			Resulting heights above mean sea level.	REMARKS.
Temperature of mercury (Fahrenheit).	Temperature of air (Fahrenheit).	Corrected readings of barometer.	Temperature of mercury (Fahrenheit).	Temperature of air (Fahrenheit).		
Degrees.	Degrees.	Inches.	Degrees.	Degrees.	Feet.	
...	24	25·736	48	48·5	5,580 a	a Mean height = 5,600 feet.
...	30	25·736	48	48·5	7,350 b	b Ditto = 7,345 ,,
...	36	25·753	46	43·8	9,430 c	c Ditto = 9,455 ,,
...	26	19·386	...	33·7	12,850 d	d Ditto = 12,930 ,,
...	14	19·386	...	33·7	10,310	
...	16	19·386	...	33·7	13,130	
...	25	19·386	...	33·7	9,280 h	h Ditto = 9,370 ,,
		At Base Station LEH.				
...	17	19·395	37·5	33·7	11,370 e	e Ditto = 11,515 ,,
...	20	19·395	37·5	33·7	14,480	
...	25	19·395	37·5	33·7	10,540	
...	10	19·395	37·5	33·7	10,100	
...	31	19·380	37·5	33·7	10,230 f	
...	32	19·504	39·3	38·4	10,160 f	f Ditto = 10,230 ,,
...	34	19·504	39·3	38·4	12,980	
...	25	19·486	39·3	38·4	14,930 g	g Ditto = 14,915 ,,
...	4	19·487		38·4	12,740	
...	19	19·504	39·3	38·4	12,970	
...	8	19·486	39·3	38·4	13,200	
...	18	19·504	39·3	38·4	12,530	
...	29	19·547	41·6	41·2	10,780	
...	31	19·562	43·8	43·9	10,800	} Ditto = 10,975 ,,
...	31	19·589	43·8	43·9	11,150	
...	...	......	Approximate.		12,000	
...	28	19·589	43·8	43·9	10,850	
...	30	19·589	43·8	43·9	10,510	
...	30	19·589	43·8	43·9	10,060	
...	37	19·589	43·8	43·9	9,110	
...	37	19·562	43·8	43·9	9,090	
...	43	19·589	47·5	46·9	9,350	
...	40	19·589	47·5	46·9	11,470	} Ditto = 11,440 ,,
...	24	19·589	47·5	46·9	11,410	
...	29	19·589	47·5	46·9	12,320	
...	54	19·589	47·5	46·9	13,120	

(358)

Observations on road from YANGI-HISSAR

Number in Alphabetical List.	Place of Observation.	Date.	Observer.	At Station — Reading of barometer or boiling point thermometer corrected for index error.
				Inches & Degrees.
178	Mazar Tupa Camp	30th April 1874	Capt. Trotter	187·48(6)
179	Victoria Lake (or Lake of Great Pamir)	1st & 2nd May 1874	,,	187·03(4)
180	Watershed on Great Pamir	2nd ,,	,,	186·52(1)
181	Shash Tupa Camp	2nd & 3rd ,,	,,	187·42(2)
182	Dahn-i-Isligh Camp	3rd ,,	,,	188·32(1)
183	Aktash Camp (on Aksu River)	5th & 6th ,,	,,	189·42(2)
184	Tagharma Plain	10th ,,	,,	A 20·42(1)
185	Neza Tash Diwan	6th ,,	,,	185·52(3)
160	TASHKURGHAN, fort and town	10th ,,	,,	193·42(2)
186	Balghun (Darschatt River)	,, ,,	,,	190·02(2)
187	Kok Mainak Pass	12th ,,	,,	184·17(2)
156	Tarbashi	13th ,,	,,	191·02(2)
155	Past Robat Camp	14th ,,	,,	194·87(2)
152	Kaskasu Pass	15th ,,	,,	188·70(2)
151	Kaskasu Camp	,, ,,	,,	192·22(2)
150	Sasak Taka Camp	16th ,,	,,	194·82(2)
149	Aktala Camp	17th ,,	,,	198·47(2)
148	Ighizyar village	18th ,,	,,	201·42(2)
110	Kizil village	19th ,,	,,	203·94(4)

(359)

to PANJAH (WAKHAN).—(Concluded.)

OF OBSERVATION.		AT BASE STATION LEH.			Resulting height above mean sea level.	REMARKS.
Temperature of mercury (Fahrenheit).	Temperature of air (Fahrenheit).	Corrected readings of barometer.	Temperature of mercury (Fahrenheit).	Temperature of air (Fahrenheit).		
Degrees.	Degrees.	Inches.	Degrees.	Degrees.	Feet.	
...	32	19·556	47·5	46·9	13,760	
...	23	19·524	49·7	49·5	13,950	
...	46	19·524	49·7	49·5	14,320	
...	33	19·524	49·7	49·5	13,760	
...	24	19·561	49·7	49·5	13,220	
...	29	19·524	49·7	49·5	12,600	
...	35	19·548	51·3	51·4	10,310	
...	42	19·524	49·7	49·5	14,900*g*	
...	51	19·508	52·8	51·9	10,270*f*	
...	30	19·548	51·3	51·4	12,240	
...	40	19·548	51·3	51·4	15,670	
...	35	19·548	51·3	51·4	11,060*e*	
...	36	19·548	51·3	51·4	9,460*h*	
...	55	19·495	52·8	51·9	13,010*d*	
...	30	19·537	52·8	51·9	10,660	
...	30	19·537	52·8	51·9	9,480*c*	
...	50	19·495	53·0	51·9	7,340*b*	
...	60	19·495	53·0	51·9	5,610*a*	
...	65	19·495	53·0	51·9	4,150	

GEOGRAPHICAL APPENDIX.

SECTION D.

ALPHABETICAL LIST OF LATITUDES, LONGITUDES, & HEIGHTS.

(362)

Alphabetical List of Latitudes

Reference number.	Name of Place.	Latitude.			Longitude.			Height.
		°	′	″	°	′	″	Feet.
64	Akkoram (or Tupa) Pass	......			......			10,465
63	Ak Masjid Camp	37	8	13	......			8,870
43	Aktagh, 1st Camp	35	59	3	......			15,960
79	Aktagh, 2nd Camp	36	0	11	78	3	20	15,330
149	Aktala Camp	38	29	18	......			7,345
183	Aktash Camp on Aksu River	37	35	13	74	53	44(c)	12,600
108a	Angche Chortan	33	41	54	......			
103	Arash Camp, bank of Keria river	35	29	54	......			16,020
115	Artysh Osten (Besak village)	39	36	50	......			5,160
114	Artysh River (bed of)	......			......			4,860
122	Artysh (Altyn)	......			......			4,100
126	Ayak Sogon Camp	40	0	6	76	40	32(c)	5,025
172	Babatangi (Pater) village	......			......			10,060
186	Balghun (Darschatt River)	......			......			12,240
158	Balghun Camp	......			......			10,540
117	Balghun Bashi	......			......			9,205
62b	Balti Polu or Karakoram Polu	35	24	26	......			
169	Baroghil Pass	......			......			12,000
125	Bash Sogon Camp	......			......			6,390
131	Belowti Pass	40	40	20	77	50	0	11,355
115	Besak village (Osten Artysh)	......			......			5,160
123	Besh Kerim village	......			......			4,130
13	Bhao or Shummal Lung Pa	34	29	6	......			17,020
121	Bibi Miriam Khan's village	......			......			4,270
177	Bilaor Bas Camp	......			......			13,120
54	Bohira village	37	37	19	......			5,340
95	Borezen Yotkan village	......			......			4,240
83	Bruchse Camp	35	4	51	......			15,920
8	Chagra Camp	34	4	59	......			15,090
118	Chakmak Fort	40	5	9	......			8,830
118a	Chakmak, three miles north of Fort	40	8	28	......			
6	Chakr Talao Camp	......			......			13,890
3	Changla or Sakti Pass	34	4	49	......			17,590
14	Changlung Burma Pass	......			......			19,280
15	Do. Nischu Camp	34	35	3	......			18,630
15a	Do. or Pangtung Pass	......			......			18,910
85	Do. spur (top of)	......			......			15,310
86 & 59b	Do. village	35	55	43	......			10,760
138	Charwagh village	......			......			3,470
43a	Chibra Camp	36	7	12	......			
44	Do. Hill	......			......			17,910
153	Chehil Gumbaz Camp	......			......			10,310
157	Chichiklik plain (pass leading into)	......			......			14,480
65a	Chiklik Camp	37	2	54	......			
1	Chinray village	......			......			11,890
98	Chira village	37	0	26	......			4,220
107	Chumik Lhakmo Camp	34	22	28	......			16,600
28	Chung Tash	35	36	56	......			15,590
116	Chungtirik (Kirghiz village)	39	47	0	......			7,000
159	Chushman village	......			......			10,100
24	Compass Wala's Pass	......			......			18,160

(c) denotes that the longitude has bee[n]

(363)

Longitudes, and Heights.

Reference number.	Name of Place.	Latitude.	Longitude.	Height.
		° ′ ″	° ′ ″	Feet.
182	Dahn-i-Isligh Camp	......	......	13,220
30a	Daktod Karpo Sumdo	35 45 48		
167	Daraz Diwan Camp	37 0 9	73 46 7(c)	10,780
61	Daulat Beguldi Camp	35 22 16	......	10,790
23	Dehra Compass Camp	......	......	17,890
89	Digar La Pass	......	......	17,930
82	Dipsang Col	......	......	18,450
97	Dol Langar village	......	......	4,420
73	Duba Camp	36 46 34	......	10,440
26	Danglung (or Shinglung)	35 9 51	......	17,030
32	Dungnagu Camp	35 51 34		
132	Faizabad town	39 29 35	76 46 10(c)	3,990
37	Fotash Camp	......	......	12,520
41a	Do. Pass	35 56 31		
63a	Fusar village	37 20 37		
165	Gazkul (see Oikul)	......	......	13,200
102	Ghubolik Camp	35 40 55	......	16,960
60a	Giapchan Kizil	35 17 54		
48b	Giazgia Camp	36 44 59		
12	Gogra Camp	34 21 4	......	15,570
38	Gulbashem Camp	36 17 28	......	12,385
90	Guma village	37 37 31	......	4,340
148	Ighiz Yar village	......	......	5,600
	Ishkashm	......	......	9,500 (Approximate.)
128	Jai Tupa Camp	......	......	4,910
130	Jigda Camp	......	......	5,095
35	Jung Chidmo Camp	36 10 32		
124	Kalti Ailak village	......	......	4,000
161	Kanshubar Camp	......	......	12,980
25	Karakash River near Compass La	......	......	17,440
94	Do. town	37 16 47	......	4,010
29	Do. river, Captain Biddulph's Camp	......	......	15,540
30	Do. do.	......	......	14,980
31	Do. do.	......	......	14,620
32	Do. do.	......	......	14,160
33	Do. Sora do.	......	......	14,000
34	Do. do.	......	......	13,670
35	Do. do.	......	......	13,120
36	Do. do.	......	......	12,910
62	Karakoram Brangsa	35 37 42	......	17,180
48a	Do. Camp	36 37 30		
81	Do. Pass	......	......	18,550
62a	Do. Nain Sing's Camp near Pass	35 33 4		
42	Karatagh Lake	......	......	16,890
41	Do. Pass	35 42 54		17,710
55	Karghalik town	37 53 15	77 27 0	4,440
113	KASHGHAR—(Yangi-shahr)	39 24 26	76 6 47	4,043

luced chronometrically from Kàshghar.

Alphabetical List

Reference number.	Name of Place.	Latitude. ° ′ ″	Longitude. ° ′ ″	Height. Feet.
134	Kashmir village	......	......	3,670
77	Kashmir Jilga Camp	36 14 54	......	14,250
151	Kaskasu Camp	38 12 0	......	10,960
152	Kaskasu Pass	......	......	12,930
104	Keria River at Bas Khiol	......	......	16,880
99	Keria Town	36 51 26	......	4,575
140b	Khanarik or Do Shamba Bazar	39 15 42	......	
51a	Khewaz Langar	37 2 47	......	
93	KHOTAN (City centre of)	37 7 36	79 59 0	4,490
78	Khufelong Camp	36 8 34	......	14,810
60	Khumdan Camp	35 8 1	......	15,290
52a	Khushtagh village	37 21 5	......	
174	Kila Panjah (Wakhan)	37 0 18	72 45 29(c)	9,090
76	Kirghiz jangal Camp	36 25 44	......	13,620
76a	Kirghiz Camp near Kirghiz jangal	36 22 9	......	
110a	Kizil Boia or Shamba Bazar	39 22 49	......	
27	Kizil Jilga Camp	35 20 42	......	16,590
110	Kizil village	38 39 23	......	4,030
163	Kogachak Camp	37 37 11	74 55 19(c)	12,740
187	Kok Mainak Pass	......	......	15,670
109	Kok Robat	38 26 5	......	3,830
19	Kotajilga Camp	34 29 25	......	16,730
69	Kugiar village	37 24 14	......	6,450
75	Kulu Naldi (on Yarkand River)	......	......	13,210
127	Kyr Bulak Camp	40 6 7	76 52 26(c)	5,335
166	Langar Camp	......	......	12,530
174a	Langarkish village	......	......	9,350
9	Lankar La (or Marsimik La)	......	......	18,420
	Leh Observatory	......	......	11,538
17	Lingzi Thung Plain (Camp on)	34 47 54	......	17,610
16	Lingzi Thung Plain (south side of)	......	......	17,680
7	Lukong village (on Pangong Lake)	34 0 6	......	14,130
137	Maralbashi Town	39 46 24	(78 11 20 Approximate.)	3,480
9	Marsimik La (or Lankar La)	......	......	18,420
65	Mazar Khoja Camp	36 50 32	......	9,355
178	Mazar Tupa Camp	37 28 53	73 34 41(c)	13,760
91	Muji village	......	......	4,290
84	Murghi Camp	......	......	15,190
185	Neza Tash Diwan	......	......	14,915
15	Nischu (Camp near)	......	......	18,630
165	Oi Kul or Lake of Little Pamir (Camp on north side)	37 14 27	74 19 40(c)	13,200
53	Oi Tugrak village	37 30 20	......	5,760
115	Osten Artysh (Besak village)	39 36 50	......	5,290
	Pamir Great, Lake of, see Victoria Lake	......	......	13,950
165	Pamir Little, Lake of, see Oi Kul	37 14 27	......	13,200
11	Pamzal Camp	......	......	14,790
59a & 87	Panamik village	37 47 10	......	10,840
20	Pangtung Camp	......	......	17,250
21	Pangtung or Chung Lung Pass	......	......	18,910
174	Panjah Kila (Wakhan)	37 0 18	72 45 29(c)	9,090
157	Pass to Chichiklik Plain	......	......	14,480
155	Past Robat Camp	......	......	9,370

atitudes, &c.—(Continued.)

Reference number.	Name of Place.	Latitude.			Longitude.			Height.
		°	′	″	°	′	″	Feet.
170	Patuch village							10,850
101	Patúr village	36	11	56				8,430
56	Posgiam village	38	11	54				4,210
10	Rimdi Camp							17,500
50	Sanju (or Grim Pass)							16,760
52	Sanju village	37	11	17				6,070
168	Sarhadd village							10,975
78a	Sasak Bulak	36	27	30				
150	Sasak Taka Camp							9,455
58	Sasser La Pass							17,820
59	Sasser Polu Camp	35	2	43				15,240
48	Shahidulla (old fort and town)	36	24	57				11,780
181	Shash Tupa Camp	37	31	39	74	15	23(c)	13,760
26	Shinglung (or Dunglung Camp)							17,030
39	Shorjilga Camp	35	41	2				16,490
40	Shorjilga (top of hill)							18,050
136	Shujeh village							3,440
13	Shummal Lungpa or Bhao							17,020
88	Shyok River at junction with Nubra River							10,760
49	Sirki Angar							13,340
71	Skatlich Camp							8,550
33	Sora Camp	36	1	9				14,000
100	Sorghak Khiang Shahi	36	39	51				7,060
47	Suget Camp	36	18	45				12,970
46	Suget hill							17,990
45	Suget Pass	36	9	53				17,610
108	Sumji Ling Camp	34	1	18				15,570
18	Sumna Camp east of Kizil Jilga	35	16	39				17,150
22	Samzumlung Pa	34	41	10				17,330
	Tagharma or Muztagh Peak	38	35	15	75	22	47	25,350
184	Tagharma Plain							10,310
51	Tam village	36	52	4				8,790
139	Tangitar Kurghan	39	56	46				5,730
5	Tanks							12,900
156	Tarbashi Camp	38	6	8				11,515
160	TASHKURGHAN Fort and Town	37	46	49	75	19	1(c)	10,230
106	Tashliak Kul (bank of Lake)	34	38	54				16,620
73a	Teshektash	36	44	18				
70	Tiznaf River (Camp on)							8,800
135	Tojha Salukh village							3,590
4	Tsultak village							15,950
140	Tughamati	40	1	52				5,975
173	Tung village							9,110
64	Tupa or Akkorum Diwan							10,465
76b	Tupa Diwan Camp	36	24	24				
154	Turat Pass							13,130
119	Turgat Bela Camp	40	23	53				11,090
120	Turgat Pass							12,760
59d	Tutialak Camp	35	0	17				
74	Uch Ughaz or Chiraghsaldi							14,940
129	Ui Bulak	40	26	14	77	35	47 (c)	6,650
164	Unkul Camp							12,970

Alphabetical List

Reference number.	Name of Place.	Latitude.			Longitude.			Height.
		°	′	″	°	′	″	*Feet.*
179	Victoria Lake, or Lake of Great Pamir (West end)	37	27	0	73	40	38	13,950
	Wahabjilga Camp	......			......			16,490
80	Wamar Fort (Junction of Murghabi and Panja River)	......			......			(Appe.) 7,500
180	Water-shed on Great Pamir	......			......			14,320
133	Yangi Awat village	......			......			3,930
66	Yangi Diwan Pass	......			......			16,000
111	Yangi Hissar Town	38	56	8	76	12	55	4,320
112	Yapchan village	39	13	31	......			4,210

Latitudes, &c.—(Concluded.)

Reference number.	Name of Place.	Latitude.			Longitude.			Height.
		°	′	″	°	′	″	*Feet.*
57	YARKAND (Yangi-shahr)	38	25	1	77	15	55	3,923
105	Yeshil Kul (Lake)							16,160
68	Yolarik	37	27	6				6,150
176	Yol Mazar Camp	37	18	7	73	5	49(c)	12,320
175	Yunkhana or Jangalik Camp							11,440
171	Yur village							10,510
96	Yurungkash town							4,370
2	Zingral Camp							15,780
92	Zawa Kurghan							4,430

GEOGRAPHICAL APPENDIX.

SECTION E.

MAGNETIC OBSERVATIONS.

MAGNETIC

Abstract of results of observations taken by Captain H. Trotter, R.E.,

Station of observation.	Date of observation.	APPROXIMATE.		
		North Latitude.	Longitude east of Greenwich.	Height above sea level.
	1873.	° ′	° ′	Feet.
On road from LEH to KASHGHAR. LEH	1st and 3rd September	34 10	77 37	11,540
Chagra Camp	21st September	34 5	78 30	15,090
Chung Tash Camp	8th October	35 37	78 40	15,590
Sanju village	1st November	37 11	78 31	6,070
Oi Toghrak village	3rd „	37 30	78 3	5,760
Karghalik town	6th „	37 53	77 41	4,370
YARKUND (Yangi-shahr)	27th „	38 25	77 16	3,923
Yangi Hissar town	1st December	38 56	76 13	4,320
Yapchan village	3rd „	39 14	76 7	4,210
KASHGHAR (Yangi-shahr)	4th and 19th December and 13th February 1874.	39 24	76 7	4,043
Ui Bulak. (On road to Ush Turfan and Aksu)	25th February	40 26	77 36	6,650
On road from KASHGHAR to WAKHAN. Ighizyar	18th May	38 40	76 12	5,600
TASHKURGHAN	31st March	37 47	75 29	10,230
Aktash	5th May	37 35	74 54	12,600
Yol Mazar Camp	28th April	37 18	73 6	12,320
Panjah (Wakhan)	18th „	37 0	72 45	9,090

The observations for Magnetic Dip were taken with Dip Circle No. 2 by Barrow (belonging to the Great "Admiralty Manual of Scientific Enquiry. The rules laid down therein were rigorously adhered to.

The observations for declination were taken with the 6-inch Transit Theodolite (by Troughton and Simms). parisons at Dehra and at Leh, both before the start and after the return of the Mission, proved that no sensible

(371)

OBSERVATIONS.

for Magnetic Inclination (Dip) and Declination (Variation) 1873-74.

Magnetic Dip north.	Magnetic Variation east.	Remarks.
° ′	° ′	
47 21·5 (Mean of two sets.)	3 43	From observations to Sun. (Two sets.)
47 22·7	3 56	From observations to Sun and to Polaris.
	3 51	From observations to Polaris.
	4 32	Ditto ditto.
	4 32	Ditto ditto.
	4 53	Ditto ditto.
53 8·0 (Mean of two sets.)	4 58	Ditto ditto.
	4 57	Ditto ditto.
	4 55	Ditto ditto.
54 31·7	5 1	Ditto ditto and to Sun. (Four sets.)
	5 40	From observations to Sun.
	4 20	From observations to β Ursæ Minoris. (Two sets.)
52 3·3	4 34	From observation to Sun ditto.
	4 24	Ditto to Polaris ditto.
	4 12	Ditto Ditto ditto.
	4 16	From observation to do. and to β Ursæ Minoris.

Remarks (right column, vertical): General Cunningham, R.E., took magnetic observations at Leh in October 1847 when the dip was found to be ... 46° 43′ 15″ and the declination ... 2° 46′ 87″ E. The Schlagintweits in July and September 1856 made dip ... 46° 51′ 88″, and the declination on July 31st ... 3° 24′ 1″ E, on September 30th ... 3° 21′ 1″ E.

Trigonometrical Survey Department). The method of observation was that recommended by General Sabine in the

The needle attached to the instrument was re-magnetized prior to the departure of the expedition from India, and com- displacement had taken place in the position of its magnetic pole.

GEOGRAPHICAL APPENDIX.

SECTION F.

METEOROLOGICAL OBSERVATIONS.

Meteorological Observations recorded by the Great Trigonometrical

Date.		Mercurial Barometer No. 720 corrected for index error.	Temperature of mercury.	Reading of aneroid barometer Solomon's uncorrected.	Temperature of Air.	
					Dry Bulb.	Wet Bulb.
		Inches.	Degrees.	Inches.	Degrees.	Degrees.
Nov. 12th, 1873,	9 A.M.	26·112	46	26·46	42	38·5
	Noon	·107	55	·46	52	47·5
	3 P.M.	·077	50	·43	48·5	44·5
	6 ,,	·007	4·65	·46	45	41
	9 ,,	·007	44·5	·47	42	39·5
,, 13th ,,	9 A.M.	·132	44	·51	42	38·5
	Noon	·127	55	·49	45	39
	3 P.M.	·077	49·5	·44	48	44
	6 ,,	·087	45	·46	45	41
	9 ,,	·087	42	·46	41	38
,, 14th ,,	9 A.M.	·147	44	·52	42	39
	Noon	·127	52	·48	48	45
	3 P.M.	·087	47·5	·45	46	42
	6 ,,	·092	46	·46	44	39·5
	9 ,,	·125	42	·50	40·8	36·5
,, 15th ,,	9 A.M.	·157	48·5	·54	41·0	37·0
	Noon	·167	58·0	·53	48	41
	3 P.M.	·142	51·5	·52	48·5	40
	6 ,,	·197	49·5	·56	43	36
	9 ,,	·237	47·5	·61	38	32
,, 16th ,,	9 A.M.	·282	47·5	·68	36	33
	Noon	·277	60·0	·66	45·3	38·8
	3 P.M.	·227	55·8	·62	50·5	43
	6 ,,	·207	48	·63	46	41·3
	9 ,,	·237	43·5	·66	42	37
,, 17th ,,	9 A.M.	·187	44·5	·61	38	34
	Noon	·157	46·5	·56	42	37·5
	3 P.M.	·107	48	·52	45·5	39
	6 ,,	·117	45	·51	40	35
	9 ,,	·037	41·5	·54	38	33
,, 18th ,,	9 A.M.	·187	43	·59	39	36
	Noon	·197	55·5	·56	47	40·3
	3 P.M.	·157	51·5	·55	48·5	41
	6 ,,	·137	47	·56	42·5	37
	9 ,,	·207	43	·58	39	34
,, 19th ,,	9 A.M.	·207	44	·63	35·5	34
	Noon	·192	57	·59	46·5	41
	3 P.M.	·162	53·5	·55	49·5	42
	6 ,,	·137	47·0	·59	45	39
	9 ,,	·187	45·0	·60	40·5	36
,, 20th ,,	Noon	·217	55·5	·61	47·5	42
	3 P.M.	·187	51·0	·57	46	39
	6 ,,	·197	45·0	·59	45	39
	9 ,,	·197	44·0	·60	41	37
,, 21st ,,	9 A.M.	·237	45·0	·65	38	32·5
	Noon	·227	47·5	·63	47	42·5
	3 P.M.	·197	52·0	·61	51	44
	6 ,,	·197	48·0	·62	42·5	38
	9 ,,	·217	43·0	·64	39	34
,, 22nd ,,	9 A.M.	·157	44·0	·58	41	36
	Noon	·127	56·5	·55	50	45

Survey Pandits at YARKAND during the winter of 1873-74.

Minimum in shade.	Maximum in shade.	Direction of wind.	Remarks.
During preceding 24 hours.			
Degrees.	Degrees.		
......	......	W.	At Yárkand the thermometers were placed in a court-yard—in the open—against a wall and at a height of five feet above the ground. The wall faced north, and the sun's rays never fell on or near it.
......	......	W.	
......	......	W.	The aneroid barometer was also suspended against the same wall.
......	......	N.	
......	......	N.	The mercurial barometer was placed in complete shade, in a porch which opened towards the north.
......	......	W.	
......	......	N.W.	On the 20th, 21st, and 22nd of every month continuous hourly observations were taken extending over a period of 48 hours, i.e., from noon on the 20th up to noon on the 22nd of each month. These observations having been reduced to diagrams, vide body of Report, it has not been thought necessary to reproduce them here.
......	......	W.	
......	......	E.	
......	......	S.W.	
......	......	W.	
......	......	S.	The thermometers were all graduated on Fahrenheit's scale.
......	......	N.	
......	......	S.	
......	......	E.	
......	......	E.	
......	......	N.E.	
......	......	S.	
......	......	E.	
......	......	N.	
......	......	S.	
......	......	S.	
......	......	N.	
......	......	E.	
......	......	W.	
......	......	N.	
......	......	N.	
......	......	W.	
......	......	E.	
......	......	E.	
......	......	S.	
......	......	E.	
......	......	W.	
......	......	N.	
......	......	E.	
......	......	S.	
......	......	E.	
......	......	S.	
......	......	E.	
......	......	S.	
......	......	W.	
......	......	S.	
......	......	S.	
......	......	N.	
......	......	S.	
......	......	N.	
......	......	N.	

(376)

Meteorological Observations recorded by the Great Trigonometrical Survey

Date.			Mercurial Barometer No. 720 corrected for index error.	Temperature of mercury.	Reading of aneroid barometer Solomon's uncorrected.	Temperature of Air.	
						Dry Bulb.	Wet Bulb.
			Inches.	Degrees.	Inches.	Degrees.	Degrees.
Nov. 22nd, 1873,		3 P.M.	26·087	53·0	26·50	52	46
		6 ,,	·087	52·5	·50	46	41
		9 ,,	·107	49·0	·53	42	38
,,	23rd ,,	9 A.M.	·127	47·0	·55	40	37
		Noon	·117	60·0	·51	53	46
		3 P.M.	·047	57·0	·46	57	49
		6 ,,	·037	50·0	·45	48	42
		9 ,,	·047	47·0	·49	44	40
,,	24th ,,	9 A.M.	·047	43·0	·50	42·3	38
		Noon	·037	58·0	·45	52	46
		3 P.M.	·002	63·0	·38	53·5	46
		6 ,,	25·962	51·0	·37	44·5	39
		9 ,,	·952	45·0	·38	40	36
,,	25th ,,	9 A.M.	·922	43·0	·35	34	31
		Noon	·932	55	·31	46·5	41
		3 P.M.	·882	52	·30	51	43
		6 ,,	·902	49	·30	45	40
		9 ,,	·942	45	·34	39	34·5
,,	26th ,,	9 A.M.	·902	45·5	·32	39	36
		Noon	·922	58	·31	45	41
		3 P.M.	·952	54	·32	49	44
		6 ,,	·952	50·5	·37	44	40·5
		9 ,,	·972	45	·40	37·5	34
,,	27th ,,	9 A.M.	26·122	45·5	·52	36	34
		Noon	·102	57	·50	49	43·3
		3 P.M.	·092	53	·49	52	44
,,	28th ,,	Noon	·422	43	·04	40	33
		3 P.M.	·427	48	·02	45	37
		6 ,,	·442	42	·06	36	32
		9 ,,	·452	37	·09	31·5	27·5
,,	29th ,,	9 A.M.	·402	28	·03	26	23
		Noon	·322	35	25·96	33	29
		3 P.M.	·272	37	·87	34	31
		6 ,,	·222	35·5	·85	28	24
		9 ,,	·212	35	·84	25	22
,,	30th ,,	9 A.M.	·102	27·5	·75	24	24
		Noon	·052	37·5	·65	36	33
		3 P.M.	·002	39·0	·63	36	32
		6 ,,	25·997	37	·62	30	27
		9 ,,	26·042	33	·66	26	25

(377)

Pandits at YARKAND during the winter of 1873-74.—(Continued.)

Minimum in shade.	Maximum in shade.	Direction of wind.	Remarks.
During preceding 24 hours.			
Degrees.	Degrees.		
......	......	E.	
......	......	W.	
......	......	S.	
......	......	N.	
......	......	N.	
......	......	E.	
......	......		
......	......	S.	
......	......	W.	
......	......	E.	
......	......	W.	
......	......	S.	
......	......	N.	
......	......	N.	
......	......	W.	
......	......	W.	
......	......	S.	
......	......	N.	
......	......	N.	
......	......	S.	
......	......	W.	For the month of November 1873.
......	......	E.	9 A.M. Noon. 3 P.M. 6 P.M. 9 P.M.
......	......	N.	
......	......	N.	Mean of Mercurial barometer No. 720 corrected to 32°... 26·143 26·149 26·115 26·109 26·126
......	......	W.	
33·5	42·5	N.E.	
......	......	N.E.	Mean of Dry Bulb Thermometer ... 37·4 45·9 48·0 42·2 38·1
......	......	N.	
......	......	N.	
16·5	44	E.	Mean of Wet Bulb Thermometer ... 34·2 40·6 41·6 37·4 34·1
......	......	S.	
......	......	E.	
......	......	W.	
......	......	S.	
14	34·8	S.W.	
......	......	W.	
......	......	E.	
......	......	N.	
......	......		

(378)

Meteorological Observations recorded by the Great Trigonometrical

Date.		Mercurial Barometer No. 720 corrected for index error.	Temperature of mercury.	Reading of aneroid barometer Solomon's uncorrected.	Temperature of Air.	
					Dry Bulb.	Wet Bulb.
		Inches.	*Degrees.*	*Inches.*	*Degrees.*	*Degrees.*
Dec. 1st, 1873,	9 A.M.	26·022	26	25·66	22	21
	Noon	·052	34·5	·68	34	31
	3 P.M.	·042	39·5	·63	37	33
	6 ,,	·042	37	·68	30	29
	9 ,,	·082	33	·71	25	24
,, 2nd ,,	9 A.M.	·152	27	·80	25	23
	Noon	·102	38	·72	36	32
	3 P.M.	·092	39	·69	36·5	34
	6 ,,	·052	36	·68	31	30
	9 ,,	·027	33	·66	25·3	25
,, 3rd ,,	9 A.M.	·042	26	·67	23	22·2
	Noon	·042	37	·67	34	30
	3 P.M.	·002	44	·64	38	35
	6 ,,	·022	39·8	·62	33	30
	9 ,,	·022	57	·65	29	26
,, 4th ,,	9 A.M.	·052	28	·68	24·5	22·3
	Noon	·027	37·5	·67	35	32
	3 P.M.	·042	42·8	·61	37·5	36
	6 ,,	·022	38	·62	30	27
	9 ,,	·032	34	·64	24	23
,, 5th ,,	9 A.M.	·022	26	·63	23	22
	Noon	....	....	·65	33	30
	3 P.M.	·027	42	·63	38	36
	6 ,,	·082	38	·69	29·5	28·3
	9 ,,	·102	33	·71	24·5	24
,, 6th ,,	9 A.M.	·202	26·5	·85	24	23
	Noon	....	....	·83	33	30
	3 P.M.	·162	40	·78	36·5	34
	6 ,,	·177	37	·80	29	28·5
	9 ,,	·167	32	·98	25	24
,, 7th ,,	9 A.M.	·192	26·3	·83	24	24
	Noon	·222	39	·86	35	32
	3 P.M.	·212	44	·83	38	34
	6 ,,	·242	40	·87	32	29
	9 ,,	·242	35·5	·88	27	24·2
,, 8th ,,	9 A.M.	·312	26·5	·95	24	23
	Noon	·307	38·5	·94	36	32
	3 P.M.	·302	44	·91	40·3	35
	6 ,,	·322	34·5	·90	34	31
	9 ,,	·282	27	·92	30	27
,, 9th ,,	9 A.M.	·182	27	·83	25	23
	Noon	·152	36	·78	34	30·8
	3 P.M.	·112	40	·70	38	34
	6 ,,	·062	37·5	·68	32·5	29
	9 ,,	·052	35	·67	29	27
,, 10th ,,	9 A.M.	·002	24	·62	21	20
	Noon	25·992	33	·61	29	26·5
	3 P.M.	·962	39·5	·57	37	32
	6 ,,	·977	36·0	·60	28	26·5
	9 ,,	26·012	32·5	·63	25·5	25·0
,, 11th ,,	9 A.M.	·122	26	·77	24	23
	Noon	·132	38	·79	32	29

Survey Pandits at YARKAND during the winter of 1873-74.—(Continued.)

Minimum in shade.	Maximum in shade.	Direction of wind.	Remarks.
During preceding 24 hours.			
Degrees.	Degrees.		
13·5	38·8	S.W.	
......	......	W.	
......	......	E.	
......	......	N.	
......	......	N.	
15·5	38·5	E.	
......	......	S.	
......	......	E.	
......	......	S.	
......	......	W.	
15·8	29·8	N.	
......	......	N.W.	
......	......	S.	
......	......	N.	
......	......	E.	
16	38	N.	
......	......	W.	
......	......	S.W.	
......	......	N.	
......	......	N.	
12	37·5	W.	
......	......	N.	
......	......	S.E.	
......	......	......	
......	......	N.E.	
13	41	N.	
......	......	N.W.	
......	......	N.	
......	......	N.W.	
......	......	S.	
12·5	35	W.	
......	......	E.	
......	......	N.	
......	......	S.W.	
......	......	W.	
11·5	37	E.S.	
......	......	N.E.	
......	......	E.	
......	......	N.	
......	......	N.	
12	38	S.E.	
......	......	W.N.	
......	......	N.E.	
......	......	W.	
......	......	E.	
10	42·5	S.	
......	......	E.	
......	......	W.	
......	......	N.	
......	......	W.	
12	34	S.W.	
......	......	S.E.	

(380)

Meteorological Observations recorded by the Great Trigonometrical Survey

Date.			Mercurial Barometer No. 720 corrected for index error.	Temperature of mercury.	Reading of aneroid barometer Solomon's uncorrected.	Temperature of Air.	
						Dry Bulb.	Wet Bulb.
			Inches.	Degrees.	Inches.	Degrees.	Degrees.
Dec. 11th, 1873,		3 P.M. ...	26·134	43	25·64	39·3	35
		6 ,, ...	·142	38	·78	31·5	28·5
		9 ,, ...	·162	32·5	·80	26	24
,,	12th ,,	9 A.M. ...	·202	28	·85	27	25
		Noon ...	·232	37	·86	37	34·3
		3 P.M. ...	·202	38·8	·82	37	33
		6 ,, ...	·202	36	·83	33	31
		9 ,, ...	·222	33	·84	27	26
,,	13th ,,	9 A.M. ...	·192	24	·84	22	21·5
		Noon ...	·182	35	·82	32	39·5
		3 P.M. ...	·152	40	·79	36	33·5
		6 ,, ...	·162	37	·78	30·5	29·5
		9 ,, ...	·172	32·5	·81	27·0	25·0
,,	14th ,,	9 A.M. ...	·162	24·5	·81	20	19·5
		Noon ...	·152	35·0	·78	32	32
		3 P.M. ...	·102	39·0	·72	36	32
		6 ,, ...	·132	35·5	·73	27	26
		9 ,, ...	·102	32·0	·72	25	22·5
,,	15th ,,	9 A.M. ...	·082	21	·71	16·5	16·0
		Noon ...	·092	33	·75	30	27
		3 P.M. ...	·062	39	·68	26	33
		6 ,, ...	·052	35	·67	26	25
		9 ,, ...	·042	30	·66	22	21·3
,,	16th ,,	9 A.M. ...	·022	25	·65	21	20
		Noon ...	25·997	36	·61	31·5	29·5
		3 P.M. ...	·952	40·5	·58	35	33
		6 ,, ...	·972	35	·59	30	29
		9 ,, ...	·952	32	·60	23	22
,,	17th ,,	9 A.M. ...	·902	23	·54	20	19
		Noon ...	·877	30·5	·53	31	29
		3 P.M. ...	·857	33·5	·59	31·3	28·5
		6 ,, ...	·862	33·0	·59	29	28
		9 ,, ...	·862	32·0	·58	28	26
,,	18th ,,	9 A.M. ...	·892	33·0	·51	30	28
		Noon ...	·902	49·3	·52	47	38
		3 P.M. ...	·892	52	·51	50	41·5
		6 ,, ...	·902	44	·52	33	31
		9 ,, ...	·927	37	·57	33	32
,,	19th ,,	9 A.M. ...	26·077	20·5	·72	17·5	16
		Noon ...	·112	32	·74	30	27
		3 P.M. ...	·102	36	·72	34	31
		6 ,, ...	·112	32	·76	25	24
		9 ,, ...	·122	26·5	·77	21	19
,,	20th ,,	9 A.M. ...	·202	23·5	·85	22	21
		Noon ...	·192	35	·84	33	30
		3 P.M. ...	·162	37	·80	36	31
		6 ,, ...	·152	32	·80	28	25
		9 ,, ...	·177	31	·82	24	22
,,	21st ,,	9 A.M. ...	·132	21	·79	17·5	16
		Noon ...	·132	30·5	·78	28	25·5
		3 P.M. ...	·102	34·5	·75	32	29
		6 ,, ...	·102	31	·72	25	23

(381)

Pandits at YARKAND during the winter of 1873-74.—(Continued.)

Minimum in shade.	Maximum in shade.	Direction of wind.	Remarks.
During preceding 24 hours.			
Degrees.	Degrees.		
......	......	N.	
......	......	N.	
......	......	N.	
18	43	S.	
......	......	N.W.	
......	......	N.E.	
......	......	N.	
......	......	S.	
10	41	N.	
......	......	N.	
......	......	S.E.	
......	......	S.	
......	......	E.	
12	34	N.	
......	......	N.W.	
......	......	N.	
......	......	W.	
......	......	S.E.	
10	33	N.W.	
......	......	W.	
......	......	E.	
......	......	W.	
......	......	S.	
10	36·5	W.	
......	......	E.	
......	......	E.	
......	......	N.	
......	......	W.	
9·8	36	N.	
......	......	S.W.	
......	......	N.	
......	......	S.	
......	......	S.	
19	35·5	S.E.	
......	......	N.	
......	......	W.	
......	......	E.	
10	49	S.	
......	......	N.E.	
......	......	N.	
......	......	N.E.	
......	......	W.	
9·5	31·5	S.	
......	......	N.	
......	......	N.	
......	......	W.	
......	......	E.	
·6	14	N.	
......	......	N.E.	
......	......	S.E.	
......	......	N.	

*a*69

Meteorological Observations recorded by the Great Trigonometrical Survey

DATE.			Mercurial Barometer No. 720 corrected for index error.	Temperature of mercury.	Reading of aneroid barometer Solomon's uncorrected.	TEMPERATURE OF AIR.	
						Dry Bulb.	Wet Bulb.
			Inches.	Degrees.	Inches.	Degrees.	Degrees.
Dec. 21st, 1873,		9 P.M.	26·092	27	25·75	21	20
,, 22nd	,,	9 A.M.	·067	20·5	·75	17·5	16·0
		Noon	·042	31·5	·67	30	27
		3 P.M.	·012	35	·65	32	29
		6 ,,	25·977	31	·61	26	24
		9 ,,	·952	28	·59	21	19·9
,, 23rd	,,	9 A.M.	·822	19·5	·48	19·5	18·5
		Noon	·772	30	·40	29	26
		3 P.M.	·712	33	·35	31	28
		6 ,,	·702	31	·35	22	20
		9 ,,	·752	30	·40	26·5	24
,, 24th	,,	9 A.M.	·942	36	·57	34·5	29·5
		Noon	·932	48	·55	47	47
		3 P.M.	·952	47	·56	47	40
		6 ,,	·952	36	·59	33	32
		9 ,,	26·002	30·5	·62	26·5	25·5
,, 25th	,,	9 A.M.	·042	19·0	·66	17	16
		Noon	·027	32	·64	31	28
		3 P.M.	25·967	36	·59	33	31
		6 ,,	·962	31·5	·58	26	24
		9 ,,	·972	28	·61	24	23
,, 26th	,,	9 A.M.	·922	20	·56	17	15·5
		Noon	·952	34	·57	32	28
		3 P.M.	·922	35	·56	32·3	29·3
		6 ,,	·952	32	·59	26	24
		9 ,,	·982	26·5	·65	21	19
,, 27th	,,	9 A.M.	26·017	21	·65	24	21·8
		Noon	·002	32	·63	31·5	28·5
		3 P.M.	25·952	36	·58	34	32
		6 ,,	·922	32	·56	27	26
		9 ,,	·942	27	·59	20	19
,, 28th	,,	9 A.M.	26·097	16	·75	12	11
		Noon	·127	29·5	·77	28	24·3
		3 P.M.	·107	33	·75	30	27
		6 ,,	·102	29·5	·73	24	22
		9 ,,	·097	24	·72	18	15·5
,, 29th	,,	9 A.M.	·022	18·5	·67	14	13
		Noon	·007	31·5	·65	29	27
		3 P.M.	·012	36	·65	33	31
		6 ,,	·027	30	·70	26	24·5
		9 ,,	·077	27	·75	21	20
,, 30th	,,	9 A.M.	·192	10	·86	9	8
		Noon	·182	23	·85	21	19
		3 P.M.	·142	28	·80	26	23
		6 ,,	·122	25	·77	18	17
		9 ,,	·102	21	·74	13	12
,, 31st	,,	9 A.M.	·052	10	·70	14	14
		Noon	·007	24·5	·66	22	21
		3 P.M.	25·952	28	·61	24	22
		6 ,,	·952	26	·61	19	18
		9 ,,	·962	22	·62	16	14

Pandits at YARKAND during the winter of 1873-74.—(Continued.)

Minimum in shade.	Maximum in shade.	Direction of wind.	Remarks.
During preceding 24 hours.			
Degrees.	Degrees.		
......	......	S.W.	
8·9	29·8	W.	
......	......	S.	
......	......	N.	
......	......	N.	
......	......	W.	
10	33	S.E.	
......	......	E.	
......	......	S.W.	
......	......	N.	
......	......	N.	
15	29·5	W.	
......	......	W.	
......	......	E.	
......	......	S.W.	
......	......	N.	
10·5	47	W.	
......	......	N.W.	
......	......	E.	
......	......	E.	
......	......	N.	
7	46·5	W.	
......	......	W.	
......	......	S.E.	
......	......	W.	
......	......	N.	
11·8	33·3	S.W.	
......	......	N.	
......	......	E.	
......	......	W.	
......	......	E.	
5	34	N.W.	
......	......	W.	
......	......	S.E.	
......	......	N.	
......	......	E.	
2·5	28	E.	
......	......	N.E.	
......	......	N.	
......	......	E.	
......	......	E.	
3	30	W.	
......	......	N.W.	
......	......	N.	
......	......	N.	
......	......	N.W.	
2	24	W.	
......	......	N.	
......	......	S.E.	
......	......	W.	
......	......	N.	

For the month of December 1873.

	9 P.M.	Noon.	3 P.M.	6 P.M.	9 P.M.
Mean of Mercurial Barometer No. 720	26·075	26·067	26·042	26·047	26·050
Mean of Dry Bulb Thermometer	21·0	32·3	35·3	28·3	24·1
Mean of Wet Bulb Thermometer	19·7	29·5	32·1	26·4	23·3
Mean of Minimum Thermometer	...		...		10·8
Mean of Maximum Thermometer in shade	...		...		35·2

(384)

Meteorological Observations recorded by the Great Trigonometrical

Date.			Mercurial Barometer No. 720 corrected for index error.	Temperature of mercury.	Reading of aneroid barometer Solomon's uncorrected.	Temperature of Air.	
						Dry Bulb.	Wet Bulb.
			Inches.	*Degrees.*	*Inches.*	*Degrees.*	*Degrees.*
Jan.	1st, 1874,	9 A.M.	25·952	10	25·61	10·3	9·3
		Noon	·952	24·8	·61	25	23
		3 P.M.	·927	28	·57	27	25
		6 ,,	·922	26	·55	21	20
		9 ,,	·932	23	·58	17·5	16
,,	2nd ,,	9 A.M.	·927	12	·60	13	12
		Noon	·932	21·5	·61	22	20
		3 P.M.	·927	26·5	·60	24·5	22
		6 ,,	·922	23	·60	19	18·5
		9 ,,	·942	20·5	·63	16	15
,,	3rd ,,	9 A.M.	26·052	11	·72	12·5	12
		Noon	·052	22·5	·72	22	19·5
		3 P.M.	·042	28·5	·70	26	23
		6 ,,	·052	24·5	·72	18·5	17
		9 ,,	·072	21	·74	15·5	14
,,	4th ,,	9 A.M.	26·062	11	25·73	11	10
		Noon	·052	25	·71	23	21
		3 P.M.	·047	28	·71	26	23
		6 ,,	·072	25	·73	21	19
		9 ,,	·082	21	·76	15	14
,,	5th ,,	9 A.M.	·117	10	·80	11	10
		Noon	·107	25	·78	23	21
		3 P.M.	·072	27·5	·72	25	23
		6 ,,	·062	25	·74	20	19
		9 ,,	·072	21	·76	16	15
,,	6th ,,	9 A.M.	·067	10	·83	8	7
		Noon	·152	23·5	·82	22	19
		3 P.M.	·127	27	·78	24	21
		6 ,,	·152	25	·80	20	18
		9 ,,	·152	22	·80	17	16
,,	7th ,,	9 A.M.	·192	11	·87	13	12
		Noon	·192	21	·86	21·5	19·5
		3 P.M.	·167	25	·81	24	21
		6 ,,	·172	23	·84	20	19
		9 ,,	·197	22	·86	19	18
,,	8th ,,	9 A.M.	·152	18·8	·81	17	16
		Noon	·117	25·8	·78	25	22·5
		3 P.M.	·077	27	·73	25·5	23
		6 ,,	·082	23·3	·74	19	18
		9 ,,	·062	20	·73	16	15
,,	9th ,,	9 A.M.	·067	10	·73	10	9
		Noon	·052	25	·70	23	21
		3 P.M.	25·992	28	·66	26	23
		6 ,,	26·007	25	·68	21	19
		9 ,,	·012	21	·69	18	16
,,	10th ,,	9 A.M.	·027	11·5	·70	10	9
		Noon	·022	26·5	·67	26	23
		3 P.M.	25·972	31	·63	29	27
		6 ,,	·972	27	·63	24	23
		9 ,,	·952	24	·61	21	19
,,	11th ,,	9 A.M.	26·202	13	·87	13	12
		Noon	·302	25	·95	23·5	20

(385)

Survey Pandits at YARKAND during the winter of 1873-74.—(Continued).

Minimum in shade.	Maximum in shade.	Direction of wind.	Remarks.
During preceding 24 hours.			
Degrees.	*Degrees.*		
0	23	N.	
......	......	S.E.	
......	......	W.	
......	......	N.	
......	......	S.	
7·5	19	W.	
......	......	S.	
......	......	S.	
......	......	N.W.	
......	......	W.	
6	29·5	S.W.	
......	......	N.	
......	......	S.E.	
......	......	W.	
......	......	N.	
2	23	N.	
......	......	N.W.	
......	......	N.	
......	......	N.	
......	......	W.	
1·8	24	N.	
......	......	N.E.	
......	......	E.	
......	......	N.	
......	......	S.E.	
1·3	25	E.	
......	......	N.E.	
......	......	E.	
......	......	W.	
......	......	W.	
3	22·5	N.W.	
......	......	W.	
......	......	S.W.	
......	......	N.E.	
......	......	N.W.	
9	26	S.W.	
......	......	E.	
......	......	S.E.	
......	......	E.	
......	......	N.	
1	29·5	S.W.	
......	......	N.E.	
......	......	E.	
......	......	E.	
......	......	W.	
3	23	S.	
......	......	N.	
......	......	W.	
......	......	W.	
......	......	N.	
4	31·5	W.	
......	......	N.E.	

Meteorological Observations recorded by the Great Trigonometrical Survey

Date.			Mercurial Barometer No. 720 corrected for index error.	Temperature of mercury.	Reading of aneroid barometer Solomon's uncorrected.	Temperature of Air.	
						Dry Bulb.	Wet Bulb.
			Inches.	Degrees.	Inches.	Degrees.	Degrees.
Jan. 11th 1874,		3 P.M.	26·352	28·3	26·01	26	23
		6 ,,	·382	24	·05	19	18
		9 ,,	·412	21	·08	14	13
,, 12th	,,	9 A.M.	·402	17·5	·05	15	14
		Noon	·342	26	·01	26	21
		3 P.M.	·302	28·5	25·94	26	23
		6 ,,	·262	23·5	·93	20	18
		9 ,,	·252	20	·90	14	13
,, 13th	,,	9 A.M.	·192	10	·85	10	8
		Noon	·152	25	·80	23·5	20
		3 P.M.	·102	28	·76	27	23
		6 ,,	·092	24·5	·75	20	17
		9 ,,	·072	19·8	·73	15	14
,, 14th	,,	9 A.M.	·052	10	·72	10	9
		Noon	·042	25	·70	24	21
		3 P.M.	·022	29	·67	27	24
		6 ,,	·032	25	·70	21	19
		9 ,,	·042	20·3	·71	17	14·5
,, 15th	,,	9 A.M.	·112	11	·80	11	10
		Noon	·107	25	·77	24	21
		3 P.M.	·102	29	·74	27	23·5
		6 ,,	·122	25	·78	20	18
		9 ,,	·152	21	·80	16	15
,, 16th	,,	9 A.M.	·207	11	·88	10	9
		Noon	·222	27	·89	26	22
		3 P.M.	·202	30	·87	28	25
		6 ,,	·242	26·5	·90	22	20
		9 ,,	·257	21	·92	17	15
,, 17th	,,	9 A.M.	26·312	12·5	26·01	13	11
		Noon	·327	27	25·98	26	22
		3 P.M.	·302	31	·95	29	26
		6 ,,	·302	27	·95	25	23
		9 ,,	·292	24	·94	20	18
,, 18th	,,	9 A.M.	·207	11	·88	13	12
		Noon	·202	27·5	·87	28	24
		3 P.M.	·107	32	·73	30	27
		6 ,,	·107	28	·77	24	22
		9 ,,	·102	24	·74	20	18
,, 19th	,,	9 A.M.	·077	12	·73	13	11
		Noon	·072	27	·72	27	23
		3 P.M.	·052	31	·69	31	28
		6 ,,	·057	28	·70	23	20
		9 ,,	·082	23	·72	18	16
,, 20th	,,	9 A.M.	·062	18·5	·71	12	10
		Noon	·052	31	·70	30	26
		3 P.M.	·052	33	·71	33	31
		6 ,,	·052	30	·73	31	28
		9 ,,	·027	27·5	·68	22	20
,, 21st	,,	9 A.M.	25·932	22	·58	21	18·5
		Noon	·927	30	·56	30·5	27·5
		3 P.M.	·862	32	·51	31	28·5
		6 ,,	·867	30	·54	28	26

(387)

Pandits at YARKAND during the winter of 1873-74.—(Continued.)

Minimum in shade.	Maximum in shade.	Direction of wind.	Remarks.
During preceding 24 hours.			
Degrees.	Degrees.		
......	......	N.W.	
......	......	W.	
......	......	S.	
3	24	S.E.	
......	......	W.	
......	......	E.	
......	......	W.	
......	......	E.	
1	23	E.	
......	......	S.E.	
......	......	N.E.	
......	......	N.W.	
......	......	N.	
0·5	23·5	S.W.	
......	......	N.E.	
......	......	S.E.	
......	......	N.	
......	......	N.	
1	25·5	W.	
......	......	N.W.	
......	......	W.	
......	......	S.	
......	......	N.	
1	25	N.	
......	......	S.	
......	......	E.	
......	......	E.	
......	......	S.	
1	25	N.W.	
......	......	S.E.	
......	......	N.E.	
......	......	E.	
......	......	N.	
2·5	27	S.W.	
......	......	W.	
......	......	S.E.	
......	......	E.	
......	......	N.E.	
4	30	E.	
......	......	N.W.	
......	......	S.	
......	......	E.	
......	......	N.E.	
7·5	33	S.W.	
......	......	S.	
......	......	E.	
......	......	S.	
......	......	W.	
10·8	34·8	S.	
......	......	N.	
......	......	N.E.	
......	......	W.	

(388)

Meteorological Observations recorded by the Great Trigonometrical

Date.			Mercurial Barometer No. 720 corrected for index error.	Temperature of mercury.	Reading of aneroid barometer Solomon's uncorrected.	Temperature of Air.	
						Dry Bulb.	Wet Bulb.
			Inches.	*Degrees.*	*Inches.*	*Degrees.*	*Degrees.*
Jan. 21st, 1874,		9 P.M.	·892	29	·56	26·5	22·5
„ 22nd	„	9 A.M.	·902	25	·55	24	21
		Noon	·912	31	·56	32	28
		3 P.M.	·912	34	·56	33·5	27
		6 „	·942	30	·60	26	23
		9 „	·947	27	·64	22·5	20·5
„ 23rd	„	9 A.M.	·952	23	·62	22	19
		Noon	·947	31·5	·58	32	27·5
		3 P.M.	·917	33	·57	33	30
		6 „	·952	31·8	·62	28	26
		9 „	·972	28·5	·67	25	24
„ 24th	„	9 A.M.	26·062	20·5	·72	19	27·3
		Noon	·062	33·5	·72	32·5	29
		3 P.M.	·052	37·5	·69	36	34·5
		6 „	·057	34·0	·73	29	28
		9 „	·072	30	·75	26	23
„ 25th	„	9 A.M.	·092	21	·75	20·5	19·5
		Noon	·042	35	·67	34·5	30·3
		3 P.M.	25·982	38	·62	37	34·5
		6 „	·972	34	·62	30	29
		9 „	·972	32	·61	29	25
„ 26th	„	9 A.M.	·992	28	·62	27	25
		Noon	·977	39	·62	40	36
		3 P.M.	·972	40	·60	38	33·5
		6 „	26·002	36	·65	31	29
		9 „	·007	30·5	·68	26	24
„ 27th	„	9 A.M.	·022	22	·69	21	19
		Noon	·042	32	·69	33	29
		3 P.M.	·017	38	·66	37	34
		6 „	·022	33·5	·69	30	28·5
		9 „	·032	29	·70	24·5	23
„ 28th	„	9 A.M.	26·132	21	·80	19	17
		Noon	·132	34	·80	33	31
		3 P.M.	·112	37·5	·75	35	30
		6 „	·122	33·5	·79	28	25
		9 „	·172	32	·84	29·5	25·3
„ 29th	„	9 A.M.	·142	28	·80	29	26
		Noon	·142	35	·81	36	32
		3 P.M.	·092	38	·73	36	31
		6 „	·102	33	·77	29	26
		9 „	·097	30	·76	24	22
„ 30th	„	9 A.M.	26·062	22·5	25·78	21	19
		Noon	·052	35·5	·68	35	31
		3 P.M.	·002	38	·64	37	31
		6 „	·007	34·5	·65	31	26
		9 „	·012	31	·66	27	24
„ 31st	„	9 A.M.	·032	22	·69	21	19
		Noon	·022	34·8	·67	33·5	29
		3 P.M.	25·997	38·5	·63	36·8	33·5
		6 „	26·002	34	·65	31	27
		9 „	·007	32	·67	29	26

(389)

Survey Pandits at YARKAND during the winter of 1873-74.—(Continued.)

Minimum in shade.	Maximum in shade.	Direction of wind.	Remarks.
During preceding 24 hours.			
Degrees.	Degrees.		
......	......	N.W.	
19	34	S.W.	
......	......	N.W.	
......	......	N.	
......	......	W.	
......	......	N.E.	
17	38	S.W.	
......	......	S.	
......	......	E.	
......	......	N.E.	
......	......	N.	
9	39	N.W.	
......	......	E.	
......	......	E.	
......	......	N.W.	
......	......	N.	
9	33.8	N.W.	
......	......	N.E.	
......	......	S.W.	
......	......	E.	
......	......	N.	
14	34.5	S.W.	
......	......	E.	
......	......	S.E.	
......	......	S.	
......	......	W.	
11	43.5	W.	
......	......	N.	
......	......	N.	
......	......	E.	
......	......	N.E.	*For the month of January 1874.*
7.8	42	N.W.	
......	......	N.E.	
......	......	N.	
......	......	S.	
......	......	E.	
17	34	W.	
......	......	E.	
......	......	S.W.	
......	......	N.	
......	......	N.E.	
11	41	S.W.	
......	......	N.E.	
......	......	N.E.	
......	......	S.	
......	......	E.	
8	34.5	S.W.	
......	......	S.E.	
......	......	S.E.	
......	......	N.	
......	......	E.	

For the month of January 1874.

	9 A.M.	Noon.	3 P.M.	6 P.M.	9 P.M.
Mean of Mercurial Barometer No. 720 corrected to 32°.	26.093	26.087	26.060	26.068	26.074
Mean of Dry Bulb Thermometer.	15.5	27.8	30.0	24.2	20.4
Mean of Wet Bulb Thermometer.	14.0	24.5	26.8	22.2	18.5

Mean of minimum thermometer ... 6°.2 6°.2
Mean of maximum thermometer in shade ... 29°.7 29°.7

(390)

Meteorological Observations recorded by the Great Trigonometrical Survey

Date.		Mercurial Barometer No. 720 corrected for index error.	Temperature of mercury.	Reading of Aneroid Barometer Solomon's uncorrected.	Temperature of Air.	
					Dry bulb.	Wet bulb.
		Inches.	Degrees.	Inches.	Degrees.	Degrees.
Feb. 1st, 1874,	9 A.M.	25·982	26	25·63	25·5	23
	Noon	·977	35	·62	36	32
	3 P.M.	·907	38	·56	37	32·5
	6 ,,	·912	34	·58	30	26
	9 ,,	·917	31	·59	26	23
,, 2nd ,,	9 A.M.	·902	20	·58	19	17
	Noon	·897	36	·56	35	31·5
	3 P.M.	·872	42	·52	41	35
	6 ,,	·892	38	·53	34	32
	9 ,,	·912	33·5	·59	28	25
,, 3rd ,,	9 A.M.	·982	24	·65	24	21
	Noon	·977	36	·62	36	32
	3 P.M.	·952	42	·58	41	35
	6 ,,	·942	38·5	·57	31	28
	9 ,,	·962	33	·62	29	26
,, 4th ,,	9 A.M.	·962	25	·62	24	21
	Noon	·962	37	·62	37	32·5
	3 P.M.	·927	42·5	·56	41	36
	6 ,,	·927	39	·58	32	28
	9 ,,	·947	33·3	·60	27	25
,, 5th ,,	9 A.M.	·952	26·5	·61	25·5	22·5
	Noon	·952	37·5	·60	37	31·5
	3 P.M.	·922	42	·55	42	36
	6 ,,	·927	39	·58	32	28
	9 ,,	·952	32·5	·61	26	23
,, 6th ,,	9 A.M.	·932	26·5	·62	26	23
	Noon	·927	36	·60	36	31
	3 P.M.	·902	42	·55	41	36
	6 ,,	·902	37·5	·55	33	29
	9 ,,	·907	33	·58	29	26
,, 7th ,,	9 A.M.	·907	25·5	·58	24	22
	Noon	·922	38	·59	38	32
	3 P.M.	·892	42·5	·52	41	34·5
	6 ,,	·892	38	·52	32	28
	9 ,,	·897	34	·55	29	26
,, 8th ,,	9 A.M.	·952	24	·50	23	20·5
	Noon	·792	36	·42	36	31
	3 P.M.	·677	41	·31	40	36
	6 ,,	·702	36	·36	33	32
	9 ,,	·722	34	·37	30	26
,, 9th ,,	9 A.M.	·732	31	·41	31·5	28
	Noon	·712	38	·36	28·	33
	3 P.M.	·712	41	·37	40	34
	6 ,,	·752	38	·40	35	31
	9 ,,	·757	35	·41	33	30
,, 10th ,,	9 A.M.	·897	31·8	·55	31	28
	Noon	·927	40·3	·57	41	36·3
	3 P.M.	·922	39	·57	38·5	34·5
	6 ,,	·947	35·5	·63	33	31
	9 ,,	·952	32	·64	31	29
,, 11th ,,	9 A.M.	·937	31·5	·59	33	31·5
	Noon	·902	37	·56	38	35·3

Pandits at YARKAND during the month of 1873-74.—(Continued).

Minimum in shade.	Maximum in shade.	Direction of wind.	Remarks.
During preceding 24 hours.			
Degrees.	*Degrees.*		
14·3	36	S.	
......	......	S.W.	
......	......	E.	
......	......	N.E.	
......	......	N.	
8·5	42	N.W.	
......	......	W.	
......	......	E.	
......	......	W.	
......	......	N.	
12·8	38·5	N.	
......	......	W.	
......	......	S.	
......	......	W.	
......	......	E.	
13	39	N.W.	
......	......	N.E.	
......	......	W.	
......	......	E.	
......	......	N.	
16·5	40	S.W.	
......	......	S.W.	
......	......	W.	
......	......	W.	
......	......	N.	
12·8	38·5	W.	
......	......	N.E.	
......	......	E.	
......	......	N.	
......	......	S.	
11	43	N.W.	
......	......	N.	
......	......	N.E.	
......	......	E.	
......	......	N.	
9·8	45	N.E.	
......	......	W.	
......	......	N.E.	
......	......	N.	
......	......	N.	
16·5	49	S.W.	
......	......	N.E.	
......	......	W.	
......	......	N.	
......	......	W.	
24·5	49·5	N.W.	
......	......	E.	
......	......	E.	
......	......	W.	
......	......	W.	
22	48	N.E.	Clouds and snow.
......	......	N.	

Meteorological Observations recorded by the Great Trigonometrical

Date.			Mercurial Barometer No. 720 corrected for index error.	Temperature of mercury.	Reading of Aneroid Barometer Solomon's uncorrected.	Temperature of Air.	
						Dry bulb.	Wet bulb.
			Inches.	Degrees.	Inches.	Degrees.	Degrees.
Feb. 11th, 1874,		3 P.M.	25·872	37·5	25·52	37	35
		6 ,,	·892	34	·55	32	30
		9 ,,	·902	30	·57	28	27
,,	12th ,,	9 A.M.	·942	30	·61	29·5	27
		Noon	·937	37	·59	35	32
		3 P.M.	·902	39·5	·54	39·3	34
		6 ,,	·902	36	·57	30	27
		9 ,,	9·12	31	·60	27	25
,,	13th ,,	9 A.M.	9·92	28	·66	26·5	25
		Noon	26·002	36	·67	35	31
		3 P.M.	25·977	45·5	·66	38	34
		6 ,,	·952	37·5	·65	30·5	28
		9 ,,	·972	31·3	·67	26·3	25
,,	14th ,,	9 A.M.	26·027	29	·68	27·5	25·5
		Noon	·002	38	·65	37	33
		3 P.M.	25·952	41	·58	39	36
		6 ,,	·912	38	·56	33	28
		9 ,,	·952	34	·63	31	26·5
,,	15th ,,	9 A.M.	26·052	34	·71	34	32
		Noon	·027	41	·69	41·3	35
		3 P.M.	·022	43	·67	41	35
		6 ,,	·022	40	·67	36	31
		9 ,,	·012	35	·67	31	27
,,	16th ,,	9 A.M.	·027	26	·71	25	22
		Noon	·042	38·5	·66	37	32
		3 P.M.	·022	43	·60	41	35
		6 ,,	25·952	40	·59	33	28
		9 ,,	·052	34	·59	30	26
,,	17th ,,	9 A.M.	·942	34·5	·57	34	31
		Noon	·927	41·5	·55	42·5	37
		3 P.M.	·912	45·5	·54	46	38·5
		6 ,,	·932	40·5	·60	35	30
		9 ,,	·972	38	·65	38	28·5
,,	18th ,,	9 A.M.	26·102	36·3	·79	36·3	31
		Noon	·102	44·5	·70	44	34
		3 P.M.	·092	48	·69	48	38
		6 ,,	·082	42	·73	39	31
		9 ,,	·102	37	·78	31·5	26
,,	19th ,,	9 A.M.	·172	26	·83	25·5	23·5
		Noon	·162	34	·76	35·5	32·3
		3 P.M.	·127	38·5	·78	38	33
		6 ,,	·127	36	·78	34	29
		9 ,,	·132	33·5	·79	32	28
,,	20th ,,	9 A.M.	·092	33·5	·74	34	30·5
		Noon	·072	40	·72	42	36
		3 P.M.	·017	43	·63	44·3	38
		6 ,,	25·997	39	·64	35	30
		9 ,,	26·002	35	·65	30	26
,,	21st ,,	9 A.M.	·042	31·5	·68	32	29
		Noon	·052	41	·70	42	35
		3 P.M.	·017	43·5	·65	43	36
		6 ,,	·032	41	·69	38	31

(393)

Survey Pandits at YARKAND during the winter of 1873-74.—(Continued).

Minimum in shade.	Maximum in shade.	Direction of wind.	Remarks.
During preceding 24 hours.			
Degrees.	Degrees.		
......	......	S.	
......	......	E.	
......	......	S.	
19·8	48	N.-W.	
......	......	N.	
......	......	N.-E.	
......	......	S.	
......	......	S.-W.	
11	41	N.	
......	......	S.	
......	......	E.	
......	......	N.	
......	......	S.	
17·5	36	N.-W.	
......	......	S.-W.	
......	......	N.-E.	
......	......	S.	
......	......	S.	
22	37	N.-W.	
......	......	N.-E.	
......	......	S.	
......	......	S.-E.	
......	......	N.	
16	47	N.	
......	......	E.	
......	......	W.	
......	......	E.	
......	......	E.	
22	40	W.	
......	......	S.-W.	
......	......	S.-E.	
......	......	N.	
......	......	S.	
21	50·5	W.	
......	......	N.	
......	......	S.-E.	
......	......	E.	
......	......	E.	
18	52	N.-W.	
......	......	W.	
......	......	S.-W.	
......	......	S.-E.	
......	......	S.	
24·5	41·5	N.-E.	
......	......	N.-E.	
......	......	S.-E.	
......	......	S.	
......	......	E.	
20	50	W.	
......	......	S.-E.	
......	......	E.	
......	......	W.	

Meteorological Observations recorded by the Great Trigonometrical

DATE.			Mercurial Barometer No. 720 corrected for index error.	Temperature of mercury.	Reading of aneroid barometer Solomon's uncorrected.	TEMPERATURE OF AIR.	
						Dry Bulb.	Wet Bulb.
			Inches.	Degrees.	Inches.	Degrees.	Degrees.
Feb. 21st,	1874,	9 P.M. ...	26·062	37	25·74	35	27
,, 22nd	,,	9 A.M. ...	·147	34·5	·82	35	31·5
		Noon ...	·152	39	·82	40·5	35·5
		3 P.M. ...	·107	38	·72	38·5	35
		6 ,, ...	·02	36	·75	35	32
		9 ,, ...	·112	33·5	·77	32	30
,, 23rd	,,	9 A.M. ...	·162	33·5	·80	33	31
		Noon ...	·142	37	·77	37·5	34
		3 P.M. ...	·092	40·3	·75	40	32
		6 ,, ...	·082	37·3	·73	33·5	29
		9 ,, ...	·077	32·5	·74	30	27
,, 24th	,,	9 P.M. ...	·052	30·5	·72	30·5	28
		Noon ...	·002	38	·65	37	34
		3 P.M. ...	25·932	40	·57	41	34
		6 ,, ...	·912	38·5	·56	36	30·5
		9 ,, ...	·902	36	·55	33	28·5
,, 25th	,,	9 A.M. ...	·852	32·5	·52	31·5	28
		Noon ...	·812	40	·47	39	34
		3 P.M. ...	·757	42	·39	42	35
		6 ,, ...	·752	39	·39	36	29
		9 ,, ...	·752	35	·39	31	26·5
,, 26th	,,	9 A.M. ...	·802	36·8	·46	36	32·5
		Noon ...	·802	48	·43	47	39
		3 P.M. ...	·772	51	·37	50·5	40·5
		6 ,, ...	·802	45·5	·44	44·5	36
		9 ,, ...	·877	40	·53	36·0	31
,, 27th	,,	9 A.M. ...	26·002	36·8	·66	36	31·5
		Noon ...	·002	44	·64	44	38
		3 P.M. ...	25·952	47	·62	46	37
		6 ,, ...	·972	44	·63	41	33
		9 ,, ...	26·002	39·8	·65	36·5	31·5
,, 28th	,,	9 A.M. ...	·002	38	·67	38	33
		Noon ...	·017	46	·66	46	37·5
		3 P.M. ...	25·992	48	·62	49	39·5
		6 ,, ...	26·002	45	·68	40	34
		9 ,, ...	·052	40	·70	37·5	31

(395)

Survey Pandits at YARKAND during the winter of 1873-74.—(Continued.)

Minimum in shade.	Maximum in shade.	Direction of wind.	Remarks.
During preceding 24 hours.			
Degrees.	Degrees.		
......	......	W.	
26·8	47·8	E.	
......	......	N.W.	
......	......	S.W.	
......	......	E.	
......	......	W.	
27	43	N.E.	
......	......	N.E.	
......	......	S.E.	
......	......	W.	
......	......	W.	
21·8	45	S.E.	
......	......	W.	
......	......	N.W.	
......	......	W.	
......	......	N.E.	
17·5	48·0	W.	
......	......	W.	
......	......	S.	
......	......	E.	
......	......	N.	
20·8	44·5	S.	
......	......	S.W.	
......	......	S.	
......	......	W.	
19·8	50·5	S.E.	
......	......	W.	
......	......	W.	
......	......	W.	
......	......	N.E.	
22	45	W.	
......	......	N.	
......	......	S.E.	
......	......	W.	
......	......	E.	

For the month of February 1874.

	9 A.M.	Noon.	3 P.M.	6 P.M.	P.M.
Mean of Mercurial Barometer No. 720.	25·980	25·971	25·935	25·936	25·952
Mean of dry bulb Thermometer	29·7	38·9	41·6	34·5	30°·7
Mean of wet bulb Thermometer	26·8	33·8	35·5	30·0	27°·0

Mean of Minimum Thermometer ... 18°·2
Mean of Maximum Thermometer in shade 44°·1

Meteorological Observations recorded by the Great Trigonometrical Survey

Date.		Mercurial Barometer No. 720 corrected for index error.	Temperature of mercury.	Reading of aneroid barometer Solomon's uncorrected.	Temperature of Air.	
					Dry Bulb.	Wet Bulb.
		Inches.	Degrees.	Inches.	Degrees.	Degrees.
March 1st, 1874,	9 A.M.	25·997	36·5	·65	36·8	32·3
	Noon	·992	45·5	·61	45·5	40
	3 P.M.	·882	50·5	·50	50·5	41
	6 ,,	·802	45·8	·43	41	34
	9 ,,	·802	41	·43	36·5	30·5
,, 2nd ,,	9 A.M.	·662	38	·32	39	33
	Noon	·612	48·3	·25	48·3	41·3
	3 P.M.	·562	52·5	·18	54	45
	6 ,,	·552	49	·16	42	35·5
	9 ,,	·542	44	·15	39	33
,, 3rd ,,	9 A.M.	·582	39	·23	40	35
	Noon	·597	48·5	·24	50·3	44
	3 P.M.	·582	50	·22	50	40·8
	6 ,,	25·652	49	25·28	47	39
	9 ,,	·682	45	·33	42	36
,, 4th ,,	9 A.M.	·832	45	·48	45	37
	Noon	·827	50	·46	51	41
	3 P.M.	·802	49·8	·43	49·3	40·8
	6 ,,	·842	46·5	·48	43	37·5
	9 ,,	·807	43	·45	40	35
,, 5th ,,	9 A.M.	·822	40	·46	39·8	35·5
	Noon	·797	49	·44	50	42
	3 P.M.	·767	51·8	·36	52	42
	6 ,,	·777	49	·45	47	39·5
	9 ,,	·782	45	·46	43	38
,, 6th ,,	9 A.M.	·832	40·5	·48	40	36
	Noon	·852	48·8	·49	50	42
	3 P.M.	·792	51	·42	51·3	41·3
	6 ,,	·767	48·8	·40	46	38
	9 ,,	·752	45	·36	43	36
,, 7th ,,	9 A.M.	·792	40·3	·44	41·5	32
	Noon	·752	47·3	·36	50	42
	3 P.M.	·652	50	·28	52	42·3
	6 ,,	·612	45·8	·22	43	37
	9 ,,	·607	42	·25	40·5	36
,, 8th ,,	9 A.M.	·597	40	·23	36	33
	Noon	·577	42	·20	43	37
	3 P.M.	·552	41·3	·18	41·3	36·8
	6 ,,	·602	40·5	·23	38	34
	9 ,,	·607	38·3	·25	36·5	33·5
,, 9th ,,	9 A.M.	·697	38	·35	39	33·5
	Noon	·692	41	·33	41	37
	3 P.M.	·677	42·8	·32	43	37·5
	6 ,,	·727	41	·36	38·5	34
	9 ,,	·772	36	·41	33	30
,, 10th ,,	9 A.M.	·877	36·5	·52	37	31·3
	Noon	·892	45·8	·53	46	39·5
	3 P.M.	·892	47·5	·53	47·3	37
	6 ,,	·932	42·5	·58	40·3	35
	9 ,,	26·002	37·5	·64	37·3	30·5
,, 11th ,,	9 A.M.	·137	34·5	·77	34	30·3
	Noon	·152	41	·82	43	40

Pandits at YARKAND during the winter of 1873-74.—(Continued.)

Minimum in shade.	Maximum in shade.	Direction of wind.	Remarks.
During preceding 24 hours.			
Degrees.	Degrees.		
19·8	49	N.W.	
......	......	N.E.	
......	......	S.	
......	......	N.	
......	......	N.	
22·3	55·5	S.W.	
......	......	S.E.	
......	......	E.	
......	......	S.	
......	......	S.W.	
24·8	56·8	W.	
......	......	W.	
......	......	S.E.	
......	......	W.	
......	......	S.E.	
34·8	57·5	N.E.	
......	......	N.E.	
......	......	N.E.	
......	......	W.	
......	......	E.	
32	57·5	W.	
......	......	S.E.	
......	......	N.	
......	......	N.E	
......	......	W.	
37	55·5	W.	
......	......	N.E.	
......	......	N.E.	
......	......	E.	
......	......	S.E.	
33·5	55·	N.E.	
......	......	S.E.	
......	......	E.	
......	......	S.W.	
......	......	N.W.	
36	58·5	W.	
......	......	E.	
......	......	N.E.	
......	......	N.E.	
......	......	N.E.	
29	44·3	W.	One inch of snow at night.
......	......	N.	
......	......	W.	
......	......	N.E.	
......	......	S.	
21	49	N.E.	
......	......	S.E.	
......	......	W.	
......	......	W.	
......	......	W.	
29·8	52	W.	
......	......	E.	

(398)

Meteorological Observations recorded by the Great Trigonometrical

DATE.		Mercurial Barometer No. 720 corrected for index error.	Temperature of mercury.	Reading of aneroid barometer Solomon's uncorrected.	TEMPERATURE OF AIR.	
					Dry Bulb.	Wet Bulb.
		Inches.	Degrees.	Inches.	Degrees.	Degrees.
March 11th, 1874,	3 P.M.	26·142	45	25·76	45	38·5
	6 ,,	·152	40·5	·81	37·5	33
	9 ,,	·162	39	·83	36	33
,, 12th ,,	9 A.M.	·147	36	·82	35·8	33
	Noon	·152	38·5	·83	39	37
	3 P.M.	·112	37·3	·77	37·8	35
	6 ,,	·107	35·3	·78	34	35
	9 ,,	·102	34·5	·77	33	30·5
,, 13th ,,	9 A.M.	·102	35	·73	36	32
	Noon	·072	41·8	·71	44	40
	3 P.M.	·057	43·5	·67	43·5	38·5
	6 ,,	·062	41	·69	37	34·5
	9 ,,	·092	39	·75	37	33·0
,, 14th ,,	9 A.M.	·122	38·8	·78	39	35
	Noon	·112	43·5	·76	45·3	40
	3 P.M.	·082	47	·71	49	42
	6 ,,	·102	42·5	·73	40·5	35·3
	9 ,,	·117	39	·76	36	33
,, 15th ,,	9 A.M.	·202	39	·86	41	37
	Noon	·197	47	·85	47·5	40
	3 P.M.	·177	48·8	·82	47	40·3
	6 ,,	·202	41·8	·84	38	34·3
	9 ,,	·207	39	·85	36	33
,, 16th ,,	9 A.M.	·247	37	·89	38	32
	Noon	·212	42	·85	43	36·3
	3 P.M.	·152	43·3	·74	43	36
	6 ,,	·152	41·5	·71	37	31
	9 ,,	·122	36·3	·73	34	30
,, 17th ,,	9 A.M.	·082	37	·67	37·5	33·5
	Noon	·002	42·5	·64	46	39·3
	3 P.M.	25·927	47	·53	49	40
	6 ,,	·902	43	·51	39	33
	9 ,,	·907	39·8	·52	37	31
,, 18th ,,	9 A.M.	·862	37·5	·52	39	34·5
	Noon	·852	46·5	·48	48	40
	3 P.M.	·807	39·3	·42	51	41
	6 ,,	·812	46·5	·44	43	36
	9 ,,	·817	42·5	·45	38·5	33
,, 19th ,,	9 A.M.	·897	39	·53	39·8	35·8
	Noon	·892	50	·52	51	41·5
	3 P.M.	·872	52·5	·49	54	44
	6 ,,	·887	50	·52	45	38
	9 ,,	·892	44·5	·53	38·5	34
,, 20th ,,	9 A.M.	26·052	39·5	·69	41	36
	Noon	·052	50·8	·69	53·3	42
	3 P.M.	·032	54·8	·65	55	43
	6 ,,	·047	51·5	·68	47	38
	9 ,,	·057	44·8	·70	43	37
,, 21st ,,	9 A.M.	25·982	43	·64	44	37
	Noon	·882	52	·58	53·5	41·5
	3 P.M.	·817	56	·47	56·3	44
	6 ,,	·762	49	·40	47	37·5

(399)

Survey Pandits at YARKAND during the winter of 1873-74.—(Continued.)

Minimum in shade.	Maximum in shade.	Direction of wind.	Remarks.
During preceding 24 hours.			
Degrees.	Degrees.		
......	......	S.E.	
......	......	N.	
29	52	N.	A fall of half an inch of snow at night.
		N.	
......	......	S.W.	
......	......	E.	
......	......	S.E.	
28	43·5	E.	
......	......	S.W.	
......	......	W.	
......	......	N.	
......	......	E.	
29	51·5	N.W.	Cloudy and slight snow.
		W.	
......	......	N.E.	
......	......	N.	
......	......	W.	
29	56·3	W.	
......	......	S.E.	
......	......	E.	
......	......	W.	
......	......	E.	
29·5	54·8	E.	
......	......	S.E.	
......	......	W.	
......	......	N.W.	
......	......	N.	
24·8	49	N.E.	
......	......	S.E.	
......	......	N.	
......	......	N.	
......	......	N.E.	
35·5	55·0	E.	
......	......	N.	
......	......	E.	
......	......	N.	
......	......	N.	
35·5	50·5	W.	
......	......	N.E.	
......	......	N.E.	
......	......	E.	
......	......	E.	
27·5	57·3	E.	
......	......	N.E.	
......	......	N.W.	
......	......	S.W.	
......	......	S.	
27	......	N.E.	
......	......	E.	
......	......	N.W.	
......	......	S.	

Meteorological Observations recorded by the Great Trigonometrical Survey

Date.			Mercurial Barometer No. 720 corrected for index error.	Temperature of mercury.	Reading of aneroid barometer Solomon's uncorrected.	Temperature of Air.	
						Dry Bulb.	Wet Bulb.
			Inches.	Degrees.	Inches.	Degrees.	Degrees.
March 21st, 1874,		9 P.M.	25·752	46	25·41	43	36
,,	22nd ,,	9 A.M.	·727	42	·34	42	37
		Noon	·752	46·5	·38	47·5	40
		3 P.M.	·742	53	·35	53	43
		6 ,,	·747	50	·35	46	39
		9 ,,	·757	44·5	·38	41	35
,,	23rd ,,	9 A.M.	·762	43·8	·41	44·5	39·8
		Noon	·762	50	·38	53	44·5
		3 P.M.	·742	52·5	·35	44·5	45
		6 ,,	·747	49	·37	45	39
		9 ,,	·752	45·8	·41	41	36
,,	24th ,,	9 A.M.	·822	49	·48	50	44
		Noon	·817	56·5	·46	60·5	50
		3 P.M.	·797	58·3	·47	60	49
		6 ,,	·802	53·8	·49	50	43
		9 ,,	·802	48	·49	43	37·5
,,	25th ,,	9 A.M.	·902	46	·53	47	42
		Noon	·872	57·8	·50	60·3	50·5
		3 P.M.	·852	60	·45	61	50
		6 ,,	·852	57	·47	54	45

Pandits at YARKAND during the winter of 1873-74.—(Concluded.)

MINIMUM IN SHADE.	MAXIMUM IN SHADE.	Direction of wind.	REMARKS.
During preceding 24 hours.			
Degrees	Degrees.		
......	......	S.	
34·5	......	S.E.	
......	......	W.	
......	......	N.W.	
......	......	N.W.	*For the month of March* 1874.
......	......	W.	9 A.M. Noon. 3 P.M. 6 P.M. 9 P.M.
35·5	......	W.	
......	......	W.	Mean of Mercurial 25·908 25·894 25·858 25·862 25·662
......	......	N.W.	Barometer No. 720
......	......	N.W.	corrected to 32°.
......	......	W.	
30·8	......	W.	Mean of Dry Bulb 40·1 48·4 49·6 42·7 37·1
......	......	N.E.	Thermometer.
......	......	W.	
......	......	N.	Mean of Wet Bulb 35·1 41·1 41·3 36·4 33·8
......	......	E.	Thermometer.
31	......	W.	
......	......	S.W.	Mean of Minimum Thermometer ... 29°·8
......	......	W.	Mean of Maximum Thermometer in shade ... 52°·5
......	......	W.	

(402)

Meteorological Observations at KASHGHAR during

Date.		Aneroid Barometer No. V., by Troughton and Simms, corrected for index error.	Aneroid Barometer by Dixey, corrected for index error.	Temperature of Air.		Maximum in Shade.	Minimum in Shade.	Minimum in Open.
				Dry bulb.	Wet bulb.	During preceding 24 hours.		
		Inches.	Inches.	Degrees.	Degrees.	Degrees.	Degrees.	Degrees.
Dec. 12th, 1873,	9 A.M.	26·07	26·09	...	...	44·0	...	15·8
	Noon	·02	·06	34·5	...	...	...	...
	3 P.M.	25·95	·02	34·5	...	...	...	...
	6 ,,	26·02	·07	...	...	...	...	...
,, 13th ,,	9 A.M.	·00	·06	...	...	38	...	5·3
	Noon	25·98	·04	33	...	...	...	...
	3 P.M.	·92	25·99	37	...	...	...	...
	6 ,,	·98	26·02	...	...	...	...	...
,, 14th ,,	9 A.M.	26·00	·05	26	...	38·5	...	10·5
	6 P.M.	25·93	25·98	...	...	...	...	...
,, 15th ,,	9 A.M.	·89	·95	20	...	37·5	...	7
	Noon	·86	·92	32	...	...	...	...
	3 P.M.	·80	·88	36	...	...	...	...
	6 ,,	·87	·90	...	...	...	...	...
,, 16th ,,	9 A.M.	·82	·88	19·5	...	37	...	6·5
	Noon	·78	·83	36·0	...	...	...	...
	3 P.M.	·74	·78	36·0	...	...	...	...
	6 ,,	·77	·80	...	...	...	...	...
,, 17th ,,	9 A.M.	·70	·76	23	...	38	...	11
	Noon	·67	·70	33	...	...	...	...
	3 P.M.	·66	·69	33	...	...	...	...
	6 ,,	·69	·72	...	...	...	...	...
,, 18th ,,	9 A.M.	·67	·74	23	...	35	...	11·5
	Noon	·67	·72	45·5	...	...	...	...
	3 P.M.	·65	·69	47·5	...	...	...	...
	6 ,,	·69	·73	...	...	...	...	...
,, 19th ,,	9 A.M.	·92	·99	...	...	50	30·5	7
	Noon	·92	·99	...	...	...	...	...
	3 P.M.	·89	·95	...	...	...	...	...
	6 ,,	·89	·95	...	...	...	...	...
,, 20th ,,	9 A.M.	·99	26·04	20	...	...	...	11
	Noon	·99	·05	36	...	...	...	...
	3 P.M.	·95	·01	32	...	...	...	...
	6 ,,	·97	·03	26·5	...	...	...	...
,, 21st ,,	9 A.M.	·93	·00	28	...	...	...	7·5
	Noon	·92	25·98	35	...	...	...	...
	3 P.M.	·89	·94	32	...	...	...	...
	6 ,,	·90	·95	27	...	...	...	...
	9 ,,	·94	·99	24	...	...	...	...
,, 22nd ,,	9 A.M.	·88	·94	25·5	...	29·5	...	8·5
	Noon	·84	·89	35	...	...	...	...
	3 P.M.	·80	·84	33	...	...	...	...
	6 ,,	·78	·82	26	...	...	...	...
,, 23rd ,,	9 P.M.	·63	·67	22	...	29	...	8·5
	Noon	·58	·60	31	...	...	...	...
	3 P.M.	·50	·54	28·5	...	...	...	...
	6 ,,	·52	·54	25·5	...	...	...	...
,, 24th ,,	9 A.M.	·72	·74	38	...	40	...	15
	Noon	·73	·75	44	...	...	...	...
	3 P.M.	·74	·76	38	...	...	...	...
	6 ,,	·80	·82	28·5	...	...	...	...
,, 25th ,,	9 A.M.	·87	·90	27	...	35	...	11·5
	3 P.M.	·78	·81	33	...	...	...	...
	6 ,,	·77	·80	26·5	...	...	...	...

the winter of 1873-74 *by Captain H. Trotter, R.E., and his Native Assistants.*

Boiling point Thermometer No. 17970, corrected for index error.	Boiling point Thermometer No. 17972, corrected for index error.	Boiling point Thermometer No. 17974, corrected for index error.	Boiling point Thermometer No. 17975, corrected for index error.	Direction of wind.	REMARKS.
Degrees.	*Degrees.*				
205·20	205·20	......	......	W.	At Kashghar the aneroid barometers and the thermometers (with the exception of the *minimum in open*) were placed in a covered porch, opening into a large court-yard and facing the east; they were completely protected from the direct rays of the sun.
......	......	......	......	W.	
205·07	205·07	......	......	S.	
......	......	......	......	W.	
205·17	205·15	......	......	W.	
......	......	......	......	E.	
205·07	205·05	......	......	N.E.	
......	......	......	......	N.	
205·12	205·10	205·07	205·07	W.	The *minimum in open* was placed on the surface of a table, raised three feet above the ground, and placed near the centre of the large court-yard.
......	......	......	......	E.	
205·02	205·00	205·02	205·02	W.	
......	......	......	......	W.	
204·87	204·85	204·77	204·77	S.W.	
......	......	......	......		The thermometers were all graduated on Fahrenheit's scale.
204·87	204·85	204·77	204·77	S.E.	
......	......	......	......	W.	
204·72	204·70	204·62	204·62	W.	
......	......	......	......	E.	
204·62	204·60	204·57	204·57	W.	
......	......	......	......	E.	
204·52	204·50	204·52	204·52	S.	
......	......	......	......	E.	
204·54	204·52	204·42	204·42	S.W.	
......	......	......	......	S.	
204·42	204·40	204·37	204·37	S.E.	
......	......	......	......	W.	
......	......	......	......	S.W.	
......	......	......	......	W.	
......	......	......	......	S.W.	
......	......	......	......	S.W.	
205·22	205·20	......	......	E.	
......	......	......	......	S.	
205·07	205·05	205·02	205·02	W.	
......	......	......	......	E.	
205·12	205·10	204·97	204·97	W.	
......	......	......	......	S.E.	
205·02	205·00	204·92	204·92	E.	
......	......	......	......	E.	
......	......	......	......	S.W.	
204·97	204·95	204·92	204·92	S.E.	
......	......	......	......	W.	
204·72	204·70	204·57	204·57	W.	
......	......	......	......	S.E.	
204·39	204·40	204·27	204·27	W.	
......	......	......	......	S.E.	
204·17	204·15	......	......	S.	
......	......	......	......	N.	
......	......	......	......	S.	
......	......	......	......	S.W.	
......	......	......	......	N.E.	
......	......	......	......	N.	
204·92	204·90	204·79	204·82	W.	
204·72	204·73	204·62	204·62	S.E.	
......	......	......	......	S.	

Meteorological Observations at KASHGHAR during the winter

Date.		Aneroid Barometer No. V., by Troughton and Simms, corrected for index error.	Aneroid Barometer by Dixey, corrected for index error.	Temperature of Air.		Maximum in Shade.	Minimum in Shade.	Minimum in Open.
				Dry bulb.	Wet bulb.	During preceding 24 hours.		
		Inches.	Inches.	Degrees.	Degrees.	Degrees.	Degrees.	Degrees.
Dec. 26th, 1873,	9 A.M.	25·74	25·77	23	...	29	...	7
	Noon	·75	·78	33	...	...	...	...
	3 P.M.	·72	·74	33	...	...	...	...
	6 ,,	·78	·80	26	...	...	...	...
,, 27th ,,	9 A.M.	·83	·86	22	...	30	...	10·5
	Noon	·78	·82	34·5	...	...	...	...
	3 P.M.	·73	·76	33	...	...	...	...
	6 ,,	·72	·76	32	...	...	...	...
,, 28th ,,	9 A.M.	·92	·97	23	...	30	...	2·5
	6 P.M.	·88	·94	26	...	...	...	...
,, 29th ,,	9 A.M.	·82	·88	24	...	29	...	0·0
	3 P.M.	·80	·85	30·5	...	...	...	...
	6 ,,	·88	·91	24·5	...	...	...	...
,, 30th ,,	9 A.M.	25·93	26·08	24	...	28·5	...	4·5
	Noon	·97	·02	29	...	...	...	...
	3 P.M.	·93	25·98	27	...	...	...	...
,, 31st ,,	9 A.M.	......	......	22·5	...	31·5	9·5	...
	Noon	......	......	30	...	...	...	...
	3 P.M.	......	......	26	...	...	...	...
	6 ,,	......	......	22	...	...	...	...

of 1873-74 by Captain H. Trotter, R.E., and his Native Assistants.—(Continued.)

Boiling point Thermometer No. 17970, corrected for index error.	Boiling point Thermometer No. 17972, corrected for index error.	Boiling point Thermometer No. 17974, corrected for index error.	Boiling point Thermometer No. 17975, corrected for index error.	Direction of wind.	Remarks.
Degrees.	Degrees.				
204·72	204·67	204·59	204·62	W.	
....	....	....	....	E.	*For the month of December* 1873.
204·64	204·62	204·57	204·57	S.W.	
....	....	....	....	S.E.	
....	....	....	....	W.	Mean of Aneroid Barometer No. V., by Troughton and Simms corrected for index error.
....	....	....	....	S.	
....	....	....	....	S.W.	
....	....	....	....	S.	
....	....	....	....	W.	
....	....	....	....	S.	Mean of Aneroid Barometer by Dixey corrected for index error.
....	....	....	....	N.	
....	....	....	....	S.E.	
....	....	....	....	E.	
....	....	....	....	N.	
....	....	....	....	N.W.	Mean of Dry Bulb Thermometer.
....	....	....	....	S.E.	
					Mean of Maximum Thermometer in shade ... 35·0
					Mean of Minimum in open ... ... 8·9
....	....	....	....	W.	
....	....	....	....	S.W.	
....	....	....	....	S.	
....	....	....	....	E.	

Mean of Aneroid Barometer No. V., by Troughton and Simms corrected for index error:

9 A.M.	Noon.	3 P.M.	6 P.M.
25·87	25·83	25·80	25·82

Mean of Aneroid Barometer by Dixey corrected for index error:

9 A.M.	Noon.	3 P.M.	6 P.M.
25·89	25·88	25·84	25·86

Mean of Dry Bulb Thermometer:

9 A.M.	Noon.	3 P.M.	6 P.M.
24·1	34·7	33·5	26·4

(406)

Meteorological Observations at KASHGHAR during the

Date.		Aneroid Barometer No. V., by Troughton and Simms, corrected for index error.	Aneroid Barometer by Dixey corrected for index error.	Temperature of air.		Maximum in shade.	Minimum in shade.	Minimum in open.
				Dry bulb.	Wet bulb.	During preceding 24 hours.		
		Inches.	Inches.	Degrees.	Degrees.	Degrees.	Degrees.	Degrees.
Jan. 1st, 1874,	9 A.M.	...	...	15·5	...	31·5	12·5	...
,, 8th ,,	9 A.M.	...	...	18	...	30·5	7·5	...
	Noon	...	...	26·5	...	...	...	...
	3 P.M.	...	...	24·5	...	...	...	...
	6 ,,	...	...	20	...	...	...	...
,, 9th ,,	9 A.M.	...	...	20	...	28·5	10	...
,, 10th ,,	9 A.M.	...	...	17·5	...	29	12·5	...
	Noon	...	...	26	...	...	...	...
	3 P.M.	...	...	25	...	...	...	...
	6 ,,	...	...	20	...	...	...	...
,, 11th ,,	9 A.M.	...	...	19	...	28·5	7·5	...
	Noon	...	...	24·5	...	...	...	...
	3 P.M.	...	...	24	...	...	...	...
	6 ,,	...	...	20·5	...	...	...	...
,, 12th ,,	9 A.M.	26·35	26·34	16·5	...	25	6	...
	Noon	·31	·30	28·5	...	...	...	...
	3 P.M.	·25	·22	26·0	...	...	...	...
,, 13th ,,	9 A.M.	·14	·13	18	...	24·5	5	...
	Noon	·08	·08	28	...	...	...	...
	3 P.M.	·06	·02	25·5	...	...	...	...
	6 ,,	·06	·02	21	...	...	...	...
,, 14th ,,	9 A.M.	·04	·00	20·5	...	28·5	7·5	...
	Noon	·01	25·97	29	...	...	...	...
	3 P.M.	25·97	·93	26·5	...	...	...	...
	6 ,,	26·01	·97	19	...	...	...	...
,, 15th ,,	9 A.M.	·08	26·07	20	...	29	7·5	...
	Noon	·05	·03	27·5	...	...	...	...
	3 P.M.	·03	·02	26·5	...	...	...	...
	6 ,,	·06	·05	19·5	...	...	...	...
,, 16th ,,	9 A.M.	·17	·17	23	...	28·5	5	...
	6 P.M.	·20	·20	21	...	...	...	...
,, 17th ,,	9 A.M.	·28	·29	25	...	30·5	6·5	−5·5
	Noon	·26	·27	28	...	...	...	...
,, 18th ,,	9 A.M.	·17	·18	23·5	...	31·5	10	+1·5
	Noon	·10	·12	31·5	...	...	...	...
	3 P.M.	·04	·05	29	...	...	...	...
	6 ,,	·05	·06	...	...	...	...	...
,, 19th ,,	9 A.M.	·00	·02	22·5	...	29·5	12	+2
,, 20th ,,	9 A.M.	25·99	·00	26·5	...	28	14·5	+5
	Noon	·97	25·97	36·5	...	...	...	...
	3 P.M.	·96	·96	33	...	...	...	...
	6 ,,	·96	·96	...	...	...	...	...
,, 21st ,,	9 A.M.	·87	·87	24	...	36	20	+10
	Noon	·82	·82	33	...	...	...	...
	3 P.M.	·77	·77	32	...	...	...	...
	6 ,,	·81	·81	27·7	...	...	...	...
,, 22nd ,,	9 A.M.	·83	·84	26·5	...	39·5	22·5	17
	Noon	·83	·84	36	...	...	...	...
	3 P.M.	·85	·86	34	...	...	...	...
	6 ,,	·86	·87	29	...	...	...	...
,, 23rd ,,	9 A.M.	·87	·88	23·5	...	36	19·5	...
,, 24th ,,	9 A.M.	26·01	26·01	33	...	35	21·5	16
	Noon	·00	·00	37·5	...	...	...	...
	6 ,,	·00	·00	...	...	...	...	...

winter of 1874-75, *by Captain H. Trotter, R.E., and his Native Assistants.*

Boiling point Thermometer No. 17450, corrected for index error.	Boiling point Thermometer No. 17972, corrected for index error.	Boiling point Thermometer No. 17974, corrected for index error.	Boiling point Thermometer No. 17975, corrected for index error.	Direction of wind.	REMARKS.
Degrees.	*Degrees.*				
……	……	……	……	S.W.	The break in the observations from 1st to 11th January caused by Captain Trotter's absence on the expedition to Chadyr-Kul.
……	……	……	……	N.E.	
……	……	……	……	S.	
……	……	……	……	N.	
……	……	……	……	N.W.	
……	……	……	……	S.	
……	……	……	……	N.	
……	……	……	……	S.	
……	……	……	……	S.W.	
……	……	……	……	W.	
……	……	……	……	N.	
……	……	……	……	N.E.	
……	……	……	……	W.	
……	……	……	……	S.	
……	……	……	……	S.	
……	……	……	……	W.	
……	……	……	……	E.	
……	……	……	……	N.W.	
……	……	……	……	S.	
……	……	……	……	S.	
……	……	……	……	S.	
……	……	……	……	N.E.	
……	……	……	……	S.W.	
……	……	……	……	S.E.	
……	……	……	……	S.	
……	……	……	……	S.W.	
……	……	……	……	S.W.	
……	……	……	……	S.E.	
……	……	……	……	S.W.	
……	……	……	……	S.W.	
……	……	……	……	W.	
……	……	……	……	S.E.	
……	……	……	……	N.E.	
……	……	……	……	W.	
……	……	……	……	S.W.	
……	……	……	……	S.	
……	……	……	……	S.E.	
……	……	……	……	S.W.	
……	……	……	……	W.	
……	……	……	……	S.	
……	……	……	……	S.W.	
……	……	……	……	N.	
……	……	……	……	W.	
204·57	204·55	204·57	204·62	S.W.	
……	……	……	……	S.E.	
……	……	……	……	W.	
……	……	……	……	S.W.	
……	……	……	……	E.	
……	……	……	……	N.E.	
……	……	……	……	S.	
……	……	……	……	N.	
……	……	……	……	W.	
……	……	……	……	S.W.	
……	……	……	……	W.	

(408)

Meteorological Observations at KASHGHAR during the winter of 1874-75,

Date.		Aneroid Barometer No. V., by Troughton and Simms, corrected for index error.	Aneroid Barometer by Dixey corrected for index error.	TEMPERATURE OF AIR.		MAXIMUM IN SHADE.	MINIMUM IN SHADE.	MINIMUM IN OPEN.
				Dry Bulb.	Wet Bulb.	During preceding 24 hours.		
		Inches.	Inches.	Degrees.	Degrees.	Degrees.	Degrees.	Degrees.
Jan. 25th, 1874,	9 A.M.	26·03	26·03	28	...	39	14·5	—5
	Noon	25·97	25·97	38·5	...	...	...	...
	6 P.M.	·92	·92	...	...	...	...	...
,, 26th ,,	9 A.M.	·93	·93	28	...	40·5	22	13
	Noon	·90	·90	35·5	...	...	...	...
	3 P.M.	·89	·89	35	...	...	...	...
	6 ,,	·92	·92	26	...	35	19·5	7·2
,, 27th ,,	9 A.M.	·99	·99	26·0	...	35	19·5	7·2
	Noon	·96	·96	34	...	...	...	...
	3 P.M.	·92	·93	35	...	...	...	...
	6 ,,	·93	·94	27	...	...	...	...
,, 28th ,,	9 A.M.	26·07	26·08	28·5	...	37·5	20	8·5
	3 P.M.	·04	·05	37	...	...	...	...
	6 ,,	·08	·08	...	...	...	...	...
,, 29th ,,	9 A.M.	·08	·10	32·5	...	42	22·5	14·5
	Noon	·02	·06	42	...	...	...	...
	3 P.M.	25·98	·02	38	...	...	...	...
	6 ,,	·98	·02	...	...	...	...	...
,, 30th ,,	9 A.M.	·96	·00	22	...	44	17·5	6·2
	Noon	·91	25·96	34·5	...	...	...	...
	3 P.M.	·90	·91	34·5	...	...	...	...
	6 ,,	·91	·92	...	...	...	...	...
,, 31st ,,	9 A.M.	·95	·98	29	...	37·5	17·5	6
	Noon	·91	·94	39	...	...	...	...
	6 P.M.	·89	·92	...	...	...	...	...

(409)

by Captain H. Trotter, R.E., and his Native Assistants.—(Continued.)

Boiling point Thermometer No. 17970, corrected values.	Boiling point Thermometer No. 17972, corrected values.	Boiling point Thermometer No. 17974, corrected values.	Boiling point Thermometer No. 17975, corrected values.	Direction of wind.	Remarks.				
Degrees.	Degrees.								
......	......	......	......	W.	*For the month of January 1874.*				
......	......	......	......	S.W.		9 A.M.	Noon.	3 P.M.	6 P.M.
......	......	......	......	N.					
......	......	......	......	N.E.					
......	......	......	......	N.E.	Mean of Aneroid Barometer No. V. by Troughton & Simms, corrected for index error.	26·04	26·01	25·97	25·98
......	......	......	......	S.E.					
......	......	......	......	S.					
......	......	......	......	N.W.					
......	......	......	......	W.					
......	......	......	......	S.					
......	......	......	......	...					
......	......	......	......	W.					
......	......	......	......	W.					
......	......	......	......	S.		9 A.M.	Noon.	3 P.M.	6 P.M.
......	......	......	......	S.E.					
......	......	......	......	E.					
......	......	......	......	W.	Mean of Aneroid Barometer by Dixey corrected for index error.	26·04	26·01	25·97	25·98
......	......	......	......	S.					
......	......	......	......	N.E.					
......	......	......	......	S.E.					
......	......	......	......	W.					
......	......	......	......	S.W.					
......	......	......	......	W.					
......	......	......	......	S.	Mean of Dry Bulb thermometer.	23·5	32·4	30·3	22·5
......	......	......	......	N.	Mean of minimum thermometer in shade.				13°·6
					Mean of maximum thermometer in shade.				33°·0
					Mean of minimum in open ...				7°·6

Meteorological Observations at KASHGHAR during the winter

Date.		Aneroid barometer No. V. by Troughton and Simms corrected for index error.	Aneroid barometer by Dixey corrected for index error.	Temperature of Air.		Maximum in Shade.	Minimum in Shade.	Minimum in Open.
				Dry Bulb.	Wet Bulb.	During preceding 24 hours.		
		Inches.	Inches.	Degrees.	Degrees.	Degrees.	Degrees.	Degrees.
Feb. 1st, 1874	9 A.M.	25·88	25·86	29	...	40·5	22	13·5
	Noon	·84	·82	38	...	...	...	...
	3 P.M.	·82	·79	35	...	...	...	...
	6 P.M.	·82	·78	...	...	...	...	...
,, 2nd ,,	9 A.M.	·82	·78	32·5	...	38·5	13·5	4
	Noon	·79	·75	38	...	...	...	...
	3 P.M.	·77	·73	38·5	...	...	...	...
	6 P.M.	·80	·77	...	...	...	...	...
,, 3rd ,,	9 A.M.	·89	·86	27·5	...	41·5	19·5	8
	Noon	·88	·85	40	...	...	...	...
	3 P.M.	·84	·80	37	...	...	...	...
	6 P.M.	·86	·82	...	...	...	...	...
,, 4th ,,	9 A.M.	·90	·86	35	...	42	19·7	9
	Noon	·86	·83	40·5	...	...	...	...
	3 P.M.	·83	·79	39	...	...	...	...
	6 P.M.	·84	·80	...	...	...	...	...
,, 5th ,,	9 A.M.	·86	·82	31	...	42	23	15
	Noon	·85	·81	41	...	...	...	...
	3 P.M.	·82	·78	40	...	...	...	...
	6 P.M.	·85	·81	...	...	...	...	...
,, 6th ,,	9 A.M.	·84	·83	32·5	...	41·5	20·5	11
	Noon	·79	·78	43·5	...	...	...	...
	3 P.M.	·76	·73	40·5	...	...	...	...
	6 P.M.	·80	·77	32	...	...	...	...
,, 7th ,,	9 A.M.	·84	·81	37	...	47·5	19·7	6·5
	Noon	·83	·80	45	...	...	...	...
	3 P.M.	·76	·75	40	...	...	...	...
	6 P.M.	·77	·76	31	...	...	...	...
,, 8th ,,	9 A.M.	·72	·73	29·5	...	44·5	20	10
	Noon	·67	·66	28	...	...	...	...
	3 P.M.	·58	·58	39	...	...	...	...
,, 9th ,,	9 A.M.	·61	·59	33·5	...	40·5	28·5	19·5
	Noon	·60	·58	39	...	...	...	...
	3 P.M.	·58	·57	39	...	...	...	...
	6 P.M.	·60	·59	34	...	...	...	...
,, 10th ,,	9 A.M.	·81	·81	39·5	...	41·5	29	24
	Noon	·83	·83	37	...	...	...	...
	3 P.M.	·81	·81	39	...	...	...	...
,, 11th ,,	9 A.M.	·80	·82	31·5	...	43·5	28·5	24·5
	Noon	·79	·79	38	...	...	...	...
	3 P.M.	·75	·76	40	...	...	...	...
	6 P.M.	·80	·81	31	...	...	...	...
,, 12th ,,	9 A.M.	·79	·82	33·5	...	46	24	15·5
	Noon	·78	·79	38·5	...	...	...	...
	3 P.M.	·76	·77	36	...	...	...	...
	6 P.M.	·76	·77	30	...	...	...	...
,, 13th ,,	9 A.M.	·83	·86	29·5	...	39·5	12·5	2
	Noon	·85	·88	36·5	...	...	...	...
	3 P.M.	·83	·84	35·5	...	...	...	...
	6 P.M.	·86	·87	31	...	...	...	...
,, 14th ,,	9 A.M.	·90	·93	30	...	38·5	21·5	12·5
	Noon	......	·89	39·5	...	...	...	...
	3 P.M.	......	·82	38	...	...	...	...

of 1874-75 by Captain H. Trotter, R. E.—(Continued.)

Boiling point thermometer No. 17970 corrected values.	Boiling point thermometer No. 17972 corrected values.	Boiling point thermometer No. 17974.	Boiling point thermometer No. 17975.	Direction of wind.	REMARKS.
Degrees.	Degrees.				
......	......	......	......	W.	
......	......	......	......	N.E.	
......	......	......	......	S.E.	
......	......	......	......	S.E.	
......	......	......	......	W.	
......	......	......	......	S.W.	
......	......	......	......	W.	
......	......	......	......	N.W.	
......	......	......	......	N.W.	
......	......	......	......	N.E.	
......	......	......	......	N.	
......	......	......	......	S.	
......	......	......	......	W.	
......	......	......	......	N.E.	
......	......	......	......	W.	
......	......	......	......	N.	
......	......	......	......	N.W.	
......	......	......	......	S.	
......	......	......	......	E.	
......	......	......	......	S.	
......	......	......	......	S.W.	
......	......	......	......	S.E.	
......	......	......	......	S.W.	
......	......	......	......	S.	
......	......	......	......	N.E.	
......	......	......	......	S.E.	
......	......	......	......	S.E.	
......	......	......	......	S.E.	
......	......	......	......	S.W.	
......	......	......	......	E.	
......	......	......	......	E.	
......	......	......	......	S.W.	
......	......	......	......	S.	
......	......	......	......	S.E.	
......	......	......	......	S.	
......	......	......	......	N.E.	
......	......	......	......	E.	
......	......	......	......	E.	
......	......	......	......	N.W.	
......	......	......	......	N.E.	
......	......	......	......	N.E.	
......	......	......	......	N.	
......	......	......	......	W.	
......	......	......	......	N.W.	
......	......	......	......	W.	
......	......	......	......	N.W.	
......	......	......	......	N.W.	
......	......	......	......	N.E.	
......	......	......	......	N.	
......	......	......	......	N.W.	
......	......	......	......	W.	The break in the readings of aneroid No. V. caused by Captain Trotter's absence in the Artysh Districts.
......	......	......	......	N.W.	
......	......	......	......	W.	

(412)

Meteorological Observations at KASHGHAR during the winter of

Date.		Aneroid barometer No. V., by Troughton and Simms corrected for index error.	Aneroid barometer by Dixey corrected for index error.	Temperature of Air.		Maximum in Shade.	Minimum in Shade.	Minimum in Open.
				Dry Bulb.	Wet Bulb.	During preceding 24 hours.		
		Inches.	Inches.	Degrees.	Degrees.	Degrees.	Degrees.	Degrees.
Feb. 15th, 1874	9 A.M.	......	25·94	31	...	42·8	25	12·5
	Noon	......	·90	42	28	...	...	...
	3 P.M.	......	·88	41	30	...	...	...
,, 16th ,,	9 A.M.	......	·95	37	33	44	23	17
	Noon	......	·91	41	33	...	...	...
	3 P.M.	......	·87	39·5	33·5	...	...	...
,, 17th ,,	9 A.M.	......	·80	34	32	42	27	15·5
	Noon	......	·79	42	33	...	...	...
	3 P.M.	......	·77	42·5	34	...	...	...
,, 18th ,,	9 A.M.	......	·99	41	32·5	44	23·5	21·5
	Noon	......	·96	45	35·6	...	...	...
	3 P.M.	......	·94	40	35	...	...	...
,, 19th ,,	9 A.M.	......	26·10	32·5	29	36·5	20	15
	Noon	......	·08	33	32	...	...	...
	3 P.M.	......	·03	31·5	32	...	...	...
,, 20th ,,	9 A.M.	......	25·98	41	31	42	22	19
	Noon	......	·93	43	32	...	...	...
	3 P.M.	......	·87	39	32	...	...	...
,, 21st ,,	9 A.M.	......	·96	32·5	29	44	22·5	14
	Noon	......	·92	42	32	...	...	...
	3 P.M.	......	·91	40	32	...	...	...
,, 22nd ,,	9 A.M.	......	26·08	31	34	42	30	12
	Noon	......	·04	34·5	32	...	...	...
	3 P.M.	......	·00	32	32	...	...	...
,, 23rd ,,	9 A.M.	......	·06	32·5	31	36	29	14
	Noon	......	·04	40	32·6	...	...	...
,, 24th ,,	9 A.M.	......	25·93	39	31	42	20	20·5
	Noon	......	·86	39·6	32·8	...	...	...
	3 P.M.	......	·84	36	32	...	...	...
,, 25th ,,	9 A.M.	......	·74	45	33	45	26	21
	Noon	......	·69	40	32	...	...	...
	3 P.M.	......	·64	32	32	...	...	...
,, 26th ,,	9 A.M.	......	·69	44	33	45	28	22
	Noon	......	·68	48	35	...	...	...
	3 P.M.	......	·67	40	36	...	...	...
,, 27th ,,	9 A.M.	......	·90	42·5	35	48	31	19
	Noon	......	·91	41	36	...	...	...
	3 P.M.	......	·89	40	36	...	...	...
,, 28th ,,	9 A.M.	......	·94	41	32	48·5	28	22
	Noon	......	·94	49	36·2	...	...	...
	3 P.M.	......	·87	45·8	35·5	...	...	...

(413)

1873-74, *by Captain H. Trotter, R.E., and his Assistants.*—(Continued.)

Boiling point thermometer No. 17970 corrected values.	Boiling point thermometer No. 17972 corrected values.	Boiling point thermometer No. 17974.	Boiling point thermometer No. 17975.	Direction of wind.	Remarks.
Degrees.	*Degrees.*				
......	......	......	......	E.	
......	......	......	......	E.S.	
......	......	......	......	W.	
......	......	......	......	W.	
......	......	......	......	N.E.	
......	......	......	......	N.	
......	......	......	......	N.E.	
......	......	......	......	W.S.	
......	......	......	......	N.E.	
......	......	......	......	S.W.	
......	......	......	......	N.W.	
......	......	......	......	S.W.	
......	......	......	......	S.W.	
......	......	......	......	E.	
......	......	......	......	S.W.	
......	......	......	......	S.	
......	......	......	......	S.	
......	......	......	......	S.E.	
......	......	......	......	S.	
......	......	......	......	E.	
......	......	......	......	S.W.	
......	......	......	......	N.E.	Slight fall of snow.
......	......	......	......	N.E.	
......	......	......	......	E.	
......	......	......	......	N.	
......	......	......	......	N.W.	
......	......	......	......	N.S.	
......	......	......	......	N.S.	
......	......	......	......	N.	
......	......	......	......	N.E.	
......	......	......	......	E.	
......	......	......	......	N.	
......	......	......	......	N.E.	
......	......	......	......	S.E.	
......	......	......	......	S.	
......	......	......	......	N.S.	
......	......	......	......	S.	

For the month of February 1874.

	9 A.M.	Noon.	3 P.M.	6 P.M.
Mean of Aneroid Barometer No. V. by Troughton and Simms	25·83	25·80	25·78	25·79
Mean of Aneroid Barometer by Dixey	25·87	25·84	25·81	25·78
Mean of Dry Bulb Thermometer	34·8	40·4	38·4	31·5
Mean of Wet Bulb Thermometer	31·9	32·8	33·2	
Mean of Minimum Thermometer in shade				23°·5
Mean of Maximum Thermometer in shade				42°·5
Mean of Minimum in open				15°·0

(414)

Meteorological Observations at KASHGHAR during the winter of 1874-75.

Date.		Aneroid barometer No. V. by Troughton and Simms corrected for index error.	Aneroid barometer by Carpenter, Westley, and Dixey corrected for index error.	Temperature of Air.		Maximum in Shade.	Minimum in Shade.	Minimum in Open.
				Dry Bulb.	Wet Bulb.	During preceding 24 hours.		
		Inches.	Inches.	Degrees.	Degrees.	Degrees.	Degrees.	Degrees.
Mar. 1st, 1874,	9 A.M.	......	25·91	49	39	49	27	20
	Noon	......	·86	51	38	...	...	...
	3 P.M.	......	·84	47	36	...	...	...
„ 2nd „	9 A.M.	......	·55	45·5	39	51·5	28	27
	Noon	......	·51	53·6	40	...	...	...
	3 P.M.	......	·44	51	41	...	...	...
„ 3rd „	9 A.M.	......	·50	40	36	55	32	21·5
	Noon	......	·49	42	38	...	...	...
	3 P.M.	......	·50	44	39	...	...	...
„ 4th „	9 A.M.	......	·74	43	40	47	36	24
	Noon	......	·71	48·5	39	...	...	...
	3 P.M.	......	·69	49·5	41	...	...	...
„ 5th „	9 A.M.	25·79	·79	43	39	50·5	37	24
	Noon	·74	·73	50	40	...	...	...
	3 P.M.	·72	·70	48·3	41	...	...	...
„ 6th „	9 A.M.	·82	·80	38·5	36	52	31	20
	Noon	·82	·78	49	41	...	...	...
	3 P.M.	·73	·73	45·5	40	...	...	...
„ 7th „	9 A.M.	·72	·73	41·2	38	54·5	37·5	...
	3 P.M.	·60	·58	45	39	...	...	...
„ 8th „	9 A.M.	·55	·54	34·5	33	48·5	34·0	28·0
	Noon	·53	·52	37·5	36	...	...	...
	3 P.M.	·51	·50	40·5	36	...	...	...
	6 P.M.	·55	·54	38	36	...	...	...
„ 9th „	9 A.M.	·63	·63	35	32·5	42	33·5	27·5
	Noon	·63	·62	40	35	...	...	...
	3 P.M.	·62	·61	44	37	...	...	...
	6 P.M.	·67	·66	37·5	34	...	...	...
„ 10th „	9 A.M.	·80	·80	43·5	36·5	44·5	27·5	22·0
	Noon	·82	·83	47	36	...	...	...
	6 P.M.	·87	·88	39·5	36	...	...	...
„ 11th „	9 A.M.	26·08	26·09	44	39	48·5	26·5	17·0
„ 12th „	9 A.M.	·12	·15	32·5	30	50	29	25
	Noon	·12	·15	39	35	...	...	...
	3 P.M.	·08	·10	40	36	...	...	...
	6 P.M.	·07	·08	37·5	36	...	...	...
„ 13th „	9 A.M.	·03	·05	39	35·5	47	30·5	26
	Noon	25·98	·00	44	38	...	...	...
	3 P.M.	·97	25·99	40	38	...	...	...
	6 P.M.	·97	·99	36·5	36	...	...	...
„ 14th „	9 A.M.	26·09	26·11	37·5	36	45	33·5	27·5
	Noon	·07	·08	46	40	...	...	...
	3 P.M.	·02	·04	41	39·5	...	...	...
	6 P.M.	·06	·08	39	37·5	...	...	...
„ 15th „	9 A.M.	·16	·19	34·5	32	47	31·5	27·5
	Noon	·15	·19	40·5	35	...	...	...
	6 P.M.	·14	·17	37·5	34·5	...	...	...
„ 16th „	9 A.M.	·20	·24	34	30	44	31·5	27
	Noon	·17	·19	41	34	...	...	...
	3 P.M.	·11	·12	44	34	...	...	...
	6 P.M.	·07	·08	38·5	35	...	...	...

by Captain H. Trotter, R.E., and his Native Assistants.—(Concluded.)

Boiling point thermometer No. 17970 corrected values.	Boiling point thermometer No. 17972 corrected values.	Boiling point thermometer No. 17974.	Boiling point thermometer No. 17975.	Direction of wind.	REMARKS.
Degrees.	Degrees.				
......	......	......	......	S.	*For the month of March* 1874.
......	......	......	......	N.	
......	......	......	......	S.	Mean of Aneroid
......	......	......	......	N.	Barometer No. 9 A.M. Noon. 3 P.M. 6 P.M.
......	......	......	......	S.	V. by Troughton
......	......	......	......	N.E.	and Simms ... 25·92 25·90 25·82 25·93
......	......	......	......	N.	Mean of Aneroid
......	......	......	......	N.	Barometer by
......	......	......	......	S.	Dixey and Car-
......	......	......	......	N.E.	penter and
......	......	......	......	N.	Westley ... 25·80 25·78 25·72
......	......	......	......	S.	Mean of Dry Bulb
......	......	......	......	S.	Thermometer... 39·7 44·9 44·6 38·0
......	......	......	......	N.	Mean of Wet Bulb
......	......	......	......	N.	Thermometer... 35·7 37·5 38·3 35·6
......	......	......	......	S.E.	Mean of minimum thermometer ... 31°·6
......	......	......	......	S.	Mean of maximum do. in shade 48°·5
......	......	......	......	N.	Mean of minimum rod in open ... 24°·9
......	......	......	......	NW.	
......	......	......	......	S.	
......	......	......	......	N.E.	
......	......	......	......	N.E.	Snow falling.
......	......	......	......	S.E.	
......	......	......	......	S.	
......	......	......	......	N.E.	Snow at night.
......	......	......	......	N.E.	
......	......	......	......	N.	
......	......	......	......	N.	
......	......	......	......	N.W.	
......	......	......	......	N.W.	
......	......	......	......	N.W.	
......	......	......	......	S.W.	
......	......	......	......	N.	
......	......	......	......	N.	
......	......	......	......	N.W.	Heavy fall of snow during night of about
......	......	......	......	N.W.	five inches.
......	......	......	......	N.W.	
......	......	......	......	N.W.	
......	......	......	......	N.W.	
......	......	......	......	N.	
......	......	......	......	N.	
......	......	......	......	N.W.	
205·25	205·25	......	......	N.W.	
......	......	......	......	N.E.	Fall of snow during night.
......	......	......	......	N.E.	
......	......	......	......	N.E.	
......	......	......	......	N.E.	
......	......	......	......	N.E.	
......	......	......	......	N.E.	
......	......	......	......	N.E.	

GEOGRAPHICAL APPENDIX.

SECTION G.

ROUTES.

GEOGRAPHICAL APPENDIX.
SECTION G.—ROUTES.
INDEX.

PART I.—*Routes traversed by members and employés of the Mission.*

Number of Route.	From.	To.	Remarks.	Authority.
I.	Yárkand	Leh (Ladakh)	*Viâ* Sánjú and Karakorum Pass.	Dr. Bellew.
II.	Ditto	Leh	*Viâ* Kugiar and Karakorum Pass.	Ditto.
III.	Leh	Shahidúlá (No. 12 of Route I.)	*Viâ* Changchenmo	Captain Biddulph.
IIIa.	Gogra	Ditto	Variation on No. III.	,, Trotter.
IV.	Yárkand	Káshghar	......	,, ,,
V.	Káshghar	Maralbáshi	......	,, Biddulph.
VI.	Ditto	Chadyr Kul	......	,, Trotter.
VII.	Ditto	Belowti Pass	On road to Ush Turfán.	,, ,,
VIII.	Yangi Hissar (No. 3 of Route IV.)	Kila Panjah (Wakhan)	*Viâ* Tashkúrghán and Little Pámír.	,, Biddulph.
IX.	Kila Panjah	Aktásh (No. 11 of Route VIII.)	*Viâ* Great Pámír.	,,
X.	Táshkúrghán (No. 9 of Route VIII.)	Yárkand	*Viâ* Charling River	,, Trotter (from Pundit Kishen Sing).
XI.	Kila Panjah	Kila Wámur (Roshan)	......	,, Trotter (from Abdul Subhan).
XII.	Yárkand	Aksú	*Viâ* Maralbáshi	,, Chapman (from Bhao Sing).
XIII.	Aksú	Kuchár	......	,, ditto.
XIV.	Karghálik (No. 2 of Route I.)	Tanksé (No. 5 of Route III.)	*Viâ* Khotan, Keria, and Polu, *vide*	,, Trotter (from Kishen Sing).
XIVa.*	Yárkand	Khotan	*Viâ* Karghálik	,, Chapman (from Ramchand).

PART II.—*Routes in Turkestan derived from verbal information supplied by natives.*

Number of Route.	From.	To.	Remarks.	Authority.	
XV.	Kuchár (Route XIII.)	Káráshahr	......	Compiled by Captain Trotter.	
XVI.	Kuchár	Túrfán	......	Ditto	ditto.
XVII.	Túrfán	Kámul, Khámil, or Hámi.	......	Ditto	Dr. Bellew.
XVIIa.	Túrfán	Orúmchí or Orumtsi	......	Ditto	ditto.
XVIII.	Urúmtsí or Orúmchí	Manás	......	Ditto	ditto.
XIX.	Manas	Yulduz	......	Ditto	ditto.
XX.	Yulduz	Ghúljá, or Kuldjá, or Ili.	......	Ditto	ditto.
XXI.	Kurla (No. 8 of Route XV.)	Lob	......	Ditto	ditto.
XXII.	Káráshahr (Route XV.)	Yuldúz Valley	......	Ditto	ditto.
XXIII.	Khotan (Route XIV.)	Aksú (Route XII.)	......	Ditto	Captain Chapman.
XXIV.	Khotan	Polu (No. 14 of Route XIV.)	......	Ditto	ditto.

* This itinerary includes some notes on Khotan, compiled by Captain Chapman.—H. T.

PART II.—*Routes in Turkestan derived from verbal information supplied by natives.*

Number of Route.	From.	To.	Remarks.	Authority.
XXV.	Khotan	Charchand	……	Compiled by Captain Trotter.
XXVI.	Kila Wamur (Roshan), Route XI.	Kila Khumb (Darwaz)	……	Ditto ditto (from Abdul Subhan.)
XXVII.	Bar Panjah (Shighnan), No. 10 of Route XI.	Káshghar (Route IV.)	……	Ditto ditto.
XXVIII.	Bughrumal Pamir (No. 4 of Route XXVII.)	Khokand	……	Ditto ditto.
XXIX.	Yúr (near Kila Panjah Route VIII.)	Chitrál	……	Ditto Captain Biddulph.
XXX.	Táshkúrghan (No. 9 of Route VIII.)	Hanza (Kanjud)	……	Ditto Dr. Bellew.
XXXI.	Sarhadd (No. 14 of Route VIII.)	Kanjud	……	Ditto ditto.
XXXII.	Yárkand	Shahidúla	*Viâ* Kilik Pass	Ditto Captain Trotter.

GEOGRAPHICAL APPENDIX.

SECTION G.

ROUTES TRAVERSED BY MEMBERS AND EMPLOYÉS OF THE MISSION.

ROUTE I.

YÁRKAND TO LEH *viâ* SÁNJÚ AND KARAKORAM PASS (DR. BELLEW, OCTOBER AND NOVEMBER 1873).

1. Yárkand to Posgám (height* 4,210 feet), 17 miles.—Across a cultivated plain covered thickly with farmsteads and traversed by numerous irrigation streams. Trees along the water-courses, and orchards round the farmsteads. Cultivation interrupted by meadows and marshes. At three miles from Posgám cross the Zarafshán river, which flows in two channels separated by patches of tamarisk jangal. Ford across a firm pebbly bed between low sandy banks four to five hundred yards apart. Posgám is a market town of about 600 houses. Called also Chársbamba Bázár.

2. Kárghalik (height 4,370 feet), 24 miles.—Cultivated plain, farmsteads and fields, with marshes and jangal patches between. At eight miles cross Tiznáf river. Ford firm and pebbly between low sandy banks 80 to 100 yards apart. At five miles on pass through Yakshamba Bazar, 300 houses. Then across thin cultivation between patches of saline encrustation, marsh, and waste to Kárghalik, 1,000 houses. A market town with widespread farmsteads. Many trees and many water-courses.

3. Borá (height 5,340 feet), 25 miles.—Soon pass beyond cultivation across a stony desert waste six miles to Besharik, or "five streams," a populous settlement of farms on the water-courses in a wide hollow running from west to east. Then cross an arid and wide waste of coarse gravel to another hollow, deeper and narrower. In this is the settlement of Borá, 30 to 40 homesteads on the course of the stream from which the cultivation is irrigated. Trees in plenty.

4. Oi-toghrák (height 5,760 feet), 12 miles.—Across an arid desert of undulating surface, coarse gravel, and wind blown ridges of sand, very scanty herbal vegetation, to a deep and winding drainage gully in which, on course of its stream, is the Oi-toghrák settlement of 15 to 20 farmsteads. Trees few.

5. Khushtagh, 19 miles.—Across an arid, undulating desert waste of sandy gravel for 18 miles; then cross a wide boulder strewn hollow with thin tamarisk jangal, and pass through a belt of tall reeds to Khushtagh settlement in a wide hollow. Farmsteads for some miles along the course of the Kilián stream which flows eastward to Gúmá.

6. Sánjú (height 6,070 feet), 25 miles.—Cross arid strip of desert as before, eight miles to a dry ravine in which are four or five farmsteads watered from springs; this is Langar, and here is a roadside rest-house and tank of water under the shade of tall poplars. From this up a steep bank and across a ridgy desert as before for 16 miles to the Sánjú valley down a steep sandy slope. The road to Gúmá branches off north-east on this desert. Sánjú is a populous settlement along the course of a river which flows towards Khotan, and is forded on a rough boulder bed. Farmsteads, orchards, and fields here extend in unbroken succession for eight or ten miles along the river.

7. Kiwaz, 13½ miles.—Pass through Sánjú settlement five or six miles to high banks of gravel and red sand; then up a narrowing valley along the Sirikia river, which runs in three or four streams and is crossed twice *en route* on a boulder bottom, to Kiwaz; six or eight scattered huts on a limited flat amongst hills.

---

* The heights throughout these routes are supplied by Captain Trotter.

8. Tám (height 8,790 feet), 16½ miles.—Up course of Sirigkya river, through a gradually narrowing valley which winds between high and bare hills of schistose slate. River crossed repeatedly *en route* on a stony bed. Banks fringed with bushes and patches of pasture grass. At 11 miles pass the Chúchú glen to the left; a narrow defile which conducts over the Chúchú ridge to Shahídula, and is taken as an alternative route when the river is unfordable during the summer floods. At Tám two houses on a small flat leave habitation behind.

9. Gachga, 10 miles.—Up narrow winding valley, and cross river repeatedly as in last stage. No cultivation or habitation. Kirghiz camps in glens and hollows in the vicinity.

10. Kichik Karákoram, 14 miles.—Up by a rapid rise through a widening and branching defile to foot of Sanjú Dawán, a sharp ridge of mica slate 16,650 feet high. Then up a steep zigzag, through a narrow and rough gap, and down another on opposite side into a very narrow, deep, rough gorge descending to Kichik Karákoram; a narrow strip of turf on a trickling stream between lofty vertical cliffs. No fuel nor pasture.

11. Pillátághách, 11½ miles.—Descend narrow, winding, dismal gorge over masses of landslip rock, down course of rivulet for four miles. Then enter valley of Karákásh river at Mírzá Abábakar camp ground at a cluster of graves on the river bank. Then follow up stream six miles by a very rough road, fording river twice *en route* to Pillátághách camp ground on a limited flat of brushwood and pasture on the river bank. Valley very narrow; hills high and bare.

12. Shahídula Khoja (height 11,780 feet), 15 miles.—Up stream by rough road in winding valley with brushwood and forage along river course; their patches interrupted by projecting moraine banks. At four miles cross Kilyán stream from the right to Korghán, a solitary mud castle at foot of a rock abutting on the river bank. At five miles on cross Toghrá stream from the right, then cross Karákásh river three times *en route* to the Fort of Shahídula Khoja, garrison 30 men; frontier post of Káshghar at the junction of the Kizil jangal glen with Karákásh valley. Fuel and forage here, and Kirghiz camps around.

13. Sugat (height 12,970 feet), 8 miles.—Up course of Karákásh river four miles. Then up course of the Sugat river to the right four miles, and, crossing several times, camp on turfy flat on right bank. Hills on left bank steep down to the river; on right bank rolling away in wide slopes to high mountains; everywhere bare schistose slate, and trap. Vegetation confined to river course.

14. Chibra, 21 miles.—Rise out of river channel and pass across wide slopes of hill to a narrow defile coming down from the left. Then up its course between bare banks of shale through a tortuous channel to foot of Sugat Pass, 17,600 feet high. Ascend by a steep path, and follow a gradual slope six miles down to camp ground at Chibra. No vegetation here. Water very scanty. Snow on Pass from September to April as on Sánjú Pass.

15. Aktágh (height 15,590 feet), 10 miles.—Over an elevated, arid, stony plateau, perfectly desert, by a path skirting banks of shale to the right. Breathing oppressed on the march. At ten miles turn slowly to right and slope down to Aktágh camping ground on a patch of turf in the wide, shallow, shingly bed of its stream. The whole region bleak, desolate, and inhospitable waste. From this down stream is the Yangi Diwán and Kugiár route to Yárkand.

16. Brangsa Karákoram, 28 miles.—Up a wide, shallow, shingly drainage bed gradually ascending between low banks of shale that roll away in wide sweeps to the mountain top. Vegetation most scanty in herbal tufts. A few antelopes met with. At half-way pass camp ground of Wahábjilga, where the Aktágh stream flows through a cutting in slate rocks. Then continue over the drainage bed to the Brangsa camp ground at the entrance of a narrow defile. No fuel and no forage in all this region. This Brangsa is also called Bálti Brangsa.

17. Daulatbeg Uldí (height 16,880 feet), 22 miles.—Through a narrow gorge up course of a little torrent for a mile; then enter a wide gully branching off amongst the hills. Soil soft and spongy, slate detritus. Rise gradually to foot of Karákoram Pass, 18,550 feet high, then up a short ascent and down a steep descent over soft clay to a hill slope along the course of a rivûlet, and cross it several times *en route* to camp. The pass is half-way on this march. Breathing affected by the elevation on this wide plateau. Surface bare gravel and clay. From Daulatbeg there are two routes towards Ladakh. One by Kúmdán, the other by Dipsang, and both meet at the Sháyok River opposite Brangsa Saser. The first is only practicable in winter, and is traversed in three stages, *viz.*—(1.) Across an undulating ravine cut plateau to Gyapshan on the upper course of the Sháyok, 15 miles. (2.) Down the bed of the stream in and out of the water repeatedly, and through a narrow straight where the river bed is very nearly blocked by a vast glacier which has slid down across it, on to a bank of loose pebbles and shingle at the foot of a lofty vertical cliff like a wall. This is Kúmdán, nine miles. (3.) Brangsa Saser. Down the river course, and through another very narrow and winding straight between a great glacier and the opposite cliffs and then down a wide river channel to camp. The passage of the straight is done on the ice or through the stream where it is broken. A difficult road under any conditions. The second and usual route is the following in continuation from Daulatbeg Uldí.

18. Kizil Langar, 20 miles.—Over the Daulatbeg plateau, across a shallow stream in a wide deep gully with muddy soft bottom in which cattle stick, and rise up to the Dipsang plain; wide undulating plateau from which the world around subsides, the highest hill tops only peering above the horizon. Soil soft and spongy, gravel and clay mixed, and, where water logged, boggy. No vegetation. Approximate altitude 17,800 feet. Breathing distressed. From this descend a steep and stony gully into a very narrow, tortuous gorge between high cliffs of red clay; and travelling along in and down its torrent half a mile, enter a wider river bed of rolled pebbles over which the stream flows in a net-work of channels. Rocks roll from the hill tops on either side into the channel. Camp at Kizil Langar, where this channel joins a wider one from the north-west. There is no fuel or forage in all this region.

19. Murghi (height 15,190 feet), 16 miles.—Route down a net-work of shallow streams on a loose pebbly bottom, crossing them continually. At four miles pass Borsa camping ground on a gravelly talus shelving to the stream bed. At a mile beyond quit river, and pass over projecting bluffs, and again meet it as a raging torrent rolling over great boulders in a tight, winding gorge, and crossing from side to side by narrow fords camp at Murghi on turfy ground, where a gully from the west joins. Road very narrow and difficult, and risk from stone avalanches.

20. Brangsa Saser, 10 miles.—Up the dry, stony gully to the west. At two miles pass Chungtásh, "Great Rock," camp ground at a great erratic boulder on a turfy flat. Then descend rapidly into a deep, dark gully and follow down its winding course till it opens into the Sháyok River; pass up its stream a mile and ford opposite Brangsa.

21. Tútyálák, 15 miles.—Up a rough gully and across a glacier at its water-shed for two or three miles. Then up and down by an extremely difficult path between the side of a vast glacier and the opposite hills, a narrow pass full of angular rocks and snow drifts, and in summer purling with torrents on all sides. At half-way pass Sartang camp ground, an open space menaced by half a dozen glaciers around. Beyond, pass along a widening valley over stretches of turf fringing the stream and sloping up the hill sides, and at a glacier projecting from a valley to the west descend into the bed of the stream flowing from it, and camp on a gravelly flat close under the glacier. Fuel scanty; pasture in plenty here. An extremely difficult march.

22. Changlung (height 10,760 feet), 11 miles.—Down left bank of river amidst granite rocks for three miles. Then cross river by a wood bridge, and pass along a steep hill slope of loose gravel and sand above the river course and rise quickly up to the Lamsa crest at eight miles on. From this descent to the secondary ridge of Karáwal Dawan,

and look down on the Nubra valley, the first green spot and inhabited country since leaving Sánjú. Drop down to it by a very steep zigzag path and camp at Changlang, a small cluster of eight or ten Tatar huts with fields around.

23. Panámik, 11 miles.—Down the valley over two long strips of gravel talus cut by the deep boulder bed of the Tútyálák River, where it joins the Nubra stream, and is crossed by timber bridge. Then along patches of turf and brushwood jangal of buckthorn, tamarisk, myricaria, and rose to the cultivation and village of Panámik—to comfort and supplies.

24. Tagar, 13 miles.—Down the left bank of the river as in last stage. Midway cross rocky ridge abutting on the stream, with the populous village of Chirása on the opposite bank.

25. Sati, 15 miles.—Down the river course, as in last stage passing villages and cultivation to its junction with the Sháyok River. Then up the right bank of the latter to Sati, passing villages and cultivation with patches of brushwood and pasture between on the way. From Sati there are two routes to Leh. First, the direct route by the Khardung Pass. Second, the river route by the Digar Pass. The first is in three stages, viz.— (1.) Cross the Sháyok by ford or boat according to the season, and pass up the narrow defile of Rong, crossing its torrent several times, four miles; then rise up to a high cultivated plateau, and at three miles more camp at Khardung village. (2.) Polú, 1 miles. Up the course of a mountain torrent, cross a tributary from the right, and pass over moraine banks to an upland turfy slope. Continue up its winding and narrowing course to the foot of the Pass. Then pass a pool and glacier, and rise over latter by very steep ascent to the crest of the Khardung Pass, nearly 18,000 feet high, and descend by a very stony, steep zigzag to Polú camp ground on a turfy flat, cut by a rivulet coming down from a glacier at the head of a glen to the right. (3.) Leh, miles. Down a winding gully, and over moraine banks, the road gradually improving to the cultivation of Leh, and then to the town itself. This is a very difficult route. The other continues down the river from Sati.

26. Digar (height 13,080 feet), 17 miles.—Cross river, and then up its left bank for 1 miles. Then rise out of river bed up to a high flat talus of bare clay and gravel. Cross it and pass round a hill spur, and ascend to fields and houses of Digar in an amphitheatre of granite hills.

27. Polú Digar, 14 miles.—Up a rising moorland amongst granite boulders and across peat beds and bogs for five miles to Polú camp ground on a spur where the ascent increases. Then up a long stony slope covered with snow patches at end of June, and rise suddenly to crest of Digar Pass, 17,900 feet high. Pass through a narrow gap, and drop by a very steep and rough path to the other side; follow a winding, turfy glen and camp at Polú huts near a thin rivulet. Some pasture here; but no fuel. Pass very difficult.

28. Leh (height 11,538 feet) or Ladákh, 10 miles.—Down the glen, across its stream, cultivation and homesteads of Sabú, and then up the valley to Leh.

ROUTE II.

YÁRKAND TO LADÁKH *via* KUGIÁR. (AUTHORITY, DR. BELLEW, JUNE 1874.

1. Yárkand to Yangichik, 12 miles.—Across a populous and cultivated plain well stocked with trees, mostly willow, poplar, mulberry, alsaguns, and orchard trees. At five miles cross Zilchak stream by rustic bridge, and at six miles on ford the Zarafshán or Yárkand river, and camp another mile on at the Yangichik Settlement.

2. Yakshamba Bázár, 18 miles.—Over cultivated plain with farmsteads, meadows, and marshes. At 13 miles pass through Posgám, and on to camp over freely irrigated tract of cultivation.

3. Kárghalik, 16 miles.—At six miles cross Tiznáf river. Country as on last stage.

4. Beshterek, 20 miles.—At three miles out quit cultivation, and cross a wide gravelly waste of arid desert, strewed with boulders and coursed from west to east by sandy ridges. Pass through a gap in these to Beshterek or "Five poplars," a cluster of 8 or 10 huts.

5. Yólarik, 12 miles.—Pass out of Beshterek gully on to a wide wind swept desert of coarse sand traversed by gravelly ridges. Camp in settlement of Yólarik, a long stretch of farmsteads on the course of a small river.

6. Kugiár, 13 miles. Cross a wide, shallow, pebbly water-run; pass over a high ridge of loose sand on summit of which is the half buried shrine of Sicheaulúe Mazár; and descend to the Kugiár gully. Follow up its course seven miles past farmsteads to camp in the centre of the settlement.

7. Ak Masjid (height 8,870 feet), 24 miles.—Continue up the gully, and cross its stream to hamlet of Fusar, six miles. Here leave cultivation and habitation behind, and enter hills up a narrow winding gully to camp ground on banks of a stream running down an open glade. Hills of shale. Vegetation scanty.

8. Chiklik, 11 miles. Up a narrow winding gully by a very steep rise between hills of loose dust, six miles, to the top of the Tupa Dawán or "Dust Pass." Then descend by a steep, dusty path down a widening gorge to the bed of the Tiznáf river, and camp on a grassy flat, under an overshading bank of rock on its right bank, near a clump of willow and poplar trees.

9. Khoja Mazár (height 9,250 feet), 14 miles.—Up the bed of the river, crossing it girth deep 24 times *en route* on a rough boulder bottom (June), in a deep winding defile, and camp on a turfy slope on its left bank. Brushwood and forage in plenty. In winter the road is over the frozen river; in summer through it, and dangerous from sudden floods. Road difficult.

10. Dúba, 6 miles.—As last stage. Camp on turfy flat at angle of junction of two torrents. Banks fringed with willow and poplar forest. Pakhpo camps in the vicinity.

11. Gurunj Káldi, 9 miles.—Up the main stream as before, crossing two tributaries from the right, and camp on turfy slope amidst boggy springs. Hills of schist and granitic trap, and perfectly bare. Marmots here.

12. Chirágh Sáldí, 11 miles.—Up stream as before through a gradually widening valley. At eight miles pass ruins of Kirghiz Tam, a former outpost of the Chinese rulers, and beyond it cross a projecting spur into the wider bed of the river, which in June is covered with a deep layer of snow over which the road passes. Camp in a patch of brushwood at junction of a tributary from the right.

13. Kúlanaldí, 11 miles.—Up a winding and narrowing gully by easy ascent to the top of Yangi Dawán, 15,800 feet high, three miles. Then down an easy descent for two miles to where a gully joins from the left. Beyond this down an extremely difficult, narrow, tortuous, and deep gorge which is blocked till June by a glacier that melts away in the next month. The passage over it very difficult down to a wider and less steep channel, of loose shingle between steep banks of moraine rubble, which opens into that of the Yárkand river. Cross the river and camp in tamarisk jangal on opposite shore. River channel half a mile wide.

14. Kúkát Aghzi, 15 miles.—Up course of Yárkand river through extensive patches of tamarisk and myricaria crossing the river girth deep five or six times *en route* on a shingly and sandy bottom, and camp in tamarisk jangal. Channel wide with high hills draining to it on each side.

15. Kashmír Jilga, 25 miles.—Up stream as before. At three miles pass ruins of an outpost fort called Nazar Beg Kurghán, at entrance to a glen on the left which leads in two stages to Shahídula by Kirghiz jangal. Beyond this through an alternately widening

(426)

and narrowing valley to a long stretch of brushwood also called Kirghiz Jangal; and through this to camp.

16. Khufelung, 11 miles.—Up stream four miles, then rise up to a shelving slope of slate and shale on right hand; follow it seven miles and drop into junction point of a stream from the right; cross its pebbly wide bed and camp on the left bank of Yárkand river in tamarisk jangal.

17. Aktágh, 20 miles.—Up course of river leaving vegetation, and passing over snow fields filling its channel (June) to Aktágh. From this onwards the route is the same as that by Sánjú.

ROUTE III.

LEH TO SHAHIDULA (NO. 12 OF ROUTE I) BY THE CHANGCHENMO ROUTE. AUTHORITY CAPTAIN BIDDULPH, SEPTEMBER AND OCTOBER 1873.

1. Tikshe, 10 miles.—Along Indus valley, road good. The village of Tikshe contains about 600 inhabitants.

2. Chimray (height 11,890 feet), 15 miles.—Along Indus valley for 10 miles, road indifferent in places. This Indus fordable in September after first six miles, turning up valley to north for five miles of pathways through cultivation to Chimray, village of about 500 inhabitants with monastery. Bad camping ground.

3. Zingral (height 15,780 feet), 8 miles.—Up valley about three miles till it forks. Up valley to eastward for 1½ miles to village of Sakti; beyond this the ascent gets steeper to Zingral; no village; good camping ground. At Zingral the valley forks to the Chang-la and Kay-la Passes, the latter saves about six miles, but is more difficult for loaded animals.

4. Tsultak (height 15,950 feet), 8 miles.—Up most northerly of the two valleys an easy but stony ascent of two miles to top of the Chang-la Pass, 17,600 feet. A very gradual descent of four miles, then turning abruptly to the east to Tsultak, a small lake; no village; good camping ground. Though the Pass is not formidable either in height or steepness, it must always prove difficult to loaded animals on account of the badness of the road which is a mere track winding through rocks and boulders.

5. Tankse (height 12,900 feet), 14 miles.—Down valley for 6¼ miles easy road, cross shoulder of hill into valley with stream running from south-east pass Durgu a small village, continue up valley to large village of Tankse, supplies of all sorts procurable, the residence of headman of the district. Behind the village is the valley coming in from the Kay-la.

6. Chakar-talab, 14 miles.—Valley above Tankse narrows to a gorge for six miles, then turns to the south and opens out, two miles further is Muglib, very small village; for three miles the valley is a grassy swamp, then narrows for two miles of gentle ascent among rocky boulders. At Chakar-talab is a small shallow pond, sometimes dry in summer; coarse grass on further side of it.

7. Lukong (height 14,130 feet), 7¼ miles.—Five miles up valley to north-west end of Pangong lake, water salt, 2 miles due north from end of the lake to Lukong small patch of cultivation with stream running into lake.

8. Chagra (height 15,090 feet), 8 miles.—1½ miles above Lukong, valley forks up one north-east-summer pasture ground of Tartars, one or two stone huts, grass plentiful and fish in the stream.

9. Rimdi (height 17,500 feet), 13 miles.—A short steep ascent out of valley half a mile due east into broad valley running east and west. Continue for 5½ miles very slight

ascent to Lunkur, stone hut, uninhabited, a little water, then steeper ascent, but not difficult to top of Lunkur-la or Marsimik Pass, 18,400 feet. Gradual descent down valley turning due north, at 3½ miles joins valley from west. Rimdi camping ground at junction; fuel scarce; water and grass plentiful.

10. Pamzal (height 14,790 feet), 13 miles.—Down valley to east; stony and narrow track for two miles along face of steep hill, valley then bends to north and road improves slightly. At nine miles, bed of stream narrows to stony gorge for a few paces, then opens out into quarter mile breadth. Very stony, brushwood plentiful, strike Changchenmo stream running east and west. Camping ground to west of junction. Fuel abundant; grass plentiful, half mile further down valley.

11. Gogra (height 15,570 feet), 12½ miles.—Up Changchenmo valley into Kugrang valley, north north-west road good; fuel plentiful; grass scarce.

12. Shummal Lungpa (height 17,020 feet), 12 miles.—Cross valley, and up Chunglung valley to north-east stream runs in narrow gorge. At 4½ miles narrow steep descent and ascent across gorge coming from north. At six miles hot springs in river bed, valley bends round to north road, winds in narrow track on hill side, several steep ascents and descents. Three miles above hot springs is large ravine leading east, up which is road over Changlung Yokma Pass on to Lingzi Thung Plain; one mile beyond is Shummal Lungpa ravine, running east; first half mile narrow and stony, then opens out; camping ground 1¼ mile from entrance; water and fuel plentiful; grass very scarce.

13. Camp near Nischu (height 18,630 feet), 14¼ miles.—Up valley about 3½ miles to fork, up ravine to eastward at head of which appears a practicable pass. At half a mile take up ravine north by west up steepish ascent across Changlung Burma Pass, 19,300 feet high. Descend low hill into broad shallow valley due east, down valley, which bends to north, and camp near black jagged hill. No grass or fuel; march throughout good for laden animals.

14. Camp Lingzi Thung (height 17,680 feet), 16½ miles.—Down main valley which makes a great sweep round to north-east, and at 6½ miles opens out into Shumshul Plain by Kala Pahar. Due north across plain for six miles cross low ridge with 200 feet rise and 700 feet descent on north side into Lingzi Thung Plain, due north for five miles and camp in water-course; fuel and water to be got by digging; no grass. From low ridge above mentioned, rocky peak at head of Kizil Jilga ravine bears 349°.

15. Jungle Camp, 17 miles.—Across plain for 9 miles, straight for rocky peak, across low ridges for 8 miles, and camp by small pond. No grass or fuel, but the latter can be collected on north side of plain where it is plentiful.

16. Camp Sumna (height 17,150 feet), 21¼ miles.—Among low hills for 3 miles into broad valley running north in which is plenty of water; keep up valley northwards for 2 miles towards smooth round hill, and turn up broad valley running in from west for 11 miles to red rock, and cross the Kizil Diwan (height 17,290 feet) at foot of it into Kizil Jilga ravine. Water, grass, and fuel obtainable 3 miles down, and more plentiful still further on.

17. Kizil Jilga (height 16,360 feet), 9 miles.—Down valley to Karakash river flowing between two huge red rocks, camping ground under southern one. Grass and fuel plentiful.

18. Khushk Maidan, 17 miles.—Down Karakash valley, at 5 miles water disappears in the ground. None to be found for 11 miles, where are numerous springs. Camp on south side of valley. Fuel abundant; grass scarce. Road excellent all the way.

19. Chung Tash (height 15,740 feet), 7 miles.—Down valley, which narrows. Huge rock on right bank. No fuel or grass. Road good.

20. Camp Sumnal (height 15,540 feet), 13 miles.—Down valley, which at 3½ miles bends round to north, and valley leading to Aktagh comes in west. The Karakash then flows

in narrow gorge and at 6 miles from Chung Tash are hot springs on right bank. A little fuel, but no grass. One mile above hot springs valley opens for a mile then closes again. Road in parts stony and bad. River has to be crossed frequently; small patches of fuel in side nullahs. Good camping ground at bend of river to east, where large nullah from west joins. Fuel and grass abundant.

21. Camp Tak Marpo (height 15,000 feet), 11 miles.—Valley opens out for 3 miles. Zinchin on right bank. Fuel and grass. Valley then narrows; road encumbered by huge boulders and masses of rubbish; very difficult for laden animals; camp under yellow rock on left bank. Fuel and grass at intervals all the way.

22. Camp Polong Karpo (height 14,600 feet), 21 miles.—Valley opens out and travelling good. At 8 miles is broad valley on left with abundant fuel, after which fuel is to be found all along in main valley; grass very scarce. At 16 miles valley narrows and turns to north, fuel becomes more plentiful. At Polong Karpo is a huge rock in bed of valley on left bank; good camping ground; grass abundant.

23. Camp Sora (height 14,000 feet).—At 5 miles river takes sharp bend to north-west into broad valley at foot of Kuen Luen. For 2 miles on either side of the bend is no fuel or grass. Ground at Sora covered with natural salt pans. Good camping ground. Fuel and grass abundant.

24. Jungle Camp, 17 miles.—Camp at mouth of small ravine. Opposite mouth of Karajilga ravine. Fuel and grass abundant.

25. Gulbashem, (height 12,390 feet), 42½ miles.—Road down valley good; and grass and fuel abundant everywhere, except for 2 miles above Gulbashem. 12 miles above Gulbashem the river is much increased by springs. Gulbashem is a favourite Kirghiz camping ground.

26. Balakchi, 10 miles.—Grass and fuel.

27. Shahidúla (height 11,780 feet), 13 miles.—Small deserted fort on left bank of the Karakash. Grass and fuel abundant. At 6 miles strike road from Sugat Pass; road good.

Though parts of the road are practicable for guns and wheeled carriage, it is on the whole only available for camels or horses.

ROUTE IIIa.

Variation on No. III. (Captain Trotter, September and October 1873). From Gogra (Station 11 of Route III) to Shahidula (No. 27 of Route III).

1. Kotajilga (height 16,730 feet), 8 miles.—Road up stream the whole way good, but somewhat difficult for loaded ponies, as there are several steep ascents and descents in crossing tributary streams, which in the autumn contain only a few inches of water. Pass ravine on right leading to Nischu as per Captain Biddulph's route. At the camp, grass, water, and wood procurable.

2. Pangtong (height 17,250 feet), 7½ miles.—Steady and gentle ascent through a broad stony ravine for four miles, then somewhat steeper. Camping ground covered with snow, but grass and an inferior fuel said to be plentiful.

3. Sumzungling (height 17,310 feet), 15 miles.—Steady and not very steep ascent to the Changlung Pass (18,910 feet). The road then passes over a high table-land for about a mile, after which it enters a ravine along which it passes for 9½ miles of execrable road crossing the stream in numerous places before reaching the camping ground at the junction of three nullas. Water and a little grass on a neighbouring hill, but no fuel, one of the worst marches on the whole road, as the number of recently dead animals that strewed the road too surely testified.

4. Dehra Kompás (height 17,890 feet), 19 miles.—Road runs nearly due north up a gentle ascent for about 5 miles, road fair, then for several miles of good road across the west edge of the Ling-zi-thang plains; crosses several easy open ravines draining eastwards descends into and crosses a branch of the Karakash river and camp at foot of a low pass; very little water to be obtained by digging; and no grass or wood.

5. Shinglung or Dunglung (height 17,030 feet), 18 miles.—Across pass, and down a ravine for 5½ miles into Karakash river, where plenty of boortsee and water, but no grass. Road follows river, which after 3 miles turns up sharp in a northerly direction, road good, but stony; boortsee abundant.

6. Kiziljilga (height 16,360 feet), 14½ miles.—Bad stony road down bed of Karakash River for the first mile, then between about two or three miles of ice bed have to be traversed, the bed extending right across the ravine, here about ¼ mile in breadth; road very slippery and difficult for laden animals. Near camp passage of Karakash difficult (in October) owing to admixture of ice and water. Fuel (boortsee), grass and water, within reach of camp down Karakash River.

7. Chungtash or Chung Tásh (height 15,740 feet), 23½ miles.—Road down Karakash River generally good but stony and bad in the latter portion. Camp badly situated, as there is neither wood nor grass both of which might have been had at Khushk Maidan, a few miles further back. Camp under a big rock near where the bed of the Karakash is very much narrowed by precipitous hills coming down near the river bank.

8. Shorjilga, 14 miles.—Road for two miles down Karakash, which takes another sudden curve to the north-east, the road goes up a tributary stream containing nearly as much water as the Karakash itself. Road bad for two or three miles owing to the number of times the frozen stream has to be crossed and recrossed, it then passes over a tolerably level plain up to a gorge at the mouth of which is Shoorjilga. In October there was no water there and camp had to be pitched half mile up the gorge at a place where the river water disappears into the ground; not a stick of wood or blade of grass.

9. Kárátágh (height 16,890 feet), 9 miles.—Up ravine for several miles, snow and ice nearly the whole way and road bad; short but sharp descent from Karatagh Pass (17,710 feet) into large flat open plain, covered with several inches of snow. Lake frozen over, but water obtained by making hole in ice; plenty of boortsee, but no grass visible.

10. Aktágh (height 15,590 feet), 22½ miles.—Road the whole way good, over a level plain, which was entirely covered by snow. About half way at east foot of low double-topped hill is a place called Tamba* sometimes used as a camping ground. Ak-tagh is at the junction of the Karakoram and Changchenmo Routes.

11. Chibra 10 miles.—Road crosses stream and goes up ravine, steady ascent with fair but stony road. No grass or wood at camp.

12. Suget (height 12,970 feet), 18 miles.—Up ravine to top of Suget Pass (17,600 feet), 4 miles. Steady ascent and road good. Descent steep through the snow down zigzag, then straight down ravine for eight miles due north. Road stony, but descent gentle. Road then turns eastward and soon leaves the nullah, which has a very rapid fall; an alternative road goes right down the nullah in which there is plenty of wood and grass, abundance of both at camp.

13. Shahidula (height 1,780 feet), 8 miles.—The road descends to Karakash River (two miles) and follows the river to camp, crossing it twice *en route*. Passage somewhat difficult. Plenty of wood and grass a few miles up the Karakash River. Shahidula is the same as Station No. 12 of Route I.

---

* On this march we lost our road and had perforce to halt at Tamba, where we found boortsee; melted snow served for water, which is not procurable here in summer.

ROUTE IV.

YARKAND TO KASHGHAR (CAPTAIN TROTTER), NOVEMBER 1873.

1. Kok Robát or "Blue Hostelry" (height 3,830 feet), 22 miles.—Pass through cultivated tracts and at 4½ miles cross the Opo or Arpi canal (from the Yárkand river) by a good bridge. A little distance beyond is the village of Kárákoram, after which the road passes through grassy swamps, followed by a desert waste. Occasional small villages are passed before reaching Kok Robát, a scattered village of about 200 houses.

2. Kizil (height 3,910 feet), 26 miles.—Pass over sandy desert, without habitations or cultivation, to Ák Robát or "White Hostelry," where are two small wells whose surface water is 98 feet below the ground level; another 13½ miles over flat waste to Kizil, a large village of about 500 houses. The dry bed of the Kizil stream is passed, coming from the Kizil Tagh on the west. The country is irrigated by small canals taken higher up from the Kizil River which in summer contains a fair supply of water.

3. Yangi Hissar or "New Fort" (height 4,320 feet), 28¼ miles. Over a flat plain irrigated by small water-courses from the Kinkol River, the scattered villages of Chemalung, Kudok, Kosh-gombaz, Tuplok and Kalpín are passed. Low sand hills on right before reaching the Yangi Hissar River, which has its chief source in springs a few miles south-west of the town of the same name, which lies two half miles beyond it. Yangi Hissar is a large town with strong fort, and contains about 4,000 houses. The Yangi Hissar River* is crossed by a two-spanned timber bridge, about 60 feet long. A low ridge of hills separates it from the town. The fort is about 600 yards to the north of the town.

4. Yapchan (height 4,210 feet), 23½ miles.—Pass at four miles the Zaikásh stream fed from springs on the west, further on cross two branches of the Saïlik canal from Kusánk. After passing the villages of Khánka Sorgoluk, and Tuglok cross by a wooden bridge a large canal from the Kusán River, and then cross the main stream of the Kusán itself by a wooden bridge. The road follows the lower bridge of the stream for about a mile, and is much cut up by branch canals. Soil generally sandy.

5. Yangi-shahr or new city of Kashghar (14½ miles).—Road passes through cultivated country and crosses several streams and canals, the largest of which are the Tazgún or Khanarik or Yamunyar and the Karasú (chiefly fed from springs). Pass the villages of Tazgún, Turmalak, and Kasr Robát. The old city of Kashghar lies about five miles from the Yangi-shahr in a north-west direction.

ROUTE V.

KASHGHAR TO MARALBASHI (AUTHORITY, CAPTAIN BIDDULPH) JANUARY 1874.

1. Sang, 19 miles. Through cultivation; at six miles village of Barin; 7½ miles Arowah, junction of road from city of Káshghar; nine miles village of Yandumba, from where goes cart road to Kizil Boia to east; cross rivers Yamunyar and Chokanak flowing into Kizil, both bridges swift streams. Sang large village.

2. Faizabad (height 4,000 feet), 16 miles.—Large village, through cultivation; at two miles cross small river; no bridge.

3. Yangi-awat, 11 miles.—Small village, cultivation almost ceases from Faizabad; at seven miles small village of Shagiat.

4. Kashmir, 28 miles.—Through bush jangal and plain; at 20 miles cross river Kizil; bridge used in summer; ice bears carts, &c. in winter. Kashmir a small post-house, no village.

5. Togha Sulukh, 13 miles.—Through tree jangal and white grass; a small post-house.

---

* Which I have known called by no less than nine different names.—H. T.

6. Shugeh, 18 miles.—A small post-house; road all the way through tree jangal.
7. Maralbashi (height   ), 14 miles.—Small village and fort; road through tree jangal and high grass. Maralbashi is at the junction of Kashghar road, with road from Yárkand to Aksu. Carts travel freely all the way.

ROUTE VI.
Kashghar to Chadyrkul, Captain Trotter.

Kashghar (Yangi-shahr) to—

1. Besák, Upper Artysh (height 5,290 feet), 26 miles.—Road leaves on left at 5½ miles the old city of Káshghar, and then crosses the Tuman (Káshghar) river by a good bridge; passes through numerous gardens into an open stony plain, and then through a gap in a low range of hills, beyond which lies the district of Osten Artysh, consisting of numerous scattered townships.
2. Chung Terek, or "Big poplar tree, (height 7,000 feet), 20 miles.—Road passes over level plain and then up the gently sloping Toyanda valley. Road good but stony; pass *en route* the old Chinese outpost of Teshektash and the small village of Tupa; a small Kirghiz village at camp.
3. Chakmák Forts (height 8,830 feet), 20 miles.—The road continues up the Toyanda valley and passes through precipitous hills rising some 3,000 feet above the bed of the stream, which has to be frequently crossed, both on this and the last march. At 12 miles pass the "Past Kurghan" or Lower Fort, garrisoned by a detachment from the larger forts at Chákmák further on. A few Kirghiz tents *en route*, but no other habitations. From Chákmák a road goes across the hills to the east to the Terekty Forts.
4. Balghùn Báshi (height 10,540 feet), 10 miles.—The road continues up stream, and at about eight miles passes the Suok outpost at the junction of two streams from the Suok and Turgat passes. The former is two days' journey in a north-west direction by a very difficult road; two miles above the outpost is the camp, where plenty of firewood, though but little or no grass.
5. Turgat Bela (height 11,090 feet), 15 miles.—Road always up stream at first through precipitous hills, which open out somewhat as the camp is approached. Occasional Kirghiz tents; plenty of grass near camp; but fuel very scarce.
6. To Chadyrkul (Lake), 20 miles.—13 miles to the crest of the Turgat Pass, a gentle ascent right up to the foot of the pass, from which to the crest (12,760 feet) there is an ascent of about 400 feet in a distance of a mile. From the pass the road passes along a spur for about three miles, and then rapidly descends to the lake, which lies about 1,500 feet lower than the pass. Plenty of grass, but little or no fuel obtainable.

The road from Kashghar to Chadyrkul is good throughout, and could with very little labour be made available for light carts and field guns. In January a little snow lay by the roadside to the north of the pass, but none whatever on the south side.

The route just described is on the main caravan route between Kashghar and Almati (Fort Vernoye), for details of which maps can be consulted.

ROUTE VII.
Kashghar to Belowti Pass, (Captain Trotter) February 1874.
(On road to Ush Turfan.)

Kashghar (Yangi-Shahr) to—

1. Altyn Artysh (height 4,100 feet), 22 miles.—Over plain for a great part of the way; road good; pass Kashghar River by wooden bridge (in cold season), and subsequently

cross two smaller streams and canals, and traverse a low ridge before entering the Artysh valley, which contains numerous villages aggregating perhaps 2,000 houses.

2. Kalti Ailák (height 3,950 feet), 22 miles.—Good road over level plain.
3. Kyr Bulak (height 5,340 feet), 33 miles.—Good road passes over plain and then through a range of low hills up the Sogon stream, on which is a military outpost, then crosses a low pass and emerges into a large plain. Camping ground is occasionally used by Kirghiz.
4. Jai Tupa (height 4,910 feet), 20 miles.—An occasional camping ground of Kirghiz; water scarce; situated near the centre of an extensive forest of stunted poplar trees; good road passing over level plain; plenty of grass and fuel.
5. Ui Bulák (height 6,650 feet), 27 miles.—Road good but stony; crosses a low spur into the Ui Bulák valley, where plenty of fire-wood and a moderate amount of grass; water scarce, but plenty of snow.
6. Tigarek, 17 miles.—Road up stream and then over a spur from the main range, stony, but otherwise not difficult. Tigarek is in a large grassy plain (no water) surrounded by hills; is sometimes used by Kirghiz as a winter pasture ground, when snow is used as a substitute for water.
7. Belowti Pass (height 11,360 feet), 9 miles.—Road crosses some low spurs and then passes up a ravine; a steady ascent of four miles followed by a sharp pull of two miles up to the pass; no high peaks near the crest, but undulating grassy ridges. The road descends on the north side of the pass in the valley of the Kokshál river. The Belowti Pass was the furthest point reached by Captain Trotter, and from it the marches to Ush Turfan were said to be as follows:—
8. Ak-chi, 10 miles, on Kokshal River.
9. Kuyok Tokai, 22 miles, down river.
10. Safr Bai.
11. Karawal, 22 miles.
12. Ush Turfan, 16 miles.

Total distance, Kashghar to Uch Turfan, 242 miles; from Safr Bai (No. 10) a road is said to go to Karakul (near the old Issigh-Kul Fort) by four difficult marches, crossing the Bedul and the Zanku passes, and the head-waters of the Naryn River. From Karakul roads go to Kuldja and to Vernoye (Almati).

ROUTE VIII.

YANGI HISSAR TO KILA PANJAH, WAKHAN, BY THE LITTLE PAMIR (CAPTAIN BIDDULPH) MARCH AND APRIL 1874.

1. Ighizyar (height 5,600 feet), 19 miles.—Large village. Road nearly due south, through sand-hills and cultivation, crossing two small streams, over soda plain for 5 miles, cross stream by village, and over stony plain for 7 miles; practicable for wheeled traffic.
2. Aktala (height 7,345 feet), 17 miles.—Kirghiz camp, south-west four miles over plain to Aktala valley, then up valley 13 miles. At six miles pass through ruined Chinese fort closing the valley. Fuel, grass, and water abundant; road good.
3. Sasak Taka (height 9,455 feet), 13 miles. Out of main valley, into side valley to south, first few miles narrow and stony, then opens out and travelling improves. Wood and grass abundant. Kirghiz camp at Sasak Taka.
4. Kaskasu (height 10,960 feet), 14 miles.—Kirghiz camp up valley; travelling good; grass plentiful, but fuel scarce. Several Kirghiz camps in the valley.
5. Chehil Gumbaz (height 10,310 feet), 8½ miles.—Kirghiz camp; half mile from Kaskasu road turns up small valley to south, and at another mile is foot of Kaskasu Pass, first 200

yards steep, then for three miles winding through undulating grassy hills round head of valley to top of pass 13,000 feet, road good half mile along narrow ridge then steep zigzag descent of 1,000 feet into Charling valley to Chehil Gumbaz at junction of two valleys. Grass and water plentiful; fuel scarce.

6. Past Robat (height 9,370 feet), 9 miles.—Road up valley to west for 2½ miles to foot of Torat Pass; 1½ mile of ascent; not difficult for laden animals to top of pass, 13,400 feet; long steep descent into narrow valley; road stony and bad; into broad valley, to south to Past Robat; Kirghiz camp at junction of two valleys; grass, fuel, and water abundant.

7. Tárbáshi (height 11,515 feet), 8 miles.—Kirghiz four miles up valley to fork. The valley to the right leads to Tashkurghan by the Yambulak Pass, only used in summer. Up valley to left for two miles along narrow gorge, among rocks and boulders, the stream having to be crossed and recrossed more than a dozen times. Many hot springs in the defile, steep ascent of 400 feet into upper valley, when road again becomes good. This route can only be used when the stream is low in winter and early spring.

8. Shindi, 17 miles.—Up the valley for eight miles of gentle ascent to the Chichiklik plain, about 1½ mile in diameter; to south-west is the Kok Moinak Pass, used in spring and summer, by which Sirikol is reached in 1½ marches; to north is the route by Yambulak Pass before mentioned. Bending to south a long descent, steep and stony, brings one to Shindi, where are a few Sarikoli huts.

9. Tashkurghan (height 10,270 feet), 19 miles.—Down valley for four miles to Yárkand River. From here a road up valley to east leads over the Shindi Dawan to Tarbashi. Continues up Yárkand River to foot of Tashkurghan. Road good all the way. Grass and fuel plentiful.

10. Kanshábúr (height 12,980 feet), 17 miles.—Due west from fort into Shingan valley. The first three miles of narrow defile strewn with boulders, very difficult travelling, after which valley opens out and road gradually improves. Fuel and grass plentiful.

11. Aktásh (height 12,600 feet), 18 miles.—Up valley to right, and after a mile up fork to left to foot of Nezatash Pass 15,000 feet. Three miles of gentle ascent, last 300 yards to top steep. Descend into valley running north-west along this for eight miles, over low spur into broad Aktash valley running south. Grass and fuel plentiful.

12. Gház Kul, or lake of Little Pamir (height 13,200 feet), 46 miles.—Down Aktash valley to south into Little Pamir due west, travelling excellent the whole way. Grass and fuel plentiful everywhere. Camp by lake. At six miles from the lake is Kabr-i-Bozai, deserted Kirghiz huts, opposite which is road leading to Kunjúd by Tagdúng-bash Pamir, over Kujroi Pass.

13. Langar (height 12,530 feet), 25 miles.—Continue due west; at 10 miles Pamir narrows into rocky valley, and travelling becomes difficult; road winding along face of hill with many small ascents and descents. At Langar deserted village; fuel and grass plentiful. Opposite Langar is road leading to Kunjoot by Bykurra Pass, closed three months in the year. This is the road generally used between Wakhan and Kunjúa.

14. Sarhadd (height 11,150 feet), 24 miles.—Down main valley, travelling bad; road much encumbered with boulders, and there are two steep ascents and three steep descents, very trying to animals. The stream has to be crossed many times, and the road in consequence of melting snow becomes impassable after 1st May. From Sarhadd road leads to south to Yassin and Chitrál by Baroghil, Darkot, and Ishkaman Passes. Sarhadd is the frontier village of Wakhan.

15. Kila Panja, 55 miles.—Down valley to foot, road good for laden animals villages at intervals the whole way; grass and fuel plentiful. By the village of Yur, 18 miles from Sarhadd, is a summer road into Mastuj. At Vost, 38 miles from Sarhadd, is a road leading into Chitrál said to be only practicable to men on foot.

ROUTE IX.

KILA PANJAH (ROUTE VIII) TO ÁKTASH BY THE GREAT PAMIR (CAPTAIN TROTTER), APRIL 1874.

Kila Panjah (Wakhan) to—

1. Langarkish village (height 9,350 feet), 6 miles.—Road lies along the banks of the main Panjah River, and then up the northern branch; pass on right bank the villages of Zang and Hissar. All supplies for the journey across the Great Pamir have to be taken from Langarkish, which is the highest village on the north branch of the Panjah river. The valley is bounded by lofty and precipitous mountains.

2. Yumkhána or Jangalik (height 11,440 feet), 18 miles.—The road follows the right bank of the river, above which it rises in many places to a height of 1,000 feet; cross the Ab-i-zer-i Zamin (River), four miles beyond which is the camp. Plenty of grass and fire-wood.

3. Yol Mazar (height 12,320 feet), 13 miles.—Road still along right bank of stream, at four miles cross the Ab-i-Matz (river) up which passes a summer road to Shighnan, two miles further is Boharak, the commencement of the Great Pamir. Plenty of grass and *boortsee*. Road good.

4. Bilaor Bas (height 13,120 feet).—March along right bank of river through a grassy plain bounded on both sides by undulating hills.

5. Mazár Túpa (height 13,760 feet), 20 miles.—Road up gentle ascent the whole way, and on the right bank of the stream.

6. Sarikol (head of the lake), (height 13,950 feet), 16½ miles.—Road up gentle grassy slope to Victoria Lake, passing along its northern edge. The lake is ten miles long and nowhere more than two miles in breadth. Camp at the east end of the lake; whole ground under snow, but very fine pasturage in summer. From Sarikol a road leads across to Langar, at the west end of the Little Pamir, crossing the Warran Pass.

7. Shash Tupa (height 13,760 feet), 19½ miles.—Cross a low water-shed a few miles from camp and then enter a valley, the stream down which flows into the Ak-su river; very gentle descent through broad open valley to camp. Roads traverse the Pámir here in all directions.

8. Dahn-i-Isligh (mouth of the Isligh River), height 13,220 feet, 18 miles.—Gentle descent through open valley, pass several broad open ravines. This camp may be considered the termination of the Great Pámir. Plenty of grass and fuel.

9. Ak-tash (height 12,600 feet), 37 miles.—Road follows the Isligh River until it joins the Ak-su, both of these streams partially frozen, but ice breaking up making journey somewhat difficult. The Isligh River passes through precipitous mountains; after entering the Ak-su valley turn south to Ak-tash, which is the same as station 11 of Route VIII.

ROUTE X.

TASHKURGHAN TO YARKAND, VIA CHARLING RIVER (CAPTAIN TROTTER, FROM KISHEN SING).

Tashkurghan (No. 9 of Route VIII) to—

3. Chehil Gumbaz (No. 5 of Route VIII), 56 miles.

4. Tashkerim, 19 miles.—Road passes down Charling River; Kirghiz encampments; wood and grass; pass on road Alumbitte Kurghan. From Tashkerim a foot-path leads across the hills to Kinkol camp.

5. Khaizak-vil, 14½ miles.—The road continues down Charling River. Pass on left bank at eight miles the small village of Bagh (30 houses), also the villages of Kiok-tash, Mirgul (25 houses), and Yoya (15 houses).

6. Arpalik, 21 miles.—Road leaves Charling River and passes up a tributary stream to small village of Yamunarik. Thence goes over two low passes, the Kara Diwan (at 11½ miles) and the Kizil Diwan.

7. Kizil-tagh, 15½ miles.—Road good for three miles to Tangitar, where the river (Kizil) passes for five miles along a very narrow ravine, very difficult to traverse in the afternoon owing to floods caused by the melting of the snow on the hills above.

8. Yak-arik, 23½ miles.—Good road over the "Shaitan kum" or "Devil's sand."

9. Yárkand, 20 miles. Road passes over a well cultivated and thickly inhabited plain.

Total distance, Tashkurghan to Yárkand, 188 miles.

ROUTE XI.

Route from Kila Panjah (WAKHAN) to Kila Wámar (ROSHAN) along the river Panjah. Authority Captain Trotter (from Abdul Subhan.)

Number of stages.	Names of places.	Country or district.	Distance in miles.	REMARKS.
1	Kila Panjah to Khandut.	Wakhán	16	A village with about 30 houses and mud fort. Road stony, passes through village of Parg at 2½ miles, Pakui at 5½ miles, and ruins of Ishmúrgh at 9 miles. From Pakui to Khandút is a dense forest of stunted poplar trees.
2	Pigish	Ditto	6	A village of 30 houses. Road good, and along left bank of river; much cultivation. Supplies plentiful.
3	Shikharbi Pareshan	Ditto	20	A scattered village of 30 houses. At 13 miles is the large village of Argund. Road bad and stony and along left bank of river. Supplies plentiful.
4	Patúr	Ditto	17	A frontier village between Wakhan and Ishkashim, subject to Mír of Wakhan, consisting of 25 houses, villages passed on road are Verg at 7 miles, Sad Ishtrag at 10 miles, and Kázideh at 11½ miles. From Sad Ishtrag a road strikes off southward to Chitrál, the capital of Káshkaro. Four miles beyond Kázideh the river turns abruptly northwards, and is dangerous here for horses, as it passes over a narrow ledge of rock overhanging the river. Road stony. Supplies plentiful.
5	Yaghduru (Doyam) or 2nd.	Shikashim	17	A village of 15 houses. Valley in this march wider and river broader. At 6 miles is the large village of Ishkashim of 60 houses. A road joins here from Faizabád. At 8 miles village of Yaghdúru (Aval) or first. Road good, and through rich cultivation. Supplies plentiful.
6	Barshár	Ghárán (Badakshán.)	9	A small village belonging to the Ghárán district situated on the right bank of river Panjah. River forded 3 miles above village of Sar-i-Shakh, left bank avoided being dangerous for horses. Road stony and bad. Supplies plentiful.
7	Nawúbád	Ditto	14	A deserted village on the left bank, river recrossed at ford near deserted village of Kázideh at a mile and half from Barshár. Another road from Badakshán to Ghárán (viâ Aghirda Pass) and to Shákh Darrah valley, crosses at the same ford. At 5 miles is the deserted village of Zich, on the opposite bank of river is a ruby mine. No supplies here. Cultivation scanty. Grass and wood plentiful.

ROUTE XI.

Route from Kila Panjah (WAKHAN) to Kila Wamar (ROSHAN) along the river Panjah. Authority Captain Trotter (from Abdul Subhan)—concluded.

Number of stages.	Names of places.	Country or district.	Distance in miles.	REMARKS.
8	Darmárakht	Shighnán	11½	Camp on the left bank. Darmárakht is on the opposite bank from whence supplies are procured by means of a wooden bridge thrown across the river, which is about 150 yards wide here. From Nawabád at 3 miles is the large village of Shekh Beg in ruins, and further on the road runs through a tunnel called Kuguz Parín, or "hole in the rock." Road bad and stony. The Kuguz Parin in the boundary between Gháran and Shighnán.
9	Viár	Ditto	14½	A scattered village of about 40 houses. At two miles from Darmárakht a large tributary of the Panjah river called Arakht is crossed by a strong wooden bridge. At 9¼ miles the road ascends and traverses the Mithinz and Tarseb passes. Road bad and stony. Supplies plentiful.
10	Kila Bar Panjah	Ditto	5½	A large town on the left bank, the capital of Shighnán. Adjacent to it stands a stone fort on the margin of the river. At Dasht-i-Khust, the river Suchán falls into the Panjah. At 3½ miles is the small village of Deh-i-Murghán. Road good. Supplies plentiful.
11	Sácharb	Ditto	9	A village of 20 houses on the right bank. Sácharb is reached by crossing the river either by ferry at Kila Bar Panjah, or by ford at the village of Dishár at 3 miles lower down. Yumj village is at 4½ miles from Sacharb. Road good. Supplies plentiful.
12	Kila Wámar	Roshan	22	A large town, the capital of Roshán, situated about 1½ miles above the junction of the Murghábi river with the Panjah. Fort and town on the high bank of the Panjah. At 13 miles is the small village of Past Khúf. At 16 miles stands the Darband tower, built on a rock. This is the boundary between Shignán and Roshan.
		Total distance	161½	

ROUTE XII.
YÁRKAND TO AKSU. AUTHORITY, CAPTAIN CHAPMAN.
BHAN SING.
FROM YÁRKAND TO AKSÚ AND ONWARDS.

1. Yárkand, *Terek Langar*, 7 *tash*,* Ek Shamba and Char Shamba Bazaars *en route*; cultivation and gardens to within one mile of the halting ground.

---

* NOTE.—A tash is the ordinary unit of measurement of distances in Eastern Turkistan, and on many of the principal roads *tash-boards* have been errected similar to the wooden sign posts, still existing in some parts of England. They were put up between Khotan and Kashghar shortly after the accession of the present Ruler, but the Yarkand road the following measurements were made by Kishen Sing Pandit :—

	Number of paces.	Average number of paces per tash.
From 1st to 5th Tash Post	36,350	9,112
,, 5th to 8th ,,	27,880	92·93
,, 8th to 11th ,,	26,800	8,933
Mean value of each tash		9,113

or almost exactly 4½ English statute miles. Theoretically the tash is equal to 12,000 paces of a riding camel, and it is by means of this measure that the distances are said to have been laid out between Yarkand and Kashghar.—[H. T.]

Terek Lángár, a village of about 40 houses, with two musjids, in every house a room for the accommodation of travellers.

2. To *Lai Lik*, 7 *tash*, through desert and low jungle; at 4 tash a deserted Lángár of the time of the Chinese; at Lailik, 22 houses, the inhabitants support themselves by the entertainment of travellers; supplies, &c.

3. To *Menut*, 4 *tash*, through a jungle of high trees. The road within one tash of Lailik (on the Yárkand side) approaches the Yárkand river; it is touched three times by the road during this stage. At Menut 16 houses in all, accommodation for travellers; supplies, water, &c.

4. To *Alaigur*, 5 *tash*, through a jungle of high trees, the river is encountered twice *en route*. At Alaigur 23 houses, accommodation in each; supplies and water; the river is nowhere crossed, but the road follows its bank.

5. To *Aksák Marál*, 3 *tash*, through jungle as during previous stage, the road approaching the river once *en route*; 14 houses at the halting stage, accommodation in each, and supplies, &c.

6. To *Shamál*, 5 *tash*. Here is only an old rest-house, but about a mile to the east on the bank of the river is a cluster of some six houses, whence the traveller may get some supplies; the entire route through jungle. From this point the river runs wide of the road.

7. To *Marálbáshi*, 3 *tash*. High jungle encountered *en route*, but in patches, there being here and there strips of sand and bog, the only water being obtained from springs. A fort, and considerable place. *Vide* Captain Biddulph's report.

8. To *Charwágh*, 3 *tash*. The spurs of a range of hills stretching out from the Tianshan are to the north of the road which runs through jungle with cultivation here and there, the drainage from this point is into the *Kashghar River* from which canals are cut to Marálbáshi and onwards; there are about 40 houses in Charwágh, each having accommodation for travellers.

9. To *Tumshuk*, 4 *tash*. Half way a hill is to the north of the road under which the road immediately runs; on the top of this hill is a Mázar and also one at the base. Captain Biddulph gives this hill the name of Pir Shereh Kuddam Múrtaza Ali Tagh, and thinks the rock must be basaltic. Beyond this hill is a fort, and at the distance of about a tash is a ruined city at the base, and on the slope of a second hill (this is one of the buried cities) the houses are of earth and not of stone. One tash further to Tumshuk, through a low jungle, a place of 32 houses, accommodation for travellers. A canal from the Kashghar river is crossed at 2 miles from Tumshuk by a bridge; this is narrow and comparatively deep, being only some 10 yards across, it runs away east.

10. To *Chadyrkul*, 3½ *tash*, through a jungle of high trees; 15 houses.

11. To *Yaka Kuduk*, 4 *tash*, through a jungle of high trees; water from a well about 30 feet deep; there is a slight drainage from this point; southwards towards the Yárkand river about 12 houses in Yarkudut, where travellers are accommodated.

At this point the road divides into two, the shorter and more direct road going by—

12. *Yazdah*, 5 *tash*. High trees during half the march when these change to low jungle. No water *en route*, spring near Yazdah itself. About eight houses in Yazdah.

13. To *Chilán*, 3 *tash*. Low jungle and sandy desert; no water *en route*; 22 houses in Chilán; two large trees at this place which are conspicuous; two tanks at Chilán supplied by springs.

The longer one by—

12 *Suget*, 4 *tash*. A deserted Lángár, but no water; no one halts here; if a halt is intended, water must be carried.

13. *Chilán*, 6 *tash*. A low jungle, but no water on the surface; but it may readily be obtained by digging. This is the easterly of the two roads.

This road is closed after the winter season when the thaw sets in and occasionally when the springs swell and bring an extra amount of water.

14. To *Chol Kuduk*, 4 *tash*. Through desert without water. At Chol Kuduk water obtained from a well, but the water is brackish. There is a large serai here with a musjid. Here is a low range of hills on the north-west, close to which the road runs, and behind which is the bed of the Kashghar Daria.

15. To *Sai Arik Langar*, 4 *tash*. Through a desert, with sand and small stones. At Sarek Lángár there are two serais, and a post for the examination of passports; some 30 or 40 houses with cultivation, &c.; water by a canal from the Kashghar Daria.

16. To *Kumush* or *Kumbásh*, 3 *tash*. The Kashghar Daria is crossed at one mile from Sai Arik Lángár. After the crossing there is a group of hamlets known as Aykol, beyond this eastwards at about one and half tash is a considerable sheet of water; in the district, which takes its name of Aykol from this, are some 2,000 houses. Cultivation may be said to extend from Sai Arik Lángár as far as Aksú; there is a bazaar held at Kum. In Aykol are two serais and a considerable bazaar (Thursday); the country is cut up by canals from the Kashghar river. The *Kum district* stretches towards Ush Turfán and eastwards; it is said to contain 8,000 houses. Kum Bazaar, which is the head-quarters of this district, is off the road some 2½ miles. At the stage of Kumbásh there is merely a Lángár.

17. To *Aksú*, 4 *tash*. After leaving Kumbásh, about two tash, the Ush Turfán river is crossed; it runs in three principal channels, one of which is crossed by a ferry during the cold season; the Kashghar Daria was crossed in four separate channels at some distance from each other, and all bridged. After leaving the Ush Turfán river the road rises to a plateau along the skirts of which it passes. It drops suddenly upon Aksú. A small stream from the north passes to the west of Aksú at about one mile distance and falls into the Aksú Daria about three miles south of the town.

Total distance 73½ tash or 75½ tash from Yárkand to Aksú.

At Terek Lángár, the first march from Yárkand, the natives are Dulans, a tribe presumably of Kálmák origin, having a distinct dialect of Turki and many customs different from those in force elsewhere; they extend as far as *Chilán*, the 13th march; they remain distinct from the natives of the Aksú and Yárkand districts.

Kokshál is the name usually given, not only to the Ush Turfán river, but to all the streams in the Aksú district, on account of the rice grown in the fields which they fertilize.

Kokshál (rice producing).

Kok really means blue, all green things springing from the ground are called Kok.

From Aksú to Ush Turfán—

1. To Sayik, 4 tash, through cultivation at the base of the hills and in the valley.
2. *Achtágh*, 6 tash.
3. *Ush Turfán*, 4 *tash*. Two serais in Ush Turfán, the last two places are in the Ush Turfán district, which is a separate command; it contains 8,000 houses, and is a highly productive district; flocks and cattle abound.

The water of Aksú is from springs, there is only one tank in the Yangi-shahr.

There is a very large sale of horses in Aksú; the Dadkhwah taxes the sale of horses, taking 12 puls on each transaction. On market day 600 loads of Indian-corn and wheat 1 tanga per charak; 300 loads of rice, 2 tangas the charak.

There are 200 dyers in Aksú.

(439)

SERAIS IN AKSU.

1. Khotan Serai, 50 rooms.
2. Kashguree Serai, 60 rooms.
3. Sheik Beg Serai.
4. Mullah Saduk Serai.
5. Dhung Serai.
6. Khona Serai.
7. Nar Kurgan Bai Serai.
8. Andijání Serai.
9. Yárkandee Serai.

There are three other serais within the walls.

Outside the walls.

1. The Custom House.
2. Charee Hakim Serai.
3. Kirghiz ditto.
4. Aíd Darogah Serai.
5. Mahomed Tokhta Bai.
6. Badshahi Serai.
7. Hají Serai.
8. Kush Najak Serai.
9. Imam Khwaja Serai.
10. Shukutlik Serai.
11. Abdullah Beg Serai.
12. Hikmut Baki Serai.
13. Eesah Kor.
14. Arjak.
15. Abdullah Bai.
16. Shah Mahomed Niaz.
17. Lalú Sheik.
18. Yanús Bai.
19. Túdi Bai.
20. Músa Akhúnd.
21. Mahomed Tej Bai.
22. Abrahim.
23. Shamsh Akhúnd.
24. Toonganee Serai.

There are altogether 33 serais outside the walls.

Inside the walls there are 84 musjids, and in the Yangi-shahr of Aksú 4 musjids.

Inside the walls 800 shops; every house is a shop almost.

Outside the walls 500 shops; 35 Coppersmiths; 33 Butchers; 22 Ashkhanas; 19 Bakers.

Outside the walls; 45 Coppersmiths; 40 Bakers; 34 Ashpaz; 50 Shoemakers.

The greater part of the population are in the suburb outside the walls.

In the entire district of Aksú there are 30,000 houses.

The principal merchants resident are—

1. *Shumsh Tar Akhoond.*—This man has agents who travel to Turfan, Úrumtsi, and Ili; he is said to be worth 500 Yamboos.

2. *Ahmed Shah Bai.*—He trades with Almati, Kashghar, Turfan, Úrumtsi; property valued at 400 Yamboos.

3. *Jait Darogah.*—Trades with all the cities before mentioned and possesses property valued at 500 Yamboos.

4. *Kassim Bai, Andijáni.*—Property valued at 1,000 Yamboos: this is the principal trader.

The tanab in Aksú district is measured in the square of 12 Kulaj (the length covered by the arms at sketch), a tanab is calculated to take 2 charaks of grain. Five tanabs make a putmun.

The tax on crops is fixed by valuation for cotton.

ROUTE No. XIII.

From Aksú to Kuchár. Authority, Captain Chapman.

From Aksú to Kuchár. The tash on this road are marked on regular Tash posts.

1. To *Jamgu*, 4 *tash*, through cultivation and past frequent habitations; watered by small canals. At Jamgu two serais and a small bazaar; about 50 houses.

2. To *Kara-Yalghán*, 3 *tash*. Kara (black) Yalghán (tamarisk), a low shrub jungle with willows, &c., tamarisk; water from springs about half way, where are a few shepherds' huts.

(440)

3. To *Yagh-Arik*, 7 *tash*. *(Oil-canal)* Through desert and low hills; at 3 tash there is a small place of shelter for cattle known as a Dhung; at the 4th tash there is a similar shelter, water procurable at both these places, streams from springs; at the 6th tash is a newly-constructed Karawul and some few houses with cultivation. About two miles to the south-east of this Karawul is a copper mine. The road here passes through a spur of the main range which is, however, very low at this point, canals. About 50 houses in Yagh Arik, a tank, gardens, &c. Yagh Arik is in the district of *Bái*.

4. To *Bai*, 7 *tash*. For 1½ tash through highly cultivated district with gardens, houses &c., to the bank of a river flowing south; the bed of the stream nearly half a mile across and very stony, the stream is rapid even in winter and is divided into three channels; the cultivation continues from the opposite bank all the way to Bai. This is a long stage and can be broken without difficulty at the hamlets *en route*. Bai is a walled town with three gates, and has its own Governor. There is a regular *urda*, four serais, musjids, &c., and three large tanks in the town; there are 62 principal shops inside the walls; there are two Madrassas and two schools. Bazaar is held on Friday after mid-day.

There is a garrison of 200 soldiers, 4 Yuzbashis, and 20 Panja Bashis.

There are six serais outside the walls of the town. It is estimated that there are 4,000 houses in the entire district of Bai.

Mahomedan population of the same type as at Aksú.

About 8 tash to the north of Bai are hot springs to which miraculous cures are attributed, the springs having been, it is said, called into existence by Hazrat Ali after a fight with infidels. There is a Ziarat at this place, and it is a place of pilgrimage; the road to it is a very difficult one.

5. To *Sairám*, 4 *tash*. The Bai district is left at about two miles from the walls; the entire road is through hamlets and cultivation, a considerable stream running through a shallow* bed immediately after leaving Bai. Sairám is larger than Bai, but there are no walls round it. The Hakim is under the orders of the Governor of Bai. There are 16 serais, 11 musjids, 4 tanks, and 75 principal shops, the population of the district is approximately the same as that of Bai. Bazaar is held on Thursday. Intermediate between Bai and Sairám and to the north about one stage, iron of a superior quality is obtained this is only worked for local purposes.

* Shah-Yar River.

Grain is exceedingly cheap, and rice is grown, but in smaller quantity than in the Aksú district.

6. To *Toga Dhung*. A single stage house, where provisions can be obtained; water procured from a distance, 5 *tash*.

The road on leaving Sairám very soon passes strips of cultivated ground and through a tamarisk jungle, 2 tash to Kizzil. Kizzil lies in a sandy strip; a stream is here encountered flowing south; there are willow trees and a few houses grouped on either bank; the bed of the stream is 40 yards across; from Kizzil to Toga Dhung a stony desert; to the south there are small sand hills, and the road here takes a more northerly direction.

7. To *Kuchár*, 6 *tash*. About two miles from Toga Dhung across a low ridge on the top of which is a serai. This gives a better halting place than the last stage, but water is obtained at the serai with great difficulty and must be paid for, the road turns southwards immediately after crossing this low ridge. There is no cultivation to within about two miles of *Kuchár*, but about 3 tash from the ridge is a Karawul in a gorge where the rocks appear to have been subject to volcanic action and are of a very dark color on a high hill to the north-east. At this point is a ruined city, the people commonly call this "Takht-i-Touran," the outskirts of these ruins are actually on the road; the

hill is of bare rock and, as before stated, presumably volcanic, but the ruins are of earth of a deep yellow color quite unlike anything on the hill itself; there are besides a large number of caves, excavated for residence; from below a high wall is visible, which is said to be the wall of an old palace. The city is said to have existed previous to the first Chinese occupation; the current story is that the city was consumed by fire sent down from heaven owing to the refusal of its ruler to adopt the Mahomedan faith, the blackened appearance of the rocks having given rise to this tale.

From the Karawul to Kuchár proper is 3 *tash*. *Kuchár* is a walled city of a circular form with four gates two of which have been lately closed.

The garrison of Kuchar is as follows:—There are two Panjsads, 20 Yuzbashis, 50 Panja Bashis, and about 600 soldiers; there are two schools and three Madrassas. The present Dadkhwah is Mahomed Tokhta Beg.

There are 205 principal shops inside the walls, 100 of which are always open, the remainder being closed except on bazar days. Four serais inside the wall; the city wall is surrounded by a ditch, which is kept full of water; there are 140 shops outside the wall, 15 serais outside. The Túngani have a separate quarter; they have 45 shops and have 9 serais; corn is ground by mills in which horses are worked; these are kept by Túnganis; the suburbs of the city are large in proportion to the rest of the town, there being only some 400 houses inside the walls, and 1,300 houses outside. The population of the district is said to be considerable, there being, according to calculated accounts, 22,000 houses in the district.

Alum and salammoniac are brought from Kuchar, and Pushum of a superior quality; it is considered the best obtainable.

Rice is grown in small quantities, but this is produced in large quantities at Shah Yart, the south of Kuchar, some 8 tash distant.

About 16 tash to north of Kuchar a large idol is said to exist, which is cut out of the rock; it is reported to be from 40 to 50 feet in height, it has 10 heads and 20 hands, and it is carved with the tongue hanging outside the mouth; the mountain behind this idol is exceedingly difficult of ascent; rumour says that it is resorted to by game of all kinds, but that the animals, owing to the protection of the idol, cannot be killed by the huntsman. A mountain lake of considerable size is said to exist in this neighbourhood, the drainage of which falls into the Yulduz and makes its way to Karashahr. The idol referred to above is said to grow thin during the daytime, but to increase in size during the night.

Salammoniac is obtained in large quantities from the neighbourhood of a volcano, which is at a distance of eight tash from Kuchar; this sells in Kuchar at 3 tangas the jing. The people of Kuchar declare that a description of rat circulates freely in the flames of this volcano without being injured; it goes by the name of Salamander. *Surrundoo (alum)* is also obtained in this neighbourhood, and sells for a half tanga the jing. The farming of the salammoniac and alum is let out for 4 *kurus* yearly.

There are copper mines between *Yagh Arik and Bai*. There is no monopoly with reference to the mining for copper ore; there are regular miners who can be hired by any one who chooses to try for copper, the agreement with them being that they are to receive one-half of what is extracted.

The copper is found in a low range of hills, and at a depth of from 30 to 36 feet; there is a smelting furnace on the spot, which is under Government supervision; the charcoal and the wages of the smelters are paid for by the finders of the ore, and from the copper extracted one-seventh goes to the Government.

It is usually calculated that the ore yields from one-ninth to one-eighth of pure copper which sells in Bai for 3½ tangas the jing.

(442)

Route XIV.

Route from Karghalik viâ KHOTAN to Tankse.

AUTHORITY CAPTAIN TROTTER FROM PUNDIT KISHEN SINGH.

Number of stage.	Names of stages.	Country or district.	Distance in miles.	REMARKS.
1	Karghalik to Yakin Langar.	Karghalik	13	A small village of four or five houses only, country well cultivated. At four miles is the village of Besharik, and at eight miles Lob village. Cart road all the way. Yakin is a halting-place for traders. Water, fuel, and supplies plentiful.
2	Chulák Langar	Gúma	20	A small village of 10 houses. At four miles is Khush Langar, and is the boundary between Karghalik and Guma. Country up to Khush Langar is cultivated, the rest of the journey is over a sandy desert, and no water except in a reservoir at Dabzokum brought daily from Chulak Langar. Supplies plentiful.
3	Gúma (height 4,340 feet).	Ditto	23	A small town and district with about 1,000 houses and a bazar of 300 shops. A Dadkwah or Governor and 200 sepoys are posted here. Two Langars or rest-houses are built on the road, viz., Silak Langar at 9½ miles, and Hajif Langar at 14 miles. The Kilian river is crossed near Guma. Road runs over a sandy plain the whole way.
4	Moji village (height 4,290 feet).	Ditto	24	A large village with a bazar. Road through a level cultivated country. At three miles the dry bed of a branch of the Kilian river, about 200 paces broad: is crossed. Súpi Khájam village is 9 miles, Cholo village of 50 houses 10 miles; Mukhila Langar at 11 miles; and the large village of Clauda at 19 miles. Road over a sandy plain. Fuel and pasture plentiful.
5	Piálma	Ditto	35½	A large village and bazar. At 2½ miles is Kosha Langar; at 10½ miles Koudla Langar; at 14 miles Jhanguia, a large place with a fort. The road from Sanju to Khotan joins at Jhanguia. The entire journey is over a sandy plain without habitation between Jhangula and Piálma. Water, fuel, and pasture plentiful.
6	Jáwá or Záwá Kúrghán (height 4,430 feet).	Khotan	25	Road over sand hills all the way. Water scarce, to be had only at Ak Robat at 15 miles, from a deep pucka well; again at Imam Salar's tomb and at Jawa Kurghán, a large village and bazar. Supplies plentiful.
7	Khotan City (Ilchi Shahr) (height 4,490 feet).	Ditto	20	Road over a cultivated country thickly inhabited throughout. The Karakash river, about half a mile wide with several channels, is crossed at 14 miles. Khotan is a large town, where a Governor and several hundred sepoys are posted. Numerous canals from the Karakash river intersect a large area of country around Khotan. At a distance of 15 miles north-west is the large commercial town of Karakash.
8	Yurung Kash (height 4,370 feet).	Ditto	3½	A large place of 500 shops. At 2½ miles the river Yurung Kash, (the same size as the Karakash) in two channels is crossed. The road for several weeks is flooded in hot weather. Jade and gold are found up the stream. Road good, and rich cultivation all round.
9	Dol Langar (height 4,420 feet).	Ditto	13	A large village of 150 houses. Excellent road, thickly inhabited, and rich cultivation all through the journey. At 10½ miles is Lob village and bazar of 50 shops.
10	Chira (height 4,220 feet).	Ditto	35	A town on the banks of a small stream with a bazar of 150 shops. Road as far as Ak Langar. The first 6 miles over a sandy plain covered with jungle. Elman Bazar 10 miles; Beshtoghrak Langar at 15 miles; Aisma Langar at 26 miles; Yakin Langar at 30 miles: all these places have rest-houses for travellers, with water and supplies. No cultivation except at Chira.

(443)

ROUTE XIV.

Route from Karghalik viâ KHOTAN to Tankse.—(Continued.)

Number of stages.	Names of stages.	Country or district.	Distance in miles.	REMARKS.
11	Kargkia Langar	Khotan	25	A small village of 10 houses. Road over an open country. At 10½ miles is the village and bazar of Gúlukma; at 16¼ miles Domaká village; from thence the country is covered with high forest. Supplies plentiful.
12	Kiria Bazar (height 4,580 feet).	Ditto	27½	A large town and bazar of 600 shops; at 5 miles is Ya Langar; at 9½ miles Siasgol; at 14½ miles Yaka Langar; at 22 miles Phundra village of about 100 houses. From Yaka Langar to Kiria country thickly populated and extensive cultivation. Felt is manufactured at Kiria. A branch road goes from Kiria to Sorghák gold fields as follows :—*1st March*, Toghrák (height 5,760 feet), 15 miles, a village of 50 houses, road over sand hills. No habitation except at Oi Toghrak. Kiria river 500 paces wide (with several channels), crossed near Kiria. *2nd March*, 15 miles, a rest-house with scanty cultivation round it. Road open and over sand hills. *3rd March*, Sorghák (height 7,000 feet), 34 miles, a place famed for its gold fields ; these fields are worked all round the year by men from Kiria, who with their wives and families sleep in temporary huts. One-fifth of the produce is paid as a tax to the ruler of Kashghar, who also purchases the remaining produce at a fixed rate.
13	Toghrak Langar	Ditto	23	A small village of 5 houses. Road through cultivation at 15 miles, the rest-house of Bughaz, to east of which, at 200 yards, is the Kiria canal here called Toghrak Ustang.
14	Polu village (height 8,430 feet).	Ditto	32	A village of 50 houses with scanty cultivation. Road runs along side the river over a plain for 8 miles, to where the river issues from a mountain gorge, up which the road passes to within 2 miles of Polu, when the river turns off to south-east. Road good.
15	Khiákde Camp	Ditto	17	Road, stony and bad, runs along the valley of the Khúrup or Polu river to Khiákde. A little fuel and grass. Gold dust is found in the stream here.
16	Ghubolik Camp (height 16,960 feet).	Ditto	25½	Camp near Ulugh Shahi Kul. A lake with sulphur mines in its neighbourhood. For 6 miles from Khiákde the road runs along the Polu stream through a narrow gorge between hills called Tangitar, then ascends the Ghubolik. At Diwan Pass, difficult for laden ponies. A gradual descent from thence for 14 miles to Ghubolik. Road bad at the pass. Grass, fuel, and water plentiful.
17	Aksu Camp	Ditto	19½	Camp on grassy plain between two small streams. At 12 miles a small pass crossed. Road good. Fuel and grass plentiful.
18	Arash Camp (height 16,020 feet).	Ditto	12	Camp on northern bank of the Kiria river. At 8 miles the Kizil Diwan pass is crossed. Road good, but stony at the pass. Grass and fuel plentiful.
19	Kiria Daria-i-bash Kul (height 16,880 feet).	Ditto	15½	Camp on small lake, the source of the Kiria river. Road stony and bad, slightly ascending to the lake. Grass scarce, and fuel plentiful.
20	Camp	Rudok	22	Camp near a small stream. Grass and wood plentiful. At 16¼ miles a pass is crossed forming boundary between Kashghar and Thibet.
21	Nikong Chumik	Ditto	17½	Camp on an extensive plain, with grass and fuel at hand. A mile from camp a pass is crossed. At 10 miles road runs along the west bank of the Yeshil Kul lake (height 16,160 feet). Grass and wood plentiful. Water scarce. Road good the whole way.
22	Daknák Camp	Ditto	25	Camp on an extensive plain. Grass and wood plentiful. Road along the banks of a dry water-course.

(444)

ROUTE XIV.

Route from Karghalik viâ KHOTAN to Tankse.—(Concluded.)

Number of stages.	Names of stages.	Country or district.	Distance in miles.	REMARKS.
23	Tashliak Kul (height 16,620 feet).	Rudok	28½	Camp on the northern edge of a fresh water lake. Two small passes are crossed, one at 10 miles and the other at 25 miles. Road good. Grass and wood plentiful.
24	Chumik Lakmo (height 16,600 feet).	Ditto	27½	Camp at the base of low hills. At 9½ miles the road runs along the eastern edge of the Mangchaka or Mangtza lake. At 13 miles ascends a low range of hills. At 19 miles passes a small lake. Road good. Water from a neighbouring spring. Wood and grass plentiful.
25	Lugrang Camp	Ditto	19	Camp between a range of hills. A pass crossed at about a couple of miles from Chumik Lakmo, from thence the road to Lugrang along bed of a partially dry stream. Water scarce. Wood and grass plentiful.
26	Sumzi Ling* (height 15,570 feet).	Ditto	17	Camp on left bank of Rudok river. At 4 miles the Kiangla (pass) is crossed, from thence along the Rudok stream to Sumzi Ling. Road stony. Fuel and grass plentiful.
27	Angche Chiortan	Ditto	31	Camp on right bank of Naichu river. Road for 8 miles good, at 10 miles ascend a pass, from thence along the river to camp. Wood and grass plentiful.
28	Noh village	Ditto	10	A small village of 25 houses on the Naichu river. Sparse cultivation. Road good and along the stream. Rudok lies about one long day's journey (by a circuitous route) to the south.
39	Pal	Ditto	20	Camp on the upper or east end of the Pangong Lake called here Chomo Ngala Ring Cho. Road in a westerly direction and along the banks of the Lake but very stony. Water good. Wood and grass plentiful.
30	Dal	Ditto	21	Camp on the Chomo Ngala Ring lake. Road stony, along the edge of the lake. Water good. Fuel and grass plentiful.
31	Aot	Ditto	12	Camp on south side of Pangong. Road crosses the lake by a shallow ford near encampment. About 2 or 3 miles north-west is the ruined fort of Kharnak. Water fuel and grass plentiful.
32	Thakung	Ladakh	29	Camp on south side of lake near a mountain stream which falls into it. Scarcity of fresh water. Road stony and along banks of the lake. Wood and grass plentiful.
33	Shushul	Ditto	8½	A village of 30 or 40 houses, with sparse cultivation. Road good, and supplies plentiful.
34	Lung Barma	Ditto	31	Good camping ground in the Lungchu valley. At 4½ miles from Shushul cross Gongta-la-pass, from thence along river bank. Road stony. Fuel and grass plentiful.
35	Tankse (Station V of Route III) (height 12,900 feet).	Ditto	24	A village of 50 or 60 houses, with some cultivation. Road stony and along Lungchu stream. Fuel and grass plentiful.
		From Tankse to Leh, *vide* Route III.		
		Total distance	742	

* The Pandit's thermometers were broken here.

ROUTE No. XIVa.

YÁRKAND TO KHOTAN.

AUTHORITY CAPTAIN CHAPMAN (COMPILED FROM NOTES BY RAMCHAND).

FROM YÁRKAND TO KHOTAN, BY KARGHÁLIK.

From Karghálik to Egun, two tash, across a ravine and for four miles across desert, and then entering cultivated land which continues for two miles, after which there is desert close up to Egun, beyond Egun desert, at three miles a Langar (Gombaz) with tank and two old tombs; eight miles beyond this through a bare desert to a place where a tank (containing about 20 mussuks of water) is prepared and covered in. Water is brought to this daily (one donkey load) from a distance of ten miles, under the orders of the Hakim of Gúma. Beyond this 10 miles through desert to Chúlák (Langar), where there is a tank. This is the usual halting-stage, and there is a post here for the examination of passports.

From Chúlák, 13 miles, to Serik Langar through desert. These Langars are all comfortably fitted up for travellers. Four miles beyond this is another Langar, where are trees and water; at this point the road divides, one going direct to Khotán and the other to the Gúma Bazaar; six miles to Gúma by taking the direct road, and not going to Gúma about four miles are saved, but all Rahdaris (passports) have to be shewn to the Hákim of Gúma.

Gúma is a considerable place; its district comprises that of Sánju. It extends from Egun to Piálmá in the Khotán direction, and southward as far as the Sánju pass. Gúma, for three miles through cultivated ground, then through desert for 12 miles to Mocha. Here is a comfortable rest-house prepared by a Mullah where travellers are entertained. A road diverges at this point to Sánju, which is distant 15 miles.

From Mocha (or Moji) for about 14 miles through desert to Zungoé or Jhanguiá; here is a small bazaar, and the place is surrounded by a wall built in the time of Habbibúlla; cultivation beyond this for some two miles, where there is a Langar, after which there is desert for 12 or 15 miles. Here there is a Langar, but no tank, only a well of extreme depth from which water is drawn. Five miles to Piálmá. Here there is a small bazaar. From Piálmá 15 miles to Ak-Robát. Here is a new rest-house prepared by the Amír's orders where travellers are entertained; there are two wells in the court-yard, which is 100 feet square: these wells are deeper than the one at the last Langar. Here there is a very high pole upon which a bell is hung, in order that during storms of sand travellers may be directed to the rest-house; during the night it is customary to place a light on the top of this pole for the same purpose. There is a regular establishment for the care of the serai. From Ak-Robát five miles to the Mazár of Imám Mahomed Shah. This stands in the middle of a desert; a large number of pigeons are kept by the Shaik custodian, for which a regular allowance of grain is made; the road is through a heavy sandy desert. There is a high pole at this point with a bell on it similar to the one at Ak-Robát. Through desert for five miles to Jawa: this is a small village of 20 houses, also surrounded by a wall in the time of Habbibúlla; there is a post for the inspection of passes and for search for gold and jade carried out of the Khotan District without permission. This is the point where the Atalik halted before the capture of Khotan, and from whence he enticed Habbibúlla into his camp. To the east of this village is a considerable stream flowing from the Sánju Diwán, which is crossed by a wooden bridge built after the fashion of Kashmir bridges. This is about 20 yards across. On the other side is a regular rest-house for the Hakim of superior construction. From this point cultivation and habitations extend uninterruptedly to Khotan at a distance of 25 miles.

Ten miles from Jawa the Kárákásh is crossed, where the breadth of the bed of the stream is about 400 yards. On the bank of the Kárákásh there is also a rest-house built to accommodate travellers detained by the rising of the river.

Seven miles short of Khotan is Do-Shamba Bazaar: this is a small village.

Marches.	Stages.
1.	Posgám.
2.	Karghálik.
3.	Egun.
4.	Chúlák.
5.	Gúma.
6.	Mocha.
7.	Zungoé or Jhanguiá.
8.	Piálmá.
9.	Ak-Robát, a short stage owing to heavy sand.
10.	Beyond Jawa, to the banks of Kárákásh.
11.	Khotan (Ilchi).

A road starting between Piálmá and Ak-Robát makes up the Kárákásh valley to the Suget pass and the Kárákorum.

To the east of Khotan and flowing close to the Yangi-shahr, 500 yards outside the wall, is the Yúrúng Kásh River; the bed of this stream is 600 yards broad, and in the dry season it flows in two channels; the road is often closed in this direction. Niaz Beg attempted the construction of a bridge, which was carried away by the stream.

From Khotan up the valley of the Yúrúng Kásh to Ladák; this was the road taken by Jumma Khan; it is said to be very difficult.

From Khotan (Ilchi) by 6 marches in a southerly direction crossing the Yúrúng Kásh at (Ilchi):—

3 tash to Sumpula.
3 ,, Hasha.
3 ,, Gunjutagh.
4 ,, Nura.
4 ,, Imám Mazár.
5 ,, Polú.

These six marches are through cultivated lands by small villages; no river encountered.

Fifteen marches from this point by a comparatively easy road to Changthang where the road between Leh and Lhassa is joined. Grass and wood during the entire route. Changthang is from 12 to 15 marches distance from Leh.

Water is procured by digging. This is a summer route; it was pursued by Nujjuf Shah, Envoy of the Maharaja of Kashmir, in 1864, with Nika, Mogul, who is now in Khotan.

The province of Khotan is divided into the following districts:—

Ilchi (Khotán proper).
Kárákásh (a Beg).
Keria (a Beg).
Chíra (a Beg).
Yúrúng Kásh united with Ilchi.
Nía united with Chíra.

The city of Khotan is of an irregular form, the circumference being approximately a mile.

The Fort and Urda of the Hakim are outside. The old Chinese wall round the town has fallen into ruin, but a wall now stands encircling the town and a large portion of the district at some considerable distance from the place itself: this is said to be some 20 miles in circuit. The gate through this on the Yárkand road is 1½ miles distant from the town.

Khotan is the great manufacturing city in the Amír's territory. The province yields very little cotton and very little grain, these being imported from Kashghar and from Gúma and Karghálik. Copper comes from Aksú and is worked into vessels, in great favor throughout the country. Rice is obtained from the same place.

Khotan is the great silk-producing province. Its gold mines and supply of jade are sources of wealth, the population, however, remain poor owing in a great measure to their indolence, work being taken up only as there is immediate necessity for the supply of daily wants. The immorality of the women of Khotan is proverbial, and the excess of women over men leads to much licentiousness. The inhabitants are chiefly artizans as distinguished from the cultivators of the other provinces of the Amír's kingdom. The resources of this province may be best arrived at by reviewing them separately.

Gold mines ... ... { Sorghák. Kappa. Chuggulaka. Charchand. Kárátagh. }

There are said to be altogether 22 places in which this mineral is found, but the above are those which are regularly worked.

3,000 people are employed at Sorghák; the mine at this place is said to be 400 feet deep.

4,000 people are employed at Kappa; the mine is said to be 100 feet deep.

At the other places there are no more than 40 or 50 workers.

The Sorghák gold is obtained in small beads and is of a red color.

At Kappa, large nuggets are obtained, but the gold is of a light color and mixed with sand. Gold is also obtained in the Yúrúng Kásh sands after the flood of the hot season has passed. The only tools used are a pick and shovel; no sieve is in use, but the soil is dug out in blocks and disintegrated by the heat of the sun.

The sieve is used in extracting gold from the sand of the Yúrúng Kásh river. On this last there is no tax paid.

The working of the mines is thus conducted. The workers are the poor of the country who sell the gold they obtain to established buyers, who keep a supply of utensils of food, &c., to meet the requirements of the workers. From these gold purchasers one-fifth of the yield is at once confiscated as the property of the Amír, who retains the right of purchasing any further quantity he may require at 120 tangas per ser (the market value being 138 tangas the ser). The whole of the gold obtained is indeed supposed to be purchased for the Amír, but a large amount finds its way surreptitiously into the market. On the road between Keria and Khotán there is a regular searching house where men are stripped if they are supposed to have concealed gold about them, women are examined and are then made to jump over a ditch, in order that any gold they have concealed may fall out. No large guard is kept at the mines, but a small detachment of soldiers watch the proceedings of the buyers.

The officials, however, even to the Beg of Keria, who is in charge, are said to be open to bribes and to study their own advantage.

The punishment for secreting gold is very light. The probable yearly yield of gold in the Khotan District is said to approach 7,000 sers, of which 5,000 sers, reach the Amír and about 2,000 are smuggled into the market.

The sale of gold is winked at, though disallowed. If a merchant is discovered to have obtained gold, no more than one-fifth will be confiscated, and the remainder is purchased at the fixed price.

Gold is readily bought up by merchants from India and Andiján.

A profit of one-eighth may be realized by conveying Khotan gold to either country.

Silver is also found in the province, but the yield was found insufficient to pay the working expenses and the mine opened has been abandoned.

Jade is obtained near the bed of the Yúrúng Kásh. There are two principal mines, one at a distance of 15 miles and the other at 25 miles from Ilchi. It is also procured from the bed of the river.

The tax on the working is one-fifth part paid into the treasury, and a tax of 1 in 40 from all traders who carry jade to other places; besides this all pieces that are of superior size and quality are bought up at a price fixed by the Dadkhwah of Khotan.

The old skilled carvers of jade have almost disappeared since the Chinese have been ejected. The mines and the working of the jade were closed until two years ago when Chinese traders began to reach Almáti. The Amír, however, allowed the market of Almáti to be flooded the first year and so much of the jade carried there from Khotan was inferior that it was not purchased, but returned to Khotan in this year.

The value of large pieces of this mineral may be judged by the following fact:—Quite lately some five men obtained a large block of a good description weighing some 40 jings; it was taken before the Dadkhwah, who purchased it as it was, in an uncut state, for 12 yamboos, the market price fixed upon it was however 60 yamboos; there was however no single merchant rich enough to purchase.

The existence of gold and jade is necessarily demoralising to the population; the number of workers in jade fluctuates, but the supply is in no wise exhausted.

Coal is said to be obtained in the Kuen Luen, but it has not been used since the Chinese were in authority; it was then brought from a considerable distance to Khotan.

Silk.—From the earliest time Khotan has been celebrated for its silk manufactures. *Sericulture* in Khotán is the same as already noted in Yangi Hissar, this is purely a domestic business: there is however a regular sale for cocoons in the market, the purchasers are regular traders who sell again to the reelers who purchase as they are in want of cocoons. There are poor people who dispose of the spun silk in the markets, which is chiefly bought by Andijáni merchants; there are however a great number of silk weavers (these color their own silks). Silk cloth made at Khotan is not exported, but spun raw silk goes in large quantities to Andiján. It is also found profitable to send the "waste" to the Almáti market, where it is purchased for Russian paper manufactories (it is a rumor that Russian notes are made from silk "waste").

Reeling does not go on during the winter season.

The white, black, and red and a fruitless mulberry are all known in Khotan, but the worms are fed only on the leaves from the fruitless tree and from that yielding a black fruit.

The produce of silk in its various stages, from the tending of the worm to the final operation, affords occupation to the bulk of the population in the Khotan province.

There are two kinds of silk, the white and the yellow, the latter being most esteemed: this is known as "Taiful," and is chiefly bought up for Andiján; the former is called "Kalawur," each of these are classed in two classes. As a rule the silk is reeled off on a single chirka, but lately an Andijáni has set up a wheel working 16 reels at one time.

Carpets.—Khotán carpets are celebrated for the excellence of their manufacture and for the variety of their patterns; they are made at three places in the Khotan province, more particularly Sumpula, Yúrúng Kásh (Char Shamba Bazaar), and at another village on the Keria road about three tash from the city (Se-Shamba Bazaar). Carpets are made of silk and of wool, gold thread is also sometimes worked into the silk carpets.

The wool used in the carpets is chiefly obtained from the hill districts through the Kirghiz; it is spun off and sold in the weekly bazaars. The dyeing is carried out by the carpet-makers.

The mordants used are—alum for dyes of yellow, brown, and red, and their various shades.

Grape juice for blues, and for mixed colors.

If green, the wool is first dyed yellow then put into an indigo solution.

If purple, it is first dyed red and then put into an indigo solution.

The dyes are indigo, madder, tookmuck (a seed), 'bukum.'

The price of labor is exceedingly cheap in the Khotan District, and the carpet makers are hired as required by those who are rich enough to purchase the materials and set up the frames.

There are two kinds of frames, standard, which are placed perpendicularly, and long flat frames near the ground; the latter are usually required for very large carpets, but the standard frames allow of better work being done.

The size of the carpets ranges from the small saddle carpet on which one man works at a time to carpets $3\frac{1}{2}$ yards wide, upon which 10 men are employed at one time. The pattern is given out by head of the party whom they term Aksakal. The patterns do not exist on paper, but are passed on from master to pupil and so remain from generation to generation. There are some 200 masters who are known for their carpet work.

It is to be noticed that in comparison with other parts of the country sheep are very abundant in the Khotan province, and that the wool is Khotan lamb skins of white color, form the linings of hats and posteens.

Men employed in carpet making under the Government receive 20 phools daily each man, and are not supplied with food; in ordinary houses, the daily wages is 10 phools and food for the day.

The copper vessels made in Khotan are superior to all others prepared in the Amír's territory; they are worked in a variety of patterns. There are about 30 shops at Khotan (Ilchi) where these are made. The copper, as previously stated, is obtained from Aksú.

Vessels for tea and for water are those principally made, the iron vessels from Russia being preferred as cooking utensils.

Patterns of various kinds are cut upon the Khotan copper work in very neat fashion.

Iron.—Iron work, stirrup irons, spoons, knife handles, &c., made of iron are inlaid with copper wire, which is usually of English manufacture and is obtained from Hindoostan; there are some 12 masters in this work at Khotan; the pattern is cut out in the iron of the stirrup, spoon or whatever article it is intended to ornament, and the wire is run into the pattern and the whole heated in the fire.

Hides.—Cow hides are largely exported from Khotan to Yárkand with sheep skins and goat. This is due rather to the existence of a large number of cattle and sheep in the Khotan province than to superiority in the manner of preparation. Skins of animals obtained in the Kuen Luen are also exported for the lining of posteens.

Sandal-wood and tea (brick) are obtained from the buried cities. The sandal is worked into beads, and the tea is sold in the market. The buried cities proper are said to be at a distance of many marches to the east of Khotan. A discovery of buried ruins has, however, lately been made quite close to the city of Khotan (Ilchi) at a distance of about four miles to the north-west. A cultivator working in his field was watering his crop; on the water suddenly disappearing into a hole and continuing to be absorbed, he dug up the place where the water disappeared and obtained a golden ornament said to have been a cow. Lately excavations have been ordered by the Dadkhwah and more gold has been found; the diggers are paid for any gold they may excavate at 110 tangas the ser. In the beginning of April 1874 a gold ornament of about eight sers weight was found by a man who had gone out in search of charcoal—this was in the shape of a small vase and had a chain attached to it. Rumours declared it to be neck ornament of the Great Afrasiab, and the finder was declared to have hit upon the spot where Afrasiab's treasure was buried; he was paid for the ornament at the rate of 100 tangas the ser, and a party was at once organized to search the neighbourhood. At present no fresh discovery has been made, and I cannot in any way fix the locality, but it is at no great distance from Khotan itself.

	PRICES.	Tangas.	Phools.
Cotton cloth, *Kám*,	per than (7 yards × $\frac{1}{2}$ yard)	1	30
" *Tulma*,	" (7 " " ")	2	25
" *Chakman*	" (22 " × $\frac{1}{4}$ ")	4	0
Kummerband (10 girras × $2\frac{1}{2}$ yards)		1	0

	MIXED CLOTHS OF COTTON AND SILK.	Tangas.	Phools.
Gazina (10 yards × 9 girras) per than	...	5	0
" (10 " " ") " No. 2	...	4	0
Mushroo (7 " × ½ yard) "	...	7	0
" (7 " " ") "	...	5	0

This is largely exported and is in general use in the province; it formerly obtained nearly double its pressent price, but the introduction of a large quantity of red chintz (Gulánár) from Russia has swamped the market. Mushroo is both dyed and stamped.

	SILKS.	Tangas.	Phools.
Dariaye (7 yards × ½ yard) per strip	...	6	0
" (7 " " ") " No. 2	...	4	0
" (7 " " ") " 3	...	3	0
Silk Chakman (13 yards × ½ yard)	...	20	0
" (13 " " ") No. 2	...	17	0

This is chiefly sold for the making up of chogas, the coloring of the strips is invariably made in pairs; the size of the than is however arranged so as to make one choga.

This silk is largely used for chogas throughout the country, but is not carried across the frontier.

	Tangas.	Phools.
Shiaye (7 yards × ½ yard), Nos. 1 and 2 ...	15	0
Dorooya (7 " " ") " "	10	0

These descriptions are largely imported from Andiján, the manufactured articles of Khotan being coarser than those from Andiján.

Numdahs for spreading on floor—

	Tangas.	Phools.
Ranging from the prayer Numdah	2	25
To large Numdahs at	20	0

They are made largely at Yúrúng Kásh.

	Tangas.	Phools.
Numdahs for packing bales of merchandize of a dark color	1	10
Rope is made from the bark of the mulberry and also from hemp, which is, however, very little grown in this province, each rope	2	0
Rope is also made of wool, per rope	2	0

There is no large sale in the Khotan market for foreign goods, nor are there established merchants in Khotan who trade across the frontier; the result is that goods are not so easily disposed of as in the Yárkand market, and there is more difficulty in obtaining by barter articles required for a return consignment.

Shrines in the Province of Khotan to which pilgrimages are made are—

Imám Akbar, Mazar, in the Kárákásh valley.
" Asgar " " "
" Assim " } Abu Bakr. } Yúrúng Kásh valley.
" Kassim "
" Iehran at Chira.
" Nasrudin ...
" Khwámudin ...
" Zahurudin ... } All at Mayartágh.
" Mayaudin ...
" Azail ... Kerai.
" Saydlik ... Nia.

Lungi Khanem, the gift of Imám Jafir Sádik, at Nia.

Imám Jáfir Sádik, in the desert beyond Nia, the principal place of pilgrimage from Khotán.

Imám Musa Kasim, at Khotán.

(451)

Trees known in the Khotan district are—

Saféda, poplar, six kinds	——Tarek Kara Tarek Kuppuk Tarek Hangi Tarek Malja Tarek Tagh Tarek	
Willow, four kinds	Suget. Tetoo Suget Kara „ Tagh „ Sirigh „	Khotan is also celebrated for its melons.
Jigda, three kinds	Jigda Khaga Jigda Kunkkisk Jigda	
Peaches, three kinds	Zard Alú Sia „ Ita „	
Plums, black and white	Yenista Khurmáni Ookcha	
Pears	Amrút.	

Quince.
Pomgranate.
Mulberries, black, white, and red berries.

Grapes of four kinds ... { Kismis or Kishmish.
Munaka,
and white Munaka.

The raisins of Khotan are exported to Yárkand and Kashghar; sugar is also made from the grape and exported.

GEOGRAPHICAL APPENDIX.

SECTION G.—ROUTES.

PART II.—*Routes in Turkestan derived from verbal information supplied by natives.*

ROUTE XV.

KUCHAR TO KARASHAHR, AUTHORITY CAPTAIN TROTTER, COMPILED FROM VARIOUS SOURCES.

Kuchar to—

1. Yakar, 4 tash. A small village.
2. Awát, 6 tash. Small village.
3. Bugar or Buigar or Bighol, 5 tash. Cross a river flowing south. Town and district containing about 100 houses, snowy mountains visible towards the north, large numbers of camel, sheep, and horses in this country.
4. Yangi-shahr, 6 tash. Cross Karatal River, road passes through sandy soil.
5. Achma Urtang, 5 tash. Country sandy; small village; cold climate; snowy mountains visible both to north and south.
6. Charchi, 5 tash. Good pasture grounds, and plenty of fuel.
7. Shákur or Ichertchou, 6 tash. Large lake in vicinity, country marshy.
8. Kurla or Koila or Kurungla, 4 tash. Large town, Kalmak population. District contains about 5,000 houses; town is situate on left bank of a large river; climate mild; and abundance of grain; grapes and other fruit in great profusion.
9. Yash Uigur, 4 tash. A post stage; coal found near.
10. Karashahr, 5 tash. Formerly an enormous city, one of, if not, the largest in East Turkestan; three days to its north is the important town and district of Lukchin, now chiefly inhabited by Kalmaks who migrate to the hills in summer. Climate cold, and much snow falls here; wheat, barley, and Indian-corn grow. There is but little fruit. A great rendezvous for merchants.

ROUTE XVI.

KARASHAHR TO TURFAN, AUTHORITY CAPTAIN TROTTER, COMPILED FROM VARIOUS SOURCES.

1. Tawalgha, 4 tash. Road through cultivation, mountains visible on north of road.
2. Tagharchi, 3 tash.
3. Ushak Tal, 3 tash. A post house.
4. Kárá Kizil, 7 tash. Road passes through sandy desert.
5. Kumush, 5 tash. Road passes through hills.
6. Ighar Bulák, 5 tash. Cross mountain ridge *en route*.
7. Subáshi, 3½ tash.
8. Takshun, 5 tash. A large town. Cross a mountain ridge *en route*.
9. Bugum, 4 tash.

(453)

10. Turfan, 4 tash. A large city. Climate hot, and fruits and grain produced in abundance. Snowy mountains on north, but at a considerable distance. Iron, copper, and gold found in neighbourhood. Water is procured from wells, and irrigation is carried on by means of underground canals.

ROUTE XVII.

TURFÁN TO KÁMÓL OR KHÁMIL OR HÁMÍ (AUTHORITY DR. BELLEW,† FROM NATIVE INFORMATION).

1. Kará Khoja, 4 tash. Town of 500 houses. Musalmán families.
2. Yangi Khhin, 4 tash. 100 houses. Water from *Kárez* or *Khhin* streams. At 2 tash is the Mazár Abúl Futtáh. 300 houses and bazar. Musalmáns.
3. Lukchun, 4 tash. Town of 2,000 houses. A stream from Ghochan Tágh north of Pichán, flows through the town on to the desert. In flood seasons it reaches Lob Nor.
4. Pichán* 4 tash. Town of 500 houses; all Musalmáns. Stream from Ghochan Tágh flows through the town. Outside is a Chinese fort.
5. Chightan, 5 tash. 100 houses. Springs. Kashghar frontier.
6. Lotu Changza, 5 tash. Camp ground at a well on Gobi desert.
7. Kosh, 6 tash. Well. Gobi desert.
8. Kudúk, 5 tash. Well. Gobi desert. Cyclones, sandstorms, and whirlwinds common on this part of the desert, and sometimes shifting sands overwhelm the traveller. Diabolical sounds and spirit calls here mislead the unwary to destruction in the trackless waste.
9. Otar Kima, 5 tash. Custom House, and 20 houses. Springs.
10. Otun Oza, 4 tash. Small village, cook-shop and restaurant. Springs.
11. Lodung, 5 tash. 50 houses of Musalmáns. Springs.
12. Shothá, 3 tash. 15 houses of Musalmáns. Springs.
13. Jighdá, 4 tash. 40 houses of Musalmáns.
14. Taghochi, 4 tash. 100 houses of Musalmáns. Bazar and fort. A river from the Kazanchi Tágh on the south flows by the city to Lupchuk and Karátaba and Lob Nor.
15. Sumcágho, 5 tash. 300 houses. Bazar and fort. Musalmáns. *Kárez* conduits. At 3 tash is Abdul Alim Fort, 2 gates; 500 houses. *Kárez*.
16. Kamul, 5 tash. Commercial city; 2,500 houses. A Chinese Governor with a Musalmán *Wang* over the Muhammadans. The city has three gates, and populous suburbs.

ROUTE XVIIa.

TURFÁN TO ORÚMCHÍ OR URUMTSÍ. (DR. BELLEW† FROM NATIVE INFORMATION.)

1. Shamál Ortang, 5 tash. Four houses. Stream from hills.
2. Dabánchi, 5 tash. Town and fort. 350 houses, in a valley amongst hills.

---

* There is an alternative road to Pichán or Pidjan passing by Sanghin and Lemtsin. There is also an alternative road from Pidjan to Kamul, lying to the south of the road here described. The southern road passes through the towns of Khoing and Khartoube.—H. T.

† I have not the means of verifying many of the routes given by Dr. Bellew, and they are inserted as given by him.—H. T.

3. Kaburghá Ortang, 4 tash. Four houses in ruins. Hilly country.
4. Dacyáyúnus, 5 tash. Ten houses and an *ortang*. Ruins of ancient city.
5. Orúmchí, 4 tash. A strong city; 8,000 houses. Double walls and four gates. Population mostly Khitáy and Tungani with Musalmán traders. Suburbs populous and extensive. Kalmák camps in hill country around.

ROUTE XVIII.
Orúmchí to Manás (Dr. Bellew).

1. Gumátur, 5 tash. Town, 500 houses of Kará Khitáy or Chinese.
2. Sánjú Ortang or Síjú, 5 tash. Ten houses. Mountainous country.
3. Sánjú, 4 tash. City and fort. 600 houses. Residence of Dáúd Khalífa.
4. Langar, 4 tash. Ten houses and an ortang.
5. Manás, 5 tash. City and fort. 800 houses; 3 gates.

ROUTE XIX.
Manás to Yuldúz (Dr. Bellew).

1. Shitáy, 4 tash. Fifty houses of Kará Khitáy and Túrgút Kalmák.
2. Kápotáy, 6 tash. 100 houses of ditto ditto.
3. Káydú, 4 tash. Town of 200 houses of ditto ditto on Káydú river.
4. Karású, 8 tash. 12,000 tents of Kará Khitáy and Kalmák of the Orúmchí District scattered about the streams all over the valley.
5. Purgáchí, 4 tash. 100 tents of the Karású camps.
6. Tomodá, 4 tash. 200 farms of Kará Khitáy of Yuldúz.
7. Tolí, 4 tash. 30 tents of Túrgút Kalmák. Salt mine in hills here.
8. Yuldúz, 5 tash. City of 1,000 houses. Capital of Kalmák Queen.

ROUTE XX.
Yuldúz to Ghúlja or Ila (Dr. Bellew).

1. Otáy, 4 tash. 100 tents of Túrgút Kalmák.
2. Tághí Yanza, 3 tash. 100 tents of Túrgút Kalmák. Wheat and barley grown here.
3. Sitáy, 4 tash. 60 tents of Chághir Kalmák of Yuldúz. Deer abound here.
4. Sintáy, 5 tash. Ten houses and an *ortang*. Ila or Ghúlja territory begins here.
5. Sarim Kol, 3 tash. The lake is two days' circuit and is fed from the Talaki hills, and has no outlet.
6. Tábahán, 1 tash. Chághir and Kará Kalmák camps on Talaki river.
7. Tálji, 7 tash. Ditto ditto ditto.
8. Chongshahr, 8 tash. Commercial town. Russian Consul resides here.
9. Ghúlja or Ila, 6 tash. Capital city. Russian frontier town and Telegraph Office. Emporium of China trade.

ROUTE XXI.
Kúrla to Lob (Dr. Bellew).

1. Yár Kurul, 4 tash. Over sandy waste with reeds, poplars, and pools.
2. Konchí, 5 tash. On the Tárim river below junction of the united streams from Kurla and Kúchá. Country desert waste. River banks belted with reeds and thickets of poplar and tamarisk; full of wild pig, stags, wolves, lynxes, and tigers.
3. Chol, 4 tash. Camp on desert of salt and reeds and pools.
4. Kará Kochún, 5 tash. Across a desert waste to the bank of Tárim river. Reed huts of Musalmán Kirghiz and Kalmák on river bank. Here the Lob district begins and extends eastward to the lake along the river course in little settlements of reed huts each with its own boats.

ROUTE XXII.
Karáshahr to Yuldúz Valley (Dr. Bellew).

1. Kará Modun, 6 tash. Ruins of a former Kalmák Khan's house.
2. Khapchigháy, 5 tash. Over a mountain pass: easy for horses and camels.
3. Bálghontáy, 5 tash. Waste country, cross low ridges and streams. Pine trees on the mountains.
4 & 5. Cross several hill ridges and camp on streams in the hollows at 5 tash each day. Vegetation very scanty. No fuel.
6. Dálan Dawán, 5 tash. Camp on snow at top of pass. No fuel nor forage.
7 & 8. Cross "Yatmish Dawán" = "Seventy Hills" by two stages of five tash each, and camp on snow. No fuel nor forage.
9. Yuldúz, 6 tash. Descend to Yuldúz valley. Meadows and streams, and Kalmák camps all over the valley.

The foregoing routes have been derived from Native traders and travellers, and are on the whole, I believe, tolerably correct, though varying in the different ideas as to distance and number of houses, and sometimes as to the nature of the road.

ROUTE XXIII.
From Khotan to Aksú.

Authority Captain Chapman, from Native information.

Khotan to—
1. Tarashi-gul. Through cultivation.
2. Lokul. Ditto.
3. Agroya. Desert.
4. Koshlush (or *Katilich*). This is the point where the Kárákásh and the Yurúngkásh Rivers unite.
5. Tagag. Desert.
6. Mazar-tágh. Sand hills.

7. Booksam (*or Bash Bonksem*).
8. Kolu.
9. Badlik Kotagh (*or Bedelik Kudok*).
10. Nurs-shakúm.
11. Balfuz-nakúm.
12. Khal.
13. Darialoe.
14. Máhtung. Here cultivation is encountered.
15. Karatal (*Kharatal*).
16. Besh-turkimirum (*Besh-arik*).
17. Aksú.

} Stages through desert

These are stages for donkeys, the chief trade being carried on with donkeys—copper, rice, iron, gold silk, and country cotton cloths going from Khotan. A trader with horses will accomplish the journey in 10 stages.

NOTE.—This route would appear to be reliable. Names in italics are found by me in Klaproth's Map.—H. T.

ROUTE XXIV.

FROM *Khotan* TO *Polu* (DIRECT). AUTHORITY CAPTAIN CHAPMAN, FROM NATIVE INFORMATION.

Khotan to—
1. Sampúla ... ... 3 tash.
2. Hásha ... ... 3 tash.
3. Ganju-tágh ... ... 3 tash. A large town.
4. Múra ... ... 4 tash.
5. Imám Mazar or Chehar Imám, 4 tash.
6. Polu ... ... 5 tash.

} These six marches are through cultivated lands with small villages. No rivers encountered.

NOTE.—This route agrees very well with another procured by me from a different source.—H. T.

ROUTE XXV.

KHOTAN TO CHARCHAND AND KURLA. AUTHORITY CAPTAIN TROTTER, COMPILED FROM VARIOUS SOURCES OF NATIVE INFORMATION.

Khotan to—
1. Dol ... 16½ Miles.
2. Chíra ... 35 ,,
3. Karákia ... 25 ,,
4. Kiria ... 27½ ,,
5. Ui Toghrak 15 ,,
6. Yessulghun.
7. Auras.

} *Vide* Route XIV.

8. Naia. At a day's journey from Naia in a southerly direction lie the Sorghák gold fields. The river, from Sorghák flows by Naia and passes in a northerly direction to Mazár Imám Jafr Sadík, a favourite place of pilgrimage, two days' journey north of Naia. From Naia to Charchand lie two roads across the desert, the northern road passes the camps of—

9. Baliklik.
10. Yer-tunguz.
11. Haidil-shah Kuduk.
12. Andhira.
13. Shiodaug.
14. Kára Buran.
15. Yantagh Kuduk.
16. Kok-muran.
17. Yang-arik.
18. Charchand.

At all these camps wells have been dug. On the alternative southern route the camping grounds are as follows:—

9. Subed (from here a road goes to Sorghák).
10. Apálik.
11. Shrine of Bibí Tujilik.
12. Moljia.
13. The Kápa gold fields.
14. Tokpai.
15. Hassan Gunj.
16. Achian.
17. Charchand.

The marches from Naia probably average between 20 and 25 miles in length.

Charchand is a place of some importance, and is said to be used as a penal settlement; a large river is said to flow through it coming from Thibet and ultimately finding its way to Lob. The geographical position of Charchand is not fixed with any degree of certainty but it is probably about equidistant from Keria (Route XIV.) and Kurla (Route XV.), to which latter place a road passes *via* Tartang and Chaktuk. Between Charchand and the Lob District are said to be oases where wandering tribes of Sokpos (Kalmaks) wander about with their flocks and herds. Near Charchand are the Khadlak gold fields, where 100 diggers are employed.

ROUTE XXVI.

KILA WÁMUR (ROSHAN) TO KILA KHUMB (DARWÁZ), AUTHORITY CAPTAIN TROTTER THROUGH ABDUL SUBHAN, FROM NATIVE INFORMATION.

Kila Wámur, chief town of Roshan.

1. Waznúd.
2. Amern.
3. Kila Chamarj.
4. Wadkhod.
5. Jarf.
6. Kila Khumb.

Road down Panjah or Amu river the whole way. Valley very narrow and precipitous, and not practicable for laden horses.

An alternative road goes in a northerly direction by which Kila Khumb may be reached in three days from Wamur.

ROUTE XXVII.

FROM BAR PANJAH (SHIGHNAN) TO KASHGHAR, AUTHORITY CAPTAIN TROTTER THROUGH ABDUL SUBHAN, FROM NATIVE INFORMATION.

From Bar Punjah—
1. Ghund village.
2. Ishtim or Wiar.
3. Charsim Fort.
4. Bugrúmal Pamir.* From here a road diverges to Khokand *via* Bartang.
5. Sasik-kul (2 lakes and Pamir).
6. Kara-su.
7. Murghabi.
8. Rang-kul.
9. Moji Chakr Arghin (Kirghiz).
10. Bulghár Pass (very high).
11. Tashbálig.
12. Káshghar.

ROUTE XXVIII.

FROM BUGRÚMAL PAMIR (NO. 4 OF ROUTE XXVII) TO KHOKAND.

1. Marjanai.
2. Sirich Fort (the capital of Bartang).
3. Kára Bulák (on Murghabi river).
4. Takhta Korum.
5. Altun Mazar, cross the Mazár Pass.
6. } Two marches in the Alai.
7. }
8.
9. Osh Kurghán by Draot (Deraout).
10. Marjilan.
11. Khokand.

NOTE.—These routes are very meagre, but have been used in conjunction with other sources of information in the compilation of my preliminary map. From Wamur there is a pathway up the Murghabi River to Sirich Fort, but so difficult that travellers nearly always go by the Ghund river in preference.—H. T.

* Probably the western prolongation of the Alichur Pamir.

(458)

ROUTE XXIX.

From Yur (see No. 15 of Route VIII) to Chitrál, authority Captain Biddulph from Native information.

Yur to—

1. Suneen.
2. Over pass.*
3. Kusht.
4. Topkhana.
5. Gazan (inhabited).
6. Manzagram.
7. Mastuch.
8. Booni.
9. Risht.
10. Ragh.
11. Chitrál.

} These are marches for a man on foot.

ROUTE XXX.

Táshkúrghán, No. 9 of Route VIII, or Saríɢh-Kúl to Hanza in Kanjúd (Dr. Bellew).

1. Davdár, 4 tash. Across valley and amongst hills to camp ground. The first stage from Táshkúrghán. No habitation.
2. Jilghar, 3 tash. Easy road amongst hills. Desert. No fuel or forage.
3. Ghajakbáy,† 4 tash. The same.
4. Rang or Zastol, 4 tash. Up a narrow gorge and over a glacier to
5. Rangal, 3 tash. Down a defile along a torrent. Road rough. Hills bare.
6. Talictáy, 4 tash. The same as last stage.
7. Lúpgal, 5 tash. Continue down the valley. Mountains high and bare.
8. Udmurkish, 4 tash. Desert country amongst hills.
9. Misgar.
10. Sás.
11. Khybar.
12. Passú.
13. Garnít.
14. Syábán.

} These are all the names of camp grounds. Each a day's journey from the other in vallies amongst hills. Streams from all sides, and scanty brushwood. Country very difficult and bare. Under snow for half the year.

15. Muhammadábád. First village from Táshkurghán. Fields and orchards on river bank.
16. Kanjúd, 3 tash. 1,000 houses and fort. Capital of Hanza on a large river. Fields and fruit trees in terraces on hill slopes.

ROUTE XXXI.

Sarhadd, No. 14 of Route VIII, Wakhán, to Kanjúd (Dr. Bellew).

1. Sháwar. In a glen. Fuel, water, and grass.
2. Langar.‡ On border of Pámir Khurd. Grass, fuel, and water.
3. Khaldarchit. In a glen of the Pamir hills. Ditto. No trees.
4. Lúptúk. A deep narrow defile in the mountains. Grass and water.
5. Irshál. Over a high mountain and a glacier down to
6. Astán. A long march down a defile along a river which flows all the way to Kanjúd.
7. Ispinj. A short march down course of the same river which is unfordable and only crossed on the ice in winter.
8. Reshit. Short march down the river.
9. Kirmín. Ditto.
10. Gírcha or Goorki. Twenty scattered houses and terraced fields.
11. Khybar. 6 houses, Ditto.
12. Passú or Basoo. 20 houses, Ditto.

---

* Closed for several months in the year.
† Probably Kila Ujadbai.—H. T.
‡ Station 13 of Route VIII.—H. T.

13. Sissúni or Sasoni. 10 houses, scattered houses and terraced fields. A very short stage to
14. Gholki. 30 houses, Ditto.
15. Gulmík or Gulmit. 100 houses on right bank of river. Leave river here and cross Durband Kotal, not high nor difficult in two stages to
17. Kanjud. 1,000 houses and a fort. Capital of the country, on a river which flows to Gilgit.

These routes, XXX. and XXXI., probably meet about Gircha. The accounts given are inconsistent, but as very little is known of the Hanza country, every contribution to a knowledge of it is valuable.—H. T.

Yárkand to Shahidula viá Kilik (Captain Trotter).

1. Yarkand to } Route I.
2. Karghálik }
3. Beshterek. 40 or 50 houses; 4 tash.
4. Balcrak Kurba. 200 houses, 2 tash.
5. Ákchik. 4 or 5 houses, 2 tash.
6. Takmà or Chakmà Camp, 4 tash. Kirghiz camp. Plenty of cattle.
7. Tupa Diwan, 4 tash. Pass. Good road.
8. Azghan or Kilik. Plenty of wood and grass.
9. Kilik Diwan. Higher than Tupa Diwan.
10. Larcha Ya Tuba, 3 tash. Good road. Plenty of grass and wood.
11. Gor Jilga, 4 tash.
12. Mazár Khoja, 2 tash. Large stream.
13. Shahidúla. (Routes I. to III.)

This road is said to be shorter and better than any other road between Yárkand and Shahidúla; grass and wood are to be found at every stage. Shahidúla can be reached by a horseman in five days from Yárkand. The man who supplied this route has tried all the roads from Yárkand and reports the road viá the Kilik Pass to be much the best for foot passengers.

CHAPTER VIII.

Section I.

A brief account of the geological structure of the Hill-ranges between the Indus Valley in Ladak and Shahidula on the frontier of Yarkand territory, by Dr. F. Stoliczka, *Geological Survey of India, Naturalist attached to the Yarkand Embassy.*

The following brief notes on the general geological structure of the hill-ranges alluded to, are based upon observations made by myself on a tour from Leh *via* Changchenmo, the high plains of Lingzi-thang, Karatagh, Aktagh to Shah-i-dula, and upon corresponding observations made by Dr. H. W. Bellew, accompanying Mr. Forsyth's camp along the Korakorum route to this place.

Before proceeding with my account, I will only notice that our journey from Leh (or Ladak) was undertaken during the second half of September and in October, and that we found the greater portion of the country north of the Changchenmo valley covered with snow, the greatest obstacle a geologist can meet on his survey. While on our journey the thermometer very rarely rose during the day above the freezing point, and hammer operations were *not easily* carried out. At night the thermometer sank as a rule to zero, or even to 8° below zero in our tents, and to 26° below zero in the open air. Adding to this the natural difficulties of the ground we had to pass through, it was occasionally not an easy matter to keep the health up to the required standard of working power.

Near Leh, and for a few miles east and west of it, the Indus flows on the boundary between crystalline rocks on the north and eocene rocks on the south. The latter consist chiefly of grey and reddish sandstones and shales, and more or less coarse conglomerates, containing an occasional *nummulite* and casts of *pelecypods*. These tertiary rocks extend from eastward south of the Pangkong lake, following the Indus either along one or both banks of the river, as far west as Kargil, where they terminate with a kind of brackish and fresh-water deposit, containing *melaniæ*.

Nearly the entire ridge north of the Indus, separating this river from the Shayok, and continuing in a south-easterly direction to the mouth of the Hanle river (and crossing here the Indus, extending to my knowledge as far as Demchock), consists of syenitic gneiss, an extremely variable rock as regards its mineralogical composition. The typical rock is a moderately fine grained syenite, crossed by veins which are somewhat richer in hornblende, while other portions contain a large quantity of schorl. Both about Leh and further eastward, extensive beds of dark, almost black, fine-grained syenite occur in the other rock. The felspar often almost entirely disappears from this fine-grained variety, and quartz remains very sparingly disseminated, so that gradually the rock passes into a hornblendic schist; and when schorl replaces hornblende, the same rock changes into layers which are almost entirely composed of needles of schorl. Again, the syenite loses in places all its hornblende, the crystals of felspar increase in size, biotite (or sometimes chlorite) becomes more or less abundant, and with the addition of quartz we have before us a typical gneiss (or protogine gneiss) without being able to draw a boundary between it and typical syenite. However, the gneissic portions, many of which appear to be regularly bedded, are decidedly subordinate to the syenitic ones. As already mentioned, the rock often has a porphyritic structure, and the felspar becomes pink instead of white, as, for instance, on the top of the Kardung pass and on the southern slope of the Chang-la, where large fragments are often met without the slightest trace of hornblende. To the north of the last mentioned pass the syenitic gneiss gradually passes into thick beds of syenite-schist, and this again into chloritic schist, by the hornblende becoming replaced by chlorite, while the other mineral constituents are gradually almost entirely suppressed. The syenitic and chloritic beds alternate with quartzose schists of great thickness. This schistose series of rocks continues from north of the Chang-la to the western end of the Pangkong lake and northwards to the Lunker-la, generally called the Marsemik pass. On the western route Dr. Bellew met similar rocks north of the Kardung pass at the village Kardung, and traced them northwards across the Shayok, up the Nubra valley to near the foot of the Sussir pass.

Intimately connected with the metamorphic schistose series just noticed, is a greenish chloritic, partly thin-bedded, partly more massive rock, which very closely resembles a similar rock found about Srinaggar. Only in this case certain layers, or portions of it, become often distinctly or even coarsely crystalline, sometimes containing bronzite sparingly disseminated, and thus passing into diallage. This chloritic rock forms the greater part of the left side of the Changchenmo valley, and also occurs south of the Sussir pass. I think we have to look upon this whole series of schistose and chloritic rocks as the representatives of the *silurian formation*.

After crossing the Changchenmo valley to Gogra, we met with a different set of rocks. They are dark, often quite black, shales alternating with sandstones. Many beds of the latter have a comparatively recent aspect, and are rather micaceous, without the least metamorphic structure, while the shales accompanying them very often exhibit a silky, sub-metamorphic appearance on the plains of facture. I observed occasionally traces of *fucoids* and other plants in these shales, but no animal fossils. On the Changchenmo route these shaly rocks forms the ridge of the Chan-lang pass, as well as the whole of the western portion of the Lingzi-thang; and they are met again after crossing these high plains and entering the Karakash valley, as far as Shinglung (or Dunglung). On the Korakorum route Dr. Bellew brought specimens of similar rocks from the Korakorum range itself. There can be but little doubt,—judging from similar rocks which I saw in Spiti, and from their geological relations to certain limestones, of which I shall presently speak—that we have in the shaly series the *carboniferous formation* represented.

In many localities along the right bank of the Changchenmo river, then at the hot springs north of Gogra, and on the southern side of the Changlang pass, we find the carboniferous beds overlain by *triassic limestone* which often has the characteristic semi-oolitic structure of the Krol-limestones south of Simla. At Gogra and several other places dolomitic beds occur; and in these, sections of *Dicerocardium Himalayaense* are not uncommon. In other places beds are met with full of *crinoid* stems. North of the Lingzi-thang plain—to the west of which the hills are mostly composed of the same triassic limestone—a red brecciated, calcareous conglomerate is seen at the foot of the Compass-lá, but this conglomerate gradually passes into the ordinary grey limestone, which forms the ridge, and undoubtedly belongs to the same group of triassic rocks. The last place where I saw the triassic limestone was just before reaching the camping ground Shinglung; here it is an almost white or light grey compact rock, containing very perfect sections of *Megalodon triqueter*, the most characteristic triassic fossil. On Mr. Forsyth's route Dr. Bellew met with similar triassic limestones on the northern declivities of the Sussir pass, and also on the Korakorum pass overlying the carboniferous shales and sandstones previously noticed. On the Korakorum the triassic limestone contains spherical corals very similar to those which had been a few years ago described by Professor Ritter von Reuss from the Hallstadt beds in the Alps, and which are here known to travellers as Korakorum stones. A description of these very remarkable corals will be given subsequently.

Returning to our Lingzi-thang route, we leave, as already mentioned, the last traces of triassic limestone at Shinglung, in the upper Karakash valley. Here the limestone rests upon some shales, and then follow immediately the same chloritic rock which we noticed on the Lunker-la, alternating with quartzose schists, both of which must be regarded as of upper palæozoic age.

At Kizil-jilga regular sub-metamorphic slates appear, alternating with a red conglomerate and red sandstones, and further on dark slate is the only rock to be seen the whole way down the Karakash, until the river assumes a north-easterly course, some fourteen miles west of the Karatagh pass. From here my route lay in a north-westerly direction towards Aktagh, and the same slaty rock was met with along the whole of this route up to the last mentioned place. Dr. Bellew also traced these slates from the northern side of the Korakorum to Aktagh. They further continue northwards across the Suget-lá, a few miles north of the pass, as well as in single patches down the Suget river to its junction with the Karakash. The irregular range of hills to the south of the portion of the Karakash river, which flows almost east-west from Shahidula, on its southern side entirely consists of these slates, while on the northern side it is composed of a fine-grained syenite, which also forms the whole of the Kuenlún range along the right bank of the Karakash river, and also is the sole rock composing the hills about the camping ground Shah-i-dula. The slates of which I spoke are, on account of the close cleavage, mostly fine, crumbling, not metamorphic, and must, I think, be referred to the silurian group. They correspond to the metamorphic schists on the southern side of the Korakorum ranges.

Thus we have the whole system of mountain ranges between the Indus and the borders of Turkistan bounded on the north and south by syenitic rocks, including between them the silurian, carboniferous, and triassic formations. This fact is rather remarkable, for, south of the Indus, we have nearly all the principal sedimentary formations represented from the silurian up to the eocene, and most of the beds abound in fossils.

The only exception to which I can allude on the Changchenmo route is near Kium, in the Changchehmo valley. Here there are on the left bank of the river some remarkably recent looking sandstones and conglomerates, dipping at an angle of about 45° to north-by-east, and at the foot of these beds rise the hot springs* of Kium. I think it probable that this conglomerate has eastward a connection with the eocene deposits, which occur at the western end of the Pangkong lake, and in the Indus valley south of it.

In the previous notes I have scarcely alluded to the dip of the rocks at the different localities. The reason is that there is indeed very great difficulty in directly observing both the dip and the strike. At the western end of the Pangkong lake the dip of the metamorphic schists is mostly a south-westerly one, but further on nearly all the rocks dip at a moderate angle to north-east, north-by-east, or to north. On the Lingzi-thang, just after crossing the Changlang, the shales are mostly highly inclined, but further on the limestones lie unconformably on them and dip to north-east. Wherever the hills consist merely of shales and slates, their sides are generally so thickly covered with débris and detritus that it becomes almost an exception to observe a rock *in situ*.

The débris is brought down in large quantities by the melting snow into the valleys, and high banks of it are everywhere observable along the water-courses. At a somewhat remote—say diluvial—period this state of things has operated on a far greater scale. Not only were the lakes, like the Pangkong, much more extensive, but valleys like the Changchenmo, or the Tanktze valley, sometimes became temporarily blocked up by glaciers, or great landslips, and the shingle and clay deposits were often accumulated in them to a thickness of two or more hundred feet. Near Aktagh similar deposits of stratified clay exist of about 160 feet thickness, and extend over an area of more than one hundred square miles. There can be but little doubt that when these large sheets of water were in existence, the climate of these now cold and arid regions was both milder and moister, and naturally more favorable to animal and vegetable life than it is now. A proof of this is given, for instance, by the occurrence of subfossil *Succineæ*, *Helices*, and *Pupæ* in the clay deposits of the Pangkong lake, while scarcely any land mollusk could exist at the present time in the same place.

SECTION II.

GEOLOGICAL NOTES ON THE ROUTE TRAVERSED BY THE YARKAND EMBASSY FROM SHAHIDULA TO YARKAND AND KASHGHAR, *by* DR. F. STOLICZKA, *Naturalist attached to the Embassy*.

IN a former communication I had already occasion to notice that the rocks composing the Kuenlún range near Shahidula, chiefly consist of syenitic gneiss, often interbedded, and alternating, with various metamorphic and quartzose schists. Similar rocks continue the

---

* The temperature of these hot springs varies from 60° to 125°. They form no deposit of gypsum, like the springs north of Gogra, but there is a good deal of soda deposit round them.

whole way down the Karakash river for about twenty-four miles. After this the road follows, in a somewhat north-westerly direction, a small stream leading to the Sanju- (or Grimm-) Pass. Here the rocks are chiefly true mica schist, in places full of garnets. Near, and on, the pass itself chloritic and quartzose schists prevail, in which veins of pale green jade occur, numerous blocks containing this mineral having been observed near the top of the pass. All the strata are very highly inclined, often vertical, the slopes of the hills, and in fact of the entire range, being on that account rather precipitous, and the crests of the ridges themselves very narrow.

To the north of the Sanju Pass we again meet with metamorphic, mostly chloritic schists, until we approach the camping place Tám, where, distinctly bedded, sedimentary rocks cap the hills of both sides of the valley. They are dark, almost black, silky slates, resting unconformably on the schists, and are overlain by a grey, partly quartzitic sandstone, passing into conglomerate. The last rock contains particles of the black slates, and is, therefore, clearly of younger age. Some of the conglomeratic beds have a remarkably recent aspect, but others are almost metamorphic. In none of the groups, the slates or sandstones or conglomerates, have any fossils been observed; but they appear to belong to some palæozoic formation. They all dip at from 40° to 50° towards north-east, extending for about one and a half miles down the Sanju valley. Here they are suddenly cut off by metamorphic schists, but the exact place of contact on the slopes of the hills is entirely concealed by débris. The schists are only in one or two places interrupted by massive beds of a beautiful porphyritic gneiss, containing splendid crystals of orthoclase and biotite; they continue for about eighteen miles to the camp Kiwáz. On the road, which often passes through very narrow portions of the valley, we often met with old river deposits, consisting of beds of gravel and very fine clay, which is easily carried off by only a moderate breeze, and fills the atmosphere with clouds of dust. These old river deposits reach in many places up to about one hundred and fifty feet above the present level of the river, which has to be waded across at least once in every mile.

At the camp Kiwáz the hills on both sides of the valley are low, composed of a comparatively recent looking conglomerate, which in a few places alternates with beds of reddish, sandy clay, the thickness of the latter varying from two to five feet only. These rocks strikingly resemble those of the supra-nummulitic group, so extensively represented in the neighbourhood of Mari. They decompose very readily, covering the slopes of the mountains with loose boulders and sand, under which very little of the original rock can be seen. Near the camp the beds dip at about 40° to north-east, but about one mile and a half further on a low gap runs parallel to the strike, and on the other side of it the beds rise again, dipping with a similar angle to south-west, thus forming a synclinal at the gap. Below the conglomerate there crops out a grey, often semi-crystalline limestone, containing in some of its thick layers large numbers of *Crinoid* stems, a *Spirifer*, very like *S. striatus*, and two species of *Fenestella*. Following the river to north by east, this carboniferous limestone again rests on chloritic schist, which, after a mile or two, is overlain by red sandstone, either in horizontal or very slightly inclined strata. Both these last named rocks are very friable, easily crumbling between the fingers, particularly the latter, from which the calcareous cement has almost entirely been dissolved out. At Sanju the red sandstones underlie coarse grey calcareous sandstones and chloritic marls, some beds of which are nearly exclusively composed of *Gryphæa vesicularis*, many specimens of this most characteristic middle cretaceous fossil being of enormous size. The *Gryphæa* beds and the red sandstones are conformable to each other, and although I have nowhere seen them interstratified near their contact, there is strong evidence of their being both of cretaceous age. Both decompose equally easily, and the *Gryphæa* beds have indeed in many places been entirely denuded. They have supplied the greater portion of the gravel and beds of shifting sand, which stretch in a north-easterly direction towards the unknown desert-land.

On the road from Sanju to Yarkand, which first passes almost due west and after some distance to north-west, we crossed extensive tracts of those gravel beds, and of low hills almost entirely composed of clay and sand, though we only skirted the true desert country. Locally, as, for instance, near Oi-tograk and Boria, pale reddish sandstones crop out from under the more recent deposits, but they appear to be younger than the cretaceous red sandstones underlying the *Gryphæa* beds; the former most probably belong to some upper tertiary group. Among the sandy and clayey deposits I was not a little surprised to find true *Loess*, as typical as it can anywhere be seen in the valleys of the Rhine or of the Danube. I might even speak of 'Berg' and 'Thal-Löss,' but I shall not enter into details on this occasion; for I may have a much better opportunity of studying this remarkable deposit. At present I will only notice that commonly we meet with extensive deposits of *Loess* only in the valleys. Its thickness varies in places from ten to eighty, and more, feet; a fine yellowish *unstratified* clay, occasionally with calcareous concretions and plant fragments. In Europe the origin of this extensive deposits was, and is up to the present date, a disputed question. Naturally, if a geologist is not so fortunate as to travel beyond the 'Rhine' or 'Donau-thal,' and is accustomed to be surrounded with the verdant beauty of these valleys, he might propose half a dozen theories, and as he advances in his experience disprove the probability of one after the other, until his troubled mind is wearied of prosecuting the object further. Here in the desert countries where clouds of fertile dust replace those of beneficial vapour, where the atmosphere is hardly ever clear and free from sand, nay occasionally saturated with it, the explanation that the *Löss is a subaerial deposit*, is almost involuntarily pressed upon one's mind. I do not think that by this I am advancing a new idea; for,—unless I am very much mistaken,—it was my friend Baron Richthofen who came to a similar conclusion during his recent sojourn in Southern China.

Yarkand lies about five miles from the river, far away from the hills, in the midst of a well cultivated land, intersected by numerous canals of irrigation; a land full of interest for the agriculturist, but where the geological mind soon involuntarily falls into repose. And what shall I say of our road from Yarkand to Kashghar? Little of geological interest, I am afraid.

Leaving Yarkand we passed for the first few miles through cultivated land, which, however, soon gave away to the usual aspect of the desert, or something very little better. A few miles south-west of Kokrabad a low ridge runs from south-east to north-west. If we are allowed to judge from the numerous boulders of red standstone and *Gryphæa* marl, some of considerable size and scarcely river-worn, we might consider the ridge as being composed of cretaceous rocks. But one hardly feels consoled with the idea, that in wading through the sand he should only cross a once cretaceous basin, and that the whole of this country should have remained free from encroachment of any of the kainozoic seas. It is very dangerous to jump to conclusions regarding the nature of a ground untouched by the geological hammer. The answer to any doubt must for the present remain a desideratum. On the fourth day of our march approaching Yangihissar, we also crossed a few very low ridges, but these consisted entirely of gravel and marly clay beds, most of them dipping with a very high angle to south by east, the strike being nearly due east and west. South of Yangihissar the ridge bent towards south-west, and there was also a distant low ridge traceable in a north-easterly direction, the whole having the appearance of representing the shore of some large inland watersheet. From Yangihissar to Kashghar we traversed only low land, as usually more or less thickly covered with a saline efflorescence, but still to a considerable extent cultivated. Here in Kashghar the distant heights of the Kuenlún, of the Pamir and Thinshan ranges, are ready to unfold their treasures, whether we go in a southerly, or westerly, or northerly direction; geological ground is even nearer to be found in some of the low ridges from twelve to thirty miles distant, while the Moralbashi forests lying eastward, invite the zoologist and sportsman. I trust we shall soon be able to see and relate some novelties from our neighbourhood.

Kashghar, 20th December 1873.

Section III.

Note regarding the occurrence of jade in the Karakash valley, on the southern borders of Turkistan, *by* Dr. F. Stoliczka, *Naturalist attached to the Yarkand Embassy.*

The portion of the Kuenlún range, which extends from Shahidula eastward towards Kotan, appears to consist entirely of gneiss, syenitic gneiss, and metamorphic rocks, these being quartzose, micaceous, or hornblendic schists. On the southern declivity of this range which runs along the right bank of the Karakash river, are situated the old jade mines, or rather quarries formerly worked by the Chinese. They are about seven miles distant from the Kirghíz encampment, Belakchi, which itself is about twelve miles south-east of Shahidula. I had the pleasure of visiting the mines in company with Dr. Bellew and Captain Biddulph, with a Yarkandee official as our guide.

We found the principal jade locality to be about one and a half miles distant from the river, and at a height of about five hundred feet above the level of the same. Just in this portion of the range a few short spurs abut from the higher hills, all of which are, however, as usually, thickly covered with débris and sand, the result of disintegration of the original rock. The whole has the appearance as if an extensive slip of the mountain-side had occurred. Viewing the mines from a little distance the place seemed to resemble a number of pigeon-holes worked in the side of the mountain, except that they were rather irregularly distributed. On closer inspection we saw a number of pits and holes dug out in the slopes, extending over a height of nearly a couple of 100 feet, and over a length of about a quarter of a mile. Each of these excavations has a heap of fragments of jade and rock at its entrance. Most of them are only from ten to twenty feet high and broad, and their depth rarely exceeds twenty or thirty feet; only a few show some approach to low galleries of moderate length, and one or two are said to have a length of eighty or a hundred feet. Looking on this mining operation as a whole, it is no doubt a very inferior piece of the miner's skill; nor could the workmen have been provided with any superior instruments. I estimated the number of holes at about hundred and twenty; but several had been opened only experimentally, an operation which had often to be resorted to on account of the superficial sand concealing the underlying rock. Several pits also which were probably exhausted at a moderate depth were again filled in; their great number, however, clearly indicates that the people had been working singly or in small parties.

The rock of which the low spurs at the base of the range are composed, is partly a thin bedded, rather sandy, syenitic gneiss, partly mica and hornblendic schist. The felspar gradually disappears entirely in the schistose beds, which on weathered planes often have the appearance of a laminated sandstone. They include the principal jade-yielding rocks, being traversed by veins of a pure white, apparently zeolitic mineral, varying in thickness from a few to about forty feet, and perhaps even more. The strike of the veins is from north-by-west to sout-by-east, or sometimes almost due east-and-west; and their dip is either very high towards north, or they run vertically. I have at present no sufficient means to ascertain the true nature of this vein-rock, as it may rather be called, being an aggregate of single crystals. The mineral has the appearance of albite, but the lustre is more silky, or perhaps rather glassy, and it is not in any way altered before the blowpipe, either by itself, or with borax or soda. The texture is somewhat coarsely crystalline, rhombohedric faces being on a fresh fracture clearly traceable. It sometimes contains iron pyrites in very small particles, and a few flakes of biotite are also occasionally observed. This zeolitic rock is again traversed by veins of nephrite, commonly called jade; which, however, also occurs in nests. There appear to be two varities of it, if the one, of which I shall presently speak, really deserves the name of jade. It is a white tough mineral, having an indistinct cleavage in two different directions, while in the other directions the fracture is finely granular or splintry, as in true nephrite. Portions of this mineral, which is apparently the same as usually called white jade, have sometimes a fibrous structure. This white jade rarely occupies the whole thickness of a vein; it usually only occurs along the sides in immediate contact with the zeolitic vein-rock, with which it sometimes appears to be very closely connected. The middle part of some of the veins and most of the others entirely consists of the common green jade, which is characterized by a thorough absence of cleavage, great toughness, and rather dull vitreous lustre. The hardness is always below 7, generally only equal to that of common felspar, or very little higher, though the polished surface of the stone appears to attain a greater hardness after long exposure to the air. The colour is very variable, from pale to somewhat darker green, approaching that of pure serpentine. The pale green variety is by far the most common, and is in general use for cups, mouth-pieces for pipes, rings and other articles used as charms and ornaments. I saw veins of the pale green jade fully amounting in thickness to ten feet; but it is by no means easy to obtain large pieces of it, the mineral being generally fractured in all directions.

Like the crystalline vein-mineral, neither the white nor the green variety of jade is affected by the blowpipe heat, with or without addition of borax or soda. Green jade of a brighter colour and higher translucency is comparatively rare, and, already on that account, no doubt much more valuable. It is usually only found in thin veins of one or a few inches; and even then it is generally full of flaws.

Since the expulsion of the Chinese from Yarkand in 1864, the jade quarries in the Karakash valley have become entirely deserted. They must have yielded a considerable portion of the jade of commerce; though no doubt the workmen made a good selection already on the spot, taking away only the best coloured and largest pieces; for even now a great number of fair fragments, measuring 12 to 15 inches in diameter, form part of the rubbish thrown away as useless.

The Belakchi locality is, however, not the only one which yielded jade to the Chinese. There is no reason to doubt the existence of jade along the whole of the Kuenlún range, as far as the mica and hornblendic schists extend. The great obstacle in tracing out the veins and following them when once discovered, is the large amount of superficial débris and shifting sand, which conceal the original rock *in situ*. However, fragments of jade may be seen among the boulders of almost every stream which comes down from the range. We also observed large fragments of jade near the top of the Sanju Pass, which on its southern side at least mostly consists of thin-bedded gneiss and hornblendic schist.

Another rich locality for jade appears to exist somewhere south of Kotan, from whence the largest and best coloured pieces are said to come; most of them are stated to be obtained as boulders in a river bed, though this seems rather doubtful. Very likely the Chinese worked several quarries south of Kotan, similar to those in the Karakash valley, and most of the jade from this last locality was no doubt brought into Kotan, this being the nearest manufacturing town. A great number of the better polished ornaments, such as rings, &c., sold in the bazaar of Yarkand, have the credit of coming from Kotan; possibly they are made there by Chinese workmen, but the art of carving seems to have entirely died away, and indeed it is not to be expected that such strict Mahomedans, as the Yarkandees mostly are, would eagerly cultivate it. If the Turkistan people will not take the opportunity of profiting by the export of jade, or if no new locality of that mineral is discovered within Chinese territory, the celestial people will feel greatly the want of the article, and good carved specimens of jade will become great rarities. The Chinese seem to have been acquainted with the jade of the Kuenlún mountains during the last two thousand years, for Kotan jade is stated to be mentioned* "by Chinese authors in the time of the dynasty under Wuti (B.C. 148—86.)"

Yarkand, 14th November 1873.

SECTION IV.

GEOLOGICAL OBSERVATIONS MADE ON A VISIT TO THE CHADERKUL, THIAN SHAN RANGE, *by* DR. F. STOLICZKA, *Naturalist attached to the Yarkand Embassy.*

AFTER a stay of nearly a month in our embassy quarters at Yangishar, near Kashgar, the diplomacy of our envoy secured us the Amir's permission for a trip to the Chaderkul, a lake situated close on the Russian frontier, about 112 miles north by west of Kashgar, among the southern branches of the Thian Shan range. Under the leadership of Colonel Gordon we, Captain Trotter and myself, left Yangishar about noon on the last day of 1873, receiving the greeting of the new year in one of the villages of the Artush valley, some 25 miles north west from our last quarters. On the 1st of January 1874 we marched up the Toyan river for about 20 miles to a small encampment of the Kirghiz, called Chungterek; and following the Toyan and passing the forts Murza-terek and Chakmák, we camped on the fifth day at Turug-at-bela, about 11 miles south of the Turug pass, beyond which five miles further on lies the Chaderkul. On the sixth we visited the lake, and on the day following retraced our steps, by the same route we came, towards Kashgar, which we reached on the 11th January.

* Yule's Marco Polo, Vol. I, p. 177.

Having had a shooting day at Turug-at-bela, and one day's halt with the King's obliging officers at the Chakmák fort, we were actually only nine days on the march, during which we accomplished a distance of about 224 miles. It will be readily understood that while thus marching, there was not much time to search for favorable sections in out-of-the-way places; but merely to note what was at hand on the road. I can, therefore, only introduce my geological observations as passing remarks.

Leaving the extensive löss-deposits of the valley of the Kashgar Daria, the plain rises very gradually towards a low ridge, of which I shall speak as the Artush range. It is remarkably uniform in its elevation, averaging about 400 feet, somewhat increasing in height towards the west and diminishing towards the east, which direction is its general strike. This range separates the Kashgar plain from the valley of the Artush river, which cuts through the ridge about eight miles nearly due north of the city. Viewed from this, the entire ridge appears very regularly furrowed and weather-worn on its slope, indicating the softness of the material of which it is composed. One would have, however, hardly fancied that it merely consists of bedded clay and sand, mostly yellowish white, occasionally reddish, and sometimes with interstratified layers of greater consistency, hardened by a calcareous or silicious cement. On the left bank, in the passage of the river through the ridge, the beds appear in dome-shape, gently dipping towards the Kashgar plain on one side, and with a considerably higher angle into the Artush valley on the other. On the right bank at the gap all the exposed beds dip southward, those on the reverse of the anticlinal having been washed away by the Artush river up to the longitudinal axis, and thus exposing almost vertical faces. These remarkably homogeneous, clayey, and sandy beds may appropriately be called *Artush beds*, and although I could nowhere find a trace of a fossil in them, it seems to me very probable that they are of marine origin and of neogene age.

The southern slopes of the ridge are on their basal half entirely covered with gravel, which in places even extends to the top, assuming here a thickness of from 10 to 15 feet. Locally the gravel beds are separated from the main range by a shallow depression, forming a low ridge which runs along the base of the higher one, and from which it is, even in the distance, clearly discernible by its dark tint. The pebbles in the gravel are mostly of small size and well river-worn; they are derived to a very large extent from grey or greenish sandstones and shales, black or white limestone, more rarely of trap, basalt, and of gneiss. With the exception of the last-named rock, all the others had been met with *in situ* in the upper Toyan valley. The pieces of gneiss belong to a group of metamorphic rock which is usually called *Protogine*. It is mainly composed of quartz and white or reddish orthoclase, with a comparatively small proportion of a green chloritic substance. The white felspar variety generally contains as an accessory mineral schorl, in short, rather thick, crystals. I shall subsequently allude to the probable source from which the protogine pebbles might have been derived.

From Artush we marched, as already stated, northwards, up the Toyan river, and for the next 22 miles one was surprised to find nothing but the same Artush—and gravel—deposits, the former constantly dipping at a high angle to north by west, and the latter resting on them in slightly inclined or horizontal strata; while among the recent river deposits in the bed of the valley itself the order of things appeared reversed. The gravels, having first yielded to denudation, were here underlying the clays derived from the Artush beds, thus preparing an arable ground for the agriculturist, whenever a favourable opportunity offered itself. A few miles south of Chungterek the laminated Artush beds entirely disappeared under the gravel, which from its greater consistency assumed here the form of a rather tough, coarse conglomerate. In the bend of the river the latter have a thickness of fully 200 feet, and are eroded by lateral rivulets into remarkably regular Gothic pillars and turrets. It is rare to meet with a more perfect imitation of nature by human art. The general surface of the gravel deposits is comparatively low, from 400 to 500 feet above the level of the river, and much denuded and intersected by minor streams and old watercourses.

At a couple of miles north of Chungterek the Koktan range begins with rather abrupt limestone cliffs, rising to about 3,000 feet above the level of the Toyan. Nearly in the middle of it are situated the forts Murzaterek and Chakmák, some ten miles distant from each other. The southern portion of this range consists at its base of undulating layers of greenish or purplish shales, overlain by dark coloured, mostly black, limestone in thick and thin strata, the latter being generally earthy. The limestone occupies all the higher elevations, and, as is generally the case, greatly adds to the ruggedness of the mountains. About five miles north of Chungterek, I found in a thick bed of limestone an abundance of *Megalodus triqueter*, a large *Pinna*, a *Spiriferina* of the type of *S. Stracheyi*, blocks full of *Lithodendron* corals, and numerous sections of various small *Gastropods*. Thinner layers of the same limestone were full of fragments of *crinoid stems*, and of a branching *Ceriopora*, the rock itself bearing a strong resemblance to the typical St. Cassian beds. In this place the shales, underlying the limestone, were partly interstratified with it, in layers of from 5 to 10 feet; and from this fact it seems to me probable that they also are of triassic age, representing a lower series of the same formation.

Proceeding in a north-westerly direction, the *Megalodus*-limestones are last seen near Murzaterek. From this place the greenish shales continue for a few miles further on, much disturbed and contorted; and at last disappear under a variety of dark coloured shales, slates, and sandstones, with occasional interstratified layers of black, earthy limestone. The strike of the beds is from east by north to west by south, and the dip either very high to north or vertical. At Chakmák the river has cut a very narrow passage through these almost vertical strata, which rise precipitously to about 3,000 feet, and to the south of the fort appear to be overlain by a lighter coloured rock. It is very difficult to say what the age of these slaty beds may be, as they seem entirely unfossiliferous, and we can at present only regard them as representing, in all probability, one of the palæozoic formations.

About five miles north-west of Chakmák a sensible decrease in the height of the range takes place, and with it a change in the geological formation. The palæozoic beds, although still crossing the valley in almost vertical strata, become very much contorted; while, unconformably on them, rest reddish and white sandstones and conglomerates, regularly bedded, and dipping to north-west with a steady slope of about 40 degrees. The rocks, though evidently belonging to a comparatively recent (kainozoic) epoch, appear to be much altered by heat, some layers having been changed into a coarse grit, in which the cement has almost entirely disappeared. I have not, however, observed any kind of organic remains in them. A little distance further on they several times alternate with successive, conformably bedded, doleritic trap. The rock is either hard and compact, being an intimate, rather fine grained mixture of felspar and augite in small thin crystals, or it decomposes into masses of various greenish and purplish hues, like some of the basic greenstones.

After leaving the junction of the Suyok and Toyan (or Chakmák) rivers, and turning northwards into the valley of the latter, the panorama is really magnificent. Shades of white, red, purple, and black compete with each other in distinctness and brilliancy, until the whole series of formations appear in the distance capped by a dark bedded rock.

Although, judging from the greater frequency of basaltic boulders, we already knew that this rock must be found further north, we hardly realized the pleasant sight which awaited us on the march of the 4th January, after having left our camp at Kulja or Bokum-bashi. The doleritic beds increased step by step in thickness, and after a few miles we passed through what appears to be the centre of an extensive volcanic eruption. Along the banks of the river columnar and massive basalt was noticed several times, with occasional small heaps of slags and scoriæ, among a few outcrops of very much altered and disturbed strata of red or white sandstone, thus adding to the remarkable contrast of the scene. In front of us, and to the right, stretched in a simicircle a regular old Somma; the almost perpendicular walls rising to about 1,500 feet above the river, and clearly exposing the stratification of the basaltic flows, which were successively dipping to north-east, east, and south-east. On our left, as well as in an almost due western direction, portions of a similar Somma were visible above the sedimentary rocks, all dipping in the opposite way from those ahead of us. The cone itself has in reality entirely disappeared by subsidence, and the cavity was filled with the rubbish of the neighbouring rocks.

Passing further north we crossed a comparatively low country, studded with small rounded hills and intercepted by short ridges with easy slopes; the average height was between 12,000 and 13,000 feet. This undulating high plateau proved to be one of the head-quarters of the *Kulja* (*Ovis Polii*), chiefly on account of the very rich grass vegetation which exists here. For this the character of the soil fully accounts. The entire ground was shown to consist of limestone gravel and pebbles of rather easily decomposing rocks, mixed with the ashes and detritus, evidently derived from the proximity of the volcanic eruption. Only rarely was an isolated basaltic dyke seen, or the tertiary sandstone cropping out from under the more recent deposits.

Viewing the country from an elevated position near our camp at Turug-at-bela, the conglomerate and gravel beds, well clad with grass vegetation, were seen to stretch far away eastwards, and in a north-easterly direction across the Turug pass; while on the south they were bounded by a continuation of the somewhat higher basaltic hills. Towards the west I traced them for about seven miles, across a low pass at which a tributary of the Toyan rises in two branches; while on the other side two similar streams flow west by south to join the Suyok river. To the north the proximity of a rather precipitously rising range shut the rest of the world out of view. For this ridge the name Terek-tagh of Humboldt's map may be retained; its average height ranges between about 16,000 and 17,000 feet. In its western extension it runs almost due east-west, composed at base of a tough limestone conglomerate of younger tertiary origin, followed by white dolomitic limestone, and then by a succession of slaty and dark limestone rocks, the former occasionally showing distinct signs of metamorphism, and changing into schist. All the beds are nearly vertical or very highly inclined, dipping to north by west, the older apparently resting on the younger ones. North of Turug-at-bela the range makes a sudden bend in an almost northerly direction, and continues to the Chaderkul, where it forms the southern boundary of the lake-plateau. By this time the white dolomitic, and afterwards the slaty beds, had entirely disappeared, and with them the height has also diminished. A comparatively low and narrow branch of the range which we visited consists here entirely of dark limestone, which in single fragments is not distinguishable from the Trias limestone of the Koktan mountains, but here it does not contain any fossils. The ridge itself, after a short stretch in a north-east-by-north direction, gradually disappears under the much younger conglomeratic beds.

Across the Chaderkul plain the true Thian Shan range was visible, a regular forest of peaks seemingly of moderate and tolerably uniform elevation. The rocks all exhibited dark tints, but most of them, as well as the hills to the west of the Chaderkul, near the sources of the Arpa, were clad in snow. The lake itself was frozen, and the surrounding plain covered with a white sheet of saline efflorescence.

Brief sketch of the geological history of the hill ranges traversed.—In order that the preceding remarks may be more easily understood, I add a few words regarding the changes which appear to have taken place at the close of the kainozoic epoch within the southern offshoots of the Thian Shan which we visited.

Short as our sojourn in the mountains was, it proved to be very interesting and equally instructive. Humboldt's account of the volcanicity of the Thian Shan, chiefly taken from Chinese sources, receives great support; but we must not speculate further beyond confiding in the expectation that both meso and kainozoic rocks will be found amply represented in it.

As far as our present researches in the physical aspect of the country extend, we may speak of three geologically different ranges: the *Terek range*, which is the northernmost, the *Koktan* in the middle, followed by the *Artush range*, below which begins the Kashghar plain. All three decrease in the same order in their absolute height, the last very much more so than the middle one. The first consists of old sedimentary rocks, the second of similar rocks in its southern parts, while younger tertiary and basaltic rocks occupy the northern portions, the third is entirely composed of young tertiary deposits. The general direction of all the ranges is from west to east, or nearly so; this direction evidently dating from the time when the whole of the Thian Shan chain was elevated. The undulating high plateau between the Terek and the Koktan is, near Turug-at-bela, about eight miles wide, the distance between the two ranges diminishing westward, while in the opposite direction it must soon more than double. Judging from the arrangement of the pebbles, which, as already noticed, are half derived from limestone, the direction of the old drainage must have been from west to east, and must have formed the headwaters of the Aksai river, which on the maps is recorded as rising a short distance east of the Chaderkul. Similarly, the gravel valley between the Koktan and Artush ranges indicates a west to east drainage, and its width appears to have approximately averaged 20 miles. About three miles north of Chungterek a secondary old valley exists, also extending from west to east, and is diametrically cut across by the Toyan river. In this valley, which was formerly tributary to the one lying more southward, the gravel beds accumulated to a thickness of fully 100 feet. As the Artush range did not offer a sufficiently high barrier, masses of the gravel passed locally over it or through its gaps into the Kashgar plain, which itself at that time formed a third large broad valley.

Thus, at the close of the volcanic eruptions in the hills north of Chakmák, we find three river systems all flowing eastward, and made more or less independent of each other by mountain ranges, about which it would, however, not be fair to theorize (in the present state of our knowlege) on the causes of their assumed relative position. It must have been at that time that the pebbles of protogine were brought down from some portion of the hills lying to the west; and it would be interesting to ascertain whether or not this rock is anywhere in that direction to be met with *in situ*. When the turbulent times of Volcan's reign became exhausted and tranquillity was restored, the whole country south of the axis of the Thian Shan must have greatly subsided, and the wider the valleys have been the more effectively was the extent of subsidence felt. To support this idea by an observation, I may notice that north of Chungterek, at the base of the Koktan range, the Artush beds have entirely disappeared in the depth, and the gravel beds overlaying them dip partially under the Trias limestone a state of things which cannot be explained by denudation, but only by subsidence and consequent overturning of the older beds above the younger ones. A similar state of things is to be observed on the Terek range, where the young tertiary limestone conglomerate is in some places of contact overlain by the much older dolomite. Now, if the broad valley of the Kashgar plain sank first, and gradually lowest, as it in all probability did, we find a more ready explanation of the large quantities of loose gravel pouring into it and accumulating at the base of the Artush range.

The sinking in of the volcanic centre north-west of Chakmák first appears to have drained off the former head of the Aksai river, making it the head of the Toyan instead; and to the north of the Terek ridge it was most probably the cause of the origin of the Chaderkul. The subsidence of the country followed in the south, making it possible for the united Suyok and Toyan rivers to force their passage right across the Koktan range, strengthen the Artush river cut with facility through the Artush range, and join the Kashghardaria. While thus indicating the course of the comparatively recent geological history of the ground, it must be however, kept in mind that this change in the system of drainage had no essential effect upon the direction of the hill ranges. This, dating from much older times, was mainly an east westerly one, following the strike of the rocks which compose the whole mountain system.

KASHGAR,
The 16th January 1874.

SECTION V.

The Altun Artush considered from a Geological point of view, by DR. F. STOLICZKA, PH.D
(Veni sed non vidi.)

As soon as the most important political business had been concluded by the signing of the Commercial Treaty by the Amir, Mr. Forsyth expressed a wish to visit the renowned tomb of Sultan Artush. The King accorded his permission, and instructed the Hakim, Mahomed Khoja, to assist us in travelling over the province under his care, to whatever extent Mr Forsyth might desire.

Under the personal guidance of our envoy we—Dr. Bellew, Captain Chapman, Captain Trotter, and myself—left Yangishar on the 14th of February reaching Altun Artush at a late hour the same day. As an introduction to the difficulties in travelling, our baggage did not arrive till next day, and we had to accommodate ourselves for the night on the carpets of the floor in a spacious but tolerably warm room. A halt of two days was desirable to enable us to make all necessary arrangements for our further movements. However, before I proceed I shall endeavour to give the reader an idea of the geographical position and limits of the country of which I shall speak in the subsequent lines. The data are derived from a general survey by Captain Trotter and from information given by the Hakim, Mahomed Khoja.

Altun Artush, which is the chief place of the province, lies approximately in east longitude 76° 8', and north latitude 39° 41', therefore about 23 miles north by east of Yangishar. It is situated in the western part of the *Yilak* on the Bugos—here called Artush river—and north of a low ridge which separates the Artush Valley from the plains. The southern boundary runs along this ridge for about ten miles west of Altun Artush, and from there almost due north to the crest of the Koktau range; then along this range eastwards of the Belauti Pass (east longitude 77° 47' and north latitude 40° 41'), and from thence in a south-eastern direction to the village of Kusltiyilak, some 15 miles north of Fyzabad in longitude 76° 42' 30" and latitude 39° 28' 30." From here the southern boundary runs close to the right bank of the Kashghar river until about opposite to where the Artush river runs into the plains.

During the first four days we all marched in company up the valley of the Bogos river to the Fort Tangitar about 23 miles to the north by west, then to a Khirghiz camp, Bashsugun, in a north-easterly direction; Tugurmatti almost eastern; and Ayaksugun in a south-eastern direction, the directions being from the last camps, respectively.

At Ayaksugun Captain Trotter and I separated from the rest of the party marching northwards along the Ushturfan road to Gaitana, and from thence across the Jigda Jilga in a north-east by east direction to the camp at Uibulak, crossing the Uibulak Pass, passing a second Jilga, and turning then for about nine miles more northwards to the Belauti Pass, beyond which lies the valley of the Kakshal or Aksai river. On our return we passed Ayaksugun, Karaul, about a mile from our former camp of the same name, and visited Kultiyilak and Fyzabad returning to Yangishar on the 3rd March.

It was not a very favorable time for travelling in these regions, not so much on account of the cold as in consequence of the heavy falls of snow which appear to occur over the whole of Tianshan during the second-half of February and first-half of March. During the last few days of February we were almost constantly wading in fresh fallen snow, though on the saline plains it melted very rapidly. The snow naturally interfered seriously with our observations. However obtaining even but a little addition to our knowledge of these hills was a better way of occupying our time than remaining in our somewhat glooming quarters. From a geological point of view the trip proved in many respects to be of considerable interest, particularly as supplementing some former observations made more to the west. Although there is not much variety in the rock formations, we may distinguish three successive series. The most southern part of the province, along the foot of the hills, is formed of alluvial gravels and sands, in whose unfathomable depths are swallowed both the Artush and Sujun rivers, before they can reach the Kashghar Daria. Wherever irrigation from the latter is possible the fields appear to be fertile, but in the contrary case the land is not much more than a mere desert covered with low and scanty scrubs of *Ephedra sp.?* The marshy grounds along the river are the breeding places of innumerable water-fowl. Brahmini ducks and pintails were already selecting sites for their nests on the 1st of March. The latter must have only just arrived. Where high grass occurs wild pigs are not uncommon.

The second series includes the low hills which extend diametrically from north to south over about 30 miles while the prevalent strike is from north-east by east to south-west by west. All these lower hills are occupied by Artush beds, of which I spoke in a former communication. They are separated into two groups. The lower beds consist of greenish or reddish clays or sandstones, and the upper ones of coarse conglomerates, which on a hill south of Tangitar have a thickness of about a thousand feet. At their contact both groups generally alternate in several layers. An anticlinal runs almost through the middle of their superficial extent. At the foot of Agaksugun it is caused by a low ridge of old dolomitic limestones on which the Artush clays and sandstones found a firm support. To the south of it the beds dip at angles of about 40°—50° towards the Kashghar plain in remarkably regular and successive layers. North of the ridge, which has no doubt a considerable subterranean extent in an east to west direction, all the beds dip towards north by west at a similar angle. Approaching the higher range more recent diluvial gravels cover most of the slopes. The geological puzzle of finding strata of young beds as a rule dipping *towards* a high range composed of comparatively much older rocks seems to me to be due, at least in this special case, to the phenomenon that the atmospheric waters which descending on the crest flow down the slopes of the high ridge, gradually soften them, and if a subterranean outlet facilitate it, the softened beds are worn away. While this process is going on the more distant beds simply subside in order to fill the vacant spaces. In some cases a sinking or rising of the main range, or even an overturn of high and precipitous cliffs, seem to go hand in hand with the action of erosion, but it is not always the case. I hope to illustrate this idea by a few diagrams, partly derived from actual observation, on some future occasion.

A third series of entirely different rocks forms the main range of hills which are a continuation of the Koktau range, and in which, more to the westward, are situated the Terek and Chakmak forts. The average height of the range is here between 12 and 1,300 feet—single peaks rising to about 1,500 feet. The whole of its southern portion consists as far as I could see of carboniferous rocks, in which, however, there is a great variety of structure. The lowest beds are very often a peculiar breccia limestone passing into regular limestone conglomerate. Above this are beds of solid grey dolomitic limestone, partly massive, partly stratified. The former possessing the character of reef limestone, and portions of it are indeed full of reef, building corals, crinoid stems, and a large *spirifer*, the sections of which when seen on the surface have a striking resemblance to those of *megalodon*.

North of Tangitar and about Bashsugun I met in several places great numbers of fossils, but they were so firmly cemented in a calcareous matrix that only a few could be extracted. Among these I could recognize a small *belerophon, productus semi-reticulatus*, and an *athyris*. A new *terebratula* was also very common. Here about Bashsugun and Tugurmatti greenish shales occurred often interstratified with the limestones, beds of which were highly carbonaceous; the shales appeared to be unfossiliferous.

The limestone hills which, as already stated, are a continuation of the Koktau range, extend in a north-easterly direction the whole way to south of the Belauti Pass, where they are overlain by a particularly well bedded dark limestone, very similar to that containing *megalodon* north of Chungterek. On this limestone rest greenish and purplish sandstones and shales which occupy the pass and the adjoining hills to the north-west of it; mineralogically these last rocks are quite identical with what we understand under the name of "*Bunter sandstein*," and it is by no means improbable that the Belauti beds are also of triassic age, as they succeed in regular layers those of the carboniferous formation.

A peculiar feature in this part of these hills consists in the occurrence of extensive plains to which the name Jilga is generally applied. It means originally, I think, merely a watercourse, and on a large scale these plains may be looked upon as water-courses of former watersheets. They occur at the base of the high range, and in some respects resemble the *doons* of the southern slopes of the Himalayas. North of Tangitar one of these large plains occurs within the limestone rocks, being surrounded by them on all sides. It must be about 30 miles long from east to west, and about 16 from north to south. Several isolated limestone hills and ridges occur in it, and it is drained off by the Bogos and Sugun rivers, the former rising in the south-west, the latter in the south-east corner. The average elevation is about 5,000 feet. The greater portion is covered with a low scrubby vegetation and, near the rivers, with high grass. The principal camping grounds are Bashsugun and Tugurmatti. The whole plain which affords a good pasturage ground is occupied by about 120 tents of Kirghiz during the summer.

The next Jilga is the Jigda Jilga. It differs considerably both in its physical situation and in its general character from the former. It stretches from west by south to east by north for about 35 miles, while the diameter of the eastern half is about 20, and that of the western about 12 miles. Save for a few low hillocks it is almost a level plain throughout. On the north-western, northern, and north-eastern side it is bounded by the Koktau range, from which several water-courses lead into it, one about the middle from the north, and one from north-east of considerable size, this containing a large quantity of crystalline pebbles, the rocks from which they are derived must be *in situ* near the axis of the ridge. A third big stream comes from the east leading from the Uibulak Pass. None of these streams had any water in them. On the south, east, and south-east the plain is bounded by the much lower hills composed of Artush beds, their slopes covered with gravel.

An elevated gap or saddle situated in the south-west corner appears to connect this Jilga with that of Tugurmatti. There is no drainage from this Jilga, all the water is absorbed by the enormous thickness of sand and mud which fills the entire basin. This accounts for the comparatively rich vegetation which exists in it. There are several stretches of regular poplar forest *(P. nigra* or *P. balsamifera)* up to 10 miles long and 4 to 5 miles in breadth. Besides which there are several places occupied by regular jungle of *tamarix, myricaria, ephedra,* and the peculiar wormwood, from the seed of which the Kirghiz prepare *satu.* The *tamarix* and poplars must absorb during their growth a very large quantity of the mineral salts with which the entire ground is saturated; the wood on being burnt gives out a strong smell of sulphur and chlorine.

The poplar trees are not healthy, they resemble oak trees covered with mistletoe. The branches are short, stumpy, and bushy. It is evident that the trees only exist in consequence of the subterranean moisture. There are a great number of springs through the forest and on its edges, but on account of the level character of the plain no flowing streams exist except where there has been a very heavy snowfall and very rapid melting.

It is satisfactory to observe that within three marches of Kashghar there is such a large supply of wood, though it is by no means good wood. I have already stated that the entire soil is very saline, and it is remarkable to see how snow melts on this saline ground. Thus about four inches of snow fell while we were there. In one day all was melted away on the saline ground, while near springs, where the saline matters has been gradually dissolved out of the ground, hardly any snow had melted. Where the soil is more moist or even swampy, and in river courses, high reed grass is abundant. The southern part of the Jilga, particularly south-east of Taitma, is lowest, and here a large quantity of pure salt in small cubical crystals is collected. The fact that there is such a large quantity of saline matter together with salt swamps in the southern part seems to prove that the Jilga at least, and probably most of the others, had been washed out by the sea, and that while others had gradually, though only partially, drained off the saline matter, this one retained it because it has at present no outlet. It is in fact a dried up saline lake, which at some remote time was cut off from the sea of which it was a fjord.

Jigda Jilga is occupied by about 150 to 170 Kirghiz tents, each tent may be taken as containing five souls. There are a few fields near Jigda camp, and if there has been a large quantity of snow the crops are said to prosper very well. During the winter the Kirghiz are encamped in small groups near the different springs. They do not keep many horses, but large number of sheep and goats and a few camels. One whole *akoi* is a light load for a camel. When packed the blankets are made into saddles over the hump of the animal.

A third Jilga is south of the Belauti Pass and north-east of the Uibulak Pass. It is about eight miles in breadth and the same in length. There are two large water-courses leading to it from the range. On the southern side it is enclosed by Artush and gravel beds, but whether an outlet exists is not known. It has no forest, nor any kind of trees or large bushes, and the grass vegetation is scanty evidently on account of the dryness. A southernly outlet very likely exists. We met a few Kirghiz encamped here from Ush-Turfan. The only supply of water they had was melted snow, and as soon as the beds about are exhausted, they have to retreat with their flocks to the Kakshal valley.

CHAPTER IX.

COMMERCE.

By Captain E. F. Chapman.

If the development of western civilization, and the growth of luxury in Europe have caused the great trade-marts of Asia, subject to Anglo-Saxon influence, to undergo change proportionate to the general progress of the age, commerce along the old trade routes to the Tartar kingdoms of Central Asia has but slightly varied through many centuries.

It is only now, as Russia from the north and west brings Moscow and St. Petersburg in close contact with Bokhara, Samarkand, and Kashghar, that a radical change is imminent in commercial dealings, which affect not only the prosperity but the political standing of the countries intermediate between Russia in Asia and British India.

According to the latest calculations goods of European manufacture may be transported from Moscow to Tashkend by Russian agency in from 70 to 90 days at an average cost per pood (36lbs.) of 90 copecks = $\frac{9}{10}$ths of a rouble, which may be said to vary from 2s. 6d. to 3s.

Hence they are distributed and carried from market to market till they meet the counterflow of British goods proper along a clearly defined line; a line which has been persistently retreating since the misfortune to British arms in Kabul checked the development of commerce, and so affected our general policy that British merchants have received but little encouragement to compete with Russian enterprise in countries lying outside our own border.

The progress of trade beyond her frontier, as a political measure, apart from its importance as a source of national wealth, has been the first consideration of Russia in her dealings with Central Asian States, whose markets have been closely studied in order that they might be made dependent on Russian commercial centres.

The systematic pursuit of a commercial policy moving hand in hand with a forward foreign policy, and not working spasmodically, marks each step of Russian progress: the wisdom which has produced those goods which are the most necessary to each locality, and has refrained from pouring articles of luxury into countries unprepared for their reception, has made her merchants amongst the most successful of her pioneers in those regions where, until lately, Europeans penetrated with infinite difficulty.

To represent fairly the commercial prospects of the country ruled over by the Amir of Kashghar, in connexion with British trade, would involve a consideration of the interests which govern and restrain our commerce along the whole of our frontier line; for, unsupported by active enterprise to other centres, the solitary effort which has lately been made to open to our merchants the markets of Kashghar, Yarkand, and Khoten is necessarily unmeaning.

The following sketch of the trade relations of those ancient cities, as far as it treats of mutual intercourse and foreign dealings, is drawn up from notes made upon the spot which are given in detail in the Appendix.

As the external trade of the country has hitherto been solely dependent upon the demand for articles which cannot be produced in the cities under the Amir's rule, and can only increase as the vast resources of the kingdom are developed by good government, and national progress creates a demand during a period of peace for western luxuries, and the arts which belong to civilization.

I propose treating, in the first instance, of trade matters which are purely local and only influence indirectly the larger questions of commerce.

The various relations of life amongst the "Osbeg Tartars" are such as involve a constant interchange of good offices; workers and consumers are of the same order, and accumulated wealth leads to no class separations such as are apparent elsewhere. The weekly market not only furnishes the weekly requirements to all, but is the great stimulus in daily life. The innate love of barter, which anticipates the market dealings, on this one day in seven, urges the matron at her spindle, and the weaver at his loom, while it stirs the cultivator and each trade apprentice alike. It is no necessity for daily bread which moves the Turk to exertion, for all are well to do and bread and meat and warm clothing reach the poorest easily; but the excitement of a bargain, the gossip at the restaurant, and the mirth and fun which circulate in crowded streets are worth living for and working for; the money comes easily and goes quickly which keeps the stream flowing.

In the various cities of Kashghar, in the capital, in Yarkand, Khoten, Aksu, Kuchar, Karashahr, and Turfan, and each smaller local centre, the scene on market day is the same, the same transfer of daily wants between "dwellers in the country" and "dwellers in the town" takes place, and the spirit of trade is kept alive.

But apart from this, the distribution of the land under cultivation, and special local advantages render one district dependant on another, and raise the shop-keeper into a merchant as his resources develop.

The grain and fruit of Yarkand are carried on donkeys, and sold to advantage in Kashghar.

Camels from Aksu similarly bring rice, pashm, salamoniac, alum, and tea (made from the leaves of the willow) to the capital, carrying back cotton cloth, and cotton from the district of Kanarik.

Aksu also, by way of the desert, supplies rice and copper to Khoten, receiving Khoten products in return.

While Khoten, the manufacturing town of all those belonging to the Amir, circulates its silks and carpets, and copper vessels, its country cloth, and its gold and ornaments throughout the kingdom.

Up to the present time the circulating medium throughout the country has been a small copper coin (*vide* Chapter XII). Gold and silver realizing only their market value; but one of the first steps following the recognition of Amir Yakúb Khan by the Porte has been the establishment of a mint at Kashghar, from which Gold Tillahs and Silver Tungas are issued. This will, naturally, influence the local markets as well as the external trade, and improve the position of the merchant, who has hitherto been restricted to the system of barter in all his transactions.

The existence of gold and silver, of copper, and coal, alum and salamoniac; the two former in the spurs of the Kuen Luen, and the remainder in the Tián Shán, has been now fully ascertained, and, when once permission is granted, the natives of the country will readily work these valuable resources: the mineral wealth of the country is, however, at present but partially developed.

There are said to be 22 places in the province of Khoten where gold is obtained, but no more than five mines are regularly worked.

1. At Káppa ... Employing 4,000 people.
2. At Soorgák ... Employing 3,000 people.
3. At Chuggulák ...
4. At Charchend ... } Employing from 50 to 100 people each.
5. At Karatagh ...

At Káppa and Soorgák the mines are reported to be of great depth.

The best gold is obtained at Soorgák, where it is found in small beads and is of a red color; at Káppa, the nuggets are larger, but the color is a pale yellow and the ore is mixed with sand.

The working of the mines is thus conducted:—The miners, men and women, are of the poor of the country, who sell the gold to licensed purchasers under the supervision of Government officials.

From the original yield a fifth part is at once appropriated by the Amir, who further reserves the right of purchasing the remainder from the regular dealers at the rate of 120 Tungas per sér, the value in the market reaching 138 Tungas—(1 sér = $3\frac{1}{2}$ tolahs).

No guard is kept at the mines, but small detachments of soldiers watch the proceedings, and there are regular searching houses, no gold being supposed to reach the market but through the authorized channel. At these searching houses the men are stripped, and women are made to jump over a broad ditch in order that any gold they may have concealed in their clothes may fall out.

The punishment for secreting gold is very light, and the whole of the officials employed are said to take bribes to allow of its being taken direct to the market, where it is in great demand by foreign traders.

If a merchant is discovered to have purchased gold irregularly, no more than a fifth part is confiscated, and the remainder is purchased at the fixed Government rate.

The gold mines in the Khoten province produce some 7,000 sérs, of which 5,000 sérs are said to reach the Amir's treasury, the remainder passing direct into the bazaar; this represents an income of 1,68,000 rupees.

Gold is readily bought up by merchants from Hindústan and Andijan.

The transport of the best gold of Khoten to India yields a profit of from 23 to 24 per cent.

Gold of an inferior quality is obtained by washing from the Yarkand river; this is allowed free entry to the market; its transport to India secures a profit of $11\frac{1}{2}$ per cent.

Sericulture in Khoten dates from the earliest times. M. Remusat's account of the introduction of the silk-worm into this place is as follows, pp. 55, 65:—

"Au sud est de la ville royale, à cinq ou six li, on voit le monastèyre de Lou-che, fondé par une ancienne reine du pays. Autrefois les habitants du royaume ne connaissaient ni les muriers ni les vers à soie. On entendit parler de ceux qu'il-y-avait dans les royaumes orientaux, et l'on envoya un ambassadeur pour en demander. Le roi d'orient se refusa a cette demande, et fit une défense très sévère aux gardiens des frontières et aux donaniers de laisser sortir ni mûriers ni semence de vers. Alors le roi de Kia-sa-tan-na fit demander une princesse en mariage. Quand le roi d'orient, plein de tendresse pour les contreés lointaines, la lui eut accordeé, le roi, chargea l'officier qui devait aller la prendre, de lui dire que dans son royaume, il n'-y-avait point d'habits de soie, parce qu'on n'-y-avait pas de muriers ni de cocons, et qu'il fallait en apporter, afin d'avoir de quoi se faire des habits. La princesse, ainsi avertie, se procura secrètement de la semence des uns et des autres, et la cacha dans l'étoffe de son bonnet. Quand le cortége fut arrivé à la frontierè, celui qui y-commandait chercha partout; il n-y-eut que le bonnet de la princesse auquel il n'osa toucher. Arrivée dans le pays de Kia-sa-tan-na, elle s'arrêta dans le lieu où a été depuis le monastère de Lou-che; et pendant que les cérémonies de sa réception se preparaient, elle déposa en ce lieu la semence de mûrier et des vers. Au printemps on planta les arbres, et la princesse alla assister elle-même aux opérations de la récolte des feuilles. On fut obliger dans le commencement de nourrir les vers à soie avec les feuilles de quelques autres arbres; mais enfin les mûriers poussèrent, et la reine fit graver sur la pierre une défense de faire perir les papillons jusqu'a ce qu'on put se procurer une quantité

N.B.—The export of gold and silver, excepting in the form of the established coinage, has lately been prohibited by the Amir.

Specimens of Galena containing a large admixture of silver are in the Mission Museum. These were obtained from Shakchu in a ravine to the S.-W. of Yarkand, known as Koohrab, about 80 miles in a direct line from Yarkand.

During the occupation of the Chinese, the silver mine from which this ore was taken, was worked for seven years; its working has been long discontinued, but the Dadkhwah of Yarkand contemplates obtaining silver once more from Shakchu.

suffisante de cocons : contrevenir à cet ordre était, disait le décret, à révolter contre la lumière et renoncer à la protection des dieux."

The quality of Khoten silk has always been considered superior; owing, however, to an inferior method of reeling, it cannot compete with the silk of Khokand, and Khoten manufactured silk is valueless as an article of export; it is, however, largely used by women in chogas, and a mixed cloth of silk and cotton, known as silk chakman (mushroo), is very commonly worn by both sexes.

The wearing of garments, made entirely of silk, by men, being prohibited by the Sheriat, such have been discontinued as articles of men's apparel since the expulsion of the Chinese.

As a rule, the silk manufacture is a purely domestic business; that is, both reeling and manufacture are carried on in the house where the eggs are hatched and the worms reared; there is, however, a sale for cocoons in the market, the purchasers being regular traders, who sell again to reelers; spun silk being again bought by Andijani merchants and others. Silk weavers laboring apart are usually employed by Andijani merchants, one of whom, last year, made some improvement in the reeling process, and arranged for the working of 15 reels by the turning of a single wheel. I refer to this in order to show that the introduction of machinery would be readily welcomed in Khoten.

In a note on sericulture placed in the Appendix, I have detailed what I have been able to gather on this subject.

Although manufactured silk is not exported, it is found profitable to send spun silk to the markets of Khokand, and the waste silk of Khoten finds a sale at Almati (Vernoe). (The paper used for the note currency in Russian Turkestan is said to be made from this.)

This year, at the request of Mr. Christie of the Sujanpúr Filature (near Gúrdaspúr in the Punjab), an order was given in Yarkand for cocoons of Khoten silk to be brought down to the Filature; it was further arranged to send a certain number of cocoons to the Filature of His Highness the Maharaja of Kashmir as an experiment. It is hoped that the money these cocoons will fetch in the markets of Kashmir and Umritsur will fully repay the cost of carriage.

Mr. R. B. Shaw, in his Trade Report of 1873-74, as British Joint Commissioner of Ladakh, paragraph 63, indicates further an opening in England for the sale of refuse silk and pierced cocoons from Khoten.

"The trade in refuse silk and cocoons also promises well. Pierced cocoons (that is, those out of which the grub has eaten its way) are considered utterly worthless in Central Asia, yet in England these same pierced cocoons are in great demand, as they are treated by carding machinery and spun into threads which are used in various fabrics. There is no silk reeling industry in England, I believe, to utilise entire cocoons. The probable price mentioned for the pierced ones in Khoten is such as to leave a hundred per cent. profit after paying all expenses when compared with the rate offered in England. When a demand springs up the Khoten rate will most likely rise, leaving only a more moderate profit."

The carpets of Khoten are celebrated for the excellence of their manufacture, and for the variety of their patterns: they are made at three places in the province, Sumpúla, Yungkásh and near Khoten itself: they are made either of silk or of wool, and gold thread is often introduced into the pattern.

The wool made use of is chiefly obtained from the Kirghiz settled in the mountain districts south of Khoten, by whom it is spun and sold in the weekly bazaars; the dyeing is carried out by the carpet manufacturer. Madder, indigo, and cochineal are amongst the imported dyes, the mordants employed being alum in the case of browns and yellows, and grape juice for blues and mixed colors.

The cost of labor in the Khoten district is very slight, and the carpet-makers are hired as required by those who are rich enough to purchase the material and set up the frames. There are two kinds of frames, the standard frame which is placed perpendicularly, and a horizontal frame which is placed near the ground; the latter is generally used with large carpets, but the perpendicular frame allows of the work being better done.

The sizes of Khoten carpets range from the small saddle carpet, on which one man work at a time, to carpets upon which ten men are employed at once: these are about three and half yards wide.

The work is carried on in all cases under the superintendence of a master who is termed Aksakál (white-beard), there being some 200 recognized masters in Khoten itself. The patterns do not exist on paper, but are passed on from master to pupil by word of mouth.

Workers employed in the manufacture of Government carpets receive a daily wage of 20 phool = 2½d. English money, while in private houses food is supplied gratis and a payment of one-half of the above is made.

Recognizing the possibility of reviving the old trade in articles of cut Jade, which under the Chinese rule was a source of wealth to the people of Khoten, the Amir has endeavoured to obtain an opening for the trade in Jade by way of Almati (Vernoe), where Chinese merchants are now appearing in search of such articles from Kashghar and Khokand as have at all times been prized in China.

M. Remusat in speaking of the appreciation in which Jade is held amongst the Chinese and others, says:—"Les peuples de L'Asie orientale attachent le plus grand prix à une espéce de pierre nommeé en Chinois iu or iu-chi. Beaucoup de voyageurs et de Missionaries ont parler de l'estime que les Chinois ont pour cette substance minérale, et des usages variés auxquels ils l'emploient."

The fact that the Jade thus spoken of is known to exist nowhere save in the valley running down from the Kuen-Luen, where the supply appears to be inexhaustible, has no doubt caused its value in the market to rise out of proportion to other minerals of a similar character and if skilful workmen could be brought from China to replace those who fell victims during the Mahomedan re-occupation, the Jade of Khoten might still be regarded as a source of wealth to the kingdom of Kashghar. The demand for highly finished cups and ornaments in this mineral is sure to be kept up, but the endeavour to sell uncut Jade at Almati (Vernoe) for transport to China and to Russia has proved a failure. Just as the mineral has acquired a special value from being found in only one locality, the art which rendered it acceptable in the market belonged solely to the Chinese Jade-cutters of Khoten.

Interesting information regarding the Jade mines in the Karakash valley will be found amongst the Geological notes of the late Dr. F. Stoliczka.

The iron ore met with by the members of the Mission can only be considered as of very inferior quality; it is chiefly obtained in the Kizzil Tagh to the north-west of Yarkand it meets certain local requirements, and is used in the manufacture of agricultural implements and horse shoes.

Copper, alum, and salamoniac are, however, unquestionably sources of wealth, and exist in sufficient quantity in the southern slopes of Tian Shan, to allow of their being largely exported towards Khokand.

There is no Government monopoly in the mining of copper ore in the districts of Aksu Bai, and Kuchar, whence it is chiefly procured. There are regular miners who can be hired by any one choosing to try for copper, the agreement with them being that they receive one half of whatever is extracted.

The copper mine between Yagh Aryk and Bai, which may be taken as a fair specimen is in a low range of hills; the ore is encountered at a depth of from 30 to 36 feet: it is usually calculated that the ore yields from one-ninth to one-eighth of pure copper. A pound of copper sells in Bai for a sum equal to about 4 pence of English money.

Although the mining is freely open to all, the smelting furnace on the spot is under Government supervision; the contractor engaged in mining paying the wages of the smelter and one-seventh of the pure copper obtained in return for the use of the furnace.

Salamoniac is obtained in large quantities from the neighbourhood of a volcano, about one day's journey to the north of Kuchar: it sells on the spot for about 11 pence the pound.

As cotton and cotton cloth of local manufacture are articles of export towards the Khanates through Khokand, and to the Russian settlement through Almati (Vernoe), it may not be uninteresting to give some account of the growth of cotton.

Throughout the entire kingdom cotton is grown for home consumption, cleaned and woven into cloth for the family use in the household of each cultivator, and for sale, as cloth, thread, or raw cotton, at the weekly bazaar.

The best cotton is unquestionably produced in the district of Kanarik, to the south-east of Kashghar.

There are three different qualities of cotton.

1st.—*Olderum or Aksakál*. The seed of this plant is said to have been originally imported from Khokand, for which reason the cotton it yields is called Andijani cotton.

The plant grows to a height of about three feet; the pod is larger than with the other two kinds, and by comparison the yield of cotton is greater, and of seed less.

This description is not grown in very large quantities, owing to the fact that the seed is not so easily obtained as that of the other cottons; its cultivation too requires special care, and the soil in which it is grown needs to be more richly manured than is usual with other crops. The first description of cotton cloth, known as Chákman, is prepared from this cotton. Chákman sells at from 1 rupee to 1-4 rupee per Thán, the length of which varies from 14 to 16 yards, and which is 11 inches wide.

2nd.—*Kara Kiwaz* is the cotton usually met with: the plant is a low one, not growing much above two feet in height; the pod is smaller than that of the Aksakál cotton, and the proportion of seed to cotton in the yield much greater. A medium description of cloth, known as Kám, is prepared from this; a Thán of Kám, 6 yards long and 18 inches broad, sells for from 6 to 8 annas.

3rd.—*Mella or Kizzil* (red) *Kiwaz*, so called from the coloring of the cotton which has a reddish tinge. This is a low plant like the previous one, and the proportion of cotton and seed in the yield is similar. The Kám prepared from this retains the reddish color spoken of, and is rarely dyed.

The usual price in the market of cleaned cotton is 3 rupees the charak of 20℔s. It occasionally rises higher, but there is really very little fluctuation, and the cottons from the three plants abovementioned obtain the same price when cleaned and exposed for sale. Where large families exist, it is more profitable to sell the cotton prepared, as thread or as Kám, than in its raw state.

Although at the present moment Chákman and Kám are readily purchased in the bazaars by the Agents of traders who export to Khokand and Almati, and Mr. Shaw refers to these descriptions of cloth as being regularly sold in the bazaars at Leh, the capital of Ladakh, it would nevertheless be a mistake to consider the districts of Kashghar as favourable to the production of cotton.

The seed is sown in April, and the crop is gathered in October and the beginning of November, there being only two pluckings at an interval of about fifteen days.

There appears to be great waste in the expenditure of seed, the plants being allowed to come up too close together, and there being no thinning of the crop.

Cotton, moreover, is rarely grown for two years running on the same land. A few years back the Chinese appear to have made an effort to encourage the further growth of cotton, but without success.

The peculiar requirements of each family necessitate the growth of a sufficient quantity on each holding to supply, as far as possible, the immediate wants of its members; but the difficulties encountered in the growth of cotton make it an unpopular crop.

The fact is that the surplus cloth and cotton of each establishment is all that finds its way into the market, whence it is collected through numerous agents for export. The producers are ignorant of the laws which should raise the price of their production, which realizes an even price, though the demand is practically unlimited.

The Pashm of Turfan and of other places in the Kashghar dominions being one of the articles of export, deserves notice amongst the products of the country; the demand for it in Kashmir and British India is however so small that it can never have much influence on the trade of the country generally.

It has been supposed that precious stones are easily obtained in the markets of Eastern Turkestan. The impression which has prevailed on this subject is erroneous, and geological investigation has made it clear that whatever precious stones exist, have been imported. Rubies, emeralds, and lapis lazuli from Badakshan, pearls from Persia, and turquoises from Khorassan (by way of Bokhara), and corals from China.

Wherever Chinese wealth has had an influence, coral, emeralds, rubies, and pearls have been used in the decoration of Chinese idols, and the ornaments of women; but few however remain in Kashghar, excepting amongst the treasures of the Amir, who is said to have successfully despoiled the palaces and temples of former Chinese rulers, and no doubt possesses considerable wealth in the form of precious stones.

No clearer review of the actual state of the trade between British India and Eastern Turkestan can be given than that contained in Mr. Shaw's last report on trade at Ladakh, and the "proceedings of the hon'ble the Lieutenant-Governor of the Punjab, in the Foreign Department," extracts from which are herein incorporated.

"It is to be remembered that, though the development of trade between Yarkand and British India has received the careful attention of the British Government for upwards of six years, though transit duties have been abolished, and special officers appointed to watch over the interests of traders, the total value of the trade with Eastern Turkestan, though the greatest on record, amounted last year to less than £60,000, a great increase compared with what it *was*, but after all an amount which must be considered altogether insignificant; and here it may be noted that the statement made in the first paragraph of the report that the trade through Ladakh increased by two lakhs of rupees, is perhaps likely to mislead. It is true that the sum total of imports and exports by the several routes increased in value from Rupees 15,84,800 to Rupees 17,76,729, but, as explained in paragraph 38, the imports and exports being the same goods, the value of the transit trade is really only half the total shown above.

"Again, it must be confessed that the greater our experience of the routes between Indian and Yarkand, the greater do the difficulties appear in the way of establishing a satisfactory trade route, owing to the length of the journey, the enormous altitudes to be traversed, the arid and unproductive character of a large portion of the country, the absence of population, and the deficiency of carriage and supplies."

The remarks which follow on the commerce of the country under the Amir's rule, and which are supported by notes in the Appendix, claim to be interesting, as resulting from observations made in the two principal markets of Eastern Turkestan which are open directly to foreign trade, *viz.*, Kashghar and Yarkand, the latter receiving its supplies principally from British India, and the former so far as foreign productions are concerned, being at present wholly dependent on Russian sources of supply through Almati (Vernoe) and Khokand.

Russian articles furnished to the markets of Eastern Turkestan are, in many respects, a close imitation of the products which from the earliest days have been in use, and are of Chinese introduction. With some of these, owing to their weight, the Indian market cannot profitably compete, but they must at all times represent a large item in the consignments from the Russian side.

I.—Iron and cast-iron vessels; the former used in the manufacture of horse shoes, and of implements of agriculture, and in the Amir's workshops, the latter in use in every household as cooking vessels.

NOTE.—From Yules' "Cathay and the way thither," preliminary Essay XLII.—(Quoting Pliny.)

"Ex omnibus autem generibus palma Serico ferro est. Seres hoc cum vestibus suis pellibus que mittunt."

Again (Julien quoted by Lassen.)

"We found cast-iron pots and pans of remarkable quality to form a chief item among the miscellaneous notions" (apart from the silk which is the staple imported by the Chinese into Ava by the Yunan road. The art of casting iron

II.—Brass vessels and candlesticks.

Although I have stated generally that it is comparatively unprofitable to carry iron from India to Yarkand across the Karakorum, I should mention that Wazir Goshaon professed to have cleared a large profit on a load of made up horse shoes sent, by way of experiment, with his caravan in 1867.

Articles of luxury being in small demand, and household furniture reduced to a minimum by the simple habits of the Turks, there remain but few articles of import, and, so far as I can ascertain, Indian traders can undersell all others when offering them to buyers in the markets I have visited. These are—

1.—Cotton piece-goods.
2.—Muslins.
3.—Chintzes.
4.—Broadcloths (a very small demand).
5.—Velvet.
6.—Kinkab.
7.—Tea.
8.—Opium.
9.—Indigo.
10.—Madder (and other dyes).
11.—Sugar.
12.—Spices.
13.—Arms.
14.—Percussion caps.
15.—Tobacco.
16.—Otter skins.
17.—Cured skins.
18.—Nick-nacks.

That the trade in these articles so far as Kashghar is concerned is in the hands of Russian traders, the following detail of a caravan which arrived from Khokand at the end of March in this year will show.

This caravan comprised 1,635 loads, of which 600 loads were piece-goods and chintzes, the remainder, 1,035 in number, being made up of madder, indigo, tobacco, iron, and steel.

The piece-goods, cloths, and chintzes were unquestionably Russian, but the indigo was said to have found its way from India viâ Bokhara, and the madder was originally obtained from Badakshan.

This caravan was a larger one than usual, owing to the fact that the merchants had been detained in Khokand in consequence of political disturbances.

The total number of loads reaching Kashghar yearly by way of Khokand may be estimated at from three to four times the amount of this single caravan, i.e., from 5,000 to 6,000 loads, more than half the goods reaching Khokand, in the first instance, directly from Tashkend.

Almati (Vernoe) is in far closer connection with the Kashghar market than Khokand and the arrival of small consignments from Russian territory, in return for which the merchants carry back cloth and cotton, gold, copper, alum, salamoniac, and churas, is pretty continuous throughout the year. The detail of merchants resident in Kashghar, which is given in the Appendix, will show that regular agencies are established between the markets of Khokand and Almati, and that of Kashghar.

The Russian consignments brought over are usually of a mixed character, comprising iron vessels, iron, steel, brass vessels, spices, sugar, honey, earthenware (Chinese), tea, otter skins, Russia leather, cloths and chintzes, bon-bons, matches, and a variety of nick-nacks. I have no data upon which to estimate accurately the total amount of trade between Almati and Kashghar, but the trade is an increasing one, and certainly exceeds that which passes by way of Khokand; to explain the nature of the return traffic along the Khokand route, I will here give the detail of the first outward caravan this season, which left Kashghar in February, taking the route across the Terek Pass.

Total horse loads 871.

	No. of loads.	Cost per load in Tangas.
Country cloth, of Kashghar, Kám and Chakman	220	600
Churas	284	800
Numdas (felts)	120	500
Carpets	25	650

is, like most Chinese arts, a very old one, and we find that, in the first century before Christ, the people of Tawan or Farghana acquired the new art of casting iron tools and utensils from Chinese deserters."

N.B.—The usual water vessels, the Aftaba and Chilumchi, are of copper, tinned over, and are made principally at Khoten, though in every large town they are made up to a certain extent.

		No. of loads.	Cost per load in tungas.
Salamoniac	... ...	12	520
Alum	... ...	200	100
Copper	... ...	10	520

Value of Cloth,	132,000	tungas.	Value of Salamoniac,	6,240	tungas.
„ Churas,	227,200	„	„ Alum,	20,000	„
„ Numdas,	7,000	„	„ Copper,	5,200	„
„ Carpets,	16,250	„			

Representing a total value of 93,378 rupees.

This consignment was divided between 50 men, of whom the eight principal had investments as under:—

Mahomed Caravan bashi	... 15 horse loads.	Mahomed Khan Bai	...	30 horse loads.
Mahomed Saleh Bai ...	... 40 ditto.	Aib Bai ...	...	20 ditto.
Mahomed Kareem Bai ...	... 50 ditto.	Mahomed Ashgar Bai	...	45 ditto.
Mir Jan Bai of Margilan	... 40 ditto.	Mahomed Ali Batcha...	...	40 ditto.

The remaining 591 loads were distributed amongst 42 men.

A certain amount of trade from Russian markets is said to reach the towns of Aksu, Bai, Sairam, Kuchar, and Turfan by way of Kuldja and the Muzart Pass, but of this I could gain no information of a reliable character, and the business transacted must, under any conditions, be comparatively insignificant.

It is very difficult to fix exactly the trade relations which unite the markets of Russian Turkestan and of Bokhara, and Khokand with Kashghar; the impetus of the trade which finds a centre in Kashghar is, however, from without. The merchants engaged are either Andijanis who have settled in the Amir's capital of late years, or the goods moving along the several trade routes are bought and sold by agents of merchants living beyond the border.

Notes of credit, or exchange transactions of money between the different markets, are quite unknown in general commercial dealings, though, between friends, arrangements are made in Kashghar for the payment of small sums in Almati and Khokand, or even in Bokhara.

The statement made before the Royal Geographical Society that there are Banks in Yarkand is quite unfounded.

Between merchants at the different places exchanges of goods are occasionally made under written authority: but there are only some three men in Kashghar, and two in Yarkand, possessing sufficient capital to allow of transactions outside the ordinary caravan trade.

The Amir's rule has not been of sufficiently long duration to attract traders of wealth, and beyond the money spent in investments for the return trip, the gains of the trader are usually spent without the country. If capital be accumulated in Kashghar, the owner of wealth is at present afraid to acknowledge his good fortune, though a more enlightened policy, and the conclusion of the commercial treaties with Russia and Great Britain, have already improved the standing of traders throughout the country.

The present condition, position, and privileges of traders in the Amir's dominions, now that these treaties are established facts, will bear favorable comparison with what is met with in any other Mahomedan country in Asia.

The enlightened treatment of traders who have reached Yarkand from India, Badakshan, and elsewhere, by the Dadkhwah Mahomed Yunus Jan, is quite exceptional; the lead that he has taken in this matter has been fully approved by the Amir, and during our intercourse with Aalish Dadkhwah, the Governor of Kashghar, we had every reason to feel satisfied that he was equally inclined to promote the interests of trade.

The removal of the disabilities under which Hindoo merchants have labored in the Mahomedan States of Central Asia by the Amir is an earnest of further progress.

N.B.—Almonds and Pistachios are brought with profit from Badakshan, and no Dasterkhwan is complete unless bon-bons with Russian mottoes are offered to the guest.

We have had practical experience of the fact that Hindoo and Mahomedan traders are treated with impartiality, and no sketch of the commercial prospects of the Amir's country would be complete which did not bring prominently to notice the absence of prejudice which rendered possible in diplomatic negociations the consideration of questions affecting Mahomedan and Hindoo traders without prejudice to the latter.

The system of barter which prevails in the markets of Eastern Turkestan is inseparable from the conditions of the trade, and the length of time occupied in passing from market to market. I have already mentioned that the evils attending it will be modified by the issue of gold and silver coinage from the Amir's Mint. In the relations of the Yarkand market with India, the length of time during which an Indian merchant trading across the frontier must be absent from his home, when once he has determined to cross the Karakorum, makes the investments for the return journey a part of the single venture which has enticed him to face the journey, and he does not count his profits until he is safe at home once more.

On reaching the city of Yarkand he secures rooms in one of the principal serais, carefully stores his goods, and then, through the medium of the Delál or Agent attached to his particular fraternity, makes known their number and quality in the market.

It is only by slow degrees that his bales are unpacked, and his wares exposed, while little by little he accumulates a store of goods for the return venture. The real skill of the merchant becomes apparent in selecting articles for the return journey, that will bring him a fair profit in the Indian markets, and in converting the copper coinage which he must necessarily receive in large quantities into gold or other portable material.

A quick return in this description of commerce is practically impossible, nor is it necessary to traders whose personal expenditure is at all times exceptionally small; but this fact must exclude European competitors from the market, or must, at any rate, place them at so great a disadvantage, as to render it unlikely that they can undertake to trade on their own account with success.

The market does not admit of any large consignment of a single description being readily disposed of, and the selection of a mixed consignment of those articles most likely to prove acceptable, requires considerable skill and experience.

It will be seen that difference of quality only in piece-goods does not assure a proportionate advantage in sale: the fact is that choice of color is of more account than quality, and fashion has a great deal to say to color.

Bright colored goods, and cloths of one color throughout, are much appreciated. With prints, the larger patterns are the most esteemed: it is however essential that goods upon which figures of men or animals are represented should not be offered for sale in the market of a Mahomedan country.

Amongst the upper classes, greys and stone colors are fashionable, being in keeping with the unostentatious costume of the Amir himself, who aims at a singular simplicity in dress, as in other matters.

Goods are often disposed of on a trust extending over two or three months, with no other than a personal security, and instances of failure in payment are not known. This is a convenience to the foreign trader, the borrower becoming practically his agent for sale.

Previous to the arrival of the Mission in Yarkand it had been supposed that green tea only was in use in Turkestan, no other having been, in former times, imported from China: it is now, however, placed beyond doubt that the black teas of our Indian plantations are highly approved of. The adulteration of China tea has, too, caused Indian teas to be sought for.

In the present condition of the market, goods of the best quality will as a rule prove the most profitable investment for merchants proceeding from India to Yarkand.

The introduction of adulterated or inferior goods from our side might destroy the confidence which has been established through the long residence of a British Mission in Kashghar.

Assuming that the most seasonable time for the passage of the mountain plateau of the Karakorum is towards the end of September, the Indian trader will leave Ladakh, if possible, by the end of August: two courses then remain open to him; he may return in the following year, either at the first opening of the passes before the snow meltings have swelled the mountain torrents, which for some time remain impassable, or at the end of the season, when he will reach Ladakh, but just in time to make his way to India before the winter snows have barred the passes in the southern Himalayas.

In the one case the period of his absence from the Punjab may extend over from 10 to 12 months, and in the latter will be lengthened out to from 16 to 18 months.

His venture must be limited to suit the period of absence intended.

In the longer period of absence it seems a fair estimate to suppose that a single trader can dispose of a consignment of from Rupees 10,000 to Rupees 20,000 and reinvest for sale at home. While if the shorter period only is allowed he will be able to sell no more than from Rupees 5,000 to 10,000 worth of goods. In either case, once he has reached the Indian markets again, his bales are quickly converted into cash and he counts the proceeds. Hitherto he has not rested satisfied with a total return of less than 100 per cent., 70 per cent. being cleared on the outward venture, and 30 per cent. on the goods brought back to India.

The facts put forward in the lists given in the Appendix would prove that, after the payment of road expenses, and a fair allowance for loss, this sanguine estimate does not far exceed what may be realized by an intelligent trader who ventures across the lofty Karakorum in search of gain.

What then are the causes which put a limit upon our trade with Eastern Turkestan?

Beyond the difficulties of the road, and the small amount of our traders, competent to undertake the adventurous journey involved, I cannot do better than quote Mr. Shaw's last report in explanation of the main difficulty which prevents an expansion of trade between British India and Yarkand, up to that point where the limit of the demand on that side the mountains, must so far reduce the profits to be realized that the venture ceases to attract. A limit to be measured by the amount of population, and the success which attends an attempt to secure some portion of the trade with Kashghar, which is now in the hands of Russian and Khokandi merchants.

Mr. Shaw in speaking of the difficulty experienced on this side in obtaining carriage for the journey, says:—

"It was almost impossible therefore to get carriage last season northward from Ladakh. The few available animals were engaged by the first comers, and, later in the year, Rupees 70 was asked and given as the hire of a baggage horse to Yarkand; whereas the rate usual in former years was Rupees 40 or 50 each. Such being the state of affairs, most of the traders from the south, including returning Yarkandis, had to wait at Ladakh till the caravan should arrive, as their only means of getting carriage. Its delay was therefore the more felt.

"Up to the year 1870 the chief difficulty in point of carriage lay between the Punjab and Ladakh; while between the latter place and Yarkand it was plentiful. Now the tables are completely turned. While the northern section of the road is reduced to such straits as are described in the last paragraph, the southern section, *viz.*, from the Punjab to Ladakh, is fully supplied. This was in the first place made possible by the construction of the excellent hill road, which now leads from the Kangra valley through Kulu and Lahoul. But the establishment of mule traffic on this road was due to the creation in 1870 of the Kulu mule train by Captain Harcourt, under the orders of Colonel Coxe, Commissioner of the Jullundur Division. The example of this train has been since followed by numerous private mule owners from the Punjab, who reap great profit from this traffic, undertaken at a time of the year (the hot weather and rains) when their business is slack in the plains. Last season the number of mules which came to Ladakh amounted to 375, against 250 the year before, and this most materially aided the local supply of carriage,—the nucleus of the mule traffic. The Kulu train also did good service last season by venturing beyond Ladakh, with provisions for Mr. Forsyth's Embassy, to the very borders of the Yarkand dominions at Shahid-ullah; thus showing the way, and a second time, over a new section of road. The carriage difficulty then seems in fair way of being solved, for the whole mule-supply of the Punjab is becoming available for employment in the Turkestan trade.

"Thanks to the improvement of the road and the removal of various impediments effected by His Highness the Maharaja, the route through Kashmir has also come into extensive use, thus providing two roads instead of one to Ladakh. This is a very hopeful circumstance, as it doubles the total of carriage available."

The return of carraige available for trade purposes in Yarkand territory which I have been able to prepare, certainly shows a very small supply with reference to what our traders require, but the number of Yarkand ponies which reach Ladakh and are available for the return journey, is measured by the amount of goods imported from Turkestan. Practically there is no limit to the pony carriage on the Yarkand side, and, when required, the supply now kept up by the Kerai-Kush (professional hirers of carriage) might be increased to any extent.

The amount of carriage required for the exportation of goods from India is necessarily greater than that demanded for the trade coming this way.

In proof of this, I cannot do better than insert the remark lately made by Mr. Shaw on this subject:—

"Proceeding to a consideration of the several headings under which the trade is grouped, the *imports from Turkestan* show a trifling increase of Rupees 8,927.

"The increase noted above consists of the balance between the greater quantity of certain articles and the smaller quantity of others that were brought down from Yarkand in the two successive years. An examination of these differences is instructive as showing the tendency of the trade. The increase is in *precious metals, horses, jade, pashm*, and *raw silk* chiefly; while the decrease is in *charras, coarse cotton goods, carpets* and *felts, furs, leather, sea-weed*, silk *fabrics* and *precious stones, &c.*; as a class, it will be observed, the former are articles of high value in proportion to their weight, or else such as carry themselves, *viz.*, horses; while the latter are chiefly (though not entirely) bulky articles of less intrinsic value.

"This seems to show that the selections made in Yarkand with the view (which we know was in fact carried out) of the owners pushing rapidly down to India without being encumbered with heavy goods. This would imply a greater anxiety to obtain English or Indian goods, than to get rid of any particular articles of Turkestan production. The same anxiety has been marked in previous years, and is an encouraging feature of the trade.

"The steady increase in the articles of *gold, shawl-wool* (pashm), *raw silk, &c.*, since the year 1867 (when a British officer was first appointed to Ladakh) is remarkable. In that year the import of *gold* (dust and 'tillas') was Rupees 3,932 worth; in 1871 it was Rupees 85,899 worth; in 1872 it was Rupees 1,04,966 worth; in 1873 it rose to Rupees 1,49,498 worth, or about 45 per cent. of the imports from Yarkand.

"*Shawl-wool (pashm)* also is steadily rising. In 1871 it stood for Rupees 28,550; in 1872 Rupees 36,330; and in 1873 Rupees 42,600, or nearly 13 per cent. of those imports.

"The value of *raw silk* imported in the year 1871 was only Rupees 3,072; in 1872 it rose to Rupees 19,012; in 1873 to Rupees 25,500, including a small quantity (Rupees 132 worth) of cocoons, or nearly 8 per cent. of the imports.

"Horses have risen from a value in 1871 of Rupees 16,650; in the year 1872 to Rupees 20,400; and in 1873 to Rupees 27,580, or over 8 per cent. of the imports. They are mostly strong hill-ponies.

"The steady progress of all these items is most encouraging, as they are of a nature calculated to put the trade on a solid foundation."

In calling attention to the necessity for giving some stimulus to the arrangements now existing for the supply of horses and mules to traders, I quote *verbatim* a short note regarding the horses and yâks now available on this side of the passes which has been given to me by Mr. Johnson, the Wazir of Ladakh.

In Kulu there are only about 40 horses to be had. In Lahoul about 200, but these are being sold off by the villagers since mules have begun to come up from the Punjab.

Four hundred mules have been generally employed on the Kulu road—they come from Kangra, Noorpúr, and Hushiarpúr. This season about 800 mules have come in.

There are a great number of horses to be procured in Kashmir, but they are mostly too weak to carry loads over the high plateau of Tibet.

There are about 600 horses in Dras and Kirgil fit for carrying loads.

The horses of Leh are particularly small and weak, there are about 250 in all through Ladakh.

The entire number of yâks fit for carriage in Ladakh is about 1,000.

Number of yâks in Nubra, Leh, &c., available for crossing the Sasair, Digar, and Khardong Passes:—

In Ladakh for carriage to Khardong and Digar	300
In Chimray for carriage over Sakti Pass	100
In Khardong and Digar for carriage of goods to Leh	100
In Nubra for carriage over Sasair Pass	120

The yâks in Nubra are very poor, and can hardly be used save in the months of August, September, and October.

Yâks as a rule cannot be used for more than a couple of marches—they get foot-sore.

One point has been clearly established by the safe passage of the late Mission, *viz.*, that mule carriage is, of all others, the best for the work in question.

The sale of the mules which accompanied the Mission at Rawul Pindee will, it is hoped, operate favorably, and induce the mulemen of the Rawul Pindee district to come forward and undertake the journey.

The incorporation of the districts of Dras, Kargil, and Zanskar in the Wazirat of Ladak would draw a certain number of good ponies from the Kashmir side into the trade, and would tend greatly to the advantage of merchants travelling through Kashmir by bringing the whole of the route on the far side of the Zogi La directly under the Ladakh authorities.

The question of employing Bactrian camels from the Yarkand side by way of the Changchemnoo has been much discussed.

The number of camels available, so far as I have been able to ascertain, are in—

Kargalik	100 camels.
Kogiar	50 "
Guma	100 "

With the wandering Papoo tribe—

(2 marches from Kogiar)	25 "

This tribe has besides some 100 horses and 200 bullocks available for traffic along the Kogiar route. Owing to the melting of the snow during the summer months, camels cannot leave Yarkand to cross the Karakorum till the end of August. The severe cold of the winter months is fatal to camels at extreme elevations, and a return from Ladakh to Yarkund during the same season would therefore be barely possible. It does not seem likely that camels can ever be used as through-carriage in the regular trade; but now that the Kogiar route has been regularly opened, the old system under which camels were employed along roads from the Yarkand side, as far as the Karakorum only, is deserving of review.

Before Kunjut raids interfered with the traffic which existed during the Chinese occupation, it was customary for the carriers of Kogiar to engage to convey loads as far as the Karakorum only, where they were met by the carriers from Nubra and Ladakh who transported the loads to Leh. Camel forage is met with throughout the bed of the Yarkand river, *i.e.*, as far as Kufelung. The distance from Kufelung to Brangsa Karakorum, 48 miles, can be performed in two days, while the Shyok is reached in two days more.

There is no known reason why camels should not make the journey to Kufelung along the bed of the Yarkand river; provided some arrangement could be made by which they could be relieved of their loads at Brangsa Karakorum, or even on reaching the Shyok river they might now be utilised. The carriers of Kogiar would enter keenly into the traffic if they were not called upon to make the through journey involving a long period of absence from home, and an extraordinary strain upon their cattle.

By the present system the animals employed in this traffic are subjected to an unnatural strain, being overladen and forced frequently to carry loads not only through from Yarkand to Ladakh, and *vice versâ*, without rest, but being pushed on to India where they arrive in an exhausted condition.

The trade with Turkestan, on its present footing even, is dependant on the carriage available; it is consequently incumbent to study closely the best means of developing and improving the system of carriage. Every encouragement and even pecuniary assistance, if required, should be given to carriers, who should be protected by regulations indicating—

*I.—The weight to be carried by each animal.

†II.—The amount of compensation to be made to the carrier on account of loss of cattle during the journey when travelling out of season.

The profits which fall to the trader will allow of the carrier being more liberally treated, and of the beast of burden meeting with a greater amount of consideration than has hitherto been shown to him.

The trader is protected by the carrier engaging to convey his loads to their destination at the risk of whatever loss in cattle.

The present difficulties in the matter of carriage are abnormal, and given a measure of encouragement, they will be removed by the actual requirements of the trade.

In crossing the Karakorum from Yarkand during the present season, every animal belonging to the British Mission was equipped with a double sack containing mixed forage for 4 days (consisting of bhoosa, chopped lucerne grass, and grain weighing some 30 lbs.), this double sack when thrown over the saddle and under the load protected the animal's ribs if properly adjusted, and the small store of provision guaranteed him against absolute starvation when crossing the Karakorum.

The additional weight of 30 lbs. thus imposed had no evil effect. A Kerai Kush in crossing from Yarkand will invariably place numdahs in a similar position upon which he intends realizing a profit in Ladakh: these however distress the animal and add to the weight of the load unnecessarily.

The construction of rough shelter houses along the Karakorum route, and the cultivation of additional grain and fodder (lucerne) in the villages of Ladakh are desiderata which would materially promote the traffic.

A proposal to establish an annual fair at Leh, the capital of Ladakh, has been made.

Leh is half-way between Yarkand and the Punjab: it was of old an emporium of trade, and with a little arrangement might be made an entrepôt of great importance. There are many merchants who would travel as far as Leh, both from India and from Yarkand, who would not care to undertake the whole journey involving the long absence from home already alluded to. Traders from India would be able to take their goods to Leh on their own mules or ponies, and on camels too, and return home the same year with the exchange commodities.

The months of August and September appear to be the best months for holding a fair at Leh. Traders visiting the fair, from either side, would thus have time to dispose of their goods and return the same season to their homes; or if their goods were not disposed of advantageously at Leh, they might pass on to Yarkand or India as the case might be.

Any one who has studied the customs of Central Asia must have noticed the very extensive resort to the system of fairs which prevails. It is a custom which commends itself at once to the mind of the Turk, and it was with a knowledge of the habits of people inhabiting those countries with which Russia desired to establish trade relations that a fair was established at Nijni Novgorod.

---

* 2 maunds 32 seers is the load accepted by carriers leaving the Punjab and Yarkand. Goods at either extremity of the route are made up to this weight: it would be impolitic to enforce the breaking up and redistribution of loads in Ladakh, consequently this appears to be the best load, but it should not be exceeded.

† A proportion only of the value, according to the season and difficulties in obtaining supply; Rupees 5 or 10 as the case may be for each horse.

At the time the Mission was leaving Yarkand, the opinion of the Dadkhwah Mahomed Yunus on this point was decided; he expressed himself to the effect that if a regular fair were established at Leh, many merchants from Yarkand who had not yet engaged in trade with India would be attracted across the Karakorum.

The only difficulty likely to arise is that of supply: it is a question whether the grain produce of Ladakh is sufficient to maintain a large assemblage of men and horses, besides its own population during the time the fair would require to be kept up.

There is however much uncultivated ground in the district of Ladakh which might be utilised, and the requirements of the fair would draw in grain from Dras and Kargil Skardo and more distant valleys. The opinions of the Joint Commissioners of Ladakh are in favor of the establishment of a fair such as is proposed, and there is every reason to suppose that the measure would be generally popular with the trade.

Articles of merchandise conveyed from Eastern Turkestan to British India.

	Weight.	Price in Yarkand.	Cost of carriage and packing.	Price in Umritsur.	Profit.	Profit per cent.	REMARKS.
		Rs. a. p.	Rs. a. p.	Rs. a. p.	Rs. a. p.		
1. Churas (Kashghar)	1 horse load	112 0 0	76 0 0	300 0 0	112 0 0	59·5	1 horse load 2 maunds 32 seers.
2. „ (Yarkand)	1 ditto	56 0 0	76 0 0	160 0 0	28 0 0	21·25	The preparation of the Kashghar churas is very superior to that of Yarkand, which is often adulterated.
3. Pashm (Kashghar)	1 ditto	112 0 0	76 0 0	225 0 0	37 0 0	29·5	
4. Shein silk of Khoten	1 charak (2 seers 10 chataks.)	15 0 0	1 8 0	18 0 0	1 8 0	9	
5. Carpets of Khoten	Per square yard	2 8 0	0 8 0	5 0 0	2 0 0	66·6	Mámirán is tested by rubbing on a blue cloth which has been dyed with indigo; if it is of good quality it should efface the color and leave a white mark.
6. Numdahs	Each	1 0 0	0 8 0	2 0 0	0 8 0	33·3	
7. Gilli flower	1 seer	3 0 0	0 8 0	5 0 0	1 8 0	42·7	
8. Mámirán-i-Khitai	1 „	0 8 0	0 8 0	2 0 0	1 0 0	100	
9. Turanjbil (gum)	1 „	0 10 0	0 8 0	2 0 0	0 8 0	33·3	Yarkand gold sells in India per tola at 15·8.
10. Gold (of Khoten)	12 tolas 9 mashas	160 0 0	......	197 0 0	37 0 0	23·25	The cost of carriage of gold is not included; it is usually distributed by the merchant throughout his various loads.
11. Gold (of Yarkand)	11 „ 6 „	160 0 0	......	178 4 0	18 4 0	11·25	

Mámirán, a yellow root, a medicine for the eyes in Hindoostan; in Turkestan it is used to flavor food.

Turanjbil (manna).

1 maund = 40 seers of 2lbs. each.

1 tola = 12 másha. 1 másha = 15 grains.

Articles of Merchandize conveyed from British India to Eastern Turkestan.

		Weight.	Cost price.	Cost of carriage and packing.	Duty at 2·5 per cent.	Price in Kashghar.	Profit.	Profit, per cent.	Remarks.
1.	Long-cloth	Per than, 4 seers	7 0 0	2 0 0	0 4 0	15 0 0	5 12 0	60	*Item No. 22, the carriage from Calcutta is included.* Many of the prices indicate a very large percentage of profit, but there are, of course, great differences in the measure of success attending individual merchants, owing to the fluctuations of the market, and the degree of talent displayed by each individual in rendering his goods acceptable to the retail dealers.
2.	Linen	"	3 0 0	0 2 0	0 1 6	6 0 0	2 12 6	75·9	
3.	Bindly	"	3 0 0	0 2 0	0 1 6	5 0 0	1 13 6	74·8	
4.	White Jaconet	"	3 8 0	0 2 0	0 1 9	6 0 0	2 4 3	44·7	
5.	Unealoured flowered muslin	"	3 0 0	0 3 0	0 1 9	4 0 0	0 11 3	20·27	
6.	Coarse sheeting	"	3 0 0	0 1 0	0 1 6	4 8 0	1 5 6	40·4	
7.	Drill	"	5 0 0	0 2 0	0 2 6	12 0 0	4 11 6	49·4	
8.	Unbleached long-cloth	"	5 8 0	0 3 0	0 2 9	12 0 0	3 10 3	29·25	
9.	Red Jaconet	"	5 0 0	0 2 0	0 2 6	16 0 0	4 11 6	66·6	
10.	Turkey-red	"	6 0 0	0 3 0	0 3 0	30 0 0	8 1 0	125	
11.	Colored Chintz	"	1 7 0	0 2 0	0 0 9	2 12 0	0 13 3	55	
12.	Stamped cotton (imitation shawl)	"	2 0 0	2 0 0	0 1 0	11 8 0	3 12 0	32·25	
13.	Cotton velvet (coarse)	"	2 0 0	0 12 0	0 1 0	4 0 0	2 0 0	100	
14.	Flowered cottons (stamped)	"	2 0 0	0 9 0	0 1 0	3 0 0	2 2 0	52·75	
15.	Broad-cloth	"	6 2 0	0 4 0	0 3 0	11 0 0	2 3 0	81·7	
16.	Alpaca	"	4 2 0	0 3 0	0 2 3	10 0 0	2 11 9	97·2	
17.	Flannel (cheap colored)	"	2 0 0	0 9 0	0 1 0	9 0 0	3 6 0	32·24	
18.	Kimab	"	1 0 0	0 9 0	0 0 6	4 0 0	1 2 6	20·6	
19.	Guarnat (thin satin with gold flowers)	"	"	98 0 0	0 4 0	12 4 0	102 0 0	35 0 0	43·78	
	plain	"	"	23 0 0	0 2 0	2 4 0	47 0 0	29 10 0	99	
20.	Enamelled leather (Igner) great skins	Per score, "	89 0 0	0 3 0	7 4 0	100 0 0	17 7 0	66·75	
21.	Otter skins (Calcutta)	"	30 0 0	0 4 0	2 0 0	45 0 0	13 6 0	107·5	*1 seer = 2 lbs. English.* A large profit is realized on the sale of Macao's plumes from Kulu, these being worn by women on the skull caps which are usually worn inside the house.
	(Kuburn)	"	8 0 0	0 0 0	0 7 6	25 0 0	12 0 6	53·6	
22.	Tea, Green (Paburgsose)	Per seer, "	4 0 0	0 6 0	0 4 0	60 0 0	29 6 0	52·9	
23.	— Black (Bombay)	"	2 0 0	0 0 0	0 2 0	150 0 0	72 14 0	100	
24.	— Soh (Calcutta)	"	1 0 0	0 0 0	0 1 0	4 2 0	1 0 2	100	
25.	Opium No. 11 (Kilfa)	Per ¼ seer,	0 6 0	0 0 0	0 0 6	2 1 0	1 7 0	107·2	
26.	No. 1 (Shaahpore)	Per 5 seers	12 0 0	0 0 0	0 12 0	21 0 0	7 2 0	98·26	
27.	Indigo (Kocja)	Per seer	8 0 0	0 0 0	0 8 0	30 0 0	18 12 0	158	
28.	Black pepper	"	0 7 0	0 0 0	0 12 0	11 0 0	Profit on 10 seers 17/8/6		
29.	Ginger	"	0 5 0	0 0 0		15 0 0			
30.	Cardamoms	"	0 6 0	0 0 0		6 0 0			
31.	Nutmeg	"	0 10 0	0 0 0	Duty on 10 seers of spices 0/14/6	1 0 0			
32.	Long pepper	"	0 4 0	0 0 0		1 0 0			
33.	Ginamon	"	1 0 0	0 0 0		4 0 0			
34.	Turmeric	"	0 0 0	0 0 0		1 0 0			
35.	Spices (Indian)	"	0 0 0	0 0 0		1 0 0			
36.	Preserves (Cannitant)	"	0 0 0	0 0 0					
37.	Money	"	3 0 0	0 0 0		6 0 0	1 7 0	Profit per cent. on spices, &c., 89.	
38.	Looking-glasses and small articles (tickle rackle) realizes a profit of								
39.	Books in Persian and Arabic find a ready sale and realize a profit of							50	
40.	Sugar, No. 1 (Schurmpore)	Per maund	13 0 0	2 2 0	0 5 0	60 0 0	33 9 0	64·5	There is a very small sale for arms, excepting when they are required by the Amir. Breech-loaders are of little value and great finish is unnecessary. Strong single barrelled rifles M.-L. of the Enfield pattern or gane-keeper's M.-L. guns are the most likely to be appreciated.
41.	No. 2 (ditto)	"	12 0 0	2 2 0	0 5 0	65 0 0	24 9 0	69	
42.	No. 3 (ditto)	"	16 0 0	2 2 0	0 6 0	98 0 0	50 6 0	319	
43.	Guns, double-barrelled	"	22 0 0	0 0 0	0 14 0	60 0 0			
44.	single do.	"	13 0 0	0 0 0	0 8 0	100 0 0			
45.	Rifles, B.-L. double-barrelled	"	130 0 0	12 12 0	3 4 0	180 0 0	35 0 0	12	
46.	ditto	"	25 0 0	12 12 0	1 12 0	100 0 0	42 8 0	12	
47.	Pistols, single barrelled	"	30 0 0	12 12 0	2 2 0	75 0 0	61 12 0	12	
48.	double do.	"	35 0 0	0 0 0	2 12 0	100 0 0	7 7 0	12	
49.	Revolvers	"	1 0 0			10 0 0		244	
50.	Percussion Caps	Per 1,000	1 0 0	0 4 0	0 1 0	10 0 0		344	

CHAPTER X.

PHOTOGRAPHY.

By Captain Chapman.

When the Mission was first formed, it was proposed to engage a qualified Native Photographer; as, however, great difficulty was experienced in securing the services of a competent man, the work of photography fell upon the officers of the Mission. Captain Trotter and Captain Chapman provided themselves, through Messrs. Lyell and Co., with $7\frac{1}{4} \times 4\frac{1}{2}$ inch cameras and with chemicals, &c., for the preparation of some 400 plates.

Messrs. Bourne and Shepherd, Photographers, Simla, were early consulted, and the ordinary wet process was adopted; at the same time a certain number of dry plates were ordered from home from the Liverpool Dry Plate Company.

Subsequently, two sets of Professor Piazzi Smith's apparatus for taking small photographs for enlargement were ordered.

Mr. Shepherd, of the Firm previously mentioned, was good enough to devote a good deal of time during May and June 1873 to Captain Chapman's instruction. Both the officers, who have been engaged in photographing, desire prominently to acknowledge the assistance they have received from this gentleman, whose advice they have followed throughout.

It was from the first decided to give up all thought of printing during the travels of the Mission, and the negatives have been regularly forwarded to Messrs. Shepherd and Bourne, by whom the photographs have been printed.

Packing.—The entire equipment was carried throughout the expedition on mules, the boxes containing chemicals, &c., being so regulated as to approximate one maund in weight: with one set, the leather trunks from the Cawnpoor Factory were provided with special fittings, and with the other, wooden boxes covered with felt and fitted with wicker cases were employed.

The experience gained during the journey leads to the conclusion that boxes arranged to weigh half a maund each (40 lbs.) would have been more useful and less liable to injury than those of the larger size; four such boxes would constitute a mule load.

Each separate bottle had a covering of its own, and was carefully stowed with cotton wool in its own partition. The greater number of the photographs obtained have been taken with Dalmayer's wide-angle lens, the slide of the $7\frac{1}{4}'' \times 4\frac{1}{2}''$ camera having warped so much under the weight of stereoscopic lenses, which were also provided, as to render them useless.

The total number of negatives obtained is 110.

The ordinary wet process, with proto-sulphate of iron developer and a pushing solution of pyro-gallic acid was employed.

Thomas' collodion in half pints, and Mawson's collodion were both brought into use, the latter being chosen as tending to density in the negative.

Triple crystalised and fused nitrate of silver was specially chosen.

The greater number of subjects being figures, the dry plates furnished with the equipment were not made use of, owing to the long exposure required with them, and as it was nearly always possible to employ the larger cameras, Professor Piazzi Smith's apparatus was not brought into use.

The possession of a certain amount of old proto-sulphate of iron which had become peroxydized was found highly advantageous as assisting the rapid preparation of developing solution when required.

The severity of the winter season and the difficulties attending photography on the line of march need to be appreciated; but in favor of the equipment and the process employed, it may be recorded that some of the negatives were obtained when the thermometer showed many degrees of frost, and that the camera was constantly used after a long march.

The prejudices which exist in all Mahomedan countries against the taking of likenesses were found to be very strongly in force on arrival, and it was only as confidence was established, and in consequence of the liberal policy of the Amir, that it became possible to secure the photographs which have been obtained.

CHAPTER XI.

Memorandum on the use of sheep carrying supplies across the Karakorum by Captain J. Biddulph.

I LEFT Tankse on 18th September, taking with me thirty sheep carrying loads of grain and flour. Wishing merely to test their marching capabilities, I looked upon the supplies they carried as extra, and their loads remained intact till within four marches of Shahidoolla, when I was forced to commence using them.

The Tartars usually make their sheep carry a load of 32lbs., and march seven or eight miles a day only, making frequent halts; as, however, I expected to be marching hard at times, I put only, a load of 20lbs. on each sheep. Beyond this I took no care of them, and they simply took their chance.

A great part of the route was over rough and stony ground, but only one sheep broke down, though many of them showed signs of footsoreness at times.

The loads secured by breast and breach ropes ride well, sinking into the fleece, and not being liable to shift.

On fair ground where they travelled with a broad front they marched at the rate of 1¾ mile an hour; a large number would no doubt travel slower, and much must depend on the breadth of the road.

The greatest difficulty they had to contend with was crossing streams, and while marching in the Karakash Valley they were sometimes obliged to cross the river three or four times in a day. Not only were their loads liable to become damaged, but the weight of water hanging in their fleeces, and on several occasions freezing, greatly impeded progress.

On the days on which they had no grass, they had literally nothing to eat, as they refused grain, not being accustomed to it.

One man was sufficient to manage the lot, and two men, I should say, could easily drive and manage an hundred.

On arrival in camp they were unloaded, and turned out to shift for themselves till dark, when they were herded for the night.

The fact that a flock of sheep carrying 20lbs. loads should be able to march 330 miles in a month with only one casualty, through a country in which forage is always scanty, and at a very inclement season of the year, is remarkable. After the first march the elevation was never less than 11,000 feet, and the thermometer at night sank to 15° and 16° below zero. The sheep, however, apparently did not feel either cold or elevation. Future exploring parties on the Karakorum will, I feel certain, find a flock of sheep a most useful addition to their camp. Not only are they very easily looked after, but they can feed themselves as they go along, which ponies cannot do, and can pick up a subsistence on the scanty pasture grounds and among the rocks where horses would starve. Besides this, when their loads are disposed of, they can themselves be eaten.

The accompanying table will show the particulars of the marches they made. I was accompanied the whole time by a Survey Pundit, who paced the distance each day.

Table showing marches taken by a flock of thirty sheep carrying loads of 20lbs.

MARCH.	DATE.	MILES.	REMARKS.
	1873.		
Tankse to Tchur-ka-talab	18th September	14	
Lukung	19th „	7¼	
Chagra	21st „	8	

Table showing marches taken by a flock, &c.—(Concluded.)

MARCH.	DATE.	MILES.	REMARKS.
	1873.		
Rimdi	22nd September	13	Cross Lunkur La, 18,400 feet.
Pamzal	23rd ,,	13	
Gogra	24th ,,	12½	
Shummal Lungpa	26th ,,	12	
Camp near Nischu	27th ,,	14¾	No grass. Cross Changlung La, 19,300 feet.
,, on Lingzi Thung	28th ,,	16½	No grass.
Camp	29th ,,	20½	No grass.
Sumnal	30th ,,	21½	Cross Kizzil Dawan, 17,600 feet; did not arrive in Camp till dark.
Kizzil Jilga	1st October	11	
Chung Tash	7th ,,	24	Grass very scarce; did not arrive till after dark.
Sumnal	9th ,,	13	
Camp	10th ,,	10¼	Grass very scarce.
,,	11th ,,	15	No grass.
,,	12th ,,	16½	No grass. One sheep broke down on march.
Sorah	13th ,,	5½	
Camp	14th ,,	13	
,,	15th ,,	18	Supplies not begun to be used till this evening.
,,	16th ,,	10½	
Gulbasher	17th ,,	18	
Shahidoolla	18th ,,	23	Total 330½ miles. The last eleven marches being down the valley of the Karakash.

CHAPTER XII.

Money, Weights, and Measures of Káshghar.

Money.

The denominations and values of the current coins are these—

  2 púl or fúl = 1 dárchin or pysa.
  25 dárchin = 1 tanga = 4 annas Indian currency.
  26 tanga = 1 tilá = 5 rupees 12 annas.
  30 tilá = 1 yámbú or kúrs = 172 rupees 8 annas.

The *púl* is a thin copper disc with a square hole in the centre for stringing. It bears a Chinese inscription on each side, and is the only copper coin current. Two of them go to a *drárchin* and fifty to a tanga. The metal appears to be much alloyed with iron, and is of Chinese mintage.

The *tanga* is a small silver coin, recently issued by the Amir, in the name of the Sultan of Turkey, 'Abdul' aziz Khan (on the obverse), as the coinage of the "protected State of Káshghar" (on the reverse). It is said to be of pure silver and worth about six pence. The *tilá* is a gold coin in the name of 'Abdul' aziz, and bears the same legend as the *tanga*, simultaneously with which it was issued. Its market value varies between five and six rupees.

The *yámbú* or *kúrs* is a silver ingot something the shape of a deep boat with projecting bow and stern. The upper surface is slightly hollowed, and stamped with a Chinese inscription. It is said to be pure silver, and to weigh fifty *ser* = 30,000 grains English. It is divided into fifths and tenths, called *on ser* and *besh ser*, respectively, which are of the same shape and stamp, and proportionate size and value.

The Kurs is really an article of merchandize and not a coin, its value depreciating as the value of silver depreciates; it may be in fact regarded as "bar silver."

Indian Rupees are, at present, but little known in the Yarkand market; like the silver Kurs they are regarded solely as articles of merchandize, and receive their value as silver in equivalent coinage (*i.e.*, the copper circulating medium).

They suffer, at present, however, from an additional disadvantage in being but little known: that is, they are affected by a variety of circumstances, and their value may fall below the value of silver.

For instance, taking the Kurs to represent 800 *Tangas* as at present, the value of a rupee would be 5 *Tangas*, whereas it realizes no more than from 4 to 4½ Tangas, and is differently priced by individuals according to circumstances.

In exchanging rupees at this moment an actual loss of from 2 annas 9 pies to 1 anna 4 pies is incurred.

Gold in the market may be thus classified:—

I.—*The Koten Régh.*—This is a small gold bead unstamped; it sells at the present time at the following rate:—

Three sérs 7 miskals, or 3 sérs 8 miskals weight, obtain 1 silver kurs of 50 sérs, *i.e.*, 800 Tangas.

This places the seller of gold at a disadvantage; should however the value of the Kurs increase so as to represent 1,000 Tangas as formerly, the buyer will then suffer.

It must however be remembered on the other hand that as much as 4 sérs of this gold have been given for a silver Kurs.

II.—*The Yarkand Régh.*—This is of gold obtained in the Yarkand river and washed on the spot; it sells as follows:—

(495)

Four sérs of gold = one Kurs silver = 800 Tangas.

The gold of China in all forms sells by weight according to the value accorded to the Koten Régh; the gold is usually in the form of Kurs, or in bar.

III.—*Gold Tillah* (Khokani)—Of the times of Allah Yar Khan and Khoda Yar Khan. These sell for 26 Tangas, 27 Tangas, or more, and the weight of gold amounts to 1½ másha.

Price paid in the Punjab from Rupees 5-11 to Rupees 5-13.

IV.—*The Bokhara Gold Tillah.*—Sells at the same rate, and is of the same weight as the Khokani Tillah, but costs in the Punjab from Rupees 6-6 to Rupees 6-8.

Gold and silver are worked in Yarkand for ornaments to meet a local demand.

Neither manufactured gold or silver are, however, exported.

Silver Kurs bought in Turkestan for Rupees 160, *i.e.*, 800 Tangas, taking the mercantile exchange to be 5 Tangas in the rupee, sell in India for Rupees 170.

Tillahs sell in the Punjab at Rupees 5-12: they may be purchased in Turkestan for 27 Tangas, which amounts to Rupees 5 annas 6⅖.

Although the actual rupee has a value often not exceeding 4½ Tangas, all mercantile transactions calculated in rupees allow them a value of 5 Tangas.

Weights.

The measures of weight and capacity used in Káshghar are these—

2 nukhud = 1 fúng = 6 grains English.
10 fúng = 1 miskál = 60 grains.
10 miskál = 1 ser = 600 grains.
16 ser = 1 jing = 20 ounces or one pound four ounces.
2 jing = 1 tártam = 2½ pounds.
4 jing = 1 ashak = 5 pounds.
4 ashak = 1 chárak = 20 pounds.
8 chárak = 1 gilbar = 160 pounds.
8 gilbar = 1 batmán = 1,280 pounds.

The *nukhud* is represented by the common chick-pea, and the others up to the *jing* by progressively larger cubes or bricks of brass on which are stamped the several values in Chinese letters; for the rest stones and measures are used. For the lesser weights up to the *jing* a small poise-beam balance is mostly used, and for the others the ordinary double scale balance. The former has the scale at one end, and the weight is shifted along the graduated beam, which is held up by a cord near the scale end, till it balances the weight.

Measures.

The linear measures in common use are these—

10 li = 1 fúng.
10 fúng = 1 sóng.
20 sóng = 1 archín = 28 inches English.
60 archín = 1 tanáb = 46 yards 24 inches.

The *archín* is the common cloth measure, and the *tanáb*, or "rope," that for land. There is another measure of cloth, called *barí*, which used in the purchase or sale of long or entire pieces. It is the width re-duplicated on the length, and the size of the square thus formed is the unit for the measurement of the whole length, which is said then to consist of so many *bar* or "breadths."

(Sd.) H. W. Bellew.

---

* The *Andijani* Charak of 16 Jings, or 20 lbs., is only used for weighing grain and fresh fruit.
The *Yarkandi* Charak is of 12½ Jings; oil, soap, sugar, meat, butter, dried fruit, &c., &c., are weighed by this charak.
Silk is sold according to two standards.
Kalawar is sold by the charak of 4 jings.
Goonji silk, a new kind of silk of superior quality, sells by the charak of 8 jings.
Cotton is usually sold by the charak of 12½ jings, but in the district of Kanarik a charak of 15 jings is a common measure.

Appendix I.

SHOPS IN YARKAND.

20th November 1873.

In the principal bazaar 190 shops are divided between cloth merchants and dealers in spices, &c., 175 being devoted to spices and minerals, and 90 to cloths; there are besides saddlers, cutlers, &c.

This bazaar is open every day of the week, business being generally transacted between 12 and 3 o'clock.

On Thursday, the fixed market day, and every evening after 3, there is a great deal of buying and selling done in the Sham or evening bazaar.

In this neighbourhood may be counted:—

100 sellers of cloths.
25 dealers in ready-made clothes, articles made up in cotton and silk; all being disposed of at separate shops.
60 boot sellers (boots for men and for women are sold at separate shops).
26 hatters, 14 for men's hats and 12 for women's. There are 34 hatters shops in addition throughout the city.
50 sellers of silk; both men and women keep these shops, and there are hawkers in addition.
20 shops where boots are supplied with nails.
25 retail dealers in spices.
50 dealers in pottery.
40 sellers of numdahs.
5 jewellers.

In addition, scattered throughout the town, are 150 butchers' shops.

There are 125 bakers, but the sellers of bread amount to 150.

There are 65 houses where soap is prepared.

There are 30 houses where candles are made.

About 100 curing houses for dressing hides, and 230 dyeing houses, 30 of which confine their work to the dyeing of silk.

22nd November 1873.

Meat.—About 600 sheep are killed daily in Yarkand, and as many as from 900 to 1,000 on market days.

Fifteen oxen are slaughtered daily, and perhaps one or two horses; these last, however, are only killed when injured by accident or worn out.

Price of Meat.

Mutton ... ... 16 puls per jing = $1\frac{1}{4}$ lbs.
Beef ... ... 14 ,, ,, ,,
Horse flesh ... ... 16 ,, ,, ,,

Bread.—A charak of grain = 20 lbs.: this is sold for $1\frac{1}{2}$ tangas; when baked, its product in bread realizes $2\frac{1}{2}$ tangas.

About 8 charaks of grain represents a fair daily consumption in one baker's shop.

(497)

CONTENTS OF A DRUGGISTS SHOP.

Local.	India.	Kashmir.	Elsewhere.
Æleagnus.	Emblica.	Violets.	Figs, dried.
Almonds.	Hareera.	Maiden's hair fern.	Raw tea.
Lithurge.	Turmeric.	Zirisk.	Tea, China.
Kantapa (root).	Ginger.	Belladonna.	Mummy wax.
Ayaldaroo.	Black pepper.		
Colchicum.	Cardamoms.		
Gum Acacia.	Cassia.		
Senna.	Cinnamon.		
Rosa Canina.	Astragolus.		
Cape Gooseberry.	Haleela.		
Cucumber seed.	Cloves.		
Corn poppy.	Sebestin.		
Rhubarb.	Gall nuts.		
Legume seed.	Carroways.		
Liquorice.	Water lilly.		
Fumitory.	Herma.		
Hurmal.	Ajwain.		
Korpa.	Kubebs.		
Dharnea.	Indian manna.		
Turkmuk.	Long pepper.		
Vetch.	Goor.		
Karksin.	Horse Chesnuts.		
Poplar bark.*	Catechu.		
Dried plums.	Glue.		
Poppy heads.	Catgut.		
Emmery (Khoten).			
Sulphate of copper.			
Antimony (Aksu).			
Alum (Aksu).			
Sesame.			
Endive.			
Fennel.			

In addition to the above exposed on the stall, the more valuable spices and medicines were carefully packed away inside the house.

Soap.—There are 65 dealers in soap.

Soap is made of lime, potash, and mutton fat, it costs 7 tangas the charak=1½ jing= 15 to 16 lbs. 1 tanga = 50 puls. 350 puls = 26 lbs. of soap, 22 to 23 puls to the pound.

Candles.—There are 30 candlemakers.

1 charak of fat mixed with about 12 miskals of wax (6 puls) produces 120 candles of ordinary size, which are sold for from 2 to 4 dacheen, *i.e.*, 4 or 8 puls, or by weight per jing 1½ tangas.

Hides.—An ox hide uncured is purchased for from 12 to 15 tangas according to size: when cured it is sold at from 22 to 25 tangas.

Ox hides are cured with quick lime and saltpetre and stained with rhubarb.

The purchase of an uncured sheepskin averages one tanga and 12 puls: when cured it sells for 1 tanga and 25 puls.

In addition to this, some portion of the wool from the skin remains with the currier this is used in the making up of ropes.

Carpets.—Are made at a village called Khiwaz (about 130 houses) about 5 miles from Yarkand. They are inferior to Khoten carpets.

    A carpet, 8 yards by 4, costs 100 tangas (8 of these make a pony load).
    A ,, 6 ditto 3 ,, 60 ,, (weight 1 charak 2 jings).
    A ,, 4 ditto 2 ,, 50 ,,
    A ,, 2 ditto 1½ ,, 25 ,,

* (Togrucho) used as a ferment in making bread.

Khoten carpets are sold in the Yarkand market at the following rates:—

A carpet, 8 yards by 4, costs 250 tangas.
A „ 4 ditto 2 „ 125 „
A „ 3 ditto 1½ „ 60 „

Dyers.—230 shops, 30 of which are occupied solely with the dyeing of silk.

Yellow dye.—From a seed name unknown.

Khakee.—From the husk of pomegranate and impure carbonate of zinc.

Red.—From Kirimiz (Cochineal) and lac from Bokhara.

Purple.—From Kirimiz and indigo.

Green.—Indigo, alum, and huldee.

Black.—Carbonate of zinc and gall-nut and sulphate of iron.

SERAIS YARKAND.

No.	Name	Rooms	No.	Name	Rooms
1.	Andijani	15 rooms.	8.	Serai Khoten	34 rooms.
2.	Ditto	14 do.	9.	„ Nur Alli	15 do.
3.	Ditto	21 do.	10.	„ Kassim	14 do.
4.	Ditto	22 do.	11.	Oil Serai (Jeger)	7 do.
5.	Serai Sugut	28 do. (Kashmiri's.)	12.	Serai Bajaori	21 do.
6.	„ Sukhan	37 do.	13.	Hindoo Serai	25 do.
7.	„ Yarkand	27 do.	14.	Serai Ghufan	20 do.

The first four are chiefly occupied by Andijani merchants; they are the most pretentious in appearance: the best have a large cellar beneath the central space of the court-yard they enclose, the rooms for accommodation of the merchants being ranged all round.

Taking No. 4 Serai as an example, the hire of a room per mensem amounted to 5 tangas, but the entire income on account of rooms and store-rooms comes to 4,000 tangas per annum.

Here you may find pig-iron from Russia (Nijni) in large quantities.

Madder from Andijan (average price 30 tungas per charak).

Cotton from Khoten and Yarkand bound for Kashghar and Andijan.

Old iron.—Average price 3 jings for 2 tangas.

Cotton.—16 jings, or 1 charak, for 4 or 6 tangas.

Grape juice—16 jings, or 1 charak, for 8 tangas.

Numdahs and carpets from Khoten are also among the goods in store.

SERAIS KASHGHAR.

No.	Name	Rooms	No.	Name	Rooms
1.	Badshahi Kona	31 rooms (The Zakatchi resides here.)	7.	Zak Mullah Bai, No. 2	63 rooms (Very small rooms.)
2.	Badshahi Nawa	30 do. (In the Chowk.)	8.	Mahomed Yusuf Bai	28 do.
3.	Serai Alum Akhun	23 do.	9.	Yusuf Bai	30 do.
4.	Ahmed Akhun	31 do.	10.	Khoda Yar Beg	40 do.
5.	Ameen Akhun Bai	17 do.	11.	Ismail Beg	22 do.
6.	Zak Mullah Bai, No. 1	21 do.			

In the best of these serais 5 tangas per mensem is paid for the hire of a room; in the second class serais the hire of a room is 3 tangas per mensem.

The remaining serais are not occupied in any way by merchants and traders, but give shelter to people without a residence of their own; camelmen, &c., &c.

SERAIS AKSU.

No.	Name		No.	Name	
1.	Khoten	Serai 50 rooms.	6.	Khoona	Serai.
2.	Kashghari	do. 60 do.	7.	Nar Kurgan Bai	do.
3.	Sheik Beg	do.	8.	Andijani	do.
4.	Mullah Saduk	do.	9.	Yarkandi	do.
5.	Dhung	do.			

There are three other serais within walls.

(499)

SERAIS OUTSIDE THE WALLS AT AKSU.

1.	The Custom House.		13.	Eesah Kor	...	Serai.
2.	Charee Hakim	... Serai.	14.	Arjuk	...	do.
3.	Kirghiz Hakim	... do.	15.	Abdullah Bai	...	do.
4.	Aid Darogah	... do.	16.	Shah Mad Niaz	...	do.
5.	Mahomed Tokhta Bai.		17.	Lalu Sheik	...	do.
6.	Badshahi	... Serai.	18.	Yanús Bai	...	do.
7.	Haji	... do.	19.	Tudi Bai	...	do.
8.	Kush Najuk	... do.	20.	Músa Akhúnd	...	do
9.	Imam Khwoja	... do.	21.	Mahomed Tej Bai	...	do.
10.	Shukutlik	... do.	22.	Ibrahim	...	do.
11.	Abdullah Beg	... do.	23.	Shamoh Akhúnd	...	do.
12.	Hikmut Baki	... do.	24.	Túngani, Serai	...	do.

There are altogether 33 serais outside the walls.

Inside the walls there are 84 Musjids, and in the Yangi-Shahr of Aksu 64 Musjids.

Outside the walls 500 shops:—

35 Copper-smiths, 33 Butchers, 22 Ash Khanas, 17 Bakers, &c., &c.

Inside the walls:—

45 Copper-smiths, 45 Bakers, 34 Ash Paz, 50 Shoe-makers, &c., &c.

PRINCIPAL MERCHANTS RESIDENT IN YARKAND AND AKSU.

	Name.	Trades with	Property.
Yarkand	Haji Dadkhwah	Ladak	80,000 Rs.
Do.	Mohamad Buksh (4 gomashtas)	do.	50,000 „
Do.	Hazrat Abdul Rahmat	do.	50,000 „
Do.	Mohomad Ján	do.	50,000 „
Do.	Haji Nasr Khan; this man goes to	Calcutta	30,000 „
Do.	Mohamad Shah	Ladak and Kashmir	30,000 „
Do.	Mohamad Akhónd	Ladak	8,000 „
Do.	Afzul Mir	Umritsur	20,000 „
Do.	Mohamad Jan Shroff (remains in the city)	Yarkand	30,000 „
Do.	Saleh Beg	Ladak	15,000 „
Do.	Mirú Kabuli	Calcutta	15,000 „
Do.	Mir Afzúl Khan	Do.	10,000 „
Do.	Safr Ali (has Agents)	Ladak	10,000 „
Do.	Mohamad Umr Bhai	Do. and Umritsur	10,000 „
Do.	Mada Shah	Do. do.	8,000 „
Do.	Abdullah Bhai	Do. do.	8,000 „
Do.	Kari Akhónd	Do. do.	5,000 „
Do.	Bahadur Bashi (remains in city)	Yarkand	5,000 „
Do.	Talúk Já (employs his son)	Ladak	5,000 „
Do.	Mir Abdullah	Do.	5,000 „

(Employing Agents)

	Name.	Trade with	Property.
Aksu	Shumsh Tar Akhónd	Turfan and Ormutsi &c.	500 Yamboos = 80,000 Rs.
Do.	Ahmed Shah Bhai	Almati, Kashghar, Turfan, Ormutsi	400 Yamboos = 64,000 „
Do.	Jait Daróga	Almati, Kashghar, Turfan, Ormutsi	500 Yamboos = 80,000 „
Do.	Kassún Bhai, Andijani	Kokand, Almati, Kashghar, Turfan, Ormutsi	1,000 Yamboos = 1,60,000 „

(500)

CARRIAGE AVAILABLE IN 1874 IN YARKAND.

List of men (Keraia Kush) possessing horses, &c., hired out for trade purposes in Yarkand, &c.

Yarkand	Toksún Bhai	20 horses.	Yarkand	Nasr Mir	20 horses, 10 camels.
Ditto	Jam Shéd	30 do.	Ditto	Ashur Mir	30 horses.
Ditto	Gul Murád	30 do.	Ditto	Mohamad Tokhta	20 do.
Ditto	Nazar Bhai Badakshi	25 do.	Ditto	Mirza Saleh Bhai	50 do.
Ditto	Sadi Bhai	15 do.	Ditto	Mada Shah	50 do.
Ditto	Nazr	15 do.	Ditto	Kadir Buksh	20 do.
Ditto	Salún	20 do.	Ditto	Taluk Jin	20 do.
Ditto	Nauroz	15 do.	Kogiar	Bagh Bhai	30 do.
Ditto	Chiring Beg Bhai	20 do.	Ditto	Mir Mullah	40 do.
Ditto	Haji Dadkhwah	40 do.	Sanju	Mohamad Beg	30 do.

If the exigencies of the trade require it, this number would probably be doubled, the Keraia Kush obtaining additions without difficulty from the local market.

In the month of April these horses are put on green food, and they are not available for transport till the end of May.

Pony carriage in Kashghar is practically unlimited, and some 2,000 camels could be engaged in Kashghar without difficulty.

MERCHANTS RESIDENT IN KASHGHAR, &c.

Mahomed Yusuf Bai, Khokandi.—Has property valued at 3,000 yamboos (Rupees 4,80,000). He has Agents in Almati, Aksu, Kuchar, Oorumchee, Yarkand, Bokhara, and Khokand. He is the owner of the principal Serai, which is called after his name.

Shah Nuzzur Bai, of Margilan.—Has property valued at 2,000 yamboos. He has Agents. In January 1874 despatched a consignment of 200 camel-loads to Almati.

Namam Bai, of Margilan.—Tash Delál.

Mohamad Khan, of Margilan.—He has Agents in Yarkand, Khoten, Aksu, and Karashahr.

Ismail Bai (Pukhta), Kashgaree.—He has Agents in Almati and Andijan.

Ibrahim Bai (Nakum).—Has property valued at 1,000 yamboos. Corresponds and trades with Almati.

Abool Russool Khwoja Akhoonzada, Kashgaree.—With property valued at 1,500 yamboos. Trades with Almati, Aksu, and Khoten. He does business through his family connection.

Akhoon Bai, Kashgaree.—Property valued at 2,000 yamboos. Has two Agents, one in Kashghar, and one in Almati.

Hajee Pulto (Argón).—Property about 40 yamboos.

Mirza Mulla, Kashgaree.—With property 150 yamboos. This man is specially occupied in trade with the Kirghiz.

Oulad Bai, Kashgaree.—Property 1,500 tillahs. Trades with Almati.

Mirza Shareef, of Oura-tippa.—Property 300 yamboos. Trades with Andijan.

Mahomed Sadik, of Oura-tippa.—Property 1,000 yamboos. Trades with Andijan.

Hajee Ismail, Kashgaree.—This man is a money changer near the cloth market.

Appendix II.

KASHGHAR ON MARKET DAY.

9th January 1874.

The length of the main street from the south gate to the north, along which the principal shops are built, is 1,475 paces double (Kurrù) approximately 2,500 yards: about half-way is a central Chowk where are two important serais and a large open space in which there is a day market.

From the Yangi Hissar (Kúm) gate as far as the Aksu Serai there are permanent shops as under:—

114 Cloth sellers.	19 Dyers.
12 Silk (skein) sellers.	28 Workers in brass, copper, and iron.
9 Numdahs and Saddle cloth sellers.	13 Cutlers.
92 Spices and general stores, soap, candles, &c.	28 Farriers.
61 Butchers.	16 Silver-smiths.
24 Saddlers and leather sellers.	61 Dealers in flour and grain.
37 Bakers.	24 Fruiterers.
9 Cleaners of steel articles.	24 Boot-makers.
	2 Barbers.

There are 13 serais for merchants and travellers outside the city gate. On the south side there are 74 shops of various kinds; outside the north gate are 149 shops of different kinds.

From the west gate to the Urda of the Dadkhwah 251 shops. In addition there are about 100 shops scattered throughout the city.

On market day commencing from outside the south gate, the business of the day was somewhat as under:—

250 stalls for selling thread, occupied by women, each woman having about 1lb. of thread to dispose of; the whole being sold, estimated total value realized 375 tangas.

150 women selling cotton, all disposed of and estimated at 337 tangas.

100 sellers of pigeons, each having about four pigeons, of which about one-half were sold, value 24 tangas; price of a pigeon 6 puls.

200 sellers of fowls, selling about 400 fowls in all 200 tangas; price of a fowl 25 puls.

200 oxen were offered for sale, of which about 90 were sold, value 1,000 tangas.

Value of a cow or heifer about 50 to 80 tangas.

Inside the Gate.—200 donkey-loads of salt about an average of 1 tanga per load = 200 tangas.

300 stalls selling flour and grain in small quantities; total sale 2,400 tangas.

Hemp seed brought on camels, 300 tangas; this was selling at 80 puls the charak.

215 fruit and vegetable sellers, total sale estimated at 860 tangas.

70 sellers of numdahs. Total sale of numdahs varying from 3 to 6 tangas each = 1,400 tangas.

30 stalls for selling country cloth, about 150 pieces exposed, all sold, 300 tangas.

40 sellers of ready made chogas; sale at an average of 30 tangas each, both of silk and cotton = 3,000 tangas.

30 sellers of old cloths and pieces for patch work.

50 sellers of cotton seed for feeding cattle (Pewá); cotton refuse after oil has been extracted (Kull) used as fodder. Sale 300 tangas.

120 hide sellers (cured) chiefly ox hides. Sale 3,000 tangas.

35 men employed in pegging and heeling boots, who realized 170 tangas.

60 women (purrí wallahs) selling bits of silk and ornaments, sale 350 tangas.

50 sellers of country cloths apart, 500 tangas.

70 carpenters and dealers in wooden articles, boxes, spoons, door-frames, &c., 280 tangas.

200 boot-sellers, about 4,000 pairs of boots exposed and one-fourth sold = 20,000 tangas.

200 hawkers of cloths and chintzes, 8,000 tangas.

30 miscellaneous stalls, 240 tangas.

200 sellers of caps, value to 30,000 tangas exposed, and one-half sold = 15,000 tangas.

10 women selling glue, 40 tangas.

2,000 loads of firewood, and grass for roofing, all sold at an average of 2 tangas = 4,000 tangas.

60 soap-sellers, 546 tangas.

50 uncured skin sellers, selling at an average of 2 tangas each = 1,000 tangas.

200 hawkers of bread and pies, 400 tangas.

LIVE-STOCK.

18 camels exposed for sale at 300 tangas to 500 tangas, none sold.

500 ponies for sale, ranging from 100 tangas to 400 tangas only, about 16 were sold = 2,400 tangas.

200 donkeys averaging 30 tangas each, 12 sold = 360 tangas.

875 sheep and goats offered for sale at an average :—

Sheep, 26 tangas } = 10,000 tangas.
Goats, 14 ,,

The butchers killed and exposed for sale (at 16 tangas per sheep) 200 sheep = 3,200 tangas.

20 oxen at an average of 50 tangas = 1,000 tangas.

10 horses, 500 tangas.

The smaller proportion of meat sold in the city, in comparison with that in the country markets, is due to the fact that the Aásh shops are always open, and that there is little store kept at home.

Intermediate hawkers selling old cloths, saddles, and every description of property on account of any one requiring cash, at least 800 men and women circulating and doing this business = 2,000 tangas.

This represents an average day's sale and purchase, in addition to the trade done by the permanent shops at 101,746 tangas, that is, something over Rupees 20,000.

The larger purchases of country cloths which have been brought from the district markets must be added to this: these transactions are however carried on in the different serais, where the merchants trading with Almati are resident.

A careful estimate of the number of persons circulating in the city on market day gives as under :—

Outside the southern gate markets for cotton, poultry	2,500 souls.
From the gate towards the Aksu Serai	500 do.
453 double paces, 80 souls in every 10 paces	3,630 do.
In the Chowk in central market	1,000 do.
From the Chowk to the Dadkhwah's Urda, 141 paces (double)	1,120 do.
In the open space in front of the Dadkhwah's Urda	1,000 do.
From this point to junction with 2nd bazaar, 300 double paces	2,400 do.
From this to the western gate, 513 double paces, at 50 men in each 10 paces	2,510 do.
Outside this gate	500 do.
From this down to the bridge over Kizzil	1,000 do.
At the horse market	500 do.
,, sheep ,,	400 do.
Separately at the thread stalls	200 do.
From the Chowk to the Aksu Serai, 140 double paces, at 25 men per 10 paces	350 do.
From the Serai along a straight gully, 172 double paces, at 30 men per 10 paces	510 do.
From this to boot bazaar, 140 paces, in every 10 paces, 200 souls (a dance crowd)	2,800 do.
Eastwards a gully, 145 double paces, at the same estimate	2,900 do.
From this point to the junction with the western gate, 243 double paces, in each 10 double paces, 150 souls	3,700 do.

This gives a total of 27,520 souls in circulation: it is further calculated one-fourth part of this number are women, and that one-third of the whole do not reside in the city which contributes from its population but two-thirds to the crowd on the market day.

Market begins at 8 o'clock and remains in full swing till mid-day, from which time till sun-down the numbers decrease.

The numbers given represent the crowd as it would actually be during the most busy time, but there is a constant influx and efflux from the city, so that comers and goers would bring the number up to something over 30,000.

The trade represented is a purely local one, and has nothing to do with the exchanges and transfers of merchandise in the larger sense.

Appendix III.

DISTRICT MARKETS, 20TH JANUARY 1874.

Tara Sing's Report.

I started on the 1st January to visit the bazaars in the Kashghar circuit.

I halted, on the night of the 1st, at the village of Yandúma about 10 miles distant from Yangi-Shahr; this is a village of some 60 houses; as far as this point I had travelled on the Aksu road.

2nd January. I reached "Shumba Bazar" about 20 miles from Yandúma; the name of the village where this bazaar is held is Jewatchí; there are about 80 houses in this village, which is in the district of Kizzil-úí; there are two serais here for travellers.

In the Kizzil-úí district there are altogether about 790 houses.

3rd January. There was a bazaar held at Jewatchí: stalls were temporarily occupied as follows:—

30 Bakers.	6 Carpenters.
4 Iron-smiths.	30 Cutlery, &c., spices.
30 Agents for buying cotton.	20 Sellers of fruit, &c.
15 Sheep butchers.	10 Purchasers of country cloth.
2 Beef ditto.	5 Basket sellers.
10 Sellers of hats.	6 Tinkers.
10 Ditto of boots.	

In addition many hawkers of silk, cotton, thread, &c.

There are only ten permanent shops in this place, and on the evening of the bazaar-day the whole of the stalls are vacated.

About 6,000 men assembled on bazaar-day.

Men collect from Kashghar, Faizabad, Artush, Yangi Hissar, and a few men from Yarkand.

SALE DURING ONE BAZAAR-DAY.

	Tangas.
* Cotton cloth, of local manufacture, 40,000 thans, average price 2 tangas	80,000
* Cotton, 50 maunds, at 8 annas per charak	2,000
Miscellaneous goods, silk, tea, &c.	1,200
Numdahs	225
† Grain	3,000
Sheep (100 sheep)	1,400
Oxen (6)	300
Fruit	400
Small articles, not included	200
	Rupees 17,745 = 88,725

The above represents an average day's business on bazaar days at Shumba Bazar.

The revenue of the Kizzil-úí district is as follows:—*One-tenth* of the produce of grain of all kinds = 38,000 charaks. With every 30 charaks of grain the Hakim will claim one donkey load of straw, or an equivalent amounting to 1 tanga 36 puls; this represents 12,664 loads, or 21,785 tangas 26 puls.

---

* Purchased for conveyance to Kashghar and Yarkand.

† Of the grain sold the *rice* had come from Aksu and Yarkand districts; it was selling at 3 tangas a charak.
Mukki from Yarkand district, 1 tanga 10 puls per charak.
Wheat from Yarkand district, 1 tanga 30 puls per charak.

Receipts on account of Cotton, &c.

From each tanab (60 paces square representing about 5 beegahs) 7 tangas 30 puls.

	Tangas.
Total revenue under this head	36,000
Melons, 7 tungas 10 phools on each tanab	12,500
Beda (fodder) 7 tungas 10 phools on each tanab	10,000
Produce of gardens, 14 tungas 10 phools per tanab	13,000

In addition to the above, the value of one-fifth levied on a small amount of tobacco grown, and upon grass lands a small tax.

The grain is collected in kind, the remainder in cash.

There is besides the tax on live-stock.

The transfers of land by sale.

The value of the land is often assessed according to the amount of seed that may be sown in it instead of by square measurement; it is usually estimated that one tanab will require four charaks of seed (of wheat).

If 70 charaks of seed are required for the sowing of a piece of land, it will be termed a puddum; similarly a half puddum and quarter puddum of land, &c., will be spoken of.

Goods of foreign manufacture were not observed in the Shumba Bazaar, with the exception of Russian chintzes.

4th January. I reached Ek-Shumba Bazaar, 10 miles from the last place: this is held at Atakchí in the Kanarik district.

The village has about 200 houses, and there are 14 permanent shops.

In the entire district of Kanarik there are 1,880 houses. On bazaar days stalls are open in Atakchí as follows:—

- 40 Purchasers of cotton cloths of local manufacture.
- 50 Ditto of cotton.
- 65 Dealers in spices, Russian chintzes, &c., tea and miscellaneous stores.
- 20 Sellers of hats.
- 20 „ of boots.
- 4 „ of baskets.
- 12 Soad dealers.
- 20 Carpenters and dealers in wooden articles.
- 10 Iron-smiths.
- 40 Tobacco sellers.
- 30 Snuff dealers.
- 40 Skein-silk sellers.
- 10 Nundah sellers.
- 20 Ready made chogas.
- 50 Prepared leather.
- 4 Oil.
- 100 Provision shops, where bread and Aásh are prepared.
- 40 Sheep butchers.
- 20 Beef butchers.

A large number of hawkers of all kinds in addition.

In one bazaar-day at this place as many as 500 sheep and 20 oxen are killed: the price of meat is 20 phools per jing for mutton; and 16 phools per jing for beef: the large expenditure of meat is accounted for by families purchasing their supply for an entire week during this cold season.

About 15,000 people assemble here on bazaar-days.

One thousand donkey loads of grain are disposed of.

The transactions on bazaar-days represent a trade equal to about double the amount of that done in the Shumba Bazaar.

Do-Shumba Bazaar.

This is held at Peinab, about 10 miles distant from Atakchí; this is a village of about 350 houses, and there are 25 permanent shops; it is in the Kanarik district.

Ek-Shumba and Do-Shumba Bazaars are under the Dadkhwah of Kanarik, Mír Mahomed (Kútchí.)

On bazaar days there are stalls as follows:—

85 Aash shops and bakers (restaurants).	15 Carpenters and sellers of wooden articles.
50 Spices, minerals, cloths, and tea.	11 Sellers of iron articles and Farriers.
30 Sellers of boots.	20 Basket sellers.
15 Hat and cap sellers.	10 Sellers of numdahs.
30 Furriers.	40 Fruit and vegetables sellers.
50 Sellers of grain and flour.	40 Sheep butchers.
40 Purchasers of country cotton cloths.	20 Beef ditto.
50 Purchasers of cotton.	

About 800 sheep and 150 oxen were in the live-stock market.

Five hundred sheep and 70 oxen were slaughtered on market day: price of meat 20 puls, for mutton, and 16 puls for beef, the jing.

Meat is dearer in the district bazaar than in the city, where it sells, mutton at 16 puls, and beef at 12 puls, the jing.

Comparing the sales in this bazaar with the preceding, they may be taken to amount to 1½ times what is realized at Ek-Shumba.

The probable number of people present on bazaar day = 18,000, all from the Amír's territories.

In the district of Kanarik there are 8 Dewan Begis (tax collectors) under the Dadkhwah.

The revenue of the Kanarik district may be estimated as under:—

From cotton at	...	... 7 tungas	10 phools the tanab	...	92,000	tangas.
„ melons at	...	... 7 „	10 ditto ditto	...	44,000	do.
„ gardens at	...	... 14 „	10 ditto ditto	...	50,000	do.
„ land under grass	... 7 „	10 ditto ditto	...	40,000	do.
„ grain $\frac{1}{10}$th = 1,40,000 charaks.						

{ A *charak* of grain is 16 jings.
{ A *charak* as applied to other articles of consumption, 12½ jings, as well as cotton, oil, butter, &c.
{ A *charak* of silk is, however, 4 jings.

Stubble in proportion; of one donkey load for every 3 charaks of grain, at 1 tanga and 36 puls the load, for which it is commuted 80,265 tangas.

In Kashghar itself this is taken in kind to supply what is required for the large number of animals in the palace and with the troops.

In addition the small tax on fallow ground; and one-fifth of the produce of tobacco.

Tax is also levied on live-stock as follows:—

On every cow, per annum	1 tunga 30 phools.
Ditto sheep or goat, per annum	12 do.
Ditto mare, according to valuation, $\frac{1}{40}$th of value during the year; the valuation being fixed yearly.	

This tax on animals is collected in the summer.

The taxes on crops, on the gathering in of the crops (in September or October).

On land under cultivation, for fruit or gardens, about the same time or at the time the crop is half-grown.

If money is wanted in the Treasury, the value of the standing corn is estimated before harvest and commuted for cash payment.

As a rule, the entire amount of grain is collected and stored; troops and employés of all kinds being paid by orders on individual Dewan Begis, who may happen to have a large supply in hand.

There is a Court Mirza (accountant) with two assistants, who records the demands on the various districts, and keeps an account of the revenue returns.

(507)

DISTRICT TRADERS OF ANY IMPORTANCE.

SHUMBA BAZAAR.

Mohamed Bai, Kashgari, purchaser of cloth.
Fuzzul Bai, spice and general dealer.
Akhún Khwoja.
Azim Khwoja. (This man trades directly with the Kirghiz of the Alai, making purchase in the bazaar on their account.)
Fuzzil Khwoja, Saudagur.
Mohamed Majur, purchaser of cloth.
Azim Bai, Baker.
Khodar Yar Bai, Butcher.

EK-SHUMBA.

Mohamad Yussúf   \
Khoda Wurdi   } Saudagurs.
Ahmed   /

DO-SHUMBA.

Mulla Jan Bai   \
Bulbul Bai   } Of Kashghar.
Mohamad Khan   — Of Kanarik.
Rozi Bai
Tokta Bai
Rozai Jan
Mulla Akhún
Hajee Yashúr   KANARIK.
Mullah Shumsúdin
Búhan Bai   These men do not trade beyond
Bukhte Chung   Kashghar, Yarkand, Khoten, and
Khwoja Beg   Aksu. They have no foreign trade.
Mohamad Meer Bai, Kashghar
Imam Allaúdin, Imam of Kanarik

REPORT ON THE ARTUSH (LOWER) BAZAAR MADE IN FEBRUARY 1874.

En route to Artush we passed Besh Kirrim, a considerable group of hamlets in the Kashghar district comprising 960 houses; this is one of the principal fruit-growing portions of the Kashghar district.

Besh Kirrim has a small bazaar of its own on Wednesdays.

From Besh Kirrim the road, which leads from the city to Lower Artush, runs through a small gap to the Artush valley on the other side of a low sand ridge: in the gorge is a small shrine to Sút Bium, the wet-nurse of Sultan Satúk Bogra Khan; the first hamlet in the Artush valley termed Lungur is 8 miles from Besh Kirrim; the road from this passes at 6 miles through the hamlet of Beh Ahmed at one mile from Artush proper.

In the entire district of Artush are some 2,000 houses, which are grouped in hamlets as follows:—

1. Altun Artush	300 houses.	11. Istachi	150 houses.		
2. Tukta Yun	200 do.	12. Tatér	100 do.		
3. Shorúk	300 do.	13. Lungur	40 do.		
4. Ogrúk	150 do.	14. Mavé	70 do.		
5. Suntuk	60 do.	15. Kulti Aylak	300 do. (a Friday bazaar.)		
6. Togúl	100 do.	16. Tók	15 do.		
7. Malid	50 do.	17. Begum	20 do.		
8. Tejún	100 do.	18. Sultán	50 do. (Kum Singi.)		
9. Beh Ahmed	150 do.	19. Wukwúk.			
10. Argúk	100 do.	20. Kurkla.			

(508)

In addition to this are 100 Kirghiz tents scattered throughout the Tiggur Mati and Sugun valleys, belonging to its different tribes and grouped permanently under the Artush Hakim.

Trades in the Artush District.

Village No. 10 Chung-oche-chung, having property ... = 1,000 kurs.
This man trades with Almati.

These men trade direct with Almati and purchase cloth made up in the district.

"	"	3 Koséh Akhún	...	...	...	500	"
"	"	10 Sufli Bai	...	...	...	700	"
"	"	10 Tursun Bai	...	...	...	300	"
"	"	1 Mahomed Tokhta	...	...	...	1,000	"
"	"	1 Mahomed Ali	...	...	...	60	"
"	"	1 Mahomed Aluneen	...	...	...	80	"
"	"	8 Hajee Alatip					
"	"	1 Abdúl Russúl					
"	"	19 Abdúl Russúl					
"	"	3 Abdúl Rehman					
"	"	11 Mullah Nax					
"	"	2 Abdúl Ghujar					

Trade is only allowed to pass to Almati by the Chakmák route, but the Kirghiz of Tiggur Mati have a direct, though difficult, line of communication with Naryn by Káramati.

Bazaar on Monday; on the 15th February the people did not collect till afternoon, and the shops did not do much business until after 1 or 2 o'clock; about 4,000 people assembled, of whom 500 were women. Shops as follow:—

24 Purchasers of country cloth.
21 Sellers of cotton.
53 Cloth, spices, and miscellaneous stores.
20 Sellers of country manufactured cloths.
10 Ditto of soap.
9 Ditto of tobacco.
20 Ditto of oil.
10 Ditto of boots, &c.
10 Ditto of leather.
3 Men employed in pegging and heeling boots.
20 Basket sellers.
15 Sellers of matting.
10 Ditto of earthenware vessels.
9 Sellers of wooden articles.
11 Ditto of country matches.
14 Ditto of spices.
10 Ditto of silk articles.
32 Ditto of grain.
48 Ditto of fruit and vegetables.
16 Ditto of hats.
9 Workers in iron.
1 Goldsmith.
1 Dyer.
28 Sheep butchers.
2 Beef ditto.
22 Bakers and Ash-paz.

About 100 sheep and 60 cattle were exposed for sale.

About 400 sellers of cotton (women) were present with thread, each woman having about 3 jings of thread, the sale of each amounting to about 6 tangas.

About 500 men presented themselves to sell country cloth.

In comparison with other bazaars the sale of cotton was very small; it would appear that scarcely any cotton is grown in the Artush district, but that it is brought from Kanarik.

The price of cotton at Artush is from 9 to $9\frac{1}{2}$ tangas the charak, in comparison with 8 to $8\frac{1}{2}$ at Kanarik.

Profit in cotton thread is as follow:—Each woman purchases about 3 tangas worth of cotton and works it into thread, about 4 jings of cotton being obtained with this amount; this produces 3 jings of thread.

This sells at the rate of 2 tangas per jing, giving the woman a profit of 3 tangas during the week; in each case the 3 tangas thus obtained would seem to be invested in necessary purchases for the week, and the remaining 3 in cotton to be worked up before the next market day.

The total sale of cotton in one day was about 63 maunds at $47\frac{1}{4}$ tangas per maund ... ... = 2,984 tangas.
Purchase of country cloths amounted to 50 horse loads, each load 2 maunds 10 seers, amounting to at 400 tangas per load to ... ... = 2,000 "

Shops.

53 Miscellaneous, tea, &c., at 40 tangas each shop			=	2,120 tangas.
20 Cloths (country) sold at 20 tangas each shop			=	400 ,,
10 Soap at	10 per shop		=	100 ,,
9 Tobacco at	2 ,,		=	18 ,,
20 Oil at	30 ,,		=	600 ,,
10 Boots, &c., at	25 ,,		=	250 ,,
10 Leather at	10 ,,		=	100 ,,
3 Heeling boots at	4 ,,		=	12 ,,
20 Basket sellers at	2 ,,		=	40 ,,
15 Matting sellers at	3 ,,		=	45 ,,
10 Earthenware sellers at	2 ,,		=	20 ,,
9 Carpenters at	6 ,,		=	54 ,,
11 Match sellers at	1 ,,		=	11 ,,
14 Spice ,, at	5 ,,		=	70 ,,
10 Silk ,, at	4 ,,		=	40 ,,
32 Flour and grain sellers at	40 ,,		=	2,120 ,,
48 Fruit sellers at	5 ,,		=	240 ,,
16 Hat sellers at	20 ,,		=	320 ,,
9 Smiths at	5 ,,		=	45 ,,
60 Sheep were sold at	21 ,,		=	1,260 ,,
4 Oxen ,, at	50 ,,		=	200 ,,
Each Ash-paz realised at the rate of 30 tangas			=	360 ,,
Sale of cotton thread			=	2,400 ,,
Transactions on market day and profits on labor in bazaars amounting to about				34,100 ,,

The sales in this bazaar in comparison with those of other places are small; it may thus fairly be urged that the population of the district is comparatively a small one.

When the crops of the district are half ready, the revenue of the district is estimated by an officer appointed by the Amir, in company with the Hakim, under whom there are 20 Dewan Begies, or tax collectors.

The proportion of the revenue at the disposal of the Hakim is the free gift of the King.

The revenue is collected in accordance with the estimate, unless special grounds are advanced for remission.

The revenue of the Artush district may be taken as under, paid in cash:—

Revenue on gardens, cotton, fodder, and melons		1,20,000 tangas.
Ditto in grain, 93,000 charaks of grain, being the 10th part of the produce, valued at an average of 2 tangas per charak	=	1,86,000 ,,
On each 3 loads of grain, 1 load of straw, giving 31,000 loads of straw, valued at 2 tangas	=	62,000 ,,
The tax on live-stock in addition.		
Tobacco is not grown in this district.		
		3,68,000 tangas.

Sujjee is made at Kulti Aylak, where a tax is levied on each house where it is prepared of 25 tangas annually.

Land of the 1st class, in which one charak of seed can be sown, realizes	100
2nd ,,	50
3rd ,,	25
From the 1st description, a crop yielding 14 charaks will be realized;	
From 2nd ditto, ditto 7 ditto; and	
From 3rd ditto, ditto 4 ditto.	

Transfers of land can only be made before the Kazee, 2 tangas per cent. being paid on the stamp.

Appendix IV.
SERICULTURE.

There are two breeds of silk-worms known in Eastern Turkestan, one producing a white and the other a yellow silk: these appear to me to be the Bombyx Mori (Lin) and Bombyx Testor (Hutton), which are referred to in the Appendix of Mr. Geogheghan's report on sericulture in Bengal.

There is but one mulberry tree which grows to a considerable height and from which the leaves are gathered three times: this is, so far as I could ascertain, the Morus Serratta of Dr. Roxborough. The tree apparently receives but little attention; it is grown along the side of the road and in small private holdings: it is pruned largely however, and cuttings are made from it in the early spring before the leaves push. These trees produce leaves for several years as food for the silk-worms.

The worms are annuals. The eggs are hatched between the 15th April and the 1st May: previous to hatching they are carried upon the persons of men and women, in the kummurbund of the men, or in the arms-pits of the women, being hatched between the 5th and 7th day by means of the heat thus afforded.

The culture of the worms, silk-reeling, weaving, and dyeing, are all carried on in the house. Whilst the worms are being tended, they are usually confided to one of the elder women of the family, and are kept apart in a room set aside for the purpose, only one individual being allowed to visit them. A pregnant woman or a girl in her courses is on no account allowed to approach them, and during the time that the eggs are being carried about the person previous to hatching, husband and wife keep apart.

The greatest cleanliness is demanded from the different members of the family during the period of education; tobacco, snuff, onions, and garlic are strictly prohibited.

During the first 10 days of feeding, the leaves are chopped into small pieces when given as food; on the 10th day the first stupor comes on, and they leave off eating for 3 days; after this period the leaves are given whole, and the worms eat for another 10 days, when their second stupor occurs. It is after the 3rd period and near the 40th day that they begin spinning. During no period of their existence is any stint placed upon their feeding, but the leaves are not too frequently renewed.

Reeling is usually carried out during the month of July: the process is exceedingly primitive, and there is great want of uniformity in the thread, owing to no attempt being made at selection in bringing the cocoons together, or in regulating the number of threads brought at one time to the reel. The work is usually done by women and children, either in the house or in the court-yard, which is a part of the humblest residences in the country.

The cocoons are placed in a large iron vessel which is filled with water: this rests on a tripod, and a fire is placed underneath it; when the temperature of the water is such as barely to allow of the fingers being dipped in it, the silk from a number of cocoons, floating on the surface of the water, is drawn together through a small iron eye which is placed immediately in front of the reel, from which the silk runs to a roller upon which it is wound by means of a fly-wheel.

The whole apparatus for reeling is of rough construction.

Previous to reeling, a prayer is offered up to the prophet Job, the patron Saint of all silk-worms, which are supposed to have had their origin in his suffering body.

I have elsewhere alluded to the introduction of silk-worms and mulberry trees having been originally made from China.

The management of the worms, &c., seems to be very similar to that adopted in China.

Great care is taken in selecting cocoons for breeding; white cocoons are kept separate from yellow ones, and with each description the best are chosen. Male and female cocoons are put together in small cloth bags which are hung on pegs round the room; when the moths are laying their eggs, great care is taken not to disturb them.

During the winter the eggs are usually placed in an old sheep-skin hat, and are deposited in a box in a fairly warm room, where there is no fear of their being frozen.

CHAPTER XIII.

The Calendar.

This is the same as the Muhammadan Almanac, the months and year being lunar, but for agricultural operations the solar months, or zodiacal signs, are used.

The names of the lunar months and their corresponding Arabic ones are these—

    'Ashúr Ay = Muharram.
    Safar Ay = Safar.
    Safar Coshini Ay = Rabí'ulawwal.
    Jamádí-ul-awwal = Rabí-'uth-thání.
    Jamádí-ul-ákhir = Jamádí-ul-awwal.
    Talásh Ay = Jamádí-uth-thání.
    Duá Ay = Rajab.
    Barát Ay = Sha'bán.
    Roza Ay = Ramazán.
    Hít ('Id) Ay = Shawál.
    Ará Ay = Zi Ca'da.
    Hít Cúrbán Ay = Zi Híjja.

The Turki cycle of years is also lunar, and every thirtieth year a month is intercalated as in the Arabic calendar. The names of the years are these—

    Sicheán yíl = Mouse year.
    'Uy yíl = Ox year.
    Yolbárs yíl = Tiger year.
    Taosheán yíl = Hare year.
    Balic yíl = Fish year.
    Yalán yíl = Serpent year.
    'At yíl = Horse year.
    Cúy yíl = Sheep year.
    Mymún yíl = Monkey year.
    Tocákhú yíl = Fowl year.
    'It yíl = Dog year.
    Tonguz yíl = Hog year.

The agricultural months are the following, beginning with the vernal equinox:—

    Duluw = February—March.
    Hút = March—April.
    Hamal = April—May.
    Thaur = May—June.
    Jauza = June—July.
    Sartám = August—September.
    Asad = September—October.
    Sumbul = October—November.
    Mízán = November—December.
    Acrab = December—January.
    Caush = January—February.
    Júdí = February—March.

(Sd.)   H. W. Bellew.

CHAPTER XIV.

Record of Meteorological observations on the march from Leh in Ladákh to Káshghar.

1873.			Thermometer.			Hygrometer.		Aneroid.	Cloud.	Wind.	Rain.	Locality.	Miles.	Remarks.
M.	D.	H.	Max.	Min.	Sun.	D.B.	W.B.							
9	25	5	...	...	...	44	38	20·70	0	N.E.	0	Leh	...	
		10	...	...	...	55	45	20·70	0	S.	0	......	...	
		12	...	...	...	59	49	20·74	0	W.	0	......	...	
		16	...	...	...	64	52	20·83	0	N.E.	0	......	...	
		20	68	42	112	57	46	20·80	0	S.	0	......	...	
	26	5	...	...	...	43	38	20·70	0	E.	0	Leh	...	
		10	...	...	...	56	47	20·70	0	S.	0	......	...	
		12	...	...	...	62	51	20·79 Cu. 2		S.	0	......	...	
		16	...	...	...	59	49	20·86 Cu. 4		S.E.	0	......	...	Camp pitched under trees in the Residency garden. Instruments under awning of a tent verandah always.
		20	68	39	...	51	44	20·81 St. 8		S.	0	......	...	
	27	6	...	...	...	41	37	20·75 Cu. 6		N.E.	0	Leh	...	
		10	...	...	...	52	44	20·77 Ci. 6		N.	0	......	...	
		12	...	...	...	55	45	20·81 Ci. 2		N.	0	......	...	
		14	...	...	...	60	49	20·87 St. 4		N.	0	......	...	
		16	...	...	...	61	49	20·90 St. 8		N.E.	0	......	...	
		18	...	...	...	53	44	20·90 St. 10		0	0	......	...	
		21	68	38	...	51	43	20·88 St. 10		0	0	......	...	
	28	6	...	...	...	38	36	20·78 St. 10		N.E.	0	Leh	...	
		10	...	...	...	...	...	...	...	...	0	......	...	
		12	...	...	...	57	47	20·78 Cu. 2		N.	0	......	...	
		16	...	...	...	58	46	20·85	0	S.	0	......	...	
		20	61	37	90	...	...	...	...	...	...	......	...	
	29	6	...	34	...	34	30	20·77	0	S.	0	Leh	...	
		14	...	...	...	...	...	18·80	...	...	0	Polu	7	At foot of rise to Khardong Pass.
		16	...	...	...	35	31	18·94 St. 8		S.	0			
		18	...	...	...	29	29	18·96 St. 10		S.E.	0			
		20	...	...	...	25	22	18·97 St. 2		0	0			
	30	6	...	15	...	24	22	18·90	0	S.E.	0	Polu.		
		16	...	...	...	54	...	19·37	...	...	0	Khardong	15	Camp on open fields near village.
		18	...	...	...	41	30	19·42 St. 8		N.	0			
		21	...	...	...	35	31	... St. 10		0	0			
10	1	6	...	25	...	26	26	18·58 Ni. 10		W.	S.	Khardong	...	Snow 4 inches.
		14	...	...	101	55	49	20·38 Cu. 5		0	0	Satti	8	
		16	59	...	...	53	49	20·36 Cu. 8		N.W.	0	......	...	During clouds of dust.
		18	...	...	...	44	38	20·36 St. 10		N.W.	0			
		21	...	...	...	42	37	20·36 St. 10		N.W.	0			
	2	6	...	26·5	...	30	29	20·33 St. 8		N.	0	Satti.		
		12	...	...	...	56	47	20·60 St. 10		N.W.	0	Tirit	7	Camp on open ground on bank of the Shayok River.
		14	...	...	...	55	45	20·52 St. 10		N.W.	0			
		16	...	...	...	47	40	20·49 Ni. 10		N.W.	0			
		18	...	...	...	39·5	36	20·52 Ni. 8		S.E.	0			
		21	70	...	...	39	35	20·52	0	S.E.	0			
	3	6	...	19·5	...	30	29	20·45	0	N.W.	0	Tirit.		
		12	...	...	89	63	49	20·51 Cu. 4		N.W.	0	Tagar	7	Nubra River.
		14	...	...	...	64	49	20·56 Cu. 8		N.W.	0			
		16	...	...	...	52	41	20·52 Cu. 8		N.W.	0			
		18	68	...	...	43	37	20·59 Ni. 10		N.W.	0			
		21	...	...	...	41	36	20·66 Ni. 10		S.W.	R.	......	...	Slight showers.
	4	6	...	26·5	...	27	27	20·62 St. 8		W.	0	Tagar.		
		14	...	...	...	44	40	20·49 C.S. 9		W.	0	Panámik	12	Nubra River.

(514)

1873.			Thermometer.			Hygrometer.		Aneroid.	Cloud.	Wind.	Rain.	Locality.	Miles.	Remarks.
M.	D.	H.	Max.	Min.	Sun.	D.B.	W.B.							
10	4	16	52	...	...	48	38	20·45	C.S. 9	N.W.	0			
		18	...	...	...	41·5	39	20·41	Ci. 3	N.	0			
		21	...	...	...	49	32	20·40	0	N.	0			
	5	6	...	...	...	32·5	31·7	20·43	0	N.	0	Panámik	...	Halt.
		8	...	...	...	38	37	20·45	Cu. 3	N.	0			
		10	...	28·5	...	44·5	41·5	20·48	Cu. 6	0	0			
		12	...	...	...	49·5	40·2	20·50	C.S. 9	N.W.	0			
		14	57	...	...	47	38	20·46	C.S. 9	N.W.	0			
		16	...	...	...	46·7	37	20·45	C.S. 9	N.W.	0			
		18	...	...	...	43	34·7	20·42	St. 10	0	0			
		20	...	...	...	40	32	20·45	St. 8	0	0			
	6	6	...	31	...	34	34	20·45	C.S. 5	N.	0	Panámik	...	Nubra River.
		16	...	...	...	48	38	19·83	C.S. 5	0	0	Changlung	12	
		18	55	...	85	35	29	19·84	0	0	0			
		21	...	...	...	32	32	19·87	0	0	0			
	7	6	...	21	...	25	23·5	19·89	0	0	0	Changlung.		
		18	37	...	...	23	18	17·38	0	N.	0	Tútyálác	16	Cross Caráwal Dawán Pass.
		21	...	12	...	21·5	20	17·39	0	N.	0	Glacier.		
	8	6	...	11	...	11	11	17·40	0	N.	0	Tútyálác.		
		18	...	...	...	21	...	16·84	0	N.W.	0	Saser	18	Cross Glacier Pass.
		21	...	...	...	19	...	16·77	0	N.W.	0	Brangsa.		
	9	6	...	6	...	9	8·5	16·80	0	S.E.	0	Saser.		
		18	43	...	...	26	21	16·75	0	S.E.	0	Kúmdán	10	Camp between two glaciers on Shayok river.
		21	...	18·5	...	21	19	16·75	0	0	0			
	10	6	...	6	...	8	8	16·74	0	0	0	Kúmdán.		
		9	...	...	...	9	9	16·75	0	S.	0			
		16	36	...	...	34	29	16·60	0	S.W.	0	Gyaptang	10	On Shayok river head waters.
		21	...	...	...	11	11	16·50	0	S.W.	0			
	11	6	...	−2	...	5	3·5	16·49	0	S.W.	0	Gyaptang.		
		16	...	...	...	27	25	15·81	0	S.W.	0	Daulatbeg	15	High plateau: on a stream.
		18	29	...	...	16	15	15·77	0	0	0			
		21	...	...	...	12	11	15·75	0	0	0			
	12	6	...	−3	...	2	1	15·71	0	W.	0	Daulatbeg.		
		18	...	...	...	20	...		St. 10	0	0	Brangsa	21	Cross Carácoram Pass. Snow.
		21	...	...	...	17	...	15·61	Ni. 10	0	S.			
	13	7	...	−2	...	2	2	15·55	Ni. 10	0	S.	Brangsa		Snow fall till 11 A.M.
		22	...	15	...	17	16	16·80	St. 10	S.E.	0	Actágh	25	
	14	6	...	−9	...	−2	−3	16·79	0	S.W.	0	Actágh	...	Halt.
	15	6	...	−15	...	...	...		0	S.W.	0	Actágh.		
	16	12	...	...	...	36	31	18·27	Cu. 8	0	0	Sugat	32	Camp on river.
		14	...	...	...	37	35	18·21	C.S. 9	0	0			
		16	...	...	...	34	34	18·22	C.S. 10	0	0			
	17	21	40	25	71	27	27	18·20	St. 10	0	0	Sugat.		
	18	19	...	...	...	32	29	19·15	St. 6	N.E.	0	Shahidulla	5	Halt. Camp on river near the Fort.
		21	...	...	...	29	27	19·17	0	N.E.	0			
	19	12	...	...	...	46	35	19·22	Cu. 2	N.E.	0	Shahidulla.		
		14	...	...	...	48	35	19·12	C.S. 6	N.E.	0			
		16	62	...	...	41	31	19·12	C.S. 6	N.E.	0			
		18	...	...	...	34	31	19·10	St. 10	N.E.	0			
		21	...	14	...	29	28	19·11	0	N.	0			
	20	7	...	...	...	15	15	19·15	0	0	0	Shahidulla.		
		10	...	...	...	37	27	19·28	0	S.W.	0			
		12	...	...	...	50	38	19·21	0	S.W.	0			
		14	...	...	...	51	36	19·15	Ci. 2	S.	0			
		16	66	...	96	49	35	19·11	0	N.	0			
		18	...	...	...	36	31	19·11	0	N.E.	0			

October.

(515)

1873.			Thermometer.			Hygrometer.		Aneroid.	Cloud.	Wind.	Rain.	Locality.	Miles.	Remarks.
M.	D.	H.	Max.	Min.	Sun.	D.B.	W.B.							
10	20	21	...	11	...	24	21	19·09	0	N.E.	0			
	21	7	...	5·5	...	12	12	19·13	0	0	0	Shahidulla.		
		12	...	...	...	49	35	19·25	Ci. 1	N.E.	0			
		15	70	...	89	47	34	19·20	Ci. 3	N.	0			
		18	...	...	...	35	24	19·18	0	N.	0			
		21	...	...	...	31	30	19·18	0	E.	0			
	22	8	...	4	...	32	32	19·25	0	E.	0	Shahidulla.		
		10	...	...	...	33	31	19·27	0	E.	0			
		12	...	...	...	45	37	19·18	Ci. 1	E.	0			
		15	61	...	...	52	39	19·12	Ci. 2	S.E.	0			
		18	...	...	...	35	28	19·13	0	0	0			
		21	...	...	...	29	25	19·11	0	N.E.	0			
	23	7	...	−3	...	21	21	19·15	0	S.	0	Shahidulla.		
		10	...	...	...	34	23	19·24	0	S.W.	0			
		12	...	...	...	47	35	19·19	0	S.E.	0			
		15	60	...	99	51	38	19·08	0	S.E.	0			
		18	...	...	...	33	25	19·06	Ci. 3	N.W.	0			
		21	...	...	...	24	21	19·05	0	N.	0			
	24	21	...	...	...	19	19	19·78	0	0	0	Pilatághách.	14	Carácásh river.
	25	7	...	12	...	18	18	19·76	0	E.S.E	0	Carácoram.	10	In defile of the Sanjú Dawán Pass.
		18	...	...	...	28	21	18·70	0	0	0			
		21	...	...	...	24	...	18·68	0	0	0			
	26	7	...	10	...	12	10	18·62	0	0	0	Carácoram.		
	27	15	...	...	...	43	...	20·20	0	N.W.	0	Gechgha	16	Sarighyár river; camp in narrow valley cross the Sánjú Pass.
		18	...	...	...	27	...	20·20	0	N.W.	0			
		22	...	...	...	20	...	20·16	0	N.W.	0			
	28	7	...	10	...	12	10	20·06	0	N.	0	Gechgha.		
		15	...	...	...	48	35	21·44	0	N.E.	0	Tam	12	Sarighyár river; camp in narrow valley.
		17	...	...	...	39	...	21·46	0	N.E.	0			
		19	...	...	...	35	35	21·48	0	0	0			
		21	...	...	...	22	22	21·48	0	0	0			
	29	8	...	8	...	15	...	21·54	0	S.W.	0	Tam.		
		18	38	...	...	31	...	22·78	0	N.E.	0	Kewaz	16	Ditto ditto Camp in open valley.
		22	...	...	...	21	...	22·75	0	S.W.	0			
	30	7	...	13	...	18	...	22·63	0	0	0	Kewaz.		
		17	...	...	...	41	32	23·64	Haze.	0	0	Sánjú	14	Camp amongst farmsteads and trees.
		19	43	...	...	30	32	23·66	Haze.	0	0			
		21	...	...	...	24	22	23·62	0	E.	0			
	31	7	...	18	...	23	21	23·62	0	0	0	Sánjú	...	Halt. Open plain at foot of hills.
		9	...	...	...	40	34	23·68	Haze.	E.	0			
		12	...	...	...	46	...	23·66	,,	E.	0			
		15	48	...	80	39	...	23·65	,,	E.	0			
		21	...	...	...	24	...	23·65	0	0	0			
11	1	9	...	18	...	36	...	23·73	0	0	0	Sánjú	...	Halt.
		12	...	...	...	40	33	23·73	0	0	0			
		15	44	...	84	42	33	23·73	0	0	0			
		18	...	...	...	29	25	23·69	0	W.	0			
		21	...	...	...	24	21	23·70	0	0	0			
	2	7	...	18	...	21	20	23·75	0	0	0	Sánjú.		
		22	...	...	...	24	...	24·13	0	0	0	Coshtác.	25	Open plain.
	3	7	...	13	...	17	16	24·15	0	0	0	,,		
		16	...	...	...	43	32	24·26	Haze.	0	0	Oe-toghrác	20	Sandy hollow on plain country.
		18	...	...	...	28	24	24·15	0	E.	0			
		21	...	...	...	19	18	24·17	0	0	0	Ditto.		
	4	7	...	9·5	...	15	14	24·15	0	0	0	Borya	12	Ditto
		15	...	9·5	...	53	42	24·61	Haze.	0	0			

October / November

(516)

1873.			Thermometer.			Hygrometer.		Aneroid.	Cloud.	Wind.	Rain.	Locality.	Miles.	Remarks.
M.	D.	H.	Max.	Min.	Sun.	D.B.	W.B.							
11	4	18	54	...	78	35	27	24·60	St. 4	0	0	......	...	Total eclipse of moon 19 h. to 23 h.
		21	...	...	...	27	24	24·62	0	0	0			
	5	6	...	14	...	20	19	24·58	0	E.	0	Borya.		
		17	...	...	...	47	40	25·47	Ci. 5	0	0	Kargalik	22	Camp in garden in the town.
		19	...	...	...	41	34	25·49	St. 8	0	0			
		21	...	...	...	37	30	25·45	St. 5	0	0			
	6	7	...	29	...	37	31	25·42	St. 9	0	0	Ditto	...	Halt. Hazy atmosphere.
		10	...	...	...	44	34	25·46	Ci. S. 6	0	0			
		12	...	...	...	54	43	25·45	Ci. S. 8	0	0			
		15	58	...	...	53	42	25·43	Ci. S.10	0	0			
		19	...	...	...	42	35	25·45	Ci. S.10	0	0			
		22	...	...	...	38	29	25·45	0	W.	0			
	7	6	...	27	...	29	...	25·45	0	0	0	Ditto.		
		18	48	26	...	33	29	25·64	Ci. S. 2	0	0	Posgám	25	Hazy air.
		21	...	...	...	32	30	25·64	Ci. 2	0	0			
	8	6	...	20	...	25	22	25·61	Ci. 2	0	0	Ditto.		
		16	53	...	...	53	42	25·77	0	0	0	Yárkand	15	Quarters in a court in the Fort of Yangishahr.
		18	...	...	...	46	43	25·78	0	0	0			
	9	9	...	25	...	27	20	25·80	0	0	0	Ditto	...	Hazy sky.
		11	...	...	...	41	33	25·86	0	0	0			
		13	...	...	...	47	36	25·86	0	0	0			Instruments in an open court on a stand in the shade of a wall, and on its north side.
		15	58	...	...	49	39	25·86	0	0	0	......	...	
		18	...	...	...	42	35	25·86	0	0	0			
		21	...	...	...	35	33	25·85	0	0	0			
	10	7	...	25	...	29	27	25·82	0	0	0			
		11	...	...	...	40	35	25·86	0	0	0			
		14	...	...	...	46	46	25·84	Ci. 4	0	0	Yárkand		Hazy weather.
		17	47	...	...	41	34	25·80	Ci. S. 8	0	0			
		21	...	...	...	33	30	25·80	St. 9	0	0	Yárkand.		
	11	7	...	26	...	30	28·5	25·75	Ci. 3	0	0	Ditto.		
		10	...	...	...	41	41	25·78	Cu. 3	0	0			
		12	...	...	...	46	46	25·76	Haze.	0	0			
		16	50	...	...	46	46	25·75	H.	0	0			
		19	...	...	...	38	38	25·76	0	0	0			
		21	...	...	...	37	36	25·75	0	0	0			
	12	7	...	27	...	33	Frozen all day	25·75	Ci. 2	0	0	Ditto.		
		10	...	...	...	48		25·79	Ci. 8	0	0			
		12	...	...	...	50		25·78	St. 6	0	0			
		16	52	...	...	44		25·78	St. 6	0	0			
		19	...	...	...	36		25·76	Cu. 4	0	0			
		21	...	...	...	34		25·75	0	0	0			
	13	7	...	25	...	29	29	25·76	0	0	0	Ditto.		
		11	...	...	...	46	37	25·79	0	0	0			
		16	52	...	...	48	39	25·77	Ci. S. 6	0	0			
		20	...	...	...	35	35	25·76	0	0	0			
	14	7	...	25·5	...	31	28	25·77	Ci. 8	0	0	Ditto.		
		10	...	...	...	42	35	25·81	Ci. S. 8	0	0			
		14	49	...	...	47	39	25·78	Ci. S.10	0	0			
		17	...	...	...	41	35	25·77	Ci. S. 8	0	0			
		21	...	...	...	33	30	25·76	0	0	0			
	15	7	...	25·5	...	30	28	25·78	Haze.	0	0	Ditto.		
		15	51	...	...	51	42	25·84	H.	0	0			
	16	7	...	24·5	...	28·5	26·5	25·90	0	0	0	Ditto.		
		11	...	...	...	47	39	25·95	Haze.	0	0			
		13	...	...	...	49	40	25·94	H.	0	0			
		16	51	...	...	50	40	25·93	H.	0	0			

November.

(517)

	1873.		THERMOMETER.			HYGROMETER.		Aneroid.	Cloud.	Wind.	Rain.	Locality.	Miles.	REMARKS.
M.	D.	H.	Max.	Min.	Sun.	D.B.	W.B.							
November	16	21	...	...	...	35	32	25·92	0	0	0			
	17	8	...	24	...	28	26	25·83	0	0	0	Yarkand ...	...	Still, hazy weather.
		12	...	...	...	43	37	25·83	St. 10	0	0			
		16	50·5	...	...	41	34	25·80	Ci.S 10	0	0			
		20	...	...	...	37	33	25·78	0	0	0			
	18	7	...	24·5	...	31	29	25·82	St. 10	0	0	Ditto ...	...	Ditto.
		14	49	...	...	48	39	25·85	Ci. 3	0	0			
		19	...	...	...	37	32	25·85	St. 10	0	0			
	19	7	...	22	...	27	25	25·85	0	0	0	Ditto ...	...	Ditto.
		12	...	...	...	44	37	25·88	Ci. 4	0	0			
		16	44	...	...	49	40	25·88	Ci. S. 8	0	0			
		21	...	...	...	32	31	25·87	0	0	0			
	20	8	...	22	...	28	26	25·87	0	0	0	Ditto ...	...	Ditto.
		12	...	...	...	48	40	25·90	0	0	0			
		17	50	...	...	45	36	25·87	St. 3	0	0			
		20	...	...	...	35	33	25·87	0	0	0			
	21	7	...	21	...	28	26	25·86	Clear blue sky all day	No wind	0	Ditto ...	...	No haze. Sky clear and still.
		11	...	...	...	41	35	25·92			0			
		14	...	...	...	49	41	25·90			0			
		16	49	...	...	46	39	25·88			0			
		18	...	...	...	38	33	25·81			0			
		21	...	...	...	33	30	25·84	0	0	0			
	22	7	...	21·5	...	27	26	25·78	0	0	0	Ditto ...	...	Clear, fine weather.
		11	...	...	...	43	34	25·82	0	0	0			
		14	...	...	...	50	41	25·78	0	0	0			
		16	53	...	...	49	41	25·77	Ci. 6	0	0			
		18	...	...	...	43	35	25·76	Ci. 4	0	0			
		20	...	...	...	36	30	25·75	0	0	0			
	23	7	...	24	...	29	28	25·75	Ci. 2	0	0	Ditto ...	...	Ditto.
		10	...	...	...	44	36	25·80	0	0	0			
		12	...	...	...	51	42	25·78	Ci. 1	0	0			
		15	55	...	...	55	44	25·75	0	0	0			
		18	...	...	...	42	35	25·72	0	0	0			
		21	...	...	...	38	32	25·72	0	0	0			
	24	7	...	26	...	31	28	25·73	St. 5	0	0	Ditto ...	...	Fine, clear weather.
		10	...	...	...	39	33	25·75	Ci. 3	0	0			
		12	...	...	...	48	39	25·72	0	0	0			
		14	...	...	...	52	42	25·69	0	0	0			
		16	52	...	...	48	40	25·67	Ci. 3	0	0			
		18	...	...	...	43	36	25·64	0	0	0			
		21	...	...	...	38	32	25·63	0	0	0			
	25	7	...	25	...	29	27	25·58	Ci. 1	0	0	Ditto ...	...	Ditto.
		12	...	...	...	46	37	25·61	Ci. 4	0	0			
		16	50	...	...	45	37	25·60	Ci. 5	0	0			
		21	...	...	...	36	31	25·58	0	0	0			
	26	7	...	26	...	31	29	25·55	Ci. 6	0	0	Ditto ...	...	Ditto.
		12	...	...	...	45	36	25·60	Cu. 4	0	0			
		16	52	...	...	49	41	25·65	0	0	0			
		21	...	...	...	35	31	25·66	0	0	0			
	27	7	...	24	...	30	28	25·75	Ci. 3	0	0	Ditto ...	...	Ditto.
		11	...	...	...	45	38	25·80	Ci. 3	0	0			
		14	51	...	...	50	44	25·79	Ci. 2	0	0			
		20	...	...	...	35	32	25·85	0	0	0			
	28	17	...	...	...	37	29	26·08	Cu. 4	N.W.	0	Kokrabát ...	25	Ditto.
		21	...	...	...	29	26	26·15	0	0	0	......	...	In rest house.
	29	7	...	14	...	18	17	26·13	Haze.	N.W.	0	Ditto.		

1873.			Thermometer.			Hygrometer.		Aneroid.	Cloud.		Wind.	Rain.	Locality.	Miles.	Remarks.
M.	D.	H.	Max.	Min.	Sun.	D.B.	W.B.								
Nov.	29	18	...	...	...	28	26	25·71	H.		0	0	Cizili	25	Hazy air.
	30	7	...	13	...	18	17	25·60	St.	10	0	0	Ditto	...	In rest house.
		17	...	...	...	33	32	25·51	Ci.	3	0	0	Yangi Hissar	32	Camp in court and garden on plain.
		19	...	...	...	30	27	25·53	Cu.	2	0	0			
		21	...	...	...	25	24	25·58	Cu.	2	0	0			
12	1	7	...	14·5	...	19	18	25·55	St.	2	0	0	Ditto	...	Halt. Hazy air.
		10	...	...	...	34	32	25·56	Ci.	5	0	0			
		14	...	...	...	38	34	25·54	St.	9	0	0			
		17	44	...	...	30	30	25·53	St.	4	0	0			
		21	...	...	...	24·5	24	25·63	0		0	0			
	2	7	...	14	...	26	26	25·70	Ci.	2	0	0	Ditto	...	Still cloudy day.
		12	...	...	...	40	34	25·61	St.	4	0	0			
		15	49	...	...	37	31	25·57	St.	9	0	0			
		20	...	...	...	28	26	25·58	Ci.	5	0	0			
	3	7	...	14	...	18	...	25·59	Ci.	3	0	0	Ditto		
		17	...	...	...	40	35	25·57	Ci.	6	0	0	Yapchang	25	Hazy sky.
		19	...	...	...	31	29	25·61	Ci.	1	0	0			
		21	...	...	...	24	24	25·66	0		0	0			
December.	4	7	...	11	...	17	16	25·65	Haze.		S.W.	0	Ditto.		
		16	...	...	...	36	33	25·60	Ci.	2	0	0	Káshghar	14	Quarters in a Residency Court on plain near the fort of Yangi-shahr.
		18	46	...	...	30	28	25·60	0		0	0			
		20	...	...	...	27	26	25·62	0		0	0			
	5	7	...	16	...	19·5	19·5	25·62	Cu.	3	0	0	Ditto.		
		10	...	...	...	31	30	25·64	Cu.	6	0	0			
		12	...	...	...	45	42	25·56	Cu.	4	W.	0	......	...	Instruments in an open Court and on north side of a wall; in the open air.
		16	...	...	...	33	30	25·64	Cu.	4	S.W.	0			
		18	55	...	...	28	27	25·71	Ci.	3	0	0			
		21	...	...	...	24	23	25·75	0		0	0			
	6	8	...	13	...	32	33	25·71	Haze.		0	0	Ditto	...	Still, hazy air.
		13	53	...	64	48	41	25·74	0		0	0			
		19	...	...	...	28	32	25·80	0		0	0			
	7	8	...	13	...	33	32	25·84	0		0	0	Ditto	...	Ditto ditto.
		12	...	...	...	42	42	25·78	0		0	0			
		16	58	...	...	42	38	25·83	0		0	0			
		20	...	...	...	32	29	25·87	0		0	0			
	8	7	...	13	...	20	20	25·93	0		0	0	Ditto	...	Ditto ditto.
		12	...	...	...	45	45	25·90	0		0	0			
		16	58	...	...	44	40	25·90	St.	2	0	0			
		19	...	...	...	29	32	25·95	0		0	0			
	9	7	...	15	...	21	20	25·81	Cu.	7	0	0	Ditto	...	Still, cloudy sky.
		14	57	...	...	44	40	25·65	Cu.	2	0	0			
		21	...	...	...	28	26	25·67	Cu.	4	0	0			
	10	7	...	17	...	22	21	25·63	Cu.	6	0	0	Ditto	...	Still, cloudcast sky.
		13	...	...	...	47	41	25·53	St.	3	0	0			
		16	56	...	...	36	30	25·57	St.	10	0	0			
		19	...	...	...	31	28	25·63	St.	10	0	0			
	11	8	...	13	...	22	...	25·75	St.	2	0	0	Ditto	...	Still air.
		12	...	...	...	45	42	25·73	St.	2	0	0			
		16	56	...	...	41	35	25·73	St.	4	0	0			
		20	...	...	...	27	26	25·80	0		0	0			
	12	8	...	13	...	26	25	25·92	St.	10	0	0	Ditto	...	Still, cloudcast sky.
		12	...	...	...	37	33	25·85	St.	10	0	0			
		16	60	...	...	35	32	25·80	St.	6	0	0			
		20	...	...	...	27	28	25·82	St.	4	0	0			

(519)

	1873.		Thermometer.			Hygrometer.		Aneroid.	Cloud.		Wind.	Rain.	Locality.	Miles.	Remarks.
M.	D.	H.	Max.	Min.	Sun.	D.B.	W.B.								
December	13	8	...	11	...	15	14	25·86	Ci.	3	0	0	Káshghar	...	Still hazy atmosphere.
		12	...	...	...	41	43	25·77	0		0	0			
		16	58	...	...	45	39	25·75	Ci.	5	0	0			
		20	...	...	...	27	26	25·74	Cu.	6	0	0			
	14	7	...	11	...	20	19	25·80	St.	6	0	0	Ditto	...	Still cold air.
		12	...	...	...	42	37	25·70	St.	8	0	0		...	Cloudy sky.
		16	54	...	...	43	39	25·70	Ci.	4	0	0			
		20	...	...	...	26	25	25·74	0		0	0			
	15	7	...	12	...	18	17	25·73	Ci.	4	0	0	Ditto	...	Still hazy and cloudy day.
		12	...	...	...	44	41	25·68	Ci.	4	0	0			
		16	53	...	...	45	40	25·65	Ci.	2	0	0			
		20	...	...	...	27	25	25·70	Ci.	6	0	0			
	16	7	...	11	...	16	15	25·68	Ci.	5	0	0	Ditto	...	Ditto.
		12	...	...	...	46	42	25·51	St.	6	0	0		...	Some sun at midday.
		16	55	...	...	37	34	25·55	St.	4	0	0			
		20	...	...	...	29	28	25·60	St.	6	0	0			
	17	7	...	13	...	22	21	25·55	St.	10	0	0	Ditto	...	Dull cloudy day.
		12	...	...	...	31	30	25·50	St.	10	0	0			No sun.
		16	39	...	...	33	31	25·48	St.	10	0	0			
		20	...	...	...	28	26	25·47	St.	10	0	0			
	18	7	...	15	...	22	21	25·50	0		0	0	Ditto	...	Clear bright sunny day.
		12	...	...	...	60	52	25·40	0		0	0			
		16	60	...	...	43	33	25·50	0		0	0		...	Haze on hills.
		20	...	...	...	35	28	25·58	0		0	0			
	19	7	...	8	...	17	16	25·75	Ci.	3	0	0	Ditto	...	Clear sunny day. Haze on hills.
		12	...	...	...	41	39	25·75	0		0	0			
		16	46	...	...	38	35	25·70	Ci.	4	0	0			
		20	...	...	...	22	21	25·75	0		0	0			
	20	7	...	7	...	18	17	25·84	St.	6	0	0	Ditto	...	Cloudy with some sunshine.
		12	...	...	...	32	28	25·84	Ci.S.	3	0	0			
		16	33	...	...	32	30	25·80	Ci.	4	0	0			
		20	...	...	...	24	20	25·84	0		0	0			
	21	7	...	6	...	20	19	25·82	St.	7	0	0	Ditto	...	Still and cloudy.
		12	...	...	...	31	29	25·75	St.	9	0	0			
		16	34	...	...	30	29	25·73	Ci.	4	0	0		...	Some sun at midday.
		20	...	...	...	20	19	25·75	0		0	0			
	22	7	...	7	...	15	14	25·75	St.	2	0	0	Ditto	...	Sunny day.
		12	...	...	...	32	30	25·65	0		0	0		...	Still, hazy air.
		16	32	...	...	32	31	25·73	St.	3	0	0			
		20	...	...	...	22	20	25·60	0		0	0			
	23	7	...	8	...	16	15	25·50	St.	10	0	0	Ditto	...	Dull, cloudy, and cold day.
		12	...	...	...	29	28	25·40	St.	10	0	0			
		16	31	...	...	27	26	25·33	St.	10	0	0			
		20	...	...	...	26	24	25·35	St.	4	0	0			
	24	7	...	8	...	29	28	25·50	St.	8	0	0	Ditto	...	Gusty wind and dust clouds at 3 P.M.
		12	...	...	...	44	35	25·50	St.	6	0	0			
		16	32	...	...	31	30	25·60	St.	9	W.	0			
		20	...	...	...	25	24	25·65	0		0	0			
	25	7	...	10	...	17	16	25·70	Cu.	4	0	0	Ditto	...	Fine weather.
		12	...	...	...	32	27	25·60	Cu.	6	E.	0			
		16	31	...	...	31	28	25·60	Cu.	8	E.	0			
		20	...	...	...	22	20	25·60	0		0	0			
	26	7	...	6	...	14	13	25·55	St.	3	0	0	Ditto	...	Cloudy day; little sun. Still air.
		12	...	...	...	30	28	25·55	St.	7	0	0			
		16	35	...	...	32	30	25·55	St.	3	0	0			
		20	...	...	...	25	23	25·64	0		0	0			

1873.			Thermometer.			Hygrometer.		Aneroid.	Cloud.		Wind.	Rain.	Locality.	Miles.	Remarks.
M.	D.	H.	Max.	Min.	Sun.	D.B.	W.B.								
December.	27	7	...	9	...	15	14	25·65	St.	2	0	0	Khasghar	...	Fine, sunny day. Still air.
		12	...	...	...	30	28	25·65	St.	3	0	0			
		16	32	...	...	32	28	25·55	0		0	0			
		20	...	...	...	22	20	25·60	0		0	0			
	28	7	...	7	...	14	14	25·73	Ci.	2	0	0	Ditto	...	Fine, sunny day. Sharp, still air.
		12	...	...	...	30	27	25·75	Ci.S.	3	0	0			
		16	32	...	...	30	26	25·74	0		0	0			
		20	...	...	...	18	16	25·75	0		0	0			
	29	7	...	−1	...	15	13	25·75	St.	6	0	0	Ditto	...	Cloudy sky. Still air.
		12	...	...	...	31	26	25·75	St.	8	0	0			
		16	31	...	...	29	27	25·75	St.	10	0	0			
		20	...	...	...	22	20	25·73	St.	5	0	0			
	30	7	...	−3	...	10	9	25·85	St.	3	0	0	Ditto	...	Sunny day. Still, frosty air.
		12	...	...	...	25	22	25·82	Ci.	2	0	0			
		16	30	...	...	23	21	25·80	0		0	0			
		20	...	...	...	16	15	25·77	0		0	0			
	31	7	...	−1	...	6	5	25·70	Ci.	4	0	0	Ditto	...	Frosty, fine day with light airs.
		12	...	...	...	25	23	25·62	St.	5	W.	0			
		16	29	...	...	23	21	25·60	St.	3	S.E.	0			
		20	...	...	...	15	14	25·61	0		0	0			
1874.															
January.	1	7	...	2	...	9	8	25·60	St.	8	0	0	Ditto	...	Dull, cloudy, still air.
		12	...	...	...	25	23	25·58	St.	10	0	0			
		16	29	...	...	23	22	25·60	St.	10	0	0			
		20	...	...	...	18	17	25·60	St.	10	0	0			
	2	7	...	9	...	16	15	25·60	St.	10	0	0	Ditto	...	Cloudcast sky. Still air. No sun.
		12	...	...	...	25	24	25·60	St.	10	0	0			
		16	29	...	...	24	22	25·59	St.	10	0	0			
		20	...	...	...	20	19	25·60	St.	10	0	0			
	3	7	...	6	...	14	13	25·70	St.	5	0	0	Ditto	...	Still, cloudy sky. Little sun.
		10	...	...	...	19	18	25·73	Ci.	4	0	0			
		12	...	...	...	27	25	25·70	Ci.	2	0	0			
		16	29	...	...	25	23	27·70	Ci.	4	0	0			
		20	...	...	...	16	15	25·72	0		0	0			
	4	7	...	7	...	16	15	25·74	Cu.	8	0	0	Ditto	...	Still, cloudy day. Little sun.
		10	...	...	...	16	18	25·75	Cu.S.	9	0	0			
		12	...	...	...	25	24	25·75	St.	6	0	0			
		16	29	...	...	25	23	25·70	St.	8	0	0			
		20	...	...	...	18	17	25·75	Cu.	8	0	0			
	5	7	...	−2	...	6	5	25·78	St.	4	0	0	Ditto	...	Ditto ditto.
		10	...	...	...	22	20	25·80	Cu.	5	0	0			
		12	...	...	...	27	25	25·70	St.	2	0	0			
		16	29	...	...	20	19	25·70	St.	4	0	0			
		20	...	...	...	15	14	25·75	0		0	0			
	6	7	...	−2	...	5	4	25·84	0		N.	0	Ditto	...	Clear, sunny day. Light airs.
		10	...	...	...	16	15	25·82	0		N.	0			
		12	...	...	...	20	19	25·82	0		0	0		...	Haze on hills.
		16	23	...	...	21	20	25·80	St.	4	0	0			
		20	...	...	...	16	15	25·82	St.	2	0	0			
	7	7	...	1	...	11	10	25·85	St.	10	0	0	Ditto	...	Dull, gloomy day. No sun.
		10	...	...	...	19	18	25·90	St.	10	0	0			
		12	...	...	...	22	21	25·85	Ni.	10	0	0			
		16	24	...	...	21	20	25·84	Ni.	10	0	0			
		20	...	...	...	18	17	25·85	St.	10	0	0			
	8	7	...	9	...	15	14	25·80	St.	10	0	0	Ditto	...	Ditto ditto.

	1874.		THERMOMETER.			HYGROMETER.		Aneroid.	Cloud.	Wind.	Rain.	Locality.	Miles.	REMARKS.
M.	D.	H.	Max.	Min.	Sun.	D.B.	W.B.							
January.	8	10	...	...	...	21	20	25·82	St. 10	0	0			
		12	...	...	...	23	21	25·82	St. 10	0	0			
		16	26	...	...	19	18	25·75	Cu. 6	0	0			
		20	...	...	...	16	15	25·72	0	0	0			
	9	7	...	−1	...	7	6	25·75	St. 6	0	0	Káshghar	...	Dull, gloomy day. No sun.
		10	...	...	...	22	21	25·67	Cu. 5	0	0			
		12	...	...	...	25	22	25·67	Cu. 6	0	0			
		16	26	...	...	22	20	25·65	Cu. 2	0	0			
		20	...	...	...	16	15	25·65	0	0	0			
	10	7	...	4	...	10	9	25·70	St. 8	0	0	Ditto	...	Cloudy, still day. Little sun.
		10	...	...	...	18	17	25·72	Cu. 9	0	0			
		12	...	...	...	27	25	25·62	St. 10	0	0			
		16	28	...	...	25	23	25·62	St. 8	0	0			
		20	...	...	...	18	17	25·62	St. 8	0	0			
	11	7	...	−2	...	7	6	25·85	St. 5	0	0	Ditto	...	Ditto.
		10	...	...	...	21	20	26·00	Cu. S. 8	0	0			
		12	...	...	...	23	22	26·00	Cu. S. 8	0	0			
		16	26	...	...	22	21	26·00	St. 4	0	0			
		20	...	...	...	15	14	26·08	0	0	0			
	12	7	...	−3	...	5	4	26·07	St. 4	0	0	Ditto	...	Ditto.
		10	...	...	...	20	18	25·00	Cu. S. 6	0	0			
		12	...	...	...	25	24	25·00	Cu. 3	0	0			
		16	26	...	...	25	23	25·97	St. 3	0	0			
		20	...	...	...	15	13	25·95	0	0	0			
	13	7	...	−4	...	4	3	25·88	St. 8	0	0	Ditto	...	Ditto.
		10	...	...	...	20	18	25·82	Cu. S. 9	0	0			
		12	...	...	...	24	22	25·80	Cu. S. 6	0	0			
		16	25	...	...	22	19	25·75	St. 4	0	0			
		20	...	...	...	14	12	25·78	0	0	0			
	14	7	...	−4	...	4	3	25·75	St. 4	0	0	Ditto	...	Ditto.
		10	...	...	...	18	17	25·75	St. 6	0	0			
		12	...	...	...	25	21	25·70	St. 8	0	0			
		16	28	...	...	24	23	25·70	St. 3	0	0			
		20	...	...	...	12	10	25·73	0	0	0			
	15	7	...	−3	...	4	3	25·78	Ci. 2	0	0	Ditto	...	Clear, sunny day. Haze on hills.
		10	...	...	...	17	16	25·78	Ci. 2	0	0			
		12	...	...	...	24	22	25·78	0	0	0			
		16	25	...	...	23	22	25·76	0	0	0			
		20	...	...	...	13	11	25·80	0	0	0			
	16	7	...	−3	...	5	4	25·90	Ci. 3	0	0	Ditto	...	Clear frosty air. Bright sun. No wind.
		10	...	...	...	25	24	25·90	Ci. 2	0	0			
		12	...	...	...	28	26	25·88	0	0	0			
		16	28	...	...	24	21	25·88	0	0	0			
		20	...	...	...	15	14	25·92	0	0	0			
	17	7	...	−3	...	5	4	26·00	Ci. S. 2	0	0	Ditto	...	Still, cold air. Some sun. Haze on hills.
		10	...	...	...	22	20	25·98	Ci. 3	0	0			
		12	...	...	...	25	23	25·98	Ci. S. 4	0	0			
		16	30	...	...	23	21	26·00	St. 8	0	0			
		20	...	...	...	18	16	26·00	0	0	0			
	18	7	...	−4	...	12	11	25·90	St. 8	0	0	Ditto	...	Ditto Little sun.
		10	...	...	...	25	24	25·90	St. 6	0	0			
		12	...	...	...	28	27	25·82	St. 9	0	0			
		16	31	...	...	28	25	25·75	St. 9	0	0			
		20	...	...	...	18	17	25·78	St. 6	0	0			
	19	7	...	−2	...	4	3	25·73	St. 4	0	0	Ditto	...	Ditto.
		10	...	...	...	22	20	25·74	St. 8	0	0			

(522)

	1874.		Thermometer.			Hygrometer.		Aneroid.	Cloud.	Wind.	Rain.	Locality.	Miles.	Remarks.
M.	D.	H.	Max.	Min.	Sun.	D.B.	W.B.							
January.	19	12	...	...	...	26	25	25·75	St. 9	0	0			
		16	31	...	...	28	25	25·70	St. 6	0	0			
		20	...	...	...	16	14	25·72	0	0	0			
	20	7	...	4·5	...	13	12	25·70	Cu. 8	0	0	Káshghar	...	Little sun.
		10	...	...	...	26	25	25·72	Cu. 5	0	0			
		12	...	...	...	35	34	25·68	St. 9	0	0			
		16	36	...	...	33	31	25·68	St. 10	0	0			
		20	...	...	...	24	23	25·72	St. 10	0	0			
	21	7	...	13	...	21	20	25·60	CuS.10	0	0	Ditto	...	Gloomy cloudcast sky Air still.
		10	...	...	...	38	36	25·60	CuS.10	0	0			
		12	...	...	...	33	32	25·52	St. 10	0	0			
		16	39	...	...	32	31	25·50	St. 10	0	0			
		20	...	...	...	26	25	25·54	St. 10	0	0			
	22	7	...	15	...	16	15	25·55	St. 10	0	0	Ditto	...	Ditto.
		10	...	...	...	33	29	25·57	St. 10	0	0			
		12	...	...	...	34	30	25·57	St. 10	0	0			
		16	37	...	...	31	30	25·56	St. 6	0	0			
		20	...	...	...	26	24	25·60	0	0	0			
	23	7	...	13	...	20	19	25·60	Cu. 10	0	0	Ditto	...	Gloomy sky. Still air No sun.
		10	...	...	...	26	25	25·60	Cu. 10	0	0			
		12	...	...	...	33	31	25·56	St. 10	0	0			
		16	35	...	...	30	28	25·56	St. 6	0	0			
		20	...	...	...	24	23	25·61	0	0	0			
	24	7	...	14·5	...	22	21	25·70	Cu. 4	0	0	Ditto	...	Still, cloudy day. Little sun.
		10	...	...	...	32	30	25·70	Cu.S. 8	0	0			
		12	...	...	...	36	33	25·70	St. 7	0	0			
		16	40	...	...	33	30	25·70	St. 4	0	0			
		20	...	...	...	24	22	25·73	0	0	0			
	25	7	...	5	...	12	11	25·74	0	0	0	Ditto	...	Sunny day. Still air Haze on hills. Starlight night.
		10	...	...	...	21	20	25·70	Ci. 3	0	0			
		12	...	...	...	35	32	25·70	Ci. 3	0	0			
		16	36	...	...	35	34	25·62	St. 6	0	0			
		20	...	...	...	28	27	25·62	0	0	0			
	26	7	...	15	...	20	19	25·60	St. 8	0	0	Ditto	...	Ditto.
		10	...	...	...	29	28	25·64	St. 2	0	0			
		12	...	...	...	34	33	25·60	Ci. 3	0	0			
		16	31	...	...	33	32	25·60	Ci. 5	0	0			
		20	...	...	...	24	23	25·68	0	0	0			
	27	7	...	9	...	16	17	25·70	St. 10	0	0	Ditto	...	Cloudy, still forenoon Some sun. Moonlight night.
		10	...	...	...	30	31	25·70	St. 10	0	0			
		12	...	...	...	32	32	25·68	Cu.S. 8	0	0			
		16	37	...	...	34	33	25·63	Cu. 4	0	0			
		20	...	...	...	24	22	25·68	Cu. 2	0	0			
	28	7	...	8	...	15	14	25·78	St. 6	0	0	Ditto	...	Some sun. Light air Hazy air.
		10	...	...	...	30	31	25·80	Cu.S. 8	0	0			
		12	...	...	...	38	39	25·80	Cu. 5	0	0			
		16	39	...	...	35	35	25·75	Cu. 5	E.	0			
		20	...	...	...	31	30	25·81	Cu.S. 7	0	0			
	29	7	...	15	...	19	19	25·82	St. 4	0	0	Ditto	...	Mild, still air. Some sun. Haze.
		10	...	...	...	33	34	25·80	St. 5	0	0			
		12	...	...	...	36	37	25·78	St. 3	0	0			
		16	37	...	...	34	34	25·70	Ci. S. 5	0	0			
		20	...	...	...	23	24	25·75	Ci. 2	0	0			
	30	7	...	7	...	15	15	25·73	Cu. 4	0	0	Ditto	...	Ditto.
		10	...	...	...	37	37	25·73	Cu.S. 6	0	0			
		12	...	...	...	39	39	25·78	Cu. 4	0	0			

(523)

	1874.		Thermometer.			Hygrometer.		Aneroid.	Cloud.		Wind.	Rain.	Locality.	Miles.	Remarks.
M.	D.	H.	Max.	Min.	Sun.	D.B.	W.B.								
January.	30	16	35	...	...	35	35	25·64	St.	5	0	0			
		20	...	...	...	23	22	25·78	Ci.	3	0	0			
	31	7	...	6	...	13	13	25·70	Cu.	3	0	0	Káshghar	...	Mild still air. Some sun. Haze.
		10	...	...	...	30	28	25·70	St.	3	0	0			
		12	...	...	...	35	31	25·65	Ci.	5	0	0			
		16	35	...	...	35	31	25·62	Ci.	3	0	0			
		20	...	...	...	24	22	25·61	Ci.	2	0	0			
2	1	7	...	13	...	20	19	25·65	Ci.S.10		0	0	Ditto	...	Gloomy sky. No wind.
		10	...	...	...	31	32	25·63	Ci.S.10		0	0			
		12	...	...	...	35	35	25·60	St.	10	0	0			
		16	38	...	...	33	33	25·55	St.	6	0	0			
		20	...	...	...	26	25	25·57	Ci.	4	0	0			
	2	7	...	5	...	11	11	25·56	0		0	0	Ditto	...	Fine sunny day. Cold air. No wind.
		10	...	...	...	29	29	25·56	0		0	0			
		12	...	...	...	37	37	25·50	St.	4	0	0			
		16	40	...	...	39	38	25·50	Cu.	6	0	0			
		20	...	...	...	30	28	25·57	Ci.	3	0	0			
	3	7	...	10	...	17	17	25·65	St.	4	0	0	Ditto	...	Mild, still air. Sunny day. Haze on hills.
		10	...	...	...	37	32	25·65	St.	1	0	0			
		12	...	...	...	38	36	25·65	St.	2	0	0			
		16	39	...	...	35	32	25·60	Ci.	3	0	0			
		20	...	...	...	30	29	25·62	Ci.	5	0	0			
	4	7	...	9	...	15	15	25·63	Cu.S.	3	0	0	Ditto	...	Ditto.
		10	...	...	...	34	34	25·60	Cu.	3	0	0			
		12	...	...	...	39	39	25·59	St.	5	0	0			
		16	49	...	...	38	33	25·55	St.	7	0	0			
		20	...	...	...	27	25	25·60	Cu.S.	8	0	0			
February.	5	7	...	15	...	22	22	25·60	St.	10	0	0	Ditto	...	Gloomy, still air. No sun.
		10	...	...	...	33	35	25·61	St.	10	0	0			
		12	...	...	...	40	38	25·58	St.	10	0	0			
		16	41	...	...	39	32	25·55	St.	8	0	0			
		20	...	...	...	28	26	25·61	Cu.	5	0	0			
	6	7	...	11	...	18	17	25·60	St.	8	0	0	Ditto	...	Still, mild air. Some sun. Haze on hills.
		10	...	...	...	38	34	25·60	St.	4	0	0			
		12	...	...	...	40	36	25·56	St.	5	0	0			
		16	41	...	...	40	34	25·50	St.	3	0	0			
		20	...	...	...	30	28	25·56	0		0	0			
	7	7	...	8	...	14	14	25·60	St.	2	0	0	Ditto	...	Fine sunny day. Still, mild air. Haze.
		10	...	...	...	35	35	25·60	St.	2	0	0			
		12	...	...	...	40	41	25·58	Cu.	5	0	0			
		16	41	...	...	38	38	25·57	Cu.S.	4	0	0			
		20	...	...	...	26	26	25·55	0		0	0			
	8	7	...	11	...	22	22	25·51	St.	10	N.W.	0	Ditto	...	Gloomy day. No sun. Light airs.
		10	...	...	...	33	34	25·50	St.	10	N.W.	0			
		12	...	...	...	37	39	25·45	St.	10	N.	0			
		16	40	...	...	35	35	25·35	St.	10	0	0			
		20	...	...	...	34	33	25·35	St.	10	0	0			
	9	7	...	23	...	29	29	25·34	St.	10	N.W.	0	Ditto	...	Gloomy day. No sun. Light air.
		10	...	...	...	35	32	25·35	St.	10	N.	0			
		12	...	...	...	39	33	25·34	St.	10	0	0			
		16	40	...	...	37	35	25·34	St.	10	0	0			
		20	...	...	...	32	29	25·40	St.	10	W.	0			
	10	7	...	24	...	38	39	25·56	Ni.	10	N.W.	0	Ditto	...	Snow began to fall 7 P.M.
		10	...	...	...	36	37	25·60	Ni.	10	S.E.	0			
		12	...	...	...	35	37	25·60	Ni.	10	N.W.	0			
		16	40	...	...	33	34	25·55	Ni.	10	0	0			

(524)

1874.			Thermometer.			Hygrometer.		Aneroid.	Cloud.		Wind.	Rain.	Locality.	Miles.	Remarks.
M.	D.	H.	Max.	Min.	Sun.	D.B.	W.B.								
February.	10	20	...	...	...	32	30	25·60	Ni.	10	0	S.	Káshghar	...	Snow in fore and afternoon. Some sun at midday. Starlight, still night.
	11	7	...	23	...	29	29	25·57	Ni.	10	N. E.	S.			
		10	...	...	...	32	33	25·60	Ni.	10	N.	S.			
		12	...	...	...	28	31	25·55	Cu.S.	9	0	0			
		16	37	...	...	30	32	25·50	Ni.	10	0	S.			
		20	...	...	...	28	28	25·60	0		0	0			
	12	7	...	14	...	21	21	25·60	St.	7	N. E.	0	Ditto	...	Clear, sunny day. Hills distinct for first time.
		10	...	...	...	25	25	25·60	Cu S.	4	E.	0			
		12	...	...	...	29	28	25·56	Cu.	2	0	0			
		16	32	...	...	31	30	25·55	0		0	0			
		20	...	...	...	20	20	25·58	0		0	0			
	13	7	...	3	...	11	11	25·64	Cu.	3	N. E.	0	Ditto	...	Ditto.
		10	...	...	...	24	24	25·66	Cu.	3	0	0			
		12	...	...	...	33	31	25·65	0		0	0			
		16	34	...	80	34	32	25·62	0		0	0			
		20	...	...	...	23	23	25·66	0		0	0			
	27	7	...	27	...	32	32		St.	10	0	0	Ditto	...	Gloomy day. Little sun. Still air.
		10	...	...	...	40	41		St.	10	0	0			
		12	...	...	...	42	43		St.	10	0	0			
		16	44	...	51	40	41		St.	10	0	0			
		20	...	...	...	33	33		St.	2	0	0			
	28	7	...	22	...	27	27	Instrument stolen.	St.	10	0	0	Ditto	...	Ditto.
		10	...	...	...	40	38		St.	10	0	0			
		12	...	...	...	44	45		St.	8	0	0			
		16	49	...	72	43	44		St.	7	0	0			
		20	...	...	...	35	35		St.	7	0	0			
March.	1	7	...	21	...	25	25		Cu.	5	0	0	Ditto	...	Sunny forenoon. Gloomy afternoon. Still air.
		10	...	...	...	42	42		Ci.	7	0	0			
		12	...	...	...	45	46		Su.	10	0	0			
		16	49	...	89	42	43		St.	10	0	0			
		20	...	...	...	35	35		St.	6	0	0			

(525)

			\multicolumn{3}{c	}{Thermometer.}	\multicolumn{2}{c	}{Hygrometer.}						
\multicolumn{3}{	c	}{1874.}									Locality.	Miles.	Remarks.
M.	D.	H.	Max.	Min.	Sun.	D.B.	W.B.	Cloud.	Wind.	Rain.			
3	2	7	...	22	...	25	25	Ci. S. 8	0	0	Káshghar	...	Still, cloudy day. Little sun.
		10	...	...	...	43	43	Cu. 6	0	0			
		12	...	...	...	49	50	Cu. 4	0	0			
		16	54	...	96	50	52	St. 6	0	0			
		20	...	...	...	38	38	St. 10	0	0			
	3	7	...	25	...	30	31	St. 10	0	0	Ditto	...	Gloomy sky. Gusts of sand blown up from the S.-E. in afternoon.
		10	...	...	...	42	44	St. 10	0	0			
		12	...	...	...	46	48	St. 10	E.	0			
		16	50	...	60	43	44	St. 10	S.E.	0			
		20	...	...	...	47	47	St. 10	W.	0			
	4	7	...	33	...	37	37	St. 10	W.	0	Ditto	...	Gloomy, damp air.
		10	...	...	...	43	41	St. 10	N.W.	0			
		12	...	...	...	44	46	St. 8	0	0			
		16	50	...	78	47	48	St. 6	0	0			
		20	...	...	...	42	42	St. 10	0	0			
	5	7	...	32	...	36	36	St. 10	N.W.	0	Ditto	...	Gloomy damp day and light breeze.
		10	...	...	...	43	45	St. 10	N.	0			
		12	...	...	...	47	49	St. 9	N.E.	0			
		16	51	...	75	44	45	St. 8	N.	0			
		20	...	...	...	39	39	St. 10	0	0			
	6	7	...	28	...	32	32	St. 10	N.	R.	Ditto	...	Gloomy day throughout. Sleet and rain in morning. Air damp and cold.
		10	...	...	...	41	40	Ni. 10	N.W.	R.			
		12	...	...	...	45	47	St. 10	0	0			
		16	49	...	...	45	45	St. 10	0	0			
		20	...	...	...	40	40	St. 10	0	0			
	7	7	...	32	...	38	38	St. 10	N.E.	0	Ditto	...	Gloomy, cold, and damp air. No rain.
		10	...	...	...	41	42	Ni. 10	N.	0			
		12	...	...	...	43	45	St. 10	0	0			
		16	46	...	...	41	41	St. 10	0	0			
		20	...	...	...	38	38	St. 10	0	0			
	8	7	...	30	...	33	34	Ni. 10	0	S.	Ditto	...	Still air, snow fell nearly all day.
		10	...	...	...	33	33	Ni. 10	0	S.			
		12	...	...	...	34	34	Ni. 10	0	S.			
		16	41	...	...	35	35	Ni. 10	0	S.			
		20	...	...	...	34	34	Ni. 10	0	S.			
	9	7	...	28	...	32	32	Ni. 10	N.W.	S.	Ditto	...	Sunny afternoon. Starlight night. Sleet and rain in forenoon.
		10	...	...	...	35	33	Cu. 10	N.	R.			
		12	...	...	...	37	38	Cu. 7	0	0			
		16	42	...	58	39	40	Cu. 5	0	0			
		20	...	...	...	33	33	0	0	0			
	10	7	...	22	...	28	28	0	N.W.	0	Ditto	...	Clear sunny day. Hills very distinct.
		10	...	...	...	40	41	0	N.W.	0			
		12	...	...	...	42	43	0	N.	0			
		16	45	...	88	41	42	Cu. 4	N.	0			
		20	...	...	...	33	33	Cu. 2	0	0			
	11	7	...	16	...	21	21	Cu. 3	N.W.	0	Ditto	...	Sunny day. Snow at nightfall.
		10	...	...	...	36	37	Cu. 3	N.W.	0			
		12	...	...	...	42	44	Cu. 5	N.	0			
		16	45	...	80	41	42	Cu. 7	0	0			
		20	...	...	...	35	35	St. 10	0	S.			
	12	7	...	25	...	29	29	Ni. 10	S.W.	S.	Ditto	...	Snow all night and till noon 10 inches deep.
		10	...	...	...	30	32	Ni. 10	S.W.	S.			
		12	...	...	...	30	33	Ni. 10	W.	S.			
		16	40	...	...	32	34	St. 10	0	0			
		20	...	...	...	30	31	St. 10	0	0			

(526)

1874.			Thermometer.			Hygrometer.		Cloud.	Wind.	Rain.	Locality.	Miles.	Remarks.
M.	D.	H.	Max.	Min.	Sun.	D.B.	W.B.						
March.	13	7	...	25	...	29	29	St. 10	W.	0	Káshghar	...	Gloomy, damp, cold day. No sun.
		10	...	...	...	33	34	St. 10	S.W.	0			
		12	...	...	...	34	37	St. 7	W.	0			
		16	43	...	54	35	36	St. 10	0	0			
		20	...	...	...	32	32	St. 10	0	0			
	14	7	...	27	...	32	32	St. 10	0	0	Ditto	...	Ditto.
		10	...	...	...	37	38	St. 10	0	0			
		12	...	...	...	39	40	St. 10	0	0			
		16	44	...	...	38	39	St. 10	0	0			
		20	...	...	...	35	35	St. 10	0	0			
	15	7	...	28	...	33	33	St. 10	E.	0	Ditto	...	Gloomy, damp day. No sun.
		10	...	...	...	35	36	St. 10	N.E.	0			
		12	...	...	...	39	40	St. 10	N.E.	0			
		16	45	...	...	40	41	St. 10	0	0			
		20	...	...	...	35	35	St. 8	0	0			
	16	7	...	28	...	32	32	St. 10	E.	0	Ditto	...	Ditto.
		10	...	...	...	34	35	St. 10	E.	0			
		12	...	...	...	40	41	St. 10	N.E.	0			
		16	44	...	...	40	41	St. 10	0	0			
		20	...	...	...	33	33	St. 10	0	0			
	17	16	...	...	...	40	38	St. 10	W.	0	Yapchang	14	Rest-house court, on sandy plain.
		18	49	...	...	38	32	Cu. 10	N.W.	0			
		20	...	...	...	33	30	Cu. 4	0	0			
	18	7	...	21	...	27	26	St. 10	N.W.	0	Ditto		
		16	...	...	...	45	41	Haze.	N.W.	0	Yáng Hissár	25	Court of Residency. Instruments in open air in shade of a N. verandah.
		19	54	...	...	40	35	H.	S.E.	0			
		21	...	...	...	35	32·5	St. 4	S.	0			
	19	8	...	25	...	36	32	St. 10	S.E.	0	Ditto		Mild air, cloudy sky and hazy atmosphere.
		10	...	...	...	48	43·5	Haze	0	0			
		12	...	...	...	45	42	Cu. 8	0	0			
		16	60	...	93	48	40	Cu. 8	0	0			
		20	...	...	...	42	41	St. 4	0	0			
	20	7	...	27	...	31	31	St. 10	0	0	Ditto	...	Ditto.
		10	...	...	...	50	47	Cu. 6	0	0			
		12	...	...	...	52	46	Cu. 6	0	0			
		16	61	...	103	50	41	Cu. 4	0	0			
		20	...	...	...	45	40	0	0	0			
	21	7	...	34	...	37	35	St. 10	N.E.	0	Ditto	...	Ditto.
		10	...	...	...	48	42	Cu. 8	E.	0			
		12	...	...	...	54	45	Cu. 6	S.E.	0			
		16	60	...	97	50	42	St. 10	0	0			
		20	...	...	...	45	39	St. 10	0	0			
	22	7	...	30	...	35	32	St. 10	E.	0	Ditto	...	Cloudy and hazy sky. Little sun and hot. Light airs from E. and S.
		10	...	...	...	44	40	St. 10	0	0			
		12	...	...	...	49	42	Cu. 8	0	0			
		16	57	...	101	52	51	Cu. 8	0	0			
		20	...	...	...	46	45	St. 10	0	0			
	23	7	...	33	...	36	36	St. 10	0	0	Ditto	...	Still, cloudy and hazy day.
		10	...	...	...	43	37	St. 10	0	0			
		12	...	...	...	46	40	St. 10	0	0			
		16	55	...	81	50	41	St. 6	0	0			
		20	...	...	...	43	41	0	0	0			
	24	7	...	31	...	51	45	Cu.S. 4	N.	0	Ditto		Sunny, spring weather. Hazy atmosphere.
		10	...	...	...	55	48	Cu. 4	N.	0			
		12	...	...	...	60	62	Ci. 5	N.E.	0			
		16	67	...	121	57	45	Ci. 3	0	0			

1874.			Thermometer.			Hygrometer.		Cloud.	Wind.	Rain.	Locality.	Miles.	Remarks.
M.	D.	H.	Max.	Min.	Sun.	D.B.	W.B.						
March	24	20				47	47	Ci. 3	0	0			
	25	7		34		41	38	Cu. 8	N.	0	Yáng Hissár.		Sunny, spring weather. Hazy atmosphere. Clouds high.
		10				54	46	Cu. 6	N.E.	0			
		12				61	51	Ci.S. 8	0	0			
		16	69		118	58	46	Ci. 5	0	0			
		20				50	43	0	0	0			
	26	7		30		35	35	CuS.10	N.	0	Ditto		Ditto.
		10				57	50	Cu. 8	E.	0			Wind in variable gusts.
		12				65	55	Ci. 5	E.	0			
		16	70		121	58	48	CuS. 8	S.W.	0			
		20				47	42	0	W.	0			
	27	7		33		40	40	St. 10	E.	0	Ditto		Ditto.
		10				53	48	St. 8	N.E.	0			Ditto.
		12				61	52	Cu. 7	N. to S.	0			
		16	65		116	54	45	Cu. 6	N.W.	0			
		20				50	44	Ci. 5	N.W.	0			
	28	7		36		43	39	Ci.S. 4	N.E.	0	Ditto		Ditto.
		10				64	54	Ci.S. 4	N.	0			
		12				68	58	Ci. 5	N.	0			
		16	75		122	60	46	Ci. 5	N.W.	0			
		20				50	42	Ci. 8	0	0			
	29	7		29		40	37	St. 8	N.	0	Ditto		Cloudy day. Cold wind. Much haze.
		10				53	42	St. 5	N.	0			
		12				60	48	St. 8	W.	0			
		16	65		91	59	46	St. 8	W.	0			
		20				45	29	St. 6	S.W.	0			
	30	7		32		43	37	St. 8	N.	0	Ditto		Sunny weather. High clouds. Gusty winds, and hazy atmosphere.
		10				65	59	Ci. 5	N.W.	0			
		12				71	60	Ci. 5	E.	0			
		16	79		113	65	65	Ci.S. 6	E.	0			
		20				56	56	Ci. 3	N.W.	0			
	31	7		39		50	43	St. 8	N.W.	0	Ditto		Ditto.
		10				60	50	Ci. 5	N.	0			
		12				63	49	Ci. 5	E.	0			
		16	73		109	65	58	St. 5	S.E.	0			
		20				55	41	Ci. 3	S.E.	0			
April	6	7		33		42	38	Ci.S. 9	0	0	Ditto		Cloudy and hazy. Breeze at sunset.
		10				67	54	Cu. 6	0	0			
		12				73	61	Ci. 4	0	0			
		16	75		125	67	52	St. 8	N.W.	0			
		20				60	60	St. 5	N.W.	0			
	7	7		41		45	39	St. 8	N.W.	0	Ditto		Breezy forenoon. Haze thick and low.
		10				74	65	St. 6	N.W.	0			
		12				78	67	Ci. 4	N.	0			
		16	79		129	70	59	Ci. 4	0	0			
		20				57	47	Cu. 6	0	0			
	8	7		31		42	38	Cu. 8	N.	0	Ditto		Ditto.
		10				58	51	Cu. 9	N.W.	0			
		12				71	62	St. 9	0	0			
		16	73		126	70	57	Ci. 3	0	0			
		20				57	47	Cu. 5	0	0			
	9	7		36		49	44	St. 10	0	0	Ditto		Dull cloudy day. Thick haze. Gusty northerly wind in evening.
		10				62	50	St. 10	N.	0			
		12				65	51	St. 10	0	0			
		16	64		87	62	53	St. 8	0	0			
		20				57	44	St. 10	N.W.	0			

(528)

1874.			Thermometer.			Hygrometer.		Cloud.	Wind.	Rain.	Locality.	Miles.	Remarks.
M.	D.	H.	Max.	Min.	Sun.	D.B.	W.B.						
April	10	7	...	34	...	45	40	St. 10	N.	0	Yáng Hissár	...	Dull cloudy day. Thick haze. Gusty northerly wind in evening. Little sun.
		10	...	...	...	57	47	St. 10	N.	0			
		12	...	...	...	61	48	St. 8	0	0			
		16	60	...	70	59	46	St. 8	N.W.	0			
		20	...	...	...	52	44	St. 10	N.W.	0			
	11	7	...	41	...	49	41	St. 10	0	0	Ditto	...	Dense haze fog. Air damp and chill.
		10	...	...	...	49	41	Haze	0	0			
		12	...	...	...	50	42	H.	N.	0			
		16	51	...	...	49	43	H.	N.	0			
		20	...	...	...	46	42	H.	N.	0			
	12	7	...	37	...	45	42	St. 10	N.	0	Ditto	...	Haze fog. Steady breeze from north. No sun.
		10	...	...	...	50	45	Haze	N.W.	0			
		12	...	...	...	52	45	H.	N.	0			
		16	55	...	...	51	44	H.	N.	0			
		20	...	...	...	50	45	H.	0	0			
	13	7	...	38	...	50	45	St. 10	N.	0	Ditto	...	Ditto. Wind cold.
		10	...	...	...	56	47	Haze	N.W.	0			
		12	...	...	...	60	50	H.	0	0			
		16	64	...	...	58	47	H.	0	0			
		20	...	...	...	53	45	H.	N.	0			
	14	7	...	42	...	50	45	St. 10	N.	0	...	...	Ditto ditto.
		10	...	...	...	61	51	Haze	0	0			
		12	...	...	...	64	51	H.	0	0			
		16	70	...	...	64	50	H.	0	0			
		20	...	...	...	58	49	H.	0	0			
	15	7	...	46	...	54	48	Haze	N.W.	0	Ditto	...	Dense haze fog. Gusty wind all day.
		10	...	...	...	60	50	H.	N.W.	0			
		12	...	...	...	65	52	H.	0	0			
		16	71	...	...	63	51	H.	N.	0			
		20	...	...	...	57	51	H.	N.W.	0			
	16	7	...	42	...	60	50	St. 10	N.W.	R.	Ditto	...	Slight rain at sunrise. Hazy forenoon. Cloudy day, and still air.
		10	...	...	...	68	55	Haze	N.W.	0			
		12	...	...	...	74	55	St. 6	0	0			
		16	86	...	127	70	51	Cu. 5	0	0			
		20	...	...	...	61	49	St. 10	0	0			
	17	7	...	32	...	54	49	Cu. 3	0	0	Ditto	...	Clear sky. Still air. Warm sunny day.
		10	...	...	...	62	54	Cu. 3	0	0			
		12	...	...	...	70	64	0	0	0			
		16	75	...	139	73	67	0	0	0			
		20	...	...	...	63	55	0	0	0			
	18	7	...	35	...	50	44	Dust.	N.W.	0	Ditto	...	Gale from N.W. Dust clouds all day. Darkness from noon to 2 P.M. Lull from 4 to 6 P.M.
		10	...	...	...	69	60	D.	N.W.	0			
		12	...	...	...	68	52	D.	N.W.	0			
		16	71	...	...	62	43	D.	0	0			
		20	...	...	...	57	49	D.	N.W.	0			
	19	7	...	33	...	54	39	0	0	0	Ditto	...	Fine clear day. Light airs. Distant haze.
		10	...	...	...	61	46	Cu. 2	N.	0			
		12	...	...	...	65	48	Cu. 3	N.W.	0			
		16	78	...	136	77	51	Cu. 6	0	0			
		20	...	...	...	55	41	Cu. 2	0	0			
	20	7	...	31	...	47	38	St. 10	N.	0	Ditto	...	Cloudy, breezy day. Little sun. Much haze.
		10	...	...	...	53	42	St. 8	N.W.	0			
		12	...	...	...	58	45	St. 6	N.W.	0			
		16	67	...	75	60	45	St. 6	N.W.	0			
		20	...	...	...	56	44	St. 8	0	0			
	21	7	...	42	...	51	45	St. 10	N.	0	Ditto	...	Ditto ditto.

(529)

1874.			THERMOMETER.			HYGROMETER.		Cloud.	Wind.	Rain.	Locality.	Miles.	REMARKS.
M.	D.	H.	Max.	Min.	Sun.	D.B.	W.B.						
April	21	10	...	...	...	58	46	Haze.	N.W.	0			
		12	...	...	...	61	50	H.	N.W.	0			
		16	68	...	88	65	49	H.	0	0			
		20	...	...	...	58	45	H.	0	0			
	22	7	...	42	...	51	48	St. 10	N.W.	0	Yáng Hissár	...	Densely hazy sky.
		10	...	...	...	59	50	H.	N.W.	0			
		12	...	...	...	63	51	H.	N.W.	0			
		16	68	...	98	65	58	H.	0	0			
		20	...	...	...	58	48	H.	0	0			
	23	7	...	39	...	55	48	St. 6	N.W.	0	Ditto	...	Sunny and cloudy day. Hazy afternoon.
		10	...	...	...	65	48	St. 8	0	0			
		12	...	...	...	70	50	Cu. 6	0	0			
		16	75	...	122	72	51	H.	S.E.	0			
		20	...	...	...	60	47	H.	0	0			
	24	7	...	39	...	52	47	St. 6	N.	0	Ditto	...	Ditto.
		10	...	...	...	67	48	H.	N.W.	0			
		12	...	...	...	71	51	H.	0	0			
		16	76	...	125	73	57	H.	S.	0			
		20	...	...	...	61	46	H.	S.E.	0			
	25	7	...	37	...	51	45	Cu. 3	N.	0	Ditto	...	Sunny, clear sky with high clouds, and steady breeze all day, with slight lulls.
		10	...	...	...	70	50	Ci. 5	N.	0			
		12	...	...	...	74	52	Ci. S. 4	N.	0			
		16	80	...	127	77	55	Ci. 3	N.	0			
		20	...	...	...	62	53	0	N.	0			
	26	7	...	40	...	55	46	H.	N.	0	Ditto	...	Hazy sky more or less all day.
		10	...	...	...	72	54	H.	0	0			
		12	...	...	...	77	56	H.	0	0			
		16	82	...	135	78	56	Cu. 8	0	0			
		20	...	...	...	69	48	Cu. 7	S.W.	0			
	27	7	...	39	...	58	53	0	0	0	Ditto	...	Still, warm, sunny day, clear sky. Lower air obscured by haze and glare.
		10	...	...	...	74	55	0	0	0			
		12	...	...	...	80	59	0	0	0			
		16	84	...	137	81	60	0	0	0			
		20	...	42	...	67	56	0	0	0			
	28	7	...	...	...	61	49	0	0	0	Ditto	...	Ditto, with light airs.
		10	...	...	...	76	54	0	N.W.	0			
		12	...	...	...	79	56	0	0	0			
		16	86	...	136	84	58	0	S.W.	0			
		20	...	...	...	69	55	0	0	0			
	29	7	...	50	...	62	56	0	0	0	Ditto	...	Ditto. Intense low haze and glare.
		10	...	...	...	76	56	0	0	0			
		12	...	...	...	80	59	0	0	0			
		16	88	...	140	85	60	Cu. 5	N.W.	0			
		20	...	...	...	70	55	Cu. 3	0	0			
	30	7	...	47	...	61	52	St. 10	N.E.	0	Ditto	...	Sunny and gusty day. With clouds and haze and dust.
		10	...	...	...	73	53	Cu. S. 8	N.E.	0			
		12	...	...	...	76	54	Cu. 5	S.E.	0			
		16	88	...	130	84	62	Cu. 6	N.W.	0			
		20	...	...	...	70	58	Cu. 3	N.W.	0			
May	1	7	...	46	...	61	53	0	S.	0	Ditto	...	Violent duststorm in afternoon from the north against a south wind.
		10	...	...	...	78	56	H.	S.	0			
		12	...	...	...	82	59	Dust.	S.	0			
		16	90	...	134	82	58	D.	N.	0			
		20	...	...	...	78	55	St. 10	N.	0			

(530)

	1874.			Thermometer.			Hygrometer.		Cloud.	Wind.	Rain.	Locality.	Miles.	Remarks.
	M.	D.	H.	Max.	Min.	Sun.	D.B.	W.B.						
May.		2	7	...	49	...	67	54	St. 10	N.	0	Yáng Hissár	...	Variable gusts of wind driving dust clouds all day, and obscuring sky.
			10	...	...	...	66	53	D.	S.-E.	0			
			12	...	...	...	66	53	D.	W.	0			
			16	83	...	91	70	54	D.	S.-W.	0			
			20	...	...	...	67	52	H.	N.-W.	0			
		3	12	...	...	...	86	56	Cu. 3	N.-W.	0	Topuluk	15	Clear sky, and hills seen distinctly. Camp on fields.
			16	95	...	130	85	57	Cu. 5	N.-W.	0			
			20	...	45	...	57	46	Cu. 2	0	0			
		4	12	...	...	...	83	57	Cu. 3	N.-W.	0	Cizili	17	Sky obscured by haze, and atmosphere by glare. Resthouse.
			16	91	...	135	78	55	H.	N.-W.	0			
			20	...	45	...	65	50	H.	S.-W.	0			
		5	3	...	42	...	56	46	Cu. 2	N.-W.	0	Ditto.		
			12	...	...	...	80	57	St. 4	N.-W.	0	Kokrabát	25	Hazy weather. Camp in resthouse.
			16	63	...	93	80	56	Ci. 6	0	0			
			20	...	...	...	72	55	Cu.S. 8	0	0			
		6	12	...	...	...	82	56	H.	N.-W.	0	Yarkand	25	Residency in fort. Instruments in shade on north side of a wall in an open court.
			16	60	...	125	79	55	Cu. 4	N.-W.	0			
			20	...	45	...	70	53	St. 8	0	0			
		7	7	...	40	...	58	50	H.	N.-W.	0	Ditto.		
			10	...	...	...	70	55	H.	N.-W.	0			
			12	...	...	...	78	56	Cu. 6	N.-W.	0			
			16	91	...	126	80	56	Cu. 5	0	0			
			20	...	...	...	67	52	St. 8	0	0			
		8	7	...	41	...	64	52	H.	0	0	Ditto	...	Warm, sunny, hazy day. Bright glare.
			10	...	...	...	73	53	St. 5	0	0			
			12	...	...	...	77	54	Cu. 3	N.	0			
			16	81	...	135	79	55	St. 5	0	0			
			20	...	...	...	67	52	St. 8	0	0			
		9	7	...	42	...	65	53	H.	0	0	Ditto	...	Gusty, dusty, hazy day. Light airs.
			10	...	...	...	73	53	H.	N.	0			
			12	...	...	...	80	56	H.	W.	0			
			16	84	...	133	80	55	H.	W.	0			
			20	...	...	...	74	52	H.	W.	0			
		10	7	...	48	...	62	52	St. 10	N.	0	Ditto	...	Hazy, gusty, dusty day. Light airs.
			10	...	...	...	77	54	H.	N.	0			
			12	...	...	...	79	56	H.	N.-W.	0			
			16	84	...	101	80	56	H.	W.	0			
			20	...	...	...	72	51	St. 10	W.	0			
		11	7	...	47	...	61	49	St. 10	N.	0	Ditto	...	Dense haze and glare. Air thick, and dusty. Winds gentle puffs.
			10	...	...	...	73	52	H.	N.-W.	0			
			12	...	...	...	80	55	H.	W.	0			
			16	89	...	108	81	56	H.	W.	0			
			20	...	...	...	72	53	H.	0	0			
		12	7	...	48	...	67	56	St. 10	0	0	Ditto	...	Hazy, thick weather.
			10	...	...	...	84	64	H.	W.	0			
			12	...	...	...	84	59	H.	N.-W.	0			
			16	93	...	123	83	59	H.	0	0			
			20	...	...	...	70	55	St. 4	0	0			
		13	7	...	53	...	63	45	St. 10	0	0	Ditto	...	Ditto.
			10	...	...	...	71	51	St. 10	N.-W.	0			
			12	...	...	...	75	54	St. 10	0	0			
			16	85	...	91	74	52	St. 10	0	0			
			20	...	...	...	69	51	St. 10	0	0			
		14	7	...	48	...	61	41	St. 10	0	0	Ditto	...	Ditto.
			10	...	...	...	70	55	H.	W.	0			
			12	...	...	...	75	55	H.	W.	0			

(531)

	1874		\multicolumn{3}{c}{Thermometer.}	\multicolumn{2}{c}{Hygrometer.}	Cloud.	Wind.	Rain.	Locality.	Miles.	Remarks.
M.	D.	H.	Max.	Min.	Sun	D.B.	W.B.						
May.	14	16	84	...	103	75	56	H.	0	0	Yarkand	...	Hazy thick weather.
		20	...	...	...	67	51	H.	0	0			
	15	7	...	48	...	61	43	St. 10	0	0			
		10	...	...	...	75	58	H.	0	0	Ditto	...	Ditto.
		12	...	...	...	79	58	H.	N.	0			
		16	86	...	106	80	56	H.	N.	0			
		20	...	...	...	68	53	H.	0	0			
	16	7	...	40	...	61	45	St. 8	N.	0	Ditto	...	Ditto.
		10	...	...	...	77	46	Cu.8.6	N.	0			
		12	...	...	...	80	56	H.	N.W.	0			
		16	86	...	128	84	57	H.	N.	0			
		20	...	...	...	72	55	Cu.S.8	0	0			
	17	7	...	46	...	63	52	St. 10	N.	0	Ditto	...	Ditto.
		10	...	...	...	76	56	H.	N.	0			
		12	...	...	...	81	56	H.	N.	0			
		16	89	...	121	81	58	H.	0	0			
		20	...	...	...	71	53	Cu. 6	0	0			
	18	10	...	40	...	80	58	St. 8	N.	0	Yangichik	12	Cloudy and warm. Air clear of haze.
		12	...	...	...	82	61	Cu. 6	N.	0			
		16	88	...	112	82	63	Cu. 4	N.W.	0			
		20	...	...	...	71	65	Cu. 2	N.W.	0			
	19	12	...	...	...	90	71		S.W.	0	Yakskanba Bazar.	18	Camp on fields.
		16	97	...	120	83	71	0	W.	0			
		20	...	41	...	78	56	St. 4	W.	0			
	20	10	...	45	...	67	55				Kargalik	16	Rest house.
		12	...	...	...	83	57	0	0	0			
		16	93	...	128	83	58	Cu. 3	N.W.	0			
		20	...	...	...	74	57	0	0	0			
	21	12	...	...	...	86	60	0	S.	0	Beshtarik	20	Camp on fields.
		16	91	...	125	84	58	0	S.	0			
		20	...	51	...	55	50	0	N.W.	0			
	22	10	...	...	...	75	57	0	S.	0	Yobaric	12	Duststorm and gusty whirls in afternoon.
		12	...	...	...	78	60	0	S.E.	0			
		16	86	...	...	71	55	Dust	Ver.	0			
		20	...	41	...	65	50	D.	Ver.	0			
	23	12	...	...	...	79	57	St. 6	S.	0	Kokyár	13	Enter hills.
		16	85	...	96	77	56	H.	S.	0			
		20	...	43	...	65	55	H.	S.W.	0			
	24	18	80	42	...	67	...	0	0	0	Acmasjid	24	Windy and dusty day.
	25	12	...	...	...	78	55	Cu. 6	S.	0	Chighligh	12	Camp on Tiznaf River. Thunder showers from noon to 2 P.M.
		16	84	...	...	65	54	St. 10	S.	R.			
		20	...	43	...	55	48	St. 10	0	0			
	26	5	...	33	...	46	42	Cu. 3	N.W.	0	Ditto.		
		16	73	...	...	67	68	Cu. 3	N.W.	0	Khoja Mazár	18	Camp in narrow valley on Tiznaf river.
		20	...	...	...	57	45	0	N.W.	0		6	
	27	10	...	32	...	75	52	Cu. 2	0	0	Duba	...	Camp on ditto at union of two streams.
		12	...	...	...	77	53	Cu. 5	0	0			
		16	81	...	...	60	51	Cu. 8	N.W.	0			
		20	...	...	...	50	43	Cu. 3	0	0	Ditto	...	Halt.
	28	7	...	25	...	46	42	Cu. 3	S.E.	0			
		10	...	...	...	71	52	Ci. 5	S.E.	0			
		12	...	...	...	72	52	Ci. 3	E.	0			
		16	80	...	...	61	46	H.	N.	0			
		20	...	...	...	55	42	Cu. 6	0	0			
	29	7	...	24	...	45	38	Cu. 3	N.W.	0	Ditto.		

	1874.		Thermometer.			Hygrometer.		Cloud.	Wind.	Rain.	Locality.	Miles.	Remarks.
M.	D.	H.	Max.	Min.	Sun.	D.B.	W.B.						
May.	29	12	...	...	...	68	49	Ci. 4	N.	0	Gurunj Cáldi	9	Camp on river bank.
		16	71	...	...	65	43	Cu. 5	S.	0			
		20	...	...	...	51	35	Ci. 2	S.E.	0			
	30	12	...	...	...	48	40	Ci. 3	N.	0	Chiragh Sáldi	14	Camp at junction of two streams
		16	68	...	...	61	51	Ci. 5	S.W.	0			
		20	...	25	...	42	32	0	S.W.	0			
	31	12	...	...	...	70	46	Ci. 3	0	0	Culánúldi	12	Cross Yangi Dawan to camp in bed of Yarkand River. Stormy night.
		16	76	...	...	64	43	Cu. 2	S.E.	0			
		20	...	22	...	54	36	0	S.E.	0			
6	1	12	...	...	...	58	45	St. 10	S.	0	Kukat Aghzi	15	Camp in river bed. Rain at sunset.
		16	69	...	...	52	39	St. 10	S.W.	0			
		20	...	31	...	40	37	Ni. 10	S.W.	R.			
	2	14	...	...	...	43	37	St. 10	N.W.	0	Kashmir Jilga	26	Thunder and lightning with hail and rain 3 to 4 p.m.
		16	60	...	...	43	37	St. 10	S.E.	R.			
		20	...	16	...	48	44	Cu. 8	0	0			
	3	12	...	...	...	65	52	Cu. 5	S.E.	0	Khapalang	12	Gusty wind. Little sun.
		16	61	...	...	52	39	St. 8	S.E.	0			
		20	...	15	...	45	34	Cu. 8	S.E.	0			
	4	12	...	...	...	66	50	Cu. 5	W.	0	Actágh	20	Camp in bed of upper course Yarkand River.
		16	59	...	...	43	39	St. 8	W.	0			
		20	...	15	...	40	35	0	N.W.	0			
	5	4	...	8	...	24	21	St. 10	S.W.	0	Ditto.		
		16	66	...	...	45	41	Cu. 3	S.	0	Brangsa	25	Camp near ascent to Caracoram Pass.
		20	...	...	...	38	30	Cu. 2	0	0	Caracoram.		
	6	18	...	...	...	57	...	0	0	0	Daulatbeg	21	
	7	4	...	10	...	26	25	Cu. 3	0	0	Ditto.		
		16	64	...	...	62	49	Cu. 3	0	0	Burcha	26	Camp in bed of tributary of Shayok River.
		20	...	...	...	43	35	0	S.E.	0			
	8	4	...	14	...	32	29	Cu. 3	0	0	Ditto.		
		12	...	...	...	58	48	St. 5	W.	0	Murgi	12	Gusty wind with snow and rain at nightfall. Camp in deep gully.
		16	68	...	...	57	47	St. 8	W.	0			
		20	...	...	...	44	35	St. 10	W.	R.			
June.	9	5	...	25	...	40	33	St. 10	W.	S.	Ditto.		
		12	...	...	...	39	35	Ni. 10	W.	S.	Brangsa Sáser	10	Snow and sleet all day, and gusty wind. Night starlight
		16	41	...	...	39	35	Ni. 10	S.	S.			
		20	...	...	...	36	33	Cu. 2	0	0			
	10	7	...	14	...	34	31	Ni. 10	S.W.	S.	Ditto	...	Halt. Snow till noon. Sunny afternoon.
		10	...	...	...	38	35	Ni. 10	S.	S.			
		12	...	...	...	37	34	Ni. 10	S.	S.			
		16	45	...	...	40	38	Cu. 5	S.	0			
		20	...	...	...	31	29	Cu. 3	0	0			
	11	5	...	10	...	25	24	Cu. 3	S.W.	0	Ditto	...	Snow in forenoon whilst crossing Saser Glacier Pass. Snow at sunset.
		17	68	...	...	47	41	Ni. 10	S.W.	S.	Tutyálác	18	
		20	...	...	...	40	33	Cu. 4	0	0	Glacier.		
	12	4	...	16	...	31	30	Cu. 3	N.	0	Tutyálác.		
		12	...	...	...	73	61	Cu. 5	N.W.	0	Changlang	16	Camp on Nubra River. Crossed Carawal Pass.
		16	80	...	...	67	49	Cu. 3	N.	0			
		20	...	...	...	55	42	0	0	0			
	13	4	...	24	...	45	41	Ci. 3	N.	0	Ditto.		
		12	...	...	...	78	68	Ci. 2	N.W.	0	Panámik	12	Clear, sunny, breezy weather. Camp on river.
		16	86	...	...	75	61	0	N.	0			
		20	...	...	...	64	57	0	N.	0			
	14	4	...	39	...	56	52	Cu. 8	N.	0	Ditto.		
		12	...	...	...	65	58	St. 10	N.W.	0	Tagar	12	Cloudy day, slight rain in afternoon.
		16	71	...	...	63	50	Ni. 10	N.W.	R.			
		20	...	...	...	56	48	Cu. 4	N.	0			

1874.			Thermometer.			Hygrometer.		Cloud.	Wind.	Rain.	Locality.	Miles.	Remarks.
M.	D.	H.	Max.	Min.	Sun.	D. B.	W. B.						
June.	15	4	...	30	...	45	42	Cu. 10	N.W.	0	Tagar.		
		12	...	...	...	69	55	Cu. 5	N.W.	0	Satti ...	14	Windy, dusty day. Camp above village, on fields.
		16	80	...	...	66	53	Cu. 3	N.W.	0			
		20	...	...	...	57	40	0	N.	0			
	16	4	...	22	...	38	30	0	E.	0	Ditto.		
		12	...	...	...	67	49	0	E.	0	Diggar ...	...	Hot, sunny forenoon.
		16	73	...	...	62	46	Cu. 8	N.E.	0			
		20	...	...	...	51	42	Cu. 8	0	0			
	17	4	...	27	...	44	39	St. 10	N.W.	0	Ditto.		
		18	64	...	...	60	48	Cu. 4	W.	0	Leh ...	24	Cross Diggar Pass. Camp Residency garden.
		20	...	...	...	52	42	Cu. 6	0	0			

In camp the instruments have always been set on a board fixed to a tripod stand, and stood in the shade at the edge of a tent verandah awning.

In quarters they have stood on the tripod in the open air of a court-yard in the shade on north side of a wall.

The higher reading of the wet bulb thermometer in frosty and very damp weather seems to be attributable to the protection afforded to the bulb against the operation of the air by a thin layer of frost or unevaporated water, in either case respectively, remaining in the meshes of its covering muslin.

(Sd.)   H. W. Bellew.

CHAPTER XV.

COMPARATIVE VOCABULARY OF SOME DIALECTS SPOKEN IN THE TERRITORY OF KASHGHAR, BY DR. H. W. BELLEW.

Parts of the body, diseases, and medicines.

English.	Yarkandi.	Kirghiz.	Sárigh Cúlí.	Wákhi.	Kalmác.
Head.	Básh.	Básh.	Kól.	Sar.	Tólgay.
Forehead.	Mangláy.	Mangláy.	Rak.	Rúkh.	Mancá.
Temple.	Cúlác-tuwí.	Chaka.	Soyá.	Zilfé.	Shul.
Face.	Yúz.	Yúz.	Pyats.	Rof.	Nyúr-Khírá.
Ear.	Cúlác.	Cúlác.	Ghaul.	Ghásh.	Chhíkin.
Nose.	Búrún.	Murun.	Nádz.	Mís.	Khamar.
Nostril.	Tushc.	Tushuc.	Dárz.	M. Sarv.	
Eye.	Kúz.	Kúz.	Tsem.	Chazhm.	Nyudun.
Eye-lash.	Kirpik.	Kirpik.	Pàtsch.	Ch. tapk.	Nyusun.
Eye-lid.	K. Capaghí.	K. Capaghi.	Ts. past.	Ch. gusht.	Negin.
Eye-brow.	Cásh.	Cásh.	Viráw.	Viraw.	Cumsún.
Eye-pupil.	Bobo.	Carágha.	Ghátsak.	Ch. Siyahí.	N. Khara.
Mouth.	Aghz.	Aghaz.	Ghov.	Ghash.	Aman.
Lip.	Calpúc.	Calpúc.	Payúz.	Lafch.	Urul.
Tongue.	Til.	Til. Dil.	Ziv.	Thík.	Khilin.
Gum.	Mulk.	Goshí.	Sharázú.	Shind.	Makhan.
Tooth.	Chish.	Chish.	Zandán.	Dandik.	Shúdun.
Tonsil.	Chilchik.	Kichik-til.	Dzá-ziv.		Zangak.
Palate.	Tamghac.	Tanglay.	Kom.	Khom.	Tangná.
Chin.	Manh.	Manh.	Zangán.	Zanakh.	Dáruk.
Cheek.	Cobz.	Cobz.	Lunj.	Put-lunj.	Khakha.
Jaw.	Ingak.	Yanghac.	Kapúz.	Zanakh.	Yajúr. Kelin.
Beard.	Sacál.	Sacál.	Bún.	Rayish.	Sacál.
Moustache.	Búrut.	Múrút.	Burut.	Zilfáyn.	Sacál.

(535)

English.	Yarkandi.	Kirghiz.	Sárigh Cúlí.	Wákhi.	Kalmác.
Neck.	Gardan.	Gal.	Gardân.	Gardán.	Khúzun.
Throat.	Bogház.	Yalcá.	Mokh?	Halc.	Khöl.
Nape.	Boyun.	Moyun.	Mokh.	Makh.	Shíl.
Gullet.	Umgach.	Halcúm.	Halcúm.	Halcúm.	Dokhtar.
Larynx.	Búghdyac.	Kekistak.	Khpârg.	Kabitok.	Khyúkun.
Clavicle.	Akhurtak.	Akhirak.	Khafgá.	Pushbar.	Khunkurka.
Scapula.	Dolú.	Dála.	Dolú.	Fayak.	Dúl.
Back.	Uchá.	Arca.	Arca.	Dam.	Arda.
Loin.	Ba-l.	Bel.	Myaz.	Máz.	Norghún.
Spine.	Umúrghá.	Omúrtca.	Wayogh.	Dam.	Norún-yásún.
Thorax.	Gokus.	Kokrac.	Púz.	Push.	Chaydin.
Breast.	Amchik.	Emchik.	Tej.	Bap.	Aymin.
Nipple.	Amchick.	Emchik.	Tejkol.	Bapsar.	Kokun.
Rib.	Cawurghá.	Cawurghá.	Pahlá.	Púrs.	Khobsún.
Flank.	Yán.	Yán. Yacca.	Pahlá.	Cabarghá.	Cabarghá.
Armpit.	Coltuc.	Coltuc.	Coltíc.	Khál.	So.
Shoulder.	Yághrin.	Kiptí.	Sefd.	Ísp.	Múr.
Arm.	Bilic.	Caráyílíc.	Charost.	Malúngerch.	Gharan.
Elbow.	Jaynac.	Chicánac.	Yorn.	Barit.	Tokhá.
Cubit.	Bilac.	Kunjilic.	Yorn-zust.	Yúrm.	Chimugin.
Wrist.	Bighish.	Banja.	Ch. band.	Bandidast.	Bagalsak.
Hand.	Cúl.	Cwal.	Zust.	Dast.	Kar.
Palm.	Alacan.	Alacan.	Alacán.	Phún.	Alakhan.
Fist.	Mush.	Mush.	Mut.	Gawust.	Noturma.
Finger.	Barmac.	Besh-ewal.	Íngyakht.	Yángl.	Kar.
Nail.	Tirnac.	Tirmác.	Nisháwr.	Digar.	Khimsin.
Abdomen.	Cúsác.	Cúrsác.	Dawr.	Dor.	Gisán.
Groin.	Ticim.	Churáy.	Chabé.	Yoghut.	Chhawih.
Anus.	Kon.	Kon.	Zúm. Thúm.	Shin.	Kosheanac.
Penis.	Sik.	Kotác.	Ghúr. Zhúkh.	Pat.	Shodo.
Vagina.	Ám.	Hom.	Kís.	Kush.	Utugun.

English.	Yarkandi.	Kirghiz.	Sárigh Cúlí.	Wákhi.	Kalmác.
Testicle.	Kaka.	Tashac.	Safúl.	Sifúl.	Bíldigin.
Hip.	Sán.	Yánbásh.	Thúmzak.	Shunj.	Shujih.
Thigh.	Yotá.	Yotá.	Sán.	Bájlang.	Kohi.
Knee.	Tiz.	Tiza.	Zún.	Barin.	Twan.
Knee-cap.	T. lapiki.	T. Kozdí.	Z. topic.	Putyerch.	Öbtuc.
Leg.	Áyágh.	Páycha.	Lang.	Barikpád.	Khúl. Bulchic.
Calf.	Páchác.	Baltar-goshi.	L: gúkht.	B: gúsht.	Shílwá.
Ankle.	Topúc.	Ciziláshic.	Pezband.	Barikband.	Shakha.
Foot.	Phut.	Phut.	Pez.	Kaf-púdz.	Shir. Khúl.
Heel.	Tápán.	Sóghánchak.	Nabúrg.	Posht.	Usca.
Sole.	Ízángúlúk.	Tapán.	Tapán.	Myána-púdz.	Thawuc.
Toe.	Barmac.	Bánji.	Ingyakht.	Yangh-púdz.	Khúl-horo.
Heart.	Zhurak.	Yúrak.	Zord.	Puznv.	Zhúrkun.
Lung.	Ópká.	Ópká.	Súl.	Shosh.	Özhkih.
Stomach.	Cúsác.	Chemarchac.	Kéch.	Ward.	Gessin.
Intestine.	Úchay.	Úchay.	Rawd.	Shingar.	Úturgessin.
Liver.	Jigar.	Bághir.	Súd.	Jigar.	Elkin.
Kidney.	Borak.	Borak.	Árwits.	Waltik.	Búr.
Spleen.	Tihil.	Taláh.	Khyanz.	Sík-tahl.	Delun.
Bladder.	Dowusac.	Towarsac.	Patafsh.		Khál.
Skin.	Tera. Teya.	Téri.	Parkhaw.	Píst.	Ársan.
Hair.	Chach.	Chách.	Kshád.	Ríp.	Lásun.
Flesh.	At.	Yét. Gósh.	Gúkht.	Gusht.	Mákhan.
Fat.	Pash. Yágh.	Yagh.	Wást.	Roghn.	Semjin.
Blood.	Cán.	Can.	Wakhín.	Wakhín.	Tsúsun.
Bone.	Sóngak.	Sóngák.	Ustukhwán.	Yerch.	Yásan.
Brain.	Mingh.	Míya.	Maghz.	Maghz.	Ehkin.
Marrow.	Zhilik.	Yilik.	Mojg.	Sirk.	Chimigin.
Vein.	Tómur.	Tómur.	Rag.	Rag.	Shúrusun.
Tendon.	Páy.	Páy.	Páy.	Rag.	Súdusun.
Cartilage.	Cumurchac.	Chumurchac.	Kartísh.	Makh.	Múrusun.

English.	Yarkandi.	Kirghiz.	Sárigh Cúlí.	Wákhi.	Kalmác.
Dung.	Puk.	Phóc.	Ghás.	Gíh.	Básun.
Urine.	Súduc.	Sídic.	Mayj.	Mízk.	Shayasin.
Flatus.	Osrác.	Osrác.	Zág.	Gand.	Onganá.
Semen.	Mani.	Sharwut.	'Ushc.	Sháwat.	Nötuc.
Milk.	Sut.	Sut.	Kshawd.	Zharj.	Ussan.
Tears.	Yásh.	Yásh.	Yúkhk.	Yashk.	Núlumsun.
Saliva.	Tupuk.	Tukruk.	Shawól.	Túf.	Tukur.
Mucus.	Pótla.	Chimkirik.	Jaráhat.	Lishp.	Khan.
Snot.	Mishrik.	Yiring.	Ghét.	Kat.	Nosun.
Pus.	Chiring.	Yiring.	Ghánd.	Chirk.	Kölsun.
Body.	Badan.	Bóy.	Ustukhwán.	Tan.	Khún.
Pulse.	Tomur.	Tomur.	Ruwj.	Rag.	Sudus.
Gall.	Ót.	Ót.	Tirách.	Tilkha.	Thosun.
Gland.	Baz.	Baz.	Bez.	Tsiland.	Nor.
Yawn.	Asnak.	Esná.	Vizám.	Zito.	Ibshyána.
Belch.	Kekik.	Kekir.	Régh.	Bok.	Kekir.
Sob.	Zhighlán.	Zhighlán.	Naw.	Nyúj.	Ulná.
Pain.	Aghrí.	Agric.	Rízd.	Ríjd.	Obdná.
Fever.	Tap.	Tepma.	Tef.	Shondr.	Chichir.
Ague.	Bazgik.	Bazgik.	Andov.	Andav.	Chichir.
Smallpox.	Chichak.	Chichak.	Gúl.	Sprug.	Chichak.
Cough.	Yútil.	Yútal.	Kyakht.	Kokh.	Khanyána.
Catarrh.	Zukám.	Phutupti.	Yóng.	Zukám.	Thomo.
Palsy.	Shal.	Shal.	Shal.	Shal.	Khachudwá.
Madness.	Saranglik.	Saranglik.	Thayú.	Lív.	Karikta
Jaundice.	Sárghiyip.	Sárigh kasal.	Zird-parwen.	Zart.	Sharla-übduá.
Wound.	Zakhm.	Zakhm.	Zakhm.	Zakhm.	Sharkha.
Ulcer.	Yará.	Yará.	Yal.		
Pustule.	Yará.	Yará.	Jósh.		Butsuruc.
Ringworm.	Táz.	Táz.	Toz.	Taz.	Khojúgúr.
Itch.	Cichísh.	Kotur.	Zijokht.	Khárish.	Khámo.

English.	Yarkandi.	Kirghiz.	Sárígh Cúlí.	Wákhi.	Kalmác.
Abscess.	Chibán.	Chícán.	Tsílond.	Tsiland.	Tsakáchí.
Goitre.	Bucác.	Pucác.	Pukhák.	Zhighár.	Bolzúr.
Physician.	Yáchi.	Tawup.	Tabíb.	Tabíb.	Emchí.
Medicine.	Dawá.	Dáré.	Dore.	Dárú.	Em.
Cupping.	Shakhak.	Khartík.	Shaw.	Shaw.	Lonkha.
Ointment.	Malham.	Malham.	Malham.	Malham.	Túrukná.
Charm.	Túmár.	Túmár.	Túmár.	Túmár.	

Terms of relationship.

English.	Yarkandi.	Kirghiz.	Sárígh Cúlí.	Wákhi.	Kalmác.
Man.	Ádam.	Er-kishi.	Adám.	Khale.	Kún.
Woman.	Agháchi.	Mazlúm.	Mazlúm.	Känd.	Bawgá.
Husband.	Er Ar.	Er.	Chor-charsu.	Shohar.	Khúrgún.
Wife.	Khâtún.	Khâtún.	Ghuju.	Zan.	Ashchiend.
Father.	Atá. Dadá.	Atá.	Atá.	Tal.	Awa.
Mother.	Aná.	Aná.	Aná.	Nan.	Eji.
Son.	Oghal.	Oghul.	Púts.	Pútr.	Khúwun.
Daughter.	Ciz.	Ciz.	Eadzen.	Zághit.	Khúyukún.
Infant.	Bálá.	Bálá.	Tsegic.	Tsakaláy.	Ölúgata.
Boy.	Yásh-bálá.	Jigit. Yásh.	Zilik.	Zamân-kash.	Zálokún.
Girl.	Chaucán.	Aghachi.	Ghâts.	Zághit.	Gíjikta.
Brother.	Áká.	Áká.	Viód.	Varit.	Akha.
Sister.	Singl. Ácha.	Eja. Síngl.	Yakh.	Khúy.	Dú.
Grandfather.	Chong-dadá.	Chong-atá.	Bâb.	Páp.	Aw.
Grandmother.	Chong-aná.	Chong-aná.	Mâm.	Mâm.	Eji.
Grandchild.	Nawera.	Nawra.	Nabús.	Napús.	Túrul.
Uncle, paternal.	Tagháy.	Taghá.	Khâlak.	Búck.	
Aunt, paternal.	Dadá-áylisí.	Táyja.	Vits.	Váck.	
Uncle, maternal.	Aná-akásí.	Aná-akásí.	Dád-ámak.	Bµck.	
Aunt, maternal.	Aná-aylisi.	Aná-aylisi.	Víts.	Váck.	
Nephew.	Áká-bálásí.	Aká-bálási.	Pútish.	Kharyan.	Akha-khuwun.
Niece.	Áká-ciz-bálásí.	Aká-ciz-bálási.	Pátish.	Kharyún.	Dú-khúyukun.

English.	Yarkandi.	Kirghiz.	Sárigh Cúlí.	Wákhi.	Kalmác.
Cousin.	Jayn.	Jayn.	Khâr.	Ritsops.	
Step-father.	Úgay-dadá.	Ugay-átá.	Pídayj.	Tatayj.	
Step-mother.	Úgay-aná.	Ugay-aná.	Mâdayz.	Nanayj.	
Step-son.	Úgay-oghal.	Ugay-bálá.	Úgay-púts.	Pútrayj.	
Step-daughter.	Úgay-ciz.	Ugay-ciz-bálá.	Úgay-radzen.	Zághtirayj.	
Widow.	Tûl-khâtún.	Tul-khátún.	Be-chor.	Bewa-zan.	Khúrgunúgá.
Widower.	Tûl-ar.	Tul-er.	Beghíyn.	Bedok.	Báwga-úgá.
Orphan.	Yatím.	Yetim.	Yatím.	Saghír.	Önchun.
Brother's wife.	Yangí.	Yanga.	Kháyun.	Khúy.	Bergin.
Sister's husband.	Cúyoghal.	Yezda.	Khaserz.	Khasírdz.	Ákhá.
Wife's sister.	Cáyin-ághá.	Cáyin-ághá.	Kháyún.	Khúy.	Ayghachi.
Wife's brother.	Khátún-ákásí.	Khátún-ákási.	Khaserz.	Khasírdz.	Kúrghun-ághá.
Husband's brother.	Ar-ákási.	Er-ákási.	Kháyún.	Vurut.	Khádim-ákha.
Husband's sister.	Ar-singlisi.	Ácha.	Khaserz.	Khúy.	Kúkun-dú.
Kinsman.	Carindásh.	Carindásh.	Khaysh.	Khísh. Khódí.	Ákhanar.
Family.	Oewńc.	Oe-úrúzgar.	Parkhokh.	Kúkht.	Gar.
Ancestors.	Ulúgh-aulád.	Yati-pusht.	Thá-pukht.	Haft-pusht.	Túrul-tosur.
Tribe.	Úrúgh.	Úrúgh.	Úlús.	Caum.	Úlús.

Household furniture and domestic animals, &c.

English	Yarkandi	Kirghiz	Sárigh Cúlí	Wákhi	Kalmác
House.	Oe.	Oy.	Chéd.	Khón.	Gir. Ger.
Wall.	Tám.	Tam.	Díwâl.	Díwál.	Bashin.
Roof.	Toyus.	Torus.	Tàm.	Kut.	Torga.
Door.	Ishik.	Ishik.	Divér.	Bar.	Öydun.
Window.	Tongluk.	Túshc.	Rézn.	Rítz.	Zokhâ.
Chimney.	Múrá.	Túnduk.	Múrí.	Rítz.	Örká.
Hearth.	Koling.	Koling.	Kholing.	Díldong.	
Court.	Háwlí.	Háwli.	Kúchá.	Aghíl.	Khúra.
Steps.	Palampáya.	Palampáyá.	Palampáya.	Wakhar.	Shotta.
Ladder.	Shotá.	Shâti.	Shattá.	Wakhar.	Shotta.
Well.	Cudúc.	Cudúc.	Cudúc.	Zhòy. Ghóv.	Cudúc.

English.	Yarkandi.	Kirghiz.	Sárígh Cúlí.	Wákhi.	Kalmác.
Bucket.	Súghí.	Sòghá.	Súghò.		Solghá.
Rope.	Aghamchi.	Arkan.	Vúkh.	Shivan.	Arghamchi.
Broom.	Spúrgú.	Shpurga.	Vidír.	Drapich.	Shulwar.
Dust heap.	Pokluk.	Kich. Kigh.	Thig.	Thart.	Ótuk.
Horse.	Át.	Át.	Vorj.	Yash.	Murun.
Mare.	Bytál.	Biyá.	Várdz.	Madán.	
Colt.	Táy.	Tày.	Táć.	Toy.	
Filly.	Tshí-táy	Cúnán.	Stir-táć.	Toy.	
Mane.	Yál.	Yál.	Yál.	Yál.	Yál.
Tail.	Coyurúc.	Cúyuruc.	Thúm.	Bichkam.	Kirghasin.
Hoof.	Túwac.	Túwac.	Phút.	Sumb.	Cöl.
Dung.	Tizik.	Tizik.	Sorn.	Shúr.	Arghasin.
Stable.	Egil.	Ákhta-khána.	Akhor.	Wanar.	Gir.
Tether.	Ishkal.	Arkan.	Kashan.	Shivan.	Ishkal.
Halter.	Nukta.	Nukta.	Nukta.	Afsár.	Nukta.
Nose bag.	Túbra.	Tobra.	Tufra.	Tufra.	Tobra.
Clothing.	Jul.	Yápúc.	Jal.	Jul.	
Saddle.	Egir.	Égar.	Bithán.	Pazn.	Emal.
Bridle.	Zhúghán.	Júgán.	Tizgín.	Jilaw.	Tizgin.
Bit.	Jojay.	Jojay.	Vizán.	Ikhán.	Ghazar.
Stirrup.	Ízángo.	Uzanga.	Padbán.	Ríkáb.	Dúra.
Girth.	Tang.	Basmayil.	Trang.	Trang.	Ulang.
Saddle bag.	Talkandán	Yághaz.	Khurjin.	Kharjin.	Daling.
,, strap.	Canjughá.	Cánchoghá.	Canjughá.	Canchaghá.	Ghánjocá.
,, pack.	Múls.	Molá.	Tucóm.	Múlá.	Tokhum.
Whip.	Camchí.	Camchí.	Camchí.	Rushúp.	Mela.
Load.	Zhúk.	Yúk.	Vúr.	Vúr.	Baran.
Horse-shoe.	Tacca.	Tagha.	Na'l.	Na'l.	Takha.
Farrier.	Tacáchí.	Tagháchi.	Na'lband.	Na'lband.	Darkhán.
Nail.	Mekh.	Mik.	Mekh.	Mekh.	Mekh.
Hammer.	Bulka.	Bulka.	Bulka.	Boliká.	Bulka.

English.	Yarkandi.	Kirghiz.	Sárígh Cúlí.	Wákhi.	Kalmác.
Knife.	Sum-tarásh.	Chim-tarash.	Sam-tarásh.	Sum-tarásh.	Yómun.
Rasp.	Aykik.	Egáw.	Akak.		Tomur-shudun.
Forceps.	Ambúr.	Ambur.	Ambur.	Ambúr.	Shudun-abdú.
Bull.	Uy.	Búcá.	Werz.	Druksh.	Bukho.
Cow.	Inak.	Inak.	Zhaw.	Thú.	Okur.
Ox.	Ugoz.	Okúz.	Khej.	Khassi.	Okúz.
Calf.	Mozó.	Torpac.	Wishk.	Wúshk.	Tughul.
Steer.	Ghonájin.	Ghonajin.	Khajak.		Er-tughul.
Heifer.	Tishí-mozé.		Stir-wíshk.		
Yak ox.	Cotás.	Cotás.	Staur.	Zúg.	Cotás.
Cow dung.	Poc.	Zámpa.	Ghash.	Sigin.	Angasir.
,, ,, dry.	Tizik.	Huyl-zámpha	Koksut.	Sigini-kok.	Corá-angasir.
Cow stall.	Egil.	Kaila-khána.	Ghijed.	Pukht.	Cáshá.
Hoof.	Túwac.	Túyac.	Kshalgak.	Sumb.	Túwuk.
Horn.	Móngúz.	Múyúz.	Shaw.	Shaw.	Öwur.
Hide.	Teya.	Tera.	Past.	Pist.	Arsin.
Udder.	Bijik.	Jaylin.	Vistân.	Bap.	Elkin.
Teat.	Amchik.	Amchík.	Tej.	Tej.	Elkin.
Milk.	Sut.	Sut.	Shevd.	Zharj.	Ussun.
Cream.	Cáymágh.	Cáymác.	Marev.	Marík.	Ussun-tósun.
Curd.	Caytic.	Cátic.	Páyí.	Páy.	Caytic.
Whey.	Caytic-Súí.	Sárigh-sú.	Kshats.	Shop.	Shar-ussun.
Butter.	Muska.	Mashka.	Maskáw.	Maska.	Tosun.
,, milk.	Dógh.	Hyrán.	Mád.	Zígh.	Dógh.
,, boiled.	Yágh.	Yágh.	Ráwun.	Róghn.	Shara-tosun.
Cheese.	Panír.	Zúghrát.	Panír.	Panír.	—
,, dry.	Cúrút.	Cúrút.	Cúrút.	Cúrút.	Shúrmuc.
Cattle.	Kalla.	Arlash.	Kalaw.	Mál.	Ökur.
Grazier.	Pátachi.	Pádáchi.	Zhúbán.	Shpún.	Pátachi.
Goat, he.	Takka.	Takka.	Buch.	Buch.	Tikka.
,, she.	Ajkú.	Ejkú.	Vaz.	Tógh.	Yamán.

English.	Yarkandi.	Kirghiz.	Sárígh Cúlí.	Wákhi.	Kalmác.
Mat.	Bórá.	Borya.	Borya.		Kolsun.
Cornbin.	Sang. Ora.	Ora.	Zhév.	Ghóv.	Ora.
Clothes.	Egin.	Égin.	Lél.	Büt.	Debil.
Box.	Sandúc.	Sandúc.	Sandúc.	Sandúc.	Abdur.
Shirt.	Komlak.	Cóynac.	Yaktá.	Yaktá.	Kiyilik.
Trowsers.	Tambal.	Tambal.	Tambán.	Tambán.	Shalwur.
Frock.	Chapan.	Chapan.	Chapán.	Chakman.	Debil.
Coat.	Pejí.	Farají.	Galim.		Kurma.
Cloak.	Thón.	Thón.	Za.		
,, fur.	Juba.	Ichik.	Warbón.	Karist.	Naka-debil.
Cap.	Búc.	Thakíya.	Khawz.	Skíz.	Torsac.
,, fur.	Tilpac.	Tilpac.	Tumâkh.		
Turban.	Salla.	Salla.	Khawd.	Salla.	
Scarf.	Bel-bágh.	Bel-bágh.	Miyónd.	Miyân.	Böz.
Veil.	Chumbal.	Chumbal.	Chumbal.	Chíl.	
Glove.	Páylay.	Páylay.	Pélay.	Pilá.	Páylay.
Boot.	Ótak.	Ótuk.	Pyakh.	Shúshk.	Ghósun.
Shoe.	Kepish.	Kawsh.	Káfksh.	Kafsh.	Shágha.
Stocking.	Páypák.	Páypák.	Padber.	Juráb.	Páypác.
Sleeve.	Yang.	Yang.	Zuyl.	Durast.	Yang.
Collar.	Yáca.	Yáca.	Zharéj.	Ghirák.	Yakhá.
Skirt.	Utuk.	Itak.	Dâman.	Dáman.	Etak.
Pocket.	Coyinú.	Chóyntác.	Yánjuc.	Jíb.	Coyún.
Button.	Tughma.	Topchi.	Tóc.	Tak.	Topcha.
Bundle.	Buchcá.	Búccha.	Bagh.		Boccha.
Spectacles.	Kúzgi.	Kúz-áynak.	Áyinak.	Áyina.	Áynak.
Pen.	Calam.	Calam.	Calam.	Calam.	Calam.
Ink.	Siyáh.	Siyáh.	Siyáhí.	Siyáhí.	Siyáh.
Paper.	Kághaz.	Kághaz.	Kághaz.	Kághaz.	Yásan.
Knife.	Bichác.	Buchác.	Châgh.	Chácur.	Ótoghur.
Spoon.	Cáshuc.	Cáshuc.	Chíp.	Kapch.	Cáshuc.

(545)

English.	Yarkandi.	Kirghiz.	Sárígh Cúlí.	Wákhi.	Kalmác.
Ladle.	Kapgír.	Chómuch.	Kamích.		Shánaghur.
Bowl.	Jam.	Áyác.	Chanók.	Cuban.	Ághih.
Cup.	Kása.	Ním-kása.	Kora.	Pil.	Ídish.
Dish.	Tacsi.	Chara.	Tasch.		Chilápcha.
Platter.	Áyac.	Tuwac.	Tabac.		Táwac.
Tray.	Khwán.	Khwán.	Khwán.	Khwáncha.	
,, cloth.	Dastúrkhwán.	Dastarkhwán.			
Tea-pot.	Chógún.	Cháeghún.	Cháyghún.	Cháyjosh.	Chogún.
,, cup.	Chíní.	Chíní.	Chíní.	Chíní.	Chíní.
Cauldron.	Cazáu.	Cazghán.	Spindeg.	Deg.	Cazán.
Saucepan.	Deg.	Deg.	Deg.	Deg.	
Gugglet.	Iwyie.	Aptáwa.	Ibric.	Lót.	Kháwuc.
Jar.	Kyup.	Chilak.	Khyup.	Lót.	Sowulgho.
Candle.	Sham.	Sham.	Sham.	Sham.	Sham.
Lamp.	Chirágh.	Chirágh.	Tsiráw.	Chirágh.	Shumur.
Wick.	Philik.	Philik.	Philik.	Philik.	Ghól.
Oil.	Yágh.	Súyí-yághí.	Rawn.	Roghn.	Usun-tosun.
Flour.	Un.	Un.	Yawj.	Yúmj.	Ghoyur.
Salt.	Túz.	Túz.	Namázj.	Namak.	Dábsún.
Onion.	Piyáz.	Piyáz.	Piyáz.	Pyáz.	Mangasir.
Garlic.	Samsác.	Samsác.	Samsác.		Swan.
Sugar.	Shakir.	Shakar.	Nabát.	Cand.	
Honey.	Asal.	Asal.	Asal.		Asal.
,, bee.	Heya.	Hárí.	Harí.		Hera.
,, wax.	Mom.	Mom.	Mom.	Múm.	Básin-asal.
Bread.	Nán.	Nán.	Shpík.	Khách.	Borsak.
Biscuit.	Cúlcha.	Takich.	Takich.	Puták.	
Porridge.	Yárma.	Yárama.	Dalya.		Kucha.
Broth.	Shorbá.	Shorwá.	Sharwa.	Shurwá.	Sholun.
Stew.	Ásh.	Ásh.	Ásh.		Khotan.

The elements and words in connection

English.	Yarkandi.	Kirghiz.	Sárígh Cúlí.	Wákhí.	Kalmác.
Fire.	Át.	Ót.	Yúts.	Rakhníl.	Ghál.
Fuel.	Otán.	Ótun.	Zhiyz.	Ghoz.	Túlan.
Flame.	Ót-ulúgh.	Ót-úlugh.	Tsirókh.		Túlan-túla.
Smoke.	Dútún.	Tútún.	Thút.	Thít.	Útan.
Ashes.	Kuyl.	Kúl.	Thér.	Parg.	Kömsun.
Charcoal.	Kúmúr.	Komúr.	Rájúr.	Skorch.	Mursun.
Spark.	Úchkún.	Úchkún.	Úchghún.		
Fireplace.	Ucháe.	Túlghá.	Ucháe.	Dildong.	Tólghur.
Poker.	Cusay.	Cusaw.	Wakharej.		Modun.
Water.	Sú.	Sú.	Khats.	Yúpk.	Ussun.
Rain.	Yámghúr.	Yaghmúr.	Áwú.	Wúr.	Khur.
Snow.	Cár.	Cár.	Zamán.	Zam.	Sásun.
Ice.	Múz.	Múz.	Shto.	Ikh.	Mösun.
Hail.	Túlá.	Dólá.	Ware.		
Cloud.	Bulút.	Bulút.	Varm.	Mór.	Ólun. Loh.
Fog.	Damán.	Yotmán.	Bús.		Salkin.
Spring.	Bulác.	Bulác.	Búlac.	Chashma.	Buloe.
River.	Daryá.	Sú.	Daryá.	Zhiráv.	Kháydic.
Lake.	Kúyl.	Kól.	Kawl.		Ókun.
Marsh.	Láylúe.	Láylie.	Góz.		
Bog.	Shlampat.	Phátik.	Shartangáz.		Sháwir.
Quicksand.	Phatik-láy.	Phatkakh.	Khámreg.		Lá-shawir.
Canal.	Aric.	Eric.	Wád.	Joé.	Búkhá.
Aqueduct.	Ustang.	Ustang.	Waspóm.	Joe.	Tugh.
Ford.	Gechid.	Kechik.	Pang.	Guzar.	Kechik.
Bridge.	Cawrue.	Koprúk.	Kapruk.	Skárd.	Takhta.
Boat.	Guni.	Kama.	Kemá.		Kima.
Air.	Hawá.		Háwú.	Hawá.	Nárin.
Sky.	Asmán.	Asmán.	Asmán.	Ásmán.	Tengir.
Wind.	Shamál.	Shamál.	Shamál.	Damá.	Sálkin.

(547)

English.	Yarkandí.	Kirghíz.	Sárígh Cúlí.	Wákhí.	Kalmác.
Storm.	Búran.	Búran.	Buran.		Kháto-sálkín.
Thunder.	Gúldú.	Kúldú.	Tandúr.		Loh-dogarwá.
Lightning.	Chácchuc.	Chácchuc.	Wadáfz.		Cháculgho.
Sun.	Kúnash.	Gún.	Khér.	Yír.	Nár.
Moon.	Áyí.	Áy.	Mást.	Zamak.	Sár.
Star.	Yuidúz.	Yildúz.	Shturj.	Stár.	Yildúz.
Night.	Gíja.	Gíja.	Kshâb.	Naghd.	Soah.
Day.	Kúndúz.	Gúndúz.	Math.	Rawár.	Ódur.
Morning.	Artigan.	Arta.	Pigánas.	Sahár.	
Noon.	Yarim-kún.	Yarim-gún.	Mathawr.	Peshín.	
Evening.	Akhshám.	Akhshám.	Shâm.	Shâm.	
To-day.	Búgún.	Búgún.	Núr.	Uthg.	Óndur.
To-morrow.	Arta.	Erta.	Pigán.	Pígah.	Mangdur.
Day after to-mor-[row].	Ógúl.	Ógún.	Fál.	Tórt.	Nakódur.
Yesterday.	Túnugún.	Túnugún.	Ghadar.	Yaz. Tost.	Echkoldur.
Day before yester-[day].	Úlúshgún.	Úchgún.	Wadír.	Tort.	
Last night.	Túnugún gíja.		Biyawr.	Shabram.	
Week.	Hapta.	Hapta.	Hafta.	Jumá.	Náminódur.
Month.	Áyí.	Áy.	Mást.	Múy.	Sár.
Year.	Yíl.	Íl.	Sâl.	Sâl.	Yíl.
Summer.	Yáz.	Yáz.	Menj.	Tábistán.	Dolán.
Autumn.	Kúz.	Kúz.	Paydz.	Tirá-máh.	Kiytin.
Winter.	Cish.	Ciysh.	Zimistân.	Zamistán.	Mösun.
Spring.	Arta-yáz.	Bahár.	Wâgh.	Bahár.	Kháwir.
Sunshine.	Aptáb.	Gúnish.	Shilwá.	Yír. Pitáo.	Nárgharwá.
Shade.	Gúlga.	Kúlaka.	Sâyá.	Sáya.	Sadur.
Land.	Yar.	Yar.	Zamâd.	Zamín.	Gházir.
Earth.	Topa.	Topa.	Sith.	Shit.	Sháwur.
Dust.	Chang.	Chong.	Sitha-khorm.		Khúyun.
Mud, clay.	Láy. Saghaz.	Láy. Saghaz.	Shartangoz.	Khat.	Chátak.
Sand.	Cúm.	Cúm.	Shush.	Liwárch.	Elsin.

English.	Yarkandi.	Kirghiz.	Sárígh Cúlí.	Wákhi.	Kalmác.
Gravel.	Gúram.	Shaghil.	Reg.		Cholí-sháwur.
Mountain.	Tágh.	Táw.	Chapâk.	Koh.	Úla.
Stone.	Tásh.	Tásh.	Zhér.	Ghar.	Cholun.
Defile.	Tárlúc.	Tang-túr.	Tang.	Tang.	Jílga.
Hill pass.	Dawán. Àeba.	Dawán.	Dawán.	Kohtal.	
Cavern.	Ghár.	Úncúr.	Ghâr.	Sumukh. Sarv.	Núkun.
Plain.	Mydán.	Conush.	Mydân.	Mydán.	Taghashi.
Meadow.	Áylác. Jilga.	Jáyláw.	Wàkhk.	Áylác.	Gázir.
Desert.	Chol.	Chol.	Dàwkht.	Dasht.	Khoyura.
Plateau.	Pámir. Sáy.	Pámir. Sáy.	Jilga.	Mydán.	Gázir.
Ravine.	Yár.	Yor.	Parend.		Írgih.
Pit.	Azgal.	Chucúr.	Azgal.	Sarv.	Nyúkun.
Earthquake.	Yar-tabridí.	Yar-tabrídur.	Zmâd-junj.	Zalanjum.	Gázir-kodilná.
Gold.	Altún.	Áltún.	Tilá.	Tilá.	Áltún.
Silver.	Komush.	Gumush.	Nucrá.	Nucra.	Saghá-mongun.
Copper.	Mis.	Mis.	Mis.	Mis.	Zis.
Iron.	Tumúr.	Tumúr.	Spín.	Yísh.	Tomur.
Lead.	Cúrghashún.	Cúrghashún.	Cúrghashún.	Surb.	Khorgholjin.
Brass.	Túch.	Túch.	Biranj.		Curac.
Sulphur.	Gógurt.	Gogut.	Gogud.	Gogird.	Shataghúl.
Antimony.	Surma.	Surma.	Khalinj.		Suzma.

Arms and armour, &c.

English.	Yarkandi.	Kirghiz.	Sárígh Cúlí.	Wákhi.	Kalmác.
Sword.	Talwár.	Calich.	Mizj.	Khingar.	Ulda.
Dagger.	Khanjar.			Bihbúdí.	
Knife.	Bichác.	Buchác.	Chogh.	Shop.	Ortucá.
Shield.	Sipar.	Calcán.	Sipar.	Sipar.	
Spear.	Neza.	Neza.		Neza.	Jída.
Club.	Gholdú.	Chomác.	Ghaldú.	Asáy.	Táyac.
Stick.	Asá.	Hássa.	Hasul.		Mundú.
Musket.	Miltic.	Miltic.	Miltic.	Miltic.	Boh.

English.	Yarkandí.	Kírghiz.	Sárígh Cúlí.	Wákhí.	Kalmác.
Powder.	Dorú.	Darú.	Dârú.	Dárú.	Dárih.
Bullet.	Óc.	Óc.	Púth.	Wúch.	Sumun.
Shot.	Másha.	Chachma.	Másha.	Sáchma.	Khetih.
Bow.	Ócyá. Yáy.	Ócyá.	Kamának.		Sáduc.
Arrow.	Óc.	Col-oc.	K. Púth.		Sumun.
Waistbelt.	Bel-bagh.	Bel-wagh.	Kamar.	Kamar.	Bûs.
Armour.	Yarác.	Yarágh.	Yarágh.	Yarágh.	Boh-úldata.
Helmet.	Durulgha.	Duwulghá.	Dabalghá.		Dówulkha.
Army.	Lashkar.	Coshún.	Cúshúm.	Lashkar.	Cherik.
Soldier, Foot.	Piyáda.	Sarbáz.	Piyáda.	Sarbáz.	Yóghún.
„ Horse.	Atlúc.	Atlic.	Suwár.	Suwár.	Murun-omná.
Banner.	Byrac.	Togh.	Byrac.	Tógh.	Tóc.
Drum.	Dumbak.	Dáwúl.	Tabl. Dól.	Dól.	Dómbur.
Trumpet.	Carnáy.	Carnáy.	Narsing.		Bíwih.
Fort.	Corghán.	Cúrghán.	Cala'.	Cala'.	Shiwa.
Tower.	Pótay.	Burj.	Kangúra.	Tip-khána.	Bulung.
Trench.	Khandac.		Khandac.		
Mine.	Taship.		Lacam.		
Barricade.	Túman.	Bótay.	Chap.	Chip.	Póta.

Agricultural terms and products.

English.	Yarkandí.	Kírghiz.	Sárígh Cúlí.	Wákhí.	Kalmác.
Town.	Kand.	Kant.	Khâr.	Shahr.	Shanco.
Village.	Yaz.	Yiz.	Tirwach.	Diyár.	Ablí.
Farm.	Yúrt.	Yúrt.	Tayij.	Búna.	Thumun.
Plough.	Bucós.	Búcursún.	Spór.	Spóndr.	Andisin.
„ share.	Tísh.	Tish.	Tísh.	Kish.	A. Tomur.
„ yoke.	Bóyun-turuk.	Móyun-turuk.	Yúgh.	Saval.	Khamit.
Harrow.	Súram.	Malla.	Nimúthg.		Ílúr.
Spade.	Katman.	Ketman.	Bel.	Bíl.	Kurza.
Shovel.	Kujak.	Kurak.	Fay.		
Hoe.	Bel.	Bel.	Ranta.		

(550)

English.	Yarkandi.	Kirghiz.	Sárígh Oúlí.	Wákhi.	Kalmác.
Prong.	Kyáki.	Áyrí.	Skawn.	Achá.	Majir.
Pickaxe.	Chácush.	Châeuch.	Matayn.		Oyli.
Sickle.	Úrghôc.	Urghac.	Zorv.	Zutr.	Khadar.
Sieve.	Ghálbír.	Ghálbír.	Parwez.	Ghalbíl.	Sezih.
Field.	Tárla.	Cirá. Átiz.	Zemz.	Wundr.	Tagh.
Turf.	Chím.	Chim.	Chím.		Undusun.
Clod.	Kesak.	Chalma.	Khalg.		
Manure.	Akhlat.	Akhlat.	Bijayn.	Thart.	Topo.
Seed.	Tukhm.	Urúgh.	Téghm.	Tukhm.	Ekin.
Stack.	Challa. Anju.	Kúp. Charkop.	Indíst.	Túdá.	Thaptsi.
Sheaf.	Bagh.	Birbagh.	Bogh.	Bâgh.	Bâduk.
Heap.	Dong.	Chach.	Song.		Tsárih.
Corn.	Bughz.	Áshlik.	Ghalla.	Zhaw.	Abba.
Wheat.	Bughdáy.	Bughdáy.	Zhandám.	Ghadún.	Chagún-taran.
Barley.	Arpa.	Arpa.	Chushch.	Yúrc.	Árawá.
Maize.	Conác.	Conác.	Conác.	Conác.	Erdnishish.
Millet.	Terik.	Tarik.	Júárí.		Khorúsuk.
Rice.	Shál.	Shál.	Shál.		Toturgha-ish.
„ grain.	Gúrúch.	Gúrunj.	Girinj.		Toturgha.
„ straw.	Palálí.	Palál.	Pakhál.		Samán.
Corn straw.	Samán.	Samán.	Wúkh.	Wush.	Samán.
Carrot.	Zardak.		Zardak.		Táwún.
Turnip.	Chamgúr.		Shám.		Lo-ung.
Cabbage.	Chilang.		Lahana.		Bísáy.
Radish.	Turup.		Turb.		Aysa.
Pumpkin.	Kapak.		Cábá.		Khábuk.
Cucumber.	Congan.				Gho.
Lucerne.	Yúrushca.	— tháb?	Beda (dry).	Ozhirk.	Ômsun.
Mustard.	Cachí.	Zághún.	Zárghún.		Shartúsun.
Hemp.	Kandír.		Kántír.		
Flax.	Zighir.		Zighir.		Tosun-tarán.
Cotton.	Kiwaz.	Kewaz.	Kawaz.		Kobun-mudun.

English.	Yarkandi.	Kirghiz.	Sárígh Cúlí.	Wákhi.	Kalmác.
Cotton seed.	Chigit.	Chighit.	Chigit.		K. Orghusun.
,, wool.	Pakhta.	Pakhta.	Pakhta.		Kobun.
Tree.	Darakht.	Darakht.	Darakht.	Darakht.	Modun.
Wood.	Aghaj.	Yagbách.	Shúng.	Ghoz.	Modun.
Branch.	Shakh.	Shakh.	Shákh.	Shalkh.	M. Úrsun.
Leaf.	Yaprác.	Yaprác.	Park.	Parch.	Bichir.
Flower.	Gul.	Chichak.	Gul.	Spraw.	Chichak.
Fruit.	Yamish.	Úrúgh.	Mewa.	Mewa.	Úrúsun.
Root.	Zhildiz.	Yildiz.	Yíldíz.	Bekh.	Úngun.
Stem.	Phutak.	Dumur.	Kunda.		Budun.
Basket.	Súwat.	Siwat.	Tsamúgh.	Wargasht.	Sawik.
Vine.	Tál.	Tál.	Tál.	Raz.	Ustá-mudun.
Grape.	Úzúm.	Uzúm.	Uzúm.	Angúr.	Ustá.
Mulberry.	Úzhma.	Uzhma.	Uzhma.		Juzum.
Æleagnus.	Jigda.	Jigda.	Jigda.		Zigda.
Jujube.	Chílán.		Chílán.		Chiwkhih.
Apple.	Almá.	Almá.	Mán.	Múr.	Almín.
Pear.	Ármút.	Ámút.	Armút.		Nashwáti.
Quince.	Biya.		Biya.		
Peach.	Shaptal.		Shaftálú.		Shaptal.
Plum.	Uruk.	Arik.	Khubáni.		Uruk.
Apricot.	Ólja.		Nósh.		
Pomegranate.	Ánár.		Anár.		Ánár.
Almond.	Bádám.	Bádám.	Bádám.	Bádám.	Bádám.
Walnut.	Yangak.	Yánghak.	Ghawz.		Yangak.
Fig.	Anjír.		Anjír.		
Thorn.	Tikan.		Shuz.	Zakh.	Chighric.
Bark.	Cóbzac.	Cawzac.	Capizók.	Píst.	Khálsin.
Gum.	Zhilim.	Yilim.	Yelim.		Zusun.
Grass.	Ót.	Ót.	Wókh.	Wukh. Sawz.	Ömsun.
Reed.	Comush. Chigh.	Comush. Chigh.	Cámish.	Chigh.	Khamsh.

Birds, beasts, and insects.

English.	Yarkandi.	Kirghiz.	Sárígh Cúlí.	Wákhi.	Kalmác.
Bird.	Cúchcách.	Cúchcách.	Tókhú.	Parinda.	Shobung.
Net.	Tor.	Tor.	Tor.		Khapkhak.
Noose.	Kildak.		Zomj.		Kiltak.
Trap.	Tozak.		Tozak.		
Eagle.	Búrghút.	Cosh. Cúsh.	Khutsúvd.		Burgút.
Hawk.	Láchín.	Láchín.	Láchín.		Lechin.
Magpie.	Saghizghan.				
Tiger.	Yolbárs.	Yolwas.	Yolbárs.		Bár.
Leopard.	Kaplán.	Kaflán.			Molun.
Wolf.	Búrí.	Búrí.	Khíthp.	Shapt.	Chhoná.
Lynx.	Súlesun.				Súlesun.
Fox.	Túlkí.		Raps.	Nakhchír.	Arátí.
Bear.	Arik.	Ayik.	Yurkh.	Naghardúm.	Ayun.
Otter.	Cáma.		Sangláví.		Kháma.
Antelope.	Jayrán.	Kiyik.	Jayrán.		Cuyosun.
Stag, male	Búghú.	Búghú.	Búghú.	Gáwaz.	Búghá.
,, female	Marál.	Marál.			Marál.
Wild goat, male	Takka.	Takka.	Yakh.	Yuksh.	Ghorásun.
,, female				Marg.	
Wild sheep, male	Ghúlja.	Ghúlja.	Raós.	Rúsh. War.	Ghúlja.
,, female			Vírokh.	Máy.	Akár.
Hare.	Táoshcán.	Toshcán.	Khktûm.	Súyí.	Túla.
Pig.	Tonguz.	Tonguz.	Khawg.	Khúg.	Ghákha.
Hedgehog.	Khirpá.		Khûrpí.		Zara.
Fish.	Balic.	Balic.	Máhí.	Máhí.	Yágbsin.

Trades and implements.

Carpenter.	Yagháchcni.		Chúbtarásh.	Ustáz.	Modunchí.
Hammer.	Bolki.	Bulka.	Bulka.	Kheyash.	Polkha.
Adze.	Cayúkí.		Wazhák.	Úzhák.	Olíh.

(553)

English.	Yarkandi.	Kirghiz.	Sárígh Cúlí.	Wákhi.	Kalmác.
Chisel.	Calam.		Nal-khán.		Calam.
Saw.	Ara.		Ará.		Hárih.
Plane.	Randa.		Randa.		
Awl.	Úshki.	Uchka.	Barma.	Barma.	Ushka.
Nail.	Mekh.	Mekh.	Makh.	Mekh.	Kázak.
Wedge.	Pána.		Fána.		Phána.
File.	Sohán.	Ekak.	Akak.		Curch.
Forceps.	Ambúr.	Ambúr.	Ambúr.	Ambúr.	
Mason.	Tamchi.		Díwálchí.	Díwálband.	
Lime.	Ahak.		Borkhák.		
Brick.	Khisht.		Karpích.	Khisht.	
Trowel.	Andawa.		Andawa.		
Ironsmith.	Túmurchí.	Túmurchí.	Ahangar.	Ústáz.	Dárkhán.
Forge.	Uchác.		Dukán.	Dukán.	Túlgui.
Bellows.	Coruc.	Korak.	Sanách.	Dam.	Korak.
Anvil.	Sandal.	Sandán.	Sandán.	Pulk.	Yakin.
Hammer.	Bazghan.		Bazghan.	Kheyisk.	Alkha.
Tongs.	Lakchagir.	Kiskach.	Lakshagir.	Lakchagir.	Chimkur.
Hone.	Bilay.	Biláw.	Pisán.	Pisán.	Búloh.
Grindstone.	Charkh.	Chác.	Chàrkh.	Charkh.	Chác.
Goldsmith.	Zargar.		Zargar.		
Ring.	Yuzak.	Yuzak.	Kachawí.	Pilangasht.	Möhr.
Seal.	Muhr.		Mehr.	Mohr.	
Bracelet.	Belázúk.	Bilazúk.	Parthust.		Boghú.
Weaver.	Khámbáp.		Wiftchoz.	Báfinda.	Böz-yásachi.
Tailor.	Sypúng.		Syfung.		Nyúdn-kún.
Thread.	Zhiyip.	Iyip.	Pitigh.	Zhútr. Tond.	Uchusun.
Cord.	Shoyina.		Padeta.		
Scissors.	Cáychí.	Cáychí.	Cáychí.	Cáychí.	Cáychi.
Thimble.	Oymac.	Oymac.	Oymác.		Oymac.
Needle.	Zhangna.		Sídz.	Síts.	Zún.

(554)

English.	Yarkandi.	Kirghiz.	Sárígh Cúlí.	Wákhi.	Kalmác.
Cobbler.	Otakchi.	Otakchi.	Kafkh-insuvj.	Shushk-ustáz.	Ghosunchi.
Knife.	Randí.		Charmbúr.	Kăzh.	Bel.
Awl.	Bighiz.		Tsorz.	Sarz.	Showugú.
Tanner.	Kwánchí.	Kwánchí.	Charmchí.		
Hide.	Teya.	Tera.	Past.	Píst.	Arsun.
Leather.	Cham.	Kwán.	Charm.	Mandítk.	Bolsun-arsun.
Dyer.	Boyakchi.		Rangchí.		Bodukchi.
Colour.	Boyak.	Boyak.	Rang.	Rang.	Boduk.
Barber.	Sátirach.	Sátirach.	Hajámatchi.	Sartarásh.	Usun-ábda-kún.
Razor.	Ustura.		Pákí.	Tegh.	Tóngúrac.
Strop.	Pásmal.	Tásmal.	Pisán.	Pisán.	Búloh.
Mirror.	Áynak.	Kúzgú.	Áynak.	Aynak.	Nyúr.
Miller.	Dagarmánchí.	Tagarmánchi.	Khadorjchí.	Asyáwán.	Teyirmachí.
Hand mill.	Yághachak.	Yaghachak.	Yárghachâc.	Dosdos.	Yághúchak.
Water „	Dagarman.	Tigirman.	Khadorj.	Khazarg.	Teyirma.
Sack.	Taghár.	Khalta.	Ghawn.	Zotsk.	Ótih.
Baker.	Nánwáy.	Náwáy.	Nánwáí.		Borsakchi.
Oven.	Tanúr.	Tándur.	Tanúr.	Dildong.	Abdor.
Yeast.	Zowuli.	Zowala.	Khámír.	Khamír.	Komach.
Kneading.	Zhúghur.	Yúghúr.	Mut-thá.	Khistá.	
„ trough.	Tánglí.	Tángla.	Khokh.	Pitkharim.	Tabashi.
Butcher.	Cassáb.		Cassáb.		Makhánchi.
Hatchet.	Pálta.	Pálta.	Baldá.	Tapár.	Tsokih.
Knife.	Bíchác.	Buchác.	Wazhác.		Otughúr.
Hook.	Cámac.	Changal.	Changul.		Cháymac.
Marriage.	Khátún-álmac.	Khátun-álmac.	Kat-khudáí.	Kat-khudáí.	Babaghay-amna.
„ feast.	Tóé.	Toy.	Tây.	Tóyit.	Gechil.
Betrothal.	Aghaz-baghlandí.	Fátiha-cilishtí.	Ráymál-bastí.	Kudáí.	
Bride.	Gelinjik.	Kelin.	Nawánz.	Stakh Bidganz.	Kelin.
Bridegroom.	Kúyáw.	Kúyáw.	Khání.	Sháhmard.	
Bridal party.	Toychi.	Toychi.	Kh-Samagh.	Toyáw.	

(555)

English.	Yarkandi.	Kirghiz.	Sárígh Cúlí.	Wákhi.	Kalmác.
Dowry.	Mahr.	Mahr.	Cáling.	Kirpa.	Cayling.
Music.	Naghma.	Naghma.	Naghma.	Báyd.	Tápshur.
Musician.	Naghmáchí.	Naghmachi.	Naghmachi.	Báydgóe.	Dáludu-kún.
Pipe.	Balaman.	Cháwr.	Taráy.	Surnáy.	Náy.
Drum.	Daff.	Daff.	Doff.	Dárya.	Dúng.

Adjectives.

English.	Yarkandi.	Kirghiz.	Sárígh Cúlí.	Wákhi.	Kalmác.
Large.	Chóng.		Lawr.	Lúp.	Ishkí.
Small.	Kichik.		Zilík.	Tskhaláy.	Pichkán.
Little.	Az.		Kam. Zuyl.	Kam.	Bagha.
Much.	Tola. Jic.	Kop, yoghán.	Húch. Púr.	Ghafch. Tkhí.	Bödun.
Heavy.	Aghir.		Girán.	Gurong.	Khundu.
Light.	Yanik.		Rindz.	Ranjk.	Gegin.
Thick.	Yúghan.		Divez.	Báj.	Bödun.
Thin.	Yangiski.		Tanúk.	Suár.	Nerkhin.
Broad.	Kyang.		Kshâdz.	Kusház.	Aynta.
Narrow.	Tár.		Tong.	Tang.	Nerkhin.
Loose.	Kyangrá.		Kshâdz.	Kusház.	Buchkhuk.
Tight.	Tárlúc.		Tong.	Tang.	Khánsun.
Long.	Uzún.		Darâz.	Varz.	Utá.
Short.	Kiská.		Kût.	Kat.	Akhir.
Open.	Achik.		Hat.	Hat.	Tarla.
Shut.	Yapighlak.		Chúst.	Gaw.	Burka.
Light.	Yoruc.	Yúrúng.	Rokhân.	Rashán.	Nárda.
Dark.	Carángo.		Kkhab.	Tárík.	Carángo.
Fast.	Zhildam.		Jald.	Jald.	Changdí.
Slow.	Gáhil.		Ahista.	Ästa.	Arghól.
Strong.	Cúchlúk.		Cúchín.	Zor.	Búcá.
Weak.	Cúchsiz.		Be-cúch.	Sust.	Cúchúgá.
Bitter.	Achchic.		Tsiyikh.	Talkh.	Cáshung.
Sweet.	Tátlúk.		Khiyig.	Khúzhg.	Amtákhin.

English.	Yarkandi.	Kirghiz.	Sárígh Cúlí.	Wákhi.	Kalmác.
Sour.	Achigh.		Tukhshp.	Turushp.	Gáshung.
Insipid.	Mazasyoc.		Be-Maza.	Trachk.	Amtunúga.
Rough.	Kotár.		Shâgh.	Shagh.	Kháto.
Smooth.	Sillik.		Pàthm.	Palam.	Sákhin.
Hard.	Cattic.		Teyáng.	Shagh.	Kháto.
Soft.	Yamúshac.		Shilét.	Palam.	Yolaghún.
Hot.	Issic.		Thiyúm.	Thín.	Khálún.
Cold.	Soghúc.		Shtó.	Súr.	Caytin.
Far.	Uzác.	Zhirác.	Thár.	Thír.	Kholá.
Near.	Yacin.	Yacín.	Nizd.	Shíkh.	Orkhun.
Rich.	Ziyátdár.	Báy.	Boy.	Daulatmand.	Báyin.
Poor.	Námyat.	Námurád.	Gadáy.	Shúm.	Uywata.
Dry.	Cúrúc.		Zyakhch.	Wusk.	Khoyrá.
Wet.	Húyl.		Khast.	Kháych.	Chikta.
Old.	Askí.		Kehna.	Kohna.	Khochun.
New.	Yángí		Núj	Shaghd.	Shina.
Aged.	Cúja.	Cárí.	Púr.	Khyár.	Kokshun.
Young.	Ganj. Yásh.	Yásh.	Júwan.	Juwán.	Zálo.
Blind.	Carágo.		Kawr.	Kor.	Tsokúr.
Lame.	Tocá.		Long.	Lang.	Dogolang.
Deaf.	Sághirgo.		Chún.	Kar.	Chikin-kháto.
Dumb.	Gacha.		Be-zív.	Gol.	Tilinúgá.
Hungry.	Aj.		Marzâng.	Marz.	Ölsuwá.
Thirsty.	Ussuz.		Túr.	Takh.	Undáswá.
Good.	Yakhshí.		Chárj.	Baf.	Sayin.
Bad.	Yamán.		Thít	Shak.	Moh.
Pretty.	Chiráylic.		Khúshrúé.	Khúshrúé.	Targhin.
Ugly.	Cokhluc.	Sahat.	Bad-súrat.	Badrúé.	Ätisin.
Fat.	Simiz.		Farbih.	Baj.	Carana.
Lean.	Oruc.		Kharâb.	Kharâb.	Kháto.
Brave.	Zhuraklú.	Bátor.	Zahráyin.	Pazívdár.	Búcá.

English.	Yarkandi.	Kirghiz.	Sárigh Cúlí.	Wákhi.	Kalmác.
Timid.	Corcác.	Corcunjác.	Be-zahrá.	Bepazív.	Aydú.
False.	Yalghán.		Fánd.	Darogh.	Khudul.
True.	Toghrú.		Rást.	Rást.	Unar.
Wild.	Yabán.	Yáwa.	Yawá.	Jangali.	Gházir-yopsun.
Tame.	Bakkan.	Cóngan.	Yakhtí.	Yokhtí.	Ger-wersun.
Straight.	Túz.	Toghrá.	Khayz.	Rást.	Tuz.
Crooked.	Agrú.		Cherz.	Kard.	Donây.
Naked.	Yalánghách.	Yúpúdak.	Chalandak.	Shilakh.	Nusugun.
Covered.	Yapighlac.		Lelin.	Batdár.	Debiltú.
Well.	A'bdan. Ságh.		Táza.	Taza.	Khochun.
Ill.	Aghric.		Bímár.	Bimár.	Khochunúga.
Nice.	A'bdan.		Chárj.	Baf.	Sáyin.
Nasty.	Yamán.		Thít.	Shak.	Moh.
Full.	Dolú.		Púr.	Takí.	Dúrún.
Empty.	Bósh.		Khálí.	Khálí.	Bacar.
Ripe.	Pishik.		Pyakhch.	Pasítk.	Bolsun.
Raw.	Khám.		Khâm.	Khám.	Túkáy.
Right.	Ong. Ságh.		Kháyz.	Rást.	Bárún.
Left.	Sól.		Chap.	Chap.	Zún.
Easy.	Ongáy.	Coláy.	Asán.	Asán.	Gigin.
Difficult.	Mushkil.	Tás.	Killá.	Mushkil	Bolkhish.
Clean.	Tamíz.	Erak.	Pák.	Pák.	Chiwar.
Dirty.	Kirlú.	Kirlú.	Nápák.	Nápák.	Kir.
Like.	Ocshash.	Tang.	Hamrang.	Kifchk.	Kádlih.
Different.	Bushka.	Bulak.	Jíthá.	Juzá.	Öngdan.
Dead.	Olak.	Ulaptor.	Mawgjanj.	Murda.	Ukuwá.
Alive.	Tirik.	Tirik.	Zinda.	Zindá.	Amda.
Black.	Cará.		Tor.	Shú.	Khárá.
White.	Ac.		Spéd.	Rokh.	Chagán.
Blue.	Kok.	Kúk.	Shayn.	Sawz.	Kok.
Yellow.	Sárigh.	Saric.	Zird	Zart.	Shara.

(558)

English.	Yarkandi.	Kirghiz.	Sárígh Cúlí.	Wákhi.	Kalmác.
Green.	Yeshil		Sawuz.	Jigari.	Noghán.
Red.	Cizil.		Rusht.	Sukr.	Ulán.
Male.	Arkak.	Er.	Ner.	Ghash.	Erih.
Female.	Dishi.	Tishí.	Stír.	Mâch.	Kokun.
Barren.	Majas.		Nazáyd.	Strínd.	Torakhish.
Fertile.	Kúchlúk.		Zádichoz.	Ghafch.	Kuchtá.
Deep.	Chúcúr.		Kars.	Gilits.	Ukun.
Erect.	Orá		Warúfj.	Tsuk.	Bússú.
Prostrate.	Yatá.		Wâkhch.	Waksht.	Unta.

Adverbs, Prepositions, &c.

English	Yarkandi	Kirghiz	Sárígh Cúlí	Wákhi	Kalmác
Above.	Óst.	Ost.	Chiter.	Uch.	Dayra.
Below.	Alt.	Alt.	Báber.	Past.	Dora.
Over.	Topúst.	Âstún.	Ter.		Derkí.
Under.	Túwan.	Túwan.	Post.		Dorkí.
Before.	Elgarí.	Aldí.	Pród.	Turpurut.	Ómna.
Behind.	Keyin.	Kötí.	Zabo.	Tarsibas.	Arda.
Inside.	Ichkiri.	Ichí.	Darún.	Pakhân.	Dokhturi.
Outside.	Táshkiri.	Tarlá.	Vách.	Tarbáhr.	Gházirso.
Here.	Búradá.	Shúyar.	Úm.	Daram.	Ándi.
There.	Óradá.	Oyar.	Awd.	Daráh.	Tändi.
Now.	Amdí.	Helí.	Shich.	Hanív.	Óda.
Then.	Yana.	Yana.	Tam. Zabó.	Sibas.	Ayir.
Again.	Yana-bir.	Yana-bir.	Wâz.	Wáz. Sibas.	Basa.
Never.	Asla-yóc.	Síra-yoc.	Tagná.	Bat.	Tung-úgá.
With.	Bilan.	Bela.	Kati.		Khâmdan.
For.	Úchún.	Úchún.	Aván.		Kichí.
All.	Hama.	Hamasi.	Jam.	Kakht.	Sughár.
None.	Hech-yóc.	Yóc.	Tag.	Hech.	Tungúga.
Whole.	Phútun.	Butún.	Durust.	Durust.	Budun.
Alone.	Yalghúz.	Yálghoz.	Îwj.	Wír.	Kangsárin.

English.	Yarkandi.	Kirghiz.	Sárígh Cúlí.	Wákhi.	Kalmác.
Without.	Amas. Siz.	Emas.	Be.	Be.	Ugá.
Amidst.	Arista.	Arási.	Mazán.	Myán.	Dongdur.
Always.	Hamesh.		Hamesha.	Harwár.	Odúr.
Another.	Bashca.	Bashka.	Dígar.	Digar.	Óngdan.
Different.	Belak.	Bulak.	Balak.	Jizá.	Tásrikáy.
Anything.	Birnamá.	Birnahmá.	Chíz.	Chíz.	Yumun.
Any one.	Birkishi.	Birkishi.	Khalc.	Koí.	Gún. Kún.
Some one.	Birkím.	Birkim.	Íkhalc.	Koí.	
No one.	Hechkimyoc.	Hechyóc.	Hechchíz.	Hechchíz.	Túngúgá.
Where?	Nayargá.	Nayaga.	Kúját.	Tarkúm.	Kharódná.
When?	Cachán.	Cánch.	Tsa-wact.	Tsi-wakht.	Khámá.
What?	Namá.	Nahmá.	Tsa-rang. Tsay.	Tsa-rangat.	Yámir.
How?	Cáydágh.	Caydagh.	Tsa-rang.	Tsa-rangat	Yámír.
Which?	Kim.	Kimasa.	Chidám.	Ko. Tsa.	Endí.
How much?	Nacha.	Nachí.	Tsóndik.	Tsómur.	Barakhta.
Thus much.	Shú-cadar.	Shú-cadar.	Dón.	Hatúm.	Kétih.
Why?	Nameshka.	Namíshga.	Tsyzir.	Chízar.	Yónúchúr.
Sometimes.	Birbira.	Bira-bira.	Égán-egán.	Kam-kam.	Ayár-ayár.
Seldom.	Biraz-biraz.	Biyaz.	Iw-iw.	Yúhóná.	Nijághát.
This way.	Shúndágh.	Múndagh.	Yámdás.	Taram.	Enibida.
That way.	Andágh.	Óldagh.	Yúdes.	Tarat.	Teríbida.
Both.	Izhkí.	Yikí.	Thaw.	Kifch.	Khóyúr.
Gratis.	Mut.		Muft.	Muft.	Bakar.
Often.	Tola-wact.	Jic-wact.	Húch-wact.	Ghafch.	Ishkí.
Formerly.	Báldí.	Burún.	Pród.	Parut.	Gizána.
Behold!	Cál.	Bác.	Chás.	Dírig.	Uzá.
Begone!	Get.	Ket.	Tez.	Ruch.	Yowá.
So be it!	Olsún.	Bolsún.	Hálda.	Nívhald.	Bolwá.
All hail!	Hármislar.	Hármáng.	Damdárata.	Damdárata.	Amarbantá.
Welcome!	Khúsh-kelding.	Khosh-kelding.	Khúshámadi.	Khúshámadí.	Sam-bolwá.
Farewell!	Yol-bolsún.	Yol-bolsún.	Khyr-bâr.	Ruch-bár.	Sambá.

English.	Yarkandi.	Kirghiz.	Sárígh Cúlí.	Wákhi.	Kalmác.
Eh!	Ha. Na.	Na.	Ha.	Hán.	Hán.
Hush!	Shuc.	Shuc.	Shóv.	Shov.	Tung-pichkí.
Yes.	Ót.	Ót.	Háhan.	Ho.	Jyá.
No.	Yóc.	Yac.	Náy.	Nay.	Ugá.
Must be.	Gark.	Garak.	Lázim.	Lázim.	Kirak.
Quickly.	Zhildam.	Zhildam.	Jald.	Jald.	Khúrdúng.
Slowly.	Yawásh.	Yávash.	Ahista.	Asta.	Arghól.
Suddenly.	Andawda.	Patrác.	Be-khalá.	Nágahán.	Ónuwá.

Numerals.

English.	Yarkandi.	Kirghiz.	Sárígh Cúlí.	Wákhi.	Kalmác.
One.	Bir.		Íw.	Iw.	Negin.
Two.	Izhki.		Tháw.	Boí.	Khoyúr.
Three.	Úch.		Haráy.	Troi.	Corghún.
Four.	Dort.		Tsavor.	Tsibúr.	Dorwun.
Five.	Besh.		Pinz.	Panz.	Tháwun.
Six.	Altí.		Khél.	Shaz.	Zúrgún.
Seven.	Yattí.		Uvd.	Húv.	Dólan.
Eight.	Sikiz.		Wókht.	Hat.	Náhaman.
Nine.	Tocuz.	Tocuz.	Néo.	Náw.	Yissin.
Ten.	On.		Théth.	Thas.	Arwún.
Eleven.	On bir.		Thethat í.	Thas-iw.	A : negin.
Twelve.	On izhkí.		Thetha-thá.	Thas-boí.	A : khóyúr.
Thirteen.	On úch.	Same as Yarkandi.	Th : haráy.	Thas-troí.	A : corghún.
Fourteen.	On dort.		Th : tsavor.	Th-tsibúr.	A : dorwun.
Fifteen.	On besh.		Th : pinz.	Th-panz.	A : tháwun.
Sixteen.	On áltí.		Th : khél.	Th-shaz.	A : zúrgún.
Seventeen.	On yattí.		Th : úvd.	Th-húv.	A : dólan.
Eighteen.	On sikiz.		Th : wókht.	Th : hat.	A : náhaman.
Nineteen.	On tocuz.	On-tocuz.	Th : néo.	Th-náw.	A : yissin.
Twenty.	Zhigirmi.		Wíst.	Bíst.	Khorun.
Twenty-one.	Zhigirmi-bir.		Wístat í.	Bíst-yak.	K : negin.

English.	Yarkandi.	Kirghiz.	Sárígh Cúlí.	Wákhi.	Kalmác.
Twenty-two.	Zh-izhki.		Wista-thá.	Bísto-boi.	K: khoyúr.
Thirty.	Otuz.		Sí.	Sí.	Cochun.
Thirty-one.	Otuz bir.		Síyat-í.	Sío-í.	C: negin.
Forty.	Circ.		Chahl.	Bo-wíst.	Dochun.
Fifty.	Ellik.		Pinjáh.	Bowísto-thas.	Thewin.
Sixty.	Altmish.		Atmish.	Trowíst.	Jirin.
Seventy.	Yatmish.		Yatmish.	Trowísto-thas.	Dâlun.
Eighty.	Siksán.		Saksan.	Tsibúr-wíst.	Nayun.
Ninety.	Tocsán.		Tocsan.	Tsibúr-wísto-thas.	Yerin.
Hundred.	Yúz.		Sad.	Panz-wíst. Sad.	Zon.
Thousand.	Ming.		Hazár.	Házer.	Mingan.

Directions for pronunciation of the vowels and certain consonants in the above vocabularies.

a	is pronounced as in	*woman.*		u	is pronounced as in	*put.*
a	,,	,,	,, *far.*	ú	,,	,,	,, *rule.*
à	,,	,,	,, *halt.*	û	,,	,,	,, *use.*
ä	,,	,,	,, *care, hare.*	aw	,,	,,	as *ou* in *house.*
ay	,,	,,	,, *day.*	áw	,,	,,	the same prolonged.
áy	,,	,,	,, *aye, aisle.*	t	,,	,,	hard and aspirated.
áy	,,	,,	,, *toy, boy.*	* th	,,	,,	hard and aspirated; each letter pronounced separately.
e	,,	,,	as *a* in *cane, hale.*	th	,,	,,	as in *those.*
ó	,,	,,	as in *tête.*	ph	,,	,,	aspirated, and each letter separately pronounced.
i	,,	,,	,, *pin.*	† kh	,,	,,	ditto. ditto.
í	,,	,,	as *ee* in *teeth.*	c	,,	,,	always hard as in *cart.*
o	,,	,,	as in *top.*	zh	,,	,,	as *j* in "*jour.*"
ó	,,	,,	,, *told.*				
ö	,,	,,	,, "*œuf.*"				

* NOTE.—This double letter is only in the Yarkandi column.
† NOTE.—This double letter is mostly in the Kalmác column.

(Sd.)   H. W. BELLEW.

VOCABULARY

OF

SIRIKOL, WAKHAN, AND KUNJOOT DIALECTS,

BY

CAPTAIN J. BIDDULPH.

The following Vocabulary was compiled during our trip to Sirikol and Wakhan.

The spelling is phonetic. The Sirikolee and Wakhee, however, contain sounds which it is impossible to render exactly in English, and much resembling sounds common in Gaelic.

	Sirikolee.	*Wakhee.*	*Kunjootee.*
Apple.	Maun.	More.	
Arm.	Yaran, Cherast.	Fekh, Yurum.	Ushuk.
Armpit.	Kultuk.	Kull.	Akut.
Ascent.	Dyoon.	Ven.	
Aunt (paternal).	Dodeh.	Bach.	
Aunt (maternal).	Mana-Verdeh.	Wach.	
All.	Fukut.	Tukkheh.	
Again.	Wuz deeger.	Tserung gokh.	
Always.		Harwar.	
Ass.	Sher.	Koor.	
Air.	Awoo.		
Animal.	Jandar.		
Afraid.	Khooj dared.	Runneh.	
Alone.		Tokha.	

	Sirikolee.	Wakhee.	Kunjootee.
Back.	Dom.	Dum.	Ashtun.
Barley.	Chusht.	Yurok.	
Beard.	Boon.	Riggish.	Ungi.
Belly.	Kecheh.	Vird.	Ool.
Black Pepper.	Tor mirich.		
Blue.	Kusheen.	Neeli	
Boat.	Ghekhit.	Kishti.	
Bread.	Khishpick, Shpeek.	Khutch.	
Breast.	Tej.	Bupp.	Amamot.
Brick.	Krich.	Khisht.	
Bride.	Zinnull.		
Bridge.	Kupprick.	Sukhoord.	
Bridle.	Wuzdun Widoon.	Akhoon.	
Brother-in-law.	Khuserez.	Khiserez.	
Bull.	Chut khej.		
Butter.	Zurd-i-on. Rown.	Rogh.	
Brother and sister.	Yakh wordeh.		
But.	Khair.		
Because.	Hutka.		
Brother.	Vurood.	Vuroot.	
Boy.		Zikat.	
Body.	Kechkal.	Yastch.	
Bullock.	Chat.	Chat.	
Bird.	Rowuhtum.	Kuppch.	
Beak.	Minkol.	Gush.	
Bone.		Yaheh.	
Branch.	Shakh.		
Boot.	Pekh.		
Blind.		Koor.	
Bad.	Jeet.	Shukk.	
Broad.	Kshoot.		

	Sirikolee.	Wakhee.	Kunjootee.
Calf of leg.	Soon.		Barun.
Canal.	Warch.	Datch.	
Cap.	Ghoza, Dopee, Tumakh.	Ascape.	
Cheek.	Peeza.	Robi.	Amookush.
Chest.	Puz.	Poshber.	Undel.
Chin.	Zina goon.	Zinnakh.	Asun.
Cloth.	Gleem.	Pallas.	
Comb.	Dolee.	Kungoo.	Uphoonun.
Cooking pot.	Dyegh.		
Cow.	Yoh.		
Cup.	Chinak.		
Child.	Ghada.	Tiffoo.	
Cloud.	Varm.	Woor.	
Copper.	Miss.		
Chair.	Koorsee.		
Clothing.	Leel.		
Cave.	Jeerboon.		
Corn.	Zan.		
Clean.	Pokuza.	Pokuza.	
Cold.	Ish.	Sur.	
Daughter.	Rezeen. Zinnal.	Thurght.	
Dust.	Seet.	Shit.	
Day.	Mass.	Rokhun.	
Dog.	Küt.	Shach.	
Deaf.	Chun.	Kar.	
Dirty.	Nopuk.	Gajt.	
Difficult.	Kilar.		
Dry.		Kishta.	
Ear.	Ol, Ghowl.	Gish.	Altootul.
Elder brother.	Lor derdo.		
Entrails.	Roda.	Shungur.	Geekun.
Ewe.	Mawul.		

	Sirikolee.	*Wakhee.*	*Kunjootee.*
Eye.	Cheem, sem.	Kizm.	Alcheen.
Eyebrow.	Warooh.	Warooh.	Altanaser.
Eyelash.	Posutch.	Teppuk.	Amolpol.
Each.	Wirfuth.		
Everywhere.	Harjoi.	Kumjairech.	
Everything.	Chaisvid.		
Evening.	Shum.	Shoom.	
East.		Mushrikh.	
Earth.	Zimad.	Zamin.	
Egg.	Burza.		
Face.	Tukkool, Pace.	Rui.	Askull.
Father.	Dood.	Tat.	
Father-in-law.	Khusoor.	Khurs.	
Felt.	Jane.	Ajane.	
Finger.	Anzekht.	Jigl or Jyigl, Yangl.	Amia nusser.
Finger-nail.	Tussoor, Nashowr.	Digger.	Uria Nusser.
Fire.	Yur, Yoots.	Rukknigh.	
Flock of sheep.	Chlo.		Alis.
Foot.	Peza, Peyr.	Poda.	Hyali.
Forehead.	Rukk.	Rukk.	
Far.	Thar.	Thir.	
From.	Uz.		
Feather.	Kunnaut.	Pür.	
Fish.	Mooee.	Mahi.	
Food.	Kugum.		
Flour.	Yogj.	Yumch.	
Flower.	Gul.	Sprüg.	
Foolish.		Akmak.	
Full.		Takhi.	
Fatigued.		Wurugneh.	
Goat.	Waz, Vas.	Togh.	
Grandfather.	Bap.	Pope.	

(566)

	Sirikolee.	*Wakhee.*	*Kunjootee.*
Grandmother.	Mam.		
Grandson.	Naboose.		
Grape.	Azom.	Angoor.	
Grass.	Dokh, Woohf.		
Green.	Soz.	Soz.	
Girl.		Zikat.	
Gold.	Tilla.	Tilla.	
Grave.	Gour.		
Great.	Lowr.	Loop.	
Good.	Charj.	Buff.	
Hair.	Kushut. Shad.	Shuffsh.	
Hand.	Vist, Zeest, Thust.	Thust.	Arin.
Head.	Kol.	Sir.	Guppal.
Heart.	Zardeh. Zord.	Pasyoo.	Us.
Herd of cattle.	Chut.		
Horse.	Voorch.	Yash.	
House.	Cheed.	Khoon.	
Husband.	Showr.		
How.	Tserang.	Tserunga vitteh.	
How much.		Tsum.	
How many.		Tsumteh. Yom.	
Half.		Chut.	
Hour.	Dum.		
Hoof.	Sum.		
Horn.	Shokh.	Shayoh.	
Hill.	Taich.	Koh.	
Helmet.	Dabulgah.		
Hot.	Jurm.	Shundr.	
Hard.		Shukk.	
Hungry.		Murz.	
Heavy.		Gorung.	
High.		Loop.	

(567)

	Sirikolee.	Wakhee.	Kunjootee.
Iron tripod.	Kurwur.		
Immediately.	Sheech dum.	Aniv dum.	
In.	Divoir.		
Iron.	Speen.	Yisht.	
Kidney.	Aroora.	Wultuk.	Asamoz.
Knee.	Zeddun, Zoon.	Bareen, Birin.	Adoomuss.
Knife.	Charg.	Kurej.	
King.	Poshow.		
Leather.	Pershyoo, Parshan.	Girdagee.	
Leg.	Pehmush, Lung.	Poty eshutch.	Geltun.
Lip.	Lucee, Pauz.	Luceeteh, Luflch.	Ile.
Little finger.			Nameel umush.
Liver.	Sod.	Jiger.	Egin.
Lucerne grass.	Buda.		
Lungs.	Sowel.	Shoosh.	Akhur poot.
Lightning.	Tundoorg thid.		
Lead.	Koorgushum.		
Lance.	Neza.	Neza.	
Lake.	Kol.		
Leaf of a tree.	Park.		
Long.	Duros.	Vurz.	
Light.		Ranjk.	
Low.		Pust.	
Mare.	Varzeh.		
Meat.	Gekhat.	Gusht.	
Melon.	Kogun.	Kurbooza.	
Middle finger.			Mukooching, Amia russer.
Milk.	Kushyood, Shivd.	Jurj.	
Mother.	Moda, Anor.	Nan.	
Mother-in-law.	Khushukh.	Khush.	
Mountain.	Tej.	Koh.	
Moustache.	Birit.	Buroot.	Sullut.

(568)

	Sirikolee.	Wakhee.	Kunjootee.
Mouth.	Ghof.	Ghush.	Rukhat.
Mud.	Ghut.	Lip.	
Many.	Ghullaba pur.	Tukkheh.	
Moon.	Most.	Jumakh.	
Morning.	Kheyr-mothoor.	Suba.	
Month.	Most.		
Man.	Choorik, Cherin.	Thai.	
Mad.		Kalundur.	
Navel.	Wunookh.	Naf.	Asooee.
Neck.	Gerdana.		Ush.
Nose.	Nauz.	Miss.	Amooposhi.
Nostril.	Nauz def.	Miss sird.	Amoltor.
Now.	Sheech.	Aniv.	
None.	Bekoor hech.	Hechiz.	
Near.	Nizd.	Drimosch.	
No.	Nai.		
Never.		Nay.	
Night.	Shob.	Naghd.	
North.		Shimmal.	
Narrow.	Tong.		
On.	Yoos.		
Out of.	Vatch.		
Other.	Deeger.		
Open.		Gush hut.	
Palate.	Tez Kurm.	Kurm.	Tull.
Pupil of eye.	Chingazik.	Chismuk.	Nunna.
Pear.	Narshbat.		
Patience.	Warofs.		
Ram.	Vairna.		
Red Pepper.	Kizzil Mirich.		
Rice.	Girinj.		
River.	Durya.	Durya.	

(569)

	Sirikolee.	Wakhee.	Kunjootee.
Road.	Poonda.	Dook.	
Rain.	Wuraij zood.		
Saddle.	Siran, Jeel.	Pushrun.	
Salt.	Ghazitch.		
Shoe.	Kuffak.	Kuffsh.	
Side.	Hullah.	Pailoo.	Apateen.
Sister.	Yakh.	Khooee.	
Sister-in-law.	Khyoon.		
Sole of foot.	Tulla Peza.	Kuff.	Alis lar.
Son.	Poora. Putz.	Putr.	
Son-in-law.	Damood.		
Spoon.	Kumach.		
Spoon, small.	Cheh.		
Stone.	Jehr.	Gehr, Ghar.	
Sweat.	Khyud.	Arak.	
Sun.	Kheyr.	Yir.	
Star.	Khutoorch.	Sittar.	
South.		Janoob.	
Servant.	Nokur.	Nokur.	
Slave.	Indeech.	Gholam.	
Sheep.	Kullob.	Kullah.	
Sky.	Usmun.	Osman.	
Silver.	Nokra.	Nokra.	
Sugar.	Shukkr.		
Soap.	Zord.		
Sword.	Mithj.	Kingar.	
Sword, straight.		Kinjar.	
Shield.	Sipar.		
Shade.	Suyah.		
Sand.	Shoosh.		
Small.	Zilikeek.	Chklai.	
Sweet.		Khosk.	

	Sirikolee.	Wakhee.	Kunjootee.
Short.	Kut.	Kurt.	
Soft.		Shillot.	
Shut.		Vandt.	
Strong.		Taiyar.	
Snow.	Zumoon.		
Tent.	Chowdyr.	Chowdyr.	
Thumb.			Lahoob umush.
Tongue.	Ziou.	Ziuck.	Owmussee.
Tooth.	Thundoon.	Dandook.	Ameh.
Town.	Khasbar.	Shahr.	
Tree.	Dutoj. Nawul.	Derakht.	
This.	Yam.	Eeum.	
That.	Yoo.	Yekhull.	
There.	Um.	Derah.	
Then.	Thom.	Dera wukht.	
To.	Hupa.		
To-day.	Noor.	Woothk. Dodakrich.	
To-morrow.	Fal.	Tortur.	
Toe.	Punja.		
Thunder.	Waraij.		
Table.	Wambone.	Sundalee.	
Tail.	Thum.		
Thirsty.		Takumsith.	
Thigh.		Shoonj.	
Uncle.	Zul dodeh.		
Under.	Vidzin.	Pusst.	
Valley.	Daroo.	Kubroo.	
Village.	Dyoor.	Dyar.	
Venison.	Gusaij.		
Water.	Khesr. Schatz.	Yupk.	
Wheat.	Arund kum.	Ghuddem.	
White.	Suppeed.	Sukhud.	

	Sirikolee.	Wakhee.	Kunjootee.
Wife.	Ghin.	Kinnat.	
Wood.	Khishung, Jeez.	Guz.	
What?	Chais.	Chiz.	
Who?	Chedoom.	Kumkalk.	
Where?	Kojaso.	Kumrut.	
When?	Chedoom wakt.	Tserung.	
Why?	Chaisir.	Tserunga.	
West.		Mughrib.	
Woman.	Abrut.	Kund.	
Wing.	Kunnaut.		
Wind.	Shamul.	Dumah.	
Wine.	Mai.		
Wise.		Hukl.	
Wet.		Hushteh.	
Yellow.	Zurd.	Zurd.	
Younger brother.	Zizul derdo.		
Yes.	Hoi-Hoi.		
Yesterday.	Pigán.	Verokh.	
Year.	Sool.	Sala.	
Young.		Shugd.	

SIRIKOLEE SENTENCES.

I will strike him.	Ata dayum.
Come here.	Owd yoth.
Go away.	Tedth.
What do you want?	Cha is kan.
I am not able to do this.	Nutch kanam.
What is your name?	Ta noom saiz.
Whence do you come?	Uz kot yot.
Where are you going?	Koj usoh.
How old are you?	Tsund sula yetsoot.
Who is that (man)?	Yoo choi.
It is a hot day.	Noor joorm.
Is this your horse?	Yum voorch taiya noh.

SIRIKOLEE SENTENCES.—(Concluded.)

This is my dog.	Yumoo küd.
How many dogs are there in the village?	Tchoond küd yost der dyör?
Bring me some milk.	Shevd meery var.
I see a man coming this way.	Awi khalk yothd awi weinam.
He is riding on a horse.	Oche voorch suvoor ka.
My house is on fire.	Moo az ched yutch izooft tooit.
How far is it to Tashkurgan?	Varsheedee tsund thar.
I do not know.	Nawuz anum.

WAKHEE SENTENCES.

Come here.	Worm ozeh.
Go away.	Rich.
Are you pleased?	Buft eea?
Where is your house?	Teh khun komur?
What is your age?	Teh sal yom?
Have you any children?	Pitr teh ten?
Eat bread.	Khech yoh.
Drink water.	Popuk yoh.
Be mounted.	Yesh sowar voi.
Load the ass.	Khoor daryur.
How far is it from here?	Yemun yom dairtch.
These mountains are very high.	Hameen kohe ghuffuch bulund.
There is much snow.	Zebum guffuch te.
There are many stones.	Gur guffuch te.
This house is old.	Hameen yesh khabir.
I want a young one.	Juwan yesh Hajjit.
Come to-morrow.	Warik wuzzeh.
Wait a week.	Aboo haftar subr yer.
Half a month ago.	Chut meh regud.
It is a month's journey.	Wokh ek mah hutteh.
Read the book.	Kitab jahi.
Have you read the Koran?	Koran jabit kit.

NUMERALS.

	Sirikolee.	Wakhee.	Kunjootee.
One.	Ee.	Yeoo.	Hen.
Two.	Thou.	Boi.	Alta.
Three.	Haroi.	Taroi.	Usko.
Four.	Savoor.	Tsavoor.	Waltoh.
Five.	Pinj.	Pans.	Zinsowur.
Six.	Khel.	Shutt.	Mushnudwur.
Seven.	Uvd.	Hüb.	Talwah.
Eight.	Wohft.	Hut.	Altamor.
Nine.	Naen.	Now.	Unchoor.
Ten.	This.	Thus.	Tormoh.
Eleven.	This-at-ee.	Thus yeoo.	Tormoh-hen.
Twelve.	This-at-tha.	Thus boi.	Tormoh-alta.
Thirteen.	This-at-haroi.	Thus taroi.	Turmoh usko.
Fourteen.	This-at-savoor.	Thus tsavoor.	Tormoh waltoh.
Fifteen.	This-at-pinj.	Thus pans.	Tormoh zinsowur.
Sixteen.	This-at-khel.	Thus shutt.	Tormoh Mushnudwur.
Seventeen.	This-at-uvd.	Thus hüb.	Tormoh talwah.
Eighteen.	This-at-wohft.	Thus hut.	Tormoh altamor.
Nineteen.	This-at-naen.	Thus now.	Tormoh unchoor.
Twenty.	Wist.	Bist.	Alter.
Thirty.	See.	See.	Altor tormoh.
Forty.	Chal.	Chil.	Altoh-altor.
Fifty.	Pinjoo.	Punja.	Altoh-altor-normoh.
Sixty.	Oltmish.	Shust.	Iski-altor.
Seventy.	Yetmish.	Huftad.	Walta-altor-tormoh.
Eighty.	Sechsan.	Hushtad.	Altmya-altor.
Ninety.	Sechsan-at-this.	Nowad.	Uncha-altor-tormoh.
Ninety-one.	Sechsan-at-this-at-ee.	Nowad yeoo.	
One hundred.	Sud.	Sud.	Teh.
One thousand.	Huzoor.	Huzar.	Huzar.

www.ingramcontent.com/pod-product-compliance
Lightning Source LLC
Chambersburg PA
CBHW081141230426
43664CB00018B/2771